Pension Distribution Answer Book

2019 Edition

by Melanie N. Aska and James E. Turpin

Pension Distribution Answer Book, 2019 Edition, provides expert guidance on the complex rules governing pension plan distributions. This comprehensive and easy-to-use resource guides the subscriber through the labyrinth of legal, administrative, and tax requirements for all types of distributions from qualified retirement plans.

Highlights of the 2019 Edition

Updated coverage in the 2019 Edition of *Pension Distribution Answer Book* includes the following:

- The changes to the 401(k) hardship withdrawal rules made by the Bipartisan Budget Act of 2018 (BBA), effective for plan years beginning after December 31, 2018 (see Qs 1:9 and 1:13).
- The Tax Cuts and Job Act's (TCJA's) narrowing of the definition of personal casualty loss under Code Section 165 and its effect upon 401(k) safe harbor hardship withdrawals, effective for taxable years 2018 to 2025 (see Q 1:11).
- The Internal Revenue Service's (IRS's) special hardship distribution rules for victims of Hurricanes Harvey, Irma, and Maria, and the California wildfires (see Q 1:14).
- The additional hardship withdrawal relief provided by the Disaster Tax Relief and Airport Airway Extension Act of 2017 (the Relief Act) for the victims of Hurricanes Harvey, Irma, and Maria (see Q 1:15).
- TCJA's "qualified 2016 disaster distribution" provisions (see Q 1:16).
- BBA's "qualified wildfire distribution" provisions (see Q 1:17).
- IRS Chief Counsel Advice Memorandum 201736022, which illustrates the participant loan cure period under Treasury Regulations § 1.72(p)-1, Q&A-10(a) (see Q 2:7).
- IRS Announcement 2017-11, which provides relief from certain participant loan verification procedures for victims of Hurricane Harvey (see Q 2:30).

- IRS Announcement 2017-13, which provides relief from certain participant loan verification procedures for victims of Hurricane Irma (see Q 2:31).
- IRS Announcement 2017-15, which provides relief from certain participant loan verification procedures for victims of Hurricane Maria and the California wildfires (see Q 2:32).
- The special plan loan rules provided under the Relief Act for victims of Hurricanes Harvey, Irma, and Maria (see Q 2:33).
- BBA's federal tax levy provisions (see Q 3:63).
- The Pension Benefit Guaranty Corporation's expanded missing participants program for plan terminations on or after January 1, 2018 (see Qs 15:42, 15:47, 15:86, and 16:56–60).
- IRS guidance on the allocation of plan assets when a plan is underfunded upon plan termination (see Q 17:41).
- TCJA and BBA exemptions from Code Section 72(t)'s 10 percent additional income tax for "qualified 2016 disaster distributions" and "qualified wildfire distributions," respectively (see Q 20:2).
- TCJA's extension of the rollover period for qualified loan offset amounts (see Q 21:28).
- The change in the system for determining voluntary correction program user fees announced in IRS Revenue Procedure 2018-4 (see Q 23:11).
- IRS Notice 2018-14, which provides federal income tax withholding rules for periodic payments when no withholding certificate (IRS Form W-4P) is furnished (see Q 24:50).
- IRS guidance on determining the fair market value of an insurance contract (see Qs 25:18 and 25:21).
- TCJA's long-term capital gain tax rates (see Q 25:35).
- 2018 Instructions for Forms 1099-R and 5498 (see Chapter 27).
- 2018 General Instructions for Forms 1097, 1098, 1099, 3921, 3922, 5498, and W-2G (see Chapter 27).

The Tables and the Index have been updated to reflect all of the changes to the text.

10/18

For questions concerning this shipment, billing, or other customer service matters, call our Customer Service Department at 1-800-234-1660.

For toll-free ordering, please call 1-800-638-8437.

Pension Distribution Answer Book

2019 Edition

Melanie N. Aska
James E. Turpin

This publication is designed to provide accurate and authoritative information in regard to the subject matter covered. It is sold with the understanding that the publisher and the author(s) are not engaged in rendering legal, accounting, or other professional services. If legal advice or other professional assistance is required, the services of a competent professional should be sought.

—From a *Declaration of Principles* jointly adopted by
a Committee of the American Bar Association and
a Committee of Publishers and Associations

Published by Wolters Kluwer in New York.

Wolters Kluwer Legal & Regulatory U.S. serves customers worldwide with CCH, Aspen Publishers and Kluwer Law International products.

Printed in the United States of America

ISBN: 978-1-5438-0049-4

1 2 3 4 5 6 7 8 9 0

About Wolters Kluwer Legal & Regulatory U.S.

Wolters Kluwer Legal & Regulatory U.S. delivers expert content and solutions in the areas of law, corporate compliance, health compliance, reimbursement, and legal education. Its practical solutions help customers successfully navigate the demands of a changing environment to drive their daily activities, enhance decision quality and inspire confident outcomes.

Serving customers worldwide, its legal and regulatory portfolio includes products under the Aspen Publishers, CCH Incorporated, Kluwer Law International, ftwilliam.com and MediRegs names. They are regarded as exceptional and trusted resources for general legal and practice-specific knowledge, compliance and risk management, dynamic workflow solutions, and expert commentary.

WOLTERS KLUWER SUPPLEMENT NOTICE

This product is updated on a periodic basis with supplements and/or new editions to reflect important changes in the subject matter.

If you would like information about enrolling this product in the update service, or wish to receive updates billed separately with a 30-day examination review, please contact our Customer Service Department at 1-800-234-1660 or email us at: *customer.service@wolterskluwer.com*. You can also contact us at:

Wolters Kluwer
Distribution Center
7201 McKinney Circle
Frederick, MD 21704

Important Contact Information

- To order any title, go to *www.WoltersKluwerLR.com* or call 1-800-638-8437.
- To reinstate your manual update service, call 1-800-638-8437.
- To contact Customer Service, e-mail *customer.service@wolterskluwer.com*, call 1-800-234-1660, fax 1-800-901-9075, or mail correspondence to: Order Department—Wolters Kluwer, PO Box 990, Frederick, MD 21705.
- To review your account history or pay an invoice online, visit *www.WoltersKluwerLR.com/payinvoices*.

For my father, John Aska (February 17, 1923–December 2, 2012)

MNA

To all of my colleagues who generously share their collective knowledge and wisdom.

JET

Preface

Pension professionals know just how challenging it is to understand the rules governing plan distributions and to administer plan distributions. *Pension Distribution Answer Book, 2019 Edition,* gives practitioners the answers to questions about developments in pension distribution rules and strategies, particularly changes brought about by federal legislation and guidance issued by the Internal Revenue Service, the Department of Labor and the Pension Benefit Guaranty Corporation.

For ease of use, *Pension Distribution Answer Book, 2019 Edition,* is divided into six major plan distribution topics:

- Part 1 In-Service Events
- Part 2 Benefit Determination
- Part 3 Plan Termination
- Part 4 Tax Treatment
- Part 5 Administrative Requirements
- Part 6 Distribution Planning

Part 1, In-Service Events, explains distributions made during employment, including withdrawals, qualified domestic relation orders, loans, minimum required distributions, corrective distributions, and the tax treatment of PS-58 costs. Part 2, Benefit Determination, covers vesting, calculation of accrued benefits in a defined benefit plan, computation of vested account balances, qualified joint and survivor requirements, death benefits, and limits on distributions to certain employees. Part 3, Plan Termination, covers the mechanics of plan termination from the very simple process for defined contribution plans to distress terminations with the Pension Benefit Guaranty Corporation for defined benefit plans. Part 4, Tax Treatment, covers the taxation of plan distributions, including excise taxes, direct rollovers, and withholding. Part 5, Administrative Requirements, reviews the administrative requirements for distributions, including withholding, tax reporting on Form 1099-R, in-kind distributions, and trustee-to-trustee transfers. Last, Part 6, Distribution Planning, analyzes participants' distribution options and suggests some planning opportunities to maximize retirement benefits for participants and their beneficiaries.

Format. The question-and-answer format, with its breadth of coverage and its plain language explanations (plus numerous illustrative examples), offers a clear and useful guide to understanding the complex area of qualified plan distributions.

Numbering System. The questions are numbered consecutively within each chapter (e.g., 1:1, 1:2, 1:3).

List of Questions. The List of Questions that follows the Table of Contents in the front of this book helps the reader to locate areas of immediate interest.

Appendixes. For the reader's convenience, a series of actuarial tables, interest rates, and information on determination of highly compensated employees are provided.

Index. A detailed topical index is provided as a further aid to locating specific information. All references in the index are to question numbers.

Use of Abbreviations. Because of the broad subject area covered, a number of terms and statutory references are abbreviated. Among the most common of these shorthand references are:

- Audit CAP—Audit Closing Agreement Program
- BAPCPA—Bankruptcy Abuse Prevention and Consumer Protection Act of 2005
- Code—The Internal Revenue Code of 1986
- DEFRA—Deficit Reduction Act of 1984
- DOL—The U.S. Department of Labor
- EGTRRA—Economic Growth and Tax Relief Reconciliation Act of 2001
- EPCRS—Employee Plans Compliance Resolution System
- ERISA—Employee Retirement Income Security Act of 1974, as amended
- ESOP—Employee Stock Ownership Plan
- FICA—Federal Insurance Contributions Act
- FUTA—Federal Unemployment Tax Act
- GATT—General Agreement on Tariffs and Trade (Uruguay Round Agreements Act of 1994)
- GUST—GATT, USERRA, SBJPA, and TRA '97
- HEART Act of 2008—Heroes Earnings Assistance and Relief Tax Act of 2008

- IRA—Individual Retirement Account
- IRC—Internal Revenue Code of 1986
- IRS—Internal Revenue Service
- JCWAA—Job Creation and Workers' Assistance Act
- MAP-21—Moving Ahead for Progress in the 21st Century Act
- MDA—Minimum Distribution Allowance
- NUA—Net Unrealized Appreciation
- OBRA '87—Omnibus Budget Reconciliation Act of 1987
- PATH Act—Protecting Americans from Tax Hikes Act of 2015
- PBGC—Pension Benefit Guaranty Corporation
- PFEA—Pension Funding Equity Act of 2004
- PPA—Pension Protection Act of 2006
- QDRO—Qualified Domestic Relations Order
- QJSA—Qualified Joint and Survivor Annuity
- QMAC—Qualified Matching Contribution
- QNEC—Qualified Nonelective Contribution
- QPSA—Qualified Preretirement Survivor Annuity
- RBD—Required Beginning Date
- REA 1984—Retirement Equity Act of 1984
- RMD—Required Minimum Distribution
- RPA—Retirement Protection Act of 1994
- RRA—IRS Restructuring and Reform Act of 1998
- SBJPA—Small Business Job Protection Act of 1996
- SCP—Self-Correction Program
- SEP—Simplified Employee Pension Plan
- SIMPLE—Savings Incentive Match Plan for Employees
- TEFRA—Tax Equity and Fiscal Responsibility Act of 1982
- TIPRA—Tax Increase Prevention and Reconciliation Act of 2005
- TRA '86—Tax Reform Act of 1986
- TRA '97—Taxpayer Relief Act of 1997
- USERRA—Uniformed Services Employment and Reemployment Rights Act of 1994

- VCO—Voluntary Correction of Operational Failures
- VCP—Voluntary Correction Program
- VCS—Voluntary Correction of Operational Failures Standardized
- VCT—Voluntary Correction of Tax-Sheltered Annuity Failures
- WRERA—Worker, Retiree, and Employer Recovery Act of 2008

Pension Distribution Answer Book is updated annually to keep you abreast of the latest developments in the field. We hope you will find it to be a useful tool in your benefits library.

Melanie N. Aska
James E. Turpin
September 2018

About the Authors

Melanie N. Aska is Counsel at the law firm of Murtha Cullina LLP, in the firm's Boston, Massachusetts office. She previously was Of Counsel at the employee benefits law firm of Parker, Brown, Macaulay & Sheerin, P.C. in Foxborough, Massachusetts. Before that, she was the Senior Benefits Compliance Officer at Harvard University. During her previous years in private law practice, she was a shareholder and head of the employee benefits practice group at Godfrey & Kahn, S.C. in Milwaukee, Wisconsin, and was an associate attorney with Ropes & Gray, LLP in Boston, Massachusetts. She has more than 30 years of experience in employee benefits law. Ms. Aska received a B.A., *summa cum laude*, Phi Beta Kappa, from Wheaton College, Norton, Massachusetts, an M.P.A. from Princeton University, and a J.D. from the University of Wisconsin. She was a co-author of *5500 Preparer's Manual* (Panel Publishers, 2001) and *Pension Distribution Answer Book: Special Supplement—Forms & Worksheets* (Panel Publishers, 1998), and was a contributing editor for *Journal of Pension Benefits* (Aspen Publishers). She has also written numerous articles on qualified plan distributions and tax-sheltered annuities.

Acknowledgments. Thanks to those who make working on this book every year a happy experience, including Michael Tuller, our patient and hardworking editor, and James Turpin, my seasoned and dedicated co-author. Thanks also to Joan Gucciardi, my former co-author, who created this book with me in 1995, and to our former editors, Susan Holt and Ellen Ros. Finally, heartfelt thanks to those in my life who lighten my day-to-day burdens throughout the year, especially when I work on this book, including my partner, Frank Feeney, my caring friends and family members, and my whimsical cat, Atticus, who helpfully naps on my research papers whenever I update my chapters.

James E. Turpin is the President and principal shareholder of The Turpin Consulting Group, Inc., which has provided actuarial, administrative, and consulting services for retirement plans since August 1981. Mr. Turpin's current professional focus is on plan design, plan compliance issues, litigation support, and expert testimony. Mr. Turpin is a May 1974 graduate of the University of Texas at Austin with a B.B.A. in Actuarial Science. In December 1975, he received an M.B.A. in Actuarial Science, also from the University of Texas, at Austin.

He is a member of the American Academy of Actuaries, a Fellow of the Conference of Consulting Actuaries, a member of the American Society of Pension Professionals and Actuaries (ASPPA), and an Enrolled Actuary under the Employee Retirement Income Security Act (ERISA) as certified by the Joint Board for Enrollment of Actuaries. He is also a member of the International Actuarial Association, the Small Business Council of America, and The Group, Inc. In addition, he has been a member of the New Mexico Employee Benefits Roundtable, the Western Pension and Benefits Association, the SouthWest Benefits Association, and the Actuaries' Club of the Southwest. Mr. Turpin has represented New Mexico on the Steering Committee for the Annual Los Angeles IRS-Practitioners Benefits Conference. He is also a past president of the New Mexico Estate Planning Council.

Mr. Turpin was Vice President-Pensions and a member of the Executive Committee for the American Academy of Actuaries (Academy) from 1999 through 2001. He was a member of the Academy Board of Directors from 1998 through 2001. As Academy Vice President for Pensions, Mr. Turpin was Chair of the Academy Pension Practice Council, which oversees the Academy's Pension, Pension Accounting, Social Insurance, and Enrolled Actuaries Meeting Committees. Prior to becoming Vice President, he was a member of the Academy Pension Committee from 1986 through 1999 and served as its Vice-Chair from 1996 through 1999, and he was also a member of the Academy Pension Practice Council from 1995 through 2001. In his capacity as Vice President-Pensions, Mr. Turpin worked closely with the staff of the Academy and ASPPA on various legislative and regulatory issues affecting the actuarial and pension profession. Mr. Turpin was the liaison between the Academy Pension Committee and the Government Affairs Committee of ASPPA from 1995 through 1998. He was an Associate Editor of the Enrolled Actuaries Report from 1995 through 1999 and was the Editor from 1999 through 2001. He also served on the Pension Committee of the Actuarial Standards Board (ASB) from 1994 through 2000 and on the ASB Editorial Advisory Committee from 1994 through 1995 and was a member of the ASB General Committee from 2011 through 2014. Mr. Turpin currently is a member of the Board of Directors of the Small Business Council of America and the Part 2 Subcommittee for the Enrolled Actuary examination. He also has been a regular contributor to *401(k) Advisor.*

Mr. Turpin has practiced as an actuary and employee benefit consultant for over 40 years and is a frequent author and lecturer on employee benefit and retirement plan issues. He has represented the pension profession in testimony before Congress and various federal regulatory agencies and is well known for his litigation support and expert testimony on actuarial and pension matters.

Acknowledgments. Thanks to my wife, Charlotte, for her support. I am honored to be part of the Wolters Kluwer author cadre. The hard work of my co-author, Melanie Aska, is greatly appreciated, as well as the work by the former authors, Joan Gucciardi, Carol Sears, and Scott Miller, who have also made *Pension Distribution Answer Book* the useful and current tool it is for today's pension professionals. Finally, my thanks to our editor, Michael Tuller, for his patience during my work on this project. And finally, to all of my colleagues who willingly share their knowledge and experience.

Contents

List of Questions xxxi

Part 1 In-Service Events

CHAPTER 1

In-Service Distributions 1-1

Profit Sharing Plans 1-2

Hardship Distributions 1-5

Pension Plans 1-23

Employee Stock Ownership Plans 1-30

CHAPTER 2

Loans 2-1

General Rule: Loans from Qualified Employer Plans Treated as Taxable Distributions 2-1

Treatment of Distributions Attributable to Qualified Retirement Plan Loans 2-13

Special Loan Rules for Certain Disaster Victims 2-29

Loans as Prohibited Transactions 2-37

Spousal Consent for Loans Made by Plans Subject to the Survivor Annuity Requirements 2-49

Federal Truth in Lending Act 2-50

CHAPTER **3**

QDROs and Other Exceptions to the Anti-Alienation Rules 3-1

General Rules and Definitions 3-2

Form or Amount of Benefits May Not Be Altered 3-16

How QDROs Affect Other Retirement Plan Benefits; Section 415 Requirements 3-20

Alternate Payee's Retirement Plan Benefits Must Be Clearly Specified 3-21

QDROs Must Specify the Benefit Period and the Retirement Plan 3-24

Retirement Plan Provisions and Written Procedures for Determining the Qualified Status of a DRO 3-25

Procedures to Follow After a Retirement Plan Receives a DRO 3-28

Taxation of Retirement Plan Distributions Made Under QDROs 3-34

Official Guidance on Drafting, Reviewing, and Administering QDROs 3-38

Permitted Offsets of Retirement Plan Benefits 3-40

CHAPTER 4

Required Minimum Distributions 4-1

Waiver of 2009 Required Minimum Distributions 4-3

Minimum Distribution Requirement in General 4-5

Distributions Beginning During a Participant's Lifetime 4-7

Death Before Required Beginning Date 4-10

Determination of the Designated Beneficiary 4-13

Required Minimum Distributions from Defined Contribution Plans 4-17

Required Minimum Distributions from Defined Benefit Plans and Annuity Contracts 4-30

Rollovers and Transfers 4-53

Special Rules 4-55

IRS Field Directive to Employee Plans (EP) Examiners 4-61

CHAPTER 5

Corrective Distributions 5-1

Excess Contributions 5-1

Excess Aggregate Contributions 5-9

Excess Elective Contributions 5-16

Excess Annual Additions 5-24

CHAPTER 6

Taxable Life Insurance Costs 6-1

Calculation of Taxable Insurance Costs 6-2

CHAPTER 7

Bankruptcy 7-1

Bankruptcy 7-1

Part 2 Benefit Determination

CHAPTER 8

Vesting 8-1

General Vesting Rules 8-2

PPA Changes Effective for Post-2006 Plan Years 8-6

Top-Heavy Rules 8-8

Determination of Top-Heavy Status 8-11

Death Benefits, Rollovers, and Plan-to-Plan Transfers 8-12

Key Employees 8-13

Top-Heavy Vesting Schedules 8-16

Determination of Years of Vesting Service 8-16

Breaks in Service 8-21

Amendments in Vesting Schedules 8-23

Forfeitures and Cash-Out Rules 8-24

Required Vesting upon Plan Termination, Partial Termination, or Complete Discontinuance of Contributions 8-30

CHAPTER 9

Administrative Determination of Benefits 9-1

Determining Account Balances in Defined Contribution Plans 9-1

Cash-Out Rules 9-5

Underfunded Defined Contribution Plans 9-9

Determining Accrued Benefits in Traditional Defined Benefit Plans 9-12

Determination of Accrual of Service 9-20

Benefit Minimums and Limitations 9-25

Lump Sum Determination 9-37

Determining Benefits in Non-Traditional Plans 9-41

CHAPTER 10

Optional Forms of Benefit and Protected Benefits 10-1

Nondiscrimination Rules Under Code Section 401(a)(4) 10-4

Permissive Aggregation of Certain Benefits, Rights, or Features 10-15

Code Section 411(d)(6) Protected Benefits 10-22

CHAPTER 11

QJSA and QPSA Rules 11-1

Overview 11-5

Retirement Plans Subject to Survivor Annuity Requirements 11-6

Transferee, Offset, Frozen, and Terminated Plans 11-12

Applying Survivor Annuity Requirements to Participants 11-13

Annuity Starting Date 11-15

Benefits 11-18

Timing of QJSA Distributions 11-19

Rules Governing the QPSA 11-20

Applying Survivor Annuity Requirements to Plan Loans 11-22

Applying Survivor Annuity Requirements to Unmarried Participants, Surviving Spouses, and Participants Who Have a Change in Marital Status 11-23

Spousal Consent Requirement 11-25

Participant's Waiver of a QPSA or QJSA 11-27

Notice Requirements 11-33

Subsidized Survivor Benefits 11-57

CHAPTER 12
Retirement, Disability, and Death 12-1

Normal Retirement 12-2

Early Retirement 12-6

Late Retirement 12-13

Phased Retirement 12-15

Longevity Annuities 12-16

Suspension of Benefits 12-17

Disability Benefits 12-18

Disability Benefits in Defined Contribution Plans 12-20

Disability Benefits in Defined Benefit Plans 12-22

Death Benefits in Defined Contribution Plans 12-24

Death Benefits in Defined Benefit Plans 12-28

Required Minimum Distribution Rules 12-36

CHAPTER 13
Other Termination of Employment Issues 13-1

General Considerations 13-2

ESOPs 13-5

Suspension of Benefits 13-8

Claims for Benefits 13-11

CHAPTER 14

Restrictions on Distributions 14-1

Historical Perspective 14-1

Application of Benefit Restriction Rules 14-4

Use of Collateral Agreements 14-10

Code Section 436 Rules on Restricted Distribution 14-12

Part 3 Plan Termination

CHAPTER 15

Plan Termination Issues 15-1

General Requirements 15-2

Defined Contribution Plans 15-4

Defined Benefit Plans 15-26

Liquidating Plan Assets 15-36

Surplus Assets 15-37

Distribution of Election Forms 15-39

Final Disclosure Forms 15-43

Abandoned Defined Contribution (Orphan) Plans 15-43

CHAPTER 16

The Termination Process for Single and Multiple Employer PBGC-Covered Plans 16-1

Coverage 16-2

PBGC Termination Steps 16-5

Notice of Intent to Terminate 16-8

Preliminary Information for PBGC 16-12

Measurement of Benefit Liabilities 16-14

Insufficiency of Plan Assets 16-18

Actions of Plan Sponsor 16-20

ERISA Section 204(h) Notice 16-21

Information Gathering 16-22

Notice of Plan Benefits 16-22

Final Stages 16-26

When the Plan Has Surplus Assets 16-27

Missing Participants 16-31

Post-Distribution Certification 16-35

Spinoff/Termination Transaction Rules 16-37

Final Returns/Reports 16-38

CHAPTER 17

Underfunded Plans 17-1

Underfunded PBGC-Covered Defined Benefit Plans 17-1

Involuntary Terminations 17-20

PPA Requirements for Distress and Involuntary Terminations 17-21

Defined Benefit Plans Not Covered by the PBGC ... 17-24

Making Contributions to Meet Plan Liabilities 17-26

Underfunded Defined Contribution Plans 17-27

Part 4 Tax Treatment

CHAPTER 18

Taxation of Periodic Payments 18-1

Understanding Basic Concepts 18-2

Simplified Method of Basis Recovery and Transition Rule 18-5

Fully Taxable Annuity Payments 18-14

CHAPTER 19

Taxation of Nonperiodic Payments 19-1

Annuity Starting Date 19-1

Various Types of Taxable Distributions and Transfers 19-4

Lump-Sum Distributions 19-9

Five-Year Forward Income Averaging 19-23

Ten-Year Forward Income Averaging 19-29

Capital Gains Treatment 19-30

Special Lump-Sum Distribution Issues 19-33

CHAPTER 20

Additional Taxes 20-1

Additional 10 Percent Income Tax on Early Distributions 20-2

Fifty Percent Excise Tax on Failure to Make Required Minimum Distributions (RMDs) ... 20-14

CHAPTER 21

Direct Rollovers 21-1

Direct Rollover Option Required 21-6

Eligible Rollover Distributions 21-22

Section 402(f) Rollover Notice 21-42

Rollover Contributions by Employees Not Yet Eligible to Participate in a Qualified Plan 21-44

Other Direct Rollover Issues 21-45

CHAPTER 22

State Income Tax Withholding and FICA and FUTA Treatment 22-1

Survey of State Income Tax Withholding Rules 22-1

FICA and FUTA Treatment of Qualified Plan Distributions 22-5

State "Source" Taxation of Retirement Benefits 22-5

CHAPTER 23

Plan Disqualification and Self-Correction Programs ... 23-1

Disqualification Events 23-4

Alternatives to Plan Disqualification—SCP, VCP, and Audit CAP 23-7

Program Eligibility 23-7

Consequences of Plan Disqualification 23-24

Part 5 Administrative Requirements

CHAPTER 24

Federal Income Tax Withholding 24-1

Federal Income Tax Withholding on Eligible Rollover Distributions That Are Not Rolled Over 24-2

Federal Income Tax Withholding on Periodic and Nonperiodic Payments That Are Not Eligible Rollover Distributions 24-9

CHAPTER 25
Distributions In-Kind 25-1

In General 25-1

Optional Form of Benefit Rules 25-2

Operational Rules 25-6

Tax Withholding Requirements 25-7

Rollover Rules 25-9

Treatment of Life Insurance and Annuity Contracts ... 25-11

Distribution of Employer Securities 25-16

CHAPTER 26
Trustee-to-Trustee Transfers 26-1

Retirement Plan Mergers, Consolidations, and Asset Transfers 26-1

Application of the Merger, Consolidation, and Transfer Requirements to Retirement Plan Spinoffs 26-2

Retirement Plan Mergers or Consolidations 26-3

CHAPTER 27
Reporting Distributions: IRS Form 1099-R 27-1

Overview 27-1

General Requirements 27-2

Line-by-Line Explanation 27-10

Electronic Filing 27-21

Correcting Form 1099-R 27-25

Combined Federal/State Filing Program 27-27

Part 6 Distribution Planning

CHAPTER **28**

Rollovers 28-1

Review of the Basics 28-1

Challenges in IRA Rollovers 28-5

Advantages and Disadvantages of IRA Rollovers 28-11

Roth IRAs 28-12

CHAPTER **29**

Lump-Sum Distributions 29-1

Review 29-1

Calculating Taxable Amounts 29-3

Economic Issues 29-9

Impact of Other Taxes 29-10

Advantages and Disadvantages of Lump-Sum Distributions 29-10

APPENDIX A

120 Percent of Federal Midterm Rate A-1

APPENDIX B

Pre-GATT Section 417(e) Interest Rates B-1

APPENDIX C

30-Year Treasury Securities Rates C-1

APPENDIX D

Single Life Table D-1

APPENDIX E

Joint Life and Last Survivor Table E-1

APPENDIX F

Mortality Tables F-1

APPENDIX G

Determination of HCEs G-1

APPENDIX H

Minimum Present Value Segment Rates H-1

Tables

Cases T-1

Internal Revenue Code Sections T-3

Treasury Regulations T-11

Index IN-1

List of Questions

Chapter 1 In-Service Distributions

Profit Sharing Plans

Q 1:1 What are the general rules for in-service distributions from profit sharing plans? 1-2

Q 1:2 In applying the withdrawal rules, what is considered a "fixed number of years"? 1-3

Q 1:3 Are there any exceptions to the two-year rule for withdrawals from profit sharing plans? 1-4

Hardship Distributions

Q 1:4 May a profit sharing or stock bonus plan distribute all or part of a participant's vested account balance because of a hardship? 1-5

Q 1:5 How is a hardship distribution from a profit sharing or stock bonus plan taxed? 1-5

Q 1:6 May a 401(k) plan make hardship distributions? 1-6

Q 1:7 When is a distribution from a 401(k) plan made on account of a hardship? 1-9

Q 1:8 Are there any other limitations on the amount that may be distributed from a 401(k) plan on account of a hardship? 1-9

Q 1:9 What is the maximum distributable amount? 1-9

Q 1:10 How is it determined whether an employee has an "immediate and heavy financial need"? 1-10

Q 1:11 Are there any instances in which the 401(k) plan need not weigh all of the relevant facts and circumstances to determine whether the employee has an immediate and heavy financial need? 1-11

Q 1:12 How does a 401(k) plan determine whether the amount of a distribution is necessary to satisfy the financial need caused by the hardship? 1-12

Q 1:13 Are there circumstances under which a 401(k) plan may deem a distribution to be necessary? 1-13

Q 1:14	Can the IRS apply special hardship rules to provide relief to taxpayers who have been adversely affected by disasters?	1-14
Q 1:15	What additional relief for victims of Hurricanes Harvey, Irma, and Maria was provided by the Disaster Tax Relief and Airport and Airway Extension Act of 2017?	1-20
Q 1:16	What relief for 2016 and 2017 distributions from eligible retirement plans due to 2016 storms and flooding was provided by the TCJA?	1-21
Q 1:17	What relief for 2017 and 2018 distributions from eligible retirement plans due to the 2017 California wildfires was provided by the BBA?	1-22

Pension Plans

Q 1:18	What are the rules for in-service distributions from pension plans?	1-23
Q 1:19	When must a participant start receiving pension benefits while still employed?	1-24
Q 1:20	Under what circumstances may in-service distributions be made from a qualified pension plan?	1-24
Q 1:21	How may in-service distributions be paid from a pension plan?	1-29
Q 1:22	Must benefits continue to accrue under a pension plan after an actively employed participant receives his or her normal retirement benefit?	1-29
Q 1:23	How must benefits continue to accrue under a defined benefit pension plan for participants who continue to work after the plan's normal retirement age?	1-29
Q 1:24	Must contributions continue to be made under a defined contribution pension plan for participants who continue to work after the plan's normal retirement age?	1-29
Q 1:25	Will a participant who receives a single-sum distribution from a pension plan after reaching normal retirement age, but before termination of employment, be entitled to lump-sum tax treatment?	1-29

Employee Stock Ownership Plans

Q 1:26	When may an ESOP make an in-service distribution?	1-30
Q 1:27	What investment diversification requirements apply to an ESOP?	1-30
Q 1:28	Who is a qualified participant for these purposes?	1-31
Q 1:29	What is the qualified election period for these purposes?	1-31
Q 1:30	How does an ESOP meet the diversification requirements?	1-31
Q 1:31	Which employer securities are subject to the diversification requirement?	1-32
Q 1:32	Are there any exceptions to the diversification requirement for employer securities acquired or contributed to a TRASOP?	1-32

Q 1:33 Are there some circumstances when employer securities acquired after December 31, 1986, are treated as acquired by, or contributed to, an ESOP on or before December 31, 1986? ... **1-32**

Q 1:34 Are there any simplified methods for determining the number of employer securities subject to the diversification rules? **1-33**

Q 1:35 Are small account balances subject to the diversification requirements? **1-34**

Q 1:36 What portion of a qualified participant's account is subject to the diversification requirement? **1-34**

Q 1:37 May an ESOP permit the diversification of amounts in excess of those required? **1-34**

Q 1:38 May the diversification requirement be satisfied by transferring shares to another defined contribution plan of the employer? ... **1-35**

Q 1:39 What are the requirements for a qualified transfer? **1-35**

Q 1:40 Must the transferee defined contribution plan comply with the safe harbor described in ERISA Section 404(c)? **1-36**

Q 1:41 How are employer securities valued for purposes of the diversification requirement? **1-36**

Q 1:42 Who is an independent appraiser? **1-36**

Q 1:43 May amounts distributed as part of the diversification election be rolled over to an eligible retirement plan? **1-36**

Q 1:44 How are dividends on employer securities handled in an ESOP? **1-36**

Q 1:45 What is the tax consequence if the employer pays dividends on employer securities directly to the participant? **1-37**

Q 1:46 How may dividends on ESOP shares be distributed to plan participants? **1-37**

Q 1:47 Are dividends paid from an ESOP to plan participants subject to the 10 percent additional income tax on early distributions? ... **1-37**

Q 1:48 Are dividends paid from an ESOP subject to spousal consent if the dividend exceeds $5,000? **1-37**

Q 1:49 Are dividends paid from an ESOP subject to mandatory withholding? **1-38**

Chapter 2 Loans

General Rule: Loans from Qualified Employer Plans Treated as Taxable Distributions

Q 2:1 What are some of the most significant plan loan rules? **2-1**

Q 2:2 What is a qualified employer plan for purposes of Code Section 72show $132#?>(p)? **2-4**

Q 2:3 If a loan from a qualified employer plan to a participant or beneficiary fails to meet the requirements of Code Section 72(p), when does a deemed distribution occur? **2-5**

Q 2:4 What limits does the Code impose on the amount of a plan loan? 2-7
Q 2:5 What restrictions does the Code impose on the term of a plan loan? 2-8
Q 2:6 What restrictions does the Code impose on plan loan repayments (amortization)? 2-9
Q 2:7 If a participant fails to make the installment payments required under the terms of a loan that satisfied all the plan loan rules when it was made, when does a deemed distribution occur, and what is the amount of the deemed distribution? 2-9
Q 2:8 Does the level amortization requirement apply when a participant is on a leave of absence without pay? 2-11
Q 2:9 Can a plan loan be accelerated if the participant terminates employment before the loan is fully repaid? 2-13
Q 2:10 Can a participant carry an outstanding loan balance even after he or she terminates employment? 2-13

Treatment of Distributions Attributable to Qualified Retirement Plan Loans

Q 2:11 Can a loan to a participant from a qualified retirement plan be taxed as a distribution? 2-13
Q 2:12 When is a distribution attributable to a plan loan an eligible rollover distribution? 2-17
Q 2:13 What is the federal income tax treatment of deemed distributions? 2-17
Q 2:14 How is the amount includible in income as a result of a deemed distribution under Code Section 72(p) required to be reported? 2-18
Q 2:15 If there is a deemed distribution under Code Section 72(p), is the interest that accrues thereafter on the amount of the deemed distribution an indirect loan for income tax purposes? 2-18
Q 2:16 Is a participant's tax basis under the plan increased if the participant repays the loan after a deemed distribution? 2-19
Q 2:17 What withholding rules apply to plan loans? 2-19
Q 2:18 May a plan loan note be transferred from one qualified plan to another when there is a transfer of assets and liabilities between plans? 2-20
Q 2:19 May a plan loan note be included in a direct rollover of an eligible rollover distribution from one qualified plan to another? 2-20
Q 2:20 What are the income tax consequences if an amount is transferred from a qualified employer plan to a participant or a beneficiary as a loan, but there is an express or tacit understanding that the loan will not be repaid? 2-21

Q 2:21 If a loan fails to satisfy the plan loan rules under Code Section 72(p) and is a prohibited transaction under Code Section 4975, is the deemed distribution of the loan under Code Section 72(p) a correction of the prohibited transaction? 2-21

Q 2:22 If a qualified employer plan maintains a program to invest in residential mortgages, are loans made pursuant to that program subject to the plan loan rules under Code Section 72(p)? 2-21

Q 2:23 May a participant refinance an outstanding loan or have more than one loan outstanding from a plan? 2-22

Q 2:24 When did Code Section 72(p) and the related final Treasury regulations become effective? 2-25

Special Loan Rules for Certain Disaster Victims

Q 2:25 Can the IRS apply special loan rules to provide relief to taxpayers who have been adversely affected by disasters? 2-29

Q 2:26 Were there any special plan loan rules that applied to taxpayers who suffered economic losses in 2005 as a result of Hurricane Katrina, Rita, or Wilma? 2-29

Q 2:27 Were there any special plan loan rules for taxpayers who were adversely affected by Hurricane Sandy in 2012 and 2013? ... 2-30

Q 2:28 Were there any special plan loan rules for taxpayers who were adversely affected by the Louisiana storms in 2016 and 2017? ... 2-31

Q 2:29 Were there any special plan loan rules for taxpayers who were adversely affected by Hurricane Matthew in 2016 or 2017? ... 2-32

Q 2:30 Were there any special plan loan rules that applied to taxpayers who were adversely affected by Hurricane Harvey in 2017 and 2018? ... 2-33

Q 2:31 Were there any special plan loan rules that applied to taxpayers who were adversely affected by Hurricane Irma in 2017 and 2018? ... 2-34

Q 2:32 Were there any special plan loan rules that applied to taxpayers who were adversely affected by Hurricane Maria or the California Wildfires in 2017 and 2018? 2-35

Q 2:33 Were there any special plan loan rules in the Disaster Tax Relief and Airport and Airway Extension Act of 2017 for taxpayers who were adversely affected by Hurricane Harvey, Hurricane Irma, or Hurricane Maria? 2-36

Loans as Prohibited Transactions

Q 2:34 What are the prohibited transaction rules under the Code that apply to loans from tax-qualified retirement plans? 2-37

Q 2:35 What are the prohibited transaction rules under ERISA that apply to plan loans from ERISA plans? 2-39

Q 2:36 What relief does ERISA Section 408(b)(1) provide from ERISA's prohibited transaction provisions? 2-40

Q 2:37 What is a participant loan for purposes of ERISA's prohibited transaction rules? 2-40

Q 2:38 When are plan loans considered to be available to participants and beneficiaries on a reasonably equivalent basis? 2-43
Q 2:39 When will plan loans not be considered disproportionately available to highly compensated employees, officers, or shareholders? 2-44
Q 2:40 Will a plan administrator's decision to disallow a participant loan based on a reasonable question concerning the legality of the loan be considered a failure to provide loans to all participants on a reasonably equivalent basis? 2-45
Q 2:41 Must a plan contain specific provisions if it has a loan program? ... 2-46
Q 2:42 When is a plan loan considered to bear a reasonable rate of interest? 2-46
Q 2:43 When is a plan loan considered to be adequately secured? ... 2-48
Q 2:44 When do participant loan repayments that are withheld from employee wages by an employer become "plan assets" subject to the prohibited transaction rules under ERISA Section 406? ... 2-48

Spousal Consent for Loans Made by Plans Subject to the Survivor Annuity Requirements

Q 2:45 Must spousal consent be obtained before a loan can be made from a plan that is subject to the survivor annuity requirements? 2-49
Q 2:46 If spousal consent is obtained (or is not required) when the plan loan is made, must it be given when the unpaid loan balance is offset against the participant's accrued benefit in the event of a default? ... 2-49
Q 2:47 If an existing plan loan is renegotiated, extended, renewed, or otherwise revised after it is made, is the renegotiation of the loan treated as the making of a new loan under the spousal consent requirements? 2-49
Q 2:48 If a plan loan is outstanding when a participant dies and the loan is secured by the participant's accrued benefit under the plan, will that affect the amount of the qualified preretirement survivor annuity (QPSA) or the survivor annuity portion of the qualified joint and survivor annuity (QJSA) that is payable on account of his or her death? 2-50

Federal Truth in Lending Act

Q 2:49 Do the federal Truth in Lending Act (TILA) and Regulation Z apply to participant loans from employer retirement plans? 2-50

Chapter 3 QDROs and Other Exceptions to the Anti-Alienation Rules

General Rules and Definitions

Q 3:1 Do the ERISA and Code rules prohibiting the assignment or alienation of a participant's benefits under a qualified retirement plan apply to QDROs? 3-2

Q 3:2 What is a DRO? ... 3-3
Q 3:3 May a QDRO be part of a divorce decree or property settlement? ... 3-3
Q 3:4 Must a DRO be issued as part of a divorce proceeding to be a QDRO? ... 3-4
Q 3:5 What is a QDRO? ... 3-4
Q 3:6 Who can be an "alternate payee"? ... 3-5
Q 3:7 May a QDRO provide for payment to the guardian of an alternate payee? ... 3-5
Q 3:8 Will a DRO fail to be a QDRO if it requires that benefits in pay status be paid to a state agency as the agent of the alternate payee? ... 3-6
Q 3:9 Can a QDRO cover more than one retirement plan? ... 3-6
Q 3:10 Will a DRO fail to be a QDRO if it does not specify the participant's or alternate payee's last known mailing address, if the plan administrator has reason to know the addresses independently of the order? ... 3-6
Q 3:11 Must all QDROs have the same provisions? ... 3-6
Q 3:12 Who determines whether an order is a QDRO? ... 3-7
Q 3:13 Who is the administrator of the retirement plan? ... 3-7
Q 3:14 Will the DOL issue advisory opinions on whether a DRO is a QDRO? ... 3-8
Q 3:15 What is the best way to divide a participant's retirement plan benefits in a QDRO? ... 3-8
Q 3:16 How much of a participant's retirement plan benefits may be provided to an alternate payee under a QDRO? ... 3-8
Q 3:17 Why are the reasons for dividing the participant's retirement plan benefits important? ... 3-8
Q 3:18 In deciding how to divide a participant's retirement plan benefits, why is understanding the type of retirement plan important? ... 3-10
Q 3:19 What are survivor benefits and why should a QDRO take them into account? ... 3-10
Q 3:20 May a QDRO specify the form in which the alternate payee's benefits will be paid? ... 3-12
Q 3:21 When may the alternate payee receive the benefits assigned under a QDRO? ... 3-13
Q 3:22 Will a DRO fail to be a QDRO solely because the DRO is issued after, or revises, another DRO or QDRO, or solely because of the time at which it is issued? ... 3-13

Form or Amount of Benefits May Not Be Altered

Q 3:23 Will a DRO be a QDRO if it alters the amount or form of benefits otherwise provided to the participant under a retirement plan? ... 3-16

Q 3:24 Are there circumstances where a QDRO may alter the payment of retirement plan benefits? 3-16
Q 3:25 What is the earliest retirement age for purposes of the rule that allows a QDRO, in certain limited circumstances, to change the timing of benefit payments under a plan? 3-17
Q 3:26 Can a QDRO require a participant's former spouse to be treated as his or her surviving spouse for purposes of determining survivor benefits under a retirement plan? 3-19

How QDROs Affect Other Retirement Plan Benefits; Section 415 Requirements

Q 3:27 Is a retirement plan required to provide additional vesting or benefits because of a QDRO? 3-20
Q 3:28 May a QDRO provide the alternate payee with a right to designate a beneficiary that is greater than the participant's? 3-20
Q 3:29 To whom is the participant's retirement plan benefit paid if the former spouse, who is treated as the current spouse under a QDRO, dies before the participant's annuity starting date? 3-21
Q 3:30 How are the annual limitations on contributions and benefits applied in cases where a participant's retirement plan benefits are awarded to an alternate payee under a QDRO? 3-21

Alternate Payee's Retirement Plan Benefits Must Be Clearly Specified

Q 3:31 Must a QDRO clearly specify the amount or percentage (or the manner of determining the amount or percentage) of a participant's benefit under a retirement plan that is to be paid to each alternate payee named in the QDRO? 3-21
Q 3:32 How is the amount available to an alternate payee under a defined contribution plan determined? 3-21
Q 3:33 How is the amount available to an alternate payee under a defined benefit plan determined? 3-23
Q 3:34 Can a DRO that changes a prior assignment of retirement plan benefits to an alternate payee reduce the amount assigned to the alternate payee and still be a QDRO? 3-24

QDROs Must Specify the Benefit Period and the Retirement Plan

Q 3:35 Must a QDRO clearly specify the number of payments or the period to which the order applies? 3-24
Q 3:36 Must a QDRO clearly specify each retirement plan to which the order applies? 3-24

Q 3:37 Will a DRO be a QDRO if it directs that retirement plan benefits must be paid to an alternate payee when those benefits have already been determined to be payable to another alternate payee under a prior QDRO? 3-25

Retirement Plan Provisions and Written Procedures for Determining the Qualified Status of a DRO

Q 3:38 Must a retirement plan document be amended to implement the QDRO rules? 3-25

Q 3:39 Must a retirement plan establish reasonable, written procedures to determine the qualified status of DROs and to administer distributions under DROs that are determined to be QDROs? 3-25

Q 3:40 Are there other matters that should be addressed in a retirement plan's written QDRO procedure? 3-26

Q 3:41 What information is a plan administrator required to provide a prospective alternate payee before the administrator receives a DRO? 3-26

Q 3:42 May a plan administrator allocate QDRO determination expenses to the retirement plan account of the participant or beneficiary seeking the determination? 3-27

Q 3:43 May a plan administrator provide parties with a model form or forms to assist in the preparation of a QDRO? 3-27

Q 3:44 In determining the qualified status of a DRO, is the plan administrator required to determine the validity of the order under state domestic relations law? 3-28

Q 3:45 Is a plan administrator required to reject a DRO as defective if the order fails to specify factual identifying information that is easily obtainable by the plan administrator? 3-28

Procedures to Follow After a Retirement Plan Receives a DRO

Q 3:46 What must the plan administrator do if a DRO is received? 3-28

Q 3:47 How long may the plan administrator take to determine whether a DRO is a QDRO? 3-29

Q 3:48 What must the plan administrator do during the determination process to protect against wrongly paying retirement benefits to the participant that would be paid to the alternate payee if the DRO had been determined to be a QDRO? 3-29

Q 3:49 What kind of notice must a plan administrator provide following a QDRO determination? 3-31

Q 3:50 What effect does an order that a plan administrator has determined to be a QDRO have on the administration of the retirement plan? 3-32

Q 3:51 What disclosure rights does an alternate payee have under a QDRO? 3-32

Q 3:52 What happens to the rights created by a QDRO if the retirement plan to which the QDRO applies is amended, merged into another plan, or is maintained by a successor employer? 3-33

Q 3:53 What happens to the rights created by a QDRO if a retirement plan is terminated? 3-33

Q 3:54 What happens to the rights created by a QDRO if a defined benefit plan is terminated and the Pension Benefit Guaranty Corporation (PBGC) becomes trustee of the plan? 3-33

Taxation of Retirement Plan Distributions Made Under QDROs

Q 3:55 Are distributions of retirement plan benefits that are paid to a participant's spouse or former spouse who is an alternate payee under a QDRO includible in the spouse's or former spouse's income? 3-34

Q 3:56 Are distributions of retirement plan benefits that are paid to a nonspouse alternate payee under a QDRO includible in his or her income? 3-35

Q 3:57 How is the investment in the contract (if any) under a retirement plan allocated between the participant and his or her spouse or former spouse who is an alternate payee under a QDRO? 3-35

Q 3:58 How is the investment in the contract (if any) allocated between the participant and any nonspouse alternate payee under a QDRO? 3-36

Q 3:59 Will the participant be liable to pay the 10 percent additional income tax on any early distributions paid to an alternate payee under a QDRO? 3-36

Q 3:60 May a spouse or former spouse alternate payee make a tax-free rollover to an eligible retirement plan of part or all of an eligible retirement distribution that is paid pursuant to a QDRO? 3-37

Q 3:61 Is a spouse or former spouse who is an alternate payee under a QDRO eligible for income-averaging treatment for any lump-sum distributions under a QDRO? 3-37

Official Guidance on Drafting, Reviewing, and Administering QDROs

Q 3:62 Is there any official guidance from the federal government on how to draft, review, and administer a QDRO? 3-38

Permitted Offsets of Retirement Plan Benefits

Q 3:63 Are there other circumstances, in addition to QDROs, in which a participant's retirement plan benefits may be assigned or alienated, despite ERISA and the Code's anti-alienation rules? 3-40

Chapter4 Required Minimum Distributions

Waiver of 2009 Required Minimum Distributions

Q 4:1 Were RMDs waived for 2009 for certain plans? **4-3**

Minimum Distribution Requirement in General

Q 4:2 What retirement plans are subject to the RMD rules? **4-5**

Q 4:3 Which employee account balances and benefits held under a Section 401(a) qualified retirement plan are subject to the RMD rules? **4-5**

Q 4:4 What specific provisions must a qualified retirement plan document contain in order to satisfy the RMD rules? **4-6**

Distributions Beginning During a Participant's Lifetime

Q 4:5 In the case of distributions beginning during a participant's lifetime, how must the participant's entire interest be distributed in order to satisfy Code Section 401(a)(9)(A)? **4-7**

Q 4:6 What does the term *RBD* mean? **4-7**

Q 4:7 When does a participant attain age 70½? **4-8**

Q 4:8 Must distributions be made before a participant's RBD satisfy the RMD rules? **4-8**

Q 4:9 If distributions have begun to a participant during the participant's lifetime in accordance with the life or life expectancy method of Code Section 401(a)(9)(A)(ii), how must distributions be made after the participant's death? **4-9**

Q 4:10 For purposes of Code Section 401(a)(9)(B), when are distributions considered to have begun to a participant in accordance with the life or life expectancy method of Code Section 401(a)(9)(A)(ii)? ... **4-9**

Death Before Required Beginning Date

Q 4:11 If a participant dies before his or her RBD, how must the participant's entire interest be distributed in order to satisfy the RMD rules of Code Section 401(a)(9)? **4-10**

Q 4:12 What is the last date for distributing a participant's entire interest in order to satisfy the five-year rule? **4-11**

Q 4:13 When must distributions begin in order to satisfy the life expectancy rule? **4-11**

Q 4:14 How is it determined whether the five-year rule or the life expectancy rule applies to a distribution? **4-11**

Q 4:15 If a participant's surviving spouse is the participant's sole designated beneficiary and the spouse dies after the participant, but before distributions have begun, how is the participant's interest to be distributed? **4-12**

Q 4:16 For these purposes, when are distributions considered to have begun to the surviving spouse? 4-12

Determination of the Designated Beneficiary

Q 4:17 Who is a designated beneficiary? 4-13
Q 4:18 Must a participant (or the participant's spouse) make an affirmative election specifying a person to be a designated beneficiary for purposes of the RMD rules? 4-13
Q 4:19 May a person other than an individual be a designated beneficiary for purposes of the RMD rules? 4-13
Q 4:20 When is the designated beneficiary determined? 4-14
Q 4:21 If a trust is named as a beneficiary of a participant, are there any circumstances that would permit the beneficiaries of the trust to be treated as the participant's designated beneficiaries for purposes of the RMD rules? 4-15
Q 4:22 When a trust is named as a beneficiary of a participant, what documentation must be provided to the plan administrator? 4-15

Required Minimum Distributions from Defined Contribution Plans

Q 4:23 If a participant's benefit is in the form of an individual account under a defined contribution plan, what is the amount required to be distributed for each calendar year? 4-17
Q 4:24 How may an annuity contract be used to satisfy the minimum distribution requirement for an individual account under a defined contribution plan? 4-18
Q 4:25 If a participant's benefit is in the form of an individual account and, in any calendar year, the amount distributed exceeds the RMD, will credit be given in subsequent calendar years for such excess distribution? 4-18
Q 4:26 What amount is used for determining a participant's RMD in the case of an individual account? 4-18
Q 4:27 What is a QLAC? 4-19
Q 4:28 What is the applicable distribution period for RMDs during a participant's lifetime? 4-22
Q 4:29 What is the applicable distribution period for RMDs after a participant's death? 4-25
Q 4:30 What life expectancies must be used for purposes of determining RMDs under Code Section 401(a)(9)? 4-26
Q 4:31 If a participant has more than one designated beneficiary, which designated beneficiary's life expectancy will be used to determine the applicable distribution period? 4-26
Q 4:32 If a portion of a participant's individual account is not vested as of the participant's RBD, how is the determination of the RMD affected? 4-29

Q 4:33 Which amounts distributed from an individual account are or are not taken into account in determining whether the RMD rules of Code Section 401(a)(9) are satisfied? 4-29

Required Minimum Distributions from Defined Benefit Plans and Annuity Contracts

Q 4:34 How must distributions under a defined benefit plan be paid in order to satisfy the RMD rules? 4-30

Q 4:35 How must distributions in the form of a life (or joint and survivor) annuity be made in order to satisfy the MDIB requirement and the distribution component of the incidental benefit requirement? 4-33

Q 4:36 How long is a period certain under a defined benefit plan permitted to extend? 4-35

Q 4:37 Will a plan fail to satisfy the RMD rules merely because distributions are made from an annuity contract purchased from an insurance company? 4-36

Q 4:38 In the case of annuity distributions under a defined benefit plan, how must additional benefits that accrue after the participant's first distribution calendar year be distributed in order to satisfy the RMD rules? 4-36

Q 4:39 If a portion of a participant's benefit is not vested as of December 31 of a distribution calendar year, how is the determination of the RMD affected? 4-37

Q 4:40 If a participant (other than a 5-percent owner) retires after the calendar year in which the participant attains age 70½, for what period must the participant's accrued benefit under a defined benefit plan be actuarially increased? 4-37

Q 4:41 What amount of actuarial increase is required? 4-38

Q 4:42 How does the actuarial increase required under Code Section 401(a)(9)(C)(iii) relate to the actuarial increase required under Code Section 411? 4-38

Q 4:43 What rule applies if distributions to a participant start on a date before the participant's RBD over a period permitted under the life or life expectancy method of Code Section 401(a)(9)(A)(ii) and the distribution form is an annuity? 4-39

Q 4:44 What rule applies if distributions start to the surviving spouse of a participant over a period permitted under Code Section 401(a)(9)(B)(iii)(II) before the date on which distributions are required to start and the distribution form is an annuity? ... 4-39

Q 4:45 In the case of an annuity contract under an individual account plan that has not yet been annuitized, how is Code Section 401(a)(9) satisfied with respect to the participant's or beneficiary's entire interest under the annuity contract for the period prior to the date annuity payments begin? 4-39

Q 4:46 When can an annuity payment period be changed? 4-40

Q 4:47 Are annuity payments permitted to increase? 4-44

Q 4:48 Are there special rules applicable to payments made under a defined benefit plan or annuity contract to a surviving child? ... **4-52**

Q 4:49 Will a governmental plan fail to satisfy the RMD rules if annuity payments under the plan do not satisfy Treasury Regulations Section 1.401(a)(9)-6? **4-52**

Q 4:50 What were the rules for determining RMDs for defined benefit plans and annuity contracts for calendar years 2003, 2004, and 2005? **4-53**

Rollovers and Transfers

Q 4:51 If an amount is distributed by one plan and rolled over to another plan, is the RMD under the distributing plan affected by the rollover? **4-53**

Q 4:52 If an amount is distributed by one plan and rolled over to another plan, how are the benefit and the RMD under the receiving plan affected? **4-53**

Q 4:53 What special rules apply for satisfying the RMD requirement or determining the participant's benefit under the transferor plan? **4-53**

Q 4:54 If a participant's benefit is transferred from one plan to another plan, how are the benefit and the RMD under the transferee plan affected? **4-54**

Q 4:55 How is a spinoff, merger, or consolidation treated for purposes of determining a participant's benefit and RMD? **4-54**

Special Rules

Q 4:56 What distribution rules apply if an individual is a participant in more than one plan? **4-55**

Q 4:57 If a participant's benefit under a defined contribution plan is divided into separate accounts (or segregated shares in the case of a defined benefit plan), do the distribution rules of Code Section 401(a)(9) apply separately to each separate account (or segregated share)? **4-55**

Q 4:58 What are separate accounts for purposes of Code Section 401(a)(9)? **4-55**

Q 4:59 Can required distributions be made even if a participant or spouse has not consented to a distribution? **4-56**

Q 4:60 Who is considered to be a participant's spouse or surviving spouse? **4-56**

Q 4:61 What special rules apply to the distribution of all or a portion of a participant's benefit payable to an alternate payee pursuant to a QDRO? **4-56**

Q 4:62 Will a plan fail to satisfy Code Section 401(a)(9) merely because it fails to distribute an amount otherwise required to be distributed during the period in which the issue of whether a domestic relations order is a QDRO is being determined? **4-58**

Q 4:63 Will a plan fail to satisfy the Code if an individual's distribution is less than the amount otherwise required because distributions are being paid under an annuity contract issued by a life insurance company in state insurer delinquency proceedings and have been reduced or suspended because of those proceedings? 4-58

Q 4:64 Will a plan fail to qualify as a pension plan solely because it permits distributions to begin on or after April 1 of the calendar year following the calendar year in which the participant attains age 70½ even though the participant has not retired or attained the normal retirement age under the plan as of that date? 4-59

Q 4:65 Is the distribution of an annuity contract a distribution for purposes of Code Section 401(a)(9)? 4-59

Q 4:66 Will a payment by a plan after the participant's death fail to be treated as a distribution because it is made to an estate or a trust? 4-59

Q 4:67 Will a plan fail to satisfy the Code if it is amended to eliminate benefit options that do not satisfy Code Section 401(a)(9)? ... 4-59

Q 4:68 Will a plan be disqualified merely because it pays benefits under a designation made before January 1, 1984, in accordance with TEFRA Section 242(b)(2)? 4-60

Q 4:69 When an amount is transferred from one plan to another plan, may the transferee plan distribute the amount transferred in accordance with a TEFRA Section 242(b)(2) election made under either plan? 4-60

Q 4:70 If an amount is distributed by one plan and rolled over into another plan, may the receiving plan distribute the amount rolled over in accordance with a TEFRA Section 242(b)(2) election? 4-61

Q 4:71 May a TEFRA Section 242(b)(2) election be revoked after the date by which distributions are required to begin? 4-61

IRS Field Directive to Employee Plans (EP) Examiners

Q 4:72 Has the IRS issued a field directive to EP examinations employees directing them not to challenge a qualified plan as failing to satisfy RMD standards if the plan has taken all of the steps listed in the field directive to pay RMDs to missing participants and beneficiaries? 4-61

Chapter 5 Corrective Distributions

Excess Contributions

Q 5:1 What are excess contributions? 5-1

Q 5:2 What are the permissible methods for correcting excess contributions? 5-2

Q 5:3 How may a combination of the permissible correction methods be employed? ... 5-2
Q 5:4 What correction methods are not permitted? ... 5-2
Q 5:5 What happens if excess distributions are not fully corrected? ... 5-2
Q 5:6 How are total excess contributions determined for a plan year? ... 5-3
Q 5:7 What excess contributions are returned to each HCE? ... 5-5
Q 5:8 Under what circumstances may excess contributions be recharacterized? ... 5-5
Q 5:9 How is the corrective distribution of excess contributions accomplished? ... 5-6
Q 5:10 How are the gains or losses allocable to excess contributions determined? ... 5-7
Q 5:11 Must gains or losses allocable to the year of the distribution be included? ... 5-7
Q 5:12 Must employee or spousal consent be obtained by the plan sponsor? ... 5-8
Q 5:13 Are corrective distributions treated as employer contributions? ... 5-8
Q 5:14 What is the tax treatment to the HCE of corrective distributions of excess contributions? ... 5-8
Q 5:15 What happens if excess contributions are not corrected on a timely basis? ... 5-8

Excess Aggregate Contributions

Q 5:16 What is an excess aggregate contribution? ... 5-9
Q 5:17 What are the permissible methods for correcting excess aggregate contributions? ... 5-9
Q 5:18 How may a combination of the correction methods be used in correcting excess aggregate contributions? ... 5-10
Q 5:19 What correction methods are not permitted? ... 5-10
Q 5:20 What happens if an excess aggregate contribution is not fully corrected? ... 5-10
Q 5:21 What is the amount of total excess aggregate contributions for HCEs? ... 5-10
Q 5:22 How are excess contributions coordinated with excess aggregate contributions? ... 5-11
Q 5:23 How are corrective distributions of excess aggregate contributions for each HCE determined? ... 5-12
Q 5:24 How is the corrective distribution of excess aggregate contributions accomplished? ... 5-13
Q 5:25 How is the gain or loss allocable to excess aggregate contributions determined? ... 5-13
Q 5:26 Must gains or losses allocable to the year of the distribution be included? ... 5-14

Q 5:27 Is employee or spousal consent required for the distribution of excess aggregate contributions? 5-14
Q 5:28 Are corrective distributions and forfeited contributions treated as employer contributions? 5-14
Q 5:29 What is the tax treatment to the HCE of corrective distributions of excess aggregate contributions? 5-15
Q 5:30 What happens if excess aggregate contributions are not corrected on a timely basis? 5-15

Excess Elective Contributions

Q 5:31 What are elective contributions for purposes of the annual limitation on elective contributions under Code Section 402(g)? 5-16
Q 5:32 What is the annual dollar limitation on an individual's elective contributions for any tax year? 5-17
Q 5:33 What is an excess elective contribution? 5-18
Q 5:34 How are excess elective contributions treated under a qualified plan? 5-18
Q 5:35 Are excess elective contributions treated as employer contributions? 5-18
Q 5:36 May excess elective contributions be distributed after the close of an individual's tax year? 5-19
Q 5:37 May excess elective contributions be distributed during the individual's tax year? 5-19
Q 5:38 Must the plan provide for the distribution of excess elective contributions? 5-20
Q 5:39 How are the gains or losses allocable to excess elective contributions determined? 5-20
Q 5:40 Must gap period gains or losses be allocated to excess elective contributions? 5-20
Q 5:41 How are excess elective contributions coordinated with the distribution or recharacterization of elective contributions? 5-21
Q 5:42 Must the plan sponsor obtain employee or spousal consent in order to distribute excess elective contributions? 5-21
Q 5:43 What is the federal income tax treatment of excess elective contributions made on or before April 15 following the close of the calendar year? 5-21
Q 5:44 What is the federal income tax treatment of excess elective contributions made after April 15 following the close of the calendar year? 5-21
Q 5:45 Does a corrective distribution of excess elective contributions reduce the required minimum distribution under Code Section 401(a)(9)? 5-22
Q 5:46 What happens if a distribution of excess elective contributions is only partially corrected? 5-22

Excess Annual Additions

Q 5:47 What is an excess annual addition, and how can it be corrected? 5-24

Q 5:48 How are excess annual additions treated for limitation years beginning on or after January 1, 2009? 5-24

Chapter 6 Taxable Life Insurance Costs

Calculation of Taxable Insurance Costs

Q 6:1 When is life insurance protection in a qualified plan subject to current taxation? 6-2

Q 6:2 Are self-employed individuals treated differently? 6-2

Q 6:3 How is the annual cost of life insurance computed? 6-2

Q 6:4 What table is available from the IRS to use in determining the taxable value of current life insurance protection? 6-2

Q 6:5 May rates other than those in the tables above be used in determining the taxable amount of insurance? 6-6

Q 6:6 What age should be used in determining the annual cost of life insurance? 6-7

Q 6:7 What happens if the life insurance is in force for less than a full year due to a termination of employment? 6-7

Q 6:8 How is the cost of life insurance computed for new life insurance contracts issued during the year? 6-7

Q 6:9 What happens if the cash value in the life insurance contract exceeds the face amount? 6-8

Q 6:10 How is the cost of life insurance computed under a universal life insurance contract? 6-8

Q 6:11 How is the annual cost of life insurance reported? 6-8

Q 6:12 How is the annual cost of life insurance computed for survivor whole life contracts? 6-8

Chapter 7 Bankruptcy

Bankruptcy

Q 7:1 How did the federal Bankruptcy Abuse Prevention and Consumer Protection Act of 2005 (BAPCPA) expand the protection for tax-favored retirement plans from creditors in bankruptcy proceedings? 7-1

Q 7:2 How did BAPCPA change the automatic stay provisions of the federal Bankruptcy Code? 7-2

Q 7:3 Under BAPCPA, can plan loans be discharged in bankruptcy? 7-2

Q 7:4 May a Chapter 13 plan materially alter the provisions of a debtor's retirement plan loan? 7-2
Q 7:5 Did BAPCPA impose a cap on the amount of traditional or Roth IRA assets that can be exempted from the debtor's bankruptcy estate? 7-3

Chapter 8 Vesting

General Vesting Rules

Q 8:1 What are the basic vesting rules under ERISA and the Code? 8-2
Q 8:2 What plans are subject to the minimum vesting standards? 8-2
Q 8:3 How are the minimum vesting rules applied? 8-3
Q 8:4 When must benefits be 100 percent vested and nonforfeitable? 8-3
Q 8:5 In determining 100 percent vesting, when does a participant reach the plan's normal retirement age? 8-3
Q 8:6 What types of contribution accounts must be 100 percent vested and nonforfeitable? 8-3
Q 8:7 How is the employee-derived accrued benefit determined in a defined benefit plan with mandatory employee contributions? 8-4
Q 8:8 What are the minimum vesting requirements for employer-derived account balances and accrued benefits? 8-4
Q 8:9 What accelerated vesting schedules applied to matching contributions? 8-5

PPA Changes Effective for Post-2006 Plan Years

Q 8:10 How did PPA change the rules for vesting under defined contribution plans? 8-6
Q 8:11 Is there a delayed effective date for collectively bargained plans? 8-6
Q 8:12 What are the vesting requirements for a qualified automatic contribution arrangement (QACA)? 8-6
Q 8:13 What are the current rules for vesting under cash balance plans? 8-6
Q 8:14 What vesting schedules apply if a portion of a participant's benefit is determined under a traditional defined benefit formula and another portion is determined under a cash balance formula? 8-7
Q 8:15 How are the minimum vesting requirements coordinated with the nondiscrimination requirements of Code Section 401(a)(4)? 8-7
Q 8:16 May vested benefits be forfeited for cause? 8-8

Top-Heavy Rules

Q 8:17 What are the minimum vesting standards for top-heavy plans? 8-8
Q 8:18 What is a top-heavy plan? 8-9

Q 8:19 What is the determination date? 8-9
Q 8:20 What if the employer maintains more than one plan? 8-9
Q 8:21 May other plans of the employer be aggregated and tested together for top-heavy purposes? 8-9
Q 8:22 In the case of an aggregation group where plans have different plan years, when must the determination of top-heavy status be made? 8-10

Determination of Top-Heavy Status

Q 8:23 How is the value of account balances determined in a defined contribution plan? 8-11
Q 8:24 How is the present value of accrued benefits determined in a defined benefit plan? 8-11
Q 8:25 What actuarial assumptions are used in computing the present value of accrued benefits in a defined benefit plan? 8-11
Q 8:26 What distributions are taken into account in determining the value of account balances and the present value of accrued benefits? 8-12
Q 8:27 Is the value of account balances and/or present value of the accrued benefits for any participant disregarded in determining top-heavy status? 8-12

Death Benefits, Rollovers, and Plan-to-Plan Transfers

Q 8:28 How are benefits paid on account of death treated? 8-12
Q 8:29 How are rollovers and plan-to-plan transfers treated? 8-13

Key Employees

Q 8:30 Who is a key employee? 8-13
Q 8:31 Who is a 5 percent owner of the employer? 8-13
Q 8:32 Who is a 1 percent owner of the employer? 8-14
Q 8:33 Who is an includible officer? 8-14
Q 8:34 What activities cause an individual to be treated as an officer? 8-15
Q 8:35 Are there limits on the number of officers included? 8-15

Top-Heavy Vesting Schedules

Q 8:36 When must the top-heavy vesting schedules be applied? 8-16
Q 8:37 What happens when a plan ceases to be top heavy? 8-16

Determination of Years of Vesting Service

Q 8:38 How is a year of service for vesting defined? 8-16
Q 8:39 May the vesting computation period be changed? 8-17
Q 8:40 How is an hour of service for vesting defined? 8-17

Q 8:41 Are there any simpler methods for determining years of vesting service? 8-18
Q 8:42 Are there any other alternatives for alleviating the record-keeping requirements? 8-18
Q 8:43 Are other equivalency methods available? 8-18
Q 8:44 May equivalencies be based on periods of employment? 8-19
Q 8:45 May different service-crediting methods be used for different classifications of employees? 8-19
Q 8:46 Must all years of service be taken into account in determining a participant's vested percentage? 8-20
Q 8:47 How are years of service before age 18 disregarded? 8-20
Q 8:48 What years are disregarded under a plan requiring mandatory employee contributions? 8-20
Q 8:49 How are years determined before a plan was maintained? 8-20
Q 8:50 What is a predecessor plan? 8-21

Breaks in Service

Q 8:51 How is vesting service determined if an employee leaves employment and then returns to work? 8-21
Q 8:52 How is a one-year break in service defined? 8-21
Q 8:53 What break-in-service rules apply in determining an employee's years of vesting service? 8-21
Q 8:54 Do maternity or paternity absences affect the determination of a one-year break in service? 8-22

Amendments in Vesting Schedules

Q 8:55 May a plan amendment reduce the vested percentage of a participant? 8-23
Q 8:56 May a plan amendment change the rate of future vesting? 8-23
Q 8:57 What is a reasonable vesting schedule election period described in Q 8:56? 8-23
Q 8:58 How do the Final Regulations under Code Section 411(d)(6) change the rules regarding the amendment of vesting schedules? 8-23

Forfeitures and Cash-Out Rules

Q 8:59 What happens with the nonvested portion of the account balance or accrued benefit? 8-24
Q 8:60 How are forfeitures treated? 8-25
Q 8:61 How are forfeitures used to increase benefits in a defined contribution plan? 8-25
Q 8:62 What are the cash-out rules? 8-26
Q 8:63 May a cash-out occur if a participant has no vested account balance or accrued benefit? 8-27

Q 8:64 How do the plan repayment provisions operate? **8-27**

Q 8:65 What interest rate is charged on amounts repaid to a defined benefit plan? **8-28**

Q 8:66 What interest rate is charged on amounts repaid to a defined contribution plan? **8-28**

Q 8:67 What sources of restoration are available to the employer in a defined contribution plan if an employee chooses to repay his or her distribution under the cash-out/repayment rules? **8-28**

Q 8:68 How are forfeitures handled in a defined contribution plan that does not contain the cash-out rules described above? **8-28**

Required Vesting upon Plan Termination, Partial Termination, or Complete Discontinuance of Contributions

Q 8:69 What vesting rules apply if a plan terminates or partially terminates or if employer contributions are completely discontinued? **8-30**

Q 8:70 When is a plan considered terminated? **8-30**

Q 8:71 Can a plan termination be reversed? **8-31**

Q 8:72 When is a plan considered partially terminated? **8-32**

Q 8:73 Do the minimum vesting standards of Title I of ERISA require 100 percent vesting when a partial termination occurs? **8-33**

Q 8:74 What is the purpose of the partial termination rule? **8-33**

Q 8:75 Does the Code or the Treasury regulations define partial termination to mean a significant reduction in the number of plan participants? ... **8-33**

Q 8:76 Despite the lack of a precise definition of partial termination, is the percentage of plan participants who separate from service a significant factor in determining whether a partial termination has indeed occurred? **8-34**

Q 8:77 What facts and circumstances have been relevant to the courts and the IRS in determining whether a partial termination has occurred? ... **8-35**

Q 8:78 How is the percentage reduction in plan participation calculated so that a determination may be made as to whether a partial termination has occurred? **8-37**

Q 8:79 How is the vested account balance or benefit of a participant who is affected by a partial termination determined? **8-39**

Q 8:80 Can a partial termination of a plan be triggered by an event other than a significant reduction in the percentage of plan participants? ... **8-40**

Q 8:81 May the sponsor of a qualified plan seek a determination from the IRS on whether a partial termination has occurred with respect to the plan? **8-41**

Q 8:82 When is a plan curtailed? **8-41**

Q 8:83 When does a complete discontinuance of plan contributions occur? **8-41**

Chapter 9 Administrative Determination of Benefits

Determining Account Balances in Defined Contribution Plans

Q 9:1 How is the accrued benefit in a defined contribution plan defined? ... 9-1
Q 9:2 What types of account balances are subject to immediate 100 percent vesting? ... 9-2
Q 9:3 How frequently are account balances updated in a defined contribution plan? ... 9-2
Q 9:4 If account balances are not valued daily, what adjustments may be made between valuation dates? ... 9-3
Q 9:5 What happens if the value of the underlying investments in the plan changes rapidly between valuation dates? ... 9-3
Q 9:6 How do outstanding participant loans affect the account balance in a defined contribution plan? ... 9-4
Q 9:7 How frequently are 401(k) account balances updated? ... 9-4
Q 9:8 How are account balances determined in a daily valued plan? ... 9-4

Cash-Out Rules

Q 9:9 What are the cash-out rules? ... 9-5
Q 9:10 May a cash-out occur if a participant has no vested accrued benefit? ... 9-6
Q 9:11 How do the plan repayment provisions operate in a defined contribution plan? ... 9-6
Q 9:12 What interest is charged on amounts repaid to a defined contribution plan? ... 9-6
Q 9:13 How does the employer restore the forfeited funds if an employee chooses to repay his or her distribution under the cash-out/ repayment rules? ... 9-7
Q 9:14 Why do some employers not have a cash-out rule? ... 9-7
Q 9:15 How is the account balance determined in a plan that does not contain cash-out rules? ... 9-7

Underfunded Defined Contribution Plans

Q 9:16 What is an underfunded defined contribution plan? ... 9-9
Q 9:17 How are account balances determined when a defined contribution plan has not fully amortized its funding waiver? ... 9-9
Q 9:18 What methods may be used in determining the adjusted account balance? ... 9-10
Q 9:19 What are the steps involved in determining a participant's account balance? ... 9-11

Determining Accrued Benefits in Traditional Defined Benefit Plans

Q 9:20 How is an accrued benefit determined in a traditional defined benefit plan? 9-12

Q 9:21 How is normal retirement age defined? 9-12

Q 9:22 What is the principal significance of the normal retirement age? ... 9-13

Q 9:23 What are the minimum accrual requirements in a defined benefit plan? 9-13

Q 9:24 How does the fractional rule operate? 9-13

Q 9:25 How does the 133⅓ percent rule work? 9-14

Q 9:26 How does the 3 percent method of benefit accrual work? 9-14

Q 9:27 What is a Section 412(e)(3) plan? 9-15

Q 9:28 How do benefits accrue under a Section 412(e)(3) plan? 9-16

Q 9:29 How do benefits accrue in a hybrid plan, such as a cash balance plan, or a floor plan? 9-16

Q 9:30 How are benefits attributable to employee contributions determined under a defined benefit plan? 9-16

Q 9:31 What portion of the accrued benefit is attributable to mandatory employee contributions? 9-16

Q 9:32 How are accumulated employee mandatory contributions determined? 9-16

Q 9:33 How are the accumulated employee mandatory contributions converted into an accrued benefit? 9-19

Q 9:34 How is the applicable interest rate under Code Section 417(e) determined? 9-19

Determination of Accrual of Service

Q 9:35 What is a year of service for benefit accrual purposes? 9-20

Q 9:36 How is an hour of service defined? 9-20

Q 9:37 Are there any simpler methods for determining years of benefit accrual? 9-20

Q 9:38 Are there any other alternatives for alleviating the recordkeeping requirements? 9-21

Q 9:39 Are other equivalency methods available? 9-21

Q 9:40 May equivalencies be based on periods of employment? 9-22

Q 9:41 May different service crediting methods be used for different classifications of employees? 9-22

Q 9:42 Must a participant who completes 1,000 hours of service receive credit for a full year of benefit accrual? 9-22

Q 9:43 May any years of service be disregarded in computing years of benefit accrual? 9-24

Q 9:44 How do the cash-out rules work in a defined benefit plan? 9-24

Q 9:45 May a cash-out occur if a participant has no vested accrued benefit? ... 9-25
Q 9:46 What interest rate is charged on cashed-out amounts repaid to a defined benefit plan? ... 9-25

Benefit Minimums and Limitations

Q 9:47 What other factors affect the computation of a participant's accrued benefit? ... 9-25
Q 9:48 What type of minimum benefit requirements may be found in defined benefit plans? ... 9-26
Q 9:49 When must a plan provide top-heavy minimum benefits? ... 9-26
Q 9:50 What is the top-heavy minimum benefit in a defined benefit plan? ... 9-27
Q 9:51 How does the defined benefit minimum of 2 percent change if it is paid in a form other than a life annuity beginning at normal retirement age? ... 9-28
Q 9:52 How does the floor-offset approach to providing top-heavy minimum benefits operate? ... 9-28
Q 9:53 How are top-heavy minimum benefits determined under the comparability approach? ... 9-29
Q 9:54 If top-heavy minimum contributions of 5 percent of pay are provided in a defined contribution plan, do top-heavy minimum benefits need to be provided? ... 9-30
Q 9:55 What happens if a plan sponsor makes a change in the benefit formula of a defined benefit plan? ... 9-30
Q 9:56 What is the maximum benefit that may be provided in a defined benefit plan? ... 9-31
Q 9:57 How is the annual benefit defined? ... 9-32
Q 9:58 Are benefits reduced if they begin early? ... 9-33
Q 9:59 Is the maximum benefit increased if it begins after age 65? ... 9-33
Q 9:60 What actuarial assumptions are used in adjusting the maximum annual benefit for optional forms of payment? ... 9-34
Q 9:61 How is average compensation defined for the maximum annual benefit? ... 9-35
Q 9:62 How is compensation defined for purposes of the Code Section 415 limits? ... 9-35
Q 9:63 Is there a reduction in the maximum benefit for short-service employees? ... 9-36
Q 9:64 Is there a minimum benefit payable from a defined benefit plan without regard to the above limitations? ... 9-37

Lump Sum Determination

Q 9:65 What interest rates and mortality table are used to determine minimum lump sums? ... 9-37
Q 9:66 How are the interest rates determined? ... 9-38

Q 9:67 How did the Retirement Protection Act of 1994 (RPA), the Small Business Job Protection Act of 1996 (SBJPA), the Pension Funding Equity Act of 2004 (PFEA), the Pension Protection Act of 2006 (PPA), and the Worker, Retiree, and Employer Recovery Act of 2008 (WRERA) change the Code Section 415 limits for lump sums? ... 9-39
Q 9:68 What mortality table must be used to make adjustments to benefits and limitations under Code Section 415(b)(2)(E)? ... 9-39
Q 9:69 How are the maximum benefit limitations under Code Section 415(b) applied to a benefit that is payable in a form subject to Code Section 417(e)(3)? ... 9-40
Q 9:70 Are fully insured plans under Code Section 412(e)(3) subject to the requirements under Code Section 415(b)? ... 9-41
Q 9:71 What are the steps necessary to compute the accrued benefit under a defined benefit plan? ... 9-41

Determining Benefits in Non-Traditional Plans

Q 9:72 Why are non-traditional plans growing in favor? ... 9-41
Q 9:73 What is a cash balance plan? ... 9-41

Cash Balance Plans

Q 9:74 What is a career average defined benefit plan? ... 9-42
Q 9:75 How does the conversion of a traditional defined benefit plan to a cash balance plan happen? ... 9-42
Q 9:76 How is the percentage of the employee's pay that is credited in a cash balance plan to his or her hypothetical account determined? ... 9-43
Q 9:77 Is the percentage of pay credited to the account actually contributed to the plan by the employer? ... 9-43
Q 9:78 What was the significance of *interest rate whipsaw*? ... 9-43
Q 9:79 How did PPA change the rules regarding the interest rate whipsaw for cash balance plans? ... 9-44
Q 9:80 How is the accrued benefit in a cash balance plan determined for purposes of nondiscrimination testing? ... 9-46
Q 9:81 What interest rate is used to increase the hypothetical account balance to normal retirement age? ... 9-46
Q 9:82 What other factors may affect the computation of the accrued benefit? ... 9-47
Q 9:83 May the benefit in a cash balance plan be paid in alternative forms at normal retirement age? ... 9-47

Floor Offset Plans

Q 9:84 What is a floor offset plan? ... 9-47
Q 9:85 What special requirements must a floor offset plan meet? ... 9-48
Q 9:86 What kind of defined contribution plan may be used to offset the defined benefit plan in a floor offset plan? ... 9-48

Q 9:87	How does a floor offset plan operate?	9-48
Q 9:88	How is a participant's vested benefit in a floor offset plan actually determined?	9-48

Code Section 414(k) Plans

Q 9:89	What is a Section 414(k) plan?	9-50
Q 9:90	How does a Section 414(k) plan differ from a cash balance plan?	9-50
Q 9:91	How are benefits determined in a Section 414(k) plan?	9-50

Pension Equity Plans

Q 9:92	What is a pension equity plan and what are its objectives?	9-51
Q 9:93	How does a pension equity plan operate?	9-51

Target Benefit Plans

Q 9:94	What is a target benefit plan?	9-52
Q 9:95	How does a target plan operate?	9-52
Q 9:96	How are benefits determined in a target plan?	9-52

Chapter 10 Optional Forms of Benefit and Protected Benefits

Nondiscrimination Rules Under Code Section 401(a)(4)

Scope and Application of the Nondiscrimination Standards

Q 10:1	What requirements must a qualified retirement plan satisfy to meet the nondiscrimination standards of Code Section 401(a)(4)?	10-4
Q 10:2	How should the nondiscrimination requirements set forth in the Treasury Regulations be interpreted?	10-5
Q 10:3	Are the nondiscrimination rules applied on the basis of the plan year?	10-5
Q 10:4	How do the minimum coverage rules under Code Section 410(b) relate to the nondiscrimination requirements under Code Section 401(a)(4)?	10-6

General Rules and Considerations

Q 10:5	What rules apply in determining whether the benefits, rights, and features, including optional forms of benefit under a qualified retirement plan, are made available in a nondiscriminatory manner?	10-8

Current Availability

Q 10:6 How is the current availability requirement satisfied? 10-8

Q 10:7 May certain age and service conditions be disregarded in determining whether a benefit, right, or feature that is subject to specified eligibility conditions is currently available to an employee? 10-8

Q 10:8 Are there any age or service conditions that may *not* be disregarded in determining whether a benefit, right, or feature that is subject to specified eligibility conditions is currently available to an employee? 10-9

Q 10:9 Are there any other conditions that may be disregarded in determining whether a right, benefit, or feature that is subject to specified eligibility conditions is currently available to an employee? 10-9

Q 10:10 Are certain implicit conditions disregarded in determining the employees to whom the benefit, right, or feature is currently available? 10-10

Q 10:11 Are other dollar limits disregarded in determining the employees to whom the benefit, right, or feature is currently available? 10-10

Q 10:12 Are certain conditions on the availability of plan loans disregarded in determining the employees to whom plan loans are currently available? 10-10

Q 10:13 Is there a special testing rule that applies when a plan is amended to eliminate a benefit, right, or feature prospectively? 10-11

Q 10:14 How is a benefit, right, or feature eliminated? 10-11

Q 10:15 Is there a different, special rule for benefits, rights, and features that are not protected benefits? 10-11

Effective Availability

Q 10:16 What is the effective availability requirement? 10-11

Special Rules

Q 10:17 Are there special testing rules that apply to a benefit, right, or feature solely available to a group of employees that is acquired as a result of a merger or acquisition? 10-13

Q 10:18 Are there also special nondiscrimination testing rules that apply to frozen participants? 10-14

Q 10:19 Are there special testing rules under the nondiscrimination regulations that apply to early retirement window benefits? ... 10-14

Permissive Aggregation of Certain Benefits, Rights, or Features

Q 10:20 May an optional form of benefit, ancillary benefit, or other right or feature be aggregated with another optional form of benefit, ancillary benefit, or other right or feature for current availability and effective availability testing purposes? 10-15

Certain Spousal Benefits, Etc.

Q 10:21 Are there any other special testing rules under the nondiscrimination regulations that apply to certain spousal benefits, employee stock ownership plans (ESOPs), and unpredictable contingent event benefits? **10-16**

Definitions

Q 10:22 What is an *optional form of benefit*? **10-17**

Q 10:23 What is an *ancillary benefit*? **10-19**

Q 10:24 What does the term *other right or feature* mean? **10-19**

Code Section 411(d)(6) Protected Benefits

In General

Q 10:25 What are protected benefits under Code Section 411(d)(6)? ... **10-22**

Q 10:26 What benefits are *not* Section 411(d)(6) protected benefits? ... **10-26**

Q 10:27 What is an *optional form of benefit* under Code Section 411(d)(6)? **10-26**

Q 10:28 Are benefits protected under Code Section 411(d)(6) only if they are provided under the terms of a plan? **10-28**

Extent to Which Section 411(d)(6) Protected Benefits May Be Reduced or Eliminated

Q 10:29 To what extent may Section 411(d)(6) protected benefits under a plan be reduced or eliminated? **10-29**

Q 10:30 Under what circumstances may Section 411(d)(6) protected benefits be eliminated or reduced? **10-32**

Q 10:31 How are multiple plan amendments that modify optional forms of benefit evaluated under the Section 411(d)(6) protected benefit rules? **10-41**

Q 10:32 Are there special circumstances under which an ESOP or a stock bonus plan will not be treated as violating the anti-cutback rules of Code Section 411(d)(6)? **10-41**

Q 10:33 Are there any limitations on the ESOP and stock bonus plan exceptions described in Q 10:32? **10-42**

Q 10:34 Does the transfer of benefits between and among defined benefit plans and defined contribution plans (or similar transactions) violate the anti-cutback rules of Code Section 411(d)(6)? **10-43**

Q 10:35 May a plan provide that the employer may, at its discretion, deny a participant a Section 411(d)(6) protected benefit for which the participant is otherwise eligible? **10-46**

Q 10:36 When will the exercise of discretion by someone other than the employer be treated as employer discretion? **10-47**

Q 10:37 May a plan condition the availability of a Section 411(d)(6) protected benefit on the satisfaction of objective conditions specifically set forth in the plan? **10-48**

Q 10:38 May a plan be amended to add employer discretion or conditions restricting the availability of a Section 411(d)(6) protected benefit? **10-49**

Reduction or Elimination of Early Retirement Benefits, Retirement-Type Subsidies, and Optional Forms of Benefit

Q 10:39 May a participant's accrued benefit be decreased by a plan amendment? **10-49**

Q 10:40 May a plan be amended to eliminate noncore optional forms of benefit if core options are offered? **10-65**

Q 10:41 May a plan be amended to eliminate or reduce Section 411(d)(6)(B) protected benefits that are burdensome and of *de minimis* value? **10-67**

Q 10:42 What is the utilization test? **10-71**

Q 10:43 Are there any examples that illustrate the application of the anti-cutback rules in Treasury Regulations Section 1.411(d)-3? **10-73**

Chapter 11 QJSA and QPSA Rules

Overview

Q 11:1 What survivor annuity requirements did the Retirement Equity Act of 1984 add to the Code and ERISA? **11-5**

Q 11:2 Must annuity contracts purchased and distributed to a participant or spouse by a retirement plan that is subject to the survivor annuity requirements of the Code also satisfy those requirements? **11-6**

Retirement Plans Subject to Survivor Annuity Requirements

Q 11:3 What qualified retirement plans are subject to the survivor annuity requirements of Code Sections 401(a)(11) and 417? **11-6**

Q 11:4 What rules apply to a participant who elects a life annuity option under a defined contribution plan, such as a profit sharing or stock bonus plan, that is not subject to the minimum funding standards of Code Section 412? **11-8**

Q 11:5 How do the QJSA and QPSA rules apply when a deferred annuity contract is purchased under a profit sharing plan? **11-8**

Transferee, Offset, Frozen, and Terminated Plans

Q 11:6 How do the survivor annuity rules of Code Sections 401(a)(11) and 417 apply to transferee plans that are defined contribution plans not subject to the minimum funding standards of Code Section 412 (e.g., profit sharing and stock bonus plans) and to offset plans? ... 11-12

Q 11:7 Must a frozen or terminated retirement plan satisfy the survivor annuity requirements of Code Sections 401(a)(11) and 417? ... 11-13

Q 11:8 If the Pension Benefit Guaranty Corporation (PBGC) is administering a retirement plan, are benefits payable in the form of a QPSA or QJSA? ... 11-13

Applying Survivor Annuity Requirements to Participants

Q 11:9 How do the survivor annuity requirements of Code Sections 401(a)(11) and 417 apply to retirement plan participants? ... 11-13

Q 11:10 May separate portions of a participant's accrued benefit under a retirement plan be subject to QPSA and QJSA requirements at any particular time? ... 11-14

Annuity Starting Date

Q 11:11 What is the relevance of the annuity starting date to the survivor annuity requirements? ... 11-15

Q 11:12 What is the annuity starting date for a survivor annuity? ... 11-15

Q 11:13 What is the annuity starting date for a disability benefit? ... 11-17

Benefits

Q 11:14 Do the survivor annuity requirements apply to retirement plan benefits derived from employer and employee contributions? ... 11-18

Q 11:15 To what retirement plan benefits do the survivor annuity requirements of Code Sections 401(a)(11) and 417 apply? ... 11-18

Q 11:16 Does the rule that permits forfeitures on account of death apply to a QPSA or to the spousal death benefit payable under defined contribution plans not subject to the survivor annuity rules? ... 11-18

Q 11:17 Can a retirement plan provide a form of benefit more valuable than the QJSA, and, if a plan offers more than one annuity option satisfying the requirements of a QJSA, is spousal consent required when the participant chooses among the various forms? ... 11-19

Timing of QJSA Distributions

Q 11:18 When must distributions to a participant under a QJSA begin? ... 11-19

Rules Governing the QPSA

Q 11:19 What is a QPSA under a defined benefit plan? **11-20**

Q 11:20 What rules apply in determining the amount and forfeitability of a QPSA? **11-21**

Q 11:21 What QPSA benefit must a defined contribution plan subject to the survivor annuity requirements of Code Sections 401(a)(11) and 417 provide? **11-21**

Q 11:22 May a defined benefit plan charge the participant for the cost of the QPSA benefit? **11-21**

Q 11:23 When must distributions to a surviving spouse under a QPSA begin? **11-22**

Applying Survivor Annuity Requirements to Plan Loans

Q 11:24 What rules under Code Sections 401(a)(11) and 417 apply to plan loans? **11-22**

Applying Survivor Annuity Requirements to Unmarried Participants, Surviving Spouses, and Participants Who Have a Change in Marital Status

Q 11:25 How do the survivor annuity requirements of Code Sections 401(a)(11) and 417 apply to participants who are not married? **11-23**

Q 11:26 How do the survivor annuity requirements apply to surviving spouses and participants who have a change in marital status? **11-24**

Spousal Consent Requirement

Q 11:27 What spousal consent requirements did REA 1984 add to the Code and ERISA? **11-25**

Q 11:28 Is a surviving spouse who had been married to a participant for less than one year entitled to full payment of the participant's vested account balance under a defined contribution plan that is not subject to the Section 412 minimum funding rules (e.g., a profit sharing, 401(k), or stock bonus plan)? **11-25**

Q 11:29 Are there circumstances when spousal consent to a participant's election to waive the QJSA or the QPSA is not required? **11-25**

Q 11:30 Does consent contained in a prenuptial agreement or similar contract entered into before a marriage satisfy the spousal consent requirements under the survivor annuity rules? **11-26**

Q 11:31 If a participant's spouse consents to the participant's waiver of a survivor annuity form of benefit, is a subsequent spouse of the same participant bound by the consent? **11-26**

Q 11:32 Does the spousal consent requirement demand that a spouse's consent be revocable? **11-26**

Q 11:33 Has the IRS provided any sample language that can be used in a spousal consent to a participant's waiver of a QJSA or QPSA? ... **11-26**

Participant's Waiver of a QPSA or QJSA

Q 11:34 What rules govern a participant's waiver of a QPSA or QJSA? ... **11-27**

Q 11:35 What rules govern a participant's waiver of the spousal benefit under a defined contribution plan not subject to the survivor annuity requirements? ... **11-28**

Q 11:36 When, and in what manner, may a participant waive the spousal benefit or a QPSA? ... **11-29**

Q 11:37 What right does a participant have to waive QJSA and QPSA benefits? ... **11-29**

Q 11:38 What additional requirements did PPA impose upon qualified retirement plans that are subject to the survivor annuity requirements of Code Section 401(a)(11)? ... **11-30**

Q 11:39 What level of spouse survivor annuity must be provided under a QOSA? ... **11-30**

Q 11:40 Must the retirement plan be amended or the plan's administration be changed in order to implement PPA's QOSA requirements? ... **11-31**

Q 11:41 If a plan that is subject to the survivor annuity requirements of Code Section 401(a)(11) provides a QJSA that is more valuable than the plan's single life annuity form of benefit, must the plan's QOSA be at least actuarially equivalent to the QJSA, or must the QOSA only be at least actuarially equivalent to the plan's single life annuity form of benefit payable at the same time as the QOSA? ... **11-31**

Q 11:42 If a participant elects to receive a distribution in the form of a QOSA, must the participant's spouse consent to the participant's election? ... **11-32**

Q 11:43 How does a plan that is subject to the survivor annuity requirements of Code Section 401(a)(11) satisfy the requirement in Code Section 417(a)(3)(i), as amended by PPA, that the plan provides to a participant a written explanation of the terms and conditions of the QOSA available to the participant? ... **11-32**

Q 11:44 Must a plan that is subject to the survivor annuity requirements of Code Section 401(a)(11) offer to participants, as an alternative to a QPSA, a pre-retirement survivor annuity that is based on a QOSA? ... **11-32**

Q 11:45 How do the PPA's plan amendment rules apply to plan amendments adopted in response to PPA's requirements? ... **11-32**

Q 11:46 What was the effective date of PPA's QOSA requirements? ... **11-33**

Notice Requirements

Q 11:47 What is the purpose of REA 1984's notice requirements, as they relate to QJSA and QPSA coverage? ... **11-33**

Q 11:48 Must written explanations of the QPSA and QJSA be provided to nonvested participants? 11-38

Q 11:49 When must a retirement plan provide the written explanation of the QPSA to a participant? 11-38

Q 11:50 How do retirement plans satisfy the requirements to provide participants with written explanations of QPSAs and QJSAs? ... 11-39

Q 11:51 What information must the Section 417(a)(3) explanation contain? ... 11-39

Q 11:52 What information must be provided in a QJSA explanation that is intended to satisfy the participant-specific information requirements? 11-40

Q 11:53 What information must be provided in a QJSA explanation that is intended to satisfy the generally applicable information requirements? 11-46

Q 11:54 Are there any examples that illustrate the application of these QJSA explanation rules? 11-48

Q 11:55 What are the effective dates for the QJSA and QPSA explanation rules? 11-54

Q 11:56 To what extent may sponsors of qualified retirement plans use new technologies to satisfy the various Code and ERISA requirements for notice, election, consent, recordkeeping, and participant disclosure? 11-55

Subsidized Survivor Benefits

Q 11:57 What are the consequences of fully subsidizing the cost of a QJSA or a QPSA? 11-57

Q 11:58 What is a fully subsidized benefit? 11-57

Chapter 12 Retirement, Disability, and Death

Normal Retirement

Q 12:1 How is normal retirement age defined in pension plans? 12-2

Q 12:2 How has the Treasury modified regulations regarding normal retirement ages in defined benefit plans? 12-2

Q 12:3 What happens if the plan provided for a normal retirement age earlier than permissible under the above Treasury regulations? 12-3

Q 12:4 What happens if the plan does not specify a normal retirement age? ... 12-5

Q 12:5 How is a participant's normal retirement date determined? 12-5

Q 12:6 What is the accrued benefit in a defined contribution plan at normal retirement age? 12-5

Q 12:7 What is the normal retirement benefit in a defined benefit plan? ... 12-5

Q 12:8 What is a qualified disability benefit? 12-6

Q 12:9 What is a Social Security supplement? 12-6

Early Retirement

Q 12:10 May employees retire early and start receiving benefits? 12-6
Q 12:11 What reasons might an employer have for providing early retirement options? 12-7
Q 12:12 What reasons might an employee have for choosing early retirement? 12-7
Q 12:13 What are typical early retirement eligibility requirements? 12-7
Q 12:14 What types of early retirement subsidies may be provided? 12-7
Q 12:15 Do some defined benefit plans provide early retirement as an option, with no subsidy? 12-8
Q 12:16 Are early retirement benefits available to employees who leave employment before reaching the plan's early retirement age? ... 12-8
Q 12:17 What is an early retirement window benefit? 12-8
Q 12:18 How does a plan satisfy the current availability requirement for early retirement window benefits? 12-9
Q 12:19 What other requirements must be met for early retirement benefits? ... 12-10
Q 12:20 How are benefits restricted in a plan that uses permitted disparity? 12-10

Late Retirement

Q 12:21 Can an employee be forced to retire at the plan's normal retirement age? 12-13
Q 12:22 What are the issues involved in determining late retirement benefits? 12-14
Q 12:23 How are retirement benefits determined for a late retiree in a defined contribution plan? 12-14
Q 12:24 What are the general requirements for accruing benefits in a defined benefit plan after normal retirement age? 12-14
Q 12:25 What adjustments may be made to the accrued benefit of an employee who has delayed retirement beyond the plan's normal retirement age? 12-15
Q 12:26 How are benefit distributions after normal retirement treated in determining delayed retirement accrued benefits? 12-15

Phased Retirement

Q 12:27 What is phased retirement? 12-15
Q 12:28 How did regulations regarding phased retirement change? 12-15

Longevity Annuities

Q 12:29 What are longevity annuities? 12-16
Q 12:30 What is a qualifying longevity annuity contract? 12-16
Q 12:31 How do the Required Minimum Distribution Rules apply to QLACs? ... 12-16

Suspension of Benefits

Q 12:32 What are the suspension-of-benefit rules? 12-17

Q 12:33 What happens if a plan does not suspend benefits in accordance with the DOL regulations? 12-18

Disability Benefits

Q 12:34 May a qualified plan provide disability benefits? 12-18

Q 12:35 How is the determination of an individual's disability made? ... 12-19

Q 12:36 What is the Social Security definition of disability? 12-19

Q 12:37 What other definitions of disability might be found in a qualified plan? 12-19

Q 12:38 What definition is most likely to be found in a plan? 12-19

Q 12:39 What other conditions might be required for disability benefits? ... 12-20

Disability Benefits in Defined Contribution Plans

Q 12:40 May a defined contribution plan provide disability benefits? 12-20

Q 12:41 What disability benefits may be found in a defined contribution plan? 12-20

Q 12:42 What are the requirements for a defined contribution plan that makes contributions for disabled participants? 12-20

Q 12:43 How is total and permanent disability defined for purposes of this special disability benefit? 12-21

Q 12:44 How is a disabled participant's compensation determined? 12-21

Q 12:45 In Letter Ruling 200031060, how did a defined contribution plan permit a participant to choose to purchase long-term disability insurance with a portion of his or her account, and what benefits were payable? 12-21

Disability Benefits in Defined Benefit Plans

Q 12:46 When do disability benefits begin in a defined benefit plan? ... 12-22

Q 12:47 How are disability benefits paid in a defined benefit plan? 12-22

Q 12:48 How is the lump-sum amount determined? 12-23

Q 12:49 How is the monthly benefit determined in the event of disability? ... 12-23

Q 12:50 What is a subsidized benefit? 12-23

Q 12:51 How are disability benefits determined if commencement does not occur until normal retirement age? 12-23

Q 12:52 Are disability benefits subject to the limitations of Code Section 415? 12-24

Death Benefits in Defined Contribution Plans

Q 12:53 How are death benefits provided in a defined contribution plan? 12-24

Q 12:54 What portion of the death benefit in a defined contribution plan is paid as a QPSA benefit to the deceased participant's spouse? 12-25
Q 12:55 What rules apply in a profit sharing plan that is not subject to the survivor annuity requirement, but that allows benefits to be paid in the form of a life annuity or permits participants to direct some or all of the investment of their elective deferral and/or matching contribution accounts into a deferred annuity contract issued by an insurance company? 12-26
Q 12:56 What is a transferee plan? 12-26
Q 12:57 What is an offset plan? 12-27
Q 12:58 How do the survivor annuity requirements apply to a defined contribution plan if the benefits are currently being paid in the form of an annuity? 12-27
Q 12:59 May a participant's account balance be subject to the QPSA and QJSA rules at the same time? 12-28

Death Benefits in Defined Benefit Plans

Q 12:60 How are death benefits provided in a defined benefit plan? 12-28
Q 12:61 What kind of death benefits are typically provided in a defined benefit plan? 12-28
Q 12:62 What is a QPSA? 12-29
Q 12:63 What is the annuity starting date? 12-30
Q 12:64 What other types of death benefits may be provided in a defined benefit plan? 12-30
Q 12:65 How is the lump-sum equivalent benefit determined? 12-31
Q 12:66 Will a death benefit be considered incidental if a plan provides a death benefit equal to 100 times the monthly pension plus a QPSA? 12-32
Q 12:67 How does a defined benefit plan sponsor provide for a death benefit of 100 times the monthly benefit without using life insurance? 12-32
Q 12:68 How does a small plan provide for death benefits? 12-32
Q 12:69 What are the requirements of a Section 412(e)(3) plan? 12-33
Q 12:70 What is the amount of the death benefit in a Section 412(e)(3) plan? 12-33
Q 12:71 What are the incidental limits for life insurance in a defined benefit plan? 12-34
Q 12:72 How is the 50 percent test satisfied for a defined benefit plan? 12-34
Q 12:73 May a defined benefit plan use the 100-times test only? 12-36

Required Minimum Distribution Rules

Q 12:74 How quickly must death benefits be paid? 12-36

Q 12:75 May distributions from a deceased participant's retirement plan be rolled over to an IRA? 12-36
Q 12:76 When must distributions begin to satisfy the life expectancy rule? 12-37
Q 12:77 When must the participant's entire interest be distributed to satisfy the five-year rule? 12-37
Q 12:78 How does a plan sponsor determine whether the life expectancy rule or the five-year rule applies? 12-38
Q 12:79 What happens if the participant has designated the estate as beneficiary? 12-39
Q 12:80 May a participant name a trust as the designated beneficiary? 12-39
Q 12:81 If an employee names a trust as his or her designated beneficiary, are the trust's beneficiaries treated as the employee's designated beneficiaries under the plan? 12-39
Q 12:82 When is the participant's designated beneficiary determined? 12-41

Chapter 13 Other Termination of Employment Issues

General Considerations

Q 13:1 How long may the plan defer payment of benefits to a terminated participant? 13-2
Q 13:2 How long may a participant defer payment of benefits? 13-2
Q 13:3 What is a participant's *required beginning date* for purposes of the RMD rules? 13-2
Q 13:4 Who is a 5 percent owner for purposes of the RMD rules? 13-3
Q 13:5 Are any participants not subject to the minimum required distribution rules? 13-3
Q 13:6 May a qualified plan require the immediate distribution of vested benefits upon termination of employment? 13-4
Q 13:7 How is the present value of the vested accrued benefit determined? 13-4

ESOPs

Q 13:8 What options must be available to a participant who is entitled to receive a distribution from an ESOP? 13-5
Q 13:9 What determines whether employer securities are readily tradable? 13-5
Q 13:10 For what length of time must a put option be offered to the participant? 13-6
Q 13:11 If the employee exercises the put option, must the employer immediately pay the employee the fair market value of the securities? 13-6
Q 13:12 What happens if the employee elects installment payments for his or her vested ESOP balance? 13-6

Q 13:13 Are there any exceptions to the put option requirements? 13-6
Q 13:14 When must distributions from an ESOP begin after termination of employment? 13-7
Q 13:15 May a participant elect to receive benefits later than the time described above? 13-8

Suspension of Benefits

Q 13:16 What are the suspension-of-benefits rules? 13-8
Q 13:17 How do the suspension-of-benefits rules apply in a multiemployer plan? 13-9
Q 13:18 How must the employee be notified of the suspension of benefits? 13-9
Q 13:19 What happens when an employee again terminates employment after payment of benefits has been suspended? 13-10
Q 13:20 Must amounts that have been withheld under the suspension-of-benefits rules be repaid to the employee? 13-10
Q 13:21 What happens if a plan does not suspend benefits in accordance with the applicable DOL regulations? 13-10

Claims for Benefits

Q 13:22 Must a participant file a claim to receive benefits under a plan? ... 13-11
Q 13:23 What are the requirements for a claims procedure? 13-11
Q 13:24 What is considered a claim for benefits? 13-12
Q 13:25 What happens if the participant's claim for retirement benefits is wholly or partially denied? 13-12
Q 13:26 What information must be provided in the claim denial? 13-12
Q 13:27 What are the standards for an electronic notice of suspension-of-benefits and a claim denial? 13-13
Q 13:28 May the participant appeal the denied claim? 13-14
Q 13:29 What is the time frame for review of the appeal of the denied claim? ... 13-14
Q 13:30 What is the penalty for failure to comply with the claims procedure requirements? 13-15
Q 13:31 What are the remedies available under ERISA? 13-15
Q 13:32 What standards do the courts apply if the participant makes a claim for benefits? 13-15

Chapter 14 Restrictions on Distributions

Historical Perspective

Q 14:1 Has the Internal Revenue Code historically contained rules restricting distribution to highly paid employees? 14-1
Q 14:2 How did the current rules evolve? 14-2

Q 14:3 What happened to a participant's benefits that were restricted under the original rules? 14-2
Q 14:4 What are the acceptable methods under the original rules of posting collateral with the plan trustee? 14-3

Application of Benefit Restriction Rules

Q 14:5 How are benefits restricted upon plan termination? 14-4
Q 14:6 How are benefits restricted on distribution? 14-4
Q 14:7 Who is a restricted employee? 14-5
Q 14:8 What benefits are included in these restrictions? 14-6
Q 14:9 Are there any exceptions to these benefit restrictions? 14-6
Q 14:10 What are current liabilities? 14-7
Q 14:11 What is the funding target? 14-8
Q 14:12 For purposes of the restricted distribution rules, how are the values of current liabilities/funding target and assets determined? 14-8
Q 14:13 How is the restricted amount recomputed each year? 14-9

Use of Collateral Agreements

Q 14:14 May a restricted employee post collateral in order to receive a distribution that is otherwise restricted? 14-10
Q 14:15 Is an IRA rollover permitted for an employee subject to the restrictions itemized in Q 14:6? 14-11
Q 14:16 How are existing collateral agreements handled? 14-11
Q 14:17 Do the rules on restricted distributions to HCEs apply to defined contribution plans? 14-11
Q 14:18 Will the use of a collateral agreement prevent treatment of the entire amount as a lump-sum distribution? 14-12
Q 14:19 What must a plan sponsor do to correct a disqualifying defect if amounts in excess of the limits have been distributed to a restricted employee? 14-12

Code Section 436 Rules on Restricted Distribution

Q 14:20 How does Code Section 436 restrict distributions to plan participants? 14-12
Q 14:21 What is a prohibited payment? 14-13
Q 14:22 How is a plan's AFTAP determined? 14-14
Q 14:23 What asset value is used in calculating the AFTAP? 14-14
Q 14:24 What is the special rule for fully funded plans? 14-14
Q 14:25 What types of security may the employer post in order to permit larger distributions from the plan? 14-15
Q 14:26 Can the 60 percent/80 percent restrictions be avoided in a manner other than by posting security? 14-16

Q 14:27 Are other plans of the plan sponsor affected by these prohibited payment rules? 14-16

Chapter 15 Plan Termination Issues

General Requirements

Q 15:1 For what reasons may a plan sponsor consider the termination of its plan? 15-2

Q 15:2 Does the termination of a qualified plan affect its qualified status? 15-2

Q 15:3 What are the valid business reasons for terminating a plan? 15-3

Q 15:4 Should every plan sponsor request a ruling from the IRS that the termination of the plan meets the qualification requirements of the Code? 15-4

Q 15:5 Must a terminated plan be amended in order to comply with all applicable qualification requirements that are in effect on the date of plan termination? 15-4

Defined Contribution Plans

Q 15:6 What procedural steps are necessary to terminate a defined contribution plan? 15-4

Q 15:7 When must the plan sponsor adopt a resolution terminating a defined contribution plan? 15-5

Q 15:8 What liability does the plan sponsor have to contribute to a defined contribution plan in the year of termination? 15-5

204(h) Notice

Q 15:9 Why is a notice required to inform participants of the cessation of benefit or contribution accruals? 15-6

Q 15:10 When must the 204(h) notice be provided? 15-6

Q 15:11 How is the 204(h) notice delivered to each participant? 15-7

Q 15:12 What are the requirements for delivering a 204(h) notice by electronic means? 15-7

Q 15:13 What are the contents of the 204(h) notice? 15-9

Q 15:14 When must notice of plan termination be provided? 15-9

Q 15:15 What are the consequences for failure to provide a 204(h) notice? 15-9

Information Gathering

Q 15:16 What information is needed to administer the plan in the year of termination? 15-10

Q 15:17 What other information should be reviewed or collected? 15-11

IRS Submission

Q 15:18 What is the purpose of submitting a terminating plan to the IRS to request a favorable determination letter? **15-12**

Q 15:19 What is the scope of a favorable determination letter? **15-12**

Q 15:20 If the plan receives a favorable determination letter from the IRS on the plan termination, is the plan protected against future audits? **15-13**

Q 15:21 What information needs to be submitted to the IRS for a favorable determination letter on the termination of the plan? **15-13**

Q 15:22 What is Form 8717, and what is the applicable user fee for a request on a plan termination? **15-14**

Q 15:23 What information is provided on Form 5310? **15-15**

Q 15:24 Who is required to file Form 6088? **15-15**

Q 15:25 How is Form 6088 completed for an underfunded defined contribution plan? **15-16**

Q 15:26 What is the purpose of Form 2848? **15-16**

Q 15:27 What additional information might the IRS request before issuing a favorable determination letter on the qualified status of the terminating plan? **15-17**

Q 15:28 How long does it take to receive a favorable determination letter from the IRS on a plan termination? **15-17**

Q 15:29 Must the participants in the plan be notified of the request for a determination letter on the termination of the plan? **15-18**

Q 15:30 Who are *interested parties*? **15-18**

Q 15:31 When must the notice to interested parties be provided? **15-18**

Q 15:32 What are the contents of the notice to interested parties? **15-18**

Q 15:33 Must any additional information be provided to interested parties? **15-19**

Problem-Solving Options

Q 15:34 What happens if operational errors or qualification defects are discovered by the IRS in the process of reviewing a plan submitted for a favorable determination letter? **15-20**

Q 15:35 When may a plan sponsor invoke SCP if the plan is currently being reviewed by the IRS? **15-20**

Q 15:36 May SCP be invoked for significant operational failure after a plan is submitted to the IRS? **15-20**

Q 15:37 What alternatives are available to a plan sponsor that is not eligible for SCP? **15-21**

Liquidating Plan Assets

Q 15:38 What is involved in the liquidation of plan assets? **15-21**

Q 15:39 When should the liquidation process be started? **15-22**

Final Stages

Q 15:40 How are account balances in a defined contribution plan updated from the last valuation date? **15-22**

Q 15:41 What benefit election forms and notices must be distributed and executed? **15-22**

Missing Participants

Q 15:42 Does a fiduciary of an ERISA plan have a duty to try to locate lost or missing participants to whom benefits or account balances are payable from the plan? **15-23**

Q 15:43 What is the IRS Letter-Forwarding Program? **15-24**

Q 15:44 What is the Social Security Administration (SSA) Letter-Forwarding Program? **15-24**

Q 15:45 What is a private locator service? **15-24**

Q 15:46 Are there any Internet resources available to plan administrators trying to locate missing participants? **15-25**

Q 15:47 What is the PBGC's missing participant program applicable to defined contribution plans? **15-25**

Q 15:48 May unclaimed benefits escheat to the state in which the plan sponsor is located? **15-26**

Final Disclosure Forms

Q 15:49 When is the final 5500 form due? **15-26**

Q 15:50 How are the distributions to participants reported? **15-26**

Defined Benefit Plans

Q 15:51 What are the steps involved in a defined benefit plan termination? **15-26**

Q 15:52 What determines whether a defined benefit plan may be terminated? **15-27**

Measurement of Plan Liabilities

Q 15:53 How are plan liabilities measured? **15-28**

Q 15:54 What are the rates for terminating plans? **15-28**

Q 15:55 How are the interest rates determined? **15-29**

Q 15:56 Can the look-back period or the stability period for the determination of interest rates be changed? **15-30**

Insufficiency of Plan Assets in a Defined Benefit Plan

Q 15:57 What happens if the plan assets are not sufficient to satisfy the plan liabilities? **15-30**

Q 15:58 What is a terminal funding contract? **15-31**

Actions of Plan Sponsor

Q 15:59 When must the plan sponsor adopt a resolution terminating a defined benefit plan? **15-31**

Q 15:60 What liability does the plan sponsor have to contribute to a defined benefit plan in the year of termination? **15-32**

Q 15:61 Do the MRC requirements under Code Section 430 apply for the entire year in the year of plan termination? **15-32**

204(h) Notice

Q 15:62 Why is a notice required to inform participants of the cessation of benefit accruals in a defined benefit plan? **15-32**

Information Gathering

Q 15:63 What data must be collected to terminate a defined benefit plan? ... **15-33**

Q 15:64 What other information should be reviewed or collected? **15-33**

IRS Submission

Q 15:65 What information needs to be submitted to the IRS for a favorable determination letter on the termination of the plan? **15-34**

Q 15:66 How is Form 6088 completed for a defined benefit plan? **15-35**

Q 15:67 How long does it take to receive a favorable determination letter from the IRS on a plan termination? **15-36**

Q 15:68 Must the participants in the plan be notified of the request for a determination letter on the termination of the plan? **15-36**

Liquidating Plan Assets

Q 15:69 What is involved in the liquidation of plan assets? **15-36**

Q 15:70 When should the liquidation process be started? **15-36**

Q 15:71 Why should the PVAB be recalculated? **15-37**

Surplus Assets

Q 15:72 What happens if a terminating defined benefit plan has surplus assets? **15-37**

Q 15:73 What is a qualified replacement plan? **15-37**

Q 15:74 May more than 25 percent of the surplus assets be transferred to a qualified replacement plan? **15-38**

Q 15:75 How large must benefit increases be in order to qualify for the reduction in the excise tax from 50 percent to 20 percent? **15-38**

Distribution of Election Forms

Q 15:76 What benefit distribution election forms and notices must be distributed and executed? **15-39**

Q 15:77 What payment options must be provided in the benefit election form? **15-39**

Q 15:78 What happens if the participant chooses a form of benefit other than the qualified joint and survivor annuity (QJSA)? **15-40**

Q 15:79 May distributions that are less than $5,000 be distributed in cash to plan participants? **15-40**

Q 15:80 Must a spouse consent to a form of benefit other than a QJSA? **15-40**

Q 15:81 What are the requirements, under Code Section 402(f), for a written explanation to recipients of distributions eligible for rollover treatment? **15-40**

Q 15:82 Has the IRS provided sample language that may be used for the Section 402(f) notice? **15-41**

Q 15:83 May language that is different from the IRS model be used? ... **15-41**

Q 15:84 When must the plan administrator provide the Section 402(f) notice to a distributee? **15-42**

Q 15:85 What options should a plan administrator consider offering to a participant covered by life insurance in a qualified plan? **15-42**

Q 15:86 What happens if a participant cannot be located? **15-43**

Final Disclosure Forms

Q 15:87 When is the final Form 5500 due? **15-43**

Q 15:88 How are distributions to participants reported? **15-43**

Abandoned Defined Contribution (Orphan) Plans

Q 15:89 What guidance is available from the DOL regarding defined contribution orphan plans? **15-43**

Q 15:90 What entity may be a QTA? **15-44**

Q 15:91 When is a defined contribution plan considered to be abandoned? **15-44**

Q 15:92 What is considered to be a reasonable effort to locate or communicate with the plan sponsor? **15-45**

Q 15:93 When is an orphan plan deemed to be terminated? **15-45**

Q 15:94 What are the contents of the QTA notice to the DOL? **15-46**

Q 15:95 What are the tasks required of the QTA in winding up the orphan plan? **15-47**

Q 15:96 What are the contents of the Special Terminal Report for Abandoned Plans? **15-49**

Chapter 16 The Termination Process for Single and Multiple Employer PBGC-Covered Plans

Coverage

Q 16:1 What determines whether a defined benefit plan is covered by the PBGC? 16-2
Q 16:2 Are any qualified plans exempt from coverage by the PBGC? ... 16-3
Q 16:3 Who is a substantial owner? 16-4
Q 16:4 What is a professional service employer? 16-4

PBGC Termination Steps

Q 16:5 What is a standard termination? 16-5
Q 16:6 What are the steps involved in a PBGC standard termination? ... 16-5
Q 16:7 What determines whether a PBGC-covered plan may be terminated? 16-8
Q 16:8 What is the proposed termination date and how is it selected? ... 16-8

Notice of Intent to Terminate

Q 16:9 What are the requirements for the NOIT? 16-8
Q 16:10 Who must receive a notice of annuity information? 16-9
Q 16:11 How is the plan administered during the termination process? ... 16-9
Q 16:12 What information must the notice of annuity information contain? 16-10
Q 16:13 What happens if the insurance company providing the annuities is not known at the time the NOIT is issued? 16-11
Q 16:14 Who are affected parties? 16-11

Preliminary Information for PBGC

Q 16:15 What information is contained in the standard termination notice? 16-12
Q 16:16 What information must be contained in PBGC Form 500 and Schedule EA-S? 16-12
Q 16:17 When must Form 500 and Schedule EA-S be filed? 16-13
Q 16:18 Why would the PBGC issue a notice of noncompliance? 16-13
Q 16:19 What happens if the PBGC does not issue a NONC? 16-14

Measurement of Benefit Liabilities

Q 16:20 How are benefit liabilities in a standard termination measured? ... 16-14
Q 16:21 What are the prescribed interest and mortality rates to be used for determining minimum amounts for non-annuity benefit liabilities in plans terminating in a standard termination? 16-15

Q 16:22 How are the interest rates determined? 16-16
Q 16:23 May the lookback period or the stability period for the determination of interest rates be changed? 16-17
Q 16:24 What is the controversy surrounding the selection of interest rates for PBGC-covered plans that terminated in a prior year but distributed benefits during a current plan year? 16-17

Insufficiency of Plan Assets

Q 16:25 What happens if the plan assets are not sufficient to satisfy the plan liabilities? 16-18
Q 16:26 Who is a majority owner? 16-18
Q 16:27 How does a majority owner waive benefits in a standard termination? 16-18
Q 16:28 What is a terminal funding contract? 16-20

Actions of Plan Sponsor

Q 16:29 When must a plan sponsor adopt a resolution terminating a defined benefit plan? 16-20
Q 16:30 What constitutes a small plan for purposes of the 204(h) notice? 16-20
Q 16:31 What liability does the plan sponsor have to contribute to a defined benefit plan in the year of termination? 16-21
Q 16:32 Do the Minimum Required Contribution requirements under Code Section 430 apply for the entire year in the year of plan termination? 16-21

ERISA Section 204(h) Notice

Q 16:33 Why is a notice required to inform participants of the cessation of benefit accruals? 16-21
Q 16:34 How is the 204(h) notice delivered to each participant? 16-21

Information Gathering

Q 16:35 What data must be collected to terminate the plan? 16-22
Q 16:36 What other information must be reviewed or collected? 16-22

Notice of Plan Benefits

Q 16:37 What is the notice of plan benefits? 16-22
Q 16:38 Does the NOPB contain the same information for all participants? 16-23
Q 16:39 What information must be provided in the NOPB? 16-23
Q 16:40 What information must be provided in the NOPB for participants in pay status? 16-24
Q 16:41 What information must be provided in the NOPB for participants who have elected to retire or who have *de minimis* benefits? ... 16-24

Q 16:42 What information must be included in the NOPB for other participants not in pay status? 16-25

Final Stages

Q 16:43 What should be considered in converting plan assets to cash in order to make distributions on termination? 16-26
Q 16:44 When should the liquidation process be started? 16-26
Q 16:45 Why is the PVAB recalculated at the time distributions are made? 16-26

When the Plan Has Surplus Assets

Q 16:46 What are the rules governing reversions in a defined benefit plan covered by the PBGC? 16-27
Q 16:47 How does the ratable distribution of surplus assets occur in a defined benefit plan with participants' mandatory after-tax contributions? 16-27
Q 16:48 Who is entitled to receive a ratable portion of the surplus? 16-28
Q 16:49 What happens if a terminating defined benefit plan has surplus assets? 16-28
Q 16:50 What is a qualified replacement plan? 16-29
Q 16:51 May more than 25 percent of the surplus assets be transferred to a qualified replacement plan? 16-30
Q 16:52 How large must benefit increases in a defined benefit plan be to qualify for the reduction in the reversion excise tax from 50 percent to 20 percent? 16-30
Q 16:53 What benefit election forms and notices must be distributed and executed? 16-30

Missing Participants

Q 16:54 What happens if a participant cannot be located? 16-31
Q 16:55 What are the requirements for purchasing an annuity from an insurance company for a missing participant? 16-31
Q 16:56 How is a diligent search defined by the PBGC? 16-32
Q 16:57 What amount is paid to the PBGC after a diligent search for a missing participant fails? 16-32
Q 16:58 What are the missing participant annuity assumptions? 16-33
Q 16:59 How are missing participant lump-sum assumptions determined? 16-34
Q 16:60 What is the most valuable benefit for a missing participant? 16-34

Post-Distribution Certification

Q 16:61 What must be provided to the PBGC after benefits are distributed? 16-35

Q 16:62 What are the penalties for failure to comply with the post-distribution certification requirements? 16-35
Q 16:63 When must the distribution be completed? 16-36
Q 16:64 May an extension of the 180-day period be granted? 16-36
Q 16:65 What if the plan administrator is unable to distribute assets for reasons other than the delay in issuance of a favorable determination letter from the IRS? 16-36
Q 16:66 Where are requests for extension submitted? 16-37

Spinoff/Termination Transaction Rules

Q 16:67 What is a spinoff/termination transaction? 16-37
Q 16:68 Who are affected participants in a spinoff/termination transaction? ... 16-37
Q 16:69 What notices must be provided to affected participants in a spinoff/termination transaction? 16-37
Q 16:70 What are the consequences of failure to provide the notices described above? 16-37

Final Returns/Reports

Q 16:71 When is the final Form 5500 due to be filed? 16-38
Q 16:72 How are the distributions to participants reported? 16-38

Chapter 17 Underfunded Plans

Underfunded PBGC-Covered Defined Benefit Plans

Q 17:1 What options are available to the plan sponsor of an underfunded Pension Benefit Guaranty Corporation (PBGC)-covered plan? 17-1
Q 17:2 How are benefit liabilities measured for plan termination purposes? 17-2
Q 17:3 What steps are necessary to terminate a defined benefit plan in a PBGC distress termination? 17-2
Q 17:4 How may the plan sponsor of a defined benefit plan qualify for a distress termination? 17-3
Q 17:5 What information must be provided to the PBGC to support the request for a distress termination? 17-4
Q 17:6 Should a plan sponsor who meets the distress criteria discussed in Q 17:4 always file for a distress termination with the PBGC? ... 17-6
Q 17:7 What information must be provided to plan participants in a distress termination? 17-6
Q 17:8 What information is contained in the NOIT? 17-6
Q 17:9 Who are affected parties? 17-7

Q 17:10 What information must be provided to the PBGC in a distress termination? **17-7**

Q 17:11 What is the next step if the PBGC determines that the plan sponsor is eligible for a distress termination? **17-10**

Q 17:12 What benefits provided in a defined benefit plan are guaranteed by the PBGC? **17-10**

Q 17:13 What are the dollar limits for each year? **17-11**

Q 17:14 Are there any adjustments to the maximum guaranteed benefits? **17-12**

Q 17:15 How are maximum guaranteed benefits actuarially adjusted? **17-12**

Q 17:16 How is the age adjustment to PBGC-guaranteed benefits made if benefits begin before or after age 65? **17-13**

Q 17:17 What adjustment factors are used for period certain and continuous annuities? **17-14**

Q 17:18 What adjustment factors are used for joint and survivor annuities (contingent basis)? **17-14**

Q 17:19 What adjustment factors are used for a joint and survivor annuity (joint basis)? **17-14**

Q 17:20 What adjustment factors are used for age differences in joint and survivor annuities? **17-14**

Q 17:21 What adjustment factors are used for step-down life annuities? **17-15**

Q 17:22 How are benefit increases treated for purposes of the PBGC maximum guarantees? **17-16**

Q 17:23 Who are majority owners? **17-17**

Q 17:24 How are a majority owner's guaranteed benefits limited by the PBGC? **17-17**

Q 17:25 How is a plan administered during the distress termination process? **17-17**

Q 17:26 What steps are involved if the plan has sufficient assets to satisfy guaranteed benefits? **17-18**

Q 17:27 What happens if the plan has insufficient assets to pay guaranteed benefits? **17-18**

Q 17:28 What happens if the funded status of the plan changes after a distribution notice is issued? **17-18**

Q 17:29 What amount is due and payable immediately upon a distress termination to the PBGC? **17-19**

Q 17:30 Will plan participants recover their unfunded benefit liabilities if the plan sponsor makes payments to the PBGC? **17-19**

Q 17:31 Because participants will generally not receive their full benefits in a distress termination, will such participants have standing to sue the plan fiduciaries? **17-19**

Q 17:32 What happens if the PBGC determines that the requirements for a distress termination are not satisfied? **17-20**

Involuntary Terminations

Q 17:33 May the PBGC initiate a plan termination? 17-20

Q 17:34 What is the liability of the plan sponsor if plan assets are insufficient to cover benefit liabilities under a PBGC-initiated involuntary termination? 17-21

PPA Requirements for Distress and Involuntary Terminations

Q 17:35 What are the rights of an affected party with respect to receipt of information submitted to the PBGC in a distress or involuntary termination? 17-21

Q 17:36 What disclosures are required of the PBGC in a PBGC-initiated termination? 17-22

Q 17:37 Does a plan sponsor owe premiums to the PBGC in the event of a distress or involuntary termination? 17-22

Q 17:38 Does a distress or involuntary termination have an impact on other plans of the plan sponsor? 17-23

Defined Benefit Plans Not Covered by the PBGC

Q 17:39 What happens if plan assets are not sufficient to satisfy the plan liabilities? 17-24

Q 17:40 When should a plan sponsor consider freezing and continuing an underfunded defined benefit plan? 17-24

Q 17:41 How does a plan sponsor terminate an underfunded defined benefit plan not subject to PBGC coverage? 17-25

Q 17:42 How are assets allocated under ERISA Section 4044? 17-25

Making Contributions to Meet Plan Liabilities

Q 17:43 May an employer make a contribution sufficient to satisfy plan liabilities? 17-26

Q 17:44 What are the normal rules governing the maximum deductible limit for a defined benefit plan? 17-26

Q 17:45 What is the special deduction limit for PBGC-covered plans with 100 or fewer participants? 17-27

Q 17:46 What is the special deduction rule for terminating plans? 17-27

Q 17:47 What happens if an amount in excess of the deductible limit is contributed to a terminated plan? 17-27

Underfunded Defined Contribution Plans

Q 17:48 What is an underfunded defined contribution plan? 17-27

Q 17:49 What interest rate is used to amortize the waived funding deficiency? 17-27

Q 17:50 What happens when a money purchase or target plan is terminated before the funding waiver is entirely paid off? **17-28**

Chapter 18 Taxation of Periodic Payments

Understanding Basic Concepts

Q 18:1 What is an annuity? **18-2**

Q 18:2 What are some common types of annuities? **18-2**

Q 18:3 When are distributions from qualified retirement plans treated as periodic payments, or "amounts received as an annuity"? **18-3**

Q 18:4 When is a variable annuity treated as periodic payments or "amounts received as an annuity"? **18-3**

Q 18:5 How are periodic payments (amounts received as an annuity) from a qualified retirement plan taxed? **18-3**

Q 18:6 What is the *exclusion ratio*? **18-4**

Q 18:7 What is the employee's *expected return* under the plan? **18-4**

Simplified Method of Basis Recovery and Transition Rule

Q 18:8 Must the simplified method of basis recovery always be used for calculating the taxable portion of annuity distributions from qualified retirement plans? **18-5**

Q 18:9 Which distributees and payors must use the simplified method of basis recovery for calculating the tax-free and taxable portions of each annuity payment made by qualified retirement plans? **18-5**

Q 18:10 How is the tax-free portion (the excluded amount) of each monthly annuity payment determined under the simplified method of basis recovery? **18-6**

Q 18:11 How is the expected number of monthly annuity payments determined under the simplified method of basis recovery? **18-7**

Q 18:12 How is the investment in the contract (i.e., basis) calculated under the simplified method of basis recovery? **18-8**

Q 18:13 Does the IRS provide any examples to illustrate how the simplified method of basis recovery is applied? **18-9**

Q 18:14 What was the effective date of the simplified method of basis recovery? **18-12**

Q 18:15 Was there a transition rule for payors and distributees who may have continued to use pre-SBJPA annuity taxation rules for annuities with annuity starting dates after November 18, 1996, and before January 1, 1997? **18-12**

Q 18:16 Are there any examples that illustrate how the transition rule described in Q 18:15 was applied? **18-13**

Fully Taxable Annuity Payments

Q 18:17 If the distributee has no investment in the contract (i.e., no basis) in his or her plan, will the annuity payments that he or she receives be fully taxable? 18-14

Q 18:18 How are distributions of deductible voluntary employee contributions (DVECs) taxed? 18-14

Chapter 19 Taxation of Nonperiodic Payments

Annuity Starting Date

Q 19:1 What is the tax treatment of a nonperiodic distribution received on or after the annuity starting date? 19-1

Q 19:2 Can part of a nonperiodic payment received on or after the annuity starting date nevertheless be excluded from gross income if its payment reduces later annuity payments? 19-2

Q 19:3 Can part of a nonperiodic payment received on or after the annuity starting date nevertheless be excluded from gross income if it is a distribution in full discharge of the plan's obligation to the participant? 19-2

Q 19:4 What is the tax treatment of a nonperiodic distribution that is received before the annuity starting date? 19-2

Q 19:5 Are there limitations or exceptions to the general allocation rule described in Q 19:4? 19-3

Various Types of Taxable Distributions and Transfers

Q 19:6 How are distributions of U.S. Savings Bonds from qualified retirement plans taxed? 19-4

Q 19:7 How are distributions of excess elective deferrals taxed? 19-4

Q 19:8 How are corrective distributions of excess elective contributions taxed? 19-5

Q 19:9 How are corrective distributions of excess aggregate contributions taxed? 19-6

Q 19:10 How are corrective distributions of excess annual additions taxed? 19-6

Q 19:11 When is a loan from a qualified retirement plan taxable as a nonperiodic distribution? 19-6

Q 19:12 How are transfers of annuity contracts treated under the nonperiodic distribution taxation rules? 19-6

Q 19:13 How are distributions of annuity contracts from qualified retirement plans taxed? 19-7

Q 19:14 What is the tax treatment of accident or health benefits provided under a qualified retirement plan? 19-7

Q 19:15 What is the tax treatment of accident or health benefits provided under a qualified retirement plan to self-employed individuals? 19-8

Q 19:16 What is the tax treatment of medical benefits provided for retired employees under qualified retirement plans? **19-8**

Q 19:17 What is the tax treatment of trustee-to-trustee transfers made between qualified retirement plans? **19-8**

Q 19:18 What is the tax treatment of distributions of deductible qualified voluntary employee contributions that were contributed to qualified plans before 1987? **19-9**

Lump-Sum Distributions

Q 19:19 What changes did the Small Business Job Protection Act of 1996 make to the rules affecting the taxation of lump-sum distributions from qualified retirement plans? **19-9**

Q 19:20 What is a lump-sum distribution from a qualified retirement plan? ... **19-10**

Q 19:21 When is a self-employed individual totally and permanently disabled for purposes of the lump-sum distribution rules? **19-10**

Q 19:22 How is the distribution of an annuity contract treated? **19-10**

Q 19:23 What distributions do not qualify as lump-sum distributions? ... **19-10**

Q 19:24 Can a distribution be a lump-sum distribution if it is not made from a tax-exempt trust that forms a part of a qualified retirement plan? **19-11**

Q 19:25 What happens if a distribution is made under a trust that is tax-exempt in the distribution year but not in a prior year? ... **19-12**

Q 19:26 Must an employee have been a plan participant for at least five years before any lump-sum distribution received during a taxable year beginning before January 1, 2000, could qualify for special forward averaging treatment? **19-12**

Q 19:27 Must a distribution represent the entire balance to the credit of an employee to qualify as a lump-sum distribution? **19-13**

Q 19:28 Which qualified retirement plans must be aggregated in determining whether a distribution represents the balance to the credit of an employee? **19-13**

Q 19:29 What amounts are excluded from the balance to the credit of an employee in determining whether a distribution qualifies as a lump-sum distribution? **19-14**

Q 19:30 Does the balance to the credit of an employee include amounts payable to an alternate payee under a QDRO? **19-14**

Q 19:31 What types of contingent plan interests are excluded from the balance to the credit of the employee in determining whether a distribution qualifies as a lump-sum distribution? **19-15**

Q 19:32 If a plan fails to distribute the balance to the credit of an employee within a single taxable year because it cannot liquidate certain illiquid assets necessary to fund the distribution, does the distribution qualify as a lump-sum distribution? **19-15**

Q 19:33 Under what circumstances will there be a recapture of any tax benefit derived from the taxation of a distribution as a lump-sum distribution? **19-17**

Q 19:34 Is a distribution a lump-sum distribution, if it otherwise qualifies, even though part of it is "restricted" under the early termination rules that affect the distribution of benefits to the 25 highest-paid employees if the plan is terminated within the first 10 years of its existence? 19-17

Q 19:35 Does a delay in distribution prevent lump-sum treatment? 19-17

Q 19:36 Are there circumstances in which additional amounts can be credited to an employee's account under a plan that will not disqualify an earlier distribution from lump-sum treatment? 19-18

Q 19:37 Under what circumstances are distributions treated as lump-sum distributions made on account of an employee's death? 19-19

Q 19:38 Under what circumstances are distributions treated as lump-sum distributions made on account of an employee's separation from service? 19-19

Q 19:39 At what time is an employee considered to have separated from his or her employer's service for purposes of the lump-sum distribution rules? 19-20

Q 19:40 If a recipient receives a lump-sum distribution from a qualified retirement plan after 1999, what are the various options for treating the taxable portion of the distribution? 19-21

Q 19:41 How are lump-sum distributions made after 1999 from qualified retirement plans taxed? 19-21

Q 19:42 What elections are available to an employee who reached age 50 before 1986? 19-21

Q 19:43 How is the tax computed for an individual who elects capital gains treatment? 19-22

Q 19:44 May more than one election of this special tax treatment be made? 19-23

Five-Year Forward Income Averaging

Q 19:45 Generally, when may the special five-year forward income averaging method have been applied to a lump-sum distribution? 19-23

Q 19:46 Could five-year forward averaging have been used for a lump-sum distribution if any portion of that distribution had been rolled over tax-free into another qualified plan or an IRA? 19-25

Q 19:47 How often was an employee permitted to elect to use five-year forward income averaging for lump-sum distributions? 19-25

Q 19:48 Who was permitted to elect to apply five-year forward income averaging to a lump-sum distribution made from a qualified retirement plan? 19-25

Q 19:49 Who was liable to pay the separate five-year averaging tax? 19-25

Q 19:50 Were estates or trusts that received lump-sum distributions from qualified retirement plans eligible to make the five-year forward averaging election? 19-26

Q 19:51 How did a recipient of a lump-sum distribution received from a qualified retirement plan elect special five-year forward income averaging? **19-26**

Q 19:52 When did the special five-year forward income averaging election have to be made with respect to a lump-sum distribution? ... **19-26**

Q 19:53 When could the special five-year forward averaging election be revoked with respect to a lump-sum distribution? **19-27**

Q 19:54 How was the separate five-year averaging tax determined with respect to a lump-sum distribution? **19-27**

Q 19:55 How was the total taxable amount of a lump-sum distribution computed? **19-28**

Q 19:56 Under what circumstances was the total taxable amount of lump-sum distribution reduced by the allocable estate tax deduction? **19-28**

Q 19:57 How was the minimum distribution allowance computed in figuring the separate five-year forward averaging tax? **19-28**

Q 19:58 How was the separate five-year averaging tax calculated when a lump-sum distribution included the distribution, received in a taxable year beginning before January 1, 1996, of an annuity contract? **19-29**

Ten-Year Forward Income Averaging

Q 19:59 What is 10-year forward income averaging? **19-29**

Q 19:60 Under what circumstances is 10-year averaging available to the recipient of a lump-sum distribution? **19-30**

Q 19:61 How is the separate 10-year forward averaging tax computed? ... **19-30**

Capital Gains Treatment

Q 19:62 Under what circumstances can an election be made to treat the portion of a lump-sum distribution attributable to pre-1974 plan participation as a capital gain, subject to the flat 20 percent capital gains tax? **19-30**

Q 19:63 How often can a recipient of a lump-sum distribution from a qualified retirement plan elect to apply capital gains treatment to the portion of the distribution attributable to pre-1974 plan participation? **19-31**

Q 19:64 What are the existing capital gains provisions that apply to recipients who elect to apply capital gains treatment to the pre-1974 portion of a lump-sum distribution? **19-31**

Q 19:65 How are the capital gains and the ordinary income portions of a lump-sum distribution determined? **19-31**

Q 19:66 What rules apply when choosing to use the special five-year or ten-year forward averaging method or the capital gain method for a lump-sum distribution from a qualified retirement plan? ... **19-32**

Q 19:67 What is the time frame for making a decision on a special method of taxation? **19-33**

Special Lump-Sum Distribution Issues

Q 19:68 What portion of a lump-sum distribution can be recovered tax-free? **19-33**

Q 19:69 Can the recipient claim a loss on his or her tax return if the lump-sum distribution he or she receives is less than his or her investment in the contract (i.e., basis) in the lump-sum distribution? **19-34**

Q 19:70 What is the tax treatment of lump-sum distributions that include employer securities? **19-34**

Q 19:71 What happens when the recipient later sells or exchanges the employer securities? **19-34**

Chapter 20 Additional Taxes

Additional 10 Percent Income Tax on Early Distributions

Q 20:1 When is the 10 percent additional income tax on early distributions from qualified retirement plans imposed? **20-2**

Q 20:2 Which distributions from qualified plans are not subject to the 10 percent additional income tax? **20-3**

Q 20:3 How is the term *disabled* defined for purposes of the exception to the 10 percent additional income tax for distributions that are attributable to an employee's becoming disabled? **20-5**

Q 20:4 What is a "series of substantially equal periodic payments" for purposes of the provision that exempts these payments from the 10 percent additional income tax on early distributions? **20-5**

Q 20:5 Will the 10 percent additional income tax be imposed, despite the exception for substantially equal periodic payments, if the series of payments is modified after it has begun? **20-8**

Q 20:6 Is a reduction in the amount of payment the kind of modification of a series of substantially equal periodic payments that would cause that exception no longer to apply? **20-9**

Q 20:7 Does the 10 percent additional income tax apply if the distribution is made after the employee separates from service after reaching age 55? **20-9**

Q 20:8 Does the 10 percent additional income tax apply to qualified reservist distributions? **20-10**

Q 20:9 Does the 10 percent additional income tax on early distributions apply to distributions from governmental defined benefit or defined contribution plans to qualified public safety employees who separate from service after age 50? **20-10**

Q 20:10 Is a distribution that is otherwise subject to the 10 percent additional income tax on early distributions exempt if it is involuntary? **20-12**

Q 20:11 Does the 10 percent additional income tax on early distributions apply to distributions that are made pursuant to a designation in effect under Tax Equity and Fiscal Responsibility Act of 1982 (TEFRA) Section 242(b)(2)? **20-12**

Q 20:12 When did the 10 percent additional income tax on early distributions become effective? **20-12**

Q 20:13 What transitional rules under TRA '86 protect certain early distributions from the application of the 10 percent additional income tax? ... **20-12**

Q 20:14 Does the 10 percent additional income tax apply if the distribution is made from a plan that is subject to an IRS levy under Code Section 6331? **20-13**

Q 20:15 How should a taxpayer report the 10 percent additional income tax on early distributions? **20-13**

Fifty Percent Excise Tax on Failure to Make RMDs

Q 20:16 Is any tax imposed on a payee if the amount distributed during the taxable year is less than the RMD for that year? **20-14**

Q 20:17 What is a qualified retirement plan for purposes of the 50 percent excise tax rules? **20-14**

Q 20:18 If a payee's interest under a qualified retirement plan is in the form of an individual account and that account is not being distributed from a purchased annuity contract, how is the RMD for a given calendar year determined for purposes of calculating the 50 percent excise tax under Code Section 4974? **20-15**

Q 20:19 If the payee's interest under a Section 401(a) qualified retirement plan is distributed in the form of an annuity, how is the RMD determined for purposes of calculating the 50 percent excise tax under Code Section 4974? **20-15**

Q 20:20 If the annuity contract (or the defined benefit plan's distribution option) provides an impermissible annuity distribution option, how is the RMD for each calendar year, for purposes of calculating the 50 percent excise tax, determined for defined benefit plans? ... **20-16**

Q 20:21 If a defined contribution plan distributes a purchased annuity contract that is an impermissible annuity distribution option, which does not pay at least the RMD for any calendar year, what rules would apply? **20-17**

Q 20:22 If there is any remaining benefit with respect to an employee after any calendar year in which his or her entire remaining benefit had to be distributed from a qualified retirement plan under the RMD rules, what is the amount of the RMD for each calendar year after that calendar year? **20-17**

Q 20:23 For which calendar year is the 50 percent excise tax imposed when the amount not distributed is an amount required to be distributed by April 1 of a calendar year? **20-17**

Q 20:24 Are there any circumstances under which the 50 percent excise tax on underpayments may be waived? **20-17**

Chapter 21 Direct Rollovers

Direct Rollover Option Required

Q 21:1 What are the direct rollover requirements under Code Section 401(a)(31)? 21-6

Q 21:2 What is a direct rollover that satisfies Code Section 401(a)(31), and how is it accomplished? 21-7

Q 21:3 Is a distribution that is directly rolled over currently includible in gross income or subject to 20 percent withholding? 21-7

Q 21:4 What procedures may a plan administrator prescribe for electing a direct rollover? 21-7

Q 21:5 May a plan administrator treat a distributee as having made an election under a default procedure when the distributee does not affirmatively elect to make or not to make a direct rollover within a certain time period? 21-8

Q 21:6 How did EGTRRA change the rules regarding the default option for mandatory distributions? 21-9

Q 21:7 What change did EGTRRA make with regard to the cash-out rule? 21-14

Q 21:8 May a plan administrator establish a deadline after which a distributee may not revoke an election to make or not make a direct rollover? 21-14

Q 21:9 Must a plan administrator permit a distributee to have a portion of an eligible rollover distribution paid to an eligible retirement plan in a direct rollover and the remainder paid to the distributee? ... 21-14

Q 21:10 Must a plan administrator allow a distributee to divide an eligible rollover distribution and have it paid in direct rollovers to two or more eligible retirement plans? 21-14

Q 21:11 May a qualified retirement plan refuse to permit a distributee to elect a direct rollover if his or her eligible rollover distributions during a year are reasonably expected to total less than $200? 21-15

Q 21:12 May a plan administrator apply a distributee's election to make (or not to make) a direct rollover with respect to one payment in a series of periodic payments to all subsequent payments in the series? 21-15

Q 21:13 Must the eligible retirement plan designated by a distributee to receive a direct rollover distribution accept the distribution? ... 21-15

Q 21:14 How is an invalid rollover contribution treated for purposes of applying the qualification requirements of Code Section 401(a) to the receiving plan? 21-16

Q 21:15 For plan qualification purposes, is an eligible rollover distribution that is paid to an eligible retirement plan in a direct rollover a distribution and rollover, or is it a transfer of assets and liabilities? 21-21

Q 21:16 Must a direct rollover option be provided for an eligible rollover distribution that is in the form of a plan loan offset amount? ... 21-21
Q 21:17 Must a direct rollover option be provided for an eligible rollover distribution from a qualified plan distributed annuity contract? ... 21-22
Q 21:18 What assumptions may a plan administrator make regarding whether a benefit is an eligible rollover distribution? ... 21-22

Eligible Rollover Distributions

Q 21:19 What rules are in effect regarding distributions that may be rolled over to an eligible retirement plan under EGTRRA? ... 21-22
Q 21:20 What rule was in effect regarding distributions that may be rolled over to an eligible retirement plan before the enactment of EGTRRA? ... 21-23
Q 21:21 What is an eligible retirement plan, and what is a qualified trust? ... 21-23
Q 21:22 What is an eligible rollover distribution? ... 21-24
Q 21:23 What amounts are not eligible rollover distributions? ... 21-24
Q 21:24 How is it determined whether a series of payments is a series of substantially equal periodic payments over a specified period? ... 21-25
Q 21:25 What types of variations in the amount of a payment cause the payment not to be part of a series of substantially equal periodic payments? ... 21-27
Q 21:26 When is a distribution from a plan an RMD under Code Section 401(a)(9)? ... 21-28
Q 21:27 How are amounts that are not includible in gross income allocated for purposes of determining the RMD? ... 21-29
Q 21:28 Can a qualified plan loan offset amount be rolled over into another eligible retirement plan or IRA? ... 21-29
Q 21:29 What is a qualified plan distributed annuity contract, and how is an amount paid under such a contract treated for purposes of Code Section 402(c)? ... 21-33
Q 21:30 If a participant contributes all or part of an eligible rollover distribution to an eligible retirement plan within 60 days, is the amount contributed not currently includible in gross income? ... 21-33
Q 21:31 How did EGTRRA modify the 60-day rule? ... 21-34
Q 21:32 How does Code Section 402(c) apply to a distributee who is not the participant? ... 21-37
Q 21:33 Must a participant's (or distributee's) election to treat a contribution of an eligible rollover distribution to an individual retirement plan as a rollover contribution be irrevocable? ... 21-38
Q 21:34 How is the $5,000 death benefit exclusion under Code Section 101(b) treated for purposes of determining the amount that is an eligible rollover distribution? ... 21-39

Q 21:35 May a participant (or distributee) roll over more than the plan administrator determines to be an eligible rollover distribution using permissible assumptions? ... 21-39

Q 21:36 How is a rollover from a qualified plan to an IRA treated for purposes of the one-year look-back rollover limitation of Code Section 408(d)(3)(B)? ... 21-39

Q 21:37 May distributions from a Code Section 401(a) qualified retirement plan be rolled over into a Roth IRA? ... 21-39

Q 21:38 Can distributions from other types of retirement plans (other than Code Section 401(a) qualified retirement plans) be rolled over into a Roth IRA? ... 21-41

Q 21:39 Does the 10 percent additional tax under Code Section 72(t) apply to a qualified rollover contribution from an eligible retirement plan other than a Roth IRA? ... 21-41

Q 21:40 Under Code Section 401(a)(31)(A), must a plan permit a distributee of an eligible rollover distribution to elect a direct rollover into a Roth IRA? ... 21-41

Q 21:41 Is the plan administrator responsible for ensuring that the distributee is eligible to make a rollover into a Roth IRA? ... 21-41

Q 21:42 What are the withholding requirements for an eligible rollover distribution that is rolled over into a Roth IRA? ... 21-41

Q 21:43 Can beneficiaries make qualified rollover contributions to Roth IRAs? ... 21-42

Section 402(f) Rollover Notice

Q 21:44 What were the requirements for a written direct rollover notice under Code Section 402(f) before the enactment of EGTRRA? ... 21-42

Q 21:45 When must a plan administrator provide the Code Section 402(f) notice to a distributee? ... 21-43

Q 21:46 Must a plan administrator provide a separate Section 402(f) notice for each distribution in a series of periodic payments that are eligible rollover distributions? ... 21-44

Q 21:47 May a plan administrator post the Section 402(f) notice as a means of providing it to distributees? ... 21-44

Q 21:48 Must the Section 402(f) notice always be a written paper document? ... 21-44

Rollover Contributions by Employees Not Yet Eligible to Participate in a Qualified Plan

Q 21:49 If employees who have not satisfied a qualified retirement plan's minimum age and service requirements are allowed to make rollover contributions to the plan, to what extent are those employees taken into account under the plan for purposes of the minimum coverage and nondiscrimination requirements? ... 21-44

Other Direct Rollover Issues

Q 21:50 If a plan separately accounts for amounts attributable to rollover contributions to the plan, will distributions of those amounts be subject to the restrictions on permissible timing that apply to distributions of other amounts from the plan? **21-45**

Q 21:51 May an ESOP direct certain rollovers of distributions of S corporation stock to an IRA in accordance with a distributee's election without terminating the corporation's S election? **21-46**

Q 21:52 Under what circumstances may a defined benefit pension plan accept a direct rollover of an eligible rollover distribution from a qualified defined contribution plan maintained by the same employer where the defined benefit plan provides an annuity resulting from the direct rollover? **21-47**

Q 21:53 What are the rules for allocating pre-tax and after-tax amounts among distributions that are made to multiple destinations from a Code Section 401(a) qualified retirement plan? **21-48**

Chapter 22 State Income Tax Withholding and FICA and FUTA Treatment

Survey of State Income Tax Withholding Rules

Q 22:1 What are the states' rules on income tax withholding? **22-1**

FICA and FUTA Treatment of Qualified Plan Distributions

Q 22:2 How are distributions from qualified plans treated? **22-5**

State "Source" Taxation of Retirement Benefits

Q 22:3 What is the State Taxation of Pension Income Act of 1995, and what effect does it have on qualified plan distributions? **22-5**

Chapter 23 Plan Disqualification and Self-Correction Programs

Disqualification Events

Q 23:1 What events may cause a qualified retirement plan to become disqualified? **23-4**

Alternatives to Plan Disqualification—SCP, VCP, and Audit CAP

Q 23:2 What programs are available to a plan sponsor who wants to lessen the financial impact of plan disqualification? **23-7**

Program Eligibility

Q 23:3 What qualified retirement plan failures may be corrected under SCP? **23-7**

Q 23:4 What qualified retirement plan failures may be corrected under VCP? **23-10**

Q 23:5 What qualified retirement plan failures may be corrected under Audit CAP? **23-12**

Self-Correction Program (SCP) Requirements

Q 23:6 How are insignificant operational failures corrected under SCP? **23-13**

Q 23:7 How are significant operational failures corrected under SCP? **23-15**

Voluntary Correction Program (VCP) Requirements

Q 23:8 What are the VCP requirements? **23-17**

Q 23:9 What special rules apply to anonymous (John Doe) submissions under VCP? **23-20**

Q 23:10 What special rules apply to group submissions under VCP? **23-21**

Q 23:11 What are the VCP user fees? **23-21**

Audit Closing Agreement Program (Audit CAP) Requirements

Q 23:12 What is the Audit CAP program? **23-21**

Q 23:13 What is the Audit CAP sanction? **23-22**

Q 23:14 How are Audit CAP sanctions paid? **23-23**

Consequences of Plan Disqualification

Q 23:15 What are the consequences of plan disqualification? **23-24**

Q 23:16 For what period of time may the IRS disqualify a previously qualified plan? **23-24**

Q 23:17 Are there any limits on retroactive plan disqualification? **23-24**

Q 23:18 What are the tax consequences to the employee if a plan is disqualified? **23-25**

Q 23:19 How are employer contributions determined for purposes of the rule discussed in Q 23:18? **23-25**

Q 23:20 How are employer contributions computed for defined benefit plans under the Section 403(b) rules? **23-25**

Q 23:21 What other methods may be used in determining employer contributions for defined benefit plans? **23-28**

Q 23:22 What does "substantially vested" mean for purposes of inclusion in gross income? **23-29**

Q 23:23 What happens if the employee's interest in the trust changes from nonvested to vested? **23-29**

Q 23:24 Are there any exceptions to the inclusion-of-income rule discussed in Q 23:18? **23-29**

Q 23:25 How are amounts previously taxed due to plan disqualification treated when amounts are later distributed from the qualified plan? **23-30**

Q 23:26 What happens if a lump-sum distribution is made from a disqualified plan? **23-30**

Chapter 24 Federal Income Tax Withholding

Federal Income Tax Withholding on Eligible Rollover Distributions That Are Not Rolled Over

Q 24:1 What are the withholding requirements under Code Section 3405 for eligible rollover distributions from qualified retirement plans? **24-2**

Q 24:2 May a distributee elect under Code Section 3405(c) not to have federal income tax withheld from an eligible rollover distribution? **24-2**

Q 24:3 May a distributee elect to have more than 20 percent federal income tax withheld from an eligible rollover distribution? **24-2**

Q 24:4 Who has responsibility for complying with Code Section 3405(c) relating to the 20 percent income tax withholding on eligible rollover distributions? **24-3**

Q 24:5 May the plan administrator shift the withholding responsibility to the payor and, if so, how? **24-3**

Q 24:6 How does the 20 percent withholding requirement under Code Section 3405(c) apply if a distributee elects to have a portion of an eligible rollover distribution paid to an eligible retirement plan in a direct rollover and to have the remainder of that distribution paid to the distributee? **24-3**

Q 24:7 Will the plan administrator be subject to liability for tax, interest, or penalties for failure to withhold 20 percent from an eligible rollover distribution that, because of erroneous information provided by a distributee, is not paid to an eligible retirement plan even though the distributee elected a direct rollover? **24-4**

Q 24:8 Is an eligible rollover distribution that is paid to a qualified defined benefit plan subject to 20 percent withholding? **24-4**

Q 24:9 If property other than cash, employer securities, or plan loans is distributed, how is the 20 percent income tax withholding required under Code Section 3405(c) accomplished? **24-4**

Q 24:10 What assumptions may a plan administrator make regarding whether a benefit is an eligible rollover distribution for purposes of determining the amount of a distribution that is subject to 20 percent mandatory withholding? **24-5**

Q 24:11 Are there any special rules for applying the 20 percent withholding requirement to employer securities and a plan loan offset amount distributed in an eligible rollover distribution? **24-5**

Q 24:12 How does the mandatory withholding rule apply to net unrealized appreciation from employer securities? 24-6

Q 24:13 Does the 20 percent withholding requirement apply to eligible rollover distributions from a qualified plan distributed annuity contract? 24-6

Q 24:14 Must a payor or plan administrator withhold federal income tax from an eligible rollover distribution for which a direct rollover election was not made if the amount of the distribution is less than $200? 24-6

Q 24:15 If eligible rollover distributions are made from a qualified retirement plan, who has responsibility for making the returns and reports required under applicable regulations? 24-7

Q 24:16 What eligible rollover distributions must be reported on Form 1099-R? 24-7

Q 24:17 Must the plan administrator, trustee, or custodian of the eligible retirement plan report amounts received in a direct rollover? ... 24-7

Q 24:18 How does the payor of an eligible rollover distribution from which federal income taxes have been withheld report those withholdings to the IRS? 24-8

Federal Income Tax Withholding on Periodic and Nonperiodic Payments That Are Not Eligible Rollover Distributions

Rules Applicable to Periodic Payments

Q 24:19 What is a *periodic payment* for purposes of the federal income tax withholding rules? 24-9

Q 24:20 How is federal income tax withheld from a periodic payment? ... 24-9

Q 24:21 Do these withholding rules apply to periodic payments made from a qualified retirement plan to the surviving spouse or other beneficiary of a deceased payee? 24-9

Q 24:22 Who is required to withhold federal income tax from periodic payments made by a qualified retirement plan? 24-10

Q 24:23 Who is a *plan administrator* for purposes of these withholding rules? 24-10

Q 24:24 How may the plan administrator of a qualified retirement plan transfer the duty to withhold federal income taxes to a payor? ... 24-10

Q 24:25 What information must the plan administrator provide to the payor in order to transfer liability for federal income tax withholding? 24-10

Q 24:26 If the plan administrator does not notify the payor of the amount of employee contributions with respect to one payee, has federal income tax liability shifted to the payor? 24-11

Q 24:27 If the plan administrator fails to supply the payor with any information concerning the existence or amount of any employee contributions, has withholding liability shifted to the payor? ... 24-11

Q 24:28 May a recipient of a periodic payment (other than an eligible rollover distribution) elect out of federal income tax withholding? **24-12**

Q 24:29 In the case of a distribution made on account of the death of an employee, who makes the election not to have federal income tax withholding apply? **24-12**

Q 24:30 Who is required to provide notice to the payee of the payee's right not to have withholding apply? **24-12**

Q 24:31 When must notice of the right to elect not to have withholding apply be given for periodic payments? **24-12**

Q 24:32 Must notice of the right to elect not to have federal income tax withholding be provided to those payees whose annual payments are less than $5,400? **24-13**

Q 24:33 Must notice of the right to elect not to have federal income tax withholding apply be provided in the same manner to all payees? ... **24-13**

Q 24:34 Must notice be attached to the first payment to satisfy the requirement that the notice be provided when making the first payment? **24-13**

Q 24:35 If a payee utilizes electronic funds transfer and notice is mailed directly to the payee at the same time the check is issued, is the notice requirement satisfied even though the payee receives the notice 15 days after the check is deposited? **24-13**

Q 24:36 If the payor of a periodic payment timely provides notice of the election not to have federal income tax withholding apply, may the payor specify a time prior to distribution by which the election must be made? **24-13**

Q 24:37 If notice is provided to a payee prior to the first payment of a periodic payment, why must it also be provided at the time of the first payment? **24-14**

Q 24:38 Must a payor provide notice if it is reasonable to believe that the entire amount payable is excludable from the payee's gross income? **24-14**

Q 24:39 What information concerning the election not to have federal income tax withholding apply must be provided by the payor to the payee? **24-14**

Q 24:40 Is there any non-required information that is desirable to include in the notice to payees? **24-15**

Q 24:41 May the plan administrator provide the notice to payees on behalf of the payor? **24-15**

Q 24:42 Is there a sample notice that can be used to satisfy the notice requirement for periodic payments? **24-15**

Q 24:43 Is there sample language that may be used to elect not to have federal income tax withholding apply or to revoke a prior election not to have withholding apply? **24-16**

Q 24:44 May the payee's election be combined with a withholding certificate (Form W-4P)? **24-16**

Q 24:45 Will a notice mailed to the payee's last-known address fulfill the notice requirement? **24-17**

Q 24:46 If the payor provides notice before making the first payment,can an abbreviated notice be used to satisfy the requirement that a notice be given when making the first payment? **24-17**

Q 24:47 Is the payor of periodic payments required to aggregate those payments with a payee's compensation to determine the amount of federal income taxes that must be withheld? **24-17**

Q 24:48 Can either the percentage method or the wage bracket method be used to determine the federal income tax withholding liability on a periodic payment? **24-18**

Q 24:49 Do rules similar to those for wage withholding apply to the filing of a withholding certificate for periodic payments? **24-18**

Q 24:50 If no withholding certificate has been filed and the payor is aware that the payee is single, is it still appropriate to base withholding on a married individual claiming three allowances? **24-18**

Q 24:51 May a payor determine whether payments to an individual are subject to withholding based on the amount of the first periodic payment for the year? **24-19**

Q 24:52 If a payment period is specified by the terms of a commercial annuity contract, must that period be used as the appropriate period for determining the amount to be withheld? **24-19**

Q 24:53 If the payor received no report from the plan administrator or beneficiary concerning the payment period, but knows the frequency of payments, can the known frequency be used as the appropriate payment period? **24-19**

Q 24:54 If a payee receives a one-time payment that is a makeup payment resulting from an insurance company's incorrect calculation of a monthly annuity amount, is the one-time payment part of a series of periodic payments? **24-20**

Rules Applicable to Nonperiodic Payments

Q 24:55 What is a nonperiodic distribution? **24-20**

Q 24:56 Must the payor of a nonperiodic distribution (other than an eligible rollover distribution) notify the payee of his or her right to elect out of the 10 percent federal income tax withholding? **24-21**

Q 24:57 What withholding rules apply to qualified retirement plan distributions that are paid outside the United States? **24-22**

Chapter 25 Distributions In-Kind

In General

Q 25:1 Who chooses to distribute in-kind? **25-1**

Q 25:2 Why would a plan sponsor choose to allow in-kind distributions? **25-1**

Optional Form of Benefit Rules

Q 25:3 Is the right to receive an in-kind distribution a protected optional form of benefit? 25-2

Q 25:4 What nondiscrimination rules apply to in-kind distributions? 25-3

Q 25:5 How is the current availability test satisfied? 25-3

Q 25:6 Who is a nonexcludable HCE or NHCE? 25-5

Q 25:7 When is the effective availability test satisfied for in-kind distributions? 25-5

Operational Rules

Q 25:8 How does the plan sponsor ensure that the nondiscriminatory availability rules for in-kind distribution are satisfied? 25-6

Q 25:9 How does a distribution in-kind work? 25-6

Q 25:10 What happens if NHCEs accept the offer of in-kind distributions and the property cannot be divided? 25-7

Q 25:11 How are assets distributed in-kind valued? 25-7

Tax Withholding Requirements

Q 25:12 What are the federal income tax withholding requirements for assets distributed in-kind? 25-7

Q 25:13 What happens if the plan administrator or trustee cannot determine the value of the property without delaying payment to the participant? 25-9

Rollover Rules

Q 25:14 Can assets distributed in-kind be rolled over into an IRA or another qualified plan? 25-9

Q 25:15 May a participant roll over in-kind assets received from a qualified plan if it is not rolled over as part of a direct rollover? 25-10

Q 25:16 May a participant who receives a distribution of property sell it and roll it over into an IRA? 25-10

Q 25:17 What if less than the full amount of the property received is rolled over? 25-10

Treatment of Life Insurance and Annuity Contracts

Q 25:18 Can life insurance and annuity contracts be distributed in-kind? 25-11

Q 25:19 What conditions must be satisfied for the sale of an insurance contract to a participant or relative to be exempt from the prohibited transaction rules? 25-11

Q 25:20 Under what circumstances would a plan typically sell a life insurance contract to a participant or a relative of the participant? 25-12

Q 25:21 How is the sale price for the purchase of the contract determined? ... 25-12

Q 25:22 Are there circumstances under which the taxable amount of the insurance contract distributed will exceed the cash surrender value? ... 25-13

Q 25:23 What are the tax consequences of distributing an insurance contract? ... 25-15

Q 25:24 May an insurance contract be rolled over into an IRA? ... 25-15

Q 25:25 May the participant roll over a life insurance contract into another qualified plan? ... 25-15

Q 25:26 May the participant surrender the life insurance contract and then roll over the proceeds into an IRA? ... 25-15

Q 25:27 May a participant receive credit for the PS-58 costs taxable in prior years? ... 25-15

Q 25:28 May an annuity contract be distributed in-kind to a participant? ... 25-16

Q 25:29 May an annuity contract be exchanged for another annuity contract with a different insurer without creating taxable income? ... 25-16

Distribution of Employer Securities

Q 25:30 May employer securities be distributed in-kind? ... 25-16

Q 25:31 What is NUA? ... 25-17

Q 25:32 May the participant choose not to have the rules on NUA apply? ... 25-17

Q 25:33 How is the cost basis determined? ... 25-17

Q 25:34 What happens if the employer securities decline in value? ... 25-19

Q 25:35 If the participant chooses to defer tax on the NUA, what taxable results occur when the employer securities are sold? ... 25-20

Chapter 26 Trustee-to-Trustee Transfers

Retirement Plan Mergers, Consolidations, and Asset Transfers

Q 26:1 What rules under the Code and ERISA apply to retirement plan mergers, consolidations, and transfers of assets? ... 26-1

Q 26:2 Are there any exceptions to the merger, consolidation, and transfer rules? ... 26-2

Application of the Merger, Consolidation, and Transfer Requirements to Retirement Plan Spinoffs

Q 26:3 Do the merger, consolidation, and transfer of asset rules apply to retirement plan spinoffs? ... 26-2

Q 26:4 How do the merger, consolidation, and transfer of asset rules apply to defined contribution plan spinoffs? ... 26-2

Q 26:5 How do the merger, consolidation, and transfer of asset rules apply to defined benefit plan spinoffs? ... 26-3

Retirement Plan Mergers or Consolidations

Q 26:6 What is a "merged" or "consolidated" retirement plan? ... 26-3
Q 26:7 How are the merger rules satisfied when two or more defined contribution plans merge? ... 26-4
Q 26:8 How are the merger rules satisfied when two or more defined benefit plans are merged? ... 26-4
Q 26:9 Must the IRS be notified if there is a retirement plan merger or consolidation, spinoff, or transfer of plan assets or liabilities? ... 26-5
Q 26:10 What is the purpose of Form 5310-A? ... 26-5
Q 26:11 Who must file Form 5310-A with the IRS? ... 26-5
Q 26:12 Are there any situations in which Form 5310-A does not have to be filed with the IRS? ... 26-6
Q 26:13 If a Form 5310-A must be filed with the IRS, when must it be filed? ... 26-8
Q 26:14 Are there penalties for filing a Form 5310-A late? ... 26-8

Chapter 27 Reporting Distributions: IRS Form 1099-R

Overview

Q 27:1 What is IRS Form 1099-R? ... 27-1
Q 27:2 Is military retirement pay reported on Form 1099-R? ... 27-2
Q 27:3 How are payments to an alternate payee under a QDRO reported? ... 27-2
Q 27:4 How are payments to nonresident aliens reported? ... 27-2

General Requirements

Q 27:5 Who must file Form 1099-R? ... 27-2
Q 27:6 When must Form 1099-R be given to the participant? ... 27-2
Q 27:7 May an extension be granted to provide Form 1099-Rs to participants? ... 27-3
Q 27:8 When must Form 1099-R and Form 1096 be filed with the IRS? ... 27-3
Q 27:9 May an extension to file Form 1099-R with the IRS be granted? ... 27-3
Q 27:10 What are the penalties for failure to file Form 1099-Rs with the IRS on a timely basis? ... 27-4
Q 27:11 Are there any exceptions to the penalties for failure to file correct Form 1099-Rs? ... 27-5
Q 27:12 What are the penalties for failure to furnish correct Form 1099-R to a participant? ... 27-6

Q 27:13 Are there any exceptions to the penalties for failure to furnish correct Form 1099-R to a participant? **27-6**
Q 27:14 Where should paper returns for Forms 1099-R and 1096 be filed with the IRS? **27-6**
Q 27:15 Where should electronic returns be filed? **27-7**
Q 27:16 How should information returns be delivered to the IRS? **27-7**
Q 27:17 What types of retirement plan distributions are reported on Form 1099-R? **27-8**
Q 27:18 How are ESOP dividends reported? **27-8**
Q 27:19 How is a distribution from a DVEC account reported? **27-9**
Q 27:20 How is a *direct rollover* reported? **27-9**
Q 27:21 Are trustee-to-trustee transfers reported on Form 1099-R? **27-9**
Q 27:22 What happens if excess contributions or excess aggregate contributions are discovered after a total distribution? **27-9**

Line-by-Line Explanation

Q 27:23 What information must be reported on Form 1099-R? **27-10**
Q 27:24 How is an employee's Social Security number reported on Form 1099-R? **27-11**
Q 27:25 How is Box 1 of Form 1099-R completed? **27-11**
Q 27:26 How is Box 2a of Form 1099-R completed? **27-12**
Q 27:27 How is Box 2b of Form 1099-R completed? **27-12**
Q 27:28 How is Box 3 of Form 1099-R completed? **27-13**
Q 27:29 How is Box 4 of Form 1099-R completed? **27-13**
Q 27:30 How is Box 5 of Form 1099-R completed? **27-13**
Q 27:31 How is Box 6 of Form 1099-R completed? **27-14**
Q 27:32 How are the codes in Box 7 of Form 1099-R determined? **27-14**
Q 27:33 How is Box 8 of Form 1099-R completed? **27-19**
Q 27:34 How is Box 9a of Form 1099-R completed? **27-20**
Q 27:35 How is Box 9b of Form 1099-R completed? **27-20**
Q 27:36 How is Box 10 completed? **27-20**
Q 27:37 How is Box 11 completed? **27-20**
Q 27:38 How are Boxes 12 through 17 of Form 1099-R completed? **27-20**

Electronic Filing

Q 27:39 May Form 1099-R be filed electronically with the IRS? **27-21**
Q 27:40 What is the due date for electronic filing of Form 1099-R? **27-21**
Q 27:41 Is there a requirement for filing electronically? **27-21**
Q 27:42 Must IRS approval be obtained to file electronically? **27-21**
Q 27:43 May a waiver from filing electronically be granted? **27-21**
Q 27:44 What is the penalty for failure to file electronically? **27-22**

Q 27:45 May Form 1099-R be furnished electronically to a plan participant? 27-22
Q 27:46 What are common errors in preparing Form 1099-R? 27-23
Q 27:47 What are the administrative rules for paper filing of Form 1099-R? 27-23
Q 27:48 What format does the IRS suggest for the completion of Form 1099-Rs? 27-24
Q 27:49 How are Form 1099-Rs submitted to the IRS? 27-25

Correcting Form 1099-R

Q 27:50 How is an incorrect Form 1099-R corrected? 27-25
Q 27:51 What are the procedures for filing corrected returns on paper? ... 27-25
Q 27:52 May an incorrect Form 1099-R be voided? 27-26

Combined Federal/State Filing Program

Q 27:53 What is the Combined Federal/State Filing Program? 27-27
Q 27:54 What is the procedure for a payer to obtain approval to use the CF/SF Program? 27-27
Q 27:55 What is the deadline for requesting approval to participate in the CF/SF Program? 27-27
Q 27:56 What states are participating in this program? 27-28

Chapter 28 Rollovers

Review of the Basics

Q 28:1 What is an eligible rollover distribution? 28-1
Q 28:2 Are there amounts that are not eligible rollover distributions? ... 28-2
Q 28:3 How is the balance to the credit of the participant defined? 28-3
Q 28:4 What happens if an eligible rollover distribution is received in cash by the participant? 28-3
Q 28:5 What is considered an eligible retirement plan under the rollover rules? 28-4
Q 28:6 What are the consequences of a rollover into an IRA more than 60 days after receipt of the distribution? 28-4
Q 28:7 May an individual other than the participant roll over funds into an IRA? 28-4

Challenges in IRA Rollovers

Q 28:8 What problems may be encountered in attempting a direct rollover to an IRA? 28-5
Q 28:9 What type of assets are IRA custodians often unwilling to accept? 28-5

Q 28:10 May an IRA custodian accept collectibles in a direct rollover? ... 28-5
Q 28:11 How do the mandatory tax withholding rules operate when collectibles are distributed in kind? ... 28-6
Q 28:12 How does an individual lose flexibility after electing a direct rollover? ... 28-7
Q 28:13 What happens if an employee who is older than age 70½ elects a direct rollover? ... 28-8
Q 28:14 How does a direct rollover affect an election under TEFRA 242(b)? ... 28-9
Q 28:15 When must distributions begin if the participant is older than age 70½ when the TEFRA Section 242(b) election is revoked? ... 28-9

Advantages and Disadvantages of IRA Rollovers

Q 28:16 What are the advantages of an IRA rollover? ... 28-11
Q 28:17 Is there an advantage in a direct rollover to an IRA for a participant who is entitled to a lump-sum distribution in a defined benefit plan? ... 28-11
Q 28:18 What are the disadvantages of an IRA rollover? ... 28-12

Roth IRAs

Q 28:19 What is a Roth IRA? ... 28-12
Q 28:20 Who qualifies for a Roth IRA rollover? ... 28-12
Q 28:21 How is an existing IRA converted into a Roth IRA? ... 28-13
Q 28:22 Is the Roth IRA conversion subject to the 10 percent additional income tax on early distributions for individuals who are younger than age 59½ at the time of conversion? ... 28-13
Q 28:23 Are investment earnings ever taxed when distributions are made from Roth IRAs? ... 28-14
Q 28:24 Does it make sense to roll over a distribution from a qualified plan to a Roth IRA? ... 28-14
Q 28:25 When might a Roth IRA conversion not make sense? ... 28-15
Q 28:26 How did the Tax Increase Prevention and Reconciliation Act of 2005 (TIPRA) and WRERA change the rules regarding Roth IRA conversions? ... 28-15

Chapter 29 Lump-Sum Distributions

Review

Q 29:1 What is a lump-sum distribution? ... 29-1
Q 29:2 How is disability defined for lump-sum purposes? ... 29-2
Q 29:3 What plans are aggregated for purposes of the lump-sum distribution rules? ... 29-2
Q 29:4 How is the balance to the credit of the participant defined? ... 29-2

Q 29:5 Is favorable tax treatment available to all individuals who qualify for lump-sum treatment? 29-2
Q 29:6 When may the participant elect special tax treatment? 29-3
Q 29:7 If an individual rolls over a portion of a lump-sum distribution to an IRA or another qualified plan, will favorable tax treatment be available for the remaining portion? 29-3

Calculating Taxable Amounts

Q 29:8 How is the total taxable amount determined? 29-3
Q 29:9 How is the minimum distribution allowance (MDA) computed? ... 29-3
Q 29:10 How does the computation change if the lump-sum distribution is paid to the beneficiary of a deceased participant? 29-4
Q 29:11 Who is eligible for grandfather treatment under TRA '86? 29-4
Q 29:12 How is the capital gains portion of the distribution determined? ... 29-5
Q 29:13 How is the capital gains portion of the distribution taxed? 29-5
Q 29:14 How is 10-year income averaging computed? 29-6
Q 29:15 How does the distribution of an annuity affect the taxation of a lump-sum distribution? 29-8

Economic Issues

Q 29:16 Should a participant take advantage of the availability of capital gains treatment or income average the entire distribution? ... 29-9

Impact of Other Taxes

Q 29:17 Must other taxes be taken into consideration when a participant receives a lump-sum distribution? 29-10
Q 29:18 How does the 10 percent additional income tax on early distributions affect the calculation of the taxes on a lump-sum distribution? 29-10

Advantages and Disadvantages of Lump-Sum Distributions

Q 29:19 What are the advantages to the participant of receiving a lump-sum distribution? 29-10
Q 29:20 What are the disadvantages of a lump-sum distribution? 29-11
Q 29:21 When does a lump-sum distribution make economic sense? ... 29-11
Q 29:22 How are employer securities in a lump-sum distribution treated? 29-12
Q 29:23 What happens if the estate of a deceased participant receives employer securities? 29-12

Part 1

In-Service Events

Chapter 1

In-Service Distributions

This chapter describes the rules for in-service distributions from qualified retirement plans. An in-service distribution is one that is made while the plan participant is still employed. Profit sharing plans (including 401(k) plans) and stock bonus plans may make in-service distributions, but defined benefit and money purchase pension plans generally may not. Employee stock ownership plan (ESOP) and tax-credit ESOP (TRASOP) in-service distributions are also discussed.

The *hardship distribution* provisions of the Pension Protection Act of 2006 (PPA) directed the Secretary of the Treasury to modify the rules relating to hardship distributions of employee elective contributions from Code Section 401(k) plans to permit such plans to treat a participant's beneficiary under the plan the same as the participant's spouse or dependent in determining whether the participant has incurred a hardship. [PPA § 826]

The *working retirement* provisions of PPA amended the Code and ERISA to permit pension plans (i.e., qualified defined benefit and money purchase pension plans) to make in-service distributions to participants who have reached age 62. These rules began to apply to such distributions made in plan years beginning after December 31, 2006 (e.g., to distributions made on or after January 1, 2007, from calendar-year pension plans). Thus, under Code Section 401(a)(36), as added by PPA, a plan would not fail to be a qualified *pension plan* under the Code or a *pension plan* under ERISA if it included a provision permitting such distributions during working retirement. [PPA § 905] On May 22, 2007, the IRS issued final regulations under Code Sections 401(a) and 411(d)(6) implementing PPA's working retirement provisions. The May 2007 IRS final regulations were generally applicable on May 22, 2007, but contained delayed effective dates for governmental plans (as defined in Code Section 414(d)) and certain collectively bargained plans. The May 2007 IRS final regulations would have applied to governmental plans for plan years beginning on or after January 1, 2009.

However, in Notice 2008-98, the IRS delayed the application of the final regulations to governmental plans until plan years beginning on or after January 1, 2011. Notice 2008-98, however, did not change the effective date of the final regulations for any plans that are not governmental plans. [Notice 2008-98, 2008-4 I.R.B. 1080] In Notice 2009-86, the IRS further delayed the application of the final regulations to governmental plans until plan years beginning on or after January 1, 2013, but it did not change the effective date of the final regulations for any non-governmental plans. [Notice 2009-86, 2009-46 I.R.B. 629]

On June 10, 2016, the IRS issued Notice 2016-39 [2016-26 I.R.B. 1068] and Revenue Procedure 2016-36 [2016-26 I.R.B. 1160]. Notice 2016-39 provides guidance as to whether payments received by an employee from a qualified retirement plan during phased retirement are "amounts received as an annuity" under Code Section 72. Revenue Procedure 2016-36 provides that the requirements of Notice 2016-39 do not apply to amounts that are received from a non-qualified contract.

On February 23, 2017, IRS/EP Examinations issued a Memorandum (a "field directive") to Employee Plans (EP) Examinations employees, providing guidelines they must follow during 401(k) plan examinations (e.g., audits and compliance checks) to determine whether distributions from plans that use the deemed (i.e., safe harbor) "immediate and heavy financial need" hardship standards have been adequately substantiated, either with source documents (for example, estimates, contract, bill, and statements from third parties) or summaries of information from source documents. The IRS Memorandum became effective on February 23, 2017.

Profit Sharing Plans 1-2
Hardship Distributions 1-5
Pension Plans 1-23
Employee Stock Ownership Plans 1-30

Profit Sharing Plans

Q 1:1 What are the general rules for in-service distributions from profit sharing plans?

In general, profit sharing plans (including 401(k) plans) and stock bonus plans may distribute all or a portion of the participant's account balance:

1. After a fixed number of years;
2. After reaching a stated age; or
3. Upon the prior occurrence of a stated event, such as layoff, illness, disability, retirement, death, or severance of employment. Under these rules, hardship withdrawals from profit sharing plans (including 401(k) plans) and stock bonus plans also are permitted.

[Treas. Reg. § 1.401-1(b)(1)(ii)]

Q 1:2 In applying the withdrawal rules, what is considered a "fixed number of years"?

The minimum time frame is two years from the date the amounts were contributed to the plan. A plan that permits withdrawal of vested monies before two years elapse is not considered to be qualified under Code Section 401(a). [Rev. Rul. 71-295, 1971-2 C.B. 184; Rev. Rul. 73-553, 1973-2 C.B. 130]

The profit sharing plan described in Revenue Ruling 71-295 [1971-2 C.B. 184] permitted a participant to withdraw any portion of the employer's contribution 18 months after it was made. The plan did not impose any other conditions upon the participant's right to withdraw. Citing Treasury Regulations Section 1.401-1(b)(1)(ii), which permits profit sharing plans to make distributions after a fixed number of years, the attainment of a stated age, or upon the prior occurrence of some event such as layoff, illness, disability, retirement, death, or severance of employment, the IRS stated that the term "fixed number of years" means at least two years, and held that the subject plan's 18-month requirement caused it to fail to be a "profit sharing plan" under Code Section 401(a).

In Revenue Ruling 73-553 [1973-2 C.B. 130], a corporation using the accrual method of accounting established a profit sharing plan intended to qualify under Code Section 401(a). Both the corporation and the plan operated on a calendar-year basis. The plan allowed participants, in November of each year, to elect to withdraw any portion of the employer contribution that was credited to their accounts during the year before the preceding year. The amount that participants elected to withdraw would be distributed in January of the year following the year of their election. The plan specified that a contribution for a year, made after the end of that year but within the period described in Code Section 404(a)(6) (i.e., the period prescribed for filing the corporation's income tax return, including extensions), was deemed to have been credited on December 31 of that year for purposes of the election to withdraw employer contributions. The plan also provided that each withdrawal the participants made would result in a six-month suspension of their participation. Code Section 404(a)(6) states that an accrual-basis taxpayer is deemed to have made a payment on the last day of the year of accrual if the payment is on account of that taxable year and is made within the time prescribed by law for filing the return for that year (including extensions). Treasury Regulations Section 1.401-1(b)(1)(ii) permits qualified profit sharing plans to make distributions upon the occurrence of several events, including after a "fixed number of years," which means at least two years. The IRS held that although Code Section 404(a)(6) provides for the deductibility of contributions that are made within a specified period after the end of a taxable year, it does not change the date on which contributions are actually made or the period during which they accumulate under the plan. The IRS observed that in the case at hand, the plan permitted amounts to be withdrawn after they were deemed to be paid under Code Section 404(a)(6), but before the requisite two-year period had been completed. For example, amounts that were contributed to the plan in March 1971 and credited for the year 1970 could be withdrawn in January 1973 if the necessary election were made in November 1972. Therefore, the plan permitted the withdrawal of amounts that had not been accumulated for at least two years. On this basis, the IRS held that the plan was not a qualified profit sharing plan under Code Section 404(a).

Example 1-1: Pamela is a participant in the Nantucket Company profit sharing plan. The plan permits the withdrawal of vested monies after two years. Pamela decides she would like to withdraw the maximum amount in April 2019. The plan has annual valuation dates, and the maximum amount available for withdrawal is Pamela's account balance as of December 31, 2016, which is $3,200. However, Pamela's current account balance is $4,000, of which only $2,000 is vested. Therefore, only $2,000 is available for withdrawal.

Q 1:3 Are there any exceptions to the two-year rule for withdrawals from profit sharing plans?

Yes. An alternate rule is provided that allows a participant who has participated in the plan for at least 60 months to withdraw his or her entire vested account balance. This withdrawal is available even though some monies may have been in the plan for less than two years. [Rev. Rul. 68-24, 1968-1 C.B. 150] A second exception is hardship withdrawals (see Qs 1:4 and 1:5).

The profit sharing plan described in Revenue Ruling 68-24 [1968-1 C.B. 150] allowed an individual who had participated in the plan for at least 60 months to withdraw his or her entire vested account balance, including employer contributions made within the last 24 months. The plan also provided that any participant who made a withdrawal had to suspend his or her participation for at least six months. The IRS observed that neither Treasury Regulations Section 1.401-1(b)(1)(ii) nor Revenue Ruling 54-231 [1954-1 C.B. 150] (which was superseded by Revenue Ruling 71-295 [1971-2 C.B. 184], described in Q 1:2) contained an exhaustive list of events, the occurrence of which would permit contributions to profit sharing plans to be distributed before they have accumulated for at least two years. The IRS found that 60 months of participation under the subject plan would result in a significant deferral of compensation, and that the completion of such a period of participation is the occurrence of an event that would permit a withdrawal within the meaning of Treasury Regulations Section 1.401-1(b)(1)(ii). Accordingly, the IRS held that the plan was a qualified profit sharing plan under Code Section 401(a).

Example 1-2: Frank, an employee of the Highland Falls Corporation, has been a participant in the company's profit sharing plan for more than five years. He needs a bit of cash to invest in a new side business, race car restoration. He may withdraw his entire vested account balance of $127,345, even though most of the contributions were made within the last two years.

Hardship Distributions

Q 1:4 May a profit sharing or stock bonus plan distribute all or part of a participant's vested account balance because of a hardship?

Yes. A profit sharing or stock bonus plan may distribute all or a portion of a participant's vested account balance in the event of a hardship. However, these three rules must be satisfied before a hardship distribution may be made:

1. The term *hardship* must be defined in the plan document;
2. Uniform and nondiscriminatory rules must be followed in determining whether a hardship exists and the amount of the distribution necessary to alleviate the hardship; and
3. The amount of the hardship distribution may not exceed the participant's vested interest under the plan.

[Rev. Rul. 71-224, 1971-1 C.B. 124]

In Revenue Ruling 71-224, the IRS deemed these rules to be satisfied when a participant submitted positive evidence to the plan's trustee, demonstrating that he was, in fact, suffering a financial hardship, which the plan defined as "circumstances of sufficient severity that a participant is confronted by present or impending financial ruin or his family is clearly endangered by present or impending want or privation." The plan set forth examples of circumstances where hardship may be found, but did not limit the finding of hardship to those listed.

Example 1-3: Frank, an employee of the Hallandale Corporation, participates in the company's profit sharing plan. The plan permits withdrawals in the event of financial hardship, which the plan defines in the same manner as the plan described in Revenue Ruling 71-224 (see above). Frank demonstrates that he is at risk of being evicted from his home in Lincoln, Rhode Island, in January (during which the average temperature is only 20 degrees). It is likely that Frank will qualify for a hardship withdrawal from the plan.

Q 1:5 How is a hardship distribution from a profit sharing or stock bonus plan taxed?

A hardship distribution from a profit sharing or stock bonus plan is a taxable distribution, and is taxed just like any other distribution from a qualified retirement plan. Hardship distributions from any qualified plan are not eligible for direct rollover treatment. [I.R.C. § 402(c)(4)(C)]

Q 1:6 May a 401(k) plan make hardship distributions?

Yes. A 401(k) plan that is a profit sharing or stock bonus plan may provide that *elective contributions* may be distributed on account of hardship. [I.R.C. § 401(k)(2)(B)(i)(IV); Treas. Reg. § 1.401(k)-1(d)(1)(ii), (3)]

PPA's 401(k) hardship withdrawal provision directed the Secretary of the Treasury to modify the rules for determining whether a participant has had a hardship for purposes of the 401(k) distribution rules to provide that if an event (including the occurrence of a medical expense) would constitute a hardship under the plan if it occurred with respect to the participant's spouse or dependent (as defined in Code Section 152), such event would, to the extent permitted under the plan, also constitute a hardship if it occurs with respect to a person who is the participant's nonspouse, nondependent beneficiary. These expanded hardship distribution rules were required to be issued within 180 days after PPA's August 17, 2006, enactment date. [PPA § 826] IRS Notice 2007-7, 2007-5 I.R.B. 395, provides that a 401(k) plan that permits hardship distributions of elective contributions to a participant only for expenses described in Treasury Regulations Section 1.401(k)-1(d)(3)(iii)(B) may, beginning August 17, 2006, permit distributions for expenses described in Treasury Regulations Section 1.401(k)-1(d)(3)(iii)(B)(1), (3), or (5) (relating to medical, tuition, and burial or funeral expenses, respectively) for a primary beneficiary under the plan. [IRS Notice 2007-7, 2007-5 I.R.B. 395, Q&A-5(a)] For this purpose, a *primary beneficiary under the plan* is an individual who is named as a beneficiary under the plan and has an unconditional right to all or a portion of the participant's account balance under the plan upon the participant's death. [IRS Notice 2007-7, 2007-5 I.R.B. 395, Q&A-5(a)] A plan that adopts these expanded hardship provisions must still satisfy all the other requirements applicable to hardship distributions, such as the requirement that the distribution be necessary to satisfy the financial need. [IRS Notice 2007-7, 2007-5 I.R.B. 395, Q&A-5(a)]

According to the IRS, the plan sponsor, even one that uses a third-party administrator (TPA) to handle participant transactions, is still ultimately responsible for obtaining and keeping the proper documentation for hardship distributions. In the IRS's view, failure to have such records available for IRS examination would be treated as a qualification failure that should be corrected using Employee Plans Compliance Resolution System (EPCRS). The IRS advises that the plan sponsor should retain the following records in paper or electronic format:

1. Documentation of the hardship request, review, and approval;
2. Financial information and documentation that substantiates the employee's immediate and heavy financial need;
3. Documentation to support that the hardship distribution was properly made in accordance with the applicable plan provisions and the Code; and
4. Proof of the actual distribution made and related Forms 1099-R. [https://www.irs.gov/Retirement-Plans/Its-Up-to-Plan-Sponsors-to-Track-Loans-Hardship-Distributions]

In the IRS's view, it is not sufficient for plan participants to keep their own records of hardship distributions, because participants may leave employment or fail to keep copies of hardship documentation, making their records inaccessible in an IRS audit. According to the IRS, electronic self-certification is not sufficient documentation of the nature of a participant's hardship, as IRS audits have shown that some TPAs allow participants to electronically self-certify that they satisfy the criteria to receive a hardship distribution. Citing Treasury Regulations Section 1.401(k)-1(d)(3)(iv)(C) and (D), the IRS has stated that self-certification is permitted to show that a distribution was the sole way to alleviate a hardship, but, because self-certification is not allowed to show the nature of the hardship, plan sponsors must request and retain additional documentation to show the nature of the hardship. [https://www.irs.gov/Retirement-Plans/Its-Up-to-Plan-Sponsors-to-Track-Loans-Hardship-Distributions]

A February 23, 2017, Memorandum ("field directive") for EP Examinations Employees (available at https://www.irs.gov/pub/foia/ig/spder/tege-04-0217-0008.pdf), issued by the Acting Director, EP Examinations, at the IRS, sets forth substantiation guidelines for EP Examinations employees examining whether a 401(k) plan hardship distribution is "deemed to be on account of a heavy financial need" under the safe harbor standards set forth in Treasury Regulations Section 1.401(k)-1(d)(3)(iii)(B). The memorandum did not address substantiation of non-safe-harbor hardship distributions under Treasury Regulations Section 1.401(k)-1(d)(3)(iii)(A). The memorandum cautioned that it was not a pronouncement of law and is not subject to use, citation or reliance as such, and that no part of the Memorandum would affect the operation of any other provision of the Code, Treasury Regulations or guidance thereunder.

As background, a 401(k) plan may distribute participants' elective deferrals on account of hardship only if the distribution is made on account of an immediate and heavy financial need of the participant and is necessary to satisfy the financial need. A distribution is "deemed to be on account of an immediate and heavy financial need" only if it is for one or more of the following:

1. Expenses for medical care deductible under Code § 213(d) for the participant or his or her spouse, children, dependents (as defined in Code § 152) or primary beneficiary under the plan;
2. Costs directly related to the purchase of the participant's primary residence;
3. Payment of tuition, related educational fees, room and board expenses for up to the next 12 months of post-secondary education for the participant or his or her spouse, children, dependents (as so defined) or primary beneficiary under the plan;
4. Payments necessary to prevent the eviction of the participant from his or her principal residence or foreclosure of the mortgage on that residence;
5. Payments for burial or funeral expenses for the participants' deceased parents, spouse, children, dependents (as so defined), or primary beneficiary under the plan; or

6. Expenses for the repair of damages to the participant's principal residence that would qualify for the casualty deduction under Code § 165.

Substantiation that a distribution is for one or more of the above items is required to determine that a hardship distribution is "deemed to be on account of an immediate and heavy financial need."

The February 23, 2017, Memorandum for EP Examinations Employees provides the following administrative guidelines that EP employees must follow when they are auditing 401(k) plans and trying to determine whether participants requesting hardship distributions have provided the substantiation required for the plan's sponsoring employer or a TPA to have determined whether the distribution is "deemed to be on account of a heavy financial need":

1. Step 1. EP employees are directed to determine whether the 401(k) plan's sponsoring employer or TPA, prior to making a distribution, obtained either source documents (e.g., estimates, contracts, bills, and statements from third parties) or a summary of the information contained in the source documents. If a summary was used, the EP employee must determine whether the employer or TPA provided required notifications to the participant before making the distribution (i.e., notification that the hardship distribution is taxable and additional taxes could apply, that the amount of the distribution cannot exceed the immediate and heavy financial need, that hardship distributions cannot be made from earnings on elective contributions, qualified nonelective contributions (QNECs) or qualified matching contributions (QMACs), and that the participant agrees to preserve source documents and to make them available at any time, upon request, to the employer or TPA).
2. Step 2. EP employees are further directed to review the source documents or summaries that an employer or TPA has obtained to determine if they substantiate the hardship distribution, and also to review any required notifications that have been provided to participants, and if those notifications are incomplete or inconsistent, to request source documents from the employer or TPA. If a summary of information is complete and consistent but shows participants who have received more than two hardship distributions in a plan year, the EP employee may request source documents from the employer or TPA (including documentation of follow-up medical or funeral expenses or tuition on a quarterly school calendar). Also, if a TPA obtained a summary of source documents, the EP employee must determine whether the TPA provided a report or other access to data to the plan's sponsoring employer, at least annually, describing the hardship distributions made during the plan year.

Finally, the February 23, 2017, Memorandum for EP Examinations Employees provides that if the EP employee determines that all applicable requirements in Steps 1 and 2 have been satisfied, the 401(k) plan should be treated as satisfying the substantiation requirement for making hardship distributions "deemed to be on account of an immediate and heavy financial need." The guidance in the

Memorandum will be incorporated into the Internal Revenue Manual by February 23, 2019. (The Internal Revenue Manual serves as the single official compilation of policies, delegated authorities, procedures, instructions, and guidelines relating to the organization, functions, administration, and operations of the IRS.)

Q 1:7 When is a distribution from a 401(k) plan made on account of a hardship?

A distribution from a 401(k) plan is made on account of a hardship if it is:

1. Made on account of the employee's immediate and heavy financial need; and
2. Necessary to satisfy the financial need.

[Treas. Reg. § 1.401(k)-1(d)(3)(i)]

Determining the existence of an immediate and heavy financial need and the amount necessary to meet that need must be done in accordance with nondiscriminatory and objective standards set forth in the plan document. [Treas. Reg. § 1.401(k)-1(d)(3)(i)]

A 401(k) plan, profit sharing plan, or stock bonus plan that permits hardship distributions may be amended to specify or modify nondiscriminatory and objective standards for determining the existence of an immediate and heavy financial need, the amount necessary to meet the need, or other conditions relating to eligibility to receive a hardship distribution without violating the anti-cutback rules under Code Section 411(d)(6) and Treasury Regulations Section 1.411(d)-4. For example, a plan will not be treated as violating those rules merely because it is amended to specify or modify the resources an employee must exhaust to qualify for a hardship distribution or to require employees to provide additional statements or representations to establish the existence of a hardship. Any such plan may also be amended to eliminate hardship distributions. [Treas. Reg. § 1.411(d)-4, Q&A-2(b)(2)(x)]

Q 1:8 Are there any other limitations on the amount that may be distributed from a 401(k) plan on account of a hardship?

Yes. As explained in Q 1:7, a hardship distribution may be made from a 401(k) plan only if it is made on account of the employee's immediate and heavy financial need and made in an amount that is necessary to satisfy that financial need. In addition, a distribution from a 401(k) plan on account of hardship may not exceed the "maximum distributable amount." [Treas. Reg. § 1.401(k)-1(d)(3)(ii)]

Q 1:9 What is the maximum distributable amount?

The maximum distributable amount referred to in Q 1:8 equals the employee's total elective contributions as of the date of the distribution, reduced by the amount of previous distributions on account of hardship. [Treas. Reg. § 1.401(k)-1(d)(3)(ii)]

Under applicable Treasury Regulations in effect before the effective date of the Bipartisan Budget Act of 2018 (BBA) [Pub. L. No. 115-123 (Feb. 2018)], as a general rule, QNECs, QMACs, and accumulated earnings could not be distributed on account of hardship. However, a plan could include a grandfather rule for earnings, QNECs, and QMACs that accrued before December 31, 1988 (or, if later, the end of the last plan year ending before July 1, 1989). This was done by determining the total of the elective contributions, QNECs, and QMACs on the applicable date and using it as a frozen amount. Losses in the participant's account after that date did not reduce the amount. [Treas. Reg. § 1.401(k)-1(d)(3)(ii); Ann. 93-105, 1993-27 I.R.B. 15; Ann. 94-101, 1994-35 I.R.B. 53]

Example 1-4: Danby, an employee of the Rowley Harness Makers Corporation, has participated in the company's 401(k) plan since 1985. Because of a financial hardship, she wants to withdraw the maximum amount available from her elective contribution account. She has not taken any hardship withdrawals previously. The plan operates on a calendar-year basis; therefore, the amount that Danby may withdraw is the sum of:

1. Her December 31, 1988, elective contribution account balance;
2. Her December 31, 1988, QNEC account balance;
3. Her December 31, 1988, QMAC account balance; plus
4. Her elective contributions made after December 31, 1988.

The BBA expanded the types of funds that may be distributed in a hardship withdrawal to include QNECs, QMACs, 401(k) safe harbor plan contributions, and all earnings (including post-December 31, 1988, earnings on participants' elective deferrals), effective with respect to plan years beginning after December 31, 2018. [IRC § 401(k)(14)(A), as added by BBA § 41114(a)]

Q 1:10 How is it determined whether an employee has an "immediate and heavy financial need"?

The 401(k) plan must determine, based upon all relevant facts and circumstances, whether an employee has an immediate and heavy financial need justifying a hardship distribution. This is called the *general standard.* Employees who apply for a hardship distribution from a 401(k) plan that uses this general standard must specify what they need and why. [Treas. Reg. § 1.401(k)-1(d)(3)(iii)(A); Ann. 93-105, 1993-27 I.R.B. 15; Ann. 94-101, 1994-35 I.R.B. 53]

For example, the need to pay the funeral expenses of a family member would constitute an immediate and heavy financial need. However, there is generally no financial need for a luxury item: a distribution made to an employee for the purchase of a boat or a television would generally not constitute a distribution made on account of an immediate and heavy financial need. [Treas. Reg. § 1.401(k)-1(d)(3)(iii)(A)]

A financial need may be immediate and heavy even if it was reasonably foreseeable or voluntarily incurred by the employee. [Treas. Reg. § 1.401(k)-1(d)(3)(iii)(A)]

Example 1-5: Doc participates in the Western Biological Laboratories Corporation 401(k) plan. He needs to withdraw funds from the 401(k) plan to make a down payment on a house in Monterey. To satisfy the general standard, Doc must state (and provide appropriate documentation) that he needs $15,000 to make a down payment on a house. This financial need may still be immediate and heavy, even though it was reasonably foreseeable and voluntarily incurred.

Q 1:11 Are there any instances in which the 401(k) plan need not weigh all of the relevant facts and circumstances to determine whether the employee has an immediate and heavy financial need?

Yes, a 401(k) plan may establish certain safe harbors for the needs test. There are six instances (sometimes called "deemed hardship" situations) in which the 401(k) plan need not weigh all of the relevant facts and circumstances to determine whether the employee is suffering from an immediate and heavy financial need. Basically, the need is presumed to exist in the six "deemed hardship" situations described below, as long as the plan has adopted the deemed hardship rules. A distribution is deemed to be on account of an immediate and heavy financial need of the employee if the distribution is for:

1. Expenses for (or necessary to obtain) medical care for the employee or the employee's spouse, children, dependents (as defined in Code Section 152 and, for taxable years beginning on or after January 1, 2005, without regard to Code Sections 152(b)(1), (b)(2), and (d)(1)(B), or primary beneficiary (as defined in Q 1:6)) that would be deductible under Code Section 213(d) (determined without regard to whether the expenses exceed 10 percent of adjusted gross income or 7.5 percent of adjusted gross income for employees who are 65 years of age or older by the end of the taxable year);
2. Costs directly related to the purchase of a principal residence for the employee (excluding mortgage payments);
3. Payment of tuition, related educational fees, and room and board expenses for up to the next 12 months of post-secondary education for the employee, or the employee's spouse, children, dependents (as defined in Code Section 152 and, for taxable years beginning on or after January 1, 2005, without regard to Code Section 152(b)(1), (b)(2), and (d)(1)(B)), or primary beneficiary (as defined in Q 1:6);
4. Payments necessary to prevent the eviction of the employee from the employee's principal residence or foreclosure on the mortgage on that residence;
5. Payments for burial or funeral expenses for the employee's deceased parent, spouse, children, dependents (as defined in Code Section 152, and, for taxable years beginning on or after January 1, 2005, without regard to Code Section 152(d)(1)(B)), or primary beneficiary (as defined in Q 1:6); or

6. Expenses for the repair of damage to the employee's principal residence that would qualify for the casualty deduction under Code Section 165 (determined without regard to whether the loss exceeds 10 percent of adjusted gross income). The Tax Cuts and Jobs Act of 2017 (TCJA) [Pub. L. No. 115-97], enacted on December 22, 2017, narrowed the personal casualty loss deduction under Code Section 165 to losses attributable to a disaster declared by the President under Section 401 of the Robert T. Stafford Disaster Relief and Emergency Assistance Act (i.e., a federally declared disaster), applicable to losses incurred in taxable years 2018 through 2025. Thus, this TCJA change in effect narrows this category of safe harbor "deemed" hardships. [IRC § 165(h)(5), as added by TCJA § 11044, effective for taxable years 2018 to 2025]

[Treas. Reg. § 1.401(k)-1(d)(3)(iii)(B)(1)–(6)]

The IRS may prescribe additional guidance of general applicability, expanding the list of deemed immediate and heavy financial needs (see 1 through 6, above) and prescribing additional methods for distributions to be deemed necessary to satisfy an immediate and heavy financial need (see Q 1:13). [Treas. Reg. § 1.401(k)-1(d)(3)(v)]

Q 1:12 How does a 401(k) plan determine whether the amount of a distribution is necessary to satisfy the financial need caused by the hardship?

Distribution May Not Exceed Amount of Need. A distribution is treated as necessary to satisfy an immediate and heavy financial need of an employee only to the extent that the amount of the distribution is not in excess of the amount required to relieve the financial need. For this purpose, the amount required to satisfy the financial need may include any amounts necessary to pay any federal, state, or local income taxes or penalties reasonably anticipated to result from the distributions. [Treas. Reg. § 1.401(k)-1(d)(3)(iv)(A)]

No Alternative Means Available. A distribution is not treated as necessary to satisfy an immediate and heavy financial need of an employee to the extent the need may be relieved from other resources that are reasonably available to the employee. This determination generally is to be made on the basis of all the relevant facts and circumstances. For these purposes, the employee's resources are deemed to include those assets of the employee's spouse and minor children that are reasonably available to the employee. Thus, for example, a vacation home owned by the employee and the employee's spouse, whether as community property, joint tenants, tenants by the entirety, or tenants in common, generally will be deemed a resource of the employee. However, property held for the employee's child under an irrevocable trust or under the Uniform Gifts to Minors Act (or comparable state law) is not treated as a resource of the employee. [Treas. Reg. § 1.401(k)-1(d)(3)(iv)(B)]

Employer Reliance on Employee Representation. An immediate and heavy financial need generally may be treated as not capable of being relieved from other resources that are reasonably available to the employee, if the employer relies upon the employee's representation (made in writing or such other form as the IRS prescribes), unless the employer has actual knowledge to the contrary, that the need cannot reasonably be relieved:

1. Through reimbursement or compensation by insurance or otherwise;
2. By liquidation of the employee's assets;
3. By cessation of elective contributions or employee contributions under the plan;
4. By other currently available distributions (including distribution of ESOP dividends under Code Section 404(k)) and nontaxable (at the time of the loan) loans, under plans maintained by the employer or by any other employer; or
5. By borrowing from commercial sources on reasonable commercial terms in an amount sufficient to satisfy the need.

[Treas. Reg. § 1.401(k)-1(d)(3)(iv)(C)]

Employee Need Not Take Counterproductive Actions. A need cannot reasonably be relieved by one of the actions described in items 1 through 5 above if the effect would be to increase the amount of the need. For example, the need for funds to purchase a principal residence cannot reasonably be relieved by a plan loan if the loan would disqualify the employee from obtaining other necessary financing. [Treas. Reg. § 1.401(k)-1(d)(3)(iv)(D)]

Q 1:13 Are there circumstances under which a 401(k) plan may deem a distribution to be necessary?

Yes. Under Code Section 401(k)(2)(B)(i)(IV) as in effect until December 31, 2018, and related Treasury Regulations, a 401(k) plan could use a safe-harbor standard, deeming a distribution to be necessary to satisfy an immediate and heavy financial need of an employee if the following two requirements were satisfied:

1. The employee had obtained all other currently available distributions (including distribution of ESOP dividends under Code Section 404(k), but not hardship distributions) and nontaxable (at the time of the loan) loans, under the plan and all other plans maintained by the employer; and
2. The employee was prohibited, under the terms of the plan or an otherwise legally enforceable agreement, from making elective contributions and employee contributions to the plan and all other plans maintained by the employer for at least six months after receipt of the hardship distribution.

[Treas. Reg. § 1.401(k)-1(d)(3)(iv)(E)]

For purposes of these rules, the phrase "plans maintained by the employer" means all qualified and nonqualified plans of deferred compensation maintained by the employer, including a cash-or-deferred arrangement that is part of a Code Section 125 cafeteria plan. However, it does not include the mandatory employee contribution portion of a defined benefit plan or a health or welfare benefit plan (including one that is part of a Section 125 cafeteria plan). In addition, for purposes of the six-month post-distribution suspension period described in item 2, above, the phrase, "plans maintained by the employer" also includes stock option, stock purchase, or similar plans maintained by the employer. [Treas. Reg. § 1.401(k)-1(d)(3)(iv)(F)]

The IRS may prescribe additional guidance of general applicability, expanding the list of deemed immediate and heavy financial needs (see Q 1:11) and prescribing additional methods for distributions to be deemed necessary to satisfy an immediate and heavy financial need (see Example 1-2, above). [Treas. Reg. § 1.401(k)-1(d)(3)(v)]

The BBA, enacted on February 9, 2018, made the following changes to the above two "deemed necessary to satisfy an immediate and heavy financial need" requirements, effective for plan years beginning after December 31, 2018:

1. The BBA removed the requirement that a participant must first request all available loans before being allowed to take a hardship withdrawal [I.R.C. § 401(k)(14)(B), as added by BBA § 41114(a), effective for plan years beginning after December 31, 2018]; and
2. The BBA also directed the Secretary of the Treasury to modify Treasury Regulations Section 1.401(k)-1(d)(3)(iv)(E), no later than one year after BBA's February 9, 2018, enactment date, to delete the six-month prohibition on post-hardship withdrawal contributions imposed by Treasury Regulations Section 1.401(k)-1(d)(3)(iv)(E)(2), effective with respect to plan years beginning after December 31, 2018 [BBA § 41113].

Q 1:14 Can the IRS apply special hardship rules to provide relief to taxpayers who have been adversely affected by disasters?

Yes. In the event of a presidentially declared disaster, the IRS can apply special hardship distribution rules to provide relief to taxpayers who have been adversely affected by those disasters. Most presidentially declared disasters have been severe storms (such as tornadoes and hurricanes), but they may also be wildfires, flooding, or earthquakes. Affected taxpayers are generally people who live in or have a business in an area directly affected by the disaster [https://www.irs.gov/retirement-plans/disaster-relief-for-retirement-plans-and-iras]. In the past, the IRS has applied the following types of special hardship distribution rules to provide relief to taxpayers affected by disasters: permitting hardship distributions for any type of hardship (not just those enumerated in the Treasury Regulations); relaxing substantiation requirements for proof of hardship; and lifting the otherwise-applicable six-month elective contribution suspension period following a hardship distribution.

Special Hardship Distribution Rules for Victims of Hurricane Sandy. In Announcement 2012-44, 2012-49 I.R.B. 663, the IRS provided relief to taxpayers who were adversely affected by Hurricane Sandy and who had retirement assets in qualified plans that they wished to use to alleviate hardships caused by that hurricane. Announcement 2012-44 provided that a qualified plan would not be treated as failing to satisfy any requirement of the Code or regulations merely because it made a hardship distribution to an employee or former employee whose principal residence on October 26, 2012, was located in one of the counties or Tribal Nations that had been identified as covered disaster areas because of the devastation caused by Hurricane Sandy or whose place of employment was located in one of those counties or Tribal Nations on that date or whose lineal ascendant or descendant, dependent, or spouse had a principal residence or place of employment in one of those counties or Tribal Nations on that date. Announcement 2012-44 further provided that plan administrators could rely upon representations from the employee or former employee as to the need for and amount of a hardship distribution, unless the plan administrator had actual knowledge to the contrary and the distribution was treated as a hardship distribution for all purposes under the Code and regulations. Announcement 2012-44 also provided that a qualified plan that did not already permit hardship or other in-service distributions nevertheless could make Hurricane Sandy-related hardship distributions pursuant to the IRS Announcement (except from QNEC or QMAC accounts or from earnings on elective contributions), provided the plan document was amended no later than the end of the first plan year beginning after December 31, 2012 (i.e., no later than December 31, 2013, for calendar-year plans). Announcement 2012-44 further provided that the relief it offered applied to any hardship, not just to the types of hardships enumerated in IRS regulations, and it lifted the post-distribution contribution restrictions (i.e., the six-month ban on post-hardship distribution contributions) that otherwise would have applied absent that relief. To qualify for the relief provided under Announcement 2012-44, a hardship distribution had to have been made due to a hardship resulting from Hurricane Sandy and had to have been made on or after October 26, 2012, and no later than February 1, 2013.

Special Hardship Distribution Rules for Victims of the Louisiana Storms in 2016 and 2017. In Announcement 2016-30, 2016-37 I.R.B. 355, the IRS provided relief from certain verification procedures that might otherwise have been required under qualified employer retirement plans for hardship distributions made on or after August 11, 2016, and no later than January 17, 2017, to an employee or former employee whose principal residence on August 11, 2016, was located in one of the parishes that were identified as part of a covered disaster area because of the devastation caused by the Louisiana storms or whose place of employment was located in one of those parishes on that date or whose lineal ascendant or descendant, dependent or spouse had a principal residence or place of employment in one of those parishes on that date. The parishes included in the covered disaster area for the Louisiana storms were identified in an IRS News Release, which can be found at https://www.irs.gov/uac/tax-relief-for-victims-of-severe-storms-flooding-in-louisiana. The relief provided in Announcement 2016-30 applied to any hardship of an affected employee, not just those enumerated in the Treasury Regulations. In addition, Announcement 2016-30 lifted the normal six-month elective contribution suspension period following hardship distributions. Announcement 2016-30 further provided that, to make a hardship distribution, a qualified retirement plan that did not provide for hardship distributions could be amended to provide for such distributions no later than the end of the first plan year beginning after December 31, 2016.

Announcement 2016-30 also provided that a qualified retirement plan would not be treated as failing to follow procedural requirements for hardship distributions imposed by the terms of the plan merely because those requirements were disregarded for any period beginning on or after August 11, 2016, and continuing through January 17, 2017, with respect to hardship distributions to individuals who qualified for relief, provided the plan administrator made a good-faith diligent effort under the circumstances to comply with those requirements. However, as soon as practicable, the plan administrator must make a reasonable attempt to assemble any foregone documentation. For example, if spousal consent were required for a distribution and the plan terms require production of a death certificate if the employee claims his or her spouse is deceased, the plan will not be disqualified for failure to operate in accordance with its terms if it made a distribution to a qualifying individual in the absence of a death certificate if it is reasonable to believe, under the circumstances, that the spouse is deceased, the distribution was made no later than January 17, 2017, and the plan administrator makes reasonable efforts to obtain the death certificate as soon as practicable. In addition, Announcement 2016-30 provided that the U.S. Department of Labor (DOL) had advised the IRS that it would not treat any person as having violated the provisions of Title I of ERISA solely because that person complied with the provisions of Announcement 2016-30. [IRS Ann. 2016-30, 2016-37 I.R.B. 355] The DOL also issued its own guidance on compliance with ERISA employee benefit rules for those adversely affected by the Louisiana Storms since August 11, 2016. [DOL News Release, available at https://www.dol.gov/newsroom/releases/ebsa/ebsa20160912; DOL FAQs for Participants and Beneficiaries Following the Louisiana Storms (Sept. 12, 2016), available at https://www.dol.gov/sites/default/files/ebsa/about-ebsa/our-activities/resource-center/faqs/for-participants-and-beneficiaries-following-louisiana-storms.pdf]

Special Hardship Rules for Victims of Hurricane Matthew in 2016 and 2017. In Announcement 2016-39, 2016-45 I.R.B. 720, the IRS provided relief from certain verification procedures that might otherwise have been required under qualified employer retirement plans for hardship distributions made on or after October 4, 2016 (October 3, 2016 for Florida) and no later than March 15, 2017, to an employee or former employee whose principal residence on October 4, 2016 (October 3, 2016 for Florida) was located in one of the counties identified for individual assistance by the Federal Emergency Management Agency (FEMA) because of the devastation caused by Hurricane Matthew or whose place of employment was located in one of those counties on that date. The counties identified for individual assistance by FEMA were in Florida, Georgia, North Carolina, and South Carolina and were found on FEMA's website at https://www.fema.gov/disasters. IRS Announcement 2016-39 provided that if additional counties in those states were identified by FEMA for individual assistance because of damage related to Hurricane Matthew, the relief provided in IRS Announcement 2016-39 would also apply from the date specified by FEMA as the beginning of the incident period, and that date should be substituted for references to October 4, 2016, in IRS Announcement 2016-39. The relief provided in Announcement 2016-39 applied to any hardship of an affected employee, not just those enumerated in the Treasury Regulations. In addition,

Announcement 2016-39 lifted the normal six-month elective contribution suspension period following hardship distributions. Announcement 2016-39 further provided that, to make a hardship distribution, a qualified retirement plan that did not provide for hardship distributions could be amended to provide for such distributions no later than the end of the first plan year beginning after December 31, 2016. Announcement 2016-39 also provided that a qualified retirement plan would not be treated as failing to follow procedural requirements for hardship distributions imposed by the terms of the plan merely because those requirements were disregarded for any period beginning on or after October 4, 2016 (October 3, 2016 for Florida), and continuing through March 15, 2017, with respect to hardship distributions to individuals who qualified for relief, provided the plan administrator made a good-faith diligent effort under the circumstances to comply with those requirements. However, as soon as practicable, the plan administrator must make a reasonable attempt to assemble any foregone documentation. For example, if spousal consent were required for a distribution and the plan terms require production of a death certificate if the employee claims his or her spouse is deceased, the plan will not be disqualified for failure to operate in accordance with its terms if it made a distribution to a qualifying individual in the absence of a death certificate if it is reasonable to believe, under the circumstances, that the spouse is deceased, the distribution was made no later than March 15, 2017, and the plan administrator makes reasonable efforts to obtain the death certificate as soon as practicable. In addition, Announcement 2016-39 provided that the DOL had advised the IRS that it would not treat any person as having violated the provisions of Title I of ERISA solely because that person complied with the provisions of Announcement 2016-39. [IRS Ann. 2016-39, 2016-45 I.R.B. 720]

Special Hardship Distribution Rules for Victims of Hurricane Harvey in 2017 and 2018. In Announcement 2017-11, 2017-39 I.R.B. 255, the IRS provided relief from certain verification procedures that might otherwise have been required under qualified employer retirement plans for hardship distributions made on or after August 23, 2017, and no later than January 31, 2018, to an employee or former employee whose principal residence on August 23, 2017, was located in one of the Texas counties identified for individual assistance by FEMA because of the devastation caused by Hurricane Harvey or whose place of employment was located in one of those counties on August 23, 2017, or whose lineal ascendant or descendant, dependent, or spouse had a principal residence or place of employment in one of those counties on that date. The counties identified for individual assistance by FEMA were found on FEMA's website at https://www.fema.gov/disasters. Announcement 2017-11 provided that if additional areas in Texas or other states were identified by FEMA for individual assistance because of damage related to Hurricane Harvey, the relief provided in Announcement 2017-11 would also apply, from the date specified by FEMA as the beginning of the incident period, and that date should be substituted for references to August 23, 2017, in Announcement 2017-11. The relief provided in Announcement 2017-11 applied to any hardship of an affected employee, not just those enumerated in the Treasury Regulations. In addition, Announcement 2017-11 lifted the then-applicable six-month elective contribution suspension period following hardship distributions. Announcement 2017-11 further provided that, to make a hardship distribution, a qualified retirement plan that did not provide for hardship distributions could be amended to provide for such distributions no later than the end of the first plan year beginning after December 31, 2017. Announcement 2017-11 also provided that a qualified retirement plan would not be treated as failing to follow procedural requirements for hardship distributions imposed by the terms of the plan merely because those requirements were disregarded for any period beginning on or after August 23, 2017, and continuing through January 31, 2018, with respect to hardship distributions to individuals who qualified for relief, provided the plan administrator made a good-faith diligent effort under the circumstances to comply with those requirements. However, as soon as practicable, the plan administrator was required to make an attempt to assemble any foregone documentation. For example, if spousal consent were required for a distribution and the plan terms required production of a death certificate if the employee claimed his or her spouse was deceased, the plan would not be disqualified for failure to operate in accordance with its terms if it made a distribution to a qualifying individual in the absence of a death certificate if it was reasonable to believe, under the circumstances, that the spouse was deceased, the distribution was made no later than January 31, 2018, and the plan administrator made reasonable efforts to obtain the death certificate as soon as practicable. In addition, Announcement 2017-11 provided that the DOL had advised the IRS that it would not treat any person as having violated the provisions of Title I of ERISA solely because that person complied with the provisions of Announcement 2017-11. [IRS Ann. 2017-11, 2017-39 I.R.B. 255]

Special Hardship Distribution Rules for Victims of Hurricane Irma in 2017 and 2018. In Announcement 2017-13, 2017-40 I.R.B. 271, the IRS provided relief from certain verification procedures that might otherwise have been required under qualified employer retirement plans for hardship distributions made on or after September 4, 2017, and no later than January 31, 2018, to an employee or former employee whose principal residence on September 4, 2017, was located in one of the Florida counties identified for individual assistance by FEMA because of the devastation caused by Hurricane Irma or whose place of employment was located in one of those counties on that date or whose lineal ascendant or descendant, dependent, or spouse had a principal residence or place of employment in one of those counties on that date. The areas identified for individual assistance by FEMA could be found on FEMA's website at https://www.fema.gov/disasters. Announcement 2017-13 provided that if additional areas were identified by FEMA for individual assistance because of damage related to Hurricane Irma, the relief provided in Announcement 2017-13 also would apply, from the date specified by FEMA as the beginning of the incident period, and that date would be substituted for references to September 4, 2017, in Announcement 2017-13. The relief provided in Announcement 2017-13 applied to any hardship of an affected employee, not just those enumerated in the Treasury Regulations. In addition, Announcement 2017-13 lifted the then-applicable six-month elective contribution suspension period following hardship distributions. Announcement 2017-13 further provided that, to make a hardship distribution, a qualified retirement plan that did not provide for hardship distributions could be amended to provide for such distributions no later than the end of the first plan year beginning after December 31, 2017. Announcement 2017-13 also provided that a qualified retirement plan would not be treated as failing to follow procedural requirements for hardship distributions imposed by the terms of the plan merely because those requirements were disregarded for any period beginning on or after September 4, 2017, and continuing through January 31, 2018, with respect to hardship distributions to individuals who qualified for relief, provided the plan administrator made a good-faith diligent effort under the circumstances to comply with those requirements. However, as soon as practicable, the plan administrator had to make a reasonable attempt to assemble any foregone documentation. For example, if spousal consent were required for a distribution and the plan terms required production of a death certificate if the employee claimed his or her spouse was deceased, the plan would not be disqualified for failure to operate in accordance with its terms if it made a distribution to a qualifying individual in the absence of a death certificate if it was reasonable to believe, under the circumstances, that the spouse was deceased, the distribution was made no later than January 31, 2018, and the plan administrator made reasonable efforts to obtain the death certificate as soon as practicable. In addition, Announcement 2017-13 provided that the DOL had advised the IRS that it would not treat any person as having violated the provisions of Title I of ERISA solely because that person complied with the provisions of Announcement 2017-13. [IRS Ann. 2017-13, 2017-40 I.R.B. 271]

Special Hardship Distribution Rules for Victims of Hurricane Maria and the California Wildfires in 2017 and 2018. In Announcement 2017-15, 2017-47 I.R.B. 534, the IRS provided relief from certain verification procedures that might otherwise have been required under qualified employer retirement plans for hardship distributions made on or after the applicable incident date (September 16, 2017, in the case of the U.S. Virgin Island, for Hurricane Maria; September 17, 2017, in the case of Puerto Rico, for Hurricane Maria; or October 8, 2018, in the case of California, for the California Wildfires) and no later than March 15, 2018, to an employee or former employee whose principal residence on the applicable incident date was located in one of the areas identified for individual assistance by FEMA because of the devastation caused by Hurricane Maria or the California Wildfires or whose place of employment was located in one of those areas on the applicable incident date or whose lineal ascendant or descendant, dependent, or spouse had a principal residence or place of employment in one of those areas on that date. The areas identified for individual assistance by FEMA could be found on FEMA's website at https://www.fema.gov/disasters. Announcement 2017-15 provided that if additional areas were identified by FEMA for individual assistance because of damage related to Hurricane Maria or the California Wildfires, the relief provided in Announcement 2017-15 would also apply, from the date specified by FEMA as the beginning of the incident period, and that date would be substituted for references to the applicable incident date in Announcement 2017-15. The relief provided in Announcement 2017-15 applied to any hardship of an affected employee, not just those enumerated in the Treasury Regulations. In addition, Announcement 2017-15 lifted the then-applicable six-month elective contribution suspension period following hardship distributions. Announcement 2017-15 further provided that, to make a hardship distribution, a qualified retirement plan that did not provide for hardship distributions could be amended to provide for such distributions no later than the end of the first plan year beginning after December 31, 2017. Announcement 2017-15 also provided that a qualified retirement plan would not be treated as failing to follow procedural requirements for hardship distributions imposed by the terms of the plan merely because those requirements were disregarded for any period beginning on or after the applicable incident date and continuing through March 15, 2018, with respect to hardship distributions to individuals who qualified for relief, provided the plan administrator made a good-faith diligent effort under the circumstances to comply with those requirements. However, as soon as practicable, the plan administrator had to make a reasonable attempt to assemble any foregone documentation. For example, if spousal consent were required for a distribution and the plan terms required production of a death certificate if the employee claimed that his or her spouse was deceased, the plan would not be disqualified for failure to operate in accordance with its terms if it made a distribution to a qualifying individual in the absence of a death certificate if it was reasonable to believe, under the circumstances, that the spouse was deceased, the distribution was made no later than March 15, 2018, and the plan administrator made reasonable efforts to obtain the death certificate as soon as practicable. In addition, Announcement 2017-15 provided that the DOL had advised the IRS that it would not treat any person as having violated the provisions of Title I of ERISA solely because that person complied with the provisions of Announcement 2017-15. [IRS Ann. 3017-15, 2017-47 I.R.B. 534]

Q 1:15 What additional relief for victims of Hurricanes Harvey, Irma, and Maria was provided by the Disaster Tax Relief and Airport and Airway Extension Act of 2017?

The Disaster Tax Relief and Airport and Airway Extension Act of 2017 (the "Relief Act"), enacted on September 29, 2017, offers relief for "qualified hurricane distributions" made from an eligible retirement plan (as defined in Code Section 402(c)(8)(B)):

1. On or after August 23, 2017, and before January 1, 2019, to an individual whose principal place of abode on August 23, 2017, was located in the Hurricane Harvey disaster area and who sustained an economic loss by reason of Hurricane Harvey;
2. On or after September 4, 2017, and before January 1, 2019, to an individual whose principal place of abode on September 4, 2017, was located in the Hurricane Irma disaster area and who sustained an economic loss by reason of Hurricane Irma; and
3. On or after September 16, 2017, and before January 1, 2019, to an individual whose principal place of abode on September 16, 2017, was located in the Hurricane Maria disaster area and who sustained an economic loss by reason of Hurricane Maria. [Relief Act § 502(a)(4)]

Qualified hurricane distributions received by qualifying individuals are not subject to the 10% additional income tax on early distributions under Code Section 72(t). [Relief Act § 502(a)(1)] The aggregate amount of qualified hurricane distributions taken by any qualified individual may not exceed $100,000 (regardless of whether received in one or more taxable years) and must be taken between the start date specified for each hurricane and January 1, 2019. [Relief Act § 502(a)(2)] A qualifying individual receiving a qualified hurricane distribution has two federal income tax options: the individual can repay all or part of the distribution to the plan within three years after receiving the distribution (which will be treated as timely rollover contributions, thus deferring federal income taxation), or the individual can elect to spread the federal income tax on the qualified hurricane distribution over that three-year period. [Relief Act § 502(a)(3) and (5)]

In addition, any individual who received a "qualified distribution," meaning—

1. A hardship withdrawal,
2. Received after February 28, 2017, and before September 21, 2017,
3. Which was used to purchase or construct a principal residence in the Hurricane Harvey disaster area, the Hurricane Irma disaster area, or the Hurricane Maria disaster area, but which was not so purchased or constructed on account of Hurricane Harvey, Hurricane Irma or Hurricane Maria,

was permitted to recontribute all or part of that withdrawal, during the period beginning on August 23, 2017, and ending on February 28, 2018, to any eligible retirement plan (as defined in Code Section 402(c)(8)(B)), and all such recontributions would be treated as timely rollover contributions. [Relief Act § 502(b)]

Q 1:16 What relief for 2016 and 2017 distributions from eligible retirement plans due to 2016 storms and flooding was provided by the TCJA?

The TCJA, enacted on December 22, 2017, provided the following federal income taxation relief for "qualified 2016 disaster distributions" of up to $100,000 made during 2016 or 2017 from an eligible retirement plan (as defined in Code Section 402(c)(8)(B)) to an individual whose principal place of abode at any time during 2016 was located in a "2016 disaster area" (i.e., any area with respect to which a major disaster had been declared by the President under Section 401 of the Robert T. Stafford Disaster Relief and Emergency Assistance Act during calendar year 2016—a Federally declared disaster area) and who had sustained an economic loss by reason of the events giving rise to the Presidential disaster declaration [TCJA § 11028(b)(1)(D)]:

1. Qualified 2016 disaster distributions are exempt from the 10 percent additional income tax on early distributions under Code Section 72(t) [TCJA § 11028(b)(1)(A)];
2. Qualified 2016 disaster distributions are not treated as eligible rollover distributions and so they are not subject to 20 percent mandatory income tax withholding or the Code Section 402(f) rollover notice requirements [TCJA § 11028(b)(1)(F)(i)];

3. Qualified 2016 disaster distributions are treated as permissible in-service distributions [TCJA § 11028(b)(1)(F)(ii)]; and
4. A qualifying individual receiving a qualified 2016 disaster distribution has two federal income tax options: the individual can repay all or part of the distribution to the plan within three years after receiving the distribution (which will be treated as timely rollover contributions, thus deferring federal income taxation), or the individual can elect to spread the federal income tax on the qualified 2016 disaster distribution over that three-year period. [TCJA § 11028(b)(1)(C) and (E)]

Plans that make qualified 2016 disaster distributions must be amended by the end of the first plan year beginning on or after January 1, 2018, or such later date as the Secretary of the Treasury prescribes. [TCJA § 11028(b)(2)(B)]

Q 1:17 What relief for 2017 and 2018 distributions from eligible retirement plans due to the 2017 California wildfires was provided by the BBA?

The BBA, enacted on February 9, 2018, provided the following federal income taxation relief for "qualified wildfire distributions" of up to $100,000 made on or after October 8, 2017, and before January 1, 2019, from an eligible retirement plan (as defined in Code Section 402(c)(8)(B)) to an individual whose principal place of abode during any portion of the period from October 8, 2017, to December 31, 2017, was located in the California wildfire disaster area and who had sustained an economic loss by reason of the wildfires to which the declaration of such area relates [BBA § 20102(a)(4)(A)]:

1. Qualified wildfire distributions are exempt from the 10 percent additional income tax on early distributions under Code Section 72(t) [BBA § 20102(a)(1)];
2. Qualified wildfire distributions are not treated as eligible rollover distributions and so they are not subject to 20 percent mandatory income tax withholding or the Code Section 402(f) rollover notice requirements [BBA § 20102(a)(6)(A)];
3. Qualified wildfire distributions are treated as permissible in-service distributions [BBA § 20102(a)(2)(B)]; and
4. A qualifying individual receiving a qualified wildfire distribution has two federal income tax options: the individual can repay all or part of the distribution to the plan within three years after receiving the distribution (which will be treated as timely rollover contributions, thus deferring federal income taxation), or the individual can elect to spread the federal income tax on the qualified wildfire distribution over that three-year period [BBA § 20102(a)(3) and (5)].

Plans that make qualified wildfire distributions must be amended by the end of the first plan year beginning on or after January 1, 2019, or such later date as the Secretary of the Treasury prescribes. [BBA § 20102(d)(2)(A)]

In addition, any individual who received a "qualified distribution," meaning—

1. A hardship withdrawal,
2. Received after March 31, 2017, and before January 15, 2018,
3. Which was to be used to purchase or construct a principal residence in the California wildfire disaster area but which was not so purchased or constructed on account of the wildfires to which the declaration of such area relates,

was permitted to recontribute all or part of that withdrawal, during the period beginning on October 8, 2017, and ending on June 30, 2018, to any eligible retirement plan (as defined in Code Section 402(c)(8)(B)), and all such recontributions would be treated as timely rollover contributions. [BBA § 20102(b)]

Pension Plans

Q 1:18 What are the rules for in-service distributions from pension plans?

Although profit sharing plans may allow for in-service distributions (see Qs 1:1–1:14), pension plans (defined benefit, money purchase, cash balance, and target benefit plans) generally may not make distributions until death, disability, separation from service, or retirement. This chapter discusses three rather limited exceptions to the rule:

1. Required minimum distributions to pension plan participants who are 5 percent owners and who continue to work after their required beginning date (RBD) (i.e., the April 1 of the calendar year following the calendar year in which the 5 percent owner reaches age 70½; (see Q 1:19)).
2. In-service distributions from pension plans to participants who have reached normal retirement age under the plan (see Q 1:20).
3. In-service distributions from pension plans to participants who have reached age 62 (see Q 1:20).

The IRS has ruled that distributions of subsidized early retirement benefits could not be made to defined benefit participants who had not yet reached age 62. In PLR 201147038, the IRS concluded that employees who "retire" on one day in order to qualify for an early benefit under the plan, with the explicit understanding between the employee and the employer that they are not separating from service with the employer, are not legitimately retired. The IRS ruled that because such employees would not actually separate from service and cease performing services for the employer when they "retire," the "retirements" would not constitute a legitimate basis to allow such participants to qualify for early retirement benefits (which would then be immediately suspended). The IRS further ruled that such "retirements" would violate Code Section 401(a) and result in plan disqualification. [PLR 201147038]

Q 1:19 When must a participant start receiving pension benefits while still employed?

The required minimum distribution rules under Code Section 401(a)(9) define the RBD on which required minimum distributions must be paid, or begin to be paid (see chapter 4).

A qualified plan participant who is a 5 percent owner (as defined in Code Section 416) must begin to receive distributions by the April 1 (the RBD) of the calendar year following the calendar year in which he or she reaches age 70½, even if he or she is still employed. [I.R.C. § 401(a)(9)(C)(ii)]

Q 1:20 Under what circumstances may in-service distributions be made from a qualified pension plan?

A qualified pension plan is a plan established and maintained by an employer primarily to provide systematically for the payment of definitely determinable benefits to its employees over a period of years, usually for life, after retirement. [Treas. Reg. § 1.401(a)-1(b)(1)(i)] A qualified pension plan generally may not distribute benefits to participants while they still are actively employed. In-service distributions may not be made from a qualified pension plan if the participant is under the plan's normal retirement age. However, in-service distributions may be made from a qualified pension plan to a participant who has reached the plan's normal retirement age. [Rev. Rul. 73-448, 1973-2 C.B. 136; Rev. Rul. 71-24, 1971-1 C.B. 114; Rev. Rul. 71-147, 1971-1 C.B.116; T.I.R.-1403, Q. M-15 (Sept. 17, 1975)]

A pension plan may allow participants to withdraw their voluntary contributions (and accumulated earnings) at any time prior to their termination of employment, however. [Rev. Rul. 60-323, 1960-2 C.B. 148; Rev. Rul. 69-277, 1969-1 C.B. 116]

Note that, because of the continuing accrual requirements (see Qs 1:22–1:24), it may make sense to design the pension plan so that it does not permit in-service distributions.

> **Example 1-6:** Elizabeth participates in the Cambridge Corporation defined benefit plan. Elizabeth continues to work after she reaches age 60, the plan's normal retirement age. She may begin receiving retirement benefits from the plan. Note that Elizabeth must continue to accrue benefits under the plan while working.

Under PPA's working retirement provisions, a pension plan (i.e., a qualified defined benefit plan or a money purchase pension plan) may provide that in-service distributions may be made to participants who have reached age 62. A plan with such a provision would not fail to be a qualified *pension plan* under the Code, nor would it fail to be a *pension plan* for ERISA purposes. A pension plan could include such an in-service provision, effective for distributions made in plan years beginning after December 31, 2006 (e.g., for distributions made on or after January 1, 2007, under calendar year pension plans). [PPA § 905]

IRS Final Regulations Permitting In-Service Distributions Upon the Attainment of Normal Retirement Age. On May 22, 2007, the IRS issued final regulations (72 Fed. Reg. 28604) under Code Sections 401(a) and 411(d)(6) permitting distributions to be made from a pension plan upon the attainment of normal retirement age prior to a participant's severance from employment with the employer maintaining the plan.

The May 2007 IRS final regulations modified existing regulations, including Treasury Regulations Section 1.401(a)-1, which generally require a pension plan (i.e., a defined benefit or money purchase pension plan) to be maintained primarily to provide systematically for the payment of definitely determinable benefits after retirement. The May 2007 regulations provided two exceptions to this general rule:

1. They clarified that a pension plan (i.e., a defined benefit or money purchase pension plan) is permitted to commence payment of retirement benefits to a participant after the participant has attained normal retirement age, in accordance with the provisions of Code Section 401(a)(36), as added by PPA's working retirement provisions. The regulations also provided rules on how low a plan's normal retirement age is permitted to be, and they included a related exception to the anti-cutback rules of Code Section 411(d)(6) to allow conforming amendments during a transitional period. [72 Fed. Reg. 28604, 28605 (May 22, 2007); Treas. Reg. § 1.401(a)-1(b)(1)(i)]
2. They reflect the provisions of Code Section 401(a)(36), as added by PPA's working retirement provisions. [72 Fed. Reg. 28604, 28605 (May 22, 2007); Treas. Reg. § 1.411(d)-4, Q&A-12]

Normal Retirement Age. The May 2007 IRS final regulations allow a pension plan (i.e., a defined benefit or money purchase pension plan) to pay benefits upon an employee's attainment of normal retirement age, even if the employee has not yet had a severance from employment with the employer maintaining the plan. [72 Fed. Reg. 28604, 28605 (May 22, 2007); Treas. Reg. § 1.401(a)-1(b)(1)(i)] The following rules apply:

1. *General rule.* The final regulations also include rules restricting a plan's normal retirement age. The general rule under the regulations is that the normal retirement age under a plan must be an age that is not earlier than the earliest age that is reasonably representative of the typical retirement age for the industry in which the covered workforce is employed. [72 Fed. Reg. 28604, 28605 (May 22, 2007); Treas. Reg. § 1.401(a)-1(b)(2)(i)]

2. *Age 62 safe harbor.* The final regulations include a safe harbor, which provides that a normal retirement age of at least age 62 is deemed to be not earlier than the typical age for the industry in which the covered workforce is employed. Thus, a plan satisfies this safe harbor if its normal retirement age is age 62 or if its normal retirement age is the later of age 62 or another specified date, such as the later of age 62 or the fifth anniversary of plan participation. However, a plan that is subject to Code Section 411 cannot provide for a normal retirement age that is later than the later of the time the participant attains

age 65 or the fifth anniversary of the time the participant commences participation in the plan. [72 Fed. Reg. 28604, 28605 (May 22, 2007); Treas. Reg. § 1.401(a)-1(b)(2)(ii)]

3. *Age 55 to age 62.* The final regulations provide that if a plan's normal retirement age is earlier than age 62, the determination of whether the age is not earlier than the earliest age that is reasonably representative of the typical retirement age for the industry in which the covered workforce is employed is based on all of the relevant facts and circumstances. If the normal retirement age is between ages 55 and 62, then it is generally expected that a good faith determination of the typical retirement age for the industry in which the covered workforce is employed that is made by the employer (or, in the case of a multiemployer plan, made by the trustees) will be given deference, assuming that the determination is reasonable under the facts and circumstances. [72 Fed. Reg. 28604, 28605 (May 22, 2007); Treas. Reg. § 1.401(a)-1(b)(2)(iii)]

4. *Under age 55.* However, a normal retirement age that is lower than age 55 is presumed to be earlier than the earliest age that is reasonably representative of the typical retirement age for the industry of the relevant covered workforce, absent facts and circumstances that demonstrate otherwise to the IRS. [72 Fed. Reg. 28604, 28605 (May 22, 2007); Treas. Reg. § 1.401(a)-1(b)(2)(iv)]

5. *Age 50 safe harbor for qualified public safety employees.* In the case of a plan where substantially all of the participants in the plan are "qualified public safety employees" (within the meaning of Code Section 72(t)(10)(B), as added by Section 828 of PPA, and as subsequently amended by Section 2 of the Defending Public Safety Employees' Retirement Act (enacted on June 29, 2015, and applicable to distributions made after December 31, 2015), and by Section 308 of the Protecting Americans from Tax Hikes (PATH) Act of 2015 (enacted on December 18, 2015, and also applicable to distributions made after December 31, 2015)), a normal retirement age of 50 or later is deemed not to be earlier than the earliest age that is reasonably representative of the typical retirement age for the industry in which the covered workforce is employed. [72 Fed. Reg. 28604, 28605 (May 22, 2007); Treas. Reg. § 1.401(a)-1(b)(2)(v)] Under Code Section 72(t)(10)(B), the term *qualified public safety employee* means (1) any employee of a state or political subdivisions of a state who provides police protection, firefighting services, or emergency medical services for any area within the jurisdiction of the state or political subdivision, or (2) any federal law enforcement officer described in Section 8331(20) or Section 8401(17) of Title 5 of the United States Code, any federal customs and border protection officer described in Section 8331(31) or Section 8401(36) of Title 5, any federal firefighter described in Section 8331(21) or Section 8401(14) of Title 5, any air traffic controller described in Section 8331(30) or Section 8401(35) of Title 5, any nuclear materials courier described in Section 8331(27) or Section 8401(33) of Title 5, any member of the United States Capitol Police, any member of the United States Supreme Court Police, or any diplomatic security special agent of the United States Department of State.

6. *Benefit distribution prior to retirement.* For purposes of the rules described in 1 through 5 above, retirement does not include a mere reduction in the

number of hours that an employee works. Accordingly, benefits may not be distributed prior to normal retirement age solely due to a reduction in the number of hours than an employee works. [Treas. Reg. § 1.401(a)-1(b)(3)]

7. *Effective date.* The rules described in 1 through 6 above generally became effective May 22, 2007. However, in the case of a governmental plan (as defined in Code Section 414(d)), those rules were to have been effective for plan years beginning on or after January 1, 2009. However, in Notice 2008-98, 2008-4 I.R.B. 1080, the IRS delayed the effective date for governmental plans until plan years beginning on or after January 1, 2011. In Notice 2009-86, 2009-46 I.R.B. 629, the IRS further delayed the effective date for governmental plans until plan years beginning on or after January 1, 2013. And, in the case of a plan maintained pursuant to one or more collective bargaining agreements that had been ratified and were in effect on May 22, 2007, those rules do not apply before the first plan year that begins after the last of such agreements terminates determined without regard to any extensions thereof (or, if earlier, May 24, 2010). Notice 2008-98 and Notice 2009-86 did not further delay the effective date for collectively bargained plans or for any other plan that is not a governmental plan. There is a special transition rule (described in "a" and "b," below) in the case of a plan's normal retirement age pursuant to the rules described in 1 through 5 above. [Treas. Reg. § 1.401(a)-1(b)(4)]

a. *Code Section 411(d)(6) relief during a transition period.* The May 2007 IRS final regulations provide an exception to the anti-cutback rules of Code Section 411(d)(6) to permit a plan to be amended during a transition period to conform to the rules (described above) concerning normal retirement age. This relief from the anti-cutback rules is limited to the elimination of a distribution option as a result of an amendment that raises the plan's normal retirement age from one that is inappropriately low to one that satisfies the requirements of Treasury Regulations Section 1.401(a)-1(a)(b)(2) (described in 1 through 5, above). Thus, a plan amendment that changes the normal retirement age under the plan to a later normal retirement age (in accordance with the May 2007 IRS final regulations) does not violate Code Section 411(d)(6) merely because the amendment eliminates the right to an in-service distribution prior to the amended normal retirement age. However, this transition rule does not provide any other relief. For example, this transition rule does not permit the amendment to reduce benefits in some manner that fails to satisfy Code Section 411(d)(6). Nor does the transition rule provide relief under Code Section 411(a)(9) (requiring that the normal retirement benefit not be less than the greater of any early retirement benefit payable under the plan or the benefit under the plan commencing at normal retirement age), Code Section 411(a)(10) (if the amendment changes the plan's vesting rules), or Code Section 4980F (or the parallel provision, ERISA Section 204(h)) (relating to amendments that reduce the rate of future benefit accrual). [72 Fed. Reg. 28604–28606 (May 22, 2007); Treas. Reg. § 1.411(d)-4, Q&A-12] This rule under Code Section 411(d)(6) permitting plan amendments during a transition period to conform to the rules (described above) concerning normal retirement age applies only to plan amendments that are adopted after May 22, 2007, and on or before the applicable remedial amendment period under Treasury Regulations Section 1.401(b)-1.

b. *Temporary Relief Under IRS Notice 2007-69.* IRS Notice 2007-69, 2007-35 I.R.B. 468 provided temporary relief, until the first day of the first plan year beginning after June 30, 2008, for certain pension plans under which the definition of normal retirement age may be required to be changed to comply with the May 2007 IRS final regulations relating to a plan's normal retirement age. IRS Notice 2007-69 also identified potential violations of the vesting and accrued benefit requirements for defined benefit plans under Code Section 411 that may arise from a definition of normal retirement age based on a minimum period of service. Finally, Notice 2007-69 requested comments from sponsors of governmental plans (as defined in Code Section 414(d)) and other plans not subject to the requirements of Code Section 411 on whether such a plan may define normal retirement age based on years of service. [IRS Notice 2007-69, 2007-35 I.R.B. 468]

IRS Guidance on the Treatment of Phased Retirement Payments Under Code Section 72. On June 10, 2016, the IRS issued guidance on the treatment of phased retirement payments under Code Section 72. Notice 2016-39, 2016-26 I.R.B. 1068, provides guidance as to whether payments received by an employee from a qualified retirement plan during phased retirement are "amounts received as an annuity" under Code Section 72. Revenue Procedure 2016-36, 2016-26 I.R.B. 1160 provides that the requirements of IRS Notice 2016-39 do not apply to amounts that are received from a non-qualified contract. Both Notice 2016-39 and Revenue Procedure 2016-36 apply to taxable years beginning on or after January 1, 2016.

1. *IRS Notice 2016-39.* Notice 2016-39 provides guidance in response to inquiries as to whether payments received by an employee from a qualified defined benefit plan during phased retirement are "amounts received as an annuity" under Code Section 72. For purposes of Notice 2016-39, "phased retirement" is an arrangement under which a participant in a qualified defined benefit plan commences the distribution of a portion of his or her retirement benefits from the plan while continuing to work on a part-time basis. Notice 2016-39 also provides guidance regarding the appropriate present value factors to be used for purposes of determining the basis recovery fraction of each payment received during phased retirement and provides guidance regarding the time for determining the basis recovery fraction for such phased retirement payments. Notice 2016-39 does not apply to amounts received from non-qualified contracts. Revenue Procure 2016-36, 2016-26 I.R.B. 1160, provides guidance on the application of Treasury Regulations Sections 1.72-2(b)(2) and 1.72-4(b)(1) to non-qualified contracts. [Notice 2016-39, 2016-26 I.R.B. 1068]

2. *IRS Revenue Procedure 2016-36.* Revenue Procedure 2016-36, 2016-26 I.R.B. 1160, provides guidance on the application of Treasury Regulations Sections 1.72-2(b)(2) and 1.72-4(b)(1) to amounts to which Code Section 72 applies that are received from a non-qualified contract. Revenue Procedure 2016-36 does not apply to amounts to which Code Section 72 applies that are received under a qualified retirement plan; Notice 2016-39 applies to such amounts. [Rev. Proc. 2016-36, 2016-26 I.R.B. 1160]

Q 1:21 How may in-service distributions be paid from a pension plan?

In-service distributions may be paid in any form permitted by the plan: single sum, joint and survivor annuity, or installments, for example (see chapter 10).

Q 1:22 Must benefits continue to accrue under a pension plan after an actively employed participant receives his or her normal retirement benefit?

Yes, benefits must continue to accrue under the plan for participants who continue to work after the plan's normal retirement age.

In a defined contribution pension plan, such as a money purchase or target benefit plan, the employer must continue to make contributions for all plan years beginning after 1987 on behalf of any such participant who has at least one hour of service in a plan year beginning after 1987.

In a defined benefit pension plan, the accrual of benefits must continue for all plan years beginning after 1987 for any such participant who has at least one hour of service in a plan year beginning after 1987. [OBRA § 9204(a)(1)]

Q 1:23 How must benefits continue to accrue under a defined benefit pension plan for participants who continue to work after the plan's normal retirement age?

See chapter 12 for the rules governing the continuation of benefit accruals under a defined benefit pension plan for participants who continue to work after the plan's normal retirement age.

Q 1:24 Must contributions continue to be made under a defined contribution pension plan for participants who continue to work after the plan's normal retirement age?

Yes. Contributions must continue to be made under a defined contribution pension plan (e.g., a money purchase pension plan), at the rate specified in the plan, for participants who continue to work after the plan's normal retirement age. In a target benefit plan, for example, the plan document will specify how contributions are determined for a participant who has reached the plan's normal retirement age.

Q 1:25 Will a participant who receives a single-sum distribution from a pension plan after reaching normal retirement age, but before termination of employment, be entitled to lump-sum tax treatment?

Only if the single-sum distribution was made before January 1, 2000, and if the participant had met each of these four requirements before the distribution was made:

1. He or she had completed at least five full years of participation in the plan;

2. He or she had reached age 59½;
3. He or she had reached the plan's normal retirement age; and
4. He or she had received, within a single taxable year, a distribution of the entire balance to his or her credit under the plan.

[Ltr. Rul. 8137048] (See chapter 19 for a detailed discussion of lump-sum treatment.)

However, pursuant to Small Business Job Protection Act of 1996 (SBJPA), favorable five-year forward averaging is not available for lump-sum distributions received in taxable years beginning after December 31, 1999. However, SBJPA retained a Tax Reform Act of 1986 (TRA'86) grandfather provision allowing individuals who were aged 50 or older as of January 1, 1986, to elect favorable 10-year forward averaging treatment. [SBJPA § 1401(c)(2)]

Employee Stock Ownership Plans

Q 1:26 When may an ESOP make an in-service distribution?

ESOPs are retirement plans that invest primarily in employer securities and operate under distribution rules that are similar to those of profit sharing plans. In-service distributions may be permitted (see Qs 1:1–1:5) and loans may be allowed (see chapter 2) under an ESOP. However, some in-service distribution rules are unique to ESOPs. For example, ESOP participants who meet certain age and service requirements must be allowed to diversify a portion of their ESOP account balances; however, as an alternative to diversification, the plan may permit an in-service distribution of the diversifiable portion of the participant's account.

In-service distributions are also available to participants in a special form of an ESOP, known as TRASOP. Although the tax benefits of TRASOPs have disappeared, some TRASOPs still exist and are subject to unique distribution rules (see Qs 1:31–1:34).

Dividends paid on employer securities held in an ESOP may be paid directly to ESOP participants, instead of being allocated to their ESOP accounts. The dividends generally are deductible by the employer and includible in participants' gross income when paid (see Qs 1:44–1:49).

Q 1:27 What investment diversification requirements apply to an ESOP?

An ESOP or TRASOP must provide that each qualified participant may elect, within 90 days after the close of each plan year within the qualified election period, to direct the plan as to the investment of at least 25 percent of his or her account balance. For the last plan year within the qualified election period, a qualified participant may elect to diversify at least 50 percent of his or her account balance. The 25 percent limit is not an annual limit; that is, once the election is made to diversify 25 percent of the account balance, another 25 percent election may not be made. [I.R.C. § 401(a)(28)(B)]

Q 1:28 Who is a qualified participant for these purposes?

A qualified participant for purposes of these ESOP diversification requirements is an employee who has completed at least 10 years of participation under the ESOP and has reached age 55. [I.R.C. § 401(a)(28)(B)(iii)]

> **Example 1-7:** Vicki participates in the Quincy Corporation ESOP. She started participation at age 45. Vicki will become a qualified participant at age 55, after she completes 10 years of participation.

Q 1:29 What is the qualified election period for these purposes?

The qualified election period, for purposes of these ESOP diversification requirements, is the six-plan-year period beginning with the later of:

1. The first plan year in which the individual first became a qualified participant; or
2. The first plan year beginning after December 31, 1986.

An exception to this general rule allows an employer to elect to treat an employee who first becomes a qualified participant in the first plan year beginning in 1987 as having become a qualified participant in the first plan year beginning in 1988. [I.R.C. § 401(a)(28)(B)(iv)]

> **Example 1-8:** Janice becomes a qualified participant in the Ferry Corporation ESOP in 2013. The ESOP's plan year begins on July 1. The qualified election period includes these six plan years:
>
> - July 1, 2013 through June 30, 2014
> - July 1, 2014 through June 30, 2015
> - July 1, 2015 through June 30, 2016
> - July 1, 2016 through June 30, 2017
> - July 1, 2017 through June 30, 2018
> - July 1, 2018 through June 30, 2019

Q 1:30 How does an ESOP meet the diversification requirements?

An ESOP may meet the diversification requirements in one of two ways:

1. The ESOP or another plan of the plan sponsor must offer at least three investment options to each participant making a diversification election and, within 90 days after the period during which the election may be made, the plan invests the portion of the participant's account covered by the election in accordance with his or her election; or
2. The portion of the participant's account covered by the election is distributed within 90 days after the period during which the election may be made.

[I.R.C. § 401(a)(28)(B)(ii)]

Example 1-9: The Hallandale Corporation ESOP must offer diversification elections to Frank. The plan may choose one of two alternatives as a means of diversification: offering three additional investment options or distributing the diversifiable shares in cash.

Q 1:31 Which employer securities are subject to the diversification requirement?

Employer securities acquired by, or contributed to, an ESOP or a TRASOP after December 31, 1986, are subject to the diversification requirement. Dividends paid to an ESOP after December 31, 1986, either in cash or stock, also are subject to the diversification requirement even if such dividends are paid with respect to employer securities acquired before December 31, 1986. [Notice 88-56, Q&A-1, 1988-1 C.B. 540]

Q 1:32 Are there any exceptions to the diversification requirement for employer securities acquired or contributed to a TRASOP?

Yes. Certain employer securities acquired by, or contributed to, a TRASOP after December 31, 1986, are deemed to be acquired or contributed to the ESOP before January 1, 1987, and, therefore, are not subject to the diversification requirement if:

- A tax credit was calculated under former Code Section 41(a) for compensation paid or accrued before January 1, 1987.
- The securities were acquired or contributed within the time period allowed under Code Sections 404(a)(6), 41(c)(2), and 41(c)(4).
- The securities were allocated no later than the last day of the plan year ending within the employer's first taxable year ending on or after December 31, 1986.

[Notice 88-56, Q&A-2, 1988-1 C.B. 540]

Example 1-10: Cambridge Novelties Corporation's fiscal year begins on July 1, but its TRASOP's plan year begins on January 1. Securities allocated to participants' accounts on or before December 31, 1987, are not subject to the diversification requirements.

Q 1:33 Are there some circumstances when employer securities acquired after December 31, 1986, are treated as acquired by, or contributed to, an ESOP on or before December 31, 1986?

Yes, under the following circumstances:

1. Cash or other assets resulting from the disposition of employer securities pursuant to a corporate reorganization or acquisition attempt (whether or not successful) that are used to purchase other employer securities, if the period between the disposition and the reinvestment does not exceed 90 days. (An extension of the 90-day period may be granted by the

IRS under rules similar to those contained in Treasury Regulations Section 1.46-8(e)(10). For dispositions after June 8, 1988, no extensions will be granted unless applied for within 90 days after the disposition.)

2. Employer securities acquired by an ESOP or TRASOP after December 31, 1986, that were purchased with contributions made to the ESOP in cash on or before December 31, 1986, if the contributions were used to purchase employer securities within 60 days after the date of the contribution.
3. Employer securities acquired by an ESOP or TRASOP after December 31, 1986, that were purchased with earnings or dividends paid in cash to an ESOP on or before December 31, 1986, if the proceeds are invested in employer securities within 60 days of the receipt of the proceeds by the ESOP.
4. Employer securities acquired by an ESOP after December 31, 1986, that were purchased with amounts transferred to an ESOP on or before December 31, 1986, pursuant to a transaction described in Code Section 4980, if the amounts are used to purchase employer securities within the time period prescribed in Code Section 4980(c)(3)(B).

[Notice 88-56, Q&A-3, 1988-1 C.B. 540]

Q 1:34 Are there any simplified methods for determining the number of employer securities subject to the diversification rules?

Yes, if the sponsor of an ESOP or TRASOP adopts the model amendments contained in IRS Notice 87-2 [1987-1 C.B. 396], the portion of a qualified participant's account balance attributable to employer securities acquired by, or contributed to, the ESOP after December 31, 1986, may be determined by multiplying the number of shares of employer securities allocated to the participant's account by this fraction:

$$\frac{\text{Number of shares acquired by or contributed to the plan after December 31, 1986}}{\text{Total number of shares held by the plan on the date nearest the qualification date}}$$

[Notice 88-56, Q&A-5, 1988-1 C.B. 540]

Example 1-11: Joanne participates in the Cambridge Novelties Corporation ESOP. The plan sponsor has adopted the model amendments discussed above and chooses to use the simplified method for determining post-1986 shares. Joanne reaches age 55 and has 10 years of participation in the plan. There are currently 1,250 shares of Cambridge Novelties stock allocated to her account. The number of shares acquired by, or contributed to, the ESOP after December 31, 1986, is 15,000 shares. On December 31, 1995, the date that Joanne became a qualified participant (eligible for diversification), the total number of shares held by the plan is 25,000. The number of shares in Joanne's account, treated as contributed or acquired after December 31, 1986, is computed as follows:

$$1{,}250 \times 15{,}000 \div 25{,}000 = 750 \text{ shares}$$

Q 1:35 Are small account balances subject to the diversification requirements?

No, if the fair market value of the employer securities allocated to a participant's account (only securities acquired or contributed after December 31, 1986) on the valuation date immediately preceding the date the participant becomes a qualified participant is $500 or less, the balance is not subject to the diversification rules. [Notice 88-56, Q&A-7, 1988-1 C.B. 540]

Q 1:36 What portion of a qualified participant's account is subject to the diversification requirement?

The portion of a qualified participant's account subject to the diversification election in the first five years of the qualified election period is equal to:

- 25 percent of the total number of shares of employer securities acquired by, or contributed to, the plan after December 31, 1986, that have ever been allocated to a qualified participant's account on or before the most recent plan allocation date, less
- The number of shares of employer securities previously distributed, transferred, or diversified pursuant to a diversification election made after December 31, 1986.

The resulting number of shares may be rounded to the nearest whole integer. In the sixth year of the qualified election period, "50 percent" is substituted for "25 percent" above. [Notice 88-56, Q&A-9, 1988-1 C.B. 540]

Example 1-12: Tim participates in the Cambridge Novelties Corporation's ESOP and has 750 shares of employer securities allocated to his account as of June 30, 2013, which are attributable to post-1986 acquisitions or contributions. The first year of the qualified election period for Tim is the plan year ending June 30, 2013. Of the 750 shares, 25 percent or 188 shares (rounded to the nearest integer) may be diversified. Tim elects the diversification option for the plan year ending June 30, 2014, and during this plan year an additional 50 shares are allocated to his account. The net number of shares in Tim's account is 612 shares (750 + 50 − 188). For the plan year ending June 30, 2015, Tim may elect to diversify an additional 12 shares, calculated as follows:

$$25\% \times (750 + 50) - 188 = 12 \text{ shares}$$

In the final year of his qualified election period, the plan year ending June 30, 2018, there are 1,075 shares allocated to Tim's account. He has previously diversified 200 shares in making a diversification election. The number of shares Tim may diversify in the final year is calculated as follows:

$$50\% \times (1{,}075 + 200) - 200 = 438$$

Q 1:37 May an ESOP permit the diversification of amounts in excess of those required?

Yes. However, if the plan complies with the diversification requirement by distributing cash to the participant (see Q 1:30), then no more than 25 percent of the post-1986 employer securities (50 percent in the final year of the qualified election period) may be distributed. [Notice 88-56, Q&A-11, 1988-1 C.B. 540]

Example 1-13: Narragansett Bay Corporation's ESOP satisfies the diversification requirement by allowing participants who reach age 55 with 10 years of participation to transfer at least 25 percent (but no more than 50 percent) of the account balance to be invested in three distinct funds. Therefore, the ESOP satisfies the diversification rules.

Example 1-14: The Limerock Grocery Store's ESOP satisfies the diversification requirement by distributing 25 percent of an eligible participant's account. The ESOP, however, will not satisfy the diversification requirements if more than 25 percent may be distributed.

Q 1:38 May the diversification requirement be satisfied by transferring shares to another defined contribution plan of the employer?

Yes, the plan may offer the option to the participant to direct the plan to transfer the diversifiable shares to another qualified defined contribution plan of the employer if the plan offers at least three distinct investment options. The transfer must be made no later than 90 days after the last day of the period during which the election can be made. The transfer must also comply with the qualification requirements of Code Sections 414(l), 411(d)(6), and 401(a)(11) (see Q 1:39). [Notice 88-56, Q&A-13, 1988-1 C.B. 540]

Q 1:39 What are the requirements for a qualified transfer?

A transfer from an ESOP to another defined contribution plan of the employer must meet these three requirements:

1. The amount credited to the account balance of the participant in the transferee defined contribution plan must be greater than or equal to the amount transferred from the ESOP. [Treas. Reg. § 1.414(l)-1(d)]
2. The distribution options available to the participant in the ESOP must continue to remain available to the participant in the other plan. [I.R.C. § 411(d)(6)]
3. The ESOP must comply with the consent requirements of Code Section 401(a)(11) (see chapter 11).

[Treas. Reg. § 1.401(a)-20, Q&A-5]

Example 1-15: Barbara participates in the ESOP of Warwick Music Stores. She is entitled to diversify 25 percent of her account balance of $352,000. Barbara is the first person in the company eligible to make the diversification election. Because Warwick Music Stores also sponsors a 401(k) plan with five distinct investment options, Barbara is offered the opportunity to transfer $88,000 to the 401(k) plan. Because the ESOP offers two forms of payment, lump sum and five-year installments, these options must continue to be available to Barbara in the 401(k) plan.

Q 1:40 Must the transferee defined contribution plan comply with the safe harbor described in ERISA Section 404(c)?

No, compliance with ERISA Section 404(c) is not required. The Secretary of the Treasury has been instructed to issue regulations defining what is a "distinct" investment option, but the regulations are yet to be issued.

Q 1:41 How are employer securities valued for purposes of the diversification requirement?

Fair market value is to be used for securities readily tradable on an established securities market. If employer securities are not readily tradable on an established securities market, an independent appraiser must handle the valuation of securities. An independent appraiser is any appraiser meeting the requirements of Treasury Regulations Section 1.170A-13(c)(5). [I.R.C. § 401(a)(28)(C)]

Q 1:42 Who is an independent appraiser?

An independent appraiser is an individual who holds himself or herself out to the public as an appraiser or performs appraisals on a regular basis and meets all of these three requirements:

1. The appraiser is qualified to make appraisals of employer securities;
2. The appraiser is not one of the following parties: the plan sponsor, an employee or former employee of the plan sponsor, a person related to an employee or former employee of the plan sponsor, or a person regularly used by the plan sponsor; and
3. The appraiser understands that an intentionally false or fraudulent overstatement of the value of the employer securities described in the appraisal or appraisal summary may subject the appraiser to civil penalties. [Treas. Reg. § 1.170A-13(c)(5)]

Q 1:43 May amounts distributed as part of the diversification election be rolled over to an eligible retirement plan?

Yes, as long as the distribution satisfies the requirement for an eligible rollover distribution (see chapter 21).

Q 1:44 How are dividends on employer securities handled in an ESOP?

Plan sponsors of ESOPs or TRASOPs, as well as participants in those plans, receive a benefit when dividends are paid on employer securities held by such plans. The plan sponsor may choose to use the dividends to purchase additional employer securities, hold the dividends in cash, reinvest in other securities, or simply pay the dividend directly to the participant.

Q 1:45 What is the tax consequence if the employer pays dividends on employer securities directly to the participant?

For the employer, the dividends paid on employer securities held in the ESOP are tax deductible, unlike other dividends paid on employer securities not held in the ESOP. For the employee, the dividends, if paid in cash, represent ordinary income. [I.R.C. §§ 404(k)(1), 72(e)]

> **Example 1-16:** Cambridge Novelties Corporation, a publicly traded corporation, declares a dividend of 20 cents per share on its common stock. Elizabeth, a participant in the ESOP, has 300 shares of Cambridge Novelties stock allocated to her account. Cambridge Novelties, the plan sponsor, chooses to distribute the dividend in cash to each participant in the ESOP. Elizabeth receives a check for $60, which will be taxable as ordinary income.

Q 1:46 How may dividends on ESOP shares be distributed to plan participants?

In accordance with the provisions of the ESOP plan document, the dividends may be:

1. Paid in cash to the ESOP's participants (or their beneficiaries);
2. Paid to the ESOP and then distributed in cash to the ESOP's participants (or their beneficiaries) not later than 90 days after the close of the plan year in which paid; or
3. At the election of the ESOP's participants (or their beneficiaries):
   (a) Paid as provided in items 1 and 2, above; or
   (b) Paid to the ESOP and reinvested in qualifying employer securities.

[I.R.C. § 404(k)(2)(A)]

Q 1:47 Are dividends paid from an ESOP to plan participants subject to the 10 percent additional income tax on early distributions?

No, they are exempt from the 10 percent additional income tax on early distributions. [I.R.C. § 72(t)(2)(A)(vi)] (See chapter 20 for a more detailed discussion of the 10 percent additional income tax on early distributions.)

Q 1:48 Are dividends paid from an ESOP subject to spousal consent if the dividend exceeds $5,000?

No. [I.R.C. § 411(a)(11)(C)] (See chapter 11 for a detailed discussion on the spousal consent rules.)

Q 1:49 Are dividends paid from an ESOP subject to mandatory withholding?

No. [I.R.C. § 3405(e)(1)(B)(iv)] (See chapter 24 for a detailed discussion of the withholding rules.)

Chapter 2

Loans

This chapter describes the Internal Revenue Code and Employee Retirement Income Security Act of 1974 (ERISA) rules that apply to loans from qualified retirement plans. Generally, under the Internal Revenue Code ("the Code"), a loan from a qualified retirement plan is treated as a taxable distribution to the participant unless it meets the requirements of Code Section 72(p). Loans that meet those requirements are not taxable. Plan loans must also satisfy other requirements under the Code and ERISA, or they will be prohibited transactions.

General Rule: Loans from Qualified Employer Plans Treated as Taxable Distributions 2-1
Treatment of Distributions Attributable to Qualified Retirement Plan Loans 2-13
Special Loan Rules for Certain Disaster Victims 2-29
Loans as Prohibited Transactions 2-37
Spousal Consent for Loans Made by Plans Subject to the Survivor Annuity Requirements 2-49
Federal Truth in Lending Act 2-50

General Rule: Loans from Qualified Employer Plans Treated as Taxable Distributions

Q 2:1 What are some of the most significant plan loan rules?

A loan from a qualified employer plan must meet several requirements under the Code and ERISA.

Plan Loan Rules Under Code Section 72(p). A loan to a participant or a beneficiary from a qualified employer plan will be treated as a taxable distribution (a "deemed distribution") under Code Section 72(p) if it fails to meet any one of these requirements:

1. The dollar amount of the loan must not exceed the amount limitations of Code Section 72(p)(2)(A).
2. The amount of the loan (when added to the outstanding balance of all other loans from the plan) may not exceed the lesser of:
   a. $50,000, reduced by the excess (if any) of:
      i. The highest outstanding balance of loans from the plan during the one-year period ending on the day before the date on which the loan was made, over
      ii. The outstanding balance of loans from the plan on the date on which the loan was made; or
   c. The greater of:
      i. One-half of the participant's vested account balance under the plan (determined without regard to any accumulated deductible employee contributions (QVECs)); or
      ii. $10,000.
3. The term of the loan must satisfy the repayment term requirement of Code Section 72(p)(2)(B), under which the loan must be repaid over five years. If, however, the loan is a home loan—that is, one used to acquire a dwelling unit that, within a reasonable period of time, is to be used (determined at the time the loan is made) as the participant's principal residence, as that term is defined in Code Section 1034—the loan may be repaid over a period exceeding five years.
4. The loan's repayment schedule must satisfy the level amortization requirement of Code Section 72(p)(2)(C), which requires that the loan be repaid in substantially level payments, made at least quarterly over the term of the loan.
5. The loan must meet the enforceable agreement requirement, which requires that the loan must be evidenced by a legally enforceable agreement (which may include more than one document), and the terms of the agreement must demonstrate compliance with the statutory requirements of Code Section 72(p)(2) (described in (1) through (3), above) as well as with the requirements of Treasury Regulations Section 1.72(p)-1. [Treas. Reg. § 1.72(p)-1, Q&A-3(b)] Thus, the loan agreement must specify the amount and date of the loan, the term of the loan, and the repayment schedule. The loan agreement does not have to be signed if the agreement is enforceable under applicable law without being signed. The agreement must be set forth either—
   a. In a written paper document;
   b. In a document that is delivered through an electronic medium that is reasonably accessible to the participant or the beneficiary and that is provided under an electronic system that satisfies the requirements of Treasury Regulations Section 1.401(a)-21 [Treas. Reg. § 1.72(p)-1, Q&A-3(b)(2)]

Under Code Section 72(p)(1), an amount received by a participant or beneficiary as a loan from a qualified employer plan is treated as having been received as a taxable distribution from the plan (a deemed distribution), unless the loan satisfies the above requirements. [I.R.C. § 72(p)(1)(A), (B)] For purposes of Code Section 72(p) and Treasury Regulations Section 1.72(p)-1, a loan made from a contract that has been purchased under a qualified employer plan (including a contract that has been distributed to the participant or beneficiary) is considered a loan made under a qualified employer plan. [I.R.C. § 72(p)(5); Treas. Reg. § 1.72(p)-1, Q&A-1(a)]

Under Code Section 72(p), if a participant or beneficiary assigns or pledges, or agrees to assign or pledge, any portion of his or her interest in a qualified employer plan as security for a loan, the portion that is assigned or pledged, or is subject to an agreement to assign or pledge, is treated as a loan from the plan to the individual, and that portion will be subject to the deemed distribution rule described above. [I.R.C. § 72(p)(1)(B)] Under Code Section 72(p) and Treasury Regulations Section 1.72(p)-1, any assignment or pledge, or agreement to assign or pledge, of any portion of a participant's or a beneficiary's interest in a contract that has been purchased under a qualified employer plan, including a contract that has been distributed to the participant or the beneficiary, will be considered an assignment or pledge of, or an agreement to assign or pledge, an interest in a qualified employer plan. However, if all or a portion of a participant's or a beneficiary's interest in a qualified employer plan is pledged or assigned as security for a loan from the plan to the participant or the beneficiary, only the amount of the loan received by the participant or beneficiary, not the amount pledged or assigned, is treated as a loan. [Treas. Reg. § 1.72(p)-1, Q&A-1(b)]

Prohibited Transaction Rules Under the Code and ERISA. For plan loans not to be prohibited transactions under the Code and ERISA, they must satisfy these five conditions:

1. They must be available to all participants and beneficiaries on a reasonably equivalent basis.
2. They must not be available to highly compensated participants in an amount greater than the amount made available to non-highly compensated participants.
3. They must be made in accordance with the plan's specific loan provisions.
4. They must bear a reasonable rate of interest.
5. They must be adequately secured.

[I.R.C. § 4975(d)(1)(A)–(E); ERISA § 408(b)(1)(A)–(E)]

Prior to the enactment of Economic Growth and Tax Relief Reconciliation Act (EGTRRA), the statutory exemptions (under the Code and ERISA) to the prohibited transaction rules for plan loans did not apply to plan loans made to owner-employees. The term *owner-employee* included a sole proprietor, a partner who owned more than 10 percent of the capital or profits interest in a partnership, an employee or officer of a Subchapter S corporation who owned more than 5 percent of the outstanding stock of the corporation, and an IRA owner, as well as certain family members of an owner-employee and certain corporations owned by an owner-employee.

EGTRRA generally eliminated the former rules relating to plan loans made to an owner-employee (other than an IRA owner). Thus, the general statutory exemption, under the Code and ERISA, began to apply to plan loans to owner-employees (other than IRA owners) made in years beginning after December 31, 2001.

IRS Documentation Requirements. According to the IRS, the plan sponsor, even one that uses a third-party administrator to handle participant transactions, is still ultimately responsible for obtaining and keeping the proper documentation for plan loans. The IRS advises that the plan sponsor should retain the following records, in paper or electronic format, for each plan loan granted to a participant:

1. Evidence of the loan application, review, and approval process;
2. An executed plan loan note;
3. If applicable, documentation verifying that the loan proceeds were used to purchase or construct a primary residence;
4. Evidence of loan repayments; and
5. Evidence of collection activities associated with loans in default and the related Forms 1099-R, if applicable.

According to the IRS, if a participant requests a loan with a repayment period in excess of five years for the purpose of purchasing or constructing a primary residence, the plan sponsor must obtain documentation of the home purchase before the loan is approved. IRS audits have found that some plan administrators impermissibly allowed participants to self-certify their eligibility for these loans. [https://www.irs.gov/Retirement-Plans/Its-Up-to-Plan-Sponsors-to-Track-Loans-Hardship-Distributions]

Q 2:2 What is a qualified employer plan for purposes of Code Section 72(p)?

For purposes of Code Section 72(p) and Treasury Regulations Section 1.72(p)-1, a *qualified employer plan* means:

1. A plan described in Code Section 401(a), which includes a trust exempt from tax under Code Section 501(a);
2. An annuity plan described in Code Section 403(a);
3. A plan under which amounts are contributed by an individual's employer for an annuity contract as described in Code Section 403(b);
4. Any plan, whether or not qualified, established and maintained for its employees by the United States, by a state or political subdivision, or by an agency or instrumentality of such governmental entities (i.e., a governmental plan); or

5. Any plan described (or determined to be described) in items 1, 2, 3, or 4 above.

[Treas. Reg. § 1.72(p)-1, Q&A-2]

Q 2:3 If a loan from a qualified employer plan to a participant or beneficiary fails to meet the requirements of Code Section 72(p), when does a deemed distribution occur?

Under Code Section 72(p), which governs the tax treatment of plan loans, a deemed distribution occurs at the first time any of the requirements described in the first list numbered (1) through (4) of Q 2:1 are not met in form or in operation. [Treas. Reg. § 1.72(p)-1, Q&A-4(a)] Thus, the deemed distribution may occur at the time the loan is made or at a later date. [Treas. Reg. § 1.72(p)-1, Q&A-4(a)]

Loans That Fail to Meet Requirements When They Are Made. If the terms of the loan do not require repayments that satisfy the repayment term requirement of Code Section 72(p)(2)(B) or the level amortization requirement of Code Section 72(p)(2)(C), or if the loan is not evidenced by an enforceable agreement that meets the requirements of Treasury Regulations Section 1.72(p)-1, Q&A-3(b), the entire amount of the loan is a deemed distribution under Code Section 72(p) at the time the loan is made. [Treas. Reg. § 1.72(p)-1, Q&A-4(a)]

However, if the loan satisfies the repayment term requirement, the level amortization requirement, and the enforceable agreement requirement, but the amount loaned exceeds the amount limitations of Code Section 72(p)(2)(A), the amount of the loan in excess of the applicable limitation is a deemed distribution at the time the loan is made. [Treas. Reg. § 1.72(p)-1, Q&A-4(a)]

Loans That Fail to Meet Requirements After They Are Made. If the loan initially satisfies the amount limitations, the repayment term requirement, the level amortization requirement, and the enforceable agreement requirement, but if payments are not made in accordance with the terms of the loan, the entire outstanding balance of the loan at the time of the failure is treated as a taxable distribution (i.e., a deemed distribution) at the time of the failure. [Treas. Reg. § 1.72(p)-1, Q&A-4(a), Q&A-10, Q&A-11]

The failure to make any installment payment when due in accordance with the terms of the loan violates the level amortization requirement of Code Section 72(p)(2)(C) and thus results in a deemed distribution at the time of such failure. However, the plan administrator may allow a cure period, and the level amortization requirement will not be treated as having been violated if the installment payment is made not later than the end of the cure period. The cure period cannot continue beyond the last day of the calendar quarter following the calendar quarter in which the required installment payment was due. [Treas. Reg. § 1.72(p)-1, Q&A-10(a)]

Examples 2-1 through 2-4 that follow illustrate how the plan loan rules apply and are based on the assumption that a bona fide loan is made to a participant from a qualified defined contribution plan pursuant to an enforceable agreement, with adequate security, and with an interest rate and repayment terms that are commercially reasonable. (The particular interest rate used is 8.75 percent, compounded annually.) In addition, unless the contrary is specified, it is assumed that the amount of the loan does not exceed 50 percent of the participant's vested account balance, the participant has no other outstanding loan (and had no prior loan) from the plan or any other plan maintained by the participant's employer or any other employer required to be aggregated with that employer under Code Section 414(b), (c) or (m), and the loan is not excluded from Code Section 72(p) as a loan made in the ordinary course of a residential mortgage investment program described in Treasury Regulations Section 1.72(p)-1, Q&A-18. [Treas. Reg. § 1.72(p)-1, Q&A-4(b)]

Example 2-1: Frank has a vested account balance of $200,000 and receives $70,000 as a loan repayable in level quarterly installments over five years. Under Code Section 72(p), Frank has a deemed distribution of $20,000 (the excess of $70,000 over $50,000) at the time of the loan, because the loan exceeds the $50,000 limit in Code Section 72(p)(2)(A)(i). The remaining $50,000 is not a deemed distribution. [Treas. Reg. § 1.72(p)-1, Q&A-4(b), Ex. 1]

Example 2-2: Meredith has a vested account balance of $30,000 and borrows $20,000 as a loan repayable in level monthly installments over five years. Because the amount of the loan is $5,000 more than 50 percent of her vested account balance, Meredith has a deemed distribution of $5,000 at the time of the loan. The remaining $15,000 is not a deemed distribution. (If the loan is secured solely by Meredith's account balance, it may be a prohibited transaction under Code Section 4975 because it does not satisfy the adequate security requirement under DOL Regulations Section 2550.408b-1(f)(2).) [Treas. Reg. § 1.72(p)-1, Q&A-4(b), Ex. 2]

Example 2-3: John has a vested account balance of $100,000 and a $50,000 loan is made to him, repayable in level quarterly installments over seven years. The loan is not eligible for the Section 72(p)(2)(B)(ii) exception for home loans. Because the repayment period exceeds the maximum five-year period in Code Section 72(p)(2)(B)(i), John has a deemed distribution of $50,000 at the time the loan is made. [Treas. Reg. § 1.72(p)-1, Q&A-4(b), Ex. 3]

Example 2-4: On August 1, 2019, Rosamond has a vested account balance of $45,000 and borrows $20,000 from a plan to be repaid over five years in level monthly installments due at the end of each month. After making monthly payments through July 31, 2020, Rosamond fails to make the payment due on August 31, 2020, or any of the payments due thereafter. The plan administrator allows a three-month cure period. As a result of her failure to satisfy the requirement that the loan be repaid in level monthly installments pursuant to Code Section 72(p)(2)(C), Rosamond has a deemed distribution on November 30, 2020, which is the last day of the three-month cure period for the August 31, 2020 installment. The amount of the deemed distribution is $17,157, which is the outstanding balance of the loan at November 30, 2020. Alternatively, if the plan administrator had allowed a cure period through the end of the next calendar quarter, there would be a deemed distribution on December 31, 2020, equal to $17,282, which is the outstanding balance of the loan at December 31, 2020. [Treas. Reg. § 1.72(p)-1, Q&A-4(b), Ex. 4, Q&A-10(c)]

The plan loan rules apply to direct and indirect loans; that is, they apply to amounts received directly or indirectly as plan loans. [I.R.C. § 72(p)(1)(A)] For example, an indirect loan is a loan from a bank to a plan participant that is contingent upon the plan making deposits at the bank equal to the loan amount. [IRS Special Ruling (Aug. 12, 1992)]

For purposes of applying the participant loan rules, plans maintained by related employers are aggregated. Plans maintained by different employers that are aggregated and treated as a single employer under Code Section 414(b), (c), or (m) (relating to controlled groups of corporations, corporations under common control, commonly controlled trades or businesses, and affiliated service groups) are aggregated and treated as a single plan. [I.R.C. § 72(p)(2)(D)]

Treating a loan as a taxable distribution does not disqualify the plan. Thus, a plan will not lose its tax-qualified status if it makes a loan that is treated as a taxable distribution. [Pub. L. No. 97-248, Senate Finance Committee Report, at 321 (TEFRA'82)]

Q 2:4 What limits does the Code impose on the amount of a plan loan?

A plan loan is not treated as a taxable distribution (i.e., a deemed distribution) to the participant or beneficiary to whom it is made if its amount (when added to the outstanding balance of all other loans from the plan and all other plans required to be aggregated with the plan) does not exceed the *lesser* of:

1. $50,000, reduced by the excess (if any) of:
   a. The highest outstanding balance of loans from the plan during the one-year period ending on the day before the date on which the loan was made, *over*
   b. The outstanding balance of loans from the plan on the date on which the loan was made; or
2. The greater of:
   a. One-half of the present value of the vested account balance of the employee under the plan, or
   b. $10,000.

[I.R.C. § 72(p)(2)(A)]

For purposes of item 2a, the vested accrued benefit is determined without regard to any accumulated deductible employee contributions (QVECs). [I.R.C. § 72(p)(2)(A)] Also, for purposes of 2a, in determining an employee's vested account balance under the plan, a valuation within the last 12 months may be used. This value must be adjusted for any distributions or contributions made after the relevant valuation date and before the date the loan is made, but it does not have to be adjusted for subsequent gains or losses after the valuation date and before the loan date. [Notice 82-22, 1982-22 C.B. 751] If an employee's outstanding loan balance is not more than one-half of the present value of his or her vested account balance under the plan immediately after the loan is made, the loan is not treated as a taxable distribution (i.e., a deemed distribution), if that present value later decreases, including a decrease because of a distribution made to the employee. [Staff of the Joint Comm. on Taxation, General Explanation of the Revenue Provisions of the Tax Equity and Fiscal Responsibility Act of 1982, H.R. 4961, 97th Cong., 2d Sess. (1982) (the "TEFRA Bluebook") at 296]

On July 26, 2017, IRS/EP Examinations issued a Memorandum (a "field directive") (https://www.irs.gov/pub/foia/ig/spder/tege-04-0717-0020.pdf), effective on its issuance date, to Employee Plans (EP) examinations employees providing two acceptable methods they could use to determine whether plans have correctly calculated the amount available for a loan when a participant with a vested account balance exceeding $100,000 has received multiple loans during the past year. The Memorandum provided the following example illustrating the two acceptable methods that a plan could use to calculate the maximum available loan amount for such a participant:

> **Example 2-5:** A plan participant borrowed $30,000 in February (which he fully repaid in April) and another $20,000 in May (which he fully repaid in July), and applied for a third loan in December. The IRS Memorandum permits the plan to determine that either:
>
> 1. No third loan may be made because the "highest outstanding loan balance" was $50,000 (i.e., $30,000 + $20,000); or
>
> 2. A third loan in the amount of $20,000 may be made because the "highest outstanding loan balance" was only $30,000.

Q 2:5 What restrictions does the Code impose on the term of a plan loan?

Under the repayment term requirement in Code Section 72(p)(2)(B), the term of a plan loan may not exceed five years unless it is used to purchase the participant's principal residence (i.e., a home loan). The term of the loan is determined at the time the loan is made. If a loan with a term of less than five years is not fully repaid at the end of its term, the amount that is left unpaid at the end of five years is treated as a taxable distribution. Also, a loan with a term exceeding five years (except a home loan) is treated as a taxable distribution even if it is repaid within five years from the date it was made. [Conference Committee Report, TEFRA'82, 97th Cong., 2d Sess. (1982)]

The one exception to the five-year repayment rule applies to home loans, which are loans used to acquire any dwelling unit that, within a reasonable time, is to be used as the participant's principal residence. [I.R.C. § 72(p)(2)(B)(ii)] The determination of whether the dwelling is to be used as the participant's principal dwelling unit is made at the time the loan is made.

For purposes of the home loan exception to the five-year repayment rule, a "dwelling unit" can be a house, condominium, or a mobile home that is not used on a transient basis. [H.R. Conf. Rpt., TEFRA'82, 97th Cong., 2d Sess. (1982), at 620]

For purposes of the home loan exception, the term *principal residence* has the same meaning as under Code Section 121 (relating to the exclusion of gain from the sale of a principal residence), and the tracing rules established under Code Section 163(h)(3)(B) (relating to interest deductions for indebtedness incurred on the acquisition of a principal residence) will be used to determine whether the home loan exception applies. [Treas. Reg. § 1.72(p)-1, Q&A-5, Q&A-7] A home loan does not have to be secured by the principal residence that is the object of the loan. [Treas. Reg. § 1.72(p)-1, Q&A-6] Also, in general, a refinancing cannot qualify as a home loan. However, a loan from a qualified employer plan that is used to repay a loan from a third party *will* qualify as a home loan, if the plan loan qualifies as a home loan without regard to the loan from the third party. [Treas. Reg. § 1.72(p)-1, Q&A-8(a)]

> **Example 2-6:** On July 1, 2019, Frank requests a $50,000 plan loan to be repaid in level monthly installments over 15 years. On August 1, 2019, he acquires his principal residence and pays a portion of the purchase price with a $50,000 bank loan. On September 1, 2019, the plan loans Frank $50,000, which he uses to repay the bank loan. Because the plan loan satisfies the requirements to qualify as a home loan (taking into account the tracing rules of Code Section 163(h)(3)(B)), the plan loan qualifies as a home loan under Code Section 72(p)(2)(B)(ii). [Treas. Reg. § 1.72(p)-1, Q&A-7 and Q&A-8(b), Ex. (unnumbered).]

It is not clear what an acceptable repayment period would be for a home loan. The Treasury Regulations do not address this point directly. However, the above example indicates that a 15-year repayment term is acceptable for a home loan.

Q 2:6 What restrictions does the Code impose on plan loan repayments (amortization)?

Generally speaking, under the level amortization requirement in Code Section 72(p)(2)(C), a plan loan must be repaid (amortized) with level payments of principal and interest, made no less frequently than quarterly, over the term of the loan. [I.R.C. § 72(p)(2)(C)]

Q 2:7 If a participant fails to make the installment payments required under the terms of a loan that satisfied all the plan loan rules when it was made, when does a deemed distribution occur, and what is the amount of the deemed distribution?

Timing of the Deemed Distribution. Failure to make any installment payment when due in accordance with the terms of the loan violates the level amortization requirement under Code Section 72(p)(2)(C) and, accordingly, results in a deemed distribution at the time of the failure. However, the plan administrator may allow a cure period, and the level amortization requirement will not be treated as having been violated if the installment payment is made not later than the end of the cure period. Any cure period cannot continue beyond the last day of the calendar quarter following the calendar quarter in which the required installment payment was due. [Treas. Reg. § 1.72(p)-1, Q&A-10(a)]

On August 30, 2017, the IRS issued Chief Counsel Advice Memorandum 201736022, which addressed how the cure period described in Treasury Regulations Section 1.72(p)-1, Q&A-10(a) would apply to a participant who failed to make installment payments required under the terms of a plan loan. The Chief Counsel Advice Memorandum addressed two different factual situations, both based upon the following assumptions:

1. The taxpayer is a participant in a Code Section 401(k) plan that permits plan loans;
2. On January 1, 2018, the participant receives a loan from the plan in an amount that does not exceed the limit provided under Code Section 72(p)(2)(A);
3. The loan, which is not a home loan, is repayable in five years (the last installment is due December 31, 2022), as required under Code Section 72(p)(2)(B);
4. Level installment payments are due at the end of each month over the repayment term of the loan (the first installment payment is due January 31, 2018), as required under Code Section 72(p)(2)(C);
5. The loan is evidenced by a legally enforceable agreement, as required under Treasury Regulations Section 1.72(p)-1, Q&A-3(b); and
6. The plan allows for a cure period, as described in Treasury Regulations Section 1.72(p)-1, Q&A-10(a), permitting a participant to make up a missed installment payment by the last day of the calendar quarter following the calendar quarter in which the required installment payment was due.

Factual Situation 1 and IRS Conclusion. In the first factual situation, the participant timely makes installment payments from January 31, 2018, through February 28, 2019. The participant misses the March 31, 2019 and April 30, 2019 installment payments. The participant makes installment payments on May 31, 2019 (which is applied to the missed March 31, 2019 installment payment) and June 30, 2019 (which is applied to the missed April 30, 2019 installment payment). On July 31, 2019, the participant makes a payment equal to three installment payments (which is applied to the missed May 31, 2019 and June 30, 2019 installment payments, as well as the required July 31, 2019 installment payment). The IRS concluded that the participant's missed installment payments did not violate the level amortization requirement under Code Section 72(p)(2)(C) because the missed installment payments were cured within the applicable cure period. Accordingly, the IRS further concluded that there was no deemed distribution of the loan due to the missed installment payments.

Factual Situation 2 and IRS Conclusion. In the second factual situation, the participant timely makes installment payments from January 31, 2018 through September 30, 2019. The participant misses the October 31, 2019, November 30, 2019, and December 31, 2019 installment payments. On January 15, 2020, the participant refinances the loan and replaces it with a new loan (the replacement loan) equal to the outstanding balance of the original loan (the replaced loan), including the three missed installment payments. Under the terms of the replacement loan, the replacement loan is to be repaid in level monthly installments at the end of each month through the end of the replaced loan's repayment term, December 31, 2022. (It also was assumed that, for purposes of this second factual situation, the replacement loan satisfied the requirements of Code Sections 72(p)(2)(A) through (C) and Treasury Regulations Section 1.72(p)-1, Q&A-3 and Q&A-20.) The IRS concluded that the participant's missed installment payments did not violate the level amortization requirement under Code Section 72(p)(2)(C) because the missed installment payments were cured within the applicable cure period by the refinancing of the loan. Accordingly, the IRS further concluded that there was no deemed distribution of the loan due to the missed installment payments.

Amount of the Deemed Distribution. If a loan satisfied all of the plan loan rules when it was made, but there is a failure to pay the installment payments required under the terms of the loan (taking into account any allowable cure period), then the amount of the deemed distribution equals the entire outstanding balance of the loan (including accrued interest) at the time of the failure. (See Q 2:3, Ex. 2-4.) [Treas. Reg. § 1.72(p)-1, Q&A-10(b); see also Notice 93-3, 1993-1 C.B. 293, § III(b), Ex. 6] For example, in *Frias v. Comm'r*, T.C. Memo. 2017-139 (2017), the U.S. Tax Court upheld the IRS's determination that the participant had received a taxable deemed distribution of the full loan amount as of the end of the first missed installment payment's cure period and that the 10 percent additional income tax on early distributions under Code Section 72(t) also applied.

Q 2:8 Does the level amortization requirement apply when a participant is on a leave of absence without pay?

Leave of Absence. The level amortization requirement of Code Section 72(p)(2)(C) does not apply for a period not longer than one year (or such longer period as may be required under Code Section 414(u), relating to veterans' reemployment rights under Uniformed Services Employment and Reemployment Rights Act (USERRA)) when a participant is on a bona fide leave of absence, either without pay from the employer or at a rate of pay (after income and employment tax withholding) that is less than the amount of the installment payments required under the terms of the loan. However, the loan (including interest that accrues during the leave of absence) must be repaid by the latest date permitted under the repayment term requirement in Code Section 72(p)(2)(B) (e.g., the suspension of payments cannot extend the term of the loan beyond five years in the case of a loan that is not a home loan), and the amount of the installments due after the leave ends (or, if earlier, after the first year of the leave or such longer period as may be required under Code Section 414(u), relating to veterans' reemployment rights under USERRA) must not be less than the amount required under the terms of the original loan. [Treas. Reg. § 1.72(p)-1, Q&A-9(a)]

> **Example 2-7:** On July 1, 2019, Scout, a participant with a vested account balance of $80,000, borrows $40,000 to be repaid in level monthly installments of $825 each over five years. The loan is not a home loan. Scout makes 9 monthly payments and begins an unpaid leave of absence that lasts for 12 months. Scout was not performing military service during this period. Thereafter, she resumes active employment and resumes making repayments on the loan until it is repaid. The amount of each monthly installment is increased to $1,130 so that the loan will be repaid by June 30, 2024.
>
> Because the loan meets the requirements of Code Section 72(p)(2), Scout does not have a deemed distribution. On the other hand, the plan loan rules would be satisfied if she continued the monthly installments of $825 after resuming active employment and, on June 30, 2024, repaid the full balance remaining due. [Treas. Reg. § 1.72(p)-1, Q&A-9(d), Ex. 1]

Military Service. In accordance with the USERRA requirements of Code Section 414(u)(4), if a plan suspends the obligation to repay a loan made to an employee from the plan for any part of a period during which the employee is performing service in the uniformed services (as defined in chapter 43 of title 38 of the United States Code), whether or not qualified military service, the suspension may not be taken into account for purposes of the plan loan rules. Thus, if a plan suspends loan repayments for any part of a period during which the employee is performing military service, the suspension will not cause the loan to be deemed distributed even if the suspension exceeds one year and even if the term of the loan is extended. However, the loan will not satisfy the repayment term requirement of Code Section 72(p)(2)(B) and the level amortization requirement of Code Section 72(p)(2)(C) unless loan repayments resume upon the completion of the period of military service. Also, the frequency of the periodic installments due during the period beginning when the military service ends and ending when the loan is repaid in full, as well as the amount of each periodic installment, may not be less than the frequency and amount of the periodic installments required under the terms of the original loan. The loan must be repaid in full (including interest that accrues during the period of military service) by the end of the period equal to the original term of the loan plus the period of military service. [Treas. Reg. § 1.72(p)-1, Q&A-9(b)]

> **Example 2-8:** The facts are the same as in Example 2-6, except Scout was on leave of absence serving in the uniformed services (as defined in chapter 43 of title 38 of the United States Code) for two years and the rate of interest charged during this period of military service is reduced to 6 percent compounded annually (under the applicable provisions of the Soldiers' and Sailors' Civil Relief Act Amendments of 1942). After her military service ends on April 2, 2022, Scout resumes active employment on April 19, 2022 continues the monthly installments of $825 thereafter, and on June 30, 2026, repays the full balance remaining due ($6,487).

Because the loan meets the requirements of Code Section 72(p)(2), Scout does not have a deemed distribution. Alternatively, Code Section 72(p)(2) would also be satisfied if the amount of each monthly installment after April 19, 2022 is increased to $930 in order to repay the loan by June 30, 2026 (without any balance remaining due then). [Treas. Reg. § 1.72(p)-1, Q&A-9(d), Ex. 2]

Q 2:9 Can a plan loan be accelerated if the participant terminates employment before the loan is fully repaid?

Yes. Loan provisions in the plan document, as well as the loan agreement and the related promissory note, can provide that the entire remaining unpaid loan balance (principal and interest) will become due and payable when the participant terminates employment, or when any other event allowing distribution occurs under the plan (e.g., disability, death, or reaching the plan's normal retirement age).

Q 2:10 Can a participant carry an outstanding loan balance even after he or she terminates employment?

Yes. It is permissible for the plan document, and the loan agreement and promissory note, to provide that a participant may carry an outstanding loan balance even after he or she terminates employment. In that case, the participant can continue to repay the loan while receiving benefit payments from the plan. However, practically speaking, the plan may be unable to collect the loan repayments when there is no easy mechanism, such as payroll deduction, to ensure timely repayments. Although there is no requirement under Code Section 72(p) that the loan be accelerated when the participant retires or otherwise terminates employment, acceleration may be desirable to avoid the problems discussed here.

Treatment of Distributions Attributable to Qualified Retirement Plan Loans

Q 2:11 Can a loan to a participant from a qualified retirement plan be taxed as a distribution?

Yes. Loans to a participant from a qualified retirement plan can give rise to two types of taxable distributions:

1. A deemed distribution pursuant to Code Section 72(p); and
2. A distribution of an offset amount.

[Treas. Reg. § 1.72(p)-1, Q&A-13(a)]

Deemed Distributions. A deemed distribution occurs when the amount requirement in Code Section 72(p)(2)(A), the repayment term requirement in

Code Section 72(p)(2)(B), the level amortization requirement in Code Section 72(p)(2)(C), or the enforceable agreement requirement under the Treasury regulations is not satisfied, either when the loan is made or at a later time. A deemed distribution is treated as a distribution to the participant or beneficiary only for certain tax purposes and is not an actual distribution of the participant's accrued benefit. [Treas. Reg. § 1.72(p)-1, Q&A-3(b), 13(a)(2)]

A deemed distribution under Code Section 72(p) is not treated as an actual distribution for purposes of the qualification requirements of Code Section 401, the distribution provisions of Code Section 402, the distribution restrictions of Code Section 401(k)(2)(B) (prohibiting or limiting distributions to an active employee) or the vesting requirements of Treasury Regulations Section 1.411(a)-7(d)(5) (which affects the application of a graded vesting schedule in cases involving a prior distribution). [Treas. Reg. § 1.72(p)-1, Q&A-12] Thus, for example, if a participant in a money purchase pension plan who is an active employee has a deemed distribution under Code Section 72(p), the plan will not be considered to have made an in-service distribution to the participant in violation of the qualification requirements for money purchase pension plans. Similarly, the deemed distribution is not eligible to be rolled over to an eligible retirement plan and is not considered an impermissible distribution of an amount attributable to elective contributions under a 401(k) plan. [Treas. Reg. §§ 1.72(p)-1, Q&A-12, 1.402(c)-2, Q&A-4(d), 1.401(k)-1(d)(5)(iii)]

Distribution of a Plan Loan Offset Amount. A distribution of a plan loan offset amount [as defined in Treas. Reg. § 1.402(c)-2, Q&A-9(b)] occurs when, under the terms governing a plan loan, the participant's or beneficiary's accrued benefit is reduced (offset) to repay the loan (including the enforcement of the plan's security interest in the participant's or beneficiary's accrued benefit). A distribution of a plan loan offset amount could occur in a variety of circumstances, such as when the terms governing the plan loan require that, in the event of the participant's request for a distribution, a loan be repaid immediately or treated as in default. [Treas. Reg. § 1.72(p)-1, Q&A-13(a)(2)]

In the event of a plan loan offset, the amount of the account balance that is offset against the loan is an actual distribution for purposes of the Code, not a deemed distribution under Code Section 72(p). Accordingly, a plan may be prohibited from making an offset under the provisions of Code Section 401(a) or 401(k)(2)(B), prohibiting or limiting distributions to an active employee. [Treas. Reg. §§ 1.72(p)-1, Q&A-13(b), 1.402(c)-2, Q&A-9(c)]

A distribution of a plan loan offset amount also occurs when, under the terms governing the plan loan, the loan is canceled, accelerated, or treated as if it were in default, for example, when the plan treats a loan as in default upon an employee's termination of employment or within a specified period thereafter. A distribution of a plan loan offset amount is an actual distribution, not a deemed distribution under Code Section 72(p). [Treas. Reg. § 1.402(c)-2, Q&A-9(b)] See Q 2:12 and Q 21:28 for a discussion of the extension of the rollover period for "qualified plan loan offset amounts" under Code Section 402(c)(3)(C)(i), as added by Section 13613(a) of the Tax Cuts and Jobs Act (TCJA), effective with respect to qualified plan loan offset amounts, which are treated as distributed in taxable years beginning after December 31, 2017.

The rules are illustrated by these examples:

Example 2-9: In 2019, Meredith has an account balance of $10,000 in the Kimbark Publishing Company plan, of which $3,000 is invested in a plan loan to Meredith that is secured by her account balance in the plan. Meredith has made no after-tax employee contributions to the plan. The plan does not provide any direct rollover option for plan loans. Upon termination of employment in 2019, Meredith, who is under age 70½, elects a distribution of her entire account balance in the plan, and her outstanding loan is offset against the account balance on distribution. Meredith elects a direct rollover of the distribution. To satisfy the direct rollover rules under Code Section 401(a)(31), the plan must pay $7,000 directly to the eligible retirement plan chosen by Meredith in a direct rollover. When Meredith's account balance was offset by the amount of the $3,000 unpaid loan balance, she received a plan loan offset amount (equivalent to $3,000) that is an eligible rollover distribution. However, the plan satisfied Code Section 401(a)(31), even though a direct rollover option was not provided for the $3,000 plan loan offset amount.

No federal income tax withholding is required under Code Section 3405(c) on account of the distribution of the $3,000 plan loan offset amount, because Meredith receives no cash or other property (other than the plan loan offset amount) from which to satisfy the withholding. Meredith may roll over $3,000 to an eligible retirement plan no later than her federal income tax return filing deadline (including extensions) for her 2019 federal income tax return provided in Code Section 402(c)(3)(C). [I.R.C. § 402(c)(3)(C), as added by TCJA § 13613(a), effective with respect to qualified plan loan offset amounts, which are treated as distributed in taxable years beginning after December 31, 2017; Treas. Reg. § 1.402(c)-2, Q&A-9(c), Ex. 1]

Example 2-10: The facts are the same as in Example 2-8, except that the terms governing the plan loan to Meredith provide that, upon termination of employment, her account balance is automatically offset by the amount of any unpaid loan balance to repay the loan. Meredith terminates employment but does not request a distribution from the plan. Nevertheless, under the terms governing the plan loan, her account balance is automatically offset by the amount of the $3,000 unpaid loan balance. The $3,000 plan loan offset amount attributable to the plan loan in this example is treated in the same manner as the $3,000 plan loan offset amount in Example 2-8. [Treas. Reg. § 1.402(c)-2, Q&A-9(c), Ex. 2]

Example 2-11: The facts are the same as in Example 2-9, except that, instead of providing for an automatic offset upon termination of employment to repay the plan loan, the terms governing the plan loan require full repayment of the loan by Meredith within 30 days of termination of employment. Meredith terminates employment, does not elect a distribution from the plan, and fails to repay the plan loan within 30 days. The plan administrator of the plan declares the plan loan to Meredith in default and executes on the loan by offsetting her account balance by the amount of the $3,000 unpaid loan balance. The $3,000 plan loan offset amount attributable to the plan loan in this example is treated in the same manner as the $3,000 plan loan offset amount in Examples 2-8 and 2-9. The result in this Example 2-10 is the same even though the plan administrator treats the loan as in default before offsetting Meredith's accrued benefit by the amount of the unpaid loan. [Treas. Reg. § 1.402(c)-2, Q&A-9(c), Ex. 3]

Example 2-12: The facts are the same as in Example 2-8, except that Meredith elects to receive the distribution of the account balance that remains after the $3,000 offset to repay the plan loan, instead of electing a direct rollover of the remaining account balance. In this case, the amount of the distribution received by Meredith is $10,000, not $3,000. Because the amount of the $3,000 offset attributable to the loan is included in determining the amount that equals 20 percent of the eligible rollover distribution received by Meredith, withholding in the amount of $2,000 (20 percent of $10,000) is required under Code Section 3405(c). The $2,000 must be withheld from the $7,000 to be distributed to Meredith in cash, so that she actually receives a check for $5,000. [Treas. Reg. § 1.402(c)-2, Q&A-9(c), Ex. 4]

Example 2-13: The facts are the same as in Example 2-11, except that the $7,000 distribution to Meredith after the offset to repay the loan consists solely of employer securities within the meaning of Code Section 402(e)(4)(E). In this case, no withholding is required under Code Section 3405(c) because the distribution consists solely of the $3,000 plan loan offset amount and the $7,000 distribution of employer securities. This is the result because the total amount that must be withheld does not exceed the sum of the cash and the fair market value of other property distributed, excluding plan loan offset amounts and employer securities. Meredith may roll over the employer securities and $3,000 to an eligible retirement plan no later than her federal income tax return filing deadline (including extensions) for her 2019 federal income tax return provided in Code Section 402(c)(3)(C). [I.R.C. § 402(c)(3)(C), as added by TCJA § 13613(a), effective with respect to qualified plan loan offset amounts, which are treated as distributed in taxable years beginning after December 31, 2017; Treas. Reg. § 1.402(c)-2, Q&A-9(c), Ex. 5]

Example 2-14: Frank, who is age 54, has an account balance in the Hallandale Beach Company profit sharing plan qualified under Code Section 401(a), which includes a qualified cash or deferred arrangement described in Code Section 401(k). The plan provides for no after-tax employee contributions. In 2019, Frank receives a loan from the plan, the terms of which satisfy Code Section 72(p)(2), that is secured by elective contributions subject to the distribution restrictions in Code Section 401(k)(2)(B). In 2025, the loan fails to satisfy Code Section 72(p)(2) because Frank stops repayment. In that year, pursuant to Code Section 72(p), Frank is taxed on a deemed distribution equal to the amount of the unpaid loan balance. The deemed distribution is not an eligible rollover distribution. Because Frank has not separated from service or experienced any other event that permits the distribution under Code

Section 401(k)(2)(B) of the elective contributions that secure the loan, the plan is prohibited from executing on the loan. Thus, there is no distribution of an offset amount that is an eligible rollover distribution in 2025. [Treas. Reg. § 1.402(c)-2, Q&A-9(c), Ex. 6; see also Notice 93-3, 1993-1 C.B. 293, § III.b.6., Exs. 1–6]

Q 2:12 When is a distribution attributable to a plan loan an eligible rollover distribution?

Deemed Distributions. A deemed distribution under Code Section 72(p) is not an eligible rollover distribution and, therefore, it may not be rolled over. [Treas. Reg. §§ 1.402(c)-2, Q&A-4(d), 1.72(p)-1, Q&A-12]

Qualified Plan Loan Offset Amounts. A distribution of a qualified plan loan offset amount is an eligible rollover distribution, provided it meets the general requirements for such distributions. [I.R.C. § 402(c)(3)(C), as added by TCJA § 13613(a), effective with respect to qualified plan loan offset amounts, which are treated as distributed in taxable years beginning after December 31, 2017; Treas. Reg. § 1.402(c)-2, Q&A-3, Q&A-9(a)] Thus, an amount equal to the qualified plan loan offset amount can be rolled over by the participant (or spousal distributee) to an eligible retirement plan within the time period required under Code Section 402(c)(3)(C) (which, is the participant's federal income tax return filing deadline, including extensions, for the taxable year during which the offset occurred), unless the plan loan offset amount fails to be an eligible rollover distribution for another reason. [Treas. Reg. § 1.402(c)-2, Q&A-9(a)]

However, a qualified plan does not have to provide a direct rollover option for an eligible rollover distribution that is in the form of a plan loan offset amount. A plan will not fail to satisfy the direct rollover rules under Code Section 401(a)(31) because the plan does not permit the distributee to elect a direct rollover of an eligible rollover distribution in the form of a plan loan offset amount. A plan administrator is permitted to allow a direct rollover of a participant note for a plan loan to another qualified plan. [Treas. Reg. § 1.401(a)(31)-1(b), Q&A-16; see also Notice 93-3, 1993-1 C.B. 293, § III.b.2]

Q 2:13 What is the federal income tax treatment of deemed distributions?

Tax Basis. If a plan loan is treated as a deemed distribution under Code Section 72(p), the amount of the deemed distribution is treated as a taxable distribution, subject to the normal annuity taxation rules under Code Section 72. If the employee's account under the plan includes after-tax contributions or other investment in the contract (i.e., basis) under Code Section 72(e), then Code Section 72 applies to a deemed distribution as if it were an actual distribution, with the result that all or a portion of the deemed distribution may not be taxable. [Treas. Reg. § 1.72(p)-1, Q&A-11(a)]

Additional 10 Percent Income Taxes. The 10 percent additional income tax on certain early distributions under Code Section 72(t) and the separate 10 percent income tax under Code Section 72(m)(5) on certain amounts received by a 5 percent owner apply to a deemed distribution under Code Section 72(p) in the same manner as if the deemed distribution were an actual distribution. [Treas. Reg. § 1.72(p)-1, Q&A-11(b)]

Q 2:14 How is the amount includible in income as a result of a deemed distribution under Code Section 72(p) required to be reported?

The amount includible in income as a result of a deemed distribution must be reported on Form 1099-R (or any other form prescribed by the IRS). [Treas. Reg. § 1.72(p)-1, Q&A-14]

Q 2:15 If there is a deemed distribution under Code Section 72(p), is the interest that accrues thereafter on the amount of the deemed distribution an indirect loan for income tax purposes?

General Rule. Except as provided below, a deemed distribution of a loan is treated as a distribution for purposes of Code Section 72. Therefore, a loan that is deemed to be distributed under Code Section 72(p) ceases to be an outstanding loan for purposes of Code Section 72, and the interest that accrues thereafter under the plan on the amount deemed distributed is disregarded in applying Code Section 72 to the participant or beneficiary. Even though interest continues to accrue on the outstanding loan (and is taken into account for purposes of determining the tax treatment of any subsequent loan in accordance with the rules described immediately below), this additional interest is not treated as an additional loan (and, thus, does not result in an additional deemed distribution) for purposes of Code Section 72(p). However, a loan that is deemed distributed under Code Section 72(p) is not considered distributed for all purposes of the Code. (See Qs 2:12, 2:13, 2:16, and 2:18.) [Treas. Reg. § 1.72(p)-1, Q&A-19(a)]

Effect on Subsequent Loans. A loan that is deemed distributed under Code Section 72(p) (including interest accruing thereafter) that has not been repaid (e.g., by a plan loan offset) is considered outstanding for purposes of applying Code Section 72(p)(2)(A) to determine the maximum amount of any subsequent loan to the participant or beneficiary. [Treas. Reg. § 1.72(p)-1, Q&A-19(b)(1)]

Additional Security for Subsequent Loans. If a loan is deemed distributed to a participant or a beneficiary under Code Section 72(p) and has not been repaid (e.g., by a plan loan offset), then no payment made thereafter to the participant or the beneficiary will be treated as a loan for purposes of Code Section 72(p)(2) unless the loan otherwise satisfies Code Section 72(p)(2) and either of the following conditions is satisfied:

1. There is an arrangement among the plan, the participant or beneficiary, and the employer, enforceable under applicable law, under which repayments will be made by payroll withholding. For this purpose, an arrangement will not fail to be enforceable merely because a party has the right to revoke the arrangement prospectively.

2. The plan receives adequate security from the participant or beneficiary that is in addition to the participant's or beneficiary's accrued benefit under the plan.

[Treas. Reg. § 1.72(p)-1, Q&A-19(b)(2)]

Conditions No Longer Satisfied. If, following a deemed distribution that has not been repaid, a payment is made to a participant or beneficiary that satisfies the conditions listed in items 1 and 2 immediately above for treatment as a plan loan and, subsequently, before repayment of the second loan, those conditions are no longer satisfied with respect to the second loan (e.g., if the loan recipient revokes consent to payroll withholding), the amount then outstanding on the second loan is treated as a deemed distribution under Code Section 72(p). [Treas. Reg. § 1.72-1(p), Q&A-19(b)(3)]

Q 2:16 Is a participant's tax basis under the plan increased if the participant repays the loan after a deemed distribution?

Repayments After Deemed Distribution. Yes. If the participant or beneficiary repays the loan after a deemed distribution of the loan under Code Section 72(p), for purposes of Code Section 72(e), the participant's or beneficiary's investment in the contract (tax basis) under the plan increases by the amount of the cash repayments that he or she makes on the loan after the deemed distribution. However, loan repayments are not treated as after-tax contributions for other purposes, including Code Sections 401(m) (matching contributions) and 415(c)(2)(B) (limitation on annual additions under defined contribution plans). [Treas. Reg. § 1.72(p)-1, Q&A-21(a)] Example 2-15 illustrates these rules and is based on the assumptions described in Q 2:3.

> **Example 2-15:** Meredith receives a $20,000 loan on January 1, 2019, to be repaid in 20 quarterly installments of $1,245 each. On December 31, 2019, the outstanding loan balance ($19,179) is deemed distributed because Meredith failed to make quarterly installment payments that were due on September 30, 2019, and December 31, 2019. On June 30, 2020, Meredith repays $5,147, which is the sum of the three installment payments that were due on September 30, 2019, December 31, 2019, and March 31, 2020, with interest thereon to June 30, 2020, plus the installment payment that was due on June 30, 2020. Thereafter, Meredith resumes making the installment payments of $1,245 from September 30, 2020, through December 31, 2023. The loan repayments made after December 31, 2019, through December 31, 2023, total $22,577. Because Meredith repaid $22,577 after the deemed distribution that occurred on December 31, 2019, she has investment in the contract (tax basis) equal to $22,577 (14 payments of $1,245 each plus a single payment of $5,147) as of December 31, 2023 [Treas. Reg. § 1.72(p)-1, Q&A-21(b), Ex.]

Q 2:17 What withholding rules apply to plan loans?

To the extent that a loan, when made, is a deemed distribution or an account balance is reduced (offset) to repay a loan, the amount includible in income is subject to withholding. If a deemed distribution of a loan or a loan repayment by benefit offset results in income at a date after the date the loan is made, withholding is required only if a transfer of cash or property (excluding employer securities) is made to the participant or beneficiary from the plan at the same time. [Treas. Reg. §§ 1.72(p)-1, Q&A-15, 31.3405(c)-1, Q&A-9, Q&A-11, 35.3405-1, Q&A F-4]

Deemed Distributions. If, and to the extent that, a loan is treated as a deemed distribution when made, withholding is accomplished by withholding tax from the amount of the loan that is treated as a distribution. For example, if a loan of $12,000 that must be repaid within five years is made to a participant with a vested account balance of $5,000, $2,000 is treated as a deemed distribution under Code Section 72(p), and the payor or plan administrator must withhold tax from the $2,000. [Treas. Reg. § 35.3405-1T, Q&A F-4] In addition, a loan that is treated as a deemed distribution under Code Section 72(p) is treated as a nonperiodic distribution other than a qualified total distribution. [Treas. Reg. § 35.3405-1T, Q&A F-5]

Plan Loan Offset Amounts. Special rules apply to the 20 percent withholding requirement when a plan loan offset amount is distributed as part of an eligible rollover distribution. The maximum amount to be withheld from the eligible rollover distribution under Code Section 3405(c) must not exceed the sum of the cash and the fair market value of property (excluding employer securities) received in the distribution. The amount of the sum is determined without regard to whether any portion of the cash or property is a designated distribution or an eligible rollover distribution. Under this rule, any plan loan offset amount [as defined in Treas. Reg. § 1.402(c)-2, Q&A-9] is treated in the same manner as employer securities. Thus, although employer securities and plan loan offset amounts must be included in the amount that is multiplied by 20 percent, the total amount required to be withheld for an eligible rollover distribution is limited to the sum of the cash and the fair market value of property received by the distributee, excluding any amount of the distribution that is a plan loan offset amount or that is distributed in the form of employer securities. For example, if the only portion of an eligible rollover distribution that is not paid in a direct rollover consists of employer securities or a plan loan offset amount, withholding is not required. [Treas. Reg. § 31.3405(c)-1, Q&A-11]

Q 2:18 May a plan loan note be transferred from one qualified plan to another when there is a transfer of assets and liabilities between plans?

Yes. Plan loan notes may be transferred in connection with a trustee-to-trustee transfer of plan assets and liabilities from one qualified plan to another. The obligee of the plan loan note would have to be changed in connection with the transfer.

Q 2:19 May a plan loan note be included in a direct rollover of an eligible rollover distribution from one qualified plan to another?

Yes. If it otherwise qualifies as an eligible rollover distribution, a direct rollover of an account balance from one qualified plan to another that includes a plan loan note will not be treated as a taxable distribution under Code Sections 72(p) and 402(a)(1). Changing the obligee on the loan, and changing the repayment schedule from weekly to twice per month, in connection with the direct rollover, would not be deemed the making of a new loan for any purpose under Code Sections 72(p), 401(a)(13), and 4975(d)(1). [Ltr. Rul. 9729042]

Also, the IRS has ruled that (1) the direct rollover of an eligible rollover distribution, including a plan loan note, from one qualified defined contribution plan to another, would not result in the distribution being treated as a taxable distribution under Code Section 402(a)(1); (2) the direct rollover of the eligible rollover distribution, including the plan loan note, would not be subject to the 20 percent withholding requirement under Code Section 3405(c)(1); and (3) the change in obligee of the plan loan note following the direct rollover would not be considered a renegotiation or revision of the loan, and the loan (which had been made before the effective date of TRA'86), would continue to be treated as a loan under Code Section 72(p) not subject to the additional requirements imposed by TRA'86 as they pertain to the renewal, renegotiation, extension, or modification of a loan after December 31, 1986. [Ltr. Rul. 9617046]

Q 2:20 What are the income tax consequences if an amount is transferred from a qualified employer plan to a participant or a beneficiary as a loan, but there is an express or tacit understanding that the loan will not be repaid?

If there is an express or tacit understanding that a loan will not be repaid (a sham loan), or, for any reason, the transaction does not create a creditor-debtor relationship or is otherwise not a bona fide loan, the amount transferred will be treated as an actual distribution from the plan for purposes of the Code and will not be treated as a loan or as a deemed distribution under Code Section 72(p). [Treas. Reg. § 1.72(p)-1, Q&A-17]

Q 2:21 If a loan fails to satisfy the plan loan rules under Code Section 72(p) and is a prohibited transaction under Code Section 4975, is the deemed distribution of the loan under Code Section 72(p) a correction of the prohibited transaction?

No. A deemed distribution will not be a correction of a prohibited transaction under Code Section 4975. [Treas. Reg. § 1.72(p)-1, Q&A-16; see Treas. Reg. §§ 141.4975-13, 53.4941(e)-1(c)(1) (relating to correction of a prohibited transaction)]

Q 2:22 If a qualified employer plan maintains a program to invest in residential mortgages, are loans made pursuant to that program subject to the plan loan rules under Code Section 72(p)?

No. Residential mortgage loans made by a plan in the ordinary course of an investment program are not subject to the plan loan rules under Code

Section 72(p) if the property acquired with the loans is the primary security for the loans and the amount loaned does not exceed the fair market value of the property. An investment program exists only if the plan has established, in advance of a specific investment under the program, that a certain percentage or amount of plan assets will be invested in residential mortgages available to persons purchasing the property who satisfy commercially customary financial criteria. Loans will not be considered as made under an investment program if:

1. Any of the loans made under the program matures upon a participant's termination from employment;
2. Any of the loans under the program is an earmarked asset of a participant's or beneficiary's individual account in the plan; or
3. The loans made under the program are made available only to participants or beneficiaries in the plan.

[Treas. Reg. § 1.72(p)-1, Q&A-18(a)]

The requirement in item 3 above does not apply to a plan that on December 20, 1995, and at all times thereafter, has had in effect a loan program under which, but for such requirement, the loans comply with applicable requirements and therefore constitute residential mortgage loans in the ordinary course of an investment program. [Treas. Reg. § 1.72(p)-1(18)(b)]

In addition, no loan that benefits an officer, director, or owner of the employer maintaining the plan, or his or her beneficiaries, will be treated as made under an investment program. [Treas. Reg. § 1.72(p)-1, Q&A-18(c)]

The Treasury regulations on plan loans under Code Section 72(p) do not provide guidance as to whether a residential mortgage loan made under a plan's investment program would result in a prohibited transaction under Code Section 4975 or as to whether such a loan made by a plan covered by Title I of ERISA would be consistent with ERISA's fiduciary standards or would result in a prohibited transaction under ERISA Section 406. [See 29 C.F.R. § 2550.408(b)-1; Treas. Reg. § 1.72(p)-1, Q&A-18(d)]

Q 2:23 May a participant refinance an outstanding loan or have more than one loan outstanding from a plan?

Refinancings and Multiple Loans—General Rule. A participant who has an outstanding loan that satisfies Code Section 72(p)(2) may refinance that loan or borrow additional amounts, if, depending on the facts and circumstances, the loans collectively satisfy the amount limitations of Code Section 72(p)(2)(A) and the prior loan and the additional loan each satisfy the repayment term requirements of Code Section 72(p)(2)(B) and the level amortization requirement of Code Section 72(p)(2)(C). For this purpose, a refinancing includes any situation in which one loan replaces another loan. [Treas. Reg. § 1.72(p)-1, Q&A-20(a)(1)]

Loans That Repay a Prior Loan and Have a Later Repayment Date. For purposes of Code Section 72(p)(2) (including the amount limitations of Code

Section 72(p)(2)(A)), if a loan that satisfies Code Section 72(p)(2) is replaced by a loan (a replacement loan) and the term of the replacement loan ends after the latest permissible term of the loan it replaces (the replaced loan), then the replacement loan and the replaced loan are both treated as outstanding on the date of the transaction. For these purposes, the latest permissible term of the replaced loan is the latest date permitted under the repayment term requirements of Code Section 72(p)(2)(B) (i.e., five years from the original date of the replaced loan, assuming that the replaced loan does not qualify for the home loan exception under Code Section 72(p)(2)(B)(ii) and that no additional period of suspension applies to the replaced loan). Thus, for example, if the term of the replacement loan ends after the latest permissible term of the replaced loan and the sum of the amount of the replacement loan plus the outstanding balance of all other loans on the date of the transaction, including the replaced loan, fails to satisfy the amount limitations of Code Section 72(p)(2)(A), then the replacement loan will result in a deemed distribution. This rule does not apply to a replacement loan if the terms of the replacement loan would satisfy Code Section 72(p)(2) determined as if the replacement loan consisted of two separate loans, the replaced loan (amortized in substantially level payments over a period ending not later than the last day of the term of the latest permissible term of the replaced loan) and, to the extent the amount of the replacement loan exceeds amount of the replaced loan, a new loan that is also amortized in substantially level payments over a period ending not later than the last day of the latest permissible term of the replacement loan. [Treas. Reg. § 1.72(p)-2, Q&A-20(a)(2)]

The following examples illustrate the rules above and are based on the assumptions described in Q 2:3.

> **Example 2-16:** Ethan Hawley, a participant with a vested account balance that exceeds $100,000, borrows $40,000 from a plan on January 1, 2019, to be repaid in 20 quarterly installments of $2,491 each. Thus, the term of the loan ends on December 31, 2023. On January 1, 2020, when the outstanding balance on the loan is $33,322, the loan is refinanced and is replaced by a new $40,000 loan from the plan to be repaid in 20 quarterly installments. Under the terms of the refinanced loan, the loan is to be repaid in level quarterly installments (of $2,491 each) over the next 20 quarters. Thus, the term of the new loan ends on December 31, 2024.
>
> Under Code Section 72(p)(2)(A), the amount of the new loan, when added to the outstanding balance of all other loans from the plan, must not exceed $50,000 reduced by the excess of the highest outstanding balance of loans from the plan during the one-year period ending on December 31, 2019, over the outstanding balance of loans from the plan on January 1, 2020. Such outstanding balance is determined immediately before the new $40,000 loan. Because the term of the new loan ends later than the term of the loan it replaces, both the new loan and the loan it replaces must be taken into account for purposes of applying Code Section 72(p)(2), including the amount limitations in Code Section 72(p)(2)(A). The amount of the new loan is $40,000, the outstanding balance on January 1, 2020, of the loan it replaces is

$33,322, and the highest outstanding balance of loans from the plan during 2019 was $40,000. Accordingly, under Code Section 72(p)(2)(A), the sum of the new loan and the outstanding balance on January 1, 2020, of the loan it replaces must not exceed $50,000 reduced by $6,678 (the excess of the $40,000 maximum outstanding loan balance during 2019 over the $33,322 outstanding balance on January 1, 2020, determined immediately before the new loan) and thus, must not exceed $43,322. The sum of the new loan ($40,000) and the outstanding balance on January 1, 2020, of the loan it replaces ($33,322) is $73,322. Because the $73,322 exceeds the $43,322 limit under Code Section 72(p)(2)(A) by $30,000, there is a deemed distribution of $30,000 on January 1, 2020.

However, no deemed distribution would occur if, under the terms of the refinanced loan, the amount of the first 16 installments on the refinanced loan was equal to $2,907, which is the sum of the $2,491 originally scheduled quarterly installment payment amount under the first loan, plus $416 (which is the amount required to repay, in level quarterly installments over five years beginning on January 1, 2020, the excess of the refinanced loan over the January 1, 2020 balance of the first loan ($40,000 minus $33,322 equals $6,678)), and the amount of the four remaining installments was equal to $416. The refinancing would not be subject to the rules described in the second paragraph above because the terms of the new loan would satisfy Code Section 72(p)(2) (including the substantially level amortization requirements of Code Section 72(p)(2)(B) and (C)) determined as if the new loan consisted of two loans, one of which is in the amount of the first loan ($33,322) and is amortized in substantially level payments over a period ending December 31, 2023 (the last day of the term of the first loan) and the other of which is in the additional amount ($6,678) borrowed under the new loan. Similarly, the transaction also would not result in a deemed distribution if the terms of the refinanced loan provided for repayments to be made in level quarterly installments (of $2,990 each) over the next 16 quarters. [Treas. Reg. § 1.72(p)-1, Q&A-20(b), Ex. 1]

Example 2-17: The facts are the same as in Example 2-15, except that the applicable interest rate used by the plan when the loan is refinanced is significantly lower because of a reduction in market rates of interest and, under the terms of the refinanced loan, the amount of the first 16 installments on the refinanced loan is equal to $2,848 and the amount of the next four installments on the refinanced loan is equal to $406. The $2,848 amount is the sum of $2,442 to repay the first loan by December 31, 2023 (the term of the first loan), plus $406 (which is the amount to repay, in level quarterly installments over the five years beginning on January 1, 2020, the $6,678 excess of the refinanced loan over the January 1, 2020 balance of the first loan).

The transaction does not result in a deemed distribution because the terms of the new loan would satisfy Code Section 72(p)(2) (including the substantially level amortization requirements of Code Section 72(p)(2)(B) and (C)) determined as if the new loan consisted of two loans, one of which is in the amount of the first loan ($33,322) and is amortized in substantially level payments over a period ending December 31, 2023 (the last day of the term of the first loan) and the other of which is in the additional amount ($6,678) borrowed under the new loan. The transaction would also not result in a deemed distribution if the terms of the new loan provided for repayments to be made in level quarterly installments (of $2,931 each) over the next 16 quarters. [Treas. Reg. § 1.72(p)-1, Q&A-20(b), Ex. 2]

Q 2:24 When did Code Section 72(p) and the related final Treasury regulations become effective?

Statutory Effective Date. Code Section 72(p) generally began to apply to assignments, pledges, and loans made after August 13, 1982. [Treas. Reg. § 1.72(p)-1, Q&A-22(a)]

Regulatory Effective Date. The final Treasury regulations that the IRS issued under Code Section 72(p) on July 31, 2000 began to apply to assignments, pledges, and loans made on or after January 1, 2002. [Treas. Reg. § 1.72(p)-1, Q&A-22(b)] The final Treasury regulations that the IRS issued under Code Section 72(p) on December 3, 2002 began to apply to assignments, pledges, and loans made on or after January 1, 2004. [Treas. Reg. § 1.72(p)-1, Q&A-22(d)] The final Treasury regulations that the IRS issued under Code Section 72(p) on December 29, 2004, began to apply to plan years beginning on or after January 1, 2006. [69 Fed. Reg. 78143] The final Treasury regulations that the IRS issued under Code Section 72(p) on October 20, 2006 began to apply to loans made on or after January 1, 2007. [71 Fed. Reg. 61877]

Loans Made Before the Regulatory Effective Date. A plan is permitted to apply the final Treasury regulations issued on July 31, 2000, to a loan made before the regulatory effective date (and after the statutory effective date described above) if there has not been any deemed distribution of the loan before the transition date or if the conditions of paragraph (2) below are satisfied with respect to the loan. [Treas. Reg. § 1.72(p)-1, Q&A-22(c)(1)]

Consistency Transition Rule for Certain Loans Deemed Distributed Before the Regulatory Effective Date. If there has been any deemed distribution of the loan before the transition date, the following rules apply. [Treas. Reg. § 1.72(p)-1, Q&A-22(c)(2)(i)]

The plan is permitted to apply the final Treasury regulations to the loan beginning on any January 1, but only if the plan reported, in Box 1 of Form 1099-R, for a taxable year no later than the latest taxable year that would be permitted under such final (if such final regulations had been in effect for all loans made after the statutory effective date described above), a gross distribution of an amount at least equal to the initial default amount. For these purposes, the initial default amount is the amount that would be reported as a gross distribution (see Qs 2:3, 2:6), and the transition date is the January 1 on which a plan begins applying the final Treasury regulations to a loan. [Treas. Reg. § 1.72(p)-1, Q&A-22(c)(2)(ii)]

If a plan applies the final Treasury regulations to such a loan, then the plan, in its reporting and withholding on or after the transition date, must not attribute investment in the contract (tax basis) to the participant or beneficiary based upon the initial default amount. [Treas. Reg. § 1.72(p)-1, Q&A-22(c)(2)(iii)]

If (1) the plan attributed investment in the contract (tax basis) to the participant or beneficiary based on the deemed distribution of the loan; (2) the plan subsequently made an actual distribution to the participant or beneficiary before the transition date; and (3) immediately before the transition date, the initial default amount (or, if less, the amount of the investment in the contract so attributed) exceeds the participant's or beneficiary's investment in the contract (tax basis), then the plan must treat the excess (the loan transition amount) as a loan amount that remains outstanding and must include the excess in the participant's or beneficiary's income at the time of the first actual distribution made on or after the transition date. [Treas. Reg. § 1.72(p)-1, Q&A-22(c)(2)(iv)]

The following examples illustrate the consistency transition rule described in Q 2:3 (and, except as specifically provided in the examples, also assume that no distributions are made to the participant and that the participant has no investment in the contract with respect to the plan). Examples 2-18, 2-19, and 2-21 illustrate the application of the consistency transition rules to a plan that, before the transition date, did not treat interest accruing after the initial deemed distribution as resulting in additional deemed distributions under Code Section 72(p). Example 2-20 illustrates the application of the consistency transition rules to a plan that, before the transition date, treated interest accruing after the initial deemed distribution as resulting in additional deemed distribution under Code Section 72(p).

Example 2-18: In 1998, when Meredith's account balance under a plan is $50,000, she receives a loan from the plan. Meredith makes the required repayments until 1999 when there is a deemed distribution of $20,000 as a result of her failure to repay the loan. For 1999, as a result of the deemed distribution, the plan reports, in Box 1 of Form 1099-R, a gross distribution of $20,000 (the initial default amount) and, in Box 2 of Form 1099-R, a taxable amount of $20,000. The plan then records an increase in Meredith's tax basis for the same amount ($20,000). Thereafter, the plan disregards, for purposes of Code Section 72, the interest that accrues on the loan after the 1999 deemed distribution. Thus, as of December 31, 2001, the total taxable amount reported by the plan as a result of the deemed distribution is $20,000, and the plan's records show that Meredith's tax basis is the same amount ($20,000). As of January 1, 2002, the plan decides to apply the final Treasury regulations the IRS issued on July 31, 2000, to the loan. Accordingly, it reduces Meredith's tax basis by the initial default amount of $20,000, so that her remaining tax basis in the plan is zero. Thereafter, the amount of the outstanding loan is not treated as part of the account balance for purposes of Code Section 72. Meredith attains age 59½ in the year 2003 and receives a distribution of the full account balance under the plan consisting of $60,000 in cash and loan receivable. At that time, the plan's records reflect an offset of the loan amount against the loan receivable in her account and a distribution of $60,000 in cash.

For the year 2003, the plan must report a gross distribution of $60,000 in Box 1 of Form 1099-R and a taxable amount of $60,000 in Box 2 of Form 1099-R. [Treas. Reg. § 1.72(p)-1, Q&A-22(c)(3), Ex. 1]

Example 2-19: The facts are the same as in Example 2-17, except that in 1999, immediately before the deemed distribution, Meredith's account balance under the plan totals $50,000 and her tax basis is $10,000. For 1999, the plan reports, in Box 1 of Form 1099-R, a gross distribution of $20,000 (the initial default amount in accordance with the final Treasury regulations the IRS issued on July 31, 2000) and reports, in Box 2 of Form 1099-R, a taxable amount of $16,000 (the $20,000 deemed distribution minus $4,000 of tax basis ($10,000 × $20,000 ÷ $50,000)) allocated to the deemed distribution. The plan then records an increase in tax basis equal to the $20,000 deemed distribution, so that Meredith's remaining tax basis as of December 31, 1999, totals $26,000 ($10,000 − $4,000 + $20,000). Thereafter, the plan disregards, for purposes of Code Section 72, the interest that accrues on the loan after the 1999 deemed distribution. Thus, as of December 31, 2001, the total taxable amount reported by the plan as a result of the deemed distribution is $16,000, and the plan's records show that Meredith's tax basis is $26,000. As of January 1, 2002, the plan decides to apply the final Treasury regulations the IRS issued on July 31, 2000, to the loan. Accordingly, it reduces Meredith's tax basis by the initial default amount of $20,000, so that her remaining tax basis in the plan is $6,000. Thereafter, the amount of the outstanding loan is not treated as part of the account balance for purposes of Code Section 72. Meredith attains age 59½ in the year 2003 and receives a distribution of the full account balance under the plan consisting of $60,000 in cash and the loan receivable. At that time, the plan's records reflect an offset of the loan amount against the loan receivable in Meredith's account and a distribution of $60,000 in cash.

For the year 2003, the plan must report a gross distribution of $60,000 in Box 1 of Form 1099-R and a taxable amount of $54,000 in Box 2 of Form 1099-R. [Treas. Reg. § 1.72(p)-1, Q&A-22(c)(3), Ex. 2]

Example 2-20: In 1993, when Meredith's account balance in a plan is $100,000, she receives a loan of $50,000 from the plan. Meredith makes the required loan repayments until 1995 when there is a deemed distribution of $28,919 as a result of her failure to repay the loan. For 1995, as a result of the deemed distribution, the plan reports, in Box 1 of Form 1099-R, a gross distribution of $28,919 (the initial default amount in accordance with the final Treasury regulations) and, in Box 2 of Form 1099-R, a taxable amount of $28,919. For 1995, the plan also records an increase in Meredith's tax basis for the same amount ($28,919). Each year thereafter through 2001, the plan reports a gross distribution equal to the interest accruing that year on the loan balance, reports a taxable amount equal to the interest accruing that year on the loan balance reduced by Meredith's tax basis allocated to the gross distribution, and records a net increase in the participant's tax basis equal to that taxable amount. As of December 31, 2001, the taxable amount reported by the plan as a result of the loan totals $44,329, and the plan's records for purposes of Code Section 72 show that Meredith's tax basis totals the same amount ($4,329). As of January 1, 2002, the plan decides to apply the final Treasury regulations. Accordingly, it reduces Meredith's tax basis by the initial default amount of $28,919, so that her remaining tax basis in the plan is $15,410 ($44,329 − $28,919). Thereafter, the amount of the outstanding loan is not treated as part of the account balance for purposes of Code Section 72. Meredith attains age 59½ in the year 2003 and receives a distribution of the full account balance under the plan consisting of $180,000 in cash and the loan receivable equal to the $28,919 outstanding loan amount in 1995 plus interest accrued thereafter to the payment date in 2003. At that time, the plan's records reflect an offset of the loan amount against the loan receivable in the participant's account and a distribution of $180,000 in cash.

For the year 2003, the plan must report a gross distribution of $180,000 in Box 1 of Form 1099-R and a taxable amount of $164,590 in Box 2 of Form 1099-R ($180,000 minus the remaining tax basis of $15,410). [Treas. Reg. § 1.72(p)-1, Q&A-22(c)(3), Ex. 3]

Example 2-21: The facts are the same as in Example 2-17, except that in 2000, after the deemed distribution, Meredith receives a $10,000 hardship distribution. At the time of the hardship distribution, Meredith's account balance under the plan totals $50,000. For 2000, the plan reports, in Box 1 of Form 1099-R, a gross distribution of $10,000 and, in Box 2 of Form 1099-R, a taxable amount of $6,000 (the $10,000 actual distribution minus $4,000 of tax basis ($10,000 × ($20,000 ÷ $50,000)) allocated to this actual distribution). The plan then records a decrease in tax basis equal to $4,000, so that Meredith's remaining tax basis as of December 31, 2000, totals $16,000 ($20,000 − $4,000). After 1999, the plan disregards, for purposes of Code Section 72, the interest that accrues on the loan after the 1999 deemed distribution. Thus, as of December 31, 2001, the total taxable amount reported by the plan as a result of the deemed distribution plus the 2000 actual distribution is $26,000 and the plan's records show that Meredith's tax basis is $16,000. As of January 1, 2002, the plan decides to apply the final Treasury regulations to the loan. Accordingly, it reduces Meredith's tax basis by the initial default amount of $20,000, so that her remaining tax basis in the plan is reduced from $16,000 to zero. However, because the $20,000 initial default amount exceeds $16,000, the plan records a loan transition amount of $4,000 ($20,000 − $16,000). Thereafter, the amount of the outstanding loan, other than the $4,000 loan transition amount, is not treated as part of the account balance for purposes of Code Section 72. Meredith attains age 59½ in the year 2003 and receives a distribution of the full account balance under the plan consisting of $60,000 in cash and the loan receivable. At that time, the plan's records reflect an offset of the loan amount against the loan receivable in Meredith's account and a distribution of $60,000 cash. [Treas. Reg. § 1.72(p)-1, Q&A-22(c)(3), Ex. 4]

Special Loan Rules for Certain Disaster Victims

Q 2:25 Can the IRS apply special loan rules to provide relief to taxpayers who have been adversely affected by disasters?

Yes. In the event of a presidentially declared disaster, the IRS can apply special loan rules to provide relief to taxpayers who have been adversely affected by those disasters. Most presidentially declared disasters have been severe storms (such as tornadoes and hurricanes), but they may also be wildfires, flooding, or earthquakes. Affected taxpayers are generally people who live in or have a business in an area directly affected by the disaster. [https://www.irs.gov/retirement-plans/disaster-relief-for-retirement-plans-and-iras] In the past, the IRS has applied the following types of special loan rules to provide relief to taxpayers affected by disasters: increasing the limits on plan loans (see Q 2:26), permitting plans to temporarily suspend loan payments (see Q 2:26), and relaxing certain verification procedures that would otherwise be required (see Qs 2:27, 2:28, and 2:29). IRS Revenue Procedure 2007-56 [2007-34 I.R.B. 388], Section 8, lists the retirement plan and IRA deadlines—including certain deadlines relating to plan loans—that the IRS may postpone because of a disaster. The IRS may postpone all or only certain deadlines listed in Revenue Procedure 2007-56 based on when the disaster occurred and its severity as well as other factors. Unless an IRS news release for a particular disaster limits the relief, all the deadlines listed in Revenue Procedure will be postponed. [https://www.irs.gov/retirement-plans/disaster-relief-for-retirement-plans-and-iras]

Q 2:26 Were there any special plan loan rules that applied to taxpayers who suffered economic losses in 2005 as a result of Hurricane Katrina, Rita, or Wilma?

Yes. The following two special loan rules applied to "qualified individuals" (as defined below):

1. *Increase in the Limits on Plan Loans*. The $50,000 limit on plan loans (see Q 2:1) was increased to $100,000. In addition, the loan limit based on 50 percent of the participant's vested account balance (see Q 2:1) was increased to 100 percent of the vested account balance. These higher limits applied only to plan loans received during the following periods:
   a. If the qualified individual's main home was located in the Hurricane Katrina disaster area, the period began on September 24, 2005 and ended on December 31, 2006.
   b. If the qualified individual's main home was located in the Hurricane Rita or Wilma disaster area, the period began on December 21, 2005 and ended on December 31, 2006.

Anyone who was a "qualified individual" based on Hurricane Katrina and another hurricane should have used the above period based on Hurricane Katrina.

1. *One-Year Suspension of Plan Loan Payments.* In addition, payments on plan loans due before 2007 could be suspended for one year by the plan administrator. To have qualified for the one-year suspension, the due date for any loan payment must have occurred during the period that began on:
   a. August 28, 2005, if the qualified individual's main home was located in the Hurricane Katrina disaster area;
   b. September 23, 2005, if the qualified individual's main home was located in the Hurricane Rita disaster area; or
   c. October 23, 2005, if the qualified individual's main home was located in the Hurricane Wilma disaster area.

Anyone who was a "qualified individual" based on more than one hurricane should have used the period above with the earliest beginning date.

Definition of "Qualified Individual." An individual was a "qualified individual" for purposes of the above-described special plan loan rules if any of the following applied:

1. The individual's main home on August 28, 2005 was located in the Hurricane Katrina disaster area and he or she had an economic loss due to Hurricane Katrina;
2. The individual's main home on September 23, 2005 was located in the Hurricane Rita disaster area and he or she had an economic loss because of Hurricane Rita; or
3. The individual's main home on October 23, 2005 was located in the Hurricane Wilma disaster area and he or she had an economic loss because of Hurricane Wilma.

Examples of an "economic loss" included, but were not limited to:

1. Loss, damage to, or destruction of real or personal property from fire, flooding, looting, vandalism, theft, wind or other cause;
2. Loss related to the qualified individual's displacement from his or her main home; or
3. Loss of livelihood due to temporary or permanent layoffs.

[Katrina Emergency Tax Relief Act of 2005 (KETRA), Pub. L. No. 19-73, Sec. 103; IRS Notice 2005-92, 2005-51 I.R.B. 1165; IRS Ann. 2005-70, 2005-40 I.R.B. 682 IRS Pub. 4492 (Jan. 2006)]

Q 2:27 Were there any special plan loan rules for taxpayers who were adversely affected by Hurricane Sandy in 2012 and 2013?

Yes. In Announcement 2012-44, 2012-49 I.R.B. 663, the IRS provided relief from certain verification procedures that might otherwise have been required under qualified employer retirement plans for plan loans made on or after October 26, 2012 until February 1, 2013 to a participant whose principal residence on October 26, 2012 was located in one of the counties or Tribal Nations that were identified as covered disaster areas because of the devastation caused by Hurricane Sandy or whose place of employment was located in one of those counties or Tribal Nations on that date or whose lineal ascendant or descendant, dependent, or spouse had a principal place of residence or place of employment in one of those counties or Tribal Nations on that date.

In Announcement 2044-12, the IRS stated that, although loans made to participants who were Hurricane Sandy victims from October 26, 2012 to February 1, 2013 had to satisfy the applicable requirements of Code Section 72(p), plans making those loans would not be treated as failing to follow procedural requirements for plan loans imposed by the terms of the plan merely because those requirements were disregarded for any period beginning on or after October 26, 2012 and continuing through February 1, 2013, provided the plan administrator made a good-faith diligent effort under the circumstances to comply with those requirements. However, as soon as practicable, the plan administrator was required to make a reasonable attempt to assemble any foregone documentation.

For example, if spousal consent were required for a plan loan and the plan terms required production of a death certificate if the employee claimed his or her spouse was deceased, the plan would not be disqualified for failure to operate in accordance with its terms if it made a loan to a participant who was a Hurricane Sandy victim in the absence of a death certificate if it was reasonable to believe, under the circumstances, that the spouse was deceased, the loan was made no later than February 1, 2013, and the plan administrator made reasonable efforts to obtain the death certificate as soon as practicable. The IRS cautioned in Announcement 2012-44, however, that, in general, the normal spousal consent rules continued to apply to plan loans made to participants who were Hurricane Sandy victims.

To make a plan loan to a participant who was a Hurricane Sandy victim during the time period described above, a qualified retirement plan that did not provide for plan loans had to have been amended to provide for loans no later than the end of the first plan year beginning after December 31, 2013 (i.e., by December 31, 2014 for a calendar plan year plan).

Q 2:28 Were there any special plan loan rules for taxpayers who were adversely affected by the Louisiana storms in 2016 and 2017?

Yes. In Announcement 2016-30, 2016-37 I.R.B. 355, the IRS provided relief from certain verification procedures that might otherwise have been required under qualified employer retirement plans for plan loans made on or after August 11, 2016 and continuing through January 17, 2017 to an employee or former employee whose principal residence on August 11, 2016 was located in one of the parishes that were identified as part of a covered disaster area because of the devastation caused by the Louisiana storms or whose place of employment was located in one of those parishes on that date or whose lineal ascendant or descendant, dependent, or spouse had a principal residence or place of employment in one of those parishes on that date. The parishes included in the covered disaster area for the Louisiana storms were identified in an IRS News Release, which can be found at https://www.irs.gov/uac/tax-relief-for-victims-of-severe-storms-flooding-in-louisiana.

Announcement 2016-30 required that, to make a loan, a qualified retirement plan that did not provide for participant loans would need to be amended to provide for loans no later than the end of the first plan year beginning after December 31, 2016. Announcement 2016-30 further required that plan loans made pursuant to its guidance must satisfy the requirements of Code Section 72(p).

Announcement 2016-30 further provided that a qualified retirement plan would not be treated as failing to follow procedural requirements for plan loans merely because those requirements were disregarded for any period beginning on or after August 11, 2016 and continuing through January 17, 2017, with respect to loans to individuals who qualified for relief, provided the plan administrator made a good-faith diligent effort under the circumstances to comply with those requirements. However, as soon as practicable, the plan administrator had to make a reasonable attempt to assemble any foregone documentation. For example, if spousal consent were required for a plan loan and the plan terms required production of a death certificate if the employee claimed his or her spouse was deceased, the plan would not be disqualified for failure to operate in accordance with its terms if it made a loan to a qualifying individual in the absence of a death certificate if it was reasonable to believe, under the circumstances, that the spouse was deceased, the loan was made no later than January 17, 2017, and the plan administrator made reasonable efforts to obtain the death certificate as soon as practicable.

In addition, Announcement 2016-30 provided that the U.S. Department of Labor (DOL) had advised the IRS that it would not treat any person as having violated the provisions of Title I of ERISA solely because that person complied with the provisions of Announcement 2016-30. [IRS Ann. 2016-30, 2016-37 I.R.B. 355] The DOL also issued its own guidance on compliance with ERISA employee benefit rules for those adversely affected by the Louisiana storms since August 11, 2016. [DOL News Release, available at https://www.dol.gov/newsroom/releases/ebsa/ebsa20160912; DOL FAQs for Participants and Beneficiaries Following the Louisiana Storms (Sept. 12, 2016), available at https://www.dol.gov/sites/default/files/ebsa/about-ebsa/our-activities/resource-center/faqs/for-participants-and-beneficiaries-following-louisiana-storms.pdf]

Q 2:29 Were there any special plan loan rules for taxpayers who were adversely affected by Hurricane Matthew in 2016 or 2017?

Yes. In Announcement 2016-39, 2016-45 I.R.B. 720, the IRS provided relief from certain verification procedures that might otherwise have been required under qualified employer retirement plans for plan loans made on or after October 4, 2016 (October 3, 2016 for Florida) and continuing through March 15, 2017 to an employee or former employee whose principal residence on October 4, 2016 (October 3, 2016 for Florida) was located in one of the counties identified for individual assistance by the Federal Emergency Management Agency (FEMA) because of the devastation caused by Hurricane Matthew or whose place of employment was located in one of those counties on that date. The counties identified for individual assistance by FEMA were in Florida, Georgia, North Carolina, and South Carolina and were found on FEMA's website at https://www.fema.gov/disasters. Announcement 2016-39 provided that if additional counties in those states were identified by FEMA for individual assistance because of damage related to Hurricane Matthew, the relief provided in Announcement 2016-39 would also apply from the date specified by FEMA as the beginning of the incident period, and that date should be substituted for references to October 4, 2016 in Announcement 2016-39.

Announcement 2016-39 required that, to make a loan, a qualified retirement plan that did not provide for participant loans would need to be amended to provide for loans no later than the end of the first plan year beginning after December 31, 2016. Announcement 2016-39 further required that plan loans made pursuant to its guidance must satisfy the requirements of Code Section 72(p).

Announcement 2016-39 further provided that a qualified retirement plan would not be treated as failing to follow procedural requirements for plan loans merely because those requirements were disregarded for any period beginning on or after October 4, 2016 (October 3, 2016 for Florida) and continuing through March 15, 2017, with respect to loans to individuals who qualified for relief, provided the plan administrator made a good-faith diligent effort under the circumstances to comply with those requirements. However, as soon as practicable, the plan administrator had to make a reasonable attempt to assemble any foregone documentation. For example, if spousal consent were required for a plan loan and the plan terms required production of a death certificate if the employee claimed his or her spouse was deceased, the plan would not be disqualified for failure to operate in accordance with its terms if it made a loan to a qualifying individual in the absence of a death certificate if it was reasonable to believe, under the circumstances, that the spouse was deceased, the loan was made no later than March 15, 2017, and the plan administrator made reasonable efforts to obtain the death certificate as soon as practicable.

In addition, Announcement 2016-39 provided that the DOL had advised the IRS that it would not treat any person as having violated the provisions of Title I of ERISA solely because that person complied with the provisions of Announcement 2016-39. [IRS Ann. 2016-39, 2016-45 I.R.B. 720]

Q 2:30 Were there any special plan loan rules that applied to taxpayers who were adversely affected by Hurricane Harvey in 2017 and 2018?

Yes. In Announcement 2017-11, 2017-39 I.R.B. 255, the IRS provided relief from certain verification procedures that might otherwise have been required under qualified employer retirement plans for plan loans made on or after August 23, 2017 and continuing through January 31, 2018 to an employee or former employee whose principal residence on August 23, 2017 was located in one of the Texas counties identified for individual assistance by FEMA because of the devastation caused by Hurricane Harvey or whose place of employment was located in one of those counties on that date or whose lineal ascendant or descendant, dependent, or spouse had a principal residence or place of employment in one of those counties on that date. The counties identified for individual assistance by FEMA were found on FEMA's website at https://www.fema.gov/disasters. Announcement 2017-11 provided that if additional areas in Texas or other states were identified by FEMA for individual assistance because of damage related to Hurricane Harvey, the relief provided in Announcement 2017-11 would also apply from the date specified by FEMA as the beginning of the incident period, and that date should be substituted for references to August 23, 2017 in Announcement 2017-11.

Announcement 2017-11 required that, to make a loan, a qualified retirement plan that did not provide for participant loans would need to be amended to provide for loans no later than the end of the first plan year beginning after December 31, 2017. Announcement 2017-11 further required that plan loans made pursuant to its guidance must satisfy the requirements of Code Section 72(p).

Announcement 2017-11 further provided that a qualified retirement plan would not be treated as failing to follow procedural requirements for plan loans merely because those requirements were disregarded for any period beginning on or after August 23, 2017 and continuing through January 31, 2018, with respect to loans to individuals who qualified for relief, provided the plan administrator made a good-faith diligent effort under the circumstances to comply with those requirements. However, as soon as practicable, the plan administrator had to make a reasonable attempt to assemble any foregone documentation. For example, if spousal consent were required for a plan loan and the plan terms required production of a death certificate if the employee claimed his or her spouse was deceased, the plan would not be disqualified for failure to operate in accordance with its terms if it made a loan to a qualifying individual in the absence of a death certificate if it was reasonable to believe, under the circumstances, that the spouse was deceased, the loan was made no later than January 31, 2018, and the plan administrator made reasonable efforts to obtain the death certificate as soon as practicable.

In addition, Announcement 2017-11 provided that the DOL had advised the IRS that it would not treat any person as having violated the provisions of Title I of ERISA solely because that person complied with the provisions of Announcement 2017-11. [IRS Ann. 2017-11, 2017-39 I.R.B. 255]

Q 2:31 Were there any special plan loan rules that applied to taxpayers who were adversely affected by Hurricane Irma in 2017 and 2018?

Yes. In Announcement 2017-13, 2017-40 I.R.B. 271, the IRS provided relief from certain verification procedures that might have otherwise been required under qualified employer retirement plans for plan loans made on or after September 4, 2017 and continuing through January 31, 2018 to an employee or former employee whose principal residence on September 4, 2017 was located in one of the Florida counties identified for individual assistance by FEMA because of the devastation caused by Hurricane Irma or whose place of employment was located in one of those counties on that date or whose lineal ascendant or descendant, dependent, or spouse had a principal residence or place of employment in one of those counties on that date. The areas identified for individual assistance by FEMA were found on FEMA's website at https://www.fema.gov/disasters. Announcement 2017-13 provided that if additional areas were identified by FEMA for individual assistance because of damage related to Hurricane Irma, the relief provided in Announcement 2017-13 would also apply from the date specified by FEMA as the beginning of the incident period, and that date would be substituted for September 4, 2017 in Announcement 2017-13.

Announcement 2017-13 required that, to make a loan, a qualified retirement plan that did not provide for participant loans would need to be amended to provide for loans no later than the end of the first plan year beginning after December 31, 2017. Announcement 2017-13 further required that plan loans made pursuant to its guidance must satisfy the requirements of Code Section 72(p).

Announcement 2017-13 further provided that a qualified retirement plan would not be treated as failing to follow procedural requirements for plan loans merely because those requirements were disregarded for any period beginning on or after September 4, 2017 and continuing through January 31, 2018, with respect to loans to individuals who qualified for relief, provided the plan administrator made a good-faith diligent effort under the circumstances to comply with those requirements. However, as soon as practicable, the plan administrator had to make a reasonable attempt to assemble to any foregone documentation. For example, if spousal consent were required for a plan loan and the plan terms required production of a death certificate if the employee claimed his or her spouse was deceased, the plan would not be disqualified for failure to operate in accordance with its terms if it made a loan to a qualifying individual in the absence of a death certificate if it was reasonable to believe, under the circumstances, that the spouse was deceased, the loan was made no later than January 31, 2018, and the plan administrator made reasonable efforts to obtain the death certificate as soon as practicable.

In addition, Announcement 2017-13 provided that the DOL had advised the IRS that it would not treat any person as having violated the provisions of Title I of ERISA solely because that person complied with the provisions of Announcement 2017-13. [IRS Ann. 2017-13, 2017-40 I.R.B. 271]

Q 2:32 Were there any special plan loan rules that applied to taxpayers who were adversely affected by Hurricane Maria or the California Wildfires in 2017 and 2018?

Yes. In Announcement 2017-15, 2017-47 I.R.B. 534, the IRS provided relief from certain verification procedures that might otherwise have been required under qualified employer retirement plans for plan loans made on or after the applicable incident date (September 16, 2017, in the case of the U.S. Virgin Islands, for Hurricane Maria; September 17, 2017, in the case of Puerto Rico, for Hurricane Maria; or October 8, 2017, in the case of California, for the California

Wildfires) and continuing through March 15, 2018 to an employee or former employee whose principal residence on the applicable incident date was located in one of the areas identified for individual assistance by FEMA because of the devastation caused by Hurricane Maria or the California Wildfires or whose place of employment was located in one of those areas on that date or whose lineal ascendant or descendant, dependent, or spouse had a principal residence or place of employment on that date. The areas identified for individual assistance by FEMA were found on FEMA's website at https://www.fema.gov/disasters. Announcement 2017-15 provided that if additional areas were identified by FEMA for individual assistance because of damage related to Hurricane Maria or the California Wildfires, the relief provided in Announcement 2017-15 would also apply from the date specified by FEMA as the beginning of the incident period and that date should be substituted for references to the incident date in Announcement 2017-15.

Announcement 2017-15 required that, to make a loan, a qualified retirement plan that did not provide for participant loans would need to be amended to provide for loans no later than the end of the first plan year beginning after December 31, 2017. Announcement 2017-15 further required that plan loans made pursuant to its guidance must satisfy the requirements of Code Section 72(p).

Announcement 2017-15 further provided that a qualified retirement plan would not be treated as failing to follow procedural requirements for plan loans merely because those requirements were disregarded for any period beginning on or after the applicable incident date and continuing through March 15, 2018, with respect to loans to individuals who qualified for relief, provided the plan administrator made a good-faith diligent effort under the circumstances to comply with those requirements. However, as soon as practicable, the plan administrator had to make a reasonable attempt to assemble any foregone documentation. For example, if spousal consent were required for a plan loan and the plan terms required production of a death certificate if the employee claimed his or her spouse was deceased, the plan would not be disqualified for failure to operate in accordance with its terms if it made a loan to a qualifying individual in the absence of a death certificate if it was reasonable to believe, under the circumstances, that the spouse was deceased, the loan was made no later than March 15, 2018, and the plan administrator made reasonable efforts to obtain the death certificate as soon as practicable.

In addition, Announcement 2017-15 provided that the DOL had advised the IRS that it would not treat any person as having violated the provision of Title I of ERISA solely because that person complied with the provisions of Announcement 2017-15. [IRS Ann. 2017-15, 2017-47 I.R.B. 534]

Q 2:33 Were there any special plan loan rules in the Disaster Tax Relief and Airport and Airway Extension Act of 2017 for taxpayers who were adversely affected by Hurricane Harvey, Hurricane Irma, or Hurricane Maria?

Yes. The Disaster Tax Relief and Airport and Airway Extension Act of 2017 (the "Relief Act"), enacted on September 29, 2017, provided special plan loan rules (and other relief) for the victims of Hurricane Harvey, Hurricane Irma, and Hurricane Maria. The relief was in addition to that already provided by the IRS and the DOL (see Q 2:30 to Q 2:32).

The special plan loan provisions in Section 502(c) of the Relief Act permitted qualified Hurricane Harvey, Hurricane Irma, or Hurricane Maria individuals to take loans in amounts greater than the maximum amount otherwise permitted under Code Section 72(p)(2)(A) and to delay repaying the loans until later than the end of the maximum loan term otherwise permitted under Code Section 72(p)(2)(B) or (C) without risking default or taxation. Qualified individuals were permitted to take plan loans from August 23, 2017 to December 31, 2018 (for qualified Hurricane Harvey individuals), from September 4, 2017 to December 31, 2018 (for qualified Hurricane Irma individuals), or from September 16, 2017 to December 31, 2018 (for qualified Hurricane Maria individuals). The maximum loan amount permitted under the Relief Act (when added to all other loans from the plan) was the lesser of $100,000 or 100 percent of the participant's vested account balance. In addition, loan repayments could be postponed for one year. Thus, a participant with an outstanding loan on or after his "qualified beginning date" (August 23, 2017 for a qualified Hurricane Harvey individual, September 4, 2017 for a qualified Hurricane Irma individual, or September 16, 2017 for a qualified Hurricane Maria individual) was permitted to delay for one year any loan repayments that were due after his or her applicable qualified beginning date and before January 1, 2019. So, for example, an installment payment originally due on September 18, 2017 was permitted to be delayed to September 18, 2018. The loan was required to be re-amortized after the end of the one-year delay period, and the one-year delay period was disregarded in determining the term of the loan. [Relief Act § 502(c)]

Loans as Prohibited Transactions

Q 2:34 What are the prohibited transaction rules under the Code that apply to loans from tax-qualified retirement plans?

Unless certain requirements are met, a loan from a tax-qualified retirement plan to a participant who is a disqualified person under Code Section 4975(e)(2) is a prohibited transaction that could subject the participant to a 15 percent initial-level excise tax and, if the prohibited transaction is not corrected in a timely fashion, a 100 percent additional excise tax as well. [I.R.C. § 4975(c)(1)(B), (d)(1)]

A loan from a tax-qualified retirement plan to a participant or beneficiary who is also a disqualified person is not a prohibited transaction only if the loan:

1. Is available to all participants and beneficiaries on a reasonably equivalent basis;
2. Is not made available to highly compensated employees, as defined under Code Section 414(q), in an amount greater than the amount made available to other employees;
3. Is made in accordance with specific provisions regarding such loans that are set forth in the plan;

4. Bears a reasonable rate of interest; and
5. Is adequately secured.

[I.R.C. § 4975(d)(1)(A)–(E)]

An employee is a *disqualified person* under the Code's prohibited transaction rules if he or she earns 10 percent or more of the employer's yearly wages or is an officer, director, 10 percent-or-more shareholder, or other person specified in Code Section 4975(e)(2). *Any* employee is a party in interest under ERISA's prohibited transaction rules. [ERISA § 3(14)(H)] A fiduciary of a tax-qualified retirement plan is both a disqualified person under the Code and a party in interest under ERISA's prohibited transaction rules.

If the loan from a tax-qualified retirement plan to a participant or beneficiary who is also a disqualified person fails to meet any of the above requirements, that loan is a prohibited transaction under the Code, and the individual receiving the loan is subject to an initial-level excise tax equal to 15 percent of the amount involved in the transaction for each tax year (or part of each tax year) in the taxable period. [I.R.C. § 4975(a)] In any case in which the 15 percent initial-level excise tax is imposed on a prohibited transaction and the transaction is not corrected during the taxable period, an additional excise tax, equal to 100 percent of the amount involved, will be imposed. [I.R.C. § 4975(b)]

The *amount involved* means, with respect to a prohibited transaction, the greater of:

- The amount of money and the fair market value of any other property given; or
- The amount of money and the fair market value of any other property received.

[I.R.C. § 4975(f)(4)]

In the case of the 15 percent initial-level excise tax, fair market value is determined as of the date on which the prohibited transaction occurs. [I.R.C. § 4975(f)(4)(A)] In the case of the additional 100 percent excise tax, fair market value is the highest fair market value during the taxable period.

The *taxable period* means, with respect to any prohibited transaction, the period beginning with the date on which the prohibited transaction occurs, and ending on the earliest of:

- The date of mailing of a notice of deficiency (a "90-day letter") for the initial-level 15 percent excise tax;
- The date on which the initial-level 15 percent excise tax is assessed; or
- The date on which correction of the prohibited transaction is completed.

[I.R.C. § 4975(f)(2)]

A prohibited transaction is corrected by undoing the transaction to the extent possible, but in any case placing the plan in a financial position not worse than that in which it would be if the disqualified person were acting under the highest fiduciary standards. [I.R.C. § 4975(f)(5)]

A prohibited transaction must be reported to the IRS on Form 5330, "Return of Excise Taxes Related to Employee Benefit Plans." Multiple prohibited transactions may occur with respect to a single plan loan because, in addition to the prohibited transaction that occurs when the loan is made, another prohibited transaction occurs on the first day of each following taxable year, or portion of a taxable year, that is within the taxable period. [Treas. Reg. § 53.4941(e)-1(e)(1)(i)]

Q 2:35 What are the prohibited transaction rules under ERISA that apply to plan loans from ERISA plans?

Any loans made by an ERISA plan to parties in interest [ERISA § 3(14)(A)] who are participants or beneficiaries of the plan are prohibited transactions and thus violate ERISA, unless the loans:

1. Are available to all participants and beneficiaries on a reasonably equivalent basis;
2. Are not made available to highly compensated employees (within the meaning of Code Section 414(q)) in an amount greater than the amount made available to other employees;
3. Are made in accordance with specific provisions regarding such loans that are set forth in the plan;
4. Bear a reasonable rate of interest; and
5. Are adequately secured.

[ERISA § 408(b); D.O.L. Reg. § 2550.408b-1(a)(1)]

Code Section 4975 contains parallel provisions to ERISA Section 408(b)(1). The Secretary of Labor has exclusive authority, under Reorganization Plan No. 4 of 1978, drawn up by the IRS and the DOL, to promulgate regulations under the prohibited transaction rules under Code Section 4975(d)(1) and ERISA Section 408(b)(1). As a result, all references to ERISA Section 408(b)(1) in this chapter should be read to include the parallel provisions of Code Section 4975(d)(1).

The term *party in interest* [ERISA § 3(14)(A)] is used in the prohibited transaction rules under ERISA Section 408(b)(1). The term *disqualified person* [I.R.C. § 4975(e)(2)] is used in the prohibited transaction rules under Code Section 4975. A loan between a plan and a party in interest generally is prohibited under ERISA and the Code. [ERISA § 406(a)(1)(B); I.R.C. § 4975(c)(1)(B)] *Any* employee is a party in interest under ERISA, and so, any plan loan to any employee might be a prohibited transaction, unless it meets the conditions of the exemption in ERISA Section 408(b)(1). However, because not all employees are disqualified persons under the Code, the 15 percent and 100 percent excise taxes might not apply to those prohibited transactions.

Q 2:36 What relief does ERISA Section 408(b)(1) provide from ERISA's prohibited transaction provisions?

ERISA Section 408(b)(1) provides an exemption from the prohibitions of ERISA Section 406(a) (the general rule forbidding fiduciaries from engaging in certain enumerated prohibited transactions with respect to any ERISA plan), ERISA Section 406(b)(1) (the prohibition against fiduciary self-dealing), and ERISA Section 406(b)(2) (the prohibition against conflicts of interest by fiduciaries) for loans by an ERISA plan to parties in interest [ERISA § 3(14)(A)] who are participants or beneficiaries of the plan, provided the loans meet the five requirements listed in Q 2:30. [D.O.L. Reg. § 2550.408b-1(a)(1)]

ERISA Section 408(b)(1) does not provide an exemption from acts described in ERISA Section 406(b)(3) (which prohibits a fiduciary from receiving any consideration for his or her own personal account from any party dealing with the plan in connection with any transaction involving plan assets). The scope of the exemption in ERISA Section 408(b)(1) is further limited by ERISA Section 408(d) (relating to transactions with owner-employees and related persons). [D.O.L. Reg. § 2550.408b-1(a)(2)]

Q 2:37 What is a participant loan for purposes of ERISA's prohibited transaction rules?

The term *participant loan* refers to a loan that is arranged and approved by the fiduciary administering the loan program primarily in the interest of the participant that otherwise satisfies the criteria set forth in the exemption under ERISA Section 408(b)(1). The existence of a participant loan or a participant loan program is determined upon consideration of all relevant facts and circumstances. Thus, for example, the mere presence of a loan document appearing to satisfy the requirements of the exemption in ERISA Section 408(b)(1) is not dispositive of whether a participant loan exists, if the subsequent administration of the loan indicates that the parties to the loan agreement did not intend the loan to be repaid. In addition, a plan containing a precondition designed to benefit a party in interest (other than the participant) is not protected by the exemptions provided by ERISA Section 408(b)(1) and the related DOL regulations. The exemption in ERISA Section 408(b)(1) recognizes that a program of participant loans, like other plan investments, must be prudently established and administered for the exclusive purposes of providing benefits to participants and beneficiaries of the plan. [D.O.L. Reg. § 2550.408b-1(a)(3)(i)]

Under these rules, the term *loan* includes any renewal or modification of an existing loan agreement, provided that, at the time of each renewal or modification, the requirements of the exemption in ERISA Section 408(b)(1) and the related DOL regulations are met. [D.O.L. Reg. § 2550.408b-1(a)(3)(ii)]

The following examples illustrate the general principles of the ERISA prohibited transaction rules for plan loans.

Example 2-22: Ethan Hawley, a trustee of the Belle Adair Company plan, has exclusive discretion over the management and disposition of plan assets. As a result, Ethan is a fiduciary of the plan under ERISA Section 3(21)(A) and a party in interest with respect to the plan under ERISA Section 3(14)(A). Ethan is also a participant in the plan. Among Ethan's duties as fiduciary is the administration of a participant loan program that meets the requirements of the exemption in ERISA Section 408(b)(1). Pursuant to strict objective criteria stated under the loan program, Ethan, who participates in all loan decisions, receives a loan on the same terms as other participants. Although the exercise of Ethan's discretion on behalf of himself would ordinarily constitute an act of self-dealing under ERISA Section 406(b)(1), the loan from the plan to Ethan will not be a prohibited transaction if the conditions of ERISA Section 408(b)(1) are otherwise satisfied. [D.O.L. Reg. § 2550.408b-1(a)(4), Ex. (1)]

Example 2-23: The Elm Street Company plan covers all the employees of the Elm Street Company, the employer who established and maintained the plan. Stonewall Jackson Smith is a fiduciary with respect to the plan and an officer of the company. The plan document gives Stonewall the authority to establish a participant loan program in accordance with ERISA Section 408(b)(1). Pursuant to an arrangement with the company, Stonewall establishes such a program, but limits the use of loan funds to investments in a limited partnership that is established and maintained by the company as general partner. Under these facts, the loan program and any loans made pursuant to this program are outside the scope of relief provided by ERISA Section 408(b)(1) because the loan program is designed to operate for the benefit of the company. Under the circumstances described, the diversion of plan assets for the company's benefit would also violate ERISA Section 403(c)(1) (the exclusive-purpose rule) and ERISA Section 404(a) (the prohibited transaction rules). [D.O.L. Reg. § 2550.408b-1(a)(4), Ex. (2)]

Example 2-24: Assume the same facts as in Example 2-22, except that Stonewall does not limit the use of loan funds. However, the company pressures its employees to borrow funds under the plan's participant loan program, and then reloan the loan proceeds to the company. Stonewall, unaware of the company's activities, arranges and approves the loans. If the loans meet all the conditions of the exemption under ERISA Section 408(b)(1), the loans will be exempt and will not be prohibited transactions. However, the company's activities would cause the entire transaction to be viewed as an indirect transfer of plan assets between the plan and the company, which is a party in interest with respect to the plan, but not the participant borrowing from the plan. By coercing the employee to engage in loan transactions for its benefit, the company has engaged in separate transactions that are not exempt under ERISA Section 408(b)(1). Accordingly, the company would be liable for the payment of excise taxes under Code Section 4975. [D.O.L. Reg. § 2550.408b-1(a)(4), Ex. (3)]

Example 2-25: Assume the same facts as in Example 2-22 except that in return for structuring and administering the loan program as indicated, the company agrees to pay Stonewall an amount equal to 10 percent of the funds loaned under the program. Such a payment would result in a separate prohibited transaction not exempt under ERISA Section 408(b)(1). The transaction would be prohibited under ERISA Section 406(b)(3), because Stonewall would be receiving consideration from a party in interest in connection with a transaction involving plan assets. [D.O.L. Reg. § 2550.408b-1(a)(4), Ex. (4)]

Example 2-26: Margie Young-Hunt is a fiduciary with respect to the Marullo Grocery Corporation retirement plan. Ethan Hawley is a party in interest with respect to the plan. ERISA Section 406(a)(1)(B) would prohibit Margie from causing the plan to lend money to Ethan. However, Margie enters into an agreement with Mary Hawley, a plan participant, whereby Margie will cause the plan to make a participant loan to Mary, with the express understanding that Mary will subsequently lend the loan proceeds to Ethan. An examination of Mary's credit standing indicates that she is not creditworthy and would not, under normal circumstances, receive a loan under the conditions established by the participant loan program. Margie's decision to approve the participant loan to Mary on the basis of Mary's prior agreement to lend the money to Ethan violates the exclusive-purpose requirements of ERISA Sections 403(c) and 404(a). In effect, the entire transaction is viewed as an indirect transfer of plan assets between the plan and Ethan, and not a loan to a participant exempt under ERISA Section 408(b)(1). Mary's lack of credit standing would also cause the transaction to fail under ERISA Section 408(b)(1)(A). [D.O.L. Reg. § 2550.408b-1(a)(4), Ex. (5)]

Example 2-27: Margie Young-Hunt is a fiduciary with respect to the Marullo Grocery Corporation retirement plan. Mary Hawley is a plan participant. Mary and Ethan Hawley are both parties in interest with respect to the plan. Margie approves a participant loan to Mary in accordance with the conditions established under the participant loan program. Upon receipt of the loan, Mary intends to lend the money to Ethan. If Margie has approved this loan solely upon consideration of those factors that would be considered in a normal commercial setting by an entity in the business of making comparable loans, Mary's subsequent use of the loan proceeds will not affect the determination of whether loans under the plan's program satisfy the conditions of ERISA Section 408(b)(1). [D.O.L. Reg. § 2550.408b-1(a)(4), Ex. (6)]

Example 2-28: H.C. Andersen is the trustee of a small defined contribution plan. Mary Hawley, the president of the plan sponsor, is also a participant in the plan. Pursuant to a participant loan program meeting the requirements of the exemption in ERISA Section 408(b)(1), Mary applies for a loan to be secured by a parcel of real property. Mary does not intend to repay the loan; rather, upon eventual default, she will permit the property to be foreclosed upon and transferred to the plan in discharge of her legal obligation to repay the loan. H.C., aware of Mary's intention, approves the loan. Mary fails to make two consecutive quarterly payments of principal and interest under the note evidencing the loan, thereby placing the loan in default. The plan then acquires the real property upon foreclosure. Such facts and circumstances indicate that the payment of money from the plan to Mary was not a participant loan eligible for the relief afforded by the exemption under ERISA Section 408(b)(1). In effect, this transaction is a prohibited sale or exchange of property between a plan and a party in interest from the time Mary receives the money. [D.O.L. Reg. § 2550.408b-1(a)(4), Ex. (7)]

Example 2-29: The Marullo Grocery Store Corporation retirement plan establishes a participant loan program. All loans are subject to the condition that the borrowed funds must be used to finance home purchases. Interest rates on the loans are the same as those charged by a local savings and loan association under similar circumstances. A loan by the plan to a participant to finance a home purchase would be subject to the relief provided by the exemption in ERISA Section 408(b)(1), provided that the conditions of ERISA Section 408(b)(1) are met. A participant loan program that is established to make loans for certain stated purposes (e.g., hardship, college tuition, or home purchases) but that is not otherwise designed to benefit parties in interest (other than plan participants) would not, in itself, cause the program to be ineligible for the relief provided by the exemption in ERISA Section 408(b)(1). However, fiduciaries are cautioned that operation of a loan program with limitations may result in loans not being made available to all participants and beneficiaries on a reasonably equivalent basis. [D.O.L. Reg. § 2550.408b-1(a)(4), Ex. (8)]

Q 2:38 When are plan loans considered to be available to participants and beneficiaries on a reasonably equivalent basis?

Plan loans will not be considered to be available to participants and beneficiaries on a reasonably equivalent basis unless:

1. The loans are available to all plan participants and beneficiaries without regard to any individual's race, color, religion, sex, age, or national origin.
2. In making such loans, consideration has been given only to those factors that would be considered in a normal commercial setting by an entity in the business of making similar types of loans. Such factors may include the applicant's creditworthiness and financial need.
3. An evaluation of all relevant facts and circumstances indicates that, in actual practice, loans are not unreasonably withheld from any applicant. [D.O.L. Reg. § 2550.408b-1(b)(i)-(iii)]

A participant loan program will not fail the reasonably equivalent basis requirement, or the requirement that the loan program not favor highly compensated employees, if the program establishes a minimum loan amount of up to $1,000, provided that the loans are adequately secured. [D.O.L. Reg. § 2550.408b-1(b)(2)]

The following examples illustrate the requirement that loans be made available to all participants and beneficiaries on a reasonably equivalent basis.

Example 2-30: H.C. Andersen, a trustee of the Belle Adair Corporation plan, has exclusive discretion over the management and disposition of plan assets. H.C.'s duties include the administration of a participant loan program that meets the requirement of the exemption in ERISA Section 408(b)(1). H.C. receives a participant loan at a lower interest rate than the rate made available to other plan participants of similar financial condition or creditworthiness with similar security. The loan by the plan to H.C. would not be covered by the relief provided by the exemption in ERISA Section 408(b)(1) because loans under the plan's program are not available to all plan participants on a reasonably equivalent basis. [D.O.L. Reg. § 2550.408b-1(b)(3), Ex. (1)]

Example 2-31: Assume the same facts as in Example 2-29, except that H.C. is a member of a committee of trustees responsible for approving participant loans. H.C. pressures the committee to refuse loans to other qualified participants in order to assure that the assets allocated to the participant loan program would be available for a loan by the plan to H.C. The loan by the plan to H.C. would not be covered by the relief provided by the exemption in ERISA Section 408(b)(1), because participant loans have not been made available to all participants and beneficiaries on a reasonably equivalent basis. [D.O.L. Reg. § 2550.408b-1(b)(3), Ex. (2)]

Example 2-32: Margie Young-Hunt is the trustee of the Marullo Grocery Store Corporation retirement plan, which covers the employees of the corporation. Ethan Hawley, Mary Hawley, and Ellen Hawley are employees of the corporation, participants in the plan, and friends of Margie. The documents governing the plan provide that Margie, at her discretion, may establish a participant loan program meeting certain specified criteria. Margie institutes such a program and tells Ethan, Mary, and Ellen of her decision. Before Margie is able to notify the plan's other participants and beneficiaries of the loan program, Ethan, Mary, and Ellen file loan applications that, if approved, will use up substantially all of the funds set aside for the loan program. Approval of these applications by Margie would represent facts and circumstances showing that loans under the plan's program are not available to all participants and beneficiaries on a reasonably equivalent basis. [D.O.L. Reg. § 2550.408b-1(b)(3), Ex. (3)]

Q 2:39 When will plan loans not be considered disproportionately available to highly compensated employees, officers, or shareholders?

Plan loans will not be considered to be made available to highly compensated employees, officers, or shareholders in an amount greater than the amount made available to other employees if, upon consideration of all relevant facts and circumstances, the program does not operate to exclude large numbers of plan participants from receiving loans under the program. [D.O.L. Reg. § 2550.408b-1(c)(1)]

A participant loan program will not fail to meet these requirements merely because the plan documents specifically governing loans set forth a maximum dollar limitation or a maximum percentage of vested accrued benefit that no loan may exceed. [D.O.L. Reg. § 2550.408b-1(c)(2)]

If the plan document sets forth a maximum percentage of vested accrued benefit that no loan may exceed, the loan program will not fail to meet this requirement solely because maximum loan amounts will vary directly with the size of the participant's accrued benefit. [D.O.L. Reg. § 2550.408b-1(c)(3)]

The following examples illustrate these rules.

Example 2-33: The documents governing the New Baytown Company retirement plan provide for the establishment of a participant loan program in which the amount of any loan under the program (when added to the outstanding balances of any other loans under the program to the same participant) does not exceed the lesser of $50,000 or one-half of the present value of that participant's vested accrued benefit under the plan (but not less than $10,000). The plan's participant loan program does not fail to meet the requirements of the exemption under ERISA Section 408(b)(1) and would be covered by the relief provided by that section if its other conditions are met. [D.O.L. Reg. § 2550.408b-1(c)(4), Ex. (1)]

Example 2-34: The documents governing the Clam Hill Corporation retirement plan provide for the establishment of a participant loan program in which the minimum loan amount would be $25,000. The documents also require that the only security acceptable under the program would be the participant's vested accrued benefit. H.C. Andersen, the plan fiduciary administering the loan program, finds that, because of the restrictions in the plan documents, only 20 percent of the plan participants, all of whom earn in excess of $75,000 a year, would meet the threshold qualifications for a loan. Most of these participants are high-level supervisors or corporate officers. Based on these facts, it appears that loans under the program would be made available to highly compensated employees in an amount greater than the amount made available to other employees. As a result, the loan program would fail to meet the requirement in ERISA Section 408(b)(1) and would not be covered by the relief provided in that section. [D.O.L. Reg. § 2550.408b-1(c)(4), Ex. (2)]

Q 2:40 Will a plan administrator's decision to disallow a participant loan based on a reasonable question concerning the legality of the loan be considered a failure to provide loans to all participants on a reasonably equivalent basis?

No. A plan administrator may deny participant loans to directors and executive officers of the sponsoring employer of the plan on the basis that such loans may violate Section 13(k) of the Securities Exchange Act of 1934, as added by the Sarbanes-Oxley Act of 2002, without contravening the requirement of ERISA Section 408(b)(2) that loans be made available to all participants on a reasonably equivalent basis. [EBSA Field Assistance Bulletin 2003-1 (Apr. 15, 2003)] Section 13(k) of the Securities Exchange Act of 1934 makes it unlawful for any subject issuer, directly or indirectly, including through any subsidiary, to extend or maintain credit, to arrange for the extension of credit, or to modify or renew an extension of credit maintained by the issuer on the date of enactment of the Sarbanes-Oxley Act of 2002, in the form of a personal loan to or for any director or executive officer (or the equivalent thereof).

Q 2:41 Must a plan contain specific provisions if it has a loan program?

Yes. For participant loans granted or renewed on or after the last day of the first plan year beginning on or after January 1, 1989, the participant loan program that is contained in the plan, or in a written document forming part of the plan, must include, without limitation:

1. The identity of the person or positions authorized to administer the plan loan program;
2. A procedure for applying for loans;
3. The basis on which loans will be approved or denied;
4. Limitations on the types and amount of loans offered;
5. The procedure under the program for determining a reasonable rate of interest;
6. The types of collateral that may secure a participant loan; and
7. The events constituting default and the steps that will be taken to preserve plan assets in the event of default.

[D.O.L. Reg. § 2550.408b-1(d)(2)(i)–(vii)]

Example 2-34 illustrates the rules.

Example 2-35: The Old Harbor Corporation retirement plan authorizes the trustee to establish a participant loan program in accordance with ERISA Section 408(b)(1). Pursuant to this explicit authority, the trustee establishes a written program that contains all of the information described above. Loans made pursuant to his authorization and the written loan program will not fail to meet the requirements under ERISA merely because the specific provisions regarding the loans are contained in a separate document forming part of the plan. The specific provisions describing the loan program, whether contained in the plan or in a written document forming part of the plan, affect the rights and obligations of the participants and beneficiaries under the plan and therefore must be disclosed in the plan's summary plan description. [D.O.L. Reg. § 2550.408b-1(d)(2)]

Q 2:42 When is a plan loan considered to bear a reasonable rate of interest?

A loan is considered to bear a reasonable rate of interest if it provides the plan with a return commensurate with the interest rates charged by persons in the business of lending money for loans that would be made under similar circumstances. [D.O.L. Reg. § 2550.408b-1(e)]

Examples 2-35 and 2-37 illustrate this rule.

Example 2-36: The Bay Hotel Corporation retirement plan makes a participant loan to Ethan Allen Hawley at the fixed rate of 8 percent for five years. The trustees, before making the loan, contacted two local banks to determine under what terms the banks would make a similar loan, taking into account Ethan's creditworthiness and the collateral offered. One bank would charge a variable rate of 10 percent adjusted monthly for a similar loan. The other bank would charge a fixed rate of 15 percent under similar circumstances. Under these facts, the loan to Ethan would not bear a reasonable rate of interest because the loan did not provide the plan with a return commensurate with interest rates charged by persons in the business of lending money for loans that would be made under similar circumstances. As a result, the loan would fail to meet the requirements of ERISA Section 408(b)(1)(D) and would not be covered by the relief provided by the exemption in ERISA Section 408(b)(1). [D.O.L. Reg. § 2550.408b-1(e), Ex. (1)]

Example 2-37: Pursuant to the provision of the High Street Company retirement plan's participant loan program, Joey Murphy, the trustee of the plan, approves a loan to Mary Hawley, a participant and party in interest with respect to the plan. At the time of execution, the loan meets all of the requirements of the exemption in ERISA Section 408(b)(1). The loan agreement provides that, at the end of two years, Mary must pay the remaining balance in full or the parties may renew for an additional two-year period. At the end of the initial two-year period, the parties agree to renew the loan for an additional two years. At the time of renewal, however, the interest rate on the loan is not adjusted to reflect current economic conditions. As a result, the interest rate on the renewal fails to provide a reasonable rate of interest as required by ERISA Section 408(b)(1)(D). Under these circumstances, the loan would not be exempt under ERISA Section 408(b)(1) from the time of renewal. [D.O.L. Reg. § 2550.408b-1(e), Ex. (2)]

Example 2-38: The documents governing the Phillips House Company retirement plan's participant loan program provide that loans must bear an interest rate no higher than the maximum interest rate permitted under the state's usury law. Pursuant to the loan program, the plan makes a participant loan to Margie Young-Hunt, a plan participant, at a time when the interest rates charged by financial institutions in the community (not subject to the usury limit) for similar loans are higher than the usury limit. Under these circumstances, the loan would not bear a reasonable rate of interest because the loan does not provide the plan with a return commensurate with the interest rates charged by persons in the business of lending money under similar circumstances. In addition, participant loans that are artificially limited to the maximum usury ceiling then prevailing call into question the status of such loans under ERISA Sections 403(c) and 404(a), since higher yielding comparable investment opportunities are available to the plan. [D.O.L. Reg. § 2550.408b-1(e), Ex. (3)]

Q 2:43 When is a plan loan considered to be adequately secured?

A plan loan is considered to be adequately secured if the security posted for the loan is something in addition to and supporting a promise to pay; moreover, the security is pledged to the plan that it may be sold, foreclosed upon, or otherwise disposed of upon default of repayment of the loan, and the value and liquidity of it is such that it may reasonably be anticipated that loss of principal or interest will not result from the loan. The adequacy of the security will be determined in light of the type and amount of security that would be required in the case of an otherwise identical transaction in a normal commercial setting between unrelated parties on arm's-length terms. A participant's vested accrued benefit under a plan may be used as security for a participant loan to the extent of the plan's ability to satisfy the participant's outstanding obligation in the event of default. [D.O.L. Reg. § 2550.408b-1(f)(1)]

Under these rules:

1. No more than 50 percent of the present value of a participant's vested accrued benefit may be considered by a plan as security for the outstanding balance of all plan loans made to that participant;
2. A plan will be in compliance with the rule in (1) if, with respect to any participant, it meets the requirements of (1) immediately after the origination of each participant loan secured in whole or in part by that participant's vested accrued benefit; and
3. Any loan secured in whole or in part by a portion of a participant's vested accrued benefit must also meet the requirements for adequate security. [D.O.L. Reg. § 2550.408b-1(f)(2)]

Q 2:44 When do participant loan repayments that are withheld from employee wages by an employer become "plan assets" subject to the prohibited transaction rules under ERISA Section 406?

Participant loan repayments made to the employer for purposes of transmittal to the plan or withheld from employee wages by the employer for transmittal to the plan, like participant contributions to the plan, become plan assets as of the earliest date on which such repayments can reasonably be segregated from the employer's general assets.

Participant contributions to a plan become "plan assets" no later than the 15th business day of the month immediately following the month in which the participant contributions are received by the employer (in the case of amounts that a participant pays to an employer) or the 15th business day of the month following the month in which such amounts would otherwise have been payable to the participant in cash (in the case of amounts withheld by an employer from a participant's wages). Although these maximum periods do not govern the repayment of participant loans, the DOL believes that holding participant loan repayments beyond such periods would raise serious questions as to whether the employer forwarded the repayments to the plan as soon as they were reasonably segregable from its general assets. [D.O.L. Adv. Op. 2002-02A (May 17, 2002)]

Spousal Consent for Loans Made by Plans Subject to the Survivor Annuity Requirements

Q 2:45 Must spousal consent be obtained before a loan can be made from a plan that is subject to the survivor annuity requirements?

Yes. A plan that is subject to the survivor annuity requirements of Code Sections 401(a)(11) and 417 does not satisfy those requirements unless the plan provides that, at the time the participant's accrued benefit is used as security for a loan, spousal consent is obtained. Consent is required even if the accrued benefit is not the primary security for the loan. No spousal consent is necessary if, at the time the loan is secured, it is established to the satisfaction of the plan representative that there is no spouse or the spouse cannot be located. Spousal consent is also not required if the plan or the participant is not subject to the survivor annuity requirements of Code Section 401(a)(11) at the time the participant's accrued benefit is used as security, or if the total accrued benefit subject to the security is not in excess of $5,000. The spousal consent must be obtained no earlier than the beginning of the 90-day period that ends on the date on which the loan is to be secured by the accrued benefit. The consent is subject to the spousal consent requirements of Code Section 417(a)(2), which means it must be in writing, must acknowledge the effect of the loan, and must be witnessed by a plan representative or a notary public. Participant consent to using the accrued benefit as security for the loan is deemed obtained at the time the participant agrees to use the accrued benefit as security for the loan. [I.R.C. § 417(a)(2)(B); Treas. Reg. §§ 1.401(a)-20, Q&A-24(a)(1), 1.417(e)-1(b)(2)]

Q 2:46 If spousal consent is obtained (or is not required) when the plan loan is made, must it be given when the unpaid loan balance is offset against the participant's accrued benefit in the event of a default?

No. If spousal consent is obtained or is not required at the time the participant's accrued benefit is used as security, spousal consent is not required at the time of any setoff of the loan against the accrued benefit resulting from a default, even if the participant is married to a different spouse at the time of the setoff. Similarly, in the case of a participant who secured a loan while unmarried, no consent is required at the time of a setoff of the loan against the accrued benefit even if the participant is married at the time of the setoff. [Treas. Reg. § 1.401(a)-20, Q&A-24(b)]

Q 2:47 If an existing plan loan is renegotiated, extended, renewed, or otherwise revised after it is made, is the renegotiation of the loan treated as the making of a new loan under the spousal consent requirements?

Yes. In obtaining any required spousal consent, any renegotiation, extension, renewal, or other revision of a loan is treated as a new loan made on the date of the renegotiation, extension, renewal, or other revision. [Treas. Reg. § 1.401(a)-20, Q&A-24(c)]

Q 2:48 If a plan loan is outstanding when a participant dies and the loan is secured by the participant's accrued benefit under the plan, will that affect the amount of the qualified preretirement survivor annuity (QPSA) or the survivor annuity portion of the qualified joint and survivor annuity (QJSA) that is payable on account of his or her death?

Yes. In determining the amount of a QPSA (qualified preretirement survivor annuity) or QJSA (qualified joint and survivor annuity), the accrued benefit of a participant is reduced by any security interest held by the plan by reason of a loan outstanding to the participant at the time of death or payment, if the security interest is treated as payment in satisfaction of the loan under the plan. A plan may offset any loan outstanding at the participant's death that is secured by his or her account balance against the spousal benefit required to be paid under a defined contribution plan that is not subject to the survivor annuity requirements. [I.R.C. § 401(a)(11)(B)(iii); Treas. Reg. § 1.401(a)-20, Q&A-24(d)]

Federal Truth in Lending Act

Q 2:49 Do the federal Truth in Lending Act (TILA) and Regulation Z apply to participant loans from employer retirement plans?

No. Prior to July 1, 2010, the federal Truth in Lending Act (TILA) [15 U.S.C. § 1601 et seq.] and its implementing regulations, known as Regulation Z, did apply to all plans that make 25 or more loans (or five or more loans secured by a dwelling) during any calendar year. The law required the plan trustee to give the participant a disclosure statement showing the amount financed, the finance charge, the annual percentage rate, the repayment procedure, and the security interest taken. However, on January 29, 2009, the Board of Governors of the Federal Reserve Bank issued final rules, amending Regulation Z, which, among other things, exempted from the Truth in Lending Act and Regulation Z any participant loan from a Code Section 401(a) qualified retirement plan, a Code Section 403(b) tax-sheltered annuity plan, or a Code Section 457(b) eligible governmental deferred compensation plan, provided that the loan is comprised of fully vested funds from the participant's account and is made in compliance with the Code. The exemption became effective on July 1, 2010. [Reg. Z, 12 C.F.R. § 226.3(g)]

Chapter 3

QDROs and Other Exceptions to the Anti-Alienation Rules

The Retirement Equity Act of 1984 (REA) amended the Employee Retirement Income Security Act of 1974 (ERISA) and the Internal Revenue Code ("the Code") to require every qualified retirement plan to pay benefits in accordance with any qualified domestic relations order (QDRO) received by the plan. This requirement began to apply to QDROs issued on or after January 1, 1985. This chapter helps plan administrators determine whether an order is a QDRO, and how plan distributions should be made to conform to the terms of the QDRO. Taxation of QDRO distributions is also discussed.

The Taxpayer Relief Act of 1997 (TRA'97) amended ERISA and the Code to add another exception to the anti-alienation rules (in addition to the existing exception for QDROs). Under TRA'97, a participant's benefit in a qualified plan may be reduced to satisfy liabilities of the participant to the plan due to certain criminal convictions, civil judgments, or administrative settlements involving the participant's misconduct with respect to the plan.

The QDRO rules under the Code and ERISA did not provide specific rules for the treatment of a domestic relations order (DRO) as a QDRO if the DRO was issued after another DRO or a QDRO (including an order issued after a divorce decree) or if the DRO revised another DRO or a QDRO. The Pension and Protection Act (PPA), enacted on August 17, 2006, directed the Secretary of Labor to issue, not later than one year after enactment, regulations to clarify the status of certain DROs. In particular, the regulations were to clarify that a DRO otherwise meeting the QDRO requirements would not fail to be treated as a QDRO solely because of the time it was issued or because it was issued after or revised another DRO or QDRO. The regulations also were to clarify that such a DRO was in all respects subject to the same requirements and protections that apply to

QDROs. For example, as under pre-PPA law, such a DRO could not require the payment of benefits to an alternate payee that are required to be paid to another alternate payee under an earlier QDRO. In addition, the pre-PPA rules regarding segregated amounts that apply while the status of a DRO as a QDRO is being determined continue to apply. The PPA provisions relating to QDROs became effective on August 17, 2006, the legislation's enactment date.

On March 7, 2007, the DOL issued interim final regulations, which became effective on April 6, 2007, implementing the PPA's directive to clarify certain timing issues with respect to DROs and QDROs under the Code and ERISA. On June 10, 2010, the DOL issued final regulations finalizing the interim final rules, effective August 9, 2010.

General Rules and Definitions 3-2
Form or Amount of Benefits May Not Be Altered 3-16
How QDROs Affect Other Retirement Plan Benefits; Section 415 Requirements 3-20
Alternate Payee's Retirement Plan Benefits Must Be Clearly Specified . . . 3-21
QDROs Must Specify the Benefit Period and the Retirement Plan 3-24
Retirement Plan Provisions and Written Procedures for Determining the Qualified Status of a DRO 3-25
Procedures to Follow After a Retirement Plan Receives a DRO 3-28
Taxation of Retirement Plan Distributions Made Under QDROs 3-34
Official Guidance on Drafting, Reviewing, and Administering QDROs 3-38
Permitted Offsets of Retirement Plan Benefits 3-40

General Rules and Definitions

Q 3:1 Do the ERISA and Code rules prohibiting the assignment or alienation of a participant's benefits under a qualified retirement plan apply to QDROs?

No. Tax-qualified retirement plans are subject to so-called anti-alienation and anti-assignment rules under ERISA and the Code, which generally provide that plan benefits may not be anticipated, assigned (either at law or in equity), alienated, or subject to attachment, garnishment, levy, execution, or other legal or equitable process. [I.R.C. § 401(a)(13); Treas. Reg. § 1.401(a)-13(b)(1)]

However, the anti-alienation and anti-assignment rules do *not* apply to the creation, assignment, or recognition of a right to any plan benefit payable with respect to a participant under a QDRO. [I.R.C. § 401(a)(13)(B); ERISA § 206(d)(3)(A)] This means that if a plan receives a DRO that it determines to be a QDRO, it must pay the participant's benefits in accordance with the QDRO's terms.

Q 3:2 What is a DRO?

A DRO is a judgment, decree, or order (including the approval of a property settlement agreement) that:

1. Relates to the provision of child support, alimony payments, or marital property rights to a spouse, former spouse, child, or other dependent (an alternate payee) of a participant; and
2. Is made pursuant to state domestic relations law (including a community property law).

A state authority, generally a court (or any state agency or instrumentality) with the authority to issue DROs, must actually issue a judgment, order, or decree or otherwise formally approve a property settlement agreement before it can be a DRO under ERISA and the Code. [D.O.L. Advisory Op. 2001-06A (June 1, 2001); FAQs About Qualified Domestic Relations Orders, available at https://www.dol.gov/agencies/ebsa/about-ebsa/our-activities/resource-center/faqs/qdro-overview] An order issued under tribal law by a family court of a federally recognized Native American tribe may constitute a DRO if it is treated or recognized as such by the law of a state that could issue a valid DRO with respect to the participant and alternate payee. [D.O.L. Advisory Op. 2011-03A (Feb. 2, 2011)]

The mere fact that a property settlement agreement is agreed to and signed by the parties will not, in and of itself, cause the agreement to be a DRO.

There is no requirement that both parties to a marital proceeding sign or otherwise endorse or approve an order. It is also not necessary that the retirement plan be brought into state court or made a party to a domestic relations proceeding for an order issued in that proceeding to be a DRO or a QDRO. Indeed, because state law is generally preempted to the extent that it relates to ERISA-subject retirement plans, the Department of Labor (DOL) takes the position that a retirement plan cannot be joined as a party in a domestic relations proceeding pursuant to state law. Moreover, retirement plans are neither permitted nor required to follow the terms of DROs purporting to assign retirement benefits unless they are QDROs.

[I.R.C. § 414(p)(1)(B); ERISA §§ 206(d)(3)(B)(ii), 514(a), 514(b)(7); FAQs About Qualified Domestic Relations Orders, available at https://www.dol.gov/agencies/ebsa/about-ebsa/our-activities/resource-center/faqs/qdro-overview]

Q 3:3 May a QDRO be part of a divorce decree or property settlement?

Yes. There is nothing in the Code or ERISA requiring that a QDRO (i.e., the provisions that create or recognize an alternate payee's interest in a participant's retirement plan benefits) be issued as a separate judgment, decree, or order. Accordingly, a QDRO may be included as part of a divorce decree or court-approved property settlement, or issued as a separate order, without affecting its qualified status. [I.R.C. § 414(p)(1); ERISA § 206(d)(3)(B); FAQs About Qualified Domestic Relations Orders, available at https://www.dol.gov/agencies/ebsa/about-ebsa/our-activities/resource-center/faqs/qdro-overview]

Q 3:4 Must a DRO be issued as part of a divorce proceeding to be a QDRO?

No. A DRO that provides for child support or recognizes marital property rights may be a QDRO, without regard to the existence of a divorce proceeding. Such an order, however, must be issued pursuant to state domestic relations law and create or recognize the rights of an individual who is an alternate payee (spouse, former spouse, child, or other dependent of a participant).

An order issued in a probate proceeding begun after a participant's death that purports to recognize an interest with respect to retirement plan benefits arising solely under state community property law, but that does not relate to the dissolution of a marriage or recognition of support obligations, is not a QDRO because the proceeding does not relate to a legal separation, marital dissolution, or family support obligation. [I.R.C. § 414(p)(1); ERISA § 206(d)(3)(B); D.O.L. Advisory Op. 90-46A; FAQs About Qualified Domestic Relations Orders, available at https://www.dol.gov/agencies/ebsa/about-ebsa/our-activities/resource-center/faqs/qdro-overview]

Q 3:5 What is a QDRO?

A QDRO is a DRO (see Q 3:2) that:

1. Creates or recognizes the existence of an alternate payee's right to receive all or some of the benefits payable to a participant under a retirement plan [I.R.C. § 414(p)(1)(A)(i); ERISA § 206(d)(3)(B)(i)(I)];
2. Clearly specifies the following information:
   - The name and last known mailing address (if any) of the participant and of each alternate payee covered by the order [I.R.C. § 414(p)(1)(A)(ii), (2)(A); ERISA § 206(d)(3)(B)(i)(II), (C)(i)];
   - The dollar amount or percentage of the participant's benefits to be paid by the plan to each alternate payee, or the manner in which that amount or percentage is to be determined [I.R.C. § 414(p)(1)(A)(ii), (2)(B); ERISA § 206(d)(3)(B)(i)(II), (3)(C)(ii)];
   - The number of payments or the period to which the order applies [I.R.C. § 414(p)(1)(A)(ii), (2)(C); ERISA § 206(d)(3)(B)(i)(II), (C)(iii)]; and
   - The name of each plan to which the order applies [I.R.C. § 414(p)(1)(A)(ii), (2)(D); ERISA § 206(d)(3)(B)(i)(II), (C)(iv)]; and

3. Meets each of the following four requirements:
   - It does not require the plan to provide an alternate payee or participant with any type or form of benefit, or any option, not otherwise provided under the plan [I.R.C. § 414(p)(1)(A)(ii), (3)(A); ERISA § 206(d)(3)(B)(i)(II), (D)(i)];
   - It does not require the plan to provide increased benefits (determined on the basis of actuarial value) [I.R.C. § 414(p)(1)(A)(ii), (3)(B); ERISA § 206(d)(3)(B)(i)(II), (D)(ii)];
   - It does not require the payment of benefits to an alternate payee which are required to be paid to another alternate payee under another order previously determined to be a QDRO [I.R.C. § 414(p)(1)(A)(ii), (3)(C); ERISA § 206(d)(3)(B)(i)(II), (D)(iii)]; and
   - It does not require the plan to pay benefits to an alternate payee in the form of a QJSA for the lives of the alternate payee and his or her subsequent spouse. [I.R.C. § 414(p)(4)(iii); ERISA § 206(d)(3)(E)(i)(III); FAQs About Qualified Domestic Relations Orders, available at https://www.dol.gov/agencies/ebsa/about-ebsa/our-activities/resource-center/faqs/qdro-overview]

Q 3:6 Who can be an "alternate payee"?

A DRO can be a QDRO only if it creates or recognizes the existence of an alternate payee's right to receive, or assigns to an alternate payee the right to receive, all or a part of a participant's retirement plan benefits. An "alternate payee" cannot be anyone other than a spouse, former spouse, child, or other dependent of a plan participant who is recognized by a DRO as having a right to receive all, or a portion of, the benefits payable under the plan with respect to that participant. [I.R.C. § 414(p)(8); ERISA § 206(d)(3)(K); FAQs About Qualified Domestic Relations Orders, available at https://www.dol.gov/agencies/ebsa/about-ebsa/our-activities/resource-center/faqs/qdro-overview] A person who is an alternate payee under a QDRO must be treated, for all relevant purposes under ERISA, as a beneficiary under the plan. [ERISA § 206(d)(3)(J)]

Q 3:7 May a QDRO provide for payment to the guardian of an alternate payee?

Yes. If an alternate payee is a minor or is legally incompetent, the QDRO can require payment to someone with legal responsibility for the alternate payee (such as a guardian or a party acting *in loco parentis* in the case of a child, or a trustee as agent for the alternate payee). [Staff of the Joint Committee on Taxation, Explanation of Technical Corrections to the Tax Reform Act of 1984 and Other Recent Tax Legislation, 100th Cong., 1st Sess. (Comm. Print 1987) at 222; FAQs About Qualified Domestic Relations Orders, available at https://www.dol.gov/agencies/ebsa/about-ebsa/our-activities/resource-center/faqs/qdro-overview] A QDRO also can require payment to a state agency, as agent for the alternate payee (see Q 3:8).

Q 3:8 Will a DRO fail to be a QDRO if it requires that benefits in pay status be paid to a state agency as the agent of the alternate payee?

No. The legislative history of the QDRO rules does not prevent the payment of amounts in pay status with respect to an alternate payee to a state agency that is the agent of the alternate payee for the payment of those amounts if the alternate payee consents to such payments. In such a case, payment to the state agency does not cause the DRO to fail to be a QDRO and, under normal principles of constructive receipt, the alternate payee is treated as having received the amounts paid under the order. [Sen. Rpt. 99-313, 99th Cong., 2d Sess. at 1103 (1986)] The DOL has advised that the fact that a DRO names a state child support enforcement agency as the party to whom payments are to be made on behalf of an alternate payee would not constitute grounds on which a plan administrator could find the DRO not to be a QDRO. [D.O.L. Advisory Op. 2002-03A (June 7, 2002)]

Q 3:9 Can a QDRO cover more than one retirement plan?

Yes. A QDRO can assign rights to benefits under more than one retirement plan of the same or different employers as long as each plan and the assignment of benefit rights under each plan are clearly specified. [I.R.C. § 414(p)(2)(D); ERISA § 206(d)(3)(C)(iv); FAQs About Qualified Domestic Relations Orders, available at https://www.dol.gov/agencies/ebsa/about-ebsa/our-activities/resource-center/faqs/qdro-overview]

Q 3:10 Will a DRO fail to be a QDRO if it does not specify the participant's or alternate payee's last known mailing address, if the plan administrator has reason to know the addresses independently of the order?

No. The legislative history of the QDRO requirements specifically states that "an order is not to be treated as failing to be a qualified order merely because the order does not specify the current mailing address of the participant and the alternate payee if the plan administrator has reason to know the addresses independently of the order." [Sen. Rpt. 98-575, 98th Cong., 2d Sess. at 20 (1984)] For example, if the plan administrator knows that the alternate payee is also a participant under the plan, and the plan's records contain a current mailing address for both participants, the plan administrator may not treat the order as failing to be a QDRO solely because it lacks current addresses.

Q 3:11 Must all QDROs have the same provisions?

No. Although every QDRO must contain certain provisions, such as the names and addresses of the participant and alternate payee(s) and the name of the plan(s) (see Q 3:5), the specific content of the rest of the QDRO will depend on the type of retirement plan, the nature of the participant's retirement benefits, the purposes for issuing the order, and the intent of the drafting parties. [FAQs About Qualified Domestic Relations Orders, available at https://www.dol.gov/agencies/ebsa/about-ebsa/our-activities/resource-center/faqs/qdro-overview]

Q 3:12 Who determines whether an order is a QDRO?

Under ERISA and the Code, the administrator of the retirement plan that provides the benefits affected by an order is the individual (or entity) initially responsible for determining whether a DRO is a QDRO. Plan administrators have specific responsibilities and duties with respect to determining whether a DRO is a QDRO. Plan administrators, as plan fiduciaries, are required to discharge their duties prudently and solely in the interest of plan participants and beneficiaries. Among other things, plans must establish reasonable procedures to determine the qualified status of DROs and to administer distributions pursuant to QDROs. Administrators are required to follow the plan's procedures for making QDRO determinations. Administrators also are required to furnish notices to participants and alternate payees of the receipt of a DRO and to furnish a copy of the plan's procedures for determining the qualified status of DROs.

It is the view of the DOL that a state court (or other state agency or instrumentality with the authority to issue DROs) does not have jurisdiction to determine whether an issued DRO constitutes a QDRO. In the view of the DOL, jurisdiction to challenge a plan administrator's decision about the qualified status of an order lies exclusively in federal court. [I.R.C. § 414(p)(6)(A)(ii); ERISA §§ 206(d)(3)(G)(i) and (ii), 404(a), 502(a)(3), 502(e), and 514; FAQs About Qualified Domestic Relations Orders, available at https://www.dol.gov/agencies/ebsa/about-ebsa/our-activities/resource-center/faqs/qdro-overview]

Q 3:13 Who is the administrator of the retirement plan?

The administrator of a retirement plan is the individual or entity specifically designated in the plan documents as the administrator. If the plan documents do not designate an administrator, the administrator is the employer maintaining the plan, or, in the case of a plan maintained by more than one employer, the association, committee, joint board of trustees, or similar group representing the parties maintaining the plan. The name, address, and telephone number of the plan administrator is required to be included in the plan's summary plan description (SPD). The SPD is a document that the administrator is required to furnish to each participant and to each beneficiary receiving benefits. The SPD summarizes the rights and benefits of participants and beneficiaries and the obligations of the plan. [I.R.C. § 414(g); ERISA § 3(16), 102(b); Treas. Reg. § 1.414(g)-1; D.O.L. Reg. § 2520.102-3(f); FAQs About Qualified Domestic Relations Orders, available at https://www.dol.gov/agencies/ebsa/about-ebsa/our-activities/resource-center/faqs/qdro-overview]

Q 3:14 Will the DOL issue advisory opinions on whether a DRO is a QDRO?

No. A determination of whether a DRO is a QDRO necessarily requires an interpretation of the specific provisions of the plan or plans to which the order applies and the application of those provisions to specific facts, including a determination of the participant's actual benefits under the plan(s). The DOL will not issue opinions on such inherently factual matters. [ERISA Procedure 76-1, 41 Fed. Reg. 36281 (1976); FAQs About Qualified Domestic Relations Orders, available at https://www.dol.gov/agencies/ebsa/about-ebsa/our-activities/resource-center/faqs/qdro-overview]

Q 3:15 What is the best way to divide a participant's retirement plan benefits in a QDRO?

There is no single best way to divide a participant's retirement plan benefits in a QDRO. What will be best in a specific case will depend upon many factors, including the type of retirement plan, the nature of the participant's benefits, and why the parties are seeking to divide those benefits.

In deciding how to divide a participant's retirement plan benefits under a QDRO, it is also important to consider two aspects of the participant's benefits: the benefit payable under the plan directly to the participant for retirement purposes (the retirement benefit), and any benefit that is payable on the participant's behalf to someone else after the participant dies (the survivor benefit). [FAQs About Drafting Qualified Domestic Relations Orders, available at https://www.dol.gov/agencies/ebsa/about-ebsa/our-activities/resource-center/faqs/qdro-drafting]

Q 3:16 How much of a participant's retirement plan benefits may be provided to an alternate payee under a QDRO?

A QDRO may provide an alternate payee with any part or all of the participant's retirement plan benefits. However, the QDRO may not require the plan to provide increased benefits (determined on the basis of actuarial value), nor may a QDRO require a plan to provide a type or form of benefit, or any option, not otherwise provided under the plan. The QDRO also may not require the payment of benefits to an alternate payee that must be paid to another alternate payee under another QDRO already recognized by the plan. [I.R.C. §§ 414(p)(1)(A)(i), 414(p)(3), 414(p)(4); ERISA §§ 206(d)(3)(B)(i)(I), 206(d)(3)(D), (E); D.O.L. Advisory Op. 2000-09A; FAQs About Drafting Qualified Domestic Relations Orders, available at https://www.dol.gov/agencies/ebsa/about-ebsa/our-activities/resource-center/faqs/qdro-drafting]

Q 3:17 Why are the reasons for dividing the participant's retirement plan benefits important?

Generally, QDROs are used either to provide support payments (temporary or permanent) to the alternate payee (who may be the spouse, former spouse, or a child or other dependent of the participant) (see Q 3:6) or to divide marital property in the course of dissolving a marriage. These differing goals often result in different choices in drafting a QDRO. There are two common approaches to drafting QDROs for these two different purposes.

One approach that is used in drafting some QDROs (called "shared payment QDROs") is to split the actual benefit payments made with respect to the participant under the plan to give the alternate payee part of each payment. This approach to dividing the participant's retirement benefits is often called the "shared payment" approach. Under this approach, the alternate payee will not receive any payments unless the participant receives a payment or is already in pay status. This approach is often used, for example, when a support order is being drafted after a participant has already begun to receive a stream of payments from the plan (such as a life annuity).

A shared payment QRDO, like any other QDRO, must specify the amount or percentage of the participant's benefit payments that is assigned to the alternate payee (or the manner in which such amount or percentage is to be determined). It must also specify the number of payments or period to which it applies. This is particularly important in the shared payment QDRO, which must specify when the alternate payee's right to share the payments begins and ends. For example, when a state authority seeks to provide support to a participant's child, an order might require payments to the alternate payee to begin as soon as possible after the order is determined to be a QDRO and to continue until the alternate payee reaches maturity. Alternatively, when support is being provided to the participant's former spouse, the QDRO might state that payments to the former spouse will end when he or she remarries. If payments are to end upon the occurrence of an event, notice and reasonable substantiation that the event has occurred must be provided for the plan to be able to comply with the terms of the QDRO.

Orders that seek to divide a participant's retirement benefit as part of the marital property upon divorce or legal separation often take a different approach to dividing the benefit. These QDROs (called "separate interest QDROs") usually divide the participant's retirement benefit (rather than just the benefit payments) into two separate portions, with the intent of giving the alternate payee a separate right to receive a portion of the participant's retirement benefit to be paid at a time and in a form different from that chosen by the participant. This approach to dividing a retirement benefit is often called the "separate interest" approach.

A separate interest QDRO must specify the amount or percentage of the participant's retirement benefit to be assigned to the alternate payee (or the manner in which that amount or percentage is to be determined). The separate interest QDRO must also specify the number of payments or period to which it applies, and such QDROs often satisfy this requirement simply by giving the alternate payee the right that the participant would have had under the plan to elect the form of benefit payment and the time at which the separate interest will be paid. Such an order would satisfy the requirements to be a QDRO.

The Code and ERISA do not require the use of either the shared payment or the shared interest approach for any specific domestic relations purpose, and it is up to the drafters of any QDRO to determine how best to achieve the purposes for which retirement plan benefits are being divided. Further, the shared payment approach and the separate interest approach can each be used for either defined benefit or defined contribution plans. However, it is important, in drafting any QDRO, to understand and follow the terms of the plan. An order that would require a plan to provide increased benefits (determined on an actuarial basis) or to provide a type or form of benefit, or an option, not otherwise available under the plan cannot be a QDRO (see Q 3:5).

In addition to determining whether or how to divide the participant's retirement benefit, it is important to consider whether or not to assign to the alternate payee a right to survivor benefits or any other benefits payable on behalf of the participant under the plan. [I.R.C. § 414(p)(2)(B)–(D); ERISA § 206(d)(3)(C)(ii)–(iv); FAQs About Drafting Qualified Domestic Relations Orders, available at https://www.dol.gov/agencies/ebsa/about-ebsa/our-activities/resource-center/faqs/qdro-drafting]

Q 3:18 In deciding how to divide a participant's retirement plan benefits, why is understanding the type of retirement plan important?

Understanding the type of retirement plan is important because the order cannot be a QDRO unless its assignment of rights or division of retirement plan benefits complies with the terms of the plan. Parties drafting a QDRO should read the plan's SPD and other plan documents to understand what retirement benefits are provided under the plan. The DOL's FAQs about drafting QDROs provide guidance on how a participant's retirement benefit may be divided based on whether the plan is a defined contribution plan or a defined benefit plan. [FAQs About Drafting Qualified Domestic Relations Orders, available at https://www.dol.gov/agencies/ebsa/about-ebsa/our-activities/resource-center/faqs/qdro-drafting]

Q 3:19 What are survivor benefits and why should a QDRO take them into account?

The Code and ERISA require all tax-qualified retirement plans, whether they are defined benefit or defined contribution plans, to provide benefits in a way that includes a survivor benefit for the participant's spouse. [I.R.C. §§ 401(a)(11) and 417; ERISA § 205] The type of survivor benefit that is required by the Code and ERISA depends on the type of retirement plan. Plans also may provide for survivor (or death) benefits that are in addition to those required by the Code and ERISA. Participants and alternate payees drafting QDROs should read the plan's current SPD and other plan documents in order to understand the survivor benefits available under the plan.

The Code and ERISA generally require that defined benefit plans and certain defined contribution plans (e.g., money purchase pension plans) pay retirement benefits to participants who were married on the participant's annuity starting date (i.e., the first day of the first period for which an amount is payable to the participant) in the form of a qualified joint and survivor annuity (QJSA) unless the participant elects a different form and the participant's spouse consents to that election. When benefits are paid as a QJSA, the participant receives a periodic payment (usually monthly) during his or her life, and the participant's surviving spouse receives a periodic payment for the rest of his or her life upon the participant's death. The Code and ERISA also generally require that, if a married participant with a vested benefit under one of these types of plans dies before his or her annuity starting date, the plan must pay the participant's surviving spouse a monthly survivor benefit, called a qualified pre-retirement survivor annuity (QPSA).

Those defined contribution plans that are not required to pay benefits to married participants in the form of a QJSA or QPSA (like most 401(k) plans) are required by the Code and ERISA to pay any balance remaining in the participant's account, after the participant dies, to his or her surviving spouse. If the spouse gives his or her written consent, the participant may elect that, upon the participant's death, any balance remaining in his or her account will be paid to a beneficiary other than the spouse (e.g., the couple's children). Under these defined contribution plans, the Code and ERISA do not require a spouse's consent to a participant's decision to withdraw any portion (or all) of his or her account balance during the participant's life.

If a participant and his or her spouse become divorced before the participant's annuity starting date, the divorced spouse loses all rights to the survivor benefit protections that the Code and ERISA require be provided to the participant's spouse. If the divorced participant remarries, his or her new spouse may acquire a right to the federally mandated survivor benefits. A QDRO, however, may change that result. To the extent that a QDRO requires that a former spouse be treated as the participant's surviving spouse for all or any part of the survivor benefits payable after the participant's death, any subsequent spouse of the participant cannot be treated as the participant's surviving spouse. For example, if a QDRO awards all of the survivor benefit rights to the participant's former spouse, and the participant remarries, the participant's new spouse will not receive any survivor benefits upon the participant's death. If such a QDRO requires that a defined benefit plan, or a defined contribution plan subject to the QJSA and QPSA requirements (e.g., a money purchase pension plan) treat the participant's former spouse as his or her surviving spouse, the plan must pay the participant's benefit in the form of a QJSA or QPSA unless the former spouse who was named as surviving spouse in the QDRO consents to the participant's election of a different form of payment.

It should also be noted that some retirement plans provide that a spouse of a participant will not be treated as married unless he or she has been married to the participant for at least a year. If the retirement plan to which the QDRO relates contains such a one-year marriage requirement, then the QDRO cannot treat the alternate payee as a surviving spouse if the marriage lasted for less than one year.

In addition, it is important to note that some retirement plans may provide for survivor benefits in addition to those required by the Code and ERISA for the benefit of the surviving spouse. Generally, however, the only way to establish a former spouse's right to survivor benefits, such as a QJSA or QPSA, is through a QDRO. A QDRO may provide that a part or all of such other survivor benefits shall be paid to an alternate payee rather than to the person who would otherwise be entitled to receive such death benefits under the plan. A spouse or former spouse can also receive a right to receive (as a separate interest or as shared payments) part of the participant's retirement benefit as well as a survivor's benefit. [I.R.C. §§ 401(a)(11), 414(p)(5), 417; ERISA §§ 205, 206(d)(3)(F); FAQs About Drafting Qualified Domestic Relations Orders, available at https://www.dol.gov/agencies/ebsa/about-ebsa/our-activities/resource-center/faqs/qdro-drafting]

Q 3:20 May a QDRO specify the form in which the alternate payee's benefits will be paid?

A separate interest QDRO may specify the form in which the alternate payee's benefits will be paid, subject to the following limitations:

1. The order may not provide the alternate payee with a type or form of payment, or any option, not otherwise provided under the plan.
2. The order may not provide any subsequent spouse of an alternate payee with the survivor benefit rights that federal law requires be provided to spouses of participants under ERISA Section 205.
3. For any tax-qualified retirement plan, the payment of the alternate payee's benefits must satisfy the requirements of Code Section 401(a)(9), respecting the timing and duration of payment of benefits. In determining the form of payment for an alternate payee, an order may substitute the alternate payee's life for the life of the participant to the extent that the form of payment is based on the duration of an individual's life. The timing and forms of benefit available to an alternate payee under a tax-qualified plan may be limited by Code Section 401(a)(9).

Alternatively, a QDRO (subject to the limitations described above) may give the alternate payee the right that the participant would have had under the plan to elect the form of benefit payment. For example, if the participant would have had the right to elect a life annuity, the alternate payee may exercise that right and choose to have the assigned benefit paid over the alternate payee's life. However, the QDRO must permit the plan to determine the amount payable to the alternate payee under any form of payment in a manner that does not require the plan to pay increased benefits (determined on an actuarial basis).

A plan may, by its own terms, provide alternate payees with additional types or forms of benefits, or options, not otherwise provided to participants, such as a lump-sum payment option, but the plan cannot prevent a QDRO from assigning to an alternate payee any type or form of benefit, or option, provided generally under the plan to the participant. [I.R.C. §§ 401(a)(9), 401(a)(13)(B), 414(p)(3), 414(p)(4)(A)(iii); ERISA §§ 206(d)(3)(A), 206(d)(3)(D), 206(d)(3)(E)(i)(III); FAQs About Drafting Qualified Domestic Relations Orders, available at https://www.dol.gov/agencies/ebsa/about-ebsa/our-activities/resource-center/faqs/qdro-drafting]

Q 3:21 When may the alternate payee receive the benefits assigned under a QDRO?

A shared payment QDRO (see Q 3:17) must specify the date on which the alternate payee will begin to share the participant's payments. That date, however, may not be earlier than the date on which the plan receives the order. A separate interest QDRO (see Q 3:17) may either specify the time (after the plan receives the order) at which the alternate payee will receive the separate interest or assign to the alternate payee the same right the participant would have had under the plan with regard to the timing of payment. In either case, a QDRO may not provide that an alternate payee will receive a benefit earlier than the date on which the participant reaches his or her earliest retirement age (see Q 3:25), unless the plan permits payments at an earlier date.

The plan itself may contain provisions permitting alternate payees to receive separate interests awarded under a QDRO at an earlier time or under different circumstances than the participant could receive the benefit. For example, a plan may provide that alternate payees may elect to receive a lump-sum payment of a separate interest at any time. [I.R.C. §§ 401(a)(9), 414(p)(2), 414(p)(3), 414(p)(4); ERISA §§ 206(d)(3)(C), 206(d)(3)(D), 206(d)(3)(E); FAQs About Drafting Qualified Domestic Relations Orders, available at https://www.dol.gov/agencies/ebsa/about-ebsa/our-activities/resource-center/faqs/qdro-drafting]

Q 3:22 Will a DRO fail to be a QDRO solely because the DRO is issued after, or revises, another DRO or QDRO, or solely because of the time at which it is issued?

No. A DRO will not fail to be a QDRO solely because the DRO is issued after, or revises, another DRO or QDRO. [D.O.L. Reg. § 2530.206(b)(1); FAQs About Qualified Domestic Relations Orders, available at https://www.dol.gov/agencies/ebsa/about-ebsa/our-activities/resource-center/faqs/qdro-overview] In addition, a DRO will not fail to be a QDRO solely because of the time at which it is issued. [D.O.L. Reg. § 2530.206(c)(1)] Any such DRO is subject to the same requirements and protections, however, that apply to all QDROs under the Code and ERISA. [D.O.L. Reg. § 2530.206(d)(1)] On March 7, 2007, the DOL issued interim final regulations [D.O.L. Reg. § 2530.206], implementing the directive contained in PPA, to clarify certain timing issues with respect to DROs and QDROs under the Code and ERISA. The DOL's interim final regulations became effective on April 6, 2007. [72 Fed. Reg. 10070 (Mar. 7, 2007)] On June 10, 2010, the DOL issued final regulations, finalizing the interim final regulations, effective August 9, 2010. [75 Fed. Reg. 32846 (June 10, 2010)]

A DRO issued after the participant's death, divorce, or annuity starting date, or subsequent to an existing QDRO will not fail to be treated as a QDRO solely because of the timing of the issuance. For example, a subsequent DRO between the same parties that revises an earlier QDRO does not fail to be a QDRO solely because it was issued after the first QDRO. Likewise, a subsequent DRO between different parties that directs apportion of the participant's previously unallocated benefits to a second alternate payee does not fail to be a QDRO solely because of the existence of the previous QDRO. Further, a DRO requiring that a portion of a participant's annuity benefit payments be paid to an alternate payee does not fail to be a QDRO solely because the DRO was issued after the annuity starting date. [FAQs About Qualified Domestic Relations Orders, available at https://www.dol.gov/agencies/ebsa/about-ebsa/our-activities/resource-center/faqs/qdro-overview]

Subsequent Domestic Relations Orders. A DRO will not fail to be treated as a QDRO solely because the DRO is issued after, or revises, another DRO or QDRO. [D.O.L. Reg. § 2530.206(b)(1)] This rule is illustrated by the following examples:

Example 3-1: *Subsequent DRO Between the Same Parties.* Participant and Spouse divorce, and the administrator of Participant's 401(k) plan receives a DRO. The administrator determines that the DRO is a QDRO. The QDRO allocates a portion of Participant's benefits to Spouse as the alternate payee. Subsequently, before benefit payments have commenced, Participant and Spouse seek and receive a second DRO. The second DRO reduces the portion of Participant's benefits that Spouse was to receive under the QDRO. The second DRO does not fail to be treated as a QDRO solely because the second DRO is issued after, and reduces the prior assignment contained in, the first QDRO. [D.O.L. Reg. § 2530.206(b)(2), Ex. (1)]

Example 3-2: *Subsequent DRO Between Different Parties.* Participant and Spouse 1 divorce and the administrator of Participant's 401(k) plan receives a DRO. The administrator determines that the DRO is a QDRO. The QDRO allocates a portion of Participant's benefits to Spouse 1 as alternate payee. Participant marries Spouse 2, and then they divorce. Participant's 401(k) plan administrator subsequently receives a DRO pertaining to Spouse 2. The DRO assigns to Spouse 2 a portion of Participant's 401(k) benefits not already allocated to Spouse 1. The second DRO does not fail to be a QDRO solely because the second DRO is issued after the plan administrator has determined that an earlier DRO pertaining to Spouse 1 is a QDRO. [D.O.L. Reg. § 2530.206(b)(2), Ex. (2)]

Timing. A DRO also shall not fail to be treated as a QDRO solely because of the time at which it is issued. [D.O.L. Reg. § 2530.206(c)(1)] This rule is illustrated by the following examples:

Example 3-3: *DRO Issued After Death.* Participant and Spouse divorce, and the administrator of Participant's plan receives a DRO, but the administrator finds the DRO deficient and determines that it is not a QDRO. Shortly thereafter, Participant dies while actively employed. A second DRO correcting the defects in the first DRO is subsequently submitted to the plan. The second DRO does not fail to be treated as a QDRO solely because it is issued after the death of Participant. The result would be the same even if no order had been issued before Participant's death; in other words, it is as though the order issued after death were the only order. [D.O.L. Reg. § 2530.206(b)(2), Ex. (1)]

Example 3-4: *DRO Issued After Divorce.* Participant and Spouse divorce. As a result, Spouse no longer meets the definition of *surviving spouse* under the terms of the plan. Subsequently, the plan administrator receives a DRO requiring that Spouse be treated as Participant's surviving spouse for purposes of receiving a death benefit payable under the terms of the plan only to a participant's surviving spouse. The DRO does not fail to be treated as a QDRO solely because, at the time it is issued, Spouse no longer meets the definition of *surviving spouse* under the terms of the plan. [D.O.L. Reg. § 2530.206(c)(2), Ex. (2)]

Example 3-5: *DRO Issued After Annuity Starting Date.* Participant retires and begins receipt of benefits in the form of a straight life annuity, equal to $1,000 per month, and with respect to which Spouse has consented to the waiver of the surviving spousal rights provided under the plan and the Code and ERISA. After the commencement of benefits (i.e., after the annuity starting date), Participant and Spouse divorce and present the plan with a DRO requiring 50 percent ($500) of Participant's future monthly annuity payments under the plan to be paid instead to Spouse, as an alternate payee (so that monthly payments of $500 are to be made to Spouse during Participant's lifetime). The order does not fail to be a QDRO solely because it is issued after the annuity starting date. If the order instead had required payments to Spouse for the lifetime of Spouse, this would constitute a reannuitization with a new annuity starting date, rather than merely allocating to Spouse a part of the determined annuity payments due to Participant, so that the order, while not failing to be a QDRO because of the timing of the order, would fail to meet the requirements of ERISA Section 206(d)(3)(D)(i) (unless the plan otherwise permits such a change after the participant's annuity starting date). [D.O.L. Reg. § 2530.206(c)(2), Ex. (3)]

Requirements and Protections. A DRO described above shall be subject to the same requirements and protections that apply to QDROs under the Code and ERISA. [D.O.L. Reg. § 2530.206(d)(1)] This rule is illustrated by the following examples:

Example 3-6: *Type or Form of Benefit.* Participant and Spouse divorce, and their divorce decree provides that the parties will prepare a DRO assigning 50 percent of Participant's benefits under a 401(k) plan to Spouse to be paid in monthly installments over a 10-year period. Shortly thereafter, Participant dies while actively employed. A DRO consistent with the decree is subsequently submitted to the 401(k) plan; however, the plan does not provide for 10-year installment payments of the type described in the DRO. The DRO does not fail to be treated as a QDRO solely because it is issued after the death of the Participant, but the DRO would fail to be a QDRO because the DRO requires the plan to provide a type or form of benefit, or any option, not otherwise provided under the plan. [D.O.L. Reg. § 2530.206(d)(2), Ex. (1)]

Example 3-7: *Segregation of Payable Benefits.* Participant and Spouse divorce, and the administrator of Participant's plan receives a DRO under which Spouse would begin to receive benefits immediately if the DRO is determined to be a QDRO. The plan administrator separately accounts for the amounts covered by the DRO, as required by the Code and ERISA. The plan administrator finds the DRO deficient and determines that it is not a QDRO. Subsequently, after the expiration of the segregation period pertaining to the DRO, the plan administrator receives a second DRO relating to the same parties under which Spouse would begin to receive benefits immediately if the second DRO is determined to be a QDRO. Notwithstanding the expiration of the first segregation period, the amounts covered by the second DRO must be separately accounted for by the plan administrator for an 18-month period, as required by the Code and ERISA. [D.O.L. Reg. § 2530.206(d)(2), Ex. (2)]

Example 3-8: *Previously Assigned Benefits.* Participant and Spouse divorce, and the administrator of Participant's 401(k) plan receives a DRO. 1 The administrator determines that the DRO is a QDRO. The QDRO assigns a portion of Participant's benefits to Spouse 1 as the alternate payee. Participant marries Spouse 2, and then they divorce. Participant's 401(k) plan administrator subsequently receives a DRO pertaining to Spouse 2. The DRO assigns to Spouse 2 a portion of Participant's 401(k) benefits already assigned to Spouse 1. The second DRO does not fail to be treated as a QDRO solely because the second DRO is issued after the plan administrator has determined that an earlier DRO pertaining to Spouse 1 is a QDRO. The second DRO, however, would fail to be a QDRO because it assigns all or a portion of Participant's benefits that are already assigned to Spouse 1 by the prior QDRO. [D.O.L. Reg. § 2530.206(d)(2), Ex. (3)]

Form or Amount of Benefits May Not Be Altered

Q 3:23 Will a DRO be a QDRO if it alters the amount or form of benefits otherwise provided to the participant under a retirement plan?

No. A DRO will not be a QDRO if it requires the retirement plan to provide any form of benefit, or any option, not otherwise provided under the plan, or to provide increased benefits (determined on the basis of actuarial value) (see Q 3:5). [I.R.C. § 414(p)(3)(A), (B); ERISA § 206(d)(3)(D)(i), (ii)]

A DRO does not require a retirement plan to provide increased benefits if it does not require benefits in excess of those to which the participant would be entitled if there were no order. [Sen. Rpt. 98-575, 98th Cong., 2d Sess. at 20 (1984)]

Q 3:24 Are there circumstances where a QDRO may alter the payment of retirement plan benefits?

Yes. Although the general rule is that an order may not alter the payment of benefits under a retirement plan, there is an exception providing that a DRO will not fail to be a QDRO solely because it requires that payment of retirement plan benefits be made to an alternate payee:

1. In the case of any payment before a participant has separated from service, on or after the date on which the participant attains (or would have attained) the earliest retirement age (see Q 3:25) under the plan [I.R.C. § 414(p)(4)(A)(i); ERISA § 206(d)(3)(E)(i)(I)];
2. As if the participant had retired on the date on which such payment is to begin under such order (but taking into account only the present value of the benefits actually accrued and not taking into account the present value of any employer subsidy for early retirement) [I.R.C. § 414(p)(4)(A)(ii); ERISA § 206(d)(3)(E)(i)(II)]; and
3. In any form in which such benefits may be paid under the plan to the participant (other than in the form of a joint and survivor annuity for the alternate payee and his or her subsequent spouse). [I.R.C. § 414(p)(4)(A)(iii); ERISA § 206(d)(3)(E)(i)(III)]

For purposes of (2), above, the interest rate assumption used in determining the present value is the rate specified in the plan, or if no rate is specified, 5 percent.

A plan that provides only normal and subsidized early retirement benefits generally would not specify a rate for determining actuarially equivalent, unsubsidized benefits. [Sen. Rpt. 98-575, 98th Cong., 2d Sess. at 21 (1984)]

If an alternate payee begins to receive benefits under the QDRO, and the participant later retires with subsidized early retirement benefits, the order may specify recalculation of the alternate payee's benefit. The payment of early retirement benefits to a participant who has not yet retired or the increase in benefits payable to the alternate payee after the recalculation will not violate the rule against QDROs providing for increased benefits. [Sen. Rpt. 98-575, 98th Cong., 2d Sess. at 21 (1984)]

Q 3:25 What is the earliest retirement age for purposes of the rule that allows a QDRO, in certain limited circumstances, to change the timing of benefit payments under a plan?

A QDRO can specify that benefit payments to the alternate payee can begin as early as the earliest retirement age under the plan, even if the participant has not yet separated from service and has not yet begun to receive his or her own benefits under the plan (see Q 3:24).

For QDROs, the Code and ERISA provide a very specific definition of earliest retirement age, which is the earliest date as of which a QDRO can order payment to an alternate payee (unless the plan permits payments at an earlier date). The earliest retirement age applicable to a QDRO depends on the terms of the retirement plan and the participant's age. The term earliest retirement age means the earlier of:

1. The date on which the participant is entitled to a distribution under the plan; or

2. The later of the date the participant reaches age 50, or the earliest date on which the participant could begin receiving benefits after separating from service with the employer.

[I.R.C. § 414(p)(4)(B); ERISA § 206(d)(3)(E)(ii); FAQs About Drafting Qualified Domestic Relations Orders, available at https://www.dol.gov/agencies/ebsa/about-ebsa/our-activities/resource-center/faqs/qdro-drafting]

Example 3-9: The Pacific Grove Corporation retirement plan provides for payment of benefits on separation from service (but not before then), and thus, the earliest date on which a QDRO can require payments to an alternate payee to begin is the date the participant separates from service. However, a QDRO could also require the plan to begin making payments to an alternate payee when the participant reaches age 50, even if he or she had not then separated from service. Because the participant could have received benefits if he or she had separated from service, he or she meets the requirements above.

The legislative history of the QDRO rules reflects Congress's intent that a participant's earliest retirement age should be determined by taking into account only the participant's actual years of service at the time of the participant's separation from service or death. [Sen. Rpt. 99-313, 99th Cong., 2d Sess. at 1097 (1986)]

Example 3-10: Under the Golden Poppy Restaurant Corporation retirement plan, a participant may not receive a benefit until he or she reaches age 65, or age 55 with 10 years of service. The earliest retirement age of a participant who dies or separates from service with only eight years of service is age 65. On the other hand, if a participant dies or separates after completing 10 years of service, the earliest retirement age occurs when the participant would have reached age 55 had the participant survived. [Sen. Rpt. 99-313, 99th Cong., 2d Sess. at 1097 (1986)]

Drafters of QDROs should consult the plan administrator and the plan documents for information on the plan's earliest retirement age. The following examples illustrate the concept of earliest retirement age.

Example 3-11: The Marullo's Grocery Store plan is a defined contribution plan that permits a participant to make withdrawals only when he or she reaches age 59½ or terminates from service. The earliest retirement age for a QDRO under this plan is the earlier of:

1. The date the participant actually terminates employment or reaches age 59½, or
2. The later of either:
    a. The date the participant reaches age 50, or
    b. The date the participant could receive the account balance if the participant terminated employment.

Because the participant could terminate employment at any time and thereby be able to receive the account balance under the plan's terms, the later of the two dates described above is age 50. The earliest retirement age formula for this plan can be simplified to read the earlier of:

1. Actually reaching age 59½ or terminating employment, or
2. Age 50.

Because age 50 is earlier than age 59½, the earliest retirement age for this plan will be the earlier of age 50 or the date the participant actually terminates from service.

Example 3-12: The Western Biological Laboratory defined benefit plan permits retirement benefits to be paid beginning when the participant reaches age 65 and terminates employment. It does not permit earlier payments. The earliest retirement age from the plan is the earlier of:

1. The date on which the participant actually reaches age 65 and terminates employment; or
2. The later of:
   a. Age 50, or
   b. The date on which the participant reaches age 65 (whether he or she terminates employment or not).

Because age 65 is later than age 50, the second part of the formula can be simplified to read age 65, so that the earliest retirement age under the simplified plan is the earlier of:

1. The date on which the participant reaches age 65 and actually terminates; or
2. The date the participant reaches age 65.

Under this plan, therefore, the earliest retirement age will be the date on which the participant reaches age 65. [I.R.C. § 414(p)(4); ERISA § 206(d)(B)–(E); FAQs About Drafting Qualified Domestic Relations Orders, available at https://www.dol.gov/agencies/ebsa/about-ebsa/our-activities/resource-center/faqs/qdro-drafting]

Q 3:26 Can a QDRO require a participant's former spouse to be treated as his or her surviving spouse for purposes of determining survivor benefits under a retirement plan?

Yes. To the extent provided in any QDRO, the participant's former spouse will be treated as his or her surviving spouse for purposes of requiring that retirement plan benefits be paid in the form of a QJSA or QPSA. But if the participant's former spouse is named for purposes of the QJSA or QPSA rules, then the participant's current spouse cannot be treated as his or her surviving spouse for these purposes. [I.R.C. § 414(p)(5)(A); ERISA § 206(d)(3)(F)(i)]

Example 3-13: Dr. Horace Dormody is divorced from Mrs. Dormody, but a QDRO provides that Dr. Dormody be treated as Mrs. Dormody's current spouse with respect to all of Mrs. Dormody's benefits under the Cafe La Ida

Company retirement plan—unless Mrs. Dormody obtains his consent to waive the QJSA or QPSA or both. The fact that Mrs. Dormody married Lee Chong after her divorce from Dr. Dormody is disregarded. If, however, the QDRO had provided that Dr. Dormody be treated as Mrs. Dormody's current spouse only with respect to benefits that accrued prior to their divorce, then Dr. Dormody's consent would be needed by Mrs. Dormody for her to waive the QPSA or QJSA with respect to benefits accrued before the divorce. Lee Chong's consent would be required with respect to the remainder of her benefits. [Treas. Reg. § 1.401(a)-13(g)(4)(i)(B)(1)]

Example 3-14: In the preceding example, if the QDRO ordered that a portion of Mrs. Dormody's benefit under the plan (either through separate accounts or a percentage of the benefit) be distributed to Dr. Dormody rather than ordering that Dr. Dormody be treated as Mrs. Dormody's spouse, the survivor annuity rules would not apply to that part of Mrs. Dormody's benefits awarded to Dr. Dormody. Instead, the terms of the QDRO would determine how Dr. Dormody's portion of Mrs. Dormody's accrued benefit is paid. Mrs. Dormody is required to obtain Lee Chong's consent if she elects to waive either the QJSA or QPSA with respect to the remaining portion of her benefit under the plan. [Treas. Reg. § 1.401(a)-13(g)(4)(i)(B)(2)]

In addition, a QDRO may specify that the participant's current spouse not be treated as his or her current spouse, even if the applicable election periods (that is, for QPSAs, the first day of the year in which the participant reaches age 35, and, for QJSAs, the 90-day period before the participant's annuity starting date) have not begun. Finally, a QDRO may provide that the participant's current spouse waive all future rights to a QJSA or QPSA under the plan. [Treas. Reg. § 1.401(a)-13(g)(4)(ii)]

How QDROs Affect Other Retirement Plan Benefits; Section 415 Requirements

Q 3:27 Is a retirement plan required to provide additional vesting or benefits because of a QDRO?

No. A retirement plan is not required to provide additional vesting or benefits to an alternate payee because of a QDRO. [Treas. Reg. § 1.401(a)-13(g)(4)(iii)(A)]

Q 3:28 May a QDRO provide the alternate payee with a right to designate a beneficiary that is greater than the participant's?

No. If an alternate payee is treated under a QDRO as having an interest in the participant's retirement plan benefit, including a separate account or percentage of the participant's account, then the QDRO may not provide the alternate payee with a greater right to designate a beneficiary than the participant's right. The QJSA and QPSA rules do not apply to the alternate payee's spouse, and so the alternate payee cannot have his or her benefit amount paid in either survivor or annuity form, with his or her current spouse as the designated beneficiary. [Treas. Reg. § 1.401(a)-13(g)(4)(iii)(B)]

Q 3:29 To whom is the participant's retirement plan benefit paid if the former spouse, who is treated as the current spouse under a QDRO, dies before the participant's annuity starting date?

Under these circumstances, any actual current spouse of the participant is treated as his or her current spouse, except as otherwise provided in a QDRO. [Treas. Reg. § 1.401(a)-13(g)(4)(iii)(C)]

Q 3:30 How are the annual limitations on contributions and benefits applied in cases where a participant's retirement plan benefits are awarded to an alternate payee under a QDRO?

Even though the participant's retirement plan benefits are awarded to an alternate payee under a QDRO, the benefits are still the participant's benefits for purposes of applying the annual limitations, under Code Section 415. [Treas. Reg. § 1.401(a)-13(g)(4)(iv)]

Alternate Payee's Retirement Plan Benefits Must Be Clearly Specified

Q 3:31 Must a QDRO clearly specify the amount or percentage (or the manner of determining the amount or percentage) of a participant's benefit under a retirement plan that is to be paid to each alternate payee named in the QDRO?

Yes. A DRO will not be recognized as a QDRO unless, among other things, it clearly specifies the amount or percentage of the participant's benefits to be paid by the retirement plan to each alternate payee named in the order, or the manner in which that amount or percentage is to be determined. [I.R.C. § 414(p)(2)(B); ERISA § 206(d)(3)(C)(ii)] The rules also provide that the order cannot require the retirement plan to pay any type or form of benefit, or any option, not otherwise available under the plan, nor can the order require the plan to provide increased benefits (determined on the basis of actuarial value). [I.R.C. § 414(p)(2)(B), (3)(A), (B); ERISA § 206(d)(3)(C)(ii), (D)(i), (ii)]

Q 3:32 How is the amount available to an alternate payee under a defined contribution plan determined?

If a QDRO requires that all or part of a participant's benefits under a defined contribution plan (e.g., money purchase pension plan, profit sharing plan, stock bonus, 401(k), or employee stock ownership plan (ESOP)) be paid to an alternate payee, the QDRO must identify both the participant's account under the plan, and the method for determining how much of it is to be paid to the alternate payee.

In the case of a defined contribution plan that provides for benefits in the form of an annuity (for example, a money purchase pension plan, which is required to provide benefits in this form, or a profit sharing, stock bonus, or 401(k) plan, which provides an annuity form, simply as a matter of plan design, and not because of any legal requirement), a QDRO requiring the plan to pay an annuity to the participant's alternate payee, for example, may specify the amount payable to the alternate payee by describing the periodic benefits payable under the annuity contract that is purchased with that portion of the participant's account that must be applied to such purpose pursuant to the order.

A QDRO dividing a retirement benefit under a defined contribution plan may adopt either a separate interest approach (see Q 3:17) or a shared payment approach (see Q 3:17), or some combination of these approaches. QDROs that provide the alternate payee with a separate interest—by assigning the alternate payee either a percentage or a dollar amount of the participant's account balance as of a certain date—often also provide that the separate interest will be held in a separate account under the plan with respect to which the alternate payee is entitled to exercise the rights of a participant. Provided that the order does not assign a right or option to an alternate payee that is not otherwise available under the plan, an order that creates a separate account for the alternate payee may qualify as a QDRO. [FAQs About Drafting Qualified Domestic Relations Orders, available at https://www.dol.gov/agencies/ebsa/about-ebsa/our-activities/resource-center/faqs/qdro-drafting]

QDROs that provide for shared payments from a defined contribution plan should clearly establish the amount or percentage of the participant's payments that will be allocated to the alternate payee and the number of payments or period of time during which the allocation to the alternate payee is to be made. A QDRO can specify that any or all payments made to the participant are to be shared between the participant and the alternate payee. [FAQs About Drafting Qualified Domestic Relations Orders, available at https://www.dol.gov/agencies/ebsa/about-ebsa/our-activities/resource-center/faqs/qdro-drafting]

In drafting QDROs and dividing benefits under a defined contribution plan, parties should also consider addressing the possibility of contingencies occurring that may affect the participant's account balance (and, therefore, the alternate payee's share) during the determination period. For example, parties might be well advised to specify the source of the alternate payee's share of the participant's account that is invested in multiple investments because there may be different methods of determining how to derive the alternate payee's share that would affect the value of that share. The parties should also consider how to allocate any income or losses attributable to the participant's account that may accrue during the determination period. If an order allocates a specific dollar amount rather than a percentage to an alternate payee as a shared payment, the order should address the possibility that the participant's account balance or individual payments might be less than the specified dollar amount when actually paid out. [FAQs About Drafting Qualified Domestic Relations Orders, available at https://www.dol.gov/agencies/ebsa/about-ebsa/our-activities/resource-center/faqs/qdro-drafting]

Q 3:33 How is the amount available to an alternate payee under a defined benefit plan determined?

A participant's benefits under a defined benefit plan are normally paid in the form of a life annuity (if unmarried, or, if married, and the QJSA form has been waived with the spouse's written consent), or in the form of a QJSA (if married, and the QJSA form of benefit has not been waived). Certain optional forms of payment may also be available under a defined benefit plan, such as a life annuity with a refund feature (for example, a 10-year certain period and life thereafter), installment payments over a term of years equal to the participant's life expectancy, or a single-sum payment. A QDRO intended to direct the payment of all or a portion of the participant's benefits under a defined benefit plan should specify not only the amount of the benefit to be paid to the alternate payee, but also its form. If the form of the benefit can be determined only after the alternate payee makes an election of the desired benefit form, then the QDRO should specify the method of determining the amount payable under each form available.

A QDRO may adopt either the shared payment (see Q 3:17) or the separate interest (see Q 3:17) approach, or a combination of the two, in dividing a participant's benefits under a defined benefit plan.

If the shared payment approach is used, the QDRO should specify the amount of each shared payment allocated to the alternate payee either by a percentage or a dollar amount. If the QDRO describes the alternate payee's share as a dollar amount, care should be taken to establish that the payments to the participant will be sufficient to satisfy the allocation, and the QDRO should indicate what is to happen if the payment is insufficient to satisfy the allocation. The QDRO must also describe the number of payments or the period of time during which the allocation to the alternate payee is to be made. This is usually done by specifying a beginning date and an ending date (or an event that will cause the allocation to the alternate payee to begin and/or end). If a QDRO specifies a triggering event that may occur outside the plan's knowledge, notice of its occurrence must be given to the plan before the plan is required to act in accordance with the QDRO. If the intent is that all payments made under the plan are to be shared between the participant and the alternate payee, the QDRO should so specify. [FAQs About Drafting Qualified Domestic Relations Orders, available at https://www.dol.gov/agencies/ebsa/about-ebsa/our-activities/resource-center/faqs/qdro-drafting]

A defined benefit plan may provide for subsidies under certain circumstances and may also provide increased benefits or additional benefits either earned through additional service or provided by way of plan amendment. A QDRO that uses the shared payment method to give the alternate payee a percentage of each payment may be structured to take into account any such future increases in the benefit paid to the participant. Such a QDRO does not need to address the treatment of future subsidies or other benefit increases, because the alternate payee automatically will receive a share of any subsidy or other benefit increases that are paid to the participant. If the parties do not wish to provide for the sharing of such subsidies or increases, the QDRO should so specify.

[FAQs About Drafting Qualified Domestic Relations Orders, available at https://www.dol.gov/agencies/ebsa/about-ebsa/our-activities/resource-center/faqs/qdro-drafting]

If a separate interest approach is taken for the alternate payee, it is important that the QDRO be based on adequate information from the plan administrator and plan documents concerning the participant's retirement benefit and the rights, options, and features provided under the plan. In particular, the drafters of a QDRO should consider any subsidies or future benefit increases that may be available with respect to the participant's retirement benefit. The QDRO may specify whether, and to what extent, an alternate payee is to receive such subsidies or future benefit increases. [FAQs About Drafting Qualified Domestic Relations Orders, available at https://www.dol.gov/agencies/ebsa/about-ebsa/our-activities/resource-center/faqs/qdro-drafting]

Q 3:34 Can a DRO that changes a prior assignment of retirement plan benefits to an alternate payee reduce the amount assigned to the alternate payee and still be a QDRO?

Yes. A state court (or other appropriate state agency or instrumentality) may alter or modify a previous DRO involving the same participant and alternate payee, as long as the new DRO itself qualifies as a QDRO. A plan administrator may determine that a DRO is a QDRO even if it would supersede or amend a pre-existing QDRO assigning the same participant's benefits to the same alternate payee. [D.O.L. Advisory Op. 2004-02A (Feb. 17, 2004)]

QDROs Must Specify the Benefit Period and the Retirement Plan

Q 3:35 Must a QDRO clearly specify the number of payments or the period to which the order applies?

Yes. Under the applicable rules, a DRO is not a QDRO unless the order clearly specifies the number of payments or period to which it applies. [I.R.C. § 414(p)(2)(C); ERISA § 206(d)(3)(C)(iii)] Of course, to specify the number of payments or period to which the order applies, the person drafting the order must know what all the available forms of benefit are under the retirement plan.

Q 3:36 Must a QDRO clearly specify each retirement plan to which the order applies?

Yes. Under the QDRO rules, a DRO is not a QDRO unless the order clearly specifies each retirement plan to which it applies. [I.R.C. § 414(p)(2)(D); ERISA § 206(d)(3)(C)(iv)] A DRO will not be a QDRO if it simply refers to "each plan of the employer in which the employee participates," and fails to identify the actual plan(s). It is possible for a DRO to be treated as a QDRO with respect to one plan, but not another. Finally, a DRO that does not identify any retirement plan in which the employee participates is not a QDRO with respect to any plan.

Q 3:37 Will a DRO be a QDRO if it directs that retirement plan benefits must be paid to an alternate payee when those benefits have already been determined to be payable to another alternate payee under a prior QDRO?

No. A DRO will not be treated as a QDRO if it requires the payment of retirement plan benefits to an alternate payee when those benefits are required to be paid to another alternate payee under another DRO previously determined to be a QDRO. [I.R.C. § 414(p)(3)(C); ERISA § 206(d)(3)(D)(iii)]

Retirement Plan Provisions and Written Procedures for Determining the Qualified Status of a DRO

Q 3:38 Must a retirement plan document be amended to implement the QDRO rules?

No. Ordinarily, it is not necessary to amend the retirement plan document to implement the QDRO rules. [Sen. Rpt. 98-575, 98th Cong., 2d Sess. at 22 (1984)]

Q 3:39 Must a retirement plan establish reasonable, written procedures to determine the qualified status of DROs and to administer distributions under DROs that are determined to be QDROs?

Yes. Under the QDRO rules, each retirement plan must establish written procedures for determining whether DROs are QDROs and for administering distributions under QDROs. [I.R.C. § 414(p)(6)(B); ERISA § 202(d)(3)(G)(ii); FAQs About Determining Qualified Status and Paying Benefits, available at https://www.dol.gov/agencies/ebsa/about-ebsa/our-activities/resource-center/faqs/qdro-determining-qualified-status-and-paying-benefits] The written QDRO procedures must:

1. Be in writing;
2. Be reasonable;
3. Provide for the notification of each person specified in a DRO as entitled to payment of benefits under the plan (at the address included in the DRO) of such procedures promptly upon receipt by the plan of the DRO; and
4. Permit an alternate payee to designate a representative for receipt of copies of notices that are sent to the alternate payee with respect to a DRO. [I.R.C. § 414(p)(6)(B); ERISA § 206(d)(3)(G)(ii); FAQs About Determining Qualified Status and Paying Benefits, available at https://www.dol.gov/agencies/ebsa/about-ebsa/our-activities/resource-center/faqs/qdro-determining-qualified-status-and-paying-benefits]

Q 3:40 Are there other matters that should be addressed in a retirement plan's written QDRO procedure?

In the DOL's view, a retirement plan's QDRO procedures should be designed to ensure that QDRO determinations are made in a timely, efficient, and cost-effective manner, consistent with the plan administrator's fiduciary duties under ERISA. The DOL believes that unnecessary administrative burdens and costs attendant to QDRO determinations and administration can be avoided with clear explanations of the retirement plan's QDRO determination process, including:

- An explanation of the information about the plan and its benefits that is available to assist prospective alternate payees in preparing QDROs, such as SPDs, plan documents, individual benefit and account statements, and any model QDROs developed for use by the plan.
- A description of the time limits set by the plan administrator for making QDRO determinations.
- A description of the steps that the plan administrator will take to protect and preserve plan assets or benefits upon receipt of a DRO (e.g., a description of when and under what circumstances plan assets will be segregated or benefit payments will be delayed or suspended).
- A description of the process provided under the plan for obtaining a review of the plan administrator's determination as to whether an order is a QDRO.

In the DOL's view, the plan administrator's adoption and use of clear QDRO procedures, coupled with the administrator's furnishing of information about the plan and its benefits upon request, will significantly reduce the difficulty and expense of obtaining and administering QDROs by minimizing confusion and uncertainty about the process. [I.R.C. §§ 414(p)(6), 414(p)(7); ERISA §§ 206(d)(3)(G), 206(d)(3)(H), 404(a); FAQs About Determining Qualified Status and Paying Benefits, available at https://www.dol.gov/agencies/ebsa/about-ebsa/our-activities/resource-center/faqs/qdro-determining-qualified-status-and-paying-benefits]

Q 3:41 What information is a plan administrator required to provide a prospective alternate payee before the administrator receives a DRO?

Congress conditioned an alternate payee's right to an assignment of a participant's retirement plan benefit on the prospective alternate payee's obtaining a DRO that satisfies specific informational and other requirements. In the DOL's view, Congress intended prospective alternate payees—spouses, former spouses, children, and other dependents of a participant who are involved in domestic relations proceedings—to have access to plan and participant benefit information sufficient to prepare a QDRO. Such information might include the SPD, relevant plan documents, and a statement of the participant's benefit entitlements.

The DOL believes that Congress did not intend to require prospective alternate payees to submit a DRO to the plan as a prerequisite to establishing the prospective alternate payee's rights to information in connection with a domestic relations proceeding. However, the DOL also takes the view that a plan administrator may condition disclosure of such information on a prospective alternate payee's providing information sufficient to reasonably establish that the disclosure request is being made in connection with a domestic relations proceeding.

Many DROs initially fail to qualify when submitted to the plan because they fail to take into account the plan's provisions or the participant's actual benefit entitlements. Affording prospective alternate payees access to plan and participant information in a timely manner will help avoid such obvious errors in preparing orders and thereby facilitate plan administration. [I.R.C. § 414(p)(1)–(3); ERISA §§ 206(d)(3)(A)–(C), 404(a); FAQs About Determining Qualified Status and Paying Benefits, available at https://www.dol.gov/agencies/ebsa/about-ebsa/our-activities/resource-center/faqs/qdro-determining-qualified-status-and-paying-benefits]

Q 3:42 May a plan administrator allocate QDRO determination expenses to the retirement plan account of the participant or beneficiary seeking the determination?

Yes. In the DOL's view, ERISA does not preclude the allocation, under a defined contribution plan, of reasonable expenses attendant to QDRO determinations to the account of the participant or beneficiary seeking the determination. [D.O.L. Field Assistance Bulletin 2003-3 (May 19, 2003), expressly superseding D.O.L. Advisory Op. 94-32A; FAQs About Determining Qualified Status and Paying Benefits, available at https://www.dol.gov/agencies/ebsa/about-ebsa/our-activities/resource-center/faqs/qdro-determining-qualified-status-and-paying-benefits] The allocation of reasonable QDRO determination expenses to the affected participant's or beneficiary's account must be disclosed in the plan's SPD. [D.O.L. Reg. § 2520.102-3(l); FAQs About Determining Qualified Status and Paying Benefits, available at https://www.dol.gov/agencies/ebsa/about-ebsa/our-activities/resource-center/faqs/qdro-determining-qualified-status-and-paying-benefits]

Q 3:43 May a plan administrator provide parties with a model form or forms to assist in the preparation of a QDRO?

Although a plan administrator is not required to do so, it may develop and make available model QDRO forms to assist in the preparation of a QDRO. Such model forms may make it easier for the parties to prepare a QDRO and reduce the time and expenses associated with a plan administrator's determination of the qualified status of an order.

Plan administrators are required to honor any DRO that satisfies the requirements to be a QDRO. In the view of the DOL, a plan may not condition its determinations of QDRO status on the use of any particular form. [FAQs About Determining Qualified Status and Paying Benefits, available at https://www.dol.gov/agencies/ebsa/about-ebsa/our-activities/resource-center/faqs/qdro-determining-qualified-status-and-paying-benefits]

Q 3:44 In determining the qualified status of a DRO, is the plan administrator required to determine the validity of the order under state domestic relations law?

No. A plan administrator is generally not required to determine whether the issuing court or agency had jurisdiction to issue an order, whether state law is correctly applied in the order, whether service was properly made upon the parties, or whether an individual identified in an order as an alternate payee is in fact a spouse, former spouse, child, or other dependent of the participant under state law. [D.O.L. Advisory Ops. 92-17A and 99-13A; FAQs About Determining Qualified Status and Paying Benefits, available at https://www.dol.gov/agencies/ebsa/about-ebsa/our-activities/resource-center/faqs/qdro-determining-qualified-status-and-paying-benefits]

Q 3:45 Is a plan administrator required to reject a DRO as defective if the order fails to specify factual identifying information that is easily obtainable by the plan administrator?

No. In many cases, a DRO that is submitted to a retirement plan may clearly describe the identity and rights of the parties, but may be incomplete only with respect to factual identifying information within the plan administrator's knowledge or easily obtained through a simple communication with the alternate payee or the participant. For example, an order may misstate the plan's name or the names of participants or alternate payees; however, the plan administrator can clearly determine the correct names. An order may omit the addresses of participants or alternate payees, but the plan administrator's records are likely to include this information. In such a case, the plan administrator should supplement the DRO with the appropriate identifying information, rather than rejecting the DRO as not qualified. [I.R.C. § 414(p)(2); ERISA §§ 206(d)(3)(C), 206(d)(3)(I); Sen. Rpt. 575, 98th Cong., 2d Sess. at 20; FAQs About Determining Qualified Status and Paying Benefits, available at https://www.dol.gov/agencies/ebsa/about-ebsa/our-activities/resource-center/faqs/qdro-determining-qualified-status-and-paying-benefits]

Procedures to Follow After a Retirement Plan Receives a DRO

Q 3:46 What must the plan administrator do if a DRO is received?

Upon receipt of a DRO, the retirement plan administrator:

1. Must promptly notify the affected participant and each alternate payee named in the order of the receipt of the DRO, and must provide a copy of the plan's procedures for determining whether the DRO is a QDRO; and
2. Must determine within a reasonable period (usually 18 months) after receipt whether the DRO is a QDRO and promptly notify the participant and each alternate payee of the determination.

[I.R.C. § 414(p)(6)(A); ERISA § 206(d)(3)(G)(i); FAQs About Determining Qualified Status and Paying Benefits, available at https://www.dol.gov/agencies/ebsa/about-ebsa/our-activities/resource-center/faqs/qdro-determining-qualified-status-and-paying-benefits]

The notices, described in (1) and (2), above, which the plan administrator must furnish, must be sent to the addresses specified in the DRO, or if the DRO fails to specify an address, to the last known mailing address of the participant or alternate payee. [Sen. Rpt. 98-575, 98th Cong., 2d Sess. at 22 (1984); FAQs About Determining Qualified Status and Paying Benefits, available at https://www.dol.gov/agencies/ebsa/about-ebsa/our-activities/resource-center/faqs/qdro-determining-qualified-status-and-paying-benefits]

Q 3:47 How long may the plan administrator take to determine whether a DRO is a QDRO?

Plan administrators must determine whether a DRO is a QDRO within a reasonable period of time after receiving the order. What constitutes a reasonable period of time will depend upon the specific circumstances. For example, a DRO that is clear and complete when submitted should require less time to review than an order that is incomplete or unclear.

Retirement plans are required to adopt reasonable procedures for determining the qualified status of DROs. Compliance with such procedures should ensure that determinations of the qualified status of a DRO take place within a reasonable period of time. Procedures that unduly inhibit or hamper the QDRO determination process will not be considered reasonable procedures. [I.R.C. § 414(p)(6)(A)(ii); ERISA § 206(d)(3)(G)(i)(II); FAQs About Determining Qualified Status and Paying Benefits, available at https://www.dol.gov/agencies/ebsa/about-ebsa/our-activities/resource-center/faqs/qdro-determining-qualified-status-and-paying-benefits]

Q 3:48 What must the plan administrator do during the determination process to protect against wrongly paying retirement benefits to the participant that would be paid to the alternate payee if the DRO had been determined to be a QDRO?

During any period in which the issue of whether a DRO is a QDRO is being determined (by a plan administrator, a court of competent jurisdiction, or otherwise), ERISA requires that the plan administrator separately account for the amounts (referred to as the segregated amounts) that would be payable to an alternate payee under the terms of the order during that period if the DRO had been determined to be a QDRO. During the period in which the status of a DRO is being determined, the plan administrator must take steps to ensure that amounts that would have been payable to the alternate payee, if the DRO were a QDRO, are not distributed to the participant or any other person.

The plan administrator's duty to separately account for and to preserve the segregated amounts is limited in time. ERISA provides that the plan administrator must preserve the segregated amounts for not longer than the end of the 18-month period beginning on the first date (after the plan receives the order) that the order would require payment to the alternate payee.

It is the view of the DOL that, in order to ensure the availability of a full 18-month protection period, the 18 months cannot begin before the plan receives a DRO. Rather, the 18-month period will begin on the first date on which a payment would be required to be made under an order following receipt by the plan.

The plan administrator must determine whether a DRO is a QDRO within a reasonable period following receipt. In the DOL's view, the 18-month period during which a plan administrator must preserve the segregated amounts is not the measure of the reasonable period for determining the qualified status of an order. In most cases, 18 months would be an unreasonably long period of time to take to review an order. [I.R.C. § 414(p)(7); ERISA § 206(d)(3)(H); FAQs About Determining Qualified Status and Paying Benefits, available at https://www.dol.gov/agencies/ebsa/about-ebsa/our-activities/resource-center/faqs/qdro-determining-qualified-status-and-paying-benefits]

It is the further view of the DOL that, during the determination period, the plan administrator, as a plan fiduciary, may not permit distributions to the participant or any other person of amounts that would be payable to the alternate payee if the DRO were determined to be a QDRO. If the DRO is determined to be a QDRO before the first date on which benefits are payable to the alternate payee, the plan administrator has a continuing duty to account for and to protect the alternate payee's interest in the plan to the same extent that the plan is obligated to account for and to protect the interests of the plan's participants. The plan administrator also has a fiduciary duty to pay out benefits in accordance with the terms of the QDRO. [ERISA §§ 206(d)(3)(H), 404(a)]

If, within the 18-month period beginning with the date (after receipt of the DRO by the plan) on which the first payment would be required to be made to an alternate payee under the DRO, the plan administrator determines that the DRO (or any modification of the DRO) is a QDRO, the plan administrator must pay the segregated amounts to the alternate payee in accordance with the terms of the QDRO. However, if the plan administrator, within the 18-month period that the DRO is *not* a QDRO, or if the status of the order is not resolved by the end of the 18-month period, the plan administrator must pay out the segregated amounts to the person(s) who would have been entitled to receive those amounts if there had not been an order in the first place. [I.R.C. § 414(p)(7); ERISA § 206(d)(3)(H); FAQs About Determining Qualified Status and Paying Benefits, available at https://www.dol.gov/agencies/ebsa/about-ebsa/our-activities/resource-center/faqs/qdro-determining-qualified-status-and-paying-benefits]

If a benefit payment is delayed pending the resolution of a dispute, then that particular payment and any other must also be segregated. If the dispute is not resolved within 18 months, then all the benefit payments that have been delayed must be paid to whoever would have been entitled to them if the DRO had not been issued. [Sen. Rpt. 99-313, 99th Cong., 2d Sess. at 1105 (1986)]

If the plan administrator determines that the DRO is not a QDRO before the 18-month period ends, several options are possible. The plan administrator may delay paying the participant's benefit until the 18-month period has ended to allow time for the participant or the alternate payee to remedy the defect(s) in the DRO. Payment of benefits may also be delayed for a reasonable time if the plan administrator is notified that a DRO is being sought. [H.R. Conf. Rpt. 99-841, 99th Cong., 2d Sess. at II-858 (1986)] A stay of execution of the order may be issued while an appeal is pending notifying the plan administrator that the parties are trying to cure the defects in the DRO. Finally, the plan administrator must obey any restraining order prohibiting the payment of the participant's benefits pending resolution of a dispute over a DRO. [Sen. Rpt. 99-313, 99th Cong., 2d Sess. at 1105 (1986)]

If the plan administrator determines after 18 months that a DRO is a QDRO, that determination can only be applied prospectively. [I.R.C. § 414(p)(7)(D); ERISA §§ 206(d)(3)(H)(iv), 404(a); FAQs About Determining Qualified Status and Paying Benefits, available at https://www.dol.gov/agencies/ebsa/about-ebsa/our-activities/resource-center/faqs/qdro-determining-qualified-status-and-paying-benefits] This means that the plan is not liable to pay the alternate payee for the period before the order was determined to be qualified. If the alternate payee has a state law cause of action against the participant for benefits paid to the participant that should have been paid to the alternate payee, the alternate payee may pursue those remedies in court, as such law permits. [Sen. Rpt. 98-575, 98th Cong., 2d Sess. at 22 (1984)]

If the alternate payee cannot be located during any period, the plan cannot forfeit the alternate payee's benefits if the plan provides for full reinstatement of those benefits when the alternate payee is finally found. [Sen. Rpt. 98-575, 98th Cong., 2d Sess. at 22 (1984)]

Q 3:49 What kind of notice must a plan administrator provide following a QDRO determination?

The plan administrator must notify the participant and each alternate payee of the administrator's determination as to whether an order constitutes a QDRO. The notice should be in writing and must be furnished promptly following a determination.

In the case of a determination that an order is not a QDRO, the notice should include the reasons for the rejection. In most instances where there has been a reasonable good-faith effort to prepare a QDRO, the parties will attempt to correct any deficiencies in the order and resubmit a corrected order for the plan administrator to review. Where a reasonable good-faith effort has been made to draft a QDRO, prudent plan administration requires the plan administrator to furnish to the parties the information, advice, and guidance that is reasonably required in order to understand the reasons for a rejection, either as part of the notification process or otherwise. Such information, advice, and guidance may serve to reduce multiple submissions of deficient orders and, therefore, the burdens and costs to plans attendant on review of such orders.

The notice of the plan administrator's determination should be written in a manner that can be understood by the parties. Multiple submissions and unnecessary expenses may be avoided by clearly communicating in the rejection notice:

- The reasons why the order is not a QDRO;
- References to the plan provisions on which the plan administrator's determination is based;
- An explanation of any time limits that apply to rights available to the parties under the plan (such as the duration of any protective actions the plan administrator will take); and
- A description of any additional material, information, or modifications necessary for the order to be a QDRO and an explanation of why such material, information, or modifications are necessary.

[I.R.C. § 414(p)(6)(A)(ii); ERISA §§ 206(d)(3)(G)(i)(II), 206(d)(3)(I); FAQs About Determining Qualified Status and Paying Benefits, available at https://www.dol.gov/agencies/ebsa/about-ebsa/our-activities/resource-center/faqs/qdro-determining-qualified-status-and-paying-benefits]

Q 3:50 What effect does an order that a plan administrator has determined to be a QDRO have on the administration of the retirement plan?

The plan administrator must act in accordance with the provisions of the QDRO as if it were a part of the retirement plan. In particular, if, under a retirement plan, a participant has the right to elect the form in which benefits will be paid, and the QDRO gives the alternate payee that right, the plan administrator must permit the alternate payee to exercise that right under the circumstances and in accordance with the terms that would apply to the participant, as if the alternate payee were the participant. [I.R.C. §§ 401(a)(13)(B), 414(p)(4)(A)(iii); ERISA §§ 206(d)(3)(A), 206(d)(3)(E)(i)(III); FAQs About Determining Qualified Status and Paying Benefits, available at https://www.dol.gov/agencies/ebsa/about-ebsa/our-activities/resource-center/faqs/qdro-determining-qualified-status-and-paying-benefits]

Q 3:51 What disclosure rights does an alternate payee have under a QDRO?

ERISA provides that a person who is an alternate payee under a QDRO generally shall be considered a beneficiary under the retirement plan for purposes of ERISA. Accordingly, upon written request, the alternate payee must be furnished with copies of various documents, including the latest SPD, the latest annual report (Form 5500), any final annual report (final Form 5500), and the bargaining agreement, trust agreement, contract, or other instrument under which the retirement plan is established or operated, and the plan administrator may impose a reasonable charge to cover the cost of furnishing such copies. In the DOL's view, at such time as benefit payments to the alternate payee begin under the QDRO, the alternate payee must be treated as a beneficiary receiving benefits under the plan and automatically furnished with the SPD, summary of material modifications (SMMs), and the plan's summary annual report (SAR). [ERISA §§ 104, 105, 206(d)(3)(J), 404(a); D.O.L. Reg. § 2520.104b-1, et seq.; FAQs About Determining Qualified Status and Paying Benefits, available at https://www.dol.gov/agencies/ebsa/about-ebsa/our-activities/resource-center/faqs/qdro-determining-qualified-status-and-paying-benefits]

Q 3:52 What happens to the rights created by a QDRO if the retirement plan to which the QDRO applies is amended, merged into another plan, or is maintained by a successor employer?

The rights of the alternate payee under a QDRO are protected in the event of retirement plan amendments, a plan merger, or a change in the sponsor of the plan to the same extent that rights of participants or beneficiaries are protected with respect to benefits accrued as of the date of the event. [I.R.C. §§ 401(a)(13)(B), 411(d)(6); ERISA §§ 204(g), 206(d)(3)(A), 403(c)(1); Staff of the Joint Committee on Taxation, Explanation of Technical Corrections to the Tax Reform Act of 1984 and Other Recent Tax Legislation, 100th Cong., 1st Sess. (Comm. Print 1987) at 224; FAQs About Determining Qualified Status and Paying Benefits, available at https://www.dol.gov/agencies/ebsa/about-ebsa/our-activities/resource-center/faqs/qdro-determining-qualified-status-and-paying-benefits]

Q 3:53 What happens to the rights created by a QDRO if a retirement plan is terminated?

The rights granted by the QDRO must be taken into account in the termination of the retirement plan as if the terms of the QDRO were part of the plan. To the extent the QDRO grants the alternate payee part of the participant's benefits, the plan administrator, in terminating the plan, must provide the alternate payee with the notification, consent, payment, or other rights that it would have provided to the participant with respect to that portion of the participant's benefits. [ERISA §§ 206(d)(3)(A), 403(d); FAQs About Determining Qualified Status and Paying Benefits, available at https://www.dol.gov/agencies/ebsa/about-ebsa/our-activities/resource-center/faqs/qdro-determining-qualified-status-and-paying-benefits]

Q 3:54 What happens to the rights created by a QDRO if a defined benefit plan is terminated and the Pension Benefit Guaranty Corporation (PBGC) becomes trustee of the plan?

The Pension Benefit Guaranty Corporation (PBGC) has special rules that apply to payment of benefits under QDROs. For example, if a QDRO is issued prior to plan termination, the PBGC will not modify the form of benefit payable to an alternate payee specified in the QDRO. If, in contrast, a QDRO is issued after plan termination, the PBGC will generally limit the form of benefit that it will pay under the QDRO to the form permitted by the PBGC in other circumstances (generally, a single life annuity). There are other special rules that apply to the administration by the PBGC of QDROs. These rules are explained in the PBGC's booklet (PBGC Publication 100), "Qualified Domestic Relations Orders & PBGC" (revised October 2012), which may be obtained from the PBGC's website at www.pbgc.gov or by calling PBGC at 1-800-400-PBGC (7242).

For information about a pension plan that PBGC has trusteed, benefit information with respect to a participant in such a plan, or information about QDROs, call PBGC's Customer Contact Center, at 1-800-400-7242, or write to:

PBGC QDRO Coordinator
P.O. Box 15170
Alexandria, VA 22315-1750

For information about terminated pension plans that the PBGC has trusteed, benefit information with respect to a participant in a PBGC-trusteed plan, or to request a copy of the PBGC's booklet, call the PBGC at 1-800-400-PBGC (7242) or visit the PBGC's website at www.pbgc.gov. [FAQs About Determining Qualified Status and Paying Benefits, available at https://www.dol.gov/agencies/ebsa/about-ebsa/our-activities/resource-center/faqs/qdro-determining-qualified-status-and-paying-benefits]

Taxation of Retirement Plan Distributions Made Under QDROs

Q 3:55 Are distributions of retirement plan benefits that are paid to a participant's spouse or former spouse who is an alternate payee under a QDRO includible in the spouse's or former spouse's income?

Yes. Generally, such retirement plan distributions are includible in the spouse's or former spouse's income. [I.R.C. § 402(a), (e)(1)(A)] The participant's spouse or former spouse who is an alternate payee treats the amount subject to the QDRO as his or her own property and is liable to pay income on the taxable portion of that amount.

Example 3-15: Lee Chong is a participant in Acme Store's profit sharing plan, a noncontributory plan. Mr. and Mrs. Chong are divorced in California, and the QDRO issued by the state court awards Mrs. Chong 50 percent of Lee's plan account as of the date of their divorce. Mrs. Chong elects to receive her QDRO account in the form of a single-sum distribution, one of the distribution forms available under the plan. If her QDRO account amounts to $100,000, and if it is paid to her as a single sum in 2019, then she will include $100,000 in her ordinary income for 2019, and no amount of that distribution will be includible in Lee's ordinary income for 2019. Because the plan is a noncontributory plan, meaning that it does not accept participant after-tax contributions, neither Mrs. Chong nor Lee has any basis (investment in the contract) under the plan, and so no part of their respective distributions is excludable as a tax-free return of basis (see Q 3:57). However, there are some exceptions to this general rule as discussed elsewhere in this chapter.

Q 3:56 Are distributions of retirement plan benefits that are paid to a nonspouse alternate payee under a QDRO includible in his or her income?

No. Unlike the situation where retirement plan benefits are paid to a spouse or former spouse alternate payee (see Q 3:55), any distribution of plan benefits paid to a nonspouse alternate payee (for example, a participant's child) under a QDRO generally is includible in the *participant's* income, and not that of the alternate payee. [Notice 89-25, 1989-1 C.B. 662, Q&A-3] This rule became effective for QDRO payments made to nonspouse alternate payees after October 22, 1986 (the effective date of the Tax Reform Act of 1986), regardless of the date the QDRO was entered.

Example 3-16: Doc Steinbeck is a retiree who is currently receiving his benefits under the Western Biological Laboratory Corporation pension plan in the form of a straight life annuity. He and his former wife, Esmerelda, divorced in 2019. Esmerelda has custody of their minor child, Meredith. Under their divorce decree, Doc is obligated to pay $500 a month in child support for Meredith's benefit. A QDRO requires that Doc pay the $500 child support from the $2,000 monthly benefit he receives from the plan. The entire $2,000 monthly benefit (including the $500 portion that the QDRO has dedicated to the payment of child support) is includible in Doc's taxable income, not Esmerelda's.

Q 3:57 How is the investment in the contract (if any) under a retirement plan allocated between the participant and his or her spouse or former spouse who is an alternate payee under a QDRO?

A participant's tax-free basis (investment in the contract) under a retirement plan gets allocated between the participant and the spouse or former spouse who is an alternate payee under a QDRO. The investment in the contract is pro rated between the present value of the distributions made to the alternate payee and the present value of all other benefits payable to the participant. [I.R.C. § 72(m)(10)] It is not clear whether the pro rata allocation is made on the date of the QDRO or on the date of the distribution, but the better approach is to make it on the date of the QDRO.

Example 3-17: Joe participates in the Old Tennis Shoes Corporation profit sharing plan, and has made voluntary after-tax contributions. Joe divorces his wife, Hazel, and their QDRO requires that 50 percent of his plan account, determined as of the date of the order, be paid to her. The value of Joe's account as of that date is $200,000, and $50,000 of that is attributable to his after-tax contributions. Joe's tax-free basis (investment in the contract) of $50,000 represents 25 percent of his $200,000 account under the plan as of the date of the QDRO. Hazel's QDRO account is $100,000 (50 percent of $200,000). Of Hazel's $100,000, $25,000 (25 percent) is attributable to Joe's after-tax contributions, and thus, $25,000 of Hazel's distribution from the plan will be excludable from her income.

Q 3:58 How is the investment in the contract (if any) allocated between the participant and any nonspouse alternate payee under a QDRO?

Unlike the situation described in Q 3:57, when the alternate payee is a nonspouse (for example, a child) of the participant, no portion of any tax-free basis (investment in the contract) the participant may have under the plan is allocated to the nonspouse alternate payee. Instead, the participant recovers all of his or her investment in the contract under the general basis recovery rules that apply. [Sen. Rpt. 99-313, 99th Cong., 2d Sess. at 1104 (1986)] Any distribution that is made to the nonspouse alternate payee under the QDRO is treated as a distribution to the participant, and therefore will consist, to the extent permitted under those rules, as a tax-free recovery of the participant's investment in the contract.

Example 3-18: Ida participates in the Palace Hotel money purchase pension plan, and receives a monthly benefit of $1,000, $200 of which represents a tax-free return of her voluntary after-tax contributions under the plan. A QDRO is entered in California state court that awards 50 percent of Ida's plan benefit to her minor daughter, Ethel. The $500 monthly benefit paid to Ethel is includible in Ida's income, and the $200 per month attributable to Ida's investment in the contract will be allocated entirely to Ida.

Q 3:59 Will the participant be liable to pay the 10 percent additional income tax on any early distributions paid to an alternate payee under a QDRO?

No. Any early distribution that is paid pursuant to a QDRO is not subject to the 10 percent additional income tax on early distributions. As a result, neither the participant nor any alternate payee (whether a spouse, former spouse, or nonspouse) is liable for that tax. [I.R.C. § 72(t)(2)(C)]

Example 3-19: Lee Chong is a participant in Acme Store's profit sharing plan. Mr. and Mrs. Chong divorce, and their QDRO directs that 50 percent of Lee's plan account be granted to Mrs. Chong. A separate account is established under the plan for her. The former Mrs. Chong, now destitute, receives a hardship distribution from her separate account under the plan. She is 50 years old when she receives the hardship distribution. The hardship distribution is includible in her ordinary income, but is not subject to the 10 percent additional income tax on early distributions.

Example 3-20: The facts are the same as in the example above, except that the QDRO requires that 50 percent of Lee's plan account be set aside for the benefit of Tse-Ping, Lee's minor daughter. Tse-Ping's guardian elects to have her separate account distributed in a single sum when Lee reaches age 50, the earliest retirement age under the plan. When the QDRO account is distributed on Tse-Ping's behalf, the 10 percent additional income tax will not be triggered, despite the fact that the distribution will be made before Lee reaches age 59½ because QDRO distributions are not subject to that tax, regardless of whether they are paid to former spouse or spouse alternate payees or to nonspouse alternate payees.

Q 3:60 May a spouse or former spouse alternate payee make a tax-free rollover to an eligible retirement plan of part or all of an eligible retirement distribution that is paid pursuant to a QDRO?

Yes. Any spouse or former spouse alternate payee under a QDRO is treated, under the direct rollover rules, as the distributee of any benefits paid pursuant to the QDRO. [I.R.C. § 402(e)(1)(A)] As a result, a spouse or former spouse alternate payee may roll over, to an eligible retirement plan, all or part of any eligible rollover distribution he or she receives pursuant to the QDRO. If the distribution was made before 1993, an alternate payee who was the participant's spouse or former spouse could roll over distributions to an IRA, but not to another qualified retirement plan. [I.R.C. § 402(a)(6)(F), before being amended by § 521(a) of the Unemployment Compensation Amendments of 1992] And, with respect to pre-1993 distributions, any spouse or former spouse alternate payee who received distributions of property pursuant to a QDRO had to roll over the actual property they received; they were not allowed to liquidate the property and roll over the sale proceeds. [I.R.C. § 402(a)(6)(F)(iii), before being amended by § 521(a) of the Unemployment Compensation Amendments of 1992] This does not apply to any property distributions made after 1992. [I.R.C. § 402(e)(1)(B), (c)(6), as amended by § 521(a) of the Unemployment Compensation Amendments of 1992]

Finally, under the mandatory income tax withholding rules, which apply to post-1992 distributions, income taxes must be withheld, at the 20 percent rate, on any distribution that is made pursuant to a QDRO and not rolled over [I.R.C. § 3405(c), as amended by § 522(b) of the Unemployment Compensation Amendments of 1992; Notice 92-48, 1992-45 I.R.B. 25]

A nonspouse alternate payee (the participant's child, for example) may not roll over his or her distribution under a QDRO. However, if the QDRO gives the participant control over that QDRO distribution, and if the distribution is otherwise eligible to be rolled over, the participant may roll it over him- or herself. [Notice 89-25, 1989-1 C.B. 662, Q&A-4]

Q 3:61 Is a spouse or former spouse who is an alternate payee under a QDRO eligible for income-averaging treatment for any lump-sum distributions under a QDRO?

Yes. The spouse or former spouse alternate payee can use income-averaging treatment, to the extent that it is otherwise available, for any lump-sum distribution received from a plan pursuant to a QDRO. [I.R.C. § 402(e)(4)(O)] However, the spouse or former spouse alternate payee cannot avail himself or herself of the capital gain and net unrealized appreciation rules. [Sen. Rpt. 98-575, 98th Cong., 2d Sess. at 22 (1984)] Any lump-sum distribution paid under a

QDRO to a nonspouse alternate payee (for example, the participant's child) will be treated as distributed to the participant, not to the nonspouse alternate payee, and so the participant, not the nonspouse alternate payee, may use income averaging for that QDRO distribution.

Pursuant to Small Business Job Protection Act of 1996 (SBJPA), favorable income-averaging is not available for lump-sum distributions made from qualified plans after December 31, 1999. However, SBJPA retained a Tax Relief Act of 1986 (TRA'86) grandfather provision allowing individuals who had reached age 50 before January 1, 1986, to elect 10-year forward income-averaging and capital gains treatment. [SBJPA § 1401(c)(2)]

Official Guidance on Drafting, Reviewing, and Administering QDROs

Q 3:62 Is there any official guidance from the federal government on how to draft, review, and administer a QDRO?

Yes. The IRS, the PBGC, and the DOL have issued guidance on how to draft, review, and administer QDROs.

IRS Guidance. IRS Notice 97-11 [1997-2 I.R.B. 50] provides information intended to help domestic relations attorneys, plan participants, spouses and former spouses of participants, and plan administrators in drafting and reviewing QDROs. Notice 97-11 provides sample language that may be included in a QDRO. The Notice also discusses a number of issues that should be considered in drafting a QDRO. Notice 97-11 was issued in response to SBJPA, which directed the Secretary of the Treasury to develop sample language for inclusion in a QDRO that meets the requirements of Code Section 414(p)(1)(A) and ERISA Section 206(d)(3)(B)(i), and whose provisions focus attention on the need to consider the treatment of any lump-sum payment, QJSA, or QPSA. Drafters who use the sample language from Notice 97-11 will need to conform it to the terms of the retirement plan to which the QDRO applies, and to specify the amounts assigned and other terms of the QDRO in order to achieve an appropriate division of marital property or level of family support. A DRO is not required to incorporate the sample language in Notice 97-11 in order to be a QDRO, and a DRO that incorporates part of the sample language may omit or modify other parts. The sample language in Notice 97-11 addresses various matters, but it is not designed to address all retirement benefit issues that may arise in each domestic relations matter or QDRO. Further, some of the sample language, while helpful in facilitating the administration of a QDRO, is not necessarily required for a QDRO. Alternative formulations would be permissible for use in drafting orders that meet the statutory requirements for a QDRO. In Notice 97-11, the IRS cautions that, in formulating a particular QDRO, it is important that the drafters tailor the QDRO to the needs of the parties and ensure that the QDRO is consistent with the terms of the retirement plan to which it applies.

Also, additional information on the rights of participants and spouses to plan benefits can be found in a two-booklet set published by the IRS, "Looking Out for #2." The booklets discuss retirement benefit choices under a defined contribution or defined benefit plan, and may be obtained by calling the IRS at 1-800-TAX-FORM, and asking for Publication 1565 (Defined Contribution Plans) or Publication 1566 (Defined Benefit Plans).

PBGC Guidance. In addition, the PBGC's booklet (PBGC Publication 100, revised October 2012), titled "Qualified Domestic Relations Orders & PBGC," discusses the special rules that apply to QDROs, which are submitted to the PBGC after a defined benefit pension plan terminates and the PBGC becomes the plan's trustee. The PBGC booklet provides four model QDROs for use in connection with such plans. The first model QDRO, the PBGC Model Separate Interest QDRO, is intended to be used when an alternate payee wishes to receive pension benefits without regard to when the participant starts payments and without regard to the form of the participant's payments. The participant's accrued benefit is divided into two separate parts—one for the participant and one for the alternate payee. The PBGC Model Separate Interest QDRO gives the alternate payee control over the timing and form of his or her benefit payments. The alternate payee can receive pension benefits over his or her lifetime rather than in the participant's lifetime, and can start his or her payments before the participant starts payments. The PBGC Model Separate Interest QDRO may only be used if the participant has not yet started to receive payments. Under the second model QDRO, the PBGC Model Shared Payment QDRO, the plan participant and the alternate payee share each benefit payment. The second model QDRO may be used regardless of whether the participant has started payments, but the alternate payee cannot start receiving benefits before the participant starts receiving benefits. Under the PBGC Model Shared Payment QDRO, the timing and duration of payments to the alternate payee are tied to the participant's payments. Payments to the alternate payee stop when the participant dies, unless the QDRO provides that the alternate payee is to receive survivor benefits. The third model QDRO, the PBGC Model Child Support Shared Payment QDRO, is used to pay a portion of the participant's monthly benefit payments as child support. The third model QDRO is designed to provide child support only. Because this model is a shared payment QDRO, payments to the alternate payee cannot start until the participant's benefit payments have started. Finally, the fourth model QDRO, the PBGC Model Treat-as-Spouse QDRO, is used if the sole purpose of the QDRO is to treat the alternate payee as the participant's spouse for a QPSA, a QJSA, or both. (To also provide an alternate payee with part of the participant's benefit, use the PBGC Model Separate Interest QDRO or the PBGC Model Shared Payment QDRO, instead of the PBGC Model Treat-as-Spouse QDRO.) The PBGC booklet includes detailed instructions on how to complete the model QDROs, and the checklist that the PBGC uses to review DROs. The PBGC's booklet may be obtained from the PBGC's website at www.pbgc.gov or by calling the PBGC at 1-800-400-PBGC (7242).

DOL Guidance. The DOL's booklet, entitled "QDROs: The Division of Retirement Benefits Through Qualified Domestic Relations Orders," clarifies how pensions are divided between participants and former spouses (or other alternate payees), and includes sample QDRO language. The booklet includes a chapter on drafting QDROs, as well as three ERISA Advisory Opinions on QDROs

(ERISA Opinion Letter Nos. 90-46A, 92-17A, and 94-32A). The booklet may be obtained from the EBSA's website at https://www.dol.gov/sites/default/files/ebsa/about-ebsa/our-activities/resource-center/publications/qdros.pdf or by calling the EBSA at 1-866-444-EBSA (3272).

Permitted Offsets of Retirement Plan Benefits

Q 3:63 Are there other circumstances, in addition to QDROs, in which a participant's retirement plan benefits may be assigned or alienated, despite ERISA and the Code's anti-alienation rules?

Yes. Under TRA'97, a participant's benefit in a qualified retirement plan may be reduced to satisfy liabilities of the participant to the plan due to:

1. The participant being convicted of committing a crime involving the plan;
2. A civil judgment (or consent order or decree) entered by a court in an action brought in connection with a violation of the fiduciary provisions of Title I of ERISA; or
3. A settlement agreement between the Secretary of Labor or the PBGC and the participant in connection with a violation of ERISA's fiduciary provisions.

The court order establishing the participant's liability must require that the participant's plan benefit be applied to satisfy the liability. If the participant is married when his or her plan benefit is offset to satisfy the liability, spousal consent to the offset is required, unless either (1) the spouse is also required to pay an amount to the plan in the judgment, order, decree, or settlement, or (2) the judgment, order, decree, or settlement provides a 50 percent survivor annuity for the spouse.

The TRA'97 rules became effective for judgments, orders, and decrees issued, and settlement agreements entered into, on or after August 5, 1997, TRA'97's enactment date. [TRA'97 § 1502, amending ERISA § 206(d) and I.R.C. § 401(a)(13)]

In addition, under Code Section 6321, the IRS may levy (i.e., seize) retirement plan assets in order to collect taxes it is owed. Code Section 6343 authorizes the IRS to release a tax levy and to return property to the person upon whom the levy was made. Section 41104 of the Bipartisan Budget Act of 2018 (Pub. L. No. 115-123, enacted on February 9, 2018), amended Code Section 6343 to provide that, if the IRS determines that a prior levy from an eligible retirement plan (as defined in Code Section 402(c)(8)(B), including a Code Section 401(a) qualified retirement plan) has been wrongful and refunds the funds to the individual on or after January 1, 2018, the individual may avoid taxation of the levy distribution by rolling back the funds (with interest) into the plan (if the plan permits such indirect rollover contributions) or to an IRA no later than the individual's federal income tax filing deadline (excluding extensions) for the year of the refund. For tax purposes, the rollover will be treated as if it occurred in the year the IRS levy against the plan resulted in a distribution.

Chapter 4

Required Minimum Distributions

In 2002, the Internal Revenue Service (IRS) issued final and temporary regulations under Section 401(a)(9) of the Internal Revenue Code ("the Code"), for required minimum distributions (RMDs) from qualified plans. The 2002 regulations finalized the rules for defined contribution plans and the basic rules regarding the determination of the required beginning date (RBD), determination of designated beneficiaries, and other general rules that apply to both defined benefit and defined contribution plans. The 2002 regulations also provided temporary regulations relating to minimum distribution requirements from defined benefit plans and annuity contracts purchased with an employee's account balance under a defined contribution plan. The 2002 final and temporary regulations became effective for determining RMDs for calendar years beginning on or after January 1, 2003. In 2004, the IRS issued final regulations, replacing the previous temporary regulations concerning RMDs from defined benefit plans and annuity contracts, effective for determining RMDs for calendar years beginning on or after January 1, 2003. This chapter focuses on how these sets of final regulations and subsequent final regulations apply to qualified plans as described in Code Section 401(a).

The Pension Protection Act of 2006 (PPA) directed the Secretary of the Treasury to issue regulations under which a qualified governmental plan (as defined in Code Section 414(d)) shall, for all years to which the RMDs rules of Code Section 401(a)(9) apply to such a plan (including years prior to the enactment of PPA), be treated as having complied with the RMD rules if the plan complies with a "reasonable good faith interpretation" of Code Section 401(a)(9). [PPA § 823] On September 8, 2009, the IRS issued final regulations implementing Section 823 of PPA.

PPA also added Section 402(c)(11) to the Code. Under Code Section 402(c)(11), beginning in 2007, if a participant in a retirement plan dies leaving his or her accrued benefit under the plan to a nonspouse designated beneficiary, the designated beneficiary may be able to roll over the inherited funds into an IRA set up to receive such funds. The rollover must be accomplished by a direct trustee-to-trustee transfer (i.e., a direct rollover). Also, the distribution must otherwise be eligible for rollover—meaning, for example, that RMDs under Code Section 401(a)(9) cannot be rolled over.

The Worker, Retiree, and Employer Recovery Act of 2008 (WRERA), Pub. L. No. 110-458, enacted on December 23, 2008, added Section 401(a)(9)(H) to the Code, which waived RMDs for 2009 for Code Section 401(a) defined contribution plans, Code Section 403(a) annuity plans, Code Section 403(b) annuity contracts and custodial accounts, Code Section 457(b) eligible deferred compensation plans sponsored by state or local governments, and IRAs. The temporary RMD waiver applied only to 2009 RMDs, not to 2008 RMDs or to RMDs for calendar years after 2009. Plan sponsors that wished to waive 2009 RMDs under their applicable plans were required to adopt conforming plan amendments by the end of the first plan year beginning on or after January 1, 2011 (for governmental plans, the amendment deadline was extended to the end of the first plan year beginning on or after January 1, 2012), and were required to operate their plans during 2009 as if the amendments had been in effect. The IRS issued Notice 2009-9, 2009-5 I.R.B. 419, to provide guidance to financial institutions on reporting RMDs after the enactment of WRERA. The IRS issued Notice 2009-82, 2009-41 I.R.B. 491, to provide additional guidance (and sample plan amendments) relating to the waiver of 2009 RMDs.

On July 2, 2014, the IRS issued final regulations relating to the use of qualifying longevity annuity contracts (QLACs) in Code Section 401(a) qualified defined contribution plans, Code Section 403(b) annuity plans, IRAs, and Code Section 457(b) eligible governmental plans. The final regulations provide guidance necessary to comply with the RMD rules applicable to a plan or IRA that holds QLACs. The final regulations became effective on July 2, 2014, and apply to QLACs purchased on or after that date. [79 Fed. Reg. 37633 (July 2, 2014)]

On July 9, 2015, the IRS issued Notice 2015-49, 2015-30 I.R.B. 79, informing taxpayers of its intent to amend the RMD regulations (specifically, Treas. Reg. § 1.401(a)(9)-6, Q&A-14(a)(4)) to address the use of lump-sum payments to replace annuity payments being paid by qualified defined benefit pension plans. The amended RMD regulations would provide that qualified defined benefit plans generally would not be permitted to replace any joint and survivor, single life, or other annuity currently being paid with a lump-sum payment or other accelerated form of distribution. The IRS intends that the amended

RMD regulations would apply as of July 9, 2015, except with respect to certain accelerations of annuity payments described in Section IV of Notice 2015-49. Notice 2015-49 effectively reversed a series of Private Letter Rulings, generally known as the "Ford/GM rulings," in which the IRS ruled that a defined benefit plan could be amended, by a so-called "de-risking" amendment, to permit a participant in pay status to elect, during a temporary "window period," to commute the remaining value of his or her annuity payments from the plan to a lump-sum payment.

On October 19, 2017, the IRS issued a memorandum (a "field directive") to its Employee Plans (EP) auditing agents directing them not to challenge a qualified plan for violating the RMD rules for the plan's failure to make or to begin RMDs to a missing participant or beneficiary to whom an RMD is due if the plan has taken all of the search steps listed in the memorandum.

Waiver of 2009 Required Minimum Distributions 4-3
Minimum Distribution Requirement in General 4-5
Distributions Beginning During a Participant's Lifetime 4-7
Death Before Required Beginning Date 4-10
Determination of the Designated Beneficiary 4-13
Required Minimum Distributions from Defined Contribution Plans 4-17
Required Minimum Distributions from Defined Benefit Plans and Annuity Contracts 4-30
Rollovers and Transfers 4-53
Special Rules 4-55
IRS Field Directive to Employee Plans (EP) Examiners 4-61

Waiver of 2009 Required Minimum Distributions

Q 4:1 Were RMDs waived for 2009 for certain plans?

Yes. The Worker, Retiree, and Employer Recovery Act of 2008 (WRERA), Pub. L. No. 110-458, enacted on December 23, 2008, waived RMDs for 2009 from Code Section 401(a) defined contribution plans, Code Section 403(a) annuity plans, 403(b) annuity contracts and custodial accounts, Code Section 457(b) eligible deferred compensation plans sponsored by state or local governments, and IRAs. [I.R.C. § 401(a)(9)(H), added by WRERA § 201(a)] Under Code Section 401(a)(9)(H), no RMDs were required for the calendar year 2009 from any of these types of retirement plans or arrangements. The next RMDs from such plans were for the calendar year 2010. The waiver of RMDs for 2009 applied to lifetime distributions to employees and IRA owners and after-death distributions to beneficiaries. [Technical Explanation of H.R. 7327, the "Worker, Retiree, and Employer Recovery Act of 2008," Joint Committee on Taxation,

JCX-85-08 (Dec. 11, 2008)] The waiver did not alter RMD requirements for 2008 or for calendar years after 2009. The inapplicability of the waiver to 2008 RMDs was confirmed in a letter sent to a member of Congress by an official of the Department of the Treasury. [Letter to the Hon. George Miller, Chairman, Comm. on Education & Labor, U.S. House of Representatives, from Kevin I. Fromer, Assistant Sec'y for Legislative Affairs, U.S. Dep't of the Treas. (Dec. 17, 2008)]

Under pre-WRERA law, in the case of an individual whose RBD was April 1, 2010 (i.e., the individual attained age 70½ in 2009), the first year for which an RMD would have been required was 2009. But, under Code Section 401(a)(9)(H), as added by Section 201(a) of WRERA, there was no RMD for 2009, and thus no distribution was required to be made by April 1, 2010. However, Code Section 401(a)(9)(H) did not change the individual's RBD for purposes of determining RMDs for calendar years after 2009. Thus, for an individual whose RBD was April 1, 2010, for example, the RMD for 2010 had to have been made by December 31, 2010. If the individual dies on or after April 1, 2010 (his or her RBD), the RMD for the individual's beneficiary would be determined using the rule for death on or after the individual's RBD. [Technical Explanation of H.R. 7327, the "Worker, Retiree, and Employer Recovery Act of 2008," Joint Committee on Taxation, JCX-85-08 (Dec. 11, 2008)]

If the five-year rule (see Q 4:11) applies to an account with respect to any decedent, under Code Section 401(a)(9)(H), the five-year period is determined without regard to the calendar year 2009. Thus, for example, for an account of an individual who died in 2007, the "five-year" period (actually, a six-year period) ended in 2013 instead of 2012. [Technical Explanation of H.R. 7327, the "Worker, Retiree, and Employer Recovery Act of 2008," Joint Committee on Taxation, JCX-85-08 (Dec. 11, 2008)]

If all or a portion of a distribution for 2009 was an eligible rollover distribution because it was no longer an RMD under Code Section 401(a)(9)(H), as added by WRERA, the distribution was not treated as an eligible rollover distribution for purposes of the direct rollover requirement and notice and written explanation of the direct rollover requirement, as well as the mandatory 20 percent income tax withholding for eligible rollover distributions, to the extent the distribution would have been an RMD for 2009 absent the waiver. Thus, for example, if a Code Section 401(a) defined contribution plan (e.g., a 401(k) plan) distributed an amount to an individual for 2009 that was an eligible rollover distribution but would have been an RMD for 2009 (but for the waiver), the plan was permitted, but not required, to offer the employee a direct rollover of that amount and provide the employee with a written explanation of the requirement. If the employee received the distribution, the distribution was not subject to mandatory 20 percent income tax withholding and the employee was able to roll over the distribution by contributing it to an eligible retirement plan within 60 days after receiving it. [Technical Explanation of H.R. 7327, the "Worker, Retiree, and Employer Recovery Act of 2008," Joint Committee on Taxation, JCX-85-08 (Dec. 11, 2008)]

Plan sponsors that wish to waive 2009 RMDs under their applicable plans were required to adopt plan amendments conforming to Code Section 401(a)(9)(H), as added by WRERA, by the end of the first plan year beginning on or after January 1, 2011 (for governmental plans, the amendment deadline is extended to the end of the first plan year beginning on or after January 1, 2012) and were required to operate their plans during 2009 as if the amendments had been in effect. [WRERA § 201(c)(2)]

The IRS issued Notice 2009-9 to provide guidance to financial institutions about reporting RMDs after the enactment of WRERA. [IRS Notice 2009-9, 2009-5 I.R.B. 419] The IRS issued further guidance (including sample plan amendments) in Notice 2009-82 relating to the waiver of 2009 RMDs. [IRS Notice 2009-82, 2009-41 I.R.B. 491]

Example 4-1: Meredith's RBD was April 1, 2009 (because she reached age 70½ in 2008) and so she had to take her 2008 RMD by April 1, 2009. However, she did not have to take an RMD for 2009 (which she otherwise would have been required to take by December 31, 2009).

Matt's RBD was April 1, 2010 (because he reached age 70½ in 2009). Matt had no RMD for 2009 and so no RMD had to be distributed by April 1, 2010. However, he had to take his 2010 RMD by December 31, 2010.

Minimum Distribution Requirement in General

Q 4:2 What retirement plans are subject to the RMD rules?

The following retirement plans are subject to the RMD rules:

1. Stock bonus, pension, and profit sharing plans qualified under Code Section 401(a);
2. Annuity plans described in Code Section 403(a);
3. Annuity contracts or custodial accounts described in Code Section 403(b);
4. Traditional IRAs under Code Section 408(a) and (b);
5. Roth IRAs under Code Section 408A (for some purposes); and
6. Eligible deferred compensation plans, described in Code Section 457(b), for employees of tax-exempt organizations or state and local governments.

[Treas. Reg. § 1.401(a)(9)-1, Q&A-1 (2002)]

Q 4:3 Which employee account balances and benefits held under a Section 401(a) qualified retirement plan are subject to the RMD rules?

In General. The RMD rules of Code Section 401(a)(9) apply to all account balances and benefits in existence on or after January 1, 1985. The 2002 final regulations apply for purposes of determining RMDs for calendar years beginning on or after January 1, 2003. [Treas. Reg. § 1.401(a)(9)-1, Q&A-2(a)]

Beneficiaries. The 2002 final regulations apply to account balances and benefits held for beneficiaries for calendar years beginning on or after January 1,

2003, even if the participant died prior to January 1, 2003. Thus, in the case of a participant who died prior to January 1, 2003, the designated beneficiary must be redetermined in accordance with the provisions of Treasury Regulations Section 1.401(a)(9)-4 and the applicable distribution period (determined under Treasury Regulations Section 1.401(a)(9)-5 or 1.401(a)(9)-6, whichever applies) must be reconstructed for purposes of determining the amount that must be distributed for calendar years beginning on or after January 1, 2003. [Treas. Reg. § 1.401(a)(9)-1, Q&A-2(b)(1)]

A designated beneficiary who is receiving payments under the five-year rule of Code Section 401(a)(9)(B)(ii), either by affirmative election or by default provisions, may, if the plan so provides, switch to using the life expectancy rule of Code Section 401(a)(9)(B)(iii). In such a case, any amounts that would have had to have been distributed under the life expectancy rule of Code Section 401(a)(9)(B)(iii) for all distribution calendar years before 2004 must be distributed by the earlier of December 31, 2003, or the end of the five-year period. [Treas. Reg. § 1.401(a)(9)-1, Q&A-2(b)(2)]

Trust Documentation. If a trust failed to meet the rule permitting the beneficiaries of the trust, and not the trust itself, to be treated as the participant's designated beneficiaries, solely because the trust documentation was not provided to the plan administrator by October 31 of the calendar year following the calendar year in which the employee died, and such documentation was provided to the plan administrator by October 31, 2003, the beneficiaries of the trust will be treated as designated beneficiaries of the employee under the plan for purposes of determining the distribution period under Code Section 401(a)(9). [Treas. Reg. § 1.401(a)(9)-1, Q&A-2(c)]

Q 4:4 What specific provisions must a qualified retirement plan document contain in order to satisfy the RMD rules?

Required Distributions. In order to satisfy the RMD rules of Code Section 401(a)(9), a qualified retirement plan document must include several written provisions reflecting Code Section 401(a)(9). First, the plan document must generally set forth the statutory rules of Code Section 401(a)(9), including the incidental death benefit requirement in Code Section 401(a)(9)(G). Second, the plan document must provide that distributions will be made in accordance with the RMD rules of Treasury Regulations Section 1.401(a)(9)-1 through 1.401(a)(9)-9. Third, the plan document must also specify that its provisions reflecting Code Section 401(a)(9) override any distribution options in the plan inconsistent with that section. Fourth, the plan document must also include any other provisions reflecting Code Section 401(a)(9) as are prescribed by the IRS in revenue rulings, notices, and other guidance published in the Internal Revenue Bulletin. [Treas. Reg. § 1.401(a)(9)-1, Q&A-3(a)] Finally, the plan document must be amended by the end of the first plan year beginning on or after January 1, 2011 (for governmental plans, the amendment deadline is extended to the end of the first plan year beginning on or after January 1, 2012) to conform to the waiver, under Code Section 401(a)(9)(H), of 2009 RMDs. [WRERA § 201(c)(2)]

Optional Provisions. A Code Section 401(a) qualified retirement plan document also may include optional provisions governing plan distributions—as long as those provisions do not conflict with Code Section 401(a)(9) and the regulations thereunder. [Treas. Reg. § 1.401(a)(9)-1, Q&A-3(b)]

Absence of Optional Provisions. Qualified retirement plan distributions beginning after a participant's death will be required to be made under the default provision set forth in Treasury Regulations Section 1.401(a)(9)-3 unless the plan document contains optional provisions that override that default. That is, if distributions have not begun to the participant at the time of the participant's death, distributions will be made automatically in accordance with the default. [Treas. Reg. § 1.401(a)(9)-1, Q&A-3(c)]

Distributions Beginning During a Participant's Lifetime

Q 4:5 In the case of distributions beginning during a participant's lifetime, how must the participant's entire interest be distributed in order to satisfy Code Section 401(a)(9)(A)?

In order to satisfy Code Section 401(a)(9)(A), the entire interest of each participant must be distributed to the participant not later than the participant's RBD (see Q 4:6) or must be distributed, beginning not later than the RBD, over the life of the participant or the joint lives of the participant and a designated beneficiary or over a period not extending beyond the life expectancy of the participant or the joint life and last survivor expectancy of the participant and the designated beneficiary. [Treas. Reg. § 1.401(a)(9)-2, Q&A-1(a)]

Code Section 401(a)(9)(G) provides that lifetime distributions also must satisfy the incidental death benefit requirements. [Treas. Reg. § 1.401(a)(9)-2, Q&A-1(b)]

The amount required to be distributed for each calendar year in order to satisfy Code Section 401(a)(9)(A) and (G) generally depends on whether a distribution is in the form of distributions under a defined contribution plan or annuity payments under a defined benefit plan or under an annuity contract. Treasury Regulations Section 1.401(a)(9)-5 provides the method of determining the RMD in accordance with Code Section 401(a)(9)(A) and (G) from an individual account under a defined contribution plan. Treasury Regulations Section 1.401(a)(9)-6 provides the method of determining the RMD in accordance with Code Section 401(a)(9)(A) and (G) in the case of annuity payments from a defined benefit plan or an annuity contract. [Treas. Reg. § 1.401(a)(9)-2, Q&A-1(c)]

Q 4:6 What does the term *RBD* mean?

Except with respect to a 5 percent owner (as defined below), the term *RBD* means April 1 of the calendar year following the later of (1) the calendar year in which the participant attains age 70½ or (2) the calendar year in which the participant retires from employment with the employer maintaining the plan. [Treas. Reg. § 1.401(a)(9)-2, Q&A-2(a)]

In the case of a participant who is a 5 percent owner, the term *RBD* means April 1 of the calendar year following the calendar year in which the 5 percent owner attains age 70½. [Treas. Reg. § 1.401(a)(9)-2, Q&A-2(b)] For these purposes, a 5 percent owner is a participant who is a 5 percent owner (as defined in Code Section 416) with respect to the plan year ending in the calendar year in which the participant attains age 70½. [Treas. Reg. § 1.401(a)(9)-2, Q&A-2(c)]

The rule for determining the RBD for 5 percent owners does not apply in the case of a governmental plan (within the meaning of Code Section 414(d)) or a church plan. For these purposes, the term *church plan* means a plan maintained by a church for church employees, and the term *church* means any church (as defined in Code Section 3121(w)(3)(A)) or qualified church-controlled organization (as defined in Code Section 3121(w)(3)(B)). [Treas. Reg. § 1.401(a)(9)-2, Q&A-2(d)] Note that, on September 8, 2009, the IRS issued final regulations permitting governmental plans to comply with the RMD rules by using, in lieu of the IRS's RMD regulations, a reasonable and good-faith interpretation of the Code's RMD rules. [Treas. Reg. §§ 1.401(a)(9)-1, Q/A-2(d), 1.401(a)(9)-6, and 1.403(b)-6(e)(2) and (e)(8), 74 Fed. Reg. 172, pp. 45993–45994]

A plan may provide that the RBD for purposes of Code Section 401(a)(9) for all participants is April 1 of the calendar year following the calendar year in which a participant attains age 70½ regardless of whether the participant is a 5 percent owner. [Treas. Reg. § 1.401(a)(9)-2, Q&A-2(e)]

Q 4:7 When does a participant attain age 70½?

A participant attains age 70½ as of the date six calendar months after the 70th anniversary of the participant's birth. For example, if a participant's date of birth were June 30, 1947, the 70th anniversary would be June 30, 2017, and the participant would become 70½ on December 30, 2017. Consequently, if the participant were a 5 percent owner or retired, the RBD would be April 1, 2018. However, if a participant's date of birth were July 1, 1947, the 70th anniversary would be July 1, 2017, and the participant would become 70½ on January 1, 2018. The participant's RBD would be April 1, 2019. [Treas. Reg. § 1.401(a)(9)-2, Q&A-3]

Q 4:8 Must distributions be made before a participant's RBD satisfy the RMD rules?

No. Lifetime distributions made before a participant's RBD for calendar years before the participant's first distribution calendar year (see Q 4:23) need not be made in accordance with the RMD rules of Code Section 401(a)(9). However, if distributions begin before a participant's RBD under a particular distribution option (e.g., an annuity), the distribution option fails to satisfy the RMD rules of Code Section 401(a)(9) at the time distributions commence if, under the terms of the particular distribution option, distributions to be made for the participant's first distribution calendar year or any subsequent distribution calendar year will fail to satisfy the RMD rules. [Treas. Reg. § 1.401(a)(9)-2, Q&A-4]

Q 4:9 If distributions have begun to a participant during the participant's lifetime in accordance with the life or life expectancy method of Code Section 401(a)(9)(A)(ii), how must distributions be made after the participant's death?

A participant's entire interest under a qualified retirement plan must either be distributed not later than his or her RBD in accordance with Code Section 401(a)(9)(A)(i) or be distributed, beginning no later than the participant's RBD, over the participant's life or the joint lives of the participant and his or her designated beneficiary (or over a period not extending beyond the participant's life expectancy or the joint life expectancy of the participant and his or her designated beneficiary) in accordance with Code Section 401(a)(9)(A)(ii). (See Q 4:5.)

Code Section 401(a)(9)(B)(i) provides that if the distribution of a participant's interest has begun in accordance with the life or life expectancy method of Code Section 401(a)(9)(A)(ii) and the participant dies before his or her entire interest has been distributed to him or her, the remaining portion of that interest must be distributed at least as rapidly as under the distribution method being used under Code Section 401(a)(9)(A)(ii) as of the date of the participant's death. The amount required to be distributed for each distribution calendar year (see Q 4:23) following the calendar year of death generally depends on whether a distribution is in the form of distributions from an individual account under a defined contribution plan or annuity payments under a defined benefit plan. [Treas. Reg. § 1.401(a)(9)-2, Q&A-5]

Q 4:10 For purposes of Code Section 401(a)(9)(B), when are distributions considered to have begun to a participant in accordance with the life or life expectancy method of Code Section 401(a)(9)(A)(ii)?

Except as otherwise provided under Treasury Regulations Section 1.401(a)(9)-6, Q&A-10 (see Q 4:43), distributions are not treated as having begun to a participant in accordance with the life or life expectancy method of Code Section 401(a)(9)(A)(ii) until the participant's RBD, without regard to whether payments have been made before that date. Thus, the "at least as rapidly" rule of Code Section 401(a)(9)(B)(i) only applies if a participant dies on or after his or her RBD. [Treas. Reg. § 1.401(a)(9)-2, Q&A-6(a)]

Example 4-2: If John Whiteside retires in 2019, the calendar year in which he attains age 65½ and begins receiving installment distributions from his profit sharing plan over a period not exceeding the joint life and last survivor expectancy of himself and his spouse, benefits are not treated as having begun in accordance with the life or life expectancy method of Code Section 401(a)(9)(A)(ii) until April 1, 2025 (the April 1 following the calendar year (2023) in which John attains age 70½). Consequently, if John dies before April 1, 2025 (his RBD), distributions after his death must be made in accordance with Code Section 401(a)(9)(B)(ii) or (iii) and (iv) and Treasury Regulations Section 1.401(a)(9)-3 (which provide the RMD rules applicable to participants who die before the distribution of their interests has begun) (see Qs 4:11–4:16), and not under the "at least as rapidly" rule of Code Section 401(a)(9)(B)(i) (which provides the RMD rules applicable to participants who die after the distribution of their interests has begun). That is so without regard to whether the plan has distributed the RMD for the first distribution calendar year (see Q 4:23) before John's death. [Treas. Reg. § 1.401(a)(9)-2, Q&A-6(a)]

If a plan provides that the RBD for purposes of Code Section 401(a)(9) for all participants is April 1 of the calendar year following the calendar year in which a participant attains age 70½ (see Q 4:6), a participant who dies after the RBD determined under the plan terms is treated as dying after the participant's distributions have begun even though the participant dies before the April 1 following the calendar year in which the participant retires. [Treas. Reg. § 1.401(a)(9)-2, Q&A-6(b)]

Death Before Required Beginning Date

Q 4:11 If a participant dies before his or her RBD, how must the participant's entire interest be distributed in order to satisfy the RMD rules of Code Section 401(a)(9)?

Except as otherwise provided under Treasury Regulations Section 1.401(a)(9)-6, Q&A-10 (see Q 4:43), if a participant dies before his or her RBD (and, thus, before distributions are treated as having begun in accordance with the life or life expectancy method of Code Section 401(a)(9)(A)(ii)), distribution of the participant's entire interest must be made in accordance with one of the following two methods:

1. *The Five-Year Rule.* One method is the five-year rule described in Code Section 401(a)(9)(B)(ii). It requires that the entire interest of the participant be distributed within five years of the participant's death regardless of who or what entity receives the distribution. (See Q 4:12.)
2. *The Life Expectancy Rule.* The other method is the life expectancy rule described in Code Section 401(a)(9)(B)(iii) and (iv), which requires that any portion of a participant's interest payable to (or for the benefit of) a designated beneficiary be distributed, commencing within one year of the participant's death, over the life of that beneficiary (or over a period not extending beyond the life expectancy of that beneficiary). Special rules apply when the designated beneficiary is the surviving spouse of the participant, including a special commencement date for distribution under Code Section 401(a)(9)(B)(iii) to the surviving spouse. (See Q 4:13.)

[I.R.C. § 401(a)(9)(B)(iv); Treas. Reg. § 1.401(a)(9)-3, Q&A-1(a)]

Q 4:12 What is the last date for distributing a participant's entire interest in order to satisfy the five-year rule?

To satisfy the five-year rule described in Code Section 401(a)(9)(B)(ii), the participant's entire interest must be distributed by the end of the calendar year that contains the fifth anniversary of the date of the participant's death. For example, if a participant dies on January 1, 2017, the entire interest must be distributed by December 31, 2022. [Treas. Reg. § 1.401(a)(9)-3, Q&A-2]

Q 4:13 When must distributions begin in order to satisfy the life expectancy rule?

Nonspouse Beneficiary. To satisfy the life expectancy rule described in Code Section 401(a)(9)(B)(iii), if the designated beneficiary is not the participant's surviving spouse, distributions must commence on or before the end of the calendar year immediately following the calendar year in which the participant died. This rule also applies to the distribution of the entire remaining benefit if another individual is a designated beneficiary in addition to the participant's surviving spouse. [Treas. Reg. § 1.401(a)(9)-3, Q&A-3(a)]

Spousal Beneficiary. To satisfy the life expectancy rule described in Code Section 401(a)(9)(B)(iii) and (iv), if the sole designated beneficiary is the participant's surviving spouse, distributions must begin on or before the later of:

1. The end of the calendar year immediately following the calendar year in which the participant died; and
2. The end of the calendar year in which the participant would have attained age 70½.

[Treas. Reg. § 1.401(a)(9)-3, Q&A-3(b)]

Q 4:14 How is it determined whether the five-year rule or the life expectancy rule applies to a distribution?

No Plan Provision. If a plan does not adopt an optional provision described below specifying the method of distribution after the death of a participant prior to his or her RBD, the distribution must be made as follows:

1. If the participant has a designated beneficiary, as determined under Treasury Regulations Section 1.401(a)(9)-4 (see Qs 4:17–4:22), distributions must be made in accordance with the life expectancy rule described in Code Section 401(a)(9)(B)(iii) and (iv) (see Qs 4:11, 4:13).
2. If the participant has no designated beneficiary, distributions must be made in accordance with the five-year rule described in Code Section 401(a)(9)(B)(ii) (see Qs 4:11, 4:12).

[Treas. Reg. § 1.401(a)(9)-3, Q&A-4(a)]

Optional Plan Provisions. A plan may adopt a provision specifying either (1) that the five-year rule described in Code Section 401(a)(9)(B)(ii) (see Qs 4:11, 4:12) will apply to certain distributions after the death of a participant even if the participant has a designated beneficiary or (2) that distribution in every case will be made in accordance with the five-year rule. A plan need not have the same method of distribution for the benefits of all participants. [Treas. Reg. § 401(a)(9)-4(b)]

Elections. A plan may adopt a provision that permits participants (or beneficiaries) to elect on an individual basis whether the five-year rule (see Qs 4:11, 4:12) or the life expectancy rule (see Qs 4:11, 4:13) applies to distributions after the death of a participant who has a designated beneficiary. Such an election must be made no later than the earlier of (1) the end of the calendar year in which distributions would be required to start in order to satisfy the requirements for the life expectancy rule or (2) the end of the calendar year that contains the fifth anniversary of the date of death of the participant. As of the last date the election may be made, the election must be irrevocable with respect to the beneficiary (and all subsequent beneficiaries) and must apply to all subsequent calendar years. If a plan provides for an election, it may also specify the method of distribution that applies if neither the participant nor the beneficiary makes the election. Further, if neither the participant nor the beneficiary elects a method and the plan does not specify which method applies, the distribution must be made in accordance with the rules, described above, that apply when the plan does not adopt an optional provision. [Treas. Reg. § 1.401(a)(9)-3, Q&A-4(c)]

Q 4:15 If a participant's surviving spouse is the participant's sole designated beneficiary and the spouse dies after the participant, but before distributions have begun, how is the participant's interest to be distributed?

Pursuant to Code Section 401(a)(9)(B)(iv)(II), if the surviving spouse is the participant's sole designated beneficiary and dies after the participant, but before distributions to the spouse have begun under the life expectancy rule described in Code Section 401(a)(9)(B)(iii) and (iv) (see Qs 4:11, 4:13), the five-year rule described in Code Section 401(a)(9)(B)(ii) (see Qs 4:11, 4:12) and the life expectancy rule described in Code Section 401(a)(9)(B)(iii) are to be applied as if the surviving spouse were the participant. In applying this rule, the date of death of the surviving spouse is to be substituted for the date of death of the participant. However, in such case, the special surviving spouse rules in Code Section 401(a)(9)(B)(iv) are not available to the surviving spouse of the deceased participant's surviving spouse. [Treas. Reg. § 1.401(a)(9)-3, Q&A-5]

Q 4:16 For these purposes, when are distributions considered to have begun to the surviving spouse?

Distributions are considered to have begun to a participant's surviving spouse (for purposes of Code Section 401(a)(9)(B)(iv)(II)), on the date, determined in accordance with Treasury Regulations Section 1.401(a)(9)-3, Q&A-3, on which distributions are required to commence to the surviving spouse, even though payments have in fact been made before that date. However, there is a special rule for annuities under Treasury Regulations Section 1.401(a)(9)-6, Q&A-11. [Treas. Reg. § 1.401(a)(9)-6, Q&A-6]

Determination of the Designated Beneficiary

Q 4:17 Who is a designated beneficiary?

A designated beneficiary is an individual who is designated as a beneficiary under the plan (see Code Section 401(a)(9)(E)).

An individual may be designated as a beneficiary under the plan either by the terms of the plan or, if the plan so provides, by an affirmative election by the participant (or the participant's surviving spouse) specifying the beneficiary. A beneficiary designated as such under the plan is an individual who is entitled to a portion of a participant's benefit, contingent on the participant's death or another specified event. For example, if a distribution is in the form of a joint and survivor annuity over the life of the participant and another individual, the plan does not satisfy Code Section 401(a)(9) unless the other individual is a designated beneficiary under the plan. A designated beneficiary need not be specified by name in the plan or by the participant in order to be a designated beneficiary—so long as the individual who is to be the beneficiary is identifiable under the plan. The members of a class of beneficiaries capable of expansion or contraction will be treated as being identifiable if it is possible, as of the date the beneficiary is determined, to identify the class member with the shortest life expectancy.

The fact that a participant's interest under the plan passes to a certain individual under a will or otherwise under applicable state law does not make that individual a designated beneficiary for purposes of the RMD rules unless the individual is designated as a beneficiary under the plan. Special rules apply to qualified domestic relations orders (QDROs) (see Q 4:61). [Treas. Reg. § 1.401(a)(9)-4, Q&A-1]

Q 4:18 Must a participant (or the participant's spouse) make an affirmative election specifying a person to be a designated beneficiary for purposes of the RMD rules?

No. A designated beneficiary is an individual who is designated as a beneficiary under the plan whether or not the designation was made by the participant (or the participant's spouse). The choice of beneficiary is subject to the requirements of Code Sections 401(a)(11), 414(p), and 417. [Treas. Reg. § 1.401(a)(9)-4, Q&A-2]

Q 4:19 May a person other than an individual be a designated beneficiary for purposes of the RMD rules?

No. Only *individuals* may be designated beneficiaries for purposes of the RMD rules under Code Section 401(a)(9). A person that is not an individual, such as the participant's estate, may not be a designated beneficiary for purposes of the RMD rules. If a person other than an individual is designated as a beneficiary of a participant's benefit, the participant will be treated as having no designated beneficiary for purposes of the RMD rules, even if there are also individuals designated as beneficiaries. However, there are special rules that apply to trusts and to separate accounts (see Q 4:21). [Treas. Reg. § 1.401(a)(9)-4, Q&A-3]

Q 4:20 When is the designated beneficiary determined?

General Rule. In order to be a designated beneficiary for purposes of the RMD rules, an individual must be a beneficiary as of the date of the participant's death. Except as provided under the special rule applicable to the participant's surviving spouse (see below) or under the RMD rules that apply to defined benefit plans and annuity contracts under Treasury Regulations Section 1.401(a)(9)-6 (see Qs 4:34–4:50), a participant's designated beneficiary for RMD purposes will be determined based on the beneficiaries designated as of the date of the participant's death who remain beneficiaries as of September 30 of the calendar year following the calendar year of the participant's death. Consequently, except as provided in Treasury Regulations Section 1.401(a)(9)-6, any person who was a beneficiary as of the date of the participant's death, but is not a beneficiary as of that September 30 (e.g., because the person receives the entire benefit to which the person is entitled before that September 30), is not taken into account in determining the participant's designated beneficiary for purposes of determining the distribution period for RMDs after the participant's death. Accordingly, if a person disclaims entitlement to the participant's benefit by that September 30, pursuant to a disclaimer that satisfies Code Section 2518, thereby allowing other beneficiaries to receive the benefit in lieu of that person, the disclaiming person is not taken into account in determining the participant's designated beneficiary for purposes of the RMD rules. [Treas. Reg. § 1.401(a)(9)-4, Q&A-4(a)]

Surviving Spouse. If the participant's spouse is the sole designated beneficiary as of September 30 of the calendar year following the calendar year of the participant's death, and the surviving spouse dies after the participant and before the date on which distributions have begun to the surviving spouse under the life expectancy rule of Code Section 401(a)(9)(B)(iii) and (iv) (see Qs 4:11, 4:13), the rule in Code Section 401(a)(9)(B)(iv)(II) will apply. That is, the relevant designated beneficiary for determining the distribution period after the death of the surviving spouse is the designated beneficiary of the surviving spouse. Similarly, such designated beneficiary will be determined based on the beneficiaries designated as of the date of the surviving spouse's death and who remain beneficiaries as of September 30 of the calendar year following the calendar year of the surviving spouse's death. If, as of that date, there is no designated beneficiary under the plan with respect to that surviving spouse, distribution must be made in accordance with the five-year rule in Code Section 401(a)(9)(b)(ii) (see Qs 4:11, 4:12), and Treasury Regulations Section 1.401(a)(9)-3, Q&A-2. [Treas. Reg. § 1.401(a)(9)-4, Q&A-4(b)]

Deceased Beneficiary. An individual who is a beneficiary as of the date of the participant's death and dies before September 30 of the calendar year following the calendar year of the participant's death without disclaiming continues to be treated as a beneficiary as of that September 30 in determining the participant's designated beneficiary for purposes of determining the distribution period for RMDs after the participant's death, without regard to the identity of the successor beneficiary who is entitled to distributions as the beneficiary of the deceased beneficiary. The same rule applies in the case of distributions to which Treasury Regulations Section 1.401(a)(9)-3, Q&A-5 applies (see Q 4:15). If an individual is designated as a beneficiary of a participant's surviving spouse as of the spouse's date of death, and dies prior to September 30 of the year following the year of the surviving spouse's death, that individual will continue to be treated as a designated beneficiary. [Treas. Reg. § 1.401(a)(9)-4, Q&A-4(c)]

Q 4:21 If a trust is named as a beneficiary of a participant, are there any circumstances that would permit the beneficiaries of the trust to be treated as the participant's designated beneficiaries for purposes of the RMD rules?

Yes. If the following requirements are met with respect to a trust that is named as the participant's beneficiary under the plan, the beneficiaries of the trust (and not the trust itself) will be treated as having been designated as beneficiaries of the participant under the plan for purposes of determining the distribution period under Code Section 401(a)(9):

1. The trust is a valid trust under state law, or would be but for the fact that there is no corpus;
2. The trust is irrevocable or will, by its terms, become irrevocable upon the death of the participant;
3. The beneficiaries of the trust who are beneficiaries with respect to the trust's interest in the participant's benefit are identifiable (see Q 4:17) from the trust instrument; and
4. Required documentation (see Q 4:22) has been provided to the plan administrator. [Treas. Reg. § 1.401(a)(9)-4, Q&A-5(a) and (b)]

Q 4:22 When a trust is named as a beneficiary of a participant, what documentation must be provided to the plan administrator?

RMDs Before Death. If a participant designates a trust as the beneficiary of his or her entire benefit and the participant's spouse is the sole beneficiary of the trust, in order to satisfy the documentation requirements so that the spouse can be treated as the sole designated beneficiary of the participant's benefits, the participant either:

1. Must provide to the plan administrator a copy of the trust instrument and agree that if the trust instrument is amended at any time in the future, the participant will, within a reasonable time, provide to the plan administrator a copy of each such amendment; or

2. Must:
   (a) Provide to the plan administrator a list of all the beneficiaries of the trust (including contingent and remaindermen beneficiaries with a description of the conditions on their entitlement sufficient to establish that the spouse is the sole beneficiary);
   (b) Certify that, to the best of the participant's knowledge, the list of beneficiaries is correct and complete and that the applicable trust requirements (see Q 4:21) are satisfied;
   (c) Agree that, if the trust instrument is amended at any time in the future, the participant will, within a reasonable time, provide to the plan administrator corrected certifications to the extent that the amendment changes any information previously certified; and
   (d) Agree to provide a copy of the trust instrument to the plan administrator upon demand.

[Treas. Reg. § 1.401(a)(9)-4, Q&A-6(a)]

RMDs After Death. In order to satisfy the documentation requirement for RMDs after the death of a participant (or spouse, if applicable), the trustee of the trust must, by October 31 of the calendar year immediately following the calendar year in which the employee died, either:

1. Provide the plan administrator with a final list of all beneficiaries of the trust (including contingent and remaindermen beneficiaries with a description of the conditions on their entitlement) as of September 30 of the calendar year following the calendar year of the participant's death; certify that, to the best of the trustee's knowledge, the list is correct and complete and that the applicable trust requirements (see Q 4:21) are satisfied; and agree to provide a copy of the trust instrument to the plan administrator upon demand; or
2. Provide the plan administrator with a copy of the actual trust document for the trust that is named as a beneficiary of the participant under the plan as of the participant's date of death.

[Treas. Reg. § 1.401(a)(9)-4, Q&A-6(b)]

Relief for Discrepancy Between Trust Instrument and Participant Certifications or Earlier Trust Instruments. If RMDs are determined based on the information provided to the plan administrator in certifications or trust instruments described above, a plan will not fail to satisfy Code Section 401(a)(9) merely because the actual terms of the trust instrument are inconsistent with the information in those certifications or trust instruments previously provided to the plan administrator—*but only if* the plan administrator reasonably relied on the information provided *and* the RMDs for calendar years after the calendar year in which the discrepancy is discovered are determined based on the actual terms of the trust instrument. [Treas. Reg. § 1.401(a)(9)-4, Q&A-6(c)(1)]

> **Note:** For purposes of determining the amount of the 50 percent excise tax under Code Section 4974, the RMD is determined for any year based on the actual terms of the trust in effect during the year. [Treas. Reg. § 1.401(a)(9)-4, Q&A-6(c)(2)]

Required Minimum Distributions from Defined Contribution Plans

Q 4:23 If a participant's benefit is in the form of an individual account under a defined contribution plan, what is the amount required to be distributed for each calendar year?

General Rule. If a participant's accrued benefit is in the form of an individual account under a defined contribution plan, the minimum amount required to be distributed for each distribution calendar year (see below) is equal to the quotient obtained by dividing the account by the applicable distribution period (see Q 4:28). However, the RMD amount will never exceed the entire account balance on the date of the distribution. (See Q 4:32 for rules that apply if a portion of the participant's account is not vested.) Further, the RMD to be distributed on or before a participant's RBD is always determined under Code Section 401(a)(9)(A)(ii) (the life or life expectancy method) and Treasury Regulations Section 1.401(a)(9)-5, Q&A-1, and not Code Section 401(a)(9)(A)(i) (which requires the participant's RMD to be distributed no later than his or her RBD) [Treas. Reg. § 1.401(a)(9)-5, Q&A-1(a)]

Distribution Calendar Year. A calendar year for which an RMD is required is a distribution calendar year. If a participant's RBD is April 1 of the calendar year following the calendar year in which the participant attains age 70½, the participant's first distribution calendar year is the year he or she attains age 70½. If a participant's RBD is April 1 of the calendar year following the calendar year in which the participant retires, the calendar year in which the participant retires is his or her first distribution calendar year. In the case of distributions to be made in accordance with the life expectancy rule [I.R.C. § 401(a)(9)(B)(iii), (iv); Treas. Reg. § 1.401(a)(9)-3], the first distribution calendar year is the calendar year containing the date described in Treasury Regulations Section 1.401(a)(9)-3, Q&A-3(a) or Q&A-3(b), whichever is applicable. [Treas. Reg. § 1.401(a)(9)-5, Q&A-1(b)]

Time for Distributions. The distribution required to be made on or before the participant's RBD is to be treated as the distribution required for the participant's first distribution calendar year. The RMD for other distribution calendar years, including the RMD for the distribution calendar year in which the participant's RBD occurs, must be made on or before the end (December 31) of that distribution calendar year. [Treas. Reg. § 1.401(a)(9)-5, Q&A-1(c)]

Minimum Distribution Incidental Benefit (MDIB) Requirement. If distributions of a participant's account balance under a defined contribution plan are made in accordance with Treasury Regulations Section 1.401(a)(9)-5 (which governs RMDs from defined contribution plans), the MDIB requirement of Code Section 401(a)(9)(G) will be satisfied. Further, with respect to the retirement benefits provided by that account balance, to the extent that the incidental benefit rules require a distribution, those rules will be deemed to be satisfied if distributions satisfy the MDIB requirement of Code Section 401(a)(9)(G) and Treasury Regulations Section 1.401(a)(9)-5. [Treas. Reg. § 1.401(a)(9)-5, Q&A-1(d)]

Q 4:24 How may an annuity contract be used to satisfy the minimum distribution requirement for an individual account under a defined contribution plan?

The RMD requirement for a defined contribution plan may be satisfied by the purchase of an annuity contract from an insurance company in accordance with Treasury Regulations Section 1.401(a)(9)-6, Q&A-4 with the participant's entire individual account. If such an annuity is purchased after distributions are required to begin, payments under the annuity contract purchased will satisfy Code Section 401(a)(9) for distribution calendar years after the calendar year of the purchase if payments under the annuity contract are made in accordance with Treasury Regulations Section 1.401(a)(9)-6. In such a case, payments under the annuity contract will be treated as distributions from the individual account for purposes of determining if the individual account satisfies Code Section 401(a)(9) for the calendar year of the purchase. A participant may also purchase an annuity contract with a portion of the participant's account under the rules of Treasury Regulations Section 1.401(a)(9)-8, Q&A-2(a)(3). [Treas. Reg. § 1.401(a)(9)-5, Q&A-1(e)]

Q 4:25 If a participant's benefit is in the form of an individual account and, in any calendar year, the amount distributed exceeds the RMD, will credit be given in subsequent calendar years for such excess distribution?

No. If, for any distribution calendar year (see Q 4:23), the amount distributed exceeds the RMD, no credit will be given in subsequent calendar years for such excess distribution. [Treas. Reg. § 1.401(a)(9)-5, Q&A-2]

Q 4:26 What amount is used for determining a participant's RMD in the case of an individual account?

The benefit used in determining the RMD for a distribution calendar year (see Q 4:23) in the case of an individual account is the account balance as of the last valuation date in the calendar year immediately preceding that distribution calendar year (valuation calendar year) adjusted in accordance with the rules described below. [Treas. Reg. § 1.401(a)(9)-5, Q&A-3(a)]

The account balance is *increased* by the amount of any contributions or forfeitures allocated to the account balance as of dates in the valuation calendar year after the valuation date. For this purpose, contributions that are allocated to the account balance as of dates in the valuation calendar year after the valuation date, but that are not actually made during the valuation calendar year, may be excluded. [Treas. Reg. § 1.401(a)(9)-5, Q&A-3(b)]

The account balance is *decreased* by distributions made in the valuation calendar year after the valuation date. [Treas. Reg. § 1.401(a)(9)-5, Q&A-3(c)]

The account balance does *not* include the value of any QLAC (as defined in Treasury Regulations Section 1.401(a)(9)-6, Q&A-17) that is held under the plan (see Q 4:27). This rule applies only to QLACs purchased on or after July 2, 2014. [Treas. Reg. § 1.401(a)(9)-5, Q&A-3(d)]

If an amount is distributed by one plan and rolled over to another plan (the receiving plan), Treasury Regulations Section 1.401(a)(9)-7, Q&A-2 provides additional rules for determining the benefit and RMD under the receiving plan (see Q 4:52). If an amount is transferred from one plan (the transferor plan) to another plan (the transferee plan) in a transfer to which Code Section 414(l) applies, Treasury Regulations Section 1.401(a)(9)-7, Q&A-3 and Q&A-4 provide additional rules for determining the amount of the RMD and the benefit under both the transferor and transferee plans (see Qs 4:53, 4:54). [Treas. Reg. § 1.401(a)(9)-3(e)]

Q 4:27 What is a QLAC?

The amount used for determining a participant's RMD from his or her individual account under a defined contribution plan does *not* include the value of any QLAC (as defined in Treasury Regulations Section 1.401(a)(9)-6, Q&A-17) that is held under the plan (see Q 4:26). This rule applies only to QLACs purchased on or after July 2, 2014. [Treas. Reg. § 1.401(a)(9)-5, Q&A-3(d)]

Definition of QLAC. A QLAC is an annuity contract purchased from an insurance company for an employee that, in accordance with the rules of application in Treasury Regulations Section 1.401(a)(9)-6, Q&A-17(d), satisfies each of the following requirements:

1. *Limitations on Premiums.* Premiums paid for a QLAC must satisfy the limitations on premiums in Treasury Regulations Section 1.401(a)(9)-6, Q&A-17(b). [Treas. Reg. § 1.401(a)(9)-6, Q&A-17 (a)(1)] In order to constitute a QLAC, the amount of premiums paid for the contract under the defined contribution plan on a date must not exceed the lesser of the dollar limitation or the percentage limitation in a. and b. below, respectively [Treas. Reg. § 1.401(a)(9)-6, Q&A-17(b)(1)]:

a. *Dollar Limitation.* The dollar limitation is an amount equal to the excess of:

i. $125,000 (as adjusted under Treasury Regulations Section 1.401(a)(9)-6, Q&A-17(d)(2)), over

ii. The sum of (A) the premiums paid before that date with respect to the contract and (B) the premiums paid on or before that date with respect to any other contract that is intended to be a QLAC and that is purchased for the employee under the plan, or any other plan, annuity or account described in Code Sections 401(a), 403(a), 403(b), 408, or eligible governmental plan under Code Section 457(b). [Treas. Reg. § 1.401(a)(9)-6, Q&A-17(b)(2)(i) and (ii)]

b. *Percentage Limitation.* The percentage limitation is an amount equal to the excess of:

i. 25 percent of the employee's account balance under the plan (including the value of any QLAC held under the plan for the employee) as of that date (determined in accordance with Treasury Regulations Section 1.401(a)(9)-6, Q&A-17(d)(1)(iii)), over

ii. the sum of (A) the premiums paid before that date with respect to the contract, and (B) the premiums paid on or before that date with respect to any other contract that is intended to be a QLAC and that is held or was purchased for the employee under the plan. [Treas. Reg. § 1.401(a)(9)-6, Q&A-17(b)(3)(i) and (ii)]

If a contract fails to be a QLAC because it does not satisfy the dollar limitation in a. above, any subsequent adjustment the IRS may make to the dollar limitation pursuant to Treasury Regulations Section 1.401(a)(9)-6, Q&A-17(d)(2)(i) will not cause the contract to become a QLAC. [Treas. Reg. § 1.401(a)(9)-6, Q&A-17(d)(2)(iii)]

For purposes of the 25 percent limitation under Treasury Regulations Section 1.401(a)(9)-6, Q&A-17(b)(3), an employee's account balance on the date on which premiums for a contract are paid is the account balance as of the last valuation date preceding the date of the premium payment, adjusted as follows: the account balance is increased for contributions allocated to the account during the period that begins after the valuation date and ends before the date the premium is paid and decreased for distributions made from the account during that period. [Treas. Reg. § 1.401(a)(9)-6, Q&A-17(d)(1)(iii)]

For purposes of both the dollar limitation and the percentage limitation on premiums described in a. and b. above, respectively, unless the plan administrator of the defined contribution plan has actual knowledge to the contrary, the plan administrator may rely on an employee's representation (made in writing or such other form as may be prescribed by the IRS) of the amount of the premiums, but only with respect to premiums that are not paid under a plan, annuity, or contract that is maintained by the employer or an entity that is treated as a single employer under the aggregation rules of Code Section 414(b), (c), (m), or (o). [Treas. Reg. § 1.401(a)(9)-6, Q&A-17(d)(1)(i)]

As a general rule, if an annuity contract fails to be a QLAC solely because a premium for the contract exceeds the dollar limitation and/or percentage limitation described in a. and b. above, respectively, then the contract is not a QLAC beginning on the date that premium payment is made, unless the excess premium is returned to the non-QLAC portion of the employee's account in accordance with Treasury Regulations Section 1.401(a)(9)-6, Q&A-17(d)(1)(ii)(B). If the contract fails to be a QLAC, then the value of the contract may not be disregarded under Treasury Regulations Section 1.401(a)(9)-5, Q&A-3(d) as of the date on which the contract ceases to be a QLAC. [Treas. Reg. § 1.401(a)(9)-6, Q&A-17(d)(1)(ii)(A)]

If the excess premium is returned (either in cash or in the form of a contract that is not intended to be a QLAC) to the non-QLAC portion of the employee's account by the end of the calendar year following the calendar year in which the excess premium was originally paid, then the contract will not be treated as exceeding the dollar limitation or the percentage limitation described in a. or b., above, respectively, at any time, and the value of the contract will not be included in the employee's account balance under Treasury Regulations Section 1.401(a)(9)-5, Q&A-3(d). If the excess premium (including the fair market value of an annuity contract that is not intended to be a QLAC, if applicable) is returned to the non-QLAC portion of the employee's account after the last valuation date for the calendar year in which the excess premium was originally paid, then the employee's account balance for that calendar year must be increased to reflect that excess premium in the same manner as an employee's account balance is increased under Treasury Regulations Section 1.401(a)(9)-7, Q&A-2 to reflect a rollover received after the last valuation date. [Treas. Reg. § 1.401(a)(9)-6, Q&A-17(d)(1)(ii)(B)]

If the excess premium is returned to the non-QLAC portion of the employee's account as described in Treasury Regulations Section 1.401(a)(9)-6, Q&A-17(d)(1)(ii)(B), it will not be treated as a violation of the requirement in Treasury Regulations Section 1.401(a)(9)-6, Q&A-17(a)(4) (described in item 4 below) that the contract did not provide a commutation benefit. [Treas. Reg. § 1.401(a)(9)-6, Q&A-17(d)(1)(ii)(C)]

2. *Limitations on Annuity Starting Date.* A QLAC must provide that distributions under the QLAC must commence not later than a specified annuity starting date that is no later than the first day of the month next following the 85th anniversary of the employee's birth. [Treas. Reg. § 1.401(a)(9)-6, Q&A-17(a)(2)] The maximum age of 85 may be adjusted to reflect changes in mortality, with any such adjusted age to be prescribed by the IRS in revenue rulings, notices, or other published guidance. [Treas. Reg. § 1.401(a)(9)-6, Q&A-17(d)(2)(ii)] If a contract fails to be a QLAC because it does not satisfy the age limitation in Treasury Regulations Section 1.401(a)(9)-6, Q&A-17(a)(2), any subsequent adjustment the IRS may make to the age requirement pursuant to Treasury Regulations Section 1.401(a)(9)-6, Q&A-17(d)(2)(ii) will not cause the contract to be a QLAC. [Treas. Reg. § 1.401(a)(9)-6, Q&A-17(d)(2)(iii)]

3. *Distribution Requirements.* A QLAC must provide that, after distributions under the QLAC commence, those distributions must satisfy the requirements of Treasury Regulations Section 1.401(a)(9)-6 (other than the requirement, in Treasury Regulations Section 1.401(a)(9)-6, Q&A-1(c), that annuity payments commence on or before the RBD). [Treas. Reg. § 1.401(a)(9)-6, Q&A-17(a)(3)]

4. *Limitations on Contract Features.* A QLAC may not make available any commutation benefit, cash surrender right, or other similar feature. [Treas. Reg. § 1.401(a)(9)-6, Q&A-17(a)(4)]

5. *Limitations on Death Benefits.* No benefits may be provided under a QLAC after the employee's death other than the benefits described in Treasury Regulations Section 1.401(a)(9)-6, Q&A-17(c). [Treas. Reg. § 1.401(a)(9)-6, Q&A-17(a)(5)]

6. *Required Contract Provision.* When the QLAC is issued, the QLAC (or a rider or endorsement with respect to that QLAC) must state that the contract is intended to be a QLAC. [Treas. Reg. § 1.401(a)(9)-6, Q&A-17(a)(6)] This requirement is satisfied if a certificate is issued under a group annuity contract and the certificate, when issued, states that the employee's interest under the group annuity contract is intended to be a QLAC. [Treas. Reg. § 1.401(a)(9)-6, Q&A-17(d)(5)]

7. *Not a Variable or Similar Contract.* Finally, a QLAC may not be a variable contract under Code Section 817, an indexed contract, or a similar contract, except to the extent the IRS, in revenue rulings, notices, or other published guidance. [Treas. Reg. § 1.401(a)(9)-6, Q&A-17(a)(7)] A contract is not treated as a variable, indexed, or similar contract merely because it is a participating contract (i.e., it provides for the payment of dividends) or merely because it provides for cost-of-living adjustments. [Treas. Reg. § 1.401(a)(9)-6, Q&A-17(d)(4)(i) and (ii)]

If a contract has a structural deficiency, that is, if the contract fails to be a QLAC at any time for a reason other than an excess premium, then as of the date of purchase the contract will not be treated as a QLAC or as a contract that is intended to be a QLAC as of the date of purchase. [Treas. Reg. § 1.401(a)(9)-6, Q&A-17(d)(3)(i)]

The QLAC requirements under Treasury Regulations Section 1.401(a)(9)-6, Q&A-17 apply to contracts purchased on or after July 2, 2014. [Treas. Reg. § 1.401(a)(9)-6, Q&A-17(e)(1)] If, on or after July 2, 2014, an existing contract is exchanged for a contract that satisfies the QLAC requirements, the new contract will be treated as purchased in the date of the exchange and the fair market value of the contract that is exchanged for a QLAC will be treated as a premium paid with respect to the QLAC. [Treas. Reg. § 1.401(a)(9)-6, Q&A-17(e)(1)] There is a delayed applicability date for the requirement in Treasury Regulations Section 1.401(a)(9)-6, Q&A-17(a)(6), described in item 6 above, that the contract state is intended to be a QLAC. [Treas. Reg. § 1.401(a)(9)-6, Q&A-17(e)(2)] Under that delayed applicability date, an annuity contract purchased before January 1, 2016, will not fail to be a QLAC merely because the contract fails to state that it is intended to be a QLAC, provided that (1) when the contract (or a certificate under a group annuity contract) is issued, the employee is notified that the annuity contract is intended to be a QLAC and (2) the contract is amended (or a rider, endorsement, or amendment to the certificate is issued) no later than December 31, 2016, to state that the annuity contract is intended to be a QLAC. [Treas. Reg. § 1.401(a)(9)-6, Q&A-17(e)(2)]

Effective with respect to QLACs purchased on or after July 2, 2014, the insurance company that issues a QLAC must file annual calendar-year reports with the IRS and must provide statements to contract holders about their QLACs. [Treas. Reg. § 1.6047-2] Code Section 6652(e) prescribes a penalty for failure to file the annual calendar-year report with the IRS. [Treas. Reg. § 1.6047-2(e)]

Q 4:28 What is the applicable distribution period for RMDs during a participant's lifetime?

General Rule. Except as provided under the rules discussed below (which apply when the participant's surviving spouse is the participant's sole designated beneficiary), the applicable distribution period for RMDs for distribution calendar years (see Q 4:23) up to and including the distribution calendar year that includes a participant's date of death generally is determined using the Uniform Lifetime Table in Treasury Regulations Section 1.401(a)(9)-9, Q&A-2 (reprinted as Table 4-1, below) for the participant's age as of the participant's birthday in the relevant distribution calendar year. If a participant dies on or after the RBD, the distribution period applicable for calculating the amount that must be distributed during the distribution calendar year that includes the participant's death is determined as if he or she had lived throughout the year. Thus, an RMD, determined as if the participant had lived throughout that year, is required for the year of the participant's death and that amount must be distributed to a beneficiary to the extent it has not already been distributed to the participant. [Treas. Reg. § 1.401(a)(9)-5, Q&A-4(a)]

Table 4-1. Uniform Lifetime Table

Age of Employee	*Distribution Period*
70	27.4
71	26.5
72	25.6
73	24.7
74	23.8
75	22.9
76	22.0
77	21.2
78	20.3
79	19.5
80	18.7
81	17.9
82	17.1
83	16.3
84	15.5
85	14.8
86	14.1
87	13.4
88	12.7
89	12.0
90	11.4
91	10.8
92	10.2
93	9.6
94	9.1
95	8.6
96	8.1
97	7.6

Age of Employee	Distribution Period
98	7.1
99	6.7
100	6.3
101	5.9
102	5.5
103	5.2
104	4.9
105	4.5
106	4.2
107	3.9
108	3.7
109	3.4
110	3.1
111	2.9
112	2.6
113	2.4
114	2.1
115 and older	1.9

[Treas. Reg. § 1.401(a)(9)-5, Q&A-4(a) and 1.401(a)(9)-9, Q&A-2]

The Uniform Lifetime Table is used for determining the distribution period for lifetime distributions to a participant in situations in which the participant's spouse is either not the sole designated beneficiary or the sole designated beneficiary but is not more than 10 years younger than the participant. [Treas. Reg. § 1.401(a)(9)-9, Q&A-2]

Spouse Is Sole Beneficiary. Except as otherwise provided under the rules relating to change in marital status (see below), if the sole designated beneficiary of a participant is the participant's surviving spouse, the applicable distribution period for RMDs during the participant's lifetime is the longer of (1) the distribution period determined in accordance with the general rule described above or (2) the joint life expectancy of the participant and spouse using their attained ages as of their birthdays in the distribution calendar year (see Q 4:23). The spouse is the sole designated beneficiary for purposes of determining the applicable distribution period for a distribution calendar year during the participant's lifetime only if the spouse is the sole beneficiary of the participant's entire interest at all times during the distribution calendar year. [Treas. Reg. § 1.401(a)(9)-5, Q&A-4(b)(1)]

The following special rule applies if there is a change in marital status. If the participant and his or her spouse are married on January 1 of a distribution calendar year (see Q 4:23) but do not remain married throughout that year (i.e., the participant or his or her spouse dies, or they become divorced during that year), the participant will not fail to have a spouse as his or her sole beneficiary for that year merely because they are not married throughout that year. If the participant's spouse dies first, the spouse will not fail to be the participant's sole beneficiary for the distribution calendar year that includes the date of the spouse's death solely because, for the period remaining in that year after the spouse's death, someone other than the spouse is named as beneficiary. However, the change in beneficiary due to the death or divorce of the spouse will be effective for purposes of determining the applicable distribution period under Code Section 401(a)(9) in the distribution calendar year following the distribution calendar year that includes the date of the spouse's death or divorce. [Treas. Reg. § 1.401(a)(9)-5 Q&A-4(b)(2)]

Q 4:29 What is the applicable distribution period for RMDs after a participant's death?

Death on or After the Participant's RBD. If a participant dies on or after his or her RBD, the applicable distribution period for distribution calendar years after the distribution calendar year containing the participant's date of death is either of the following:

1. If the participant has a designated beneficiary as of the date his or her designated beneficiary is determined (see Q 4:20), the longer of:
   a. the remaining life expectancy of the participant's designated beneficiary, determined in accordance with the rules described in items 1 and 2 below; or
   b. the remaining life expectancy of the participant, determined in accordance with the rules described in item 3, below; or
2. If the participant does not have a designated beneficiary as of the date his or her designated beneficiary is determined (see Q 4:20), the remaining life expectancy of the participant is determined in accordance with the rules described in item 3, below.

[Treas. Reg. § 1.401(a)(9)-5, Q&A-5(a)]

Death Before a Participant's RBD. If a participant dies before his or her RBD, the applicable distribution period for distribution calendar years after the distribution calendar year containing the date of death is determined in accordance with the rules described in items 1, 2, and 3, below. [Treas. Reg. § 1.401(a)(9)-5, Q&A-5(b)]

Life Expectancy.

1. *Nonspouse Designated Beneficiary.* The applicable distribution period measured by the beneficiary's remaining life expectancy is determined using the beneficiary's age as of the beneficiary's birthday in the calendar

year immediately following the calendar year of the participant's death. In subsequent calendar years, the applicable distribution period is reduced by one for each calendar year that has elapsed after the calendar year immediately following the calendar year of the participant's death. [Treas. Reg. § 1.401(a)(9)-5, Q&A-5(c)(1)]

2. *Spouse Is Designated Beneficiary.* If the participant's surviving spouse is his or her sole beneficiary, the applicable distribution period is measured by the surviving spouse's life expectancy using his or her birthday for each distribution calendar year after the calendar year of the participant's death up through the calendar year of the spouse's death. For calendar years after the calendar year of the spouse's death, the applicable distribution period is the life expectancy of the spouse using his or her age as of his or her birthday in the calendar year of the spouse's death, reduced by one for each calendar year that has elapsed after the calendar year of the spouse's death. [Treas. Reg. § 1.401(a)(9)-5, Q&A-5(c)(2)]
3. *No Designated Beneficiary.* If the participant does not have a designated beneficiary, the applicable distribution period measured by the participant's remaining life expectancy is the life expectancy of the participant using his or her age as of his or her birthday in the calendar year of the participant's death. In subsequent calendar years, the applicable distribution period is reduced by one for each calendar year that has elapsed after the calendar year of the participant's death. [Treas. Reg. § 1.401(a)(9)-5, Q&A-5(c)(3)]

Q 4:30 What life expectancies must be used for purposes of determining RMDs under Code Section 401(a)(9)?

Life expectancies for purposes of determining RMDs under Code Section 401(a)(9) must be computed using the Single Life Table in Treasury Regulations Section 1.401(a)(9)-9, Q&A-1 and the Joint and Last Survivor Table in Treasury Regulations Section 1.401(a)(9)-9, Q&A-3. [Treas. Reg. § 1.401(a)(9)-5, Q&A-6]

Q 4:31 If a participant has more than one designated beneficiary, which designated beneficiary's life expectancy will be used to determine the applicable distribution period?

General Rule. Except as otherwise provided below under the rules relating to successor beneficiaries, if more than one individual is designated as a beneficiary with respect to a participant as of the applicable date for determining the designated beneficiary, the designated beneficiary with the shortest life expectancy will be the designated beneficiary for purposes of determining the applicable distribution period. [Treas. Reg. § 1.401(a)(9)-5, Q&A-7(a)(1)] The rules of Treasury Regulations Section 1.401(a)(9)-4, Q&A-3 apply if a person other than an individual is designated as a beneficiary. In addition, special rules under Treasury Regulations Section 1.401(a)(9)-8, Q&A-2 and 3 apply if a participant's benefit under a plan is divided into separate accounts and the beneficiaries with respect to a separate account differ from the beneficiaries of another separate account. [Treas. Reg. § 1.401(a)(9)-5, Q&A-7(a)(2)]

Contingent Beneficiary. Except as otherwise provided below under the rules relating to successor beneficiaries, if a beneficiary's entitlement to a participant's benefit after the participant's death is a contingent right, such contingent beneficiary is nevertheless considered to be a designated beneficiary for purposes of determining which designated beneficiary has the shortest life expectancy. [Treas. Reg. § 1.401(a)(9)-5, Q&A-7(b)]

Successor Beneficiary. A person will not be considered a beneficiary for purposes of determining who is the beneficiary with the shortest life expectancy under the general rule described above, or whether a person who is not an individual is a beneficiary, merely because the person could become the successor to the interest of one of the participant's beneficiaries after that person's death. However, this rule does not apply to a person who has any right (including a contingent right) to a participant's benefit beyond being a mere potential successor to the interest of one of the participant's beneficiaries upon that beneficiary's death. Thus, for example, if the first beneficiary has a right to all income with respect to a participant's individual account during that beneficiary's life and a second beneficiary has a right to the principal but only after the death of the first income beneficiary (any portion of the principal distributed during the life of the first income beneficiary to be held in trust until that first beneficiary's death), both beneficiaries must be taken into account in determining the beneficiary with the shortest life expectancy and whether only individuals are beneficiaries. [Treas. Reg. § 1.401(a)(9)-5, Q&A-7(c)(1)]

If the individual beneficiary whose life expectancy is being used to calculate the distribution period dies after the September 30 of the calendar year following the calendar year of the participant's death, such beneficiary's remaining life expectancy will be used to determine the distribution period without regard to the life expectancy of the subsequent beneficiary. [Treas. Reg. § 1.401(a)(9)-5, Q&A-7(c)(2)]

The successor beneficiary rules are illustrated by the following examples.

Example 4-3: The Pastures of Heaven Company maintains the POH Defined Contribution Plan. George Battle, an employee of the Company, died in 2019 at the age of 55, survived by his spouse, Myrtle, who was 50 years old. Before George's death, the Company had established an account balance for George in the plan. George's account balance is invested only in productive assets. George named a testamentary trust established under his will as the beneficiary of all amounts payable from his account in the plan after his death. A copy of the trust and a list of the trust beneficiaries were provided to the plan administrator of the plan by October 31 of the calendar year following the calendar year of George's death. As of the date of George's death, the trust was irrevocable and was a valid trust under the laws of the state of George's domicile. George's account balance in the plan was includible in George's gross estate under Code Section 2039.

Under the terms of the trust, all trust income is payable annually to Myrtle, and no one has the power to appoint the trust principal to any person other than Myrtle. George's children, who are all younger than Myrtle, are the sole remainder beneficiaries of the trust. No other person has a beneficial interest in the trust. Under the terms of the trust, Myrtle has the power, exercisable annually, to compel the trustee to withdraw from George's account balance in the plan an amount equal to the income earned on the assets held in George's account in the plan during the calendar year and to distribute that amount through the trust to Myrtle. The plan contains no prohibition on withdrawal from George's account of amounts in excess of the annual RMDs under Code Section 401(a)(9). In accordance with the terms of the plan, the trustee of the trust elects, in order to satisfy Code Section 401(a)(9), to receive annual RMDs using the life expectancy rule in Code Section 401(a)(9)(B)(iii) for distributions over a distribution period equal to Myrtle's life expectancy. If Myrtle exercises the withdrawal power, the trustee must withdraw from George's account under the plan, the greater of the amount of income earned in the account during the calendar year or the RMD. However, under the terms of the trust, and applicable state law, only the portion of the plan distribution received by the trustee equal to the income earned by George's account in the plan is required to be distributed to Myrtle (along with any other trust income).

Because some amounts distributed from George's account in the plan to the trust may be accumulated in the trust during Myrtle's lifetime for the benefit of George's children (as remaindermen beneficiaries of the trust), even though access to those amounts is delayed until after Myrtle's death, George's children are beneficiaries of George's account in the plan in addition to Myrtle and Myrtle is not the sole beneficiary of George's account. Thus, the designated beneficiary used to determine the distribution period from George's account in the plan is the beneficiary with the shortest life expectancy. Myrtle's life expectancy is the shortest of all the potential beneficiaries of the testamentary trust's interest in George's account in the plan (including remainder beneficiaries). The distribution period for purposes of Code Section 401(a)(9)(B)(iii) is therefore Myrtle's life expectancy. Because Myrtle is not the sole beneficiary of the testamentary trust's interest in George's account in the plan, the special rule in Code Section 401(a)(9)(B)(iv) is not available and the annual RMDs from the account to the trust must begin no later than the end of the calendar year immediately following the calendar year of George's death. [Treas. Reg. § 1.401(a)(9)-5, Q&A-7(c)(3) Ex. 1]

Example 4-4: The facts are the same as in Example 4-3, except that the testamentary trust instrument provides that all amounts distributed from George's account in the POH Plan to the trustee while Myrtle is alive will be paid directly to Myrtle upon receipt by the trustee.

In this case, Myrtle is the sole beneficiary of George's account in the plan for purposes of determining the designated beneficiary under Code Section 401(a)(9)(B)(iii) and (iv). No amounts distributed from George's account in the plan to the trust are accumulated in the trust during Myrtle's lifetime for the benefit of any other beneficiary. Therefore, the residuary beneficiaries of the trust are mere potential successors to Myrtle's interest in the plan. Because Myrtle is the sole beneficiary of the testamentary trust's interest in George's account in the plan, the annual RMDs from George's account to the trust must begin no later than the end of the calendar year in which George would have attained age 70½, rather than the calendar year immediately following the calendar year of George's death. [Treas. Reg. § 1.401(a)(9)-5, Q&A-7(c)(3), Ex. 2]

Q 4:32 If a portion of a participant's individual account is not vested as of the participant's RBD, how is the determination of the RMD affected?

If a participant's benefit is in the form of an individual account, the benefit used to determine the RMD for any distribution calendar year will be determined without regard to whether or not all of the participant's benefit is vested. Further, if any portion of a participant's benefit is not vested, distributions will be treated as being paid from the vested portion of the benefit first.

If, as of the end of a distribution calendar year (or as of a participant's RBD, in the case of a participant's first distribution calendar year), the total amount of the participant's vested benefit is less than the RMD for the calendar year, only the vested portion, if any, of the participant's benefit is required to be distributed by the end of the calendar year (or, if applicable, by the participant's RBD). The RMD for the subsequent distribution calendar year must be increased, however, by the sum of amounts not distributed in prior calendar years because the participant's vested benefit was less than the RMD. [Treas. Reg. § 1.401(a)(9)-5, Q&A-8]

Q 4:33 Which amounts distributed from an individual account are or are not taken into account in determining whether the RMD rules of Code Section 401(a)(9) are satisfied?

General Rule. With some exceptions (see below), all amounts distributed from an individual account are taken into account in determining whether the RMDs rules of Code Section 401(a)(9) are satisfied, regardless of whether the amount is includible in income. For example, amounts that are excluded from income as a recovery of investment in the contract (i.e., basis) under Code Section 72 are taken into account for purposes of determining whether Code Section 401(a)(9) is satisfied for a distribution calendar year. Similarly, amounts excluded from income as net unrealized appreciation on employer securities also are amounts distributed for purposes of determining if Code Section 401(a)(9) is satisfied. [Treas. Reg. § 1.401(a)(9)-5, Q&A-9(a)]

Exceptions. The following amounts are *not* taken into account in determining whether the RMD has been distributed for a calendar year:

1. Elective deferrals and employee contributions that, pursuant to Treasury Regulations Section 1.415-6(b)(6)(iv), are returned (together with the income allocable to these corrective distributions) as a result of the application of the Code Section 415 limitations;

2. Corrective distributions of excess deferrals as described in Treasury Regulations Section 1.402(g)-1(e)(3), together with the income allocable to these distributions;
3. Corrective distributions of excess contributions under a 401(k) plan under Code Section 401(k)(8) and excess aggregate contributions under Code Section 401(m)(6), together with income allocable to these distributions;
4. Loans that are treated as deemed distributions pursuant to Code Section 72(p);
5. Dividends described in Code Section 404(k) that are paid on employer securities. (Amounts paid to the plan that, pursuant to Code Section 404(k)(2)(A)(iii)(II), are included in the account balance and subsequently distributed from the account lose their character as dividends.);
6. The costs of life insurance coverage (PS 58 costs); and
7. Similar items designated by the IRS in revenue rulings, notices, and other guidance published in the Internal Revenue Bulletin.

[Treas. Reg. § 1.401(a)(9)-5, Q&A-9]

Required Minimum Distributions from Defined Benefit Plans and Annuity Contracts

Q 4:34 How must distributions under a defined benefit plan be paid in order to satisfy the RMD rules?

General Rules. In order to satisfy the RMD rules of Code Section 401(a)(9) (with exceptions described below), distributions of the participant's entire interest under a defined benefit plan must be paid in the form of periodic annuity payments for the participant's life (or the joint lives of the participant and his or her beneficiary) or over a period certain that does not exceed the maximum length of the period certain determined under the rules described in Q 4:36. The interval between payments for the annuity must be uniform over the entire distribution period and must not exceed one year. Once payments have begun over a period, the period may not be changed except in certain limited circumstances. Life (or joint and survivor) annuity payments must satisfy the MDIB requirements described in Q 4:35. All payments (whether paid over a participant's life, joint lives, or a period certain) must either be nonincreasing or may increase only in accordance with one or more of the following:

1. With an annual percentage increase that does not exceed the annual percentage increase in an eligible cost-of-living index (as defined in Treasury Regulations Section 1.401(a)(9)-6, Q&A-14(b)) for a 12-month period ending in the year during which the increase occurs or the prior year;
2. With a percentage increase that occurs at specified times (for example, at specified ages) and does not exceed the cumulative total of annual

percentage increases in an eligible cost-of-living index (as defined in Treasury Regulations Section 1.401(a)(9)-6, Q&A-14(b)) since the annuity starting date, or if later, the date of the most recent percentage increase. However, in cases providing such a cumulative increase, an actuarial increase may not be provided to reflect the fact that the increases were not provided in the interim years;

3. To the extent of the reduction in the amount of the participant's payments to provide for a survivor benefit, but only if there is no longer a survivor benefit because the beneficiary whose life was being used to determine the period described in Code Section 401(a)(9)(A)(ii) over which payments were being made dies or is no longer the participant's beneficiary pursuant to a QDRO within the meaning of Code Section 414(p);
4. To pay increased benefits that result from a plan amendment;
5. To allow a beneficiary to convert the survivor portion of a joint and survivor annuity into a single-sum distribution upon the participant's death; or
6. To the extent increases are permitted under Treasury Regulations Section 1.401(a)(9)-6, Q&A-14(c) or (d).

[Treas. Reg. § 1.401(a)(9)-6, Q&A-1(a) and Q&A-14]

Life Annuity with Period Certain. The annuity may be a life annuity (or joint and survivor annuity) with a period certain if the life (or lives, if applicable) and period certain each meet the general rules described above. For these purposes, if distributions are permitted to be made over the lives of the participant and his or her designated beneficiary, references to a life annuity include a joint and survivor annuity. [Treas. Reg. § 1.401(a)(9)-6, Q&A-1(b)]

Annuity Commencement. Annuity payments must begin on or before the participant's RBD. The first payment, which must be made on or before the RBD, must be the payment required for one payment interval. The second payment need not be made until the end of the next payment interval even if that payment interval ends in the next calendar year. Similarly, in the case of distributions beginning after the participant's death in accordance with Code Section 401(a)(9)(B)(iii) and (iv), the first payment, which must be made on or before the date determined under Treasury Regulations Section 1.401(a)(9)-3, Q&A-3(a) or (b), whichever applies, must be the payment which is required for one payment interval. Payment intervals are the periods for which payments are received (e.g., bimonthly, monthly, semiannually, or annually). All benefit accruals as of the last day of the first distribution calendar year must be included in the calculation of the amount of annuity payments for payment intervals ending on or after the participant's RBD. [Treas. Reg. § 1.401(a)(9)-6, Q&A-1(c)]

Example 4-5: The Salinas Company Defined Benefit Plan provides monthly annuity payments of $500 for the life of unmarried participants with a 10-year period certain. Raymond Banks, an unmarried, retired participant in the plan, attains age 70½ in 2019. The first monthly payment of $500 must be made on behalf of Raymond on or before April 1, 2020, and the payments must continue to be made in monthly payments of $500 thereafter for the life and 10-year period certain. [Treas. Reg. § 1.401(a)(9)-6, Q&A-1(c), Ex. unnumbered]

Single-Sum Distributions. In case of a single-sum distribution of a participant's entire accrued benefit during a distribution calendar year (see Q 4:23), the amount that is the RMD for the distribution calendar year (and thus not eligible for rollover under Code Section 402(c)) is determined using either of the rules described in items 1 and 2 below:

1. The portion of the single-sum distribution that is an RMD is determined by treating the single-sum distribution as a distribution from an individual account plan and treating the amount of the single-sum distribution as the participant's account balance as of the end of the relevant valuation calendar year. If the single-sum distribution is being made in the calendar year containing the RBD and the RMD for the participant's first distribution calendar year has not been distributed, the portion of the single-sum distribution that represents the RMD for the participant's first and second distribution calendar years is not eligible for rollover. [Treas. Reg. § 1.401(a)(9)-6, Q&A-1(d)(1)]
2. The portion of the single-sum distribution that is an RMD may be determined by expressing the participant's benefit as an annuity with an annuity starting date as of the first day of the distribution calendar year for which the RMD is being determined, and treating one year of annuity payments as the RMD for that year, and not eligible for rollover. If the single-sum distribution is being made in the calendar year containing the RBD and the RMD for the participant's first distribution calendar year has not been made, the benefit must be expressed as an annuity with an annuity starting date as of the first day of the first distribution calendar year and the payments for the first two calendar years would be treated as RMDs, and not eligible for rollover. [Treas. Reg. § 1.401(a)(9)-6, Q&A-1(d)(2)]

Death Benefits. The rule prohibiting increasing payments under an annuity applies to payments made upon the death of the participant. However, an ancillary death benefit described below may be disregarded in applying that rule. Such an ancillary death benefit is excluded in determining a participant's entire interest and the rules prohibiting increasing payments do not apply to such an ancillary benefit. A death benefit with respect to a participant's benefit is an ancillary death benefit for these purposes if:

1. It is not paid as part of the participant's accrued benefit or under any optional form of the participant's benefit; and
2. The death benefit, together with any other potential payments with respect to the participant's benefit that may be provided to a survivor, satisfies the incidental benefit requirement of Treasury Regulations Section 1.401-1(b)(1)(i). [Treas. Reg. § 1.401(a)(9)-6, Q&A-1(e)]

Additional Guidance. Additional guidance regarding how distributions under a defined benefit plan must be paid in order to satisfy the RMD rules of Code Section 401(a)(9) may be issued by the IRS in revenue rulings, notices, or other guidance published in the Internal Revenue Bulletin. [Treas. Reg. § 1.401(a)(9)-6, Q&A-1(f)]

Q 4:35 How must distributions in the form of a life (or joint and survivor) annuity be made in order to satisfy the MDIB requirement and the distribution component of the incidental benefit requirement?

Life Annuity for Participant. If the participant's benefit is paid in the form of a life annuity for the life of the participant satisfying Code Section 401(a)(9) without regard to the MDIB requirement, the MDIB requirement of Code Section 401(a)(9)(G) will be satisfied. [Treas. Reg. § 1.401(a)(9)-6, Q&A-2(a)]

Joint and Survivor Annuity, Spouse Beneficiary. If the participant's sole beneficiary, as of the annuity starting date for annuity payments, is the participant's spouse and the distributions satisfy Code Section 401(a)(9) without regard to the MDIB requirement, the distributions to the participant will be deemed to satisfy the MDIB requirement of Code Section 401(a)(9)(G). For example, if a participant's benefit is being distributed in the form of a joint and survivor annuity for the lives of the participant and the participant's spouse and the spouse is the sole beneficiary of the participant, the amount of the periodic payment payable to the spouse would not violate the MDIB requirement if it were 100 percent of the annuity payment payable to the participant regardless of the difference in the ages between them. [Treas. Reg. § 1.401(a)(9)-6, Q&A-2(b)]

Joint and Survivor Annuity, Nonspouse Beneficiary. If distributions begin under a distribution option that is in the form of a joint and survivor annuity for the joint lives of the participant and a beneficiary other than the participant's spouse, the MDIB requirement will not be satisfied as of the date distributions start unless the distribution option provides that annuity payments to be made to the participant on and after the participant's RBD will satisfy the conditions described here. The periodic annuity payment payable to the survivor must not at any time on and after the participant's RBD exceed the applicable percentage of the annuity payment payable to the participant using Table 4-2. The applicable percentage is based on the adjusted participant/beneficiary age difference. The adjusted participant/beneficiary age difference is determined by first calculating the excess of the age of the participant over the age of the beneficiary based on their ages on their birthdays in a calendar year. Then, if the participant is younger than age 70, the age difference is reduced by the number of years that the participant is younger than age 70 on the participant's birthday in the calendar year that contains the annuity starting date. In the case of an annuity that provides for increasing payments, the increase must be determined in the same manner for the participant and the beneficiary.

Table 4-2. Applicable Percentage of Annuity Payments

Adjusted Participant/ Beneficiary Age Difference	*Applicable Percentage*
10 years or less	100
11	96
12	93
13	90
14	87
15	84
16	82
17	79
18	77
19	75
20	73
21	72
22	70
23	68
24	67
25	66
26	64
27	63
28	62
29	61
30	60
31	59
32	59
33	58
34	57
35	56
36	56
37	55
38	55
39	54
40	54
41	53
42	53
43	53
44 and greater	52

[Treas. Reg. § 1.401(a)(9)-6, Q&A-2(c)(2)]

Example 4-6: Distributions begin on January 1, 2019, to participant John Whiteside, born March 1, 1953, after his retirement at age 65. John's daughter Alice, born February 5, 1983, is John's beneficiary. The distributions are in the form of a joint and survivor annuity for the lives of John and Alice with payments of $500 a month to John and upon John's death of $500 a month to Alice; that is, the projected monthly payment to Alice is 100 percent of the monthly amount payable to John. The adjusted participant/beneficiary age difference is calculated by taking the excess of the participant's age over the beneficiary's age and subtracting the number of years the participant is younger than age 70. In this case, John is 30 years older than Alice is and is beginning distributions four years before attaining age 70, so the adjusted participant/beneficiary age difference is 26 years. Under Table 4-2, the applicable percentage for a 26-year adjusted participant/beneficiary age difference is 64 percent. As of January 1, 2019 (the annuity starting date), the plan does not satisfy the MDIB requirement because, as of that date, the distribution option provides that, as of John's RBD, the monthly payment to Alice upon John's death will exceed 64 percent of John's monthly payment. [Treas. Reg. § 1.401(a)(9)-6, Q&A-2(c)(3), Ex. unnumbered]

Period Certain and Annuity Features. If a distribution form includes a period certain, the amount of the annuity payments payable to the beneficiary need not be reduced during the period certain, but in the case of a joint and survivor annuity with a period certain, the amount of the annuity payments payable to the beneficiary must satisfy the requirements of Treasury Regulations Section 1.401(a)(9)-6, Q&A-2(c), described above, after the expiration of the period certain. [Treas. Reg. § 1.401(a)(9)-6, Q&A-2(d)]

Deemed Satisfaction of Incidental Benefit Rule. Except in the case of distributions with respect to a participant's benefit that include an ancillary death benefit, to the extent the incidental benefit requirement of Treasury Regulations Section 1.401-1(b)(1)(i) requires a distribution, that requirement is deemed to be satisfied if distributions satisfy the MDIB requirement of Treasury Regulations Section 1.401(a)(9)-6, Q&A-2. If the participant's benefits include an ancillary death benefit, the benefits (including the ancillary death benefit) must be distributed in accordance with the incidental benefit requirement described in Treasury Regulations Section 1.401-1(b)(1)(i) and must also satisfy the MDIB requirement of Treasury Regulations Section 1.401(a)(9)-6, Q&A-2. [Treas. Reg. § 1.401(a)(9)-6, Q&A-2(e)]

Q 4:36 How long is a period certain under a defined benefit plan permitted to extend?

Distributions Starting During the Participant's Life. The period certain for any annuity distributions starting during the participant's life with an annuity starting date on or after the participant's RBD generally is not permitted to exceed the applicable distribution period for the participant (determined in accordance with the Uniform Lifetime Table in Treasury Regulations

Section 1.401(a)(9)-9, Q&A-2) for the calendar year that contains the annuity starting date. The rule for annuity payments with an annuity starting date before the RBD appears in Treasury Regulations Section 1.401(a)(9)-6, Q&A-10. However, if the participant's sole beneficiary is the participant's spouse and the annuity provides only a period certain and no life annuity, the period certain may be as long as the joint life and last survivor expectancy of both, if longer than the applicable distribution period for the participant, provided the period certain is not provided is conjunction with a life annuity. [Treas. Reg. § 1.401(a)(9)-6, Q&A-3(a)]

Distributions Starting After the Participant's Death. If annuity distributions start after the death of the participant under the life expectancy rule (under Code Section 401(a)(9)(B)(iii) or (iv)), the period certain for any distributions starting after death cannot exceed the applicable distribution period determined under Treasury Regulations Section 1.401(a)(9)-5, Q&A-5(b) for the distribution calendar year that contains the annuity starting date. [Treas. Reg. § 1.401(a)(9)-6, Q&A-3(b)(1)]

If the annuity starting date is in a calendar year before the first distribution calendar year, the period certain may not exceed the life expectancy of the designated beneficiary using the beneficiary's age in the year that contains the annuity starting date. [Treas. Reg. § 1.401(a)(9)-6, Q&A-3(b)(2)]

Q 4:37 Will a plan fail to satisfy the RMD rules merely because distributions are made from an annuity contract purchased from an insurance company?

No. A plan will not fail to satisfy the RMD rules of Code Section 401(a)(9) merely because distributions are made from an annuity contract that is purchased with the participant's benefit by the plan from an insurance company, as long as the payments satisfy the requirements of Treasury Regulations Section 1.401(a)(9)-6. If the annuity contract is purchased after the RBD, the first payment interval must begin on or before the purchase date and the payment required for one payment interval must be made no later than the end of such payment interval. If the payments actually made under the annuity contract do not meet the requirements of Code Section 401(a)(9), the plan fails to satisfy Code Section 401(a)(9). [Treas. Reg. § 1.401(a)(9)-6, Q&A-4(a)]

Q 4:38 In the case of annuity distributions under a defined benefit plan, how must additional benefits that accrue after the participant's first distribution calendar year be distributed in order to satisfy the RMD rules?

In the case of annuity distributions under a defined benefit plan, if any additional benefits accrue in a calendar year after the participant's first distribution calendar year (see Q 4:23), distribution of that amount must begin with the first payment interval ending in the calendar year immediately following the calendar year in which such amount accrues.

A plan will not fail to satisfy the RMD rules merely because there is an administrative delay in the start of the distribution of the additional benefits accrued in a calendar year, provided that the actual payment of such amount starts as soon as practicable. However, payment must start no later than the end of the first calendar year following the calendar year in which the additional benefit accrues, and the total amount paid during such first calendar year must be no less than the total amount that was required to be paid during that year. [Treas. Reg. § 1.401(a)(9)-6, Q&A-5]

Q 4:39 If a portion of a participant's benefit is not vested as of December 31 of a distribution calendar year, how is the determination of the RMD affected?

In the case of annuity distributions from a defined benefit plan, if any portion of the participant's benefit is not vested as of December 31 of a distribution calendar year (see Q 4:23) the portion that is not vested as of that date will be treated as not having accrued for purposes of determining the RMD for that distribution calendar year. When an additional portion of the participant's benefit becomes vested, such portion will be treated as an additional accrual. [Treas. Reg. § 1.401(a)(9)-6, Q&A-6]

Q 4:40 If a participant (other than a 5-percent owner) retires after the calendar year in which the participant attains age 70½, for what period must the participant's accrued benefit under a defined benefit plan be actuarially increased?

Actuarial Increase Starting Date. If a participant in a defined benefit plan (other than a 5-percent owner) retires after the calendar year in which he or she attains age 70½, the participant's accrued benefit under the plan must be actuarially increased to take into account any period after age 70½ in which the participant was not receiving any benefits under the plan. The required actuarial increase must be provided for the period starting on the April 1 following the calendar year in which the employee attains age 70½, or January 1, 1997, if later. [Treas. Reg. § 1.401(a)(9)-6, Q&A-7(a)]

Actuarial Increase Ending Date. The period for which the actuarial increase must be provided ends on the date on which benefits begin after retirement in an amount sufficient to satisfy Code Section 401(a)(9). [Treas. Reg. § 1.401(a)(9)-6, Q&A-7(b)]

Nonapplication to Plan Providing Same RBD for All Participants. If a plan provides that the RBD for purposes of Code Section 401(a)(9) for all participants is April 1 of the calendar year following the calendar year in which the participant attains age 70½ (regardless of whether the participant is a 5-percent owner) and the plan makes distributions in an amount sufficient to satisfy Code

Section 401(a)(9) using that RBD, no actuarial increase is required. [Treas. Reg. § 1.401(a)(9)-6, Q&A-7(c)]

Nonapplication to Governmental and Church Plans. The required actuarial increase does not apply to governmental plans (within the meaning of Code Section 414(d)) or church plans. For these purposes, the term church plan means a plan maintained by a church for church employees, and the term church means any church (as defined in Code Section 3121(w)(3)(A)) or qualified church-controlled organization (as defined in Code Section 3121(w)(3)(B)). [Treas. Reg. § 1.401(a)(9)-6, Q&A-7(d)] Note that, on September 8, 2009, the IRS issued final regulations permitting governmental plans to comply with the RMD rules by using, in lieu of the IRS's RMD regulations, a reasonable and good-faith interpretation of the Code's RMD rules. [Treas. Reg. §§ 1.401(a)(9)-1, Q/A-2(d), 1.401(a)(9)-6, and 1.403(b)-6(e)(2) and (e)(8); 74 Fed. Reg. 172, pp. 45993–45994]

Q 4:41 What amount of actuarial increase is required?

In order to satisfy Code Section 401(a)(9)(C)(iii), the retirement benefits payable with respect to a participant as of the end of the period for actuarial increases must be no less than: the actuarial equivalent of the participant's retirement benefits that would have been payable as of the date the actuarial increase must begin if benefits had started on that date; plus the actuarial equivalent of any additional benefits accrued after that date; reduced by the actuarial equivalent of any distributions made with respect to the participant's retirement benefits after that date. Actuarial equivalence is determined using the plan's assumption for determining actuarial equivalence for purposes of satisfying Code Section 411. [Treas. Reg. § 1.401(a)(9)-6, Q&A-8]

Q 4:42 How does the actuarial increase required under Code Section 401(a)(9)(C)(iii) relate to the actuarial increase required under Code Section 411?

In order for any of a participant's accrued benefit to be nonforfeitable as required under Code Section 411, a defined benefit plan must make an actuarial adjustment to an accrued benefit, the payment of which is deferred past normal retirement age. The only exception to this rule is that generally no actuarial adjustment is required to reflect the period during which a benefit is suspended as permitted under ERISA Section 203(a)(3)(B). The actuarial increase required under Code Section 401(a)(9)(C)(iii) is generally the same as, and not in addition to, the actuarial increase required under Code Section 411 to reflect any delay in the payment of retirement benefits after normal retirement age. However, unlike the actuarial increase required under Code Section 411, the actuarial increase required under Code Section 401(a)(9)(C)(iii) must be provided even during any period during which an employee's benefit has been suspended in accordance with ERISA Section 203(a)(3)(B). [Treas. Reg. § 1.401(a)(9)-6, Q&A-9]

Q 4:43 What rule applies if distributions to a participant start on a date before the participant's RBD over a period permitted under the life or life expectancy method of Code Section 401(a)(9)(A)(ii) and the distribution form is an annuity?

General Rule. If distributions to a participant start on a date before the participant's RBD over a period permitted under Code Section 401(a)(9)(A)(ii) and the distribution form is an annuity under which distributions are made in accordance with the provisions of applicable Treasury regulations, the annuity starting date will be treated as the RBD. Thus, for example, the designated beneficiary distributions will be determined as of the annuity starting date. Similarly, if the participant dies after the annuity starting date but before the RBD, after the participant's death, the remaining portion of the participant's interest must continue to be distributed over the remaining period over which distributions began (single or joint lives or period certain, as applicable). [Treas. Reg. § 1.401(a)(9)-6, Q&A-10(a)]

Period Certain. If, as of the participant's birthday in the year that contains the annuity starting date, the participant is under 70, the following rule applies. The applicable distribution period for the participant is the distribution period for age 70 using the Uniform Lifetime Table (see Q 4:28) plus the excess of 70 over the age of the participant as of the participant's birthday in the year that contains the annuity starting date. [Treas. Reg. § 1.401(a)(9)-6, Q&A-10(b)]

Q 4:44 What rule applies if distributions start to the surviving spouse of a participant over a period permitted under Code Section 401(a)(9)(B)(iii)(II) before the date on which distributions are required to start and the distribution form is an annuity?

If distributions start to the surviving spouse of a participant over a period permitted under Code Section 401(a)(9)(B)(iii)(II) before the date on which distributions are required to start and the distribution form is an annuity, distributions will be considered to have begun on the actual starting date for purposes of Code Section 401(a)(9)(B)(iv)(II). [Treas. Reg. § 1.401(a)(9)-6, Q&A-11]

Q 4:45 In the case of an annuity contract under an individual account plan that has not yet been annuitized, how is Code Section 401(a)(9) satisfied with respect to the participant's or beneficiary's entire interest under the annuity contract for the period prior to the date annuity payments begin?

General Rule. As a general rule, prior to the date that an annuity contract under an individual account plan is annuitized, the interest of a participant or beneficiary under that contract is treated as an individual account for purposes of Code Section 401(a)(9). Thus, the RMD for any year with respect to that interest is determined under Treasury Regulations Section 1.401(a)(9)-5 (which provides the rules for determining RMDs from defined contribution plans) rather than Treasury Regulations Section 1.401(a)(9)-6 (which provides the rules for determining RMDs from defined benefit plans and annuity contracts).

Entire Interest. For purposes of applying the rules in Treasury Regulations Section 1.401(a)(9)-5, the entire interest under the annuity contract as of December 31 of the relevant valuation calendar year is treated as the account balance for the valuation calendar year. [Treas. Reg. § 1.401(a)(9)-6, Q&A-12(a)] The entire interest under an annuity contract is the dollar amount credited to the participant or beneficiary under the contract plus the actuarial present value of any additional benefits (e.g., survivor benefits in excess of the dollar amount credited to the participant or beneficiary) that will be provided under the contract. However, certain additional benefits may be disregarded in determining the participant's entire interest under the annuity contract. The actuarial present value of any additional benefits is determined using reasonable actuarial assumptions, including reasonable assumptions as to future distributions, and without regard to the individual's health. [Treas. Reg. § 1.401(a)(9)-6, Q&A-12(b)]

Exclusions. The actuarial present value of any additional benefits provided under an annuity contract may be disregarded if the sum of the dollar amount credited to the participant or beneficiary under the contract and the actuarial present value of the additional benefits is no more than 120 percent of the dollar amount credited to the participant or beneficiary under the contract and the contract provides only for the following additional benefits:

1. Additional benefits that, in the case of a distribution, are reduced by an amount sufficient to ensure that the ratio of such sum to the dollar amount credited does not increase as a result of the distribution; and
2. An additional benefit that is the right to receive a final payment upon death that does not exceed the excess of the premiums paid less the amount of prior distributions.

[Treas. Reg. § 1.401(a)(9)-6, Q&A-12(c)(1)]

If the only additional benefit provided under the contract is the additional benefit described in (2), above, the additional benefit may be disregarded regardless of its value in relation to the dollar amount credited to the participant or beneficiary under the contract. [Treas. Reg. § 1.401(a)(9)-6, Q&A-12(c)(2)]

The IRS may provide guidance on additional benefits that may be disregarded. [Treas. Reg. § 1.401(a)(9)-6, Q&A-12(c)(3)]

Q 4:46 When can an annuity payment period be changed?

In General. An annuity payment period may be changed in accordance with the provisions set forth below or in association with an annuity payment increase described in Q 4:47.

Reannuitization. If, in a stream of annuity payments that otherwise satisfies the RMD requirements of Code Section 401(a)(9), the annuity payment period is changed and the annuity payments are modified in association with that change, this modification will not cause the distributions to fail to satisfy the RMD requirements provided the conditions described below are satisfied, and either:

1. The modification occurs at the time that the participant retires or in connection with a plan termination;
2. The annuity payments prior to modification are annuity payments paid over a period certain without life contingencies; or
3. The annuity payments after modification are paid under a qualified joint and survivor annuity (QJSA) over the joint lives of the participant and a designated beneficiary, the participant's spouse is the sole designated beneficiary, and the modification occurs in connection with the participant becoming married to that spouse.

[Treas. Reg. § 1.401(a)(9)-6, Q&A-13(b)]

Conditions. In order to modify a stream of payments in accordance with the reannuitization rules described above, the following conditions must be satisfied:

1. The future payments under the modified stream satisfy the RMD rules in Code Section 401(a)(9) and Treasury Regulations Section 1.401(a)(9)-6 (determined by treating the date of the change as a new annuity starting date and the actuarial present value of the remaining payments prior to modification as the entire interest of the participant);
2. For purposes of Code Sections 415 and 417, the modification is treated as a new annuity starting date;
3. After taking into account the modification, the annuity stream satisfies Code Section 415 (determined at the original starting date using the interest rates and mortality tables applicable to that date); and
4. The end point of the period certain, if any, for any modified payment period is not later than the end point available under Code Section 401(a)(9) to the participant at the original annuity starting date.

[Treas. Reg. § 1.401(a)(9)-6, Q&A-13(c)]

Examples. For the following examples, assume that the Applicable Interest Rate throughout the period from 2005 through 2008 is 5 percent and throughout 2009 is 4 percent, that the Applicable Mortality Table throughout the period from 2005 to 2009 is the table provided in Revenue Ruling 2001-62 (2001-2 C.B. 632), and that the Code Section 415 limit in 2005 at age 70 for a straight life annuity is $255,344.

> **Example 4-7:** Doc, who has 10 years of participation in the frozen Monterey Corporation Defined Benefit Plan, attains age 70½ in 2005. Doc is not retired and elects to receive distributions from the Plan in the form of a straight life (i.e., level payment) annuity with annual payments of $240,000 per year beginning in 2005 at a date when Doc has an attained age of 70. The Plan offers non-retired participants in pay status the opportunity to modify their annuity payments due to an associated change in the payment period at

retirement. The Plan treats the date of the change in payment period as a new "annuity starting date" for the purposes of Code Sections 415 and 417. Thus, for example, the Plan provides a new QJSA election and obtains spousal consent.

The Plan determines modifications of annuity payment amounts at retirement such that the present value of future new annuity payment amounts (taking into account the new associated payment period) is actuarially equivalent to the present value of future pre-modification annuity payments (taking into account the pre-modification annuity payment period). Actuarial equivalency for this purpose is determined using the Applicable Interest Rate and the Applicable Mortality Table as of the date of modification.

Doc retires in 2009 at the age of 74 and, after receiving four annual payments of $240,000, elects to receive his remaining distributions from the Plan in the form of an immediate final lump-sum payment (calculated at 4 percent interest) of $2,399,809.

Because payment of retirement benefits in the form of an immediate final lump-sum payment satisfies (in terms of form) the RMD rules of Code Section 401(a)(9), the condition set forth in Treasury Regulations Section 1.401(a)(9)-6, Q&A-13(c)(1), described above, is met.

Because the Plan treats a modification of an annuity payment stream at retirement as a new annuity starting date for purposes of Code Sections 415 and 417, the condition under Treasury Regulations Section 1.401(a)(9)-6, Q&A-13(c)(2), described above, is met.

After taking into account the modification, the annual stream determined as of the original annuity starting date consists of annual payments beginning at age 70 of $240,000, $240,000, $240,000, $240,000, and $2,399,809. This benefit stream is actuarially equivalent to a straight life annuity at age 70 of $250,182, an amount less than the Code Section 415 limit determined at the original annuity starting date, using the interest and mortality rates applicable to that date. Thus, the condition under Treasury Regulations Section 1.401(a)(9)-6, Q&A-13(c)(3), described above, is met. [Treas. Reg. § 1.401(a)(9)-6, Q&A-13(d), Ex. 1]

Example 4-8: The facts are the same as in Example 4-7 except that the straight life annuity payments are paid at a rate of $250,000 per year and, after Doc retires, the lump-sum payment at age 75 is $2,499,801. Thus, after taking into account the modification, the annuity stream determined as of the original annuity starting date consists of annual payments beginning at age 70 of $250,000, $250,000, $250,000, $250,000, and $2,499,801. This benefit stream is actuarially equivalent to a straight life annuity at age 70 of $260,606, an amount greater than the Code Section 415 limit determined at the original annuity starting date, using the interest and mortality rates applicable to that date. Thus, the lump-sum payment to Doc fails to satisfy the condition under Treasury Regulations Section 1.401(a)(9)-6, Q&A-13(c)(3), described above. Therefore, the lump-sum payment to Doc fails to meet the requirements of Treasury Regulations Section 1.401(a)(9)-6, Q&A-13, and thus fails to satisfy the RMD requirements of Code Section 401(a)(9). [Treas. Reg. § 1.401(a)(9)-6, Q&A-13, Ex. 2]

Example 4-9: George Battle, who has 10 years of participation in the frozen Pastures of Heaven Defined Benefit Plan, attains age 70½ and retires in 2005 at a date when his attained age is 70. George was born in 1935. George elects to receive annual distributions from the Plan in the form of a 27-year period certain annuity (i.e., a 27-year annuity payment period without a life contingency) paid at a rate of $37,000 per year beginning in 2005, with future payments increasing at a rate of 4 percent per year (i.e., the 2006 payment will be $38,480, the 2007 payment will be $40,019, and so on). The Plan offers participants in pay status whose annuity payments are in the form of a term-certain annuity the opportunity to modify their payment period at any time and treats such modifications as a new annuity starting date for the purposes of Code Sections 415 and 417. Thus, for example, the Plan provides a new QJSA election and obtains spousal consent.

The Plan determines modifications of annuity payment amounts such that the present value of future new annuity payment amounts (taking into account the new associated payment period) is actuarially equivalent to the present value of future pre-modification annuity payments (taking into account the pre-modification annuity payment period). Actuarial equivalency for this purpose is determined using 5 percent and the Applicable Mortality Table as of the date of modification.

In 2008, George, after receiving annual payments of $37,000, $38,480, and $40,019, elects to receive his remaining distributions from the Plan in the form of a straight life annuity paid with annual payments of $92,133 per year.

Because payment of retirement benefits in the form of a straight life annuity satisfies (in terms of form) the RMD requirements of Code Section 401(a)(9), the condition under Treasury Regulations Section 1.401(a)(9)-6, Q&A-13(c)(1), described above, is met.

Because the Plan treats a modification of an annuity payment stream at retirement as a new annuity starting date for purposes of Code Sections 415 and 417, the condition under Treasury Regulations Section 1.401(a)(9)-6, Q&A-13(c)(2), described above, is met.

After taking into account the modification, the annuity stream determined as of the original annuity starting date consists of annual payments beginning at age 70 of $37,000, $38,480, $40,019, and a straight life annuity beginning at age 73 of $92,133. This benefit stream is equivalent to a straight life annuity at age 70 of $82,539, an amount less than the Code Section 415 limit determined at the original annuity starting date, using the interest and mortality rates applicable to such date. Thus, the condition in Treasury Regulations Section 1.401(a)(9)-6, Q&A-13(c)(3), described above, is met.

Thus, because a stream of annuity payments in the form of a straight life annuity satisfies the RMD requirements of Code Section 401(a)(9), and because each of the conditions under Treasury Regulations Section 1.401(a)(9)-6, Q&A-13 are satisfied, the modification of annuity payments to George, described above, meets the requirements of Treasury Regulations Section 1.401(a)(9)-6, Q&A-13. [Treas. Reg. § 1.401(a)(9)-6, Q&A-13, Ex. 3]

Q 4:47 Are annuity payments permitted to increase?

General Rule. Except as otherwise permitted in Treasury Regulations Section 1.401(a)(9)-6, Q&A-14, all annuity payments (whether paid over a participant's life, joint lives, or a period certain) must be nonincreasing or increase only in accordance with one or more of the following:

1. With an annual percentage increase that does not exceed the percentage increase in an eligible cost-of-living index, as defined below, for a 12-month period ending in the year during which the increase occurs or the prior year;
2. With a percentage increase that occurs at specified times (e.g., at specified ages) and does not exceed the cumulative total of annual percentage increases in an eligible cost-of-living index, as defined below, since the annuity starting date or, if later, the date of the most recent percentage increase. However, in cases providing such a cumulative increase, an actuarial increase may not be provided to reflect the fact that increases were not provided in the interim years;
3. To the extent of the reduction in the amount of the employee's payments to provide for a survivor benefit, but only if there is no longer a survivor benefit because the beneficiary whose life was being used to determine the period certain described in Code Section 401(a)(9)(A)(ii) over which payments were being made dies or is no longer the participant's beneficiary pursuant to a QDRO within the meaning of Code Section 414(p);
4. To pay increased benefits that result from a plan amendment;
5. To allow a beneficiary to convert the survivor portion of a joint and survivor annuity into a single-sum distribution upon the participant's death; or
6. To the extent increased are permitted in accordance with Treasury Regulations Section 1.401(a)(9)-6, Q&A-14(c) or (d), described below.

[Treas. Reg. § 1.401(a)(9)-6, Q&A-14(a)(1)–(6)]

Note, however, that on July 9, 2015, the IRS issued Notice 2015-49, 2015-30 I.R.B. 79, informing taxpayers of its intent to amend the RMD regulations (specifically, Treasury Regulation § 1.401(a)(9)-6, Q&A-14(a)(4), reflected in 4., above) to address the use of lump-sum payments to replace annuity payments being paid by qualified defined benefit pension plans. The amended RMD regulations would provide that qualified defined benefit plans generally would not be permitted to replace any joint and survivor, single life, or other annuity currently being paid with a lump-sum payment or other accelerated form of distribution. The IRS intends that the amended RMD regulations would apply as of

July 9, 2015, except with respect to certain accelerations of annuity payments described in Section IV of Notice 2015-49. Notice 2015-49 effectively reversed a series of Private Letter Rulings, generally known as the "Ford/GM rulings," in which the IRS ruled that a defined benefit plan could be amended, by a so-called "de-risking" amendment, to permit a participant in pay status to elect, during a temporary "window period," to commute the remaining value of his or her annuity payments from the plan to a lump-sum payment.

Eligible Cost-of-Living Index. An eligible cost-of-living index is:

1. A consumer price index that is based on prices of all items (or all items excluding food and energy) and issued by the Bureau of Labor Statistics, including an index for a specific population (such as urban consumers or urban wage earners and clerical workers) and an index for a geographical area or areas (such as a given metropolitan area or state)
2. A percentage adjustment based on a cost-of-living index described in (1) above, or a fixed percentage if less. In any year when the cost-of-living index is lower than the fixed percentage, the fixed percentage may be treated as an increase in an eligible cost-of-living index, provided it does not exceed the sum of:
   a. The cost-of-living index for that year; and
   b. The accumulated excess of the annual cost-of-living index from each prior year over the fixed annual percentage used in that year (reduced by any previously utilized amount).
3. A percentage adjustment based on the increase in compensation for the position held by the participant at the time of retirement, and provided under either the terms of a governmental plan within the meaning of Code Section 414(d) or under the terms of a nongovernmental plan as in effect on April 17, 2002.

[Treas. Reg. § 1.401(a)(9)-6, Q&A-14(b)]

Additional Permitted Increases for Annuity Payments Under Annuity Contract Purchased from Insurance Companies. In the case of annuity payments paid from an annuity contract purchased from an insurance company, if the total future expected payments exceed the total value being annuitized, the payments under the annuity will not fail to satisfy the nonincreasing payment requirement of Treasury Regulations Section 1.401(a)(9)-6, Q&A-1(a) merely because the payments are increased in accordance with one or more of the following:

1. By a constant percentage applied not less frequently than annually;
2. To provide a final payment upon the death of the participant that does not exceed the excess of the total value being annuitized over the total of payments before the death of the participant;
3. As a result of divided payments or other payments that result from actuarial gains, but only if actuarial gain is measured no less frequently than annually and the resulting dividend payments or other payments are either paid no later than the year following the year for which the

actuarial experience is measured or paid in the same form as the payment of the annuity over the remaining period of the annuity (beginning no later than the year following the year for which the actuarial experience is measured); and

4. An acceleration of payments under the annuity.

[Treas. Reg. § 1.401(a)(9)-6, Q&A-14(c)]

Additional Permitted Increases for Annuity Payments from a Qualified Trust. In the case of annuity payments paid under a defined benefit plan qualified under Code Section 401(a) (other than annuity payments under an annuity contract purchased from an insurance company that satisfy Treasury Regulations Section 1.401(a)(9)-6, Q&A-14(c)), the payments under the annuity will not fail to satisfy the nonincreasing payment requirement of Treasury Regulations Section 1.401(a)(9)-6, Q&A-1(a) merely because the payments are increased in accordance with one of the following:

1. By a constant percentage, applied not less frequently than annually, at a rate that is less than 5 percent per year;
2. To provide a final payment upon the death of the participant that does not exceed the excess of the actuarial present value of the participant's accrued benefit (within the meaning of Code Section 411(a)(7)) calculated as of the annuity starting date using the applicable interest rate and the applicable mortality table under Code Section 417(e) (or, if greater, the total amount of employee contributions) over the total of payments before the death of the participant; or
3. As a result of dividend payments or other payments that result from actuarial gains, as defined below, but only if:
    a. Actuarial gain is measured no less frequently than annually;
    b. The resulting dividend payments or other payments are either paid no later than the year following the year for which the actuarial experience is measured or paid in the same form as the payment of the annuity over the remaining period of the annuity (beginning no later than the year following the year for which the actuarial experience is measured);
    c. The actuarial gain taken into account is limited to actuarial gain from investment experience;
    d. The assumed interest used to calculate such actuarial gains is not less than 3 percent; and
    e. The payments are not increasing by a constant percentage, as described in Treasury Regulations Section 1.401(a)(9)-6, Q&A-14(d)(1).

[Treas. Reg. § 1.401(a)(9)-6, Q&A-14(d)]

Definitions. For purposes of the rules described in this question, the following definitions apply:

1. *Total value being annuitized* means:
   [Treas. Reg. § 1.401(a)(9)-6, Q&A-14(e)(1)]
   a. In the case of annuity payments under a Code Section 403(a) annuity plan or under a deferred annuity purchased by a Code Section 401(a) trust, the value of the participant's entire interest being annuitized (valued as of the date annuity payments commence);
   b. In the case of annuity payments under an immediate annuity contract purchased by a trust for a defined benefit plan qualified under Code Section 401(a), the amount of the premiums used to purchase the contract; and
   c. In the case of a defined contribution plan, the value of the participant's account balance used to purchase an immediate annuity under the contract.
2. *Actuarial gain* means the difference between an amount determined using the actuarial assumptions (i.e., investment return, mortality, expense, and other similar assumptions) used to calculate the initial payments before adjustment for any increases and the amount determined under the actual experience with respect to those factors. Actuarial gain also includes differences between the amount determined using actuarial assumptions when an annuity as purchased or commenced and such amount determined using actuarial assumptions used in calculating payments at the time the actuarial gain is determined. [Treas. Reg. § 1.401(a)(9)-6, Q&A-14(e)(2)]
3. *Total future expected payments* mean that total future payments expected to be made under the annuity contract as of the date of the determination, calculated using the Single Life Table in Treasury Regulations Section 1.401(a)(9)-9, Q&A-1 (or, if applicable, the Joint and Last Survivor Table in Treasury Regulations Section 1.401(a)(9)-9, Q&A-3) for annuitants who are still alive, without regard to any increases in annuity payments after the date of determination, and taking into account any remaining period certain. [Treas. Reg. § 1.401(a)(9)-6, Q&A-14(e)(3)]
4. *Acceleration of payments* means a shortening of the payment period with respect to an annuity or a full or partial commutation of the future annuity payments. An increase in the payment amount will be treated as an acceleration of payments in the annuity only if the total future expected payments under the annuity (including the amount of any payment made as a result of the acceleration) is decreased as a result of the change in the payment period. [Treas. Reg. § 1.401(a)(9)-6, Q&A-14(e)]

Examples. The rules of Treasury Regulations Section 1.401(a)(9)-6, Q&A-14(c) are illustrated by the following examples.

Example 4-10: *Variable Annuity*. Doc, a retired participant in the Monterey Corporation Defined Contribution Plan, attains age 70 on March 5, 2019, and, thus, attains age 70½ in 2019. Doc elects to purchase an annuity contract from the Salinas Valley Insurance Company in 2019. The contract is a single life annuity contract with a 10-year period certain. The contract provides for an initial annual payment calculated with an assumed interest rate (AIR) of 3 percent. Subsequent payments are determined by multiplying the prior year's payment by a fraction, the numerator of which is 1 plus the actual return on the separate account assets underlying the contract since the preceding payment and the denominator of which is 1 plus the AIR during that period. The value of Doc's account balance in the plan at the time of purchase is $105,000, and the purchase price of the contract is $105,000. The contract provides Doc with an initial payment of $7,200 at the time of purchase in 2019. The total future expected payments to Doc under the contract are $122,400, calculated as the initial payment of $7,200 multiplied by the age 70 life expectancy of 17 provided in the Single Life Table of Treasury Regulations Section 1.401(a)(9)-9, Q&A-1. Because the total future expected payments on the purchase date exceed the total value used to purchase the contract and payments may increase only as a result of actuarial gain, with such increases, beginning no later than the next year, paid in the same form as the payment of the annuity over the remaining period of the annuity, distributions received by Doc from the contract meet applicable requirements. [Treas. Reg. § 1.401(a)(9)-6, Q&A-14(f), Ex. 1]

Example 4-11: *Participating Annuity.* Frank, a retired participant in the Pastures of Heaven Defined Contribution Plan, attains age 70 on May 1, 2019, and, thus, attains age 70½ in 2018. Frank elects to purchase an annuity contract from the Salinas Valley Insurance Company in 2019. The contract is a participating single life annuity contract with a 10-year period certain. The contract provides for level annual payments with dividends paid in a lump sum in the year after the year for which the actuarial experience is measured or paid out levelly beginning in the year after the year for which the actuarial gain is measured over the remaining lifetime and period certain, that is, the period certain ends at the same time as the original period certain. Dividends are determined annually by the Board of Directors of the Insurance Company based upon a comparison of actual actuarial experience to expected actuarial experience in the past year. The value of Frank's account balance in the Plan at the time of purchase is $265,000, and the purchase price of the contract is $265,000. The contract provides Frank with an initial payment of $16,000 in 2019. The total future expected payments to Frank under the contract are calculated as the annual initial payment of $16,000 multiplied by the age 70 life expectancy of 17 provided in the Single Life Table of Treasury Regulations Section 1.401(a)(9)-6, Q&A-1 for a total of $272,000. Because the total future expected payments on the purchase date exceeds the account value used to purchase the contract and payments may increase only as a result of actuarial gain, with such increases, beginning no later than the next year, paid in the same form as the payment of the annuity over the remaining period of the annuity, distributions received by Frank from the contract meet applicable requirements. [Treas. Reg. § 1.401(a)(9)-6, Q&A-14(f), Ex. 2]

Example 4-12: *Participating Annuity with Dividend Accumulation.* The facts are the same as in Example 4-11 except that the annuity provides a dividend accumulation option under which Frank may defer receipt of the dividends to a time selected by him. Because the dividend accumulation option permits dividends to be paid later than the end of the year following the year for which the actuarial experience is measured or as a stream of payments that increase only as a result of actuarial gain, with such increases beginning no later than the next year, paid in the same form as the payment of the annuity over the remaining period of the annuity in Example 4-11, the dividend accumulation option does not meet applicable requirements. Neither does the dividend accumulation option fit within any of the other permissible increases. Accordingly, the dividend accumulation option causes the contract, and consequently any distributions from the contract, to fail to meet the requirements of Treasury Regulation Section 1.401(a)(9)-6, Q&A-14 and thus fail to satisfy the minimum distribution requirements of Code Section 401(a)(9). [Treas. Reg. § 1.401(a)(9)-6, Q&A-14(f), Ex. 3]

Example 4-13: *Participating Annuity with Dividends Used to Purchase Additional Death Benefits*. The facts are the same as in Example 4-11 except that the annuity provides an option under which actuarial gain under the contract is used to provide additional death benefit protection for Frank. Because this option permits payments as a result of actuarial gain to be paid later than the end of the year following the year for which the actuarial experience is measured or as a stream of payments that increase only as a result of actuarial gain, with such increases beginning no later than the next year, paid in the same form as the payment of the annuity over the remaining period of the annuity in Example 4-11, the option does not meet the requirements of Treasury Regulations Section 1.401(a)(9)-6, Q&A-14(c)(3). Neither does the option fit within any of the other permissible increases described in Treasury Regulations Section 1.401(a)(9)-6, Q&A-14(c). Accordingly, the addition of the option causes the contract, and consequently any distributions from the contract, to fail to meet the requirements of Treasury Regulations Section 1.401(a)(9)-6, Q&A-14 and thus fail to satisfy the minimum distribution requirements of Code Section 401(a)(9). [Treas. Reg. § 1.401(a)(9)-6, Q&A-14(f), Ex. 4]

Example 4-14: *Annuity with a Fixed Percentage Increase*. Raymond Banks, a retired participant in the Wide River Defined Contribution Plan, attains age 70½ in 2019. Raymond elects to purchase an annuity contract from the Salinas Valley Insurance Company. The contract is a single life annuity contract with a 20-year period certain (which does not exceed the maximum permitted period certain) with fixed annual payments increasing 3 percent each year. The value of Raymond's account balance in the Plan at the time of purchase is $110,000, and the purchase price of the contract is $110,000. The contract provides Raymond with an initial payment of $6,000 at the time of purchase in 2019. The total future expected payments to Raymond under the contract are $120,000, calculated as the initial annual payment of $6,000 multiplied by the period certain of 20 years. Because the total future expected payments on the purchase date exceed the account value used to purchase the contract and payments increase only as a constant percentage applied not less frequently than annually, distributions received by

Raymond from the Salinas Valley contract meet the requirements of Treasury Regulations Section 1.401(a)(9)-6, Q&A-14. [Treas. Reg. § 1.401(a)(9)-6, Q&A-14(f), Ex. 5]

Example 4-15: *Annuity with Excessive Increases.* The facts are the same as in Example 4-14 except that the initial payment is $5,400 and the annual rate of increase is 4 percent. In this example, the total future expected payments are $108,000, calculated as the initial payment of $5,400 multiplied by the period certain of 20 years. Because the total future expected payments are less than the account value of $110,000 used to purchase the contract, distributions received by Raymond do not meet the requirements of Treasury Regulations Section 1.401(a)(9)-6, Q&A-14, and thus fail to meet the minimum distribution requirements of Code Section 401(a)(9). [Treas. Reg. § 1.401(a)(9)-6, Q&A-14(f), Ex. 6]

Example 4-16: *Annuity with Full Commutation Feature.* Doc, a retired participant in the Palace Flophouse Defined Contribution Plan, attains age 78 in 2019. Doc elects to purchase a contract from the Salinas Valley Insurance Company. The contract provides for a single life annuity with a 10-year period certain (which does not exceed the maximum permitted period certain) with annual payments. The contract provides that Doc may cancel the contract at any time before he attains age 84 and receive, on his next payment due date, a final payment in an amount determined by multiplying the initial payment amount by a factor obtained from a Table in the contract using Doc's age as of his birthday in the calendar year of the final payment. The value of Doc's account balance in the Plan at the time of the purchase is $450,000, and the purchase price of the contract is $450,000. The contract provides Doc with an initial payment in 2019 of $40,000. The factors in the Table in the contract are as follows:

Age at Final Payment	*Factor*
79	10.5
80	10.0
81	9.5
82	9.0
83	8.5
84	8.0

The total future expected payments to Doc under the contract are $456,000, calculated as the initial payment of $40,000 multiplied by the age 78 life expectancy of 11.4 provided in the Single Life Table of Treasury Regulations Section 1.401(a)(9)-9, Q&A-1. Because the total future expected payments on the purchase date exceed the total value being annuitized (i.e., the $450,000 used to purchase the contract), the permitted increases set forth in Treasury Regulations Section 1.401(a)(9)-6, Q&A-14(c) are available. Furthermore, because the factors in the Table above are less than the life expectancy of each of the ages in the Single Life Table in Treasury Regulations Section 1.401(a)(9)-6, Q&A-1, the final payment is always less than the total future expected payments. Thus, the final payment is an acceleration of payments within the meaning of Treasury Regulations Section 1.401(a)(9)-6, Q&A-14(c)(4).

As an illustration of the above, if Doc were to elect to cancel the contract on the day before he was to attain age 84, his contractual final payment would be $320,000. This amount is determined as $40,000 (the annual payment due under the contract) multiplied by 8.0 (the factor in the Table for the next payment due date, age 84). The total future expected payments under the contract at age 84 before the final payment is $324,000, calculated as the initial payment amount multiplied by 8.1, the age 84 life expectancy provided in the Single Life Table in Treasury Regulations Section 1.401(a)(9)-9, Q&A-1. Because $320,000 (the total future expected payments under the annuity contract, including the amount of the final payment) is less than $324,000 (the total future expected payments under the annuity contract, determined before the election), the final payment is an acceleration of payments within the meaning of Treasury Regulations Section 1.401(a)(9)-6, Q&A-14(c)(4). [Treas. Reg. § 1.401(a)(9)-6, Q&A-14(f), Ex. 7]

Example 4-17: *Annuity with Partial Commutation Feature.* The facts are the same as in Example 4-16 except that the annuity provides that Doc may request, at any time before he attains age 84, an ad hoc payment on his next payment due date with future payments reduced by an amount equal to the ad hoc payment divided by the factor obtained from the Table in Example 4-16 corresponding to Doc's age at the time of the ad hoc payment. Because, at each age, the factors in the Table are less than the corresponding life expectancies in the Single Life Table in Treasury Regulations Section 1.401(a)(9)-9, Q&A-1, total future expected payments under the contract will decrease after an ad hoc payment. Thus, ad hoc distributions received by Doc from the contract will satisfy the requirements under Treasury Regulations Section 1.401(a)(9)-6, Q&A-14(c)(4).

As an illustration, if Doc were to request, on the day before he was to attain age 84, an ad hoc payment of $100,000 on his next payment due date, his recalculated annual payment amount would be reduced to $27,500. This amount is determined as $40,000 (the amount of Doc's next annual payment) reduced by $12,500 (his $100,000 ad hoc payment divided by the Table factor at age 84 of 8.0). Thus, Doc's total future expected payments after the ad hoc payment (and including the ad hoc payment) are equal to $322,750 ($100,000 plus $27,500 multiplied by the Single Life Table value of 8.1). Note that this $322,750 amount is less than the amount of Doc's total future expected payments before the ad hoc payment ($324,000, determined as $40,000 multiplied by 8.1) and the requirements of Treasury Regulations Section 1.401(a)(9)-6, Q&A-14(c)(4) are satisfied. [Treas. Reg. § 1.401(a)(9)-6, Q&A-14(f), Ex. 8]

Example 4-18: *Annuity with Excessive Increases*. Doc, a retired participant in the Monterey Bay Defined Contribution Plan, attains age 70½ in 2019. Doc elects to purchase an annuity contract from the Biological Laboratory Insurance Company in 2019 with a premium of $1,000,000. The contract is a single life annuity contract with a 20-year period certain. The contract provides for an initial payment of $200,000, a second payment one year from the time of purchase of $40,000, and 18 succeeding annual payments each increasing at a constant percentage rate of 4.5 percent from the preceding payment.

The contract fails to meet the RMD requirements of Code Section 401(a)(9) because the total future expected payment without regard to any increases in the annuity payment, calculated as $200,000 in year one and $40,000 in each of years 2 through 20, is only $960,000 (i.e., an amount that does not exceed the total value used to purchase the annuity). [Treas. Reg. § 1.401(a)(9)-6, Q&A-14(f), Ex. 9]

Q 4:48 Are there special rules applicable to payments made under a defined benefit plan or annuity contract to a surviving child?

Yes. Under Code Section 401(a)(9)(F), payments under a defined benefit plan or annuity contract that are made to a participant's child until the child reaches the age of majority (or dies, if earlier) may be treated, for purposes of the RMD rules of Code Section 401(a)(9), as if such payments were made to the surviving spouse to the extent they become payable to the surviving spouse upon cessation of the payments to the child. For these purposes, a child may be treated as having not reached the age of majority if the child has not completed a specified course of education and is under the age of 26. In addition, a child who is disabled within the meaning of Code Section 72(m)(7) when he or she reaches the age of majority may be treated as having not reached the age of majority so long as the child continues to be disabled. Thus, when the payments described above become payable to the surviving spouse because the child attains the age of majority, recovers from a disabling illness, or completes a specified course of education, there is not an increase in benefits within the meaning of Treasury Regulations Section 1.401(a)(9)-6, Q&A-1. Likewise, the age of the child receiving such payments is not taken into consideration for purposes of the MDIB requirements. [Treas. Reg. § 1.401(a)(9)-6, Q&A-15]

Q 4:49 Will a governmental plan fail to satisfy the RMD rules if annuity payments under the plan do not satisfy Treasury Regulations Section 1.401(a)(9)-6?

No. On September 8, 2009, the IRS issued final regulations permitting governmental plans to comply with the RMD rules by using, in lieu of the IRS's RMD regulations, a reasonable and good-faith interpretation of the Code's RMD rules. [Treas. Reg. §§ 1.401(a)(9)-1, Q/A-2(d), 1.401(a)(9)-6, and 1.403(b)-6(e)(2) and (e)(8); 74 Fed. Reg. 172, pp. 45993–45994]

Q 4:50 What were the rules for determining RMDs for defined benefit plans and annuity contracts for calendar years 2003, 2004, and 2005?

A distribution from a defined benefit plan or annuity contract for calendar years 2003, 2004, and 2005 would not have failed to satisfy the RMD rules of Code Section 401(a)(9) merely because the payments did not satisfy Treasury Regulations Section 1.401(a)(9)-6, Q&A-1 through Q&A-15, provided the payments satisfied Code Section 401(a)(9) based on a reasonable and good-faith interpretation of that section. [Treas. Reg. § 1.401(a)(9)-6, Q&A-16]

Rollovers and Transfers

Q 4:51 If an amount is distributed by one plan and rolled over to another plan, is the RMD under the distributing plan affected by the rollover?

No. If an amount is distributed by one plan (distributing plan) and rolled over to another plan, the amount distributed is still treated as a distribution by the distributing plan for purposes of Code Section 401(a)(9), notwithstanding the rollover. [Treas. Reg. § 1.401(a)(9)-7, Q&A-1]

Q 4:52 If an amount is distributed by one plan and rolled over to another plan, how are the benefit and the RMD under the receiving plan affected?

If an amount is distributed by one plan (distributing plan) and rolled over to another plan (receiving plan), the participant's benefit under the receiving plan is increased by the amount rolled over for purposes of determining the RMD for the calendar year following the calendar year in which the amount rolled over is distributed. If the amount rolled over is received after the last valuation date in the calendar year under the receiving plan, the participant's benefit as of such valuation date, as adjusted, will be increased by the rollover amount valued as of the date of receipt. In addition, if the amount rolled over is received in a different calendar year from the calendar year in which it is distributed, the amount rolled over is deemed to have been received by the receiving plan in the calendar year in which it was distributed. [Treas. Reg. § 1.401(a)(9)-7, Q&A-2]

Q 4:53 What special rules apply for satisfying the RMD requirement or determining the participant's benefit under the transferor plan?

When there is a transfer of an amount of a participant's benefit from one plan (transferor plan) to another plan (transferee plan), the transfer is not treated as a distribution by the transferor plan for purposes of Code

Section 401(a)(9). Instead, the participant's benefit under the transferor plan is decreased by the amount transferred. However, if any portion of a participant's benefit is transferred in a distribution calendar year with respect to that participant, in order to satisfy Code Section 401(a)(9), the transferor plan must determine the amount of the participant's RMD for the calendar year of the transfer using the participant's benefit under the transferor plan before the transfer. Also, if any portion of a participant's benefit is transferred in the second distribution calendar year but on or before the participant's RBD, the transferor plan must determine the amount of the RMD for the participant's first distribution calendar year based on the participant's benefit under the transferor plan before the transfer.

The transferor plan may satisfy the minimum distribution requirement for the calendar year of the transfer (and the prior year if applicable) by segregating the amount that must be distributed from the participant's benefit and not transferring that amount. Such amount may be retained by the transferor plan and distributed on or before the date required under Code Section 401(a)(9). [Treas. Reg. § 1.401(a)(9)-7, Q&A-3(a)]

For purposes of determining any RMD for the calendar year immediately following the calendar year in which the transfer occurs, when the transfer occurs after the last valuation date for the calendar year of the transfer under the transferor plan, the participant's benefit as of such valuation date, as adjusted, will be decreased by the amount transferred, valued as of the date of the transfer. [Treas. Reg. § 1.401(a)(9)-7, Q&A-3(b)]

Q 4:54 If a participant's benefit is transferred from one plan to another plan, how are the benefit and the RMD under the transferee plan affected?

In the case of a transfer from one plan (transferor plan) to another (transferee plan), the participant's benefit under the transferee plan is increased by the amount transferred in the same manner as if it were a plan receiving a rollover contribution under Treasury Regulations Section 1.401(a)(9)-7, Q&A-2 (see Q 4:47). [Treas. Reg. § 1.401(a)(9)-7, Q&A-4]

Q 4:55 How is a spinoff, merger, or consolidation treated for purposes of determining a participant's benefit and RMD?

For purposes of determining a participant's benefit and RMD under Code Section 401(a)(9), a spinoff, a merger, or a consolidation (as defined in Treasury Regulations Section 1.414(l)-1) will be treated as a transfer of the benefits of the employees involved. Consequently, the benefit and RMD of each participant involved under the transferor and transferee plans will be determined in accordance with the rules of Treasury Regulations Section 1.401(a)(9)-7, Q&A-3 and Q&A-4 (see Qs 4:48, 4:49). [Treas. Reg. § 1.401(a)(9)-7, Q&A-5]

Special Rules

Q 4:56 What distribution rules apply if an individual is a participant in more than one plan?

If an individual is a participant in more than one plan, those plans are not permitted to be aggregated for purposes of testing whether the minimum distribution requirements of Code Section 401(a)(9) are met. The distribution of the participant's benefit under *each* plan must separately meet the requirements of Code Section 401(a)(9). For this purpose, a plan described in Code Section 414(k) is treated as two separate plans—a defined contribution plan to the extent benefits are based on an individual account and a defined benefit plan with respect to the remaining benefits. [Treas. Reg. § 1.401(a)(9)-8, Q&A-1]

Q 4:57 If a participant's benefit under a defined contribution plan is divided into separate accounts (or segregated shares in the case of a defined benefit plan), do the distribution rules of Code Section 401(a)(9) apply separately to each separate account (or segregated share)?

In general, if a participant's account under a defined contribution plan is divided into separate accounts (or into segregated shares in the case of a defined benefit plan) under the plan, the separate accounts (or segregated shares) will be aggregated for purposes of satisfying the rules of Code Section 401(a)(9). Thus, all separate accounts, including a separate account for nondeductible employee contributions (under Code Section 72(d)(2)), will be aggregated for purposes of Code Section 401(a)(9). [Treas. Reg. § 1.401(a)(9)-8, Q&A-2(a)(1)] However, there are a number of exceptions to this general rule. [Treas. Reg. § 1.401(a)(9)-8, Q&A-2(a)(2)]

Q 4:58 What are separate accounts for purposes of Code Section 401(a)(9)?

For purposes of Code Section 401(a)(9), separate accounts are separate portions of the participant's benefit for which separate accounting is maintained. Each portion reflects the separate interests of each beneficiary under the plan as of the date of the participant's death. The accounting must allocate all post-death investment gains and losses, contributions, and forfeitures, for the period before the establishment of the separate accounts on a pro rata basis in a reasonable and consistent manner. However, once the separate accounts are actually established, the accounting can provide for separate investments for each account under which gains and losses from the investment of the account are only allocated to that account, or investment gain or loss can continue to be allocated among the separate accounts on a pro rata basis. A separate accounting must allocate any post-death distribution to the separate account of the beneficiary receiving that distribution. [Treas. Reg. § 1.401(a)(9)-8, Q&A-3]

Q 4:59 Can required distributions be made even if a participant or spouse has not consented to a distribution?

Yes. Although it is true that Code Sections 411(a)(11) and 417(e) require participant and spousal consent to certain distributions of plan benefits while such benefits are immediately distributable, if a participant's normal retirement age is later than the RBD for the commencement of distributions under Code Section 401(a)(9) (and therefore benefits are still immediately distributable), the plan must distribute benefits to the participant (or, where applicable, to the spouse) in a manner that satisfies the requirements of Code Section 401(a)(9). Indeed, Code Section 401(a)(9) must be satisfied even though the participant (or spouse, where applicable) fails to consent to the distribution.

In such a case, the plan may distribute the benefits in the form of a QJSA or in the form of a qualified pre-retirement survivor annuity (QPSA), as applicable, and the consent requirements of Code Sections 411(a)(11) and 417 are deemed to be satisfied if the plan has made reasonable efforts to obtain consent from the participant (or spouse) and if the distribution otherwise meets the requirements of Code Section 417(e).

If, because of Code Section 401(a)(11)(B), the plan is not required to make distributions in the form of a QJSA to a participant or a QPSA to a surviving spouse, the plan may distribute the RMD at the time required to satisfy Code Section 401(a)(9), and the consent requirements of Code Sections 411(a)(11) and 417(e) are deemed to be satisfied if the plan has made reasonable efforts to obtain consent from the participant (or spouse) and if the distribution otherwise meets the requirements of Code Section 417. [Treas. Reg. § 1.401(a)(9)-8, Q&A-4]

Q 4:60 Who is considered to be a participant's spouse or surviving spouse?

For purposes of Code Section 401(a)(9), an individual is a spouse or surviving spouse of a participant if such individual is treated as the participant's spouse under applicable state law (except in the case of distributions of a portion of a participant's benefit payable to a former spouse pursuant to a QDRO). In the case of distributions after the death of a participant, for purposes of determining whether under the life expectancy rule [I.R.C. § 401(a)(9)(B)(iii) and (iv)], the provisions of Code Section 401(a)(9)(B)(iv) apply, the participant's spouse is determined as of the date of the participant's death. [Treas. Reg. § 1.401(a)(9)-8, Q&A-5]

Q 4:61 What special rules apply to the distribution of all or a portion of a participant's benefit payable to an alternate payee pursuant to a QDRO?

A former spouse to whom all or a portion of a participant's benefit is payable pursuant to a QDRO (as defined in Code Section 414(p)) will be treated as a spouse (including a surviving spouse) of the participant for purposes of Code

Section 401(a)(9), including the MDIB requirements, regardless of whether the QDRO specifically provides that the former spouse is treated as the spouse for purposes of Code Sections 401(a)(11) and 417. [Treas. Reg. § 1.401(a)(9)-8, Q&A-6(a)]

Further, if a QDRO provides that a participant's benefit is to be divided and a portion is to be allocated to an alternate payee, such portion will be treated as a separate account (or segregated share) that separately must satisfy the requirements of Code Section 401(a)(9) and may not be aggregated with other separate accounts (or segregated shares) of the participant for purposes of satisfying Code Section 401(a)(9). In general, distribution of such a separate account allocated to an alternate payee pursuant to a QDRO must be made in accordance with Code Section 401(a)(9). For example, in general, distribution of such an account will satisfy Code Section 401(a)(9)(A) if RMDs from such an account during the participant's lifetime begin not later than the participant's RBD and the RMD for each distribution calendar year is determined using an applicable distribution period based on the age of the participant or the surviving spouse.

The determination of whether distributions from such an account after the death of the participant to the alternate payee will be made in accordance with Code Section 401(a)(9)(B)(i) or Code Section 401(a)(9)(B)(ii) or (iii) and (iv) will depend on whether distributions have begun. For example, if the alternate payee dies before the participant and distribution of the separate account allocated to the alternate payee pursuant to the QDRO is to be made to the alternate payee's beneficiary, that beneficiary may be treated as a designated beneficiary for purposes of determining the minimum distribution required. [Treas. Reg. § 1.401(a)(9)-8, Q&A-6(b)(1)]

Distribution of the separate account allocated to an alternate payee pursuant to a QDRO satisfies the requirements of Code Section 401(a)(9)(A)(ii) if the account is to be distributed, beginning not later than the participant's RBD, over the life of the alternate payee (or over a period not extending beyond the life expectancy of the alternate payee). Also, if the plan permits the participant to elect whether distribution upon his or her death will be made in accordance with the five-year rule in Code Section 401(a)(9)(B)(ii) or the life expectancy rule in Code Section 401(a)(9)(B)(iii) and (iv), the election may be made only by the alternate payee for purposes of distributing the separate account allocated to the alternate payee pursuant to the QDRO. If the alternate payee dies after distribution of the separate account allocated to the alternate payee pursuant to a QDRO has begun but before the participant dies, the distribution of the remaining portion of that portion of the benefit allocated to the alternate payee must be made in accordance with the rules for distributions during the life of the participant. Only after the death of the participant is the amount of the RMD determined in accordance with the rules of Code Section 401(a)(9)(B). [Treas. Reg. § 1.401(a)(9)-8, Q&A-6(b)(2)]

If a QDRO does not provide that a participant's benefit is to be divided but provides that a portion of a participant's benefit (otherwise payable to the participant) is to be paid to an alternate payee, that portion will not be treated as a separate account (or segregated share) of the participant. Instead, that portion will be aggregated with any amount distributed to the participant and will be treated as having been distributed to the employee for purposes of determining whether the minimum distribution requirement has been satisfied with respect to that participant. [Treas. Reg. § 1.401(a)(9)-8, Q&A-6(c)]

Q 4:62 Will a plan fail to satisfy Code Section 401(a)(9) merely because it fails to distribute an amount otherwise required to be distributed during the period in which the issue of whether a domestic relations order is a QDRO is being determined?

No. A plan will not fail to satisfy Code Section 401(a)(9) merely because it fails to distribute a required amount during the period in which the issue of whether a domestic relations order is a QDRO is being determined pursuant to Code Section 414(p)(7), provided that the period does not extend beyond the 18-month period described in Code Section 414(p)(7)(E). To the extent that a distribution otherwise required under Code Section 401(a)(9) is not made during this period, any segregated amounts (as defined in Code Section 414(p)(7)(A)) will be treated as though they are not vested during the period and any distributions with respect to such amounts must be made under the relevant rules for nonvested benefits under Treasury Regulations Section 1.401(a)(9)-5, Q&A-8 or 1.401(a)(9)-6, Q&A-6, as applicable. [Treas. Reg. § 1.401(a)(9)-8, Q&A-7]

Q 4:63 Will a plan fail to satisfy the Code if an individual's distribution is less than the amount otherwise required because distributions are being paid under an annuity contract issued by a life insurance company in state insurer delinquency proceedings and have been reduced or suspended because of those proceedings?

No. A plan will not fail to satisfy Code Section 401(a)(9) merely because an individual's distribution from the plan is less than the amount otherwise required to satisfy Code Section 401(a)(9) because distributions are being paid under an annuity contract issued by a life insurance company in state insurer delinquency proceedings and have been reduced or suspended by reasons of those state proceedings. To the extent that a distribution otherwise required under Code Section 401(a)(9) is not made during the state insurer delinquency proceedings, that amount and any additional amount accrued during that period will be treated as though it is not vested during the period, and any distributions with respect to such amounts must be made under the relevant rules for nonvested benefits under Treasury Regulations Section 1.401(a)(9)-5, Q&A-8 or 1.401(a)(9)-6, Q&A-6, as applicable. [Treas. Reg. § 1.401(a)(9)-8, Q&A-8]

Q 4:64 Will a plan fail to qualify as a pension plan solely because it permits distributions to begin on or after April 1 of the calendar year following the calendar year in which the participant attains age 70½ even though the participant has not retired or attained the normal retirement age under the plan as of that date?

No. A plan will not fail to qualify as a pension plan within the meaning of Code Section 401(a) solely because it permits distributions to begin on or after April 1 of the calendar year following the calendar year in which the participant attains age 70½ even though the employee has not retired or attained the normal retirement age under the plan as of that date. This rule applies whether or not the participant is a 5 percent owner with respect to the year ending in the calendar year in which distributions commence. [Treas. Reg. § 1.401(a)(9)-8, Q&A-9]

Q 4:65 Is the distribution of an annuity contract a distribution for purposes of Code Section 401(a)(9)?

No. The distribution of an annuity contract is not a distribution for purposes of Code Section 401(a)(9). [Treas. Reg. § 1.401(a)(9)-8, Q&A-10]

Q 4:66 Will a payment by a plan after the participant's death fail to be treated as a distribution because it is made to an estate or a trust?

No. A payment by a plan after the participant's death will not fail to be treated as a distribution for purposes of Code Section 401(a)(9) solely because it is made to an estate or a trust. As a result, the estate or trust that receives a payment from a plan after the participant's death need not distribute the amount of such payment to the beneficiaries of the estate or trust in accordance with Code Section 401(a)(9)(B). However, distributions to the estate must satisfy the five-year rule in Code Section 401(a)(9)(B)(iii) if distributions to the participant had not begun as of the participant's date of death. Further, an estate may not be a designated beneficiary. [Treas. Reg. § 1.401(a)(9)-8, Q&A-11]

Q 4:67 Will a plan fail to satisfy the Code if it is amended to eliminate benefit options that do not satisfy Code Section 401(a)(9)?

No. Pursuant to Code Section 411(d)(6)(B), a plan will not fail to satisfy Code Section 411(d)(6) merely because the plan is amended to eliminate the availability of an optional form of benefit to the extent that the optional form does not satisfy Code Section 401(a)(9). A plan must provide that, notwithstanding any other plan provision, it will not distribute benefits under any option that does not satisfy Code Section 401(a)(9). [Treas. Reg. § 1.401(a)(9)-8, Q&A-12]

Q 4:68 Will a plan be disqualified merely because it pays benefits under a designation made before January 1, 1984, in accordance with TEFRA Section 242(b)(2)?

No. Even though the distribution requirements added by TEFRA were retroactively repealed by the Tax Reform Act of 1984 (TRA '84), the transitional election rule in TEFRA Section 242(b) was preserved. Satisfaction of the spousal consent requirements of Code Section 417(a) and (e) (added by the Retirement Equity Act of 1984) will not be considered a revocation of the pre-1984 designation. Nevertheless, Code Sections 401(a)(11) and 417 must be satisfied with respect to any distribution subject to those sections. [Treas. Reg. § 1.401(a)(9)-8, Q&A-13]

Q 4:69 When an amount is transferred from one plan to another plan, may the transferee plan distribute the amount transferred in accordance with a TEFRA Section 242(b)(2) election made under either plan?

When an amount is transferred from one plan (transferor plan) to another plan (transferee plan), the amount transferred may be distributed in accordance with a TEFRA Section 242(b)(2) election made under the transferor plan if the participant did not elect to have the amount transferred and if the amount transferred is separately accounted for by the transferee plan. However, only the benefit attributable to the amount transferred, plus earnings thereon, may be distributed in accordance with the TEFRA Section 242(b)(2) election made under the transferor plan. If the participant elected to have the amount transferred, the transfer will be treated as a distribution and rollover of the amount transferred. [Treas. Reg. § 1.401(a)(9)-8, Q&A-14(a)]

On the other hand, when an amount is transferred from one plan to another plan, the amount transferred may not be distributed in accordance with a TEFRA Section 242(b)(2) election made under the transferee plan. If a TEFRA Section 242(b)(2) election was made under the transferee plan, the amount transferred must be separately accounted for. If the amount transferred is not separately accounted for under the transferee plan, the TEFRA Section 242(b)(2) election under the transferee plan is revoked and Code Section 401(a)(9) will apply to subsequent distributions by the transferee plan. [Treas. Reg. § 1.401(a)(9)-8, Q&A-14(b)]

A merger, spinoff, or consolidation, as defined in Treasury Regulations Section 1.414(l)-1(b), will be treated as a transfer for purposes of the TEFRA Section 242(b)(2) election. [Treas. Reg. § 1.401(a)(9)-8, Q&A-14(c)]

Q 4:70 If an amount is distributed by one plan and rolled over into another plan, may the receiving plan distribute the amount rolled over in accordance with a TEFRA Section 242(b)(2) election?

No. If an amount is distributed by one plan (distributing plan) and rolled over into another plan (receiving plan), the receiving plan must distribute the amount rolled over in accordance with Code Section 401(a)(9) whether or not the participant made a TEFRA Section 242(b)(2) election under the distributing plan. Further, if the amount rolled over was not distributed in accordance with the election, the election under the distributing plan is revoked and Code Section 401(a)(9) will apply to all subsequent distributions by the distributing plan. Also, if the participant made a TEFRA Section 242(b)(2) election under the receiving plan and that election is still in effect, the amount rolled over must be separately accounted for under the receiving plan and distributed in accordance with Code Section 401(a)(9). If amounts rolled over are not separately accounted for, any TEFRA Section 242(b)(2) election under the receiving plan is revoked and Code Section 401(a)(9) will apply to subsequent distributions by the receiving plan. [Treas. Reg. § 1.401(a)(9)-8, Q&A-15]

Q 4:71 May a TEFRA Section 242(b)(2) election be revoked after the date by which distributions are required to begin?

Yes. A TEFRA Section 242(b)(2) election may be revoked after the date by which distributions are required to begin in order to satisfy Code Section 401(a)(9). However, if the TEFRA Section 242(b)(2) election is revoked after that date and the total amount of the distributions that would have been required to be made before the date of the revocation in order to satisfy Code Section 401(a)(9), but for the TEFRA Section 242(b)(2) election, have not been made, the plan must distribute, by the end of the calendar year following the calendar year in which the revocation occurs, the total amount not yet distributed that was required to have been distributed and continue distributions in accordance with the requirements of Code Section 401(a)(9). [Treas. Reg. § 1.401(a)(9)-8, Q&A-16]

IRS Field Directive to Employee Plans (EP) Examiners

Q 4:72 Has the IRS issued a field directive to EP examinations employees directing them not to challenge a qualified plan as failing to satisfy RMD standards if the plan has taken all of the steps listed in the field directive to pay RMDs to missing participants and beneficiaries?

Yes. On October 19, 2017, the IRS issued a memorandum (a "field directive") to its EP examinations employees directing them not to challenge a Code Section 401(a) qualified plan for violating the RMD standards for the plan's failure to make or commence an RMD to a missing participant or beneficiary to whom an RMD is due, provided the plan has taken all of the search steps set forth in the memorandum, specifically:

1. The plan has searched plan and related plan, sponsor and publicly available records or directories for alternative contact information;
2. The plan has used any of the following search methods:
   a. A commercial locator service;
   b. A credit reporting agency; or
   c. A proprietary Internet search toll for locating individuals.
3. The plan has attempted contact via United States Postal Service (USPS) certified mail to the last known mailing address and through appropriate means for any address or contact information (including email addresses and telephone numbers).

If a plan has not completed the above steps, IRS EP examiners may challenge a Code Section 401(a) qualified plan for violation of the RMD standards for the failure to make or commence a distribution to a missing participant or beneficiary to whom an RMD is due. The IRS field directive applies to examinations open on and after the date of issuance (Oct. 19, 2017), and its guidance will be incorporated into Internal Revenue Manual (IRM) 4.71.1 by October 19, 2019.

Chapter 5

Corrective Distributions

This chapter explains and illustrates the rules permitting the distribution from qualified plans of: (1) excess contributions to correct failures of the actual deferral percentage (ADP) test under Code Section 401(k); (2) excess aggregate contributions to correct failures of the actual contribution percentage (ACP) test under Code Section 401(m); (3) excess elective contributions to correct violations of the annual limitation on elective contributions under Code Section 402(g); and (4) excess annual additions to correct violations of the limitation on annual additions under Code Section 415(c).

Excess Contributions 5-1
Excess Aggregate Contributions 5-9
Excess Elective Contributions 5-16
Excess Annual Additions 5-24

Excess Contributions

Q 5:1 What are excess contributions?

Excess contributions are elective contributions (including designated Roth contributions), qualified nonelective contributions (QNECs), and qualified matching contributions (QMACs) that are treated as elective contributions, on behalf of eligible highly compensated employees (HCEs) that exceed the amount of contributions permitted for the plan year to satisfy the ADP test. [I.R.C. § 401(k)(8)(B); Treas. Reg. § 1.401(k)-2(b)(2)(ii)(A)] (See Appendix G for information on the determination of HCEs.)

Q 5:2 What are the permissible methods for correcting excess contributions?

Excess contributions (see Q 5:1) may be corrected by one of the following methods:

1. Contributing sufficient amounts of QNECs or QMACs (that are treated as elective contributions) for non-highly compensated employees (NHCEs) to satisfy the ADP test;
2. Recharacterizing the excess contributions as employee after-tax contributions;
3. Returning excess contributions plus earnings to HCEs by use of corrective distributions; or
4. Any combination of items (1), (2), or (3).

[Treas. Reg. § 1.401(k)-2(b)(1)(i)]

Q 5:3 How may a combination of the permissible correction methods be employed?

A 401(k) plan may use any of the correction methods described in Q 5:2. If use of a combination of these methods is desired to correct excess contributions, each applicable method would be used for a portion of the excess contribution. For example, a portion of the excess contributions for an HCE may be recharacterized as an employee after-tax contribution, and the remaining portion of the excess contribution may be distributed to the HCE in a corrective distribution. A plan may permit an HCE to elect whether any excess contributions are to be recharacterized or distributed. A plan may also permit an HCE to choose a split of pre-tax and designated Roth elective contributions that make up any necessary distribution. [Treas. Reg. § 1.401(k)-2(b)(1)(ii)]

Alternatively, a plan may proactively limit elective contributions throughout the plan year in a manner designed to prevent excess contributions.

Q 5:4 What correction methods are not permitted?

Excess contributions for a plan year may neither remain unallocated nor be allocated to a suspense account for allocation to one or more employees in any future plan year. Excess contributions may not be corrected retroactively under the correction rules of Treasury Regulations Section 1.401(a)(4)-11(g). [Treas. Reg. § 1.401(k)-2(b)(1)(iii)]

Q 5:5 What happens if excess distributions are not fully corrected?

Any distribution of less than the entire amount of excess contributions with respect to any HCE is treated as a pro rata distribution of excess contributions and allocable gain or loss. [Treas. Reg. § 1.401(k)-2(b)(2)(vii)(D)]

Q 5:6 How are total excess contributions determined for a plan year?

The total excess contribution for an HCE is the amount that must be returned to an HCE that would result in the revised ADP equaling the highest permitted ADP under the plan.

The steps to determine the total excess contributions to be returned to the applicable HCEs are:

1. *Calculate the dollar amount of excess contributions for each HCE.* The amount of excess contributions attributable to a given HCE for a plan year is the amount (if any) by which the HCE's contributions taken into account must be reduced for the HCE's actual deferral ratio (ADR) to equal the highest permitted ADR under the plan. To calculate the highest permitted ADR under a plan, the ADR of the HCE with the highest ADR is reduced by the amount required to cause that HCE's ADR to equal the ADR of the HCE with the next highest ADR. The process is repeated until the remainder ADRs achieve the highest permitted ADP for the plan year. If a lesser reduction would enable the plan to pass the ADP test at any point in this repetition, only this lesser reduction is used, and the process ceases.
2. *Determine the amount of total excess contributions.* The sum of all reductions for all HCEs determined in Step 1 is the amount of total excess contributions for the plan year.
3. *Satisfaction of ADP.* A cash or deferred arrangement satisfies the ADP test if the ADR for each HCE were determined after the reductions described in item 1 above.

[Treas. Reg. § 1.401(k)-2(b)(2)(ii)]

Example 5-1: ABC Widgets sponsors a 401(k) plan for its employees. For the plan year ended December 31, 2017, the following elective contributions were made. The table below shows the HCEs and NHCEs, their testing compensation, their elective contributions, their ADRs, and the ADP of the HCE and NHCE groups:

Employee	*Status*	*Testing Compensation*	*Elective Contributions*	*ADR*	*ADP*
A	HCE	$275,000	$18,500	6.73%	
B	HCE	$230,000	$18,500	8.04%	
C	HCE	$125,000	$16,000	12.80%	9.19%
D	NHCE	$80,000	$4,000	5.00%	
E	NHCE	$50,000	$5,000	10.00%	
F	NHCE	$30,000	$1,500	5.00%	
G	NHCE	$20,000	$0	0.00%	5.00%

The ADP of the HCE group (9.19 percent) exceeds 7 percent, which reflects the maximum allowable spread of 2 percent over the ADP of the NHCE group (5 percent). Using the leveling process, HCE C (the HCE with the largest ADR) must be reduced first to the level of the HCE with the next highest ADR, HCE B. HCE C's ADR is reduced to 8.04 percent. The results of the first step in the leveling process are shown below. The HCE ADP still exceeds the allowable 7 percent.

Employee	*Status*	*Testing Compensation*	*Elective Contribution*	*ADR*	*ADP*
A	HCE	$275,000	$18,500	6.73%	
B	HCE	$230,000	$18,500	8.04%	
C	HCE	$125,000	$10,050	8.04%	7.60%
D	NHCE	$80,000	$4,000	5.00%	
E	NHCE	$50,000	$5,000	10.00%	
F	NHCE	$30,000	$1,500	5.00%	
G	NHCE	$20,000	0	0.00%	5.00%

The leveling process then continues by reducing HCEs B and C to the point at which the ADP test is passed; that is, the ADP for HCEs is 7 percent. To accomplish this, the ADRs for HCEs B and C are both reduced to 7.13 percent. Note that HCE A's ADR needs no reduction because their ADR of 6.73 percent is less than the 7.13 percent for HCEs B and C.

Employee	*Status*	*Testing Compensation*	*Elective Contribution*	*ADR*	*ADP*
A	HCE	$275,000	$18,500	6.73%	
B	HCE	$230,000	$16,399	7.13%	
C	HCE	$125,000	$8,913	7.13%	7.00%
D	NHCE	$80,000	$4,000	5.00%	
E	NHCE	$50,000	$5,000	10.00%	
F	NHCE	$30,000	$1,500	5.00%	
G	NHCE	$20,000	0	0.00%	5.00%

The amounts of the excess contributions are shown below:

HCE	*Original Total Elective Contributions*	*Maximum Elective Contributions*	*Excess Elective Contributions*
A	$18,500	$18,500	$0
B	$18,500	$16,399	$2,101
C	$16,000	$8,913	$7,087
Totals	$53,000	$43,812	$9,188

Note that the excess contributions listed above are *not* the amounts to be returned to the corresponding HCEs. Rather, the total amount to be returned is $9,188 distributed as determined in Q 5:7 below.

Q 5:7 What excess contributions are returned to each HCE?

The total excess contributions are determined in the manner described in Q 5:6. In a leveling process similar to that demonstrated in Example 5-1 in Q 5:6, except that it is based on dollars rather than percentages, the HCE with the highest dollar elective contribution is reduced first. The amount of their reduction is that amount necessary to cause the remainder elective contribution to equal the next highest elective contribution deferred by an HCE. This process is repeated until the total excess contributions are fully allocated. [I.R.C. § 401(k)(8)(C); Treas. Reg. § 1.401(k)-2(b)(iii)]

Example 5-2: In Example 5-1 above, excess contributions of $9,188, adjusted by allocable gains or losses (which is assumed to be $0 in this example), must be returned to HCEs. The leveling process starts with HCEs A and B, the HCEs with the highest dollar elective contribution. The steps to follow are:

1. Reduce each of HCEs A and B from $18,500 to $16,000 (the elective contribution of the HCE with the next highest elective contribution).
2. Remaining excess contributions left to be refunded are now $4,188 ($9,188 − $2,500 − $2,500).
3. Reduce HCE A to $14,604, HCE B to $14,604, and HCE C to $14,604 (3 x $14,604 = $43,812).

Table of Refunds

HCE	*Amount of Corrective Distribution Refund*
A	$3,896
B	$3,896
C	$1,396
Total	$9,188

Q 5:8 Under what circumstances may excess contributions be recharacterized?

General Rule. Excess contributions may be recharacterized as after-tax contributions only if the excess contributions are treated as described below and all of the conditions set forth below are also satisfied. Excess contributions may be recharacterized only if the plan permits after-tax contributions.

Treatment of Recharacterized Excess Contributions. Recharacterized excess contributions are includible in the HCE's gross income on the earliest date that the HCE would have received any elective contribution made on his or her behalf during the plan year, had the HCE originally elected to receive their recharacterized excess contributions in cash. The recharacterized excess contributions must be treated as employee contributions for purposes of the taxation rules of Code Section 72, the nondiscrimination rules of Code Section 401(a)(4), the ACP test under Code Section 401(m), and the distribution limitation rules (including hardship distribution rules) applicable to Section 401(k) plans. This particular requirement is not satisfied unless:

1. The payor or plan administrator reports the recharacterized excess contributions as employee contributions to the IRS and the employees by:
   a. Timely providing the appropriate forms to the employer and to employees whose excess contributions have been recharacterized;
   b. Timely taking any other action that the IRS requires; and
2. The plan administrator accounts for the amounts as employee contributions for purposes of the distribution taxation rules of Code Section 72.

Recharacterized excess contributions continue to be treated as elective contributions for all other purposes under the Internal Revenue Code, including Code Section 401(a) (except for the nondiscrimination rules of Code Section 401(a)(4) and the ACP test under Code Section 401(m)), the deduction rules of Code Section 404, the tax credit employee stock ownership plan rules under Code Section 409, the minimum vesting standards of Code Section 411, the minimum funding standards of Code Section 412, the annual limitations under Code Section 415, the top-heavy requirements of Code Section 416, and the minimum survivor annuity requirements of Code Section 417.

Time of Recharacterization. Excess contributions may not be recharacterized later than 2½ months after the close of the plan year to which the recharacterization relates.

Effectiveness of Recharacterization. Recharacterization of excess contributions as after-tax employee contributions is often ineffective because the recharacterized contributions are then subject to the ACP test, which might not be passed. [Treas. Reg. § 1.401(k)-2(b)(3)]

Q 5:9 How is the corrective distribution of excess contributions accomplished?

Excess contributions, adjusted by allocable gains or losses, are distributed in accordance with these rules only if they are designated by the employer as a distribution of excess contributions, adjusted by allocable gains or losses, and are distributed to the appropriate HCEs within 12 months after the close of the plan year in which the excess contributions arose. In the event of a complete termination of the plan during the plan year in which an excess contribution arose, the corrective distribution must be made as soon as administratively feasible after the date of termination of the plan, but in no event later than 12 months after the date of termination. If the entire account balance of the HCE is distributed during the plan year in which an excess contribution arose, the distribution is deemed to have been a corrective distribution of excess contributions, adjusted by allocable gains or losses, to the extent that a corrective distribution would otherwise have been required. If the distribution was transferred directly to an IRA or another qualified plan, the amount must be removed from the IRA or other plan and distributed to the participant. [Treas. Reg. § 1.401(k)-2(b)(2)(v)]

Example 5-3: ABC Widgets' 401(k) plan is terminated on June 30, 2018, and the plan assets are distributed to participants on September 30, 2018. Beth, the only HCE, receives a distribution of her entire account balance of $250,000. It is determined that $2,500 of this distribution is an excess contribution, as adjusted by allocable gains or losses. Thus, $247,500 is eligible as an IRA or plan-to-plan rollover, and the $2,500 excess contribution must be distributed to Beth in cash as a taxable distribution.

Q 5:10 How are the gains or losses allocable to excess contributions determined?

General Rule. The gains or losses allocable to excess contributions are equal to the allocable gains or losses for the plan year. [Treas. Reg. § 1.401(k)-2(b)(2)(iv)(A)]

Method of Allocating Gains or Losses. A plan may use any reasonable method for computing the gains or losses allocable to excess contributions, provided that the method does not violate the nondiscrimination rules of Code Section 401(a)(4), is used consistently for all participants and for all corrective distributions under the plan for the plan year, and is used by the plan for allocating gains or losses to participants' accounts. [Treas. Reg. § 1.401(k)-2(b)(2)(iv)(B)]

Alternative Method of Allocating Plan Year Gains or Losses. A plan may allocate gains or losses to excess contributions for the plan year by multiplying the gains or losses for the plan year allocable to the elective contributions and other amounts (including contributions made for the plan year), by a fraction, the numerator of which is the excess contributions for the employee for the plan year, and the denominator of which is the sum of:

1. The account balance attributable to elective contributions and other contributions as of the beginning of the plan year, and
2. Any additional amount of such contributions made for the plan year.

[Treas. Reg. § 1.401(k)-2(b)(2)(iv)(C)]

Example 5-4: ABC Widgets' 401(k) plan fails the ADP test for the plan year ended December 31, 2018. Alex, who is an HCE, has an excess contribution of $5,000. The portion of Alex's 2018 plan year total gain attributable to his $5,000 excess contribution is $500. Thus, $5,500 is the corrective distribution due to Alex.

Q 5:11 Must gains or losses allocable to the year of the distribution be included?

No. Such gains or losses are known as *gap period gains or losses*. Effective for plan years beginning in 2008, gap period gains or losses are not required to be distributed by the plan. [I.R.C. § 401(k)(8)(A)(i); Treas. Reg. § 1.401(k)-2(b)(2)(iv)(D)]

Q 5:12 Must employee or spousal consent be obtained by the plan sponsor?

No. A corrective distribution of excess contributions, adjusted by applicable gains or losses, may be made under the terms of the plan without any employee or spousal consent otherwise required under the rules of Code Sections 411(a)(11) and 417. [Treas. Reg. § 1.401(k)-2(b)(2)(vii)(A)]

Q 5:13 Are corrective distributions treated as employer contributions?

Yes. Excess contributions are treated as employer contributions under the deduction rules of Code Section 404 and the annual limitations under Code Section 415, even if they are distributed from the plan. Note that elective contributions are generally not counted toward the deductible limits under Code Section 404. [I.R.C. § 404(n); Treas. Reg. § 1.401(k)-2(b)(2)(vii)(B)]

Q 5:14 What is the tax treatment to the HCE of corrective distributions of excess contributions?

Effective for plan years beginning in 2008 or after, excess contributions are taxed in the year of distribution. [I.R.C. § 4979(f)(2)] Regardless of when the corrective distribution is made, it is not subject to the 10 percent additional income tax on early distributions under Code Section 72(t). [Treas. Reg. § 1.401(k)-2(b)(2)(vi)(A)] A distribution of excess contributions is not includible in gross income to the extent it represents a distribution of designated Roth contributions. However, any gain allocable to a corrective distribution of excess contributions that are designated Roth contributions is included in gross income for income tax purposes. [Treas. Reg. § 1.401(k)-2(b)(2)(vi)(C)]

Example 5-5: ABC Widgets' 401(k) plan fails the ADP test for the plan year ended December 31, 2018. Scott, the only HCE, has an excess contribution of $4,000. The entire excess contribution is attributable to a designated Roth contribution. The 2018 gain attributable to Scott's $4,000 excess contribution is $200. Thus, $4,200 must be distributed to Scott. Because $4,000 is a designated Roth contribution that has already been taxed, only $200 of the corrective distribution is taxable to Scott.

Q 5:15 What happens if excess contributions are not corrected on a timely basis?

Failure to Correct Within 2½ Months After the End of the Plan Year. If a plan does not correct excess contributions within 2½ months (six months for an eligible automatic contribution arrangement within the meaning of Code Section 414(w)(3) for plan years beginning in 2008 or later) after the close of the plan year for which they were made, the employer will be liable for a 10 percent excise tax on the amount of the excess contributions. [Treas. Reg. § 1.401(k)-2(b)(5)(i); I.R.C. § 4979; Treas. Reg. § 54.4979-1]

Rule for Eligible Automatic Contribution Arrangements. Effective for plan years beginning in 2008 and later, a plan with an eligible automatic contribution arrangement as defined in Code Section 414(w)(3) will have six months after the close of the plan year to return excess contributions. [I.R.C. § 4979(f)(1); Treas. Reg. § 1.401(k)-2(b)(5)(iii)]

Failure to Correct Within 12 Months After the End of the Plan Year. If excess contributions are not corrected within 12 months after the close of the plan year for which they were made, the Section 401(k) arrangement will fail to satisfy the ADP test and will be disqualified for the plan year for which the excess contributions are not timely distributed and for all subsequent plan years during which the excess contributions remain in the plan. [Treas. Reg. § 1.401(k)-2(b)(5)(ii)] However, one of the available IRS correction programs under Employee Plans Compliance Resolution System (EPCRS) may be used as an alternative to disqualification (see chapter 23).

Example 5-6: ABC Widgets' 401(k) plan fails the ADP test for the plan year ended December 31, 2018. The 401(k) plan is an eligible automatic contribution arrangement within the meaning of Code Section 414(w)(3). Shannon, the only HCE, has an excess contribution of $3,000. The gain attributable to her $3,000 excess contribution for the 2018 plan year is $300. Thus, $3,300 must be distributed to Shannon. Because the plan contains an eligible automatic contribution arrangement, the plan has until June 30, 2019, to make the distribution to Shannon without incurring a 10 percent excise tax. If the plan did not have an eligible automatic contribution arrangement, the excess contribution (plus gains) would have to be distributed by March 15, 2019, to avoid a 10 percent excise tax.

Excess Aggregate Contributions

Q 5:16 What is an excess aggregate contribution?

An excess aggregate contribution means the aggregate amount of employee after-tax and employer matching contributions (and any appropriate qualified nonelective contribution or elective contributions taken into account in computing the ACP) actually made on behalf of HCEs for the plan year that exceeds the maximum contributions permitted under the ACP test described in Code Section 401(m)(2)(A). QMACs that are treated as elective contributions are disregarded. [Treas. Reg. §§ 1.401(m)-2(b)(2)(ii)(A); 1.401(m)-5]

Q 5:17 What are the permissible methods for correcting excess aggregate contributions?

The following methods are permissible in correcting excess aggregate contributions:

1. If the plan so provides, the employer may make QNECs or QMACs that, in combination with employee after-tax and matching contributions already made, satisfy the ACP test;

2. If the plan so provides, excess aggregate contributions on behalf of HCEs, adjusted by allocable gains or losses, may be distributed in a corrective distribution;
3. Alternatively, excess aggregate contributions, adjusted by allocable gains or losses, may be forfeited; or
4. Any combination of items (1), (2), or (3).

[Treas. Reg. § 1.401(m)-2(b)(1)(i)]

Q 5:18 How may a combination of the correction methods be used in correcting excess aggregate contributions?

A 401(k) plan may use any of the correction methods described in Q 5:17. If use of a combination of these methods is desired to correct excess aggregate contributions, each applicable method would be used for a portion of the excess aggregate contribution. For example, a portion of the excess aggregate contributions for an HCE may be distributed to the HCE in a corrective distribution, and the remaining portion of the excess aggregate contribution may be forfeited. [Treas. Reg. § 1.401(m)-2(b)(1)(ii)]

Q 5:19 What correction methods are not permitted?

Excess aggregate contributions may not be corrected by forfeiting vested matching contributions, distributing nonvested matching contributions, recharacterizing matching contributions, or not making matching contributions required under the terms of the plan. Excess aggregate contributions for a plan year may neither remain unallocated nor be allocated to a suspense account for allocation to one or more employees in any future year. In addition, excess aggregate contributions may not be corrected retroactively. [Treas. Reg. § 1.401(m)-2(b)(1)(iii)]

Q 5:20 What happens if an excess aggregate contribution is not fully corrected?

Any distribution of less than the entire amount of excess aggregate contributions, adjusted by allocable gains or losses, is treated as a pro rata distribution of excess aggregate contributions and gain or loss. [Treas. Reg. § 1.401(m)-2(b)(3)(iv)]

Q 5:21 What is the amount of total excess aggregate contributions for HCEs?

The following steps must be followed to determine the amount of excess aggregate contributions to be returned to the applicable HCEs:

1. *Calculate the dollar amount of excess aggregate contributions for each HCE.* The amount of excess aggregate contributions attributable to an

HCE for a plan year is the amount (if any) by which the HCE's contributions must be reduced for the HCE's actual contribution ratio (ACR) to equal the highest permitted ACR under the plan. To calculate the highest permitted ACR under the plan, the ACR of the HCE with the highest ACR is reduced by the amount required to cause that HCE's ACR to equal the ACR of the HCE with the next highest ACR. This process is repeated until the remainder ACRs would satisfy the ACP test. If a lesser reduction within any step of the process would enable the plan to satisfy the ACP test, only this lesser reduction applies.

2. *Determine the amount of total excess aggregate contributions.* The sum of all reductions for all HCEs determined under item 1 above is the amount of total excess aggregate contributions for the plan year.
3. *Satisfaction of ACP.* A plan satisfies the ACP test if the ACRs for each HCE, after any applicable reduction, pass the ACP test.

[Treas. Reg. § 1.401(m)-2(b)(2)]

Q 5:22 How are excess contributions coordinated with excess aggregate contributions?

Excess aggregate contributions for an HCE for a plan year are calculated after determining the excess contributions (see Q 5:2) to be recharacterized as employee after-tax contributions for the plan year. [Treas. Reg. § 1.401(m)-2(a)(4)(ii)]

Example 5-7: ABC Widgets' 401(k) plan provides for matching contributions equal to 75 percent of the first 10 percent of pay deferred as elective contributions. The plan contains a vesting schedule equal to 25 percent per year of service. Mary Lou, the only HCE, has compensation equal to $180,000 and is 50 percent vested in her matching contributions. The ADPs and ACPs for the HCE and the NHCE group are shown below:

	ADP	*ACP*
HCEs	10.0%	7.5%
NHCEs	5.0%	3.0%

To satisfy the ADP test, Mary Lou's actual deferral ratio must be reduced to 7 percent. A corrective distribution equal to $5,400 (3% × $180,000) must be made. Gains or losses relating to the $5,400 must also be determined and distributed, if applicable. Mary Lou's employer match must also be reduced so that the remainder matching contribution is appropriate according to the plan's matching formula (75 percent of 7 percent, or 5.25 percent) and reduced further, if necessary, to pass the ACP test, which is 5 percent in this example. By reducing the ACP for Mary Lou from 7.5 percent to 5 percent, her remainder matching contribution will be no more than is necessary to satisfy the matching formula and pass the ACP test. The plan provides that the 2.5 percent excess aggregate contribution for Mary Lou be forfeited.

The ADPs and ACPs after correction are shown below:

	ADP	*ACP*
HCEs	7.0%	5.0%
NHCEs	5.0%	3.0%

Q 5:23 How are corrective distributions of excess aggregate contributions for each HCE determined?

Total excess aggregate contributions are determined in a leveling process similar to that used in Q 5:21, except based on dollars rather than percentages. The dollar-based leveling process starts with the HCE with the highest dollar amount of employer matching and after-tax employee contributions. [I.R.C. § 401(m)(6)]

Example 5-8: ABC Widgets' 401(k) plan provides for matching contributions equal to 50 percent of elective contributions up to the first 12 percent of pay. There are two HCEs, and both HCEs are fully vested. The ADRs for the HCEs (both of whom are 5 percent owners) are shown below:

The two HCEs, Roanne and Judy, have ADRs of 9 percent and 11 percent, respectively. The ADP for NHCEs is 5 percent. The two HCEs, Roanne and Judy have ACRs of 4.5 percent and 5.5 percent, respectively, while the ACP of the NHCEs is 2 percent. The excess contributions and refunds are calculated as follows:

Calculation of Excess Contributions and Refunds

	Testing Compensation	*Original Elective Contribution*	*ADR*	*Excess Contribution*	*Level Down*
Roanne	$100,000	$9,000	9.00%	$2,000	$3,050
Judy	$70,000	$7,700	11.00%	$2,800	$1,750
Totals		$16,700		$4,800	$4,800

The excess aggregate contributions (EAC) and refunds are calculated as follows:

Calculation of Excess Aggregate Contributions (EAC) and Refunds

	Testing Compensation	*Original Match*	*ACP*	*EAC*	*Level Down*	*Match After Refund*
Roanne	$100,000	$4,500	4.50%	$500	$1,100	$3,400
Judy	$ 70,000	$3,850	5.50%	$1,050	$450	$3,400
Totals		$8,350		$1,550	$1,550	$6,800

Although different ADRs and ACRs would be computed if these ratios were calculated after the refunds, the final 401(k) regulations permit the use of the deemed results.

Deemed ADP and ACP

	ADP	*ACP*
HCEs	7.00%	4.00%
NHCEs	5.00%	2.00%

Q 5:24 How is the corrective distribution of excess aggregate contributions accomplished?

Excess aggregate contributions, adjusted by allocable gains or losses, are distributed in a corrective distribution only if the excess aggregate contributions, adjusted by allocable gains and losses, are designated by the employer as a distribution of excess aggregate contributions, adjusted by allocable gains and losses, and are distributed to the appropriate HCEs within 12 months after the close of the plan year in which the excess aggregate contributions arose. If there is a complete termination of the plan during the plan year in which the excess aggregate contributions arose, the corrective distribution must be made as soon as administratively feasible after the date the plan terminates, but not later than 12 months after the termination date. If the entire account balance of an HCE is distributed during the plan year in which the excess aggregate contribution arose, the distribution is deemed to have been a corrective distribution of excess aggregate contributions, adjusted by allocable gains and losses, if a corrective distribution would otherwise have been required. If the distribution was transferred directly to an IRA or another qualified plan, the amount should be removed from the IRA or other plan and distributed to the participant. [Treas. Reg. § 1.401(m)-2(b)(2)(v); Rev. Proc. 2013-12, § 6.06]

Q 5:25 How is the gain or loss allocable to excess aggregate contributions determined?

General Rule. The gain or loss allocable to excess aggregate contributions is the amount for the applicable plan year. [Treas. Reg. § 1.401(m)-2(b)(2)(iv)(A)] Effective for plan years beginning in 2008, gap period gains or losses for the year of distribution are not required to be distributed by the plan. [I.R.C. § 401(m)(6)(A); Treas. Reg. § 1.401(m)-2(b)(2)(iv)(D)] (See Q 5:26.)

Method of Allocating Gains or Losses. A plan may use any reasonable method for computing the gains or losses allocable to excess aggregate contributions, provided that the method does not violate the nondiscrimination requirements of Code Section 401(a)(4), is used consistently for all participants and for all corrective distributions under the plan for the plan year, and is used by the plan for allocating gains or losses to participants' accounts. [Treas. Reg. § 1.401(m)-2(b)(2)(iv)(B)]

Alternative Method of Allocating Gains or Losses for the Plan Year. A plan may allocate gains or losses to excess aggregate contributions for the plan year by multiplying the gains or losses for the plan year allocable to employee contributions, matching contributions, and other amounts (including the contributions for the year), by a fraction, the numerator of which is the excess aggregate contributions for the employee for the plan year, and the denominator of which is the sum of the:

1. Account balance attributable to employee contributions and matching contributions and other amounts as of the beginning of the plan year; and
2. Any additional such contributions for the plan year. [Treas. Reg. § 1.401(m)-2(b)(2)(iv)(C)]

Allocable Gains or Losses for Recharacterized Elective Contributions. If recharacterized elective contributions are distributed as excess aggregate contributions, the gains or losses allocable to the excess aggregate contributions are determined as if recharacterized elective contributions had been distributed as excess contributions. Thus, the gains or losses must be allocated to the recharacterized amounts distributed using the methods described under Treasury Regulations Section 1.401(k)-2(b)(2)(iv). [Treas. Reg. § 1.401(m)-2(b)(2)(iv)(E)] (See Q 5:8.)

Example 5-9: ABC Widgets' 401(k) plan fails the ACP test for the plan year ended December 31, 2018. Alex has an excess aggregate contribution of $5,000. The gain attributable for the 2018 plan year based on Alex's account is $500. The plan provides that excess aggregate contributions are forfeited. Thus, $5,500 must be forfeited and utilized as specified by the terms of the plan.

Q 5:26 Must gains or losses allocable to the year of the distribution be included?

No. Such gains or losses are known as *gap period gains or losses*. Effective for plan years beginning in 2008, gap period gains or losses are not required to be distributed by the plan. [I.R.C. § 401(k)(8)(A)(i); Treas. Reg. § 1.401(m)-2(b)(2)(iv)(D)]

Q 5:27 Is employee or spousal consent required for the distribution of excess aggregate contributions?

No. A distribution of excess aggregate contributions and allocable gains or losses may be made under the terms of the plan without any notice or consent otherwise required under Code Sections 411(a)(11) and 417. [Treas. Reg. § 1.401(m)-2(b)(3)(i)]

Q 5:28 Are corrective distributions and forfeited contributions treated as employer contributions?

Yes. Excess aggregate contributions, including forfeited matching contributions, are treated as employer contributions under the deduction rules under Code Section 404 and the annual limitations under Code Section 415, even if distributed from the plan. Forfeited matching contributions reallocated to the accounts of other participants for the plan year in which the forfeiture occurs are treated under Code Section 415 as annual additions for the participants to whose accounts they are reallocated and for the participants from whose accounts they are forfeited. [Treas. Reg. § 1.401(m)-2(b)(3)(ii)]

Q 5:29 What is the tax treatment to the HCE of corrective distributions of excess aggregate contributions?

Effective for plan years beginning in 2008, excess aggregate contributions are taxed in the year of distribution. [I.R.C. § 4979(f)(2)] A distribution of excess aggregate contributions is not includible in gross income to the extent it represents a distribution of designated Roth contributions. However, any gains allocable to a corrective distribution of excess aggregate contributions that are designated Roth contributions are included in gross income. [Treas. Reg. § 1.401(k)-2(b)(2)(vi)(A)]

Regardless of when the corrective distribution is made, it is not subject to the 10 percent additional income tax on early distributions under Code Section 72(t). [Treas. Reg. § 1.401(m)-2(b)(2)(vi)(A)]

A distribution of excess aggregate contributions and allocable gains or losses is not treated as a distribution for purposes of determining whether the plan satisfies the minimum distribution requirements of Code Section 401(a)(9). [Treas. Reg. § 1.401(m)-2(b)(3)(iii)]

A matching contribution that is an excess aggregate contribution may be distributed in a corrective distribution, as described above. However, a matching contribution may not be distributed merely because the contribution to which it relates is treated as an excess contribution (see Q 5:1), excess aggregate contribution (see Q 5:16), or excess elective contribution (see Q 5:31). Such related matching contributions must generally be forfeited. [Treas. Reg. § 1.401(m)-2(b)(3)(v)]

Q 5:30 What happens if excess aggregate contributions are not corrected on a timely basis?

Failure to Correct Within 2½ Months After the End of the Plan Year. If a plan does not correct excess aggregate contributions within 2½ months (six months for an eligible automatic contribution arrangement for plan years beginning in 2008 or later) after the end of the plan year for which they are made, the employer will be liable for a 10 percent excise tax on the amount of the excess aggregate contributions. [I.R.C. § 4979; Treas. Reg. § 54.4979-1] QNECs that are taken into account for purposes of the ACP for a plan year may enable a plan to avoid having excess aggregate contributions, even if the contributions are made after the close of the 2½-month period. [Treas. Reg. § 1.401(m)-2(b)(4)(i)]

Rule for Eligible Automatic Contribution Arrangements. Effective for plan years beginning in 2008, a plan with an eligible automatic contribution arrangement as defined in Code Section 414(w)(3) will have six months after the close of the plan year to return excess aggregate contributions. [I.R.C. § 4979(f)(2); Treas. Reg. § 1.401(m)-2(b)(4)(iii)]

Failure to Correct Within 12 Months After the End of the Plan Year. If excess aggregate contributions are not corrected within 12 months after the close of the plan year for which they were made, the plan will fail to meet the nondiscrimination requirements of Code Section 401(a)(4) for the plan year for which the excess aggregate contributions were made and for all subsequent plan years in which the excess aggregate contributions remain in the plan. The plan, therefore, will be disqualified. However, one of the available IRS correction programs under EPCRS may be used as an alternative to disqualification (see chapter 23). [Treas. Reg. § 1.401(m)-2(b)(4)(ii)]

Excess Elective Contributions

Q 5:31 What are elective contributions for purposes of the annual limitation on elective contributions under Code Section 402(g)?

Annual Limitation on Elective Contributions—General Rule. Code Section 402(g) imposes an annual limitation on the income exclusion for elective contributions. The excess of an individual's elective contributions for any tax year of that individual (not for the plan year of the plan) over the applicable limit for the year may not be excluded from his or her federal gross income. Thus, an individual's elective contributions in excess of the applicable limit for a tax year—his or her excess elective contributions—must be included in gross income for the year. [Treas. Reg. § 1.402(g)-1(a)]

Elective Contributions Defined. An individual's elective contributions for a tax year are the sum of the following:

1. Any elective contribution under qualified Section 401(k) arrangements to the extent not includible in the individual's gross income for the tax year;
2. Any employer contribution to a SEP (Simplified Employee Pension) or SIMPLE (Savings Incentive Match Plan for Employees) plan to the extent not includible in the individual's gross income for the tax year;
3. Any employer contribution, made pursuant to a salary reduction agreement, to an annuity contract or custodial account under a Section 403(b) arrangement, to the extent not includible in the individual's gross income for the tax year; and
4. Any employee contribution designated as a deduction under a Section 501(c)(18) trust (a trust underlying a pension plan funded solely through employee contributions).

[Treas. Reg. § 1.402(g)-1(b)]

Certain One-Time Irrevocable Elections. An employer contribution is not treated as an elective contribution under the above definition if the contribution is made pursuant to a one-time irrevocable election by the employee:

1. For an annuity contract or custodial account under Code Section 403(b), at the time of initial eligibility to participate in the salary reduction agreement;

2. For a Section 401(k) arrangement, at a time when the election is not treated as a cash or deferred election under Treasury Regulations Section 1.401(k)-1(a)(3)(iv); or
3. For a trust described under Code Section 501(c)(18) (a trust underlying a pension plan funded solely through employee contributions).

[Treas. Reg. § 1.402(g)-1(c)]

Q 5:32 What is the annual dollar limitation on an individual's elective contributions for any tax year?

The annual dollar limitation on an individual's elective contributions (see Q 5:31) for 1987 and subsequent taxable years is as follows:

Year	*Annual Dollar Limitation on Elective Contributions*
1987	$7,000
1988	$7,313
1989	$7,627
1990	$7,979
1991	$8,475
1992	$8,728
1993	$8,994
1994	$9,240
1995	$9,240
1996	$9,500
1997	$9,500
1998	$10,000
1999	$10,000
2000	$10,500
2001	$10,500
2002	$11,000
2003	$12,000
2004	$13,000
2005	$14,000
2006	$15,000
2007	$15,500
2008	$15,500
2009	$16,500
2010	$16,500
2011	$16,500
2012	$17,000

Year	Annual Dollar Limitation on Elective Contributions
2013	$17,500
2014	$17,500
2015	$18,000
2016	$18,000
2017	$18,000
2018	$18,500

[I.R.C. § 402(g)(1)]

In the case of taxable years beginning after December 31, 2006, the $15,000 limitation is adjusted for cost-of-living increases, in increments of $500. [I.R.C. § 402(g)(4)]

Starting in 2002, eligible participants who reach at least age 50 by the end of the year are permitted to make catch-up contributions over and above the limit on elective contributions. The catch-up limit will be adjusted for cost-of-living increases, in $500 increments. The 2018 catch-up limit is still $6,000.

[Treas. Reg. §§ 1.402(g)-1(d), 1.414(v)-1; I.R.C. § 414(v)]

Q 5:33 What is an excess elective contribution?

The term *excess elective contributions* means the amount of an individual's elective contributions for any tax year that exceeds the dollar limit under Code Section 402(g)(1) (see Q 5:32).

Q 5:34 How are excess elective contributions treated under a qualified plan?

A plan will not be qualified if it fails to provide that for any participant, the amount of elective contributions under the plan, plus the amount of elective contributions under any other retirement plan, may not exceed the annual limitation of such elective contributions under Code Section 402(g). [Treas. Reg. § 1.402(g)-1(e)(1)(i)]

Q 5:35 Are excess elective contributions treated as employer contributions?

Yes. For other plan qualification purposes under the Code, including the nondiscrimination rules under Code Section 401(a)(4), the ADP test under Code Section 401(k)(3), the deduction rules under Code Section 404, the minimum vesting rules under Code Section 411, the minimum funding standards of Code Section 412, and the top-heavy rules of Code Section 416, excess elective contributions (see Q 5:31) must be treated as employer contributions even if they are distributed in a corrective distribution (see Q 5:43). However, excess elective contributions of an NHCE are not taken into account under the ADP test for the year in question. Excess elective contributions are also treated as employer contributions for purposes of the annual limitations rules under Code Section 415, unless they are distributed in a corrective distribution. [Treas. Reg. § 1.402(g)-1(e)(1)(ii)]

Q 5:36 May excess elective contributions be distributed after the close of an individual's tax year?

If excess elective contributions are includible in the gross income of an individual who is participant for a tax year, a plan may provide that:

1. Not later than the first April 15 (or an earlier date specified in the plan) following the close of the individual's tax year in which the excess occurred, the individual may notify each of his or her plans of the amount of excess elective contributions received by that plan. This notification must include the portion of excess elective contributions that are designated Roth contributions. A plan may instead provide that the applicable employer may notify the plan on behalf of the individual. [Treas. Reg. § 1.402(g)-1(e)(2)(i)]
2. Not later than the first April 15 following the close of the applicable tax year in which the excess occurred, the plan may distribute to the individual the amount of excess elective contributions, adjusted by allocable gains or losses. [Treas. Reg. § 1.402(g)-1(e)(2)(ii)]

Q 5:37 May excess elective contributions be distributed during the individual's tax year?

Yes. A plan may provide that an individual who has excess elective contributions for a tax year may receive a corrective distribution of excess elective contributions during the same taxable year. This corrective distribution may be made only if each of the following conditions are satisfied:

1. The individual designates the distribution as an excess elective contribution. A plan may provide that an individual is deemed to have so designated the distribution to the extent that the individual calculates excess elective contributions for the tax year to include only elective contributions under this plan and other plans of the same employer. A plan may instead provide that the employer may make the designation on behalf of the individual. [Treas. Reg. § 1.402(g)-1(e)(3)(i)(A)]
2. The corrective distribution is made after the date on which the plan received the excess elective contributions. [Treas. Reg. § 1.402(g)-1(e)(3)(i)(B)]
3. The plan designates the distribution as a distribution of excess elective contributions. [Treas. Reg. § 1.402(g)-1(e)(3)(i)(C)]

Example 5-10: Harry is a 62-year-old participant in ABC Widgets' 401(k) plan. In January 2018, Harry withdraws $5,000 from the plan. From February 2018 through September 2018, Harry defers elective contributions of $1,000 per month ($8,000). On October 1, 2018, Harry leaves ABC Widgets and joins CDE Gadgets (unrelated to the ABC Widgets). During the remainder of 2018,

Harry defers a total of $18,500 under the CDE Gadgets 401(k) plan. In January 2019, Harry realizes that he has deferred a total of $26,500 in 2018 and, therefore, has a $2,000 excess elective contribution ($26,500 less $24,500 [$18,500 elective contribution plus $6,000 catch-up for 2018]). That $2,000 must be distributed to Harry before April 15, 2019, to correct the excess elective contribution. The $5,000 withdrawal did not correct the excess elective contribution because it occurred before the excess elective contribution was made. [Treas. Reg. § 1.402(g)-1(e)(3)(ii)]

Q 5:38 Must the plan provide for the distribution of excess elective contributions?

Yes. To make a corrective distribution of excess elective contributions for any tax year, a plan must contain language permitting such corrective distributions. A plan may require the participant notification described above to be in writing and may require that the employee certify or otherwise establish that the designated amount is an excess elective contribution. A plan need not permit distribution of excess elective contributions. [Treas. Reg. § 1.402(g)-1(e)(4)]

Q 5:39 How are the gains or losses allocable to excess elective contributions determined?

General Rule. The gains or losses allocable to excess elective contribution are equal to the sum of the allocable gain or loss for the tax year of the individual. [Treas. Reg. § 1.402(g)-1(e)(5)(i)]

Method of Allocating Gains or Losses. A plan may use any reasonable method for computing the gains or losses allocable to excess elective contributions if the method does not violate the nondiscrimination requirements of Code Section 401(a)(4), is used consistently for all participants and for all corrective distributions under a plan for the plan year, and is used by the plan for allocating gains or losses to participants' accounts. [Treas. Reg. § 1.402(g)-1(e)(5)(ii)]

Alternative Method of Allocating Gains or Losses. A plan may allocate gains or losses to excess elective contributions by multiplying the gains or losses for the tax year allocable to elective contributions by the following fraction—the employee's excess elective contributions for the tax year divided by the sum of:

1. The employee's total account balance attributable to elective contributions as of the beginning of the tax year *plus*
2. The employee's elective contributions for the tax year.

[Treas. Reg. § 1.402(g)-1(e)(5)(iii)]

Q 5:40 Must gap period gains or losses be allocated to excess elective contributions?

No. A 401(k) plan distributing excess elective contributions must calculate gains or losses attributable to the excess elective contributions for the calendar year to which the excess elective contributions relate, but not to the calendar year of distribution. [I.R.C. § 402(g)(2)(A)(ii)]

Q 5:41 How are excess elective contributions coordinated with the distribution or recharacterization of elective contributions?

The amount of excess elective contributions that may be distributed in a corrective distribution under the rules for an employee for a tax year is reduced by any excess contributions previously distributed or recharacterized for the employee (see Q 5:1) for the plan year beginning with or during the tax year. If the amount of excess elective contributions that may be distributed under the rules is reduced, the amount of excess contributions includible in gross income of the employee and reported by the employer as a distribution of excess contributions is reduced by the same amount. In no case may an individual receive from a plan as a corrective distribution for a tax year an amount in excess of the individual's total elective contributions under the plan for the same tax year. [Treas. Reg. § 1.402(g)-1(e)(6)]

Q 5:42 Must the plan sponsor obtain employee or spousal consent in order to distribute excess elective contributions?

No. A corrective distribution of excess elective contributions, adjusted by allocable gains or losses, may be made under the terms of the plan without regard to any notice or consent otherwise required under Code Section 411(a)(11) or Section 417. [Treas. Reg. § 1.402(g)-1(e)(7)]

Q 5:43 What is the federal income tax treatment of excess elective contributions made on or before April 15 following the close of the calendar year?

A corrective distribution of excess elective contributions made on or before April 15 following the close of the tax year for which they were made is excludable from the employee's gross income in the year received because it is taxable in the year deferred. However, the gains or losses allocable to excess elective contributions are includible in the employee's gross income for the tax year in which the allocable gains and losses are distributed. The corrective distribution of excess elective contributions, adjusted by allocable gains or losses, is not subject to the 10 percent additional income tax on early distributions under Code Section 72(t). [Treas. Reg. § 1.402(g)-1(e)(8)(i)]

Q 5:44 What is the federal income tax treatment of excess elective contributions made after April 15 following the close of the calendar year?

If excess elective contributions, adjusted by allocable gains or losses, for a tax year are not distributed within the correction period, they may only be distributed when permitted under the rules of Code Section 401(k)(2)(B). The amounts are includible in gross income when distributed and are treated for purposes of the distribution rules as elective contributions and gains excludable from the individual's gross income under Code Section 402(g). Thus, any amount includible in gross income for any tax year that is not distributed by April 15 of the following tax year is not treated as a tax-free return of basis for purposes of Code Section 72 and is includible in the employee's gross income when distributed from the plan (therefore, it is taxed twice). Excess elective contributions that are distributed under the rules are treated as employer contributions under the annual limitations of Code Section 415 when they are contributed to the plan. [Treas. Reg. § 1.402(g)-1(e)(8)(iii)]

Q 5:45 Does a corrective distribution of excess elective contributions reduce the required minimum distribution under Code Section 401(a)(9)?

No. A corrective distribution of excess elective contributions is not treated as a distribution in determining whether the plan meets the minimum distribution requirements of Code Section 401(a)(9). [Treas. Reg. § 1.402(g)-1(e)(9)]

Q 5:46 What happens if a distribution of excess elective contributions is only partially corrected?

Any corrective distribution of less than the entire amount of excess elective contributions, adjusted by allocable gains or losses, is treated as a pro rata distribution of excess elective contributions and related earnings. [Treas. Reg. § 1.402(g)-1(e)(10)]

Example 5-11: Peter is a 60-year-old HCE participating in the ABC Widgets' 401(k) plan. From January through September 2018, Peter contributed $18,500 to the plan in elective contributions. During the same period, Peter also contributed $7,500 in elective contributions under a plan for an unrelated employer. In December 2018, Peter made a permitted and taxable withdrawal of $1,000 from the ABC Widgets's 401(k) plan, but did not designate it as a withdrawal of an excess elective contribution. In January 2019, Peter notified ABC Widgets of an excess elective contribution, specifying a distribution of $1,500 for 2018. To correct the excess elective contribution, Peter must receive this additional $1,500, adjusted by allocable gains or losses, even though he has already withdrawn $1,000 for 2018. Peter may exclude from his 2018 taxable income only $24,500, the calendar-year limit on elective contributions, plus allowable catch-up contribution in 2018. However, if the $1,500 is distributed by April 15, 2019, the distribution is excludable from Peter's gross income in 2019 (it would be included in taxable income for 2018). Even if Peter withdraws the $1,500, ABC Widgets must take into account the entire $18,500 in computing Peter's actual deferral ratio for 2018. [Treas. Reg. § 1.402(g)-1(e)(11)]

Example 5-12: CDE Gadgets maintains a 401(k) plan. The plan year is the calendar year. For plan year 2018, all 10 of the corporation's employees are eligible to participate in the plan. The employees' testing compensation, elective contributions, and ADRs are shown in the following table:

Employee	*Status*	*Testing Compensation*	*Elective Contribution*	*Actual Deferral Ratio*
A	HCE	$140,000	$ 7,000	5.0%
B	HCE	$100,000	$10,000	10.0%
C	HCE	$100,000	$10,000	10.0%
D	NHCE	$45,000	$ 2,250	5.0%
E	NHCE	$40,000	$ 4,000	10.0%
F	NHCE	$35,000	$ 1,750	5.0%
G	NHCE	$35,000	$ 350	1.0%
H	NHCE	$30,000	$ 3,000	10.0%
I	NHCE	$17,500	0	0.0%
J	NHCE	$17,500	0	0.0%

The actual deferral percentages for the HCEs and NHCEs are 8.33 percent and 4.43 percent, respectively. These percentages do not satisfy the ADP test under Code Section 401(k)(3)(A)(ii). The actual deferral percentage for the HCEs must not exceed 6.43 percent (2 percent greater than the actual deferral percentage for NHCEs).

The plan reduces the actual deferral ratios of HCEs B and C to 7.14 percent by distributing $2,860 ($10,000 − [7.14% × $100,000]) to each in January 2019. The ADP test, therefore, is satisfied.

In February 2019, B notifies CDE Gadgets that B made elective contributions totaling $9,500 under a 401(k) plan maintained by an unrelated employer in 2018 and requests a corrective distribution of $1,000 from the CDE Gadgets 401(k) plan. However, because B has already received a distribution of $2,860 to meet the ADP test, additional amounts are neither required nor permitted to be distributed to B as excess elective contributions by the CDE Gadgets 401(k) plan, and the prior distribution of excess contributions corrects the excess elective contributions too. CDE Gadgets must report $1,000 as a distribution of an excess deferral to B and $1,860 as a distribution of an excess contribution to B. [Treas. Reg. § 1.402(g)-1(e)(11)]

Example 5-13: Employee Ed has excess elective contributions of $1,000 for 2018. The 2018 gain attributable to excess elective contributions is $100. Ed properly notifies his employer and requests a distribution of the excess elective contributions and allocable gain on February 1, 2019. The plan distributes $1,000 to Ed by April 15, 2019. The plan did not distribute any additional amount as gain. Thus, $909 is treated as a distribution of excess elective contribution, and $91 is treated as a distribution of gain. With respect to amounts remaining in the account, ($1,000 − $909) $91 is treated as an elective contribution and not tax-free basis for purposes of Code

Section 72(t). Because it was not distributed by the required date, the $91 is includible again in Ed's gross income at his future distributable event. [Treas. Reg. § 1.402(g)-1(e)(11), Ex. 3]

Excess Annual Additions

Q 5:47 What is an excess annual addition, and how can it be corrected?

An excess annual addition is the amount allocated to a participant's account in a defined contribution plan that exceeds the lesser of:

1. 100 percent of the participant's compensation or
2. The dollar amount of annual addition limitation ($54,000 for limitation years ending in 2018).

[Treas. Reg. § 1.415(c)-1(a)]

The final 415 regulations do not specify the correction methods for excess annual additions. [Treas. Reg. § 1.415(c)-1] Revenue Procedure 2013-12 should be used in correcting excess annual additions. Acceptable correction methods follow the terms of the plan document with regard to forfeitures and include reallocating excess annual additions to other participants' contributions or reducing employer contributions. If excess annual additions were part of a distribution into an IRA or another qualified plan, corrective action includes returning the excess to the plan and following plan provisions. [Rev. Proc. 2013-12, § 6.06(2) as updated by Rev. Proc. 2015-27]

Q 5:48 How are excess annual additions treated for limitation years beginning on or after January 1, 2009?

Revenue Procedure 2013-12 as updated by Revenue Procedure 2015-27 provides that excess annual additions under Code Section 415 are corrected by using the Reduction of Account Balance Correction Method. Under this method, the account balance of an employee who received an excess annual addition is reduced by the amount of the excess annual addition, adjusted by allocable gains or losses, attributable to the excess annual addition.

If the excess annual addition was attributable to employer contributions, then the excess annual addition, adjusted by allocable gains or losses, is reallocated to other employees in accordance with the plan's allocation formula. If such excess annual addition would not have been allocable to other employees in accordance with the plan's allocation formula (e.g., under a money purchase plan), then such excess amounts, adjusted by allocable gains or losses are placed in an unallocated account and used to reduce employer contributions in the current or succeeding plan years. While such amounts remain in the unallocated account, the employer is not permitted to make contributions to the plan other than elective contributions, if any.

If the excess annual addition is attributable to an employee's elective or after-tax employee contribution, such excess amount, adjusted by allocable gains or losses, is distributed to the participant. Such amounts attributable to employee's elective or after-tax employee contributions are not considered for the following purposes:

1. The 402(g) limit on elective contributions (see Q 5:33);
2. The 415(c) limit on maximum annual additions (see Q 5:47);
3. The ADP test of Code Section 401(k)(3) (see Q 5:1);
4. The ACP test of Code Section 401(m)(2) (see Q 5:16).

If the excess annual addition is attributable to both an employee's elective (or after-tax) contribution and an employer's contribution, the correction occurs in the following order:

1. Returning the employee's elective (or after-tax) contribution that is not matched by the employer;
2. Returning the employee's elective (or after-tax) contribution that is matched by the employer;
3. Forfeiting the employer matching contribution attributable to the returned elective (or after-tax) contribution;
4. Reallocating or reducing employer contributions to extent needed to satisfy Code Section 415(c).

[Rev. Proc. 2013-12, § 6.06(2) and Appendix A, § .08, Rev. Proc. 2015-27, § 2.15 amending Appendix A, § .08]

Example 5-14: Jean participates in the ABC Widgets' 401(k) plan and has an excess annual addition of $500 for the plan year ending December 31, 2018. She contributed $10,500 in elective contributions for 2018. ABC Widgets did not match her elective contributions. To correct the excess annual addition, $500 of her elective contributions plus allocable gains is returned and is taxable to Jean.

Example 5-15: Jack participates in the CDE Gadgets' money purchase plan. The plan provides a formula of 25 percent of pay. Jack earns $275,000 in 2018, and the company contributes $68,750 to his account, which is in excess of the Code Section 415(c) annual additions limit of $55,000. The error is discovered in early 2019 and $13,750, adjusted by allocable gains or losses, is removed from Jack's account. Because the money purchase contribution had already been deposited for all participants for 2018, the excess amount of $13,750, adjusted by allocable gains or losses, is used to reduce the company contribution obligation for 2019.

Chapter 6

Taxable Life Insurance Costs

Qualified plans are designed to provide retirement benefits, but they may also provide ancillary benefits, including life insurance protection for plan participants. A plan may purchase life insurance to fund pre-retirement death benefits offered under the plan. Both the employer and the participant receive tax benefits; the employer may treat the life insurance premiums as tax-deductible contributions to the plan, and the deceased participant's beneficiary may exclude the pure death benefit from his or her gross income.

However, the participant must include in his or her gross income, for each taxable year during which the plan holds a life insurance contract on his or her life, the current value of life insurance protection (also called PS-58 costs). The participant is taxed each year on the PS-58 costs because he or she derives an economic benefit from the life insurance contract—specifically, the tax-free life insurance proceeds payable to the participant's beneficiary after the participant dies.

Either Table 2001 or the insurers published premium rates may be used in determining the taxable income of a participant who is covered by a life insurance contract in a qualified plan. This chapter discusses the inclusion of life insurance protection costs in the participant's gross income.

Calculation of Taxable Insurance Costs 6-2

Calculation of Taxable Insurance Costs

Q 6:1 When is life insurance protection in a qualified plan subject to current taxation?

The cost of life insurance protection provided by contracts purchased by employer or pre-tax employee contribution (e.g., 401(k) elective contributions) accounts in a qualified plan are subject to taxation in the year of each premium payment. This cost of insurance protection used to be referred to as PS-58 costs. The cost of insurance is taxable because the participant is receiving a current economic benefit—the current life insurance protection. Only the cost of the current life insurance protection is taxable, not the entire premium paid. The costs of life insurance paid entirely with accumulated after-tax employee contributions are not subject to taxation. If the contract is funded with funds from employer or 401(k) accounts, in addition to after-tax employee contributions, a proration to determine the taxable amount of the insurance cost must be done. [Treas. Reg. § 1.72-16(b)]

Q 6:2 Are self-employed individuals treated differently?

Yes. Self-employed individuals are not subject to "PS-58" cost taxation directly. Self-employed individuals are sole proprietors who carry on a trade or business or are partners in a partnership. These individuals are not allowed to deduct the portion of the life insurance premiums that is attributable to PS-58 costs. This produces an effect similar to that of having the PS-58 costs become taxable income. [I.R.C. §§ 72(m)(3)(B), 404(e); Treas. Reg. §§ 1.404(e)-1A(g), 1.72-16(b)(4)]

Q 6:3 How is the annual cost of life insurance computed?

The annual cost of life insurance is the difference between the face amount of the life insurance and the insurance cash value, multiplied by the annual rate of term insurance cost as shown in the table in Q 6:12, and divided by 1,000. The rate depends on the age of the participant during the year of reporting. [Treas. Reg. § 1.72-16(b)(3)]

Q 6:4 What table is available from the IRS to use in determining the taxable value of current life insurance protection?

In IRS Notice 2002-8, the IRS published a table that could be used in determining the taxable amount of life insurance for plan years beginning after December 31, 2000. [IRS Notice 2002-8 (revoking IRS Notice 2001-10, which rendered obsolete Rev. Rul. 55-747); Rev. Rul. 66-110; Rev. Rul. 67-154]

This table, called Table 2001, which uses updated mortality rates, yields significantly less taxable income than the prior table. Table 2001 is shown in Table 6-1 below.

Table 6-1. Table 2001

Age	Rate per $1,000 of Face Amount
0	$0.70
1	$0.41
2	$0.27
3	$0.19
4	$0.13
5	$0.13
6	$0.14
7	$0.15
8	$0.16
9	$0.16
10	$0.16
11	$0.19
12	$0.24
13	$0.28
14	$0.33
15	$0.38
16	$0.52
17	$0.57
18	$0.59
19	$0.61
20	$0.62
21	$0.62
22	$0.64
23	$0.66
24	$0.68
25	$0.71
26	$0.73
27	$0.76
28	$0.80
29	$0.83
30	$0.87
31	$0.90
32	$0.93
33	$0.96
34	$0.98

Table 6-1. Table 2001 ***(cont'd)***

Age	Rate per $1,000 of Face Amount
35	$0.99
36	$1.01
37	$1.04
38	$1.06
39	$1.07
40	$1.10
41	$1.13
42	$1.20
43	$1.29
44	$1.40
45	$1.53
46	$1.67
47	$1.83
48	$1.98
49	$2.13
50	$2.30
51	$2.52
52	$2.81
53	$3.20
54	$3.65
55	$4.15
56	$ 4.68
57	$ 5.20
58	$ 5.66
59	$ 6.06
60	$ 6.51
61	$ 7.11
62	$ 7.96
63	$ 9.08
64	$10.41
65	$11.90
66	$13.51
67	$15.20
68	$16.92
69	$18.70

Table 6-1. Table 2001 (*cont'd*)

Age	*Rate per $1,000 of Face Amount*
70	$20.62
71	$22.72
72	$25.07
73	$27.57
74	$30.18
75	$33.05
76	$36.33
77	$40.17
78	$44.33
79	$49.23
80	$54.56
81	$60.51
82	$66.74
83	$73.07
84	$ 80.35
85	$ 88.76
86	$ 99.16
87	$110.40
88	$121.85
89	$133.40
90	$144.30
91	$155.80
92	$168.75
93	$186.44
94	$206.70
95	$228.35
96	$250.01
97	$265.09
98	$270.11
99	$281.05

Example 6-1: Bernie, age 40, is covered by the ABC Plastics' profit sharing plan. Her life insurance contract under the plan has a face amount of $120,000 and cash value of $20,000 as of December 31, 2019. The rate per

$1,000 according to Table 2001 (see Table 6-1) is $1.10. The taxable cost of insurance for Bernie is calculated as follows:

($120,000 − $20,000) × 1.10 ÷ 1,000 = $110

Therefore, $110 will be reported as ordinary income to Bernie for 2019.

Q 6:5 May rates other than those in the tables above be used in determining the taxable amount of insurance?

Yes. If the insurance company that issues the life insurance contracts has uniform one-year term premium rates that are lower than the Table 2001 rates, they may be used. [Rev. Rul. 66-110] Many insurance companies have developed products specifically to take advantage of this rule and produce very low taxable income for individuals purchasing their contracts. However, those rates may only be used if they represent initial issuance insurance available to all standard risks. [Rev. Rul. 67-154]

In IRS Notice 2002-8, the IRS responded to this approach by insurers indicating that taxpayers may continue to determine the value of current life insurance protection by using the insurer's lower published premium rates that are available to all standard risks for initial issue one-year term insurance. The use of the insurer's rates is subject to the following limitations:

1. For taxable years after December 31, 2003, the IRS will not consider an insurer's published premium rates to be available to all standard risks who apply for term insurance unless:
   a. The insurer generally makes the availability of such rates known to persons who apply for term insurance coverage from the insurer;
   b. The insurer regularly sells term insurance at such rates to individuals who apply for term insurance coverage from the insurer; and
   c. The insurer does not more commonly sell term insurance at higher premium rates to individuals that the insurer classifies as standard risks under the definition of standard risk most commonly used by the insurer for the issuance of term insurance.
2. For life insurance contracts issued after March 1, 2001, the IRS provides no assurance that such published premium rates may be used to determine the value of life insurance protection for periods after the later of December 31, 2003, or December 31 of the year in which further guidance relating to the valuation of current life insurance protection is published.

This Notice is in the format of interim guidance, so taxpayers can expect that updated tables will be provided sometime in the future. [Notice 2002-8]

Example 6-2: First National Insurance Company has one-year renewable term rates that are lower than the rates in Table 2001 for all ages between 15 and 81, inclusive. Such lower rates may be used without limitation for life insurance contracts under the First National Insurance Company that are held in pension or profit sharing plans as long as the rates meet the requirements set forth in IRS Notice 2002-8.

Q 6:6 What age should be used in determining the annual cost of life insurance?

There is no specific guidance; however, it is generally considered appropriate to use a determination date for age applied on a reasonable and consistent basis. Common methods include:

- The participant's attained age as of the beginning of the calendar year
- The participant's age on his or her birthday nearest the policy anniversary date
- The participant's age on his or her birthday nearest the end of the plan year ending within the calendar year or
- The participant's attained age as of the end of the calendar year.

Q 6:7 What happens if the life insurance is in force for less than a full year due to a termination of employment?

If a participant terminates employment, his or her life insurance may be in force for only a portion of the year. In that case, the full annual term cost of the life insurance protection must be included in his or her gross income for the year of termination. However, if an amount is returned to the plan representing a refund of the premium paid for that year, the amount of the credit will reduce the amount includible in the participant's gross income. [Rev. Rul. 69-490]

Example 6-3: Norman becomes eligible for the ABC Plastics' pension plan on September 1, 2018. Life insurance is purchased for his benefit with a face amount of $150,000 (with no cash value in the policy in the first year). The cost of life insurance for Norman, who is age 30, for 2018 is computed as follows using the annual rate of term insurance cost as shown in Table 2001 in Q 6:4:

$$(\$150{,}000 - 0) \times 0.87 \div 1{,}000 = \$130.50$$

Norman terminates employment on December 1, 2018, and the insurance company issues a premium refund of $100. The net taxable amount reported to Norman is $30.50 ($130.50 − $100) for 2018.

Q 6:8 How is the cost of life insurance computed for new life insurance contracts issued during the year?

Generally, a full year's cost of life insurance is computed, despite the fact that the insurance policy has not been in force for an entire year. However, in the case of premiums that are payable other than annually, the cost of life insurance is prorated for the portion of the year covered by the premiums. For example, if two monthly premiums are paid during the calendar year, the cost of life insurance is 2/12 of the calculated amount. [Rev. Rul. 69-490]

Q 6:9 What happens if the cash value in the life insurance contract exceeds the face amount?

This happens in later policy years with a type of insurance contract known as a retirement income or retirement endowment contract. These contracts are no longer available, but might still exist in older plans. Under this type of contract, in years that the cash value exceeds the face amount, no taxable cost of life insurance is reportable, because there would be no income tax-free death benefit.

Q 6:10 How is the cost of life insurance computed under a universal life insurance contract?

Generally, under a universal life insurance contract, the face amount (or death benefit) may vary, depending on the premiums that are paid. The costs of life insurance are calculated in the same manner as under any other contract, based on the actual face amount and actual cash value for the contract.

Q 6:11 How is the annual cost of life insurance reported?

The annual cost of life insurance is reported annually to the participant and the IRS on Form 1099-R. (See chapter 27 for the details on reporting cost of life insurance.)

Q 6:12 How is the annual cost of life insurance computed for survivor whole life contracts?

Some profit sharing or 401(k) plans allow the purchase of a special type of insurance contract commonly referred to as survivor whole life, or "second-to-die" life insurance. This type of life insurance provides a death benefit only upon the death of the second covered individual. Since the payment of proceeds is contingent upon the death of two individuals, premium rates are substantially lower, and greater life insurance protection can be provided. In determining the current taxation of these contracts, a lower government table is used, the U.S. Life Table 38. If the participant's spouse (or other covered individual) dies while the policy is held in the plan, the Table 2001 costs will be applicable thereafter. [Information Letter from Norman Greenberg, Chief of the Actuarial Branch, Aug. 10, 1983, Department of Treasury, to Morton Greenberg Advanced Underwriting Director and Counsel, The Manufacturers Life Insurance Company, Ltr. Rul. 9709027] Sample rates from the U.S. Life Table 38 are shown in Table 6-2.

Table 6-2. One-Year Term Premiums for $1,000 of Joint and Survivor Life Insurance Protection

Age	5	10	15	20	25	30	35	40	45	50
5	0.00	0.00	0.00	0.00	0.00	0.00	0.00	0.01	0.01	0.01
10	0.00	0.00	0.00	0.00	0.00	0.00	0.00	0.00	0.01	0.01
15	0.00	0.00	0.00	0.00	0.00	0.00	0.00	0.01	0.01	0.01
20	0.00	0.00	0.00	0.00	0.00	0.00	0.01	0.01	0.01	0.02
25	0.00	0.00	0.00	0.00	0.00	0.00	0.01	0.01	0.01	0.02
30	0.00	0.00	0.00	0.00	0.00	0.01	0.01	0.01	0.02	0.02
35	0.00	0.00	0.00	0.01	0.01	0.01	0.01	0.01	0.02	0.03
40	0.01	0.00	0.01	0.01	0.01	0.01	0.01	0.02	0.03	0.04
45	0.01	0.01	0.01	0.01	0.01	0.02	0.02	0.03	0.04	0.06
50	0.01	0.01	0.01	0.02	0.02	0.02	0.03	0.04	0.06	0.09
55	0.02	0.01	0.02	0.02	0.03	0.03	0.05	0.06	0.09	0.13
60	0.03	0.02	0.03	0.03	0.04	0.05	0.07	0.09	0.13	0.20
65	0.04	0.03	0.04	0.05	0.06	0.08	0.10	0.14	0.20	0.30
70	0.06	0.04	0.06	0.08	0.10	0.12	0.16	0.22	0.31	0.45
75	0.09	0.06	0.10	0.12	0.14	0.18	0.24	0.33	0.47	0.69
80	0.14	0.09	0.14	0.18	0.22	0.28	0.37	0.50	0.72	1.05
85	0.21	0.14	0.22	0.28	0.33	0.42	0.55	0.76	1.08	0.16
90	0.31	0.21	0.32	0.41	0.49	0.61	0.81	1.12	1.59	2.33
95	0.44	0.30	0.46	0.59	0.70	0.88	1.17	1.61	2.29	3.36
100	0.61	0.42	0.64	0.81	0.98	1.23	1.62	2.23	3.18	4.66

Age	55	60	65	70	75	80	85	90	95	100
5	0.02	0.03	0.04	0.06	0.09	0.14	0.21	0.31	0.44	0.61
10	0.01	0.02	0.03	0.04	0.06	0.09	0.10	0.21	0.30	0.42
15	0.02	0.03	0.04	0.06	0.10	0.14	0.20	0.32	0.46	0.64
20	0.02	0.03	0.05	0.08	0.12	0.18	0.28	0.41	0.59	0.81
25	0.03	0.04	0.06	0.10	0.14	0.23	0.33	0.49	0.70	0.98
30	0.03	0.05	0.08	0.12	0.18	0.28	0.42	0.61	0.88	1.23
35	0.05	0.07	0.10	0.16	0.24	0.37	0.50	0.81	1.17	1.62
40	0.06	0.09	0.14	0.22	0.33	0.50	0.76	1.12	1.61	2.23
45	0.09	0.13	0.20	0.31	0.47	0.72	1.08	1.99	2.29	3.18
50	0.13	0.20	0.30	0.45	0.69	1.05	1.16	2.33	3.35	4.66
55	0.19	0.29	0.44	0.68	1.03	1.56	2.35	3.47	5.00	6.94
60	0.29	0.44	0.67	1.02	1.56	2.36	3.54	5.74	7.55	10.47

Table 6-2. One-Year Term Premiums for $1,000 of Joint and Survivor Life Insurance Protection (*cont'd*)

Age	5	10	15	20	25	30	35	40	45	50
65	0.44	0.67	1.02	1.55	2.37	3.59	5.39	7.96	11.47	15.92
70	0.68	1.02	1.55	2.37	3.61	5.47	8.22	12.14	17.49	24.28
75	1.08	1.56	2.37	3.61	5.50	8.33	12.52	18.50	26.65	37.00
80	1.56	2.36	3.59	5.47	8.33	12.64	18.98	28.05	40.42	56.10
85	2.35	3.54	5.39	8.22	12.52	18.98	28.52	42.13	60.70	84.26
90	3.47	5.24	7.96	12.14	18.50	28.05	42.13	62.26	89.70	124.52
95	5.00	7.55	11.47	17.49	26.65	40.42	60.70	89.70	129.26	179.42
100	6.94	10.47	15.92	24.28	37.00	56.10	84.26	124.52	179.42	249.02

Chapter 7

Bankruptcy

This chapter describes the effect of a participant's bankruptcy on his or her benefits under a tax-favored retirement plan.

Bankruptcy 7-1

Bankruptcy

Q 7:1 How did the federal Bankruptcy Abuse Prevention and Consumer Protection Act of 2005 (BAPCPA) expand the protection for tax-favored retirement plans from creditors in bankruptcy proceedings?

Bankruptcy Abuse Prevention and Consumer Protection Act of 2005 (BAPCPA) expanded the protection for tax-favored retirement plans or arrangements that were not already protected under Bankruptcy Code Section 541(c)(2) pursuant to *Patterson v. Shumate* [504 U.S. 753 (1992)] or other state or federal law.

BAPCPA amended Section 522 of the Bankruptcy Code to permit a debtor to exempt certain retirement funds from the debtor's bankruptcy estate to the extent those monies are in a fund or account that is exempt from taxation under Code Sections 401 (qualified retirement plans), 403 (tax-sheltered annuities), 408 (traditional IRAs), 408A (Roth IRAs), 414 (church plans, governmental plans, and multiemployer plans), 457 (deferred compensation plans of state and local governments and tax-exempt organizations), or 501(a) (tax-exempt organizations) and that has received a favorable determination letter from the IRS pursuant to Code Section 7805 that is in effect as of the date of the filing of the petition in the bankruptcy case. If the retirement monies are in a retirement fund that has not received a favorable IRS determination letter, those monies will be exempt from the debtor's bankruptcy estate if the debtor demonstrates that (1) no prior determination to the contrary has been made by a court or the IRS and

(2) the retirement fund is in substantial compliance with the applicable requirements of the Code; or if the retirement fund fails to be in substantial compliance with the applicable requirements of the Code, the debtor is not materially responsible for the failure.

BAPCPA also resolved the question of how direct transfers and rollover distributions are treated in bankruptcy. Direct transfers under Code Section 401(a)(31) from tax-exempt retirement funds described in Code Sections 401, 403, 408, 408A, 414, 457, or 501(a) are exempt from the debtor's bankruptcy estate.

Similarly, eligible rollover distributions, including eligible rollover distributions under Code Section 402(c), remain exempt from the debtor's bankruptcy estate as long as they are deposited into another tax-exempt retirement fund within 60 days after they have been distributed.

[Bankruptcy Code § 522, as amended by BAPCPA]

Q 7:2 How did BAPCPA change the automatic stay provisions of the federal Bankruptcy Code?

BAPCPA amended Section 362(b) of the federal Bankruptcy Code to except from the automatic stay the withholding of income from a debtor's wages pursuant to an agreement authorizing such withholding for the benefit of a pension, profit sharing, stock bonus, or other employer-sponsored plan established under Code Sections 401, 403, 408, 408A, 414, 457, or 501(c) to the extent that the amounts withheld are used solely to repay a loan from a plan as authorized by ERISA Section 408(b)(1) or subject to Code Section 72(p) or with respect to a loan from certain thrift savings plans. This exception from the automatic stay may not be used to cause any loan made under a Code Section 414(d) governmental plan or a Code Section 403(b) tax-sheltered annuity to be construed to be a claim or debt within the meaning of the Bankruptcy Code.

Q 7:3 Under BAPCPA, can plan loans be discharged in bankruptcy?

No. BAPCPA amended Section 523(a) of the Bankruptcy Code to except from discharge any amounts owed by the debtor to a pension, profit sharing, stock bonus, or other plan established under Code Sections 401, 403, 408, 408A, 414, 457, or 501(c) under a loan authorized by ERISA Section 408(b)(1) or subject to Code Section 72(p) or with respect to a loan from certain thrift savings plans. This exception to discharge may not be used to cause any loan made under a Code Section 414(d) governmental plan or a Code Section 403(b) tax-sheltered annuity to be construed to be a claim or debt within the meaning of the Bankruptcy Code.

Q 7:4 May a Chapter 13 plan materially alter the provisions of a debtor's retirement plan loan?

No. BAPCPA amended Section 1322 of the Bankruptcy Code to provide that a Chapter 13 plan may not materially alter the terms of a debtor's retirement plan loan, and that any amounts required to repay such a loan shall not constitute "disposable income" under Section 1325 of the Bankruptcy Code.

Q 7:5 Did BAPCPA impose a cap on the amount of traditional or Roth IRA assets that can be exempted from the debtor's bankruptcy estate?

Yes. BAPCPA amended Section 522 of the Bankruptcy Code to impose a $1 million cap (periodically adjusted pursuant to Section 104 of the Bankruptcy Code to reflect changes in the Consumer Price Index) on the value of the debtor's interest in a traditional IRA described in Code Section 408 or a Roth IRA described under Code Section 408A (but not a Code Section 408(b) SEP account or a Code Section 408(p) SIMPLE retirement account) that a debtor may claim as exempt property in bankruptcy. This limit applies without regard to any amounts attributable to rollover contributions made pursuant to Code Sections 402(c), 402(e)(6), 403(a)(4), 403(a)(5), or 403(b)(8) and earnings thereon. The cap may be increased if required in the interest of justice.

Part 2

Benefit Determination

Chapter 8

Vesting

The Employee Retirement Income Security Act of 1974 (ERISA) and the Internal Revenue Code ("the Code"), as amended, require that plans comply with rules on how long it takes participants to earn vested benefits. This chapter explores the vesting rules including permissible vesting schedules, top-heavy accelerated vesting rules, methods for determining vesting service, and the mechanism for changing vesting schedules. The timing of forfeitures and methods for restoring forfeited amounts are also examined.

Certain plan events, such as plan termination or partial termination, and other analogous events, such as complete discontinuance of employer contributions, will cause an otherwise nonvested or partially vested participant to become 100 percent vested in his or her account balance or accrued benefit under the plan.

General Vesting Rules 8-2
PPA Changes Effective for Post-2006 Plan Years 8-6
Top-Heavy Rules 8-8
Determination of Top-Heavy Status 8-11
Death Benefits, Rollovers, and Plan-to-Plan Transfers 8-12
Key Employees 8-13
Top-Heavy Vesting Schedules 8-16
Determination of Years of Vesting Service 8-16
Breaks in Service 8-21
Amendments in Vesting Schedules 8-23
Forfeitures and Cash-Out Rules 8-24
Required Vesting upon Plan Termination, Partial Termination, or Complete Discontinuance of Contributions 8-30

General Vesting Rules

Q 8:1 What are the basic vesting rules under ERISA and the Code?

ERISA and the Code contain five basic rules on the vesting of benefits:

1. An employee's right to his or her normal retirement benefit must be 100 percent vested and nonforfeitable upon attainment of normal retirement age.
2. An employee's own contributions must be 100 percent vested and nonforfeitable at all times.
3. An employee's right to employer contributions must vest at a rate that is at least as rapid as the minimum vesting schedules prescribed in ERISA and the Code.
4. Certain events may lead to a forfeiture of benefits.
5. Certain events may require 100 percent vesting.

[I.R.C. § 411(a)]

Q 8:2 What plans are subject to the minimum vesting standards?

Generally, most qualified plans are subject to the minimum vesting standards of ERISA and the Code. However, the following types of plans are exempt from these rules:

1. Governmental plans established and maintained for its employees by the U.S. government, by the government of any state or political subdivision, or by any agency or instrumentality of any of the foregoing. Governmental plans also include any plan to which the Railroad Retirement Act of 1935 or 1937 applies and that is financed by contributions required under that Act and any plan of an international organization that is exempt from tax by reason of the International Organizations Immunities Act. [I.R.C. § 414(d)]
2. A plan established and maintained for its employees by a religious denomination that is exempt from tax under Code Section 501. [I.R.C. § 414(e)(1)] In some cases, the otherwise exempt plan sponsor may have made an election under Code Section 410(d)(1) to be subject to ERISA and the Code. In that case, the plan will be subject to the minimum vesting rules described in this chapter.
3. A plan that has not, at any time after September 2, 1974, provided for employer contributions.
4. A plan established and maintained by a fraternal beneficiary society, order, or association, if none of the contributions is made by employers of the participants.

[I.R.C. § 411(e)(1)]

Q 8:3 How are the minimum vesting rules applied?

In a defined contribution plan, vesting is applied to the participant's account balances to determine the portion to which he or she is entitled as of a particular determination date. In a defined benefit plan, vesting is applied to the participant's accrued benefit as of a particular determination date to determine the portion to which he or she is entitled as of that particular determination date.

Q 8:4 When must benefits be 100 percent vested and nonforfeitable?

Generally, benefits must be 100 percent vested and nonforfeitable when:

- The participant reaches the plan's normal retirement age (see Q 8:5)
- The benefits are attributable to an employee's own contributions (see Q 8:6)
- The participant completes the requisite number of years of vesting service under the plan's vesting schedule to become 100 percent vested (see Q 8:8)
- A plan termination or partial termination occurs (see Qs 8:69–8:81)
- Contributions are completely discontinued, in the case of a plan that is not subject to the minimum funding standards of Code Section 412 (see Qs 8:26–8:83)
- The plan requires more than one year of service for participation (e.g., the plan's eligibility requirement is two years of service)

[Treas. Reg. § 1.411(a)-1(a)]

Q 8:5 In determining 100 percent vesting, when does a participant reach the plan's normal retirement age?

The term *normal retirement age* means the earlier of:

1. The time specified in the plan document at which the participant attains normal retirement age; or
2. The later of the time a plan participant attains age 65, or the fifth anniversary of the time a plan participant commenced participation in the plan.

[I.R.C. § 411(a)(8)]

Example 8-1: ABC Toys' defined benefit plan document defines normal retirement age as 62. Nancy retires on April 15, 2019, her 62nd birthday. Nancy is 100 percent vested in her accrued benefit (regardless of her number of accumulated years of vesting service) because she has attained the plan's normal retirement age.

Q 8:6 What types of contribution accounts must be 100 percent vested and nonforfeitable?

In a defined contribution plan under which separate accounts are maintained, account balances attributable to the following types of contributions must be 100 percent vested at all times:

- Elective contributions [I.R.C. § 401(k)]
- Qualified nonelective contributions [Treas. Reg. § 1.401(k)-6]
- Qualified matching contributions [Treas. Reg. § 1.401(k)-6]
- Voluntary after-tax employee contributions [I.R.C. § 411(a)(1)]
- Mandatory after-tax employee contributions [I.R.C. § 411(a)(1)]
- Rollover contributions [I.R.C. § 411(a)(1)]

If separate accounts are not maintained (rarely the case), the account balance attributable to employee contributions is determined by multiplying the total account balance by this fraction:

$$\frac{\text{Total employee contributions under the plan less withdrawals}}{\text{Total employee contributions under the plan less withdrawals plus total employer contributions (on behalf of such employee) less withdrawals}}$$

[I.R.C. § 411(c)(2)(A)]

Q 8:7 How is the employee-derived accrued benefit determined in a defined benefit plan with mandatory employee contributions?

A special formula and conversion factors are used in determining the portion of the accrued benefit attributable to mandatory employee contributions in a defined benefit plan. (See Qs 9:31–9:34.) [Treas. Reg. § 1.411(c)-1(c)]

Q 8:8 What are the minimum vesting requirements for employer-derived account balances and accrued benefits?

Before 2007, the general rule was that employer-derived account balances and accrued benefits must vest at a rate at least as rapid as one of these two minimum schedules:

1. *Five-year cliff vesting.* An employee who completes at least five years of vesting service is 100 percent vested.
2. *Three- to seven-year graded vesting.* An employee's nonforfeitable rights vest at the following rate:

Years of Service	Nonforfeitable Annual Percentage
3	20%
4	40%
5	60%
6	80%
7 or more	100%

[I.R.C. §§ 411(a)(2)(A), 411(a)(2)(B)]

Exceptions to the pre-2007 minimum vesting rules are applied to:

1. Matching employer contributions made for plan years beginning after December 31, 2001:
2. Top-heavy plans:

After 2006, only traditional defined benefit plans may abide by pre-PPA minimum vesting rules.

Example 8-2: ABC Toys' profit sharing plan has adopted a vesting schedule that provides for no vesting for the first three years and 100 percent vesting at the end of the fourth year. The plan is not top heavy. This schedule complies with the pre-2007 minimum vesting standards, because it vests more rapidly than the five-year cliff schedule.

Example 8-3: CDE Games has adopted the following vesting schedule:

Years of Vesting Service	*Vesting Percentage*
3	0%
4	40%
5	60%
6	80%
7 or more	100%

This vesting schedule does not comply with the pre-2007 minimum vesting standards. It is not as rapid as the five-year cliff schedule because it yields a vested percentage of only 60 percent (rather than 100 percent) after five years. Similarly, it is not as rapid as the three- to seven-year graded schedule because it yields a vested percentage of zero percent (rather than 20 percent) at the end of the third year.

Q 8:9 What accelerated vesting schedules applied to matching contributions?

The minimum vesting schedules applicable to top-heavy plans applied to pre-2007 matching employer contributions. The plan sponsor, at its option, applied these rules only to matching contributions made for plan years beginning after December 31, 2001. [I.R.C. § 411(a)(12) (stricken after 2006)]

Example 8-4: ABC Toys sponsors a 401(k) plan that was not top heavy. The plan document provided that matching employer contributions were subject to a five-year cliff vesting schedule (full vesting upon the completion of five years of vesting service). The plan was amended, effective for plan years beginning after December 31, 2001, to provide that all matching contribution accounts (inclusive of past and future contributions and related earnings) were subject to three-year cliff vesting. Alternatively, the company could have amended the plan, effective for plan years beginning after December 31, 2001, to provide that any matching contributions (and attributable earnings) made after December 31, 2001, were subject to three-year cliff vesting.

The portion of the matching contribution account attributable to matching contributions made on or before December 31, 2001, would have then remained subject to the five-year cliff vesting schedule.

PPA Changes Effective for Post-2006 Plan Years

Q 8:10 How did PPA change the rules for vesting under defined contribution plans?

Effective for plan years beginning in 2007, the top-heavy minimum schedules apply to defined contribution plans. These minimum schedules apply to employees who have at least one hour of service after the plan year that begins in 2006. [PPA § 904; I.R.C. § 411(a)(2)(B); ERISA § 203(a)]

Q 8:11 Is there a delayed effective date for collectively bargained plans?

In the case of a plan maintained pursuant to one or more collective bargaining agreements between employee representatives and one or more employers, ratified before the enactment of PPA, the vesting schedule changes shall not apply to contributions on behalf of employees covered by any such agreement for plan years beginning before the earlier of:

1. The later of:
    a. The date on which the last of such collective bargaining agreements terminates (determined without regard to any extension on or after the enactment of PPA); or
    b. January 1, 2007; and
2. January 1, 2009.

These minimum schedules apply to employees who have at least one hour of service after the applicable effective date of the vesting schedule change. [PPA § 904(c); I.R.C. § 411(a); ERISA § 203(a)]

Q 8:12 What are the vesting requirements for a qualified automatic contribution arrangement (QACA)?

Employer contributions made to support a Code Section 401(k)(13) QACA requirements must be fully vested for each employee who has completed at least two years of vesting service.

[I.R.C. § 401(k)(13)(D)(iii)(I)]

Q 8:13 What are the current rules for vesting under cash balance plans?

For cash balance plans (or similar hybrid plans) established after June 29, 2005, the vesting schedule must be at least as rapid as three-year cliff vesting.

For cash balance plans in existence on June 29, 2005, the vesting schedule must be, or be amended to be, at least as rapid as the three-year cliff vesting schedule for plan years beginning after 2007, unless the plan sponsor elects an earlier application of a compliant vesting schedule.

[PPA § 701(a); ERISA § 203(f); I.R.C. § 411(a)(13)]

Example 8-5: ABC Toys adopted a cash balance plan for the plan year ended December 31, 2005. The plan was adopted on December 10, 2005, but was effective as of January 1, 2005. Because the plan was not in existence on June 29, 2005, the plan must provide a vesting schedule that is at least as rapid as the three-year cliff vesting schedule. The business decides to use the following schedule for all years:

Years of Vesting Service	*Vested Percentage*
0	0%
1	0%
2	20%
3	100%

Q 8:14 What vesting schedules apply if a portion of a participant's benefit is determined under a traditional defined benefit formula and another portion is determined under a cash balance formula?

The three-year cliff minimum vesting schedule applies to the participant's entire accrued benefit. [Prop. Reg. § 1.411(a)(13)-1(c)(1)]

Example 8-6: ABC Toys adopted a traditional defined benefit plan in 1991 and converted it to a cash balance plan in 2013. Shannon has an accrued benefit under the old traditional formula equal to $500 per month payable commencing at age 65. She also has a current hypothetical accumulation account of $10,200 under the cash balance portion of the plan. Shannon terminates employment in 2018. Under the rules discussed above, the plan is subject to the three-year cliff vesting for all of Shannon's benefits. Because Shannon has more than three years of vesting service when she terminates employment, she is 100 percent vested in both her traditional and cash balance accrued benefits.

Q 8:15 How are the minimum vesting requirements coordinated with the nondiscrimination requirements of Code Section 401(a)(4)?

A plan that satisfies the minimum vesting requirements is generally treated as satisfying the nondiscrimination requirements of Code Section 401(a)(4) unless:

1. There has been a pattern of abuse under the plan, such as the dismissal of employees before their benefits become vested, which tends to discriminate

in favor of highly compensated employees (HCEs). (See Appendix G for rules determining HCEs.)

2. There have been, or there is a reason to believe that there will be, an accrual of benefits or forfeitures tending to discriminate in favor of employees who are highly compensated. [I.R.C. § 411(d)(1)]

Example 8-7: ABC Toys maintains a profit sharing plan with a five-year cliff vesting schedule. Over the last 10 years, while the plan has been in force, a number of lower-paid employees with four years of vesting service have been fired. The DOL may view this as a pattern of abuse.

Q 8:16 May vested benefits be forfeited for cause?

If a plan document has specific provisions, a plan may provide that vested benefits in excess of the minimum required vesting under Code Section 411 can be forfeited for cause (e.g., theft or other dishonest behavior related to the employer or in situations where an employee leaves employment with the employer and goes to work for a competitor). These types of plan provisions are commonly known as "bad boy" forfeiture clauses. [Treas. Reg. §§ 1.411(a)-4(a), 1.411(a)-4(c)]

Example 8-8: ABC Toys' pension plan (a traditional, non-top-heavy defined benefit plan) has a vesting schedule of 20 percent per year of service. An alternative vesting schedule, the five-year cliff vesting schedule, applies if an employee commences employment with a competitor business within one year of termination of employment. After he completes four years of vesting service, Fred terminates employment and immediately begins working for a competitor of ABC Toys. Therefore, based upon the plan provisions and because the plan is not top heavy, Fred is nonvested, because he is subject to the alternative vesting schedule rather than being 80 percent vested under the plan's normal vesting schedule.

Top-Heavy Rules

Q 8:17 What are the minimum vesting standards for top-heavy plans?

All top-heavy plans must provide for a vesting schedule that is at least as rapid as follows:

1. *Three-year cliff vesting.* An employee who completes at least three years of vesting service is 100 percent vested.
2. *Six-year graded vesting.* An employee's nonforfeitable rights must vest at the rate of 20 percent per year starting after two years of vesting service, so that the employee is 100 percent vested after six years of vesting service.

[I.R.C. § 416(b)(1)]

Q 8:18 What is a top-heavy plan?

A plan is considered top heavy if, as of the determination date:

1. In a defined benefit plan, more than 60 percent of the present value of all accrued benefits is attributable to key employees.
2. In a defined contribution plan, more than 60 percent of the value of all account balances is attributable to key employees.
3. See Q 8:20 for determining top-heavy status if an employer maintains more than one plan.

[I.R.C. § 416(g)(1)]

Q 8:19 What is the determination date?

The determination date is the last day of the prior plan year. However, for the first year of a plan, the determination date is the last day of the first plan year. [I.R.C. § 416(g)(4)(C)]

Q 8:20 What if the employer maintains more than one plan?

If a key employee participates in more than one plan of the employer, all plans in which a key employee participates are aggregated for top-heavy testing purposes. In addition, if a plan relies on another plan for purposes of the minimum coverage rules of Code Section 410(b) or the nondiscrimination requirements of Code Section 401(a)(4), all such plans must be aggregated and tested together. [I.R.C. § 416(g)(2)(A)(i)] Such plans are called a required aggregation group (RAG). If the RAG is top heavy, all plans that are part of the RAG are considered to be top heavy and are required to provide a vesting schedule at least as rapid as the schedules discussed in Q 8:17. If the RAG is not top heavy, none of the plans in the RAG is top heavy. [I.R.C. § 416(g)(1)(B)]

Q 8:21 May other plans of the employer be aggregated and tested together for top-heavy purposes?

Yes, certain plans may be combined with other plans of the employer to form a permissive aggregation group (PAG). An employer may aggregate a plan covering only non-key employees with a plan covering one or more key employees under these two conditions:

1. When aggregating all plans in the PAG, the combined plans pass the minimum coverage requirements of Code Section 410(b); and
2. When aggregating all plans in the PAG, the nondiscrimination requirements of Code Section 401(a)(4) are satisfied; that is, the amounts of contributions and benefits do not discriminate in favor of HCEs.

If the PAG is not top heavy, none of the plans in the PAG is top heavy. If the PAG is top heavy, only the plans in the RAG are top heavy. [Treas. Reg. § 1.416-1, Q&A T-7]

Example 8-9: ABC Toys maintains three qualified plans: a traditional defined benefit plan, a money purchase plan, and a profit sharing plan. The defined benefit plan covers only union employees. No key employees participate in the defined benefit plan, and, therefore, it is not part of the RAG and it is not considered top heavy (because there are only non-key employees participating in the plan). The money purchase plan and the profit sharing plan are part of a RAG, because each plan has at least one key employee covered. For the 2018 plan year, the RAG is tested as of the determination date, December 31, 2017, and is found to be top heavy. Therefore, both of the plans in the RAG—the money purchase plan and the profit sharing plan—are top heavy for the 2018 plan year and are subject to the top-heavy minimum vesting schedule. [Treas. Reg. § 1.416-1, Q&A T-7]

However, all plans of the employer may be permissively aggregated if the combined plans satisfy the minimum coverage rules of Code Section 410(b) and the nondiscrimination requirements of Code Section 401(a)(4). Because the defined benefit plan provides very generous benefits, it makes sense to permissively aggregate the plans. If the PAG is not top heavy, none of the plans in the PAG are top heavy and the top-heavy minimum vesting schedules are not required for any of the plans. If the PAG were top heavy, the defined benefit plan would still not be considered top heavy, because only plans in the RAG—the money purchase plan and profit sharing plan—are treated as top heavy under the permissive aggregation rules.

Q 8:22 In the case of an aggregation group where plans have different plan years, when must the determination of top-heavy status be made?

When two or more plans constitute a RAG or PAG, this two-step method should be used in determining top-heavy status:

1. Step 1. Determine the present value of accrued benefits in a defined benefit plan and value of account balances in a defined contribution plan, separately for each plan as of the applicable plan's determination date.
2. Step 2. Add the results together, using the determination dates that fall within the same calendar year.

[Treas. Reg. § 1.416-1, Q&A T-23]

Example 8-10: ABC Toys maintains a defined benefit plan, with a plan year ending June 30, 2018, and a determination date of June 30, 2017. The 401(k) plan has a plan year ending December 31, 2018, with a determination date of December 31, 2017. Using the determination dates (June 30, 2017 and December 31, 2017) that fall within the same calendar year (2017), the present value of the accrued benefits and value of account balances, as applicable, can be determined separately for each plan in the RAG and then combined to determine the top-heavy results.

Determination of Top-Heavy Status

Q 8:23 How is the value of account balances determined in a defined contribution plan?

The value of account balances as of the determination date for any individual is the sum of:

1. The account balance as of the most recent valuation date occurring within the 12-month period ending on the determination date; in most instances, the determination date and the most recent valuation date will be the same date; plus
2. An adjustment for contributions not made as of the determination date but allocated to the participant's account as of the determination date, if either of two conditions exists:
   a. The plan is a money purchase plan, target plan, or other defined contribution plan subject to minimum funding standards under Code Section 412; or
   b. The plan is a profit sharing plan (including a 401(k) plan) or stock bonus plan, and a top-heavy determination is made for the first plan year.

[Treas. Reg. § 1.416-1, Q&A T-24]

Q 8:24 How is the present value of accrued benefits determined in a defined benefit plan?

The present value is calculated as of the most recent valuation date that falls within a 12-month period ending on the determination date. In the first plan year of a plan, the accrued benefit for a current employee is determined either:

1. As if the participant terminated employment as of the determination date; or
2. As if the participant terminated employment as of the valuation date, but taking into account the estimated accrued benefit as of the determination date.

The valuation date is the same as the valuation date used by the plan's enrolled actuary in computing plan costs for minimum funding. [Treas. Reg. § 1.416-1, Q&A T-25]

Q 8:25 What actuarial assumptions are used in computing the present value of accrued benefits in a defined benefit plan?

No specific actuarial assumptions are prescribed. The assumptions that are used, however, must be reasonable, but they need not be the same as the assumptions used for minimum funding or used in the plan document for determining actuarial equivalence. Plan documents are required to contain provisions specifying actuarial assumptions to be used for determining top-heavy status. The present value must be computed using an interest and a post-retirement mortality assumption. Pre-retirement mortality may be used, as well as future cost of living adjustments (not to exceed the maximum dollar limit permitted by Code Section 415). Assumptions about future withdrawals or future salary increases may not be used. [Treas. Reg. § 1.416-1, Q&A T-26]

Q 8:26 What distributions are taken into account in determining the value of account balances and the present value of accrued benefits?

Distributions, other than in-service distributions, made within the plan year that includes the determination date are added to the present value of the value of account balances and/or accrued benefits for key and non-key employees. In-service distributions made within the plan year that includes the determination date and within the four preceding plan years are also added to the value of account balances and/or to the present value of accrued benefits for key and non-key employees. A rollover to a related plan is disregarded, because the rollover will likely be counted as an account balance in the related plan (see Q 8:29). [Treas. Reg. § 1.416-1, Q&As T-30, T-32; I.R.C. § 416(g)(3)]

Q 8:27 Is the value of account balances and/or present value of the accrued benefits for any participant disregarded in determining top-heavy status?

Yes, the value of account balances and/or present value of the accrued benefits are disregarded in the following situations:

1. If a participant was a key employee in a prior plan year, but ceases to be a key employee in the current plan year; or
2. If the employee has not performed services for the employer at any time during the one-year period ending on the determination date.

[I.R.C. § 416(g)(4)(B), (E)]

Death Benefits, Rollovers, and Plan-to-Plan Transfers

Q 8:28 How are benefits paid on account of death treated?

In determining top-heavy status, death benefits are treated as distributions except to the extent the death benefit exceeds the value of account balances and/or present value of the accrued benefits immediately before death. [Treas. Reg. § 1.416-1, Q&A T-31]

Example 8-11: ABC Toys maintains a defined benefit plan. A death benefit is paid to the widow of Toby, a deceased participant. The death benefit payable is $150,000, although the present value of the accrued benefit immediately before Toby's death was $45,600. In determining top-heavy status, $45,600 is treated as a distribution to Toby's spouse.

Q 8:29 How are rollovers and plan-to-plan transfers treated?

The treatment of rollovers and plan-to-plan transfers depends upon whether the transactions are related. A rollover or plan-to-plan transfer is related if:

1. It is not initiated by the participant; or
2. It is made between plans of the same employer.

If it is initiated by the participant or made between plans of different employers, the transaction is considered to be unrelated. The chart shows whether a transaction is included in the value of account balances and/or present value of accrued benefits for top-heavy determination:

	Transferee Plan	*Transferor Plan*
Related Rollover or Plan-to-Plan Transfer	Yes	No
Unrelated Rollover or Plan-to-Plan Transfer	No	Yes

[Treas. Reg. § 1.416-1, Q&A T-32]

Key Employees

Q 8:30 Who is a key employee?

A key employee is any employee (including a deceased or terminated employee) who meets one or more of the following criteria during the plan year:

1. A "5 percent owner" of the employer;
2. A "1 percent owner" of the employer, earning annual compensation from the employer that is greater than $150,000; or
3. An "includible officer" of the employer. (See Q 8:33.)

[I.R.C. § 416(i)(1)(A)]

Q 8:31 Who is a 5 percent owner of the employer?

An employee is a 5 percent owner if during the plan year or any of the four preceding plan years, the employee is a 5 percent owner as defined in the top-heavy rules of Code Section 416. A 5 percent owner is defined as an individual who:

1. If the employer is a corporation, the individual owns (or is considered as owning under the stock attribution rules of Code Section 318) *more* than 5 percent of the outstanding stock of the corporation or stock possessing more than 5 percent of the total combined voting power of all stock of the corporation; or
2. If the employer is not a corporation, any individual who owns *more* than 5 percent of the capital or profits interest in the employer.

Although the attribution rules in Code Section 318(a)(2) require that 50 percent or more of the value of the stock be owned by an individual before the attribution rules apply, the 5 percent owner rules lower this threshold to 5 percent. Also, in determining the 5 percent threshold, only ownership in a single entity is considered; the controlled group and affiliated service group rules of Code Section 414(b), (c), and (m) are ignored. [I.R.C. §§ 416(i)(1), 318(a)(2)(C)]

Example 8-12: Brianna owns 6 percent of the stock of ABC Toys, which is a part of a controlled group with CDE Games. Although Brianna owns less than 2 percent of the value of all stock in the controlled group of corporations, she is considered a 5 percent owner because she owns more than 5 percent of the stock of ABC Toys.

Example 8-13: Jack owns 4 percent of the stock of ABC Toys. His children, Ben and Grace, also own stock in the corporation: Ben owns 2 percent and Grace owns 1 percent. Jack is considered a 5 percent owner, because he owns his 4 percent plus the 3 percent owned by his children. Ben also is considered a 5 percent owner, because the stock of his father is attributed to him (4 percent plus 2 percent); Grace's stock is not attributable to Ben as a sibling. Grace is not considered a 5 percent owner because the stock attributable to her is not greater than 5 percent (4 percent plus 1 percent).

Q 8:32 Who is a 1 percent owner of the employer?

The same rules described in Q 8:31 apply in determining 1 percent owners; merely substitute "1 percent" for "5 percent." However, a 1 percent owner must have annual compensation that is greater than $150,000 to be a key employee. Compensation includes compensation within the meaning of Code Section 414(q)(4). [I.R.C. § 416(i)(1)(D)]

Example 8-14: In Example 8-13, Grace is not considered a 5 percent owner, because she owns or is considered to own exactly 5 percent of the stock of ABC Toys. However, because she earns annual compensation of $225,000 per year and owns more than 1 percent of the company, she is considered to be a key employee.

Q 8:33 Who is an includible officer?

An employee is an includible officer if these two criteria are met:

1. The employee is an officer of the employer at any time during the plan year.
2. During the plan year, the employee received compensation greater than $130,000 indexed annually.

The $130,000 limit (as in effect in 2004) will be adjusted for cost of living at the same time and in the same manner as under Code Section 415(d). The base period for the adjustment will be the calendar quarter beginning July 1, 2001, and any increase less than $5,000 will not cause an adjustment. Any such increase shall be rounded to the next lowest multiple of $5,000. The adjusted limit for 2018 is $175,000.

[I.R.C. § 416(i)]

Q 8:34 What activities cause an individual to be treated as an officer?

Whether an individual is an officer is determined on the basis of all facts, including, for example, the source of the individual's authority, the term for which he or she is elected or appointed, and the nature and extent of his or her duties. Generally, the term *officer* means an administrative executive who is in regular and continued service. The term implies continuity of service and excludes those employed for a special and single transaction. An employee who has the title but not the authority of an officer is not treated as an officer under these rules. If the sponsoring employer is part of a controlled or affiliated service group (under Code Section 414(b), (c), or (m)), determining whether the individual is an officer rests upon the duties that the individual performs for the company by which he or she is employed, rather than the group as a whole. A partner in a partnership is not treated as an officer merely because he or she owns a capital or profits interest in the partnership and exercises voting rights as a partner. [Treas. Reg. § 1.416-1, Q&A T-13]

Example 8-15: Bernie is a teller for the FGH Bank. Bernie is named as assistant vice president. She has no supervisory authority and no authority to transact business for the bank outside of the scope of her duties as a teller. Bernie is not an officer for purposes of determining key employees.

Q 8:35 Are there limits on the number of officers included?

There is no minimum number of includible officers, but there is a maximum, as shown below:

Number of Employees	*Maximum Number of Includible Officers*
500 or more employees	50
30 or more employees, but fewer than 500 employees	10% of the number of employees
Fewer than 30 employees	3

[I.R.C. § 416(i)(1)(A)]

If the number of includible officers is greater than the maximum number of includible officers, the includible officers with the greatest amount of compensation during the plan year in the determination period are treated as key employees. [Treas. Reg. § 1.416-1, Q&A T-14]

Top-Heavy Vesting Schedules

Q 8:36 When must the top-heavy vesting schedules be applied?

The minimum vesting schedules described in Q 8:17 must be applied for all plan years in which the plan is top heavy. If a participant does not have an hour of service after the plan becomes top heavy, the account balances or accrued benefits of that participant are not subject to the minimum top-heavy vesting schedules. [Treas. Reg. § 1.416-1, Q&A V-3]

Q 8:37 What happens when a plan ceases to be top heavy?

When a plan ceases to be top heavy, the vesting schedule may be changed to a schedule that is at least as rapid as one of the non-top-heavy minimum schedules. The vested status of a participant at the time the plan ceased to be top heavy must not be reduced. Any employee with three or more years of service must also be given the opportunity to remain on the top-heavy vesting schedule. From a practical standpoint, this option applies only to traditional defined benefit plans, and most of these plans that change from top-heavy to non-top-heavy status rarely change their vesting schedules. [Treas. Reg. §§ 1.416-1, Q&A V-7, 1.411(a)-8T]

> **Example 8-16:** CDE Games sponsors a traditional defined benefit plan that is top heavy for the plan year ended December 31, 2018. The plan uses a vesting schedule of 20 percent per year of service, starting with the second year of service (full vesting after six years). Because of the significant number of new non-key participants entering the plan during 2018, the plan is not top heavy on the determination date, December 31, 2018, for the plan year ending December 31, 2019. The plan adopts a five-year cliff vesting schedule for the plan year ending December 31, 2019. Dale has two years of vesting service as of December 31, 2018. Although she would not be vested under the new vesting schedule, Dale must remain under the old vesting schedule for her accrued benefit determined as of December 31, 2018, but the new vesting schedule would apply to any benefit accrued after 2018.

Determination of Years of Vesting Service

Q 8:38 How is a year of service for vesting defined?

A year of service for vesting purposes means a calendar year, plan year, or other 12-consecutive-month period designated by the plan (and not prohibited by the Secretary of Labor) during which the participant has completed 1,000 hours of service. This is known as a vesting computation period. A plan may define a year of service for vesting purposes to require fewer than 1,000 hours. [I.R.C. § 411(a)(5)(A)]

Q 8:39 May the vesting computation period be changed?

A plan may be amended to change the vesting computation period to a different 12-consecutive-month period, provided that no employee's vested percentage is less on any date after the change than it would have been had the change not occurred. A vesting computation period other than an initial or final short plan year may never be less than 12 months. In the event of a change, there will be two overlapping 12-month periods. If a participant is credited with 1,000 hours in both vesting computation periods, the participant is credited with two years of service for vesting purposes. [D.O.L. Reg. § 2530.203-2(c)]

Example 8-17: CDE Games maintains a defined benefit plan with a vesting computation period based on the calendar year. In 2018, CDE Games decides to change the vesting computation period to coincide with the fiscal year of the corporation, which ends March 31, 2019. The two overlapping periods used for vesting service are:

1. January 1, 2018 to December 31, 2018 and
2. April 1, 2018 to March 31, 2019.

A participant who is credited with 1,000 hours in each of these two periods is credited with two years of service for vesting purposes.

Q 8:40 How is an hour of service for vesting defined?

Hours of service are defined as:

1. Each hour for which an employee is paid, or entitled to payment, for the performance of duties for the employer. These hours are credited to the employee for the computation period in which the duties are performed.
2. Each hour for which an employee is paid, or entitled to payment, by the employer on account of a period of time during which no duties are performed (irrespective of whether the employment relationship has terminated) because of vacation, holiday, illness, incapacity (including disability), layoff, jury duty, military duty, or leave of absence. No more than 501 hours of service should be credited for these purposes for any single continuous period.
3. Each hour for which back pay, irrespective of mitigation of damages, is awarded or agreed to by the employer. The same hours of service may not be credited under paragraph (1) or (2) and under this paragraph (3). These hours are credited to the employee for the computation period in which the award, agreement, or payment is made.

Hours of service must be credited for employment with other members of an affiliated service group (under Code Section 414(m)), a controlled group of corporations (under Code Section 414(b)), or a group of trades or businesses under common control (under Code Section 414(c)) of which the adopting employer is a member, and any other entity required to be aggregated with the employer under Code Section 414(o). [D.O.L. Reg. §§ 2530.200b-2, 2530.210(b)]

Q 8:41 Are there any simpler methods for determining years of vesting service?

Yes, a plan may use a method known as "elapsed time," in which it is not necessary to count hours of service. Under that method, an employee earns a year of vesting service for each whole year of service. The time period begins on the employee's first day of employment (i.e., the first day an hour of service is performed) and ends on the date of severance. Periods of less than a whole year may be disregarded. The disadvantage of the elapsed time approach is that periods of employment in which the employee works fewer than 1,000 hours must be counted as years of service for vesting purposes. [Treas. Reg. § 1.410(a)-7(d)(1)]

Example 8-18: CDE Games maintains a defined benefit pension plan on a calendar year basis that uses the elapsed time method for determining years of vesting. The vesting schedule used by the plan is the five-year cliff. Nancy was employed on April 5, 2013, and quit on February 10, 2018. Because Nancy did not work for five full years, she is not vested at the time of her severance of employment.

Q 8:42 Are there any other alternatives for alleviating the record-keeping requirements?

Yes, a plan document may compute equivalent total hours of service by counting only hours worked or regular time hours. If a plan uses the hours-worked method of determining vested service (counting only actual hours worked and excluding vacation, sick time, etc.), the 1,000-hour requirement is reduced to 870 hours, and the number of hours required for a break in service is reduced from 500 hours to 435 hours. [D.O.L. Reg. § 2530.200b-3(d)(1)] If the plan counts only regular time hours (excluding overtime), the 1,000-hour and 500-hour requirements are reduced to 750 and 375 hours, respectively. [D.O.L. Reg. § 2530.200b-3(d)(2)]

Q 8:43 Are other equivalency methods available?

Yes, in the case of an employee whose compensation is based on an hourly rate, a plan may determine the number of hours to be credited during the computation period on the basis of earnings if:

1. The employee receives credit for the number of hours computed as: total earnings during the period divided by the lowest hourly rate during the period.
2. Using this method, the 1,000-hour and 500-hour thresholds are reduced to 870 and 435 respectively.

[D.O.L. Reg. § 2530.200b-3(f)(1)]

In the case of an employee whose compensation is determined on a basis other than an hourly rate, a plan may determine that the number of hours credited to an employee be computed on a basis that reduces the threshold of earnings from 1,000 and 500 hours to 750 and 375 hours, respectively, if one of the following two rules is met:

1. For any employee whose compensation is determined on the basis of a fixed rate for a specified period of time (a day, week, or month), the employee's hours are determined by dividing total earnings during the computation period by the lowest rate of compensation during the period/hours regularly.
2. For an employee whose compensation is not determined on the basis of a fixed rate of time, the employee's hours are determined as in (1) above, using the lowest hourly rate of compensation payable to employees in the same job classification, or, if no employees in the same job classification have an hourly rate, the minimum wage currently in effect.

[D.O.L. Reg. § 2530.200b-3(f)(2), (3)]

Example 8-19: CDE Games employs teachers who generally work only during the summer. Al, a summer employee, is paid $100 per day and is regularly scheduled to work approximately 12 hours per day. Over the vesting computation period running from January 1, 2018, to December 31, 2018, Al is paid $6,500. In computing his vesting service, Al is credited with 780 hours (6,500 × (100/12)) and receives a year of vesting service because he is credited with more than 750 hours.

Q 8:44 May equivalencies be based on periods of employment?

Yes. The DOL regulations allow a simplified computation method that credits the following number of hours for each unit worked:

1. *Days.* An employee is credited with ten hours of service for each day the employee would be required to be credited with at least one hour of service.
2. *Weeks.* An employee is credited with 45 hours of service for each week the employee would be required to be credited with at least one hour of service.
3. *Semimonthly period.* An employee is credited with 95 hours of service for each semimonthly payroll period the employee would be required to be credited with at least one hour of service.
4. *Months.* An employee is credited with 190 hours of service for each month for which the employee would be required to be credited with at least one hour of service.

[D.O.L. Reg. § 2530.200b-3(e)(1)]

Q 8:45 May different service-crediting methods be used for different classifications of employees?

Yes, different methods may be used if, on the basis of all the relevant facts and circumstances, the crediting of service does not discriminate in favor of HCEs. Thus, a plan could count actual hours for hourly employees and use one of the equivalency methods described above for salaried employees. [Treas. Reg. § 1.401(a)(4)-11(d)(2)]

Q 8:46 Must all years of service be taken into account in determining a participant's vested percentage?

No. The following years of service may be disregarded:

1. Years of service before age 18 (see Q 8:47);
2. Years of service during a period for which the employee declined to contribute to a plan requiring mandatory employee contributions (see Q 8:48);
3. Years of service with the employer during which the employer did not maintain the plan or a predecessor plan (see Q 8:50); and
4. Certain years of service before a one-year break in service (see Q 8:47).

[I.R.C. § 411(a)(4); Treas. Reg. § 1.411(a)-5]

Q 8:47 How are years of service before age 18 disregarded?

Although the regulations have not been changed to reflect the fact that the previous standard of age 22 has been changed to age 18, the principles in the regulations can be applied. All years of service completed before the attainment of age 18 may be disregarded. [Treas. Reg. § 1.411(a)-5(b)(1)]

Example 8-20: Jim, who has been employed by CDE Games since age 16, was hired on January 2, 2017. He was born on December 5, 2000, and he turned age 18 during the plan year ending December 31, 2018. The plan years ending December 31, 2017 and December 31, 2018 may be disregarded in determining Jim's vested percentage in the profit sharing plan.

Q 8:48 What years are disregarded under a plan requiring mandatory employee contributions?

If a plan requires mandatory contributions, a plan year in which the participant failed to make any mandatory contributions may be disregarded. If contributions were made for any part of the year, that year may not be disregarded. [Treas. Reg. § 1.411(a)-5(b)(2)]

Q 8:49 How are years determined before a plan was maintained?

In general, an employee's years of service with an employer may be disregarded for any period during which the employer did not maintain the plan or a predecessor plan. A plan is treated as established on the first day of the plan year in which the plan is adopted. Service with a predecessor employer that maintained the plan of the current employer is treated as service with the current employer. Also, certain service with a predecessor employer that did not maintain the plan of the current employer is treated as service with the current employer. [Treas. Reg. § 1.411(a)-5(b)(3); I.R.C. § 414(a)(1)]

Q 8:50 What is a predecessor plan?

If a plan is established within a five-year period immediately preceding or following the date another qualified plan is terminated, the other qualified plan is considered a predecessor plan. [Treas. Reg. § 1.411(a)-5(b)(3)(v)]

Example 8-21: ABC Toys terminates its money purchase plan effective December 31, 2014. On April 1, 2019, the corporation adopts a profit sharing plan. The money purchase plan is considered to be a predecessor plan, and vesting service under the money purchase plan must be counted for vesting purposes under the profit sharing plan.

Breaks in Service

Q 8:51 How is vesting service determined if an employee leaves employment and then returns to work?

All years of vesting service, before and after the break, must be counted, unless the plan uses break-in-service rules described in Q 8:53. [Treas. Reg. § 1.411(a)-5(a)]

Q 8:52 How is a one-year break in service defined?

A one-year break in service means a 12-consecutive-month period (vesting computation period) during which the participant does not complete more than 500 hours of service with the employer. [D.O.L. Reg. § 2530.200b-4(a)(1)]

Q 8:53 What break-in-service rules apply in determining an employee's years of vesting service?

A qualified plan may contain the following three basic rules:

1. *One-year holdout rule.* For a participant who has incurred a one-year break in service, years of vesting service before the break do not count until the participant has completed a year of service after resuming employment. Once an employee completes a year of service, all prior years of service are credited in determining vesting service, assuming no other such rules are in the plan. [I.R.C. § 411(a)(6)(B)]
2. *Rule of parity.* This rule only applies to nonvested participants. For a participant who has five or more consecutive one-year breaks in service, the participant's pre-break service counts in determining the vesting of the employer-derived account balance or accrued benefit only if upon returning to service, the number of consecutive one-year breaks in service is less than the number of years of service. [I.R.C. § 411(a)(6)(D)]
3. *Five-year rule.* This rule only applies to defined contribution plans or certain defined benefit plans funded exclusively by insurance contracts (Section 412(e)(3) plans). For a participant who has five or more

consecutive one-year breaks in service, all service after the breaks in service is disregarded in determining the vesting in the employer-derived account balance or accrued benefit that accrued before the breaks in service. The participant's pre-break service counts in determining the vesting of the post-break employer-derived account balance or accrued benefit only if either—

a. The participant has any nonforfeitable interest in the account balance or accrued benefit attributable to employer contributions at the time of separation from service; or

b. Upon returning to service, the number of consecutive one-year breaks in service is less than the number of years of service. [I.R.C. § 411(a)(6)(C)]

For a defined contribution plan, separate accounts should be maintained for the participant's pre-break and post-break employer-derived account balance. Both accounts should share in the earnings and losses of the fund. [Treas. Reg. § 1.411(b)-1(e)(2)]

Example 8-22: Mary, a participant in the ABC Toys defined benefit plan, terminates employment after six years of vesting service and is 80 percent vested. She receives a distribution of $4,000 from her otherwise full lump sum of $5,000. She does not work for ABC Toys for the next five plan years and thus experiences five consecutive one-year breaks in service. She then returns to work for ABC Toys and works for two more years before terminating employment again. In determining her vested percentage in the current accrued benefit (net of the benefit already paid her), her pre-break years are counted because the number of consecutive one-year breaks in service (five) is less than the number of years of service worked during her original period of employment (six). Thus, Mary has a total of eight years of vesting service: six pre-break years and two post-break years.

Q 8:54 Do maternity or paternity absences affect the determination of a one-year break in service?

Yes, *solely* for the purposes of avoiding a one-year break in service for the first year in which a break might occur, an employee absent from work due to a maternity or paternity leave of absence must be credited with hours not to exceed 501 hours of service. The number of hours credited during the absence would be the hours normally credited. If the number of hours normally credited cannot be determined, eight hours of service per day of absence should be credited. These rules apply to an employee absent from work for any of the following four reasons:

1. Pregnancy of the employee;
2. Birth of a child of the employee;
3. Placement of a child with the employee in conjunction with the adoption of the child; or
4. Caring for the child for a period immediately following the birth or placement.

The plan administrator may require that the employee furnish timely information to establish that the reason for the absence is one of those listed above and the number of days for which there was such an absence. [I.R.C. § 411(a)(6)(E)]

Amendments in Vesting Schedules

Q 8:55 May a plan amendment reduce the vested percentage of a participant?

No. A plan amendment changing any vesting schedule under the plan will not be treated as satisfying the minimum vesting requirements, if the vested percentage of the account balance or accrued benefit derived from employer contributions (determined as of the later of the date the amendment is adopted or the date the amendment is effective) of any participant is less than the vested percentage computed under the plan before the amendment. [I.R.C. § 411(a)(10)(A)]

Q 8:56 May a plan amendment change the rate of future vesting?

A plan amendment may change the rate of future vesting if each participant with three or more years of service is permitted to irrevocably elect, within a reasonable period after adoption of the amendment, to have his or her vested percentage computed under the old vesting schedule. [I.R.C. § 411(a)(10)(B)] However, plan sponsors must retain the prior vesting schedule with respect to benefits accrued as of the date of amendment. [Treas. Reg. § 1.411(d)-3(a)(3)]

Q 8:57 What is a reasonable vesting schedule election period described in Q 8:56?

The election period under the plan must begin no later than the date the plan amendment is adopted and end no earlier than the latest of these dates:

1. 60 days after the date the plan amendment is adopted;
2. 60 days after the date the plan amendment becomes effective; or
3. 60 days after the date the participant is issued written notice of the plan amendment by the employer or plan administrator.

[Treas. Reg. § 1.411(a)-8T(b)(2)]

Q 8:58 How do the Final Regulations under Code Section 411(d)(6) change the rules regarding the amendment of vesting schedules?

In *Heinz v. Central Laborers' Pension Fund* [303 F.3d 802 (7th Cir. 2002)], the Supreme Court agreed with the Seventh Circuit that a:

> ... participant's benefits cannot be understood without reference to the conditions imposed after a benefit has accrued, and an amendment

placing materially greater restrictions on the receipt of the benefit "reduces" the benefit just as surely as a decrease in the size of the monthly benefit.

The Treasury interpreted this case to mean that, in the case of an amendment to a plan's vesting schedule, from the amendment date forward, with regard to a participant's account balance (and future related earnings) or accrued benefit on the date of the amendment, a participant's vesting percentage must be no less than the greater of the vesting percentages under the two vesting schedules. This change in the application of the vesting rules is effective with respect to plan amendments adopted after August 9, 2006. [Treas. Reg. § 1.411(d)-3(a)(3), Ex. 4]

Example 8-23: CDE Games sponsors a target benefit plan with a five-year cliff vesting schedule. Effective December 31, 2018, a plan amendment changes the vesting schedule to 20 percent per year, starting with the second year. Greg, an employee with four years of vesting service (nonvested) must be given the opportunity to remain under the old vesting schedule. If Greg elects to remain under the old vesting schedule, he will retain his current vested percentage of zero and become 100 percent vested after five years of vesting service. However, if Greg moves over to the new vesting schedule, he will become 60 percent vested immediately, 80 percent vested in the fifth year, and 100 percent vested after six years. However, with respect to Greg's account balance as of December 31, 2018, Greg will become 100 percent vested in this account balance (including earnings) if he completes one more year of vesting service (based upon the five-year cliff vesting schedule).

Lisa has only two years of service. She need not be given an election to remain under the old vesting schedule because she has less than three years of service. She becomes 20 percent vested now in her total account balance and continues to vest at the rate of 20 percent per year. However, her account balance as of December 31, 2018 (including future related earnings) will be subject to the five-year cliff vesting schedule, and she will become fully vested (based on the original five-year cliff vesting schedule) in this portion of the account balance if she completes three more years of vesting service (a total of five years of vesting service).

Forfeitures and Cash-Out Rules

Q 8:59 What happens with the nonvested portion of the account balance or accrued benefit?

The nonvested portion of the account balance or accrued benefit for a terminated participant will be forfeited. Generally, the forfeiture occurs at the earlier of:

1. The plan year in which the participant receives a distribution of the vested account balance or accrued benefit (if the plan uses the cash-out rules; see Q 8:60); or
2. After the participant incurs five consecutive one-year breaks in service (see Q 8:52).

[I.R.C. § 411(a)(6)(C)]

Q 8:60 How are forfeitures treated?

The treatment of forfeitures depends upon the type of plan:

Defined Benefit Plan. Forfeitures must not be applied to increase benefits for any participant. [I.R.C. § 401(a)(8)]

Target Plan. Available forfeitures must be applied to reduce future contributions of the employer in a plan designed to meet the safe harbor requirements. [Treas. Reg. § 1.401(a)(4)-8(b)(3)(i)(B)]

All Other Plans. Available forfeitures may be applied to reduce future contributions of the employer, to pay eligible plan-related expenses, or to increase the benefits of the remaining participants, depending on the terms of the plan document.

Q 8:61 How are forfeitures used to increase benefits in a defined contribution plan?

In a defined contribution plan (other than a target plan), the following methods are typically used to allocate forfeitures:

1. *Pro rata based on compensation.* Each participant receives an allocation of the forfeitures based on the ratio of his or her compensation to total covered compensation.
2. *Additional contribution.* The forfeited amounts are added to the employer's contribution and allocated based on the plan's allocation formula.
3. *Pro rata based on account balances.* Each participant receives an allocation of forfeitures based on the ratio of his or her account balance to the total of account balances for all active participants. This method is fairly unusual, but is allowed as long as the allocation does not discriminate in favor of HCEs. The principles of the regulations under Code Section 401(a)(4) are used in demonstrating nondiscrimination. [Rev. Rul. 81-10]

Example 8-24: CDE Games is reallocating $10,000 of forfeitures to the employees actively participating in its profit sharing plan. The plan covers no HCEs. The plan document may allow the reallocation of forfeitures in one of the following ways:

1. **Pro Rata Based on Compensation**

Name	*Compensation*	*Forfeitures*	*Percentage of Total*
Art	$30,000	$1,500	15.00%
Bart	$45,000	$2,250	22.50%
Shelly	$45,000	$2,250	22.50%
Mark	$35,000	$1,750	17.50%
Brenda	$45,000	$2,250	22.50%
Totals	$200,000	$10,000	100.00%

2. **As an Additional Contribution** (A $20,000 contribution is made with $10,000 in forfeitures, and the allocation formula is not pro rata based on compensation.)

Name	*Compensation*	*Contributions Plus Forfeitures*	*Percentage of Total*
Art	$30,000	$4,177	13.92%
Bart	$45,000	$6,911	23.04%
Shelly	$45,000	$6,911	23.04%
Mark	$35,000	$5,090	16.96%
Brenda	$45,000	$6,911	23.04%
Totals	$200,000	$30,000	100.00%

3. **Pro Rata Based on Account Balances**

Name	*Account Balance*	*Forfeitures*	*Percentage of Total*
Art	$160,000	$ 3,200	32.00%
Bart	$130,000	$ 2,600	26.00%
Shelly	$150,000	$ 3,000	30.00%
Mark	$25,000	$500	5.00%
Brenda	$35,000	$700	7.00%
Totals	$500,000	$10,000	100.00%

Q 8:62 What are the cash-out rules?

The cash-out rules allow an employer to disregard pre-break service in determining future additional vesting in pre-break amounts if each of the following conditions are met:

1. The employee receives a distribution of the present value of his or her entire vested benefit or account balance at the time of the distribution;

2. If the distribution is greater than $5,000, the participant consents to the distribution (see chapter 11); [I.R.C. § 411(a)(11)]
3. The distribution is made because of the termination of the employee's participation in the plan;
4. The distribution is made, or would have been made had the distributable amount been less than the cash-out limit in effect, no later than the close of the second plan year following the plan year in which the employee's termination of participation occurs; and
5. The plan has a repayment provision that meets the requirements discussed in Q 8:68.

The purpose of the cash-out rules is administrative simplicity. If the employer makes an immediate distribution to a participant at the time of termination of employment, then forfeitures occur immediately, and the employer does not need to maintain the forfeited amounts in suspense for a five-year period. [Treas. Reg. § 1.411(a)-7(d)(4)]

Example 8-25: ABC Toys maintains a profit sharing plan. Mark, a participant in the plan, terminates employment with an account balance of $10,000. Under the plan's vesting schedule, Mark's vested percentage is 60 percent and he is entitled to a distribution of $6,000. Mark and his spouse consent to the distribution of $6,000, and the remaining $4,000 will be forfeited. Mark later returns to work for ABC Toys, and his vesting percentage increases to 80 percent. Only if he repays the $6,000 distribution, as directed by the plan document, will Mark be entitled to a greater share of the $10,000 pre-break account balance.

Q 8:63 May a cash-out occur if a participant has no vested account balance or accrued benefit?

Yes. Generally, a plan document will provide that a participant with a vested percentage of zero will be deemed to be cashed out. This allows the forfeiture of unvested account balance or accrued benefits to occur immediately at severance of employment. [G.C.M. 39310]

Q 8:64 How do the plan repayment provisions operate?

The forfeited account balance or accrued benefit of a participant is restored to the plan if the participant repays the full amount of the distribution. All optional forms of benefit and subsidies relating to the benefit must also be restored. The plan is not required to allow repayment unless the following conditions are met:

1. The individual received a distribution that was less than the present value of his or her full account balance or accrued benefit;
2. The individual resumes employment covered under the plan;
3. For a defined benefit plan, the individual repays the full amount of the distribution with interest; and
4. For a defined contribution plan, the individual repays the full amount of the distribution.

The repayment must be made before the earlier of (a) five years after the date of reemployment or (b) the first period of five consecutive one-year breaks in service commencing after the date of distribution.

[I.R.C. § 411(a)(7)(C)]

Q 8:65 What interest rate is charged on amounts repaid to a defined benefit plan?

The *maximum* interest rate that may be charged is 120 percent of the federal midterm rate in effect on the first day of the plan year during which repayment occurs. (See Appendix A for a listing of historical federal midterm rates.) [Treas. Reg. § 1.411(a)-7(d)(2)(ii)(B)]

Example 8-26: Phyllis terminates employment and receives a distribution from ABC Toys, which maintains a defined benefit plan. She is 50 percent vested and receives a distribution of the present value of her vested accrued benefit of $6,000 (with appropriate spousal consent) on December 31, 2017. Phyllis returns to work for ABC Toys on December 31, 2018 and wishes to repay the distribution plus interest by December 31, 2019, in order to have her forfeited accrued benefit restored. Assume that, for the plan year ending December 31, 2019, 120 percent of the federal midterm rate in effect on January 1, 2019, is 3 percent. If Phyllis repays $6,000 plus interest ($6,365 in total) on December 31, 2019, her forfeited accrued benefit will be restored to her.

Q 8:66 What interest rate is charged on amounts repaid to a defined contribution plan?

No interest is charged; the exact amount distributed to the participant must be repaid to the plan. Similarly, the amount restored to the participant's account is not credited with interest. [Treas. Reg. § 1.411(a)-7(d)(4)(v)]

Q 8:67 What sources of restoration are available to the employer in a defined contribution plan if an employee chooses to repay his or her distribution under the cash-out/repayment rules?

The permissible sources for restoration of the account balance in a defined contribution plan are forfeitures, employer contributions, and available plan income. The employer has until the end of the plan year following the plan year of repayment to make the restoration. [Treas. Reg. § 1.411(a)-7(d)(6)(iii)(C)]

Q 8:68 How are forfeitures handled in a defined contribution plan that does not contain the cash-out rules described above?

First, forfeitures are not reallocated or applied to reduce employer contributions until the participant experiences five consecutive one-year breaks in service. Then, for employees who return to service and increase their vested percentage (but not up to 100 percent), their vested account is determined by one of the following methods:

Method 1. The current vested account balance, X, is determined by this formula:

$$X = P \times [AB + (R \times D)] - (R \times D)$$

where X = Current vested account balance
P = Current vested percentage
AB = Current account balance
D = Amount of the distribution
R = Current account balance/Account balance after distribution

[Treas. Reg. § 1.411(a)-7(d)(5)(iii)(A)]

Method 2. The current vested account balance, X, is determined by this formula:

$$X = P \times (AB + D) - D$$

where X = Current vested account balance
P = Current vested percentage
AB = Current account balance
D = Amount of the distribution

[Treas. Reg. § 1.411(a)-7(d)(5)(iii)(B)]

Example 8-27: CDE Games sponsors a profit sharing plan. Mike, a participant in the plan, terminates employment with an account balance of $10,000. Under the plan's vesting schedule, his vested percentage is 40 percent and he is entitled to, and takes a distribution of, $4,000. The remaining $6,000 will be forfeited after five consecutive one-year breaks in service because the plan does not have a cash-out provision. Mike returns to work after three years, when the previous unvested account balance has grown from $6,000 to $9,000. Mike works another year and becomes 60 percent vested and then terminates employment again. His account balance at the time of his second termination of employment is $9,000. His vested portion may be determined in accordance with either of these two methods, as defined in the plan document.

Method 1. The current vested account balance, X, is determined by:

$$R = \$9{,}000/\$6{,}000 \times 150\%$$

$$\begin{aligned} X &= P \times [AB + (R \times D)] - (R \times D) \\ &= 60\% \times [\$9{,}000 + (150\% \times \$4{,}000)] - (150\% \times \$4{,}000) \\ &= 60\% \times (\$9{,}000 + \$6{,}000) - \$6{,}000 \\ &= \$3{,}000 \end{aligned}$$

Method 2. The current vested account balance, X, is determined by:

$$X = P \times (AB + D) - D$$
$$= 60\% \times (\$9{,}000 + \$4{,}000) - \$4{,}000$$
$$= 60\% \times (\$13{,}000) - \$4{,}000$$
$$= \$3{,}800$$

Required Vesting upon Plan Termination, Partial Termination, or Complete Discontinuance of Contributions

Q 8:69 What vesting rules apply if a plan terminates or partially terminates or if employer contributions are completely discontinued?

A plan will not be qualified unless it provides that the rights of each employee to the amounts credited to his or her account or accrued benefit are nonforfeitable at the time any of the following events occur:

1. Plan termination (see Q 8:75),
2. Partial termination (see Qs 8:72–8:81), or
3. Complete discontinuance of contributions under the plan (see Qs 8:82–8:83) (applicable only in the case of a plan (such as a profit sharing or stock bonus plan) to which the minimum funding standards of Code Section 412 do not apply).

[I.R.C. § 411(d)(3); Treas. Reg. § 1.411(d)-2(a)(1)]

Q 8:70 When is a plan considered terminated?

The Treasury regulations do not specifically define when a plan is considered to be terminated. Whether a plan has terminated depends on all of the facts and circumstances of a particular case.

A pension, profit sharing, or stock bonus plan under which benefit accruals have ceased is not terminated if, after an amendment is adopted to terminate the plan, the plan assets are not distributed as soon as administratively feasible. If such assets are held in a trust that remains in existence in order to make distributions when employees become entitled to receive payments as provided under the terms of the plan they are considered undistributed. [Rev. Rul. 89-87]

In order to terminate a plan, the date of termination must be established, the benefits of plan participants and other liabilities under the plan must be determined with respect to the date of plan termination, and all plan assets must be distributed to satisfy those liabilities in accordance with the terms of the plan as soon as administratively feasible after the date of termination. Generally, the date of plan termination for a single-employer plan under ERISA Title IV will also be the date of plan termination for purposes of the Code. In addition, a single-employer plan to which Title IV applies that has not been terminated under Title IV, even though its assets have been distributed, will not have terminated for purposes of the Code.

A plan that is amended to terminate and to cease benefit accruals or contributions has not, in fact, been terminated under the Code, if the assets are not distributed as soon as reasonably feasible after the stated date of plan termination, regardless of whether the plan is treated as terminated under other federal law, including Title IV. Termination of a multiemployer plan under Title IV generally does not result in plan assets being distributed as soon as administratively feasible after the date of plan termination. Accordingly, such a plan will not be treated as terminated under Code Section 401(a) and will have to continue to meet the requirements of Code Section 401(a) to retain its qualified status. In the case of a single-employer plan that is terminated for purposes of Title IV, if plan assets are not distributed as soon as administratively feasible after the date of plan termination under Title IV, the plan will not be treated as terminated for purposes of the Code, except that the plan will be considered as terminated for purposes of Treasury Regulations Section 1.411(d)-2(c). [Rev. Rul. 89-87]

Whether a distribution is made as soon as administratively feasible is to be determined under all the facts and circumstances of the given case; generally, however, a distribution that is not completed within one year following the date of plan termination specified by the employer will be presumed not to have been made as soon as administratively feasible. Such a plan is an ongoing plan and must meet the requirements of Code Section 401(a) in order to continue its qualified status. Such a plan remains subject to the minimum funding requirements of Code Section 412, where applicable. Also, in any year in which the trust assets have not been distributed, the plan is subject to the information reporting requirements of Code Section 6057 (e.g., annual registration) and Code Section 6058 (information required in connection with certain plans of deferred compensation) and, in the case of a defined benefit plan, the actuarial reporting requirements of Code Section 6059 (periodic report of actuary). [Rev. Rul. 89-17]

In *Borda v. Hardy, Lewis, Pollard and Page, P.C.* [138 F.3d 1062 (6th Cir. 1998)], the Court of Appeals for the Sixth Circuit held that a former plan participant who quit his job and did not withdraw his vested share of plan assets was not entitled to his nonvested share when the employer dissolved three and one-half years later, before the end of the five-year forfeiture period.

Q 8:71 Can a plan termination be reversed?

In *Carter v. Pension Plan of A. Finkl & Sons Co. for Eligible Office Employees* [2010 WL 3516079 (N.D. Ill. 2010)], the court held that a plan that was in the process of terminating could reverse the termination and avoid 100 percent vesting participants even though the proper participant notifications of the plan termination had been given. The plan sponsor in this case sought both IRS and Pension Benefit Guaranty Corporation (PBGC) approval for the reversal and was granted the same. The plan was allowed to continue operations, including vesting in accordance with the schedule in the plan document, as though the plan termination commencement had never begun, without violation of the anti-cutback rule in Code Section 411(d)(6).

Q 8:72 When is a plan considered partially terminated?

A partial termination of a qualified plan generally is a significant reduction in the number of participants covered by the plan, sometimes referred to as a vertical partial termination. For defined benefit plans, a horizontal partial termination is a cessation or decrease in future benefit accruals; for profit sharing and stock bonus plans, a horizontal partial termination is a complete discontinuance of contributions. A partial termination typically is triggered by a distinct event, or a series of distinct events, such as plant closings, reductions in force, sales of subsidiaries or unincorporated divisions or other business units, or plan amendments.

As a condition of qualification, Code Section 411(d)(3) requires that, on a plan's termination or partial termination, the rights of all affected employees to benefits accrued to the date of such termination or partial termination (to the extent funded, as determined under ERISA Section 4044 for defined benefit plans, as of such date) or the amounts credited to the employees' accounts must be completely nonforfeitable (i.e., 100 percent vested). [I.R.C. § 411(d)(3); Treas. Reg. § 1.411(d)-2]

General rule. As a general rule, whether or not a partial termination of a qualified plan has occurred (and the time it occurred) is determined based on all the facts and circumstances in a particular case, including:

1. The exclusion, by reason of a plan amendment or severance by the employer, of a group of employees that has previously been covered by the plan; and
2. Plan amendments that adversely affect the rights of employees to vest in benefits under the plan.

[Treas. Reg. § 1.411(d)-2(b)(1)]

Special rule for defined benefit plans. Under a special rule that applies only to defined benefit plans, a partial termination is deemed to occur if a defined benefit plan ceases or decreases future benefit accruals under the plan and, as a result of the cessation or decrease, a potential reversion to the employer or employers maintaining the plan (determined as of the date the cessation or decrease is adopted) is created or increased. If no employer reversion is created or increased, a partial termination is deemed not to occur by reason of the cessation or decrease. A partial termination of a defined benefit plan may occur nevertheless under the general rule described above for reasons other than the cessation or decrease of future benefit accruals under the plan. [Treas. Reg. § 1.411(d)-2(b)(2)]

Effect of a partial termination. If a partial termination of a qualified plan occurs, the 100 percent vesting requirement of Code Section 411(d)(3) applies only to the part of the plan that is terminated (that is, only the employees who are affected by the partial termination become 100 percent vested in their account balances or accrued benefits under the plan, to the extent the benefits are funded, as determined under ERISA Section 4044 for defined benefit plans, as of the date the partial termination occurs). [Treas. Reg. § 1.411(d)-2(b)(3)] When a complete termination of a qualified plan occurs, however, all participants must become 100 percent vested in their account balances or accrued benefits under the plan, to the extent those benefits are funded (as determined under ERISA Section 4044 for defined benefit plans) as of the date the termination occurs. [I.R.C. § 411(d)(3)]

Q 8:73 Do the minimum vesting standards of Title I of ERISA require 100 percent vesting when a partial termination occurs?

No. The concept of the partial termination of a qualified plan and its consequences (i.e., 100 percent vesting in account balances or accrued benefits of affected participants, to the extent the benefits are funded (as determined under ERISA Section 4044 for defined benefit plans) as of the date the partial termination occurs) is found only in Code Section 411(d)(3) as one of the many conditions for keeping the plan qualified. There is no analog in the minimum vesting standards of Title I of ERISA to Code Section 411(d)(3)'s concept of partial termination. Thus, partial termination is a tax qualification requirement only.

Q 8:74 What is the purpose of the partial termination rule?

The IRS created the partial termination rule as an extension of the pre-ERISA Code Section 401(a)(7) rule that required full vesting on complete termination. [Pre-ERISA Treas. Reg. § 1.401-6(b)(2) (1963), superseded by post-ERISA Treas. Reg. § 1.411(d)-2(b) (1977)] The IRS issued pre-ERISA Treasury Regulations Section 1.401-6(b)(2) in 1963 out of concern about possible discrimination against rank-and-file employees whose years of vesting service would not be sufficient to satisfy pre-ERISA vesting schedules at the time a partial termination occurred. [Rev. Rul. 55-186, modified by Rev. Rul. 56-596, declared obsolete by Rev. Rul. 72-92]

Q 8:75 Does the Code or the Treasury regulations define partial termination to mean a significant reduction in the number of plan participants?

No. Neither Code Section 411(d)(3) nor Treasury Regulations Section 1.411(d)-2(b) defines partial termination to any degree. The legislative history of Code Section 411(d)(3), which ERISA added to the Code, is somewhat helpful in that it states: "[E]xamples of a partial termination might include, under certain circumstances, a large reduction in the workforce, or a sizable reduction in benefits under the plan." [S. Rep. No. 93-383, at 50 (1973); see also H.R. Rep. No. 93-779, at 64 (1974); H.R. Rep. No. 93-807, at 65 (1974)]

Treasury Regulations Section 1.411(d)-2(b) does not define partial termination, but merely states the following:

> (b) Partial termination—(1) General rule. Whether or not a partial termination of a qualified plan occurs (and the time of such event) shall be determined by the Commissioner with regard to all the facts and circumstances in a particular case. Such facts and circumstances include: the exclusion, by reason of a plan amendment or severance by the employer, of a group of employees who have previously been covered by the plan; and plan amendments which adversely affect the rights of employees to vest in benefits under the plan. (2) Special rule. If a defined benefit plan ceases or decreases future benefit accruals under the plan, a partial termination shall be deemed to occur if, as a result of such cessation or decrease, a potential reversion to the employer, or employers, maintaining the plan (determined as of the date such cessation or decrease is adopted) is created or increased. If no such reversion is created or increased, a partial termination shall be deemed not to occur by reason of such cessation or decrease. However, the Commissioner may determine that a partial termination of such a plan occurs pursuant to subparagraph (1) of this paragraph for reasons other than such cessation or decrease. (3) Effect of partial termination. If a termination of a qualified plan occurs, the provisions of Section 411(d)(3) apply only to the part of the plan that is terminated.

In 2007, the IRS issued Revenue Ruling 2007-43 [I.R.B. 2007-48] to clarify the definition of a partial plan termination. This ruling formalizes a presumption that has been in effect since before ERISA that a partial plan termination occurs when the total number of participants decreases by at least 20 percent. Under the ruling, voluntary terminations by participants are not included in the 20 percent turnover figure, although there is some question about how the phrase "voluntary terminations" is to be interpreted. In general, if there is a turnover of 20 percent or more, the burden of proof seems to shift to the employer to show that a partial termination has not occurred.

Q 8:76 Despite the lack of a precise definition of partial termination, is the percentage of plan participants who separate from service a significant factor in determining whether a partial termination has indeed occurred?

Yes. A significant factor in the courts' and the IRS's determinations of whether a partial termination of a qualified plan has occurred is the percentage of plan participants who separate from service covered by the plan, either over a relatively short period of time or as a result of a distinct event. The only situations in which significant reductions in the percentage of plan participants have occurred but partial terminations were found not to have occurred have been situations in which plan participants separated from service voluntarily rather than involuntarily. As discussed in Q 8:75, this rule has been continued under Revenue Procedure 2007-43.

Treasury Regulations Section 1.411(d)-2(b) does not set any numerical percentage standard for triggering a partial termination. Rather, it states simply that a "group of employees previously covered by the plan" must separate from service.

The key question is how large a percentage constitutes a significant reduction, and thus a partial termination of the plan. Both court decisions and IRS rulings demonstrate that partial terminations generally occur when at least 20 percent to 30 percent of the plan's participants involuntarily separate from service covered by the plan. [See, e.g., Rev. Rul. 69-24 (98.2 percent reduction); Rev. Rul. 73-284 (80 percent reduction); Rev. Rul. 72-439 (70.6 percent reduction); Rev. Rul. 81-27; Ltr. Rul. 72-021-86880A (57.8 percent reduction); Collingnon v. Reporting Servs. Co., 796 F. Supp. 1136 (C.D. Ill. 1992) (83.3 percent reduction); Tipton & Kalmbach, Inc. v. Commissioner, 83 T.C. 154 (1984) (51.2 percent reduction); *In re* Gulf Pension Litig., 764 F. Supp. 1149 (S.D. Tex. 1991), *aff'd on another issue sub nom.* Borst v. Chevron Corp., 36 F.3d 1308 (5th Cir. 1994), *cert. denied,* 514 U.S. 1066 (1995) (45.2 percent reduction); Weil v. Retirement Plan Admin. Comm. of the Terson Co., No. 82 Civ. 8468 (JEL), 1988 U.S. Dist. LEXIS 5802 (S.D.N.Y. June 15, 1988), *aff'd on reh'g,* 933 F.2d 106 (2d Cir. 1991) (34.2 percent reduction)] For purposes of determining whether a partial termination of a qualified pension plan has occurred, the Seventh Circuit Court of Appeals, in *Matz v. Household International Tax Reduction Investment Plan* [388 F.3d 570 (7th Cir. 2004)], sometimes referred to as *Matz III*, accepted a rebuttable presumption that a 20 percent or greater reduction in total plan participants (fully vested and not) is a partial termination and that such a reduction below 20 percent is not. However, a reduction below 10 percent is conclusively presumed not to result in a partial termination, and above 40 percent a partial termination is conclusively presumed to have occurred. Revenue Ruling 2007-43 adopts the 20 percent standard.

Q 8:77 What facts and circumstances have been relevant to the courts and the IRS in determining whether a partial termination has occurred?

Notwithstanding the attempt to institute a bright line rule in Revenue Ruling 2007-43, the IRS acknowledges that there may be facts and circumstances that rebut the presumption of the presence of a partial plan termination. As a result, it remains instructive to review the positions taken by the IRS in prior guidance and by the courts. The plan's turnover rate appears to be the primary measuring tool for the analysis. The turnover rate of a plan is determined by dividing the employer-initiated terminations by the sum of the total participants at the start of the period and the participants added during the period. [IRM § 7.12.1.2.7 (Jan. 1, 2003); Tipton & Kalmbach, Inc. v. Commissioner, 83 T.C. 154 (1984); Weil v. Terson Co. Ret. Plan Comm., 750 F.2d 10 (2d Cir. 1984)] If there is a significant increase in the turnover rate for a period and a partial termination of the plan, with the employer failing to fully vest (to the extent funded, as determined under ERISA Section 4044 for defined benefit plans) all affected participants upon the partial termination, then it is reasonable to expect that the plan will not be qualified when it subsequently terminates. [IRM § 7.7.2.2.7 (Apr. 20, 1999)]

In general, the IRS's position is that fully vested terminated employees are included in determining whether there has been a partial termination. [IRM § 7.12.1.2.7. (Jan. 1, 2003); *Weil*, 750 F.2d 10] Employer-initiated terminations are counted even if caused by an event outside the employer's control, such as terminations due to depressed economic conditions. [IRM § 7.12.1.2.7.2 (Jan. 1, 2003)]

Additional factors bearing directly on the issue of whether a partial termination has occurred include (1) whether a potential for reversion has been created or increased as a result of participant turnover and (2) whether the possibility of prohibited discrimination has been increased. [IRM § 7.12.1.2.7.2 (Jan. 1, 2003)]

Example 8-28: The employer ceases future accruals in a defined benefit plan at a time when the fair market value of the assets is greater than the present value of the accrued benefits for all the participants. A potential for reversion exists because any forfeitures would be likely to cause assets to further exceed the present value of accrued benefits. These events may cause the IRS to treat this cessation of future accruals as a partial termination. [IRM § 7.12.1.2.7.2, Ex. 1 (Jan. 1, 2003)]

Example 8-29: A corporation that has a qualified profit sharing plan decides to relocate to another state. Although it offers to pay for moving expenses, the only employees who decide to move are HCEs. The IRS might conclude that the termination of non-highly compensated employees (NHCEs) was not employer-initiated and, based solely on this, a partial termination has not occurred. However, the forfeitures from the rank and file who do not move could go to the remaining participants who are all HCEs, and, therefore, a partial termination might be deemed to occur because of the potential discrimination. [IRM § 7.12.1.2.7.2, Ex. 2 (Jan. 1, 2003)]

It should be noted that the possibility of reversion, prohibited discrimination, or a reduction in the number of employees covered by the plan may not, when each factor is considered individually, reflect that a partial termination has occurred. However, when those factors are considered collectively, they may interrelate in such a way as to reflect a partial termination. [IRM § 7.12.1.2.7.2 (Jan. 1, 2003)]

Examples of situations in which the IRS or the federal courts have ruled that partial terminations indeed have occurred include the following:

1. Revenue Ruling 81-27. Discharge by the employer of 95 out of 165 participants under the plan in connection with the dissolution of one division of the employer's business. [1981-1 CB 228]
2. Revenue Ruling 73-284. Discharge of 12 out of 15 participating employees who refused to transfer to the employer's new business location when the old location was closed. [1973-2 CB 139]
3. *Tipton & Kalmbach, Inc. v. Commissioner*. Reductions in the participation of 34 percent and 51 percent in consecutive years where adverse business conditions beyond the employer's control resulted in such reductions. [83 T.C. 154 (1984)]

4. *Weil v. Terson Co. Retirement Plan Committee.* Reduction of two of an employer's 16 divisions resulting in the termination of over 75 percent of the employees in the affected divisions (a termination of 27 percent of the total plan participants). [750 F.2d 10 (2d Cir. 1984)]

The Internal Revenue Manual notes that in the situations described in items 1 through 4, above, a significant percentage of employees were, in effect, excluded from participating in the plan. There is no fixed turnover rate that determines whether a partial termination has occurred, but the rate must be substantial. The facts and circumstances must be considered in each case, and may include the extent to which terminated employees are replaced and the normal turnover rate in a base period. The base period ordinarily would be a set of consecutive plan years (at least two) from which the normal turnover rate can be determined, and it should reflect a period of normal business operations rather than one of unusual growth or reduction. Generally, the plan years selected for inclusion in the base period should be those immediately preceding the period in question. [IRM § 7.12.1.2.7.1 (Jan. 1, 2003)]

Revenue Procedure 2007-43 indicates that information about the turnover rate in other periods, and the extent to which terminated employees were actually replaced, whether the new employees performed the same functions, had the same job classification or title, and received comparable compensation, are relevant to determining whether the turnover is routine for the employer.

Q 8:78 How is the percentage reduction in plan participation calculated so that a determination may be made as to whether a partial termination has occurred?

The court cases and the IRS rulings in this area show that the key elements in the calculation are:

1. The period of time over which the percentage reduction in plan participation has occurred, and
2. The number of employees who are included in the numerator and the denominator of the fraction that, when expressed as a percentage, quantifies the actual decline in participation over the relevant period.

Measuring period. In general, the court cases and IRS rulings involve reductions in plan participation that occur over relatively short periods of time, such as a year or two, and are caused by distinct events, such as reductions in force, plant closings, layoffs, and the like. In some situations, however, reductions in plan participation occurring over several years will be considered. For example, in one unpublished technical advice memorandum, the IRS examined the reduction in participation under the Great Atlantic & Pacific Tea Co.'s plan from 1975 through 1981. The percentage declines over those years ranged from a low of 8.8 in 1981 to a high of 24.3 in 1979. [Unpublished IRS TAM 1992 (A&P partial termination)] The IRS viewed all seven years of declining plan participation as triggered by a single corporate event, which A&P had intentionally initiated in 1975, and held that the employees that A&P had intentionally terminated in each of the years from 1975–1981 as part of its gradual reduction in force had been affected by a partial termination and, as a result, were entitled to 100 percent vesting of their accrued funded benefits.

Determining the percentage reduction in plan participation. There is some controversy as to which terminations are included in the numerator and denominator of the turnover rate. One Tax Court case, *Halliburton Co. v. Commissioner* [100 T.C. 216 (1993), *aff'd per curiam*, 25 F.3d 1043 (5th Cir. 1994), *cert. denied sub nom.* Nash v. Halliburton Co., 513 U.S. 989 (1994)], illustrates a complex analysis of which participants must be included in the numerator and denominator of the fraction that, when expressed as a percentage, shows the actual decline in plan participation over the relevant measuring period. In 1986, the Halliburton Co., which was adversely affected by the drop in oil prices, instituted a voluntary early retirement program and then laid off a large number of employees. In that year, the company's profit sharing plan lost 7,720 participants for the following reasons: death (22 participants), normal retirement (38 participants), early retirement (1,141 participants), terminations for cause (264 participants), transfers to affiliated companies (443 participants), voluntary separations from service (797 participants), involuntary separations of fully vested participants (224 participants), involuntary separations of partially vested participants (4,560 participants), and involuntary separations of participants with no account balances (231 participants). The plan had 19,017 participants at the beginning of the year and added 581 participants during the year, for a total of 19,598. In 1987 and 1988, 1,124 of the participants who had been involuntarily terminated were rehired. The rehired group consisted of 45 participants who were fully vested when they were terminated, 1,039 participants who were partially vested, and 40 participants who were not vested at all.

The Tax Court held that the numerator and the denominator of the fraction would exclude participants who had died, had taken normal retirement, or had been terminated for cause during 1986, because those terminations of employment would have occurred regardless of the company's economic health. The Tax Court further held that the following participants also should be excluded from the numerator, but not from the denominator, of the fraction:

1. Participants who were involuntarily terminated in 1986 but rehired in 1987 and 1988;
2. Participants who had voluntarily separated from employment, including those who had accepted the company's offer of early retirement; and
3. Participants who had left the plan because they had transferred to other jobs with other members of the company's controlled group.

The Tax Court held that, with those adjustments, the company's plan had experienced a net reduction in participation of 19.85 percent (3,891 out of 19,598), which was not significant enough to cause it to hold that a partial termination had occurred.

In *Administrative Committee of the Sea Ray Employees' Stock Ownership & Profit Sharing Plan v. Daniel Robinson* [164 F.3d 981 (6th Cir. 1999)], the Sixth Circuit held that an employee benefit plan administrator's determination that the plan had not experienced a partial plan termination was not arbitrary and capricious, despite the claim that the administrator should have included in the partial termination calculation former employees who left the company in anticipation of an involuntary layoff.

The Seventh Circuit Court of Appeals, in *Matz v. Household International Tax Reduction Investment Plan* [388 F.3d 570 (7th Cir. 2004)] (*Matz III*), reviewed the various courts' analysis of how the relevant percentage was determined, and rejected the idea that the percentage was anything more sophisticated than the number of terminated participants in a given period, divided by the number of participants at the beginning of the period.

Revenue Ruling 2007-43 provides that the turnover rate calculation should include all participants, whether or not they are vested, thereby aligning with the *Matz* decision.

Q 8:79 How is the vested account balance or benefit of a participant who is affected by a partial termination determined?

When there is a partial termination of a defined contribution plan, participants who are affected by the partial termination must become fully vested in their account balances. When there is a partial termination of a defined benefit plan, affected participants must fully vest in their accrued benefits, but only to the extent those benefits are funded as of the date the partial termination occurs (as determined under ERISA Section 4044 for defined benefit plans).

Defined contribution plans. A participant's account balance under a defined contribution plan is determinable as of any specified date. Some defined contribution plans, however, hold unallocated assets, such as unallocated forfeitures. Unallocated assets generally must be allocated to all participants' accounts under the plan when the plan terminates or partially terminates in order for the plan to remain qualified. [Treas. Reg. § 1.411(d)-2(a)(2)(i)] When there is a partial termination of such a plan, the affected participants' accounts, including their allocated forfeitures, must become 100 percent vested.

However, some unallocated assets are not allocated to participants' accounts when there is a partial termination of a defined contribution plan. The unallocated assets that remain unallocated even when a partial termination occurs are those that are not required to be used to satisfy the liabilities under the plan. [Treas. Reg. § 1.411(d)-2(a)(2)(iii)] For example, unallocated shares of employer stock that are held in a suspense account under a leveraged employee stock ownership plan (ESOP) may not be released from suspense and allocated to participants' accounts until loan repayments release them. Consequently, if there is a partial termination of such an ESOP, the unallocated shares of employer stock will not be allocated to plan participants.

Defined benefit plans. Treasury Regulations Section 1.411(d)-2(a)(2)(ii) requires that when a partial termination of a defined benefit plan occurs, affected participants must be fully vested in their accrued benefits to the extent the benefits are funded as of the date the partial termination occurs. The extent to which a defined benefit plan is funded when a partial termination occurs is determined under ERISA Section 4044, as if the plan were terminating. [Treas. Reg. § 1.411(d)-2(a)(2)(ii)] A court has held that for purposes of determining the extent to which a defined benefit plan is funded when a partial termination occurs, plan assets must be valued at fair market value, not actuarial value, and must be increased by the amount of unamortized minimum funding waivers. [Weil v. Retirement Plan Admin. Comm. of the Terson Co., No. 82 Civ. 8468 (JEL), 1988 U.S. Dist. LEXIS 5802 (S.D.N.Y. June 15, 1988), *aff'd*, 933 F.2d 106 (2d Cir. 1991)]

Q 8:80 Can a partial termination of a plan be triggered by an event other than a significant reduction in the percentage of plan participants?

Yes. Treasury Regulations Section 1.411(d)-2(b)(2) envisions that a decrease or a cessation of benefit accruals under a defined benefit plan could trigger a partial termination. It provides:

> (2) Special rule. If a defined benefit plan ceases or decreases future benefit accruals under the plan, a partial termination shall be deemed to occur if, as a result of such cessation or decrease, a potential reversion to the employer, or employers, maintaining the plan (determined as of the date such cessation or decrease is adopted) is created or increased. If no such reversion is created or increased, a partial termination shall be deemed not to occur by reason of such cessation or decrease. However, the Commissioner may determine that a partial termination of such a plan occurs pursuant to subparagraph (1) of this paragraph for reasons other than such cessation or decrease.

This Treasury regulation, which was issued after ERISA was enacted, expanded on its pre-ERISA counterpart, which had provided as follows:

Whether or not a partial termination occurs when benefits or employer contributions are reduced, or the eligibility or vesting requirements under the plan are made less liberal, will be determined on the basis of all the facts and circumstances. [Treas. Reg. § 1.401-6(b)(2) (1973)]

ERISA's legislative history includes, as an example of a partial termination, "a sizeable reduction in benefits under the plan," but the Conference Report on ERISA does not contain this language. [S. Rep. No. 93-383, at 50 (1973). Contrast H.R. Rep. No. 93-1280, at 277–78 (1974)] [IRM 7753 § 252(9)(c)]

A leading horizontal partial termination case involving a defined benefit plan is *In re Gulf Pension Litigation*. [764 F. Supp. 1149 (S.D. Tex. 1991), *aff'd on another issue sub nom.* Borst v. Chevron Corp., 36 F.3d 1308 (5th Cir. 1994), *cert. denied*, 514 U.S. 1006 (1995)] It is the only reported case in which participants have succeeded in their claim that a horizontal partial termination has occurred. In that case, Gulf Oil and Chevron Oil merged, and the companies' two defined benefit plans also were merged. The merger resulted in a number of changes in the benefits formerly provided under the Gulf Oil plan, including an increase in the lump-sum present value of death benefits; an actuarial reduction for disability benefits; the elimination of unreduced, early retirement benefits beginning at age 60, with respect to benefits accrued after the merger; the freeze of a post-retirement survivor annuity whose value exceeded the required qualified joint and survivor annuity (QJSA) benefit; and the elimination of Social Security bridge benefits with respect to post-merger service. The former Gulf participants sued, claiming, among other things, that the benefit changes constituted a horizontal partial termination, entitling them to full vesting of benefits to the extent then funded. The court agreed, holding that a horizontal partial termination had occurred. The court's conclusion and its reasoning have been criticized, however.

Q 8:81 May the sponsor of a qualified plan seek a determination from the IRS on whether a partial termination has occurred with respect to the plan?

Yes. Determinations involving the partial termination of a qualified plan are within the jurisdiction of the appropriate IRS office. The IRS National Office, however, will not issue a letter ruling on the partial termination of a qualified plan. [Rev. Proc. 2008-4, 2008-1 C.B. 121, § 8.03]

Q 8:82 When is a plan curtailed?

A plan is curtailed when benefits or employer contributions are reduced or when vesting or eligibility rules are tightened. [Rev. Proc. 69-24, 1969-1 C.B. 110] Narrowing the plan's coverage or eliminating and returning employee contributions is also a curtailment. The Treasury regulations under Code Section 411, which govern partial terminations, do not refer to curtailments specifically. The events that constitute curtailments, however, are among the facts and circumstances that the IRS will consider when determining whether a partial termination has occurred. [IRM § 7.12.1.2.6 (Jan. 1, 2003)]

Q 8:83 When does a complete discontinuance of plan contributions occur?

This issue applies only to defined contribution plans. A determination that contributions have been discontinued and a determination of the date upon which such discontinuance occurred require consideration of all of the relevant facts and circumstances. [Treas. Reg. § 1.411(d)-2(d)(1); IRM § 7.12.1.2.6 (Jan. 1, 2003)] A discontinuance of contributions may occur even when the employer makes some contributions but those amounts are not substantial enough to continue to maintain the plan. [Treas. Reg. § 1.411(d)-2(d); IRM § 7.12.1.2.6 (Jan. 1, 2003)] If the employer has failed to make substantial contributions in three out of five years and there is a pattern of profits earned, the IRS will consider whether a discontinuance of contributions has occurred. [IRM § 7.12.1.2.6 (Jan. 1, 2003)]

If the employer has failed to make significant contributions in years before the proposed year of plan termination, the IRS will consider whether an earlier discontinuance of contributions has occurred. [IRM § 7.12.1.2.6 (Jan. 1, 2003)]

A temporary cessation of contributions in a profit sharing or stock bonus plan may not constitute a discontinuance of contributions. However, if it becomes a discontinuance, the discontinuance becomes effective not later than the last day of the taxable year of the employer for which a substantial contribution was made under the plan, if the plan is a single-employer plan. In the case of a plan maintained by more than one employer, the discontinuance is effective not later than the last day of the plan year following the plan year within which any employer made the last substantial contribution. [Treas. Reg. § 1.411(d)-2(d); IRM § 7.12.1.2.6 (Jan. 1, 2003)]

Chapter 9

Administrative Determination of Benefits

Once a participant's vested percentage has been determined, the next task is to determine the vested benefit to which he or she is entitled. Vesting schedules are applied to the account balances in non-safe harbor sources of company contributions in defined contribution plans and employer-provided accrued benefits in defined benefit plans.

Determining Account Balances in Defined Contribution Plans 9-1
Cash-Out Rules 9-5
Underfunded Defined Contribution Plans 9-9
Determining Accrued Benefits in Traditional Defined Benefit Plans 9-12
Determination of Accrual of Service 9-20
Benefit Minimums and Limitations 9-25
Code Section 415 Limits 9-31
Lump Sum Determination 9-37
Determining Benefits in Non-Traditional Plans 9-41
Cash Balance Plans 9-41
Floor Offset Plans 9-47
Code Section 414(k) Plans 9-50
Pension Equity Plans 9-51
Target Benefit Plans 9-52

Determining Account Balances in Defined Contribution Plans

Q 9:1 How is the accrued benefit in a defined contribution plan defined?

According to Code Section 411(a)(7)(A)(ii), *accrued benefit* means the balance in the employee's account. The regulations define accrued benefit slightly differently, as the balance to the credit of the participant's account. [Treas. Reg. § 1.411(b)-1(a)(1)] Thus, the accrued benefit in a defined contribution plan is a participant's account balance.

Q 9:2 What types of account balances are subject to immediate 100 percent vesting?

In a defined contribution plan, account balances attributable to these types of contributions must be 100 percent vested at all times:

1. Elective contributions, including designated Roth Contribution [I.R.C. § 401(k)];
2. Voluntary after-tax employee contributions;
3. Mandatory after-tax employee contributions;
4. Rollover contributions;
5. Qualified nonelective contributions [Treas. Reg. § 1.401(k)-(6)];
6. Qualified matching contributions [Treas. Reg. § 1.401(k)-(6)];
7. Safe harbor matching contributions [I.R.C. § 401(k)(12)(B)]; and
8. Safe harbor nonelective contributions [I.R.C. § 401(k)(12)(C)].

If separate accounts are not maintained, the account balance attributable to employee contributions is determined by multiplying the total account balance by this fraction:

$$\frac{\text{Total employee contributions under the plan less withdrawals}}{\text{Total employee contributions less withdrawals plus employer contributions (on behalf of employee)}}$$

[Treas. Reg. § 1.411(c)-1(b)]

Example 9-1: ABC Builders maintains a profit sharing plan. The plan does not maintain separate accounts for the employer and employee contributions made to the plan. Les, a participant in the plan, has made voluntary after-tax contributions totaling $5,000. The corporation has made total employer contributions for Les in the amount of $20,000. The current account balance, including earnings, is $40,000. Of this account, 20 percent or $8,000 ([$5,000 ÷ ($20,000 + $5,000)] × $40,000) is the account balance attributable to Les's voluntary after-tax contributions.

Q 9:3 How frequently are account balances updated in a defined contribution plan?

The underlying investments in a defined contribution plan must be valued at least annually in order to allocate applicable gain or loss to the account balances of participants. [Rev. Rul. 65-178] Defined contribution plans can permit participants to select a blend of investments from a menu of investment choices, and the plan's record keeper will update each investment within each participant contribution source with applicable gain or loss. These are commonly referred to as participant-directed plans. Alternatively, the plan sponsor or trustee can select the blend of investment choices that are applied to all participant accounts in a pooled account. Defined contribution plans, especially participant-directed plans, often perform gain or loss allocation on a daily basis, but can perform the gain or loss allocation on any frequency as long as it is done at least as frequently as annually.

Q 9:4 If account balances are not valued daily, what adjustments may be made between valuation dates?

Certain transactions have a significant impact on a participant's account balance. The plan document generally describes the adjustments appropriate for activities occurring between valuation dates. Plans that permit the purchase of individual life insurance contracts typically indicate that insurance premiums paid after the valuation date are subtracted from the non-insurance portion of the participant's account balance. The participant's total account consists of adjusted non-insurance account balance plus any cash value in the insurance contract. Other plans may permit in-service withdrawals; any withdrawals made after the valuation date are reflected in the adjusted account balance. Contributions applicable to periods before a valuation date but credited after a valuation date are added to the participant's account balance.

Example 9-2: ABC Builders sponsors a profit sharing plan that allows participants the option to purchase life insurance. Account balances are valued on an annual basis. Pauline, a participant in the plan, has an account balance of $2,500 on December 31, 2018. She agrees to purchase a life insurance contract with an annual premium of $500 on March 4, 2019. Pauline's account balance until the next valuation date of December 31, 2019, is $2,000 ($2,500 − $500) plus the cash value in the insurance contract.

Q 9:5 What happens if the value of the underlying investments in the plan changes rapidly between valuation dates?

Many defined contribution plans that are not valued daily have a provision that permits the trustee to make an interim valuation and update account balances to reflect a significant change in the plan's asset value. By requiring this interim valuation, the plan spreads the impact of a sudden decline or increase in the market value of assets among all participants. However, daily valuation is the only gain or loss allocation method that assigns actual daily gain or loss to each investment within each participant's account.

Example 9-3: ABC Builders sponsors a profit sharing plan with an annual valuation date of June 30. The plan permits the trustee to authorize an interim valuation if plan assets change significantly in value. The account balances as of June 30, 2018, for the three participants in the plan are:

Participants	*Account Balance*
Lu	$350,000
Dave	$125,000
Tom	$175,000

Dave leaves employment on December 15, 2018. Between June 30, 2018, and December 15, 2018, the plan assets experienced a dramatic 50 percent increase in value. Although Dave's account balance is $125,000 as of June 30, 2018 (the last valuation date), if he received only $125,000, the other participants in the plan would be allocated the entire gain. Likewise, if the plan assets declined 50 percent in value, Dave would share in none of the loss if he received the June 30, 2018, account balance of $125,000. In either situation, the plan trustee would likely authorize an interim valuation and update Dave's account balance.

Q 9:6 How do outstanding participant loans affect the account balance in a defined contribution plan?

An outstanding loan represents an obligation of the participant to the plan. Upon termination of employment, if the participant has not paid back the outstanding loan, the plan may treat the outstanding loan as an immediate distribution to the participant (see chapter 2). In essence, the obligation of the participant is used to reduce the participant's remaining account balance. [Ltr. Rul. 8103063]

> **Example 9-4:** Deena, a terminated participant in the CDE Plumbers profit sharing plan, has a vested account balance of $10,000. Of this amount, $7,500 is the sum of the account balances in her chosen investments, and $2,500 is her outstanding loan balance. The plan provides that an outstanding loan is deemed to be a distribution upon termination of employment or other distributable event. Deena chooses a single-sum distribution; 20 percent of the taxable amount, or $2,000 (20% × $10,000), must be withheld for taxes. Deena will receive $5,500 in cash ($7,500 − $2,000), in addition to the deemed distribution of her outstanding loan. She will be subject to income tax plus any applicable early distribution additional income tax on the entire $10,000 distribution. The $2,000 withheld from her distribution for taxes will be treated as prepaid taxes. Note that if Deena had chosen to have $7,500 directly transferred to her IRA or new employers' plan, no withholding would have been necessary. A plan need not withhold more than the actual cash distribution released to the participant, which in this case is $0. [Treas. Reg. § 31.3405(c)-1 Q11]

Q 9:7 How frequently are 401(k) account balances updated?

Because at least some contributions, such as salary deferrals, are deposited frequently in 401(k) plans (salary deferrals must be deposited as soon as feasible following each applicable payroll period), valuations are generally more frequent. Frequencies include semiannual, quarterly, and monthly, but daily valuations are the most common.

Q 9:8 How are account balances determined in a daily valued plan?

Typically, funding vehicles such as mutual funds, life insurance company variable annuities, bank collective funds, or employer securities (that are easily unitized) are used in such plans. Units are credited or deducted, as appropriate, to a participant's account when any transaction occurs. Transactions include contributions, loan payments, withdrawals, loans, distributions, dividends, and transfers. The value of the account balance changes on a daily basis and can be obtained by multiplying the number of units in the account by the price per unit.

Example 9-5: Mike, a participant in CDE Plumbers 401(k) plan, has 125.649 units in the High Risk Equity Fund. On July 24, 2018, the unit price of this mutual fund is $12.31. The value of the portion of Mike's account balance invested in this fund on July 24, 2018, is $1,546.74 (125.649 × $12.31).

Cash-Out Rules

Q 9:9 What are the cash-out rules?

The cash-out rules allow pre-break service to be disregarded in determining future additional vesting on pre-break account balances or accrued benefits if the following conditions are met:

1. The employee receives the present value of his or her entire vested accrued benefit at the time of the distribution;
2. If the distribution, optionally exclusive of rollover account balances, is greater than $5,000, the participant consents to the distribution (see chapter 11) [I.R.C. § 411(a)(11)];
3. The distribution is made because of the termination of the employee's participation in the plan;
4. The distribution is made no later than the close of the second plan year following the plan year in which the employee's termination of participation occurs; and
5. The plan has a repayment provision that meets the conditions discussed in Q 9:11.

If the pre-break vested benefit is paid back in accordance with the repayment provisions discussed in Q 9:11 when and if participation in the plan begins again, the participant becomes entitled to continue to increase his or her vested percentage in the total pre-break accrued benefit (vested and non-vested) based upon the participant's combined pre- and post-break vesting service (see Q 9:11).

The purpose of the cash-out rules is administrative simplicity. If the employer makes an immediate distribution to a participant at the time of severance of employment, then forfeitures may occur immediately, and the thus employer does not need to maintain the forfeited amounts in a suspense account for a five-year period. [Treas. Reg. § 1.411(a)-7(d)(4)]

Example 9-6: Mark, a participant in the ABC Builders profit sharing plan, terminates employment with a total account balance of $10,000. The plan contains the cash-out rules discussed above. Mark has no elective (i.e., 401(k) salary deferral) contribution accounts. Under the plan's vesting schedule, his vested percentage is 60 percent, and he is entitled to an immediate distribution of $6,000. He and his spouse consent to the distribution of $6,000, and the remaining $4,000 will be forfeited. If Mark later returns to work for CDE Plumbers, his vested percentage may increase. However, Mark will not be entitled to a greater share of the $10,000 pre-break account balance, unless he first repays the $6,000 distribution. Regardless, he will retain his pre-break vesting service credit with respect to accounts created after his return to work.

Q 9:10 May a cash-out occur if a participant has no vested accrued benefit?

Yes, generally a plan document will provide that a participant with a vested percentage of zero percent is deemed to be cashed out immediately after terminating employment. This allows the forfeiture of all unvested accrued benefits to occur immediately upon severance of employment. [FSA 1992-1023-1]

Q 9:11 How do the plan repayment provisions operate in a defined contribution plan?

The forfeited (non-vested) accrued benefit of a participant is restored to the plan if the participant repays the full amount of his or her vested distribution. All optional forms of benefit and subsidies relating to the benefit must also be restored. The plan is not required to allow repayment unless these conditions are met:

1. The individual received a distribution that was less than the full account balance;
2. The individual resumes employment covered under the plan; and
3. The individual repays the full amount of the distribution before the earlier of (a) five years after the date of reemployment or (b) the first period of five consecutive one-year breaks in service following the date of distribution (see Qs 8:51–8:52).

[Treas. Reg. §§ 1.411(a)-7(d)(4)(iv), 1.411(a)-7(d)(4)(vi)]

Q 9:12 What interest is charged on amounts repaid to a defined contribution plan?

No interest is charged; the exact amount distributed to the participant must be repaid to the plan, without recognition of any related gains or losses the participant may have experienced. Similarly, the pre-break non-vested amount restored to the participant's account upon repayment is not credited with interest. [Treas. Reg. § 1.411(a)-7(d)(4)(v)]

Q 9:13 How does the employer restore the forfeited funds if an employee chooses to repay his or her distribution under the cash-out/repayment rules?

The permissible sources for restoration of the non-vested accrued benefit in a defined contribution plan are plan income, forfeitures, or employer contributions. The employer has until the end of the plan year following the plan year of repayment to make the restoration. [Treas. Reg. § 1.411(a)-7(d)(6)(iii)(C)]

Example 9-7: Mary Ann leaves employment at ABC Builders. At the time she leaves, she is 40 percent vested in her account balance of $20,000 and is entitled to her vested account balance in the profit sharing plan of $8,000. She receives her $8,000 on January 15, 2018. Because the plan contains a cash-out provision, the non-vested balance of $12,000 is forfeited and redistributed to the remaining participants for the plan year ended December 31, 2018. Mary Ann returns to work in 2019 and becomes eligible immediately to enter the plan. She chooses to repay the distribution of $8,000. Her previously non-vested account balance of $12,000 must be restored to her.

ABC Builders must determine, as of December 31, 2019, in accordance with the provisions of the plan, what source or sources to use: earnings, forfeitures, or an employer contribution. Because the plan is daily valued, earnings may not be used, as all the gains or losses have already been allocated to participants' accounts for the year. ABC Builders chooses to use forfeitures for the 2019 year of $10,000 to restore Mary Ann's account. The $2,000 remainder due Mary Ann is contributed by ABC Builders.

Q 9:14 Why do some employers not have a cash-out rule?

Some plans will not have a cash-out rule, because the plan sponsors are not willing to be forced to contribute additional amounts if previously partially vested employees return to service and repay their distribution.

Q 9:15 How is the account balance determined in a plan that does not contain cash-out rules?

First, a partially vested participant's forfeitures are not reallocated or applied to reduce employer contributions until that participant experiences five consecutive one-year breaks in service. Then, the vested account for employees who return to service, do not repay their prior distribution, and increase their vested percentage (but not up to the full 100 percent) is determined by one of the following two methods (as provided in the plan document).

Method 1. The current vested account balance, X, may be determined by this formula:

$$X = P \times [AB + (R \times D)] - (R \times D),$$

where X	=	Current vested account balance
P	=	Current vested percentage
AB	=	Current account balance
D	=	Amount of the distribution
R	=	Current account balance/Account balance after the distribution

[Treas. Reg. § 1.411(a)-7(d)(5)(iii)(A)]

Method 2. The current vested account balance, X, may also be determined by this formula:

$$X = P \times (AB + D) - D,$$

where X	=	Current vested account balance
P	=	Current vested percentage
AB	=	Current account balance
D	=	Amount of the distribution

[Treas. Reg. § 1.411(a)-7(d)(5)(iii)(B)]

Example 9-8: CDE Plumbers sponsors a target benefit plan. Jean, a participant in the plan, terminates employment with an account balance of $10,000. Under the plan's vesting schedule, her vested percentage is 60 percent, and she is entitled to, and takes a distribution of $6,000. She and her spouse consent to the distribution of $6,000, and the remaining $4,000 will be forfeited after five consecutive one-year breaks in service, because the plan does not have a cash-out provision. Jean returns to work after three years, does not repay her prior distribution of $6,000, and the previous unvested account balance has grown from $4,000 to $7,500. Jean works another year and becomes 80 percent vested and then quits again. Her total account balance at the time of her second termination of employment is $9,000. Her vested portion may be determined in accordance with one of two possible methods contained in the plan document:

Method 1. The current vested account balance, X, may be determined by this formula, if the plan document so provides:

$$X = P \times [AB + (R \times D)] - (R \times D)$$
$$R = \$9,000/\$4,000 = 2.25$$
$$X = 80\% \times [\$9,000 + (2.25 \times \$6,000)] - [(2.25) \times \$6,000]$$
$$= 80\% \times (\$9,000 + \$13,500) - \$13,500$$
$$= \$4,500$$

Method 2. The current vested account balance, X, may also be determined by the following formula, if the plan document so provides:

$$\begin{aligned} X &= P \times (AB + D) - D \\ &= 80\% \times (\$9{,}000 + \$6{,}000) - \$6{,}000 \\ &= 80\% \times \$15{,}000 - \$6{,}000 \\ &= \$6{,}000 \end{aligned}$$

Underfunded Defined Contribution Plans

Q 9:16 What is an underfunded defined contribution plan?

In a defined contribution plan, the general rule is that, as of the valuation date, the market value of plan assets (including receivable contributions) is equal to plan liabilities. In other words, the sum of the account balances for all participants is exactly equal to the market value of assets in the plan. If the plan sponsor does not deposit the receivable contributions, the plan will be underfunded.

However, in the case of money purchase and target benefit plans, which are subject to the minimum funding requirements of Code Section 412, plan sponsors may request a waiver of the minimum funding requirements from the IRS. This waiver, if it is granted, is not a permanent forgiveness of the contribution requirement. The plan sponsor is required to amortize the waived amount in annual installments over five years (15 years in the case of a multiemployer plan). [I.R.C. § 412(b)(2)(C)] The interest rate used for the amortization payment is 150 percent of the federal mid-term rate in effect for the first month of the plan year of amortization. [I.R.C. § 412(d)(1)(A)] In such a case, the market value of plan assets will be less than the sum of the account balances for all participants.

Example 9-9: CDE Plumbers sponsors a target benefit plan that had a contribution requirement of $75,000 for the plan year that ended December 31, 2018. Because of financial hardship, CDE Plumbers applies for a waiver of the funding standards and receives approval from the IRS National Office. The $75,000 funding deficiency must be amortized over five plan years. Assuming that 150 percent of the federal mid-term rate in effect on January 1, 2019 (the first month of the plan year of amortization), is 3.00 percent, the annual installment required to repay the funding deficiency is $16,377, which is the annual amortization of $75,000 over five years at 3.00 percent interest.

Q 9:17 How are account balances determined when a defined contribution plan has not fully amortized its funding waiver?

The plan sponsor must maintain two account balances for each participant: an actual account balance and an adjusted account balance. The actual account balance for all plan participants on any valuation date is exactly equal to the plan assets as of that date. The adjusted account balance is the theoretical account balance of the participant, had the plan sponsor made the contribution required under the funding standards. If not specified in the plan document, the plan must be amended at the time of waiver to specify the method used in determining the adjusted account balance. [Rev. Rul. 78-223; Ltr. Rul. 9224052]

Q 9:18 What methods may be used in determining the adjusted account balance?

Three basic methods for determining the adjusted account balance are described in Revenue Ruling 78-223. Other methods may be available. Some of the methods listed below may not be appropriate in a given situation or may be discriminatory under Code Section 401(a)(4):

1. *Immediate allocation method.* Waiver payments, adjusted for investment gains or losses, are allocated immediately to the actual account balances of participants entitled to allocations of employer contributions at the time the waiver was granted. The adjusted account balance of a participant may exceed the participant's actual account balance. The plan's distribution provisions limit the distribution of the vested portion of the actual account balance. Participants, therefore, receive less than their entire vested account balance, but are entitled to subsequent distributions when future waiver payments are made to the plan.
2. *Suspense account method.* Waiver payments, adjusted for investment gains or losses, are credited immediately to a suspense account. The adjusted account balance of each affected participant may exceed that participant's actual account balance. The plan provides that, if the vested portion of the participant's adjusted account balance exceeds that participant's actual account balance at the time of distribution, that participant receives the largest amount, to the extent that there are funds in the unallocated suspense account to cover the excess. Thus, some participants may not be able to receive a total distribution of the vested portion of their entire adjusted account balances. These participants would receive subsequent distributions derived from future waiver payments adjusted for investment gains or losses. When the total of plan assets equals the sum of the adjusted account balances, the suspense account is allocated to the affected participants so that the actual account balance of each affected participant equals that participant's adjusted account balance.
3. *Unrestricted distribution method.* The waiver payments, adjusted for investment gains or losses, become part of the plan's general assets, and actual account balances are not maintained. When a participant is entitled to a distribution, that participant receives the entire non-forfeitable portion of the adjusted account balance, to the extent that the plan's assets are sufficient to make the payment. Some participants may not be able to receive a total distribution of the vested portion of their entire adjusted account balances. These participants would receive subsequent distributions derived from future waiver payments adjusted for investment experience gains or losses. Caution should be taken in applying this method as the results may cause discrimination in favor of highly compensated employees.

[Rev. Rul. 78-223]

Example 9-10: Maxine is a participant in ABC Builders money purchase plan. The plan has an outstanding funding waiver, and the plan sponsor uses the immediate allocation method. When Maxine retires, her actual account balance is $122,348, and her adjusted account balance (increased by the funding waiver amount) is $165,478. Maxine elects a lump-sum distribution and will receive $122,348. As ABC Builders continues to pay off its funding waiver, Maxine will receive additional amounts that apply toward the difference of $43,130 ($165,478 − $122,348) plus investment gains or losses.

Example 9-11: Alex, a participant in CDE Plumbers target benefit plan, terminates employment while the plan has an outstanding funding waiver. The suspense account method is used. Alex's actual vested account balance is $4,500, and his adjusted vested account balance is $6,000. As waiver payments are made to repay the funding waiver, those payments are immediately credited to a suspense account. At the time of Alex's termination, the suspense account totals $24,000. If he requests a lump-sum distribution, Alex may receive his entire adjusted account balance of $6,000, because the suspense account has sufficient funds to pay him the shortfall.

Pamela retires a few months after Alex quits. Her vested actual account balance is $145,000, and her vested adjusted account balance is $180,000. Because there is not enough in the suspense account ($22,500) to cover the shortfall of $35,000, Pamela will only receive a distribution of $167,500 ($145,000 + $22,500). The balance will be paid to Pamela as funding waiver payments are credited to the suspense account.

Example 9-12: Tim terminates from ABC Builders. He participated in the money purchase plan to which ABC Builders is currently paying off a funding waiver. The plan uses the unrestricted distribution method. Tim's vested account balance is $23,459, and he is entitled to receive this distribution, to the extent that plan assets exceed $23,459. Plan assets are $123,948, so Tim may receive his full distribution.

The next day, Janet also terminates, and her vested account balance is $156,798. However, the plan assets are insufficient to pay the full benefit to Janet, so she receives only $100,489 ($123,948 − $23,459). The balance will be paid to Janet as the funding waiver is paid off.

Q 9:19 What are the steps involved in determining a participant's account balance?

To summarize, the following steps should be taken in determining a participant's vested account balances at the time of retirement or other termination of employment:

Step 1. Verify the frequency of valuation in the plan document.

Step 2. Confirm that account balances were determined as of the appropriate valuation date.

Step 3. Determine whether adjustments, if applicable to the plan, need to be made to any of the account balances after the last valuation date because of payment of insurance premiums, withdrawals, or significant market fluctuations.

Step 4. Determine which of the account balances are attributable to any of the contribution sources listed in Q 9:2 and, therefore, 100 percent vested.

Step 5. Determine whether there is an outstanding loan balance and to which account balance it belongs.

Step 6. Research the plan's history to find out if any distributions were previously paid to the participant.

Step 7. If the plan is a money purchase or target benefit plan, find out if there is an outstanding funding deficiency. If a deficiency exists as the result of a waiver of the minimum funding standards, determine the adjusted account balance accordingly.

Step 8. Determine vested percent and apply to the applicable account balances.

Determining Accrued Benefits in Traditional Defined Benefit Plans

Q 9:20 How is an accrued benefit determined in a traditional defined benefit plan?

The method for determining an accrued benefit is defined in the plan document and in a traditional defined benefit plan is expressed in the form of a periodic benefit beginning at normal retirement age. Typically, accrued benefits are stated in monthly benefit form, because benefits are generally paid on a monthly basis.

Q 9:21 How is normal retirement age defined?

Normal retirement age means the earlier of:

1. The time a plan participant attains normal retirement age under the plan; or
2. The later of the time a plan participant attains age 65 or the fifth anniversary of the time a plan participant began participation in the plan. [I.R.C. § 411(a)(8)(B)(i)]

Example 9-13: ABC Builders sponsors a defined benefit plan with a normal retirement age of the earlier of either (1) the later of age 55 or 20 years of service or (2) the later of age 65 or the fifth anniversary of plan entry. Greg starts working for the company at age 50 and enters the plan at age 51. His normal retirement age is the earlier of either (1) the later of age 55 or age 70 (age 50 plus 20 years of service) or (2) the later of age 65 or 56 (fifth anniversary of age at entry). Therefore, Greg's normal retirement age under the plan is 65.

Q 9:22 What is the principal significance of the normal retirement age?

A plan must provide that an employee's right to his or her normal retirement benefit is 100 percent vested when he or she reaches normal retirement age. [I.R.C. § 411(a)]

Q 9:23 What are the minimum accrual requirements in a defined benefit plan?

Benefits must accrue under a method that is at least as fast as determined under one of these four methods:

1. Fractional rule;
2. 133⅓ percent rule;
3. Three percent method; or
4. Fully insured method. [I.R.C. § 412(e)(3)]

[I.R.C. § 411(b)(1)]

Q 9:24 How does the fractional rule operate?

A plan satisfies the fractional rule if the accrued benefit that any participant is entitled to upon separation from service is not less than the following fraction, multiplied by the annual benefit at normal retirement age:

$$\frac{\text{Total number of years of participation as of the date of separation from service}}{\text{Total number of years of participation if separated from service at normal retirement age}}$$

This fraction may not exceed one. The normal retirement benefit is based on the plan provisions in effect on the date of separation from service and is based on average compensation, as defined in the plan (if the benefit is based on average compensation). No more than 10 years of service immediately preceding separation from service may be considered in determining average compensation. Social Security benefits and all other relevant factors used in computing benefits are treated as remaining constant (as of the separation year) for all years after the separation year. [I.R.C. § 411(b)(1)(C)] A defined benefit plan may use years of service rather than participation in determining the accrued benefit.

> **Example 9-14:** Marissa is a participant in the defined benefit plan sponsored by CDE Plumbers. The plan uses the fractional accrual method in determining accrued benefits. Marissa became a participant at age 40 and has a normal retirement age of 65. She separates from service at age 55 after 15 years of participation in the plan. Based on the plan formula and her average compensation, her normal retirement benefit, if she were to remain in service until age 65, is $1,000 per month. Her accrued benefit is obtained by multiplying her normal retirement benefit of $1,000 by the fraction described above: 15/25. Her accrued benefit is $600 ($1,000 × 15/25).

Q 9:25 How does the 133⅓ percent rule work?

The accrued benefit payable to a participant working to normal retirement age must be equal to the normal retirement benefit. In addition, for any plan year, the annual rate at which any individual (who is, or could be, a participant) can accrue benefits cannot be more than 133⅓ percent of the annual rate for any plan year beginning for any earlier plan year. Under the 133⅓ percent rule, these four assumptions apply:

1. Any amendment to the plan that is in effect for the current year is treated as in effect for all other plan years;
2. Any change in an accrual rate that does not apply to any individual who is, or could be, a participant in the current year is disregarded;
3. The fact that benefits under the plan may be payable to certain employees before normal retirement age is disregarded; and
4. Social Security and all other relevant factors used to compute benefits are treated as remaining constant as of the current year for all years after the current year.

[I.R.C. § 411(b)(1)(B)]

Example 9-15: ABC Builders sponsors a defined benefit plan. The plan has an accrual formula that states that benefits accrue at the rate of 3 percent per year for the first 20 years of service and 4 percent per year for the next 10 years. The ratio of the accrual rate (4 percent) to the earliest accrual rate (3 percent) does not exceed 133⅓ percent (4%/3% = 133⅓%). Thus, as long as the plan provides that the normal retirement benefit is payable upon reaching normal retirement age, this plan satisfies the 133⅓ percent accrual rule.

Phil is entitled to receive an annual benefit of $18,000 at age 65. His annual accrued benefit at the end of 10 years is calculated as:

$$\$18{,}000 \times 3\% \times 10 = \$5{,}400$$

His annual accrued benefit at the end of 25 years is calculated as:

$$(\$18{,}000 \times 3\% \times 20) + (\$18{,}000 \times 4\% \times 5)$$
$$= \$10{,}800 + \$3{,}600 = \$14{,}400$$

Q 9:26 How does the 3 percent method of benefit accrual work?

The accrued benefit to which each participant is entitled upon separation from service is not less than:

> 3 percent of the normal retirement benefit to which he or she would be entitled if he or she began participation at the earliest possible entry age under the plan and worked continuously until the earlier of age 65 or the normal retirement age specified under the plan, multiplied by the number of years (not in excess of 33⅓) of his or her participation in the plan.

For a defined benefit plan providing compensation-based benefits during any period, the normal retirement benefit to which a participant would be entitled is determined as if he or she continued to earn annually the average rate of compensation that he or she earned during consecutive years of service, not in excess of 10, for which his or her compensation was the highest. Under this rule, social security benefits and all other relevant factors used in computing benefits are treated as remaining constant as of the current year for all years after the current year. [I.R.C. § 411(b)(1)(A)]

Example 9-16: CDE Plumbers traditional defined benefit plan provides a flat retirement benefit of $500 per month at age 65. The plan uses the 3 percent method for accrual of benefits. Mary enters the plan at age 40 and leaves at age 55. The accrued benefit is calculated as:

$$\$500 \times 3\% \times 15 = \$225$$

Q 9:27 What is a Section 412(e)(3) plan?

A Section 412(e)(3) plan, sometimes known as a *fully insured plan*, is a plan funded exclusively with insurance contracts. Such a plan used to be known as a Section 412(i) plan. In the case of a top-heavy plan, a small investment fund may be used in conjunction with the insurance contracts in order to provide the top-heavy minimum benefit to non-key employees. A Section 412(e)(3) plan must satisfy these requirements to receive an exemption from the minimum funding requirements of Code Sections 412 and 430:

1. The plan is funded exclusively with individual or group insurance contracts.
2. The contracts must provide for level annual premium payments to be paid from the time the participant becomes eligible for the plan until the plan's normal retirement age.
3. The benefits provided by the plan are equal to the benefits provided under the insurance contracts at normal retirement age (to the extent premiums have been paid).
4. Premiums for the current plan year and all prior plan years must be paid before lapse of the contracts or there must be a reinstatement of the policy.
5. No rights under the contracts may be subject to a security interest at any time during the plan year.
6. No policy loans are outstanding at any time during the plan year.

[I.R.C. § 412(e)(3)]

Example 9-17: ABC Builders sponsors a qualified defined benefit plan that is intended to meet the requirements of 412(e)(3). Amanda, the only participant, is entitled to a lifetime monthly benefit of $8,000 at normal retirement age. The plan purchases life insurance and annuity contracts from MM Insurance Company with a death benefit of $800,000 and annual premiums of $42,780. The contracts will provide a monthly retirement benefit of $8,000 to

Amanda when she retires at age 65, if all premiums have been paid. Assuming that premiums are paid on a timely basis, that no policy loans are taken, and that no rights under the contracts have been assigned, this plan should meet the requirements of Code Section 412(e)(3).

Q 9:28 How do benefits accrue under a Section 412(e)(3) plan?

The accrued benefit is equal to the cash surrender value of all contracts for an employee. [Treas. Reg. § 1.411(b)-1(d)(2)] In the event that the plan is top heavy and provides top-heavy minimum benefits, the cash surrender value of the contracts may be insufficient to satisfy the top-heavy minimum requirements (see Q 9:50). In that event, an investment fund may be established to ensure that the top-heavy minimum accrued benefit is provided. [Treas. Reg. § 1.416-1, M-17]

Q 9:29 How do benefits accrue in a hybrid plan, such as a cash balance plan, or a floor plan?

See Qs 9:75–9:88.

Q 9:30 How are benefits attributable to employee contributions determined under a defined benefit plan?

The treatment of these benefits depends on the source of the employee contributions. If the employee contributions are voluntary, a separate account is set up and the account is treated the same as if it existed within a defined contribution plan. [I.R.C. § 411(d)(5)] If the plan requires mandatory employee contributions, a portion of the accrued benefit is attributable to the mandatory employee contributions. [I.R.C. § 411(c)(2)(B)]

Q 9:31 What portion of the accrued benefit is attributable to mandatory employee contributions?

The employee portion of the accrued benefit is equal to the employee's accumulated mandatory employee contributions (as of the determination date; see Q 9:32) expressed as an equivalent periodic benefit, beginning at normal retirement age, using an interest rate prescribed in Code Section 417(e)(3). [I.R.C. § 411(c)(2)(B)]

Q 9:32 How are accumulated employee mandatory contributions determined?

Accumulated employee mandatory contributions are the sum of the following amounts:

1. All mandatory contributions made by the employee;
2. Interest compounded annually at 5 percent for periods before the first plan year beginning after December 31, 1987;

3. Interest compounded annually at 120 percent of the federal mid-term rate for years beginning with the first plan year beginning after December 31, 1987, and ending with the determination date (see Appendix A for historical federal mid-term rates); and
4. Interest compounded at the Code Section 417(e) interest rates for the period beginning on the determination date and ending with the normal retirement date (see Appendices B, C, and H for historical Code Section 417(e) interest rates).

For plan years beginning on or after January 1, 2008, the accumulated employee mandatory contributions are calculated using the three-tier segment rates under PPA.

[I.R.C. § 411(c)(2)(C); 2008 Enrolled Actuaries Meeting Gray Book, Q&A 34]

Example 9-18: Kevin, a participant in the CDE Plumbers contributory defined benefit plan, terminates employment in 2011 and opts to receive a distribution of his vested accrued benefit in a lump sum at the end of 2015 (his normal retirement age). The plan year runs from January 1 through December 31. Kevin's historical mandatory employee contributions are shown in Table 9-1.

Table 9-1.

Year	*Mandatory Contribution Amounts*
1987	$ 600
1988	$ 650
1989	$ 700
1990	$ 750
1991	$ 800
1992	$ 850
1993	$ 900
1994	$ 950
1995	$ 980
1996	$1,000
1997	$1,200
1998	$1,100
1999	$1,300
2000	$1,400
2001	$1,500
2002	$1,600
2003	$1,800
2004	$2,000
2005	$2,200

Table 9-1. (*cont'd*)

Year	*Mandatory Contribution Amounts*
2006	$2,400
2007	$3,000
2008	$3,500
2009	$3,500
2010	$4,000
2011	$4,500

For 1987, a 5 percent interest rate is used for accumulation purposes. For years 1988 through 2010, 120 percent of the federal mid-term rate is used. For years 2011 through 2015 (Kevin reaches normal retirement age at the end of 2015), the Code Section 417(e) segment interest rate percent is used. The accumulated mandatory contributions are calculated as shown in Table 9-2.

Table 9-2. Mandatory Employee Contributions

Year	*Mandatory Contribution Amounts*	*Interest Rate*	*Interest Credit*	*Accumulated Balance*
1987	600	5.00%	30	630
1988	650	10.61%	136	1,416
1989	700	11.11%	235	2,351
1990	750	9.57%	297	3,398
1991	800	9.78%	411	4,609
1992	850	8.10%	442	5,901
1993	900	7.63%	519	7,319
1994	950	6.40%	529	8,798
1995	980	9.54%	932	10,711
1996	1,000	6.89%	807	12,518
1997	1,200	7.34%	1,007	14,725
1998	1,100	7.13%	1,128	16,953
1999	1,300	5.59%	1,020	19,273
2000	1,400	7.47%	1,544	22,217
2001	1,500	6.75%	2,312	26,029
2002	1,600	5.40%	1,492	29,121
2003	1,800	4.12%	1,274	32,194
2004	2,000	4.23%	1,446	35,640
2005	2,200	4.53%	1,714	39,554
2006	2,400	5.39%	2,261	44,215

Table 9-2. Mandatory Employee Contributions (*cont'd*)

Year	*Mandatory Contribution Amounts*	*Interest Rate*	*Interest Credit*	*Accumulated Balance*
2007	3,000	5.51%	2,602	49,817
2008	3,500	4.31%	2,298	55,615
2009	3,500	2.48%	1,466	60,581
2010	4,000	2.95%	1,905	66,486
2011	4,500	2.45%	1,739	72,725
2012	0	1.84%	1,338	74,063
2013	0	1.00%	741	74,804
2014	0	1.24%	928	75,732
2015	0	1.33%	1,007	76,739

The 2011 through 2015 rates represent the first segment rate of the three-segment tier for Code Section 417(e) minimum present values under PPA. The accumulated contributions for Kevin as of his normal retirement date are $76,739.

Q 9:33 How are the accumulated employee mandatory contributions converted into an accrued benefit?

The accumulated employee mandatory contributions are converted into an accrued benefit by using the actuarial equivalence factors as stated in the plan document. However, the converted benefit may never be less than the benefit computed using the applicable Code Section 417(e) rates. [Treas. Reg. § 1.417(e)-1(d)(3)]

Q 9:34 How is the applicable interest rate under Code Section 417(e) determined?

For plan years beginning before January 1, 2008, the applicable interest rate is the annual interest rate on 30-year Treasury securities. For plan years beginning on or after January 1, 2008, the applicable interest rates are from the three-tier segment rate set that is associated with the length of time to when a payment is to be made (typically beginning at normal retirement). [Treas. Reg. § 1.417(e)-1(d)(3)]

Example 9-19: In Example 9-18, the value of Kevin's accumulated contributions was $76,739. Using the 2015 applicable mortality table and three-tier segment rates of 1.33%, 3.46%, and 4.40%, respectively, the conversion to a monthly life only annuity commencing at age 65 would result in a monthly benefit of $460. Thus, $460 is the portion of the accrued benefit attributable to Kevin's employee mandatory contributions.

Determination of Accrual of Service

Q 9:35 What is a year of service for benefit accrual purposes?

A plan must contain language specifying a 12-month accrual computation period. An employee who completes 1,000 hours of service during an accrual computation period must, under certain circumstances, be credited with at least a partial year of service for benefit accrual. A full year of credit need not be given unless the employee is credited with the number of hours of service required under the plan for a full year of benefit accrual. [D.O.L. Reg. § 2530.200b-1(a)]

Q 9:36 How is an hour of service defined?

Hour of service is defined as:

1. Each hour for which an employee is paid, or entitled to payment, for the performance of duties for the employer. These hours are credited to the employee for the computation period in which the duties are performed.
2. Each hour for which an employee is paid, or entitled to payment, by the employer on account of a period of time during which no duties are performed (irrespective of whether the employment relationship has terminated) because of vacation, holiday, illness, incapacity (including disability), layoff, jury duty, military duty, or leave of absence. No more than 501 hours of service may be credited for these purposes for any single continuous period.
3. Each hour for which back pay, irrespective of mitigation of damages, is either awarded or agreed to by the employer. The same hours of service are not to be credited under paragraph 1 or 2 *and* under this paragraph 3. These hours are credited to the employee for the computation period in which the award, agreement, or payment is made.

Hours of service are credited for employment with other members of an affiliated service group (under Code Section 414(m)), a controlled group of corporations (under Code Section 414(b)), or a group of trades or businesses under common control (under Code Section 414(c)), of which the adopting employer is a member, and any other entity required to be aggregated with the employer under Code Section 414(o). [D.O.L. Reg. § 2530.200b-2, b-3]

Q 9:37 Are there any simpler methods for determining years of benefit accrual?

Yes, a plan may use a method known as *elapsed time,* in which case it is not necessary to count hours of service. Under this method, the number of years of service is treated as the number of whole years of the employee's period of service. The time period begins on the employee's first day of employment (the first day an hour of service is performed) and ends on the date of termination. Periods of less than a whole year may be disregarded. The disadvantage of the elapsed time approach is that periods of employment in which the employee works fewer than 1,000 hours must be counted as years of service for benefit accrual purposes. However, an employee who is credited with more than 1,000 hours of service, but works less than 365 days, is not credited with any service for that period of time. [D.O.L. Reg. § 2530.200b-3(b)]

Q 9:38 Are there any other alternatives for alleviating the recordkeeping requirements?

Yes, a plan document may compute equivalent total hours of service by counting only hours worked or regular time hours. If a plan uses the hours-worked method of determining accrual service (counting only actual hours worked and excluding vacation, sick time, and so forth), then the 1,000-hour requirement is reduced to 870 hours and the number of hours required for a break in service is reduced from 500 hours to 435 hours. [D.O.L. Reg. § 2530.200b-3(d)(1)] If the plan counts only regular time hours (excluding overtime), then the 1,000-hour and 500-hour requirements are reduced to 750 and 375 hours, respectively. [D.O.L. Reg. § 2530.200b-3(d)(2)]

Q 9:39 Are other equivalency methods available?

Yes, for an employee whose compensation is based on an hourly rate, a plan may determine the number of hours to be credited during the computation period on the basis of earnings if:

1. The employee receives credit for the number of hours computed as the total of the employee's earnings from time to time during the computation period divided by the employee's hourly rate in effect at such times during the computation period, or equal to the employee's total earnings for the performance of duties during the computation period divided by the employee's lowest hourly rate of compensation during the computation period, or by the lowest hourly rate of compensation payable to an employee in the same, or similar, job classification, reasonably defined.
2. The 1,000-hour and 500-hour thresholds are reduced to 870 and 435 respectively. [D.O.L. Reg. § 2530.200b-3(f)(1)]

For an employee whose compensation is determined on a basis other than an hourly rate, a plan may determine the number of hours to be credited to the employee as a computation period on the basis of earnings, if the 1,000-hour and 500-hour thresholds are reduced to 750 and 375, and one of these two rules is met:

1. For any employee whose compensation is determined on the basis of a fixed rate for a specified period of time (e.g., day, week, or month), the employee's hours are determined as the employee's hourly rate of compensation (the employee's lowest rate of compensation during a computation period for such specified period of time) divided by the number of hours regularly scheduled for the performance of duties during such period of time.

2. For any employee whose compensation is not determined on the basis of a fixed rate of time, the employee's hours are determined as above, using the lowest hourly rate of compensation payable to employees in the same job classification or, if no employees in the same job classification have an hourly rate, the minimum wage currently in effect. [D.O.L. Reg. §§ 2530.200b-3(f)(2), 2530.200b-3(f)(3)]

Example 9-20: ABC Builders employs laborers who generally work only during the summer. Jack, a summer employee, is paid $200 per day and is regularly scheduled to work 12 hours per day. Over the accrual computation period running from January 1, 2018, to December 31, 2018, Jack is paid $13,000. In computing his accrual service, Jack is credited with 780 hours (13,000 ÷ (200 ÷ 12)) and receives a year of benefit accrual because he is credited with more than 750 hours.

Q 9:40 May equivalencies be based on periods of employment?

The DOL regulations allow a simplified computation method that credits the following number of hours for each unit worked:

Days. An employee is credited with 10 hours of service for each day the employee would be required to be credited with at least one hour of service.

Weeks. An employee is credited with 45 hours of service for each week the employee would be required to be credited with at least one hour of service.

Semimonthly Period. An employee is credited with 95 hours of service for each semimonthly payroll period the employee would be required to be credited with at least one hour of service.

Months. An employee is credited with 190 hours of service for each month for which the employee would be required to be credited with at least one hour of service.

[D.O.L. Reg. § 2530.200b-3(e)(1)]

Q 9:41 May different service crediting methods be used for different classifications of employees?

Yes, different methods may be used if, on the basis of all the relevant facts and circumstances, the crediting of service does not discriminate in favor of highly compensated employees. Thus, for example, a plan could count actual hours for hourly employees and use one of the equivalency methods described above for salaried employees. [Treas. Reg. § 1.401(a)(4)-11(d)(2)]

Q 9:42 Must a participant who completes 1,000 hours of service receive credit for a full year of benefit accrual?

No, the DOL regulations indicate that up to 2,000 hours may be used as a requirement for a full year's accrual. However, a participant who works 1,000 or more hours must receive at least a pro rata accrual for the year. The DOL regulations also provide an example in which a participant must complete more than 1,800 hours of service in order to earn a full year of benefit accrual. Partial accrual is based on Table 9-3.

Table 9-3. Partial Accrual

Hours of Service Credited	*Percentage of Full Year of Service Credited*
1,000	50%
1,001 to 1,200	60%
1,201 to 1,400	70%
1,401 to 1,600	80%
1,601 to 1,800	90%
1,801 and above	100%

The DOL regulations also prohibit a double proration for defined benefit plans where, for example, the plan benefits are based on compensation.

[D.O.L. Reg. § 2530.204-2(c), (d)]

Example 9-21: Mr. Rogers is a participant in the CDE Plumbers Defined Benefit Plan. The plan uses the following schedule to prorate for the hours less than 1,800:

Hours of Service Credited	*Percentage of Full Year of Service Credited*
1,000	50%
1,001 to 1,200	60%
1,201 to 1,400	70%
1,401 to 1,600	80%
1,601 to 1,800	90%
1,801 and above	100%

Mr. Rogers works 1,000 hours in 2018 and is entitled to an accrual based on 50 percent of full year of service. The plan provides for an annual accrual of 2 percent of pay. If Mr. Rogers earns $30,000 in 2018, his annual benefit accrued during 2018 will need to be adjusted so that it reflects the pay he would have received had he worked 2,000 hours rather than 1,000 hours—or $60,000 ($30,000 × 2) to avoid a double reduction for working less than full-time:

$$2\% \times (\$30{,}000 \times 2) \times 50\% = \$600$$

Q 9:43 May any years of service be disregarded in computing years of benefit accrual?

Any rules that disregard certain periods of services must be contained in the plan document. Years of service before an employee becomes eligible to participate may be disregarded. In addition, the first two years of service (in which the employee completes more than 1,000 hours of service) may be disregarded until the employee completes two years of service. Once the participant completes two years of service, the plan must go back and retroactively count those disregarded years. [Treas. Reg. § 1.411(b)-1(d)(1)] Also, years of service in excess of the limits imposed by the plan may be disregarded. [I.R.C. § 411(b)(1)(H)(ii)]

> **Example 9-22:** Roger, an employee of ABC Builders, becomes a participant in the defined benefit plan on January 1, 2017. The plan disregards years of service until the completion of two years of service. He completes a year of service in 2017 by working more than 1,000 hours. He quits in April 2018 prior to completing 1,000 hours of service. Because Roger did not complete two years of service prior to termination, his year of service in 2017 is disregarded, and he will earn no benefit accrual. If, however, he comes back to work in June of 2018 and completes 1,000 hours in 2018, Roger will receive credit for two years of benefit accrual.

> **Example 9-23:** Barry, an employee of ABC Builders, has worked there for 35 years. The plan formula provides a benefit of 1 percent of average compensation multiplied by years of service, up to a maximum of 30 years. For benefit accrual purposes, five years of Barry's service may be disregarded because he has reached the maximum number of years of service.

Q 9:44 How do the cash-out rules work in a defined benefit plan?

The cash-out rules allow a plan sponsor to disregard pre-break service in determining future additional vesting for pre-break amounts if the five conditions discussed in Q 9:9 are met.

> **Example 9-24:** Matthew, a participant in the CDE Plumbers defined benefit plan, terminates employment in 2018 with an accrued benefit of $625, a vested percentage of 80 percent, and, therefore, a vested accrued benefit of $500 per month, payable commencing at age 65. The plan contains a lump-sum distribution provision, and Matthew elects, with his spouse's consent, to receive the current actuarially equivalent vested lump-sum distribution on December 31, 2018. Unless Matthew returns to work and repays the lump-sum distribution with interest (see Q 9:46), the plan will no longer consider Matthew's non-vested benefit of $125 per month as a plan obligation.

Q 9:45 May a cash-out occur if a participant has no vested accrued benefit?

Yes, generally a plan document will provide that a participant with a vested percentage of zero percent is deemed cashed out immediately after terminating employment. This permits the forfeiture of all unvested accrued benefits to occur immediately upon termination of employment. Some plan administrators may confirm the cash-out in writing to the plan participant.

Q 9:46 What interest rate is charged on cashed-out amounts repaid to a defined benefit plan?

The plan may provide that interest be paid on the cashed-out amounts in a defined benefit plan. If this is done, the amount to be repaid is determined as the sum of:

1. The initial amount distributed to the participant and
2. Interest compounded annually at 120 percent of the federal mid-term rate for years from the date of such distribution to the date of repayment (See Appendix A for historical federal mid-term rates).

[Treas. Reg. § 1.411(a)-7(d)(4)(iv)(C); Treas. Reg. § 1.411(a)-7(d)(2)(ii); I.R.C. § 411(c)(2)(C)]

> **Example 9-25:** Assume that Matthew (see Example 9-24) returns to employment in 2019. The amount to be repaid (if he chooses to do so) by December 31, 2020, consists of the cashed-out amount, plus interest for the 2019 and 2020 plan years. If the applicable rate for 2019 is 1.30 percent and for 2020 is 1.50 percent, and Matthew's repayment amount is his 2018 lump-sum payment × 1.013 × 1.015.
>
> After repayment, all Matthew's prior years of service will be counted in determining his accrued benefit at his next distributable event.

Benefit Minimums and Limitations

Q 9:47 What other factors affect the computation of a participant's accrued benefit?

By determining the number of years of benefit accrual and applying the plan's benefit formula, an initial determination may be made of the participant's accrued benefit. However, a number of factors (imposed by the plan or the Code) may change the calculation of the accrued benefit, including:

1. A minimum benefit established in the plan document;
2. Top-heavy minimum benefits (if the plan, or the required or permissive aggregation group of plans is top heavy and the defined benefit plan specifies that it will provide any applicable top-heavy minimum);

3. The preservation of a prior accrued benefit floor because of a change in the plan formula, normal retirement age, or actuarial equivalence factors; and
4. A cap on the maximum benefit because of the limits of Code Section 415.

Q 9:48 What type of minimum benefit requirements may be found in defined benefit plans?

A plan document may provide a minimum benefit. For example, a plan may provide a minimum benefit of $30 per month to ensure that participants receive at least a nominal benefit from the plan. In some cases, the minimum benefit formula may be based on years of service in order to reward long-service employees. Or, the minimum benefit may be set at a flat amount such as $10 per month per year of service.

Example 9-26: ABC Builders provides a defined benefit plan for its eligible employees. The plan's regular benefit formula is 2 percent of average pay multiplied by years of service. The minimum benefit formula is $30 per month per year of service. Charles has worked 20 years for the company, his average monthly pay is $1,000, and he has reached the normal retirement age. Under the plan's regular benefit formula, his monthly accrued benefit is:

$$2\% \times \text{Average pay} \times \text{Years of service}$$
$$= 2\% \times \$1{,}000 \times 20$$
$$= \$400$$

His minimum accrued benefit is:

$$\text{Minimum benefit} \times \text{Years of service}$$
$$= \$30 \times 20$$
$$= \$600$$

Charles's monthly accrued benefit is the greater of $400 or his minimum benefit of $600. Thus, Charles is entitled to begin receiving a monthly benefit of $600.

Q 9:49 When must a plan provide top-heavy minimum benefits?

If the plan is top heavy, or the required or permissive aggregation group of plans is top heavy, top-heavy minimum benefits must be provided to non-key employees. (See chapter 8 for a discussion on determining top-heavy status and key employees.) If the employer or related employers maintain only a defined benefit plan, each non-key employee who is a participant must receive the defined benefit minimum from that plan. If the employer or related employers maintain multiple plans, top-heavy minimums need not be provided in each plan. There are four alternatives for providing top-heavy minimums to non-key employees if the employer or related employers maintain a mix of defined benefit and defined contribution plans:

1. Provide full defined benefit plan top-heavy minimum benefits within the defined benefit plans.
2. Use a floor-offset approach [Rev. Rul. 76-259] under which the defined benefit minimum in the applicable year provided in the defined benefit plan is the otherwise full defined benefit top-heavy minimum offset by the benefits equivalent to the contributions provided under the defined contribution plan.
3. Use a comparability analysis to demonstrate that the combination of the defined benefit plan and the defined contribution plan are providing at least the top-heavy minimum. [Rev. Rul. 81-202]
4. Provide a minimum contribution (employer contributions plus forfeitures) of 5 percent of compensation within the defined contribution plans.

[Treas. Reg. § 1.416-1, M-12]

Q 9:50 What is the top-heavy minimum benefit in a defined benefit plan?

The top-heavy minimum benefit is equal to an employee's average annual compensation for the period of consecutive years (not exceeding five) when the employee had the highest aggregate compensation from the employer, multiplied by 2 percent per year of service, up to a maximum of 10 years. The following years of service may be disregarded:

- Years of service before the employee became a participant
- Years of service when the plan was not top heavy
- Years of service completed in a plan year beginning before January 1, 1984
- Years of service when the employee did not earn a year of accrual service under the terms of the plan
- Years in which no key employees benefit for purposes of the minimum coverage rules in Code Section 410(b).

The defined benefit minimum described above is payable as a life annuity (with no ancillary benefits), beginning at normal retirement age of the later of age 65 or the fifth anniversary of plan entry. If the normal form of benefit is other than a life annuity, or the retirement is other than the later of age 65 or the fifth anniversary of the entry date, the minimum benefit may be adjusted (see Q 9:51).

The top-heavy minimum benefit is a minimum benefit, not an "add-on" benefit. To the extent that the accrued benefit as determined under the plan's regular benefit formula is not sufficient to satisfy the top-heavy minimum, additional benefits must accrue. Accrued benefits attributable to mandatory employees contributions are ignored (see Qs 9:30–9:34). [Treas. Reg. § 1.416-1, M-2; I.R.C. § 416(c)(1)(C)]

Example 9-27: Todd, a non-key participant in the CDE Plumbers defined benefit plan, has accrued a benefit under the plan's regular benefit formula of $475 per month based on his 15 years of accrual service. The plan is top heavy and provides a top-heavy minimum benefit of 2 percent of average compensation per applicable years of participation in the plan. The plan has been top heavy for five years. Todd has average monthly compensation for top-heavy purposes of $3,000. The top-heavy minimum benefit for Todd is:

top-heavy average compensation × 2% × top-heavy years
= $3,000 × 2% × 5
= $300

Since Todd's regular accrued benefit exceeds his top-heavy minimum benefit, Todd's monthly accrued benefit is $475, without any increase due to the plan being top heavy. Had the plan formula provided Todd a monthly accrued benefit less than $300, Todd's monthly accrued benefit would have been increased to be the top-heavy minimum of $300.

Q 9:51 How does the defined benefit minimum of 2 percent change if it is paid in a form other than a life annuity beginning at normal retirement age?

If the benefit is paid in a form other than a life annuity, the top-heavy minimum benefit is the actuarial equivalent of the life-only top-heavy minimum benefit. Similarly, if the benefit begins before the later of age 65 or the fifth anniversary of plan entry, the earlier top-heavy minimum benefit is the reduced benefit that is the actuarial equivalent of the benefit that would commence at the later of age 65 or the fifth anniversary of plan entry. If the benefit begins after the later of age 65 or the fifth anniversary of plan entry, the actuarially equivalent top-heavy minimum benefit will be actuarially increased. No assumptions are specified by the IRS for use in the actuarial equivalent computations, although the assumptions must be reasonable. [Treas. Reg. § 1.416-1, M-3]

Q 9:52 How does the floor-offset approach to providing top-heavy minimum benefits operate?

The defined benefit plan document must define the top-heavy minimum benefit as the otherwise minimum, offset by the actuarially equivalent benefit provided by the participant's employer-provided defined contribution accounts. The defined benefit plan document must also indicate the actuarial assumptions to be used to convert the account balance into the actuarially equivalent benefit. [Rev. Rul. 76-259]

> **Example 9-28:** CDE Plumbers sponsors both a defined benefit and a profit sharing plan. The plans form a top-heavy required aggregation group, and both of the plan documents provide that a floor-offset arrangement is used to provide top-heavy minimum benefits. Jim terminates employment. Jim had 10 years of top-heavy service and average monthly compensation of $4,000. His accrued benefit under the regular defined benefit plan formula is $225 per month beginning at age 65 and payable for his lifetime. His top-heavy minimum accrued benefit (before offset by the profit sharing plan equivalent benefit) is $800 per month ($4,000 × 2% × 10 years). Jim is age 45 and has a profit sharing account balance of $27,000. Both plans provide that the actuarial assumptions used in the conversion of the profit sharing plan's employer contributions account balances are 5 percent interest, no pre-retirement mortality, the current Section 417(e) applicable mortality table for post-retirement periods, and an annuity purchase rate of $125. The calculation of the offset to the top-heavy minimum benefit is as follows:
>
> $$\$27{,}000 \times (1.05)^{20} \div 125 = \$573$$
>
> (Note that 20 is the number of years from current age to Jim's normal retirement age of 65.)
>
> Jim's accrued benefit in the defined benefit plan is the greater of the regular accrued benefit of $225 per month, or the top-heavy minimum benefit of $800 offset by the profit sharing plan equivalent benefit of $573, or $227 ($800 − $573). Because the top-heavy benefit after the offset of the profit sharing plan equivalent benefit is greater than the regular benefit by formula, Jim's current accrued benefit is $227 per month beginning at age 65 payable for his lifetime (or any other form of actuarially equivalent benefit specified by the plan) from the defined benefit plan, plus his account balance of $27,000 in the profit sharing plan.

Q 9:53 How are top-heavy minimum benefits determined under the comparability approach?

The comparability approach operates in much the same way that the floor-offset approach does. The account balance in the defined contribution plan is actuarially converted to a benefit and added to the accrued benefit in the defined benefit plan. If the sum of the two benefits is greater than the top-heavy minimum requirement, the top-heavy minimum is satisfied. If the benefit is less than the top-heavy minimum, the benefit difference must accrue in the defined benefit plan. [Treas. Reg. § 1.416-1, M-12/Rev. Rul. 81-202 as modified by Rev. Rul. 83-110]

Q 9:54 If top-heavy minimum contributions of 5 percent of pay are provided in a defined contribution plan, do top-heavy minimum benefits need to be provided?

If non-key employees (who benefit in both defined benefit and defined contribution plans within a top-heavy aggregation group) are allocated at least 5 percent of pay in employer contributions and forfeitures in defined contribution plans, additional top-heavy minimum benefits are not necessary in the defined benefit plans. If the defined contribution plans participant allocations are insufficient, the employer or related employers have two options:

1. Contribute additional contributions so that at least 5 percent of pay is allocated for each non-key participant in order to satisfy the top-heavy requirement; or
2. Provide top-heavy minimum benefits in the defined benefit plan (if allowed for in the plan documents). [Treas. Reg. § 1.416-1, M-13]

It should be noted that a non-key participant who benefits in defined benefit plans, but not in a defined contribution plan, will need to accrue a full defined benefit plan top-heavy minimum benefit. If a non-key employee benefits only in the defined contribution plans, the top-heavy minimum contribution is generally equal to 3 percent of pay. When relying on the 5% contribution to a defined contribution plan for non-key employees who are also in a defined benefit plan, it is important to watch for participants who might be entitled to a top-heavy benefit in the defined benefit plan in a year in which 5 percent is not allocated to the participant in the defined contribution plan, such as the year in which the participant terminates employment.

Q 9:55 What happens if a plan sponsor makes a change in the benefit formula of a defined benefit plan?

A defined benefit plan sponsor may increase, reduce, or freeze a plan's benefit formula. Defined benefit plan sponsors may also convert a traditional defined benefit plan into a statutory hybrid plan (e.g., cash balance plan). The final regulations for statutory hybrid plans are effective for plan years beginning on or after January 1, 2011. For conversion amendments that occurred between June 29, 2005, and January 1, 2011, a plan sponsor is permitted to rely on the proposed statutory hybrid plan regulations and other existing guidance. The proposed and final regulations are similar. Additional final regulations and new proposed regulations were issued in October 2014. Affected participants must generally be provided with a benefit after the conversion that is at least equal to the sum of the benefits accrued through the date of the conversion plus benefits earned after the conversion. [Treas. Reg. § 1.411(b)(5)-1(c)]

Example 9-29: Sally, age 45, is a participant in the ABC Builders Defined Benefit Plan. The plan is converted to a cash balance plan effective January 1, 2013. Sally's monthly accrued benefit as of December 31, 2012, is $500. The opening balance in the cash balance plan for Sally is the actuarially equivalent lump sum as of January 1, 2013, to her $500 benefit deferred to age 65 or $26,700.

However, prior to conversion, the defined benefit plan provided a fully subsidized early retirement benefit at age 55 for employees with 30 years of service. Sally retires at age 55 and has more than 30 years of service. The lump sum actuarial equivalent to her $500 benefit commencing immediately on her 55th birthday is $87,500. The portion of her cash balance account attributable to her opening balance is $43,500. The difference, or $44,000, must be credited to Sally's cash balance account. This example assumes that the lump-sum distribution under the prior traditional defined benefit plan was based on an immediate annuity at early retirement, as opposed to being determined as a deferred benefit payable at normal retirement age.

Code Section 415 Limits

Q 9:56 What is the maximum benefit that may be provided in a defined benefit plan?

Code Section 415 limits the benefits that may be provided in a defined benefit plan and limits the benefits or contributions when an employee participates in a defined benefit plan and a defined contribution plan. The maximum annual benefit payable from a defined benefit plan at any age between 62 and 65 may not exceed the lesser of:

1. $90,000, as indexed (dollar limit); or
2. 100 percent of the participant's average compensation for his or her highest-paid three consecutive years (percentage limit).

Table 9-4 shows the indexed limits (dollar limits) since 1987:

Table 9-4.

Year	*Maximum Annual Dollar Benefit*
1987	$ 90,000
1988	$ 94,023
1989	$ 98,064
1990	$102,582
1991	$108,963
1992	$112,221
1993	$115,641
1994	$118,800
1995	$120,000
1996	$120,000
1997	$125,000

Table 9-4. (*cont'd*)

Year	*Maximum Annual Dollar Benefit*
1998	$130,000
1999	$130,000
2000	$135,000
2001	$140,000
2002	$160,000
2003	$160,000
2004	$165,000
2005	$170,000
2006	$175,000
2007	$180,000
2008	$185,000
2009	$195,000
2010	$195,000
2011	$195,000
2012	$200,000
2013	$205,000
2014	$210,000
2015	$210,000
2016	$210,000
2017	$215,000
2018	$220,000

[I.R.C. § 415(b)(1)]

Q 9:57 How is the annual benefit defined?

Annual benefit means a benefit payable annually in the form of a straight life annuity (with no ancillary benefits) under a plan to which employees do not contribute and under which no rollover contributions are made. A straight life annuity pays benefits for the life of the participant; once the participant dies, all payments cease. If the benefit under the plan is payable in a form other than a straight life annuity, the maximum benefit described in Q 9:56 is an actuarially equivalent benefit. However, if the benefit is payable in the form of a qualified joint and survivor annuity, no actuarial reduction is necessary. The annuity benefit or any portion of such benefit provided from a direct rollover of an eligible rollover distribution from a qualified defined contribution plan maintained by the same employer is not included in the annual benefit subject to Code Section 415(b) if the benefit provided from the rollover is the actuarially equivalent immediate annuity using the applicable interest rate and applicable mortality table under Code Section 417(e). If other conversion factors are used, some of the benefits may be included in the annual benefit subject to Code Section 415(b). [I.R.C. § 415(b)(2)(A), (B); Rev. Rul. 2012-4]

Q 9:58 Are benefits reduced if they begin early?

The dollar limit is not reduced if benefits begin on or after a normal retirement age that is between ages 62 and 65 (see Q 9:56). If benefits begin before age 62, an actuarial reduction is applied to maximum benefits. Note that maximum benefit limits are determined at the plan's normal retirement age and reduced for early commencement or optional benefit forms, including joint and survivor adjustments, according to plan terms. This adjusted benefit is subject to the pre-age 62 limits, if less. [I.R.C. § 415(b)(2)(C); Treas. Reg. § 1.415(b)-1(b)(1)(i); 2013 Enrolled Actuaries Meeting, Gray Book Question 6]

Q 9:59 Is the maximum benefit increased if it begins after age 65?

Yes, the maximum benefit is actuarially increased to the actual benefit commencement age if it begins after age 65. [I.R.C. § 415(b)(2)(D)]

Table 9-5 shows sample Code Section 415 dollar limits at various retirement ages, assuming the plan document contains an interest rate of 5 percent and Code Section 417(e) 2018 Applicable Mortality Table as the actuarial equivalence factors.

Table 9-5.

Retirement Age	*Maximum Dollar Limit in 2018*
55	$138,729
56	$147,854
57	$157,678
58	$168,277
59	$179,724
60	$192,102
61	$205,497
62	$220,000
63	$220,000
64	$220,000
65	$220,000
66	$236,361
67	$254,193
68	$270,000
69	$270,000
70	$270,000

Table 9-5. (*cont'd*)

Retirement Age	*Maximum Dollar Limit in 2018*
71	$270,000
72	$270,000
73	$270,000
74	$270,000
75	$270,000

Under final Treasury Regulations, the Code Section 401(a)(17) limit on compensation would be applied to limit the benefit payable after age 65 to no more than the percentage limit. For example, the benefit payable at age 68 would be limited to $270,000 in 2018 (the average of the compensation limits for 2016, 2017, and 2018 of $265,000, $270,000, and $275,000). [Treas. Reg. § 1.415(b)-1(a)(5)]

Example 9-30: Meredith retires from CDE Plumbers in 2018. She has participated in the defined benefit plan for 10 years, and her three-year highest-paid average (2015–2017) compensation is $280,000, with each year's compensation in excess of the Code Section 401(a)(17) limit. She is 70 years old. The plan document contains an actuarial equivalence factor of 5 percent and the current Code Section 417(e) Applicable Mortality Table. The maximum annual dollar limit benefit payable to Meredith from the defined benefit plan is $220,000 actuarially increased to age 70 or $318,443. However, under the final Code Section 415 regulations, Meredith's benefit would be limited to her percentage limit or $266,667, which is the average compensation limit for 2015, 2016, and 2017 under Code Section 401(a)(17).

Q 9:60 What actuarial assumptions are used in adjusting the maximum annual benefit for optional forms of payment?

In adjusting for a normal form other than a life annuity or for benefits beginning before age 62, the required interest rate is equal to the greatest of:

1. 5½ percent;
2. The rate that would provide a benefit of not more than 105 percent of the benefit that would be provided if the Code Section 417(e)(3) rate were used; or
3. The actuarial equivalence rate specified in the plan.

Option 2 above does not apply for plans sponsored by eligible employers. The term *eligible employer* means, with respect to any year, an employer that had no more than 100 employees who received at least $5,000 of compensation from the employer for the preceding year.

[I.R.C. §§ 415(b)(2)(E)(vi); 408(p)(2)(C)(i)]

Q 9:61 How is average compensation defined for the maximum annual benefit?

Average compensation is an employee's highest-paid three years of service, based on the period of three consecutive 12-month periods during which the employee had the greatest aggregate compensation from the employer. For an employee who completes less than three years of service, the actual number of consecutive years with the employer should be used. The plan may use any 12-month period (limitation year) in determining average compensation, provided that it is uniformly and consistently applied. [Treas. Reg. § 1.415(b)-1(a)(1)(ii)]

> **Example 9-31:** Charlotte is a participant in the CDE Plumbers defined benefit plan. During 2017, her first year of employment, she earns $120,000, and during 2018, she earns $150,000. She terminates employment in late 2018. For purposes of the maximum benefit limit, Charlotte's average compensation is $135,000 [($150,000 + $120,000) ÷ 2].

Q 9:62 How is compensation defined for purposes of the Code Section 415 limits?

Generally, compensation includes all taxable compensation paid to the participant during the limitation year. Amounts specifically included as compensation are:

1. The employee's wages, salaries, fees for professional services, and other amounts received (in cash or in kind) for personal services actually rendered in the course of employment with the employer maintaining the plan, to the extent that such amounts are included in gross income (including, for example, commissions paid to sales personnel, compensation for services on the basis of profits, commissions on insurance premiums, tips, bonuses, taxable fringe benefits, and reimbursements or other expense allowances under an expense reimbursement arrangement);
2. In the case of a self-employed individual, the employee's earned income (as described in Code Section 401(c)(2)), which generally equals:
   a. Net income from self-employment, as reported on IRS Form 1040, Schedule C or E, *minus*
   b. 50 percent of self-employment taxes payable by the individual, *minus*
   c. Qualified plan contributions made for the individual.
3. Accident or health benefits, to the extent that such benefits are includible in the individual's taxable income;
4. Amounts paid or reimbursed by the employer for moving expenses, as long as it is reasonable to believe that such amounts are not deductible by the employee under Code Section 217;
5. The value of a nonqualified stock option granted to an employee by the employer, but only to the extent that the value of the option is includible in the employee's income for the taxable year in which it is granted; and

6. The amount includible in the employee's income upon making an election under Code Section 83(b); or
7. Amounts that are includible in the gross income of an employee under a nonqualified deferred compensation arrangement under Code Section 409A or 457(f)(1)(A).

The following amounts are *not includible* as compensation:

1. Employer contributions to a simplified employee pension (SEP) plan, SIMPLE IRA, regular IRA, or 457 plan;
2. Amounts realized from the exercise of a nonqualified stock option, or when restricted stock (or property) held by an employee either becomes freely transferable or is no longer subject to a substantial risk of forfeiture [I.R.C. § 83];
3. Amounts realized from the sale, exchange, or other disposition of stock acquired under a qualified stock option;
4. Other amounts that receive special tax benefits, including premiums for group-term life (to the extent includible in taxable income), or contributions made by an employer to a Code Section 403(b) annuity contract (regardless of whether such amounts are excludable from the gross income of the employee), including salary-reduction contributions made on a pre-tax basis to a cafeteria or Code Section 125 plan; or
5. Other items of remuneration that are similar to any of the items described above.

[Treas. Reg. § 1.415(c)-2(b)]

Q 9:63 Is there a reduction in the maximum benefit for short-service employees?

Yes, in the case of the dollar limitation ($220,000 for 2018), the maximum benefit is prorated for an employee who has fewer than 10 years of participation. In the case of the percentage limitation (100 percent), the maximum benefit is prorated for an employee who has less than 10 years of service. [I.R.C. § 415(b)(5)(A), (B)]

Example 9-32: Louise participates in the ABC Builders defined benefit plan and retires in 2018, when she is age 65. Her average compensation (based on her highest-paid three years) is $180,000. When Louise retires in 2018, she has five years of participation and eight years of service. The maximum annual benefit payable in life annuity form to Louise is the lesser of:

1. *Dollar limit:* $220,000 × 5/10 = $110,000 or
2. *Percentage limit:* 100% × $180,000 × 8/10 = $144,000

The maximum annual benefit payable to Louise is $110,000.

Q 9:64 Is there a minimum benefit payable from a defined benefit plan without regard to the above limitations?

Yes. A defined benefit plan may pay a minimum annual benefit of $10,000 to a participant if all of the following conditions are met:

1. The employer has not at any time maintained a defined contribution plan in which the participant participated;
2. The retirement benefits payable to the participant under the defined benefit plan and under all other defined benefit plans of the employer do not exceed $10,000; and
3. If the participant has fewer than 10 years of service with the employer, the $10,000 benefit is reduced pro rata for each year of service less than 10.

[I.R.C. § 415(b)(4); Treas. Reg. § 1.415(b)-1(f)]

It is important to note that the $10,000 minimum represents the maximum amount that may be paid in a year under this provision in the law. Thus, for example, the $10,000 benefit could not be converted to a lump sum and paid to a participant who retires or terminates employment.

Treas. Reg. § 1.415(b)-1(f)(2)]

Example 9-33: CDE Plumbers provides a minimum benefit of $10,000 per year and has never maintained another defined contribution or defined benefit plan. Joanne retires at age 60 after working for eight years, with average compensation of $5,000. The minimum benefit of $10,000 is reduced as follows:

$$\$10{,}000 \times 8 \div 10 = \$8{,}000$$

Joanne would not be able to elect a lump sum on this benefit. Alternatively, the plan could purchase an annuity for her to pay her a monthly benefit of $666.66 ($8,000 ÷ 12) or pay her a lump sum on the benefit calculated by the plan formula without regard to the minimum benefit.

Lump Sum Determination

Q 9:65 What interest rates and mortality table are used to determine minimum lump sums?

With respect to applicable interest rates, a three-segment rate approach is used. A phase-in of prior (30-year Treasury securities rates) and new rates (corporate bond yield curve prescribed by the Secretary of the Treasury) applied from 2008 to 2011. The phase-in period is expired for minimum lump sum calculations after the 2011 plan year.

The applicable minimum lump sum value interest rates are the first, second, and third segment rates, for the month before the date of distribution or such other time as prescribed by Treasury regulations. The adjusted first, second, and third segment rates are derived from a corporate bond yield curve prescribed by the Secretary of the Treasury for such month which reflects the yields on investment grade corporate bonds with varying maturities (rather than a 24-month average, as under the minimum funding rules). Thus, the interest rate that applies depends upon how many years in the future a participant's annuity payment will be made. Typically, a higher interest applies for payments made further out in the future.

Prior to 2008, the applicable minimum lump sum interest rate was the annual rate of interest on 30-year Treasury securities, for the month before the date of distribution or such other time as prescribed by Treasury regulations. An applicable interest rate transition rule applied for distributions in 2008 through 2011. For distributions in 2008 through 2011, interest rates used to determine minimum lump sum values were the weighted average of two values:

1. The pre-2008 single applicable interest rate; and
2. The post-2007 applicable first, second, and third segment rates.

For distributions in plan years 2008, 2009, 2010, and 2011, the weighting factor is shown in the table below:

Year	*Pre-2008 Rate Weighting*	*Post-2007 Rate Weighting*
2008	80%	20%
2009	60%	40%
2010	40%	60%
2011	20%	80%

The mortality table that must be used for calculating minimum lump sums is based on the mortality table required for minimum funding purposes, modified as appropriate by the Secretary of the Treasury. The Secretary has prescribed gender-neutral tables for use in determining minimum lump sums. (See Appendix F.)

[PPA § 302; ERISA § 205(g)(3); I.R.C. § 417(e)(3); Prop. Treas. Reg. § 1.417(e)-1(d)(7)]

Q 9:66 How are the interest rates determined?

The applicable interest rate for distributions made during a month is the annual rate of interest for the month before the date of distribution. However, the regulations permit selection of a monthly, quarterly, or annual period during which the applicable interest rate remains constant. Permitting selection of a quarterly or annual stability period allows plans to offer greater benefit stability than is provided by the statutory rule, under which the applicable interest rate changes monthly. The regulations provide that the applicable interest rate for the stability period may be determined as the rate for any one of the five calendar months preceding the first day of the stability period. Permitting this "look back" of up to five months provides added flexibility and gives plan administrators and participants more time to comply with applicable notice and election requirements (see chapter 11) using the actual interest rate rather than an estimate. Thus, a plan may change the applicable interest rate monthly, quarterly, or annually and may determine the rate with reference to one of the five months preceding the month, quarter, or year. [Treas. Reg. § 1.417(e)-1(d)(3), (4)]

> **Example 9-34:** ABC Builders sponsors a defined benefit plan with a calendar plan year, uses the same interest rate for all distributions in the plan year (i.e., the annual stability period). The plan provides that the applicable interest rate for the entire plan year is the set of interest rates specified by the Commissioner for the prior August (i.e., five calendar months before January 1, the first day of the plan year).

Q 9:67 How did the Retirement Protection Act of 1994 (RPA), the Small Business Job Protection Act of 1996 (SBJPA), the Pension Funding Equity Act of 2004 (PFEA), the Pension Protection Act of 2006 (PPA), and the Worker, Retiree, and Employer Recovery Act of 2008 (WRERA) change the Code Section 415 limits for lump sums?

These laws made significant changes to the calculation of the Code Section 415 limits discussed in Qs 9:56–9:64 for all forms of benefit except non-decreasing annuity benefits payable for the life of the participant or the joint lives of the participant and spouse. A mandatory interest rate is applied in the calculation of such benefits. For all practical purposes, it applies to lump-sum distributions and installment payments. A non-decreasing annuity includes a qualified joint and survivor annuity (QJSA), a qualified pre-retirement survivor annuity (QPSA), and an annuity that decreases merely because of the cessation or reduction of Social Security supplements or qualified disability payments (see chapter 11).

[Treas. Reg. § 1.415(b)-1(c)(3)(i); I.R.C. § 415(b)(2)(E)]

Q 9:68 What mortality table must be used to make adjustments to benefits and limitations under Code Section 415(b)(2)(E)?

For plan years beginning on or after January 1, 2008, the IRS has published mortality tables to determine present value under Code Section 417(e) for 2009 through 2018. [Notice 2008-85 for 2008 through 2013, Notice 2013-49 for 2014 and 2015, Notice 2015-53 for 2016, Notice 2016-50 for 2017, and Notice 2017-60 for 2018] The tables are reproduced in Appendix F.

The mortality table in Revenue Ruling 2001-62 must be used for distribution with annuity starting dates after December 31, 2002, and for plan years beginning before January 1, 2008. [Rev. Rul. 2001-62; Rev. Rul. 2007-67] (See Appendix F.)

Q 9:69 How are the maximum benefit limitations under Code Section 415(b) applied to a benefit that is payable in a form subject to Code Section 417(e)(3)?

In general, to determine whether a benefit satisfies the Code Section 415(b) limitations, compare the greater actuarially equivalent annual benefit determined in Step 1 with the lesser of the adjusted dollar limit determined in Step 2 and the Code Section 415(b) compensation limitation determined in Step 3. If necessary, the lesser of the Step 2 or Step 3 benefit will become an upper limit for the greater benefit in Step 1 and serve as a limit to the Code Section 417(e)(3) benefit amount payable.

Step 1. Determine the annual benefit in the form of a straight life annuity commencing at the same age that is actuarially equivalent to the yet-unlimited Code Section 417(e)(3) plan benefit (generally, the lump sum benefit). This equivalent annual benefit is the greatest of:

1. The actuarially equivalent immediate straight life annual benefit computed using the interest rate and mortality table, or tabular factor, specified in the plan for actuarial equivalence, or
2. The actuarially equivalent immediate straight life benefit computed using a 5.5 percent interest rate assumption and the Code Section 417(e) applicable mortality table, or
3. The actuarially equivalent immediate straight life benefit computed using the applicable Code Section 417(e)(3) interest rates and applicable mortality table, divided by 1.05. However, the Worker, Retiree, and Employer Recovery Act of 2008 amended the Code to eliminate this step for plans sponsored by eligible employers. The term *eligible employer* means, with respect to any year, an employer that had no more than 100 employees who received at least $5,000 of compensation from the employer for the preceding year.

Step 2. Determine the Code Section 415(b) dollar limitation that applies at the age the benefit is payable (age-adjusted dollar limit). The age-adjusted dollar limit is the straight life annual benefit that is actuarially equivalent to an annual benefit equal to the Code Section 415(b) dollar limitation as discussed in Qs 9:56–9:64.

Step 3. Determine the participant's Code Section 415(b) compensation limitation. This limitation is equal to the participant's compensation averaged over the consecutive three-year period producing the highest average, as provided in Code Section 415(b)(3) and discussed in Qs 9:61 and 9:62.

The plan does not satisfy the Code Section 415(b) limitations unless the equivalent annual straight life benefit determined in Step 1 is limited to the lesser of the age-adjusted dollar limit determined in Step 2 and the compensation limitation determined in Step 3.

[Treas. Reg. § 1.415(b)-1; I.R.C. § 415(b)(2)(E)]

Q 9:70 Are fully insured plans under Code Section 412(e)(3) subject to the requirements under Code Section 415(b)?

Yes, fully insured plans (see Qs 9:27, 9:28) are subject to all of the requirements of Code Section 415.

Q 9:71 What are the steps necessary to compute the accrued benefit under a defined benefit plan?

Although the rules and limitations may be overwhelming to a plan sponsor or administrator, the steps necessary to compute an accrued benefit under a defined benefit plan can be summarized as follows:

Step 1. Compute the accrued benefit based on the terms of the plan, taking into account the applicable data as of the determination date, such as the number of years of benefit accrual service and average compensation.

Step 2. Check to see whether any minimum benefits are provided in the plan.

Step 3. Determine whether any prior accrued benefit is greater than the current accrued benefit; if so, determine if it must be preserved.

Step 4. Determine whether the plan is top heavy; if so, determine whether the top-heavy minimum benefit is greater.

Step 5. Verify that the applicable defined benefit plan limits under Code Section 415 have not been exceeded.

Determining Benefits in Non-Traditional Plans

Q 9:72 Why are non-traditional plans growing in favor?

A driving force behind non-traditional plan designs is a perception that traditional defined benefit plans do not meet the needs of today's workforce; there is also a perception that it is too difficult to anticipate required funding from year to year. Often, non-traditional plans provide a higher level of benefits than traditional plans to employees who will spend fewer than 25 to 30 years with a company; however, the relative complexity of non-traditional plans has made the calculation of benefits far more difficult. This section will briefly describe some non-traditional plans available today and focus on the calculation of accrued benefits in these plans. The following plans are discussed: cash balance plans, floor plans, 414(k) plans, pension equity plans, and target benefit plans.

Cash Balance Plans

Q 9:73 What is a cash balance plan?

A hybrid of a defined benefit and a defined contribution plan, a cash balance plan provides benefits similar to those provided under a career average defined benefit plan (see Q 9:74). However, benefits are generally communicated as an account balance (referred to as a hypothetical account), and the normal form of benefit is generally a lump-sum benefit. The hypothetical account balance is determined in a manner similar to a defined contribution plan. The previous year's account balance is increased by employer contribution credits and earnings determined using the defined interest-crediting rate. Cash balance plans are sometimes known as individual account pension plans, guaranteed account balance plans, and pension equivalent reserve credit plans. [Treas. Reg. § 1.401(a)(4)-8(c)(3)(i)]

Q 9:74 What is a career average defined benefit plan?

A career average defined benefit plan bases the benefits on compensation earned by the participant throughout his or her career. Contrast such a plan with a final average plan that averages the highest consecutive years' compensation earned during a defined period, commonly three or five years. For example, a typical career average formula might be 1 percent of pay for each year of service; that is, the year's annual pay is multiplied by 1 percent and added to the prior year's accrued benefit.

Q 9:75 How does the conversion of a traditional defined benefit plan to a cash balance plan happen?

At the conversion date, the accrued benefit of each employee in the traditional defined benefit plan is determined, based on the terms of the existing plan (see Qs 9:20–9:55). The actuarially equivalent present value of the accrued benefit is calculated as of the conversion date, and that generally will become the opening balance of the participant's account, known as the hypothetical account. During each future plan year after the conversion to a cash balance plan, a percentage of the employee's pay and plan-defined interest credits are added to the participant's hypothetical account. At the retirement distribution date, the accumulated hypothetical account balance may be available as a lump sum or converted and paid out as an annuity. Because a cash balance plan is a type of defined benefit plan, the qualified joint and survivor annuity must be the automatic form of distribution, unless appropriate elections and waivers are made (see chapter 11).

The final regulations applicable to cash balance conversions are effective for plan years beginning on or after January 1, 2011. There were no special additional rules or regulations that covered conversions prior to June 29, 2005. For plan conversions that occurred between June 29, 2005, and January 1, 2011, a plan sponsor was permitted to rely on the proposed regulations and other existing guidance. The proposed and final regulations are very similar. Affected participants must generally be provided with a benefit after the conversion that is at least equal to the sum of the benefits accrued through the date of the conversion plus benefits earned after the conversion. Final regulations issued in October 2014 further limited the options for conversion, essentially eliminating the "set and forget" approach to opening balances. [Treas. Reg. § 1.411(b)(5)-1(c)] (See Q 9:55 and Example 9-29.)

Q 9:76 How is the percentage of the employee's pay that is credited in a cash balance plan to his or her hypothetical account determined?

The percentage is defined in the plan document. It may be a flat percentage of pay or a flat dollar amount, or it may be integrated with social security. The percentage or amount need not be the same for all employees

Example 9-35: ABC Builders' cash balance plan provides a monthly credit to a participant's account based on years of service, according to the following schedule:

Years of Service	*Percentage of Pay*
10 or less	3%
10 to 20	3.5%
20 or more	4%

Charlie has worked for the ABC Builders for 25 years and earns $2,000 during the month. He currently has a contribution credit of $80 ($2,000 × 4%) to his cash balance account for each month.

Q 9:77 Is the percentage of pay credited to the account actually contributed to the plan by the employer?

No. Because the plan is a defined benefit plan, employer contributions are actuarially determined. Thus, although a plan may credit, for example, 2 percent of pay to a participant's hypothetical account plus 5 percent interest per annum, the plan sponsor may be required to contribute an amount larger or smaller than 2 percent of pay. All other things being equal, if the plan earnings exceed the required interest credit, lesser amounts will need to be contributed. Alternatively, if the actual earnings of the plan are less than the required credit, the employer may need to contribute more than the percentage of pay required to be credited to the participant's account. The employer bears the entire investment risk in a cash balance plan, with the participants being credited with a plan-defined interest rate credit.

Q 9:78 What was the significance of *interest rate whipsaw*?

Cash balance plans generally state that the participant can receive his or her accumulated cash balance account as a lump sum at termination of employment or other distributable event. Until Code and regulation changes made to accommodate the Pension Protection Act and subsequent laws, most pension rules did not contemplate cash balance plans. The accrued benefit and lump sum distribution rules associated with qualified defined benefit plans were historically premised on the concept that a defined benefit plan's primary form of benefit was an annuity beginning at normal retirement age, which is often age 65.

In order to make a lump-sum distribution under a traditional defined benefit plan, the annuity benefit is actuarially converted into an equivalent present value amount using approved mortality tables and interest rates. [I.R.C. § 411(a)(11); I.R.C. § 417(e)]

In order to calculate the lump-sum payment of a cash balance plan, the IRS had required a two-step calculation. [Notice 96-8; Treas. Reg. § 1.401(a)(4)-8(c)(3)(vi); Treas. Reg. § 1.401(a)(4)-8(c)(3)(vii)]

1. The participant's cash balance accumulation account was projected to normal retirement age using the interest credits specified in the plan and converted into an actuarially equivalent annuity.
2. The actuarially equivalent present value of the annuity calculated in step one was determined using the applicable interest rates prescribed by Code Section 417(e).

The lump-sum distribution was then the greater of the participant's hypothetical account balance or the amount calculated in step 2. This is called an *interest rate whipsaw*, because the comparatively low interest rates specified by Code Section 417(e) often required the plan to pay a lump-sum amount that was larger than the balance in the participant's cash balance accumulation account.

Example 9-36: In 2000, CDE Plumbers Cash Balance Plan provided for interest credits at a fixed rate of 8 percent per annum, and for conversions into optional annuity benefit forms using the Code Section 417(e) applicable interest rate and mortality table. Andrea, a fully vested employee with a hypothetical account balance of $45,000, terminated employment at age 45 and elected an immediate lump-sum distribution. At the time of Andrea's termination, the Section 417(e) applicable interest rate was 6.5 percent.

The amount of Andrea's current cash balance accumulation account projected to age 65 using 8 percent was $209,743. Using the interest rate of 6.5 percent, as then required by Code Section 417(e), the discounted actuarially equivalent present value of the projected hypothetical account for Andrea to age 45 was $59,524. The plan suffered an interest rate whipsaw, because it had to pay Andrea $14,524 ($59,524 − 45,000) more than her actual cash balance accumulation account.

Q 9:79 How did PPA change the rules regarding the interest rate whipsaw for cash balance plans?

Under PPA, a statutory hybrid plan may define the normal form of benefit as a lump sum equal to the vested hypothetical cash balance accumulation account. The interest rate whipsaw will not come into play provided that the statutory hybrid plan provides that a participant's hypothetical account may never be less than the sum of the contribution credits to date and the defined interest credits (credited no less frequently than annually), where the interest credits are based on one of the following (or are the greater of a combination of two or more of the following):

1. The interest rate on long-term investment grade corporate bonds (i.e., the third segment rate for Section 417(e)(3) or 430(h)(2)(C)(iii))
2. The rate of interest plus associated margins from the following list:

Interest Rate Bond Index	*Associated Margin*
Discount rate on 3-month Treasury Bills	175 basis points
Discount rate on 12-month or shorter Treasury Bills	150 basis points
Yield on 1-year Treasury Constant Maturities	100 basis points
Yield on 3-year or shorter Treasury bonds	50 basis points
Yield on 7-year or shorter Treasury bonds	25 basis points
Yield on 30-year or shorter Treasury bonds	0 basis points
First segment rate for Section 417(e)(3)(D) or 430(h)(2)(c)	0 basis points
Second segment rate for Section 417(e)(3)(D) or 430(h)(2)(c)	0 basis points

3. The actual rate of return on the aggregate assets of the plan, if the plan's assets are diversified so as to minimize volatility (or an appropriate subset of plan assets), or the rate of return on an appropriately structured annuity contract for the participant.

The final regulations issued in October 2014 address a fixed rate of return not to exceed 6 percent and the registered investment company (RIC) option. The proposed regulations as updated in December 2010 supported a 5 percent fixed rate, but the final regulations provide for a maximum fixed rate of 6 percent.

These rules are generally effective for plan years beginning after December 31, 2007, except that the plan sponsor may elect to have such rules apply for any period after June 29, 2005. For plan years that begin before January 1, 2012, statutory hybrid plans may utilize a rate that is permissible under the 2010 final regulations or the 2010 proposed regulations.

[ERISA § 204(b)(5); I.R.C. § 411(b)(5)(B); Treas. Reg. § 1.411(b)(5)-1(d); Prop. Reg. published in Fed. Reg., Dec. 28, 2010 [75FR 81543]]

Example 9-37: ABC Builders sponsors a cash balance plan that provides an annual interest credit equal to the return for a calendar year based on the actual rate of return on the aggregate assets of the plan. Kara has a hypothetical account balance of $5,000 as of December 31, 2017. The 2018 interest credit is a negative 1 percent. Therefore, Kara's 2017 interest credit will be – $50 ($5,000 × – 1%). Her December 31, 2018, hypothetical account balance will be the greater of [$5,000 – $50 + her 2018 hypothetical contribution credit] or the sum of all the hypothetical contribution credits through December 31, 2018.

Q 9:80 How is the accrued benefit in a cash balance plan determined for purposes of nondiscrimination testing?

The accrued benefit is an annuity beginning at normal retirement age, which is the actuarial equivalent of the employee's hypothetical cash balance accumulation account projected to normal retirement age. In other words, the hypothetical account balance is increased with interest from the participant's current age to normal retirement age and then converted into a monthly annuity beginning at normal retirement age. [Treas. Reg. § 1.401(a)(4)-8(c)(3)(vi)]

Q 9:81 What interest rate is used to increase the hypothetical account balance to normal retirement age?

If the interest rate specified in the plan is a variable interest rate, the plan must specify that the determination of the interest rate is made by assuming that the current value of the variable interest rate for all future periods is:

1. The current value of the variable interest rate for the current period or
2. The average of the current value of the variable interest rate for the current period and one or more periods immediately preceding the current period, not to exceed five years in the aggregate.

If the interest rate in the plan is fixed, then the fixed rate is used. A mortality table must also be specified in the plan for the determination of the actuarial equivalence. [Notice 96-8]

Example 9-38: Claudia participates in CDE Plumbers' cash balance plan. Her hypothetical account balance on December 31, 2018, is $10,400. The plan's 2018 interest-crediting rate is a fixed 5 percent and defines the mortality table for this purpose to be the Applicable Mortality Table used for Internal Revenue Code Section 417(e) minimum lump-sum determination purposes. Claudia is age 45, and her normal retirement age is 65. The monthly annuity payable to Claudia at age 65 for purposes of nondiscrimination testing is computed as follows:

$$\text{Monthly Annuity} = \text{Hypothetical account balance} \times (1 + i)^n \div \text{Annuity purchase rate}$$

$$= \$10{,}400 \times (1.05)^{20} \div 151.7833$$

$$= \$181.80$$

Q 9:82 What other factors may affect the computation of the accrued benefit?

If the cash balance plan was converted from an existing traditional defined benefit plan, the accrued benefit as of the date of conversion must be protected (see Q 9:55). In addition, the plan sponsor may be concerned about employees who were close to retirement age as of the date of conversion who will get lower future annual accruals under the cash balance plan design. To address this concern, the prior defined benefit plan projected benefits may be guaranteed for certain individuals (e.g., those within 10 years of normal retirement age). If the plan is top heavy, top-heavy minimums may also need to be provided (see Qs 9:49–9:54). The plan sponsor may also establish minimum benefit levels to ensure that all participants receive a minimum accrued benefit from the plan.

> **Example 9-39:** Dino, a participant in the ABC Builders statutory hybrid cash balance plan, retires at age 65 with a hypothetical cash balance accumulation account of $364,463. Based on the terms of the plan, Dino's hypothetical cash balance accumulation account is actuarially equivalent to a life only annuity benefit of $3,250 per month. At the time that ABC Builders converted from a traditional defined benefit plan to a statutory hybrid cash balance plan, it was anticipated that participants within 10 years of normal retirement age might suffer a loss in projected benefits as a result of the conversion. Hence, ABC Builders decided to provide a minimum benefit for such participants equal to 60 percent of average monthly pay. Dino's average monthly pay is $6,500. Thus, his minimum monthly life only benefit from the plan is $3,900 per month ($6,500 × 60%).

Q 9:83 May the benefit in a cash balance plan be paid in alternative forms at normal retirement age?

Yes. Most cash balance plans define an immediate lump sum as the normal form of benefit. If this is the case, the plan must also offer an immediate annuity beginning at the participant's current age. Qualified Joint and Survivor Annuities must be offered in any defined benefit plan. The gamut of optional benefits available in any traditional defined benefit plan may also be included in a statutory hybrid plan. (See chapter 10 for a discussion of optional forms of benefit.)

Floor Offset Plans

Q 9:84 What is a floor offset plan?

A floor offset plan is a combination of a defined benefit and a defined contribution plan, where each plan defines accruals by considering the other. The objective of combining these disparate plans is to assure a minimum level of benefits to all employees. By using this approach, a plan sponsor will generally reduce costs when compared to maintaining two independent plans. In a floor offset plan, benefits in the defined benefit plan are generally defined as the formula offset by the actuarial equivalent of the defined contribution plan account balance.

Q 9:85 What special requirements must a floor offset plan meet?

A floor offset plan must meet these special requirements:

1. The defined benefit portion of the arrangement must provide definitely determinable benefits.
2. The plan must specify the actuarial basis for converting defined contribution account balances to benefits.
3. The pre-offset defined benefit accrual formula must meet the accrual rules of Code Section 411 (see Q 9:23).
4. In the process of converting account balances to benefits, vested account balances plus prior withdrawals must be used (although the plan may specify that only a certain portion of the account balance be used for offset purposes).

[Rev. Rul. 76-259]

Q 9:86 What kind of defined contribution plan may be used to offset the defined benefit plan in a floor offset plan?

Any type of defined contribution plan (other than an employee stock ownership plan (ESOP)) may be used, although an employee's elective contributions under a 401(k) plan may not be used. Similarly, matching contributions in a 401(k) plan may not be used as an offset. [Treas. Reg. § 1.401(a)(4)-8(d)(1)(vii)]

Q 9:87 How does a floor offset plan operate?

The plan sponsor determines a minimum threshold of benefits, or floor, to be provided under the defined benefit and defined contribution plan. The defined benefit plan will state that objective in its plan formula; for example, the objective might be 2 percent of final average pay multiplied by years of service, up to a maximum of 30 years. The plan document will specify the conversion factors used to convert the defined contribution account balance into a benefit upon termination of employment or retirement. To the extent that the converted defined contribution vested account balance exceeds the benefit guarantee, no benefits are payable from the defined benefit plan. If the vested account balance in the defined contribution plan is insufficient to provide the promised benefits, a portion of the benefits will be paid from the defined benefit plan.

Q 9:88 How is a participant's vested benefit in a floor offset plan actually determined?

The following steps are used to determine the accrued benefit in a floor offset plan:

Step 1. Determine the vested accrued benefit before any offset in the defined benefit plan. (See chapter 8 for vesting rules and Qs 9:20–9:55 on determining accrued benefits.)

Step 2. Determine the vested account balance in the defined contribution plan. (See Qs 9:1–9:19 for the calculation of account balances.)

Step 3. Accumulate the vested account balance in the defined contribution plan with interest to the plan's normal retirement age, using the interest factor specified in the plan document.

Step 4. Convert the accumulated vested account balance to a monthly accrued benefit, using the interest and mortality factors in the plan document.

Step 5. If step 4 is greater than step 1, no benefits are due from the defined benefit plan. The vested account balance may be distributed to the participant. If step 1 is greater than step 4, the participant is entitled to the vested account balance in the defined contribution plan plus the difference between step 1 and step 4 from the defined benefit plan.

Example 9-40: CDE Plumbers sponsors a floor offset plan. The plan provides a minimum benefit in the defined benefit plan of 1.5 percent of average pay per year of service, up to a maximum of 30 years. The benefit in the defined benefit plan is offset by the vested account balance in a profit sharing plan. Bob retires in 2018 at age 65 and is entitled to a floor benefit of $2,500 per month in the form of a life annuity. He currently has an account balance of $150,000 in the profit sharing plan. The plans provide that account balances are converted at 5 percent interest, using the Applicable Mortality Table used for Internal Revenue Code Section 417(e) minimum lump-sum determination purposes. Bob is 100 percent vested in both plans, because he has reached the plan's normal retirement age. Bob's defined benefit plan benefit is calculated below:

1. Floor vested accrued benefit in the defined benefit plan: $2,500 per month.
2. Vested account balance in the defined contribution plan: $150,000.
3. Accumulated vested account balance in the defined contribution plan with interest to the plan's normal retirement age: $150,000.
4. Converted accumulated vested account balance: $150,000 ÷ 151.7833 = $988 per month.
5. Because the defined contribution plan will provide $988 of the floor $2,500 benefit in the defined benefit plan, only the balance, or $1,512 ($2,500 − $988), will be provided by the defined benefit plan.

Example 9-41: Patty also participates under CDE Plumbers' floor offset plan. Patty terminates employment with the company at age 45 when she is 40 percent vested in the defined benefit plan and 60 percent vested in the profit sharing plan. Her floor accrued benefit in the defined benefit plan is $800 per month, and she has an account balance of $45,000 in the profit sharing plan. Patty's defined benefit plan benefit is calculated below:

1. Floor vested accrued benefit under the defined benefit plan: $800 × 40% = $320 per month.
2. Vested account balance under the defined contribution plan: $45,000 × 60% = $27,000.
3. Accumulated vested account balance under the defined contribution plan with interest to the plan's normal retirement age: $27,000 × $(1.05)^{20}$ = $71,639.

4. Converted accumulated vested account balance: $71,639 ÷ 151.7833 = $472 per month.
5. Since the defined contribution will provide a benefit greater than the floor defined benefit plan benefit of $320, Patty is simply entitled to her vested account balance of $27,000. No benefits will be due her from the defined benefit plan.

Code Section 414(k) Plans

Q 9:89 What is a Section 414(k) plan?

A Section 414(k) plan is a defined benefit plan that provides a benefit derived from employer contributions that is partly based on the balance of the separate account of a participant. To the extent that benefits are based on a participant's separate account balance, the plan is treated as a defined contribution plan. All other benefits paid from the plan are treated as if paid from a defined benefit plan. [I.R.C. § 414(k)]

Q 9:90 How does a Section 414(k) plan differ from a cash balance plan?

In a cash balance plan, the hypothetical account balance is credited with earnings based on an interest rate specified in the plan. The actual earnings of the plan may not have an impact on the benefits paid to participants. In a Section 414(k) plan, however, the earnings credited to the separate account of the participant are based on the plan's actual experience—identical to the operation of a defined contribution plan.

Q 9:91 How are benefits determined in a Section 414(k) plan?

To the extent that benefits are in a separate account, the plan is treated as a defined contribution plan, and the plan's vesting schedule is applied to the participant's balance in the separate account. The plan's benefit accrual formula determines the amount of a participant's accrued benefit for all employer-derived benefits that are not in a separate account.

> **Example 9-42:** ABC Builders sponsors a defined benefit plan. A provision contained in the plan allows participants who reach the plan's normal retirement age, 60, to segregate the present value of their accrued benefit in a separate account, which will be credited with the actual earnings of the account. This is a type of Section 414(k) plan. Jean retires at age 60 and opts to have her benefit segregated in a separate account. Future benefits will be paid to Jean based on her account balance, and the plan will look very much like a defined contribution plan to Jean. Joe leaves employment at age 40 and is not entitled to segregate the present value of his accrued benefit in a separate account. The plan, in this case, operates as a defined benefit plan.

Pension Equity Plans

Q 9:92 What is a pension equity plan and what are its objectives?

Like a cash balance plan, a pension equity plan provides benefits in the form of a lump sum. Participants accumulate lump-sum credits that are determined based on their final average pay and years of service. As in any defined benefit plan, the lump-sum credits may be converted to an annuity. The objectives of plan sponsors in adopting a pension equity plan may include the following:

- To accommodate the needs of a diverse workforce with significantly different career patterns than in the past
- To limit the cost of the current defined benefit plan
- To provide the employees with easily understood, tangible, and portable benefits
- To offer a reasonable standard of living after retirement for long-service employees

Q 9:93 How does a pension equity plan operate?

A participant in a pension equity plan receives credits each year toward a lump-sum benefit at retirement. Those credits are pay-based and may include additional credits above the social security integration level. The credits may increase as an employee's years of service increase. When a participant terminates employment or retires, the credits are accumulated and may be paid in the form of a lump sum or an annuity.

Example 9-43: CDE Plumbers sponsors a pension equity plan that bases its annual benefit accruals on age, according to the following schedule:

Age	*Percentage of Pay*
20–34	4%
35–44	5%
45–54	6%
55–59	8%
60–65	10%

Paul retires at age 65, with final average earnings of $20,000. He started working for CDE Plumbers at age 45. His lump-sum benefit is computed as follows:

Age	*Credits*	*Benefit Amount*
45–54	6% × 20,000 × 10	$12,000
55–59	8% × 20,000 × 5	$8,000
60–65	10% × 20,000 × 6	$12,000
Total Benefit		$32,000

Paul may opt to receive a lump-sum distribution at age 65 of $32,000. Or he may elect a joint and 50 percent survivor annuity of $203 per month.

Target Benefit Plans

Q 9:94 What is a target benefit plan?

A target benefit plan is a type of defined contribution plan. Contributions to a target benefit plan are determined actuarially, however, as the annual amount necessary to fund the "target" benefit for each participant. Once the determination of the annual target contribution is made, the contribution amount is tested to determine whether it exceeds the limits of Code Section 415(c), the limits on contributions to defined contribution plans. If the plan is top heavy and provides top-heavy minimum contributions to non-key employees, testing must be done to ensure that the minimum contribution is provided.

Q 9:95 How does a target plan operate?

Each year, the target benefit is computed for each eligible participant. The actuarial present value of the target benefit at retirement age is computed. The theoretical reserve at retirement age (the annual contributions and interest earnings made to date, accumulated with interest at the assumed rate) is subtracted from the actuarial present value or the target benefit. The difference is funded on a level annual basis from the participant's current age to normal retirement age. The level annual contribution is tested to determine whether it exceeds the limits of Section 415(c) and whether it meets the top-heavy minimum requirements, if applicable. From that point on, the target plan operates as an ordinary defined contribution plan.

Q 9:96 How are benefits determined in a target plan?

Benefits are based solely on the account balance of the participant. The participant bears the investment risk in a target plan. (See Qs 9:1–9:19 for a discussion of the determination of account balances in a defined contribution plan.)

Chapter 10

Optional Forms of Benefit and Protected Benefits

The nondiscrimination rules under Code Section 401(a)(4) generally provide that a retirement plan is a qualified plan only if the contributions or benefits provided under the plan do not discriminate in favor of highly compensated employees (HCEs). These rules require, in part, that the benefits, rights, and features, including optional forms of benefit under the plan, be available to HCEs and non-highly compensated employees (NHCEs) on a nondiscriminatory basis. Whether a plan satisfies the nondiscrimination requirements, including the requirement that benefits, rights, and features, including optional forms of benefit, be available to HCEs and NHCEs on a nondiscriminatory basis, depends upon the form of the plan and on its effect in operation. Intent is irrelevant to this determination. Treasury Regulations Sections 1.401(a)(4)-1 through 1.401(a)(4)-13 set forth the exclusive rules for determining whether a plan satisfies the nondiscrimination requirements of Code Section 401(a)(4). A plan that complies, in form and operation, with those regulations therefore satisfies Code Section 401(a)(4).

The anti-cutback rules of Code Section 411(d)(6) generally protect accrued benefits, early retirement benefits, retirement-type subsidies, and optional forms of benefit under qualified retirement plans and provide that such benefits, to the extent they have accrued, cannot be reduced or eliminated by plan amendment, except to the extent permitted by Treasury Regulations. Treasury Regulations Section 1.411(d)-4, issued in 1988, specifies circumstances under which a plan is permitted to be amended to reduce or eliminate an optional form of benefit. The Economic Growth and Tax Relief Reconciliation Act (EGTRRA) amended Code Section 411(d)(6) and Internal Revenue Code and Employee Retirement Income Security Act (ERISA) Section 204(g) to direct the Secretary of the Treasury to issue regulations providing that the anti-cutback rules of

Code Section 411(d)(6) do not apply to any plan amendment that reduces or eliminates early retirement benefits or retirement-type subsidies that create significant burdens or complexities for the plan and its participants unless the amendment adversely affects the rights of any participant in a more than *de minimis* manner. EGTRRA also amended Code Section 4980F and ERISA Section 204(h) to require a plan administrator to give notice of a plan amendment to affected plan participants and beneficiaries when the plan amendment provides for a significant reduction in the rate of future benefit accrual or the elimination or significant reduction of an early retirement benefit or a retirement-type subsidy. Treasury Regulations Section 1.411(d)-3, as amended in 2005, responded to the EGTRRA directive and specified the circumstances under which a plan may be amended to reduce or eliminate early retirement benefits, retirement-type subsidies, and optional forms of benefit (Section 411(d)(6) protected benefits). The circumstances specified in Treasury Regulations Section 1.411(d)-3 were designed to implement EGTRRA's directive to permit reduction or elimination of Section 411(d)(6) protected benefits that create significant burdens or complexities for the plan and its participants, but only if the elimination does not adversely affect the rights of any participant in a more than *de minimis* manner.

Treasury Regulations Section 1.411(d)-3, relating to the permissible elimination of Section 411(d)(6) protected benefits, is in addition to Treasury Regulations Section 1.411(d)-4, which permits a plan to be amended to eliminate optional forms of benefit and which was also amended, in 2005, to conform to Treasury Regulations Section 1.411(d)-3 (including amendments to the definition of *optional form of benefit* and the multiple amendment rule). In 2012, Treasury Regulations Section 1.411(d)-4 was amended to provide an additional, limited exception to the anti-cutback rules to permit a plan sponsor that is a debtor in a bankruptcy proceeding to amend its single-employer defined benefit plan to eliminate a single-sum distribution option (or other optional form of benefit providing for accelerated payments) under the plan if certain specified conditions are met.

Treasury Regulations Section 1.411(d)-3 provides two permitted methods for eliminating or reducing Section 411(d)(6) protected benefits under the EGTRRA directive: (1) elimination of redundant optional forms of benefit, and (2) elimination of non-core optional forms of benefit where core options are offered. Either of these two alternative methods can be applied with respect to any optional form of benefit. Treasury Regulations Section 1.411(d)-3, as amended in 2005, also included general guidance on Code Section 411(d)(6) (including the meaning of terms used therein), the scope of the Code Section 411(d)(6)(A) protection against plan amendments decreasing a participant's accrued benefit, and the scope of the Code Section 411(d)(6)(B) protection for early retirement benefits, retirement-type subsidies, and optional forms of benefit.

In 2005, the IRS also amended Treasury Regulations Section 54.4980F-1(b), relating to the notice requirement for certain plan amendments that eliminate or significantly reduce early retirement benefits or retirement-type subsidies. In 2006, the IRS issued final Treasury Regulations Section 1.411(d)-3 to provide guidance on the application of the anti-cutback rules of Code Section 411(d)(6) to a plan amendment that places greater restrictions or conditions on a participant's right to Code Section 411(d)(6) protected benefits, even if the amendment merely adds a restriction or condition that is permitted under the vesting rules of Code Sections 411(a)(3) through (11). The 2006 final regulations were intended to reflect the holding in *Central Laborers' Pension Fund v. Heinz*, 541 U.S. 739 (2004). (In that case, the United States Supreme Court, holding on behalf of the plaintiff participants, ruled that ERISA Section 204(g) prohibits a plan amendment expanding the categories of post-retirement employment that result in suspension of the payment of early retirement benefits already accrued.) In Revenue Procedure 2005-23, 2005-18 I.R.B. 991, the IRS addressed the application of *Heinz* and provided examples of how plans can comply with the revenue procedure and avoid plan disqualification. The 2006 final regulations also set forth standards for the *utilization test*, which is a permitted method of eliminating optional forms of benefit that are burdensome to the plan and of minimal value to plan participants.

Nondiscrimination Rules Under Code Section 401(a)(4) 10-4
- Scope and Application of the Nondiscrimination Standards 10-4
- General Rules and Considerations 10-8
- Current Availability 10-8
- Effective Availability 10-11
- Special Rules 10-13

Permissive Aggregation of Certain Benefits, Rights, or Features 10-15
- Certain Spousal Benefits, Etc. 10-16
- Definitions 10-17

Code Section 411(d)(6) Protected Benefits 10-22
- In General 10-22
- Extent to Which Section 411(d)(6) Protected Benefits May Be Reduced or Eliminated 10-29
- Reduction or Elimination of Early Retirement Benefits, Retirement-Type Subsidies, and Optional Forms of Benefit 10-49

Nondiscrimination Rules Under Code Section 401(a)(4)

Scope and Application of the Nondiscrimination Standards

Q 10:1 What requirements must a qualified retirement plan satisfy to meet the nondiscrimination standards of Code Section 401(a)(4)?

A qualified retirement plan must satisfy each of the following requirements:

1. *Nondiscriminatory amount of contributions or benefits*. First, the contributions or the benefits provided under the plan must be nondiscriminatory in amount. It need not be shown that *both* the contributions and the benefits provided are nondiscriminatory in amount, but only that *either* the contributions alone or the benefits alone are nondiscriminatory in amount. Also, a defined benefit plan may demonstrate that, on a contributions basis, it does not discriminate. Similarly, a defined contribution plan may demonstrate that, on a benefits basis, it does not discriminate. [Treas. Reg. § 1.401(a)(4)-1(b)(2)]

   IRS Notice 2014-5 [2014-2 I.R.B. 276], provided temporary nondiscrimination relief for certain "closed" defined benefit plans (i.e., defined benefit plans that provide ongoing accruals but that have been amended to limit those accruals to some or all of the employees who participated in the plan on a specified date). Specifically, for plan years beginning before 2016, IRS Notice 2014-5 permitted a defined benefit/defined contribution plan that included a closed defined benefit plan (that was closed before December 13, 2013) and that satisfied certain conditions set forth in IRS Notice 2014-5 to demonstrate satisfaction of the nondiscrimination in amount requirement of Treasury Regulations Section 1.401(a)(4)-1(b)(2) on the basis of equivalent benefits even if the defined contribution/defined benefit plan did not meet any of the existing eligibility conditions for testing on that basis under Treasury Regulations Section 1.401(a)(4)-9(b)(2)(v). IRS Notice 2015-28 [2015-14 I.R.B. 848], extended the temporary nondiscrimination relief provided in IRS Notice 2014-5 for an additional year by applying that relief to plan years beginning before 2017 if the conditions of IRS Notice 2014-5 are satisfied. During the period for which the extension applies, the remaining provisions of the nondiscrimination regulations under Code Section 401(a)(4) continue to apply. IRS Notice 2016-57 [2016-40 I.R.B. 432] further extended the temporary nondiscrimination relief for closed defined benefit plans provided in IRS Notice 2014-5 by making that relief available for plan years beginning before 2018 if the conditions of IRS Notice 2014-5 are satisfied.

   IRS Notice 2014-5 also requested comments on whether the nondiscrimination regulations under Code Section 401(a)(4) should be amended to provide additional alternatives that would allow an aggregated defined benefit/defined contribution (DB/DC) plan to satisfy the nondiscrimination in amount requirements on the basis of equivalent benefits, and whether certain other permanent changes should be made to the nondiscrimination regulations, such as modifications to the rules regarding nondiscriminatory benefits, rights, and features. The comments the IRS received in response to ITS Notice 2014-5 generally supported these types of changes. In addition, all of the commenters requested permanent changes to the nondiscrimination requirements in order to make it easier for closed plans to continue to satisfy the nondiscrimination requirements. On January 29, 2016, the IRS issued Proposed Regulations (81 Fed. Reg. 4976) relating to the nondiscrimination requirements applicable to qualified plans under Code Section 401(a)(4) [REG-125761-14, 2016-7 I.R.B. 322], but on May 2, 2016, in Announcement 2016-16, the IRS announced that it was withdrawing certain provisions of those Proposed Regulations—specifically, the provisions in the Proposed Regulations that would have modified §§ 1.401(a)(4)-2(c) and 1.401(a)(4)-3(c)—because after the IRS issued the Proposed Regulations, it gave additional consideration to the effects of those proposed modifications on the adoption and continued maintenance of qualified retirement plans with a variety of designs and concluded that further consideration would be needed with respect to issues relating to those provisions.

2. *Nondiscriminatory availability of benefits, rights, and features.* Second, all benefits, rights, and features provided under the plan must be made available under the plan in a nondiscriminatory manner. The rules for determining whether this requirement is met are set forth in Treasury Regulations Section 1.401(a)(4)-4, and are one of the two major focuses of this chapter. [Treas. Reg. § 1.401(a)(4)-1(b)(3)]
3. *Nondiscriminatory effect of plan amendments and terminations.* Finally, the timing of plan amendments must not have the effect of discriminating significantly in favor of HCEs (see Appendix G). [Treas. Reg. § 1.401(a)(4)-1(b)(4)] There are also additional nondiscrimination requirements regarding plan termination (see chapter 15).

Q 10:2 How should the nondiscrimination requirements set forth in the Treasury Regulations be interpreted?

The nondiscrimination requirements set forth in Treasury Regulations Sections 1.401(a)(4)-1 through 1.401(a)(4)-13 must be interpreted in a reasonable manner consistent with the purpose of preventing discrimination in favor of HCEs. [Treas. Reg. § 1.401(a)(4)-1(c)(2)]

Q 10:3 Are the nondiscrimination rules applied on the basis of the plan year?

Yes. The nondiscrimination requirements are generally applied on the basis of the plan year, and on the basis of the terms of the plan in effect during the plan year. Thus, unless otherwise provided under the Treasury regulations, the compensation, contributions, benefit accruals, and other items used to apply the nondiscrimination requirements must be determined for the plan year being tested. However, Treasury Regulations Section 1.401(a)(4)-11(g) provides rules allowing for corrective amendments made after the close of the plan year to be taken into account in satisfying certain nondiscrimination requirements. [Treas. Reg. § 1.401(a)(4)-1(c)(3)]

Q 10:4 How do the minimum coverage rules under Code Section 410(b) relate to the nondiscrimination requirements under Code Section 401(a)(4)?

To be qualified, a retirement plan must satisfy both the minimum coverage rules under Code Section 410(b) and the nondiscrimination requirements of Code Section 401(a)(4). The minimum coverage rules require that a plan benefit a nondiscriminatory group of employees, and the nondiscrimination rules require that the contributions or benefits provided to employees benefiting under the plan not discriminate in favor of HCEs. Consistent with this requirement, the "plan" subject to nondiscrimination testing under Code Section 401(a)(4) is the same as the "plan" subject to minimum coverage testing under Code Section 410(b), that is, it is the plan determined *after* applying the mandatory disaggregation rules of Treasury Regulations Section 1.410(b)-7(c) and the permissive aggregation rules of Treasury Regulations Section 1.410(b)-7(d). In addition, whatever testing option is used for the plan year for minimum coverage testing purposes (for example, quarterly testing) must also be used for purposes of determining whether the plan satisfies the nondiscrimination rules under Code Section 401(a)(4) for the plan year. [Treas. Reg. § 1.401(a)(4)-1(c)(4)(i)]

Special Rules for Certain Aggregated Plans. There are special rules, under Treasury Regulations Section 1.401(a)(4)-9(b), for applying the nondiscriminatory amount and availability requirements to a plan that includes one or more defined benefit plans and one or more defined contribution plans that have been permissively aggregated under Treasury Regulations Section 1.410(b)-7(d). [Treas. Reg. § 1.401(a)(4)-1(c)(4)(ii)]

Restructuring. In certain cases, a plan may be restructured on the basis of employee groups and treated as two or more plans, each treated as a separate plan that must independently satisfy the nondiscrimination requirements of Code Section 401(a)(4) and the minimum coverage requirements of Code Section 410(b). The rules relating to restructuring plans for purposes of applying the nondiscrimination requirements are found in Treasury Regulations Section 1.401(a)(4)-9(c). [Treas. Reg. § 1.401(a)(4)-1(c)(4)(iii)]

Collectively Bargained Plans. A collectively bargained plan that automatically satisfies the minimum coverage requirements of Code Section 410(b) [see Treas. Reg. § 1.410(b)-2(b)(7)] will be treated as satisfying the nondiscrimination requirements of Code Section 401(a)(4). [Treas. Reg. § 1.401(a)(4)-1(c)(5)]

Former Employees. In applying the nondiscriminatory amount and nondiscriminatory availability requirements under the nondiscrimination rules, former employees are tested separately from active employees, unless the Treasury regulations provide otherwise. The rules for applying these requirements to former employees are set forth in Treasury Regulations Section 1.401(a)(4)-10. [Treas. Reg. § 1.401(a)(4)-1(c)(6)]

Employee-Provided Contributions and Benefits. In applying the nondiscriminatory amount requirement of Treasury Regulations Section 1.401(a)(4)-(b)(2), employee-provided contributions and benefits are tested separately from employer-provided contributions and benefits, unless otherwise provided. [Treas. Reg. § 1.401(a)-1(c)(7)]

Allocation of Earnings. Notwithstanding any other provision of the Treasury regulations under Code Section 401(a)(4), a defined contribution plan will not satisfy the nondiscrimination requirements if the manner in which income, expenses, gains, or losses are allocated to accounts under the plan discriminates in favor of HCEs or former HCEs. [Treas. Reg. § 1.401(a)-1(c)(8)]

Rollovers, Transfers, and Buy-Backs. In applying the nondiscrimination requirements, rollover contributions (including direct rollovers), elective transfers [Treas. Reg. § 1.411(d)-4, Q&A-3(b)], transfers of assets and liabilities [I.R.C. § 414(l)], and employee buy-backs are treated in accordance with the nondiscrimination rules set forth in Treasury Regulations Section 1.401(a)(4)-11(b). [Treas. Reg. § 1.401(a)(4)-1(c)(9)]

Vesting. A plan does not satisfy the nondiscriminatory amount requirement of Treasury Regulations Section 1.401(a)(4)-1(b)(2) unless it meets applicable requirements (set forth in Treasury Regulations Section 1.401(a)(4)-11(c)) with respect to the manner in which employees vest in their accrued benefits. [Treas. Reg. § 1.401(a)(4)-1(c)(10)]

Crediting Service. A plan does not satisfy the nondiscriminatory amount requirement or the nondiscriminatory availability requirement unless it satisfies the specific nondiscrimination rules under Treasury Regulations Section 1.401(a)(4)-11(d), which govern the manner in which employees' service is credited under the plan. Imputed service, that is, service other than actual service with the employer, may not be taken into account. [Treas. Reg. § 1.401(a)(4)-1(c)(11)]

Governmental Plans. The Treasury regulations under Code Section 401(a)(4) provide that, with certain exceptions, the nondiscrimination requirements apply to governmental plans described in Code Section 414(d). [Treas. Reg. § 1.401(a)(4)-1(c)(12)] However, the Taxpayer Relief Act of 1997 (TRA'97) permanently exempted state and local governmental plans from both the minimum participation rules under Code Section 401(a)(26) and the nondiscrimination rules under Code Section 401(a)(4) (including the actual deferral percentage (ADP) and the actual contribution percentage (ACP) tests). The permanent moratorium became effective for taxable years beginning on or after August 5, 1997, TRA'97's enactment date. In addition, TRA'97 deemed governmental plans to have satisfied the minimum coverage and nondiscrimination requirements for all taxable years beginning before August 5, 1997. [TRA'97 § 1505]

Effective Dates and Fresh-Start Rules. Generally, the nondiscrimination requirements set forth in Treasury Regulations Section 1.401(a)(4)-1 through 1.401(a)(4)-13 apply to plan years beginning on or after January 1, 1994. However, the Tax Reform Act of 1986 (TRA'86) provided an earlier effective date (plan years beginning on or after January 1, 1989) for these requirements. To assure employers and practitioners that their plans would not violate the nondiscrimination rules during the transition period between the effective date of TRA'86 and the effective date of the Treasury regulations, the IRS created a reasonable, good faith compliance standard for determining whether a plan had been operating in a way that meets the nondiscrimination rules under Code Section 401(a)(4). Good faith interpretation of the rules generally is determined on the basis of all relevant facts and circumstances, including the extent to which an employer has resolved unclear issues in its favor. [Treas. Reg. §§ 1.401(a)(4)-1(c)(16), 1.401(a)(4)-1(c)(13)]

General Rules and Considerations

Q 10:5 What rules apply in determining whether the benefits, rights, and features, including optional forms of benefit under a qualified retirement plan, are made available in a nondiscriminatory manner?

Benefits, rights, and features provided under a qualified retirement plan include all optional forms of benefit (see Q 10:21), ancillary benefits (see Q 10:22), and other rights and features available to any employee under the plan. They are made available to employees in a nondiscriminatory manner only if they satisfy the current availability requirement described in Treasury Regulations Section 1.401(a)(4)-4(b) *and* the effective availability requirement described in Treasury Regulations Section 1.401(a)(4)-4(c). Special rules for applying the current availability and effective availability requirements are found in Treasury Regulations Section 1.401(a)(4)-4(d). "Optional form of benefit," "ancillary benefit," and "other right or feature" are defined in Treasury Regulations Section 1.401(a)(4)-4(e). [Treas. Reg. § 1.401(a)(4)-4(a)]

Current Availability

Q 10:6 How is the current availability requirement satisfied?

Generally, the current availability requirement is satisfied if the group of employees to whom a benefit, right, or feature is currently available during the plan year satisfies the minimum coverage rules under Code Section 410(b) (determined without regard to the average benefit percentage (ABP) test described in Treasury Regulations Section 1.410(b)-5). In determining whether the group of employees satisfies the minimum coverage requirements, an employee is treated as benefiting only if the benefit, right, or feature is currently available to the employee. [Treas. Reg. § 1.401(a)(4)-4(b)(1)]

Generally, whether a benefit, right, or feature that is subject to specified eligibility conditions is currently available to an employee is determined based on the current facts and circumstances with respect to the employee (for example, his or her current compensation, accrued benefit, position, or net worth). [Treas. Reg. § 1.401(a)(4)-4(b)(2)(i)]

Q 10:7 May certain age and service conditions be disregarded in determining whether a benefit, right, or feature that is subject to specified eligibility conditions is currently available to an employee?

Yes. Notwithstanding the general rule described in Q 10:6, any specified age or service condition with respect to an optional form of benefit or a social security supplement is disregarded in determining whether the optional form of benefit or the social security supplement is currently available to an employee.

For example, an optional form of benefit that is available to all employees who terminate employment on or after age 55 with at least 10 years of service is treated as currently available without regard to the employee's current age or years of service, and without regard to whether the employee could potentially meet the age and service conditions before attaining the plan's normal retirement age. [Treas. Reg. § 1.401(a)(4)-4(b)(2)(ii)(A)(1)]

Q 10:8 Are there any age or service conditions that may *not* be disregarded in determining whether a benefit, right, or feature that is subject to specified eligibility conditions is currently available to an employee?

Yes. Notwithstanding the rules described in Q 10:7, an age or service condition is *not* disregarded in determining the current availability of an optional form of benefit or social security supplement if the condition must be satisfied within a limited period of time. However, the age and service of employees may be projected to the last date by which the age condition or service condition must be satisfied in order to be eligible for the optional form of benefit or social security supplement under the plan.

For example, an optional form of benefit that is available only to employees who terminate employment between July 1, 2019 and December 31, 2019, after attaining age 55 with at least 10 years of service is treated as currently available to an employee only if the employee could satisfy those age and service conditions by December 31, 2019. [Treas. Reg. § 1.401(a)(4)-4(b)(2)(ii)(A)(2)]

Q 10:9 Are there any other conditions that may be disregarded in determining whether a right, benefit, or feature that is subject to specified eligibility conditions is currently available to an employee?

Yes. The following conditions may be disregarded in determining the employees to whom the benefit, right, or feature is currently available:

- Specified conditions on the availability of a benefit, right, or feature requiring a specified percentage of the employee's accrued benefit to be vested;
- Termination of employment;
- Death;
- Satisfaction of a specified health condition (or failure to meet such condition);
- Disability;
- Hardship;
- Family status;
- Default on a plan loan secured by a participant's account balance;

- Execution of a covenant not to compete;
- Application for benefits or similar ministerial or mechanical acts;
- Election of a benefit form;
- Execution of a waiver of rights under the Age Discrimination in Employment Act or other federal or state law; and
- Absence from service.

In addition, if a multiemployer plan includes a reasonable condition that limits its eligibility for an ancillary benefit, or other right or feature, to those employees who have recent service under the plan (e.g., a condition or death benefit that requires an employee to have a minimum number of hours credited during the last two years) and the condition applies to all employees in the multiemployer plan (including the collectively bargained employees) to whom the ancillary benefit, or other right or feature, is otherwise currently available, then the condition is disregarded in determining the employees to whom the ancillary benefit, or other right or feature, is currently available. [Treas. Reg. § 1.401(a)(4)-4(b)(2)(ii)(B)]

Q 10:10 Are certain implicit conditions disregarded in determining the employees to whom the benefit, right, or feature is currently available?

Yes. In the case of a plan that provides for mandatory cash-outs of all terminated employees who have a vested accrued benefit with an actuarial present value less than or equal to a specified dollar amount (not to exceed $5,000), the implicit condition on any other benefit, right, or feature is disregarded. [Treas. Reg. § 1.401(a)(4)-4(b)(2)(ii)(C)]

Q 10:11 Are other dollar limits disregarded in determining the employees to whom the benefit, right, or feature is currently available?

Yes. A condition that the amount of an employee's vested accrued benefit or the actuarial present value of that benefit be less than or equal to a specified dollar amount is disregarded in determining to whom the benefit, right, or feature is currently available. [Treas. Reg. § 1.401(a)(4)-4(b)(2)(ii)(D)]

Q 10:12 Are certain conditions on the availability of plan loans disregarded in determining the employees to whom plan loans are currently available?

Yes. In the case of an employee's right to a loan from a plan, the condition that an employee must have an account balance sufficient to be eligible to receive a minimum amount specified in the plan (not to exceed $1,000) is disregarded in determining the employees to whom plan loans are currently available (see chapter 2). [Treas. Reg. § 1.401(a)(4)-4(b)(2)(ii)(E)]

Q 10:13 Is there a special testing rule that applies when a plan is amended to eliminate a benefit, right, or feature prospectively?

Yes. Notwithstanding the currently available requirement described in Q 10:6 and Q 10:7, a plan may be amended to eliminate a benefit, right, or feature with respect to benefits accrued *after* the later of the eliminating amendment's adoption or effective date (the elimination date). However, if that right, benefit, or feature is retained for benefits accrued as of the elimination date, and if it prospectively satisfies the current availability test as of the elimination date, then it will be treated as satisfying that requirement for all future periods. However, this special rule does not apply if the features of the benefit, right, or feature (including the employees to whom it is available) are changed after the elimination date. [Treas. Reg. § 1.401(a)(4)-4(b)(3)(i)]

Q 10:14 How is a benefit, right, or feature eliminated?

For purposes of the special testing rule described in Q 10:13, a benefit, right, or feature provided to an employee is eliminated with respect to benefits accrued after the elimination date (see Q 10:13) if the amount or value of the benefit, right, or feature depends solely on the amount of the employee's accrued benefit as of the elimination date, including subsequent income, expenses, gains, and losses with respect to that benefit in the case of a defined contribution plan. [Treas. Reg. § 1.401(a)(4)-4(b)(3)(ii)(A)]

Q 10:15 Is there a different, special rule for benefits, rights, and features that are not protected benefits?

Yes. Notwithstanding the special testing rule described in Q 10:14, there is another special rule that says that in the case of a benefit, right, or feature under a defined contribution plan that is *not* a protected benefit (within the meaning of Code Section 411(d)(6) and Treasury Regulations Section 1.411(d)-4, Q&A-1), for example, the availability of plan loans, each employee's accrued benefit as of the elimination date (see Q 10:13) may be treated, on a uniform basis, as consisting exclusively of the dollar amount of the employee's account balance as of the elimination date. [Treas. Reg. § 1.401(a)(4)-4(b)(3)(ii)(B)]

Effective Availability

Q 10:16 What is the effective availability requirement?

Generally, the effective availability rule requires that, based upon all of the relevant facts and circumstances, the group of employees to whom a benefit, right, or feature is effectively available must not substantially favor HCEs. [Treas. Reg. § 1.401(a)(4)-4(c)(1)]

> **Example 10-1:** The Cannery Row Corporation maintains a defined benefit plan that covers both of the corporation's highly compensated nonexcludable

employees and nine of its 12 non-highly compensated nonexcludable employees. The plan provides for a normal retirement benefit payable as an annuity and based on a normal retirement age of 65, and an early retirement benefit payable upon termination in the form of an annuity to employees who terminate on or after age 55 with 30 or more years of service. Both HCEs of the corporation currently meet the age and service requirement, or will have 30 years of service by the time they reach age 55. All but two of the nine NHCEs who are covered by the plan were hired on or after age 35 and, thus, cannot qualify for the early retirement benefit. Even though the group of employees to whom the early retirement benefit is currently available satisfies the ratio percentage test under the minimum coverage rules [Treas. Reg. § 1.410(b)-2(b)(2)] when age and service are disregarded, absent other facts, the group of employees to whom the early retirement benefit is effectively available substantially favors HCEs. [Treas. Reg. § 1.401(a)(4)-4(c)(2), Ex. 1]

Example 10-2: The Western Biological Corporation maintains a defined benefit plan that provides for a normal retirement benefit payable as an annuity and based on a normal retirement age of 65. Western Biological Corporation amends the plan effective December 1, 2019, to provide an early retirement benefit that is available only to employees who terminate employment before December 15, 2019, and who are at least age 55 with 30 or more years of service. All employees were hired before attaining age 25, and the group of employees who have, or will have, attained age 55 with 30 years of service by December 15, 2019 satisfy the ratio percentage test under the minimum coverage rules. [Treas. Reg. § 1.410(b)-2(b)(2)] However, the corporation takes no steps to inform all eligible employees of the early retirement option on a timely basis and the only employees who terminate during the two-week period in which the early retirement benefit is available are HCEs. Given these facts, the group of employees to whom this early retirement window is effectively available substantially favors HCEs. [Treas. Reg. § 1.401(a)(4)-4(c)(2), Ex. 2]

Example 10-3: The Palace Hotel and Grill Company amends its retirement plan on June 30, 2019, to provide for a single-sum distribution as an optional form of benefit for employees who terminate after June 30, 2019 and before January 1, 2020. The availability of this single-sum distribution is conditioned on the employees having a particular disability at the time of termination of employment. The only employee of the company who meets this disability requirement at the time of the amendment and thereafter through December 31, 2019 is an HCE. Under the rule described in Q 10:5, the disability condition is disregarded in determining the current availability of the single-sum optional form of benefit. Nevertheless, given these facts, the group of employees to whom the single-sum distribution is effectively available substantially favors HCEs. [Treas. Reg. § 1.401(a)(4)-4(c)(2), Ex. 3]

Special Rules

Q 10:17 Are there special testing rules that apply to a benefit, right, or feature solely available to a group of employees that is acquired as a result of a merger or acquisition?

Yes. Under special testing rules, acquired employees are treated as satisfying the current availability and effective availability requirements under the nondiscrimination rules during the period of time that each of the following requirements is satisfied:

1. The benefit, right, or feature must satisfy the current availability and effective availability requirements (determined without regard to the special rules for certain dispositions or acquisitions described in Code Section 410(b)(6)(C)) on the date that is selected by the employer as the latest date by which an employee must be hired or transferred into the acquired trade or business for an employee to be included in the acquired group of employees. This determination is made with reference to the plan of the current employer and its nonexcludable employees.
2. The benefit, right, or feature must be available under the plan of the current employer after the transaction on the same terms as under the plan of the prior employer. This requirement is not violated merely because of a change made to the benefit, right, or feature that is permitted by Code Section 411(d)(6), provided that—
   a. The change is a replacement of the benefit, right, or feature with another that is available to the same employees as the original and is of inherently equal or greater value, or
   b. The change is made before January 12, 1993.

This special testing rule applies only to benefits, rights, and features for benefits accruing under the plan of the current employer, and not to those accrued under the plan of the prior employer (unless, pursuant to the transaction, the plan of the prior employer becomes the plan of the current employer, or the assets and liabilities with respect to the acquired group of employees under the plan of the prior employer are transferred to the plan of the current employer in a plan merger, consolidation, or other transfer described in Code Section 414(l)). [Treas. Reg. § 1.401(a)(4)-4(d)(1)]

> **Example 10-4:** The Bear Flag Restaurant Corporation maintains a defined benefit plan, with a single-sum optional form of benefit for all employees. The Palace Hotel Corporation acquires the Bear Flag Restaurant Corporation and merges the Bear Flag defined benefit plan into the Palace Hotel defined benefit plan, which does not otherwise provide a single-sum optional form of benefit. The Palace Hotel Corporation continues to provide the single-sum optional form of benefit under its plan on the same terms as offered under the Bear Flag defined benefit plan to all employees who were acquired in the transaction (but to no other employees). The optional form of benefit satisfies the current availability and effective availability requirements immediately after the transaction (determined without taking into account the

special rules for certain dispositions or acquisitions described in Code Section 410(b)(6)(C)) when tested with reference to the Palace plan and the Palace Corporation's nonexcludable employees. Given these facts, the Palace plan is treated as satisfying the special testing rule that applies in the case of mergers and acquisitions with respect to the single-sum optional form of benefit for the plan year of the transaction and all subsequent plan years. [Treas. Reg. § 1.401(a)(4)-4(d)(1)(iii)]

Q 10:18 Are there also special nondiscrimination testing rules that apply to frozen participants?

Yes. A plan must satisfy the nondiscriminatory availability requirements under the Treasury regulations not only for benefits, rights, and features provided to employees who are currently benefiting under the plan, but also separately for benefits, rights, and features provided to nonexcludable employees with accrued benefits who are not currently benefiting under the plan (frozen participants). Thus, each benefit, right, and feature available to any frozen participant under the plan is separately subject to the nondiscrimination requirements. A plan satisfies the current availability and the effective availability requirements for a benefit, right, or feature available to any frozen participant under the plan only if at least one of the following requirements is satisfied:

1. The benefit, right, or feature must be one that would satisfy those requirements if it were not available to any employee currently benefiting under the plan.
2. The benefit, right, or feature must be one that would satisfy the requirements if all frozen participants were treated as employees currently benefiting under the plan.
3. No change in the availability of the benefit, right, or feature may have been made that is first effective in the current plan year with respect to a frozen participant.
4. Any change in the availability of the benefit, right, or feature that is first effective in the current plan for a frozen participant must be made in a nondiscriminatory manner. Thus, any expansion in the availability of the benefit, right, or feature to any highly compensated frozen participant must be applied on a consistent basis to all non-highly compensated frozen participants. Similarly, any contraction in the availability of the benefit, right, or feature that affects any non-highly compensated frozen participant must be applied on a consistent basis to all highly compensated frozen participants.

[Treas. Reg. § 1.401(a)(4)-4(d)(2)]

Q 10:19 Are there special testing rules under the nondiscrimination regulations that apply to early retirement window benefits?

Yes. If a benefit, right, or feature is an early retirement window benefit [Treas. Reg. § 1.401(a)(4)-3(f)(4)(iii)], it is disregarded for purposes of applying the nondiscrimination rules for an employee for all plan years other than the first plan year in which the benefit is currently available to the employee. [Treas. Reg. § 1.401(a)(4)-4(d)(3)]

An early retirement window benefit is an early retirement benefit, retirement-type subsidy, qualified social security supplement (QSUPP), or other optional form of benefit under a plan that is available only to (or a change in the plan's benefit formula that is applicable only to) employees who terminate employment within a limited period specified by the plan (not to exceed one year) under circumstances specified by the plan. A benefit will still be applicable if, for bona fide business reasons, employment is terminated within a reasonable period *after* the end of the limited period. An amendment to an early retirement window benefit that merely extends the early retirement period is not treated as a separate early retirement window benefit, provided that the periods, as extended, do not exceed one year. However, any other amendment to an early retirement window benefit creates a separate early retirement window benefit. [Treas. Reg. § 1.401(a)(4)-3(f)(4)(iii)]

Permissive Aggregation of Certain Benefits, Rights, or Features

Q 10:20 May an optional form of benefit, ancillary benefit, or other right or feature be aggregated with another optional form of benefit, ancillary benefit, or other right or feature for current availability and effective availability testing purposes?

Yes. Generally, an optional form of benefit, ancillary benefit, or other right or feature may be aggregated with another optional form of benefit, ancillary benefit, or other right or feature, respectively, and the two may be treated as a single unit for purposes of testing whether the current availability and effective availability requirements are met. Such aggregation is permitted only if *both* of the following requirements are satisfied:

1. One of the two optional forms of benefit, ancillary benefit, or other rights or features must in all cases be of inherently equal or greater value than the other. For this purpose, one benefit, right, or feature is of inherently equal or greater value than another only if, at any time and under any conditions, it is impossible for any employees to receive a smaller amount or a less valuable right under the first benefit, right, or feature than under the second.
2. The optional form of benefit, ancillary benefit, or other right or feature of inherently equal or greater value must separately satisfy the current availability and effective availability requirement, without regard to these permissive aggregation rules.

Permissive aggregation may be applied more than once. For example, an optional form of benefit may be aggregated with another optional form of benefit that itself constitutes two separate optional forms that are aggregated and treated as a single optional form of benefit. [Treas. Reg. § 1.401(a)(4)-4(d)(4)]

Example 10-5: The Western Biological Corporation maintains a defined benefit plan that provides a single-sum optional form of benefit to all employees. The single-sum optional form of benefit is available on the same terms to all employees, except that for employees in the tidal pool division, a 5 percent discount factor is applied, and for employees of the laboratory testing division, a 7 percent discount factor is applied. Under the definition of optional form of benefit in Treasury Regulations Section 1.401(a)(4)-4(e)(1), this constitutes two separate optional forms of benefit. The single-sum optional form of benefit available to employees of the tidal pool division separately satisfies the current availability and the effective availability requirements, without taking into account the permissive aggregation rules. Because a lower discount factor is applied to employees of the tidal pool division than is applied to employees of the laboratory testing division, the first single-sum optional form of benefit is of inherently greater value than the second. Given these facts, these two single-sum optional forms of benefit may be aggregated and treated as a single optional form of benefit for purposes of the permissive aggregation rules. [Treas. Reg. § 1.401(a)(4)-4(d)(4)(iii), Ex. 1]

Example 10-6: The facts are the same as in Example 10-5, except that in order to receive the single-sum optional form of benefit, employees of the tidal pool division (but not employees of the laboratory testing division) must have completed at least 20 years of service. This means that the benefit available to employees of the tidal pool division is not of inherently equal or greater value than the benefit available to employees of the laboratory testing division, because an employee of the tidal pool division who terminates employment with fewer than 20 years of service would receive a smaller single-sum amount (that is, zero) than a similarly situated employee of the laboratory testing division who terminates employment with fewer than 20 years of service. In this case, the two single-sum optional forms of benefit may not be aggregated and treated as one for purposes of the permissive aggregation rules. [Treas. Reg. § 1.401(a)(4)-4(d)(4)(iii), Ex. 2]

Certain Spousal Benefits, Etc.

Q 10:21 Are there any other special testing rules under the nondiscrimination regulations that apply to certain spousal benefits, employee stock ownership plans (ESOPs), and unpredictable contingent event benefits?

Yes. There are special testing rules under the nondiscrimination regulations that apply to certain spousal benefits, employee stock ownership plans (ESOPs), and unpredictable contingent event benefits, as explained below.

Special Testing Rule for Certain Spousal Benefits. In the case of a plan that includes two or more plans that have been permissively aggregated under

Treasury Regulations Section 1.410(b)-7(d) (permissive aggregation for the ratio percentage and nondiscriminatory classification tests under the minimum coverage rules), the aggregated plan satisfies the current availability and effective availability requirements for the availability of any nonsubsidized qualified joint and survivor annuities (QJSAs), qualified preretirement survivor annuities (QPSAs), or spousal death benefits described in Code Section 401(a)(11), if each plan that is part of the aggregated plan satisfies Code Section 401(a)(11). (See chapter 11 for a discussion of the QJSA and QPSA requirements.) Whether a benefit is considered subsidized for this purpose may be determined using any reasonable actuarial assumptions. For purposes of this special testing rule, a QJSA, QPSA, or spousal death benefit is deemed to be nonsubsidized if it is provided under a defined contribution plan. [Treas. Reg. § 1.401(a)(4)-4(d)(5)]

Special Testing Rule for ESOPs. An ESOP does not fail to satisfy the current availability and effective availability requirements under the nondiscrimination regulations merely because it makes an investment diversification right or feature or a distribution option available solely to all qualified participants [I.R.C. § 401(a)(28)(B)(iii)], or merely because the restrictions of Code Section 409(n) (relating to securities received in certain ESOP transactions) apply to certain individuals. [Treas. Reg. § 1.401(a)(4)-4(d)(6)]

Special Testing Rule for Unpredictable Contingent Event Benefits. A benefit, right, or feature that is contingent on the occurrence of an unpredictable contingent event (within the meaning of Code Section 412(l)(7)(B)(ii), such as a plant closing, for example, that gives rise to subsidized early retirement benefits) is tested under the current availability and effective availability tests as if the event had occurred. Thus, the current availability of a benefit that becomes an optional form of benefit upon the occurrence of an unpredictable contingent event is tested by deeming the event to have occurred and by disregarding age and service conditions on eligibility to the extent permitted for optional forms of benefit. [Treas. Reg. § 1.401(a)(4)-4(d)(7)]

Definitions

Q 10:22 What is an *optional form of benefit*?

Generally, an *optional form of benefit* is a distribution alternative (including the normal form of benefit) that is available under a plan for accrued benefits that may not be decreased by plan amendment [I.R.C. § 411(d)(6)(A)] or a distribution alternative that is an early retirement benefit or retirement-type subsidy [I.R.C. § 411(d)(6)(B)(i)], including a QSUPP. Different optional forms of benefit exist if a distribution alternative is not payable on substantially the same terms as another distribution alternative (exceptions are described below). The relevant terms include all terms affecting the value of the optional form, such as the method of benefit calculation and the actuarial assumptions used to determine the amount distributed. Thus, for example, different optional forms of benefit may result from differences in terms relating to the payment schedule, timing, commencement, medium of distribution (for example, cash or in kind), election rights, differences in eligibility requirements, or the portion of the benefit to which the distribution alternative applies. [Treas. Reg. § 1.401(a)(4)-4(e)(1)(i)]

There are exceptions to this general definition, however, as the following discussion indicates.

Differences in Benefit Formula or Accrual Method. A distribution alternative available under a defined benefit plan does not fail to be a single optional form of benefit merely because the benefit formulas are different for different employees. Such formulas may vary in accrual methods, other underlying factors (including service-computation methods and definitions of compensation), the manner in which employees vest in, or how the accrued benefit is paid. Notwithstanding this, differences in the normal retirement ages of employees or in the form in which the accrued benefit of employees is payable at normal retirement age under a plan *are* taken into account in determining whether a distribution alternative constitutes one or more optional forms of benefit. [Treas. Reg. § 1.401(a)(4)-4(e)(1)(ii)(A)]

Differences in Allocation Formula. A distribution alternative available under a defined contribution plan does not fail to be a single optional form of benefit merely because the allocation formula is different for different employees. Other factors may differ, including service-computation methods; definitions of compensation; the manner in which income, expenses, gains, and losses attributable to the balance in an employee's account are allocated; or the manner in which employees vest in the accrued benefit that is paid in the form of the distribution alternative. [Treas. Reg. § 1.401(a)(4)-4(e)(1)(ii)(B)]

Differences Attributable to Uniform Normal Retirement Age. A distribution alternative available under a defined benefit plan does not fail to be a single optional form of benefit, to the extent that the differences are attributable to differences in normal retirement dates among employees, provided that the differences do not prevent the employees from having the same uniform normal retirement age under the definition in Treasury Regulations Section 1.401(a)(4)-12. [Treas. Reg. § 1.401(a)(4)-4(e)(1)(ii)(D)]

The following examples illustrate the optional form of benefit.

Example 10-7: The Lee Chong Corporation maintains a defined benefit plan for all employees of the frozen foods and fresh fish divisions of the company. The plan offers a qualified joint and 50 percent survivor annuity at normal retirement age, calculated by multiplying an employee's single life annuity payment by a factor. For an employee of the frozen foods division whose benefit starts at age 65, the plan provides a factor of 0.90, but for a similar employee of the fresh fish division, the plan provides a factor of 0.85. The qualified joint and survivor annuity is not available to employees of the frozen foods and fresh fish divisions on substantially the same terms, and thus it constitutes two separate optional forms of benefit. [Treas. Reg. § 1.401(a)(4)-4(e)(1)(iii), Ex. 1]

Example 10-8: The Western Biological Corporation maintains a defined benefit plan for all employees of the research and marketing divisions. The plan offers a single-sum distribution alternative available on the same terms and determined using the same actuarial assumptions, to all employees. However, different benefit formulas apply to employees of each division. Under the exception to the general optional form of benefit definition, described above ("Differences in Benefit Formula or Accrual Method"), the single-sum optional form of benefit available to employees of the research division is not a separate optional form of benefit from the single-sum optional form of benefit available to employees of the marketing division. [Treas. Reg. § 1.401(a)(4)-4(e)(1)(iii), Ex. 2]

Example 10-9: The Palace Hotel maintains a defined benefit plan that provides an early retirement benefit based on a schedule of early retirement factors that is a single optional form of benefit. The plan is amended to provide an early retirement window benefit that consists of a temporary change in the plan's benefit formula (the addition of five years of service to an employee's actual service under the benefit formula) applicable in determining the benefits for certain employees who terminate employment within the next six months. Under the exception described above ("Differences in Benefit Formula or Accrual Method"), the early retirement optional form of benefit available to window-eligible employees is *not* a separate optional form of benefit from the early retirement optional form of benefit available to the other employees. [Treas. Reg. § 1.401(a)(4)-4(e)(1)(iii), Ex. 3]

Q 10:23 What is an *ancillary benefit*?

Ancillary benefits are Social Security supplements (other than QSUPPs), disability benefits (not in excess of a qualified disability benefit described in Code Section 411(a)(9)), ancillary life insurance and health insurance benefits, death benefits under a defined contribution plan, pre-retirement death benefits under a defined benefit plan, shut-down benefits not protected under Code Section 411(d)(6), and other similar benefits. Different ancillary benefits exist if an ancillary benefit is not available on substantially the same terms as another ancillary benefit. [Treas. Reg. § 1.401(a)(4)-4(e)(2)]

Q 10:24 What does the term *other right or feature* mean?

Generally, the term *other right or feature* means any right or feature applicable to employees under the plan. Different rights or features exist if a right or feature is not available on substantially the same terms as another right or feature. [Treas. Reg. § 1.401(a)(4)-4(e)(3)(i)]

There are exceptions to this general definition, however. Notwithstanding the general definition above, a right or feature is *not* considered an *other right or feature* if it:

1. Is an optional form of benefit or an ancillary benefit under the plan;
2. Is one of the terms that are taken into account in determining whether separate optional forms of benefit or ancillary benefits exist, or that would

be taken into account but for the exceptions described in Q 10:22 (for example, benefit formula or the manner in which benefits vest); or

3. Cannot reasonably be expected to be of meaningful value to an employee (for example, administrative details).

Examples of other rights and features include, but are not limited to:

1. Plan loan provisions (other than those relating to a distribution of an employee's accrued benefit upon default under a loan);
2. The right to direct investments;
3. The right to a particular form of investment, including, for example, a particular class or type of employer securities (taking into account, in determining whether different forms of investment exist, any differences in conversion, dividend, voting, liquidation preference, or other rights conferred under the security) (on October 23, 2014, the IRS issued Notice 2014-66, 2014-66 I.R.B. 820, which provided guidance enabling defined contribution plan to provide lifetime income—without violating applicable nondiscrimination requirements—by offering, as investment options, a series of target date funds (TDFs) that include deferred annuities among their assets, even if some of the TDFs within the series are available only to older participants);
4. The right to make each rate of elective contributions described in Treasury Regulations Section 1.401(k)-6 (determining the rate based on the plan's definition of compensation out of which the elective contributions are made (regardless of whether that definition satisfies Code Section 414(s)), but also treating different rates as existing if they are based on definitions of compensation or other requirements or formulas that are not substantially the same);
5. The right to make after-tax employee contributions to a defined benefit plan that are not allocated to separate accounts;
6. The right to make each rate of after-tax employee contributions described in Treasury Regulations Section 1.401(m)-1(a)(3) (determining the rate based on the plan's definition of compensation out of which the after-tax employee contributions are made, regardless of whether that definition satisfies Code Section 414(s), but also treating different rates as existing if they are based on definitions of compensation or other requirements or formulas that are not substantially the same);
7. The right to each rate of allocation of matching contributions described in Treasury Regulations Section 1.401(m)-1(a)(2) (determining the rate using the amount of matching, elective, and after-tax employee contributions determined after any corrections under Treasury Regulation Sections 1.401(k)-1(f)(1)(i), 1.401(m)-1(e)(1)(i), and 1.401(m)-2(c), but also treating different rates as existing if they are based on definitions of compensation or other requirements or formulas that are not substantially the same);
8. The right to purchase additional retirement or ancillary benefits under the plan; and
9. The right to make rollover contributions and transfers to and from the plan.

[Treas. Reg. § 1.401(a)(4)-4(e)(3)(ii)(A)–(I)]

On October 23, 2014, the IRS issued Notice 2014-66, 2014-46 I.R.B. 820, which provides a special rule that enables qualified defined contribution plans to provide lifetime income by offering, as investment options, a series of TDFs that include deferred annuities among their assets, even if some of the TDFs within the series are available only to older participants. This special rule provides that, if certain conditions are satisfied, a series of TDFs in a defined contribution plan is treated as a single right or feature for purposes of the nondiscrimination requirements of Code Section 401(a)(4). The special rule in Notice 2014-66 permits the TDFs to satisfy those nondiscrimination requirements as they apply to rights or features even if one or more of the TDFs considered on its own would not satisfy those requirements. Under the special rule in Notice 2014-66, a series of TDFs under a defined contribution plan in which participation in some TDFs is restricted to participants in particular age-bands is permitted to be treated as a single "other right or feature" for purposes of Treasury Regulations Section 1.401(a)(4)-4, provided the following conditions are satisfied:

1. The series of TDFs is designed to serve as a single integrated investment program under which the same investment manager manages each TDF and applies the same generally accepted investment theories across the series of TDFs. Thus, the only difference among the TDFs is the mix of assets selected by the investment manager, which difference results solely from the intent to achieve the level of risk appropriate for the age-band of individuals participating in each TDF. In accordance with the consistent investment strategy used to manage the series of TDFs, the design for the series is for the mix of assets in a TDF currently available for older participants to become available to each younger participant as the asset mix of each TDF for younger participants changes to reflect the increasing age of those participants.
2. Some of the TDFs available to participants in older age-bands include deferred annuities, and none of the deferred annuities provide a guaranteed lifetime withdrawal benefit (GLWB) or guaranteed minimum withdrawal benefit (GMWB) feature.
3. The TDFs do not hold employer securities, as described in ERISA Section 407(d)(1), that are not readily tradable on an established securities market.
4. Each TDF in the series is treated in the same manner with respect to rights or features other than the mix of assets. For example, the fees and administrative expenses for each TDF are determined in a consistent manner, and the extent to which those fees and expenses are paid from plan assets (rather than by the employer) is the same.

The DOL informed the Department of the Treasury that the use of unallocated deferred annuity contracts as fixed income investments would not cause the TDFs to fail to meet the requirements of Section 2550.404c-5(e)(4)(i) of the DOL's qualified default investment alternative (QDIA) regulation. It is also the

DOL's view that the distribution of annuity certificates as each TDF dissolves on its target date, as described in the example in Section IV of IRS Notice 2014-66, is consistent with Section 2550.404c-5(e)(4)(vi) of the DOL's QDIA regulations. [Letter to J. Mark Iwry at the Department of the Treasury (Oct. 23, 2014) from Phyllis C. Borzi, available at https://www.dol.gov/agencies/ebsa/employers-and-advisers/guidance/information-letters/10-23-2014]

Code Section 411(d)(6) Protected Benefits

In General

Q 10:25 What are protected benefits under Code Section 411(d)(6)?

Code Section 411(d)(6) provides that, in general, a qualified retirement plan will not satisfy the minimum vesting standards of Code Section 411 if the accrued benefit of a participant is decreased by an amendment of the plan, other than an amendment described in Code Section 412(c)(8) (relating to certain retroactive plan amendments), or ERISA Section 4281. Code Section 411(d)(6) also provides that a plan amendment that has the effect of eliminating or reducing an early retirement benefit or a retirement-type subsidy or eliminating an optional form of benefit, with respect to benefits attributable to service before the amendment, shall be treated as impermissibly reducing accrued benefits. In the case of a retirement-type subsidy, this rule applies only with respect to a participant who satisfies (either before or after the amendment) the pre-amendment conditions for the subsidy. The Secretary of the Treasury must provide, by regulations, that the anti-cutback rule will not apply to any plan amendment that reduces or eliminates benefits or subsides that create significant burdens or complexities for the plan and plan participants, unless the amendment adversely affects the rights of a participant in a more than *de minimis* manner. [I.R.C. § 411(d)(6)(A) and (B)]

General Rule. A Section 411(d)(6) protected benefit includes any benefit that falls into one or more of the following categories:

1. Benefits described in Code Section 411(d)(6)(A) that cannot be decreased by plan amendment;
2. Early retirement benefits (as defined in Treasury Regulations Section 1.411(d)-3(g)(6)(i)) and retirement-type subsidies (as defined in Treasury Regulations Section 1.411(d)-3(g)(6)(iv)); and
3. Optional forms of benefit described in Code Section 411(d)(6)(B)(ii).

[Treas. Reg. § 1.411(d)-4, Q&A-1]

Such benefits, to the extent they have accrued, are subject to the protection of Code Section 411(d)(6) and cannot, therefore, be reduced, eliminated, or made subject to employer discretion except to the extent provided by applicable Treasury regulations. [Treas. Reg. § 1.411(d)-4, Q&A-1] This authority does not extend to a plan amendment that would have the effect of eliminating or reducing an early retirement benefit or retirement-type subsidy (see preamble to final Treasury Regulations Section 1.411(d)-4). [Treas. Reg. § 1.411(d)-4, Q&A-1-3; Notice 98-29, 1998-22 I.R.B. 5] ERISA Section 204(g)(2) provides a parallel rule to Code Section 411(d)(6)(B) that applies under Title I and authorizes the Secretary of the Treasury to provide exceptions to this parallel ERISA requirement. Thus, Treasury regulations issued under Code Section 411(d)(6)(B) apply as well for purposes of ERISA Section 204(g)(2).

In Notice 98-29, the IRS and the Treasury Department announced that they were considering further guidance exercising this authority in order to provide possible relief for defined contribution plans that are amended to eliminate optional forms of benefit. Most of the public comments received in response to Notice 98-29 indicated that, particularly for defined contribution plans, the Code Section 411(d)(6)(B) requirement that a plan continue to offer all existing payment options often imposes significant administrative burdens that are disproportionate to any corresponding benefit to participants. [65 Fed. Reg. 53902]

After considering these comments, the IRS and Treasury issued proposed regulations on March 29, 2000, to relieve defined contribution plans from the requirements of Code Section 411(d)(6)(B) in a wide range of circumstances. [65 Fed. Reg. 16546] The final regulations that were issued on September 6, 2000 [65 Fed. Reg. 53901] generally provide for additional circumstances under which a defined contribution plan may be amended to eliminate or restrict a participant's right to receive payment of accrued benefits under certain optional forms of benefit. A defined contribution plan may be amended to eliminate or restrict a participant's right to receive payment of accrued benefits under a particular optional form of benefit without violating the Code Section 411(d)(6) anti-cutback rules if, once the plan amendment takes effect for a participant, the alternative forms of payment that remain available to the participant include payment in a single-sum distribution form that is otherwise identical to the optional form of benefit that is being eliminated or restricted. The final regulations apply to any plan amendment that is adopted on or after September 6, 2000. However, any such amendment cannot apply to any distribution that has an annuity starting date earlier than the 90th day after the date the participant receiving the distribution has been given a summary of material modifications (SMM) that reflects the amendment and satisfies the requirements of DOL Regulations Section 2520.104b-3 (or, if earlier, the first day of the second plan year following the plan year in which the amendment is adopted). [Treas. Reg. § 1.411(d)-4, Q&A-2(e)] The final regulations also:

1. Significantly liberalized existing Code Section 411(d)(6) relief for distributable event transfers; and
2. Provided new Code Section 411(d)(6) relief for transfers in connection with certain corporate mergers and acquisitions or changes in the participant's employment status, known as transaction transfers and employment change transfers, respectively, effective for transfers made on or after September 6, 2000.

EGTRRA, enacted on June 7, 2001, further changed the extent to which Code Section 411(d)(6) protected benefits may be reduced or eliminated under a defined contribution plan. With respect to plan transfers, for example, a defined contribution plan (the transferee plan) to which benefits are transferred from another defined contribution plan (the transferor plan) will not be treated as reducing a participant's protected benefits even though it does not provide all of the forms of distribution previously available under the transferor plan if:

1. The transferee plan receives from the transferor plan a direct transfer of the participant's benefit accrued under the transferor plan or the transferee plan results from a merger or other transaction that has the effect of a direct transfer;
2. Both the transferee and transferor plans authorize the transfer;
3. The transfers occur pursuant to a voluntary election by the participant that is made after he or she receives a notice describing the consequences of making that election; and
4. The transferee plan allows the participant to receive distribution of his or her benefit under the transferee plan in the form of a single-sum distribution.

[I.R.C. § 411(d)(6)(D)]

EGTRRA did not modify existing survivor annuity rules under Code Section 417. Therefore, a plan that is a transferee of a plan subject to the QJSA and QPSA rules is also subject to those rules.

With respect to plan amendments, EGTRRA also provided that, except to the extent provided in Treasury regulations, a defined contribution plan would not be treated as reducing a participant's accrued benefit in violation of Code Section 411(d)(6) if:

1. A plan amendment eliminates a form of distribution previously available under the plan;
2. A single-sum distribution is available to the participant at the same time(s) as the form of distribution eliminated by the amendment; and
3. The single-sum distribution is based on the same or greater portion of the participant's accrued benefit as the form of distribution eliminated by the amendment.

[I.R.C. § 411(d)(6)(E)]

Code Section 411(d)(6)(E), as added by EGTRRA, is similar to final Treasury Regulations Section 1.411(d)-4, Q&A-2(e) that was issued on September 6, 2000 (described above), but it eliminated the regulations' advance notice condition.

On July 8, 2003, the IRS issued proposed regulations [68 Fed. Reg. 40581] that would have amended the 2000 final Treasury Regulations Section 1.411(d)-4, Q&A-2(e), described above, to reflect the addition of Code Section 411(d)(6)(E) by EGTRRA, including the elimination of the final regulations' 90-day advance notice requirement. Those proposed regulations were finalized, without any changes, on January 25, 2005, effective on that same date. [70 Fed. Reg. 3475]

On March 24, 2004, the IRS issued proposed regulations [69 Fed. Reg. 13769] that would have revised existing final Treasury Regulations Section 1.411(d)-3. The 2004 proposed regulations, among other things, would have permitted plan amendments that eliminate "redundant" optional forms of benefit with respect to benefits accrued before the date of the amendment, if certain requirements are met. On August 12, 2005, the IRS issued final Treasury Regulations Section 1.411(d)-3, which responded to the EGTRRA directive for purposes of both Code Section 411(d)(6) and ERISA Section 204(g) by specifying the circumstances under which a plan may be amended to reduce or eliminate retirement benefits, retirement-type subsidies, and optional forms of benefit. The 2005 final Treasury Regulations Section 1.411(d)-3 reserved two topics for later guidance—a utilization test (described below) and the interaction of the permitted forfeiture rules under Code Section 411(a) with the anti-cutback rules under Code Section 411(d)(6) after taking into account the decision in *Central Laborers' Pension Fund v. Heinz*, 541 U.S. 739 (2004). (In that case, the U.S. Supreme Court, holding on behalf of the plaintiff participants, ruled that ERISA Section 204(g) prohibits a plan amendment from expanding the categories of post-retirement employment that result in suspension of the payment of early retirement benefits already accrued.) In Revenue Procedure 2005-23, 2005-18 I.R.B. 991, the IRS addressed the application of *Heinz* and provided examples of how a plan can comply with the revenue procedure and avoid plan disqualification. In 2006, the IRS issued final Treasury Regulations Section 1.411(d)-3 to provide guidance on the application of the anti-cutback rules of Code § 411(d)(6) to a plan amendment that places greater restrictions or conditions on a participant's right to Code § 411(d)(6) protected benefits, even if the amendment merely adds a restriction or condition that is permitted under the vesting rules of Code Sections 411(a)(3) through (11). The 2006 final regulations are intended to reflect the holding in *Central Laborers*. The 2006 final regulations also set forth standards for the *utilization test*, which is a permitted method of eliminating optional forms of benefit that are burdensome to the plan and of minimal value to plan participants.

On November 8, 2012, the IRS issued final Treasury Regulations Section 1.411(d)-4, Q&A-2(b)(2)(xii), which provides an additional, limited exception to the anti-cutback rules to permit a plan sponsor that is a debtor in a bankruptcy proceeding to amend its single-employer defined benefit plan to eliminate a single-sum distribution option (or other optional form of benefit providing for accelerated payments) under the plan if certain specified conditions are satisfied. Those final regulations apply to plan amendments that are adopted and effective after November 8, 2012.

On April 18, 2013, the IRS issued Notice 2013-17, 2013-20 I.R.B. 1082, which provides relief from the anti-cutback requirements of Code Section 411(d)(6) for plan amendments that eliminate a distribution option described in Code Section 401(a)(28)(B)(ii)(I) (setting forth the distribution method of meeting the diversification requirements of Code Section 401(a)(28)(B)(i)) from an ESOP that becomes subject to the diversification requirements of Code Section 401(a)(35), which apply to certain defined contribution plans that hold (or are treated as holding) publicly traded employer securities.

Q 10:26 What benefits are *not* Section 411(d)(6) protected benefits?

The following benefits are examples of items that are *not* Section 411(d)(6) protected benefits:

1. Ancillary life insurance protection;
2. Accident or health insurance benefits;
3. Social Security supplements described in Code Section 411(a)(9), except QSUPPs, as defined in Treasury Regulations Section 1.401(a)(4)-12;
4. The availability of loans (other than the distribution of an employee's accrued benefit upon default under a loan);
5. The right to make after-tax employee contributions or elective deferrals described in Code Section 402(g)(3);
6. The right to direct investments;
7. The right to a particular form of investment (for example, investment in employer stock or securities or investment in certain types of securities, commercial paper, or other investment vehicles);
8. The allocation dates for contributions, forfeitures, and earnings, the time for making contributions (but not the conditions for receiving an allocation of contributions or forfeitures for a plan year after such conditions have been satisfied), and the valuation dates for account balances;
9. Administrative procedures for distributing benefits, such as provisions relating to the particular dates on which notices are given and by which elections must be made; and
10. Rights that derive from administrative and operational provisions, such as mechanical procedures for allocating investment experience among accounts in defined contribution plans.

[Treas. Reg. § 1.411(d)-4, Q&A-1(d)]

Q 10:27 What is an *optional form of benefit* under Code Section 411(d)(6)?

The term *optional form of benefit* has the same meaning as in Treasury Regulations Section 1.411(d)-3(g)(6)(ii) (see Q 10:39). Under this definition, different forms of benefit exist if a distribution alternative is not payable on substantially the same terms as another distribution alternative. Thus, for example, different optional forms of benefit may result from differences in terms relating to the payment schedule, timing, commencement, medium of distribution (e.g., in cash or in kind), election rights, differences in eligibility requirements, or the portion of the benefit to which the distribution alternative applies. [Treas. Reg. § 1.411(d)-4, Q&A-1(b)(1)]

The following examples illustrate the meaning of the term optional form of benefit. Other issues, such as the requirement that the optional forms satisfy the nondiscrimination requirements of Code Section 401(a)(4), are not addressed in the following examples, and no inferences should be drawn from them about those requirements. Assume that the distribution forms, including those not described in these examples, provided under the plan in each example are identical in all respects.

Example 10-10: The Bear Flag Restaurant maintains a retirement plan that permits each participant to receive his or her benefit under the plan in one of the following ways: as a single-sum distribution; a level monthly distribution schedule over 15 years; a single life annuity; a joint and 50 percent survivor annuity; a joint and 75 percent survivor annuity; a joint and 50 percent survivor annuity with a benefit increase for the participant if the beneficiary dies before a specified date; and a joint and 50 percent survivor annuity with a 10-year certain feature. Each of these benefit distribution options is an optional form of benefit (without regard to whether the values of these options are actuarially equivalent). [Treas. Reg. § 1.411(d)-4, Q&A-1(b)(2), Ex. 1]

Example 10-11: The Palace Hotel maintains a retirement plan that permits each participant who is employed by the restaurant division to receive his or her benefit in a single-sum distribution payable upon termination of employment, and each participant who is employed by the housekeeping division to receive his or her benefit in a single-sum distribution payable upon termination of employment on or after attaining age 50. This plan provides two single-sum optional forms of benefit. [Treas. Reg. § 1.411(d)-4, Q&A-1(b)(2), Ex. 2]

Example 10-12: The Western Biological Laboratory maintains a retirement plan that permits each participant to receive his or her benefit in a single life annuity that begins in the month after the participant's termination of employment, or in a single life annuity that begins upon the completion of five consecutive one-year breaks in service. These are two optional forms of benefit. [Treas. Reg. § 1.411(d)-4, Q&A-1(b)(2), Ex. 3]

Example 10-13: The Lee Chong Corporation maintain a profit sharing plan that permits each participant who is employed by the produce division to receive an in-service distribution upon the satisfaction of objective criteria set forth in the plan designed to determine whether the participant has a heavy and immediate financial need. Each participant who is employed by the meats and poultry division is allowed to receive an in-service distribution upon the satisfaction of objective criteria set forth in the plan designed to determine whether the participant has a heavy and immediate financial need attributable to extraordinary medical expenses. These in-service distribution options are two optional forms of benefit. [Treas. Reg. § 1.411(d)-4, Q&A-1(b)(2), Ex. 4]

Example 10-14: The Great Tidal Pool Corporation maintains a profit sharing plan that permits each participant who is employed by the mollusk division to receive an in-service distribution up to $5,000. Each participant who is employed by the algae division may receive an in-service distribution of up to his or her total vested benefit. These in-service distribution options differ as to the portion of the accrued benefit that may be distributed in a particular form and are, therefore, two optional forms of benefit. [Treas. Reg. § 1.411(d)-4, Q&A-1(b)(2), Ex. 5]

Example 10-15: The La Ida Company maintains a profit sharing plan that provides for a single-sum distribution on termination of employment. The plan is amended in 2019 to eliminate the single-sum optional form of benefit on benefits accrued after the date of amendment. This single-sum optional form of benefit continues to be a single optional form of benefit, although, over time, the percentage of various employees' accrued benefits potentially payable under this single sum may decrease because the form is only available on benefits accrued up to and including the date of amendment. [Treas. Reg. § 1.411(d)-4, Q&A-1(b)(2), Ex. 6]

Example 10-16: The Carmel Valley Company maintains a profit sharing plan that permits each participant to receive a single-sum distribution of his or her benefit in cash or in the form of a specified class of employer stock. This plan provides two single-sum distribution optional forms of benefit. [Treas. Reg. § 1.411(d)-4, Q&A-1(b)(2), Ex. 7]

Example 10-17: The Waters Corporation maintains a stock bonus plan that permits each participant to receive a single-sum distribution of his or her benefit in cash or in the form of the property in which it was invested before the distribution. This plan's single-sum distribution option provides two optional forms of benefit. [Treas. Reg. § 1.411(d)-4, Q&A-1(b)(2), Ex. 8]

Example 10-18: The Gate Corporation maintains a defined benefit plan that provides for an early retirement benefit payable upon termination of employment after attaining age 55 and either 10 years of service, or if earlier, upon plan termination, to employees of the wrought iron division, and provides for an identical early retirement benefit payable on the same terms with the exception of payment on plan termination to employees of the filigree division. This plan provides for two optional forms of benefit. [Treas. Reg. § 1.411(d)-4, Q&A-1(b)(2), Ex. 9]

Example 10-19: The Hatton Fields Company maintains a profit sharing plan that provides for loans secured by an employee's account balance. In the event of default on such a loan, there is an execution on those account balances. Such execution is a distribution of the employee's accrued benefits under the plan. A distribution of an accrued benefit contingent on default under a plan loan secured by such accrued benefits is an optional form of benefit under the plan. [Treas. Reg. § 1.411(d)-4, Q&A-1(b)(2), Ex. 10]

Q 10:28 Are benefits protected under Code Section 411(d)(6) only if they are provided under the terms of a plan?

Generally, benefits described in Code Section 411(d)(6)(A) (that is, accrued benefits that cannot be decreased by plan amendment), early retirement benefits, retirement-type subsidies, and optional forms of benefit are Section 411(d)(6) protected benefits only if they are provided under the terms of the plan. However, if an employer establishes a pattern of repeated plan amendments providing for similar benefits in similar situations for substantially consecutive, limited periods of time, those benefits also will be treated as provided under the terms of the plan, despite the limited periods of time, to the extent necessary to carry out the purposes of the anti-cutback rules under Code Section 411(d)(6) and, where applicable, the definitely determinable requirement described in Code Section 401(a), including Code Section 401(a)(25), which sets forth the requirement that actuarial assumptions must be specified in the plan.

A pattern of repeated plan amendments providing that a particular optional form of benefit is available to certain named employees for a limited period of time is within the scope of this rule and may result in such optional form of benefit being treated as provided under the terms of the plan to all employees covered under the plan. [Treas. Reg. § 1.411(d)-4, Q&A-1(c)(1)]

Extent to Which Section 411(d)(6) Protected Benefits May Be Reduced or Eliminated

Q 10:29 To what extent may Section 411(d)(6) protected benefits under a plan be reduced or eliminated?

Reduction or Elimination of Section 411(d)(6) Protected Benefits. A plan is not permitted to be amended to eliminate or reduce a Section 411(d)(6) protected benefit that has already accrued, except as provided in Treasury Regulations Section 1.411(d)-3 or -4. This is generally the case even if such elimination or reduction is contingent upon the employee's consent. However, a plan may be amended to eliminate or reduce Section 411(d)(6) protected benefits with respect to benefits not yet accrued as of the later of the amendment's adoption date or effective date without violating Section 411(d)(6). [Treas. Reg. § 1.411(d)-4, Q&A-2(a)(1)]

Selection of Optional Forms of Benefit. A plan generally may treat a participant as receiving his or her entire nonforfeitable accrued benefit under the plan if the participant receives his or her benefit in an optional form of benefit in an amount determined under the plan that is at least the actuarial equivalent of the employee's nonforfeitable accrued benefit payable at normal retirement age under the plan. This is true even though the participant could have elected to receive an optional form of benefit with a greater actuarial value than the value of the optional form received, such as an optional form including retirement-type subsidies, and without regard to whether the other, more valuable optional form could have begun immediately or could have become available only upon the employee's future satisfaction of specified eligibility conditions. [Treas. Reg. § 1.411(d)-4, Q&A-2(a)(2)(i)]

Election of an Optional Form. Except as provided under the so-called buy-back rule, discussed below, a plan does not violate the anti-cutback rules under Code Section 411(d)(6) merely because an employee's election to receive a portion of his or her nonforfeitable accrued benefit in one optional form of benefit precludes him or her from receiving that portion of the benefit in another form. That employee retains all Section 411(d)(6) protected rights on the entire portion of nonforfeitable accrued benefit for which no distribution election was made. For purposes of this rule, an elective transfer (see Q 10:30) of an otherwise distributable benefit is treated as the selection of an optional form of benefit. [Treas. Reg. § 1.411(d)-4, Q&A-2(a)(2)(ii)]

Buy-Back Rule. Notwithstanding the above, an employee who received a distribution of his or her nonforfeitable benefit from a plan that is required to provide a repayment opportunity to the employee if he or she returns to service within the applicable period under Code Section 411(a)(7) and who, upon later reemployment, repays the full amount of that distribution in accordance with the rules of Code Section 411(a)(7)(C), must be reinstated with the full array of Section 411(d)(6) protected benefits that existed for that benefit before it was distributed. [Treas. Reg. § 1.411(d)-4, Q&A-2(a)(2)(iii)]

Example 10-20: The Presidio Corporation maintains a defined benefit plan that provides, among its optional forms of benefit, for a subsidized early retirement benefit payable solely in the form of an annuity and available to employees who terminate employment on or after their 55th birthday. In addition, the plan provides for a single-sum distribution available upon termination of employment or termination of the plan. The single-sum distribution is determined on the basis of the present value of the accrued normal retirement benefit and does not take the early retirement subsidy into account. The plan is terminated on December 31, 2019. Eva Flanagan, age 47, Dora Flood, age 55, and Josh Billings, age 47, all continue working for the corporation. Sam Malloy, age 47, Agnes Malloy (Sam's wife), age 55, and Lee Chong, age 47, terminate employment during 2019. Eva Flanagan and Dora Flood elect to take the single-sum optional form of distribution at the time of plan termination. Sam Malloy and Agnes Malloy elect to take the single-sum distribution on termination of employment. The elimination of the subsidized early retirement benefit for Eva, Dora, and Sam and Agnes Malloy is not a violation of the anti-cutback rules of Code Section 411(d)(6). This is the result even though Eva and Sam had not yet satisfied the conditions for the subsidized early retirement benefit. Because Josh Billings and Lee Chong have not selected an optional form of benefit, they continue to have a Section 411(d)(6) protected right to the full array of Section 411(d)(6) protected benefits provided under the plan, including the single-sum distribution form and the subsidized early retirement benefit. [Treas. Reg. § 1.411(d)-4, Q&A-2(a)(2)(iv), Ex. 1]

Example 10-21: Joe Green is a partially vested employee who receives a single-sum distribution of the present value of his entire nonforfeitable benefit when he separates from service under Bear Flag Restaurant Corporation's defined benefit plan. The plan includes a repayment provision. Upon reemployment with the corporation, Joe repays the required amount, in accordance with the buy-back rules of Code Section 411(a)(7). Joe may, upon subsequent termination of employment, elect to take such repaid benefits in any optional form that was offered under the plan at the time of his *initial* separation from service. If the plan were amended before that repayment, to eliminate the single-sum optional form of benefit for benefits accrued after the date of the amendment, the participant has a Section 411(d)(6) protected right to take distribution of the repaid benefit in the form of a single-sum distribution. [Treas. Reg. § 1.411(d)-4, Q&A-2(a)(2)(iv), Ex. 2]

Plan Mergers and Benefit Transfers. The prohibition against the reduction or elimination of Section 411(d)(6) protected benefits that have already accrued applies to plan mergers, spinoffs, transfers, and transactions amending, or having the effect of amending, a plan or plans to transfer plan benefits. For example, if Plan A, a profit sharing plan that provides for distribution of plan benefits in annual installments over 10 or 20 years, is merged with Plan B, a profit sharing plan that provides for distribution of plan benefits in annual installments over life expectancy at time of retirement, the merged plan must retain the 10- or 20-year installment option for participants on benefits already accrued under Plan A as of the merger and the installments over life expectancy for participants with benefits already accrued under Plan B. Similarly, if an employee's benefit under a defined contribution plan is transferred to another defined contribution plan (whether or not of the same employer), the optional forms of benefit available on the employee's benefit accrued under the transferor plan may not be eliminated or reduced, except as otherwise permitted under the Treasury regulations promulgated under Code Section 411(d)(6). [Treas. Reg. § 1.411(d)-4, Q&A-2(a)(3)(i)] The IRS has ruled that Section 411(d)(6) protected benefits that may be eliminated by plan amendment may also be eliminated by trustee-to-trustee transfer. [Ltr. Rul. 9743045]

Annuity Contracts. The protection provided by the anti-cutback rules of Code Section 411(d)(6) generally may not be avoided by the use of annuity contracts. Thus, Section 411(d)(6) protected benefits already accrued may not be eliminated or reduced merely because a plan uses annuity contracts to provide such benefits, whether or not the plan, a participant, or a beneficiary of a participant holds the contract or whether such annuity contracts are purchased as a result of the termination of the plan. However, to the extent that an annuity contract constitutes payment of benefits in a particular optional form elected by the participant, the plan does not violate the anti-cutback rules of Code Section 411(d)(6) merely because it provides that other optional forms are no longer available to that participant. [Treas. Reg. § 1.411(d)-4, Q&A-2(a)(3)(ii)]

In general, the right of a participant to receive a benefit in the form of cash payments from the plan and the right of a participant to receive that benefit in the form of the distribution of an annuity contract that provides for cash payments that are identical in all respects to the cash payments from the plan except with respect to the source of the payments are not separate optional forms of benefit. Therefore, for example, if a plan includes an optional form of benefit under which benefits are distributed in the medium of an annuity contract that provides for cash payments, that optional form of benefit may be modified by a plan amendment that substitutes cash payments from the plan for the annuity contract, where those cash payments from the plan are identical to the cash payments payable from the annuity contract in all respects except with respect to the source of the payments. [Treas. Reg. § 1.411(d)-4, Q&A-2(a)(3)(ii)]

Example 10-22: The Monterey Bay Corporation maintains a profit sharing plan that is being terminated. It satisfies the anti-cutback rules of Code Section 411(d)(6) only if it makes available to participants annuity contracts that provide for all Section 411(d)(6) protected benefits under the plan that may not otherwise be reduced or eliminated. The plan provided for a single-sum distribution upon attainment of early retirement age, and a provision for payment in the form of 10 equal annual installments. The plan satisfies the anti-cutback rules of Code Section 411(d)(6) only if participants have the opportunity to elect either of those two options. [Treas. Reg. § 1.411(d)-4, Q&A-2(a)(3)(ii)(B), Ex. 1]

Example 10-23: The Western Biological Laboratory Corporation maintains a defined benefit plan that permits each participant who separates from service on or after age 62 to receive a QJSA or a single life annuity beginning 45 days after termination of employment. For a participant who separates from service before age 62, payments under these optional forms of benefit begin 45 days after the participant's 62nd birthday. Under the plan, a participant must elect among these optional forms of benefit during the 90-day period preceding the annuity starting date. However, during that period, a participant may defer both benefit commencement and the election of a particular benefit form to any later date, subject to the minimum required distribution requirements of Code Section 401(a)(9). In January 2019, the corporation decides to terminate the plan as of July 1, 2019. The plan will not satisfy the anti-cutback rules of Code Section 411(d)(6) unless the optional forms of benefit provided under the plan are preserved under the annuity contract purchased on plan termination. Then that annuity contract must offer participants the same optional benefit commencement rights that the plan provided. In addition, the annuity contract must provide the same election rights on those benefit options. This is the case even if, for example, in conjunction with the termination of the plan, the corporation amended the plan to permit participants to elect a QJSA, single life annuity, or single-sum distribution beginning on July 1, 2019. [Treas. Reg. § 1.411(d)-4, Q&A-2(a)(3)(ii)(B), Ex. 2]

Benefits Payable to a Spouse or Beneficiary. Section 411(d)(6) protected benefits may not be eliminated merely because they are payable to a spouse or other beneficiary, instead of to the participant. [Treas. Reg. § 1.411(d)-4, Q&A-2(a)(4)]

Q 10:30 Under what circumstances may Section 411(d)(6) protected benefits be eliminated or reduced?

Permitted Cutback in Section 411(d)(6) Protected Benefits. The IRS may provide for the elimination or reduction of Section 411(d)(6) protected benefits that have already accrued only to the extent that such elimination or reduction does not result in the loss to plan participants of either a valuable right or an employer-subsidized optional form of benefit unless a comparable subsidy is provided and is consistent with the requirements of Treasury Regulations

Section 1.411(d)-4. The IRS may also provide for such elimination or reduction if it is necessary to accomplish compliance with other requirements of Code Section 401 (for example, the nondiscrimination rules of Code Section 401(a)(4), the minimum required distribution rules of Code Section 401(a)(9), or the limitations on contributions and benefits under Code Section 415). The IRS may exercise this authority only through the publication of revenue rulings, notices, and other documents of general applicability. [Treas. Reg. § 1.411(d)-4, Q&A-2(b)(1)]

Section 411(d)(6) Protected Benefits That May Be Eliminated or Reduced. The elimination or reduction of certain Section 411(d)(6) protected benefits that have already accrued does *not* violate the anti-cutback rules of Code Section 411(d)(6) in the situations described below. The rules with respect to possible eliminations and reductions of Section 411(d)(6) protected benefits generally became effective January 20, 1986. However, the rules in Treasury Regulations Section 1.411(d)-4, Q&A-2(b)(2)(iii)(A) (relating to in-kind distributions payable under defined contribution plans in the form of marketable securities other than employer securities) and Q&A-2(b)(2)(iii)(B) (relating to amendments in defined contribution plans to specify the medium of distribution) are effective for plan amendments that are adopted and effective on or after September 6, 2000. In addition, the rules in Treasury Regulations Section 1.411(d)-4, Q&A-2(b)(2)(xii) (providing an additional, limited exception to the anti-cutback rules to permit a plan sponsor that is a debtor in a bankruptcy proceeding to amend its single-employer defined benefit plan to eliminate a single-sum distribution option (or other optional form of benefit providing for accelerated payments) under the plan if certain specified conditions are satisfied) are effective for plan amendments that are adopted and effective after November 8, 2012. [Treas. Reg. § 1.411(d)-4, Q&A-2(b)(2)]

Change in Statutory Requirement. A plan may be amended to eliminate or reduce a Section 411(d)(6) protected benefit if the following three requirements are met:

1. The amendment constitutes timely compliance with a change in law affecting plan qualification;
2. There is an exercise of Section 7805(b) relief (relating to retroactive regulations or rulings) by the IRS; and
3. The elimination or reduction is made only to the extent necessary to enable the plan to continue to satisfy the requirements for qualified plans.

In general, the elimination or reduction of a Section 411(d)(6) protected benefit will not be treated as necessary if other modifications to the plan (for example, by expanding the availability of an optional form of benefit to additional employees) would make it possible to satisfy the applicable qualification requirement. [Treas. Reg. § 1.411(d)-4, Q&A-2(b)(2)(i)]

Joint and Survivor Annuity. A plan that provides a range of three or more actuarially equivalent joint and survivor annuity options may be amended to eliminate any of those options, except those with the largest and smallest optional survivor payment percentages, even if the effect of the amendment is to change which of the options is the qualified joint and survivor annuity under Code Section 417.

Example 10-24: A money purchase pension plan provides three joint and survivor annuity options with survivor payments of 50 percent, 75 percent, and 100 percent that are uniform with respect to age and are actuarially equivalent. The employer may eliminate the option with the 75 percent survivor payment, even if this option had been the qualified joint and survivor annuity under the plan. [Treas. Reg. § 1.411(d)-4, Q&A-2(b)(2)(ii)]

In-Kind Distributions Payable Under Defined Contribution Plans in the Form of Marketable Securities Other Than Employer Securities. If a defined contribution plan includes an optional form of benefit under which benefits are distributed in the form of marketable securities, other than securities of the employer, that optional form of benefit may be modified by a plan amendment that substitutes cash for the marketable securities as the medium of distribution. For such purposes, the term *marketable securities* means marketable securities as defined in Code Section 731(c)(2), and the term *securities of the employer* means securities of the employer as defined in Code Section 402(e)(4)(E)(ii). [Treas. Reg. § 1.411(d)-4, Q&A-2(b)(2)(iii)(A)] This rule applies to plan amendments that are adopted and effective on or after September 6, 2000. [Treas. Reg. § 1.411(d)-4, Q&A-2(b)(2)(iii)(A)]

Amendments to Defined Contribution Plans to Specify Medium of Distribution. If a defined contribution plan includes an optional form of benefit under which benefits are distributable to a participant in a medium other than cash, the plan may be amended to limit the types of property in which distributions may be made to the participant to the types of property specified in the amendment. For this purpose, the types of property specified in the amendment must include all types of property (other than marketable securities that are not securities of the employer) that are allocated to the participant's account on the effective date of the amendment and in which the participant would be able to receive a distribution immediately before the effective date of the amendment if a distributable event occurred. In addition, a plan amendment may provide that the participant's right to receive a distribution in the form of specified types of property is limited to the property allocated to the participant's account at the time of distribution that consists of property of those specified types. [Treas. Reg. § 1.411(d)-4, Q&A-2(b)(2)(iii)(B)] This rule applies to plan amendments that are adopted and effective on or after September 6, 2000. [Treas. Reg. § 1.411(d)-4, Q&A-2(b)(2)(iii)(B)]

In-Kind Distributions After Plan Termination. If a plan includes an optional form of benefit under which benefits are distributed in specified property, that optional form of benefit may be modified for distributions after plan termination by substituting cash for the specified property as the medium of distribution to the extent that, on plan termination, an employee has the opportunity to receive the optional form of benefit in the form of the specified property. This exception is not available, however, if the employer that maintains the terminating plan also maintains another plan that provides an optional form of benefit under which benefits are distributed in the specified property. [Treas. Reg. § 1.411(d)-4, Q&A-2(b)(2)(iii)(C)]

Example 10-25: The Hazel & Mack Company maintains a profit sharing plan under which participants may direct the investment of their accounts. One investment option available to participants is a fund invested in common stock of the employer. The plan provides that the participant has the right to a distribution in the form of cash upon termination of employment. In addition, the plan provides that, to the extent a participant's account is invested in the employer stock fund, he or she may receive an in-kind distribution of employer stock upon termination of employment. On October 18, 2019, the plan is amended, effective on January 1, 2020, to remove the fund invested in employer common stock as an investment option under the plan and to provide for the stock held in the fund to be sold. The amendment permits participants to elect how the sale proceeds are to be reallocated among the remaining investment options and provides for amounts not so reallocated as of January 1, 2020, to be allocated to a specified investment option.

The plan does not fail to satisfy Code Section 411(d)(6) solely on account of the amendment eliminating the employer stock investment option, which is not a Section 411(d)(6) protected benefit. Moreover, because the plan did not provide for distributions of employer securities, except to the extent participants' accounts were invested in the employer stock fund, the plan is not required operationally to offer distributions of employer securities following the amendment. In addition, the plan would not fail to satisfy Code Section 411(d)(6) on account of a further plan amendment, effective after the plan has ceased to provide for an employer stock fund investment option (and participants' accounts have ceased to be invested in employer securities), to eliminate the right to a distribution in the form of employer stock. [Treas. Reg. § 1.411(d)-4, Q&A-2(b)(2)(iii)(D), Ex. 1]

Example 10-26: The Hazel & Mack Company maintains a profit sharing plan under which a participant, upon termination of employment, may elect to receive benefits in a single-sum distribution either in cash or in kind. The plan's investments are limited to a fund invested in employer stock, a fund invested in XYZ mutual funds (which are marketable securities), and a fund invested in shares of PQR limited partnership (which are not marketable securities).

The following alternative plan amendments would not cause the plan to fail to satisfy Code Section 411(d)(6):

1. A plan amendment that limits noncash distributions to a participant on termination of employment to a distribution of employer stock and shares of PQR limited partnership.
2. A plan amendment that limits noncash distributions to a participant on termination of employment to a distribution of employer stock and shares of PQR limited partnership that also provides that only participants with employer stock allocated to their accounts as of the effective date of the amendment have the right to distributions in the form of employer stock

and that only participants with shares of PQR limited partnership allocated to their accounts as of the effective date of the amendment have the right to distributions in the form of shares of PQR limited partnership. To comply with the plan amendment, the plan administrator retains a list of participants with employer stock allocated to their accounts as of the effective date of the amendment and a list of participants with shares of PQR limited partnership allocated to their accounts as of the effective date of the amendment.

3. A plan amendment that limits noncash distributions to a participant on termination of employment to a distribution of employer stock and shares of PQR limited partnership to the extent that those assets are allocated to the participant's account at the time of the distribution.
4. A plan amendment that limits noncash distributions to a participant on termination of employment to a distribution of employer stock and shares of PQR limited partnership. The amendment must also specify that only participants with employer stock allocated to their accounts as of the effective date of the amendment have the right to distributions in the form of employer stock. Further, only participants with shares of PQR limited partnership allocated to their accounts as of the effective date of the amendment have the right to distributions in the form of shares of PQR limited partnership. Distribution of that stock or those shares may be available only to the extent that those assets are allocated to those participants' accounts at the time of the distribution. To comply with the plan amendment, the plan administrator retains a list of participants with employer stock allocated to their accounts as of the effective date of the amendment and a list of participants with shares of PQR limited partnership allocated to their accounts as of the effective date of the amendment.

[Treas. Reg. § 1.411(d)-4; Q&A-2(b)(2)(iii)(D), Ex. 2]

Example 10-27: The Hazel & Mack Company maintains a stock bonus plan under which a participant, upon termination of employment, may elect to receive benefits as a single-sum distribution in employer stock. This is the only plan maintained by the employer under which distributions in employer stock are available. The employer decides to terminate the stock bonus plan. If the plan makes available a single-sum distribution in employer stock on plan termination, the plan will not fail to satisfy Code Section 411(d)(6) solely because the optional form of benefit providing a single-sum distribution in employer stock on termination of employment is modified to provide that such distribution is available only in cash. [Treas. Reg. § 1.411(d)-4, Q&A-2(b)(2)(iii)(D), Ex. 3]

Permitted Plan Amendments Affecting Alternative Forms of Payment Under Defined Contribution Plans. A defined contribution plan does not violate the requirements of Code Section 411(d)(6) merely because the plan is amended to eliminate or restrict the ability of a participant to receive payment of accrued benefits under a particular optional form of benefit for distributions with annuity starting dates after the date the amendment is adopted if, after the plan amendment is effective with respect to the participant, the alternative forms of payment available to the participant include payment in a single-sum distribution form that is otherwise identical to the optional form of benefit that is being eliminated or restricted. [Treas. Reg. § 1.411(d)-4, Q&A-2(e)(1)]

A single-sum distribution form is "otherwise identical" to an optional form of benefit that is eliminated or restricted only if it is identical in all respects to the eliminated or restricted optional form of benefit (or would be identical except that it provides greater rights to the participant), except for the timing of payments after commencement. For example, a single-sum distribution form is not otherwise identical to a specified installment form of benefit if the single-sum distribution form is not available for distribution on the date on which the installment form would have been available for commencement, if it is not available in the same medium of distribution as the installment form, or if it imposes any condition of eligibility that did not apply to the installment form. However, an otherwise identical distribution form need not retain rights or features of the optional form of benefit that is eliminated or restricted to the extent that those rights or features would not be protected from elimination or restriction under Code Section 411(d)(6). [Treas. Reg. § 1.411(d)-4, Q&A-2(e)(2)]

Example 10-28: Hazel is a participant in the Hazel & Mack Company Plan, a qualified calendar-year profit sharing plan that is invested in mutual funds. The distribution forms available to Hazel under the plan include a distribution of Hazel's vested account balance under the plan in the form of various annuity contracts, including a single life annuity and a joint and survivor annuity. The annuity payments under the annuity contract forms begin as of the first day of the month following Hazel's severance from employment (or as of the first day of any subsequent month, subject to the minimum distribution requirements of Code Section 401(a)(9)). Hazel has not previously elected payment of benefits in the form of a life annuity, and the plan is not a direct or indirect transferee of any plan that is a defined benefit plan or a defined contribution plan that is subject to the minimum funding requirements of Code Section 412. The plan provides that distributions on the death of a participant are made in accordance with Code Section 401(a)(11)(B)(iii)(I). On September 2, 2019, the plan is amended so that, effective for payments that begin on or after November 1, 2019, Hazel is no longer entitled to any distribution in the form of an annuity contract. However, after the amendment is effective, Hazel is entitled to receive a single-sum cash distribution of her vested account balance payable on the first day of the month following her severance from employment (or as of the first day of any subsequent month, subject to the minimum distribution requirements of Code Section 401(a)(9)).

The plan does not violate the requirements of Code Section 411(d)(6) (or Code Section 401(a)(11)) merely because, as of November 1, 2019, the plan amendment has eliminated Hazel's option to receive a distribution in any of the various annuity contract forms previously available. [Treas. Reg. § 1.411(d)-4, Q&A-2(e)(3), unnumbered Ex.]

Coordination with Diversification Requirement. A tax credit ESOP (as defined in Code Section 409(a)) or an ESOP (as defined in Code Section 4975(e)(7)) may be amended to provide that a distribution is not available in employer securities to the extent that an employee elects to diversify benefits pursuant to Code Section 401(a)(28) (additional qualification requirements relating to ESOPs). [Treas. Reg. § 1.411(d)-4, Q&A-2(b)(2)(iv)] (See chapter 1.)

On April 19, 2013, the IRS issued Notice 2013-17, 2013-20 I.R.B. 1082, which provides relief from the anti-cutback rules for plan amendments that eliminate a Code Section 401(a)(28)(B)(ii)(1) distribution option from an ESOP that becomes subject to the diversification requirements of Code Section 401(a)(35), which apply to certain defined contribution plans that hold (or are treated as holding) publicly traded employer securities. Notice 2013-17 also addresses the circumstances in which an ESOP that satisfied the diversification requirements of Code Section 401(a)(28)(B)(i) by allowing a distribution of a portion of a participant's benefit has become subject to the diversification requirements of Code Section 401(a)(35). Because the ESOP became subject to Code Section 401(a)(35), Code Section 401(a)(28)(B) no longer applies, and such an ESOP is no longer able to make distributions that (in the absence of the applicability of Code Section 401(a)(28)(B)(i)) would be impermissible under other rules restricting the distribution of plan benefits before termination of employment or the occurrence of certain other events. Thus, under current rules for such plans, some in-service distribution options used to satisfy the diversification requirements under Code Section 401(a)(28)(B) are no longer permissible. The relief provided in Notice 2013-17 allows amendment of an ESOP to eliminate all in-service distribution options previously used to satisfy the diversification requirements of Code Section 401(a)(28)(B)(i). The relief applies to amendments that are both adopted and put into effect under a plan by the last day of the first plan year beginning on or after January 1, 2013, or by the time the plan must be amended to satisfy Code Section 401(a)(35), if later. In cases in which an ESOP has been timely amended to satisfy Code Section 401(a)(35) and the remedial amendment period with respect to that amendment expires before the ending date of Code Section 411(d)(6) relief, Notice 2013-17 also extends the remedial amendment period to the last day of the first plan year beginning on or after January 1, 2013 to permit the adoption of an amendment to the ESOP eliminating a distribution option described in Code Section 401(a)(28)(B)(ii)(1).

Involuntary Distributions. A plan may be amended to provide for the involuntary distribution of an employee's benefit to the extent that it is permitted under Code Sections 411(a)(11) and 417(e). For example, an involuntary distribution provision may be amended to require that an employee who terminates receives a single-sum distribution in the event that the present value of the employee's benefit is not more than $3,500, by substituting the cash-out limit in effect under Treasury Regulations Section 1.411(a)-11(c)(3)(ii) (i.e., $5,000) for $3,500, without violating the anti-cutback rules of Code Section 411(d)(6). In addition, for example, the employer may amend the plan to reduce the involuntary distribution threshold from the cash-out limit in effect under Treasury Regulations Section 1.411(a)-11(c)(3)(ii) to any lower amount or to eliminate the involuntary single-sum option for employees with benefits between the cash-out limit in effect under Treasury Regulations Section 1.411(a)-11(c)(3)(ii) and the lower amount without violating the anti-cutback rules. This rule does not permit a plan provision permitting employer discretion on optional forms of benefit for employees the present value of whose benefit is less than the cash-out limit in effect under Treasury Regulations Section 1.411(a)-11(c)(3)(ii). [Treas. Reg. § 1.411(d)-4, Q&A-2(b)(2)(v)]

Distribution Exception for Certain Profit Sharing Plans. Generally, if a defined contribution plan that is not subject to the minimum funding requirements of Code Section 412 (for example, a profit sharing or stock bonus plan) and does not provide for an annuity option is terminated, the plan may be amended to provide for the distribution of a participant's accrued benefit upon termination in a single sum without the participant's consent. This rule does not apply, however, if the employer maintains any other defined contribution plan (other than an ESOP).

Example 10-29: The Bear Flag Restaurant Corporation maintains a defined contribution plan that is not subject to the minimum funding requirements of Code Section 412. The plan provides for distribution in the form of equal installments over five years or equal installments over 20 years. The corporation maintains no other defined contribution plans. The corporation terminates its defined contribution plan after amending it to provide for the distribution of all participants' accrued benefits in the form of single-sum distributions, without first obtaining the participants' consent. Because of the rule described above, this plan amendment does not violate the anti-cutback requirements of Code Section 411(d)(6). [Treas. Reg. § 1.411(d)-4, Q&A-2(b)(2)(vi)(B), Ex. 1]

Example 10-30: Western Biological Laboratory Corporation and Monterey Peninsula Corporation are members of a controlled group of corporations. Both corporations maintain defined contribution plans. Western Biological's plan, that is *not* subject to the minimum funding requirements of Code Section 412, covers only employees working for Western Biological. Monterey Peninsula's plan, which *is* subject to the minimum funding requirements of Code Section 412, covers only employees who work for Monterey Peninsula. Western Biological terminates its defined contribution plan. Because the controlled group of corporations maintains another defined contribution plan, Western Biological's plan may *not* distribute participants' accrued benefits upon termination without participants' consent. [Treas. Reg. § 1.411(d)-4, Q&A-2(b)(2)(vi)(B), Ex. 2]

Distribution of Benefits on Default of Loans. Despite the fact that the distribution of benefits caused by an execution on an account balance securing a plan loan on which there has been a default is an optional form of benefit under the nondiscrimination rules of Section 401(a)(4), a plan may be amended to eliminate or change a plan's loan provisions, even if loans would be secured by an employee's account balance under the plan (see chapter 2). [Treas. Reg. § 1.411(d)-4, Q&A-2(b)(2)(vii)]

Provision for Transfer of Benefits Between and Among Defined Contribution Plans and Defined Benefit Plans. A plan may be amended to eliminate provisions permitting the transfer of benefits between and among the employer's defined contribution plans and defined benefit plans. [Treas. Reg. § 1.411(d)-4, Q&A-2(b)(2)(viii)]

De Minimis *Change in the Timing of an Optional Form of Benefit.* A plan may be amended to modify an optional form of benefit by changing the timing of its availability if, after the change, it is available within two months of the time it was available before the amendment. To the extent the optional form of benefit is available before termination of employment, six months may be substituted for two months in the preceding sentence. For example, a plan that makes in-service distributions available to employees once every month may be amended to make those in-service distributions available only once every six months. This exception to the anti-cutback rules under Code Section 411(d)(6) relates only to the timing of the availability of the optional form of benefit. Other aspects of an optional form of benefit may *not* be modified and the value of that optional form may not be reduced merely because of an amendment permitted by this exception. [Treas. Reg. § 1.411(d)-4, Q&A-2(b)(2)(ix)]

Amendment of Hardship Distribution Standards. A 401(k) plan that permits hardship distributions may be amended to specify or modify nondiscriminatory and objective standards for determining the existence of an immediate and heavy financial need, or other conditions relating to eligibility to receive a hardship distribution. For example, a plan will not be treated as having violated the anti-cutback rules of Code Section 411(d)(6) merely because it is amended to specify or modify the resources that an employee must exhaust to qualify for a hardship distribution, or to require employees to provide additional statements or representations to establish the existence of a hardship. A 401(k) plan may also be amended to eliminate hardship distributions. These rules also apply to profit sharing or stock bonus plans that permit hardship distributions, whether or not the hardship distributions are limited to the safe harbor hardship events described in Treasury Regulations Section 1.401(k)-1(d)(3). [Treas. Reg. § 1.411(d)-4, Q&A-2(b)(2)(x)]

Section 415 Benefit Limitations. Accrued benefits that exceed the benefit limitations under Code Section 415(b) effective on the first day of the plan's first limitation year beginning after December 31, 1986, because of a change in the terms and conditions of the plan made after May 5, 1986, or the establishment of a plan after that date, may be reduced to the level permitted under Code Section 415, without violating the anti-cutback rules of Code Section 411(d)(6). [Treas. Reg. § 1.411(d)-4, Q&A-2(b)(2)(xi)]

Amendment of Single-Employer Defined Benefit Plans to Eliminate a Single-Sum Distribution Option (or Other Accelerated Payment Option) If the Plan Sponsor Is in Bankruptcy. A single-employer defined benefit plan may be amended, effective for a plan amendment that is both adopted and effective after November 8, 2012, to eliminate an optional form of benefit that includes a prohibited payment described in Code Section 436(d)(5), provided the following conditions are satisfied on the applicable amendment date (as defined in Treasury Regulations Section 1.411(d)-3(g)(4)):

1. The plan's enrolled actuary has certified that the plan's adjusted funding target attainment percentage (as defined in Code Section 436(j)(2)) for the plan year that contains the applicable amendment date is less than 100 percent;

2. The plan is not permitted to pay any prohibited payment, due to the application of Code Section 436(d)(2) and ERISA Section 206(g)(3)(B), because the plan sponsor is a debtor in a bankruptcy case (that is, a case under Title 11, United States Code, or under similar federal or state law);
3. The court overseeing the bankruptcy has issued an order, after notice to the affected parties (as defined in ERISA Section 4001(a)(21)) and a hearing, within the meaning of 11 U.S.C. 102(1), finding that the adoption of the amendment eliminating that optional form of benefit is necessary to avoid a distress termination of the plan pursuant to ERISA Section 4041(c) or an involuntary termination of the plan pursuant to ERISA Section 4042 before the plan sponsor emerges from bankruptcy (or before the bankruptcy case is otherwise completed); and
4. The Pension Benefit Guaranty Corporation (PBGC) has issued a determination that:
   a. The adoption of the amendment eliminating that optional form of benefit is necessary to avoid a distress or involuntary termination of the plan before the plan sponsor emerges from bankruptcy (or before the bankruptcy case is otherwise completed); and
   b. The plan is not sufficient for guaranteed benefits within the meaning of ERISA Section 4041(d)(2). [Treas. Reg. § 1.411(d)-4, Q&A-2(b)(2)(xii)]

Q 10:31 How are multiple plan amendments that modify optional forms of benefit evaluated under the Section 411(d)(6) protected benefit rules?

A plan amendment violates the requirements of Code Section 411(d)(6) if it is one of a series of plan amendments that, when taken together, have the effect of reducing or eliminating a Section 411(d)(6) protected benefit in a manner that would be prohibited by Code Section 411(d)(6) if accomplished through a single amendment. [Treas. Reg. § 1.411(d)-4, Q&A-2(c)(1)]

For these purposes, generally, only plan amendments adopted within a three-year period are taken into account. But see Q 10:28 for rules relating to repeated plan amendments. [Treas. Reg. § 1.411(d)-4, Q&A-2(c)(2)]

Q 10:32 Are there special circumstances under which an ESOP or a stock bonus plan will not be treated as violating the anti-cutback rules of Code Section 411(d)(6)?

The answer to this question is, in general, yes. Subject to the limitations described below, a tax credit ESOP (as defined in Code Section 409(a)) or an ESOP (as defined in Code Section 4975(e)(7)) will not be treated as violating the anti-cutback rules merely because of any of the circumstances described in (1) through (4), below. In addition, a stock bonus plan that is not an ESOP will not be treated as violating the anti-cutback rules merely because of any of the circumstances described in (2) and (4), below.

1. Single-sum or installment optional forms of benefit.
   The employer eliminates, or retains the discretion to eliminate, with respect to all participants, a single-sum optional form or installment optional form with respect to benefits that are subject to Code Section 409(h)(1)(B) (regarding participants who are entitled to a distribution from the plan in the form of employer securities, and if those securities are not readily tradable on an established market, has a right to require that the employer repurchase the securities under a fair valuation formula). [Treas. Reg. § 1.411(d)-4, Q&A-2(d)(1)(i)]
2. Employer becomes substantially employee-owned or is an S corporation. In cases in which either:
   a. The employer becomes substantially employee-owned or
   b. For taxable years of the employer beginning after December 31, 1997, the employer is an S corporation (as defined in Code Section 1361)
3. Employer securities become readily tradable.
   In cases in which the employer securities become readily tradable, the employer eliminates (or retains the discretion to eliminate), for all participants, optional forms of benefit by substituting distributions in the form of employer securities for distributions in cash for benefits that are subject to Code Section 409(h). [Treas. Reg. § 1.411(d)-4, Q&A-2(d)(1)(iii)]
4. Employer securities cease to be readily tradable or certain sales.
   The employer eliminates, or retains the discretion to eliminate, for all participants, optional forms of benefit by substituting cash distributions for distributions in the form of employer stock for benefits that are subject to Code Section 409(h) in the following circumstances—
   a. The employer stock ceases to be readily tradable; or
   b. The employer stock continues to be readily tradable, but there is a sale of substantially all of the stock of the employer or a sale of substantially all of the assets of a trade or business of the employer and, in either situation, the purchasing employer continues to maintain the plan.

In the situation described in (4), above, the employer may also substitute distributions in the purchasing employer's stock for distributions in the form of employer stock of the predecessor employer. [Treas. Reg. § 1.411(d)-4, Q&A-2(d)(1)(iv)]

Q 10:33 Are there any limitations on the ESOP and stock bonus plan exceptions described in Q 10:32?

Yes, there are two basic limitations, although, as noted above, final Treasury Regulations have not yet been amended to reflect EGTRRA.

Nondiscrimination Requirement. Plan amendments and the retention and exercise of discretion permitted (see Q 10:32 (1)) must meet the nondiscrimination requirements of Code Section 401(a)(4). [Treas. Reg. § 1.411(d)-4, Q&A-2(d)(2)(i)]

ESOP Investment Requirement. Except as provided in Q 10:32 (3), benefits provided by ESOPs will not escape the application of the anti-cutback rules under Code Section 411(d)(6) unless the benefits have been held in a tax credit ESOP or an ESOP subject to Code Section 409(h) for the five-year period prior to the exercise of employer discretion or any amendment affecting those benefits. Under these rules, if benefits held by an ESOP are transferred to a plan that is an ESOP at the time of the transfer, then the consecutive periods under the transferor and transferee ESOPs may be aggregated for purposes of meeting the five-year requirement. If the benefits are held in an ESOP throughout the entire period of their existence, and that total period of existence is less than five years, then that lesser period may be substituted for the five-year requirement. [Treas. Reg. § 1.411(d)-4, Q&A-2(d)(2)(ii)]

Q 10:34 Does the transfer of benefits between and among defined benefit plans and defined contribution plans (or similar transactions) violate the anti-cutback rules of Code Section 411(d)(6)?

Section 411(d)(6) protected benefits may not be eliminated because of transfers. For example, an employer who maintains a money purchase pension plan that provides for a single-sum optional form of benefit may not establish another plan that does not provide this form of benefit and then transfer participants' account balances to the new plan. [Treas. Reg. § 1.411(d)-4, Q&A-3(a)(1)]

Defined Benefit Feature and Separate Account Feature. The defined benefit feature of a defined benefit plan and the separate account feature of a defined contribution plan are Section 411(d)(6) protected benefits. For example, the elimination of an employee's benefit under a defined benefit plan through transfer of benefits to a defined contribution plan will violate the anti-cutback rules of Code Section 411(d)(6). [Treas. Reg. § 1.411(d)-4, Q&A-3(a)(3)]

Waiver Prohibition. In general, a participant may not elect to waive Section 411(d)(6) protected benefits. There are some exceptions under the rules that apply to elective transfers of benefits between defined contribution plans (see below). However, eliminating the defined benefit feature of a defined benefit plan by transferring such benefits to a defined contribution plan at a time when the benefit is not distributable to the participant violates Code Section 411(d)(6). [Treas. Reg. § 1.411(d)-4, Q&A-3(a)(3)]

Direct Rollovers. A direct rollover described in Treasury Regulations Section 1.401(a)(31)-1, Q&A-3, that is paid to a qualified plan is not a transfer of assets and liabilities that must satisfy the Section 414(l) requirements. It is not a transfer of benefits for purposes of applying the anti-cutback requirements under Code Section 411(d)(6) and Treasury Regulations Section 1.411(d)-4, Q&A-3(a)(1), which provide that protected benefits may not be eliminated because of transfers. Therefore, if such a direct rollover is made to another qualified plan, the receiving plan is not required to provide the same optional forms of benefit as the plan that made the direct rollover. [Treas. Reg. § 1.411(d)-4, Q&A-3(a)(4); see Treas. Reg. § 1.401(a)(31)-1, Q&A-14]

Elective Transfers of Benefits Between Defined Contribution Plans. A transfer of a participant's entire benefit between qualified defined contribution plans (other than any direct rollover as described in Treasury Regulations Section 1.401(a)(31)-1, Q&A-3) that results in the elimination or reduction of protected benefits does not violate Code Section 411(d)(6) if the following requirements are met:

1. *Voluntary Election.* The plan from which the benefits are transferred must verify that the transfer is a voluntary, fully informed election by the participant to transfer the participant's entire benefit to the other qualified defined contribution plan. As an alternative to the transfer, the participant must be offered the opportunity to retain his or her Section 411(d)(6) protected benefits under the plan (or, if the plan is terminating, to receive any optional form of benefit for which the participant is eligible under the plan as required by Code Section 411(d)(6)). [Treas. Reg. § 1.411(d)-4, Q&A-3(b)(1)(i)]
2. *Types of Plans to Which Transfers May Be Made.* If benefits are transferred from a money purchase pension plan, the receiving plan must be a money purchase pension plan. If the benefits being transferred are part of a qualified cash or deferred arrangement under Code Section 401(k), they must be transferred to a qualified cash or deferred arrangement under Code Section 401(k). If the benefits being transferred are part of an ESOP as defined in Code Section 4975(e)(7), they must be transferred to another ESOP. Benefits transferred from a profit sharing plan other than from a qualified cash or deferred arrangement, or from a stock bonus plan other than an ESOP, may be transferred to any type of defined contribution plan. [Treas. Reg. § 1.411(d)-4, Q&A-3(b)(1)(ii)]
3. *Circumstances Under Which Transfers May Be Made.* Transfers must be made either in connection with an asset or stock acquisition, merger, or other similar transaction involving a change in employer of the employees of a trade or business (i.e., an acquisition or disposition within the meaning of Treasury Regulations Section 1.410(b)-2(f)) or in connection with the participant's change in employment status resulting in loss of entitlement to additional allocations under the transferor plan. Such transfers are often referred to as "transaction transfers" and "employment change transfers," respectively. [Treas. Reg. § 1.411(d)-4, Q&A-3(b)(1)(iii)]

Applicable Qualification Requirements. An elective transfer of benefits between defined contribution plans is a transfer of assets or liabilities within the meaning of Code Section 414(l)(1) and must satisfy the requirements of Code Section 414(l). In addition, Treasury Regulations Section 1.411(d)-4, Q&A-3(b) only provides relief under Code Section 411(d)(6); an elective transfer of benefits between defined contribution plans must satisfy all other applicable qualification requirements. Thus, if the survivor annuity requirements of Code Sections 401(a)(11) and 417 apply to the plan from which the benefits are transferred, but do not otherwise apply to the receiving plan, those requirements must be met with respect to the transferred benefits under the receiving plan. In addition, the vesting provisions under the receiving plan must satisfy the requirements of Code Section 411(a)(10) with respect to the amounts transferred. [Treas. Reg. § 1.411(d)-4, Q&A-3(b)(2)]

Status of Elective Transfer as Other Right or Feature. A right to a transfer of benefits from a plan pursuant to the elective transfer rules is an *other right or feature* within the meaning of Treasury Regulations Section 1.401(a)(4)-4(e)(3), the availability of which is subject to the nondiscrimination requirements of Code Section 401(a)(4) and Treasury Regulations Section 1.401(a)(4)-4. However, for purposes of applying those rules, the following conditions are to be disregarded in determining the employees to whom the other right or feature is available:

1. A condition restricting the availability of the transfer to benefits of participants who are transferred to a different employer in connection with a specified asset or stock disposition, merger, or other similar transaction involving a change in employer of the employees of a trade or business (i.e., a disposition within the meaning of Treasury Regulations Section 1.410(b)-2(f)) or in connection with any such disposition, merger, or other similar transaction. [Treas. Reg. § 1.411(d)-4, Q&A-3(b)(3)(i)]
2. A condition restricting the availability of the transfer to benefits of participants who have a change in employment status resulting in loss of entitlement to additional allocations under the transferor plan. [Treas. Reg. § 1.411(d)-4, Q&A-3(b)(3)(ii)]

Elective Transfers of Certain Distributable Benefits Between Qualified Plans. A transfer of a participant's benefits between qualified plans that results in the elimination or reduction of Section 411(d)(6) protected benefits does not violate Code Section 411(d)(6) if it meets all of the following requirements (such a transfer is often referred to as a "distributable event transfer"):

1. The transfer occurs when the participant's benefits are distributable;
2. The transfer occurs when the participant is not eligible to receive an immediate distribution of his or her entire nonforfeitable accrued benefit in a single-sum distribution that would consist entirely of an eligible rollover distribution within the meaning of Code Section 401(a)(31)(C) (for transfers that occur on or after January 1, 2002);
3. The voluntary election requirements described above are met;
4. The participant is fully vested in the transferred benefit in the transferee plan;
5. In the case of a transfer from a defined contribution plan to a defined benefit plan, the defined benefit plan provides a minimum benefit for each participant whose benefits are transferred, equal to the benefit and expressed as an annuity payable at normal retirement age, that is derived solely on the basis of the amount transferred with respect to such participant; and
6. The amount of the benefit transferred, together with the amount of any contemporaneous Section 401(a)(31) direct rollover to the transferee plan, equals the entire nonforfeitable accrued benefit under the transferor plan

of the participant whose benefit is being transferred, calculated to be at least the greater of the single-sum distribution provided for under the plan for which the participant is eligible (if any) or the present value of the participant's accrued benefit payable at normal retirement age (calculated by using interest and mortality assumptions that satisfy the requirements of Code Section 417(e) and subject to the limitations imposed by Code Section 415).

[Treas. Reg. § 1.411(d)-4, Q&A-3(c)(i)-(vi)]

A transfer of benefits under the elective transfer rules generally is treated as a distribution for purposes of Code Section 401(a). For example, the transfer is subject to the cash-out rules of Code Section 411(a)(7), the early termination requirements of Code Section 411(d)(2), and the survivor annuity requirements of Code Sections 401(a)(11) and 417. A transfer pursuant to such elective transfer rules is not treated as a distribution for purposes of the minimum distribution requirements of Code Section 401(a)(9). [Treas. Reg. § 1.411(d)-4, Q&A-3(c)(2)(i)]

A right to a transfer of benefits from a plan pursuant to Treasury Regulations Section 1.411(d)-4, Q&A-3(c), is an optional form of benefit under Code Section 411(d)(6), the availability of which is subject to the nondiscrimination requirements of Code Section 401(a)(4) and Treasury Regulations Section 1.401(a)(4)-4. [Treas. Reg. § 1.411(d)-4, Q&A-3(C)(3)(ii)]

For purposes of the general rule described above, a participant's benefits are distributable on a particular date if, on that date, the participant is eligible, under the terms of the plan from which the benefits are transferred, to receive an immediate distribution of these benefits (e.g., in the form of an immediately commencing annuity) from that plan under provisions of the plan not inconsistent with Code Section 401(a). [Treas. Reg. § 1.411(d)-4, Q&A-3(c)(3)]

Q 10:35 May a plan provide that the employer may, at its discretion, deny a participant a Section 411(d)(6) protected benefit for which the participant is otherwise eligible?

Apart from exceptions that apply to certain ESOPs described in Q 10:29, a plan that permits the employer, either directly or indirectly, through the exercise of discretion, to deny a participant a Section 411(d)(6) protected benefit under the plan for which the participant is otherwise eligible (but for the employer's exercise of discretion) violates the anti-cutback rules of Code Section 411(d)(6). A plan provision that makes a Section 411(d)(6) protected benefit available only to those employees the employer may designate is also prohibited. For example, a plan provision under which only employees who are designated by the employer are eligible to receive a subsidized early retirement benefit constitutes an impermissible provision under Code Section 411(d)(6). In addition, a pension plan that permits employer discretion to deny the availability of a Section 411(d)(6) protected benefit violates the definitely determinable requirement of Code Section 401(a), including Code Section 401(a)(25) (regarding the requirement that actuarial assumptions be specified). This is the result even if the plan specifically limits the employer's discretion to choose among Section 411(d)(6) protected benefits, including optional forms of benefit, that are actuarially equivalent. However, the provisions of Code Sections 411(a)(11) and 417(e) that allow a plan to make involuntary distributions of certain amounts are excepted from this limitation on employer discretion. For example, a plan may not permit employer discretion on whether benefits will be distributed involuntarily in the event that the present value of the employee's benefit is not more than $5,000 within the meaning of Code Sections 411(a)(11) and 417(e). [Treas. Reg. § 1.411(d)-4, Q&A-4(a)] TRA'97 increased the limit on involuntary cash-outs from $3,500 to $5,000, effective for plan years beginning after August 5, 1997, TRA'97's enactment date.

Exception for Administrative Discretion. A plan may permit limited discretion in the ministerial or mechanical administration of the plan, including the application of objective plan criteria specifically set forth in the plan. Such plan provisions do not violate the anti-cutback rules of Code Section 411(d)(6) or the definitely determinable requirement of Code Section 401(a), including the requirement that actuarial assumptions be specified. [I.R.C. § 401(a)(25)] For example, these requirements are not violated by the following provisions that permit limited administrative discretion:

1. Commencement of benefit payments as soon as administratively feasible after a stated date or event;
2. Employer authority to determine whether objective criteria specified in the plan (for example, to identify employees with a heavy and immediate financial need or to determine whether an employee has a permanent and total disability) have been satisfied; and
3. Specific guidelines set forth in the plan giving the employer authority to determine whether the participant or spouse is dead or cannot be located.

[Treas. Reg. § 1.411(d)-4, Q&A-4]

Q 10:36 When will the exercise of discretion by someone other than the employer be treated as employer discretion?

For purposes of applying Code Section 411(d)(6)'s anti-cutback rules and the nondiscrimination rules under Code Section 401(a)(4), the term employer includes plan administrator, fiduciary, trustee, actuary, independent third party, and other persons. If the plan permits any person, other than the participant (or the participant's spouse), the discretion to deny or limit the availability of a Section 411(d)(6) protected benefit for which the employee is otherwise eligible under the plan (but for the exercise of such discretion), that plan violates the requirements of Code Section 401(a), including the anti-cutback rules of Code Section 411(d)(6) and, where applicable, the definitely determinable requirement of Code Section 401(a), including Code Section 401(a)(25) (regarding the requirement that actuarial assumptions be specified). [Treas. Reg. § 1.411(d)-4, Q&A-5]

Q 10:37 May a plan condition the availability of a Section 411(d)(6) protected benefit on the satisfaction of objective conditions specifically set forth in the plan?

Certain Objective Conditions Permissible. The availability of a Section 411(d)(6) protected benefit may be limited to employees who satisfy certain objective conditions, provided the conditions are ascertainable, clearly set forth in the plan, and not subject to the employer's discretion except to the extent reasonably necessary to determine whether they have been met. Also, the availability of the Section 411(d)(6) protected benefit must meet the nondiscrimination requirements of Code Section 401(a)(4) (see Qs 10:1–10:24). [Treas. Reg. § 1.411(d)-4, Q&A-6(a)(1)]

The following are examples of permissible conditions that may be imposed upon the availability of Section 411(d)(6) protected benefits:

- A plan may deny a single-sum distribution form to employees for whom life insurance is not available at standard rates as defined under the terms of the plan at the time the single-sum distribution would otherwise have been payable.
- A plan may provide that a single-sum distribution is available only if the employee is in extreme financial need as defined under the terms of the plan at the time the distribution would otherwise be payable.
- A plan may condition the availability of a single-sum distribution on the execution of a covenant not to compete, provided that objective conditions of the terms of such covenant and the employees and circumstances requiring execution of such covenant are set forth in the plan.

[Treas. Reg. § 1.411(d)-4, Q&A-6(a)(2)]

Conditions Based on Factors Within the Employer's Discretion Are Generally Impermissible. A plan may not limit the availability of Section 411(d)(6) protected benefits on objective conditions that are within the employer's discretion. For example, the availability of Section 411(d)(6) protected benefits in a plan may not be conditioned on a determination of the level of the plan's funded status, because the amount of plan funding is within the employer's discretion. However, a plan may limit the availability of a Section 411(d)(6) protected benefit (for example, a single-sum distribution) in an objective manner, such as:

1. Single-sum distributions of $25,000 and less are available without limit;
2. Single-sum distributions in excess of $25,000 are available for a year only if the total amount of such distributions for the year is not greater than $5 million; and
3. An objective and nondiscriminatory method for determining which particular single-sum distributions will not be available during a year in order for the $5 million limit to be satisfied is set forth in the plan.

[Treas. Reg. § 1.411(d)-4, Q&A-6(b)]

Q 10:38 May a plan be amended to add employer discretion or conditions restricting the availability of a Section 411(d)(6) protected benefit?

No. The addition of employer discretion or objective conditions for a Section 411(d)(6) protected benefit that has already accrued violates the anti-cutback rules of Code Section 411(d)(6). Also, the addition of conditions (whether or not objective) or any change to existing conditions of Section 411(d)(6) protected benefits that results in any further restriction violates Code Section 411(d)(6). However, the addition of objective conditions to a Section 411(d)(6) protected benefit may be made for benefits accrued after the later of the adoption or effective date of the amendment. In addition, objective conditions may be imposed on Section 411(d)(6) protected benefits accrued as of the date of an amendment where permitted under the transitional rules under the nondiscrimination regulations under Code Section 401(a)(4) and the transitional rules under Treasury Regulations Section 1.411(d)-4, Q&A-8. Finally, objective conditions may be imposed on Section 411(d)(6) protected benefits to the extent permitted by the permissible benefit cutback provisions of Treasury Regulations Section 1.411(d)-4, Q&A-2, described in Q 10:26. [Treas. Reg. § 1.411(d)-4, Q&A-7]

Reduction or Elimination of Early Retirement Benefits, Retirement-Type Subsidies, and Optional Forms of Benefit

Q 10:39 May a participant's accrued benefit be decreased by a plan amendment?

Generally, no. Code Section 411(d)(6) generally prohibits any decrease in a participant's accrued benefit by means of a plan amendment. Code Section 411(d)(6)(B) generally prohibits the elimination or reduction of an early retirement benefit or a retirement-type subsidy or the elimination of an optional form of benefit, but, as amended by EGTRRA, allows the IRS to issue regulations permitting plan amendments that reduce or eliminate benefits or subsidies that create significant burdens or complexities for the plan and plan participants.

Protection of Code Section 411(d)(6)(A) Accrued Benefits

1. *General Rule.* Under Code Section 411(d)(6)(A), a plan is not a qualified plan (and a trust forming a part of such plan is not a qualified trust) if a plan amendment decreases the accrued benefit of any plan participant, except as provided in Code Section 412(c)(8), ERISA Section 4281, or other applicable law. For these purposes, a plan amendment includes any changes to the terms of a plan, including changes resulting from a merger, consolidation, or transfer (as defined in Code Section 414(l)) or a plan termination. The protection of Code Section 411(d)(6) applies to a participant's entire accrued benefit under the plan as of the applicable amendment date, without regard to whether the entire accrued benefit was accrued before a participant's severance from employment or whether any portion was the result of an increase in the accrued benefit of the

participant pursuant to a plan amendment adopted after the participant's severance from employment. [Treas. Reg. § 1.411(d)-3(a)(1)]

2. *Plan Provisions Taken into Account*

   a. *Direct or Indirect Reduction in Accrued Benefit.* For purposes of determining whether a participant's accrued benefit is decreased, all of the amendments to the provisions of a plan affecting, directly or indirectly, the computation of accrued benefits are taken into account. Plan provisions indirectly affecting the computation of accrued benefits include, for example, provisions relating to years of service and compensation. [Treas. Reg. § 1.411(d)-3(a)(2)(i)]

   b. *Amendments Effective with the Same Applicable Amendment Date.* In determining whether a reduction in a participant's accrued benefit has occurred, all plan amendments with the same applicable amendment date are treated as one amendment. Thus, if two amendments have the same applicable amendment date and one amendment, standing alone, increases participants' accrued benefits and the other amendment, standing alone, decreases participants' accrued benefits, the amendments are treated as one amendment and will only violate Code Section 411(d)(6) if, for any participant, the net effect is to decrease participants' accrued benefit as of that applicable amendment date. [Treas. Reg. § 1.411(d)-3(a)(2)(ii)]

   c. *Multiple Amendments.* In general, a plan amendment violates the requirements of Code Section 411(d)(6) if it is one of a series of plan amendments that, when taken together, has the effect of reducing or eliminating a Code Section 411(d)(6) protected benefit in a manner that would be prohibited by Code Section 411(d)(6) if accomplished through a single amendment. For purposes of applying this rule, generally only plan amendments adopted within a three-year period are taken into account. [Treas. Reg. § 1.411(d)-3(a)(2)(iii)]

   The term *Section 411(d)(6) protected benefit* means the accrued benefit of a participant as of the applicable amendment date described in Code Section 411(d)(6)(A) and any Code Section 411(d)(6)(B) protected benefit. [Treas. Reg. § 1.411(d)-3(g)(14)] The term *applicable amendment date*, with respect to a plan amendment, means the later of the effective date of the amendment or the date the amendment is adopted. [Treas. Reg. § 1.411(d)-3(g)(4)]

3. *Application of Code Section 411(a) Nonforfeitability Provisions with Respect to Code Section 411(d)(6) Protected Benefits*

   a. *In General.* The anti-cutback rules apply to a plan amendment that decreases a participant's accrued benefits or otherwise places greater restrictions or conditions on a participant's right to Code Section 411(d) protected benefits, even if the amendment merely adds a restriction or condition that is permitted under the vesting rules in Code Sections 411(a)(3) through (11). However, such an amendment does not violate Code Section 411(d)(6) to the extent that it applies with respect to benefits that accrue after the applicable amendment date. (Additional rules relating to changes in a plan's vesting schedule are found in Code Section 411(a)(10) and Treasury Regulations Section 1.411(a)-8. [Treas. Reg. § 1.411(d)-3(a)(3)(i)]

b. *Exception for Changes in a Plan's Vesting Computation Period.* Notwithstanding the rules discussed above, a plan amendment that satisfies the applicable requirements of DOL Regulations Section 2530.203-2(c) (i.e., rules relating to vesting computation periods) does not fail to satisfy the requirements of Code Section 411(d)(6) merely because the plan amendment changes the plan's vesting computation period. [Treas. Reg. § 1.411(d)-3(a)(3)(ii)]

4. *Examples.* The following examples illustrate the application of these rules:

Example 10-31: The Bear Flag Restaurant Corporation Plan provides an annual benefit of 2 percent of career average pay times years of service commencing at normal retirement age (age 65). The Plan is amended on November 1, 2019, effective as of January 1, 2020, to provide for an annual benefit of 1.3 percent of final pay times years of service, with final pay computed as the average of a participant's highest three consecutive years of compensation. As of January 1, 2020, participant Frank Battle has 16 years of service, his career average pay is $37,500, and the average of his highest three consecutive years of compensation is $67,308. Thus, Frank's accrued benefit as of the applicable amendment date is increased from $12,000 per year at normal retirement age (2 percent times $37,500 times 16 years of service) to $14,000 per year at normal retirement age (1.3 percent times $67,308 times 16 years of service). As of January 1, 2020, participant Fred Marullo has six years of service, his career average pay is $50,000, and the average of his highest three consecutive years of compensation is $51,282. Fred's accrued benefit as of the applicable amendment date is decreased from $6,000 per year at normal retirement age (2 percent times $50,000 times six years of service) to $4,000 per year at normal retirement age (1.3 percent times $51,282 times six years of service).

While the plan amendment increases Frank's accrued benefit, the plan amendment fails to satisfy the requirements of Code Section 411(d)(6)(A) because the amendment decreases Fred's accrued benefit below the level of his accrued benefit immediately before the applicable amendment date. [Treas. Reg. § 1.411(d)-3(a)(4), Ex. 1]

Example 10-32: The facts are the same as Example 10-31, except that the Plan includes a provision under which Fred's accrued benefit cannot be less than what it was immediately before the applicable amendment date (so that Fred's accrued benefit could not be less than $6,000 per year at normal retirement age).

The plan amendment does not violate the requirements of Code Section 411(d)(6)(A) with respect to Frank (whose accrued benefit has been increased) or with respect to Fred (although Fred would not accrue any benefits until the point in time at which the new formula amount would exceed the amount payable under the minimum provision, approximately three years after the amendment becomes effective). [Treas. Reg. § 1.411(d)-3(a)(4), Ex. 2]

Example 10-33: Marullo's Grocery Store maintains a qualified defined benefit plan under which an employee becomes a participant upon completion of one year of service and is vested in 100 percent of the employer-derived accrued benefit upon completion of five years of service. The plan provides that a former employee's years of service prior to a break in service will be reinstated upon completion of one year of service after being rehired. The plan has participants who have fewer than five years of service and who are accordingly zero percent vested in their employer-derived accrued benefits. On December 31, 2019, effective January 1, 2020, the plan is amended, in accordance with Code Section 411(a)(6)(D), to provide that any nonvested participant who has at least five consecutive one-year breaks in service and whose number of consecutive one-year breaks in service exceeds his or her number of years of service before the break will have his or her pre-break service disregarded in determining vesting under the plan.

The plan amendment does not satisfy the requirements of Treasury Regulations Section 1.411(d)-3(a), and thus it violates the anti-cutback rules of Code Section 411(d)(6), because the amendment places greater restrictions or conditions on the rights to Code Section 411(d)(6) protected benefits, as of January 1, 2020, for participants who have fewer than five years of service, by restricting the ability of those participants to receive further vesting protections on benefits accrued as of that date. [Treas. Reg. § 1.411(d)-3(a)(4), Ex. 3]

Example 10-34: Under the Octavio Fish Market Profit Sharing Plan, each employee has a nonforfeitable right to a percentage of his or her employer-derived accrued benefit based on the following vesting schedule:

Completed Years of Service	*Vested Percentage*
Fewer than 3	0%
3	20%
4	40%
5	60%
6	80%
7	100%

In January 2019, Octavio's Fish Market acquires the Belair Company, which maintains the Belair Company Profit Sharing Plan, under which each employee who has completed five years of service has a nonforfeitable right to 100 percent of his or her employer-derived accrued benefit. In 2020, the Belair Company Profit Sharing Plan is merged into the Octavio Fish Market Profit Sharing Plan. On the effective date of the merger, the Octavio Fish Market Profit Sharing Plan is amended to provide that the vesting schedule for participants of the Belair Company Profit Sharing Plan is the seven-year graded vesting schedule of the Octavio Fish Market Profit Sharing Plan. In accordance with Code Section 411(a)(10)(A), the plan amendment provides that any participant of the Belair Company Profit Sharing Plan who had completed five years of service prior to the amendment is fully vested. In addition, as required under Code Section 411(a)(10)(B), the amendment provides that any participant in the Belair Company Profit Sharing Plan who has at least three years of service prior to the amendment is permitted to make an irrevocable election to have the vesting of his or her nonforfeitable right to his or her employer-derived accrued benefit determined under either the five-year cliff vesting schedule or the seven-year graded vesting schedule. Participant George, who has an account balance of $10,000 on the applicable amendment date, is a participant in the Belair Company Profit Sharing Plan with two years of service as of the applicable amendment date. As of the date of the plan merger, George's nonforfeitable right to his employer-derived accrued benefit is zero percent under both the seven-year graded vesting schedule of the Octavio Fish Market Profit Sharing Plan and the five-year cliff vesting schedule of the Belair Company Profit Sharing Plan.

The plan amendment does not satisfy Treasury Regulations Section 1.411(d)-3(a) and violates the anti-cutback rules of Code Section 411(d)(6), because the amendment places greater restrictions or conditions on the right to Code Section 411(d)(6) protected benefits with respect to George and any participant who has fewer than five years of service and who elected (or was made subject to) the new vesting schedule. A method of avoiding a Code Section 411(d)(6) violation with respect to account balances accrued as of the applicable amendment date and earning thereon would be for the Octavio Fish Market Profit Sharing Plan to provide for the vested percentage of George and each other participant in the Belair Company Profit Sharing Plan to be no less than the greater of the vesting percentages under the vesting schedule (for example, for George and each other participant in the Belair Company Profit Sharing Plan to be 20 percent vested upon the completion of three years of service, 40 percent upon completion of four years of service, and fully vested (100 percent) upon completion of five years of service) for those account balances and earning. [Treas. Reg. § 1.411(d)-3(a)(4), Ex. 4]

Protection of Code Section 411(d)(6)(B) Protected Benefits

1. *General Rule*

   a. *Prohibition Against Plan Amendments Eliminating or Reducing Code Section 411(d)(6)(B) Protected Benefits*. Except as otherwise provided in Treasury Regulations Section 1.411(d)-3, a plan is treated as decreasing an accrued benefit if it is amended to eliminate or reduce a Code Section 411(d)(6)(B) protected benefit. The term *Section 411(d)(6)(B) protected benefit* means the portion of an early retirement benefit, a retirement-type subsidy, or an optional form of benefit attributable to benefits accrued before the applicable amendment date. [Treas. Reg. § 1.411(d)-3(g)(15)] Code Section 411(d)(6)(B)'s protections apply to participants who satisfy (either before or after the plan amendment) the pre-amendment conditions for a Section 411(d)(6)(B) protected benefit. [Treas. Reg. § 1.411(d)-3(b)(1)(i)]

b. *Contingent Benefits*. The rules described immediately above apply to participants who satisfy (either before or after the plan amendment) the pre-amendment conditions for the Section 411(d)(6)(B) protected benefit even if the condition on which the eligibility for the Section 411(d)(6)(B) protected benefit depends is an unpredictable contingent event (e.g., a plant shutdown). [Treas. Reg. § 1.411(d)-3(b)(1)(ii)]

c. *Application of General Rules to Section 411(d)(6)(B) Protected Benefits*. For purposes of determining whether a participant's Section 411(d)(6)(B) protected benefit is eliminated or reduced, the general rules protecting Section 411(d)(6) protected benefits apply to Section 411(d)(6)(B) protected benefits in the same manner as they apply to accrued benefits described in Code Section 411(d)(6)(A). For example, if there are two amendments with the same applicable amendment date and one amendment increases accrued benefits and the other amendment decreases the early retirement factors that are used to determine the early retirement annuity, the amendments are treated as one amendment and only violate Code Section 411(d)(6) if, after the two amendments, the net dollar amount of any early retirement annuity with respect to the accrued benefit of any participant as of the applicable amendment date is lower than it would have been without the two amendments. By way of further example, a series of amendments made within a three-year period that, when taken together, has the effect of reducing or eliminating early retirement benefits or retirement-type subsidies in a manner that adversely affects the rights of any participant in a more than *de minimis* manner violates Code Section 411(d)(6)(B) even if each amendment would otherwise be permissible. [Treas. Reg. § 1.411(d)-3(b)(1)(iii)]

2. *Permissible Elimination of Section 411(d)(6)(B) Protected Benefits*

The term *optional form of benefit*, in general, means a distribution alternative (including the normal form of benefit) that is available under the plan with respect to an accrued benefit or a distribution alternative with respect to a retirement-type benefit. Different optional forms of benefit exist if a distribution alternative is not payable on substantially the same terms as another distribution alternative. The relevant terms include all terms affecting the value of the optional form, such as the method of benefit calculation and the actuarial factors or assumptions used to determine the amount distributed. Thus, for example, different optional forms of benefit may result from differences in terms relating to the payment schedule, timing, commencement, medium of distribution (e.g., in cash or in kind), election rights, differences in eligibility requirements, or the portion of the benefit to which the distribution alternative applies. Likewise, differences in the normal retirement ages of employees or in the form in which the accrued benefit of employees is payable at normal retirement age under a plan are taken into account in determining whether a distribution alternative constitutes one or more optional forms of benefit. [Treas. Reg. § 1.411(d)-3(g)(6)(ii)(A)]

If a death benefit is payable after the annuity starting date for a specific optional form of benefit and the same death benefit would not be provided if another optional form of benefit were elected by a participant, then that death benefit is part of the specific optional form of benefit and is thus protected under Code Section 411(d)(6). A death benefit is not treated as part of a specific optional form of benefit merely because the same benefit is not provided to a participant who has received his or her entire accrued benefit prior to death. For example, a $5,000 death benefit that is payable to all participants except any participant who has received his or her accrued benefit in a single-sum distribution is not part of a specific optional form of benefit. [Treas. Reg. § 1.411(d)-3(g)(6)(ii)(B)] The term *retirement-type benefit* means (1) the payment of a distribution alternative with respect to an accrued benefit or (2) the payment of any other benefit under a defined benefit plan (including a QSUPP as defined in Treasury Regulation Section 1.401(a)(4)-12) that is permitted to be in a qualified pension plan, continues after retirement, and is not an ancillary benefit. [Treas. Reg. § 1.411(d)-3(g)(6)(iii)]

a. *In General.* A plan is permitted to be amended to eliminate a Section 411(d)(6)(B) protected benefit if the elimination is in accordance with Treasury Regulations Section 411(d)-3 or Section 1.411(d)-4. [Treas. Reg. § 1.411(d)-3(b)(2)]

b. *Increases in Payment Amounts Do Not Eliminate an Optional Form of Benefit.* An amendment is not treated as eliminating an optional form of benefit or eliminating or reducing an early retirement benefit or retirement-type subsidy under the plan, if, effective after the plan amendment, there is another optional form of benefit available to the participant under the plan that is of inherently equal or greater value (within the meaning of Treasury Regulations Section 1.401(a)(4)-4(d)(4)(i)(A)). Thus, for example, a change in the method of calculating a joint and survivor annuity from using a 90 percent adjustment factor on account of the survivorship payment at particular ages for a participant and a spouse to using a 91 percent adjustment factor at the same ages is not treated as an elimination of an optional form of benefit. Similarly, a plan that offers a subsidized qualified joint and survivor annuity option for married participants under which the amount payable during the participant's lifetime is not less than the amount payable under the plan's straight life annuity is permitted to be amended to eliminate the straight life annuity option for married participants. [Treas. Reg. § 1.411(d)-3(b)(2)(ii)]

3. *Permissible Elimination of Benefits That Are Not Section 411(d)(6) Protected Benefits*

a. *In General.* Code Section 411(d)(6) does not provide protection for benefits that are ancillary benefits, other rights and features, or any other benefits that are not described in Code Section 411(d)(6). (See Treasury Regulation Section 1.411(d)-4, Q&A-1(d).) However, a plan may not be amended to recharacterize a retirement-type benefit as an ancillary benefit. Thus, for example, a plan amendment to recharacterize any portion of an early retirement subsidy as a social security supplement that is an ancillary benefit violates Code Section 411(d)(6). [Treas. Reg. § 1.411(d)-3(b)(3)(i)] The term *ancillary benefit* means: [Treas. Reg. § 1.411(d)-3(g)(2)]

b. A social security supplement under a defined benefit plan (other than a QSUPP as defined in Treasury Regulation Section 1.401(a)(4)-12)

c. A benefit payable under a defined benefit plan in the event of disability (to the extent that the benefit exceeds the benefit otherwise payable), but only if the total benefit payable in the event of disability does not exceed the maximum qualified disability benefit, as defined in Code Section 411(a)(9)

d. A life insurance benefit

e. A medical benefit described in Code Section 401(h)

f. A death benefit under a defined benefit plan other than a death benefit that is a part of an optional form of benefit, or

g. A plant shutdown benefit or other similar benefit in a defined benefit plan that does not continue past retirement age and does not affect the payment of the accrued benefit, but only to the extent that such plant shutdown benefit, or other similar benefit (if any), is permitted in a qualified pension plan (see Treasury Regulation Section 1.401-1(b)(1)(i))

h. *No Protection for Future Benefit Accruals*. Code Section 411(d)(6) protects only benefits that accrue before the applicable amendment date. Thus, a plan is permitted to be amended to eliminate or reduce an early retirement benefit, a retirement-type subsidy, or an optional form of benefit with respect to benefits that accrue after the applicable amendment date without violating Code Section 411(d)(6). However, Code Section 4980F(e) and ERISA Section 204(h) require notice of an amendment to an applicable pension plan that either provides for a significant reduction in the rate of future benefit accrual or that eliminates or significantly reduces an early retirement benefit or a retirement-type subsidy. (See Treasury Regulation Section 54.4980F-1.) [Treas. Reg. § 1.411(d)-3(b)(3)(ii)]

4. *Examples*. The following examples illustrate the application of these rules:

Example 10-35: *Facts Involving Amendments to an Early Retirement Subsidy*. The Western Biological Laboratory Corporation Plan provides an annual benefit of 2 percent of career average pay times years of service commencing at normal retirement age (age 65). The Plan is amended on November 1, 2019, effective as of January 1, 2020, to provide for an annual benefit of 1.3 percent of final pay times years of service, with final pay computed as the average of a participant's highest three consecutive years of compensation. Participant Frank Battle is age 50, he has 16 years of service, his career average pay is $37,500, and the average of his highest three consecutive years of compensation is $67,308. Thus, Frank's accrued benefit as of the effective date of the amendment is increased from $12,000 per year at normal retirement age (2 percent times $37,500 times 16 years of service) to $14,000 per year at normal retirement age (1.3 percent times $67,308 times 16 years of service). (These facts are similar to the facts in Example 10-31.) Before the amendment, the Plan permitted a former employee to commence distribution of benefits as early as age 55 and, for a participant with at least 15 years of service, actuarially reduced the amount payable in the form of a straight life annuity commencing before normal retirement age by 3 percent per year from age 60 to age 65 and by 7 percent per year from age 55 through age 59. Thus, before the amendment, the amount of Frank's early retirement benefit that would be payable for commencement at age 55 was $6,000 per year ($12,000 per year minus 3 percent for five years and minus 7 percent for five more years). The amendment also alters the actuarial reduction factor so that, for a participant with at least 15 years of service, the amount payable in a straight life annuity commencing before normal retirement age is reduced by 6 percent per year. As a result, the amount of Frank's early retirement benefit at age 55 becomes $5,600 per year after the amendment ($14,000 minus 6 percent for 10 years).

Conclusion. The straight life annuity payable under the Plan at age 55 is an optional form of benefit that includes an early retirement subsidy. The plan amendment fails to satisfy the requirements of Code Section 411(d)(6)(B) because the amendment decreases the optional form of benefit payable to Frank below the level that he was entitled to receive immediately before the effective date of the amendment. If, instead, the Plan had included a provision under which Frank's straight life annuity payable at any age could not be less than what it was immediately before the amendment (so that Frank's straight life annuity payable at age 55 could not be less than $6,000 per year), then the amendment would not fail to satisfy the requirements of Section 411(d)(6)(B) with respect to Frank's straight life annuity payable at age 55 (although the straight life annuity payable to Frank at age 55 would not increase until the point in time at which the new formula amount with the new actuarial reduction factors exceeds the amount payable under the minimum provision, approximately 14 months after the amendment becomes effective). [Treas. Reg. § 1.411(d)-3(b)(4), Ex. 1]

Example 10-36: *Facts Involving Plant Shutdown Benefits.* The Bear Flag Restaurant Corporation Plan permits participants who have a severance from employment before normal retirement age (age 65) to commence distributions at any time after age 55 with the amount payable to be actuarially reduced using reasonable actuarial assumptions regarding interest and mortality specified in the Plan, but provides that the annual reduction for any participant who has at least 20 years of service and who has a severance from employment after age 55 is only 3 percent per year (which is a smaller reduction than would apply under reasonable actuarial reductions). The Plan also provides two plant shutdown benefits to participants who have a severance of employment as a result of a plant shutdown. First, the favorable 3 percent per year actuarial reduction applies for commencement of benefits after age 55 and before age 65 for any participant who has at least 10 years of service and who has a severance from employment as a result of a plant shutdown.

Second, all participants who have at least 20 years of service and who have a severance from employment after age 55 (and before normal retirement age at age 65) as a result of a plant shutdown will receive supplemental payments. Under the supplemental payments, an additional amount equal to the participant's estimated old-age insurance benefit under the Social Security Act is payable until age 65. The supplemental payments are not a QSUPP, as defined in Treasury Regulations Section 1.401(a)(4)-12, because the Plan's terms do not state that the supplement is treated as an early retirement benefit that is protected under Code Section 411(d)(6).

Conclusion with Respect to Plant Shutdown Benefits. The benefits payable with the 3 percent annual reduction are retirement-type benefits. The excess of the actuarial present value of the early retirement benefit using the 3 percent annual reduction over the actuarial present value of the normal retirement benefit is a retirement-type subsidy and the right to receive payments of the benefit at age 55 is an early retirement benefit. These conclusions apply not only with respect to the rights that apply to participants who have at least 20 years of service, but also to participants with at least 10 years of service who have a severance from employment as a result of a plant shutdown. Thus, the right to receive benefits based on a 3 percent annual reduction for participants with at least 10 years of service at the time of a plant shutdown is an early retirement benefit that provides a retirement-type subsidy and is a Section 411(d)(6)(B) protected benefit (even though no plant shutdown has occurred). Therefore, a plan amendment cannot eliminate this benefit with respect to benefits accrued before the applicable amendment date, even before the occurrence of the plant shutdown. Because the plan provides that the supplemental payments cannot exceed the OASDI benefit under the Social Security Act, the supplemental payments constitute a social security supplement (but not a QSUPP as defined in Treasury Regulation Section 1.401(a)(4)-12), which is an ancillary benefit that is not a Section 411(d)(6)(B) protected benefit and accordingly is not taken into account in determining whether a prohibited reduction has occurred).

[Treas. Reg. § 1.411(d)-3(b)(4), Ex. 2]

Example 10-37: The Electricians' Pension Plan, a multiemployer defined benefit plan in which participation is limited to electricians in the construction industry, provides that a participant may elect to commence distribution only if the participant is not currently employed by a participating employer and provides that, if the participant has a specified number of years of service and attains a specified age, the distribution is without any actuarial reduction for commencement before normal retirement age. Since its inception, the Plan has provided for suspension of pension benefits during periods of disqualifying employment (i.e., ERISA § 203(a)(3)(B) service). Before 2019, the Plan defined disqualifying employment to include any job as an electrician in the particular industry and geographic location to which the Plan applies. This definition of disqualifying employment did not cover a job as an electrician supervisor. In 2017, participant Eduardo, having rendered the specified number of years of service and attained the specified age to retire with a fully subsidized early retirement benefit, retires from his job as an electrician with the Yerkes Electrical Company and starts a position with the Zephos Electrical Company as an electrician supervisor. The Zephos Electrical Company is not a participating employer in the Electricians' Pension Plan but is an employer in the same industry and geographic location as the Yerkes Electrical Company. When Eduardo left service with the Yerkes Electrical Company, his position as an electrician supervisor was not disqualifying employment for purposes of the Electricians' Pension Plan suspension of pension benefits provision, and Eduardo elected to commence benefits in 2017. In 2018, effective January 1, 2019, the Plan is amended to expand the definition of disqualifying employment to include any job (including supervisory positions) as an electrician in the same industry and geographic location to which the Plan applies. The Plan's definition of disqualifying employment satisfies the requirements of Code Section 411(a)(3)(B). On January 1, 2019, Eduardo's pension benefits are suspended because of his disqualifying employment as an electrician supervisor.

The 2019 Plan amendment violates the anti-cutback rules of Code Section 411(d)(6), because the amendment places greater restrictions or conditions on a participant's rights to Code Section 411(d)(6) protected benefits to the extent it applies with respect to benefits that accrued before January 1, 2019. The result would be the same even if the amendment did not apply to former employees and instead applied only to participants who were actively employed at the time of the applicable amendment. [Treas. Reg. § 1.411(d)-3(b)(4), Ex. 3]

Permissible Elimination of Optional Forms of Benefit That Are Redundant

1. *General Rule.* Except as otherwise provided below, a plan is permitted to be amended to eliminate an optional form of benefit for a participant with respect to benefits accrued before the applicable amendment date if:
   a. The optional form of benefit is redundant with respect to a retained optional form of benefit, as described below;
   b. The plan amendment is not applicable with respect to an optional form of benefit with an annuity commencement date that is earlier than the number of days in the maximum QJSA explanation period after the date the amendment is adopted; and the *maximum QJSA explanation period* is the maximum number of days before an annuity starting date for a QJSA for which a written explanation relating to the QJSA would satisfy the timing requirements of Code Section 417(a)(3) and Treasury Regulations Section 1.417(e)-1(b)(3)(ii); see Treasury Regulation Section 1.411(d)-3(g)(9); and
   c. The requirements relating to permissible plan amendments eliminating or reducing Section 411(d)(6)(B) permitted benefits that are burdensome and of *de minimis* value are satisfied in any case in which either:
      i. The retained optional form of benefit for the participant does not commence on the same annuity commencement date as the optional form of benefit that is being eliminated, or

ii. As of the date the amendment is adopted, the actuarial present value of the retained optional form of benefit for the participant is less than the actuarial present value of the optional form of benefit that is being eliminated.

2. *Similar Types of Optional Forms of Benefit Are Redundant*

An annuity does not fail to be a core option (e.g., a joint and contingent annuity or a 10-year term certain and life annuity) as a result of differences intended to comply with applicable law, such as limitations on death benefits to comply with the incidental benefit requirement of Treasury Regulations Section 1.401-1(b)(1)(i) or on account of the spousal consent rules of Code Section 417.

In general, except as provided below, the term *most valuable option for a participant with a short life expectancy* means, for an annuity starting date, the optional form of benefit that is reasonably expected to result in payments that have the largest actuarial present value in the case of a participant who dies shortly after the annuity starting date, taking into account both payments due to the participant prior to the participant's death and any payments due after the participant's death. For this purpose, a plan is permitted to assume that the spouse of the participant is the same age as the participant. In addition, a plan is permitted to assume that the optional form of benefit that is the most valuable option for a participant with a short life expectancy when the participant is age 70½ also is the most valuable option for a participant with a short life expectancy at all older ages, and that the most valuable option for a participant with a short life expectancy at age 55 is the most valuable option for a participant with a short life expectancy at all younger ages. Under the following safe harbor hierarchy, a plan is permitted to treat a single-sum distribution option with an actuarial present value that is not less than the actuarial present value of any optional form of benefit eliminated by the plan amendment as the most valuable option for a participant with a short life expectancy for all of a participant's annuity starting dates if such single-sum distribution option is available at all such dates, without regard to whether the option was available before the plan amendment.

If the plan before the amendment does not offer a single-sum distribution option as described above, a plan is permitted to treat a joint and contingent annuity with a continuation percentage that is at least 75 percent and that is at least as great as the highest continuation percentage available before the amendment as the most valuable option for a participant with a short life expectancy for all of a participant's annuity starting dates if such joint and contingent annuity is available at all such dates, without regard to whether the option was available before the plan amendment.

If the plan before the amendment offers neither a single-sum distribution option described above, nor a joint and contingent annuity with a continuation percentage as described above, a plan is permitted to treat a term certain and life annuity with a term certain period no less than 15 years as the most valuable option for a participant with a short life expectancy for each annuity starting date if such 15-year term certain and life annuity is available at all annuity starting dates, without regard to whether the option was available before the plan amendment.

[Treas. Reg. § 1.411(d)-3(g)(5)]

a. *General Rule.* An optional form of benefit is redundant with respect to a retained optional form of benefit if, after the amendment becomes applicable:

   i. There is a retained optional form of benefit available to the participant that is in the same family of optional forms of benefit, as described below, as the optional form of benefit being eliminated; and

   ii. The participant's rights with respect to the retained optional form of benefit are not subject to materially greater restrictions (such as conditions relating to eligibility, restrictions on a participant's ability to designate the person who is entitled to benefits following the participant's death, or restrictions on a participant's right to receive an in-kind distribution) than applied to the optional form of benefit being eliminated.

b. *Special Rule for Core Options.* An optional form of benefit that is a core option (as defined below) may not be eliminated as a redundant benefit under these rules unless the retained optional form of benefit and the eliminated core option are identical except for differences described in paragraph (3)(a) below. Thus, for example, a particular 10-year term certain and life annuity may not be eliminated by plan amendment unless the retained optional form of benefit is another 10-year term certain and life annuity. [Treas. Reg. § 1.411(d)-3(c)(2)(ii)]

   i. A straight life annuity generalized optional form under which the participant is entitled to a level life annuity with no benefit payable after the participant's death

   ii. A 75 percent joint and contingent annuity generalized optional form under which the participant is entitled to a life annuity with a survivor annuity for any individual designated by the participant (including a nonspousal contingent annuitant) that is 75 percent of the amount payable during the participant's life (but there is a special rule relating to the joint and contingent annuity core option)

   iii. A 10-year term certain and life annuity generalized optional form under which the participant is entitled to a life annuity with a guarantee that payments will continue to any person designated by the participant for the remainder of a fixed period of 10 years if the participant dies before the end of the 10-year period, and

   iv. The most valuable option for a participant with a short life expectancy (as described below).

3. *Family of Optional Forms of Benefit*

The term *social security leveling feature* means a feature with respect to an optional form of benefit commencing prior to a participant's expected commencement of social security benefits that provides for a temporary period of higher payments that is designed to result in an approximately level amount of income when the participant's estimated old age benefits from social security are taken into account. [Treas. Reg. § 1.411(d)-3(g)(16)]

The term *refund of employee contributions feature* means a feature with respect to an optional form of benefit that provides for employee contributions and interest thereon to be paid in a single sum at the annuity starting date with the remainder to be paid in another form beginning on that date. [Treas. Reg. § 1.411(d)-3(g)(11)]

Finally, the term *retroactive annuity starting date* feature means a feature with respect to an optional form of benefit under which the annuity starting date for the distribution occurs on or before the date the written explanation required by Code Section 417(a)(3) is provided to the participant. [Treas. Reg. § 1.411(d)-3(g)(13)]

a. *In General.* Paragraph (4) below describes certain families of optional forms of benefits. Not every optional form of benefit that is offered under a plan necessarily fits within a family of optional forms of benefit, as described below. Each optional form of benefit that is not included in any particular family of optional forms of benefit listed in paragraph (4) below is in a separate family of optional forms of benefit with other optional forms of benefit that would be identical to that optional form of benefit but for certain differences that are disregarded as described immediately below. [Treas. Reg. § 1.411(d)-3(c)(3)(i)]

b. *Certain Differences Among Optional Forms of Benefit*

   i. *Differences in Actuarial Factors and Annuity Starting Dates.* The determination of whether two optional forms of benefit are within a family of optional forms of benefit is made without regard to actuarial factors or annuity starting dates. Thus, any optional forms of benefit that are part of the same generalized optional form are in the same family of optional forms of benefit. (The term *generalized optional form* means a group of optional forms of benefit that are identical except for differences due to the actuarial factors that are used to determine the amount of the distributions under those optional forms of benefit and the annuity starting dates. [Treas. Reg. § 1.411(d)-3(g)(8)]) For example, if a plan has a single-sum distribution option for some participants that is calculated using a 5 percent rate and a specific mortality table (but no less than the minimum present value as determined under Code Section 417(e)) and another single-sum distribution option for other participants that is calculated using the applicable interest rate as defined in Code Section 417(e)(3)(A)(ii)(II) and the applicable mortality table as defined in Code Section 417(e)(3)(A)(ii)(I), both single-sum distribution options are part of the same generalized optional form and thus in the same family of optional forms of benefit. However, differences in actuarial factors and annuity starting dates are taken into account. [Treas. Reg. § 1.411(d)-3(c)(3)(ii)(A)]

ii. *Differences in Pop-Up Provisions and Cash Refund Features for Joint and Contingent Options.* The determination of whether two optional forms of benefit are within a family of optional forms of benefit relating to joint and contingent families (as described below) is made without regard to the following features: [Treas. Reg. § 1.411(d)-3(c)(2)(ii)]

- Pop-up provisions (under which payments increase upon the death of the beneficiary or another event that causes the beneficiary not to be entitled to a survivor annuity)
- Cash refund features (under which payment is provided upon the death of the last annuitant in an amount that is not greater than the excess of the present value of the annuity at the annuity starting date over the total of payments before the death of the last annuitant), or
- Term-certain provisions for optional forms of benefit within a joint and contingent family.

iii. *Differences in Social Security Leveling Features, Refund of Employee Contributions Features, and Retroactive Annuity Starting Date Features.* The determination of whether two optional forms of benefit are within a family of optional forms of benefit is made without regard to social security leveling features, refund of employee contributions features, or retroactive annuity starting date features. There are special rules, discussed below, relating to social security leveling, refund of employee contributions, and retroactive annuity starting date features in optional forms of benefit. [Treas. Reg. § 1.411(d)-3(c)(3)(ii)(C)]

4. *List of Families.* The following are families of optional forms of benefit for purposes of these rules:

   a. *Joint and Contingent Options with Continuation Percentages of 50 Percent to 100 Percent.* An optional form of benefit is within the 50 percent or more joint and contingent family if it provides a life annuity to the participant and a survivor annuity to an individual that is at least 50 percent and no more than 100 percent of the annuity payable during the joint lives of the participant and the participant's survivor. [Treas. Reg. § 1.411(d)-3(c)(4)(i)]

   b. *Joint and Contingent Options with Continuation Percentages Less Than 50 Percent.* An optional form of benefit is within the less than 50 percent joint and contingent family if it provides a life annuity to the participant and a survivor annuity to an individual that is less than 50 percent of the annuity payable during the joint lives of the participant and the participant's survivor. [Treas. Reg. § 1.411(d)-3(c)(4)(ii)]

   c. *Term Certain and Life Annuity Options with a Term of 10 Years or Less.* An optional form of benefit is within the 10 years or less term certain and life family if it is a life annuity with a guarantee that payments will continue to the participant's beneficiary for the remainder of a fixed period that is 10 years or less if the participant dies before the end of the fixed period. [Treas. Reg. § 1.411(d)-3(c)(4)(iii)]

d. *Term Certain and Life Annuity Options with a Term Longer Than 10 Years*. An optional form of benefit is within the longer than 10 years term certain and life family if it is a life annuity with a guarantee that payments will continue to the participant's beneficiary for the remainder of a fixed period that is in excess of 10 years if the participant dies before the end of the fixed period. [Treas. Reg. § 1.411(d)-3(c)(4)(iv)]

e. *Level Installment Payment Options over a Period of 10 Years or Less*. An optional form of benefit is within the 10 years or less installment family if it provides for substantially level payments to the participant for a fixed period of at least two years and not in excess of 10 years with a guarantee that payments will continue to the participant's beneficiary for the remainder of the fixed period if the participant dies before the end of the fixed period. [Treas. Reg. § 1.411(d)-3(c)(4)(v)]

f. *Level Installment Payment Options over a Period of More than 10 Years*. An optional form of benefit is within the more than 10 years installment family if it provides for substantially level payments to the participant for a fixed period that is in excess of 10 years with a guarantee that payments will continue to the participant's beneficiary for the remainder of the fixed period if the participant dies before the end of the fixed period. [Treas. Reg. § 1.411(d)-3(c)(4)(vi)]

5. *Special Rules for Certain Features Included in Optional Forms of Benefit*. For purposes of applying these rules, to the extent an optional form of benefit that is being eliminated includes either a social security leveling feature or a refund of employee contributions feature, the retained optional form of benefit must also include that feature, and, to the extent that the optional form of benefit that is being eliminated does not include a social security leveling feature or a refund of employee contributions feature, the retained optional form of benefit must not include that feature. For purposes of applying these rules, to the extent an optional form of benefit that is being eliminated does not include a retroactive annuity starting date feature, the retained optional form of benefit must not include the feature. [Treas. Reg. § 1.411(d)-3(c)(5)]

6. *Separate Application of Redundancy Rules for Bifurcated Benefits*. If a plan permits the participant to make different distribution elections with respect to two or more separate portions of the participant's benefit, the rules of Treasury Regulations Section 1.411(d)-3(c) are permitted to be applied separately to each portion of the participant's benefit as if that portion were the participant's entire benefit. Thus, for example, if one set of distribution elections applies to a portion of the participant's accrued benefit and another set of distribution elections applies to the other portion of the participant's accrued benefit, then with respect to one portion of the participant's benefit, the determination of whether any optional form of benefit is within a family of optional forms of benefit is permitted

to be made disregarding elections that apply to the other portion of the participant's benefit. Similarly, if a participant can elect to receive any portion of the accrued benefit in a single sum and the remainder pursuant to a set of distribution elections, the rules of Treasury Regulations Section 1.411(d)-3(c) are permitted to be applied separately to the set of distribution elections that apply to the portion of the participant's accrued benefit that is not paid in a single sum. (For example, for the portion of a participant's benefit that is not paid in a single sum, the determination of whether any optional form of benefit is within a family of optional forms of benefit is permitted to be made disregarding the fact that the other portion of the participant's benefit is paid in a single sum.) [Treas. Reg. § 1.411(d)-3(e)(6)]

Q 10:40 May a plan be amended to eliminate noncore optional forms of benefit if core options are offered?

General Rule. Yes, as a general rule, except as otherwise provided under the special rules described below, a plan is permitted to be amended to eliminate an optional form of benefit for a participant with respect to benefits accrued before the applicable amendment date if:

1. After the amendment becomes applicable, each of the core options described below is available to the participant with respect to benefits accrued before and after the amendment;
2. The plan amendment is not applicable with respect to an optional form of benefit with an annuity commencement date that is earlier than four years after the date the amendment is adopted; and
3. The requirements (described in Q 10:41 below) that apply to plan amendments that eliminate or reduce Section 411(d)(6)(B) protected benefits that are burdensome and of *de minimis* value are satisfied in any case in which either:
    a. One or more of the core options are not available commencing on the same annuity commencement date as the optional form of benefit that is being eliminated, or
    b. As of the date the amendment is adopted, the actuarial present value of the benefit payable under any core option with the same annuity commencement date is less than the actuarial present value of benefits payable under the optional form of benefit that is being eliminated. [Treas. Reg. § 1.411(d)-3(d)(1)]

Special Rules

1. *Treatment of Certain Features Included in Optional Forms of Benefit.* For purposes of applying these rules, to the extent an optional form of benefit that is being eliminated includes either a social security leveling feature or a refund of employee contributions feature, at least one of the core options must also be available with that feature, and, to the extent that the optional form of benefit that is being eliminated does not include

a social security leveling feature or a refund of employee contributions feature, each of the core options must be available without that feature. For purposes of applying this rule, to the extent an optional form of benefit that is being eliminated does not include a retroactive annuity starting date feature, each of the core options must be available without that feature. [Treas. Reg. § 1.411(d)-3(d)(2)(i)]

2. *Eliminating the Most Valuable Option for a Participant with a Short Life Expectancy.* For purposes of applying these rules, if the most valuable option for a participant with a short life expectancy is eliminated, then, after the plan amendment, an optional form of benefit that is identical, except for certain permitted differences, must be available to the participant. However, such a plan amendment cannot eliminate a refund of employee contributions feature from the most valuable option for a participant with a short life expectancy. [Treas. Reg. § 1.411(d)-3(d)(2)(ii)]

3. *Single-Sum Distributions.* A plan amendment is not treated as satisfying these rules if it eliminates an optional form of benefit that includes a single-sum distribution that applies with respect to at least 25 percent of the participant's accrued benefit as of the date the optional form of benefit is eliminated. (But see Treasury Regulations Section 1.411(d)-4, Q&A-2(b)(2)(v), relating to involuntary single-sum distributions for benefits with a present value not in excess of the maximum dollar amount in Section 411(a)(11).) [Treas. Reg. § 1.411(d)-3(d)(2)(iii)]

4. *Application of Multiple Amendment Rule to Core Option Rule.* If a plan is amended to eliminate an optional form of benefit using the core options rule (described in Q 10:40), then the employer must wait three years after the first annuity commencement date for which the optional form of benefit is no longer available before making any changes to the core options offered under the plan (other than a change that is not treated as an elimination). Thus, for example, if a plan amendment eliminates an optional form of benefit for a participant using the core options rule, with an adoption date of January 1, 2012 and an effective date of January 1, 2016, the plan would not be permitted to be amended to make changes to the core options offered under the plan (and the core options would continue to apply with respect to the participant's accrued benefit) until January 1, 2019. [Treas. Reg. § 1.411(d)-3(d)(2)(iv)]

5. *Special Rule for Joint and Contingent Annuity Core Option.* If a plan offers joint and contingent annuities under which a participant is entitled to a life annuity with a survivor annuity for the individual designated by the participant (including a nonspousal contingent annuitant) with continuation percentage options of both 50 percent and 100 percent (after certain permitted adjustments), the plan is permitted to treat both of these options as core options, in lieu of a 75 percent joint and contingent annuity. Thus, such a plan is permitted to use the core options rules if the plan satisfies all of the requirements of such rules other than the requirement of offering a 75 percent joint and contingent annuity. [Treas. Reg. § 1.411(d)-3(d)(2)(v)]

Q 10:41 May a plan be amended to eliminate or reduce Section 411(d)(6)(B) protected benefits that are burdensome and of *de minimis* value?

Generally, yes. Such a plan amendment may be made if:

1. The amendment eliminates Section 411(d)(6)(B) protected benefits that create significant burdens or complexities for the plan and its participants (as described below); and
2. The amendment does not adversely affect the rights of any participant in a more than *de minimis* manner (as described below).

[Treas. Reg. § 1.411(d)-3(e)(1)]

Plan Amendments Eliminating Section 411(d)(6)(B) Protected Benefits That Create Significant Burdens and Complexities

1. *Facts and Circumstances Analysis.*
   a. *In General.* The determination of whether a plan amendment eliminates Section 411(d)(6)(B) protected benefits that create significant burdens or complexities for the plan and its participants is based on facts and circumstances. [Treas. Reg. § 1.411(d)-3(e)(2)(i)(A)]
   b. *Early Retirement Benefits.* In the case of an amendment that eliminates an early retirement benefit, relevant factors include whether the annuity starting dates under the plan considered in the aggregate are burdensome or complex (e.g., the number of categories of early retirement benefits, whether the terms and conditions applicable to the plan's early retirement benefits are difficult to summarize in a manner that is concise and readily understandable to the average plan participant, and whether those different early retirement benefits were added to the plan as a result of a plan merger, transfer, or consolidation) and whether the effect of the plan amendment is to reduce the number of categories of early retirement benefits. [Treas. Reg. § 1.411(d)-3(e)(2)(i)(B)]
   c. *Retirement-Type Subsidies and Actuarial Factors.* In the case of a plan amendment eliminating a retirement-type subsidy or changing the actuarial factors used to determine optional forms of benefit, relevant factors include whether the actuarial factors used for determining optional forms of benefit available under the plan considered in the aggregate are burdensome or complex (e.g., the number of different retirement-type subsidies and other actuarial factors available under the plan, whether the terms and conditions applicable to the plan's retirement-type subsidies are difficult to summarize in a manner that is concise and readily understandable to the average plan participant, whether the plan is eliminating one or more generalized optional forms, whether the plan is replacing a complex optional form of benefit that contains a retirement-type subsidy with a simpler form, and whether the different retirement-type subsidies and other actuarial factors were added to the plan as a result of a plan merger, transfer, or consolidation), and whether the effect of the plan amendment is to

reduce the number of categories of retirement-type subsidies or other actuarial factors. [Treas. Reg. § 1.411(d)-3(e)(2)(i)(C)]

The following example illustrates the application of these rules:

Example 10-38: *Facts*. The Monterey Bay Corporation Plan is a defined benefit plan under which employees may select a distribution in the form of a straight life annuity, a straight life annuity with cost-of-living increases, a 50 percent qualified joint and survivor annuity with a pop-up provision, or a 10-year term certain and life annuity. On January 15, 2019, the Plan is amended, effective June 1, 2019, to eliminate the 50 percent qualified joint and survivor annuity with a pop-up provision and replace it with a 50 percent qualified joint and survivor annuity without the pop-up provision (and using the same actuarial factor).

Conclusion. The Plan satisfies applicable requirements because, based on the relevant facts and circumstances (e.g., the amendment replaces a complex optional form of benefit with a simpler form), the amendment eliminates Section 411(d)(6)(B) protected benefits that create significant burdens and complexities. Accordingly, the plan amendment is permitted to eliminate the pop-up provision, provided that the plan amendment satisfies all other applicable requirements. For example, the plan amendment must not eliminate the most valuable option for a participant with a short life expectancy, and the plan amendment must not adversely affect the rights of any participant in a more than *de minimis* manner, taking into account the actuarial factors for the joint and survivor annuity with the pop-up provision and the joint and survivor annuity without the pop-up provision. [Treas. Reg. § 1.411(d)-3(e)(2)(i)(D), unnumbered Example]

1. *Presumptions for Certain Amendments*
   a. *Presumption for Amendments Eliminating Certain Annuity Starting Dates*. If the annuity starting dates under the plan considered in the aggregate are burdensome or complex, then elimination of any one of the annuity starting dates is presumed to eliminate Section 411(d)(6)(B) protected benefits that create significant burdens or complexities for the plan and its participants. However, if the effect of a plan amendment with respect to a set of optional forms of benefit is merely to substitute one set of annuity starting dates for another set of annuity starting dates, without any reduction in the number of different annuity starting dates, then the plan amendment does not satisfy applicable requirements. [Treas. Reg. § 1.411(d)-3(e)(2)(ii)(A)]
   b. *Presumption for Amendments Changing Certain Actuarial Factors*. If the actuarial factors used for determining benefit distributions available under a generalized optional form considered in the aggregate are burdensome or complex, then replacing some of the actuarial factors for the generalized optional form is presumed to eliminate Section 411(d)(6)(B) protected benefits that create significant burdens or complexities for the plan and its participants. However, if the effect is merely to substitute one set of actuarial factors for another set of actuarial factors, without any reduction in the number of different

actuarial factors or the complexity of those factors, then the plan amendment does not satisfy applicable requirements unless the change of actuarial factors is merely to replace one or more of the plan's actuarial factors for determining optional forms of benefit with new actuarial factors that are more accurate (e.g., reflecting more recent mortality experience or more recent market rates of interest). [Treas. Reg. § 1.411(d)-3(e)(2)(ii)(B)]

2. *Restrictions Against Creating Burdens or Complexities*. A plan amendment does not eliminate a Section 411(d)(6)(B) protected benefit that creates burdens and complexities for a plan and its participants if, less than three years earlier, a plan was previously amended to add another retirement-type subsidy in order to facilitate the elimination of the original retirement-type subsidy, even if the elimination of the other subsidy would not adversely affect the rights of any plan participant in a more than *de minimis* manner. [Treas. Reg. § 1.411(d)-3(e)(2)(iii)]

Elimination of Early Retirement Benefits or Retirement-Type Subsidies That Are De Minimis

1. *Rules for Retained Optional Forms of Benefit*. For purposes of these rules, the elimination of an optional form of benefit does not adversely affect the rights of any participant in a more than *de minimis* manner if:
   a. The retained optional form of benefit has substantially the same annuity commencement date as the optional form of benefit that is being eliminated; and
   b. Either the actuarial present value of the benefit payable in the optional form of benefit that is being eliminated does not exceed the actuarial present value of the benefit payable in the retained optional form of benefit by more than a *de minimis* amount, or the amendment satisfies the requirements described below relating to a delayed effective date. [Treas. Reg. § 1.411(d)-3(e)(3)(i)]
2. *Rules for Core Options.* The elimination of an optional form of benefit does not adversely affect the rights of any participant in a more than *de minimis* manner if, with respect to each of the core options:
   a. The core option is available after the amendment with substantially the same annuity commencement date as the optional form of benefit that is being eliminated; and
   b. Either the actuarial present value of the benefit payable in the optional form of benefit that is being eliminated does not exceed the actuarial present value of the benefit payable under the core option by more than a *de minimis* amount, or the amendment satisfies the requirements discussed below, relating to a delayed effective date. [Treas. Reg. § 1.411(d)-3(e)(3)(ii)]

Definition of Substantially the Same Annuity Starting Dates

For purposes of applying these rules, annuity starting dates are considered substantially the same if they are within six months of each other. [Treas. Reg. § 1.411(d)-3(e)(4)]

Definition of De Minimis *Difference in Actuarial Present Value*

For purposes of applying these rules, a difference in actuarial present value between the optional form of benefit being eliminated and the retained optional form of benefit or core option is not more than a *de minimis* amount if, as of the date the amendment is adopted, the difference between the actuarial present value of the eliminated optional form of benefit and the actuarial present value of the retained optional form of benefit or core option is not more than the greater of:

1. 2 percent of the present value of the retirement-type subsidy (if any) under the eliminated optional form of benefit prior to the amendment; or
2. 1 percent of the greater of the participant's compensation (as defined in Code Section 415(c)(3)) for the prior plan year or the participant's average compensation for his or her high three years (within the meaning of Code Sections 415(b)(1)(B) and (b)(3)). [Treas. Reg. § 1.411(d)-3(e)(5)]

Delayed Effective Date

1. *General Rule.* An amendment that eliminates an optional form of benefit satisfies the delayed effective date requirements if the elimination of the optional form of benefit is not applicable to any annuity commencement date before the end of the expected transition period for that optional form of benefit. [Treas. Reg. § 1.411(d)-3(e)(6)(i)]
2. *Determination of Expected Transition Period*
   a. *General Rule.* The expected transition period for a plan amendment eliminating an optional form of benefit is the period that begins when the amendment is adopted and ends when it is reasonable to expect, with respect to a Section 411(d)(6)(B) protected benefit (i.e., not taking into account benefits that accrue in the future), that the form being eliminated would be subsumed by another optional form of benefit after taking into account expected future benefit accruals. [Treas. Reg. § 1.411(d)-3(e)(6)(ii)]
   b. *Determination of Expected Transition Period Using Conservative Actuarial Assumptions.* The expected transition period for a plan amendment eliminating an optional form of benefit must be determined in accordance with actuarial assumptions that are reasonable at the time of the amendment and that are conservative (i.e., reasonable actuarial assumptions that are likely to result in the longest period of time until the eliminated optional form of benefit would be subsumed). For this purpose, actuarial assumptions are not treated as conservative unless they include assumptions that a participant's compensation will not increase and that future benefit accruals will not exceed accruals in recent periods. [Treas. Reg. § 1.411(d)-3(e)(6)(ii)(B)]
   c. *Effect of Subsequent Amendments Reducing Future Benefit Accruals on the Expected Transition Period.* If, during the expected transition period for a plan amendment eliminating an optional form of benefit, the plan is subsequently amended to reduce the rate of future benefit accrual (or otherwise to lengthen the expected transition period), that

subsequent plan amendment must provide that the elimination of the optional form of benefit is void or must provide for the effective date for elimination of the optional form of benefit to be further extended to a new expected transition period that satisfies the delayed effective date rules taking into account the subsequent amendment. [Treas. Reg. § 1.411(d)-3(e)(6)(ii)(C)]

3. *Applicability of the Delayed Effective Date Rule Limited to Employees Who Continue to Accrue Benefits Through the End of Expected Transition Period.* An amendment eliminating an optional form of benefit must be limited to participants who continue to accrue benefits under the plan through the end of the expected transition period. Thus, for example, the plan amendment may not apply to any participant who has a severance from employment during the expected transition period. [Treas. Reg. § 1.411(d)-3(e)(6)(iii)]

Q 10:42 What is the utilization test?

General Rule. A plan is permitted to be amended to eliminate all of the optional forms of benefit that comprise a generalized optional form (as defined in Treasury Regulations Section 1.411(d)-3(g)(8)) for a participant with respect to benefits accrued before the applicable amendment date if:

1. None of the optional forms of benefit being eliminated is a core option, as defined in Treasury Regulations Section 1.411(d)-3(g)(5);
2. The plan amendment is not applicable with respect to an optional form of benefit with an annuity commencement date that is earlier than the number of days in the maximum QJSA explanation period (as defined in Treasury Regulations Section 1.411(d)-3(g)(9)) after the date the amendment is adopted; and
3. During the look-back period:
   a. The generalized optional form has been available to at least the applicable number of participants who are taken into account under the rules described below; and
   b. No participant has elected any optional form of benefit that is part of the generalized optional form with an annuity commencement date that is within the look-back period.

[Treas. Reg. § 1.411(d)-3(f)(1)]

The term "generalized optional form" means a group of optional forms of benefit that are identical except for differences due to the actuarial factors that are used to determine the amount of the distribution under those optional forms of benefit and the annuity starting dates. [Treas. Reg. § 1.411(d)-3(g)(8)]

The term "maximum QJSA explanation period" means the maximum number of days before the annuity starting date for a QJSA for which a written explanation relating to the QJSA would satisfy the timing requirements of Code § 417(a)(3) and Treasury Regulations § 1.417(e)-1(b)(3)(ii). [Treas. Reg. § 1.411(d)-3(g)]

Look-Back Period.

1. *In General.* For these purposes, the "look-back period" is the period that includes:
   a. The portion of the plan year in which such plan amendment is adopted that precedes the date of adoption (the pre-adoption period); and
   b. The two plan years immediately preceding the pre-adoption period.
2. *Special Look-Back Period Rules.*
   a. *Twelve-Month Plan Year.* In the look-back period, at least one of the plan years must be a twelve-month plan year.
   b. *Permitted Three-Month Exclusion in the Pre-Adoption Period.* A plan is permitted to exclude from the look-back period the calendar month in which the amendment is adopted and the preceding one or two calendar months to the extent those preceding months are contained within the pre-adoption period.
   c. *Permission to Extend the Look-Back Period.* In order to have a look-back period that satisfies the minimum applicable numbers of participants described above, the look-back period is permitted to be expanded, so as to include the three, four, or five plan years immediately preceding the plan year in which the amendment is adopted. Thus, in determining the look-back period, a plan is permitted to substitute the three, four, or five plan years immediately preceding the pre-adoption period for the two plan years described above. However, if a plan does not satisfy the minimum applicable number of participants requirement using the pre-adoption period and the immediately preceding five plan years, the plan is not permitted to be amended in accordance with the utilization test.

[Treas. Reg. § 1.411(d)-3(f)(3)]

Participants Taken into Account. A participant is taken into account for these purposes only if the participant was eligible to elect to commence payment of an optional form of benefit that is part of the generalized optional form being eliminated with an annuity commencement date that is within the look-back period. However, a participant is not taken into account if the participant—

1. Did not elect any optional form of benefit with an annuity commencement date that was within the look-back period;
2. Elected an optional form of benefit that included a single-sum distribution that applied with respect to at least 25 percent of the participant's accrued benefit;
3. Elected an optional form of benefit that was available only during a limited period of time and that contained a retirement-type subsidy where the subsidy that is part of the generalized optional form being eliminated was not extended to any optional form of benefit with the same annuity commencement date; or
4. Elected an optional form of benefit with an annuity commencement date that was more than 10 years before normal retirement age.

[Treas. Reg. § 1.411(d)-3(f)(3)]

Determining the Applicable Number of Participants. For purposes of applying these rules, the applicable number of participants is 50 participants. However, a plan is permitted to take into account any participant who elected an optional form of benefit that included a single-sum distribution that applied with respect to at least 25 percent of the participant's accrued benefit, but only if the applicable number of participants is increased to 1,000 participants. [Treas. Reg. § 1.411(d)-3(f)(4)]

Default Elections. For these purposes, an election includes the payment of an optional form of benefit that applies in the absence of an affirmative election. [Treas. Reg. § 1.411(d)-3(f)(5)]

Q 10:43 Are there any examples that illustrate the application of the anti-cutback rules in Treasury Regulations Section 1.411(d)-3?

Yes, the following examples illustrate the application of the anti-cutback rules in Treasury Regulations Section 1.411(d)-3:

> **Example 10-39:** (1) *Facts Involving Elimination of Optional Forms of Benefit as Redundant.* The Pastures of Heaven Corporation Plan is a defined benefit plan under which employees may elect to commence distributions at any time after the later of termination of employment or attainment of age 55. At each potential annuity commencement date, the Plan permits employees to select, with spousal consent where required, a straight life annuity or any of a number of actuarially equivalent alternative forms of payment, including a straight life annuity with cost-of-living increases and a joint and contingent annuity with the participant having the right to select any beneficiary and any continuation percentage from 1 percent to 100 percent, subject to modification to the extent necessary to satisfy the requirements of the incidental benefit requirement of Treasury Regulations Section 1.401-1(b)(1)(i). The amount of any alternative payment is determined as the actuarial equivalent of the straight life annuity payable at the same age using reasonable actuarial assumptions. On June 2, 2019, the Plan is amended to delete all continuation percentages for joint and contingent options other than 25 percent, 50 percent, 75 percent, or 100 percent, effective with respect to annuity commencement dates that are on or after January 1, 2020.
>
> (2a) *Conclusion for Categorization of Family Members Under the Redundancy Rule.* The optional forms of benefit described in paragraph (1) of this Example 10-39 are members of four families: a straight life annuity; a straight life annuity with cost-of-living increases; joint and contingent options with continuation percentages of less than 50 percent; and joint and contingent options with continuation percentages of 50 percent or more. The amendment does not affect either of the first two families, but affects the two families relating to joint and contingent options.
>
> (2b) *Conclusion for Elimination of Optional Forms of Benefit as Redundant.* The amendment satisfies applicable requirements. First, the eliminated

optional forms of benefit are redundant with respect to the retained optional forms of benefit because each eliminated joint and contingent annuity option with a continuation percentage of less than 50 percent is redundant with respect to the 25 percent continuation option and each eliminated joint and contingent annuity option with a continuation percentage of 50 percent or higher is redundant with respect to any one of the retained 50 percent, 75 percent, or 100 percent continuation options. In addition, to the extent that the optional form of benefit that is being eliminated does not include a social security leveling feature, return of employee contribution feature, or retroactive annuity starting date feature, the retained optional form of benefit does not include that feature. Second, the amendment is not effective with respect to annuity commencement dates before September 1, 2018. Third, the plan amendment does not eliminate any available core option, including the most valuable option for a participant with a short life expectancy, treating a joint and contingent annuity with a 100 percent continuation percentage as this optional form. Finally, the amendment need not satisfy the delayed effective date requirements because the retained optional forms of benefit are available on the same annuity commencement dates and have the same actuarial present value as the optional forms of benefit that are being eliminated. [Treas. Reg. § 1.411(d)-3(h), Ex. 1]

Example 10-40: (1) *Facts Involving Elimination of Optional Forms of Benefit as Redundant if Additional Restrictions Are Imposed.* The facts are the same as Example 10-39, except that the Plan amendment also restricts the class of beneficiaries that may be elected under the four retained joint and contingent annuities to the employee's spouse.

(2) *Conclusion.* The amendment fails to satisfy applicable requirements because the retained joint and contingent annuities have materially greater restrictions on the beneficiary designation than did the eliminated joint and contingent annuities. Thus, the joint and contingent annuities being eliminated are not redundant with respect to the retained joint and contingent annuities. In addition, the amendment fails to satisfy the requirements of the core option rules because the amendment fails to be limited to annuity commencement dates that are at least four years after the date the amendment is adopted, the amendment fails to include a core option (i.e., the 75 percent joint and contingent annuity generalized optional form) because the participant does not have the right to designate any beneficiary, and the amendment fails to include another core option (i.e., the 10-year certain and life annuity generalized optional form) because the plan does not provide a 10-year term certain and life annuity. [Treas. Reg. § 1.411(d)-3(h), Ex. 2]

Example 10-41: (1) *Facts Involving Elimination of a Social Security Leveling Feature and a Period Certain Annuity as Redundant.* The Monterey Bay Corporation Plan is a defined benefit plan under which participants may elect to commence distributions in the following actuarially equivalent forms, with spousal consent if applicable: a straight life annuity; a 50 percent, 75 percent, or 100 percent joint and contingent annuity; a 5-year, 10-year, or a 15-year term certain and life annuity; and an installment refund annuity (i.e., an optional form of benefit that provides a period certain, the duration of which is based on the participant's age), with the participant having the right to select any beneficiary. In addition, each annuity offered under the plan, if payable to a participant who is less than age 65, is available both with and without a social security leveling feature. The social security leveling feature provides for an assumed commencement of social security benefits at any age selected by the participant between age 62 and 65. The Plan is amended on June 2, 2019, effective as of January 1, 2020, to eliminate the installment refund form of benefit and to restrict the social security leveling feature to an assumed social security commencement age of 65.

(2) *Conclusion*. The amendment satisfies the requirements of paragraph (c) of this section. First, the installment refund annuity option is redundant with respect to the 15-year certain and life annuity (except for advanced ages where, because of shorter life expectancies, the installment refund annuity option is redundant with respect to the five-year certain and life annuity and also redundant with respect to the 10-year certain and life annuity). Second, with respect to restricting the social security leveling feature to an assumed social security commencement age of 65, straight life annuities with social security leveling features that have different social security commencement ages are treated as members of the same family as straight life annuities without social security leveling features. To the extent an optional form of benefit that is being eliminated includes a social security leveling feature, the retained optional form of benefit must also include that feature, but it is permitted to have a different assumed age for commencement of social security benefits. Third, to the extent that the optional form of benefit that is being eliminated does not include a social security leveling feature, a return of employee contribution feature, or retroactive annuity starting date feature, the retained optional form of benefit must not include that feature. Fourth, the plan amendment does not eliminate any available core option, including the most valuable option for a participant with a short life expectancy, treating a joint and contingent annuity with a 100 percent continuation percentage as this optional form of benefit. Fifth, the amendment is not effective with respect to annuity commencement dates before September 1, 2017, as required under applicable rules. The amendment need not satisfy the delayed effective date requirements because the retained optional forms of benefit are available on the same annuity commencement dates and have the same actuarial present value as the optional forms of benefit that are being eliminated. [Treas. Reg. § 1.411(d)-3(h), Ex. 3]

Example 10-42: (1) *Facts Involving Elimination of Noncore Options*. The Bear Flag Restaurant Corporation sponsors the Bear Flag Corporation Plan, a defined benefit plan that permits every participant to elect payment in the following actuarially equivalent optional forms of benefit (the Plan's uniformly available options), with spousal consent if applicable: a straight life annuity; a 50 percent, 75 percent, or 100 percent joint and contingent annuity with no restrictions on designation of beneficiaries; and a 5-year, 10-year, or 15-year term certain and life annuity. In addition, each can be elected in conjunction with a social security leveling feature, with the participant permitted to select a social security commencement age from age 62 to age 67. None of the Plan's uniformly available options include a single-sum distribution. The Plan has been in existence for over 30 years, during which time the Corporation has acquired a large number of other businesses, including merging over 20 defined benefit plans of acquired entities into the Plan. Many of the merged plans offered optional forms of benefit that were not among the Plan's uniformly available options, including some plans funded through insurance products, often offering all of the insurance annuities that the insurance carrier offers, and with some of the merged plans offering single-sum distributions. In particular, under the XYZ acquisition that occurred in 1998, the XYZ-acquired plan offered a single-sum distribution option that was frozen at the time of the acquisition. On April 1, 2019, each single-sum distribution option applies to less than 25 percent of the XYZ participants' accrued benefits. The Corporation has generally, but not uniformly, followed the practice of limiting the optional forms of benefit for an acquired unit to an employee's service before the date of the merger, and has uniformly followed this practice with respect to each of the early retirement subsidies in the acquired unit's plan. As a result, as of April 1, 2020, the Plan includes a large number of generalized optional forms that are not members of families of optional forms of benefit identified above, but there are no participants who are entitled to any early retirement subsidies because any subsidies have been subsumed by the actuarially reduced accrued benefit. The Plan is amended in April 2020 to eliminate all of the optional forms of benefit that the Plan offers other than the Plan's uniformly available options, except that the amendment does not eliminate any single-sum distribution option except with respect to XYZ participants and permits any commencement date that was permitted under the Plan before the amendment. The Plan also eliminates the single-sum distribution option for XYZ participants. Further, each of the Plan's uniformly available options has an actuarial present value that is not less than the actuarial present value of any optional form of benefit offered before the amendment. The amendment is effective with respect to annuity commencement dates that are on or after May 1, 2024.

(2) *Conclusion.* The amendment satisfies applicable requirements. First, the Plan, as amended, does not eliminate any single-sum distribution option except for single-sum distribution options that apply to less than 25 percent of a plan participant's accrued benefit as of the date the option is eliminated (May 1, 2024). Second, the Plan, as amended, includes each of the core options, including offering the most valuable option for a participant with a short life expectancy (treating the 100 percent joint and contingent annuity as this benefit). The 100 percent joint and contingent annuity option (and not the grandfathered single-sum distribution option) is the most valuable option for a participant with a short life expectancy because the grandfathered single-sum distribution option is not available with respect to a participant's entire accrued benefit. In addition, as required under applicable rules, to the extent an optional form of benefit that is being eliminated includes either a social security leveling feature or a refund of employee contributions

feature, at least one of the core options is available with that feature and, to the extent that the optional form of benefit that is being eliminated does not include a social security leveling feature or a refund of employee contributions feature, each of the core options is available without that feature. Third, the amendment is not effective with respect to annuity commencement dates that are less than four years after the date the amendment is adopted. Finally, the amendment need not satisfy the delayed effective date requirements because the retained optional forms of benefit are available on the same annuity commencement date and have the same actuarial present value as the optional forms of benefit that are being eliminated. The conclusion that the amendment satisfies applicable requirements assumes that no amendments are made to change the core options before May 1, 2026. [Treas. Reg. § 1.411(d)-3(h), Ex. 4]

Example 10-43: (1) *Facts Involving Reductions in Actuarial Present Value.*

(a) The Western Biological Laboratory Corporation Plan is a defined benefit plan providing an accrued benefit of 1 percent of the average of a participant's highest three consecutive years' pay times years of service, payable as a straight life annuity beginning at the normal retirement age at age 65. The Plan permits employees to elect to commence actuarially reduced distributions at any time after the later of termination of employment or attainment of age 55. At each potential annuity commencement date, the Plan permits employees to select, with spousal consent, either a straight life annuity, a joint and contingent annuity with the participant having the right to select any beneficiary and a continuation percentage of 50 percent, 66 percent, 75 percent, or 100 percent, or a 10-year certain and life annuity, with the participant having the right to select any beneficiary, subject to modification to the extent necessary to satisfy the requirements of the incidental benefit requirement of Treasury Regulations Section 1.401-1(b)(1)(i). The amount of any joint and contingent annuity and the 10-year certain and life annuity is determined as the actuarial equivalent of the straight life annuity payable at the same age using reasonable actuarial assumptions. The Plan covers employees at four divisions, one of which, Division X, was acquired on January 1, 2012. The Plan provides for distributions before normal retirement age to be actuarially reduced, but, if a participant retires after attainment of age 55 and completion of 10 years of service, the applicable early retirement reduction factor is 3 percent per year for the years between age 65 and age 62 and 6 percent per year for the ages from 62 to 55 for all employees at any division, except for employees who were in Division X on January 1, 2012, for whom the early retirement reduction factor for retirement after age 55 and 10 years of service is 5 percent for each year before age 65. On June 2, 2019, effective January 1, 2020, the Plan is amended to change the early retirement reduction factors for all employees of Division X to be the same as for other employees, effective with respect to annuity commencement dates that are on or after January 1, 2021, but only with respect to participants who are employees on or after January 1, 2021, and only if the Plan continues accruals at the current rate through January 1, 2021 (or the effective date of the change in reduction factors is delayed to reflect the change in the accrual rate). For purposes of this Example 10-43, it is assumed that an actuarially equivalent early retirement factor would have a reduction shown in column 4 of the following table, which compares the reduction factors for Division X before and after the amendment:

1	2	3	4	5
Age	*Old Division X Factor (as a %)*	*New Factor (as a %)*	*Actuarially Equivalent Factor (as a %)*	*Column 3 minus Column 2*
65	NA	NA	NA	NA
64	95	97	91.1	+2
63	90	94	83.2	+4
62	85	91	76.1	+5
61	80	85	69.8	+5
60	75	79	64.1	+4
59	70	73	59.0	+3
58	65	67	54.3	+2
57	60	61	50.1	+1
56	55	55	46.3	0
55	50	49	42.8	−1

(b) On January 1, 2020, the employee with the largest number of years of service is Frank Battle, who is age 54 and has 20 years of service. For 2019, Frank's compensation is $80,000, and the compensation for his highest three consecutive years of pay on January 1, 2020 is $75,000. Frank's accrued benefit as of the January 1, 2020 effective date of the amendment is a life annuity of $15,000 per year at normal retirement age (1 percent times $75,000 times 20 years of service) and his early retirement benefit commencing at age 55 has a present value of $91,397 as of January 1, 2020. It is assumed for purposes of this example that the longest expected transition period for any active employee does not exceed five months (20 years and five months, times 1 percent times 49 percent exceeds 20 years times 1 percent times 50 percent). Finally, it is assumed for purposes of this example that the amendment reduces optional forms of benefit that are burdensome or complex.

(2) *Conclusion Concerning Application of Section 411(d)(6)(B)*. The amendment reducing the early retirement factors has the effect of eliminating the existing optional forms of benefit (where the amount of the benefit is based on pre-amendment early retirement factors in any case where the new factors result in a smaller amount payable) and adding new optional forms of benefit (where the amount of benefit is based on the different early retirement factors). Accordingly, the elimination must satisfy applicable requirements if the amount payable at any date is less than would have been payable under the plan before the amendment.

(3) *Conclusion Concerning Application of Redundancy Rules*. The amendment satisfies applicable requirements. First, with respect to each eliminated optional form of benefit (i.e., with respect to each optional form of benefit with the Old Division X Factor), after the amendment there is a retained optional form of benefit that is in the same family of optional forms of benefit (i.e., the optional form of benefit with the New Factor). Second, the amendment is not effective with respect to annuity commencement dates that are less than the time period required under paragraph (c)(1)(ii) of this section. Third, to the extent that the plan amendment eliminates the most valuable option for a participant with a short life expectancy, the retained optional form of benefit is identical except for differences in actuarial factors.

(4) *Conclusion Concerning Application of the Delayed Effective Date Requirements*. The plan amendment must satisfy the delayed effective date requirements because, as of the June 2, 2019 adoption date, the actuarial present value of the early retirement subsidy is less than the actuarial present value of the early retirement subsidy being eliminated. The plan amendment satisfies applicable requirements because the amendment eliminates optional forms of benefit that create significant burdens or complexities for the plan and its participants.

(5) *Conclusion Concerning Application of* De Minimis *Rules*. The amendment does not satisfy applicable requirements because the reduction in the actuarial present value is more than a *de minimis* amount. For example, for Frank, the amount of the joint and contingent annuity payable at age 55 is reduced from $7,500 (50 percent of $15,000) to $7,350 (49 percent of $15,000) and the reduction in present value as a result of the amendment is $1,828 ($91,397 − $89,569). In this case, the retirement-type subsidy at age 55 is the excess of the present value of the 50 percent early retirement benefit over the present value of the deferred payment of the accrued benefit, or $13,921 ($97,269 − $83,348) and the present value at age 54 of the retirement-type subsidy is $13,081. The reduction in present value is more than the greater of 2 percent of the present value of the retirement-type subsidy and 1 percent of Frank's compensation because the reduction in present value exceeds $800 (the greater of $262, which is 2 percent of the present value of the retirement-type subsidy for the benefit being eliminated, and $800, which is 1 percent of Frank's compensation of $80,000).

(6) *Conclusion Involving Application of* De Minimis *Rules Relating to Expected Transition Period*. The amendment satisfies these rules. First, as assumed under the facts above, the amendment reduces optional forms of benefit that are burdensome or complex. Second, the plan amendment is not effective for annuity commencement dates before January 1, 2020, and that date is not earlier than the longest expected transition period for any participant in the Plan on the date of the amendment. Third, the amendment does not apply to any participant who has a severance from employment during the transition period. If, however, a later plan amendment reduces accruals under the Plan, the initial plan amendment will no longer satisfy the delayed effective date requirements (and must be voided) unless, as part of the later amendment,

the expected transition period is extended to reflect the reduction in accruals under the Plan. [Treas. Reg. § 1.411(d)-3(h), Ex. 5]

Example 10-44: Facts Involving Elimination on Noncore Options Using the Utilization Test. The Grafton Company Plan is a calendar-year defined benefit plan under which participants may elect to commence distributions after termination of employment in the following actuarially equivalent forms, with spousal consent, if applicable: a straight life annuity; a 50 percent, 75 percent, or 100 percent joint and contingent annuity; or a 5-year, 10-year, or 15-year term certain and life annuity. A participant is permitted to elect a single-sum distribution if the present value of the participant's nonforfeitable accrued benefit is not greater than $5,000. The annuities offered under the Plan are generally available both with and without a social security leveling feature. The social security leveling feature provides for an assumed commencement of social security benefits at any age elected by the participant between the ages of 62 and 67. Under the Plan, the normal retirement age is defined as age 65.

In 2019, the Grafton Company, after reviewing participants' benefit elections, determines that, during the period from January 1, 2017 through June 30, 2019, no participant has elected a five-year term certain and life annuity with a social security leveling option. During that period, the Plan has made the five-year term certain and life annuity with a social security leveling option available to 142 participants who were at least age 55 and who elected optional forms of benefit with annuity commencement dates within that period. In addition, during that period, 20 of the 142 participants elected a single-sum distribution and there was no retirement-type subsidy available for a limited period of time. The Plan, in accordance with Treasury Regulations Section 1.411(d)-1(f)(1), is amended on September 15, 2019, effective as of January 1, 2020, to eliminate all five-year term certain and life annuities with a social security leveling option for annuity commencement dates on or after January 1, 2020.

The amendment satisfies the requirements of the utilization test. First, the five-year term certain and life annuity with a social security leveling option is not a core option as defined in Treasury Regulations Section 1.411(d)-1(g)(5). Second, the plan amendment is not applicable with respect to an optional form of benefit with an annuity commencement date that is earlier than the number of days in the maximum QJSA explanation period after the date the amendment is adopted. Third, the five-year term certain and life annuity with a social security leveling option has been available to at least 50 participants who are taken into account during the look-back period. Finally, during the look-back period, no participant elected any optional form that is part of the generalized optional form being eliminated (for example, the five-year term certain and life annuity with a social security leveling option). [Treas. Reg. § 1.411(d)-3(h), Ex. 6]

Chapter 11

QJSA and QPSA Rules

This chapter summarizes the survivor annuity rules under the Internal Revenue Code of 1986 ("the Code") and the Employee Retirement Income Security Act of 1974 (ERISA). These rules require all defined benefit pension plans, defined contribution plans that are subject to the minimum funding standards of Code Section 412 (e.g., money purchase pension plans), and certain other defined contribution plans to pay, in the form of a qualified joint and survivor annuity (QJSA), the vested accrued benefit of a participant who lives at least until his or her annuity starting date. The rules also require these plans to pay the vested accrued benefit of a participant who dies before his or her annuity starting date to his or her surviving spouse (if any), in the form of a qualified pre-retirement survivor annuity (QPSA). The annuity starting date is the reference point for determining whether a participant's vested accrued benefit is to be paid in the form of a QJSA or a QPSA.

Any plan that is subject to the survivor annuity requirements under the Code, and that fails to pay benefits in these required forms, will be disqualified. A participant in a plan that is subject to the survivor annuity rules may elect not to receive his or her vested accrued benefit in the form of a QPSA or QJSA, but only if the applicable notice, election, and spousal consent requirements are met. If the participant is married, any election he or she makes not to receive his or her vested accrued benefit in the form of a QPSA or QJSA will be ineffective, unless his or her spouse consents to this election in writing.

The survivor annuity requirements apply to benefits that are attributable to both employer and employee contributions. However, vested accrued benefits do not have to be paid in the form of a QPSA or QJSA if, at the time of the participant's death or the date his or her benefits otherwise became distributable under the plan, his or her entire vested accrued benefit was attributable to employee contributions, and his or her death or the distribution occurred before October 11, 1986.

On December 17, 2003, the IRS issued final regulations governing the contents of QJSA and QPSA explanations. [68 Fed. Reg. 70141] The 2003 final regulations became effective on December 17, 2003, and they would have applied to all QJSA distributions with annuity starting dates on or after October 1, 2004, and to all QPSA explanations provided on or after July 1, 2004. [68 Fed. Reg. 70141] However, on June 30, 2004, the IRS announced a delay in the effective date, from October 1, 2004, until February 1, 2006, for certain QJSA explanations. [Ann. 2004-58, 2004-29 I.R.B. 66] That delay was reflected in final regulations issued by the IRS on March 24, 2006. [71 Fed. Reg. 14798] Nevertheless, the original October 1, 2004, effective date was retained for QJSA explanations of any optional form of benefit that is subject to Code Section 417(e)(3) cash-out rules (e.g., a lump-sum payment), if the actuarial present value of that optional form is less than that of the QJSA. In addition, Announcement 2004-58 and the 2006 final regulations retained the July 1, 2004, effective date for all QPSA explanations.

Under the Taxpayer Relief Act of 1997 (TRA'97), Congress directed the Department of Labor (DOL) and the Treasury Department to issue guidance facilitating the use of electronic media for qualified retirement plan purposes.

On February 8, 2000, the IRS issued final regulations setting forth applicable standards for the transmission of certain notices and consents required in connection with distributions from retirement plans through electronic media. The 2000 final regulations did not permit the use of electronic media for any notice or election required under Code Section 417 with respect to a waiver of a QJSA. On October 20, 2006, the IRS issued final regulations on the use of electronic media for providing employee benefit notices and making employee benefit elections and consents. The 2006 final regulations are generally applicable to notices provided, and participant elections made, on or after January 1, 2007. The participant election rules in the 2006 final regulations extend the use of electronic media to the notice and election rules applicable to plans that are subject to the QJSA requirements of Code Section 417. Accordingly, a qualified retirement plan subject to the QJSA requirements is permitted to provide the notice required by Code Section 417 to a participant through the use of electronic media as long as the plan complies with either of the two methods (i.e., the consumer consent method or the alternative method), described in the 2006 final regulations, for providing electronic notices. Similarly, a participant's consent to a distribution is permitted to be provided through the use of electronic media if the plan complies with the standards set forth in the 2006 final regulations, subject to obtaining valid spousal consent. Code Section 417 requires any spousal consent to a waiver of a QJSA to be witnessed by a plan representative or a notary public. In accordance with Section 101(g) of E-SIGN, the 2006 final regulations authorize the use of an electronic acknowledgment or notarization if the standards of Section 101(g) of E-SIGN and state law applicable to notary publics are satisfied. The 2006 final regulations require that the signature of a spouse be witnessed in the physical presence of the plan representative or notary public.

The Pension and Protection Act (PPA) revised the QJSA rules under the Code and ERISA to require that, at the participant's election, benefits will be paid in the form of a *qualified optional survivor annuity (QOSA)*. A QOSA is an annuity for the life of the participant, with a survivor annuity for the life of the participant's spouse, which is equal to the applicable percentage of the annuity that is (1) payable during the joint lives of the participant and the spouse and (2) the actuarial equivalent of a single annuity for the life of the participant. If the survivor annuity provided by the QJSA under the plan is less than 75 percent of the annuity payable during the joint lives of the participant and spouse, the "applicable percentage" is 75 percent. If the survivor annuity provided by the QJSA under the plan is greater than or equal to 75 percent of the annuity payable during the joint lives of the participant and spouse, the "applicable percentage" is 50 percent. So, for example, if the survivor annuity provided by the QJSA under the plan is 50 percent, the survivor annuity provided under the QOSA must be 75 percent. As a further example, if the survivor annuity provided by the QJSA under the plan is 75 percent, the survivor annuity provided under the QOSA must be 50 percent. The written explanation required to be provided to participants explaining the terms and conditions of the QJSA must also include the terms and conditions of the QOSA. The PPA provision pertaining to the QOSA applies generally to plan years beginning after December 31, 2007 (i.e., in the case of calendar-year plans, to plan years beginning on January 1, 2008). In the case of collectively bargained plans, the new PPA provision applies to plan years beginning on or after the earlier of (1) the later of January 1, 2008, and the last date on which an applicable collective bargaining agreement terminates (without regard to extensions) and (2) January 1, 2009. [PPA § 1004]

PPA also expanded the applicable election period from 90 to 180 days, ending on the annuity starting date, within which participants may elect to waive the QJSA. (The same change also was made to the rollover notice rules under Code Section 402(f) and the general consent rules under Code Section 411(a)(11)). These PPA changes apply to plan years beginning after December 31, 2006. PPA also directed the Secretary of the Treasury to modify the regulations under Code Sections 402(f), 411(a)(11), and 417 (as well as the regulations under ERISA Sections 203(e) and 205) by substituting "180 days" for "90 days" each place "90 days" appears in those regulations. [PPA § 1102]

On January 10, 2007, the IRS issued Notice 2007-7, 2007-5 I.R.B. 395, which provides guidance in the form of questions and answers with respect to certain provisions of PPA that are primarily related to distributions and that became effective beginning in 2007 or earlier, including PPA Section 1102, which made the above-described changes to the notice requirements related to distributions.

On March 5, 2008, the IRS issued Notice 2008-30, 2008-12 I.R.B. 638, which provides guidance in the form of questions and answers with respect to certain distribution-related provisions of PPA that became effective in 2008, including PPA Section 1004, relating to the QOSA option described above.

On October 9, 2008, the IRS issued proposed regulations pursuant to PPA which stipulated that the notice required under Code Section 401(a)(11) to be provided to a participant of his or her right, if any, to defer receipt of an immediately distributable benefit must also describe the consequences of failing to defer receipt of the distribution (i.e., taking an immediate distribution). The proposed regulations would also provide that the applicable election period for waiving the QJSA under Code Section 417 is the 180-day period ending on the annuity starting date, and that a notice required to be provided under Code Section 402(f), 411(a)(11), or 417 may be provided to a participant as much as 180 days before the annuity starting day (or for a notice under Code Section 402(f), the distribution date). [Prop. Reg. §§ 1.401(a)-13, 1.401(a)-20, 1.402(f), 1.411(a)-11, and 1.417(e)-1, 73 Fed. Reg. 59575 (Oct. 9, 2008)]

On February 21, 2012, the IRS issued Revenue Ruling 2012-3, 2012-8 I.R.B. 383, describing how the QJSA and QPSA rules apply when a deferred annuity contract is purchased under a profit sharing plan.

On September 9, 2016, the IRS issued final regulations under Code Section 417(e) providing guidance relating to the minimum present value requirements applicable to certain defined benefit pension plans. The final regulations change the existing regulations regarding the minimum present value requirements for defined benefit plan distributions to permit plans to simplify the treatment of certain optional forms of benefit that are partly paid in the form of an annuity and partly in a single sum or other more accelerated form. [81 Fed. Reg. 62359] The final regulations apply to distributions with annuity starting dates in plan years beginning on or after January 1, 2017. On November 25, 2016, the IRS issued proposed regulations that would amend the September 9, 2016 final regulations in several areas. [81 Fed. Reg. 85190] Specifically, the proposed regulations would update the final regulations for changes made by PPA'06 to eliminate certain obsolete provisions and make other clarifying changes. [81 Fed. Reg. 85190, 85191]

Overview 11-5
Retirement Plans Subject to Survivor Annuity Requirements 11-6
Transferee, Offset, Frozen, and Terminated Plans 11-12
Applying Survivor Annuity Requirements to Participants 11-13
Annuity Starting Date 11-15
Benefits 11-18
Timing of QJSA Distributions 11-19
Rules Governing the QPSA 11-20
Applying Survivor Annuity Requirements to Plan Loans 11-22
Applying Survivor Annuity Requirements to Unmarried Participants, Surviving Spouses, and Participants Who Have a Change in Marital Status 11-23
Spousal Consent Requirement 11-25
Participant's Waiver of a QPSA or QJSA 11-27
Notice Requirements 11-33
Subsidized Survivor Benefits 11-57

Overview

Q 11:1 What survivor annuity requirements did the Retirement Equity Act of 1984 add to the Code and ERISA?

The Retirement Equity Act of 1984 (REA 1984) added qualified joint and survivor annuity (QJSA) and qualified pre-retirement survivor annuity (QPSA) rules to the Code and ERISA. Retirement plans that are subject to the rules must provide a QJSA and a QPSA to remain qualified. The survivor annuity requirements apply to any benefit payable under a subject plan, including a benefit payable to a participant under a contract purchased by the plan and paid by a third party. [Treas. Reg. § 1.401(a)-20, Q&A-1]

REA 1984 was meant to address a variety of issues thought to be of special concern to spouses. REA 1984 amended the Code and ERISA to introduce mandatory spousal rights in certain qualified retirement plans, so that the choice of the form of benefit received from the plan was no longer solely the participant's. The legislative history of REA 1984 reflects that Congress viewed the marriage relationship as a partnership, and the retirement benefit resulting from that partnership as deriving from the contributions of both spouses. Before the enactment of REA 1984, the spouse of a participant had very few rights to share in that participant's retirement plan benefit. [Ann. 95-33, 1995-19 I.R.B. 14]

REA 1984 greatly augmented the nonemployee spouse's interests by creating the right to choose a survivorship annuity as the form in which benefits are distributed from the plan. If the participant survives until retirement age, REA 1984 generally requires that the participant's annuity be a QJSA, under which payments continue for the lives of the employee and the nonemployee spouse. If the participant dies before retirement and is vested, REA 1984 makes the nonemployee spouse a plan beneficiary, with an interest called a QPSA, which survives the participant's death. These automatic forms of benefit (the QJSA and the QPSA) may be waived by the nonemployee spouse. [Ann. 95-33, 1995-19 I.R.B. 14]

REA 1984 added Section 417 to the Code and made amendments to Code Section 401(a). Its provisions generally became effective for the first plan year beginning in 1985. Technical and other corrections were made to REA 1984 by the Tax Reform Act of 1986 (TRA '86). Final regulations provide additional guidance under Code Sections 401(a)(20), 411, and 417.

Q 11:2 Must annuity contracts purchased and distributed to a participant or spouse by a retirement plan that is subject to the survivor annuity requirements of the Code also satisfy those requirements?

Yes. The survivor annuity requirements and the rights and benefits that they confer may not be eliminated or reduced merely because (1) an annuity contract is held by a participant or spouse instead of a plan trustee, or (2) annuity contracts are distributed upon plan termination. Thus, the survivor annuity requirements of Code Sections 401(a)(11) and 417 apply to payments under the annuity contracts, not to the distributions of the contracts by a plan. [Treas. Reg. § 1.401(a)-20, Q&A-2]

Note that in Revenue Ruling 2012-3, 2012-8 I.R.B. 383 (Feb. 21, 2012), the IRS described how the QJSA and QPSA rules apply when a deferred annuity contract is purchased under a profit sharing plan (see Q 11:5).

Retirement Plans Subject to Survivor Annuity Requirements

Q 11:3 What qualified retirement plans are subject to the survivor annuity requirements of Code Sections 401(a)(11) and 417?

Code Section 401(a)(11) provides that the QJSA and QPSA requirements apply to all defined benefit plans and any defined contribution plan to which

Code Section 412 minimum funding requirements apply (which includes money purchase pension plans but excludes profit sharing plans). [I.R.C. § 401(a)(11); Ann. 95-33, 1995-19 I.R.B. 14] The QJSA and QPSA requirements also apply to certain other defined contribution plans, unless certain conditions are met. [Treas. Reg. § 1.401(a)-20, Q&A-3(a)]

Defined Benefit Plans. The QJSA and QPSA requirements apply to any defined benefit plan. Under a defined benefit plan, the survivor annuity requirements apply only to benefits in which a participant was vested immediately before he or she died. They do not apply to benefits, to which a participant's beneficiary becomes entitled by reason of the participant's death, or to the proceeds of a life insurance contract, to the extent those proceeds exceed the present value of the participant's nonforfeitable benefits that existed immediately before he or she died. [Treas. Reg. § 1.401(a)-20, Q&A-3(a) and Q&A-12(a)]

Defined Contribution Plans Subject to the Minimum Funding Standards of Code Section 412. The survivor annuity requirements also apply to all nonforfeitable benefits payable under a defined contribution plan that is subject to the funding standards of Code Section 412 (e.g., a money purchase pension plan, but not a profit sharing plan or a stock bonus plan), whether nonforfeitable before or upon death, including the proceeds of insurance contracts. [Treas. Reg. § 1.401(a)-20, Q&A-3(a) and Q&A-12(b)]

Certain Other Defined Contribution Plans. The survivor annuity requirements also apply to any participant in a defined contribution plan that is not subject to the minimum funding standards of Code Section 412 (e.g., a profit sharing plan or a stock bonus plan), unless these three conditions are satisfied:

1. The plan provides that the participant's nonforfeitable accrued benefit (minus any security interest that the plan holds relating to a participant's outstanding loan) is payable in full upon the participant's death to the participant's surviving spouse or to a designated beneficiary if there is no spouse or if the surviving spouse consents in the manner described in Code Section 417(a)(2), which stipulates, among other requirements, that the spouse's consent be in writing. [I.R.C. § 401(a)(11)(B)(iii)(I)]
2. The participant does not elect the payment of benefits in the form of a life annuity. [I.R.C. § 401(a)(11)(B)(iii)(II)] and
3. With respect to the participant, the plan is not a "transferee plan" or an "offset plan" [I.R.C. § 401(a)(11)(B)(iii)(III)] (see Q 11:6).

[Treas. Reg. § 1.401(a)-20, Q&A-3(a)(1)–(3)]

A defined contribution plan that is not subject to the minimum funding standards of Code Section 412 will not be treated as satisfying the requirement described in item 1, above, unless these two additional conditions are met:

- The benefit is available to the surviving spouse within a reasonable time after the participant's death. Availability within the 90-day period after the date of death is deemed to be reasonable; the reasonableness of longer periods is determined based on the particular facts and circumstances. A time period longer than 90 days, however, is deemed unreasonable if it is less favorable to the surviving spouse than any time period under the plan that is applicable to other distributions. For example, it would be unreasonable to require distribution to be made to the surviving spouse by the close of the plan year during which the participant died, if distributions to employees who separate from service are required to be made within 90 days of separation. [Treas. Reg. § 1.401(a)-20, Q&A-3(b)(1)]

- The benefit payable to the surviving spouse is adjusted for gains or losses occurring after the participant's death in accordance with plan rules governing the adjustment of account balances for other distributions. For example, distributions of an account balance to a surviving spouse may not be determined as of the last day of the quarter in which the participant's death occurred without allowing for adjustments for gains or losses after death, if the plan provides for such adjustments for a participant who separates from service within a quarter. [Treas. Reg. § 1.401(a)-20, Q&A-3(b)(2)]

Q 11:4 What rules apply to a participant who elects a life annuity option under a defined contribution plan, such as a profit sharing or stock bonus plan, that is not subject to the minimum funding standards of Code Section 412?

If a participant elects at any time a life annuity option under such a plan, the survivor annuity requirements of Code Sections 401(a)(11) and 417 will always thereafter apply to all of the participant's benefits under that plan, unless there is a separate accounting of the account balance subject to the election. If a participant elects a life annuity option, the plan must satisfy the written explanation, consent, election, and withdrawal rules of Code Section 417, including waiver of the QJSA within 180 days before the annuity starting date (see Q 11:37). If a participant selecting such an option dies, his or her surviving spouse must be able to receive the QPSA benefit, described in Code Section 417(c)(2), which is a life annuity, the actuarial equivalent of which is not less than 50 percent of the nonforfeitable account balance (adjusted for loans, as described in Q 11:24). The remaining account balance may be paid to a designated nonspouse beneficiary. [I.R.C. § 417(a)(6)(A); Treas. Reg. § 1.401(a)-20, Q&A-4; Prop. Reg. § 1.401(a)-20, Q&A-4; IRS Notice 2007-7, 2007-5 I.R.B. 395]

Q 11:5 How do the QJSA and QPSA rules apply when a deferred annuity contract is purchased under a profit sharing plan?

On February 21, 2012, the IRS issued Revenue Ruling 2012-3, 2012-8 I.R.B. 383, describing how the QJSA and QPSA rules apply when a deferred annuity contract is purchased under a profit sharing plan in the three different fact situations described below:

Situation 1. In the first fact situation, participants in a Code Section 401(k)/profit sharing plan were permitted to direct the investment of their elective deferral and matching contribution accounts among the plans available investment options, including a deferred annuity contract issued by an insurance company. The plan separately accounted for all amounts by investment and contribution source. No other annuity options were available under the plan, and the plan was not an indirect or direct transferee plan (see Q 11:6).

Amounts invested for a plan participant in a deferred annuity contract were applied at the time of the investment to purchase an annuity contract providing for payments commencing generally by the first day of the month beginning after the day the participant retired or attained age 65. The amount payable under the deferred annuity contract was fixed on the first day of the first period for which an amount was paid under the contract (the annuity starting date), and depended upon the amount accumulated under the contract on the annuity starting date and the actuarial assumptions (including interest rate and mortality assumptions) used to determine the annuity purchase rate on that date, subject to a minimum-purchase-rate guarantee set forth in the contract. Amounts invested in the deferred annuity contract could be transferred to other investments at any time before the annuity starting date.

Generally, the deferred annuity contract paid benefits in one of various life annuity forms that could be elected during the 180-day period ending on the annuity starting date, but the participant could instead elect, at any time before the annuity starting date, to have a single-sum payment. If the participant failed to elect a form of payment, the form of payment would be a straight life annuity for a participant who was not married on the annuity starting date and an actuarially equivalent 50 percent joint and survivor annuity (with the participant's surviving spouse as the joint annuitant) for a participant who was married on the annuity starting date. If a participant was married on the annuity starting date, the notarized consent of his or her spouse had to be obtained if the participant elected a life annuity form other than a joint and survivor annuity with the surviving spouse as the joint annuitant and the survivor annuity not less than 50 percent or more than 100 percent of the joint annuity amount. (So, for example, no spousal consent would be required if a participant elected a QOSA (see Q 11:38).)

The plan provided that if a participant died before the annuity starting date under the deferred annuity contract, the participant's surviving spouse (or if none, the participant's designated beneficiary) would receive a death benefit equal to the vested accrued benefit under the deferred annuity contract as of the date of death. For a married participant, the death benefit would be paid to the surviving spouse in the form of an annuity for the life of the surviving spouse (unless the surviving spouse elected a single-sum payment).

For amounts not invested in a deferred annuity contract, the plan provided that, upon the participant's death, his or her vested accrued benefit (reduced by any security interest held by the plan on account of an outstanding loan) would be payable in full to the participant's surviving spouse (or, if none, or if the surviving spouse gave his or her notarized consent, to the participant's designated beneficiary).

In the first fact situation posited in Revenue Ruling 2012-3, the participant invested portions of his or her elective deferral and matching contribution accounts in the deferred annuity contract on various dates from age 45 to 65, and then retired at age 65. The annuity starting date for the participant's benefit under the deferred annuity contract was the first day of the month after he or she retired.

Code Section 401(a)(11)(B)(iii) provides that the QJSA and QPSA requirements apply to a participant under a defined contribution plan that is not subject to the funding standards under Code Section 412 (i.e., a profit sharing or stock bonus plan) unless the following three conditions are satisfied:

1. The plan provides that the participant's vested accrued benefit (reduced by any security interest held by the plan on account of an outstanding loan) is payable in full, on the participant's death, to his or her surviving spouse (or, if none, or if the surviving spouse consents, to the participant's designated beneficiary); [I.R.C. § 401(a)(11)(B)(iii)(I)]
2. The participant does not elect a payment of benefits in the form of a life annuity; [I.R.C. § 401(a)(11)(B)(iii)(II)] and
3. With respect to the participant, the plan is not a direct or indirect transferee (in a post-1984 transfer) of a plan that was subject to the QJSA and QPSA requirements with respect to the participant. [I.R.C. § 401(a)(11)(B)(iii)(III)]

The IRS ruled, based on these facts, that:

1. The plan satisfied the first condition, in Code Section 401(a)(11)(B)(iii)(I), because a participant's entire vested accrued benefit, including amounts attributable to the deferred annuity contract, was payable in full, upon the participant's death prior to the annuity starting date, to the participant's surviving spouse (or, if none, to the participant's designated beneficiary);
2. The plan satisfied the third condition, in Code Section 401(a)(11)(B)(iii)(III), because the plan was not a direct or indirect transferee of a plan that was subject to the QJSA and QPSA requirements with respect to any participant; and
3. The plan also satisfied the second condition, in Code Section 401(a)(11)(B)(iii)(II), that the participant not elect a payment of benefits in the form of a life annuity. Although a life annuity was the default payment under the deferred annuity contract, a participant could elect another form of payment before the annuity starting date under the contract, either by transferring amounts invested in the contract to another investment option (with respect to which other forms of distribution were available) or by electing a single-sum payment under the contract. Thus, in the absence of an affirmative election of a life annuity during the 180-day period ending on the annuity starting date, the participant did not elect a life annuity under the deferred annuity contract until his or her annuity starting date with respect to the contract. Because the participant did not elect a life annuity under the deferred annuity contract until his or her annuity starting date with respect to the contract, the plan was not subject to the QPSA requirements before the annuity starting date. However, at the annuity starting date, if the participant had not previously elected to receive another form of payment, the plan became subject to the QJSA requirements with respect to the deferred annuity. But, because the plan separately accounted for the deferred annuity contract, the remainder of the plan was not subject to the QJSA and QPSA requirements.

The IRS ruled, under the facts in Situation 1, that the plan qualified for the exception in Code Section 401(a)(11)(B)(iii) and thus was not subject to the QJSA and QPSA requirements with respect to the participant's deferred annuity contract until the participant's annuity starting date under the deferred annuity contract.

Situation 2: The facts in this situation were the same as in Situation 1, except as described below.

A plan participant who invested amounts in a fixed deferred annuity contract could not subsequently transfer those amounts out of the contract and could not elect to take those amounts in the form of a single-sum payment. Thus, amounts invested in the deferred annuity contract were paid in the form of a life annuity, without an option for the participant to accelerate payment of the amounts in the form of a single-sum payment.

In addition, the amount payable under the deferred annuity contract on a plan participant's annuity starting date in the form of a straight life annuity that was attributable to an amount invested in the contract was fixed on the date the investment was made. Thus, the amount payable under the fixed annuity contract depended on the amount invested in the contract on the date the investment was made and the actuarial assumptions, including interest rate and mortality assumptions, used to determine the annuity purchase rate on that date.

The IRS ruled, in Situation 2, that the plan was generally subject to the QJSA and QPSA requirements with respect to the participant's benefits under the deferred annuity contract beginning when the participant first invested in the contract. The deferred annuity contract did not qualify for the exception under Code Section 401(a)(11)(B)(iii) because, at the time the participant invested amounts in the contract, he or she had elected a life annuity.

The IRS further ruled that the death benefit under the deferred annuity contract in Situation 2 satisfied the QPSA requirements. In addition, because the QPSA was fully subsidized (i.e., no charge was imposed for the coverage) and because the plan did not allow the participant to waive the QPSA or to select a nonspouse beneficiary, the plan was not required to obtain spousal consent with respect to the QPSA.

Situation 3: The facts in this situation were the same as in Situation 2, except as follows.

A plan participant who invested amounts in a deferred annuity contract could make an election to have no benefits payable under the contract with respect to amounts invested in the contract that were attributable to matching contributions in the event of death before the annuity starting date. If the participant made this election, then the participant's spouse, if any, was required to give notarized consent to the election.

The IRS ruled, in Situation 3, that the plan was generally subject to the QJSA and QPSA requirements with respect to the participant's benefits under the deferred annuity contract beginning when the participant first invested in the contract.

However, unlike in Situation 2, the IRS further ruled that the plan in Situation 3 was required to comply with the written explanation and spousal consent rules of Code Section 417(a) with respect to the participant's waiver of the QPSA. This is because the Code Section 417(a)(5)(A) exception from the written explanation and spousal consent requirements of Code Section 417(a) impose two conditions: (1) that the benefit not be waived and (2) that the benefit be fully subsidized. In Situation 3, unlike in Situation 2, the plan allowed a participant to waive the QPSA and thus was required to provide a written explanation and obtain notarized spousal consent to any such waiver. [Rev. Rul. 2012-3. 2012-8 I.R.B. 383 (Feb. 21, 2012)]

Transferee, Offset, Frozen, and Terminated Plans

Q 11:6 How do the survivor annuity rules of Code Sections 401(a)(11) and 417 apply to transferee plans that are defined contribution plans not subject to the minimum funding standards of Code Section 412 (e.g., profit sharing and stock bonus plans) and to offset plans?

Transferee Plans. Although the survivor annuity requirements of Code Sections 401(a)(11) and 417 generally do not apply to defined contribution plans, such as profit sharing and stock bonus plans, that are not subject to the minimum funding standards of Code Section 412, those plans are subject to the survivor annuity requirements to the extent that they are transferee plans with respect to any participant. A defined contribution plan is a transferee plan with respect to any participant if it is a direct or indirect transferee of the participant's benefits held on or after January 1, 1985, by:

1. A defined benefit plan;
2. A defined contribution plan, such as a money purchase pension plan, that is subject to the minimum funding standards of Code Section 412; or
3. A defined contribution plan that is subject to the survivor annuity requirements of Code Sections 401(a)(11) and 417 with respect to that participant.

If, through a merger, spin-off, or other transaction having the effect of a transfer, benefits subject to the survivor annuity requirements of Code Sections 401(a)(11) and 417 are held under a plan that is not otherwise subject to those requirements, those benefits will nevertheless be subject to the survivor annuity requirements. However, even if a plan satisfies the survivor annuity requirements, other rules apply to these transactions between plans; for example, the anti-cutback rules of Code Section 411(d)(6) and the related Treasury Regulations (see chapter 10).

A transfer made before January 1, 1985 and any rollover contribution made at any time are not transactions that subject the transferee plan to the survivor annuity requirements with respect to a participant. If a plan is a transferee plan with respect to a participant, the survivor annuity requirements do not apply to other plan participants solely because of the transfer. [Treas. Reg. § 1.401(a)-20, Q&A-5(a)]

Offset Plans. If a plan would not otherwise be subject to the survivor annuity requirements of Code Sections 401(a)(11) and 417, but its benefits are used to offset benefits in a plan that is subject to those requirements, the offset plan is subject to the survivor annuity requirements for those participant's whose benefits are offset. Thus, if a stock bonus or profit sharing plan offsets benefits under a defined benefit plan, the stock bonus or profit sharing plan is subject to the survivor annuity requirements. [Treas. Reg. § 1.401(a)-20, Q&A-5(a)]

Benefits Covered. The survivor annuity requirements apply to all accrued benefits held for a participant with respect to whom the plan is a transferee plan, unless there is an acceptable separate accounting between the transferred benefits and all other benefits under the plan. A separate accounting is not acceptable unless gains, losses, withdrawals, contributions, forfeitures, and other credits or charges are allocated on a reasonable and consistent basis between the accrued benefits subject to the survivor annuity requirements and other benefits. If there is an acceptable separate accounting between transferred benefits and any other benefits under the plan, only the transferred benefits are subject to the survivor annuity requirements. [Treas. Reg. § 1.401(a)-20, Q&A-5(b)]

Q 11:7 Must a frozen or terminated retirement plan satisfy the survivor annuity requirements of Code Sections 401(a)(11) and 417?

In general, benefits provided under a retirement plan subject to the survivor annuity requirements of Code Sections 401(a)(11) and 417 must be provided in accordance with those requirements, even if the plan is frozen or terminated. However, any plan that terminated before September 17, 1985, and that distributed all remaining assets as soon as administratively feasible after the termination date, is not subject to the survivor annuity requirements of Code Sections 401(a)(11) and 417. [Treas. Reg. § 1.401(a)-20, Q&A-6]

Q 11:8 If the Pension Benefit Guaranty Corporation (PBGC) is administering a retirement plan, are benefits payable in the form of a QPSA or QJSA?

Yes. The Pension Benefit Guaranty Corporation (PBGC) will pay benefits in the form of a QPSA or QJSA. [Treas. Reg. § 1.401(a)-20, Q&A-7]

Applying Survivor Annuity Requirements to Participants

Q 11:9 How do the survivor annuity requirements of Code Sections 401(a)(11) and 417 apply to retirement plan participants?

Payment in the Form of QPSA or QJSA. If a retirement plan participant dies before his or her annuity starting date with vested benefits attributable to employer or employee contributions (or both), benefits must be paid to his or her surviving spouse in the form of a QPSA. If a participant survives until his or her annuity starting date with vested benefits attributable to employer or employee contributions (or both), benefits must be provided to the participant in the form of a QJSA. [Treas. Reg. § 1.401(a)-20, Q&A-8(a)]

Waiving the QPSA or QJSA. A participant may waive the QPSA or the QJSA (or both) if the notice, election, and spousal consent requirements of Code Section 417 are satisfied. [Treas. Reg. § 1.401(a)-20, Q&A-8(b)]

Benefits Not Required to Be Paid as a QPSA or QJSA. Benefits are not required to be paid in the form of a QPSA or QJSA if, at the time of death or distribution, the participant was vested only in employee contributions, and he or she died, or the distribution commenced, before October 22, 1986. [Treas. Reg. § 1.401(a)-20, Q&A-8(c)]

Certain Mandatory Distributions. A distribution may occur without satisfying the spousal consent requirements of Code Section 417(a) and (e) if the present value of the participant's nonforfeitable benefit does not exceed the cash-out limit in effect under Treasury Regulations Section 1.411(a)-11(c)(3)(ii) (i.e., $5,000 for dates in plan years beginning on or after August 6, 1997). [Treas. Reg. § 1.401(a)-20, Q&A-8(d)]

Q 11:10 May separate portions of a participant's accrued benefit under a retirement plan be subject to QPSA and QJSA requirements at any particular time?

Yes. One portion of a participant's retirement plan benefit may be subject to the QPSA requirements and another portion to the QJSA requirements at the same time.

For example, for a money purchase pension plan to distribute any portion of a married participant's benefit to the participant, the plan must distribute that portion in the form of a QJSA (unless the plan satisfies the consent requirements of Code Section 417(a) and (e) for that portion of the participant's benefit). This rule applies even if the distribution is merely an in-service distribution attributable to voluntary employee contributions and regardless of whether the participant has reached the normal retirement age under the plan. The QJSA requirements apply to such a distribution because the participant's annuity starting date has occurred for that portion of his or her benefit. If the participant dies after his or her benefit has begun to be distributed in the form of a QJSA, the remaining payments must be made to his or her surviving spouse under the QJSA. In addition, the plan must satisfy the QPSA requirements for any portion of the participant's benefits for which his or her annuity starting date has not yet occurred. [Treas. Reg. § 1.401(a)-20, Q&A-9(a)]

Example 11-1: George, age 60, has a $100,000 account balance under the Pastures of Heaven Corporations money purchase pension plan. George makes an in-service withdrawal of $20,000 attributable to voluntary employee contributions. The QJSA requirements apply to George's withdrawal of the $20,000. Unless George properly waives payment in the form of a QJSA, the $20,000 must be distributed in the form of a QJSA. George's remaining account balance ($80,000) remains subject to the QPSA requirements because his annuity starting date has not yet occurred for the $80,000. If George survives until his annuity starting date, the $80,000 would be subject to the QJSA requirements. If George died on the day after his annuity starting date for the withdrawal, his wife would be entitled to a QPSA with a value equal to at least $40,000 for the $80,000 account balance, in addition to any survivor benefit on the $20,000 withdrawal. If the $20,000 payment to George had been the first payment of an annuity purchased with the entire $100,000 account balance (see Q 11:2) rather than an in-service distribution, the QJSA requirements would apply to the entire account balance at the time of George's annuity starting date. In that event, the plan would have no obligation to provide George's wife with a QPSA benefit upon George's death. George's wife would receive the QJSA benefit (if the QJSA had not been waived) based on the full $100,000. [Treas. Reg. § 1.401(a)-20, Q&A-9(b)]

Annuity Starting Date

Q 11:11 What is the relevance of the annuity starting date to the survivor annuity requirements?

The annuity starting date is relevant in determining whether retirement plan benefits are payable as a QJSA, a QPSA, or another selected optional form of benefit available under the plan. If a participant is alive on his or her annuity starting date, his or her benefits must be payable as a QJSA. If the participant is not alive on his or her annuity starting date, his or her surviving spouse must receive a QPSA.

The annuity starting date is also used to determine when a spouse may consent to, and a participant may waive, a QJSA. A waiver is effective only if it is made within 180 days before the annuity starting date. Thus, a deferred annuity cannot be selected and a QJSA waived until within 180 days before payments begin under the deferred annuity (see Q 11:37). In some cases, the annuity starting date will have occurred for a portion of the participant's accrued benefit and will not have occurred for the remaining portion (see Q 11:10). [I.R.C. § 417(a)(6)(A); Treas. Reg. § 1.401(a)-20, Q&A-10(a); Notice 2007-7, 2007-5 I.R.B. 395]

Q 11:12 What is the annuity starting date for a survivor annuity?

General Rule. Under Code Sections 401(a)(11), 411(a)(11), and 417, the annuity starting date is the first day of the first period for which an amount is paid as an annuity or in any other form. [Treas. Reg. § 1.401(a)-20, Q&A-10(b)(1)]

IRS Notice 93-26 [1993-18 C.B. 11], however, permits a plan administrator to treat the date of distribution as the annuity starting date in the case of distributions that are not in the form of an annuity and that were also not subject to the survivor annuity requirements. [Ann. 95-33, 1995-19 I.R.B. 14]

The term *annuity starting date* is important initially because it distinguishes the period of time when the QPSA coverage ends and the QJSA coverage begins. Before the annuity starting date, the spouse is protected by the QPSA coverage. Once the annuity starting date is reached, the spouse is protected under the QJSA requirements. [Ann. 95-33, 1995-19 I.R.B. 14]

The annuity starting date is also important because it is used to determine the notice and election periods for the QJSA. A participant and spouse must be provided with notice of the right to elect among optional forms of benefits, in lieu of the QJSA, during a period that is no less than 30 days and no more than 180 days before the annuity starting date. Also, if the participant and spouse decide not to receive the QJSA, an election by the participant and spouse must be made within a 180-day period ending on the annuity starting date (see Q 11:37). [I.R.C. § 417(a)(6)(A); Notice 2007-7, 2007-5 I.R.B. 395; Ann. 95-33, 1995-19 I.R.B. 14]

Annuity Payments. The annuity starting date is the first date for which an amount is paid, not the actual date of payment. Thus, if a participant is to receive annuity payments as of the first day of the first month after retirement but does not receive any payments until three months later, his or her annuity starting date is the first day of the first month.

For example, if an annuity is to begin on January 1, then January 1 is the annuity starting date, even though the annuity payment for January is not actually made until a later date. In the case of a deferred annuity, the annuity starting date is the date for which the annuity payments are to begin, not the date that the deferred annuity is elected or the date the deferred annuity contract is distributed. [Treas. Reg. § 1.401(a)-20, Q&A-10(b)(2)]

Administrative Delay. A payment is not considered to occur after the annuity starting date merely because actual payment is reasonably delayed in order to calculate the benefit amount, if all payments are actually made. [Treas. Reg. § 1.40(a)-20, Q&A-10(b)(3)]

Forfeitures on Death. Before the annuity starting date, a plan can permit forfeitures of a participant's benefit on account of death, except in the case of a QPSA or the spousal death benefit payable under a defined contribution plan that is not subject to the survivor annuity requirements. Once the annuity starting date has occurred, even if actual payment has not yet been made, a plan must pay the benefit in the distribution form that has been elected. [Treas. Reg. § 1.401(a)-20, Q&A-10(b)(4)]

Surviving Spouses and Alternate Payees. The definition of *annuity starting date* for surviving spouses, other beneficiaries, and alternate payees under qualified domestic relations orders (QDROs) is the same as that for participants. [Treas. Reg. § 1.401(a)-20, Q&A-10(b)(5)]

Q 11:13 What is the annuity starting date for a disability benefit?

General Rule. The annuity starting date for a disability benefit is the first day of the first period for which the disability benefit becomes payable, unless the disability benefit is an auxiliary benefit. The payment of any auxiliary disability benefit is disregarded in determining the annuity starting date. A disability benefit is an auxiliary benefit if it is paid to a participant upon reaching early or normal retirement age and if it satisfies the accrual and vesting rules of Code Section 411 without taking into account the disability benefit payments up to that date. [Treas. Reg. § 1.401(a)-20, Q&A-10(c)]

> **Example 11-2:** Participant Edward Wicks at age 45 is entitled under the South County Oil Corporations retirement plan to a vested accrued benefit of $100 per month beginning at age 65 in the form of a joint and survivor annuity. If, before reaching age 65, Edward receives a disability benefit under the plan, and the payment of the benefit does not reduce his retirement benefit of $100 per month beginning at age 65, any disability benefits paid to Edward between ages 45 and 65 are auxiliary benefits. Thus, Edward's annuity starting date does not occur until he reaches age 65. Mrs. Wicks would be entitled to receive a QPSA if Edward died before age 65. Mrs. Wicks would be entitled to receive the survivor portion of a QJSA, unless it has been waived, if Edward died after age 65. The QPSA payable to Mrs. Wicks upon Edward's death before age 65 would be computed by reference to the QJSA that would have been payable to Mr. and Mrs. Wicks had Edward survived to age 65. [Treas. Reg. § 1.401(a)-20, Q&A-10(c)(2)(i)]
>
> If Edward's benefit payable at age 65 is reduced from $100 to $90 per month because a disability benefit is provided to him before age 65, the disability benefit would not be an auxiliary benefit. The benefit of $90 per month payable to him at age 65 would not, without taking into account disability benefit payments he received before age 65, satisfy the minimum vesting and accrual rules of Code Section 411. The first day of the first period for which the disability payments are to be made to Edward would be his annuity starting date, and any benefit paid to him would have to be paid in the form of a QJSA (unless he waived the QJSA with his wife's consent). [Treas. Reg. § 1.401(a)-20, Q&A-10(c)(2)(ii)]

Other Rules—Suspension of Benefits. If benefit payments are suspended after the annuity starting date under the benefit suspension rules of Code Section 411(a)(3)(B) after an employee separates from service, the date that benefit payments recommence after the suspension is not treated as a new annuity starting date, unless the plan provides otherwise (see chapter 9). In that case, the plan administrator is required neither to provide new notices nor to obtain new waivers for the recommenced distributions, if the form of distribution is the same as the form that was selected before benefits were suspended. If benefits are suspended for an employee who continues in service without a separation and who never receives payments, the date when payments commence after the period of suspension is treated as the participant's annuity starting date, unless the plan provides otherwise. [Treas. Reg. § 1.401(a)-20, Q&A-10(d)(1)]

Other Rules—Additional Accruals. An annuity starting date that occurs on or after normal retirement age applies to any additional accruals after the annuity starting date, unless the plan provides otherwise. For example, if a participant who continues to accrue benefits elects to have benefits paid in an optional form at normal retirement age, the additional accruals must be paid in the optional form selected, unless the plan provides otherwise. An annuity starting date that occurs before normal retirement age does not apply to any additional accruals after that date. [Treas. Reg. § 1.401(a)-20, Q&A-10(d)(2)]

Benefits

Q 11:14 Do the survivor annuity requirements apply to retirement plan benefits derived from employer and employee contributions?

Yes. Retirement plan benefits are not required to be paid in the form of a QPSA or QJSA if the participant was vested only in employee contributions at the time of his or her death or the distribution, and if his or her death or the distribution occurred before October 22, 1986. All benefits provided under a retirement plan, including benefits attributable to rollover contributions, are subject to the survivor annuity requirements. [Treas. Reg. § 1.401(a)-20, Q&A-11]

Q 11:15 To what retirement plan benefits do the survivor annuity requirements of Code Sections 401(a)(11) and 417 apply?

Defined Benefit Plans. Under a defined benefit plan, the survivor annuity requirements of Code Sections 401(a)(11) and 417 apply only to benefits in which a participant was vested *immediately before his or her death.* They do not apply to benefits to which a participant's beneficiary becomes entitled by reason of death or to the proceeds of a life insurance contract to the extent those proceeds exceed the present value of the participant's vested benefits immediately before death. [Treas. Reg. § 1.401(a)-20, Q&A-12(a)]

Defined Contribution Plans. The survivor annuity requirements of Code Sections 401(a)(11) and 417 apply to all vested benefits (whether vested before or upon death) payable under a defined contribution plan to which those requirements apply, including the proceeds of insurance contracts. [Treas. Reg. § 1.401(a)-20, Q&A-12(b)]

Q 11:16 Does the rule that permits forfeitures on account of death apply to a QPSA or to the spousal death benefit payable under defined contribution plans not subject to the survivor annuity rules?

No. Code Section 411(a)(3)(A) permits forfeitures on account of death before all the events fixing payment occur. However, this rule does not operate to deprive a surviving spouse of a QPSA or the spousal benefit, described in Code

Section 401(a)(11)(B)(iii), payable under a defined contribution plan that is not subject to the survivor annuity rules. [Treas. Reg. § 1.401(a)-20, Q&A-13]

Q 11:17 Can a retirement plan provide a form of benefit more valuable than the QJSA, and, if a plan offers more than one annuity option satisfying the requirements of a QJSA, is spousal consent required when the participant chooses among the various forms?

For an unmarried participant, the QJSA may be less valuable than other optional forms of benefit payable under the plan. For a married participant, the QJSA must be at least as valuable as any other optional form of benefit payable under the plan at the same time. Thus, if a plan has two joint and survivor annuities that would satisfy the requirements for a QJSA, but one has a greater actuarial value than the other, the more valuable joint and survivor annuity is the QJSA. If two or more actuarially equivalent joint and survivor annuities satisfy the requirements for a QJSA, the plan must designate which one is the QJSA and, therefore, the automatic form of benefit payment. However, a plan may allow a participant to elect out of such a QJSA, without spousal consent, in favor of another actuarially equivalent joint and survivor annuity that satisfies the QJSA conditions. Such an election is not subject to the requirement that it be made within the 180-day period before the annuity starting date (see Q 11:37).

For example, if a plan designates a joint and 100 percent survivor annuity as the QJSA and offers an actuarially equivalent joint and 50 percent survivor annuity that would satisfy the requirements of a QJSA, the participant may elect the joint and 50 percent survivor annuity without spousal consent. However, the participant does need spousal consent to elect a joint and survivor annuity that is not actuarially equivalent to the automatic QJSA. A plan does not fail to meet this requirement merely because the amount payable under an optional form of benefit that is subject to the minimum present value requirement of Code Section 417(e)(3) is calculated using the applicable interest rate (and, for periods when required, the applicable mortality table under Code Section 417(e)(3)). [I.R.C. § 417(a)(6)(A); Treas. Reg. § 1.401(a)-20, Q&A-16; Notice 2007-7, 2007-5 I.R.B. 395]

Timing of QJSA Distributions

Q 11:18 When must distributions to a participant under a QJSA begin?

QJSA Benefits upon Earliest Retirement Age. A retirement plan must allow a participant to receive a distribution in the form of a QJSA when he or she reaches the earliest retirement age under the plan. The participant's written consent is required, but the consent of the participant's spouse is not. However, any payment not in the form of a QJSA is subject to spousal consent.

For example, if the participant separates from service under a plan that allows for distributions upon separation from service, or if a plan allows for in-service distributions, the participant may receive a QJSA without spousal consent. Payments in any other form, including a single sum, would require a waiver of the QJSA by the participant's spouse. [Treas. Reg. § 1.401(a)-20, Q&A-17(a)]

Earliest Retirement Age. The term *earliest retirement age* can have several meanings under the survivor annuity rules, as described below.

For a plan providing for voluntary distributions that begin upon the participant's separation from service, earliest retirement age is the earliest age at which a participant could separate from service and receive a distribution. The participant's death is treated as a separation from service. [Treas. Reg. § 1.401(a)-20, Q&A-17(b)(2)]

For a plan that provides for in-service distributions, earliest retirement age is the earliest age at which those distributions can be made. [Treas. Reg. § 1.401(a)-20, Q&A-17(b)(3)]

For any other plan, earliest retirement age is the early retirement age determined under the plan or, if there is no early retirement age, the normal retirement age determined under the plan. If the participant dies or separates from service before that age, then only the participant's actual years of service at the time of his or her separation from service or death are taken into account. So, in the case of a plan under which benefits are not payable until age 65, or at age 55 after completion of ten years of service, the earliest retirement age of a participant who died or separated from service after eight years of service is age 65 (if he or she had survived to that age). On the other hand, if the participant died or separated from service after ten years, the earliest retirement age is age 55 (if he or she had survived to that age). [Treas. Reg. § 1.401(a)-20, Q&A-17(b)(4)]

Rules Governing the QPSA

Q 11:19 What is a QPSA under a defined benefit plan?

A QPSA under a defined benefit plan is an immediate annuity for the life of the participant's surviving spouse. Each payment under a QPSA under a defined benefit plan may not be less than the payment that would have been made to the survivor under the QJSA payable under the plan if (1) in the case of a participant who dies after reaching the plans earliest retirement age, the participant had retired with a QJSA on the day before his or her death; and (2) in the case of a participant who dies on or before the earliest retirement age under the plan, the participant had separated from service at the earlier of the actual time of separation or death, survived until the earliest retirement age, retired at that time with a QJSA, and died on the next day. If, before his or her annuity starting date, the participant elects a form of joint and survivor annuity that satisfies the requirements for a QJSA and then dies before his or her annuity starting date, the form of benefit he or she elected is treated as the QJSA, and the QPSA, payable to his surviving spouse, must be based on that form. [Treas. Reg. § 1.401(a)-20, Q&A-18]

In essence, the survivor portion of the QJSA is the QPSA in a defined benefit plan, because the QPSA cannot be less than the survivor portion of the QJSA. Ann. 95-33, 1995-19 I.R.B. 14]

Q 11:20 What rules apply in determining the amount and forfeitability of a QPSA?

The QPSA is calculated as of the earliest retirement age if the participant dies before that time or at death if the participant dies after the earliest retirement age. The plan must make reasonable actuarial adjustments to reflect a payment earlier or later than the earliest retirement age. A defined benefit plan may provide that the QPSA is forfeited if the spouse does not survive until the date prescribed for commencement of the QPSA (i.e., the earliest retirement age). Similarly, if the spouse survives past the participant's earliest retirement age (or other QPSA distribution date under the plan) and elects, after the participant's death, to defer the commencement of the QPSA, a defined benefit plan may provide for a forfeiture of the QPSA benefit, if the spouse does not survive until the deferred commencement date. The account balance in a defined contribution plan may not be forfeited, even if the spouse does not survive until the time the account balance is used to purchase the QPSA. [Treas. Reg. § 1.401(a)-20, Q&A-19]

Q 11:21 What QPSA benefit must a defined contribution plan subject to the survivor annuity requirements of Code Sections 401(a)(11) and 417 provide?

A defined contribution plan subject to the survivor annuity requirements of Code Sections 401(a)(11) and 417 must provide a QPSA with a value of not less than 50 percent of the participant's vested account balance as of the date of his or her death. If only 50 percent of the participant's account balance is used to purchase an annuity, the remaining portion of the account balance can be paid to other beneficiaries of the participant without the consent of the spouse. [Ann. 95-33, 1995-19 I.R.B. 14] If a contributory defined contribution plan has a forfeiture provision on account of death, as permitted by Code Section 411(a)(3)(A), no more than a proportional percentage of the account balance attributable to contributions that may not be forfeited at death (e.g., employee and 401(k) contributions) may be used to satisfy the QPSA benefit. For example, if the QPSA benefit is to be provided from 50 percent of the account balance, not more than 50 percent of the vested contributions may be used for the QPSA. [Treas. Reg. § 1.401(a)-20, Q&A-20]

Q 11:22 May a defined benefit plan charge the participant for the cost of the QPSA benefit?

Before the plan allows the participant to waive the QPSA (or provides notice that the participant can do so—whichever is later), a defined benefit plan may not charge the participant for the cost of the QPSA by reducing the participant's plan benefits or by any other method. (This rule does not apply to any charges before the first plan year beginning after December 31, 1988.) Once the participant is given the opportunity to waive the QPSA or receives notice that he or she can do so (whichever is later), the plan may charge the participant for the cost of the QPSA. A charge for the QPSA that reasonably reflects the cost of providing the QPSA will satisfy the requirements of Code Section 411, even if it reduces the participant's accrued benefit. [Treas. Reg. § 1.401(a)-20, Q&A-21]

Q 11:23 When must distributions to a surviving spouse under a QPSA begin?

Defined Benefit Plan. A defined benefit plan must permit the surviving spouse to direct payments under the QPSA to begin no later than the month in which the participant would have reached the earliest retirement age. However, the plan may permit the payments to begin at an earlier date. [Treas. Reg. § 1.401(a)-20, Q&A-22(a)]

Defined Contribution Plan. A defined contribution plan must permit the surviving spouse to direct payments under the QPSA to begin within a reasonable time after the participant's death. [Treas. Reg. § 1.401(a)-20, Q&A-22(b)]

Applying Survivor Annuity Requirements to Plan Loans

Q 11:24 What rules under Code Sections 401(a)(11) and 417 apply to plan loans?

Consent Rules. A retirement plan that is subject to the survivor annuity requirements of Code Sections 401(a)(11) and 417 will not satisfy them unless it provides that, at the time the participant's accrued benefit is used as security for a loan, spousal consent is obtained. Consent is required even if the accrued benefit is not the primary security for the loan. (See chapter 2 for a discussion of loans.)

No spousal consent is necessary if, at the time the loan is secured, no consent would be required for a distribution under Code Section 417(a)(2)(B) (because the participant was unmarried at the time or because his or her spouse could not be located). Spousal consent is not required if the plan or the participant is not subject to the survivor annuity rules at the time the accrued benefit is used as security, or if the total accrued benefit subject to the security interest is $5,000 or less. The spousal consent must be obtained no earlier than the beginning of the 180-day period that ends on the date on which the loan is to be so secured (see Q 11:37). The consent is subject to the requirements of Code Section 417(a)(2) and, therefore, it must be in writing, must acknowledge the effect of the loan, and must be witnessed by a plan representative or a notary public. [I.R.C. § 414(a)(6)(A); Treas. Reg. § 1.401(a)-20, Q&A-24(a)(1); Notice 2007-7, 2007-5 I.R.B. 395]

Participant (as opposed to spousal) consent is deemed to be obtained at the time the participant agrees to use his or her accrued benefit as security for a loan. [Treas. Reg. § 1.401(a)-20, Q&A-24(a)(2)]

Change in Status. If spousal consent is obtained or is not required at the time the participant's accrued benefit is used as security for the loan, spousal consent is not required at the time of any setoff of the loan against the accrued benefit resulting from a default, even if the participant is married to a different spouse at the time of the setoff. Similarly, if a participant secured a loan while unmarried, no consent is required at the time of the setoff of the loan against his or her accrued benefit, even if the participant is married at the time of the setoff. [Treas. Reg. § 1.401(a)-20, Q&A-24(b)]

Renegotiation. In obtaining any required spousal consent, any renegotiation, extension, renewal, or other revision of a loan is treated as a new loan made on the date of the renegotiation, extension, renewal, or other revision. [Treas. Reg. § 1.401(a)-20, Q&A-24(c)]

Effect on Benefits. In determining the amount of a QPSA or QJSA, the accrued benefit of a participant is reduced by any security interest held by the plan because of a loan outstanding to the participant at the time of death or payment, if the security interest is treated as payment in satisfaction of the loan under the plan. A plan may offset any loan secured by the participant's account balance and outstanding at the participant's death against the spousal benefit required to be paid under a defined contribution plan not subject to the survivor annuity rules. [Treas. Reg. § 1.401(a)-20, Q&A-24(d)]

Effective Date. Loans made before August 19, 1985 are deemed to satisfy the consent requirements described above. [Treas. Reg. § 1.401(a)-20, Q&A-24(e)]

Applying Survivor Annuity Requirements to Unmarried Participants, Surviving Spouses, and Participants Who Have a Change in Marital Status

Q 11:25 How do the survivor annuity requirements of Code Sections 401(a)(11) and 417 apply to participants who are not married?

Unmarried Participant Rule. Retirement plans that are subject to the survivor annuity requirements of Code Sections 401(a)(11) and 417 must satisfy the requirements for QJSA, even for participants who are not married. A QJSA for a participant who is not married is an annuity for the life of the participant. Thus, an unmarried participant must be provided with the written QJSA explanation (see Qs 11:32–11:41) and a single life annuity, unless the participant elects another form of benefit. An unmarried participant is deemed to have waived the QPSA requirements. However, this deemed waiver becomes null and void if the participant later marries. [Treas. Reg. § 1.401(a)-20, Q&A-3, Q&A-25(a); Ann. 95-33, 1995-19 I.R.B. 14]

Q 11:26 How do the survivor annuity requirements apply to surviving spouses and participants who have a change in marital status?

Remarriage. If a participant was married on the date he or she dies, payments to his or her surviving spouse under a QPSA or a QJSA must continue, even if the surviving spouse remarries. [Treas. Reg. § 1.401(a)-20, Q&A-25(b)(1)]

One-Year Marriage Rule. A retirement plan is not required to treat a participant as married unless he or she and his or her spouse have been married throughout the one-year period ending on the earlier of the participant's annuity starting date or the date of the participant's death. Nevertheless, a participant and his or her spouse must be treated as married throughout the one-year period ending on the participant's annuity starting date, even if they had been married for less than one year before the annuity starting date, if they remain married for at least one year. If a plan adopts a one-year marriage rule, it must treat the participant and spouse who are married on the annuity starting date as married and must provide benefits that begin on the annuity starting date in the form of a QJSA, unless the participant (with spousal consent) elects another form of benefit. The plan is not required to provide the participant with a new or retroactive election or to provide the spouse with a new consent when the one-year marriage period requirement is satisfied. If the participant and the spouse do not remain married for at least one year, the plan may treat the participant as not having been married on the annuity starting date. In that event, the plan may provide that the spouse loses any right to survivor benefits. No retroactive correction of the amount paid to the participant is required. [Treas. Reg. § 1.401(a)-20, Q&A-25(b)(2)(i)]

Example 11-3: The Russian Hill Corporation retirement plan provides that participants who are married for less than one year on the annuity starting date are treated as unmarried participants. The plan provides benefits in the form of a QJSA or an optional single-sum distribution. Participant Helen Van Deventer was married six months before her annuity starting date. The plan must treat Helen as married and must begin payments to her in the form of a QJSA, unless she elects another form of benefit with her spouse's consent. If a QJSA is paid, and Helen is divorced from her spouse, Hubert, within the first year of their marriage, Hubert will no longer have any survivor rights under the annuity (unless a QDRO provides otherwise). If Helen remains married to Hubert and Helen dies within the one-year period, the plan may treat Helen as unmarried, and Hubert forfeits the QJSA benefit payable to him. [Treas. Reg. § 1.401(a)-20, Q&A-25(b)(2)(ii)]

Divorce. If a participant divorces his or her spouse before his or her annuity starting date, any elections made while the participant was married to the former spouse remain valid, unless otherwise provided in a QDRO, or unless the participant changes them or remarries. If a participant dies after his or her annuity starting date, the spouse to whom he or she was married on that date is entitled to the QJSA protection under the plan. The spouse is entitled to this protection (unless the participant has waived it and the spouse has consented) even if the participant and spouse are not married on the date of the participant's death, unless otherwise provided in a QDRO. [Treas. Reg. § 1.401(a)-20, Q&A-25(b)(3)]

Spousal Consent Requirement

Q 11:27 What spousal consent requirements did REA 1984 add to the Code and ERISA?

REA 1984 added the requirement of spousal consent before a participant may take a distribution, so that a nonemployee spouse would have some control over the form of benefit chosen by the participant and would, at the very least, be aware that retirement benefits existed. [Ann. 95-33, 1995-19 I.R.B. 14]

Spousal consent is not necessary for distributions made in the form of a QJSA. [Treas. Reg. § 1.401(a)-20, Q&A-17]

However, spousal consent is required at all other times for payment of benefits in a form other than a QJSA, even when payments are no longer immediately distributable. [Ann. 95-33, 1995-19 I.R.B. 14]

Q 11:28 Is a surviving spouse who had been married to a participant for less than one year entitled to full payment of the participant's vested account balance under a defined contribution plan that is not subject to the Section 412 minimum funding rules (e.g., a profit sharing, 401(k), or stock bonus plan)?

It depends on whether the plan provides that a spouse who has not been married to a participant throughout the one-year period ending on the earlier of the participant's annuity starting date or the date of the participant's death is not treated as a surviving spouse and is not entitled to receive the vested participant's account balance. [Treas. Reg. § 1.401(a)-20, Q&A-26]

Q 11:29 Are there circumstances when spousal consent to a participant's election to waive the QJSA or the QPSA is not required?

Yes. If it is established to the satisfaction of a plan representative that there is no spouse, or that the participant's spouse cannot be located, spousal consent to waive the QJSA or the QPSA is not required. If the spouse is legally incompetent to give consent, the spouse's legal guardian, even if the guardian is the participant, may give consent. Also, if the participant is legally separated or the participant has been abandoned (within the meaning of local law) and the participant has a court order to that effect, spousal consent is not required, unless a QDRO provides otherwise. Similar rules apply to a defined contribution plan not subject to the minimum funding standards of Code Section 412, which pays the participant's vested accrued benefit to the surviving spouse upon the participant's death. [Treas. Reg. § 1.401(a)-20, Q&A-27]

A participant may elect out of the QJSA in favor of an actuarially equivalent alternative joint and survivor annuity that satisfies the conditions to be a QJSA, without spousal consent. [Treas. Reg. § 1.401(a)-20, Q&A-16; Notice 2007-7, 2007-5 I.R.B. 395, Q&A-11] (See Q 11:17.) Because a QOSA (see Qs 11:38–11:46), by definition, satisfies the conditions to be a QJSA, no spousal consent is required if a plan participant elects a QOSA that is actuarially equivalent to the plans QJSA. If the QOSA is not actuarially equivalent to the QJSA, spousal consent is required for the participant to waive the QJSA and elect the QOSA. [Notice 2007-7, 2007-5 I.R.B. 395, Q&A-11]

Q 11:30 Does consent contained in a prenuptial agreement or similar contract entered into before a marriage satisfy the spousal consent requirements under the survivor annuity rules?

No. An agreement entered into before marriage (a prenuptial agreement) does not satisfy the spousal consent requirements, even if the agreement is executed within the election period. [Treas. Reg. § 1.401(a)-20, Q&A-28]

Q 11:31 If a participant's spouse consents to the participant's waiver of a survivor annuity form of benefit, is a subsequent spouse of the same participant bound by the consent?

No. Consent by one spouse is binding only on that spouse. [Treas. Reg. § 1.401(a)-20, Q&A-29]

Q 11:32 Does the spousal consent requirement demand that a spouse's consent be revocable?

No. A plan may preclude a spouse from revoking consent once it has been given. On the other hand, a plan may also permit a spouse to revoke consent after it has been given and thereby render ineffective the participant's prior election not to receive a QPSA or QJSA. However, a participant must always be allowed to change his or her election during the election period. Spousal consent is never required for a QPSA or a QJSA. [Treas. Reg. § 1.401(a)-20, Q&A-30]

Q 11:33 Has the IRS provided any sample language that can be used in a spousal consent to a participant's waiver of a QJSA or QPSA?

Yes. IRS Notice 97-10 includes sample language designed to make it easier for spouses of plan participants to understand their rights to survivor annuities under qualified retirement plans. [1997-2 I.R.B. 41] The sample language can be included in a form used for a spouse to consent to a participant's waiver of a QJSA or QPSA, or to a participant's choice of a nonspouse beneficiary in a defined contribution plan that is not subject to the QJSA and QPSA requirements. The sample language is designed to assist plan administrators in preparing spousal consent forms that meet the statutory requirements. No one is required to use the sample language, and plan administrators who choose to use it are free to incorporate all or any part of it in their spousal consent forms. The four appendixes to Notice 97-10 contain four sets of sample language as follows:

1. *Appendix A* contains sample language that can be included in a spouse's consent to a participant's waiver of a QJSA. This language can be used for a defined benefit plan and for a defined contribution plan to the extent that it is subject to Code Section 401(a)(11).
2. *Appendix B* contains language that can be included in a spouse's consent to a participant's waiver of a QPSA and, if the plan so provides, to the participant's choice of a beneficiary other than the spouse to receive any survivor benefit. This language can be used for a defined benefit plan.
3. *Appendix C* contains sample language that can be included in a spouse's consent to a participant's waiver of a QPSA and, if the plan so provides, to the participant's choice of a beneficiary other than the spouse to receive any survivor benefit. This language can be used for a defined contribution plan to the extent that it is subject to Code Section 401(a)(11).
4. *Appendix D* contains sample language that can be included in a spouse's consent to a participant's choice of a beneficiary other than the spouse for a participant's account balance. This language can be used for a defined contribution plan to the extent that it is not subject to Code Section 401(a)(11).

Participant's Waiver of a QPSA or QJSA

Q 11:34 What rules govern a participant's waiver of a QPSA or QJSA?

Specific Beneficiary. The participant's waivers of a QPSA and a QJSA, and the spouse's consent to those waivers, must state the specific nonspousal beneficiary, including any class of beneficiaries or any contingent beneficiaries, who will receive the benefit. [Treas. Reg. § 1.401(a)-20, Q&A-31(a)]

> **Example 11-4:** If Helen Van Deventer consents to husband-participant Hubert's election to waive a QPSA and to have any benefits payable upon his death before his annuity starting date paid to his children, Hubert may not change beneficiaries later without Helen's consent (except if the change is a return to a QPSA). If Hubert's designated beneficiary is a trust, Helen need only consent to the designation of the trust and need not consent to the designation of trust beneficiaries or any changes of trust beneficiaries. [Treas. Reg. § 1.401(a)-20, Q&A-31(a)]

Optional Form of Benefit—QJSA. The participant's waiver of a QJSA and any required spousal consent to that waiver must specify the particular optional form of benefit. The participant who has, with his or her spouse's consent, waived a QJSA in favor of another form of benefit, may not later change the optional form of benefit without obtaining the spouse's consent (except if the change is a return to a QJSA). The participant may change the form of benefit, if the plan so provides, after the spouse's death or a divorce (other than as provided in a QDRO). A participant's waiver of a QJSA (and any required spousal consent to that waiver) made before the first plan year beginning after December 31, 1986, is not required to specify the optional form of benefit. [Treas. Reg. § 1.401(a)-20, Q&A-31(b)(1)]

Optional Form of Benefit—QPSA. A participant's waiver of a QPSA and the spouse's consent to that waiver are not required to specify the optional form of any pre-retirement benefit. Thus, a participant who waives the QPSA with spousal consent may later change the form of the pre-retirement benefit, but not the nonspousal beneficiary, without obtaining the spouse's consent. [Treas. Reg. § 1.401(a)-20, Q&A-31(b)(2)]

Optional Form of Benefit—Change in Form. After the participant's death, a beneficiary may change the optional form of survivor benefit as permitted by the plan. [Treas. Reg. § 1.401(a)-20, Q&A-31(b)(3)]

General Consent. A plan may permit a spouse to execute a general consent that satisfies the requirements specified below. A general consent permits the participant to waive a QPSA or QJSA and to change the designated beneficiary or the optional form of benefit payment without further consent by the spouse. A general consent is not valid unless it acknowledges the spouse's right to limit consent to a specific beneficiary and to a specific optional form of benefit and the spouse's election to relinquish both of those rights. Notwithstanding this rule, a spouse may execute a general consent that is limited to certain beneficiaries or forms of benefit payment. A general consent, including a limited general consent, is not effective unless it is made during the election period. A general consent executed before October 22, 1986 does not have to satisfy the specific beneficiary requirements described above. [Treas. Reg. § 1.401(a)-20, Q&A-31(c)]

Q 11:35 What rules govern a participant's waiver of the spousal benefit under a defined contribution plan not subject to the survivor annuity requirements?

Application. In a defined contribution plan not subject to the survivor annuity requirements of Code Sections 410(a)(11) and 417, a participant may waive the spousal benefit payable to the surviving spouse upon the participant's death only if certain conditions are satisfied. (In general, a spousal benefit is the vested account balance on the participant's date of death.) [Treas. Reg. § 1.401(a)-20, Q&A-32(a)]

Conditions. In general, the same requirements, other than the age-35 requirement, that apply to the participant's waiver of a QPSA and the spouse's consent to that waiver, apply to the participant's waiver of the spousal benefit under a defined contribution plan not subject to the survivor annuity requirement. Thus, the participant's waiver of that spousal benefit must state the specific nonspousal beneficiary who will receive the benefit. The waiver is not required to specify the optional form of benefit. The participant may change the optional form of benefit, but may not change the nonspousal beneficiary without obtaining the spouse's consent. [Treas. Reg. § 1.401(a)-20, Q&A-32(b)]

Q 11:36 When, and in what manner, may a participant waive the spousal benefit or a QPSA?

Plans Not Subject to the Survivor Annuity Requirements. A participant in a retirement plan that is not subject to the survivor annuity requirements of Code Section 401(a)(11) (because it is a defined contribution plan, not subject to the minimum funding standards of Code Section 412, that pays the participant's entire vested account balance to the surviving spouse) may waive the spousal benefit at any time, provided that no such waiver will be effective unless the spouse consents to it. The spouse may consent to a waiver of the spousal benefit at any time, even before the participant reaches age 35. No spousal consent is required for a payment to the participant or to the use of the accrued benefit as security for a plan loan to the participant. [Treas. Reg. § 1.401(a)-20, Q&A-33(a)]

Plans Subject to the Survivor Annuity Requirements. A participant in a plan subject to the survivor annuity requirements of Code Section 401(a)(11) generally may waive the QPSA requirement (with spousal consent) only on or after the first day of the plan year in which the participant reaches age 35. However, a plan may provide for an earlier waiver (with spousal consent), provided that the participant receives a written explanation of the QPSA and that the waiver becomes invalid upon the beginning of the plan year in which the participant attains age 35. If there is no new waiver after that date, the participant's spouse must receive the QPSA benefit upon the participant's death. [Treas. Reg. § 1.401(a)-20, Q&A-33(b)]

Q 11:37 What right does a participant have to waive QJSA and QPSA benefits?

A retirement plan participant has the right to make a revocable election to waive a QJSA or QPSA. [I.R.C. § 417(a)(1); Ann. 95-33, 1995-19 I.R.B. 14]

In general, any waiver will not be effective unless:

1. The participant's spouse consents in writing to the election;
2. The election designates a beneficiary that may not be changed without spousal consent (unless the spouse expressly permits designation by the participant without any further spousal consent);
3. The election designates a form of benefit that may not be changed without spousal consent;
4. The spouse's consent acknowledges the effect of the election; and
5. The spouse's consent is witnessed by a plan representative or notary public.

[I.R.C. § 417(a)(2); Ann. 95-33, 1995-19 I.R.B. 14]

For plan years beginning on or after January 1, 2007, the election to waive the QJSA must be made within the 180-day period ending on the annuity starting date. [I.R.C. §§ 417(a)(1)(A)(i); 417(a)(6)(A)]

The same types of requirements apply to QPSA, except that once the spouse consents to the participant's election not to receive a QPSA, the participant can change the form of the benefit without again getting the spouse's consent. [Ann. 95-33, 1995-19 I.R.B. 14] Also, the election period for the QPSA is considerably longer (see Q 11:49).

Q 11:38 What additional requirements did PPA impose upon qualified retirement plans that are subject to the survivor annuity requirements of Code Section 401(a)(11)?

PPA amended Code Section 417 to require a qualified retirement plan that is subject to the survivor annuity requirements of Code Section 401(a)(11) (see Q 11:3) to offer to participants a specified optional form of benefit as an alternative to the QJSA. In particular, a plan that is subject to the survivor annuity requirements of Code Section 401(a)(11) must provide to a participant who waives the QJSA (1) an opportunity to elect a QOSA during the applicable election period and (2) a written explanation of the terms and conditions of the QOSA. [I.R.C. § 417(g), as added by PPA § 1004, effective generally for plan years beginning after December 31, 2007; Notice 2008-30, 2008-12 I.R.B. 638]

A QOSA is defined as an annuity for the life of the participant with a survivor annuity for the life of the participant's spouse that is equal to a specified applicable percentage (see Q 11:39) of the amount of the annuity that is payable during the joint lives of the participant and the spouse and that is the actuarial equivalent of a single annuity for the life of the participant. A QOSA also includes a distribution option in the form of having the effect of such an annuity. [I.R.C. § 417(g), as added by PPA § 1004, effective generally for plan years beginning after December 31, 2007; Notice 2008-30, 2008-12 I.R.B. 638]

Q 11:39 What level of spouse survivor annuity must be provided under a QOSA?

The level of spouse survivor annuity that must be provided under a QOSA depends upon the level of spouse survivor annuity provided under a plan's QJSA (i.e., the QJSA form of benefit that is provided to a married participant in the absence of a waiver of such form of benefit).

If the QJSA for a married participant provides a survivor annuity for the life of the participant's spouse that is less than 75 percent of the amount of the annuity payable during the joint lives of the participant and the participant's spouse, the QOSA must provide a spouse survivor annuity percentage of 75 percent.

If the QJSA for a married participant provides a survivor annuity for the life of the participant's spouse that is greater than or equal to 75 percent of the amount of the annuity that is payable during the joint lives of the participant and the participant's spouse, the QOSA must provide a spouse survivor annuity percentage of 50 percent. [I.R.C. § 417(g), as added by PPA § 1004, effective generally for plan years beginning after December 31, 2007; Notice 2008-30, 2008-12 I.R.B. 638]

Q 11:40 Must the retirement plan be amended or the plan's administration be changed in order to implement PPA's QOSA requirements?

No. If, both before and after the effective date of PPA's QOSA requirements (generally, plan years beginning after December 31, 2007), a retirement plan that is subject to the survivor annuity requirements of Code Section 401(a)(11) offers, in addition to the QJSA, an optional joint and spouse survivor annuity that is at least actuarially equivalent to the plan's single life annuity form of benefit payable at the same time as the optional joint and spouse survivor annuity and that provides a spouse survivor annuity percentage equal to the spouse survivor annuity percentage required to be provided under the QOSA, the plan need not be amended nor must the plan's administration be changed in order to implement PPA's QOSA requirements.

The plan must provide an optional joint and survivor annuity that:

1. Is at least actuarially equivalent to the plan's single life annuity form of benefit payable at the same time as the optional joint and spouse survivor annuity; and
2. Provides a spouse survivor annuity percentage that is equal to the spouse survivor annuity percentage required to be provided under a QOSA.

The plan need not be amended so that the optional joint and survivor spouse annuity is designated as a QOSA, and its administrative procedures need not be revised to designate the optional form of benefit as a QOSA. For example, a plan that, both before and after the effective date of PPA's QOSA requirements (generally, plan years beginning after December 31, 2007), provides a QJSA for a married participant that includes a spouse survivor annuity percentage of 50 percent, and also provides an optional joint and spouse survivor annuity that includes a spouse survivor annuity percentage of 75 percent and is at least actuarially equivalent to the plan's single life annuity form of benefit payable at the same time as the optional joint and spouse survivor annuity, complies with PPA's QOSA requirements without the need for any plan amendment or other administrative change. [Notice 2008-30, 2008-12 I.R.B. 638]

Q 11:41 If a plan that is subject to the survivor annuity requirements of Code Section 401(a)(11) provides a QJSA that is more valuable than the plan's single life annuity form of benefit, must the plan's QOSA be at least actuarially equivalent to the QJSA, or must the QOSA only be at least actuarially equivalent to the plan's single life annuity form of benefit payable at the same time as the QOSA?

A retirement plan that is subject to the survivor annuity requirements of Code Section 401(a)(11) must provide a QOSA that is at least actuarially equivalent to the plan's form of benefit that is a single life annuity for the life of the participant payable at the same time as the QOSA. The QOSA need not be actuarially equivalent to the plan's QJSA. [Notice 2008-30, 2008-12 I.R.B. 638]

Q 11:42 If a participant elects to receive a distribution in the form of a QOSA, must the participant's spouse consent to the participant's election?

In general, spousal consent is required for a participant to waive a plan's QJSA form of distribution and elect an alternative distribution form. However, Treasury Regulations Section 1.401(a)-20, Q&A-16 provides that a participant may elect out of the QJSA in favor of an actuarially equivalent joint and survivor annuity that satisfies the conditions to be a QJSA, without spousal consent (see Q 11:17). Because a QOSA, by definition, satisfies the conditions to be a QJSA, no spousal consent is required if a plan participant elects a QOSA that is actuarially equivalent to the plan's QJSA. If the QOSA is not actuarially equivalent to the QJSA, however, spousal consent is required for the participant to waive the QJSA and elect the QOSA. [Notice 2008-30, 2008-12 I.R.B. 638]

Q 11:43 How does a plan that is subject to the survivor annuity requirements of Code Section 401(a)(11) satisfy the requirement in Code Section 417(a)(3)(i), as amended by PPA, that the plan provides to a participant a written explanation of the terms and conditions of the QOSA available to the participant?

A retirement plan that is subject to the survivor annuity requirements of Code Section 401(a)(11) can satisfy the requirement that it provides to a participant a written explanation of the terms and conditions of the QOSA available to the participant by satisfying the written explanation requirements of Treasury Regulations Section 1.417(a)(3)-1 (see Qs 11:50–11:56). In satisfying the written explanation requirements, the plan must treat the QOSA as an optional form of benefit presently available to participants under the plan. The written explanation need not designate the optional form of benefit as the plan's QOSA. [Notice 2008-30, 2008-12 I.R.B. 638]

Q 11:44 Must a plan that is subject to the survivor annuity requirements of Code Section 401(a)(11) offer to participants, as an alternative to a QPSA, a pre-retirement survivor annuity that is based on a QOSA?

No. A retirement plan that is subject to the survivor annuity requirements of Code Section 401(a)(11) must offer participants a QOSA that is an alternative form of distribution to the QJSA. There is no requirement that the plan offer to participants, as an alternative to a QPSA, a pre-retirement survivor annuity that is based on a QOSA. [Notice 2008-30, 2008-12 I.R.B. 638]

Q 11:45 How do the PPA's plan amendment rules apply to plan amendments adopted in response to PPA's requirements?

If a retirement plan that is subject to the survivor annuity requirements of Code Section 401(a)(11) is amended to implement a QOSA within the PPA amendment period (established in PPA Section 1107(b)(2)(A)), and the plan is operated as if the amendment were in effect during the period from the effective date of the changes made to Code Section 417 by PPA Section 1004 (generally, the changes became effective for plan years beginning after December 31, 2007) until the date of the amendment, the plan will be treated pursuant to PPA's plan amendment rules (in PPA Section 1107) as being operated in accordance with its terms during such period, and the amendment will be treated as adopted on the effective date of such changes made to Code Section 417. However, an amendment that implements a QOSA is not eligible for any relief (pursuant to PPA's amendment rules in PPA Section 1107) from the anti-cutback requirements of Code Section 411(d)(6). Thus, for example, a plan amendment that implements a QOSA may eliminate a distribution form or reduce or eliminate a subsidy with respect to a distribution form only to the extent such reduction or elimination is permitted under Treasury Regulations Section 1.411(d)-3. [Notice 2008-30, 2008-12 I.R.B. 638]

Q 11:46 What was the effective date of PPA's QOSA requirements?

In general, PPA's QOSA requirements (i.e., found in Code Section 417(g), as added by PPA Section 1004) began to apply to distributions from a retirement plan subject to Code Section 401(a)(11)'s survivor annuity rules with annuity starting dates in plan years beginning after December 31, 2007. However, in the case of a plan subject to the survivor annuity requirements of Code Section 401(a)(11) and maintained pursuant to one or more collective bargaining agreements between employee representatives and one or more employers ratified on or before August 17, 2006 (PPA's enactment date), PPA's QOSA requirements began to apply to distributions with annuity starting dates during plan years beginning on or after the earlier of (1) January 1, 2008 or, if later, the date on which the last collective bargaining agreement related to the plan terminates (determined without regard to any extensions to a collective bargaining agreement made after August 17, 2006) or (2) January 1, 2009. [Notice 2008-30, 2008-12 I.R.B. 638]

Notice Requirements

Q 11:47 What is the purpose of REA 1984's notice requirements, as they relate to QJSA and QPSA coverage?

REA 1984 notice rules are intended to ensure that participants and their spouses are made aware of their retirement benefit options, and the consequences of any elections they make concerning these options. This information is to be made available at a time when the consequences of the elections will be of immediate, rather than remote, concern to the participant and spouse, and at a time when they would best be able to make sound decisions concerning their retirement benefits. To achieve those goals, REA 1984 requires that the participant and spouse receive two notices (the QJSA and QPSA notices) about retirement benefits before benefits begin under the plan. [Ann. 95-33, 1995-19 I.R.B. 14]

The QJSA and QPSA notices (which are written explanations of QJSA and QPSA coverage) inform the participant and the spouse of:

1. Their right to receive a QJSA, a QPSA, or other optional forms of benefits;
2. The option of selecting alternate beneficiaries; and
3. Spousal consent requirements.

[Ann. 95-33, 1995-19 I.R.B. 14]

For the QJSA, for plan years beginning after December 31, 2007, Code Section 417(a)(3) requires the employer to provide each participant with a written explanation of the QJSA, describing:

1. The terms and conditions of the QJSA and the QOSA (see Qs 11:38–11:46);
2. The participant's right to make, and the effect of, an election to waive the QJSA;
3. The rights of the participant's spouse; and
4. The right of the participant to make, and the effect of, a revocation of an election.

[I.R.C. § 417(a)(3)(A)]

The QJSA notice may be provided as much as 180 days before the annuity starting date. [I.R.C. § 417(a)(6)(A); IRS Notice 2007-7, 2007-5 I.R.B. 395, Q&A-31]

Comparable information must be provided for the QPSA. [I.R.C. § 417(a)(3)(B)]

The QPSA notice must be provided within the "applicable period" (see Q 11:49). [I.R.C. § 417(a)(3)(B)(ii)]

In general, the opportunity to elect among the various plan options must be provided, in the case of the QJSA, within a 180-day period that ends on the annuity starting date, and, in the case of the QPSA, beginning on the first day of the plan year in which the participant reaches age 35. [I.R.C. § 417(a)(1)(A)(i); § 417(a)(6)]

Written consent of the participant and his or her spouse to the distribution must be made not more than 180 days before the annuity starting date and except as otherwise provided below, no later than the annuity starting date. [Treas. Reg. § 1.417(e)-1(b)(3)(i); Prop. Reg. § 1.417(e)-1(b)(3)(i)]

A plan must provide participants with the written explanation of the QJSA required by Code Section 417(a)(3) no less than 30 days and no more than 180 days before the annuity starting date, except as provided below regarding retroactive annuity starting dates. [I.R.C. § 417(a)(1)(A)(i); § 417(a)(6); IRS Notice 2007-7, 2007-5 I.R.B. 395, Q&A-31] However, if the participant, after having received the written explanation of the QJSA, affirmatively elects a form of distribution and his or her spouse consents to that form of distribution (if necessary), a plan will not fail to satisfy the requirements of Code Section 417(a) merely because the written explanation was provided to the participant in less than 30 days before the annuity starting date, provided that the following conditions are met:

1. The plan administrator provides information to the participant clearly indicating that he or she has a right to take at least 30 days to consider whether to waive the QJSA and consent to a form of distribution other than the QJSA. [Treas. Reg. § 1.417(e)-1(b)(3)(ii)(A)]
2. The participant is permitted to revoke an affirmative distribution election at least until the annuity starting date, or, if later, at any time before the expiration of the seven-day period that begins the day after the written explanation of the QJSA is provided to the participant. [Treas. Reg. § 1.417(e)-1(b)(3)(ii)(B)]
3. The annuity starting date is after the date that the explanation of the QJSA is provided to the participant. [Treas. Reg. § 1.417(e)-1(b)(3)(ii)(C)]
4. Distribution in accordance with the affirmative election does not commence before the expiration of the seven-day period that begins the day after the QJSA notice is provided to the participant. [Treas. Reg. § 1.417(e)-1(b)(3)(ii)(D)]

The plan may permit the annuity starting date to be before the date that any affirmative distribution election is made by the participant (and before the date that distribution is permitted to commence), provided that, except as otherwise provided under the rules regarding administrative delay, distributions commence not more than 180 days after the explanation of the QJSA is provided. [Treas. Reg. § 1.417(e)-1(b)(iii)]

Retroactive Annuity Starting Dates. Notwithstanding the general requirements of Code Section 417, pursuant to Code Section 417(a)(7), a defined benefit plan is permitted to provide benefits based on a retroactive annuity starting date if the requirements described below are satisfied. A defined benefit plan is not required to provide for retroactive annuity starting dates. If a plan does provide for a retroactive annuity starting date, it may impose additional conditions on the availability of a retroactive annuity starting date, provided that imposition of those additional conditions does not violate any of the rules applicable to qualified plans. For example, a plan that includes a single-sum payment as a benefit option may limit the election of a retroactive annuity starting date to those participants who do not elect the single-sum payment. A defined contribution plan is not permitted to have a retroactive annuity starting date. [Treas. Reg. § 1.417(e)-1(b)(iv)(A)]

For these purposes, a "retroactive annuity starting date" is an annuity starting date affirmatively elected by a participant that occurs on or before the date the written explanation required by Code Section 417(a)(3) is provided to the participant. In order for a plan to treat a participant as having elected a retroactive annuity starting date, future periodic payments with respect to a participant who elects a retroactive annuity starting date must be the same as the future periodic payments, if any, that would have been paid with respect to the participant had payments actually commenced on the retroactive annuity starting date. The participant must receive a make-up payment to reflect any missed payment or payments for the period from the retroactive annuity starting date to the date of the actual make-up payment (with an appropriate adjustment for interest from the date the missed payment or payments would have been made to the date of the actual make-up payment). Thus, the benefit determined as of the retroactive annuity starting date must satisfy the requirements of Code Section 417(e)(3), if applicable, and Code Section 415 with the applicable interest rate and applicable mortality table determined as of that date. Similarly, a participant is not permitted to elect a retroactive annuity starting date that precedes the date upon which the participant could have otherwise started receiving benefits (e.g., in the case of an ongoing plan, the earlier of the participant's termination of employment or the participant's normal retirement age) under the terms of the plan in effect as of the retroactive annuity starting date. A plan does not fail to treat a participant as having elected a retroactive annuity starting date merely because the distributions are adjusted to the extent necessary to satisfy the requirements relating to Code Sections 415 and 417(e)(3). [Treas. Reg. § 1.417(e)-1(b)(iv)(B)]

If the participant's spouse as of the retroactive annuity starting date would not be the participant's spouse determined as if the date distributions commence were the participant's annuity starting date, consent of that former spouse is not needed to waive the QJSA with respect to the retroactive annuity starting date, unless otherwise provided under a QDRO (as defined in Code Section 414(p)). [Treas. Reg. § 1.417(e)-1(b)(iv)(C)]

A distribution payable pursuant to a retroactive annuity starting date election is treated as excepted from the present value requirements if the distribution form would have met those requirements had the distribution actually commenced on the retroactive annuity starting date. Similarly, annuity payments that otherwise satisfy the requirements of a QJSA under Code Section 417(b) will not fail to be treated as a QJSA for purposes of Code Section 415(b)(2)(B) merely because a retroactive annuity starting date is elected and a make-up payment is made. Also, for purposes of Code Section 72(t)(2)(A)(iv), a distribution that would otherwise be one of a series of substantially equal periodic payments will be treated as one of a series of substantially equal periodic payments notwithstanding the distribution of a make-up payment. [Treas. Reg. § 1.417(e)-1(b)(iv)(D)]

The following Example 11-5 illustrates the application of these rules.

Example 11-5: Under the terms of the Pastures of Heaven defined benefit plan, George Battle is entitled to a QJSA with a monthly payment of $1,500 beginning as of his annuity starting date. Due to an administrative error, the QJSA explanation is provided to George after the annuity starting date. After receiving the QJSA explanation George elects a retroactive annuity starting date. Pursuant to this election, George begins to receive a monthly payment of $1,500 and also receives a make-up payment of $10,000. Under these circumstances, the monthly payments may be treated as a QJSA for purposes of Code

Section 415(b)(2)(B). In addition, the monthly payments of $1,500 and the make-up payment of $10,000 may be treated as part of a series of substantially equal periodic payments for purpose of Code Section 72(t)(2)(A)(iv). [Treas. Reg. § 1.417(e)-1(b)(3)(iv)(E)]

Requirements Applicable to Retroactive Annuity Starting Dates. A distribution is permitted to have a retroactive annuity starting date with respect to a participant's benefit only if the following requirements are met:

1. The participant's spouse (including an alternate payee who is treated as the spouse under a QDRO, as defined in Code Section 414(p)), determined as if the date distributions commence were the participant's annuity starting date, consents to the distribution in a manner that would satisfy the requirements of Code Section 417(a)(2). The spousal consent requirement is satisfied if such spouse consents to the distribution. The spousal consent requirement does not apply if the amount of such spouses survivor annuity payments under the retroactive annuity starting date election is no less than the amount that the survivor payments to such spouse would have been under an optional form of benefit that would satisfy the requirements to be a QJSA under Code Section 417(b) and that has an annuity starting date after the date that the explanation was provided. [Treas. Reg. § 1.417(e)-1(b)(3)(v)(A)]
2. The distribution (including appropriate interest adjustments) provided based on the retroactive annuity starting date would satisfy the requirements of Code Section 415 if the date the distribution commences is substituted for the annuity starting date for all purposes, including for purposes of determining the applicable interest rate and the applicable mortality table. However, in the case of a form of benefit that would have been excepted from the present value requirements if the distribution had actually commenced on the retroactive annuity starting date, the requirement to apply Code Section 415 as of the date distribution commences does not apply if the date distribution commences is 12 months or less from the retroactive annuity starting date. [Treas. Reg. § 1.417(e)-1(b)(3)(v)(B)]
3. In the case of a form of benefit that would have been subject to Code Section 417(e)(3) if distributions had commenced as of the retroactive annuity starting date, the distribution is no less than the benefit produced by applying the applicable interest rate and the applicable mortality table determined as of the date the distribution commences to the annuity form that corresponds to the annuity form that was used to determine the benefit amount as of the retroactive annuity starting date. Thus, for example, if a distribution paid pursuant to an election of a retroactive annuity starting date is a single-sum distribution that is based on the present value of the straight life annuity payable at normal retirement age, then the amount of the distribution must be no less than the present value of the annuity payable at normal retirement age, determined as of the distribution date using the applicable mortality table and applicable interest rate that apply as of the distribution date. Likewise, if a distribution paid pursuant to an election of a retroactive annuity starting date is a single-sum distribution that

is based on the present value of the early retirement annuity payable as of the retroactive annuity starting date, then the amount of the distribution must be no less than the present value of the early retirement annuity payable as of the distribution date, determined as of the distribution date using the applicable mortality table and applicable interest rate that apply as of the distribution date. [Treas. Reg. § 1.417(e)-1(b)(3)(v)(C)]

Timing of Notice and Consent Requirements in the Case of Retroactive Annuity Starting Dates. In the case of a retroactive annuity starting date, the date of the first actual payment of benefits based on the retroactive annuity starting date is substituted for the annuity starting date for purposes of satisfying the timing requirements for giving consent and providing an explanation of the QJSA, with certain exception. [Treas. Reg. § 1.417(e)-1(b)(3)(vi)]

Q 11:48 Must written explanations of the QPSA and QJSA be provided to nonvested participants?

Written explanations of the QPSA and QJSA benefits must be provided to nonvested participants who are employed by an employer maintaining the retirement plan but not to nonvested participants who are no longer employed by the employer. [Treas. Reg. § 1.401(a)-20, Q&A-34]

Q 11:49 When must a retirement plan provide the written explanation of the QPSA to a participant?

General Rule. A retirement plan must provide written explanation of the QPSA to a participant within the "applicable period." Except as provided below, under the discussion of "Separations Before Age 35," the applicable period for any participant is whichever of the following periods ends latest:

1. The period beginning with the first day of the plan year in which the participant reaches age 32 and ending with the close of the plan year preceding the plan year in which the participant reaches age 35.
2. A reasonable period ending after the individual becomes a participant.
3. A reasonable period ending after the QPSA is no longer fully subsidized.
4. A reasonable period ending after the survivor annuity rules first apply to the participant. The survivor annuity rules would first apply when a benefit is transferred from a plan that is not subject to those requirements to a plan that is or at the time a participant elects to have his benefit paid in the form of an annuity under a defined contribution plan, such as a profit sharing or stock bonus plan, that has been designed to be exempt from the survivor annuity requirements.

[I.R.C. § 417(a)(3)(B); Treas. Reg. § 1.401(a)-20, Q&A-35(a); Ann. 95-33, 1995-19 I.R.B. 14]

Separations Before Age 35. For a participant who separates from service before reaching age 35, the applicable period is the period beginning one year before the separation from service and ending one year after that separation. If such a participant returns to service, then the plan must also comply with the general rule described above. [I.R.C. § 417(a)(3)(B); Treas. Reg. § 1.401(a)-20, Q&A-35(b); Ann. 95-33, 1995-19 I.R.B. 14]

Reasonable Period. In applying the general rule described above, a reasonable period ending after any of the events listed in paragraphs (2), (3), or (4), above, is the end of the one-year period beginning with the date the event occurs. The applicable period for any of those events begins one year before that event occurs. [Treas. Reg. § 1.401(a)-20, Q&A-35(c); Ann. 95-33, 1995-19 I.R.B. 14]

Q 11:50 How do retirement plans satisfy the requirements to provide participants with written explanations of QPSAs and QJSAs?

General Rule. A qualified retirement plan meets the survivor annuity requirements of Code Section 401(a)(11) only if the plan meets the written explanation requirements of Code Section 417(a)(3) and Treasury Regulations Section 1.417(a)(3)-1 regarding the written explanation (a "Section 417(a)(3) explanation") required to be provided to a participant with respect to either a QJSA or a QPSA. There is an exception to the written explanation requirement in the case of a fully subsidized QPSA or QJSA (see Treas. Reg. § 1.401(a)-20, Q&A-37). [Treas. Reg. § 1.417(a)(3)-1(a)(1)]

Time for Providing the Section 417(a)(3) Explanation. The rules governing the timing of the QJSA and QPSA explanations are found in Treasury Regulations Sections 1.417(e)-1(b)(3)(ii) and 1.401(a)-20, Q&A-35, respectively. [Treas. Reg. § 1.417(a)(3)-1(a)(2)]

Required Method for Providing Section 417(a)(3) Explanation. A Section 417(a)(3) explanation must be a written explanation. First-class mail to the last-known address of the participant is an acceptable delivery method for a Section 417(a)(3) explanation. Likewise, hand delivery is acceptable. However, posting the explanation is not acceptable. [Treas. Reg. § 1.417(a)(3)-1(a)(3); But see Treas. Reg. § 1.401(a)-21 for rules permitting the use of electronic media to provide the Code § 417(a)(3) explanation.]

Understandability. A Section 417(a)(3) explanation must be written in a manner calculated to be understood by the average participant. [Treas. Reg. § 1.417(a)(3)-1(a)(4)]

Q 11:51 What information must the Section 417(a)(3) explanation contain?

Content of the QPSA Explanation. The QPSA explanation must contain a general description of the QPSA, the circumstances under which it will be paid if elected, the availability of the election of the QPSA, and, except as provided in Q 11:52 (regarding permitted estimates), a description of the financial effect of the election of the QPSA on the participant's benefits (i.e., an estimate of the reduction to the participant's estimated normal retirement benefit that would result from an election of the QPSA). [Treas. Reg. § 1.417(a)(3)-1(b)(1)]

Content of the QJSA Explanation: The QJSA explanation must provide either participant-specific information satisfying the requirements of Treasury Regulations Section 1.417(a)(3)-1(c) or generally applicable information satisfying the requirements of Treasury Regulations Section 1.417(a)(3)-1(d). [Treas. Reg. § 1.417(a)(3)-1(b)(2)] Under the participant-specific information requirements (see Q 11:52), the QJSA must contain certain specific information relating to the benefits available under the plan to the particular participant. Alternatively, under the generally applicable information requirements (see Q 11:53), the QJSA explanation can contain generally applicable information in lieu of specific participant information, provided that the participant has the right to request additional information regarding the participant's benefits under the plan. [Treas. Reg. § 1.417(a)(3)-1(b)] (See Q 11:43 for a discussion on how a plan that is subject to the Code Section 401(a)(11) survivor annuity requirements would provide a participant with a written explanation of the terms and conditions of the QOSA available to the participant.)

Q 11:52 What information must be provided in a QJSA explanation that is intended to satisfy the participant-specific information requirements?

In General. A QJSA explanation satisfies the participant-specific information requirements if it provides the following information with respect to each of the optional forms of benefit presently available to the participant (i.e., optional forms of benefit for which the QJSA explanation applies that have an annuity starting date after the providing of the QJSA explanation and optional forms of benefit with retroactive annuity starting dates that are available with payments commencing at that same time):

1. A description of the optional form of benefit;
2. A description of the eligibility conditions for the optional form of benefit;
3. A description of the financial effect of electing the optional form of benefit (i.e., the amounts and timing of payments to the participant under the form of benefit during the participant's lifetime, and the amounts and timing of payment after the participant's death);
4. In the case of a defined benefit plan, a description of the relative value of the optional form of benefit compared to the value of the QJSA (in the manner described below and in Treasury Regulations Section 1.417(a)(3)-1(c)(2)); and
5. A description of any other material features of the optional form of benefit.

[Treas. Reg. § 1.417(a)(3)-1(c)(1)(i)-(v)]

Requirement for Numerical Comparison of Relative Values. In the case of a defined benefit plan, a participant-specific QJSA explanation must provide a description of the relative value of the optional form of benefit compared to the value of the QJSA (see item 4, above).

1. *In General.* The description of the relative value of an optional form of benefit compared to the value of the QJSA provided in a participant-specific QJSA explanation under a defined benefit plan must be expressed to the participant in a manner that provides a meaningful comparison of the relative economic values of the two forms of benefit without the participant having to make calculations using interest or mortality assumptions. Thus, in performing the calculations necessary to make this comparison, the benefits under one or both optional forms of benefit must be converted, taking into account the time, value of money, and life expectancies, so that the values of both optional forms of benefit are expressed in the same form. For example, such a comparison may be expressed to the participant using any of the following techniques:
   a. Expressing the actuarial present value of the optional form of benefit as a percentage or factor of the actuarial present value of the QJSA;
   b. Stating the amount of the annuity that is the actuarial equivalent of the optional form of benefit and that is payable at the same time and under the same conditions as the QJSA; or
   c. Stating the actuarial present value of both the optional form of benefit and the QJSA.
   [Treas. Reg. § 1.417(a)(3)-1(c)(2)]
2. *Use of One Form for Both Married and Unmarried Individuals.* In lieu of providing different QJSA explanations for married and unmarried individuals, the defined benefit plan may provide a QJSA explanation that does not vary based on the participant's marital status. [Treas. Reg. § 1.417(a)(3)-1(c)(2)(ii)(A)]

   For a married participant, in lieu of comparing the value of each optional form of benefit presently available to the participant to the value of the QJSA, the defined benefit plan can compare the value of each optional form of benefit (including the QJSA) to the value of a QJSA for an unmarried participant (i.e., a single life annuity), but only if that same single life annuity is available to that married participant. [Treas. Reg. § 1.417(a)(3)-1(c)(2)(ii)(B)]

   For an unmarried participant, in lieu of comparing the value of each optional form of benefit presently available to the participant to the value of the QJSA for that individual (which is a single life annuity), the defined benefit plan can compare the value of each optional form of benefit (including the single life annuity) to the value of the joint and survivor annuity that is the QJSA for a married participant, but only if that same joint and survivor annuity is available to that unmarried participant. [Treas. Reg. § 1.417(a)(3)-1(c)(2)(ii)(C)]
3. *Simplified Presentations Are Permitted.* Two more optional forms of benefit that have approximately the same value may be grouped for purposes of a required numerical comparison described in Q 11:52. For this purpose, two or more optional forms of benefit have approximately the same

value if none of these optional forms of benefit vary in relative value in comparison to the value of the QJSA by more than five percentage points when the relative value comparison is made by expressing the actuarial present value of each of those optional forms of benefit as a percentage of the actuarial present value of the QJSA. For such a group of optional forms of benefit, the requirement relating to disclosing the relative value of each optional form of benefit compared to the value of the QJSA can be satisfied by disclosing the relative value of any one of the optional forms in the groups compared to the value of the QPSA, and disclosing that the other optional forms of benefit in the groups are of approximately the same value. If a single-sum distribution is included in such a group of optional forms of benefit, the single-sum distribution must be the distribution form that is used for purposes of this comparison. [Treas. Reg. § 1.417(a)(3)-1(c)(2)(iii)(A)]

If two or more optional forms of benefits are grouped under the rules described above, the relative values for all of the optional forms of benefit in the group can be stated using a representative relative value as the approximate relative value for the entire group. For this purpose, a representative relative value is any relative value that is not less than the relative value of the member of the group of optional forms of benefit with the lowest relative value and is not greater than the relative value of the member of that group with the highest relative value when measured on a consistent basis. For example, if three grouped optional forms have relative values of 87.5 percent, 89 percent, and 91 percent of the value of the QJSA, all three optional forms can be treated as having a relative value of approximately 90 percent of the value of the QJSA. As required under the group rules described above, if a single-sum distribution is included in the group of optional forms of benefit, the 90 percent relative factor of the value of the QJSA must be disclosed as the approximate relative value of the single sum, and the other forms can be described as having the same approximate value as the single sum. [Treas. Reg. § 1.417(a)(3)-1(c)(2)(iii)(B)]

There is a special rule for optional forms of benefit that are close in value to the QJSA. Under this special rule, the relative value of all optional forms of benefit that have an actuarial present value that is at least 95 percent of the actuarial present value of the QJSA and no greater than 105 percent of the actuarial present value of the QJSA is permitted to be described by stating that those optional forms of benefit are approximately equal in value to the QJSA, or that all of those forms of benefit and the QJSA are approximately equal in value. [Treas. Reg. § 1.417(a)(3)-1(c)(2)(iii)(C)]

4. *Actuarial Assumptions Used to Determine Relative Values*. For the purpose of providing a numerical comparison of the value of an optional form of benefit to the value of an immediately commencing QJSA, the following rules apply.

   If an optional form of benefit is subject to the requirements of Code Section 417(c)(3) and Treasury Regulations Section 1.417(e)-1(d) (relating to the determination of present value for purposes of the rules restricting cash-outs), any comparison of the value of the optional form of benefit to the value of the QJSA must be made using the applicable mortality table and the applicable interest rate as defined in Treasury Regulations Sections 1.417(e)-1(d)(2) and (3) (or, at the option of the plan, another reasonable interest rate and reasonable mortality table used under the plan to calculate the amount payable under the optional form of benefit). [Treas. Reg. § 1.417(a)(3)-1(c)(2)(iv)(A)]

In addition, all other optional forms of benefit payable to the participant must be compared with the QJSA using a single set of interest and mortality assumptions that are reasonable and that are applied uniformly with respect to all such optional forms payable to the participant (regardless of whether those assumptions are actually used under the plan for purposes of determining benefit payments). For this purpose, the reasonableness of interest and mortality assumptions is determined without regard to the circumstances of the individual participant. In addition, the applicable mortality table and the applicable interest rate as defined in Treasury Regulations Sections 1.417(e)-1(d)(2) and (3) are considered reasonable actuarial assumptions for this purpose and thus are permitted (but not required) to be used. [Treas. Reg. § 1.417(a)(3)-1(c)(2)(iv)(B)]

5. *Required Disclosure of Assumptions*. The notice must provide an explanation of the concept of relative value, communicating that the relative value comparison is intended to allow the participant to compare the total value of distributions paid in different forms, that the relative value comparison is made by converting the value of the optional forms of benefit presently available to a common form (such as the QJSA or a single-sum distribution), and that this conversion uses interest and life expectancy assumption. The explanation of relative value must include a general statement that all comparisons provided are based on average life expectancies and that the relative value of payments ultimately made under an annuity optional form of benefit will depend on actual longevity. [Treas. Reg. § 1.417(a)(3)-1(c)(2)(v)(A)]

   A required numerical comparison of the value of the optional form of benefit to the value of the QJSA is required to include a disclosure of the interest rate that was used to develop the comparison. [Treas. Reg. § 1.417(a)(3)-1(c)(2)(v)(B)]

   If the plan does not disclose the actuarial assumptions used to calculate the required numerical comparison, then the notice must be accompanied by a statement that includes an offer to provide, upon the participant's request, the actuarial assumptions used to calculate the relative value of optional forms of benefit under the plan. [Treas. Reg. § 1.417(a)(3)-1(c)(2)(v)(C)]

Permitted Estimates of Financial Effect and Relative Value. In general, for purposes of providing, in a participant-specific notice, a description of the financial effect of the distribution forms available to a participant, and for purposes of providing, in such a notice, a description of the relative value of an optional form of benefit compared to the value of the QJSA, the plan is permitted to provide reasonable estimates (e.g., estimates based on data as of an earlier date than the annuity starting date, a reasonable assumption for the age of the participant's spouse or, in the case of a defined contribution plan, reasonable estimates of amounts that would be payable under a purchased annuity contract), including reasonable estimate of the applicable interest rate under Code Section 417(e)(3). [Treas. Reg. § 1.417(a)(3)-1(c)(3)(i)]

If a QJSA notice uses a reasonable estimate, the QJSA explanation must identify the estimate and explain that the plan will, upon the request of the participant, provide a more precise calculation, and the plan must provide the participant with a more precise calculation if so requested. Thus, for example, if a plan provides an estimate of the amount of the QJSA that is based on a reasonable assumption concerning the age of the participant's spouse, the participant can request a calculation that takes into account the actual age of the spouse, as provided by the participant. [Treas. Reg. § 1.417(a)(3)-1(c)(3)(ii)]

If a more precise calculation materially changes the relative value of an optional form compared to the value of the QJSA, the revised value of that optional form must be disclosed, regardless of whether the financial effect of selecting the optional form is affected by the more precise calculation. For example, if a participant provides a plan with the age of the participant's spouse and that information materially changes the relative value of an optional form of benefit (such as a single sum) compared to the value of the QJSA, then the revised relative value of the optional form of benefit and the value of the QJSA must be disclosed, regardless of whether the amount of the payment under that optional form of benefit is affected by the more precise calculation. [Treas. Reg. § 1.417(a)(3)-1(c)(3)(iii)]

Special Rules for Disclosure of Financial Effect for Defined Contribution Plans. For a participant-specific written explanation provided by a defined contribution plan, the required description of financial effect with respect to an annuity form of benefit must include a statement that the annuity will be provided by purchasing an annuity contract from an insurance company with the participant's account balance under the plan. If the description of the financial effect of the optional form of benefit is provided using estimates rather than by assuring that an insurer is able to provide the amount disclosed to the participant, the written explanation must also disclose this fact. [Treas. Reg. § 1.417(a)(3)-1(c)(4)]

Simplified Presentations of Financial Effect and Relative Value to Enhance Clarity for Participants. In general, it is permissible, in certain cases in which a plan offers a range of optional forms of benefit, to use certain simplified presentations of financial effect and relative value of optional forms of benefit so that more useful presentations of information may be provided to participants. Simplified presentations of financial effect and relative value are permitted for a plan that offers a significant number of substantially similar optional forms of benefit. Simplified presentations of financial effect and relative value are permitted for a plan that permits the participant to make separate benefit elections with respect to parts of a benefit. [Treas. Reg. § 1.417(a)(3)-1(c)(5)(ii)]

1. *Disclosure for Plans Offering a Significant Number of Substantially Similar Optional Forms of Benefit.* In general, if a plan offers a significant number of substantially similar optional forms of benefit (as described below) and disclosing the financial effect and relative value of each such optional

form of benefit would provide a level of detail that could be overwhelming rather than helpful to participants, then the financial effect and relative value of those optional forms of benefit can be disclosed by disclosing the relative value and financial effect of a representative range of examples of those optional forms of benefit (as described below), if certain requirements, described below, relating to additional information available upon request, are satisfied. [Treas. Reg. § 1.417(a)(3)-1(c)(5)(ii)(A)]

For these purposes, optional forms of benefit are "substantially similar" if they are identical except for a particular feature or features (with associated adjustment factors) and the feature or features vary linearly. For example, if a plan offers joint and survivor annuity options with survivor payments available in every whole number percentage between 50 percent and 100 percent, those options are substantially similar optional forms of benefit. Similarly, if a participant is entitled under the plan to receive a particular form of benefit with an annuity starting date that is the first day of any month beginning three years before commencement of a distribution and ending on the date of commencement of the distribution, those forms of benefit are substantially similar optional forms of benefit. [Treas. Reg. § 1.417(a)(3)-1(c)(5)(ii)(B)]

A range of examples with respect to substantially similar optional forms of benefit is representative only if it includes examples illustrating the financial effect and relative value of the optional forms of benefit that reflect each varying feature at both extremes of its linear range, plus at least one example illustrating the financial effect and relative value of the optional forms of benefit that reflects each varying feature at an intermediate point. However, if one intermediate example is insufficient to illustrate the pattern of variation in relative value with respect to a varying feature, examples sufficient to illustrate such pattern must be provided. Thus, for example, if a plan offers joint and survivor annuity options with survivor payments available in every whole number percentage between 50 percent and 100 percent, and if all such optional forms of benefit would be permitted to be disclosed as approximately equal in value, the plan could satisfy the requirement to disclose the financial effect and relative value of a representative range of examples of those optional forms of benefit by disclosing the financial effect and relative value with respect to the joint and 50 percent survivor annuity, the joint and 75 percent survivor annuity, and the joint and 100 percent survivor annuity. [Treas. Reg. § 1.417(a)(3)-1(c)(5)(ii)(C)]

If a QJSA explanation discloses the financial effect and relative value of substantially similar optional forms of benefit by disclosing the financial effect and relative value of a representative range of examples, the QJSA explanation must explain that the plan will, upon the request of the participant, disclose the financial effect and relative value of any particular optional form of benefit from among the substantially similar optional forms of benefit and the plan must provide the participant with the financial effect and relative value of any such optional form of benefit if the participant so requests. [Treas. Reg. § 1.417(a)(3)-1(c)(5)(ii)(D)]

2. *Separate Presentations Permitted for Elections That Apply to Parts of a Benefit.* If a plan permits a participant to make separate benefit elections with respect to two or more portions of the participant's benefit, the description of the financial effect and relative values of optional forms of benefit can be made separately for each such portion of the benefit, rather than for each optional form of benefit (i.e., each combination of possible elections). [Treas. Reg. § 1.417(a)(3)-1(c)(5)(iii)]

Q 11:53 What information must be provided in a QJSA explanation that is intended to satisfy the generally applicable information requirements?

Forms of Benefit Available. In lieu of providing the required information described in (1) through (4) under the "In General" heading of Q 11:52 for each optional form of benefit presently available to the participant in a participant-specific QJSA explanation (see Q 11:52), a generally applicable QJSA explanation can be provided that may contain such required information for the QJSA and each other optional form of benefit generally available under the plan, along with a reference to where a participant may readily obtain such required information for any other optional forms of benefit that are presently available to the participant. [Treas. Reg. § 1.417(a)(3)-1(d)(1)]

Financial Effect and Comparison of Relative Values. In lieu of providing a statement of the financial effect of electing an optional form of benefit or a comparison of relative values as required for the participant-specific QJSA explanation (see Q 11:52), based on the actual age and benefit of the participant, the QJSA explanation is permitted to include a chart (or other comparable device) showing the financial effect and relative value of optional forms of benefit in a series of examples specifying the amount of the optional form of benefit payable to a hypothetical participant at a representative range of ages and the comparison of relative values at those same representative ages. Each example in the chart must show the financial effect of electing the optional form of benefit, and a comparison of the relative value of the optional form of benefit to the value of the QJSA, using reasonable assumptions for the age of the hypostatized participant's spouse and any other variables that affect the financial effect, or relative value, of the optional form of benefit. The requirement to show the financial effect of electing an optional form can be satisfied through the use of other methods (e.g., expressing the amount of the optional form as a percentage or a factor of the amount payable under the normal form of benefit), provided that the method provides sufficient information so that a participant can determine the amount of benefits payable in the optional form. The chart (or other comparable device) must be accompanied by disclosures explaining the concept of relative value and disclosing certain interest assumptions. In addition, the chart (or other comparable device) must be accompanied by a general statement describing the effect of significant variations between the assumed ages or other variables on the financial effect of electing the optional form of benefit and the comparison of the relative value of the optional form of benefit to the value of the QJSA. [Treas. Reg. § 1.417(a)(3)-1(d)(2)(i)]

The generalized notice will satisfy these requirements only if the notice includes either the amount payable to the participant under the normal form of benefit or the amount payable to the participant under the normal form of benefit adjusted for immediate commencement. For this purpose, the normal form of benefit is the form in which payments due the participant under the plan are expressed under the plan, prior to adjustments for form of benefit. For example, assuming that a plan's benefit accrual formula is expressed as a straight life annuity, the generalized notice must provide the amount of either the straight life annuity commencing at normal retirement age or the straight life annuity commencing immediately. Reasonable estimates may be used to determine the amount payable to the participant under the normal form of benefit. [Treas. Reg. § 1.417(a)(3)-1(d)(2)(ii)]

The generalized notice must be accompanied by a statement that includes an offer to provide, upon the participant's request, a statement of financial effect and a comparison of relative values that is specific to the participant for any presently available optional form of benefit, and a description of how a participant may obtain this additional information. [Treas. Reg. § 1.417(a)(3)-1(d)(2)(iii)]

Financial Effect of QPSA Election. In lieu of providing a specific description of the financial effect of the QPSA election, the QPSA explanation may provide a general description of the financial effect of the election. Thus, for example, the description can be in the form of a chart showing the reduction to a hypothetical participant's normal retirement benefit at a representative range of participant ages as a result of the QPSA election (using a reasonable assumption for the age of the hypothetical participant's spouse relative to the age of the hypothetical participant). In addition, this chart must be accompanied by a statement that includes an offer to provide, upon the participant's request, an estimate of the reduction to the participant's estimated normal retirement benefit, and a description of how a participant may obtain this additional information. [Treas. Reg. § 1.417(a)(3)-1(d)(3)]

Additional Information Required to Be Furnished at the Participant's Request. The generalized notice must be accompanied by a statement that includes an offer to provide, upon the participant's request, the information described below and a description of how a participant may obtain this additional information. [Treas. Reg. § 1.417(a)(3)-1(d)(4)]

1. *Explanation of QJSA*. If the content of a QJSA explanation does not include all the items described in Q 11:53, then, upon a participant's request, the plan must furnish such information with respect to one or more presently available optional forms. Thus, with respect to those optional forms of benefit, the participant must receive a QJSA explanation specific to the participant that is based on the participant's actual age and benefit. Further, if the plan does not disclose the actuarial assumptions used to calculate the numerical comparison, then, upon request, the plan must provide the actuarial assumptions used to calculate the relative value of optional forms of benefit under the plan. [Treas. Reg. § 1.417(a)(3)-1(d)(4)(i)]
2. *Explanation of QPSA*. If the content of a QPSA explanation does not include all the required information, then, upon a participant's request, the plan must furnish an estimate of the reduction to the participant's

estimated normal retirement benefit that would result from a QPSA election. [Treas. Reg. § 1.417(a)(3)-1(d)(4)(ii)]

Use of Participant-Specific Information in Generalized Notice. A QJSA explanation does not fail to satisfy the generalized notice requirements merely because it contains an item of participant-specific information in place of the corresponding generally applicable information. [Treas. Reg. § 1.417(a)(3)-1(d)(5)]

Q 11:54 Are there any examples that illustrate the application of these QJSA explanation rules?

Yes. The following examples illustrate the application of the QJSA explanation rules. Solely for the purposes of these examples, the applicable interest rate that applies to any distribution that is subject to the rules of Code Section 417(e)(3) is assumed to be 5½ percent, and the applicable mortality table under Code Section 417(e)(3) and Treasury Regulations Section 1.417(e)-1(d)(2) is assumed to be the table that applies as of January 1, 2003. In addition, solely for the purposes of these examples, assume that a plan that determines actuarial equivalence using 6 percent interest and the applicable mortality table under Code Section 417(e)(3) and Treasury Regulations Section 1.417(e)-1(d)(2) that applies as of January 1, 1995, is using reasonable actuarial assumptions. The examples are as follows:

Example 11-6: Participant Tom Joad participates in the Grapes of Wrath Corporation Plan, a qualified defined benefit plan. Under the Plan, the QJSA is a joint and 100 percent survivor annuity, which is actuarially equivalent to the single life annuity determined using 6 percent interest and the Code Section 417(e)(3) applicable mortality table that applies as of January 1, 2010. On October 1, 2019, Tom will terminate employment at age 55. When Tom terminates employment, he will be eligible to elect an unreduced early retirement benefit, payable as either a single life annuity or the QJSA. Tom will also be eligible to elect a single-sum distribution equal to the actuarial present value of the single life annuity payable at normal retirement age (age 65), determined using the applicable mortality table and the applicable interest rate under Code Section 417(e)(3).

Tom is provided with a QJSA explanation that describes the single life annuity, the QJSA, and single-sum distribution options under the Plan, and any eligibility conditions associated with these options. Tom is married when the explanation is provided. The explanation indicates that, if Tom commenced benefits at age 55 and had a spouse age 55, the monthly benefit under an immediately commencing single life annuity is $3,000, the monthly benefit under the QJSA is estimated to be 89.96 percent of the monthly benefit under the immediately commencing single life annuity or $2,699, and the single sum is estimated to be 74.7645 times the monthly benefit under the immediately commencing single life annuity, or $224,293.

The QJSA explanation indicates that the single life annuity and the QJSA are of approximately the same value, but that the single-sum option is equivalent in value to a monthly benefit under the QJSA of $1,215. (This amount is 45 percent of the value of the QJSA at age 55 ($1,215 divided by 89.96 percent of $3,000 equals 45 percent).) The explanation states that the relative value comparison converts the value of the single life annuity and the single-sum options to the value of each if paid in the form of the QJSA and that this conversion uses interest and life expectancy assumptions. The explanation specifies that the calculations relating to the single-sum distribution were prepared using 5.5 percent interest and average life expectancy, that the other calculations were prepared using a 6 percent interest rate and that the relative value of actual annuity payments for an individual can vary depending on how long the individual and spouse live. The explanation notes that the calculation of the QJSA assumed that the spouse was age 55, that the amount of the QJSA will depend on the actual age of the spouse (e.g., annuity payments will be significantly lower if the spouse is significantly younger than the participant), and that the amount of the single-sum payment will depend on the interest rates that apply when the participant actually takes a distribution. The explanation also includes an offer to provide a more precise calculation to the participant taking into account the spouse's actual age.

Tom requests a more precise calculation of the financial effect of choosing a QJSA taking into account that his spouse is 50 years of age. Using the actual age of Participant, Tom's spouse, the Plan determines that the monthly payments under the QJSA are 87.62 percent of the monthly payments under the single life annuity, or $2,628.60 per month, and provides this information to Tom. The Plan is not required to provide an updated calculation of the relative value of the single sum because the value of the single sum continues to be 45 percent of the value of the QJSA. [Treas. Reg. § 1.417(a)(3)-1(e), Ex. 1]

Example 11-7: The facts are the same as in Example 11-6, except that the comparison of the relative values of optional forms of benefit to the value of the QJSA is not expressed as a percentage of the actuarial present value of the QJSA, but instead is expressed by disclosing the actuarial present values of the optional forms and the QJSA. In addition, the Plan uses the applicable interest rate and the applicable mortality table under Code Section 417(e)(3) for all comparison purposes.

Accordingly, the QJSA explanation indicates that the QJSA has an actuarial present value of $498,089, while the single-sum payment has an actuarial present value of $224,293 (i.e., the amount of the single sum is $224,293) and that the single life annuity is approximately equal in value to the QJSA. The explanation states that the relative value comparison converts the value of single life annuity and the QJSA into an amount payable in the form of the single-sum option (even though a single-sum distribution in that amount is not available under the plan) and that this conversion uses interest and life expectancy assumptions. The explanation specifies that the calculations were prepared using 5.5 percent interest and average life expectancy, and that the relative value of actual annuity payments for an individual can vary depending on how long the individual and spouse live. The explanation notes that the calculation of the QJSA assumed that the spouse was of age 55, that the amount of the QJSA will depend on the actual age of the spouse (e.g., annuity payments will be significantly lower if the spouse is significantly younger than the participant), and that the amount of the single-sum payment will depend on the interest rates that apply when the participant actually takes a distribution. The explanation also includes an offer to provide a more precise calculation to the participant taking into account the spouse's actual age. [Treas. Reg. § 1.417(a)(3)-1(e), Ex. 2]

Example 11-8: The facts are the same as in Example 11-6, except that, in lieu of providing information specific to Tom in the QJSA notice, the plan satisfies the QJSA explanation requirement by providing Tom with a statement that Tom's monthly benefit under an immediately commencing single life annuity (which is the normal form of benefit under the plan, adjusted for immediate commencement) is $3,000, along with the following chart. The chart shows the financial effect of electing each optional form of benefit for a hypothetical participant with a $1,000 benefit and a spouse who is the same age as the participant. Instead of showing the relative value of these optional forms of benefit compared to the value of the QJSA, the chart shows the relative value of these optional forms of benefit compared to the value of the single life annuity. Separate charts are provided for ages 55, 60, and 65 as follows:

Age 55 Commencement

Optional Form	*Amount of Distribution per $1,000 of Immediate Single Life Annuity*	*Relative Value*
Life Annuity	$1,000 per month	N/A
QJSA (Joint and 100% survivor annuity)	$900 per month ($900 per month for survivor annuity)	Approximately the same value as the Life Annuity
Lump sum	$74,764	Approximately 45% of the value of the Life Annuity

Age 60 Commencement

Optional Form	*Amount of Distribution per $1,000 of Immediate Single Life Annuity*	*Relative Value*
Life Annuity	$1,000 per month	N/A
QJSA (Joint and 100% survivor annuity)	$878 per month ($878 per month for survivor annuity)	Approximately the same value as the Life Annuity
Lump sum	$99,792	Approximately 66% of the value of the Life Annuity

Age 65 Commencement

Optional Form	*Amount of Distribution per $1,000 of Immediate Single Life Annuity*	*Relative Value*
Life Annuity	$1,000 per month	N/A
QJSA (Joint and 100% survivor annuity)	$852 per month ($852 per month for survivor annuity)	Approximately the same value as the Life Annuity
Lump sum	$135,759	Approximately the same value as the Life Annuity

When Tom requests specific information regarding the amounts payable under the QJSA, the joint and 100 percent survivor annuity, and the single-sum distribution and provides the age of his spouse, the Plan determines that Tom's QJSA is $2,628.60 per month and the single-sum distribution is $224,293. The actuarial present value of the QJSA (determined using the 5.5 percent interest and the Code Section 417(e)(3) applicable mortality table) is $498,896, and the actuarial present value of the single life annuity is $497,876. Accordingly, the specific information discloses that the single-sum distribution has a value that is 45 percent of the value of the single life annuity available to Tom on October 1, 2019. The QJSA notice provides that the QJSA is of approximately the same value as the single life annuity. [Treas. Reg. § 1.417(a)(3)-1(e), Ex. 3]

Example 11-9: The facts are the same as in Example 11-6, except that under the Plan, the single-sum distribution is determined as the actuarial present value of the immediately commencing single life annuity. In addition, the Plan provides a joint and 75 percent survivor annuity that is reduced from the single life annuity and that is the QJSA under the Plan. For purposes of determining the amount of the QJSA, if the participant is married, the reduction is only half of the reduction that would normally apply under the actuarial assumptions specified in the Plan for determining actuarial equivalence of optional forms.

In lieu of providing information specific to Tom in the QJSA notice as set forth in paragraph (c) of this section, the Plan satisfies the QJSA explanation requirement in accordance with paragraph (d)(2) of this section by providing Tom with a statement that Tom's monthly benefit under an immediately commencing single life annuity (which is the normal form of benefit under the Plan, adjusted for immediate commencement) is $3,000, along with the following chart showing the financial effect and the relative value of the optional forms of benefit compared to the QJSA for a hypothetical participant with a $1,000 benefit and a spouse who is three years younger than the participant. For each optional form generally available under the Plan, the chart shows the financial effect and the relative value, using the grouping rules. Separate charts are provided for ages 55, 60, and 65, as follows:

Age 55 Commencement

Optional Form	*Amount of Distribution per $1,000 of Immediate Single Life Annuity*	*Relative Value*
Life Annuity	$1,000 per month	Approximately the same value as the QJSA
QJSA (Joint and 75% survivor annuity for a participant who is married)	$956 per month ($717 per month for survivor annuity)	N/A
Joint and 100% survivor annuity	$886 per month ($886 per month for survivor annuity)	Approximately the same value as the QJSA
Lump sum	$165,959	Approximately the same value as the QJSA

Age 60 Commencement

Optional Form	*Amount of Distribution per $1,000 of Immediate Single Life Annuity*	*Relative Value*
Life Annuity	$1,000 per month	Approximately 94% of the value of the QJSA
QJSA (Joint and 75% survivor annuity for a participant who is married)	$945 per month ($709 per month for survivor annuity)	N/A
Joint and 100% survivor annuity	$859 per month ($859 per month for survivor annuity)	Approximately 94% of the value of the QJSA
Lump sum	$151,691	Approximately the same value as the QJSA

Age 65 Commencement

Optional Form	*Amount of Distribution per $1,000 of Immediate Single Life Annuity*	*Relative Value*
Life Annuity	$1,000 per month	Approximately 93% of the value of QJSA
QJSA (Joint and 75% survivor annuity for a participant who is married)	$932 per month ($699 per month for survivor annuity)	N/A
Joint and 100% survivor annuity	$828 per month ($828 per month for survivor annuity)	Approximately 93% of the value of the QJSA
Lump sum	$135,759	Approximately 93% of the value of the QJSA

The chart disclosing the financial effect and the relative value of the optional forms specifies that the calculations were prepared assuming that the spouse is three years younger than the participant, that the calculations relating to the single-sum distribution were prepared using 5.5 percent interest and average life expectancy, that the other calculations were prepared using a 6 percent interest rate, and that the relative value of actual payments for an individual can vary depending on how long the individual and spouse live. The explanation states that the relative value comparison converts the single life annuity, the joint and 100 percent survivor annuity, and the single-sum options to the value of each if paid in the form of the QJSA and that this conversion uses interest and life expectancy assumptions. The explanation notes that the calculation of the QJSA depends on the actual age of the spouse (e.g., annuity payments will be significantly lower if the spouse is significantly younger than the participant) and that the amount of the single-sum payment will depend on the interest rates that apply when the participant actually takes a distribution. The explanation also includes an offer to provide a calculation specific to the participant upon request and an offer to provide mortality tables used in preparing calculations upon request.

Tom requests specific information regarding the amounts payable under the QJSA, the joint and 100 percent survivor annuity, and the single sum.

Based on the information about the age of Tom's spouse, the Plan determines that Tom's QJSA is $2,856.30 per month, the joint and 100 percent survivor annuity is $2,628.60 per month, and the single sum is $497,876. The actuarial present value of the QJSA (determined using the 5.5 percent interest and the

Code Section 417(e)(3) applicable mortality table, the actuarial assumptions required under Section 417) is $525,091. Accordingly, the value of the single-sum distribution available to Tom on October 1, 2019, is 94.8 percent of the actuarial present value of the QJSA. In addition, the actuarial present value of the life annuity and the 100 percent joint and survivor annuity are 95 percent of the actuarial present value of the QJSA.

The Plan provides Tom with a QJSA explanation that incorporates these more precise calculations of the financial effect and relative value of the optional forms for which Tom requested information. [Treas. Reg. § 1.417(a)(3)-1(e), Ex. 4]

Q 11:55 What are the effective dates for the QJSA and QPSA explanation rules?

General Effective Date for QJSA Explanations. In general, except as otherwise provided below, the QJSA explanation rules apply to a QJSA explanation with respect to any distribution with an annuity date starting date that is on or after February 1, 2006. [Treas. Reg. § 1.417(a)(3)-1(f)(1)(i)]

Under a reasonable, good-faith transition rule, except with respect to any portion of a QJSA explanation that is subject to the earlier (October 1, 2004) effective date rule described below, a reasonable, good-faith effort to comply with the new QJSA explanation rules in Treasury Regulations Section 1.417(a)(3)-1 will be deemed to satisfy the requirements of those regulations for QJSA explanations provided before January 1, 2007, with respect to distributions with annuity starting dates that are on or after February 1, 2006. For this purpose, a reasonable, good-faith effort to comply with the new QJSA explanation regulations includes substantial compliance with Treasury Regulations Section 1.417(a)(3)-1 as it appeared in 26 C.F.R. Part 1 revised April 1, 2004. [Treas. Reg. § 1.417(a)(3)-1(f)(1)(ii)]

Special Effective Date for Certain QJSA Explanations.

1. *Application to QJSA Explanations with Respect to Certain Optional Forms That Are Less Valuable than the QJSA.* The new QJSA rules also apply to any distribution with an annuity starting date that is on or after October 1, 2004, and before February 1, 2006, if the actuarial present value of any optional form of benefit is less than the actuarial present value of the QJSA. For these purposes, the actuarial present value of an optional form is treated as not less than the actuarial present value of the QJSA if:
    a. Using the applicable interest rate and applicable mortality table under Treasury Regulations Sections 1.417(e)-1(d)(2) and (3), the actuarial present value of that optional form is not less than the actuarial present value of the QJSA for an unmarried participant; and
    b. Using reasonable actuarial assumptions, the actuarial present value of the QJSA for an unmarried participant is not less than the actuarial present value of the QJSA for a married participant.
    [Treas. Reg. § 1.417(a)(3)-1(f)(2)(i)]

2. *Requirement to Disclose Differences in Value for Certain Optional Forms.* A QJSA explanation with respect to any distribution with an annuity starting date that is on or after October 1, 2004, and before February 1, 2006, is only required to be provided under this section with respect to:
   a. An optional form of benefit that is subject to the requirements of Code Section 417(e)(3) (the rules requiring the use of the applicable mortality table and the applicable interest rate to determine present value) and that has an actuarial present value that is less than the actuarial present value of the QJSA; and
   b. The QJSA.
   [Treas. Reg. § 1.417(a)(3)-1(f)(2)(ii)]
3. *Application to QJSA Explanations with Respect to Optional Forms That Are Approximately Equal in Value to the QJSA.* The new rules in Treasury Regulations Section 1.417(a)(3)-1(c)(2)(iii)(C), relating to disclosures of optional forms of benefit that are permitted to be described as approximately equal in value to the QJSA, do not apply to the QJSA explanation provided before January 1, 2007. Previously issued rules (specifically, Treasury Regulations Section 1.417(a)(3)-1(c)(2)(iii)(C), as it appeared in 26 C.F.R. Part 1 revised April 1, 2004) apply to a QJSA explanation with respect to any distribution with an annuity starting date that is on or after October 1, 2004 and that is provided before January 1, 2007. [Treas. Reg. § 1.417(a)(3)-1(f)(2)(iii)]

Effective Date for QPSA Explanations. The new QPSA explanation rules apply to any QPSA explanation provided on or after July 1, 2004. [Treas. Reg. § 1.417(a)(3)-1(j)(4)]

Q 11:56 To what extent may sponsors of qualified retirement plans use new technologies to satisfy the various Code and ERISA requirements for notice, election, consent, recordkeeping, and participant disclosure?

Before the enactment of TRA'97, it was not clear whether sponsors of qualified retirement plans could use new technologies (e.g., telephonic response systems, computers, e-mail) to satisfy the various Code and ERISA requirements for notice, election, consent, recordkeeping, and participant disclosure.

Under TRA'97, Congress directed the DOL and the Treasury Department to issue guidance facilitating the use of new technologies for qualified plan purposes. The guidance is to be designed to (1) interpret the notice, election, consent, disclosure, and time requirements (and related recordkeeping requirements) under the Code and ERISA relating to retirement plans as applied to the use of new technologies by plan sponsors and administrators, while maintaining the protection of the rights of participants and beneficiaries, and (2) clarify the extent to which writing requirements under the Code will be interpreted to permit paperless transactions. Congress required the guidance to be issued no later than December 31, 1998. In IRS Ann. 98-62 [1998-29 I.R.B. 13], the IRS and the Treasury Department invited public comment relating to the use of paperless technologies in the administration of retirement plans, but noted therein that comments received to date indicated that the possible use of such technologies in the administration of the spousal consent requirements that apply to QJSAs and QPSAs raised a number of significant legal and practical issues relating to adequate protection of persons who are not plan participants or current or former employees. Consequently, initial guidance on paperless technologies is unlikely to address issues involving spousal consent.

On February 8, 2000, the IRS issued final regulations (the "2000 regulations") setting forth applicable standards for the transmission of certain notices and consents required in connection with distributions from retirement plans through electronic media. In the preamble to those regulations the IRS and the Treasury Department noted that—regarding notices, elections, and spousal consents governed by Code Sections 401(a)(11) and 417—the statutory requirement that spousal consent be witnessed either by a notary public or a plan representative appears to presuppose that a spouse is to be in the physical presence of the notary public or the plan representative at the time consent is given. The IRS and the Treasury Department further noted that such statutory requirement appeared to place significant limitations on the utility of electronic media in effecting spousal consent and stated that it was unclear what guidance the IRS and the Treasury Department could issue that would meaningfully facilitate paperless distributions in the case of plans subject to the QJSA and QPSA requirements of Code Section 401(a)(11) and 417. [65 Fed. Reg. 6004] The 2000 regulations did not permit the use of electronic media for any notice or election required under Code Section 417 with respect to a waiver of a QJSA.

On October 20, 2006, the IRS issued final regulations (the 2006 regulations) on electronic employee plan notices, elections, and consents. The 2006 regulations set forth standards for electronic systems that make use of an electronic medium to provide a notice to a recipient, or to make a participant election or consent, with respect to a retirement plan, an employee benefit arrangement, or an IRA. The 2006 regulations reflect the provisions of E-SIGN. The 2006 regulations apply to notices provided, and participant elections made, on or after January 1, 2007. However, a plan, arrangement, or IRA that provided an applicable notice or made a participant election that complied with the 2006 regulations on or after October 1, 2000, and before January 1, 2007, will not be treated as failing to provide an applicable notice or make a participant election merely because the notice or election was not in writing or written form. [71 Fed. Reg. 61877 (Oct. 20, 2006); Treas. Reg. § 1.401(a)-21(g)]

The participant election rules in the 2006 regulations extend the use of electronic media to the notice and election rules applicable to plans that are subject to the QJSA requirements of Code Section 417. Accordingly, a plan subject to the QJSA requirements is permitted to provide the notice required by Code 417 to a participant through use of electronic media as long as the plan complies with either of two methods described in the 2006 regulations for providing notices. Similarly, a participant's consent to a distribution is permitted to be provided through the use of electronic media if the plan complies with the standards set forth in the 2006 regulations. [71 Fed. Reg. 61877 (Oct. 20, 2006); Treas. Reg. §§ 1.401(a)-21, 1.417(a)(3)-1(a)(3)]

Code Section 417 requires any spousal consent to a waiver of a QJSA to be witnessed by a plan representative or a notary public. In accordance with Section 101(g) of E-SIGN, the 2006 regulations authorize the use of an electronic acknowledgment or authorization if the standards of Section 101(g) of E-SIGN and state law applicable to notary publics are satisfied. The 2006 regulations retain the requirement that the signature of the spouse be witnessed in the physical presence of a plan representative or notary public and do not permit the use of a spousal PIN to sign a spousal consent electronically. [71 Fed. Reg. 6177 (Oct. 20, 2006); Treas. Reg. § 1.401(a)-21(f), Ex. 3 (spousal consent, to a plan loan, via electronic notarization)]

Subsidized Survivor Benefits

Q 11:57 What are the consequences of fully subsidizing the cost of a QJSA or a QPSA?

If a retirement plan fully subsidizes a QJSA or QPSA and does not allow a participant to waive the QJSA or QPSA or to select a nonspousal beneficiary, the plan need not provide the written explanation otherwise required. However, if the plan offers an election to waive the benefit or designate a beneficiary, it must satisfy the election, consent, and notice requirements for the subsidized QJSA or QPSA. [Treas. Reg. § 1.401(a)-20, Q&A-37]

Q 11:58 What is a fully subsidized benefit?

QJSA. Generally, a fully subsidized QJSA is one under which no increase in cost to, or decrease in actual amounts received by, the participant may result from the participant's failure to elect another form of benefit. [Treas. Reg. § 1.401(a)-20, Q&A-38(a)(1)]

> **Example 11-10:** Salinas Corporation maintains a retirement plan that provides a joint and survivor annuity and a single-sum option. The plan does not fully subsidize the joint and survivor annuity, regardless of the actuarial value of the joint and survivor annuity, because, in the event of the participant's early death, the participant would have received less under the annuity than he or she would have received under the single-sum option. [Treas. Reg. § 1.401(a)-20, Q&A-38(a)(2), Ex. 1]

> **Example 11-11:** If the Monterey Bay Company's retirement plan provides for a life annuity of $100 per month and a joint and survivor benefit of $90 per month, the plan does not fully subsidize the joint and survivor benefit. [Treas. Reg. § 1.401(a)-20, Q&A-38(a)(2), Ex. 2]

QPSA. A QPSA is fully subsidized if the amount of the participant's benefit is not reduced because of the QPSA coverage and if the participant under the plan is not charged for the coverage. Thus, a QPSA is fully subsidized in a defined contribution plan. [Treas. Reg. § 1.401(a)-20, Q&A-38(b)]

Chapter 12

Retirement, Disability, and Death

Determining benefits payable at retirement, death, or upon disability is a simple matter in the case of defined contribution plans, because the amount payable is generally the account balance at each event. However, for defined benefit plans, benefits can vary quite dramatically, depending upon whether the individual is disabled or is at early, late, or at normal retirement age. Benefits may be actuarially adjusted or subsidized. Some plans allow plan participants to ease into retirement by reducing their work hours and starting to receive their retirement benefits gradually. This transition into retirement is commonly referred to as phased retirement. Different types of retirement benefits are discussed.

Until the passage of the Employee Retirement Income Security Act (ERISA) in 1974, a significant number of pension plans provided no death benefits to the spouses of deceased participants. The drafters of ERISA were concerned about protecting the surviving widow or widower and, therefore, introduced the concepts of protecting the spouse before retirement with the qualified preretirement survivor annuity (QPSA) and after retirement with the qualified joint and survivor annuity (QJSA). Participants could elect, however, to waive survivor benefits and frequently did so. The Retirement Equity Act of 1984 made changes to ERISA's QPSA and QJSA requirements by mandating that the QPSA or QJSA be paid automatically unless consent to an alternative choice is obtained from the spouse in addition to the participant. The death benefit provisions typically found in retirement plans, how life insurance is used to provide enhanced death benefits, and the technical requirements for payment of death benefits to a participant under the incidental death benefit rules are discussed.

Normal Retirement 12-2
Early Retirement 12-6
Late Retirement 12-13
Phased Retirement 12-15
Longevity Annuities 12-16
Suspension of Benefits 12-17
Disability Benefits 12-18
Disability Benefits in Defined Contribution Plans 12-20
Disability Benefits in Defined Benefit Plans 12-22
Death Benefits in Defined Contribution Plans 12-24
Death Benefits in Defined Benefit Plans 12-28
Required Minimum Distribution Rules 12-36

Normal Retirement

Q 12:1 How is normal retirement age defined in pension plans?

For purposes of the minimum vesting standards (see chapter 8), normal retirement age is the earlier of (1) the time a plan participant reaches normal retirement age under the terms of the plan, or (2) the later of (a) the time a participant reaches age 65, or (b) the fifth anniversary of the time a plan participant began participating in the plan. [I.R.C. § 411(a)(8)] Each plan defines its normal retirement age.

It is important to note that the plan may set an actual retirement age later than the normal retirement age as defined for vesting purposes as described above. In one case, a plan sponsor amended its plan to change the normal retirement age from 65 to 67, while preserving all early retirement benefits, including subsidies that accrued prior to the effective date of amendment. The U.S. Court of Appeals for the Tenth Circuit decided that such a provision does not violate ERISA's vesting and benefit accrual requirements. The U.S. Supreme Court has declined to review this case. [Lindsay v. Thiokol Corp., 112 F.3d 1068 (10th Cir. 1997), *cert. denied*, 522 U.S. 863, 118 S. Ct. 168, 139 L. Ed. 2d 111 (1997)]

Q 12:2 How has the Treasury modified regulations regarding normal retirement ages in defined benefit plans?

The Treasury modified its regulations to provide that the normal retirement age under a plan must be an age that is not earlier than the earliest age that is reasonably representative of the typical retirement age for the industry in which the covered workforce is employed. A safe harbor is established whereby a normal retirement age of 62 or later is deemed permissible (i.e., age 62 or later is deemed reasonably representative of the typical retirement age for any industry).

If the normal retirement age is between ages 55 and 62, the plan sponsor must demonstrate, based on all of the relevant facts and circumstances, that the normal retirement age is reasonably representative of the typical retirement age for the industry in which the covered workforce is employed.

A normal retirement age earlier than 55 is generally not permissible, unless the Commissioner determines that, under the facts and circumstances, the normal retirement age is reasonably representative of the typical retirement age for the industry in which the covered workforce is employed.

An exception to the age 55 rule is granted for qualified public safety employees to allow a normal retirement age of 50. *Qualified public safety employee* means any employee of a state or political subdivision of a state who provides police protection, firefighting services, or emergency medical services for any area within the jurisdiction of such state or political subdivision.

These rules are generally effective May 22, 2007. In the case of a governmental plan under Code Section 414(d), these rules are effective for plan years beginning on or after January 1, 2009. In the case of a collectively bargained plan, these rules do not apply before the first plan year that begins after the last of such agreements terminated, but no later than May 22, 2010.

[Treas. Reg. § 1.401(a)-1(b)(2), (4); I.R.C. § 72(t)(10)(B)]

> **Example 12-1:** ABC Farms sponsors a defined benefit plan with a normal retirement age of 58. Under the new regulations, this normal retirement age does not meet the safe harbor. The company must demonstrate to the IRS that the normal retirement age of 58 is reasonably representative of the typical retirement age for employees who work on farms.

Q 12:3 What happens if the plan provided for a normal retirement age earlier than permissible under the above Treasury regulations?

Generally, a defined benefit plan may permit in-service distributions once a participant has attained his or her normal retirement age. If the normal retirement age in a plan was earlier than permissible under the new Treasury regulations, it was necessary to amend the plan to eliminate the right to in-service distributions before age 62, or such other normal retirement age that is reasonably representative of the covered workforce.

Treasury regulations provided an exception to anti-cutback rules in Code Section 411(d)(6), which generally protected the right to in-service distributions. However, this relief did not apply to any other requirements including:

1) Code Section 411(a)(9), which requires that the normal retirement benefit be not less than the greater of any early retirement benefit or the benefit commencing at normal retirement age (see Q 12:7);
2) Code Section 411(a)(10), which does not permit a reduction of a participant's vesting percentage due to a plan amendment. Therefore, for example, if the normal retirement age before the amendment was 45, a participant who was at least age 45 at the time of the amendment would remain

100 percent vested even though normal retirement age was amended to a later age. In addition, any participant who was less than age 45 at the time of the amendment, but had at least three years of service at the time of the amendment, was permitted to elect, within a reasonable period after the adoption of such amendment, to have his or her nonforfeitable percentage computed under the plan without regard to such amendment.

3) Code Section 411(d)(6), which protects accrued benefits earned prior to a plan amendment (other than the right to an in-service distribution as discussed above);
4) Code Section 4980F, relating to participant notices and due dates for amendments that reduce the rate of future benefit accrual.

[Treas. Reg. § 1.411(d)-4, Q&A-12]

Example 12-2: CDE Livestock has a defined benefit plan that had a normal retirement age of 45 before May 22, 2007. For employees who continued employment after attainment of age 45, the plan provided for benefits to continue to accrue and permitted benefits to commence at any time, with an actuarial increase in benefits to apply to the extent benefits did not commence by normal retirement age.

On February 18, 2008, the plan was amended, retroactively effective to May 21, 2007, to change its normal retirement age to age 65. The amendment provided 100 percent vesting for any participating employee who was employed on May 21, 2007, and who terminates employment on or after attaining age 45. The amendment provided that employees who ceased employment before age 65 are entitled to a vested benefit with the right to commence benefits at any date after age 45. The plan amendment also revised the plan's benefit accrual formula so that the benefit for prior service (payable commencing at the revised normal retirement age or any other age after age 45) is not less than would have applied under the plan's formula before the amendment (also payable commencing at the corresponding dates), based on the benefit accrued on May 21, 2007. It also provided for service thereafter to have the same rate of future benefit accrual. Thus, for any participant employed on May 21, 2007, with respect to benefits accrued for service after May 21, 2007, the amount payable under the plan (as amended) at any benefit commencement date after age 45 is the same amount that would have been payable at that benefit commencement date under the plan prior to amendment. The plan amendment also eliminated the right to an in-service distribution between ages 45 and 65. The plan has been operated since May 21, 2007, in conformity with the amendment adopted on February 18, 2008.

Such plan amendment did not violate the anti-cutback rules in Code Section 411(d)(6) because it was relief eligible. Although the amendment eliminated the right to commence in-service benefits between ages 45 and 65, the amendment was made before the last day of the remedial amendment period applicable to the plan under Treasury Regulations Section 1.401(b)-1. Further, the amendment did not result in a reduction in any benefit for service after May 21, 2007. Thus, the amendment did not result in a reduction in any benefit for future service. Advance notice of a significant reduction in the rate of future benefit accrual was not required under ERISA Section 204(h).

Q 12:4 What happens if the plan does not specify a normal retirement age?

If the plan does not specify a normal retirement age, normal retirement age is the earliest age beyond which the participant's benefits under the plan do not increase solely on account of age or service. [Treas. Reg. § 1.411(a)-7(b)(1)]

Q 12:5 How is a participant's normal retirement date determined?

Most plans determine a participant's normal retirement date as one of the following:

1. The first day of the plan year after the participant reaches normal retirement age;
2. The first day of the month after the participant reaches normal retirement age;
3. The actual date the participant reaches normal retirement age; or
4. The first day of the plan year nearest the participant's normal retirement age.

If the normal retirement date is after the normal retirement age, full vesting must be granted at the time the participant reaches normal retirement age. [Rev. Rul. 81-211]

Example 12-3: Shannon participates in the High-Tech Repair Center's profit sharing plan, which specifies the normal retirement date as January 1 after the participant reaches age 65. Shannon turns age 65 on August 19, 2018, and her normal retirement date is January 1, 2019. In determining her vested percentage, Shannon is 100 percent vested in her account balance on August 19, 2018 (the date she attains her normal retirement age).

Q 12:6 What is the accrued benefit in a defined contribution plan at normal retirement age?

The accrued benefit is the entire account balance attributed to the participant. (See chapter 9 for determination of the account balance in a defined contribution plan.)

Q 12:7 What is the normal retirement benefit in a defined benefit plan?

The normal retirement benefit is the greater of the periodic benefit under the plan beginning at early retirement (if any) or at normal retirement age. If normal and early retirement benefits are payable in the same form, for example, as a life annuity, the dollar amounts of the benefits are compared. If the normal and early retirement benefits are payable in different forms, the greater benefit is determined by converting the annuity benefit payable at early retirement age to the same form as the normal retirement benefit, and then comparing the dollar amounts. Ancillary benefits not directly related to retirement benefits, such as medical benefits or disability benefits not in excess of the qualified disability benefit, are disregarded (see Q 12:8). The early retirement benefit is determined without regard to any Social Security supplement (see Q 12:9). [Treas. Reg. § 1.411(a)-7(c)]

Example 12-4: CDE Livestock sponsors a defined benefit plan that provides a benefit at normal retirement age (age 65) equal to $750 per month payable in the form of a life annuity. The early retirement benefit is equal to $900 per month, beginning on or after age 57 (if the employee has 20 years of service) and payable in the form of a life annuity. Kara retires at age 65 with 20 years of service; therefore, her normal retirement benefit is $900 per month, that is, the greater of the early retirement or normal retirement benefit.

Q 12:8 What is a qualified disability benefit?

A qualified disability benefit is a benefit payable upon disability that does not exceed the amount of benefit that would have been payable to the participant if he or she separated from service at normal retirement age. [Treas. Reg. § 1.411(a)-7(c)(3)]

Q 12:9 What is a Social Security supplement?

A Social Security supplement is a benefit that begins and ends before a participant reaches Social Security retirement age and that does not exceed the amount of the Social Security benefit. [Treas. Reg. § 1.411(a)-7(c)(4)] The supplement, also referred to as a "bridge benefit," is intended to provide extra benefits for a short period of time between retirement under the plan and when actual Social Security benefits begin.

Early Retirement

Q 12:10 May employees retire early and start receiving benefits?

Defined benefit and defined contribution plans can provide an opportunity for employees to retire before the plan's normal retirement age. The significance of an early retirement provision in a defined contribution plan is that the early retirement age becomes the time at which the participant becomes fully vested, regardless of the vesting percentage earned so far. The decision to insert an early retirement provision becomes more significant in a defined benefit plan, because the plan will likely provide certain incentives or retirement subsidies.

Q 12:11 What reasons might an employer have for providing early retirement options?

An employer may wish to encourage employees to retire early through the use of early retirement options for various business reasons, such as the need for restructuring and downsizing.

Q 12:12 What reasons might an employee have for choosing early retirement?

The availability of subsidized benefits may be an important factor for a participant in making the choice to retire early. Other economic factors may play a significant role, including the improved economic status of some older employees. The causes of the improved economic status include dual wage-earning households, improved Social Security benefits, and the explosive growth of defined contribution plans, particularly 401(k) plans. Poor health may play a role—if an employee is not eligible to receive disability benefits, the availability of an early retirement incentive may be more attractive than the prospect of continuing to work. Changes in job descriptions that are not appealing may also be an incentive to retire early. Finally, family and friends may be a significant incentive: the desire to spend more time with grandchildren or with a spouse or friends who have already retired.

Q 12:13 What are typical early retirement eligibility requirements?

Both age and service requirements are common. The age requirement might typically be between ages 55 and 65, although earlier early retirement ages are allowed but require that the participant actually separate from employment to receive the benefit. The service requirement commonly varies between 10 and 30 years of service. In some cases, there might be a service requirement only (e.g., early retirement after 25 years of service, regardless of age). In addition, a specific number (e.g., 75 or 80) that is a sum of age and years of credited service might be used.

Q 12:14 What types of early retirement subsidies may be provided?

Any type of early retirement benefit that exceeds the actuarial equivalent of the accrued benefit deferred to normal retirement age is considered to be subsidized. Common types of subsidies are:

1. A flat percentage reduction for each year preceding normal retirement age, for example, 4 percent per year reduction for each year preceding age 65;
2. A graded reduction for years preceding normal retirement age, for example, a 1/15th reduction for the first five years preceding age 65, and a 1/30th reduction for the next five years;
3. A Social Security supplement (see Q 12:9) that provides additional, temporary benefits in those years that the participant is not yet eligible for Social Security benefits;

4. No reduction for early start of benefits if specified age and service requirements are met; and
5. An early retirement window program (see Qs 12:17, 12:18).

Example 12-5: Doug retires at age 57 with 30 years of service from ABC Farms. Normal retirement age is 65, and the pension plan provides that early retirement benefits are payable any time after a participant attains age 55 with 30 or more years of service. The defined benefit plan's early retirement reduction is 3 percent per year of service preceding age 62. Doug's accrued benefit, deferred to commence at age 65 in the form of a life annuity, is $4,000. The reduced early retirement benefit payable to Doug at age 57 in the form of a life annuity is $3,400 per month [$4,000 × (1 − (3% × 5))].

Q 12:15 Do some defined benefit plans provide early retirement as an option, with no subsidy?

Yes. Some defined benefit plans provide that a participant, who retires early, as defined in the plan document, may defer commencement of his or her normal retirement benefit until normal retirement age, or commence an actuarially equivalent reduced benefit at an early retirement age. These plans usually accelerate vesting to 100 percent if early retirement criteria are met.

Q 12:16 Are early retirement benefits available to employees who leave employment before reaching the plan's early retirement age?

Yes. If the employee has met the service requirement but not the age requirement, benefits must be available to the employee when he or she reaches the early retirement age. However, the amount of the benefit available need not be the subsidized early retirement benefit. The minimum amount available to the employee is the benefit the employee would be entitled to receive, reduced in accordance with reasonable actuarial assumptions. [Treas. Reg. § 1.401(a)-14(c)]

Example 12-6: Peter retires at the age of 50, with 22 years of service. The early retirement age in the CDE Livestock defined benefit plan is age 55 with 20 years of service. The CDE Livestock defined benefit plan provides subsidized early retirement benefits only to those retirees who retire after completing both the age and service criteria. Upon reaching age 55, Peter may apply for benefits and receive an actuarially reduced benefit beginning at age 55. The plan is not required to permit Peter to receive subsidized early retirement benefits that may be available to those who work until reaching early retirement eligibility.

Q 12:17 What is an early retirement window benefit?

An early retirement window benefit is an additional, subsidized early retirement benefit made available to a limited group of employees for a limited period of time. Early retirement window benefits may resemble early retirement benefits (see Q 12:14) or may take the form of a credit to the participant of additional benefits, age or years of service to be used in calculating their benefits. The fact that a plan may be amended repeatedly to provide different or additional early retirement window benefits does not violate the requirement that benefits in a defined benefit plan be definitely determinable as long as these windows are not expected to become an ongoing feature. [Treas. Reg. § 1.401-1(b)(1)(i); Rev. Rul. 92-66] An early retirement window benefit, as an optional form of benefit, must generally be "currently available" to substantially all employees (see Q 12:18). [Treas. Reg. § 1.401(a)(4)-3(b)(2)(iii)] (See chapter 10 for a discussion of optional forms of benefit.)

Example 12-7: ABC Farms provides a temporary early retirement benefit boost during a specified window of time to employees who are at least age 57 and are credited with 25 years of service or more. The subsidized benefit adds five years of service credit to the otherwise early retirement benefit formula. The early retirement time window is open from January 1, 2019, through June 30, 2019.

Q 12:18 How does a plan satisfy the current availability requirement for early retirement window benefits?

Substantially all employees within the plan or applicable component plans must meet eligibility for the early retirement window by the end of the window period or the plan is deemed to fail the current availability requirement. The plan may be restructured into two (or more) component plans, one comprising the employees eligible for the early retirement window and the other comprising the employees not eligible for the window. If the restructured component plan satisfies the minimum coverage requirements of Code Section 410(b), using the more favorable percentages in the nondiscriminatory classification test of Treasury Regulations Section 1.410(b)-4(c)(4) without having to first pass the average benefits test, the plan as a whole is deemed to satisfy the current availability requirement. [Treas. Reg. § 1.401(a)(4)-3(b)(2)(iii); Treas. Reg. § 1.401(a)(4)-4(b)(2)]

Example 12-8: The early retirement window for ABC Farms is currently available, as of June 30, 2019, to one of the firm's highly compensated employees (HCEs) and six of the firm's 200 non-highly compensated employees (NHCEs). Ten employees are HCEs participants, and 200 are NHCEs participants. The NHCE concentration percentage for ABC Farms is 95.24 percent (200 ÷ 210). The applicable Treasury Regulations Section 1.410(b)-4(c)(4) safe harbor minimum coverage percentage is 23.75 percent. The early retirement window is not available to substantially all nonexcludable employees in the whole plan. However, the plan may be restructured into two component plans, one comprising the employees eligible for the early retirement window, or seven eligible employees (Plan A), and the other comprising the other 203 (200 + 10 − 7) employees (Plan B). The coverage percentage for Plan A, in which all employees meet early retirement window eligibility, is 30 percent ((6/200) ÷ (1/10)), which exceeds 23.75 percent and satisfies the coverage requirements of Code Section 410(b) applicable to current availability testing. The coverage percentage for Plan B is 108 percent ((194/200) ÷ (9/10)), which exceeds the basic 70 percent minimum coverage threshold. Therefore, the early retirement window is deemed to satisfy the current availability requirement. Note that for the purposes of current availability testing it is not necessary to perform the average benefits test to rely upon the nondiscriminatory classification safe harbor percentage.

Q 12:19 What other requirements must be met for early retirement benefits?

The limitations of Code Section 415 apply (see chapter 9), and a plan that uses a safe harbor permitted disparity benefit formula must restrict the benefits in accordance with the applicable regulations (see Q 12:20). [Treas. Reg. § 1.401(l)-3(e)(2)] Moreover, the plan, or restructured component plans, must satisfy the rules of Code Section 401(a)(4) in demonstrating that the early retirement benefits do not discriminate in favor of HCEs (see chapter 10). [Treas. Reg. § 1.401(a)(4)-3(f)(4)]

Q 12:20 How are benefits restricted in a plan that uses permitted disparity?

A defined benefit plan that relies on a safe harbor formula to satisfy nondiscrimination requirements may use permitted disparity to provide greater benefits to participants whose compensation exceeds certain amounts, called *covered compensation*. A defined benefit plan that relies on the general test to satisfy nondiscrimination requirements need not adhere to formulaic rules. A typical safe harbor formula might read: the sum of 0.65 percent of all pay plus 0.65 percent of pay in excess of covered compensation, multiplied by years of service.

Generally speaking, the maximum permitted disparity factor is 0.75 percent; that is, the maximum spread between benefits above and below covered compensation. However, if benefits begin before or after the Social Security retirement age, the factor of 0.75 percent is adjusted according to the following tables:

Table 12-1. Social Security Retirement Age 67

Age at Which Benefits Commence	*Annual Factor in Maximum Excess Allowance and Maximum Offset Allowance*
70	1.002%
69	0.908%
68	0.825%
67	0.750%
66	0.700%

Table 12-1. Social Security Retirement Age 67 (*cont'd*)

Age at Which Benefits Commence	*Annual Factor in Maximum Excess Allowance and Maximum Offset Allowance*
65	0.650%
64	0.600%
63	0.550%
62	0.500%
61	0.475%
60	0.450%
59	0.425%
58	0.400%
57	0.375%
56	0.344%
55	0.316%

Table 12-2. Social Security Retirement Age 66

Age at Which Benefits Commence	*Annual Factor in Maximum Excess Allowance and Maximum Offset Allowance*
70	1.101%
69	0.998%
68	0.907%
67	0.824%
66	0.750%
65	0.700%
64	0.650%
63	0.600%
62	0.550%
61	0.500%
60	0.475%
59	0.450%
58	0.425%
57	0.400%
56	0.375%
55	0.344%

Table 12-3. Social Security Retirement Age 65

Age at Which Benefits Commence	*Annual Factor in Maximum Excess Allowance and Maximum Offset Allowance*
70	1.209%
69	1.096%
68	0.996%
67	0.905%
66	0.824%
65	0.750%
64	0.700%
63	0.650%
62	0.600%
61	0.550%
60	0.500%
59	0.475%
58	0.450%
57	0.425%
56	0.400%
55	0.375%

Table 12-4. Simplified Table
(Available for use as an alternative to Tables 12-1 to 12-3)

Age at Which Benefits Commence	*Annual Factor in Maximum Excess Allowance and Maximum Offset Allowance*
70	1.048%
69	0.950%
68	0.863%
67	0.784%
66	0.714%
65	0.650%
64	0.607%
63	0.563%
62	0.520%
61	0.477%
60	0.433%
59	0.412%

Table 12-4. Simplified Table
(Available for use as an alternative to Tables 12-1 to 12-3)
(cont'd)

Age at Which Benefits Commence	*Annual Factor in Maximum Excess Allowance and Maximum Offset Allowance*
58	0.390%
57	0.368%
56	0.347%
55	0.325%

If benefits begin before the employee attains age 55, the 0.75 percent factor in the maximum excess allowance and in the maximum offset allowance is further reduced (on a monthly basis to reflect the month in which benefits begin) to a factor that is the actuarial equivalent of the 0.75 percent factor, as adjusted under the tables above, applicable to a benefit commencing in the month in which the employee attains age 55. In determining actuarial equivalence for this purpose, a reasonable interest rate must be used. In addition, a reasonable mortality table must be used to determine the actuarial present value (as defined in Treasury Regulations Section 1.401(a)(4)-12) of the benefits commencing at age 55 and at the earlier commencement age. A reasonable mortality table may also be used to determine the actuarial present value at the earlier commencement age of the benefits commencing at age 55. A standard interest rate and a standard mortality table, as defined in Treasury Regulations Section 1.401(a)(4)-12, are considered reasonable. [Treas. Reg. § 1.401(l)-3(e)(3)]

Late Retirement

Q 12:21 Can an employee be forced to retire at the plan's normal retirement age?

Generally no. Effective in 1979, the Age Discrimination in Employment Act (ADEA) was amended to raise the allowable mandatory retirement age from 65 to 70. ADEA was again amended, effective January 1, 1987, to eliminate any mandatory retirement age, except for certain individuals who are executives or in high policymaking positions. For defined contribution plan sponsors, ADEA required that contributions could not cease regardless of the normal retirement age.

Until the passage of the Omnibus Budget Reconciliation Act of 1986 (OBRA '86), working after normal retirement age was not a problem for many defined benefit plan sponsors, as the rules merely required that employees be given a suspension of benefits notice, and benefits calculated as of the plan's normal retirement age were payable without adjustment at a later retirement age. OBRA '86 instituted requirements that benefits in a defined benefit plan must continue to accrue beyond the plan's normal retirement age. When these requirements were combined with the ADEA amendments, plan sponsors were faced with significantly different calculations of retirement benefits for late retirees. [I.R.C. § 411(b)(1)(H)]

Q 12:22 What are the issues involved in determining late retirement benefits?

Issues that need to be addressed in determining a late retiree's benefits include:

1. The late retiree may have already started to receive benefits. This is especially possible if the retiree is over age 70½, as required minimum distributionsunder Code Section 401(a)(9) may have commenced (see chapter 4).
2. The plan may provide for actuarial increases or it may follow the suspension-of-benefit rules. A late retiree could receive significantly different benefits, depending on the terms of the plan.
3. Additional service credit and increased compensation may have increased the participant's accrued benefit.

Q 12:23 How are retirement benefits determined for a late retiree in a defined contribution plan?

For any defined contribution plan, the benefits are 100 percent of the account balance of the participant. Contributions must continue to be made after normal retirement age if the participant continues to satisfy the requirements necessary to receive a contribution. The account balance may have been reduced in the past by prior distributions, such as required minimum distributions under Code Section 401(a)(9). (See chapter 4 for a discussion of required minimum distributions.)

Q 12:24 What are the general requirements for accruing benefits in a defined benefit plan after normal retirement age?

A participant's benefit accrual may not stop, nor may the rate of benefit accrual be reduced, because he or she has reached any normal retirement age. In addition, a participant's compensation may not cease to be considered because he or she has reached normal retirement age. If the benefit formula includes a limit on the number of years of service, that limit may be considered. [I.R.C. § 411(b)(1)(H); Prop. Treas. Reg. § 1.411(b)-2(b)(1)(i)]

Example 12-9: The CDE Livestock's pension plan provides a benefit equal to $30 per month per year of service, with a provision that for determining benefits, years of service cannot exceed 30 years. Ted retires at age 70, after working for 35 years. His benefit by formula (without consideration of actuarial increases, which are not required if the plan document provides for suspension of benefits and provided the applicable notices) is $900 per month at age 70, although he would have received the same benefit at age 65 because he had already worked the 30 maximum years of service for benefit purposes at age 65. This provision does not violate the requirement of Code Section 411(b) because it is permissible to cap the number of years for benefit accrual purposes.

Q 12:25 What adjustments may be made to the accrued benefit of an employee who has delayed retirement beyond the plan's normal retirement age?

The benefit accruals that would otherwise be required due to the delayed retirement may be offset by (1) the actuarial equivalent of certain benefit distributions previously made and (2) the amount of any actuarial adjustment to benefits due to the delay in paying benefits after normal retirement age. [I.R.C. § 411(b)(1)(H)(iii)]

Q 12:26 How are benefit distributions after normal retirement treated in determining delayed retirement accrued benefits?

The post-normal retirement benefit accrual rate for a plan year may be reduced, but not below zero, by the actuarial equivalent of benefit distributions made to the participant by the close of the plan year. [Prop. Treas. Reg. § 1.411(b)-2(b)(4)]

Phased Retirement

Q 12:27 What is phased retirement?

Phased retirement is a written, employer-adopted program pursuant to which employees may reduce the number of hours they customarily work, beginning on or after the normal retirement date specified under the program. In-service retirement benefits will commence and are phased in based on the number of hours worked. [I.R.C. § 401(a)(36)]

Q 12:28 How did regulations regarding phased retirement change?

Under the final Treasury regulations, retirement does not include a mere reduction in the number of hours that an employee works. Thus, benefits may not be distributed prior to normal retirement age solely due to a reduction in the number of hours worked. Effective May 22, 2007 (with exceptions for governmental plans and collectively bargained plans), a phased retirement program may not permit in-service distributions earlier than the normal retirement age in the plan. [Treas. Reg. § 1.401(a)-1(b)(3)]

Example 12-10: ABC Farms sponsors a defined benefit plan with a normal retirement age of 62. The plan provides for phased retirement benefits to commence, once an employee's hours drop below 1,500. The phased-in benefits depend on the number of hours worked:

Hours Worked	*Percentage of Normal Retirement Benefit*
1,250–1,500	20%
1,000–1,249	40%
750–999	60%
1–749	80%

Longevity Annuities

Q 12:29 What are longevity annuities?

A longevity annuity is a periodic benefit for life that is deferred to commence at a later age.

Q 12:30 What is a qualifying longevity annuity contract?

A qualifying longevity annuity contract (QLAC) is a non-variable annuity contract that is purchased from an insurance company for an employee under a tax-qualified defined contribution plan, Section 403(b) plan, IRA, or Section 457 governmental plan that satisfies the following criteria:

1. Accumulated premiums do not exceed the lesser of $125,000 or 25 percent of the participant's account balance;
2. Benefit payments must commence not later than the first day of the next month following the participant's 85th birthday and be payable for the lifetime of the participant (no term certain distributions may be provided);
3. The annuity is not a variable annuity (or any annuity with an account balance—no cash surrender values), although the benefit can be adjusted for cost of living increases; however, the annuity may pay experience dividends; and
4. The only death benefit is a joint and survivor annuity or a return of premium provision. A survivor's life annuity may be provided to a surviving spouse or a nonspousal designated beneficiary within prescribed age dependent benefit limits.

[Amendment to Treas. Reg. § 1.401(a)(9)-6]

Q 12:31 How do the Required Minimum Distribution Rules apply to QLACs?

The account balance used to determine any applicable year's required minimum distribution does not include the value of any QLAC for distribution calendar years beginning on or after January 1, 2013.

[Amendment to Treas. Reg. § 1.401(a)(9)-5]

Suspension of Benefits

Q 12:32 What are the suspension-of-benefit rules?

The suspension-of-benefit rules allow a plan to stop paying retirement benefits to a participant who is reemployed after the start of retirement benefits. The rules also apply to a participant who remains in service after reaching the plan's normal retirement age. Generally, benefits may be suspended for each calendar month (or during a four- to five-week payroll period ending in a calendar month) in which a participant is reemployed for 40 or more hours. A plan that wants to suspend benefits must notify participants, in the summary plan description and at the time the benefits are to be suspended, in order for the suspension to be effective. [D.O.L. Reg. § 2530.203-3] (See chapter 13 for a discussion of the suspension-of-benefit rules as they apply to participants who have not reached retirement age.)

Under proposed Treasury regulations, a defined benefit plan does *not* satisfy the minimum vesting standards of Code Section 411(a) if, either directly or indirectly, because of the attainment of any age:

1. A participant's accrual of benefits is discontinued or the rate of a participant's accrual of benefits is decreased, or
2. A participant's compensation after the attainment of such age is not taken into account in determining the participant's accrual of benefits.

[Prop. Treas. Reg. § 1.411(b)-2]

In determining the rate of a participant's accrual of benefits under the plan, the following are disregarded:

1. The subsidized portion of an early retirement benefit (whether provided on a temporary or permanent basis),
2. A Social Security supplement (see Q 12:9), and
3. A qualified disability benefit (see Q 12:8).

[Treas. Reg. § 1.411(d)-3(a)(3); (j)(3)(i)]

Example 12-11: ABC Farms provides a defined benefit plan with a benefit formula equal to $20 per month per year of credited service. The plan sponsor complied with the suspension-of-benefit rules and informed Chuck when he reaches age 65 (the plan's normal retirement age) that benefits were being suspended. At age 65, Chuck had 15 years of service. Chuck continued to work and is now age 70. He accrued an additional $20 per month in benefits for the five years between ages 65 and 70. Chuck retires at age 70 and is entitled to receive a benefit of $400 ($20 × 20 years) per month.

Example 12-12: CDE Livestock provides a defined benefit plan, with a benefit formula equal to $20 per month per year of participation. The plan sponsor complies with the suspension-of-benefit rules and informs Ginny when she is age 65 (when her accrued benefit is $600 per month) that benefits are being suspended. Ginny, now age 70, continues to work and has accrued an additional benefit $100 per month benefit. Her accrued benefit is now $700 per month ($600 + $100).

Q 12:33 What happens if a plan does not suspend benefits in accordance with the DOL regulations?

The plan must grant to the participant an additional accrued benefit each year equal to the greater of the actuarially increased benefit *or* the increased benefit due to accruals per the benefit formula in plan years ending after the participant reaches normal retirement age. Alternatively, the plan may provide that the participant is granted both an actuarial increase to prior year's accrued benefit plus the accrual increment by formula for such plan years. If the plan is silent, both the actuarial increase and the accrual by formula are granted. [2009 Enrolled Actuaries Conference Gray Book Q39] If benefits have begun while the participant is still employed, the actuarial value of the benefits paid during the plan year may be used to offset the additional accrued benefit. [Prop. Treas. Reg. § 1.411(b)-2(b)(4)]

Example 12-13: ABC Farms' pension plan provides that normal retirement benefits will be actuarially increased for late retirement. Normal retirement age in the plan is 65. The benefit formula provides a monthly retirement benefit equal to $20 per year of service. Jim's benefit at age 65 is $600 per month ($20 × 30 years). After Jim works an additional year, his accrued benefit at age 66 is the greater of the actuarially increased benefit of $672 ($600 actuarially increased by one year) or $620 ($20 × 31 years). Jim's accrued benefit at age 66 is $672. Jim continues to work and accrues another year's worth of benefits. His accrued benefit at age 67 is the greater of the actuarially increased benefit of $756 ($672 actuarially increased by one year) or $640 ($20 × 32 years). Jim's accrued benefit at age 67 is $756.

Example 12-14: ABC Farms' defined benefit plan does not provide for the suspension of benefits, nor does it grant actuarial increases for benefit payments due to late retirement. The plan provides that benefits will begin at age 65, regardless of whether or not the participant actually retires. Sophie reaches age 65 and starts receiving her monthly benefit of $600. Sophie continues to work through age 66 and accrues an additional benefit of $20 per month. The total benefit payments made to Sophie in the first plan year after she reaches age 65 are $7,200 ($600 × 12). The actuarially increased single-sum value of those payments at age 66 is $7,559. The single sum of $7,559 produces a life annuity benefit of $72 per month at age 66. Because the $72 converted benefit exceeds the increased accrual of $20, Sophie's benefit remains at $600 per month.

Disability Benefits

Q 12:34 May a qualified plan provide disability benefits?

Yes. In addition to providing retirement benefits in a qualified plan, many plan sponsors provide special benefits if a participant in the plan becomes disabled. While the options are generally limited to 100 percent of the account balance in a defined contribution plan, more generous benefits are often available in a defined benefit plan. A common example of a disability benefit in a defined benefit plan is an immediate benefit payable monthly and continuing until the earliest of the date the participant reaches normal retirement age, the time the disability ceases, or death. In some cases, an immediate lump sum of the present value of the accrued benefit may be payable. Other plans may defer the payment of any benefits until the individual reaches normal retirement age. Some sponsors may use a more liberal definition of disability than the standard of qualifying for Social Security disability benefits (see Q 12:33). In nearly all cases, qualified plans that include disability benefits provide benefits to disabled participants that exceed the benefits they would have received had they ceased employment for any other reason. Disability benefits are not protected benefits and can be reduced or removed from the plan at any time. [Treas. Reg. § 1.411(d)-3(b)(3)]

Q 12:35 How is the determination of an individual's disability made?

The plan document defines the conditions necessary for an individual to be considered disabled. Some plan sponsors attempt to coordinate the definition of disability in the retirement plan with the definition used for their long-term disability plan.

Q 12:36 What is the Social Security definition of disability?

The Social Security Act defines disability as a physical or mental impairment that can be expected to result in death or be of long-continued and indefinite duration. Rather than apply this standard, plan sponsors may leave the determination to the Social Security Administration and require that an individual qualify for Social Security disability benefits before being eligible for disability benefits from the qualified plan. [I.R.C. § 72(m)(7)]

Q 12:37 What other definitions of disability might be found in a qualified plan?

Some plans use a definition that is quite liberal, defining disability as inability to perform the customary duties of the employee. Other plans use this definition for a period of time, for example, two years, and then proceed to a more narrow definition of disability. More narrow definitions may include:

- Inability to perform any occupation for which the individual is suited by education and training; and
- Inability to perform any substantial gainful activity.

Q 12:38 What definition is most likely to be found in a plan?

The Social Security definition is most likely to be used. One reason for this may be that a more liberal definition may not qualify the individual for an exemption from the 10 percent early distribution penalty (see chapter 20). Also, if there is subjectivity in applying the standard, the plan administrator could become exposed to litigation. [I.R.C. § 72(t)]

Q 12:39 What other conditions might be required for disability benefits?

A plan sponsor may make an age or service requirement a condition for payment of disability benefits. Benefits may be payable, for example, only if the individual has reached age 55, or has completed 10 years of service.

Disability Benefits in Defined Contribution Plans

Q 12:40 May a defined contribution plan provide disability benefits?

Yes, but a defined contribution plan has little room to provide additional disability benefits to a participant. Because benefits payable from a defined contribution plan are based solely on an individual's account balance, any benefits that the employer wants to pay in excess of the account balance must generally come from sources other than the qualified plan (see chapter 9). However, some defined contribution plans permit the purchase of long-term disability coverage by the participant (see Q 12:45).

Q 12:41 What disability benefits may be found in a defined contribution plan?

Typically, a defined contribution plan will provide that a participant's account balance will become 100 percent vested if he or she becomes disabled (see chapter 8), regardless of whether the participant is 100 percent vested according to the vesting schedule. In some cases, a plan may provide that disabled NHCEs may continue to be allocated employer contributions based on their current rate of earnings at the time of their disability (see Q 12:42).

Example 12-15: Alice is a participant in CDE Livestock's profit sharing plan. The vesting schedule is a five-year cliff schedule; that is, there is no vesting until the completion of five Years of Service. Alice has completed three years of vesting service at the time of her disability. However, the plan provides for 100 percent vesting if the participant meets the plan's definition of disability. If Alice meets this definition, her vested percentage is accelerated to 100 percent.

Q 12:42 What are the requirements for a defined contribution plan that makes contributions for disabled participants?

The following rules must be satisfied for a plan sponsor to make contributions for a disabled employee:

1. The employee is totally and permanently disabled (see Q 12:43);
2. The employee is not a HCE (see Appendix G);

3. The contribution does not exceed the lesser of 100 percent of the participant's compensation (see Q 12:41) or $55,000 (for 2018); and
4. Any such contributions are 100 percent vested.

[I.R.C. § 415(c)(3)(C)]

Q 12:43 How is total and permanent disability defined for purposes of this special disability benefit?

An individual is permanently and totally disabled if he or she is unable to engage in any substantial gainful activity due to any medically determinable physical or mental impairment that can be expected to result in death or that has lasted, or can be expected to last, for a continuous period of not less than 12 months. [I.R.C. § 22(e)(3)]

Q 12:44 How is a disabled participant's compensation determined?

In providing employer contributions for a disabled participant after the participant has ceased providing services due to a disability, compensation is the amount the participant would have received for the year if the participant had been paid at the rate of compensation paid immediately before becoming permanently and totally disabled. [I.R.C. § 415(c)(3)(C)]

> **Example 12-16:** Ethan, a NHCE, is a participant in the ABC Farms' Money Purchase Plan. The plan provides for an annual contribution equal to 10 percent of pay and provides that a disabled participant will be entitled to an annual contribution based on his or her rate of pay at the time of disability. Ethan becomes disabled at a time when his annual rate of pay is $24,000. The corporation will make annual contributions to Ethan's account equal to $2,400 ($24,000 × 10%) during his disability and the contributions will be 100 percent vested.

Q 12:45 In Letter Ruling 200031060, how did a defined contribution plan permit a participant to choose to purchase long-term disability insurance with a portion of his or her account, and what benefits were payable?

In Letter Ruling 200031060 (Aug. 26, 2000), the IRS ruled that a qualified profit sharing plan with a 401(k) feature could permit participants to acquire a long-term disability insurance contract. If a participant elected to purchase such coverage, monthly premiums would be deducted from the participant's plan account. The plan, rather than the participant, would become the policyholder. Upon the participant's disability, any policy benefits would be paid directly to the plan and allocated to the account of the participant.

Under the terms of the long-term disability contract, if a participant became disabled and met a one-year waiting period, the plan's trust would thereafter receive a monthly amount (from the policy) equal to 1/12 of the participant's elective deferrals, employer matching contributions and qualified nonelective contributions that were made to the plan on behalf of the participant for the plan year immediately preceding the year in which the participant became disabled. These payments would continue until the earliest of:

- The participant's recovery from disability
- The participant's death
- The termination of the plan
- The participant's withdrawal of all or a portion of his or her account attributable to the policy benefits or
- The maximum payment period determined at the inception of the disability (e.g., age 65).

The plan positioned the long-term disability policy as an investment alternative and any policy benefits were treated as investment earnings that were to be allocated to the disabled participant's account. [Ltr. Rul. 200031060]

Example 12-17: Mary, a participant in the CDE Livestock 401(k) plan, opts to purchase a long-term disability insurance contract with a portion of her elective contributions to the 401(k) plan. Mary's account is reduced by $20 per month, which is the monthly premium for this contract. Mary becomes disabled in 2018 at age 50 and is entitled to benefits under the contract. Starting in 2019 (after the one-year waiting period), the contract pays a monthly benefit to the plan equal to $800, which is 1/12 of Mary's elective contributions and the company's matching contribution made in 2017. Mary recovers in 2019 after 12 monthly payments have been made. The total payments of $9,600 plus earnings are included in Mary's 401(k) account.

Disability Benefits in Defined Benefit Plans

Q 12:46 When do disability benefits begin in a defined benefit plan?

Generally, disability benefits begin at the onset of the disability. There may be a waiting period of six months from the onset of disability to allow time for a determination that the disability is total and permanent or to ensure that the participant is indeed eligible for Social Security disability benefits. In other cases, disability benefits may be paid as a retirement benefit commencing at normal retirement age.

Q 12:47 How are disability benefits paid in a defined benefit plan?

Disability benefits may be paid in the following forms:

- As a monthly benefit beginning at the time of determination of disability and continuing until the earliest of cessation of disability, death, or normal retirement age, or
- As a lump sum

Q 12:48 How is the lump-sum amount determined?

Generally, the lump sum payable at the time of disability is equal to the present value of the accrued benefit (see chapter 9).

Example 12-18: Nick is a participant in the ABC Farms' defined benefit plan. Nick becomes disabled at age 45, and his accrued benefit at the time of his disability is $525 per month. The plan provides for 100 percent vesting and an actuarially equivalent lump sum of the regular deferred accrued benefit earned as of the disability date. Based on the actuarial equivalence assumptions contained in the plan document, Nick is entitled to a current lump-sum distribution of $106,600. Both Nick and his spouse must consent to receive the distribution in the form of a lump sum (see chapter 11). If this is not the case, the qualified joint and survivor rules will apply to the benefit payment.

Q 12:49 How is the monthly benefit determined in the event of disability?

The amount of the monthly benefit depends upon the formula in the plan. Generally, the benefit equals the accrued benefit beginning immediately and payable until attainment of normal retirement age. In other cases, the accrued benefit may be actuarially reduced to provide a lesser benefit that is not so heavily subsidized. The benefit may be a flat amount or a flat percentage of pay, taking into account the possibility that the individual will likely be entitled to Social Security benefits.

Q 12:50 What is a subsidized benefit?

A subsidized benefit is any benefit payable from a defined benefit plan that exceeds the actuarial equivalent of the accrued benefit.

Q 12:51 How are disability benefits determined if commencement does not occur until normal retirement age?

In the case of an unsubsidized disability benefit, the benefit payable at normal retirement age is simply the accrued benefit of the participant determined at the time of disability. In the case of a subsidized disability benefit, the benefit payable may be determined under the assumption that the disabled participant continues to earn salary at the same rate of pay from the date of disability until normal retirement age.

Example 12-19: ABC Farms sponsors a defined benefit plan with unsubsidized disability benefits that begin at normal retirement age. Tully becomes disabled at age 50 and has a current accrued benefit of $725 per month beginning at normal retirement age of 62. Tully will be entitled to $725 per month starting at age 62.

Example 12-20: The pension plan of CDE Livestock provides a subsidized disability benefit. Shelly becomes disabled at age 40 and is earning compensation at a rate of $60,000 per year. The plan benefit formula is 1 percent of average annual compensation (based on the five consecutive highest paid years) multiplied by years of service. At the time of Shelly's disability, she has completed 10 years of service. The plan provides that, upon determination of disability, the participant will be entitled to additional compensation and service credit based on the compensation rate at the time of disability. If Shelly continues to be disabled until she reaches age 65, her benefit payable commencing at age 65 will be equal to a benefit based on 25 additional years of service and average annual compensation of $60,000:

$60,000 × 1% × 35 years ÷ 12 = $1,750 per month

Q 12:52 Are disability benefits subject to the limitations of Code Section 415?

Code Section 415 limits benefits that may be payable from a defined benefit plan (see chapter 9). To the extent that the disability benefit exceeds the normal or early retirement benefit in the plan, it is subject to the provisions of Code Section 415.

In the case of larger monthly benefits, Code Section 415 may require the reduction of benefits to which the participant is otherwise entitled. [Treas. Reg. 1.415-3(c)(2)(ii); Ltr. Rul. 9237042] Note that the plan could provide for cost-of-living adjustments on the disability benefits, based on the cost-of-living adjustments made to the defined benefit limits (see chapter 9). [Treas. Reg. § 1.415-3(c)(2)(iii); I.R.C. § 415(d)]

Example 12-21: ABC Farms sponsors a defined benefit plan that provides a disability benefit of $2,000 per month at the time of disability. Janie becomes disabled and is entitled to a disability benefit. The accrued benefit payable to Janie, based on her current salary of $20,000 per year and years of credited service to date, is $1,000 per month. Because the disability benefit exceeds the normal retirement benefit in the plan, the disability benefit is limited by Code Section 415. The maximum benefit under Section 415 payable to Janie is 100 percent of her three consecutive highest paid years of pay, reduced for each year of service less than 10. If her three-year average pay is $20,000, the maximum disability benefit payable to Janie is $1,666.67 per month (20,000 ÷ 12).

Death Benefits in Defined Contribution Plans

Q 12:53 How are death benefits provided in a defined contribution plan?

Typically, a defined contribution plan provides that the account of a deceased participant (who has died as an active participant) becomes fully vested and is paid in full to the participant's beneficiary. In some cases, the defined contribution plan may merely pay the vested account balance to the beneficiary. In very rare cases, all but the QPSA is forfeited. [I.R.C. § 411(a)(3)(A)]

Example 12-22: Judy, a participant in the CDE Livestock's profit sharing plan, dies when her vested interest is only 20 percent. However, the plan provides that participants become fully vested at death. Thus, Judy's beneficiary receives 100 percent of Judy's account balance.

Q 12:54 What portion of the death benefit in a defined contribution plan is paid as a QPSA benefit to the deceased participant's spouse?

The answer depends on the type of plan and whether it is subject to the QPSA rules. For profit sharing plans that are not subject to the QPSA requirements (see chapter 11), a QPSA need not be paid if the following conditions are satisfied:

1. The plan provides that the participant's vested account balance is payable in full upon the participant's death to the participant's surviving spouse, unless the participant chooses (with spousal consent) to pay the benefits instead to a designated beneficiary.
2. The participant does not elect payment of benefits in the form of a life annuity. This may be a moot point if the plan does not allow benefits in the form of a life annuity (see Q 12:55).
3. With respect to the participant, the plan is not a transferee or an offset plan (see Qs 12:56, 12:54).

[Treas. Reg. § 1.401(a)-20, Q&A-3]

For defined contribution plans that are subject to the survivor annuity requirements of Code Sections 401(a)(11) and 417, a preretirement survivor annuity must be provided. The value of the annuity must be at least 50 percent of the vested account balance of the participant as of the date of the participant's death. [Treas. Reg. § 1.401(a)-20, Q&A-20]

Example 12-23: Sam, a participant in CDE Livestock's target benefit plan (a plan subject to the survivor annuity requirements), dies with a vested account balance of $15,000. At least $7,500 of the account balance must be used to provide a preretirement survivor annuity for his wife, Cheryl, unless Cheryl chooses an alternative payout permitted by the plan.

For defined contribution plans that forfeit the nonvested employer's portion of the accrued benefit at death and that allow for after-tax or pre-tax contributions, no more than a proportionate percentage of the after-tax and pre-tax contributions may be used to satisfy the QPSA benefit. [Treas. Reg. § 1.401(a)-20, Q&A-20]

Example 12-24: Dave, a participant in the CDE Livestock's money purchase pension plan (a plan that contains a required joint and survivor annuity option), dies with an account balance of $20,000, of which $12,000 is attributable to employer-provided contributions and $8,000 to mandatory after-tax contributions made by Dave. The plan provides that the nonvested portion of the employer-provided benefit is forfeited at death. Dave is 50 percent vested in the employer-provided contributions; therefore, $6,000 of the account balance is forfeited, and $14,000 ([$12,000 × 50%] + $8,000) is available for distribution to Dave's beneficiary or beneficiaries. Dave has named his sister, Chris, as beneficiary. However, a QPSA must be paid to Dave's wife, Mary, unless Mary waives the annuity benefit. The amount of the QPSA is equal to $7,000, and no more than $4,000 ($8,000/$14,000 × $7,000) of the QPSA may be provided by Dave's after-tax contributions. Chris will receive the remaining $7,000.

Q 12:55 What rules apply in a profit sharing plan that is not subject to the survivor annuity requirement, but that allows benefits to be paid in the form of a life annuity or permits participants to direct some or all of the investment of their elective deferral and/or matching contribution accounts into a deferred annuity contract issued by an insurance company?

If a participant chooses at any time to receive a life annuity, the survivor annuity requirements (see chapter 11) always apply to all of the participant's benefits under the plan, unless there is a separate accounting of the account balance subject to the election. If there is a separate account, only the separate account balance applied to the life annuity is subject to survivor annuity requirements. If the participant selecting such an option dies, the surviving spouse must be able to elect to receive a life annuity that is equivalent in value to 50 percent of the vested account balance of the participant. Any remaining balance may be paid to a designated nonspousal beneficiary if the plan permits. Note that the spouse may waive the death benefit and consent to an alternate beneficiary. [Treas. Reg. § 1.401(a)-20, Q&A-4]

If the participant chooses to invest his or her elective deferrals or matching accounts into a deferred annuity, if permitted within the plan, the survivor annuity requirements depend upon the revocability of the annuity and the preretirement death benefit. Only the separate account balances applied to the deferred annuity have to be subject to the QPSA and QJSA requirements.

[Rev. Rul. 2012-3]

Q 12:56 What is a transferee plan?

A defined contribution plan is a transferee plan with respect to any participant if the plan is a direct or indirect transferee of the participant's benefits held on or after January 1, 1985, by:

- A defined benefit plan;
- A money purchase or target benefit plan; or
- A defined contribution plan that is subject to the survivor annuity requirements.

The survivor annuity requirements apply to all accrued benefits held for a participant with respect to whom the plan is a transferee plan unless there is an acceptable separate accounting between the transferred benefits and all other benefits under the plan. A separate accounting is not acceptable unless gains, losses, withdrawals, contributions, forfeitures, and other credits or charges are allocated on a reasonable and consistent basis between the accrued benefits subject to the survivor annuity requirements and other benefits. If there is an acceptable separate accounting between transferred benefits and any other benefits under the plan, only the transferred benefits are subject to the survivor annuity requirements. [Treas. Reg. § 1.401(a)-20, Q&A-5]

Example 12-25: DEF Grain money purchase plan was merged into the ABC Farms' profit sharing plan. The plan does not separately account for the account balances from the money purchase plan. ABC Farms' profit sharing plan is considered a transferee plan and subject to the survivor annuity requirements of Code Sections 401(a)(11) and 417.

Q 12:57 What is an offset plan?

Sometimes called a floor plan or a floor-offset plan (see Qs 9:85–9:89), such a plan is part of an arrangement that includes a defined benefit and a defined contribution plan. Under the floor-offset arrangement, benefits under the defined benefit plan are reduced by the actuarial equivalent of all or a part of an employee's account balance in the defined contribution plan. A defined contribution plan which might otherwise be exempt from the survivor annuity requirements (see Q 12:54) will be required to satisfy the survivor annuity requirements if it is part of a floor-offset plan. [Treas. Reg. § 1.401(a)(4)-8(d)(1)]

Q 12:58 How do the survivor annuity requirements apply to a defined contribution plan if the benefits are currently being paid in the form of an annuity?

As discussed in Q 12:52, if a defined contribution plan allows benefits to be paid in the form of a life annuity, it must also allow the participant to choose a QJSA as an option for the payment of retirement benefits. Depending on the form of benefit chosen, benefits may be continued to the spouse after the participant's death. If the participant had elected the life annuity benefit and the consent of the spouse was obtained, no further benefits would be due to the spouse after the participant's death. Note that it is typical for such a defined contribution plan to purchase an annuity from an insurance carrier and have the insurance carrier assume responsibility for the payment of future benefits to the participant.

Some defined contribution plan sponsors allow the transfer of the defined contribution account balance into the sponsor's defined benefit plan and have the defined benefit plan make the annuity distributions.

Example 12-26: Sara retires at age 55 from CDE Livestock. Her 401(k) plan has an account balance of $1.3 million. She and her husband, Jason, are both quite healthy and concerned that they may outlive their income if she rolls the money into an IRA and draws out benefits from that account. Therefore, as permitted by the plans, they choose to transfer Sara's account balance directly from the CDE Livestock 401(k) plan to the CDE Livestock defined benefit plan. Using the actuarial factors contained in the defined benefit plan, the account balance of $1.3 million is converted to a joint and 100 percent survivor annuity paying Sara and Jason $6,700 per month for the rest of their lives.

Q 12:59 May a participant's account balance be subject to the QPSA and QJSA rules at the same time?

Yes, a defined contribution plan that is subject to the survivor annuity requirements and allows in-service distributions (see chapter 1) has to treat portions of the account balance differently. A typical case is a profit sharing plan that contains the survivor annuity requirements and that allows hardship withdrawals. The portion of the account balance that is withdrawn as a hardship withdrawal is subject to the QJSA requirements and, therefore, must be paid as a QJSA unless the spouse consents to the immediate distribution. The other portion of the non-distributed account is subject to the QPSA requirements until it is withdrawn or distributed. [Treas. Reg. § 1.401(a)-20, Q&A-9]

Death Benefits in Defined Benefit Plans

Q 12:60 How are death benefits provided in a defined benefit plan?

Traditional defined benefit plans must provide at least the required minimum death benefit. In a traditional defined benefit pension plan, the minimum required death benefit is less valuable than full accrued benefit at the date of death. Statutory hybrid cash balance plans often provide 100 percent of the hypothetical account balance, which is more valuable than the required minimum and is analogous to the typical defined contribution plan.

Q 12:61 What kind of death benefits are typically provided in a defined benefit plan?

For benefits that are not in pay status (i.e., currently being paid or have been paid out completely), a traditional defined benefit plan often provides the QPSA as the preretirement death benefit. For benefits in pay status, the selected optional form of benefit determines whether any kind of death benefit is payable to the surviving spouse or other designated beneficiary. The annuity starting date is the date that determines whether a preretirement (QPSA) or postretirement (QJSA) death benefit is applicable.

For benefits that have commenced, the amount of the death benefit is determined by the optional form of benefit elected by the participant at the time of retirement. It is important to keep in mind that the spouse must have consented to any form of benefit other than the QJSA (see chapter 11). The table below shows some typical optional benefit forms found in defined benefit plans and the corresponding death benefit:

Form of Benefit	*Death Benefit*
Lump sum	None
Life annuity	None
Life annuity with period certain	If the period certain has not expired, the balance of payments for the remaining portion of the period certain is paid to the designated beneficiary.
Joint and *X* percent survivor annuity	Life annuity equal to *X* percent of the participant's life annuity to the surviving beneficiary.
Refund annuity	If the accumulated payments to date made to the participant are less than the refund amount, the balance is paid to the designated beneficiary.

Q 12:62 What is a QPSA?

A QPSA is payable to the spouse of a participant who dies before the annuity starting date. The amount of the benefit payable for life to the surviving spouse is at least equal to the payments that would be made to the surviving spouse under the QJSA had the participant severed employment at the date of death. The amount depends on whether the individual has reached the earliest retirement age under the plan.

For a participant who dies after reaching the plan's earliest retirement age, the QPSA payable immediately to the spouse is equal to the QJSA that would have been paid had the participant retired with an immediate QJSA on the day before the date of death.

For a participant who dies before reaching the plan's earliest retirement age, the QPSA is calculated under these four assumptions:

1. The participant separated from service on the date of death;
2. The participant survived to the earliest retirement age;
3. The participant retired with an immediate QJSA at the earliest retirement age; and
4. The participant died on the day after reaching the plan's earliest retirement age.

[I.R.C. § 417(c)(1)]

An additional survivor annuity option must be offered to plan participants. This additional option is called a qualified optional survivor annuity (QOSA). If the QJSA option is less than 75 percent, a 75 percent survivor annuity option must be offered as the QOSA. If the QJSA is greater than or equal to 75 percent, then a 50 percent QOSA must be offered. This provision is effective for plan years beginning after December 31, 2007.

For example, defined benefit plans often offer a joint and 50 percent survivor annuity as the QJSA. For such a plan, it must also offer a joint and 75 percent survivor annuity as a QOSA. [PPA § 1004, I.R.C. § 417(a)(3)(A)(i); ERISA § 205(c)(3)(A)(i)]

The plan need not provide a QOSA that is actuarially equivalent to the QJSA. The QOSA must be actuarially equivalent to the single life annuity form. The plan need not provide a QPSA that is equivalent to the QOSA. [Notice 2008-30 Q&A-8–13]

Example 12-27: Bob, age 57, dies in 2019 while a participant in the CDE Livestock's defined benefit plan. The earliest retirement age in the plan is age 55. Had Bob retired on the day before his death, the plan would have provided to a joint with 50 percent QJSA of $1,200 per month. Therefore, Bob's spouse is now entitled to a life annuity of $600 per month beginning immediately. Bob's spouse need not be provided an election for an alternate preretirement survivor annuity that is equivalent to the joint with 75 percent QOSA.

Example 12-28: Christine has been a participant in the CDE Livestock's defined benefit plan. She dies at age 52, before reaching the plan's early retirement age. Had she separated from service on the day before her death, she would have been entitled to receive a joint with 50 percent QJSA of $1,240 per month, beginning at her age 55. Her husband, Jerry, is 10 years younger and is entitled to receive $620 (50% × $1,240) per month for his life, deferred to commence at his age 45 (the time when Christine would have reached age 55).

Q 12:63 What is the annuity starting date?

The annuity starting date is the first day of the first period for which an amount is due to be paid as an annuity or in any other form. Administrative delays may often cause payments to be delayed beyond the annuity starting date. The annuity starting date is critical, since certain benefits may be forfeited if the annuity starting date has not yet occurred. [Treas. Reg. § 1.401(a)-20, Q&A-10]

Example 12-29: Sue retired from ABC Farms upon reaching early retirement at age 57. Her early retirement date is June 1, 2019, and, because of administrative delays, benefits do not begin until August 1, 2019. The annuity starting date under the survivor annuity rules is June 1, 2019. If Sue were to die between June 1, 2019, and August 1, 2019, the plan would be required to pay benefits in the form that Sue has elected. If she had chosen a joint and 50 percent survivor annuity, a 50 percent survivor annuity would be paid to her spouse.

Q 12:64 What other types of death benefits may be provided in a defined benefit plan?

Among the various alternatives are:

1. An actuarially equivalent survivor life annuity to the participant's vested accrued benefit payable in the normal form;

2. An actuarially equivalent survivor life annuity to 100 percent of the participant's accrued benefit payable in the normal form (regardless of the participant's vesting based on the plan's vesting schedule);
3. A lump sum actuarial equivalent of (1) or (2); and
4. A lump-sum benefit equal to 100 times (or some lesser multiple) of the participant's monthly accrued or projected benefit;

A lump-sum benefit (such as in items (3) and (4) above) may be funded with life insurance: such as whole life, term, retirement endowment, or universal. If an enhanced death benefit is offered in a defined benefit plan, the benefit may also be paid to a beneficiary other than the surviving spouse. The surviving spouse must be entitled to at least the QPSA or QJSA portion, unless waived. Death benefits must be incidental to the primary purpose of the plan, which is to provide retirement benefits. [Treas. Reg. § 1.401-1(b)(1)(i)]

Q 12:65 How is the lump-sum equivalent benefit determined?

Defined benefit plans that provide a lump-sum actuarial equivalent of the accrued benefit to the designated beneficiary of a deceased participant specify the factors used for actuarial equivalence in the plan document. The factors include interest and mortality assumptions. Different factors may be used for preretirement and postretirement periods. In some cases, no mortality discount may apply on a preretirement basis. Regardless of the factors contained in the plan, other issues may affect the lump-sum actuarial equivalent of the accrued benefit death benefit payable. For example:

- Code Section 417(e) prescribes the applicable interest rates and mortality table for use in the minimum lump-sum calculation (see chapter 9); and
- Code Section 415 may limit the maximum lump sum (see chapter 9)

Because the factors may vary from year to year or from month to month, it is generally best that plan sponsors not provide estimated single-sum death benefits on the annual statement provided to participants in a defined benefit plan.

Example 12-30: Ralph, age 55, a participant in the ABC Farms' defined benefit plan, is fatally injured while on the job. The plan provides that a single-sum death benefit equal to the actuarial equivalent of the accrued benefit be paid to the surviving spouse. Ralph's accrued benefit payable as a QJSA is $2,400 per month, beginning at age 65. The plan provides no early retirement benefits, and the actuarial equivalence factors in the plan document are 5 percent interest and postretirement mortality based upon the 1994 GAR table. If the Section 417(e) prescribed minimum lump-sum rates are ignored for purposes of this illustration, the single-sum equivalent is calculated as follows:

Accrued benefit × Annuity factor × Interest discount = Single-sum equivalent

$$\$2{,}400 \times 141.5291 \times 1.05^{-10} = \$208{,}528$$

According to the terms of the plan, Ralph's spouse, Cindy, is entitled to receive a single-sum benefit in the amount of $208,528. Alternatively, Cindy may elect to receive a QPSA equal to $1,200 per month deferred to commence at what would have been Ralph's 65th birthday or an immediate actuarially equivalent QPSA benefit dependent upon her current age.

Q 12:66 Will a death benefit be considered incidental if a plan provides a death benefit equal to 100 times the monthly pension plus a QPSA?

No, such a benefit will not necessarily be deemed to be incidental within the meaning of Treasury Regulations Section 1.401-1(b)(1)(i). The plan could be amended to ensure that the death benefit remains incidental by either of the following methods:

1. Amend the plan to remove the preretirement death benefit of 100 times the monthly pension. Note that death benefits are not covered by the anti-cutback rules of Code Section 411(d)(6).
2. Amend the plan to provide a death benefit equal to 100 times the monthly pension, but no less than the actuarial equivalent of the QPSA, in which case the QPSA may be paid to the surviving spouse and the remaining death benefit paid to the designated beneficiary.

[Rev. Rul. 85-15]

Q 12:67 How does a defined benefit plan sponsor provide for a death benefit of 100 times the monthly benefit without using life insurance?

Plan sponsors often provide a death benefit of this type without using life insurance. Life insurance is a way to transfer the financial exposure risk, but the risk does not have to be transferred. In essence, the plan sponsor self-insures this death benefit in the same way that the plan's retirement, termination, or disability benefits are self-insured.

Q 12:68 How does a small plan provide for death benefits?

A small plan does not have the advantage of the law of large numbers and, therefore, might consider using insurance company policies if it wants to provide a significant preretirement death benefit. Smaller defined benefit plans (fewer than 100 participants) were commonly funded extremely conservatively from the 1940s through the mid-1960s. Plan sponsors relied on an insurance company to provide retirement and death benefits through insurance contracts. The contracts, called retirement income or retirement endowment contracts, provided the retirement benefit at the plan's normal retirement age, as well as the plan's other ancillary benefits. Contributions were the premiums for such contracts. ERISA recognized the existence of these types of plans and established certain requirements in Code Section 412(i), now superseded by Code Section 412(e)(3).

Q 12:69 What are the requirements of a Section 412(e)(3) plan?

A Section 412(e)(3) plan, sometimes known as a fully insured plan, is a plan funded exclusively with insurance contracts. In the case of a top-heavy plan, a small side fund may be used in conjunction with the insurance contracts to provide top-heavy minimums (see chapter 9). A Section 412(e)(3) plan must satisfy the following requirements to receive an exemption from the otherwise minimum funding requirements of Code Section 430:

1. The plan is funded exclusively with individual or group insurance contracts.
2. The contracts provide for level annual premium payments to be paid from the time the participant becomes eligible for the plan until the plan's normal retirement age.
3. Benefits provided by the plan are equal to the benefits provided under the contracts at normal retirement age (to the extent premiums have been paid).
4. Premiums for the current plan year and all prior plan years are paid before lapse of the contracts, or there is a reinstatement of the policy.
5. No rights under the contracts are subject to a security interest at any time during the plan year.
6. No policy loans are outstanding at any time during the plan year.

[I.R.C. § 412(e)(3)]

Example 12-31: CDE Livestock sponsors a qualified defined benefit plan that is intended to satisfy the requirements of Code Section 412(e)(3). Ed, the only participant, is entitled to a monthly benefit of $8,000 per month. The plan purchases a retirement income contract from MM Insurance Company. The contract will pay either a monthly retirement benefit of $8,000 to Ed when he retires at age 65 or a preretirement death benefit of $800,000. Level annual premiums to the earlier of Ed's death or age 65 are $42,780. Assuming that premiums are paid on a timely basis, no policy loans are taken, and no rights under the contracts have been assigned, this plan should meet the requirements of Code Section 412(e)(3).

Q 12:70 What is the amount of the death benefit in a Section 412(e)(3) plan?

The death benefit in a Section 412(e)(3) plan that is funded with retirement income or retirement endowment contracts is the greater of:

1. The face amount of the life insurance contract, or
2. The cash value in the life insurance contract.

A Section 412(e)(3) plan may also be funded with a combination of whole life or term life contracts, and annuity contracts. Such a plan is designed to provide similar benefits to retirement income or endowment contracts. The death benefit with this design is the sum of:

1. The face amount of the life insurance contracts, plus
2. The cash value in the annuity contracts.

In some cases, flexible premium annuities are the sole vehicle used in funding a Section 412(e)(3) plan, and the death benefit is simply the cash value in the contract.

Q 12:71 What are the incidental limits for life insurance in a defined benefit plan?

A plan that funds the death benefit with life insurance may provide a death benefit equal to the greater of:

1. The proceeds of the ordinary life insurance policies providing a death benefit of 100 times the anticipated monthly normal retirement benefit; or
2. The sum of the reserve under the ordinary life insurance policies, plus the participant's account in the auxiliary fund.

Such a plan satisfies the incidental test if less than 50 percent of the employer contribution credited to each participant is used to purchase ordinary life insurance policies on behalf of the participant. [Rev. Rul. 74-307]

Q 12:72 How is the 50 percent test satisfied for a defined benefit plan?

The IRS, in a list of required modifications (LRMs), defines the maximum permissible death benefit plan as:

> The qualified preretirement survivor annuity plus, if a positive amount, the incidental reserve. The incidental reserve equals the proceeds of insurance policies purchased on a participant's life plus the theoretical individual level premium (ILP) (an actuarial funding method) reserve minus the sum of the present value of the qualified pre-retirement survivor annuity and the cash value of the policies purchased.

The limit expressed by the IRS is 66 percent of the theoretical contribution if whole life insurance is used, and 33 percent if term or universal life insurance is used. The theoretical ILP reserve is the amount that would be available at the time of death if, for each year of plan participation, a contribution was made on behalf of the participant equal to the theoretical contribution.

The theoretical contribution is the amount of the contribution that would have been made on behalf of the participant, using the ILP funding method from the age at which participation began to normal retirement age, to fund the participant's entire retirement benefit without regard to preretirement ancillary benefits. The entire retirement benefit for this purpose is based upon a straight life annuity and assumes continuation of current salary (i.e., with no salary escalation assumption). [LRMs, Master and Prototype Defined Benefit (Feb. 2000) No. 52]

A sample calculation of the theoretical contribution and the theoretical reserve is shown below:

Step No.	*Description*	*Year 1*	*Year 2*	*Year 3*	*Explanation*
1	Age	35	36	37	
2	Projected monthly benefit	2,000	2,100	2,250	Retirement benefit calculated based on current salary without salary increase.
3	Annuity rate	146.1078	146.1078	146.1078	Annuity factor using 5% interest, 2016 Applicable mortality life annuity at age 65.
4	Prior-year cash at retirement	0	292,216	306,826	#2 × #3 from prior year
5	Normal cost factor	69.761	65.439	61.323	Future value of $1 per year; 5% interest, no mortality.
6	Incremental normal cost	4,189	223	357	(#2 × #3 − #4) ÷ #5
7	Theoretical contribution	4,189	4,412	4,769	#7 (prior year) + #6
8	Accumulated theoretical contribution	4,189	8,601	13,370	#8 (prior year) + #7
9	Accumulated incidental limit	2,793	5,734	8,913	2/3 × #8
10	Theoretical reserve at beginning of year	4,189	8,810	14,020	#10 (prior year) × 1.05 + #7

The table represents the individual calculations necessary for each participant in a defined benefit plan that wants to use the higher incidental limits. This shows the first three years for an individual age 35 at the time of the inception of the plan. To satisfy this test at the end of the third year, no more than $8,913 (number 9 in the third year) may have been used to pay whole life insurance premiums for this individual. If the individual dies at the end of the third year, the maximum death benefit would be equal to:

Insurance proceeds + Theoretical reserve − Insurance cash value =
$225,000 + $13,964 − Insurance cash value

If term or universal life insurance were used, no more than $4,457 (1/3 × $13,370) could be used to purchase term or universal life, since a one-third rather than a two-thirds test would be used.

Q 12:73 May a defined benefit plan use the 100-times test only?

Yes, many defined benefit plans that use life insurance to fund the preretirement death benefits use the much simpler 100-times incidental benefits test for providing a death benefit.

Required Minimum Distribution Rules

Q 12:74 How quickly must death benefits be paid?

Required timings of benefit payments upon the participant's death are in the required minimum distribution (RMD) rules of Code Section 401(a)(9) (see chapter 4). The rules deal with two situations: when the participant is in pay status and when the participant has not yet begun receiving benefits.

Two methods of making minimum required distributions are allowed if the participant dies before the required beginning date (see chapter 4):

1. *Life expectancy rule.* The life expectancy rule requires that any portion of a participant's interest payable to, or for the benefit of, a designated beneficiary, be distributed beginning within one year after the participant's death, over the beneficiary's life or over a period not exceeding the beneficiary's life expectancy. Special rules apply if the participant's designated beneficiary is his or her spouse, including a special commencement date for the distribution of benefits. Under these rules, distributions need not begin to the spouse until the later of the date the participant would have reached age 70½ (had he or she survived) or December 31 of the year after the employee's death. Also, if the surviving spouse dies before distributions to the spouse are required to begin, the rules are generally applied as if the surviving spouse were the employee.
2. *Five-year rule.* The five-year rule requires that the participant's entire interest under the plan be distributed within five years after his or her death, regardless of to whom the distribution is made.

[Treas. Reg. § 1.401(a)(9)-3, Q&A 1]

Q 12:75 May distributions from a deceased participant's retirement plan be rolled over to an IRA?

Yes. Spouse and nonspouse beneficiaries may roll over death benefits from a plan. If a direct trustee-to-trustee transfer is made from the qualified plan to an IRA established to receive the distribution on behalf of the beneficiary, then:

1. The transfer is treated as an eligible rollover distribution;
2. The transferee IRA is treated as an inherited IRA; and
3. The required minimum distribution (RMD) rules that are applicable when the participant dies before the entire interest is distributed also apply to the transferee IRA.

Before the passage of the Worker, Retiree, and Employer Recovery Act of 2008 (WRERA), this provision for a nonspouse beneficiary rollover was a permissible but not required amendment for a qualified plan. WRERA provides that, effective for plan years beginning after December 31, 2009, employer-sponsored plans must offer the rollover option to a designated nonspouse beneficiary. (See Q 21:32 for more details regarding this rollover issue.)

[I.R.C. §§ 402(c)(11), 402(f)(2)(A)]

Q 12:76 When must distributions begin to satisfy the life expectancy rule?

The commencement date depends upon whether distributions are made to a spouse or nonspouse:

1. If distributions are being made to a spouse under the life expectancy rule, they must begin by December 31 of the later of the year after the participant died, or the calendar year in which the participant would have attained age 70½ if the participant had lived.
2. If distributions are being made to a nonspousal beneficiary under the life expectancy rule, they must begin on or before December 31 of the calendar year immediately following the calendar year in which the participant died.

[Treas. Reg. § 1.401(a)(9)-3, Q&A-3]

> **Example 12-32:** Ronnie named his wife, Chris, as his designated beneficiary. Ronnie was born on January 15, 1949, and died on December 15, 2017. Under the life expectancy rule, distributions must begin by December 31, 2019, to Ronnie's spouse, because Ronnie would have attained age 70½ in the year 2019.

> **Example 12-33:** Amal named his best friend, Anthony, as beneficiary of his interest in the ABC Farms profit sharing plan. Amal died on January 2, 2018. Under the life expectancy rule, Anthony must start to receive Amal's interest in the plan on or before December 31, 2018.

Q 12:77 When must the participant's entire interest be distributed to satisfy the five-year rule?

The participant's entire interest under the plan must be distributed by December 31 of the calendar year that contains the fifth anniversary of the participant's death. [Treas. Reg. § 1.401(a)(9)-3, Q&A-2]

Example 12-34: Ralph, a participant in the ABC Farms' profit sharing plan, died on March 29, 2018. His entire interest in the profit sharing plan must be distributed by December 31, 2023 in order to satisfy the five-year rule.

Q 12:78 How does a plan sponsor determine whether the life expectancy rule or the five-year rule applies?

The specific provisions within a particular plan document determine which rule applies.

Optional plan provisions. The plan may adopt a provision specifying either that:

1. The five-year rule applies to certain distributions after the death of the employee even if the employee has a designated beneficiary, or
2. Distributions in every case will be made in accordance with the five-year rule.

A plan need not have the same method of distribution for the benefits of all employees in order to satisfy Code Section 401(a)(9).

Elections. A plan may adopt a provision that permits employees (or beneficiaries) to elect, on an individual basis, whether the five-year rule or the life expectancy rule applies to distributions after the death of an employee who has a designated beneficiary. Such an election must be made no later than the earlier of:

1. The end of the calendar year in which distributions would be required to commence in order to satisfy the requirements for the life expectancy rule, or
2. The end of the calendar year that contains the fifth anniversary of the date of death of the employee.

The election of the distribution method must be irrevocable (as of the last date the election may be made) with respect to the beneficiaries (and all subsequent beneficiaries) and must apply to all subsequent calendar years. If the plan provides for the election, the plan may also specify the method of distribution that applies if neither the employee nor the beneficiary makes the election. If neither the employee nor the beneficiary elects a method and the plan does not specify which method applies, distribution must be made as if the plan had no provision.

No plan provision. If a plan does not adopt an optional provision specifying the method of distribution after the death of an employee, distribution must be made as follows:

1. If the employee has a designated beneficiary, distributions are to be made in accordance with the life expectancy rule.
2. If the employee has no designated beneficiary, distributions are to be made in accordance with the five-year rule.

[Treas. Reg. § 1.401(a)(9)-3, Q&A-4]

Q 12:79 What happens if the participant has designated the estate as beneficiary?

If a participant designates the estate as beneficiary, he or she will be treated as if no beneficiary was designated for purposes of the required minimum distribution rules. This will be the case even if individuals (in addition to the estate) are named as beneficiaries. An exception to this rule applies if there are separate accounts in the plan and separate beneficiaries are named. Thus, the five-year rule discussed in Q 12:73 applies. [Treas. Reg. § 1.401(a)(9)-4, Q&A-3; Treas. Reg. § 1.401(a)(9)-8 Q&A-2, Q&A-3]

> **Example 12-35:** Marjorie is a participant in the CDE Livestock's profit sharing plan. She has named her estate as beneficiary of a separate account in the plan representing a rollover from a prior employer's plan. Her daughter, Phyllis, is named as beneficiary of the regular profit sharing account. Upon Marjorie's death, the separate rollover account will be treated as if no designated beneficiary has been named. The regular profit sharing account will be distributed to Phyllis in accordance with the terms of the plan.

Q 12:80 May a participant name a trust as the designated beneficiary?

Yes. In certain cases the employee may name a trust as designated beneficiary (see Q 12:81 for the special rules that apply to trusts). [Treas. Reg. § 1.401(a)(9)-4, Q&A-5]

Q 12:81 If an employee names a trust as his or her designated beneficiary, are the trust's beneficiaries treated as the employee's designated beneficiaries under the plan?

Generally, only an individual may be a designated beneficiary for purposes of the required minimum distribution rules. Consequently, a trust itself may not be the designated beneficiary despite being named as a beneficiary. However, if the requirements listed below are met, distributions made from a qualified plan to the trust will be treated as paid to the beneficiaries of the trust, and the beneficiaries of the trust will be treated as having been designated as beneficiaries of the employee under the plan for purposes of determining the distribution period under the required minimum distribution rules. If, as of any date on or after the employee's required beginning date, a trust is named as a beneficiary and the requirements listed below are not met, the employee will be treated as not having a designated beneficiary under the plan for purposes of the required minimum distribution rules. In that case, for calendar years beginning after that date, distributions must be made over the employee's life (or over the period which would have been the employee's remaining life expectancy determined as if no designated beneficiary had been designated as of the employee's required beginning date). Distribution must be made in accordance with the five-year rule under Code Section 401(a)(9)(B)(ii).

Requirements that must be met are the following:

1. The trust is a valid trust under state law, or would be except for the fact that there is no corpus;
2. The trust is irrevocable or will, by its terms, become irrevocable upon the death of the employee;
3. The trust beneficiaries who are beneficiaries with respect to the trust's interest in the employee's benefit under the plan are identifiable from the trust instrument under the rules described below; and
4. The documentation described below has been provided to the plan administrator.

[Treas. Reg. § 1.401(a)(9)-4, Q&A-5]

The same rules also apply if a trust is named as a beneficiary of the employee's surviving spouse. [Treas. Reg. § 1.401(a)(9)-4, Q&A-6]

Required distributions commencing before death. In order to satisfy the requirements for distributions required under Code Section 401(a)(9) to commence before the death of an employee, the employee must comply with either item (1) or (2) as follows:

1. The employee provides to the plan administrator a copy of the trust instrument and agrees that if the trust instrument is amended at any time in the future, the employee will, within a reasonable time, provide to the plan administrator a copy of each such amendment.
2. The employee:
    a. Provides to the plan administrator a list of all of the beneficiaries of the trust (including contingent and remainderman beneficiaries with a description of the conditions on their entitlement);
    b. Certifies that, to the best of the employee's knowledge, this list is correct and complete and that certain other requirements are satisfied;
    c. Agrees to provide corrected certifications to the extent that an amendment changes any information previously certified; and
    d. Agrees to provide a copy of the trust instrument to the plan administrator upon demand.

[Treas. Reg. § 1.401(a)(9)-4, Q&A-6]

Required distributions after death. In order to satisfy the documentation requirement for required distributions after death, by the end of the calendar year following the calendar year of the employee's death, the trustee of the trust must either:

1. Provide the plan administrator with a final list of all of the beneficiaries of the trust (including contingent and remainderman beneficiaries with a description of the conditions on their entitlement) as of the date of death; certify that, to the best of the trustee's knowledge, this list is correct and complete and that certain other requirements are met as of the date of

death; and agree to provide a copy of the trust instrument to the plan administrator upon demand; or

2. Provide the plan administrator with a copy of the actual trust document for the trust that is named as a beneficiary of the employee under the plan as of the employee's date of death.

Relief for discrepancy between trust instrument and employee certifications or earlier trust instruments. If required minimum distributions are determined based on the information provided to the plan administrator in certifications or trust instruments described above, a plan will not fail to satisfy Code Section 401(a)(9) merely because the actual terms of the trust instrument are inconsistent with the information in those certifications or trust instruments previously provided to the plan administrator, but only if the plan administrator reasonably relied on the information provided and the minimum required distributions for calendar years after the calendar year in which the discrepancy is discovered are determined based on the actual terms of the correct trust instrument.

For purposes of determining the amount of the 50 percent excise tax under Code Section 4974 for a distribution that is less than the minimum required distribution for a particular year, the minimum required distribution is determined for any year based on the actual terms of the trust in effect during the year. [Treas. Reg. § 1.401(a)(9)-4, Q&A-6]

Q 12:82 When is the participant's designated beneficiary determined?

Unless the designated beneficiary is the surviving spouse, the participant's designated beneficiary will be determined based on the beneficiaries designated as of the date of death who remain beneficiaries as of September 30 of the calendar year following the calendar year of the employee's death. Consequently, any person who was a beneficiary as of the date of the participant's death, but is not a beneficiary as of September 30 (e.g., because such person disclaims the benefit in favor of another beneficiary or because such person receives the entire benefit before that date), is not taken into account in determining the participant's designated beneficiary for purposes of determining the distribution period for required minimum distributions after the participant's death.

Surviving spouse. If the participant's spouse is the sole designated beneficiary as of September 30 of the calendar year following the calendar year of the participant's death, and the surviving spouse dies after the participant and before the date on which distributions have begun to the spouse, the relevant designated beneficiary for determining the distribution period is the designated beneficiary of the surviving spouse. Such designated beneficiary will be determined as of September 30 of the calendar year following the calendar year of the surviving spouse's death. If, as of September 30, there is no designated beneficiary under the plan with respect to that surviving spouse, distribution must be made in accordance with the five-year rule discussed in Q 12:71.

Deceased beneficiary. An individual who is a beneficiary as of the date of the employee's death and dies before September 30 of the calendar year following the calendar year of the employee's death without disclaiming, continues to be treated as a beneficiary. That individual is the employee's designated beneficiary for purposes of determining the distribution period for required minimum distributions after the employee's death, without regard to the identity of the successor beneficiary who is entitled to distributions. The same rule applies so that, if an individual is designated as a beneficiary of an employee's surviving spouse as of the spouse's date of death and dies prior to September 30 of the year following the year of the surviving spouse's death, that individual will continue to be treated as a designated beneficiary. [Treas. Reg. § 1.401(a)(9)-4, Q&A-4]

Example 12-36: Emil, a participant in the ABC Farms' profit sharing plan, has designated his wife, Emily, as his beneficiary. Emil, born on November 14, 1945, died on June 15, 2003. Had Emil lived, he would have attained age 70½ during the calendar year 2016 and payments to Emily would have to start by December 31, 2016. However, Emily died on August 15, 2014, without a designated beneficiary. Emily's interest must be distributed under the five-year rule and must be entirely distributed by December 31, 2019.

Chapter 13

Other Termination of Employment Issues

Participants who wish to delay the payment of their retirement benefits for as long as possible are subject to certain rules. These rules as well as their interrelationship with the required minimum distribution (RMD) rules (see chapter 4), are discussed. The mandatory cash-out rules are also discussed.

Employee stock ownership plans (ESOPs) have their own unique benefit distribution rules. ESOPs, plans that are designed to invest primarily in employer securities, generally require that terminated participants have a right to demand that benefits be received in the form of employer securities. If the employer securities are not readily tradable, the employee has a right to require the employer to repurchase the securities at their fair market value. In addition, ESOPs require that distributions be paid to terminated participants on an accelerated basis, unless the participant elects otherwise. The other rules relating to in-service distributions for ESOPs are described in chapter 1.

Defined benefit plans (or any retirement plan that allows periodic distribution of benefits), which are not generally permitted to make in-service contributions, may have participants in pay status who later return to work. The rules permitting the suspension of benefits generally allow the plan to stop paying benefits until the participant again terminates employment.

Knowledge of the plan's benefit claims and appeals procedure is crucial for both participants and plan sponsors. Without knowing the appropriate procedures, a plan participant cannot make a claim for benefits or appeal a denial of his or her claims. The plan sponsor should know, and carefully follow the plan's claim and appeal procedures to ensure that the participant is treated fairly and to minimize the risk of litigation. In an important case, the U.S. Supreme Court upheld its *Firestone Tire & Rubber Co. v. Bruch* [489 U.S. 101 (1989)] standard in providing deference to the plan administrator in interpreting the provisions in the plan. [Conkright v. Frommert, 559 U.S. 506 (2010)]

General Considerations 13-2
ESOPs 13-5
Suspension of Benefits 13-8
Claims for Benefits 13-11

General Considerations

Q 13:1 How long may the plan defer payment of benefits to a terminated participant?

Unless the participant elects otherwise as permitted by the terms of the plan, the payment of benefits may not begin later than the latest of the 60th day after the close of the plan year in which:

1. The participant attains the earlier of age 65 or the normal retirement age specified under the plan,
2. The participant's tenth anniversary of participation in the plan, or
3. The participant terminates employment with the employer.

[I.R.C. § 401(a)(14)] (See Qs 13:14, 13:15 for an exception to this rule for ESOPs.)

Example 13-1: John participates in the ABC Painters' pension plan. The plan specifies a normal retirement age as the later of age 65 or 20 years of service. John became a participant under the plan at age 55. The plan may delay paying benefits to John only until he reaches age 65 (the tenth anniversary of his participation in the plan), even though his normal retirement age under the plan is 75. Note that for vesting purposes, normal retirement age cannot be later than age 65 or the fifth anniversary of plan participation (Q 12:1).

Q 13:2 How long may a participant defer payment of benefits?

A participant may defer payment of benefits until his or her required beginning date. [I.R.C. § 401(a)(9)] (See chapter 4 for a detailed discussion of these rules.) However, plan sponsors may require immediate payment if the present value of benefits is $5,000 or less (see chapter 11).

Q 13:3 What is a participant's *required beginning date* for purposes of the RMD rules?

The required beginning date for employees (other than 5 percent owners) is the April 1st of the calendar year following the later of the calendar year in which the employee attains age 70½ or the calendar year in which the employee retires. For 5 percent owners, the required beginning date is April 1st of the calendar year following the calendar year in which the employee attains age 70½, even if the employee has not retired. [I.R.C. § 401(a)(9)(C)]

Q 13:4 Who is a 5 percent owner for purposes of the RMD rules?

A 5 percent owner is an employee who is a 5 percent owner (as defined in Code Section 416) with respect to the plan year ending in the calendar year in which the employee attains age 70½. [Treas. Reg. § 1.401(a)(9)-2, Q&A-2]

Under Code Section 416, a 5 percent owner is defined as an individual who:

1. If the employer is a corporation, the individual owns (or is considered as owning under the stock attribution rules of Code Section 318) more than 5 percent of the outstanding stock of the corporation or stock possessing more than 5 percent of the total combined voting power of all stock of the corporation; or
2. If the employer is not a corporation, any individual who owns more than 5 percent of the capital or profits interest in the employer.

Although the attribution rules in Code Section 318(a)(2) require that 50 percent or more of the value of the stock be owned by an individual before the attribution rules apply, the 5 percent owner rules reduce this threshold to 5 percent. Also, in determining the 5 percent threshold, only ownership in a single entity is considered; the controlled group and affiliated service group rules of Code Section 414(b), (c), and (m) are ignored. [I.R.C. §§ 416(i)(1); 318(a)(2)(C)]

> **Example 13-2:** Susan owns 100 percent of the stock of CDE Tailors. Her husband, Dennis, is considered a 5 percent owner of the corporation (he is attributed the ownership of his wife). Dennis turns age 70½ on June 9, 2018. Although he has not retired from CDE Tailors, his required beginning date is April 1, 2019, because he is considered a 5 percent owner of the corporation.

Q 13:5 Are any participants not subject to the minimum required distribution rules?

Yes. Any participant who made a special election under Section 242(b)(2) of the Tax Equity and Fiscal Responsibility Act of 1982 (TEFRA) may delay payment of his or her benefits until after the deadline described in Q 13:3. Instead, his or her benefits will be paid in accordance with the special election. If the participant's benefits are accelerated so that they are paid more rapidly than the TEFRA Section 242(b)(2) election specifies, the participant will be deemed to have revoked that election and will have to receive "make-up" distributions in the year of the revocation that satisfy the rules (see chapter 4). [Treas. Reg. § 1.401(a)(9)-8, Q&A-13]

Example 13-3: Bob, who is a 50 percent owner of ABC Painters, was born on September 15, 1947. He reached age 70½ on March 15, 2018, and his required beginning date would have been April 1, 2019. However, Bob made a valid election before January 1, 1984, under TEFRA Section 242(b)(2) that provides that benefits will begin at age 80 in the year 2027. Thus, benefits may be deferred until the year 2027. If Bob elects to receive benefits before the year 2027, the minimum required distribution rules may apply to him retroactively and he may be required to receive make-up distributions for all years back to 2019. It is possible to structure an in-service distribution that would not be considered a distribution under Code Section 401(a)(9) and avoid revoking the TEFRA Section 242(b) election.

Q 13:6 May a qualified plan require the immediate distribution of vested benefits upon termination of employment?

Although a participant who is younger than age 70½ may have some control over the timing of benefit payment from his or her retirement plan, the plan can mandate distribution of the participant's vested benefit if its present value is $5,000 or less. [I.R.C. § 411(a)(11)]

Q 13:7 How is the present value of the vested accrued benefit determined?

Under a defined contribution plan, the participant's vested account balance is considered to be the present value of the vested accrued benefit. (See chapters 8 and 9 for determination of vesting and account balances.) In a defined benefit plan, the starting point is the determination of the accrued benefit. (See chapter 9 for the determination of the accrued benefit.) The actuarially equivalent present value of the accrued benefit is determined by using defined interest rates and mortality tables. The interest rates and mortality tables used for these purposes are called *actuarial equivalence* rates and must be specified in the plan document. However, the plan must also provide that in no event may the present value of any vested accrued benefit be less than the present value obtained by using the applicable interest rate and applicable mortality table. [I.R.C. § 417(e)] (See chapter 9 for a detailed discussion on determining the applicable interest rates and present value.)

Example 13-4: Tony participates in the ABC Painters' defined benefit plan. He terminates employment in 2018, and his vested accrued benefit under the plan is $150 per month, payable as a life annuity commencing at age 65. Because the plan contains a mandatory immediate distribution provision, Tony's only optional benefit is to receive the present value of his benefit, $3,780, as an immediate payment, because that value is $5,000 or less. If Tony does not make an affirmative and timely election, the plan may specify that it will transfer the $3,780 to an appropriate IRA in his name.

ESOPs

Q 13:8 What options must be available to a participant who is entitled to receive a distribution from an ESOP?

A special rule applies to ESOPs, which must invest primarily in employer securities. A participant who is entitled to a distribution from an ESOP may receive the distribution in the form of employer securities. In many cases, the employee might want to receive cash instead of securities. In certain cases, rules that allow the employee to sell securities back to his or her employer enable the employee to receive the distribution in the form of cash.

A participant who is entitled to receive a distribution from an ESOP must have two distribution options under the plan:

1. He or she may demand that the ESOP distribution consist of employer securities.
2. He or she must be given the right (via a put option) to require the employer to repurchase the employer securities at fair market value if the employer securities are not readily tradable (see Q 13:9) on an established market.

[I.R.C. § 409(h)(1)]

The Taxpayer Relief Act of 1997 (TRA '97) provided that, for taxable years beginning after 1997, an S-corporation ESOP may distribute cash to plan participants in lieu of distributing employer securities. [I.R.C. § 409(h)(2)(B)]

A U.S. District Court case ruled that an ESOP violated Employee Retirement Income Security Act of 1974 (ERISA) when it terminated the right of its employees to receive put options for in-kind distributions of non-public stock distributed from an ESOP. Such termination of rights was a violation of the anti-cutback rules under Code Section 411(d)(6). [Kelli Goodin v. Innovative Technical Solutions, Inc., 489 F. Supp. 1157 (D. Haw. 2007)]

Q 13:9 What determines whether employer securities are readily tradable?

Employer securities are not readily tradable if they are not publicly traded or are subject to a trading limitation at the time of distribution. A publicly traded security is either:

- Listed on a national securities exchange registered under Section 6 of the Securities Exchange Act of 1934; or
- Quoted on a system sponsored by a national securities association registered under Section 15A(b) of the Securities Exchange Act.

A trading limitation on an employer security is a restriction under any federal or state securities law, any securities regulation, or an agreement affecting the security that would make the security not as freely tradable as one not subject to that restriction. [Treas. Reg. § 54.4975-7(b)(1)(iv), (10)]

Q 13:10 For what length of time must a put option be offered to the participant?

The put option, or right to require the employer to repurchase the employer securities in the ESOP, must be offered for a period of at least 60 days after the date of distribution, and for an additional period of at least 60 days in the following plan year. [I.R.C. § 409(h)(4)]

Example 13-5: Dula is a participant in the CDE Tailors' ESOP, a plan that operates on a calendar-year basis. CDE Tailors is owned entirely by the ESOP. Shares are not publicly traded. Dula terminates employment on September 1, 2018, and receives 150 shares of CDE Tailors on September 15, 2018. Dula has 60 days after the distribution, until November 14, 2018, to require CDE Tailors to repurchase her 150 shares. If she does not make the election, Dula must receive another 60-day period to make the election in the 2019 calendar year. Thus, CDE Tailors must offer Dula the opportunity to make the election again during any 60-day period in 2019.

Q 13:11 If the employee exercises the put option, must the employer immediately pay the employee the fair market value of the securities?

No. The employer may pay the option price to the participant in at least substantially equal annual payments over a period of five years or less. Such payments must commence within 30 days after the exercise of the put option. The employer must provide adequate security to the employee and pay reasonable interest on unpaid amounts if the employer elects to defer payment of the option price. [I.R.C. § 409(h)(5)]

Example 13-6: Dula exercises her put option to sell her 150 shares back to CDE Tailors. The fair market value of the shares as of March 15, 2019 (the exercise date) is $75,000. CDE Tailors is lacking liquidity at that time and opts to pay Dula in five annual installments of $15,000 each. In addition to the $15,000 principal payment each year, Dula will be paid the prime rate on the unpaid balance each year. CDE Tailors also opens an escrow account in Dula's name as security for the unpaid balance.

Q 13:12 What happens if the employee elects installment payments for his or her vested ESOP balance?

If the put option is exercised for an installment payment, the employer must pay the option price within 30 days after the exercise of the option. There is no option for the employer to pay in further installments (see Q 13:11). [I.R.C. § 409(h)(6)]

Q 13:13 Are there any exceptions to the put option requirements?

The put option requirement does not apply to distributions from a Tax Reduction Act stock ownership plan (TRASOP) or payroll stock ownership plan

(PAYSOP) that is established and maintained by certain banks or similar financial institutions; certain banks or financial institutions may be prohibited by law from buying their own securities. If the ESOP provides that participants who are entitled to a distribution from the plan have the right to receive the distribution in cash, a put option need not apply. TRASOPs and PAYSOPs were forms of ESOPs permitted before 1987, which enabled corporations to receive a payroll-based tax credit for contributions. The tax credit has since been repealed, but such plans may still be in existence. [I.R.C. § 409(h)(3)]

Q 13:14 When must distributions from an ESOP begin after termination of employment?

An ESOP participant must begin receiving benefits no later than one year after the later of:

- The end of the plan year in which he or she separates from service because of reaching normal retirement age, disability, or death; or
- The fifth plan year after the plan year in which he or she separated from service for any other reason, unless such participant is reemployed during the five-year period.

[I.R.C. § 409(o)(1)(A)]

An exception exists for the amount of the participant's account balance attributable to an outstanding loan balance in a leveraged ESOP—any such amount need not be distributed until the end of the plan year in which the loan is repaid. [I.R.C. § 409(o)(1)(B)] Another exception exists for account balances that exceed $800,000. To the extent that the account balance is attributable to stock acquired after December 31, 1986, the five-year period discussed above may be extended by one year for each $160,000 (or part thereof) by which the account balance exceeds $800,000. The maximum payout period is 10 years. The $800,000 and $160,000 limits are indexed for inflation as follows:

Year	*$800,000 Indexed Amount*	*$160,000 Indexed Amount*
2002	$ 800,000	$160,000
2003	$ 810,000	$160,000
2004	$ 830,000	$165,000
2005	$ 850,000	$170,000
2006	$ 885,000	$175,000
2007	$ 915,000	$180,000
2008	$ 935,000	$185,000
2009–2011	$ 985,000	$195,000
2012	$1,015,000	$200,000
2013	$1,035,000	$205,000
2014	$1,050,000	$210,000

Year	*$800,000 Indexed Amount*	*$160,000 Indexed Amount*
2015	$1,070,000	$210,000
2016	$1,070,000	$210,000
2017	$1,080,000	$215,000
2018	$1,105,000	$220,000

[I.R.C. § 409(o)(1)(C)]

For example, the distribution period for distributions beginning in 2018 would be extended as shown in the table below:

Account Balance Attributable to Employer Securities	*Distribution Period*
Up to $1,105,000	5 years
$1,105,001–$1,325,000	6 years
$1,325,001–$1,545,000	7 years
$1,545,001–$1,765,000	8 years
$1,765,001–$1,985,000	9 years
More than $1,985,000	10 years

Q 13:15 May a participant elect to receive benefits later than the time described above?

Yes. A participant may elect in writing to receive benefits at a later time, subject to the RMD rules described in chapter 4.

Suspension of Benefits

Q 13:16 What are the suspension-of-benefits rules?

The suspension-of-benefits rules allow a plan to stop paying retirement benefits to a participant who is reemployed after retirement benefits have begun to be paid. The rules also apply to a participant who remains in service after reaching the plan's normal retirement age. Generally, benefits may be suspended for each calendar month (or during a four- to five-week payroll period ending in a calendar month) in which a participant is reemployed for 40 or more hours. For the suspension to be effective, a plan that wants to suspend benefits must include the required language in the plan document and summary plan description (SPD) as well as properly notify each affected participant during the first calendar month or pay period in which the benefits are to be suspended. [D.O.L. Reg. § 2530.203-3]

The final regulations under Code Section 411(d)(6) retroactively apply the requirement that a plan cannot add or expand a suspension-of-benefits provision back to June 7, 2004. Plans that adopted such an amendment prior to June 7, 2004, must adopt a reforming plan amendment, comply operationally with the reforming amendment, and provide notice to affected participants of their right to elect to retroactively commence payment of benefit and complete all these actions by January 1, 2007.

[Treas. Reg. §§ 1.411(d)-3(a)(3), 1.411(d)-3(j)(3)(i)]

Example 13-7: Dawn began receiving benefits at age 57 of $542 per month from the ABC Painters' defined benefit plan. She returned to work at age 60. If the plan has a suspension-of-benefits provision that has been explained in the SPD and the provisions are again properly explained to Dawn when she returns to work, the plan sponsor may cease paying benefits to Dawn when she returns to work.

Q 13:17 How do the suspension-of-benefits rules apply in a multiemployer plan?

The rules described in Q 13:16 apply when an employee is reemployed in the same industry or the same trade or craft, and in the same geographic area covered by the plan, as when the benefits began. [I.R.C. § 411(a)(3)(B)]

Example 13-8: John is employed by ABC Tailors and retires at age 55 with a monthly retirement benefit of $550 from the Tailors Union Local No. 52 pension plan. The Tailors Union Local No. 52 pension plan contains suspension-of-benefits provisions. John decides to go back to work at age 60 for DEF Tailors. DEF Tailors is located in the same city as ABC Tailors. The suspension-of-benefits rules will apply to John if he will again be covered under the Tailors Union Local No. 52 pension plan and he is given the proper notices.

Q 13:18 How must the employee be notified of the suspension of benefits?

The plan must notify the employee via first-class mail, by electronic delivery (see Q 13:27), or by personal delivery during the first calendar month or payroll period in which the plan stops paying benefits. The notice must contain this information:

- A description of specific reasons why benefits are being suspended
- A general description of the plan provisions on suspension of benefits
- A copy of the part of the plan containing the suspension-of-benefits rules
- A statement of where the applicable Department of Labor (DOL) regulations may be found and
- A description of the plan's provisions that allow for review of the rules

The rules may also be provided in the SPD, provided the notice of suspension of benefits refers to the SPD, the employee is advised how to obtain a copy of the SPD, and the SPD is provided within 30 days after an employee's request. A requested SPD must be supplied even if it was already furnished to the employee. [D.O.L. Reg. § 2530.203-3(b)(4); and D.O.L. Reg. § 2520.104b-1]

Q 13:19 What happens when an employee again terminates employment after payment of benefits has been suspended?

Benefit payments must resume no later than the first day of the third calendar month after the calendar month in which the employee ceases to be employed in employment covered by the plan. However, the employee must notify the plan sponsor that his or her employment has ended. This is an obvious event in a single-employer plan, but it may not be readily known in the case of a multiemployer plan. [D.O.L. Reg. § 2530.203-3(b)(2)]

Example 13-9: ABC Painters provides a defined benefit plan with a benefit formula equal to $20 per month, per year of participation. Ginny retires at age 65 and starts receiving a monthly benefit of $600 per month. At age 67, Ginny decides that she will return to work for ABC Painters. The plan sponsor complies with the suspension-of-benefits rules and informs Ginny that benefits are being suspended. Ginny retires again at age 70 on January 15, 2019, and has accrued an additional benefit equal to $60 per month. Her accrued benefit is now $660 per month ($600 + $60). Ginny must commence receiving her benefits again by April 1, 2019 (the first day of the third calendar month following her most recent termination of employment).

If an employee with suspended benefits retires after the calendar year in which he or she attains age 70½, the employee's accrued benefit under a defined benefit plan must be actuarially increased to take into account any period after age 70½ in which the employee was not receiving any benefits under the plan. The actuarial increase must be provided for the period starting on the April 1 following the calendar year in which the employee attains age 70½. The period for which the actuarial increase must be provided ends on the date on which benefits commence after retirement in an amount sufficient to satisfy Code Section 401(a)(9). [Treas. Reg. § 1.401(a)(9)-6, Q&A-7 and Q&A-9; I.R.C. § 401(a)(9)(C)(iii)]

Q 13:20 Must amounts that have been withheld under the suspension-of-benefits rules be repaid to the employee?

No. [D.O.L. Reg. § 2530.203-3(b)(1); Treas. Reg. § 1.411(a)-4(b)(2)]

Q 13:21 What happens if a plan does not suspend benefits in accordance with the applicable DOL regulations?

If benefits have not begun, the benefits payable at normal retirement age must be actuarially increased for each plan year during the delayed retirement. When benefits commence, the plan may pay the participant either an accrued benefit equal to the greater of the actuarially increased benefit or the increased benefit that results from increase in accruals calculated for each of the plan years between reaching normal retirement age and benefit commencement age. (This comparison must be performed on an annual basis to determine each year's accrued benefit or both the actuarial increase and the formulaic increase. In the event the plan is silent about the type of increase, it must pay both the actuarial and formulaic increases.) [Rev. Rul. 81-140; 2009 Enrolled Actuaries Conference Gray Book, Q&A 39]

If benefits have begun, the actuarial value of the benefits paid during the plan year is used to offset the adjusted accrued benefit, but not below the benefit in pay status. [Prop. Treas. Reg. § 1.411(b)-2(b)(4)]

Claims for Benefits

Q 13:22 Must a participant file a claim to receive benefits under a plan?

No. Not all plans require participants to file applications for benefits in order to begin receiving them. Some plans do require participants to apply for benefits in order to begin receiving benefits. Generally, if anyone believes that he or she is entitled to a benefit under a plan, but does not receive it, he or she can file a claim under the plan's claim procedure. If a claim is denied, in whole or in part, the participant may appeal.

Q 13:23 What are the requirements for a claims procedure?

Every retirement plan that is subject to ERISA must establish a claims procedure, describe it in the SPD, and inform participants who are making claims of the proper timing during all phases of the process. The claims procedure must not contain any provision, and must not be administered in a fashion, that "unduly inhibits or hampers the initiation or processing of plan claims." The claims procedure must not preclude an authorized representative of a claimant from acting on behalf of such claimant in pursuing a benefit claim or appealing an adverse benefit determination. Nevertheless, a plan may establish reasonable procedures for determining whether an individual has been authorized to act on behalf of a claimant. The claims procedure should contain administrative processes and safeguards designed to ensure and to verify that benefit claim determinations are made in accordance with governing plan documents and that the plan provisions have been applied consistently with respect to similarly situated claimants.

Special rules apply for a plan maintained pursuant to a collective bargaining agreement. A plan will be deemed to comply with the rules if the collective bargaining agreement contains:

- Provisions concerning the filing of benefit claims and the initial disposition of benefit claims; and
- A grievance and arbitration procedure for the denial of claims.

[D.O.L. Reg. § 2560.503-1(b)]

Q 13:24 What is considered a claim for benefits?

A claim for benefits is a request for a plan benefit or benefits made by a claimant in accordance with a plan's reasonable procedure for filing benefit claims.

[D.O.L. Reg. § 2560.503-1(e)]

> **Example 13-10:** Pat terminates employment and has an accrued benefit with a present value of $12,000 in the ABC Painters' defined benefit plan. Pat writes to the trustee of the plan and explains that she would like to receive her benefits under the plan. This is considered to be the filing of a claim for benefits.

Q 13:25 What happens if the participant's claim for retirement benefits is wholly or partially denied?

The plan administrator must notify the participant of the denial within a reasonable period of time after the plan administrator receives the claim for benefits. A reasonable period is deemed to be no more than 90 days after receipt of the claim, unless special circumstances require an extension of time for processing the claim. If an extension is needed, written notice of the extension must be provided to the participant before the end of the 90-day period. The notice of the extension must contain the reasons necessitating the extension as well as the date on which a final decision is expected. The extension must not exceed 90 days. [D.O.L. Reg. § 2560.503-1(f)]

Q 13:26 What information must be provided in the claim denial?

The plan administrator must provide the participant whose claim has been denied with a written or electronic notice of any adverse benefit determination. Any electronic notice must satisfy the standards discussed in Q 13:27. The notice must contain the following information:

- The specific reason or reasons for the denial
- Specific reference to pertinent plan provisions on which the denial is based
- A description of any additional material or information necessary for the claimant to perfect the claim and an explanation of why such material or information is necessary, and
- A description of the plan's review procedures and the time limits applicable, including a statement of the participant's rights to bring a civil action under ERISA Section 502(a) following an adverse benefit determination

[D.O.L. Reg. § 2560.503-1(g)]

> **Example 13-11:** In Example 13-10, the trustee writes to Pat (within 90 days) and explains that she did not complete five years of service and, because the plan contains a five-year cliff vesting schedule, she is 0 percent vested and thus has no benefits due under the plan. This notice of denial of benefits should contain the following information:

- The reason for the denial: that is, Pat is not vested in any benefits because she has not completed five years of vesting service in the plan,
- The sections in the plan document that discuss vesting and the computation of vesting years of service,
- The steps Pat must take to ask for a review of the claim and notice that a response must be received from Pat in 60 days, and
- A notice that Pat may file a civil action under ERISA if she believes that she received an adverse benefit determination.

Q 13:27 What are the standards for an electronic notice of suspension-of-benefits and a claim denial?

A plan administrator furnishing documents through electronic media must meet the following requirements:

- All reasonable measures to ensure that the system for furnishing documents—
  - — Results in actual receipt of transmitted information (e.g., using return-receipt or notice of undelivered electronic mail features, conducting periodic reviews or surveys to confirm receipt of the transmitted information); and
  - — Protects the confidentiality of personal information relating to the individual's accounts and benefits (e.g., incorporating into the system measures designed to preclude unauthorized receipt of or access to such information by individuals other than the individual for whom the information is intended);
- The electronically delivered notice is prepared and furnished in a manner that is consistent with the style, format, and content requirements (as discussed in Qs 13:18 and 13:26).
- A notice is provided to the participant in electronic or non-electronic form, at the time a document is furnished electronically, that apprises the participant of the significance of the document when it is not otherwise reasonably evident as transmitted (e.g., the attached document describes changes in the benefits provided by your plan) and of the right to request and obtain a paper copy of such document; and
- Upon request, the participant is furnished, free of charge, a paper version of the electronically furnished documents.

Electronic notices may only be furnished to the following individuals:

- An individual who has the ability to effectively access documents furnished in electronic form at any location where the participant is reasonably expected to perform his or her duties as an employee; and
- With respect to whom access to the employer's or plan sponsor's electronic information system is an integral part of those duties.

[D.O.L. Reg. § 2520.104b-1(c)(1)]

Q 13:28 May the participant appeal the denied claim?

Yes. Every retirement plan must establish and maintain a procedure that allows a participant or a participant's representative a reasonable opportunity to appeal a denied claim. The procedure must also provide for a full and fair review by a named fiduciary of the plan. Such procedures must:

- Provide participants with at least 60 days to file an appeal following notice of an adverse benefit determination;
- Provide participants with the opportunity to submit written comments, documents, records, and other information relating to the claim for benefits;
- Provide that a participant may receive, upon request and free of charge, copies of all documents, records, and other information relevant to the claimant's claim for benefits;
- Provide for a review that takes into account all comments, documents, records, and other information submitted by the claimant relating to the claim, without regard to whether such information was submitted or considered in the initial benefit determination.

[D.O.L. Reg. § 2560.503-1(h)]

Q 13:29 What is the time frame for review of the appeal of the denied claim?

The fiduciary of the plan must respond to the appeal within 60 days after receipt of the notice from the participant. An extension may be allowed if there are special circumstances, such as the need to hold a hearing; the extension, however, may not exceed 60 days. If an extension of time is required, written notice must be provided to the participant before the extension starts. The decision on the review of the appeal must:

- Be in writing;
- Include the specific reasons for the decision;
- Be written in a manner calculated to be understood by the participant; and
- Include specific references to the pertinent plan provisions on which the decision is based.

[D.O.L. Reg. § 2560.503-1(i)]

Example 13-12: Pat decides to appeal the denied claim from Example 13-11. She appeals the denial and attaches her records showing that she received credit for 1,000 hours in each of the last five plan years of her employment. The trustee responds within 60 days and agrees with Pat that she is entitled to her vested accrued benefit (100 percent vested) of $12,000 and distributes the vested amount to Pat.

Q 13:30 What is the penalty for failure to comply with the claims procedure requirements?

Because the claims procedures are not a requirement for qualification, the plan will not be disqualified. However, the plan will be subject to the general remedies for noncompliance with ERISA provided under ERISA Section 502. [ERISA § 510]

Q 13:31 What are the remedies available under ERISA?

Criminal penalties apply to any person who willfully violates ERISA. For an individual, the penalty may be a fine up to $100,000 or 10 years in prison, or both. For a non-individual, the fine may be up to $500,000. [ERISA § 501, as amended by § 904 of the Sarbanes-Oxley Act of 2002] Civil enforcement is also possible, and any complaint by a participant or beneficiary for the purpose of recovering benefits due under the plan must also be served upon the Secretary of Labor and the Secretary of the Treasury by certified mail. Either Secretary has the right, at his or her discretion, to intervene in any action. [ERISA § 502(h)]

Q 13:32 What standards do the courts apply if the participant makes a claim for benefits?

If a participant files a claim in court when his or her benefits have been denied, the court applies a standard of deference when reviewing the determination of the plan administrator. Two standards for review have evolved in the courts:

1. The de novo standard; and
2. The arbitrary and capricious standard.

The de novo standard provides very little deference to the plan administrator; the court must review not only the decisions of the plan administrator, but also all the facts and related plan documents. By contrast, if a court applies the arbitrary and capricious standard, the plan administrator's decision is overridden by the court only if the decision is an abuse of discretion, arbitrary and capricious, or in violation of law. Under this standard, the court defers to the decision of the fiduciary, even if the court itself would have reached a different result. [Firestone Tire & Rubber Co v. Bruch, 489 U.S. 101 (1989); T. Ferrera, *ERISA Fiduciary Answer Book*, 8th ed. (Wolters Kluwer Law & Business, 2019) Q 11:29]

A more recent case, *Conkright v. Frommert*, involved an ERISA action based on a plan administrator's interpretation of a benefits plan. The Supreme Court reversed the Second Circuit's order affirming the district court's order declining to apply a deferential standard to the administrator's interpretation. The administrator had arrived at a mistaken interpretation, and the Supreme Court recognized that, in a complicated area, mistakes may be made. [559 U.S. 506 (2010)]

Chapter 14

Restrictions on Distributions

The nondiscrimination rules of Code Section 401(a)(4) and Treasury Regulations Section 1.401(a)(4)-5(b) restrict amounts that may be distributed to certain highly compensated employees (HCEs) in defined benefit (and certain money purchase) plans. The purpose of the rules is to prevent higher-paid employees from drawing significant benefits from a defined benefit plan, leaving only the lower-paid employees exposed to possible insufficient assets and reduced benefits.

Additionally, Code Section 436 requires plans with specified funding percentages that are less than 80 percent (or plans of bankrupt sponsors with specified funding percentages that are less than 100 percent) to restrict distributions to any participant other than in the form of a life annuity until specified funding percentages rise.

Historical Perspective 14-1
Application of Benefit Restriction Rules 14-4
Use of Collateral Agreements 14-10
Code Section 436 Rules on Restricted Distribution 14-12

Historical Perspective

Q 14:1 Has the Internal Revenue Code historically contained rules restricting distribution to highly paid employees?

Yes. In Mimeograph 5717, published in 1944, the IRS first discussed the qualification rules relating to limitations on distributions to highly paid employees. The rules were later incorporated into the regulations at Treasury Regulations Section 1.401-4(c) and subsequently modified (interim rules). This regulation was then replaced when final regulations under Code Section 401(a)(4) were issued in 1993. The current rules are discussed in the rest of this chapter.

Although the original rules under Mimeograph 5717 and Treasury Regulations Section 1.401-4(c) are now obsolete, escrow agreements established while these rules were in effect may still exist.

Q 14:2 How did the current rules evolve?

Code Section 401(a)(4) as amended by the Tax Reform Act of 1986 (TRA '86) is rather brief and contains the requirement that:

> A trust created or organized in the United States and forming part of a stock bonus, pension, or profit sharing plan of an employer for the exclusive benefit of his employees or their beneficiaries shall constitute a qualified trust under this section—
>
> If the contributions or benefits provided under the plan do not discriminate in favor of highly compensated employees . . .

Treasury has issued substantial regulations explaining the meaning of this single sentence. Those regulations deal with nondiscrimination in retirement plans and address issues including:

1. Amounts of benefits or contributions;
2. Benefits, rights, and features; and
3. Plan amendments and plan terminations.

The restrictions on distributions to HCEs are contained in the plan amendments and terminations section of the regulations. Those restrictions apply to most defined benefit plans and, in some cases, target benefit and money purchase plans. The impact of the rules on plan sponsors and affected HCEs are discussed.

The final regulations under Code Section 401(a)(4) changed early plan termination rules. A defined benefit plan is deemed to discriminate significantly in favor of HCEs unless it incorporates provisions restricting benefits and distributions in the plan document. The early plan termination rules contained in the regulations restrict benefits upon plan termination or upon distribution following severance of employment. [Treas. Reg. § 1.401(a)(4)-5(b)(1)]

Q 14:3 What happened to a participant's benefits that were restricted under the original rules?

In the event of a plan termination, a substantial owner's benefits may have been limited in accordance with the original rules. In circumstances other than plan termination, a participant restricted under the old (or interim) rules may have chosen one of the following options:

1. To defer payment of the vested accrued benefit until the earlier of attainment of normal retirement age, age 70½, or plan termination;
2. To receive the benefit in the normal form of annuity provided by the plan;
3. To receive a distribution of unrestricted funds and defer payment of restricted funds until the restrictions expired; that is, until full current costs have been met or a 10-year period expires;

4. To receive the maximum annual distribution of $20,000 per year; or
5. To receive a distribution after posting collateral with the plan trustee (see Q 14:4).

Q 14:4 What are the acceptable methods under the original rules of posting collateral with the plan trustee?

The IRS has indicated that the following methods of posting collateral are acceptable:

Depository Option. The employee enters into an agreement with the plan administrator. The agreement states that, in the event of plan termination within the first 10 years of establishment of the plan or if the full current costs of the plan have not been met, the employee (or at the employee's death, the employee's estate) agrees to repay any restricted amounts to the plan. The employee agrees to deposit with an acceptable depository, property with a fair market value equal to 125 percent of the amount repayable to the plan. The employee further agrees that if the fair market value falls below 110 percent of the amount repayable to the plan, additional property will be deposited to bring the value up to the 125 percent level. Upon certification from the plan administrator, the depository will release the collateral to the employee. The participant may receive the net income derived from the property, as long as the property continues to have a fair market value of at least 125 percent of the restricted amount. [Rev. Rul. 92-76; Ltr. Rul. 8845060]

Individual Retirement Account (IRA) Escrow Option. The employer may have permitted the present value of the terminated employee's accrued benefit to be rolled over into an IRA. The plan would have entered into an escrow agreement with the custodial trustee of the IRA. If the plan terminated while the employee's benefits were subject to the early plan termination rules, the employee and IRA trustee agreed to repay the plan the restricted amount by transferring sufficient assets from the IRA to the plan. If the assets rolled over into the IRA did not have a fair market value of at least 125 percent of the restricted amount, the employee agreed to secure the obligation with personal assets by transferring the assets to the plan. [Ltr. Ruls. 8408063, 8436065, 8440070, 8514093, 8525148, 8801060, 8805021, 9151047, 9514028]

Letter of Credit Option. The terminated participant who is subject to the early plan termination restrictions obtained a letter of credit issued by a bank or similar financial institution for an amount equal to at least 125 percent of the restricted amount in favor of the trustee of the plan. The terminated participant entered into a separate agreement with a financial institution whereby the financial institution is directed to pay to the plan any amount the participant failed to repay under the agreement. The agreement could be structured to allow the reduction in the amount of the letter of credit due to a reduction in the restricted amount. [Ltr. Ruls. 8805060, 8805061, 8845060] In one ruling, the IRS stated that a letter of credit of at least 100 percent of the restricted amount, used in conjunction with a security agreement, would be acceptable. [Rev. Rul. 92-76; Ltr. Rul. 9210037]

Bond Option. The terminated participant obtained a bond or other undertaking furnished by an insurance company, bonding company, or other surety approved by the U.S. Treasury with a face value of at least 110 percent of the restricted amount for the benefit of the trustee of the plan. The terminated participant entered into a separate agreement with the surety, whereby the surety was directed to pay to the plan any amount the participant failed to repay under the repayment agreement. The face value of the bond could be reduced on an annual basis to reflect any reduction in the restricted amount. [Ltr. Ruls. 8805060, 8805061, 8845060]

A combination of any of the above options would not appear to be an acceptable alternative. [Ltr. Rul. 8805060]

Example 14-1: John is entitled to a lump-sum distribution of $880,000. The restricted amount is $800,000. If John wants to roll over the entire lump sum into an IRA, the trustee of the plan and the IRA custodian could enter into an escrow agreement in order to repay the restricted amount to the plan in the event of plan termination. However, the distribution of $880,000 is insufficient to satisfy the 125 percent requirement discussed above, because $1,000,000 is needed (125% × $800,000). Thus, John would need to deposit the difference, or $120,000, with the plan trustee to satisfy the escrow requirements. Each year, if the restricted amount decreases, funds may be released back to John.

Application of Benefit Restriction Rules

Q 14:5 How are benefits restricted upon plan termination?

A plan must provide that the benefit of any HCE or highly compensated former employees (HCFE) is limited to a benefit that is nondiscriminatory under Code Section 401(a)(4). [Treas. Reg. § 1.401(a)(4)-5(b)(2)] (See chapter 15 for a detailed discussion of the plan termination rules.) Unlike the original rules that eventually expire with the passage of time, these rules never expire. (See Appendix G for detailed definitions of HCE and HCFE.)

Q 14:6 How are benefits restricted on distribution?

A plan must provide that, in any year, the payment of benefits to, or on behalf of, a restricted employee must not exceed an amount equal to the payments that would be made to, or on behalf of, the restricted employee in that year under:

1. A straight life annuity that is the actuarial equivalent of the accrued benefit and other benefits to which the restricted employee is entitled under the plan (other than a Social Security supplement); plus
2. A Social Security supplement, if any, that the restricted employee is entitled to receive.

It should be noted that a restricted employee's alternate payee under a qualified domestic relations order (QDRO) is also subject to the benefit restrictions above.

[Treas. Reg. § 1.401(a)(4)-5(b)(3)(i)]

Q 14:7 Who is a restricted employee?

The term *restricted employee* refers to any HCE or HCFE if the employee is one of the 25 (or a larger number chosen by the employer) nonexcludable employees and former employees of the employer with the largest amount of compensation in the current or any prior year. Plan provisions defining or altering this group can be amended at any time without violating the anti-cutback provision of Code Section 411(d)(6). [Treas. Reg. § 1.401(a)(4)-5(b)(3)(ii)]

In a private letter ruling, the Treasury has opined that the "high 25" limit is determined on an employer-by-employer basis in a multiple employer plan, where none of the members are in a controlled or affiliated service group (under Section 414(b), (c), (m), or (o)) with another employer in the plan. [Ltr. Rul. 200449043]

In another private letter ruling, the Treasury has opined that the "high 25" limit is determined on an employer-wide basis, regardless of the fact that a qualified separate lines of business (QSLOB) election has been made by the plan sponsor. [Ltr. Rul. 200248029]

Example 14-2: Art is an HCE for the plan year ending December 31, 2018, because he earned $125,000 working for ABC Restaurant in 2017. Art terminates employment in 2018. ABC Restaurant wants to determine if Art is a restricted employee. Toby, the benefits manager, makes a list of all HCEs for the years 1995 (the year the business started) through 2018. This list is arranged in order of compensation, using the highest compensation earned for each HCE. Art is number 30 on the list and is, therefore, not a restricted employee.

Example 14-3: Gladys earned $95,100 in 2007 and was one of the five HCEs. She is considered an HCE for 2008. She participates in ABC Restaurant's Defined Benefit Plan. In 2009 and 2010, Gladys is no longer considered an HCE, because she earned $80,000 in 2008 and 2009. Gladys terminates employment in 2018, but is still considered a restricted employee because she was an HCE in 2008 and is one of the 25 nonexcludable employees and former employees with the largest amount of compensation.

Example 14-4: CDE Cafe participates in a multiple employer plan called the Cafes of New York Defined Benefit Plan. Two hundred separate employers participate in the plan. Bryan is the only HCE working for CDE Cafe and is, therefore, a restricted employee, regardless of the fact that there are approximately 100 HCEs covered by the entire plan from among unrelated employers.

Q 14:8 What benefits are included in these restrictions?

Restricted benefits include the following:

1. Loans in excess of the amounts in Code Section 72(p)(2)(A) (the taxable limit of the lesser of 50 percent of vested account balance or $50,000);
2. Any periodic income;
3. Any withdrawal values payable to a living employee or former employee (lump sums); or
4. Any death benefits not provided for by insurance on the employee's or former employee's life.

[Treas. Reg. § 1.401(a)(4)-5(b)(3)(iii)]

Q 14:9 Are there any exceptions to these benefit restrictions?

Yes. Amounts in excess of a life annuity (and Social Security supplement, if applicable) may be paid to a restricted employee if any one of the following requirements is satisfied:

1. After taking into account all payments due to, or on behalf of, the restricted employee, the value of plan assets equals or exceeds 110 percent of the value of current liabilities, as defined in Code Section 412(l)(7);
2. The value of the benefits payable to, or on behalf of, the restricted employee is less than 1 percent of the value of current liabilities before distribution; or
3. The value of the benefits payable to, or on behalf of, the restricted employee does not exceed $5,000.

Under these rules, any reasonable and consistent method may be used in determining the value of plan assets and current liabilities. [Treas. Reg. § 1.401(a)(4)-5(b)(3)(iv), (v)]

In a private letter ruling, the Treasury has opined that, in a multiple employer plan where all plan assets are available to pay benefits to employees covered by the plan and their beneficiaries, the 1 percent rule discussed above applies on a plan-wide basis. [Ltr. Rul. 200449043]

> **Example 14-5:** ABC Restaurant sponsors a defined benefit plan. As of the last actuarial valuation date, current liabilities were approximately $450 million. Because the largest possible lump-sum distribution for an individual is approximately $2.5 million, it would be nearly impossible for a lump-sum distribution to exceed 1 percent of the value of current liabilities ($4.5 million). Hence, HCEs are not subject to restrictions on their lump-sum distributions.

> **Example 14-6:** DEF Bistros sponsors a defined benefit plan. Four of the restricted HCEs are retiring at age 62, with each eligible to receive a lump-sum distribution of $1.5 million. Current liabilities in the plan are equal to $300 million as of the last actuarial valuation date. Because each restricted HCE is eligible to receive a distribution that is less than 1 percent of the value of current liabilities ($3 million), each restricted HCE may receive his or her

full lump-sum distribution without restriction. Because this exception is tested on a per participant basis, these distributions are permitted even though the aggregate of distributions to the four restricted HCEs will be $6 million (4 × $1.5 million), more than 1 percent of the value of current liabilities.

Example 14-7: CDE Cafe participates in a multiple employer plan called Cafes of New York Defined Benefit Plan. There are 150 employers participating in the defined benefit plan, and liabilities of the plan total $450 million. Grace, a restricted employee, terminates employment and wishes to receive a lump-sum distribution of approximately $2 million. Because all plan assets in the Cafes of New York Defined Benefit Plan are available to pay benefits of any participant in the plan, Grace may receive a lump-sum distribution because her benefit is less than 1 percent of the total liabilities in the plan ($4.5 million).

Q 14:10 What are current liabilities?

For plan years prior to 2008, current liabilities were computed on an annual basis by the defined benefit plan's enrolled actuary and were used in limiting the amount that could be contributed to the plan, as well as computing additional contributions required by the employer.

Current liabilities are defined as the present value of all liabilities of the defined benefit plan to employees and their beneficiaries. However, unpredictable contingent event (UCE) benefits may not be taken into account until the event on which the benefit is contingent occurs. A UCE benefit is any benefit contingent on an event other than:

- Age
- Service
- Compensation
- Death
- Disability
- Any event that is reasonably and reliably predictable

Thus, for example, a defined benefit plan may provide additional benefits to participants in the event of a plant shutdown. Such additional benefits were not to be taken into account in computing current liabilities. [I.R.C. § 412(l)(7)]

Effective with 2008 plan years, the term *current liability* is no longer defined in the Code. Informal guidance received from the IRS indicates that the following may be used: the current liability using pre-2008 rules; the *funding target* with regular segment rates; or the *funding target* with the Moving Ahead for Progress in the 21st Century Act (MAP-21) threshold segment rates as adjusted by the Highway and Transportation Funding Act of 2014 (HATFA) (see Q 14:11):

> Until additional guidance is used, it would be reasonable for the sponsor to continue to use a method consistent with prior practice (i.e., continue to use a current liability type approach). It would also be reasonable for the sponsor to assume current liability can be replaced with the "funding target" concept introduced by PPA. See § 1.401(a)(4)-5(b)(3)(v)

which states that "any reasonable and consistent method may be used for determining the value of current liabilities and the value of plan assets."

[2008 Enrolled Actuaries Meeting, Gray Book, Q&A 30; 2013 Enrolled Actuaries Meeting, Gray Book, Q&A 8]

Q 14:11 What is the funding target?

The funding target is equal to the present value of all benefit liabilities accrued at the beginning of the plan year. [I.R.C. § 430(d)(1)] This present value is determined using the Treasury-prescribed segment interest rates (as modified by the Moving Ahead for Progress in the 21st Century Act (MAP-21) rates for plan years beginning in 2012 or 2013 or HATFA for 2013 and later years) and prescribed mortality tables.

Q 14:12 For purposes of the restricted distribution rules, how are the values of current liabilities/funding target and assets determined?

Any reasonable and consistent method may be used for determining the value of current liabilities/funding targets and the value of plan assets. [Treas. Reg. § 1.401(a)(4)-5(b)(3)(v)] For example, the value of funding target and assets reported on the Schedule SB of Form 5500 applicable to the beginning of the year or end of the prior year of the potential distribution could be used. A re-determination of the value of current liabilities/funding targets and assets could be made as of the projected distribution date for the restricted employee. Another reasonable method would be to project the current liabilities/funding targets and assets from the date of the last actuarial valuation to the projected distribution date.

The IRS has interpreted the consistency requirement to mean that the current liability/funding target must be calculated on a consistent basis within the plan year for any lump-sum distributions during the plan year. The methodology for the calculation of the current liability/funding target may be changed from year to year. [2005 Enrolled Actuaries Meeting, Gray Book, Q. 32]

> **Example 14-8:** Tom, the 100 percent owner of ABC Restaurants, retires in 2018 and wants to receive a lump-sum distribution equal to the present value of his accrued benefit of $800,000. As the only HCE of ABC Restaurants, Tom is subject to the restricted distribution rules described above. In the 2018 Schedule SB prepared by the enrolled actuary for the plan year ended December 31, 2018, the funding target was $1 million. Plan assets were valued at $1.15 million.
>
> Immediately after the distribution to Tom, the funding target would be equal to $300,000, after subtracting out the funding target attributable to Tom. Similarly, after subtracting out the distribution to Tom, net plan assets equal $350,000. Because the plan assets (after distribution) of $350,000 are greater than 110 percent of current liabilities, $330,000 (110% × $300,000), Tom may receive the lump-sum distribution.

Had plan assets been less than 110 percent of current liabilities, Tom would be restricted to an annual distribution of the actuarial equivalent of a life annuity benefit or may use a collateral agreement as described in Qs 14:14–14:19 below.

Q 14:13 How is the restricted amount recomputed each year?

During a plan year, the amount that may be required to be repaid to the plan is the restricted amount. (See Table 14-1.) The restricted amount is the excess of the accumulated amount of distributions made to the employee over the accumulated amount of the employee's unrestricted limit. The employee's unrestricted limit is equal to the payments that could have been distributed to the employee, commencing when distribution started to the employee, had the employee received payments in the form described in Treasury Regulations Sections 1.401(a)(4)-5(b)(3)(i)(A) and (B) (i.e., a single life annuity plus any social security supplement). An *accumulated amount* is the amount of a payment increased by a reasonable amount of interest from the date the payment was made (or would have been made) until the date for the determination of the restricted amount. [Rev. Rul. 92-76]

The restricted amount is reduced by the unrestricted amount each year.

Example 14-9: Larry, a restricted HCE, is entitled to a life annuity of $2,000 a month from the CDE Cafe's Defined Benefit Plan. He receives a lump sum of $283,059, based on a 5 percent interest rate and the 1994 Group Annuity Reserving mortality table. An interest rate of 5 percent is used in the calculation of the restricted and unrestricted amounts. For simplicity, this assumes that the Code Section 417(e) prescribed rates and mortality table would have produced a smaller lump sum and would not be applicable.

Table 14-1. Computing Restricted Amounts

Year	*Unrestricted Amount*	*Unrestricted Amount with Interest*	*Lump Sum Adjusted with Interest*	*Remaining Restricted Amount*
1	$ 24,000	$ 24,600	$283,059	$258,459
2	$ 48,000	$ 50,430	$297,212	$246,782
3	$ 72,000	$ 77,552	$312,073	$234,521
4	$ 96,000	$106,029	$327,676	$221,647
5	$120,000	$135,931	$344,060	$208,129
6	$144,000	$167,327	$361,263	$193,936
7	$168,000	$200,293	$379,326	$179,033
8	$192,000	$234,908	$398,292	$163,384
9	$216,000	$271,253	$418,207	$146,954
10	$240,000	$309,416	$439,117	$129,701
11	$264,000	$349,487	$461,073	$111,586

Table 14-1. Computing Restricted Amounts (*cont'd*)

Year	*Unrestricted Amount*	*Unrestricted Amount with Interest*	*Lump Sum Adjusted with Interest*	*Remaining Restricted Amount*
12	$288,000	$ 391,561	$484,127	$ 92,566
13	$312,000	$ 435,739	$508,333	$ 72,594
14	$336,000	$ 482,126	$533,750	$ 51,624
15	$360,000	$ 530,833	$560,437	$ 29,605
16	$384,000	$ 581,974	$588,459	$ 6,485
17	$408,000	$ 635,673	$617,882	$ 0
18	$432,000	$ 692,057	$648,776	$ 0
19	$456,000	$ 751,259	$681,215	$ 0
20	$480,000	$ 813,422	$715,276	$ 0
21	$504,000	$ 878,694	$751,040	$ 0
22	$528,000	$ 947,228	$788,592	$ 0
23	$552,000	$1,019,190	$828,021	$ 0
24	$576,000	$1,094,749	$869,422	$ 0
25	$600,000	$1,174,087	$912,894	$ 0

Using the above projections, the lump-sum distribution is not subject to restrictions after the 16th year, and any collateral agreement may be terminated.

Use of Collateral Agreements

Q 14:14 May a restricted employee post collateral in order to receive a distribution that is otherwise restricted?

Yes. The plan may permit distributions in excess of the limits discussed above, provided that an agreement has been established to secure repayment to the plan of any amount necessary for the distribution of assets on plan termination.

The following alternatives are available to secure an employee's repayment obligation:

1. The employee must agree that, upon distribution, he or she will deposit in escrow with an acceptable depositary, property with a fair market value equal to at least 125 percent of the restricted amount;
2. The employee may collateralize the obligation by posting a bond, furnished by an approved surety, equal to at least 100 percent of the restricted amount; and
3. The employee's obligation under the repayment agreement can be secured by a bank letter of credit in an amount equal to at least 100 percent of the restricted amount.

A depositary may not redeliver any property held under such an agreement (other than amounts in excess of 125 percent of the restricted amount), and a surety or bank may not release any liability on a bond or letter of credit unless the plan administrator certifies that the employee (or the employee's estate) is no longer obligated to repay any amount under the agreement. [Rev. Rul. 92-76]

Q 14:15 Is an IRA rollover permitted for an employee subject to the restrictions itemized in Q 14:6?

Yes. An employee may roll over the entire distribution to an IRA. A number of private letter rulings have been issued permitting employees whose benefits are restricted (as described in this chapter) to roll over the present value of their accrued benefit to an IRA. The steps needed to accomplish the rollover are listed below:

1. The participant rolls over at least 125 percent of the restricted amount;
2. If the amount of the rollover from the defined benefit plan is insufficient to satisfy the 125 percent rule, the participant would need to provide additional collateral, either from another IRA or from personal funds;
3. The IRA trustee executes a collateral agreement agreeing to hold 125 percent of the restricted amount for the benefit of the plan to repay the plan in the event of insufficiency upon plan termination;
4. The IRA trustee agrees to notify the plan's trustee if the assets in the IRA (and other assets, if applicable) decline in value to 110 percent or less of the restricted amount; and
5. The plan participant agrees to establish an escrow account to bring the total value of the escrowed amount up to the 125 percent threshold, in the event that the IRA declines in value to 110 percent or less.

[Rev. Rul. 92-76; Ltr. Ruls. 9743051, 9151047, 8850046, 8639068, 8615094, 8612079, 9514028]

Q 14:16 How are existing collateral agreements handled?

The plan administrator may make a determination about whether the individual is a restricted employee as discussed in Q 14:7. If the individual is a restricted employee, the plan's enrolled actuary may make a re-determination about whether the distribution is subject to the rules under Treasury Regulations Section 1.401(a)(4)-5. If the employee is not restricted, or if the distribution is no longer subject to the restrictions, the plan trustee may instruct the depositary to redeliver any property held under the agreement or instruct the surety or bank to release any liability on a bond or letter of credit. [Ltr. Ruls. 9419040, 9417031]

Q 14:17 Do the rules on restricted distributions to HCEs apply to defined contribution plans?

Generally, no. However, a money purchase or target benefit plan that has an accumulated funding deficiency or an unamortized funding waiver must comply with the restrictions discussed in Q 14:5 and Q 14:6. Such a plan does not fail to satisfy the anti-cutback provisions of Code Section 411(d)(6) merely because of the restrictions imposed by these rules. [Treas. Reg. § 1.401(a)(4)-5(b)(4)] (See chapter 17 for a further discussion of underfunded defined contribution plans.)

Q 14:18 Will the use of a collateral agreement prevent treatment of the entire amount as a lump-sum distribution?

If the benefits paid to the participant represent his or her entire accrued benefit, the participant is considered to have received the balance to his or her credit in a single taxable year. Such distributions are considered lump-sum distributions within the meaning of Code Section 402(e)(4)(D) and, thus, are entitled to special tax treatment regardless of the fact that certain amounts are subject to the restrictions of Treasury Regulations Section 1.401(a)(4)-5(b) and may have to be repaid to the plan in the future. [Rev. Rul. 92-76]

Q 14:19 What must a plan sponsor do to correct a disqualifying defect if amounts in excess of the limits have been distributed to a restricted employee?

This disqualifying defect could likely be corrected through Employee Plans Compliance Resolution System (EPCRS) (see chapter 23). Likely solutions include the following:

1. Request that the restricted HCE repay the restricted amounts to the plan.
2. Have the plan sponsor make a sufficient contribution to ensure that the restrictions are no longer applicable.
3. Use one of the options discussed in Q 14:4 and require the restricted employee to post collateral with the plan trustee.

Code Section 436 Rules on Restricted Distribution

Q 14:20 How does Code Section 436 restrict distributions to plan participants?

Code Section 436 restricts distributions to plan participants that exceed the amount of a monthly life annuity that varies according to the plan's adjusted funding target attainment percentage (AFTAP). Amounts in excess of the monthly life annuity are known as prohibited payments. (See Q 14:21.) These distribution restrictions were first effective for plan years beginning after 2007.

Plans funded below a 60 percent threshold. Distributions in excess of the monthly life annuity payable under the plan when the plan's AFTAP is less than 60 percent are prohibited (see Q 14:22). This also applies if the employer is in bankruptcy, unless the plan's AFTAP is 100 percent or greater. The employer could put up security to permit larger distributions to be made (see Q 14:24).

Plans funded at a 60 percent level or higher, but below an 80 percent level. A limited payout, rather than a prohibition on any distribution in excess of the monthly life annuity, is allowed if a plan's AFTAP is at least 60 percent, but below 80 percent. The employer could put up security to permit larger distributions to be made (see Q 14:24). Plans at least 60 percent but less than 80 percent funded can make lump-sum payments limited to the lesser of:

1. 50 percent of the amount that would have been paid without restriction; or
2. The present value of the participant's Pension Benefit Guaranty Corporation (PBGC) guaranteed benefit (see chapter 16).

Note. The PBGC.gov website contains a table of the present value of guaranteed benefits for the current year. These values apply to benefits with annuity starting dates in the current year. For example, the 2018 table was developed using the 417(e) segment rates (without application of HATFA or MAP-21 rates) for August 2017 (1.93%, 3.53%, and 4.36%, respectively) and the Code Section 417(e) applicable mortality table for 2018. The table can be found at:

http://www.pbgc.gov/prac/mortality-retirement-and-pv-max-guarantee/present-guarantee.html

Sample amounts for 2018 are shown in the table below:

Age	*Present Value of PBGC Maximum Guarantee*
25	$149,687
30	$185,444
35	$229,796
40	$284,858
45	$353,332
50	$459,281
55	$583,832
60	$733,668
65	$932,228

[PPA §§ 102, 103, 113; ERISA § 206(g); I.R.C. § 436(b); Treas. Reg. § 1.436-1(d)(3)(iii)(C)]

Q 14:21 What is a prohibited payment?

The following types of payments are prohibited when a plan's AFTAP (see Q 14:22) is below 60 percent or for a plan sponsor in bankruptcy if the plan's AFTAP is below 100 percent:

1. Any payment in excess of the monthly amount under a single life annuity (plus any Social Security supplement) to a participant or beneficiary whose annuity starting date occurs during the period of prohibition;

2. Any payment for the purchase of an irrevocable commitment from an insurer to pay benefits (e.g., annuity contract);
3. Any other payment specified by the Secretary of the Treasury by regulations.

The rules on prohibited payments do not apply to a plan year if the terms of the plan (as in effect for the period beginning on September 1, 2005) provide for no benefit accruals with respect to any participant during the period.

[PPA § 103(a); ERISA § 206(g)(3)(E); I.R.C. § 436(d)(5); Treas. Reg. §§ 1.436-1(j)(6), 1.436-1(d)(4)]

Q 14:22 How is a plan's AFTAP determined?

A plan's funding target attainment percentage (FTAP) is the following ratio:

$$\frac{\text{Assets} - \text{Funding Standard Carryover} - \text{Pre-Funding Credit Balance}}{\text{Target Liability (disregarding the plan's at-risk status)}}$$

The AFTAP reflects plan assets and funding target liabilities as increased by the aggregate amount of annuity purchases made for non-highly compensated employees by the plan during the preceding two plan years.

$$\frac{\text{Assets} - \text{Funding Standard Carryover} - \text{Pre-Funding Balance} + \text{Annuity Purchases}}{\text{Target Liability (disregarding the plan's at-risk status)} + \text{Annuity Purchases}}$$

There is a special rule for fully funded plans (see Q 14:24). [PPA §§ 102, 103, 113; ERISA § 206(g)(9)(B); I.R.C. § 436(j)(2); Treas. Reg. § 1.436-1(j)(1)]

Q 14:23 What asset value is used in calculating the AFTAP?

The actuarial value of assets used for purposes of the minimum funding requirements under Code Section 430 is used. If the asset value changes after the actuarial valuation is completed, then the AFTAP must be updated.

[Treas. Reg. § 1.436-1(j)(2); 2008 Enrolled Actuaries Meeting, Gray Book, Q&A 20]

Q 14:24 What is the special rule for fully funded plans?

Under a special rule for fully funded plans, if the following ratio is at least 100 percent,

$$\frac{\text{Assets}}{\text{Target Liability (disregarding the plan's at-risk status)}}$$

then the funding standard carryover and the pre-funding balance will not reduce the AFTAP. Thus, the AFTAP for a fully funded plan is calculated as follows:

$$\frac{\text{Assets} + \text{Annuity Purchases}}{\text{Target Liability (disregarding the plan's at-risk status)} + \text{Annuity Purchases}}$$

Under a transition rule for the years 2007 through 2010, the 100 percent requirement was reduced:

Year	*Applicable Percentage*
2007	92
2008	94
2009	96
2010	98

However, if the AFTAP falls below the applicable percentage in any year, the special rule was accelerated to 100 percent.

[PPA §§ 102, 103, 113; ERISA § 206(g); I.R.C. § 436(d); Treas. Reg. § 1.436-1(j)(1)(ii)(B), (D)]

Q 14:25 What types of security may the employer post in order to permit larger distributions from the plan?

The following types of security are permitted:

1. Surety bond;
2. Cash;
3. Certain U.S. government obligations;
4. Other form satisfactory to Secretary of the Treasury.

The securities listed above are treated as plan assets. Any such securities may be perfected and enforced at any time after the earlier of:

1. The date on which the plan terminates;
2. If the plan sponsor fails to make a required contribution, on the due date of the contribution;
3. If the plan's AFTAP is less than 60 percent for a consecutive period of seven years, on the valuation date for the last year in the seven-year period.

[PPA §§ 103, 113; ERISA § 206(g)(5); I.R.C. § 436(f); Treas. Reg. § 1.436-1(f)(2), (3)]

Q 14:26 Can the 60 percent/80 percent restrictions be avoided in a manner other than by posting security?

Yes, a plan sponsor can irrevocably waive credit balances in order to improve the AFTAP. The plan sponsor would apply the funding standard carryover (pre-2008 credit balance) first and then apply any pre-funding credit balance.

The plan sponsor may also make a contribution sufficient to bring the AFTAP up to the 60 percent/80 percent threshold.

[PPA §§ 103, 113; ERISA § 206(g)(5); I.R.C. § 436(f); Treas. Reg. § 1.436-1(g)(2)(ii)]

Q 14:27 Are other plans of the plan sponsor affected by these prohibited payment rules?

Yes, nonqualified deferred compensation arrangements are subject to an excise tax if amounts are set aside for applicable covered employees during the restricted period. The restricted period is defined as:

1. Any period during which the plan is in at-risk status (as defined in Code Section 430(i));
2. Any period during which the plan sponsor is a debtor in a case under title 11, U.S. Code, or similar federal or state law; and
3. The 12-month period beginning on the date that is six months before the termination date of the plan if, as of the termination date, the plan is not sufficient for benefit liabilities (within the meaning of ERISA Section 4041). (See chapter 17.)

In general, applicable covered employees include:

1. The chief executive officer (or individual acting in such capacity);
2. The four highest compensated officers for the taxable year (other than the chief executive officer); and
3. Individuals subject to Section 16(a) of the Securities Exchange Act of 1934.

An applicable covered employee includes any:

1. Covered employee of a plan sponsor;
2. Covered employee of a member of a controlled group which includes the plan sponsor; and
3. Former employee who was a covered employee at the time of termination of employment with the plan sponsor or a member of a controlled group that includes the plan sponsor.

A nonqualified deferred compensation plan is any plan that provides for the deferral of compensation other than a qualified employer plan or any bona fide vacation leave, sick leave, compensatory time, disability pay, or death benefit plan.

Any subsequent increases in the value of, or any earnings with respect to, transferred or restricted assets are treated as additional transfers of property. Interest at the underpayment rate plus one percentage point is imposed on the underpayments that would have occurred had the amounts been includible in income for the taxable year in which first deferred or, if later, the first taxable year not subject to a substantial risk of forfeiture. The amount required to be included in income is also subject to an additional 20 percent tax.

If an employer provides directly or indirectly for the payment of any federal, state, or local income taxes with respect to any compensation required to be included in income under the provision, interest is imposed on the amount of such payment in the same manner as if the payment were part of the deferred compensation to which it related. As under present law, such payment is included in income. In addition, such payment is subject to a 20 percent additional tax. The payment is also nondeductible by the employer. [PPA § 116; I.R.C. § 409A(b)(3)]

Part 3

Plan Termination

Chapter 15

Plan Termination Issues

Terminating a retirement plan, whether it is a defined contribution or a defined benefit plan, can be an arduous process. This chapter reviews the technical and administrative requirements for plan terminations, other than multiemployer plan terminations. Because the processes differ quite dramatically, defined contribution plans are discussed separately from defined benefit plans. Chapter 16 discusses the Pension Benefit Guaranty Corporation (PBGC) requirements for covered defined benefit plans. Chapter 17 discusses the issues unique to underfunded terminating single or multiple employer plans. For a thorough guide to plan termination rules and procedures, including for multiemployer plans, see the *Plan Termination Answer Book, Fifth Edition*. [Bitzer; Wolters Kluwer Law & Business, 2014]

General Requirements 15-2
Defined Contribution Plans 15-4
204(h) Notice 15-6
Information Gathering 15-10
IRS Submission 15-12
Problem-Solving Options 15-20
Liquidating Plan Assets 15-21
Final Stages 15-22
Missing Participants 15-23
Final Disclosure Forms 15-26
Defined Benefit Plans 15-26
Measurement of Plan Liabilities 15-28
Insufficiency of Plan Assets in a Defined Benefit Plan 15-30
Actions of Plan Sponsor 15-31
204(h) Notice 15-32
Information Gathering 15-33
IRS Submission 15-34
Liquidating Plan Assets 15-36
Surplus Assets 15-37
Distribution of Election Forms 15-39
Final Disclosure Forms 15-43
Abandoned Defined Contribution (Orphan) Plans 15-43

General Requirements

Q 15:1 For what reasons may a plan sponsor consider the termination of its plan?

A plan sponsor may consider the termination of its plan for a number of reasons. One or more of the following may be reasons for considering the termination of the plan:

1. The plan is too costly to maintain;
2. The plan no longer meets the needs or expectations of the employer's changing workforce;
3. The plan cannot be converted into another type of plan, so the plan must be terminated and another type of plan must be established (e.g., the termination of a defined benefit plan and the establishment of a 401(k) plan);
4. The plan sponsor is in bankruptcy or is insolvent;
5. The plan sponsor has gone out of business;
6. The stock or assets of the company have been sold and neither the seller nor the buyer wishes to continue to maintain the plan after the sale;
7. The plan sponsor has been merged into another company and the surviving company does not want to continue to maintain the plan after the merger;
8. Changes in the law make the existing plan unnecessary;
9. The plan was maintained pursuant to a collective bargaining or other contractual agreement, and the union has been decertified or the contract has been terminated.

Although a plan sponsor may wish to terminate its plan, it is another matter to secure a favorable determination letter from the IRS. The plan sponsor may be putting the qualified status of its plan at risk if it does not comply with IRS requirements.

Q 15:2 Does the termination of a qualified plan affect its qualified status?

Termination or curtailment of a qualified pension, profit sharing, stock bonus, or annuity plan that is intended to meet the qualification requirements of Code Section 401(a) may affect its qualified status, depending on the facts and circumstances of the case. A *curtailment* of a plan consists of a modification reducing benefits or employer contributions or making the eligibility or vesting requirements less liberal. Principles that affect the determination of whether plan termination will create plan qualification issues include:

1. The existence of a valid business reason for the termination, consistent with the assumption that the plan, from its inception, has been a bona fide program for the exclusive benefit of employees in general and intended to be a permanent program; and

2. Compliance with the requirements of Code Section 401(a), not only at the time of the adoption of the plan, but also throughout its entire operation, inclusive of the plan termination.

[Rev. Rul. 69-24]

Although it is not required, a plan sponsor may choose to apply to the IRS for a determination of whether the termination adversely affects the plan's qualified status. The application is made on IRS Form 5310.

Q 15:3 What are the valid business reasons for terminating a plan?

Treasury Regulations Section 1.401-1(b)(2) provides that the term *plan* implies a permanent, as distinguished from a temporary, program. Thus, although the employer may reserve the right to change or terminate the plan, and to discontinue benefit accruals or contributions under the plan, the abandonment of the plan for any reason other than business necessity within a few years after it has taken effect may be considered evidence that the plan from its inception was not a bona fide program for the exclusive benefit of employees in general. [Treas. Reg. § 1.401-1(b)(2)]

If a plan has been in existence for more than 10 years, termination without a valid business reason has been held not to affect its qualification. [Treas. Reg. § 1.401-1(b)(2); Rev. Rul. 72-239; IRM § 7.12.1.2.5 (Jan. 1, 2003)]

If a plan is terminated within a few years after its adoption, there is a presumption that it was not intended as a permanent program from its inception. Unless business necessity required the termination, it may be concluded that the plan did not qualify from its inception. Generally to be considered valid, the business necessity for termination must have been unforeseen when the plan was adopted and not within the control of the employer. [Treas. Reg. § 1.401-1(b)(2); Rev. Rul. 69-25; IRM § 7.12.1.2.5 (Jan. 1, 2003)] Whatever the reason given for the termination of the plan, the facts and circumstances leading to its termination must indicate that the taxpayer intended that the plan be permanent. [IRM § 7.12.1.2.5 (Jan. 1, 2003)]

Bankruptcy, insolvency, or discontinuance of the business of the employer would ordinarily be considered as prima facie evidence of the type of business necessity that would justify the termination of the employer's plan. [IRM § 7.12.1.2.5 (Jan. 1, 2003)] Business necessity also includes other valid business reasons that significantly impair the attractiveness of a plan as a means of providing employee compensation. Other acceptable reasons for terminating a plan may, depending on the circumstances, include:

1. Substantial change in stock ownership;
2. Merger;
3. Substitution of another type of plan;
4. Financial inability to continue the plan;
5. Employee dissatisfaction with the plan; or
6. Substantial change in the law affecting retirement plans.

[IRM § 7.12.1.2.5 (Jan. 1, 2003)]

What constitutes a valid business reason for a plan termination depends on the facts and circumstances of the case. If a plan sponsor desires certainty as to the effect that plan termination or a plan amendment resulting in curtailment of a plan will have on the plan's qualified status under Code Section 401(a), it should apply for an IRS favorable determination letter (see Q 15:18) and be prepared to explain why the termination or curtailment is taking place. [Rev. Ruls. 69-24, 69-25]

Q 15:4 Should every plan sponsor request a ruling from the IRS that the termination of the plan meets the qualification requirements of the Code?

While it is not a requirement that a plan sponsor seek a favorable determination letter upon plan termination, it is highly recommended. By requesting a favorable determination letter, the plan sponsor is asking the IRS to rule on whether the plan meets the qualification requirements at the time of termination. One of the major qualification requirements for any retirement plan is that the plan be a permanent, not temporary, program. A favorable determination letter assures the plan sponsor that the plan has met the qualification requirements, including the permanency requirement, even if a remedial amendment period has not expired. [Rev. Procs. 2015-6, 2016-6, 2017-4, 2018-4]

Q 15:5 Must a terminated plan be amended in order to comply with all applicable qualification requirements that are in effect on the date of plan termination?

Yes, the plan document must be amended to comply with all applicable qualification requirements that are in effect on the date of plan termination. [Rev. Procs. 2015-6, 2016-6, 2017-4, 2018-4]

> **Example 15-1:** The 401(k) plan of ABC Consulting was terminated as of June 30, 2018. Even though the plan has been timely restated and amended, the employer must amend the plan to comply with all qualification requirements in effect on June 30, 2018, even though adoption of these amendments may not yet be required as of June 30, 2018, for ongoing plans.

Defined Contribution Plans

Q 15:6 What procedural steps are necessary to terminate a defined contribution plan?

Terminating a defined contribution plan generally includes the following steps:

1. A resolution terminating the plan is adopted by the plan sponsor. The plan sponsor may also adopt an amendment that brings the plan document up to date with all applicable law changes through the date of termination and that formalizes the termination itself.

2. Participants are notified of the plan termination.
3. Information is collected, including employee census, plan asset information, and insurance policy cash value information.
4. Notice is given to interested parties, informing them of the upcoming application for an IRS favorable determination letter, if applicable.
5. The plan termination information is submitted to the IRS for its review and approval, if a favorable determination letter is desired.
6. The IRS favorable determination letter is received, if applicable.
7. Benefit distribution election forms are furnished to participants and processed by the plan.
8. The plan assets are liquidated if they will not be distributed in kind.
9. Participants' account balances are updated to the date of distribution.
10. Benefits are distributed to participants according to their valid elections.
11. The final Form 5500 (or 5500-SF or 5500-EZ) is prepared and filed.
12. Income tax reporting on Forms 945 and 1099-R is completed.

Q 15:7 When must the plan sponsor adopt a resolution terminating a defined contribution plan?

If the plan is a profit sharing plan or other defined contribution plan not subject to the minimum funding standards, the resolution by the plan sponsor may be adopted at any time prior to the desired termination date. If the plan is a money purchase or target benefit plan, the plan cannot be terminated until accrual of contributions is ceased. A resolution must generally be adopted at least 45 days (or 15 days for a small plan) in advance of the cessation of contributions, with the termination date being the same date or later (see Q 15:9). Thus, the resolution not only should terminate the money purchase or target benefit plan, but should also state that no further benefits will accrue to participants, if this was not previously done. A timely accrual cessation notice must be given to participants as well (see Q 15:9). [ERISA § 204(h)]

Q 15:8 What liability does the plan sponsor have to contribute to a defined contribution plan in the year of termination?

The answer depends on the provisions in the terminating plan's document. For instance, if a profit sharing (including 401(k)) plan document has a 1,000-hour requirement and a last-day provision (requiring that participants be employed on the last day of the plan year to receive an allocation of all types of employer's contribution), it appears that the plan may generally be terminated at any time prior to the last day of the plan year without the plan sponsor incurring a liability for contributions (see Q 15:9). However, the IRS, in public pronouncements, has taken the position that a money purchase or target plan must cease accruals effective before any participant accrues the requisite number of hours and also provide affected participants with required 204(h) notice at least 45 (or 15 for a small plan) days before the cessation data in order to avoid all employer contributions.

> **Example 15-2:** ABC Consulting wants to terminate its money purchase plan but cannot afford to make the required 10 percent contribution for its plan year ending December 31, 2019. Although the plan has a 1,000-hour requirement and a last-day provision, ABC Consulting decides to terminate the plan on March 31, 2019 (before any participant accrues 1,000 hours), to ensure that they will not have a contribution requirement for the 2019 plan year. ABC Consulting delivers the 204(h) notice to affected participants by February 14, 2019, to permit the March 31, 2019, accrual cessation as well.

204(h) Notice

Q 15:9 Why is a notice required to inform participants of the cessation of benefit or contribution accruals?

The Employee Retirement Income Security Act (ERISA) requires that a defined benefit, money purchase, or target plan (not a profit sharing or stock bonus plan) may not be amended to provide for a significant reduction in the rate of future benefit or contribution accruals unless, after adoption of the plan amendment and within a defined time period (see Q 15:10) before the effective date of the plan amendment, the plan administrator provides a written notice (commonly called a 204(h) notice) setting forth the effect of the plan amendment and its effective date to:

1. Each affected participant in the plan;
2. Each affected beneficiary who is an alternate payee under a qualified domestic relations order (QDRO) (see chapter 3); and
3. Each employee organization representing participants in the plan.

[ERISA § 204(h)]

Employees who have not yet become participants in a plan at the time an amendment to the plan is adopted are not taken into account in applying ERISA Section 204(h) with respect to the amendment. [Treas. Reg. § 54.4980F-1, Q&A-10]

> **Example 15-3:** ABC Consulting has decided to terminate the ABC Consulting Money Purchase Plan. The plan covers salaried employees, as well as members of the Clerical Employees Local Union #59. ABC Consulting must provide the 204(h) notice described above to each participant in the plan and to the Clerical Employees Local Union #59, which represents the union employees covered by the plan.

Q 15:10 When must the 204(h) notice be provided?

Generally, the 204(h) notice must be provided at least 45 days before the effective date of the cessation of benefit or contribution accruals. In the case of a small plan, the 204(h) notice must be provided at least 15 days before the effective date of the cessation of benefit or contribution accruals. A small plan is defined as one that the plan administrator reasonably expects to have fewer than 100 participants who have an accrued benefit or account balance under the plan (on the effective date of the plan termination). In the case of a multiemployer plan, the 204(h) notice must be provided at least 15 days before the effective date of any ERISA Section 204(h) amendment. A multiemployer plan means a multiemployer plan as defined in Code Section 414(f).

The date the notice is considered to be issued depends on how it is delivered to the participant:

1. Hand delivery: The notice is considered provided on the date it is delivered.
2. First-class mail: The notice is considered provided as of the date of the U.S. Postal Service postmark stamped on the envelope.
3. Electronic method: The notice is considered provided either as of the date the electronic notice is sent or the date it is actually received by the participant, depending on the situation (see Q 15:12).

[Treas. Reg. § 54.4980F-1, Q&A-9, Q&A-13(a)]

Q 15:11 How is the 204(h) notice delivered to each participant?

A plan administrator (including a person acting on behalf of the plan administrator, such as the employer or plan trustee) must provide the 204(h) notice using a method reasonably calculated to ensure that the participant actually receives it. The 204(h) notice must be provided either as a paper document or in an electronic format that satisfies certain requirements (see Q 15:12). First-class mail to the last-known address of the participant is an acceptable delivery method. Likewise, hand delivery is acceptable. However, posting of the 204(h) notice is not permitted. The 204(h) notice may be enclosed with or combined with another notice. [Treas. Reg. § 54.4980F-1, Q&A-13]

Q 15:12 What are the requirements for delivering a 204(h) notice by electronic means?

General Rule. A 204(h) notice may be provided to a participant using an electronic method (other than an oral communication or a recording of an oral communication), provided that all of the following requirements are met:

1. Either the notice is actually received by the participant or the plan administrator takes appropriate and necessary measures reasonably calculated to ensure that the method for providing the 204(h) notice results in actual receipt by the participant.
2. The plan administrator provides the participant with a clear and conspicuous statement, in electronic or non-electronic form, that the participant has a right to request and obtain a paper copy of the 204(h) notice without charge.

3. The other requirements under the Treasury Regulations Section 54.4980F-1 are satisfied. For example, a 204(h) notice provided through an electronic method must be delivered on or before the date discussed in Q 15:10 and must satisfy the content requirements of Q 15:13.

If all of the requirements in the above general rule are met, the notice is considered received on the date it is sent. If all of the requirements are not met, the notice is considered received on the date the participant actually receives the notice.

Example 15-4: On July 1, 2018, Bernie, a plan administrator of the CDE Advisors' target plan, sends a notice intended to satisfy 204(h) to Dolly, an employee of the company and a participant in the plan. The notice is sent to Dolly's e-mail address on the company's electronic information system. Accessing the company's electronic information system is not an integral part of Dolly's duties. Bernie sends the e-mail with a request for a computer-generated notification that the message was received and opened. Bernie receives notification indicating that the e-mail was received and opened by Dolly on July 9, 2018. Although Bernie has failed to take appropriate and necessary measures reasonably calculated to ensure that the method for providing the 204(h) notice results in actual receipt of the notice, Bernie is deemed to have provided the notice on July 9, 2018, which is when Dolly actually receives the notice.

Safe harbor in case of consent. The notice requirements are deemed to be satisfied with respect to a participant if the 204(h) notice is provided electronically to a participant, and:

1. Prior to the notice being provided, the participant has affirmatively consented electronically, or confirmed consent electronically, in a manner that reasonably demonstrates the participant's ability to access the information in an electronic format and has not withdrawn such consent;
2. The participant has provided, if applicable, in electronic or non-electronic form, an address for the receipt of electronically furnished documents;
3. Prior to consenting, the participant has been provided, in electronic or non-electronic form, a clear and conspicuous statement indicating:
   a. That the consent can be withdrawn at any time without charge;
   b. The procedures for withdrawing consent and for updating the address or other information needed to contact the applicable individual;
   c. Any hardware and software requirements for accessing and retaining the documents; and
   d. The fact that the participant may request a paper copy of the 204(h) notice.
4. After consenting, if a change in hardware or software requirements needed to access or retain electronic records creates a material risk that the participant will be unable to access or retain the 204(h) notice:
   a. The applicable individual is provided with a statement of the revised hardware and software requirements for access to and retention of the 204(h) notice and is given the right to withdraw consent without the imposition of any fees for such withdrawal and without the imposition

of any condition or consequence that was not disclosed at the time of the initial consent; and

b. The requirement of paragraph 3 above is again complied with.

[Treas. Reg. § 54.4980F-1, Q&A-13]

Q 15:13 What are the contents of the 204(h) notice?

The contents of the 204(h) notice for a terminating plan should include the following information:

1. Name of the plan;
2. A description of the benefit or contribution formula;
3. A statement that after the date of cessation of benefit or contribution accruals no participant will earn any further benefits or contributions; and
4. The effective date of the amendment.

[Treas. Reg. § 54.4980F-1, Q&A-11]

Example 15-5: Maintaining the CDE Advisors' money purchase plan is becoming cost prohibitive. The president of CDE Advisors decides that he wants to stop making future contributions to the plan. He provides a letter on March 1, 2019, to each affected participant that satisfies the 204(h) notice content rules. The letter states: "CDE Advisors has decided to cease making contributions to CDE Advisors' Money Purchase Plan, effective as of April 30, 2019. Before contributions are ceased, the company will provide contributions equal to 10 percent of year-to-date compensation."

Q 15:14 When must notice of plan termination be provided?

Unlike the cessation of benefit and contribution accruals (see Q 15:9) for defined benefit, money purchase and target benefit plan rules, which requires an advance 204(h) participant notice, notice of plan termination can be provided at any time on or before the date of the plan termination. A plan termination date cannot precede the date benefits or contribution accruals have ceased in a defined benefit, money purchase, or target benefit plan. If benefits or contribution accruals are coincident with plan termination (which will occur whether specified or not in the termination amendment unless the cessation amendment properly occurred as of a prior date), the 204(h) notice timing requirements will apply for the plan termination amendment and a single combined notice that addresses both requirements may be provided.

Q 15:15 What are the consequences for failure to provide a 204(h) notice?

In the case of any egregious failure to meet the 204(h) notice requirements with respect to the amendment ceasing benefit or contribution accruals, the amendment is invalid, and the pre-amendment plan provisions are applied so that all participants are entitled to the benefits and contributions provided under the plan, ignoring the amendment. An egregious failure is defined as a failure to meet the notice requirements if:

1. The failure to provide the required notice is within the control of the plan sponsor, and
2. Is either an intentional failure or a failure, whether or not intentional, to provide most of the individuals with most of the information they are entitled to receive. For this purpose, an intentional failure includes any failure to promptly provide the required 204(h) notice or information after the plan administrator discovers an unintentional failure to meet the requirements.

If the failure to provide the 204(h) notice is not egregious, the amendment terminating the plan or freezing the benefit accruals or contributions is still effective with respect to all plan participants. However, affected plan participants who have not received the notice may still have recourse under ERISA Section 502. [Treas. Reg. § 54.4980F-1(b), Q&A-14(a)(2)]

There is a penalty for failure to provide a 204(h) notice. The penalty is $100 for each day in the noncompliance period with respect to any applicable individual. The *noncompliance period* is the period beginning on the first day of the failure and ending on the date the notice is given or the failure is otherwise corrected.

Applicable individuals are defined to include:

1. Each participant in the plan, and
2. Any beneficiary who is an alternate payee under an applicable QDRO:

whose rate of future benefit accrual or contributions under the plan may reasonably be expected to be significantly reduced by the termination of the plan.

The penalty will not apply where any person subject to liability did not know that the failure existed and exercised reasonable diligence to meet the notice requirements. Furthermore, a person who exercised reasonable diligence and provided the notice within a 30-day period beginning on the first date such person knew, or exercising reasonable diligence would have known that such failure existed, will not be subject to the penalty tax.

[Treas. Reg. § 54.4980F-1(b), Q&A-15(b)]

There is a cap on the penalty of $500,000 for persons who exercised reasonable diligence in attempting to provide the notice. The Secretary of the Treasury may waive part of or the entire penalty to the extent that the payment would be excessive or otherwise inequitable relative to the failure involved. [I.R.C. § 4980F(c)(3)]

Information Gathering

Q 15:16 What information is needed to administer the plan in the year of termination?

The information needed depends on the type of plan being terminated, the frequency of valuation, and use of life insurance contracts:

1. *401(k) plans*. It is necessary to collect information on elective contributions from the beginning of the plan year to the date of termination, as well as matching employer contributions and nonelective employer contributions. Compensation data is also needed for the entire plan year or for the period of participation. For example, if a calendar-year 401(k) plan terminates on June 30, 2019, and the definition of compensation provided in the plan is compensation earned while an employee is a participant, compensation from April 1, 2019, through June 30, 2019, would be needed for a participant who entered the plan on April 1, 2019.
2. *Discretionary profit sharing plans*. It may not be necessary to collect any compensation data if no profit sharing contribution is made. Because participants become 100 percent vested upon plan termination (see chapter 8), it is not necessary for vesting purposes to collect information on the hours worked during the plan year of termination. On the other hand, if the plan sponsor elects to make a profit sharing contribution for the year of termination or if there are forfeitures to be allocated, it is necessary to collect information required to determine the allocation of contributions and/or forfeitures.
3. *Money purchase or target plans*. To the extent that contributions are earned (see Q 15:8) or if there are forfeitures to be allocated, it is necessary to collect information required to determine the allocation of contributions and/or forfeitures.
4. *Frequency of valuation*. No special efforts are needed for defined contribution plans that are valued daily. However, a plan that is valued less frequently than daily must be updated from the last valuation date to the date of distribution (see Q 15:41).
5. *Individual insurance contracts*. Special care needs to be taken to properly handle individual insurance contracts. Although the plan sponsor clearly has authority to surrender such contracts, it may make sense from an employee relations standpoint to offer participants the opportunity to personally continue the life insurance protection through a distribution (see chapter 25).

Q 15:17 What other information should be reviewed or collected?

Of particular importance are the plan documents. The plan documents should be reviewed and amended as they are needed to ensure compliance with all applicable laws, regulations, and other applicable guidance.

The termination of a plan ends the plan's remedial amendment period and thus will generally shorten the remedial amendment cycle for the plan. Accordingly, any retroactive remedial plan amendments or other required plan amendments for a terminating plan must be adopted in connection with the plan termination (i.e., plan amendments required to be adopted to reflect qualification requirements that apply as of the date of termination regardless of whether such requirements are included on the most recently published Cumulative List).

It is always helpful to review the plan's compliance history for at least the last five to six years to spot problems before the plan is submitted to the IRS. If problems are discovered, the plan sponsor may be able to correct them using one of several IRS voluntary compliance programs (see chapter 23). These IRS programs should also be used as part of the termination process if the plan sponsor failed to adopt one or more required amendments.

[Rev. Procs. 2016-51, 2015-28, 2015-27, 2015-6, 2014-6, 2013-12, 2013-8, 2013-6, 2013-1, 2007-44, 2008-56, 2009-36, 2012-50; Notices 2009-97, 2010-77; Anns. 2012-3, 2011-82]

IRS Submission

Q 15:18 What is the purpose of submitting a terminating plan to the IRS to request a favorable determination letter?

It is valuable to request an IRS determination regarding the qualified status (under Section 401(a) or Section 403(a)) of a pension, profit sharing, or other deferred compensation plan upon plan termination in order to clearly protect the tax-sheltered status of the termination distributions and the deductibility of company contributions. After the IRS completes its review, if everything is satisfactory, the IRS will provide a letter (commonly referred to as a favorable determination letter or FDL) advising that it has determined that termination of the plan does not adversely affect the plan's qualification for federal tax purposes. If, during its review, the IRS finds problems, or thinks that changes should be made, the IRS will advise of its findings and of the changes needed. If an FDL is not obtained and the terminated plan is audited, it may be more difficult or expensive to make changes required by the IRS in order to protect the plan's qualification status. The plan must comply with all applicable qualification and documentation requirements, even if the remedial amendment period has not expired. [Rev. Procs. 2007-44, § 8, 2015-6, 2014-6, 2013-6, 2013-1]

> **Example 15-6:** The 401(k) plan of ABC Consulting was terminated as of June 30, 2018. Even though the remedial amendment period for existing required law changes had not yet expired for the plan, ABC Consulting must review their plan and amend the plan to comply with all qualification requirements not yet documented, that are in effect on June 30, 2018.

Q 15:19 What is the scope of a favorable determination letter?

A determination letter applies only to qualification requirements regarding the form of the qualified plan, not its operation. In addition, the applicant may request that the IRS review other non-form qualification requirements, including the following:

- That the formula is a non-design-based safe-harbor formula as defined in Code Section 1.401(a)(4)-2(b) or 1.401(a)(4)-3(b)
- That the applicable requirements of Code Sections 401(k) and 401(m) are satisfied

- Whether the employer is a member of an affiliated service group within the meaning of Code Section 414(m)
- Whether leased employees are deemed employees of the employer within the meaning of Code Section 414(n)

For example, a determination letter does not consider nondiscrimination requirements (other than non-design-based safe harbors), minimum coverage requirements, minimum participation requirements, whether actuarial assumptions are reasonable for funding purposes, or whether a specific contribution is deductible. The determination as to whether a retirement plan qualifies is made from the information in the written plan document and the supporting information submitted by the employer. Therefore, the determination letter may not be relied upon if:

1. There has been a misstatement or omission of material facts;
2. The facts subsequently developed are materially different from the facts on which the determination was made; or
3. There is a change in applicable law.

In addition, the determination letter applies only to the employer and its participants on whose behalf the determination letter was issued. A determination letter may include one or more caveats that affect the scope of reliance represented by the letter. [Rev. Procs. 2015-6, 2014-6, 2013-6, 2013-1; Anns. 2013-13, 2013-15, 2011-82]

Q 15:20 If the plan receives a favorable determination letter from the IRS on the plan termination, is the plan protected against future audits?

No, the IRS may audit the plan at any time prior to the expiration of the statute of limitations.

Example 15-7: ABC Advisors terminates its profit sharing plan effective January 1, 2019, and seeks a favorable determination letter from the IRS. The favorable letter is received on June 15, 2019. Later that year, in October 2019, ABC Advisors receives a letter from the IRS stating that it will be auditing the 2017 and 2018 plan years. ABC Advisors calls their ERISA pension consultants for help with the audit.

Q 15:21 What information needs to be submitted to the IRS for a favorable determination letter on the termination of the plan?

The following information is needed:

1. Form 8717, *User Fee for Employee Plan Determination Letter* and appropriate user fee (see Q 15:22);
2. Form 5310, *Application for Determination for Terminating Plan* with applicable information (see Qs 15:23, 15:24);
3. A copy of the plan document;

4. A copy of the latest determination letter from the IRS;
5. A copy of all amendments since the last determination letter;
6. A statement explaining how the amendments affect or change the plan or any other plan maintained by the employer;
7. A copy of the latest opinion letter for a standardized master or prototype plan, if applicable;
8. A copy of the latest opinion or advisory letter for a master or prototype plan or volume submitter plan on which the employer is entitled to rely, if applicable;
9. Copies of all records of all actions taken to terminate the plan;
10. Copy of any compliance statements or closing agreements made since the last determination letter.
11. Form 8905, *Certification of Intent to Adopt a Pre-Approved Plan*, if an employer intends to switch from the five-year remedial amendment cycle to the six-year remedial amendment cycle by meeting one of the eligibility requirements for the six-year remedial amendment cycle;
12. Form 6088, *Distributable Benefits from Employee Pension Benefit Plans*, if required with sample calculations; and
13. Form 2848, *Power of Attorney and Declaration of Representative*, if the representative appointed by the employer is an attorney, certified public accountant (CPA), enrolled agent, or enrolled actuary. Otherwise, Form 8821, *Tax Information Authorization*, should be used.

[Instructions to Form 5310, rev. Dec. 2013]

Q 15:22 What is Form 8717, and what is the applicable user fee for a request on a plan termination?

Form 8717, *User Fee for Employee Plan Determination Letter Request*, is the form used to transmit IRS user fees along with the determination letter application. The user fee is $2,300. [Form 8717, Sept. 2017, Rev. Proc. 2017-4]

Certain employers will receive an exemption from the user fee in requesting a determination letter on a plan termination, if the determination letter is requested within the first five years of the plan's existence or, if later, the end of the remedial amendment period that begins within the first five plan years.

An eligible employer is defined as an employer that had no more than 100 employees who received at least $5,000 in compensation from the employer for the preceding year. In addition, an eligible employer must have at least one employee who is a non-highly compensated employee and who is participating in the plan.

Employers that are exempt from the user fee should complete only the Certification line.

[Form 8717, Sept. 2017]

For multiple employer plans, the fee depends on the number of Forms 5310 submitted. Generally, one Form 5310 must be submitted for each employer maintaining the plan. The fee is $4,000, regardless of the number of participants.

[Form 8717, Sept. 2017, Rev. Proc. 2017-4]

Q 15:23 What information is provided on Form 5310?

Form 5310, *Application for Determination for Terminating Plan*, gives the reviewing agent a road map to determine whether qualification failures occurred in recent years. Form 5310 is a computer-read (optical character recognition) form and must either be typed or produced by software pre-approved by the IRS. Key questions contained on the form include:

Question Number	*Question*
3a	Is this a pre-approved plan (prototype or volume submitter)?
3c	Is this an individually designed plan?
3d	Has the plan received a favorable determination letter?
3e	Has the plan been amended since the last favorable letter was received?
4c	Will funds be, or have any funds been, returned to the employer?
8a	Have interested parties received the required notification (see Qs 15:32–15:34)?
14	Reason for the plan termination.
16a	Show a six-year history of participation in the plan, including the number of participants added and dropped during each plan year (used to determine whether a partial termination occurred).
17	Miscellaneous qualification questions.
18	Does the plan have any issues pending with the IRS, DOL, PBGC, a court, or under VCRP of EPCRS?
19	Show the employer contribution and forfeiture history for the current plan year and five prior years.
20	Indicate the form of distributions to be made after the plan is terminated (e.g., single sums, annuities, etc.).
21	Statement of net assets available to pay benefits.

[Form 5310, *Application for Determination for Terminating Plan*, and instructions, rev. Dec. 2013]

Q 15:24 Who is required to file Form 6088?

A plan sponsor or administrator of a defined benefit or an underfunded defined contribution plan (money purchase or target plan that has not met minimum funding requirements in any prior year) must file Form 6088. In addition, the plan sponsor or administrator of a collectively bargained underfunded defined contribution plan must file if the plan benefits employees who are not collectively bargained employees [Treas. Reg. § 1.410(b)-6(d)] or more than 2 percent of the employees covered by the plan are professional employees. [Treas. Reg. § 1.410(b)-9] A separate Form 6088 must be filed for each employer participating in a multiple employer defined benefit or underfunded multiple employer defined contribution plan as described in Code Section 413(c). [Instructions to Form 6088, rev. Mar. 2008]

Q 15:25 How is Form 6088 completed for an underfunded defined contribution plan?

The form requests the following items:

Column	*Information Required*
(a)	Name
(b)	HCE status (see Appendix G)
(c)	Not applicable.
(d)	Not applicable.
(e)	Compensation: Enter the participant's compensation for the current 12-month period. The current 12-month period can be the last calendar or plan year ending on or before the plan termination date. For participants who are no longer employed as of the date of plan termination, compensation is the compensation received for the applicable period immediately before the earlier of retirement or separation from employment.
(f)	Not applicable.
(g)(1)	Enter the total assets distributable to each participant attributable to mandatory and voluntary employee contributions and rollover contributions.
(g)(2)	Not applicable.
(g)(3)	Enter the total assets distributable to each participant attributable to employer contributions, including elective deferrals to a 401(k) plan and matching contributions.
(h)	Enter the account balance of each participant.

Q 15:26 What is the purpose of Form 2848?

Form 2848, *Power of Attorney and Declaration of Representative*, is used by the plan sponsor to designate a third party to represent the plan sponsor in the determination letter request to the IRS. Representatives will generally include only attorneys, CPAs, enrolled agents, enrolled retirement plan agents, and enrolled actuaries. Form 2848 is used to notify the IRS that an individual who is licensed to practice before the IRS will be representing a given taxpayer. Individuals who are licensed to practice before the IRS include attorneys, CPAs, enrolled agents, enrolled retirement plan agents, and enrolled actuaries.

Other practitioners, called "unenrolled individuals," can represent taxpayers only in relation to returns that the unenrolled individual prepared and only under limited circumstances. In particular, unenrolled preparers are never able to represent taxpayers in appeals, collection, or functions other than examination on the return they prepared. (There are exceptions to these limitations if the unenrolled preparer has a special relationship with the taxpayer, such as a family member of an individual, an officer, partner, or employee of a corporation, or a fiduciary of a trust or individual.)

The IRS considers "practice before the IRS" to be:

- Communicating with the IRS for a taxpayer regarding the taxpayer's rights, privileges, or liabilities under laws and regulations administered by the IRS;
- Representing the taxpayer at conferences, hearings, or meetings with the IRS; or
- Preparing and filing necessary documents with the IRS for a taxpayer.

Filing a tax return, furnishing information to the IRS upon its request, or appearing as a witness are not considered to constitute "practice before the IRS."

Historically, when the IRS received a Form 2848 from an unenrolled preparer for a purpose for which he or she was not qualified, it would be treated as if it were a Form 8821. Form 8821, contrary to popular belief, is not an authorization for representation by an unenrolled preparer. It is simply an authorization to permit the IRS to furnish information to the unenrolled preparer.

[Instructions to Form 2848, rev. July 2018]

Q 15:27 What additional information might the IRS request before issuing a favorable determination letter on the qualified status of the terminating plan?

The IRS examiner of the terminating plan generally looks at operational issues. Of particular importance are compliance with the minimum coverage rules of Code Section 410(b), the maximum contribution limits of Code Section 415, the top-heavy requirements of Code Section 416, participant loans, and hardship withdrawals (only in a profit sharing or 401(k) plan). In addition, historical demographic information is reviewed in determining whether a partial termination or curtailment occurred in past years, resulting in greater vested amounts for previously terminated employees (see chapter 8).

Q 15:28 How long does it take to receive a favorable determination letter from the IRS on a plan termination?

The IRS has 270 days to review the plan and issue its findings. Depending on its workload, the processing period may be shorter. [I.R.C. § 7476(b)(3)]

Q 15:29 Must the participants in the plan be notified of the request for a determination letter on the termination of the plan?

Yes, a notice to interested parties must be provided. The purpose of the notice is to inform interested parties of their right to:

1. Receive notice that an application for an advance determination will be filed about the qualification of plans described in Code Section 401;
2. Submit written comments about the qualification of the plans to the IRS;
3. Request the U.S. Department of Labor (DOL) to submit a comment to the IRS on behalf of the interested parties; and
4. Submit written comments to the IRS on matters about which the DOL was requested to comment but declined.

[Rev. Proc. 2018-4, §§ 17, 18]

Q 15:30 Who are *interested parties*?

Interested parties for purposes of plan termination are generally all employees eligible for the plan, including retirees receiving benefit payments from the plan, vested terminated employees who have not yet received their entire vested accrual benefits under the plan, and beneficiaries of deceased former employees currently receiving benefits under the plan. [Treas. Reg. § 1.7476-1(b)(5)]

Q 15:31 When must the notice to interested parties be provided?

The notice must be given not less than 10 days and not more than 24 days before the request is filed. [Treas. Reg. § 1.7476-1; Rev. Procs. 2015-6, 2016-6, 2017-4, 2018-4]

Q 15:32 What are the contents of the notice to interested parties?

The notice to interested parties must contain this information:

1. A brief description identifying the class or classes of interested parties to whom the notice is addressed (e.g., all present employees of the employer and all present employees eligible to participate);
2. The name of the plan, the plan identification number, and the name of the plan administrator; and
3. The name and taxpayer identification number of the applicant for a determination;
4. A statement that an application for a determination on the qualified status of the plan is to be made to the IRS and that it applies to a plan termination, or a partial termination, and the address of the IRS;
5. A description of the class of employees eligible to participate in the plan;
6. A statement of whether or not the IRS has issued a previous determination about the qualified status of the plan;

7. A statement that any person to whom the notice is addressed is entitled to submit, or request the DOL to submit, to the IRS Key District Director, a comment on the question of whether the plan meets the qualification requirements of Code Section 401(a); that two or more individuals may join in a single comment or request; that if those individuals request the DOL to submit a comment but the DOL declines to do so on one or more matters raised in the request, those individuals may still submit a comment to the IRS Key District Director on the matters about which the DOL declined to comment (the PBGC may also submit comments); and that in every instance when there is a final adverse termination or a distress termination, the IRS will formally notify the PBGC for comments;
8. The specific dates by which a comment to the IRS Key District Director or a request to the DOL must be received to preserve the right of comment;
9. The number of interested parties needed for the DOL to comment; and
10. A description of a reasonable procedure for interested parties to obtain additional information.

The following documents must be available to all interested parties:

1. An updated copy of the plan and the related trust agreement (if any); and
2. The application for determination.

[Rev. Proc. 2018-4, § 18]

Q 15:33 Must any additional information be provided to interested parties?

If there are fewer than 26 participants in the plan, a document containing the following information may be made available to interested parties in lieu of item 10 in Q 15:32:

1. A description of the plan's requirements respecting eligibility for participation and benefits and the plan's benefit formula;
2. A description of the provisions providing for nonforfeitable benefits;
3. A description of the circumstances that may result in ineligibility or denial or loss of benefits;
4. A description of the source of financing of the plan and the identity of any organization through which benefits are provided;
5. A description of any optional forms of benefits described in Code Section 411(d)(6) that have been reduced or eliminated by plan amendment (see chapter 10); and
6. Any coverage schedule or other demonstration submitted with Form 5310 to show that the plan meets the requirements of Code Sections 401(a)(4) and 410(b).

[Rev. Proc. 2018-4, § 18]

Problem-Solving Options

Q 15:34 What happens if operational errors or qualification defects are discovered by the IRS in the process of reviewing a plan submitted for a favorable determination letter?

Depending upon the error or defect, the plan sponsor or administrator may want to first attempt to persuade the examining agent that such error or defect can be corrected under the self-correction program (SCP) (see Qs 15:36, 15:37). None of the voluntary correction programs (VCPs) are available to a plan sponsor once the plan has been submitted to the IRS (see chapter 23 for a detailed discussion of these programs). [Rev. Proc. 2013-12, as modified by Rev. Procs. 2015-27, 2015-28, and 2016-51]

Q 15:35 When may a plan sponsor invoke SCP if the plan is currently being reviewed by the IRS?

A plan under audit is entitled to make self-correction of operational failures under SCP if the plan had procedures in place to avoid the failures and if the failures are deemed to be insignificant. The factors to be considered in determining whether or not an operational failure under a plan is insignificant include, but are not limited to:

1. Whether other failures occurred during the period being examined (for this purpose, a failure is not considered to have occurred more than once merely because more than one participant is affected by the failure);
2. The percentage of plan assets and contributions involved in the failure;
3. The number of years the failure occurred;
4. The number of participants affected relative to the total number of participants in the plan;
5. The number of participants affected as a result of the failure relative to the number of participants who could have been affected by the failure;
6. Whether correction was made within a reasonable time after discovery of the failure; and
7. The reason for the failure (e.g., data errors such as errors in the transcription of data, the transposition of numbers, or minor arithmetic errors).

No single factor is determinative. Factors 2, 4, and 5 should not be interpreted to exclude small businesses. [Rev. Proc. 2013-12, § 8]

Q 15:36 May SCP be invoked for significant operational failure after a plan is submitted to the IRS?

No. The correction period for significant operational failure ends on the first date the plan or plan sponsor is under examination. However, if the plan sponsor recognized the significant operational failure before the plan was submitted to the IRS and had started to correct the failure, the operational failure is deemed to be corrected by the time the plan is submitted if either paragraph (1) or (2) below is satisfied:

1. Before the plan is submitted, the plan sponsor is reasonably prompt in identifying the operational failure, formulating a correction method, and initiating correction in a manner that demonstrates a commitment to completing correction of the operational failure as expeditiously as practicable, and the plan sponsor completes correction of the operational failure within 120 days after the plan is submitted.
2. Before the plan is submitted, correction is completed with respect to 65 percent of all participants affected by the operational failure, and the plan sponsor completes correction of the operational failure with respect to the remaining affected participants in a diligent manner thereafter.

[Rev. Proc. 2013-12, § 9]

Example 15-8: CDE Advisors' 401(k) plan is terminated on September 15, 2018. Before the plan is submitted to the IRS, Jean discovers that the ADP test was not satisfied for the plan year ended December 31, 2016. Jean, with the help of her new service provider, identifies the amount of the qualified nonelective contributions (QNECs) necessary to assure passage of the ADP test for the December 31, 2016, plan year. On November 1, 2018, the plan is submitted to the IRS for a favorable determination letter. If corrections are completed on or before March 1, 2019, Jean should be able to invoke SCP.

Q 15:37 What alternatives are available to a plan sponsor that is not eligible for SCP?

Audit CAP is an audit correction program available for all types of disqualifying defects (plan document defects, operational defects, and demographic defects) found on IRS examination. The sanction amounts are discussed in chapter 23. [Rev. Proc. 2013-12, as modified by Rev. Procs. 2015-27, 2015-28 Part VI, and 2016-51]

Liquidating Plan Assets

Q 15:38 What is involved in the liquidation of plan assets?

The liquidation of plan assets could be a time-consuming process, depending on the types of assets in the plan. It is also possible to distribute assets in kind if the plan provides (see chapter 25). If the plan assets are invested in marketable securities such as common stocks or mutual funds, the liquidation process may take a week or less. If some of the plan assets are invested in life insurance contracts or guaranteed investment contracts (GICs) with insurance companies, the liquidation process could be significantly longer. Some of the contracts may have significant penalties for early withdrawals. If the assets are not readily marketable (that is, limited partnerships, real estate, or closely held employer stock), the plan sponsor may have to find a willing buyer.

Q 15:39 When should the liquidation process be started?

In general, an investment advisor should be consulted before the liquidation of assets is needed so that cash is available as of the expected distribution date (except for assets being distributed in kind). Assets that are not readily marketable will generally take longer to liquidate, so additional liquidation time should be anticipated.

Final Stages

Q 15:40 How are account balances in a defined contribution plan updated from the last valuation date?

The plan document describes the method for allocating earnings. Generally, the earnings (gains or losses) are allocated on a pro rata basis to all participants' accounts in the plan, or if the plan uses unit or daily accounting, the value of the units on the liquidation date becomes the updated account balance.

Example 15-9: CDE Advisors terminates its profit sharing plan and liquidates assets totaling $115,000 as of April 1, 2019. The profit sharing plan document provides that earnings are allocated annually on a pro rata basis, using the account balance as of the beginning of the year. The account balances as of December 31, 2018, totaled $100,000. Earnings of $15,000 are allocated, and the account balances are updated as follows:

Name	*December 31, 2018, Account Balance*	*Allocation of Earnings*	*April 1, 2019, Account Balance*
Liz	$ 70,000	$10,500	$ 80,500
Lee	$ 30,000	$ 4,500	$ 34,500
Totals	$100,000	$15,000	$115,000

Q 15:41 What benefit election forms and notices must be distributed and executed?

The following election forms are discussed in detail later in this chapter and include:

- Form of Benefit Election
- Waiver of Joint and Survivor Annuity and Spousal Consent, if applicable
- Tax Notice and Withholding Election
- Life Insurance Election Form, if applicable

When the forms are completed and properly executed, distributions may be made to the participants, or direct transfers may be made to the participant's IRA or other qualified plan (see Qs 15:76–15:84; chapter 21).

Missing Participants

Q 15:42 Does a fiduciary of an ERISA plan have a duty to try to locate lost or missing participants to whom benefits or account balances are payable from the plan?

Yes. Under ERISA, plan administrators and other fiduciaries have the following general duties:

- To protect the plan's benefits for participants and beneficiaries
- To discharge his or her duties with respect to a plan solely in the interest of its participants and beneficiaries and for the exclusive purpose of providing benefits to them
- To discharge his or her duties with the care, skill, prudence, and diligence that a prudent person acting in a like capacity and familiar with such matters would use in the conduct of an enterprise of a like character and like aims, and
- To discharge his or her duties in accordance with the documents and instruments governing the plan insofar as they are consistent with the provisions of Title I and Title IV of ERISA

[ERISA § 404]

In addition, ERISA Section 404(d) contains specific fiduciary requirements in the case of plan termination, including carrying out all duties in relation to the payment of benefits, the reversion of assets, transferring assets to a qualified replacement plan, and increasing benefits to participants.

How the plan administrator or other fiduciary discharges his or her fiduciary duties under ERISA with respect to lost or missing participants and beneficiaries is not directly addressed by ERISA. The DOL, however, has provided guidance on what a fiduciary should do to locate a missing participant on plan termination in DOL Field Assistance Bulletin 2004-02. The DOL indicated that the following steps are mandatory in order for a fiduciary to fulfill its ERISA duties:

- Send a letter to the last known mailing address by certified mail
- Review records of other benefit plans (such as the health plan) to determine whether there is an updated address
- Check with the designated beneficiary as to the participant's whereabouts
- Utilize the Social Security letter-forwarding program

The DOL guidance also encourages the fiduciary to take further action where warranted (such as the use of Internet search tools, a private locator service, or credit reporting agencies). If the cost of the search is to be charged to the participant's account, the size of the account in relation to the cost of these additional services should be considered.

PBGC-covered plans can also consider the PBGC missing participant program. The Pension Protection Act of 2006 (PPA) expanded the PBGC missing participant program to also include non-PBGC-covered plans and the regulations required to implement the expanded program are applicable to plan terminations after January 1, 2018.

Q 15:43 What is the IRS Letter-Forwarding Program?

The IRS Letter-Forwarding Program was established under Revenue Procedure 94-22, which is superseded by Revenue Procedure 2012-35. Effective August 31, 2012, and because several alternatives now exist, this program is no longer available to locate a missing taxpayer who may be entitled to a retirement plan payment.

[Rev. Proc. 2013-12, as modified by Rev. Procs. 2015-27, 2015-28, and 2016-51, Rev. Proc. 2012-35]

Q 15:44 What is the Social Security Administration (SSA) Letter-Forwarding Program?

The Social Security Administration (SSA) Letter-Forwarding Program was similar to the prior IRS Letter-Forwarding Program (see Q 15:43). The SSA discontinued its letter-forwarding program in May 2014.

Q 15:45 What is a private locator service?

A private (or commercial) locator service is another resource available to plan administrators that need to find missing participants in order to pay them their plan benefits. These services are called *private locator services* or *commercial locator services* to distinguish them from the locator services and letter-forwarding programs provided by federal governmental agencies, such as the PBGC missing participants program (see Q 15:47; chapter 16) and the former letter-forwarding programs of the IRS and SSA (see Qs 15:43 and 15:44). Using a private locator service can ease the plan administrator's burden of trying to find missing participants who are owed benefits from a plan. It is important to note that one of the requirements for using the PBGC missing participants program is that plan administrators that used private locator services may not charge the missing participant for the cost of using the private locator service or reduce the participant's plan benefits to compensate for any charges. [PBGC Reg. § 4050.4(b)(3)] The cost of using a private locator service or any other investigative service is considered an operating expense of the plan.

Private locator services, according to the PBGC, are "cost-effective, timely and thorough." [Preamble to PBGC Reg. Pt. 4050, 60 Fed. Reg. 61740] By contrast, according to the PBGC, the SSA program simply forwarded letters, and a missing participant who received a letter may or may not contact the plan. Furthermore, SSA letter-forwarding times varied, and the forwarding area may in some cases be limited to one region of the country. [Preamble to PBGC Reg. Pt. 4050, 60 Fed. Reg. 61740]

There are many private locator services from which a plan administrator may choose. Private locator services are listed under such headings or search words as *missing persons, locators, or finding and searching*. Companies that operate private locator services as a sideline to their regular business are usually listed under headings such as *private investigators, detectives*, or *investigators*. Unlike the former SSA Letter-Forwarding Program, a private locator service will confirm to the plan administrator whether or not the missing participant has been found (or is deceased) and will confirm his or her address. The private locator service's primary search tool is a comprehensive computer search. Typically, such a search is all that is needed to find a missing participant or confirm that he or she is deceased. The cost of using a private locator service varies by the scope of the computer search and the quality of the information that the plan administrator provides to the private locator service. The cost of using a private locator service can often be outweighed by the advantages of the results it produces: paying plan benefits to missing participants, cleaning up plan records, not having to pay PBGC per participant premiums in terminating plans or for deceased participants, eliminating concerns over fraudulent uses of benefit checks that were unknowingly sent to deceased participants, and avoiding escheat of participant benefits to the state. Private locator services compile their computer databases from many sources, including state and other government records (e.g., birth certificates, death certificates, marriage licenses, divorce records, motor vehicle department registrations, property records, voter registration lists, and court records), as well as telephone company listings, credit checks, liens, and state limited partnership and corporation filings.

Q 15:46 Are there any Internet resources available to plan administrators trying to locate missing participants?

Yes. Use of Internet resources, however, will not satisfy the PBGC's requirement that the plan administrator use a private locator service before availing itself of the PBGC's missing participant program (see Q 15:47; chapter 16). The plan administrator must assess the cost of using an Internet resource and evaluate the quality of the data available on the Internet before using such a resource to locate missing participants.

Q 15:47 What is the PBGC's missing participant program applicable to defined contribution plans?

The PBGC's missing participant program (see Q 16:54) was extended to terminated defined contribution plans. The administrators of these plans are not required to participate in the missing participant program, but would have the option to do so. Such transfers are now available for plan terminations after January 1, 2018. If benefits are transferred to the PBGC and the missing participant is located, then the PBGC shall transfer to the participant or beneficiary:

1. A single sum plus interest from the date of PBGC's receipt of the funds, or
2. Another form of benefit as is specified in PBGC regulations.

[PPA § 410; ERISA § 4050(d)]

Example 15-10: ABC Consulting terminates its profit sharing plan and distributes assets to all participants, with the exception of a former employee, Kathy, who cannot be located. Assuming that the PBGC has issued regulations, the plan administrator pays Kathy's account balance to the PBGC. The PBGC will then conduct and search for Kathy and pay her account balance plus interest when it locates Kathy.

Q 15:48 May unclaimed benefits escheat to the state in which the plan sponsor is located?

No, the DOL has long expressed the opinion that state escheat laws that treat assets of an ERISA-covered plan as unclaimed property are preempted by ERISA Section 514(a). [ERISA Op. Letter 79-30A (May 14, 1979); 94-41A (Dec. 7, 1994)] The Seventh Circuit held, in *Commonwealth Edison Co. et al. v. Sarah D. Vega*, that ERISA preempts an Illinois law that requires pension plans to transfer to the state any benefits payable that are not claimed by a plan beneficiary within five years. [174 F.3d 870, 22 Emp. Benefits Cas. (BNA) 2794 (7th Cir. 1999)]

Final Disclosure Forms

Q 15:49 When is the final 5500 form due?

Form 5500, Form 5500-SF, or 5500-EZ is used. The form is due on the last day of the seventh month following the date all assets were distributed. A 2½-month extension may be obtained by timely filing Form 5558 with the IRS.

Example 15-11: ABC Consulting terminates its 401(k) plan and distributes all assets to participants on August 3, 2018. Form 5500 is due on or before March 31, 2019, the last day of the seventh month following the distribution of assets. If ABC Consulting seeks an extension, they have until June 15, 2019, to file Form 5500.

Q 15:50 How are the distributions to participants reported?

Form 1099-R is used to report distributions to participants. Form 1099-R must be provided to participants by January 31 in the calendar year following the calendar year of distribution. The plan reports income tax withholding on Form 945, which is also due by January 31 in the calendar year following the calendar year of distribution. (See chapter 27 for a detailed discussion of distribution reporting.)

Defined Benefit Plans

Q 15:51 What are the steps involved in a defined benefit plan termination?

The termination of a defined benefit plan *not covered* by the PBGC generally involves the following steps (see chapter 16 for a discussion of the PBGC process):

1. The plan determines whether the plan, in fact, may be terminated.
2. A resolution terminating the plan, including the cessation of benefit accruals, is adopted by the plan sponsor. The plan sponsor may also adopt an amendment that brings the plan document up to date with all applicable law changes through the date of termination and that formalizes the termination itself.
3. Participants are notified of the plan termination.
4. Information is collected—employee census, plan asset information, and insurance policy cash value.
5. Notice is given to interested parties, informing them of the upcoming application to IRS requesting a favorable determination letter, if applicable.
6. The plan termination information is submitted to the IRS for its review and approval, if a determination letter is desired.
7. The IRS favorable determination letter is received, if applicable.
8. The plan assets are liquidated.
9. The accrued benefits are calculated as of the date benefits ceased to accrue, and optional forms of payment are calculated as of the expected date of distribution.
10. If assets are insufficient to pay all benefits, the assets are allocated pursuant to the plan terms.
11. If assets exceed the amount needed to pay benefits and the excess is to be allocated to participants, such allocation is done.
12. Benefit distribution election forms are furnished to participants, returned, and processed by the plan.
13. Benefits are distributed to the participants.
14. If assets exceed the amount needed to pay benefits and the excess is to be reverted to the employer, such reversion is done and/or excess assets are transferred to a qualified replacement plan.
15. The final Form 5500, 5500-SF or 5500-EZ is prepared and filed with the Employee Benefits Security Administration (EBSA).
16. Income tax reporting to participants and the IRS on Form 1099-R and Form 945 is completed.

Q 15:52 What determines whether a defined benefit plan may be terminated?

Generally speaking, plan assets must be sufficient to cover plan liabilities. (Plan liabilities are measured on a termination basis, using factors in the plan document and Code Section 417(e) (see Qs 15:53–15:55).) In certain cases, an underfunded plan may still be terminated. (See chapter 17 for a discussion of underfunded plans.) If the plan is covered by the PBGC, the plan must qualify as a standard termination or a distress termination in order to be terminated. In some cases, the PBGC may take over the plan in an involuntary termination. (See chapter 16 for a discussion of PBGC termination procedures.)

Measurement of Plan Liabilities

Q 15:53 How are plan liabilities measured?

Generally speaking, plan liabilities are equal to the present value of the accrued benefit of all participants as of the date of termination (chapter 9 discusses the determination of the accrued benefit in a defined benefit plan). The present value of accrued benefits (PVAB) is computed by applying the actuarial equivalence factors contained in the plan document. The factors are limited to pre- and post-retirement interest and mortality assumptions. (Note that there is a floor on the single-sum actuarial equivalent of the accrued benefit as established by Code Section 417(e).)

Q 15:54 What are the rates for terminating plans?

Mandatory interest and mortality rates are imposed. Notice 2008-85 provides the static mortality tables that applicable pension plans will use to calculate their minimum funding obligations for 2009 through 2013 plan years. The Notice also includes a modified "unisex" version of the mortality tables to be used for calculating lump-sum distributions during that same period. The unisex mortality tables are shown in Appendix F. [Notice 2008-85] The mortality tables for 2014 and 2015 are also included in Appendix F as they appeared in Notice 2013-49 along with the mortality table for 2016 from Notice 2015-53, the 2017 mortality table as it appears in Notice 2016-50 and the 2018 mortality table from Notice 2017-60.

For plan terminations occurring in plan years beginning before 2008, the mandatory mortality table is the 1994 Group Annuity Reserving Table, as shown in Appendix F. The mandatory interest rate is the rate on 30-year Treasury securities, adjusted monthly. The applicable rates are shown in Appendix C.

The Code Section 417(e) three-segment rate set, with a phase-in of 20 percent a year from 2008 through 2011, contains the applicable interest rates for terminating plans. Note that Moving Ahead for Progress in the 21st Century Act (MAP-21) and Highway and Transportation Funding Act of 2014 (HATFA) did not change Code Section 417(e) rates.

The minimum lump-sum value is calculated using the first, second, and third segment rates for the month before the date of distribution or such other time as prescribed by Treasury regulations. The adjusted first, second, and third segment rates are derived from a corporate bond yield curve prescribed by the Secretary of the Treasury for such month that reflects the yields on investment grade corporate bonds with varying maturities (rather than a 24-month average, as under the minimum funding rules). Thus, the interest rate that applies depends on how many years in the future a participant's annuity payments will be made. Typically, a higher interest applies for payments made further out in the future.

A transition rule applies for distributions in 2008 through 2011. For distributions in 2008 through 2011, minimum lump-sum values are determined as the weighted average of two values:

1. The value of the lump sum determined under the methodology under pre-2008 law (the "old" methodology); and
2. The value of the lump sum determined using the methodology applicable for 2008 and thereafter (the "new" methodology).

For distributions in 2008–2012 plan years, the weighting factor is shown in the table below:

Plan Years Beginning in	*"Old" Methodology Weighting*	*"New" Methodology Weighting*
2008	80%	20%
2009	60%	40%
2010	40%	60%
2011	20%	80%
2012 or after	0%	100%

In December 2008, the PBGC issued Technical Update 08-4, Minimum Lump-Sum Assumptions for Single-Employer Plans That Terminate in a Plan Year Beginning on or After January 1, 2008. The Technical Update takes the position that the termination date, not the distribution date, determines which set of rules legally governs the calculation of minimum values. The minimum value of a participant's accrued benefit is calculated by applying plan provisions that reflect the law in effect on the plan's termination date, but the actual assumptions to be used are determined by reference to the date of distribution.

[PPA § 302; ERISA § 205(g)(3); I.R.C. § 417(e)(3); Treas. Reg. § 1.417(e)-1]

Example 15-12: CDE Consulting's defined benefit plan (with a calendar plan year) has a termination date of July 1, 2018. The plan has a two-month look-back and the plan year as the stability period. The plan is ready to make distributions in 2019. The lump sums paid in 2019 are calculated based on applicable mortality table for 2019 and the November 2018 rates. Accordingly, a lump sum paid in 2019 would be determined using 100 percent of the November 2018 segment rates, since the phase-in has ended.

Q 15:55 How are the interest rates determined?

The regulations permit selection of a monthly, quarterly, or annual period during which the applicable interest rate remains constant. Permitting selection of a quarterly or annual period allows plans to offer greater benefit stability than is provided by the statutory rule, under which the applicable interest rate changes monthly. The regulations provide that the applicable interest rate for the stability period may be determined as the interest rate for any one of the five calendar months preceding the first day of the stability period. Permitting this "lookback" of up to five months provides added flexibility and gives plan administrators and participants more time to comply with applicable notice and election requirements (see chapter 11) using the actual interest rate rather than an estimate. Thus, a plan may change the applicable interest rate monthly, quarterly, or annually, and may determine the rate with reference to one of the five months preceding the month, quarter, or year. [Treas. Reg. § 1.417(e)-1(d)(4)]

Example 15-13: CDE Advisors sponsors a defined benefit plan with a calendar-year plan and uses the same interest rate for all distributions in the plan year. The plan provides that the applicable interest rate for the entire plan year is the interest rates specified by the Commissioner for the prior August (i.e., five calendar months before January 1, the first day of the plan year).

Q 15:56 Can the look-back period or the stability period for the determination of interest rates be changed?

Yes. However, for a one-year period starting with the effective date of the amendment, the present value must be determined by using the greater of:

1. The present value determined using the interest rate determined before such amendment; or
2. The present value determined using the interest rate determined after such amendment.

[Treas. Reg. § 1.417(e)-1(d)(10)(ii)]

Example 15-14: CDE Advisors' defined benefit plan uses a one-month stability period and a one-month lookback for the determination of interest rates under Code Section 417(e). CDE Advisors desires to make a change, effective January 1, 2019, to use an annual stability period. For any distribution during the 2019 plan year (January 1, 2019, to December 31, 2019), the present value is determined by using the greater of:

1. The interest rate in effect for the month immediately preceding the month of the distribution, or
2. The interest rate in effect for December 2018.

Insufficiency of Plan Assets in a Defined Benefit Plan

Q 15:57 What happens if the plan assets are not sufficient to satisfy the plan liabilities?

The plan sponsor's options if plan assets are insufficient include:

1. Make a contribution in an amount equal to the unfunded portion of the liability.
2. Continue the plan and continue making contributions to make the plan sufficient. In most cases, it is desirable to cease future benefit accruals so that the liabilities do not continue to increase.

3. If the plan is not covered by the PBGC, determine whether the plan may use the rules described in chapter 17, Q 17:41.
4. If the plan is not severely underfunded and does not allow for lump-sum distributions, the plan sponsor may be able to find an annuity carrier to provide the accrued benefits to all participants through the use of a terminal funding contract (see Q 15:58) or the plan sponsor may amend the plan to permit lump-sum distributions if the value of lump-sum distributions will be less than the premium for a terminal funding contract.

Q 15:58 What is a terminal funding contract?

A terminal funding contract is a collection of individual annuity contracts purchased by the plan to guarantee the payment of accrued benefits at normal retirement age for a defined benefit plan. Once the contract is purchased, the plan ceases to be liable for the payment of benefits, and the insurance carrier promises to pay the benefits to participants when they reach normal or early retirement age.

Example 15-15: ABC Consulting has a frozen defined benefit plan that does not contain a lump-sum distribution optional form of benefit. The plan sponsor has decided to terminate the plan because it no longer meets their retirement program goals. The actuary calculates the PVAB and determines that the liabilities of the plan are equal to $375,000 as of May 17, 2018. However, the plan assets as of May 17, 2018, are only $335,000. ABC Consulting does not want to contribute anything further to the plan or to continue the plan. On the advice of its pension consultant, ABC Consulting seeks competitive bids from insurance companies for a terminal funding contract to provide the benefits accrued in the plan. ABC Consulting receives the following bids:

Insurance Carrier	*Terminal Funding Quote*
MLIC	$345,000
FBN	$312,000
TIC	$327,000

Although FBN has the lowest bid, ABC Consulting chooses TIC because its rating is the highest among the insurance carriers in the industry.

Actions of Plan Sponsor

Q 15:59 When must the plan sponsor adopt a resolution terminating a defined benefit plan?

If benefit accruals were properly ceased as of a prior date, the plan termination resolution may be adopted at any time before the desired termination date.

However, the plan termination will automatically cease benefit accruals. Therefore, if benefit accruals cessation did not previously occur, the plan sponsor will need to cease future benefit accruals coincident with plan termination. Therefore, a resolution both ceasing benefit accruals and terminating the plan must generally be adopted on a date that precedes the date on which participants are given their ERISA 204(h) notice (at least 45 days for single/multiple employer plans with 100 or more participants, or 15 days for single/multiple employer plans with less than 100 participants, or any multi-employer plan). [ERISA § 204(h); Treas. Reg. § 54.4980F-1, Q&A-9)]

Q 15:60 What liability does the plan sponsor have to contribute to a defined benefit plan in the year of termination?

That depends on the funded status of the plan. If the plan is overfunded (i.e., plan assets exceed plan liabilities), it is quite likely that the plan sponsor will not be required to make a contribution. In any event, an actuarial valuation must be performed in the year of termination to determine the minimum required contribution (MRC) requirements in the year of termination. Funding actuarial valuations are not required for plan years after the year of termination.

Q 15:61 Do the MRC requirements under Code Section 430 apply for the entire year in the year of plan termination?

Yes. For 2008 plan years and later, generally, the MRC consists of a target normal cost plus shortfall bases amortization. Both components are calculated based on the benefits accrued at the beginning of the plan year and the benefits accrued (or projected to be accrued) during the plan year. The benefits projected to be accrued may be affected by the plan's termination amendment. [I.R.C. § 430(b); Treas. Reg. § 1.430(d)-1(b)(1)]

204(h) Notice

Q 15:62 Why is a notice required to inform participants of the cessation of benefit accruals in a defined benefit plan?

ERISA requires that a defined benefit plan may not be amended to provide for a significant reduction in the rate of future benefit accruals unless, after adoption of the plan amendment and not less than 45 days (15 days for small plans) before the effective date of the plan amendment, the plan administrator provides a written notice (commonly called a 204(h) notice), setting forth the plan amendment and its effective date, to:

1. Each affected participant in the plan;
2. Each affected beneficiary who is an alternate payee under a QDRO (see chapter 3); and

3. Each employee organization representing participants in the plan.

(See Qs 15:9–15:15.)

[ERISA § 204(h)]

Information Gathering

Q 15:63 What data must be collected to terminate a defined benefit plan?

The information needed is dependent upon the type of defined benefit plan being terminated, whether the plan is top heavy, and whether there is use of life insurance contracts:

1. *Flat dollar plans*. It will be necessary to obtain the years or partial years of credited service.
2. *Percentage of pay plans*. Current year's pay (based on the plan's definition of compensation) as well as credited service should be obtained.
3. *Individual insurance contracts*. Special care needs to be taken to properly handle individual insurance contracts. Although the plan sponsor clearly has authority to surrender such contracts, it may make sense from an employee relations standpoint to offer participants the opportunity to continue the life insurance protection through a distribution (see chapter 25).
4. *Top-heavy plans*. If the plan or required aggregation group of plans is top heavy, then top-heavy minimum benefits may need to be provided to non-key participants in the plan for the plan year that includes the date of termination. The top-heavy minimum accrual is usually 2 percent of average pay multiplied by years of participation, up to a maximum of 10 (see chapter 9). Note that for plan years beginning after December 31, 2001, top-heavy minimums need not be provided in plans where benefit accruals have been hard frozen. [I.R.C. § 416(c)(1)(C)(iii)]

Q 15:64 What other information should be reviewed or collected?

Of particular importance are the plan documents. The plan documents should be reviewed and amended as needed, to ensure compliance with all applicable laws.

The termination of a plan ends the plan's remedial amendment period and thus will generally shorten the remedial amendment cycle for the plan. Accordingly, any retroactive remedial plan amendments or other required plan amendments for a terminating plan must be adopted in connection with the plan termination (i.e., plan amendments required to be adopted to reflect qualification requirements that apply as of the date of termination regardless of whether such requirements are included on the most recently published Cumulative List).

It is always helpful to review the plan's compliance history for at least the last five to six years to spot problems before the plan is submitted to the IRS. If problems are discovered, the plan sponsor may be able to correct them using one of several IRS voluntary compliance programs (see chapter 23). These IRS programs may also be used if the plan sponsor failed to adopt one or more required amendments.

[Rev. Procs. 2016-51, 2015-28, 2015-27, 2015-06, 2014-06, 2013-12, 2013-8, 2013-6, 2013-1, 2007-44, 2008-56, 2009-36, 2012-50; Notices 2009-97, 2010-77; Anns. 2012-3, 2011-82]

IRS Submission

Q 15:65 What information needs to be submitted to the IRS for a favorable determination letter on the termination of the plan?

The following information is needed to request a favorable determination letter on the termination of a plan:

1. Form 8717, *User Fee for Employee Plan Determination Letter* and appropriate user fee (see Q 15:22);
2. Form 5310, *Application for Determination for Terminating Plan* (see Q 15:23);
3. A copy of the plan document;
4. A copy of the latest determination letter from the IRS;
5. A copy of all amendments since the last determination letter;
6. A statement explaining how the amendments affect or change the plan or any other plan maintained by the employer;
7. A copy of the latest opinion letter for a standardized master or prototype plan, if applicable;
8. A copy of the latest opinion or advisory letter for a master or prototype plan or volume submitter plan on which the employer is entitled to rely, if applicable;
9. Copies of all records of all actions taken to terminate the plan;
10. Copy of any compliance statements or closing agreements made since the last determination letter.
11. Form 8905, *Certification of Intent to Adopt a Pre-Approved Plan,* if an employer intends to switch from the five-year remedial amendment cycle to the six-year remedial amendment cycle by meeting one of the eligibility requirements for the six-year remedial amendment cycle;
12. Form 6088, *Distributable Benefits from Employee Pension Benefit Plans,* if required; and
13. Form 2848, *Power of Attorney and Declaration of Representative,* if the representative appointed by the employer is an attorney, CPA, enrolled agent, or enrolled actuary. Otherwise, Form 8821, *Tax Information Authorization,* should be used.

[Instructions to Form 5310, rev. Dec. 2013]

Q 15:66 How is Form 6088 completed for a defined benefit plan?

The form itself requests the following items:

Column	*Information Required*
(a)	Name.
(b)	HCE status (see Appendix G).
(c)	Years of participation: List years of participation from date of initial participation until the earliest of the date of (1) plan termination, (2) retirement, or (3) separation from service.
(d)	Age as of the date of plan termination date.
(e)	Compensation: Enter the participant's average compensation for the three highest years. Average compensation means the participant's average compensation determined on an annual basis for the period of consecutive calendar years (but not more than three) during which the participant was both an active plan participant and had the greatest aggregate compensation from the employer (or earned income if the participant is self-employed or an owner-employee). For participants no longer employed as of the proposed termination date, use compensation and years of participation before the earliest of the proposed date of plan termination, retirement, or separation from service.
(f)	Accrued benefit: List the accrued benefit, as of the date of plan termination, of each participant (in the normal form payable at normal retirement age under the plan), excluding any benefits attributable to voluntary employee contributions (including roll-overs). For participants in pay status (currently receiving annuity or installment benefits from the plan), the accrued benefit currently being paid may be entered with an asterisk, and the form of payment should be described in an attachment to Form 6088.
(g)(1)	Leave blank if plan assets exceed liabilities. If not, see chapter 17.
(g)(2)	Leave blank if plan assets exceed liabilities. If not, see chapter 17.
(g)(3)	Leave blank if plan assets exceed liabilities. If not, see chapter 17.
(h)	Enter the present value of the participant's total benefit liabilities (whether or not vested) at the date of distribution of the plan assets. Present value is the single-sum distribution amount provided under the terms of the plan. However, if the plan does not provide for a single-sum distribution or the participant's benefits are provided by an annuity contract, present value is the cost (or estimated cost if actual cost is not available) of the annuity. Attach a statement explaining how the present values were determined. This statement should indicate the interest rates used to compute single-sum distributions.

A separate Form 6088 must be filed for each employer participating in a multiple employer defined benefit plan as described in Code Section 413(c). Sample calculations are also required.

[Instructions to Form 6088 (Rev. Mar. 2008)]

Q 15:67 How long does it take to receive a favorable determination letter from the IRS on a plan termination?

The IRS has 270 days to review the plan and issue its findings. Depending on its workload, the processing period may be shorter, but is often longer than 270 days. [I.R.C. § 7476(b)(3)]

Q 15:68 Must the participants in the plan be notified of the request for a determination letter on the termination of the plan?

Yes, a notice to interested parties must be provided. The purpose of the notice is to inform interested parties of their rights to:

1. Receive notice that an application for an advance determination will be filed about the qualification of plans described in Code Section 401;
2. Submit written comments about the qualification of the plans to the IRS;
3. Request the DOL to submit a comment to the IRS on behalf of the interested parties; and
4. Submit written comments to the IRS on matters about which the DOL was requested to comment but declined.

[Rev. Procs. 2015-6, 2016-6, 2017-4, 2018-4]

(The contents of the notice are described in Qs 15:32 and 15:33.)

Liquidating Plan Assets

Q 15:69 What is involved in the liquidation of plan assets?

The liquidation of plan assets could be a time-consuming process, depending on the types of assets in the plan. It is also possible to distribute assets in kind (see chapter 25). If the plan assets are invested in marketable securities such as common stocks or mutual funds, the liquidation process may take a week or less. If some of the plan assets are invested in life insurance contracts or GICs with insurance companies, the liquidation process could be significantly longer. Some of the contracts may have significant penalties for early withdrawals. If the assets are not readily marketable (that is, limited partnerships, real estate, or closely held employer stock), the plan sponsor may have to find a willing buyer.

Q 15:70 When should the liquidation process be started?

In general, the plan's investment advisor should be notified as to the expected timeframe for distributions so that an appropriate timeframe for asset liquidation can occur for cash to be available as of the expected distribution date (except for assets being distributed in kind). Assets that are not readily marketable will generally take longer to liquidate, so additional liquidation time should be anticipated.

Q 15:71 Why should the PVAB be recalculated?

There are several reasons why the PVAB may need to be recalculated between the date of plan termination and the date of distribution:

1. A number of months may intervene between the date of termination and the approval of the termination by the IRS, and the participants' age may have changed.
2. The plan assets may change in value. If surplus plan assets are to be redistributed to plan participants, a nondiscriminatory allocation of the surplus must occur. [Rev. Rul. 80-229]
3. Applicable interest rates and mortality tables may change. [I.R.C. § 417(e)]

Surplus Assets

Q 15:72 What happens if a terminating defined benefit plan has surplus assets?

The plan document must define how surplus assets (the excess, if any, of plan assets over liabilities) are treated in the event of a plan termination. If such language is not in the plan or has not been in the plan document for at least five years, surplus assets must be distributed to participants in a nondiscriminatory manner. [Rev. Rul. 80-229] If the plan permits surplus assets to revert to the employer, and a reversion takes place, there is a 50 percent excise tax on the reversion. The reversion excise tax may be reduced to 20 percent if any of these events occurs:

1. The employer establishes or maintains a qualified replacement plan;
2. The plan provides benefit increases to participants in the terminating defined benefit plan; or
3. The employer is in Chapter 7 bankruptcy liquidation or in a similar court proceeding on the plan termination date.

[I.R.C. § 4980(d)(1)]

Q 15:73 What is a qualified replacement plan?

A qualified replacement plan is a qualified plan established or maintained by the employer that meets the following requirements:

1. At least 95 percent of the active participants in the terminated plan (who remain as employees of the employer after the termination) are active participants in the replacement plan.
2. A direct transfer is made from the terminated plan to the replacement plan before any employer reversion. This transfer is an amount equal to the excess (if any) of:

   a. 25 percent of the maximum amount the employer could receive as a reversion minus
   b. The present value of benefit increases granted to participants in the terminated defined benefit plan (see Q 15:77).
3. In the case of a defined contribution qualified replacement plan, the amount transferred is either:
   a. Allocated to the accounts of plan participants in the year the transfer occurs; or
   b. Credited to a suspense account and allocated over a period not to exceed seven years.

[I.R.C. § 4980(d)(2); Rev. Rul. 2003-85]

Example 15-16: ABC Consulting sponsors a defined benefit plan that is in the process of terminating. The liabilities of the plan are $500,000, and the plan assets are $1 million. The plan allows for the reversion of surplus assets to the plan sponsor, but ABC Consulting wants to avoid paying a 50 percent excise tax of $250,000 on the reversion of $500,000. By transferring $125,000 (25% × $500,000) to a qualified replacement plan, ABC Consulting reduces the excise tax to $75,000 (20% × ($500,000 − $125,000)).

Q 15:74 May more than 25 percent of the surplus assets be transferred to a qualified replacement plan?

More than 25 percent of the surplus assets may be transferred to a qualified replacement plan. In a significant change in position, the IRS ruled that a transfer in excess of 25 percent of the surplus assets in a terminated defined benefit plan will not result in an imposition of the 20 percent reversion excise tax under Code Section 4980 on the transferred proceeds. Only the actual amount returned to the plan sponsor as a reversion will be subject to the 20 percent reversion excise tax. Furthermore, the amount transferred will not be subject to corporate tax, nor will the plan sponsor be allowed a tax deduction under Code Section 404 for the transferred proceeds. [Rev. Rul. 2003-85]

Q 15:75 How large must benefit increases be in order to qualify for the reduction in the excise tax from 50 percent to 20 percent?

As an alternative to the qualified replacement plan, the plan may provide benefit increases to participants in the terminating plan, if the aggregate present value of the increases is not less than 20 percent of the maximum reversion. [I.R.C. § 4980(d)(3)] Note that the allocation of the surplus assets must not discriminate in favor of highly compensated employees. [Rev. Rul. 80-229]

Example 15-17: In Example 15-16, ABC Consulting decides that it does not want to institute a qualified replacement plan. It also does not want to pay the 50 percent reversion excise tax ($250,000). To avoid this significant excise tax, ABC Consulting decides to provide benefit increases to the participants in the terminating defined benefit plan in order to reduce the excise tax to 20 percent. As long as the aggregate present value of the benefit increases is at least $100,000 (20% × $500,000) and the nondiscrimination tests are passed, the reversion excise tax will be reduced to 20 percent.

Distribution of Election Forms

Q 15:76 What benefit distribution election forms and notices must be distributed and executed?

Required election forms include:

- Form of Benefit Election, including Relative Value Disclosure
- Waiver of Joint and Survivor Annuity and Spousal Consent
- Tax Notice and Withholding Election
- Life Insurance Election Form, if applicable

When the forms are completed and properly executed, distributions may be made to the participants, annuities may be purchased, or direct transfers may be made to the participants' IRAs or other qualified plans.

Q 15:77 What payment options must be provided in the benefit election form?

All optional forms of benefit available in the plan document must be disclosed on the election form upon termination of the plan, because benefit options are each protected benefits under Code Section 411(d)(6) (see chapter 10). An exception occurs if a defined contribution plan terminates and the plan does not offer an annuity option. In this case, the plan may distribute the participant's accrued benefit without the participant's consent. This does not apply, however, if the employer, or any entity within the same controlled group as the employer, maintains another defined contribution plan, other than an employee stock ownership plan (ESOP). In such a case, the participant's accrued benefit may be transferred without the participant's consent to the other plan if the participant does not consent to an immediate distribution from the terminating plan. [Treas. Reg. § 1.411(a)-11(e)(1)]

Example 15-18: Tom, a participant in the profit sharing plan sponsored by CDE Advisors is eligible to receive a distribution due to the termination of the plan. The plan document allows a participant to defer payment of benefits until age 60. Tom, who is 45, wants to defer distribution of his benefits until age 60. However, the terminating plan may force Tom to receive a distribution of benefits, because it does not provide for benefits in annuity form. Tom may elect a direct rollover to an IRA in order to defer benefits until age 60.

If a plan does provide an annuity option and the participant chooses to defer payments of benefits, the plan sponsor may purchase a commercial annuity that defers payment of the participant's benefit until the time requested. However, the participant may also defer taxable receipt of benefits by choosing a direct rollover to an IRA instead (see chapter 21).

Q 15:78 What happens if the participant chooses a form of benefit other than the qualified joint and survivor annuity (QJSA)?

In plans that provide for distributions in the form of a qualified joint and survivor annuity (QJSA) (see chapter 11), the participant must formally waive the QJSA if he or she wants to receive benefits in a form other than the QJSA. The plan administrator must explain the terms and conditions of the QJSA and explain the effect of making or revoking an election to waive the QJSA. If the present value of the vested accrued benefit (or vested account balance) is less than $5,000, the participant may be cashed out without his or her consent if the plan so provides. [Treas. Reg. § 1.417(e)-1(b)(1)]

Q 15:79 May distributions that are less than $5,000 be distributed in cash to plan participants?

In the case of a plan that provides for involuntary distributions, an eligible rollover distribution that exceeds $1,000 must be directly rolled over to an IRA or individual retirement annuity. Some plans may wish to avoid the automatic rollover rule and will reduce the cash-out threshold from $5,000 to $1,000. [I.R.C. § 401(a)(31)(B)] (See chapter 21 for a discussion of the automatic rollover requirements.)

Q 15:80 Must a spouse consent to a form of benefit other than a QJSA?

Yes. If a plan provides for a QJSA, the spouse must consent to the participant's election to waive the QJSA or the qualified optional survivor annuity (QOSA), if the value of the benefit is greater than $5,000 (see chapter 11). [I.R.C. § 417(a)(2)]

Q 15:81 What are the requirements, under Code Section 402(f), for a written explanation to recipients of distributions eligible for rollover treatment?

Under Code Section 402(f), the plan administrator of a qualified plan is required, within a reasonable period of time (see Q 15:84) before making an eligible rollover distribution, to provide the distributee with the written explanation described in Code Section 402(f) (the Section 402(f) notice). The Section 402(f) notice must be designed to be easily understood and must explain the following:

1. The rules under which the distributee may have the distribution paid in a direct rollover to an eligible retirement plan;
2. The rules that require the withholding of tax on the distribution if it is not paid in a direct rollover;

3. The rules under which the distributee will not be subject to tax if the distribution is contributed in a rollover to an eligible retirement plan within 60 days of the distribution; and
4. If applicable, certain special rules on the taxation of the distribution as described in Code Section 402(d) and (e).

In addition, a distributee must be informed if his or her election with respect to a rollover periodic payment will apply to all subsequent payments in the series unless the distributee changes the election, and that treatment must be explained in the Section 402(f) notice. [Treas. Reg. § 1.402(f)-1, Q&A-1]

Q 15:82 Has the IRS provided sample language that may be used for the Section 402(f) notice?

Yes. The IRS has created a model Section 402(f) notice, also called the "safe-harbor explanation." [Treas. Reg. § 1.402(f)-1(b)] The safe-harbor explanation meets the requirements of Code Section 402(f) if the plan administrator provides it to the recipient of an eligible rollover distribution within a reasonable time before the distribution is made (see chapter 21). The IRS issued an updated model tax notice for qualified plans to provide to recipients of eligible rollover distributions from an employer plan. A model Section 402(f) tax notice was issued in 2002. Notice 2009-68 contains a version of the model notice that applies to the distribution of designated Roth contributions and one that applies to the distribution of traditional contributions. These updated model Section 402(f) tax notices reflect changes in the law since 2002 and reorganize and simplify the presentation of information. The model notices in Notice 2009-68 have been updated in Notice 2014-74.

A plan administrator may customize the safe-harbor explanation by omitting any inapplicable portions. For example, if the plan does not hold after-tax employee contributions, the paragraph in the safe-harbor explanation headed "Non-Taxable Payments" could be eliminated. Similarly, if the plan does not provide for distributions of employer stock or other employer securities, the paragraph headed "Employer Stock or Securities" could be eliminated. Other paragraphs in the safe-harbor explanation that may not be relevant to a particular plan include, for example, "Payments Spread Over Long Periods," "Direct Rollover of a Series of Payments," and "Special Tax Treatment." A plan administrator also may provide additional information with the safe-harbor explanation if the information is not inconsistent with it. [IRS Notices 2009-68 and 2014-74]

Q 15:83 May language that is different from the IRS model be used?

Yes. A plan administrator can satisfy Code Section 402(f) by providing distributees with a 402(f) notice that is different from the safe-harbor notice. Any notice must contain the information required by Code Section 402(f) and must be written in a manner designed to be easily understood. [Treas. Reg. § 1.402(f)-1, Q&A-1] It is important that the plan administrator be aware of required notice changes so that the notice the administrator distributes is updated to reflect current law.

Q 15:84 When must the plan administrator provide the Section 402(f) notice to a distributee?

The plan administrator must provide the Section 402(f) notice to a distributee within a reasonable period of time, which is defined as no earlier than 180 days and no later than 30 days before the distribution is made. However, the distributee may waive the 30-day period (but not the 180-day period) in the manner described below. As modified by the permitted waiver of the 30-day requirement, the 180/30-day rule ensures that participants receive timely notice of their options and the related tax consequences of taking a distribution, before they elect whether or not to roll over their distribution. The plan administrator is thus not required to enforce a 30-day waiting period against a participant who has had the opportunity to make an informed decision. [Treas. Reg. § 1.402(f)-1 as modified by PPA]

If a participant, after having received the Section 402(f) notice, affirmatively elects to make or not to make a direct rollover, the reasonable-time requirement of Code Section 402(f) is not violated merely because the election is implemented less than 30 days after the Section 402(f) notice was given, provided that these requirements are met:

1. The participant must be given the opportunity to consider the decision of whether or not to elect a direct rollover for at least 30 days after the notice is provided; and
2. The plan administrator must provide information to the participant clearly indicating that the participant has a right to this period for making the decision.

If these conditions are met and the participant affirmatively elects a distribution, the plan administrator may make the distribution. [IRS Notice 93-26]

The plan administrator may use any method to inform the participant of the relevant time period, provided that the method is reasonably designed to attract the participant's attention. For example, this information could be provided either in the Section 402(f) notice itself or stated in a separate document (e.g., attached to the election form) that is provided at the same time as the Section 402(f) notice. The rules permitting participants to waive the 30-day waiting period apply to any distribution from a qualified plan, including one subject to the consent requirements of Code Section 411(a)(11) but not the QJSA rules. [Treas. Reg. § 1.402(f)-1, Q&A-2]

Q 15:85 What options should a plan administrator consider offering to a participant covered by life insurance in a qualified plan?

The plan administrator should consider offering participants the opportunity to continue their life insurance protection on an individual basis. Because life insurance coverage is not a protected benefit under Code Section 411(d)(6) (see chapter 10), the plan administrator could surrender the contracts at the time of plan termination. However, because a participant may need continuous life insurance protection, it makes sense to consider offering the participant the option of continuing the insurance personally. (See chapter 25 for a discussion of distributing life insurance policies.)

Q 15:86 What happens if a participant cannot be located?

Below are some methods that can be used to locate lost or missing participants:

1. Private locator services;
2. Internet resources; and
3. PBGC-covered plans can also consider the PBGC missing participant program. PPA has expanded the PBGC's missing participant program for plan terminations after January 1, 2018, to include non-PBGC-covered plans and participants who are not missing, but are nonresponsive.

(See Qs 15:41–15:47 for more detailed information.)

Final Disclosure Forms

Q 15:87 When is the final Form 5500 due?

The final Form 5500, 5500-SF, or 5500-EZ is due on the last day of the seventh month following the date all assets were distributed. A 2½-month extension may be obtained by filing Form 5558 with the IRS.

Q 15:88 How are distributions to participants reported?

Form 1099-R is used to report distributions to participants. Form 1099-R must be provided to participants by January 31 in the calendar year following the calendar year of distribution. The plan reports income tax withholding on Form 945, which is also due by January 31 in the calendar year following the calendar year of distribution. (See chapter 27 for a detailed discussion of distribution reporting.)

Abandoned Defined Contribution (Orphan) Plans

Q 15:89 What guidance is available from the DOL regarding defined contribution orphan plans?

On March 10, 2005, the DOL's EBSA issued three proposed regulations authorizing a qualified termination administrator (QTA) to determine that a defined contribution plan has been abandoned and to take certain actions to facilitate the plan's termination and the distribution of plan benefits. At the same time that the proposed regulations were issued, EBSA also issued notice of a proposed class prohibited transaction exemption that would permit the QTA of an orphan defined contribution plan to select and pay fees to itself or to an affiliate for performing services to the plan in connection with the plan's termination. The regulations were finalized in April 2006.

The purpose of the regulations is to establish standards and procedures under Title I of ERISA that will facilitate the voluntary, safe, and efficient termination of orphan plans, increasing the likelihood that participants and beneficiaries receive the greatest retirement benefit under the circumstances. Specifically, the regulations establish standards for determining:

- When a plan may be considered abandoned and deemed terminated;
- Procedures for winding up the affairs of the plan and distributing benefits to participants and beneficiaries; and
- Guidance on who may initiate and carry out the winding-up process.

[Preamble to D.O.L. Reg. § 2578.1]

Q 15:90 What entity may be a QTA?

A QTA must meet the following requirements:

1. It must be eligible to serve as a trustee or issuer of an IRA under Code Section 7701(a)(37) (e.g., bank, trust company, mutual fund, investment house, and so forth);
2. It must hold the assets of the orphan defined contribution plan.

[D.O.L. Reg. § 2578.1(g)]

In December 2012, EBSA issued proposed amendments to the abandoned plan regulations, which would permit bankruptcy trustees to be QTAs.

Q 15:91 When is a defined contribution plan considered to be abandoned?

A QTA may find a defined contribution plan to be abandoned (an orphan plan) when either:

1. No contributions to, or distributions from, the plan have been made for a period of 12 consecutive months immediately preceding the date of determination; or
2. Other facts and circumstances (e.g., a filing by or against the plan sponsor for liquidation under Title 11 or communications from participants and beneficiaries regarding distributions) known to the QTA suggest that the plan is or may become abandoned by the plan sponsor.

The QTA must make reasonable efforts to locate or communicate with the plan sponsor. Following such efforts, the QTA may determine that the plan sponsor either:

1. No longer exists;
2. Cannot be located; or
3. Is unable to maintain the plan.

[D.O.L. Reg. § 2578.1(b)(1)(ii)]

Q 15:92 What is considered to be a reasonable effort to locate or communicate with the plan sponsor?

A QTA is considered as making a reasonable effort if the QTA sends to the last-known address of the plan sponsor (if the plan sponsor is a corporation, to the address of the person designated as the corporation's agent for service of legal process) by registered mail a notice containing the following information:

1. The name and address of the QTA;
2. The name of the plan;
3. The account number or other identifying information relating to the plan;
4. A statement that the plan may be terminated and benefits distributed pursuant to DOL Regulations Section 2578.1 if the plan sponsor fails to contact the QTA within 30 days;
5. The name, address, and telephone number of the person, office, or department that the plan sponsor must contact regarding the plan;
6. A statement that, if the plan is terminated pursuant to DOL Regulations Section 2578.1, notice of such termination will be furnished to the DOL's EBSA;
7. The following statement: "The U.S. Department of Labor requires that you be informed that, as a fiduciary or plan administrator or both, you may be personally liable for costs, civil penalties, excise taxes, etc. as a result of your acts or omissions with respect to this plan. The termination of this plan will not relieve you of your liability for any such costs, penalties, taxes, etc."; and
8. A statement that the plan sponsor may contact the DOL for more information about the federal law governing the termination and winding-up process for abandoned plans and the telephone number of the appropriate EBSA contact person.

[D.O.L. Reg. § 2578.1(b)]

Q 15:93 When is an orphan plan deemed to be terminated?

If a QTA determines that a defined contribution plan has been abandoned, the plan shall be deemed to be terminated on the 90th day following the date on which such notice of plan abandonment has been furnished to the DOL. However, within the 90-day period preceding the date of deemed termination, the DOL may notify the QTA that it:

1. *Objects to the termination of the plan.* The plan shall not be deemed terminated until the QTA is notified that the DOL has withdrawn its objection;
2. *Waives the 90-day period described above.* The plan shall be deemed to be terminated upon the QTA's receipt of such notification.

[D.O.L. Reg. § 2578.1(c)]

Q 15:94 What are the contents of the QTA notice to the DOL?

The QTA must furnish a notice of plan abandonment that is signed and dated by the QTA containing the following information:

1. The name, employer identification number (EIN), address, and telephone number of the QTA, including the address, e-mail address, and telephone number of the person signing the notice;
2. A statement that the person is a QTA under the definition described in Q 15:92 and elects to terminate and wind up the plan in accordance with the requirements of the DOL;
3. An identification as to whether the QTA or an affiliate is, or within the past 24 months has been, the subject of an investigation, examination, or enforcement action by the DOL, IRS, or SEC concerning such entity's conduct as a fiduciary or party-in-interest with respect to any plan covered by ERISA;
4. Plan information:
   a. The name, EIN, address, and telephone number, account number, and plan number of the plan for which the entity is serving as QTA;
   b. The name and last-known address and telephone number of the plan sponsor;
   c. The estimated number of participants in the plan.
5. A statement of the QTA regarding its findings, including an explanation of the basis for its findings, and a description of the specific steps taken by the QTA to locate or communicate with the plan sponsor;
6. Plan asset information as follows:
   a. The estimated value of the plan's assets held by the QTA;
   b. The length of time plan assets have been held by the person electing to be the QTA, if such period of time is less than 12 months;
   c. An identification of any assets with respect to which there is no readily ascertainable fair market value, as well as information, if any, concerning such assets;
   d. An identification of known delinquent contributions.
7. Service provider information:
   a. The name, address, and telephone number of known service providers (e.g., recordkeeper, accountant, attorney, other asset custodians to the plan);
   b. An identification of any services considered necessary to wind up the plan, the name of the service provider(s) expected to provide such services, and an itemized estimate of expenses to be paid out of plan assets by the QTA;
8. A statement that the information being provided in the notice is true and complete based on the knowledge of the person electing to be the QTA, and that the information is being provided by the QTA under penalty of perjury.

[D.O.L. Reg. § 2578.1(c)(3)]

Q 15:95 What are the tasks required of the QTA in winding up the orphan plan?

If the orphan plan is deemed to be terminated under the requirements discussed above, the QTA shall take steps necessary or appropriate to wind up the affairs of the plan and distribute benefits to the plan's participants and beneficiaries. The tasks include:

1. Maintenance of plan records:
   a. The QTA shall undertake reasonable and diligent efforts to locate and update plan records necessary to determine the benefits payable under the terms of the plan to each participant and beneficiary;
   b. A QTA shall not have failed to make reasonable and diligent efforts to update the plan records merely because the administrator determines in good faith that updating the records is either impossible or involves significant cost to the plan in relation to the total assets of the plan.
2. Calculation of benefits: The QTA shall use reasonable care in calculating the benefits payable to each participant and beneficiary based on the plan records described in item 1;
3. Report delinquent contributions by notifying EBSA of any known contributions (employer or employee) owed to the plan;
4. Engage service providers: The QTA shall engage, on behalf of the plan, such service providers as are necessary for the QTA to wind up the affairs of the plan and distribute benefits to plan participants and beneficiaries;
5. Pay reasonable expenses: The QTA shall pay, from plan assets, the reasonable expenses of carrying out the QTA's authority and responsibility under the DOL requirements. Expenses shall be considered as reasonable solely for purposes of these rules if:
   a. Such expenses are for services necessary to wind up the affairs of the plan and distribute benefits to the plan participants and beneficiaries;
   b. Such expenses are consistent with industry rates for such similar services (based on the experience of the QTA), are not in excess of rates charged by the QTA (or affiliate) for the same or similar services provided to non-orphan plans, and the payment of such expenses would not constitute a prohibited transaction under ERISA Section 408.
6. Notification to plan participants: Furnish to each participant or beneficiary of the plan a notice containing the following:
   a. The name of the plan;
   b. A statement that the plan has been determined to be abandoned by the plan sponsor and, therefore, has been terminated pursuant to regulations issued by the DOL;
   c. A statement of the account balance and the date on which it was calculated by the QTA, and the following statement: "The actual amount of your distribution may be more or less than the amount stated in this letter depending on investment gains or losses and the administrative cost of terminating your plan and distributing your benefits."

d. A description of the distribution options available under the plan and a request that the participant or beneficiary elect a form of distribution and inform QTA (or its designee) of that election;

e. A statement explaining that, if a participant or beneficiary fails to make an election within 30 days from receipt of the notice, the QTA (or its designee) will roll over the account balance of the participant or beneficiary directly to an IRA or other account and the account balance will be invested in an investment product designed to preserve principal and provide a reasonable rate of return and liquidity;

f. A statement of the fees, if any, that will be paid from the participant or beneficiary's individual retirement plan, if such information is known at the time of the furnishing of this notice;

g. The name, address, and phone number of the individual retirement plan provider, if such information is known at the time of the furnishing of this notice; and

h. The name, address, and telephone number of the QTA and, if different, the name, address, and phone number of a contact person (or entity) for additional information concerning the termination and distribution of benefits. A notice shall be furnished to each participant or beneficiary to the last-known address of the participant or beneficiary. In the case of a notice that is returned to the plan as undeliverable, the QTA shall, consistent with the duties of a fiduciary under ERISA Section 404(a)(1), take steps to locate and provide notice to the participant or beneficiary prior to making a distribution. If, after such steps, the QTA is unsuccessful in locating and furnishing notice to a participant or beneficiary, the participant or beneficiary shall be deemed to have been furnished the notice and to have failed to make an election within the 30-day period described below.

7. Distribute benefits: The QTA shall:

   a. Distribute benefits in accordance with the form of distribution elected by each participant or beneficiary.

   b. If the participant or beneficiary fails to make an election within 30 days from receipt of the notice described above, distribute benefits in the form of a direct rollover.

   c. For purposes of such distributions, the QTA may designate itself (or an affiliate) as the transferee of such proceeds and invest such proceeds in a product in which it (or an affiliate) has an interest, only if such designation and investment is exempted from the prohibited transaction provisions of ERISA Section 408(a).

8. File a Special Terminal Report (see Q 15:98).

9. The following information should be provided to EBSA no later than two months after the end of the month in which the QTA satisfies all the above requirements in a signed and dated notice:

   a. The name, EIN, address, e-mail address, and telephone number of the QTA, including the address and telephone number of the person signing the notice (or other contact person, if different from the person signing the notice);

b. The name, account number, EIN, and plan number of the plan with respect to which the person served as the QTA;

c. A statement that the plan has been terminated and that all assets held by the QTA have been distributed to the plan's participants and beneficiaries on the basis of the best available information;

d. A statement that the Special Terminal Report for Abandoned Plans is attached to this notice;

e. A statement that plan expenses were paid out of plan assets by the QTA in accordance with the requirements described above;

f. If fees and expenses paid to the QTA (or its affiliate) exceed by 20 percent or more the estimate provided to the DOL, a statement that actual fees and expenses exceeded estimated fees and expenses and the reasons for such additional costs; and

g. A statement that the information being provided in the notice is true and complete based on the knowledge of the QTA, and that the information is being provided by the QTA under penalty of perjury.

[D.O.L. Reg. § 2578.1(d)]

Q 15:96 What are the contents of the Special Terminal Report for Abandoned Plans?

The QTA shall provide the following information to EBSA in its terminal report:

1. Identification information concerning the QTA and the plan being terminated.
2. The total assets of the plan as of the date the plan was deemed terminated, prior to any reduction for termination expenses and distributions to participants and beneficiaries.
3. The total termination expenses paid by the plan and a separate schedule identifying each service provider and amount received, itemized by expense.
4. The total distributions made to plan participants and beneficiaries and a statement regarding whether any such distributions were direct rollovers for plan participants and beneficiaries that could not be located.

The terminal report is attached to the most recent Form 5500.

[D.O.L. Reg. § 2520.103-13]

Chapter 16

The Termination Process for Single and Multiple Employer PBGC-Covered Plans

The Pension Benefit Guaranty Corporation (PBGC), a wholly owned government corporation, was established in 1974 by Title IV of the Employee Retirement Income Security Act (ERISA) to ensure that participants in covered defined benefit plans receive benefits promised to them when a plan terminates if the plan itself does not have sufficient assets. Plan sponsors of PBGC-covered defined benefit plans pay annual premiums to purchase insurance for the promised benefits. The original provisions of Title IV were amended by the Single-Employer Pension Plan Amendments Act (SEPPAA) in 1986, the Retirement Protection Act (RPA) in 1994, the Small Business Job Protection Act of 1996 (SBJPA), the Job Creation and Workers' Assistance Act of 2002 (JCWAA), and the Pension Protection Act of 2006 (PPA). For a thorough guide to aspects of plan termination rules and procedures, including for multiemployer plans, see the *Plan Termination Answer Book, Fifth Edition* [Bitzer; Wolters Kluwer Law & Business, 2014]

A plan administrator of a single-employer plan that is covered by PBGC's termination program and has sufficient plan assets to satisfy all plan benefit obligations may terminate the plan voluntarily in a standard termination. The plan administrator must follow specific steps and meet specific deadlines. The procedures and deadlines are discussed in this chapter.

A plan administrator may voluntarily terminate a plan that does not have sufficient plan assets to satisfy all plan benefit obligations if the plan sponsor, and all members of any applicable controlled group to which they belong, meets certain criteria for a distress termination. The specific steps and deadlines for a distress termination are also discussed in this chapter.

The PBGC may act to terminate a plan involuntarily if it determines that the PBGC's ultimate liabilities will increase if steps are not taken. The PBGC may also restore a plan that has previously been involuntarily terminated or is in the process of either a standard or a distress termination.

Coverage 16-2
PBGC Termination Steps 16-5
Notice of Intent to Terminate 16-8
Preliminary Information for PBGC 16-12
Measurement of Benefit Liabilities 16-14
Insufficiency of Plan Assets 16-18
Actions of Plan Sponsor 16-20
ERISA Section 204(h) Notice 16-21
Information Gathering 16-22
Notice of Plan Benefits 16-22
Final Stages 16-26
When the Plan Has Surplus Assets 16-27
Missing Participants 16-31
Post-Distribution Certification 16-35
Spinoff/Termination Transaction Rules 16-37
Final Returns/Reports 16-38

Coverage

Q 16:1 What determines whether a defined benefit plan is covered by the PBGC?

ERISA Title IV covers defined benefit plans established or maintained by:

- An employer engaged in commerce or in any industry or activity affecting commerce and/or
- Any employee organization, or organization representing employees, engaged in commerce or in any industry or activity affecting commerce.

Any covered plan must be a qualified plan meeting the requirements of Code Section 401(a). Hence, a plan that becomes disqualified (see chapter 23) could lose its PBGC-covered status. A successor plan is considered to be a continuation of a predecessor plan if it covers a group of employees that includes substantially the same employees as a previously established plan and provides substantially the same benefits as that plan provided. [ERISA § 4021(a)]

Q 16:2 Are any qualified plans exempt from coverage by the PBGC?

Yes, the following plans are not covered by the PBGC:

1. Defined contribution plans under which benefits are based solely on the account balance of the participant;
2. Plans established and maintained by the U.S. government, any state government, or political subdivision, or any agency or instrumentality of the foregoing;
3. Plans that are subject to the Railroad Retirement Act of 1935 or 1937, which are financed by contributions required under that act;
4. Church plans as defined in Code Section 414(e), unless the plan has made an election under Code Section 410(d) to be subject to ERISA and has notified the PBGC of that election;
5. Plans established and maintained by a society, order, or association described in Code Section 501(c)(8) or (9) if no part of the contributions are made by employers of the participants in the plans;
6. Plans containing a trust described in Code Section 501(c)(18) that was created before June 25, 1959, and that permit elective contributions on the part of participants;
7. Plans that have not, at any time after September 9, 1974, permitted employer contributions;
8. Plans that are unfunded and maintained by an employer primarily for the purpose of providing deferred compensation for a select group of management or highly compensated employees;
9. Plans established and maintained outside of the United States primarily for the benefit of individuals, substantially all of whom are nonresident aliens;
10. Excess benefit plans, established solely for the purpose of providing benefits for certain employees in excess of the limits on benefits and contributions imposed by Code Section 415;
11. Plans established and maintained exclusively for substantial owners (see Q 16:3);
12. Plans maintained solely for the purpose of complying with workers' compensation, unemployment compensation, or disability insurance laws;
13. Plans maintained by an international organization that is exempt from taxation under the International Organizations Immunity Act;
14. Any portion of a defined benefit plan that bases benefits solely on account balances; and
15. Plans established and maintained by a professional service employer that do not, at any time after September 9, 1974, have more than 25 active participants (see Q 16:4).

[ERISA § 4021(b)]

In addition, the following types of plans are not covered by the PBGC:

1. Individual retirement account or annuity (IRA) plans under Code Section 408(a) or (b); [PBGC Op. Letter 75-13 (Jan. 6, 1975)]
2. Unwritten plans; [PBGC Op. Letter 75-55 (Nov. 10, 1975); PBGC Op. Letter 76-56 (Jan. 19, 1976)]
3. Target plans that do not guarantee benefits in the event that contributions are insufficient to provide the target benefit; [PBGC Op. Letter 74-17 (Nov. 14, 1974)]
4. Employee welfare benefit plans as defined in ERISA Section 3(1). [PBGC Op. Letter 75-40 (Aug. 12, 1975); PBGC Op. Letter 76-7 (Jan. 14, 1976)]

Plan sponsors who are unsure whether their plans are covered by the PBGC may send an e-mail to standard@pbgc.gov.

[www.pbgc.gov contact information]

Q 16:3 Who is a substantial owner?

A substantial owner is any of the following:

- An individual who owns the entire interest in an unincorporated trade or business;
- In the case of a partnership, a partner who owns directly or indirectly 50 percent or more of the capital interest or the profits interest in the partnership; or
- In the case of a corporation, an individual who owns directly or indirectly 50 percent or more in value of either the voting stock or all the stock of the corporation.

The constructive ownership rules of Code Section 1563(e) apply, determined without regard to Code Section 1563(e)(3)(C). [ERISA § 4022(b)(5)(A)]

> **Example 16-1:** ABC Grocery sponsors a defined benefit plan that covers only the two partners of the business, each of whom owns 50 percent of the partnership's capital interest. This plan is not covered by the PBGC because it covers substantial owners only. If non-owners become eligible for the plan, the plan will become subject to PBGC coverage.

Q 16:4 What is a professional service employer?

A professional service employer is any proprietorship, partnership, corporation, or other association or organization that meets both of these requirements:

1. It is owned or controlled by professional individuals or by executors or administrators of professional individuals; and
2. The principal business of the organization is the performance of professional services.

The term *professional individuals* includes, but is not limited to, physicians, dentists, chiropractors, osteopaths, optometrists, other licensed practitioners of the healing arts, attorneys, public accountants, public engineers, architects, draftsmen, actuaries, psychologists, social or physical scientists, and performing artists. [ERISA § 4021(c)(2)]

Example 16-2: ABC Architects sponsors a defined benefit plan. ABC Architects employs approximately 75 individuals, but 55 of them work part-time and do not qualify for the plan. Because the plan has never had more than 25 active participants, it is exempt from PBGC coverage provided it meets the criteria for a professional service employer.

PBGC Termination Steps

Q 16:5 What is a standard termination?

A standard termination (for a single-employer plan) is one in which the plan administrator fulfills the following conditions:

1. Provides an advance notice of intent to terminate (NOIT) to all affected parties (see Qs 16:9–16:13);
2. Issues a notice of plan benefits (NOPB) to all affected parties entitled to plan benefits (see Qs 16:33–16:38);
3. Files a standard termination notice with the PBGC (see Q 16:15);
4. Distributes the plan's assets in satisfaction of plan benefits; and
5. In the case of a spinoff/termination transaction (see Q 16:64), issues the required notices (see Q 16:66).

[PBGC Reg. § 4041.21(a)]

Q 16:6 What are the steps involved in a PBGC standard termination?

A PBGC standard termination involves the following steps:

1. Select a proposed termination date (see Q 16:8);
2. Issue a NOIT to affected parties (other than PBGC) at least 60 days and no more than 90 days before the proposed termination date (see Q 16:9);
3. Issue a NOPB to each participant, beneficiary of deceased participant, and alternate payee no later than the time the plan administrator files the Standard Termination Notice (PBGC Form 500) with PBGC (see Qs 16:37–16:42);
4. File a Standard Termination Notice (PBGC Form 500, including the enrolled actuary's Schedule EA-S) with PBGC on or before the 180th day after the proposed termination date (see Q 16:15);

5. If any benefits may be distributed in annuity form, provide a Notice of Annuity Information to affected parties (other than PBGC) no later than 45 days before the distribution date (see Qs 16:10, 16:13);
6. Distribute plan assets to satisfy all plan benefit obligations by the distribution deadline. The deadline is the later of:
   a. 180 days after the expiration of PBGC's 60-day review period, or
   b. 120 days after receipt of a favorable Internal Revenue Service (IRS) determination letter (see chapter 15), but only if the request for an IRS letter (see chapter 15) is made on or before the date of filing of Form 500;
7. If the plan has missing participants, follow the PBGC rules for the location and distribution of benefits to missing participants (see Qs 16:51–16:57);
8. Provide a Notice of Annuity Contract to participants receiving their plan benefits in the form of any annuity no later than 30 days after the contract is available;
9. File a Post-Distribution Certification (PBGC Form 501) with PBGC no later than 30 days after all plan benefits are distributed (see Qs 16:58–16:60).

The PBGC standard termination timetable is shown graphically in Figure 16-1.

[PBGC Standard Termination Filing Instructions]

Figure 16-1. Standard Termination Timeline

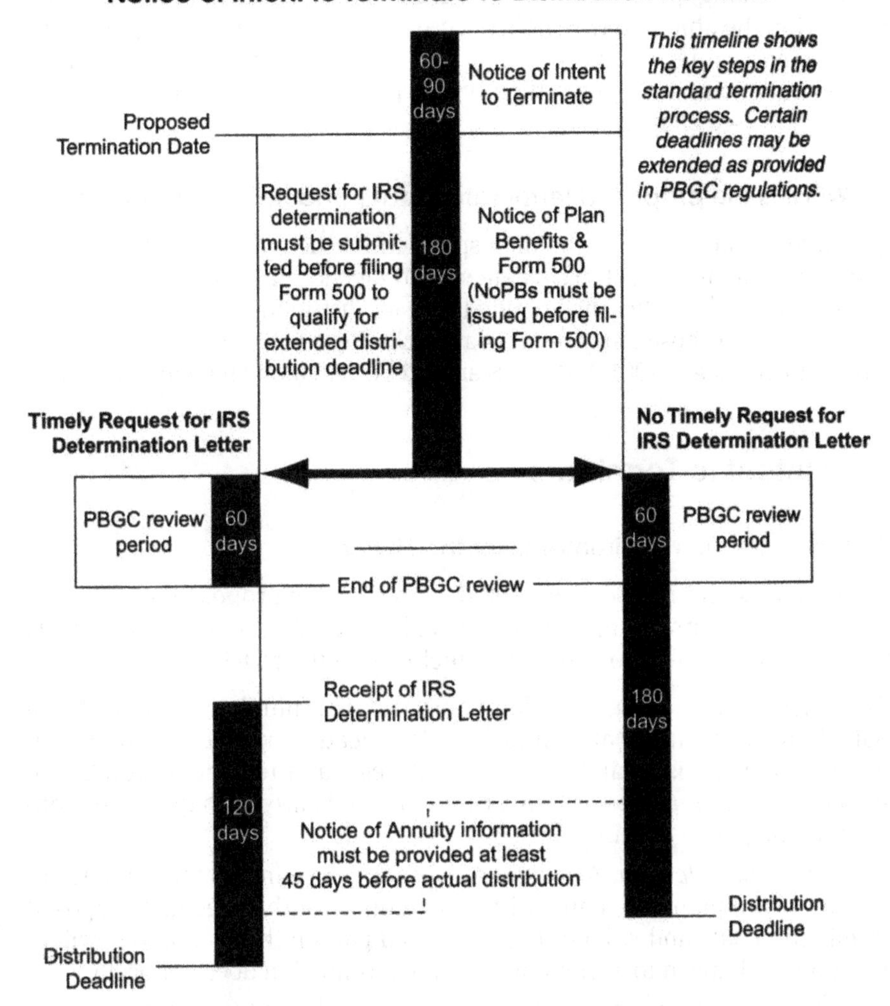

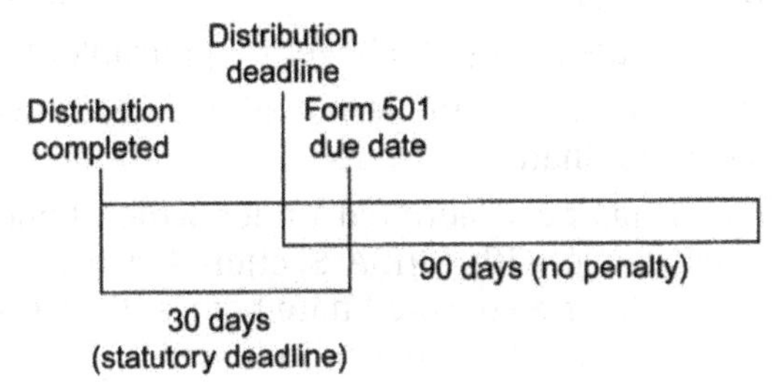

Q 16:7 What determines whether a PBGC-covered plan may be terminated?

Generally speaking, plan assets must be sufficient to cover plan liabilities on termination (i.e., be able to pay benefits accrued to date); that is, the plan must qualify as a standard termination (see Q 16:5). In some cases where the plan sponsor is experiencing financial difficulty, the plan may be terminated in a distress termination (see chapter 17).

Q 16:8 What is the proposed termination date and how is it selected?

Proposed termination date is the date specified by the plan administrator of a single-employer plan in a NOIT. This date should be chosen to be at least 60 days but no more than 90 days after the intended date for distribution to affected parties of the NOIT. The date chosen may be any day, including a Saturday, Sunday, or federal holiday. [PBGC Reg. § 4001.2; PBGC Standard Termination Filing Instructions]

Notice of Intent to Terminate

Q 16:9 What are the requirements for the NOIT?

At least 60 days and no more than 90 days before the proposed termination date, the plan administrator must issue to each affected party a written NOIT. All of the following information should be included in the NOIT:

1. *Identifying information.* The plan name and plan number (used for Form 5500 filings), the name and employer identification number (EIN) of each contributing sponsor, and the name, address, and telephone number of the person who may be contacted by an affected party with questions concerning the plan's termination;
2. *Intent to terminate plan.* A statement that the plan administrator intends to terminate the plan in a standard termination as of the specified proposed termination date and will notify the affected party if the proposed termination date is changed to a later date or if the termination does not occur;
3. *Sufficiency requirement.* A statement that, in order to terminate in a standard termination, plan assets must be sufficient to provide all plan benefits under the plan;
4. *Cessation of accruals.* A statement (whichever is applicable) that:
    a. Benefit accruals will cease as of the termination date, but will continue if the plan does not terminate,
    b. A plan amendment has been adopted under which benefit accruals will cease, in accordance with ERISA Section 204(h), as of the proposed termination date or a specified date before the proposed termination date, whether or not the plan is terminated, or
    c. Benefit accruals ceased, in accordance with ERISA Section 204(h), as of a specified date before the NOIT was issued;

5. *Annuity information.* If required (see Q 16:10) because annuity contracts are being distributed to irrevocably provide benefits under the plan, plan participants must be furnished with the information contained in Q 16:12;
6. *Benefit information.* A statement that each affected party entitled to plan benefits will receive a written notification regarding his or her plan benefits;
7. *Summary plan description (SPD).* A statement as to how an affected party can obtain the latest updated SPD under ERISA Section 104(b);
8. *Continuation of monthly benefits.* For persons who are in pay status (currently receiving annuity or installment benefits for at least one year) as of the proposed termination date, a statement (as applicable) explaining:
   a. That their monthly (or other periodic) benefit amounts will not be affected by the plan's termination; or
   b. How their monthly (or other periodic) benefit amounts will be affected under plan provisions;
9. *Extinguishment of guarantee.* A statement that the PBGC no longer guarantees that a participant's or beneficiary's plan benefits after plan assets have been distributed in full satisfaction of all plan benefits under the plan, either by the purchase of irrevocable commitments (annuity contracts) or by an alternative form of distribution provided for under the plan.

A model NOIT is contained in the PBGC Standard Termination Filing Instructions, Appendix B.

[PBGC Reg. § 4041.23(b); PBGC Standard Termination Filing Instructions]

Q 16:10 Who must receive a notice of annuity information?

Any participant who is entitled to plan benefits, other than a participant who is receiving a *de minimis* benefit, must receive a notice of annuity information. Generally, this is provided as part of the NOIT (see Q 16:9). If the insurance carrier was not known at the time the NOIT was issued, however, the NOIT must contain a statement that the annuity information about the selected insurer will be provided in a supplemental notice of annuity information at least 45 days in advance of the distribution (see Q 16:12). A failure to provide a required supplemental notice to an affected party will be deemed to be a failure to comply with the NOIT requirements. [PBGC Reg. § 4041.27]

Q 16:11 How is the plan administered during the termination process?

Neither purchases of irrevocable commitments to provide any plan benefits nor any plan benefits attributable to employer contributions (other than death benefits) in any form other than an annuity may be made during the following time frame:

1. Earliest date: the first day the plan administrator issues a NOIT, and
2. Latest date: the last day of the PBGC's 60-day review period.

An exception exists if the participant has terminated employment or is otherwise permitted under the Code to receive the distribution. As long as the distribution is consistent with prior practice and is not reasonably expected to jeopardize the plan's sufficiency for benefits, irrevocable commitments may be made.

[PBGC Standard Termination Filing Instructions; PBGC Reg. § 4041.22]

The PBGC has two substantial concerns when a plan purchases irrevocable commitments before initiating a related standard termination:

1. A participant whose plan benefits are fully satisfied through the purchase of an irrevocable commitment prior to the issuance of a NOIT will not receive the disclosures required as a part of the standard termination process, including advance notice of the plan termination, advance information about the insurer, and a statement that the PBGC no longer guarantees his or her plan benefits. Such participants may not have the same opportunity to correct personal information used to calculate their benefits or provide personal data not available to the plan. In addition, the PBGC would not receive the information necessary to determine whether participants received their correct benefits.
2. Plan assets could be insufficient for plan benefits at the time of any distribution upon termination, because plan assets used to purchase irrevocable commitments would no longer be available to pay other plan benefits. To a certain extent, this concern is alleviated by the restrictions on benefits under Code Section 436, which would treat the purchase of such irrevocable commitments as a prohibited payment if the plan's funded percentage was below 80 percent (or 100 percent in the case of a plan sponsor's bankruptcy). (See chapter 12.)

[Preamble to Proposed PBGC Regulations § 4041, Nov. 18, 2009]

Q 16:12 What information must the notice of annuity information contain?

The plan administrator must include:

1. *Identity of insurers.* The name and address of the insurer or insurers from whom (if known), or (if not) from among whom, the plan administrator intends to purchase irrevocable commitments (annuity contracts);
2. *Change in identity of insurers.* A statement that if the plan administrator later decides to select a different insurer, affected parties will receive a supplemental notice no later than 45 days before the distribution date; and
3. *State guaranty association coverage information.* A statement informing the affected party that:
    a. Once the plan distributes a benefit in the form of an annuity purchased from an insurance company, the insurance company takes over the responsibility for paying that benefit;

b. All states, the District of Columbia, and the Commonwealth of Puerto Rico have established guaranty associations to protect policyholders in the event of an insurance company's financial failure;

c. A guaranty association is responsible for all, part, or none of the annuity if the insurance company cannot pay;

d. Each guaranty association has dollar limits on the extent of its guaranty coverage, along with a general description of the applicable dollar coverage limits;

e. In most cases, the policyholder is covered by the guaranty association for the state where he or she lives at the time the insurance company fails to pay; and

f. How to obtain the addresses and telephone numbers of guaranty association offices from the PBGC.

A model notice of state guaranty association coverage of annuities is contained in the PBGC Standard Termination Filing Instructions, Appendix C and can be accessed on the Internet at

www.pbgc.gov/docs/500_instructions.pdf

[PBGC Reg. § 4041.27(b); PBGC Standard Termination Filing Instructions]

Q 16:13 What happens if the insurance company providing the annuities is not known at the time the NOIT is issued?

If the identity of the insurance company is not known, a supplemental notice must be provided to an affected party no later than 45 days before the distribution date. In lieu of the notice of annuity information, the following must be provided with the NOIT:

- A statement that irrevocable commitments (annuity contracts) may be purchased from an insurer to provide some or all of the benefits under the plan,
- A statement that the insurer or insurers have not yet been identified, and
- A statement that affected parties will be notified at a later date (but no later than 45 days before the distribution date) of the name and address of the insurer or insurers from whom the plan administrator intends to purchase irrevocable commitments (annuity contracts).

[PBGC Reg. § 4041.27(c), (d)]

Q 16:14 Who are affected parties?

Affected parties—that is, those who must receive the NOIT—fall into the following categories:

1. Each participant;
2. Each beneficiary of a deceased participant;

3. Each alternate payee under a qualified domestic relations order (QDRO) (see chapter 3);
4. Each employee organization that currently represents any group of participants;
5. For any group of participants not currently represented by an employee organization, the employee organization, if any, that last represented the group of participants within the last five years; and
6. The PBGC.

If an affected party has designated in writing that another individual is to receive the notice, the designated individual is the affected party. [ERISA § 4001(a)(21); PBGC Reg. § 4001.2]

Preliminary Information for PBGC

Q 16:15 What information is contained in the standard termination notice?

In accordance with the rules set forth in PBGC Regulations Section 4041.3(a) and (b), the standard termination notice that the plan administrator must file with the PBGC must contain:

1. PBGC Form 500 (see Q 16:16);
2. The enrolled actuary's certification form, Schedule EA-S (see Q 16:16); and
3. Designation of Representative, Form REP-S, if the plan administrator desires to designate an individual to represent it before the PBGC.

[PBGC Reg. § 4041.25; Standard Termination Filing Instructions]

Q 16:16 What information must be contained in PBGC Form 500 and Schedule EA-S?

Key elements of Form 500 include the reason(s) for plan termination, whether the termination was associated with changes in the plan sponsor, the number of plan participants, whether participants will be covered by another plan, and whether there will be a reversion to the plan sponsor (see chapter 15). The PBGC Form 500 contains blanks for the e-mail addresses of the plan administrator as well as the person to be contacted for more information. If the e-mail address is completed, the PBGC will acknowledge the receipt of the standard termination notice via e-mail.

Key items on Schedule EA-S, the certification by the enrolled actuary, include the following:

1. Estimated value of plan assets as of the proposed distribution date;
2. Estimated value of plan liabilities as of the proposed distribution date (see Qs 16:19–16:21); and

3. Total residual assets and whether the residual assets are to be returned to the plan sponsor or distributed to plan participants.

[ERISA § 4041(b)(2)(A)(ii); PBGC Form 500, Schedule EA-S]

Q 16:17 When must Form 500 and Schedule EA-S be filed?

Form 500 and Schedule EA-S must be completed and filed on or before the 180th day after the proposed termination date. The plan administrator may select a proposed termination date that is later than the date selected in the NOIT (see Qs 16:8, 16:9), provided that it is not later than 90 days after the earliest date on which a NOIT was issued to any affected party. [PBGC Reg. § 4041.25; PBGC Standard Termination Filing Instructions]

> **Example 16-3:** ABC Grocery is terminating its PBGC-covered defined benefit plan. The plan administrator, Susan, had originally selected a proposed termination date of July 1, 2018. The NOIT was distributed to interested parties on April 15, 2018, which was within the 60- to 90-day timeframe required. Because of delays in issuing the NOPB to participants, Form 500 cannot be filed until February 15, 2019 (more than 180 days after the proposed termination date). If the proposed termination date is delayed to October 1, 2018, a new NOIT must be issued no earlier than July 3, 2018 (90 days before the proposed termination date).

Q 16:18 Why would the PBGC issue a notice of noncompliance?

Within 60 days after receiving the NOIT, the PBGC may issue a notice of noncompliance (NONC) if:

1. The plan administrator failed to properly issue the NOIT to all affected parties (other than the PBGC);
2. The plan administrator failed to properly issue a NOPB (see Q 16:6) to all affected parties entitled to plan benefits;
3. The plan administrator failed to properly file the standard termination notice, Form 500;
4. As of the distribution date proposed in the standard termination notice, plan assets are not sufficient to meet the plan's benefit liabilities; or
5. In the case of a spinoff/termination transaction, the plan administrator failed to properly issue any required notice.

The PBGC may decide not to issue an NONC based on a failure to meet the notice requirement in items (1), (2), (3), or (5) above if the PBGC determines that issuance of the NONC would be inconsistent with the interests of participants and beneficiaries;

The plan administrator and the PBGC may agree to extend the 60-day review period by written agreement signed before the expiration of the original 60-day review period. Subsequent written agreements may extend this period further.

After the end of the PBGC's review period, the PBGC may still issue an NONC or suspend a termination proceeding for a failure to meet any of the requirements above, if the PBGC determines that such action is necessary to carry out the purposes of Title IV. The NONC could even be issued after a PBGC audit.

The PBGC may also issue an NONC at any time if the plan administrator fails to properly complete the final distribution of plan assets. For example, the following failures may cause the PBGC to issue an NONC:

- Failing to satisfy the requirements for providing plan benefits in the form of an irrevocable commitment, or
- Failing to complete the distribution before the distribution deadline

[ERISA § 4041(b)(2)(C); PBGC Standard Termination Filing Instructions]

Q 16:19 What happens if the PBGC does not issue a NONC?

The plan administrator may begin to distribute assets pursuant to the standard termination of the plan as soon as practicable after the 60-day period expires. The plan administrator must complete the distribution of plan assets by the later of:

1. 180 days after the PBGC review period ends (generally 240 days after the PBGC receives a complete and valid Form 500 filing), or
2. 120 days after the plan's receipt of a favorable IRS determination letter.

The IRS determination letter deadline described above is available only if, on or before the time the plan administrator files the Form 500 with the PBGC, the plan administrator submits a valid request for a determination letter with respect to the plan's tax-qualification status upon termination. (See chapter 15 for a discussion of the IRS determination letter request.) Final distribution may occur only if the plan's assets are sufficient to meet its benefit liabilities. [ERISA § 4041(b)(2)(D); PBGC Standard Termination Filing Instructions]

Measurement of Benefit Liabilities

Q 16:20 How are benefit liabilities in a standard termination measured?

Generally speaking, plan liabilities are equal to the present value of the accrued benefit of all participants as of the date of termination. (Chapter 9 discusses the determination of the accrued benefit in a defined benefit plan.) The present value of plan benefits that will be provided through the purchase of annuity contracts is either the actual quoted cost by the selected insurer or a reasonable estimate of the expected annuity contract cost. The present value of non-annuity benefits (e.g., lump sums) is computed by applying the actuarial equivalence factors contained in the plan document. The factors are based upon defined pre- and post-retirement interest and mortality assumptions. Note that regulations and Code Section 417(e) provide that lump sums be at least as great as the prescribed minimum.

Q 16:21 What are the prescribed interest and mortality rates to be used for determining minimum amounts for non-annuity benefit liabilities in plans terminating in a standard termination?

For plan years beginning before 2008, the mandatory interest rate was the rate on 30-year Treasury securities, adjusted monthly as shown in Appendix C, and the mandatory mortality table was the 1994 Group Annuity Reserving Table, as shown in Appendix F.

IRS Revenue Ruling 2007-67 provides the applicable mortality table for annuity starting dates in 2008, and IRS Notice 2008-85 includes a modified "unisex" version of the static mortality tables (used to calculate minimum funding obligations for 2009 through 2013 plan years) that are to be used for calculating minimum lump-sum distributions during that same period. The mortality tables for 2014 and 2015 are found in Notice 2013-49. The mortality table for 2016 is found in Notice 2015-53, the 2017 mortality table is found in Notice 2016-50, and the 2018 mortality table from Notice 2017-60. The applicable unisex mortality tables are shown in Appendix F.

Also for years beginning after 2007, the prescribed interest rates are those used for purposes of the minimum lump sum under Code Section 417(e). A three-segment rate approach is used, with a phase-in of prior rates to new rates at 20 percent a year from 2008 through 2011. The corridor rates imposed on minimum funding requirements by the Moving Ahead for Progress in the 21st Century Act (MAP-21) and Highway and Transportation Funding Act of 2014 (HATFA) did not alter the rates applicable for Code Section 417(e) or standard termination liabilities.

The minimum lump-sum value is calculated using the first, second, and third segment rates for the month before the date of distribution or such other time as prescribed by Treasury regulations. The adjusted first, second, and third segment rates are derived from a corporate bond yield curve prescribed by the Secretary of the Treasury for such month that reflects the yields on investment grade corporate bonds with varying maturities (rather than a 24-month average, as under the minimum funding rules). Thus, the interest rate that applies depends on how many years in the future a participant's annuity payment will be made. Typically, a higher interest applies for payments made further out in the future.

A transition rule applied for distributions in 2008 through 2011. For distributions in 2008 through 2011, minimum lump-sum values were determined as the weighted average of two values:

1. The value of the lump sum determined under the methodology under pre-2008 law (the "old" methodology); and
2. The value of the lump sum determined using the methodology applicable for 2008 and thereafter (the "new" methodology).

The phase-in for years 2008 through 2012 is shown in the following table:

Plan Year	*Weighting Factor "Old" 417(e) Rates*	*Weighting Factor "New" PPA Rates*
2008	80%	20%
2009	60%	40%
2010	40%	60%
2011	20%	80%
2012 and later	0%	100%

Note that statutory hybrid plans (e.g., cash balance or pension equity plans) (see chapter 9) are not treated as failing to meet the present value requirements of Code Section 417(e) if the plans provide that the present value of the accrued benefit is equal to the participants' hypothetical account balances or accumulated percentages of final average compensation as applicable, provided such plans also meet certain other requirements under PPA.

[PPA § 302; ERISA § 205(g)(3); I.R.C. § 417(e)(3); Treas. Reg. § 1.430(h)-1; I.R.C. § 411(a)(13)(A); PBGC Standard Termination Filing Instructions]

Q 16:22 How are the interest rates determined?

The regulations permit selection of a monthly, quarterly, or annual period during which the applicable interest rate remains constant. Permitting selection of such a quarterly or annual stability period allows plans to offer greater benefit stability than is provided by the statutory rule, under which the applicable interest rate changes monthly. The temporary regulations provide that the applicable interest rate for the stability period may be determined as the interest rate for any one of the five calendar months preceding the first day of the stability period. Permitting this "lookback" of up to five months provides added flexibility and gives plan administrators and participants more time to comply with notice and election requirements. Thus, a plan may change the applicable interest rate monthly, quarterly, or annually, and may determine the rate with reference to one of the five months preceding the month, quarter, or year. [Treas. Reg. § 1.417(e)-1(d)(4)]

Example 16-4: ABC Grocery sponsors a defined benefit plan with a calendar-year plan and uses the same interest rate for all distributions in the plan year (i.e., the annual stability period) and provides 120 days for employee notices based on the actual interest rate. The plan provides that the applicable interest rate for the entire plan year is the interest rate specified by the Commissioner for the prior August (i.e., five calendar months before January 1, the first day of the plan year).

Q 16:23 May the lookback period or the stability period for the determination of interest rates be changed?

Yes. However, for a one-year period starting with the effective date of the amendment, the present value must be determined by using the greater of:

1. The present value determined using the interest rate determined before such amendment; or
2. The present value determined using the interest rate determined after such amendment.

[Treas. Reg. § 1.417(e)-1(d)(10)(ii)]

Example 16-5: ABC Grocery Defined Benefit Plan uses a one-month stability period and a one-month lookback for the determination of interest rates under Code Section 417(e). Prior to January 1, 2019, ABC Grocery amends the Plan to use an annual stability period beginning January 1, 2019. For any distribution during the 2019 plan year (January 1, 2019–December 31, 2019), the present value is determined by using the greater of:

1. The interest rates in effect for the month immediately preceding the month of the distribution or
2. The interest rates in effect for December 2018.

Q 16:24 What is the controversy surrounding the selection of interest rates for PBGC-covered plans that terminated in a prior year but distributed benefits during a current plan year?

There was confusion about a plan with a termination date in a prior plan year that actually makes distributions in a current plan year. In December 2008, the PBGC issued Technical Update 08-4, Minimum Lump Sum Assumptions for Single-Employer Plans that Terminate in a Plan Year Beginning on or After January 1, 2008. [https://www.pbgc.gov/prac/other-guidance/tu/technical-update-08-4-minimum-lump-sum-assumptions-single-employer-plans] The Update takes the position that the termination date, not the distribution date, determines which set of rules legally governs the calculation of minimum values. The minimum value of a participant's accrued benefit is calculated by applying plan provisions that reflect the law in effect on the plan's termination date, but the actual assumptions to be used are determined by reference to the date of distribution.

Example 16-6: ABC Grocery Defined Benefit Plan (with a calendar plan year) has a termination date of July 1, 2018. The plan has a two-month lookback and uses the plan year as the stability period. The plan is ready to make distributions in 2019. The lump sums paid in 2019 are calculated based on the November 2018 rates. Accordingly, a lump sum paid in 2019 would be determined using the November 2018 segment rates.

Insufficiency of Plan Assets

Q 16:25 What happens if the plan assets are not sufficient to satisfy the plan liabilities?

The plan sponsor has five options if plan assets are insufficient:

1. Make a contribution in an amount equal to the difference between benefit liabilities and plan assets. A model commitment to make the plan sufficient for plan benefits is contained in the PBGC Standard Termination Filing Instructions, Appendix D, and can be accessed at https://www.pbgc.gov/documents/500-instructions.pdf
2. Continue the plan and increase contributions to bring the plan up to the point at which it can be terminated in a standard termination. In most cases, it is generally desirable to cease future benefit accruals so that the liabilities do not increase due to these additional accruals.
3. Determine whether a majority owner or owners, if any, would like to waive a portion of their accrued benefits in order for the plan to qualify as a standard termination (see Qs 16:26, 16:27).
4. Find an annuity carrier to provide the accrued benefits to all participants through the use of a terminal funding contract (see Q 16:28), if the plan is not severely underfunded and does not allow for lump-sum distributions, or amend the plan to permit lump-sum distributions if the rates for lump-sum distributions would produce a lower liability than the annuity purchase rates.
5. Determine whether the plan sponsor qualifies for a distress termination (see chapter 17).

Q 16:26 Who is a majority owner?

In the case of a single-employer plan, a majority owner is an individual who directly or indirectly owns 50 percent or more of:

- An unincorporated trade or business,
- The capital interest or the profits interest in a partnership, or
- The voting stock of a corporation or the value of all of the stock of a corporation.

For these purposes, the constructive ownership rules of Code Sections 414(b) and (c) apply, which attribute ownership to certain individuals.

Note that the PBGC definition is not impacted by the majority owner definition used for guaranteed benefit phase-in.

[PBGC Reg. § 4041.2; 2013 Enrolled Actuaries Meeting Blue Book Q5]

Q 16:27 How does a majority owner waive benefits in a standard termination?

To facilitate the termination of the plan and distribution of assets in a standard termination, a majority owner may agree to forgo receipt of all or part of his or her benefit up to the point at which the benefit liabilities of all non-majority owners have been satisfied. Such an agreement is valid only under these four conditions:

1. The agreement is in writing;
2. In any case in which the total value of the benefit is greater than $5,000, the spouse of the majority owner consents, in writing, to the alternative treatment of the benefit;
3. The majority owner makes the election, and the spouse consents, during the time period beginning with the date of issuance of the NOIT and ending with the date of the last distribution; and
4. The agreement by the majority owner and the consent of the spouse is not inconsistent with a QDRO (see chapter 3).

[PBGC Reg. § 4041.21(b)(2)]

A sample waiver form follows.

Waiver of Benefits

I, ________, being a majority owner of ________, and a participant in the ________ plan, hereby agree to accept a benefit that is lower than my accrued benefit under the terms of the Plan if, upon termination of the Plan and allocation of assets pursuant to plan section ________, assets are insufficient to cover all such benefits.

I understand that my signature on this form will release the plan and the Pension Benefit Guaranty Corporation from any and all liability to myself or my beneficiaries with respect to my benefits under the above-mentioned plan.

Date: ________________ Signed: ________________

Participant/Majority Owner

Married: ☐ Yes ☐ No

As the spouse of the majority owner mentioned above, I also agree to release the plan and the Pension Benefit Guaranty Corporation from any liability to myself or my beneficiaries with respect to benefits under the above-mentioned plan. I understand that by signing this form I may be giving up valuable benefits under the plan.

Date:________________ Signed:________________

Date:________________

Signed:________________

(Witness or Notary)

Q 16:28 What is a terminal funding contract?

A terminal funding contract is a group annuity contract purchased by the plan to guarantee the payment of accrued benefits at normal retirement age for a defined benefit plan. Once the contract is purchased, the plan ceases to be liable for the payment of benefits, and the insurance carrier irrevocably promises to pay the benefits to participants when they reach normal or early retirement age.

Example 16-7: ABC Grocery has a frozen defined benefit plan and does not permit participants to receive lump-sum distributions. The plan sponsor has decided to terminate the plan because it no longer meets their business needs. The actuary calculates the present value of accrued benefits (PVAB) and determines that the liabilities of the plan are equal to $375,000 as of May 17, 2018. However, the plan assets as of May 17, 2018, are only $335,000. ABC Grocery does not wish to contribute anything further to the plan or continue the plan. On the advice of its pension consultant, ABC Grocery seeks competitive bids from insurance companies for a terminal funding contract to provide the benefits accrued in the plan. ABC Grocery receives the following bids:

Insurance Carrier	*Terminal Funding Quote*
MLIC	$345,000
FBN	$312,000
TIC	$327,000

Although FBN has the lowest bid, ABC Grocery chooses TIC because its rating is the highest among insurance carriers in the industry.

Actions of Plan Sponsor

Q 16:29 When must a plan sponsor adopt a resolution terminating a defined benefit plan?

The termination resolution can be adopted at any time prior to the proposed termination date, as long as a plan amendment ceasing benefit accruals was already timely adopted. Since plan amendments ceasing benefit accruals must be adopted at least 45 days (15 days for a small plan) in advance of the cessation of benefit accruals (see Q 16:33), this must be considered when adopting a proposed termination date when benefit accruals have not already been ceased. [ERISA § 204(h)]

Q 16:30 What constitutes a small plan for purposes of the 204(h) notice?

A small plan is defined as one that the plan administrator reasonably expects to have fewer than 100 participants who have an accrued benefit under the plan (on the effective date of the plan termination). [Treas. Reg. § 54.4980F-1 Q&As-3, -9]

Q 16:31 What liability does the plan sponsor have to contribute to a defined benefit plan in the year of termination?

That depends on the funded status of the plan. If the plan is overfunded—that is, plan assets exceed plan liabilities—it is quite likely that contributions by the plan sponsor will not be required. In any event, an actuarial valuation must be performed in the year of termination to determine the minimum funding requirements in the year of termination.

Q 16:32 Do the Minimum Required Contribution requirements under Code Section 430 apply for the entire year in the year of plan termination?

For 2008 plan years and later, generally, the Minimum Required Contribution (MRC) consists of a target normal cost plus shortfall bases amortization. Both components are calculated based on the benefit accrued at the beginning of the plan year and the benefit accrued (or projected to be accrued) during the plan year. Therefore, no special rules apply in the year of termination. However, the benefit accrued in the year of termination may be affected by the termination amendment. [I.R.C. § 430(b); Treas. Reg. § 1.430(d)-1(b)(1)]

For plan years that began before 2008, the charges and credits to the funding standard account are adjusted ratably to reflect the portion of the plan year from the first day of the plan year to the date of termination. [Prop. Reg. § 1.412(b)-4(b)]

ERISA Section 204(h) Notice

Q 16:33 Why is a notice required to inform participants of the cessation of benefit accruals?

ERISA requires that a defined benefit plan may not be amended to provide for a significant reduction in the rate of future benefit accruals unless, after adoption of the plan amendment and not less than 45 days (15 days for small plans) before the effective date of the plan amendment, the plan administrator provides a written notice (commonly referred to as a 204(h) notice) setting forth the plan amendment and its effective date, to:

- Each affected participant in the plan,
- Each affected beneficiary who is an alternate payee under a QDRO (see chapter 3), and
- Each employee organization representing participants in the plan.

[ERISA § 204(h)]

Q 16:34 How is the 204(h) notice delivered to each participant?

A plan administrator (including a person acting on behalf of the plan administrator, such as the employer or plan trustee) must provide the 204(h) notice using a method reasonably calculated to ensure that the participant actually receives it (see Qs 15:9–15:15 for further information on 204(h) notices). [Treas. Reg. § 54.4980F-1, Q&A-13]

Information Gathering

Q 16:35 What data must be collected to terminate the plan?

The data needed depends on the type of defined benefit plan being terminated, whether the plan is top heavy, and the use of life insurance contracts:

- *Flat-dollar benefit plan.* It will be necessary to obtain the years or partial years of credited service.
- *Percentage-of-pay benefit plan.* Pay earned during the plan's compensation averaging period (based on the plan's definition of compensation) as well as credited service should be obtained.
- *Individual insurance contracts.* Special care needs to be taken to dispose of individual insurance contracts. Although the plan sponsor clearly has authority to surrender the contracts, it may be appropriate to offer participants the opportunity to continue the life insurance protection (see chapter 25).

Q 16:36 What other information must be reviewed or collected?

Of particular importance are the plan documents. The plan documents should be reviewed and amended, if necessary, to ensure compliance with all existing laws.

If benefits accrue during the plan year of termination, the accruals should be reviewed to ensure compliance with the requirements of Code Section 401(a)(4). It is also generally helpful to review the plan's compliance history for at least the last five to six years to spot problems before the plan is submitted to the IRS to request a favorable determination letter on the termination of the plan. If problems are discovered, the IRS voluntary compliance program may offer alternative solutions (see chapter 23).

Notice of Plan Benefits

Q 16:37 What is the notice of plan benefits?

The NOPB provides detailed information about the benefit entitlement and its calculation to each affected party. The NOPB must be issued to each affected party who, as of the proposed termination date, falls into one of the following categories:

- A participant,
- A beneficiary of a deceased participant, or

- An alternate payee under a QDRO.

The NOPB must be issued no later than the time the plan administrator files the standard termination notice (Form 500 and Schedule EA-S) with the PBGC. After the proposed termination date and on or before the distribution date, the NOPB must also be issued to a person who becomes a beneficiary of a deceased participant or an alternate payee.

[PBGC Reg. § 4041.24(a); PBGC Standard Termination Filing Instructions]

Q 16:38 Does the NOPB contain the same information for all participants?

No. A NOPB must contain both general information and specific additional information for three categories of affected parties:

1. Persons in pay status (currently receiving annuity or installment benefits for at least one year) as of the proposed termination date;
2. Persons not in pay status as of the proposed termination date, but who have made valid benefit elections or for whom the plan administrator has determined that the benefit will be payable as a lump sum (e.g., individuals who are below the $5,000 cash-out threshold); and
3. All other participants not in pay status.

[PBGC Reg. § 4041.24]

Q 16:39 What information must be provided in the NOPB?

The plan administrator must include the following information in each NOPB:

1. The name of the plan, the EIN of the contributing sponsor, and the plan number (PN);
2. The name, address, and telephone number of the person who may be contacted to answer questions on a participant's or beneficiary's benefit;
3. The proposed termination date and any extended proposed termination date;
4. If the amount of the plan benefits in the notice is an estimate, a statement that the amount is an estimate and that benefits paid may be greater than or less than the estimate;
5. Except for participants or beneficiaries in pay status for one year or more as of the proposed termination date, a statement containing the following information:
   a. The specific personal data used to calculate the plan benefits (e.g., date of birth, date of hire, credited service, salary history);
   b. A statement requesting that the affected party promptly correct any information he or she believes to be incorrect;

c. If any of the personal data needed to calculate the affected party's plan benefits is not available, the best available data, along with a statement informing the affected party of the data not available and affording him or her the opportunity to provide it; and

d. Any other applicable information.

6. Specific information depending on the status of the participant or beneficiary (see Qs 16:40–16:42)

[PBGC Reg. § 4041.24(b)]

Q 16:40 What information must be provided in the NOPB for participants in pay status?

For persons in pay status (currently receiving annuity or installment benefits for at least one year) as of the proposed termination date, the NOPB must contain the following information:

1. The amount and form of the participant's or beneficiary's plan benefits payable as of the proposed termination date;
2. The amount and form of benefit, if any, payable to a beneficiary upon the participant's death and the name of the beneficiary (generally applicable to joint and survivor or term certain annuities); and
3. The amount and date of any increase or decrease in the benefit scheduled to occur after the proposed termination date (or that has already occurred) and an explanation of the increase or decrease, including a reference to the pertinent plan provision.

[PBGC Reg. § 4041.24(c)]

Q 16:41 What information must be provided in the NOPB for participants who have elected to retire or who have *de minimis* benefits?

For participants who have elected to retire, and have made a valid election of a starting date and form of benefits, but have not yet begun to receive benefits or for participants who are receiving a *de minimis* benefit (a lump-sum benefit of less than $5,000) and the plan contains non-consensual lump-sum distributions, the NOPB must include:

1. The projected benefit starting date and the amount and form of the participant's plan benefits payable as of that date;
2. The amount and form of benefit, if any, payable to a beneficiary upon the participant's death and the name of the beneficiary (generally applicable to joint and survivor or term certain annuities);
3. The amount and date of any increase or decrease in the benefit scheduled to occur after the proposed termination date (or that has already occurred) and an explanation of the increase or decrease, including a reference to the pertinent plan provision;

4. If benefits are payable in a form other than a lump sum, the age at which the plan benefits will be paid, and if the age differs from the age stated in the plan, the age stated in the plan (with reference to pertinent plan provisions) as well as any age adjustment factors;
5. If benefits are payable in a form other than a lump sum, the form in which benefits will be paid, and if the form of benefits differs from the form stated in the plan, the form stated in the plan (with reference to pertinent plan provisions) as well as any form adjustment factors; and
6. If benefits are payable in a lump sum:
   a. An explanation of when a lump sum may be paid without the consent of the participant or the participant's spouse
   b. A description of the mortality table used to convert the benefit to a lump sum (with reference to pertinent plan provisions)
   c. A description of the interest rate(s) used to convert the benefit to a lump sum (with pertinent plan provision)
   d. An explanation of how interest rates are used to calculate lump sums
   e. A statement that the use of a higher interest rate results in a smaller lump-sum amount, and
   f. A statement that the applicable interest rate may change before the distribution date

[PBGC Reg. § 4041.24(d)]

Q 16:42 What information must be included in the NOPB for other participants not in pay status?

For all other participants not in pay status, the NOPB must include:

1. The amount and form of the participant's plan benefits payable at normal retirement age in any form permitted under the plan;
2. The availability of any alternative benefit forms, including those payable to a beneficiary upon the participant's death either before or after retirement, and, for any benefits to which the participant is or may become entitled that would be payable before normal retirement age, the earliest benefit commencement date, the amount payable, and after that date, whether the benefit would be subject to future reduction;
3. Specific personal data used to calculate the plan benefits described in Q 16:39, 5a, including:
   a. The participant's age at retirement
   b. The spouse's age
   c. The participant's length of service
   d. For Social Security offset plans, the participant's actual (or, if unknown, estimated) Social Security benefits (or, if estimated benefits, the assumptions used for the participant's earnings history); and

4. In order for the plan benefits to be paid as a lump sum, the following are needed:
   a. A description of the mortality table used to convert the monthly benefit to a lump sum
   b. A description of the interest rate used to convert the monthly benefit to a lump sum
   c. An explanation of how interest rates are used to calculate the lump sums
   d. A statement that the higher the interest rate used, the smaller the lump-sum amount, and
   e. A statement that the lump-sum amount given is an estimate because the applicable interest rate may change before the distribution date

[PBGC Reg. § 4041.24(e)]

Final Stages

Q 16:43 What should be considered in converting plan assets to cash in order to make distributions on termination?

The liquidation of plan assets could be a time-consuming process, depending on the types of assets in the plan. It is also possible to distribute assets in kind (see chapter 25), if the plan document allows such a distribution. If the plan assets are invested in marketable securities such as common stocks or mutual funds, the liquidation process may take a week or less. If some of the plan assets are invested in life insurance contracts or guaranteed investment contracts (GICs) with insurance companies, the liquidation process could be significantly longer. Some of the contracts may have significant penalties for early withdrawals. If the assets are not readily marketable (i.e., limited partnerships, real estate, closely held employer stock), the plan sponsor may have to find a willing buyer.

Q 16:44 When should the liquidation process be started?

In general, an investment advisor should be consulted before the liquidation of assets is needed so that cash is available as of the expected distribution date (except for assets being distributed in kind). Assets that are not readily marketable will generally take longer to liquidate, so additional liquidation time should be anticipated.

Q 16:45 Why is the PVAB recalculated at the time distributions are made?

There are several reasons why the PVAB may need to be recalculated between the date of plan termination and the date of distribution:

1. A number of months may intervene between the date of termination and the approval of the termination by the IRS, and thus the participants' ages may have changed.
2. The plan assets may change in value. If surplus plan assets are to be redistributed to plan participants, a nondiscriminatory allocation of the surplus must occur. [Rev. Rul. 80-229]
3. Applicable interest rates and mortality tables may have changed. [I.R.C. § 417(e)]

When the Plan Has Surplus Assets

Q 16:46 What are the rules governing reversions in a defined benefit plan covered by the PBGC?

If the plan requires mandatory after-tax contributions, surplus assets must be ratably distributed to participants' after-tax contribution accounts (see Q 8:6). Any residual assets of a single-employer plan may be distributed to the employer if:

1. All liabilities of the plan to participants and their beneficiaries have been satisfied;
2. The distribution does not contravene any provision of law;
3. The plan provides for a distribution to the employer in these circumstances; and
4. Any amendment to the plan permitting a reversion has been adopted on a timely basis (see Q 16:49).

[ERISA § 4044(d)(1)]

Q 16:47 How does the ratable distribution of surplus assets occur in a defined benefit plan with participants' mandatory after-tax contributions?

The portion of the surplus assets attributable to participants' mandatory after-tax contributions is the product of the following:

1. The market value of the surplus assets; and
2. A fraction:
   a. The numerator of which is the present value of all portions of the accrued benefits with respect to participants (see chapter 5) that are derived from participants' mandatory after-tax contributions, and
   b. The denominator of which is the present value of all benefits with respect to which assets are allocated under priority categories (2) through (6) of ERISA Section 4044 (see chapter 2).

[ERISA § 4044(d)(3)]

Example 16-8: ABC Architects terminates its contributory defined benefit plan as of September 30, 2018. The present value of all liabilities in the plan as of September 30, 2018, is broken down as follows:

Source	*Present Value*
Accrued benefits from mandatory after-tax employee contributions	$1,000,000
Benefits provided by employer	$4,000,000
Total benefit liabilities	$5,000,000

As of the distribution date, the market value of plan assets is $5.5 million. Therefore, there is a potential $500,000 available to the corporation. Because of the mandatory after-tax employee contributions, a portion of the surplus must be allocated to such employee-provided benefits. That portion is calculated by multiplying the potential reversion, $500,000, by the following fraction:

$$\frac{\$1{,}000{,}000}{\$5{,}000{,}000}$$

Thus, employees must receive a 20 percent pro rata portion of the surplus or $100,000.

Q 16:48 Who is entitled to receive a ratable portion of the surplus?

Each participant whose vested accrued benefit is or was attributable to his or her mandatory after-tax contributions is entitled to receive a ratable portion of the surplus funds. This includes individuals who are participants as of the plan termination date, as well as individuals who have received, during the three-year period ending with the termination date, a distribution from the plan of their entire vested accrued benefit in the form of a single-sum distribution or in the form of an annuity purchased by the plan. [ERISA § 4044(d)(3)(C)]

Example 16-9: The facts are the same as in the Example 16-8 in Q 16:47, including the fact that ABC Architects has terminated its defined benefit plan. Brianna received a distribution of her entire vested accrued benefit in the form of a lump-sum distribution in 2016, two years before the plan terminated. A portion of her vested accrued benefit was attributable to mandatory employee contributions. Brianna is entitled to share in a portion of the surplus, as if she were an active employee at the time of plan termination.

Q 16:49 What happens if a terminating defined benefit plan has surplus assets?

The plan document must define how surplus assets (the excess, if any, of plan assets over liabilities) are treated in the event of a plan termination. If such language is not in the plan or has not been in the plan document for the lesser of five years or the life of the plan, surplus assets must be distributed to participants in a nondiscriminatory manner. [ERISA § 4044(d)]

If the plan permits surplus assets to revert to the employer, there is a 50 percent excise tax on the reversion. The excise tax may be reduced to 20 percent if one of these events occurs:

1. The employer establishes or maintains a qualified replacement plan;
2. The plan provides benefit increases to participants in the terminating defined benefit plan; or
3. The employer is in Chapter 7 bankruptcy liquidation or in a similar court proceeding on the plan termination date.

[I.R.C. § 4980(d)(1)]

Q 16:50 What is a qualified replacement plan?

A qualified replacement plan is a qualified plan established or maintained by the employer that meets the following requirements:

1. At least 95 percent of the active participants in the terminated plan (who remain as employees of the employer after the termination) are active participants in the replacement plan.
2. A direct transfer is made from the terminated plan to the replacement plan before any employer reversion. This transfer is an amount equal to the excess (if any) of:
   a. At least 25 percent of the maximum amount the employer could receive as a reversion, *minus*
   b. The present value of benefit increases, if any, granted to participants in the terminated defined benefit plan (see Q 16:49).
3. For a defined contribution qualified replacement plan, the amount transferred is either:
   a. Allocated to the accounts of plan participants in the year the transfer occurs, *or*
   b. Credited to a suspense account and allocated over a period not to exceed seven years.

[I.R.C. § 4980(d)(2)]

Example 16-10: ABC Grocery sponsors a defined benefit plan that is in the process of terminating. The liabilities of the plan are $500,000, and the plan assets are $1 million. The plan allows for the reversion of surplus assets to the plan sponsor, but ABC Grocery wants to avoid paying a 50 percent excise tax of $250,000 on the reversion of $500,000. By transferring $125,000 (25% × $500,000) to a qualified replacement plan, ABC Grocery reduces the excise tax on the remainder reversion to $75,000 (20% × [$500,000 − $125,000]).

Q 16:51 May more than 25 percent of the surplus assets be transferred to a qualified replacement plan?

Yes, more than 25 percent of the surplus assets may be transferred to a qualified replacement plan. In a significant change in position, the IRS ruled that a transfer in excess of 25 percent of the surplus assets in a terminated defined benefit plan will not result in an imposition of the 20 percent excise tax under Code Section 4980 on the transferred proceeds. Only the amount returned to the plan sponsor will be subject to the 20 percent excise tax. Furthermore, the amount transferred will not be subject to corporate tax, nor will the plan sponsor be allowed a tax deduction under Code Section 404 for the transferred proceeds. [Rev. Rul. 2003-85]

Q 16:52 How large must benefit increases in a defined benefit plan be to qualify for the reduction in the reversion excise tax from 50 percent to 20 percent?

As an alternative to the qualified replacement plan, in order to reduce the reversion excise tax from 50 percent to 20 percent, the plan may provide benefit increases to participants in the terminating defined benefit plan. To reduce the excise tax, the aggregate present value of the increases must not be less than 20 percent of the maximum potential reversion. [I.R.C. § 4980(d)(3)] The allocation of the surplus assets must not discriminate in favor of highly compensated employees. [Rev. Rul. 80-229]

Example 16-11: In Example 16-10, ABC Grocery decides not to establish a qualified replacement plan. Still wanting to be able to reduce the $250,000 reversion tax, ABC Grocery decides to provide benefit increases to the participants in the terminating defined benefit plan to reduce the excise tax to 20 percent. As long as the aggregate present value of the benefit increases is at least $100,000 (20% × $500,000), the excise tax on the remainder reversion to ABC Grocery will be reduced to 20 percent.

Q 16:53 What benefit election forms and notices must be distributed and executed?

These election forms include the following:

- Form of Benefit Election and Statement of Relative Value;
- Waiver of Joint and Survivor Annuity and Spousal Consent;
- Tax Notice and Withholding Election; and
- Life Insurance Election Form, if applicable.

When the forms are completed and properly executed, distributions may be made to the participants or direct transfers may be made to the participants' IRAs or other qualified plans. (See chapter 15 for a discussion of these forms.)

Missing Participants

Q 16:54 What happens if a participant cannot be located?

These methods can be used to locate lost or missing participants:

1. *Private locator services.* Unlike the former SSA program, this type of service will generally provide the address to the plan sponsor. This is more expensive than the former SSA or IRS programs, but will likely provide a faster turnaround.
2. *Internet resources.*

(For more information on items 1 and 2, see chapter 15.)

3. *PBGC missing participant program.* If the plan administrator has made a diligent search (see Q 16:56) for the participants and cannot still locate them, the plan administrator may:
   a. Purchase an annuity in the participant's name (an irrevocable commitment that satisfies the requirements of PBGC Regulations Section 4041.28(c) from an insurance company); or
   b. Pay the designated benefit to the PBGC.

[PBGC Reg. § 4050; www.pbgc.gov/sites/default/files/form-mp100-instructions.pdf]

Q 16:55 What are the requirements for purchasing an annuity from an insurance company for a missing participant?

The selection of an insurance company to provide an annuity must satisfy the same standards used for other participants, including:

1. The plan administrator must select the insurer in accordance with the fiduciary standards of Title I of ERISA.
2. In the case of a plan in which any residual assets will be distributed to participants, a participating annuity contract may be purchased to satisfy the requirement that annuities be provided by the purchase of irrevocable commitments only if the portion of the price of the contract that is attributable to the participation feature:
   a. Is not taken into account in determining the amount of residual assets; and
   b. Is not paid from residual assets allocable to participants.

[PBGC Reg. § 4041.28(c), (d)]

This may be an impractical solution, because insurance carriers may decline to issue an annuity contract without the participant's signature. Thus, paying the designated benefit to the PBGC (after a diligent search) may be the only solution.

Q 16:56 How is a diligent search defined by the PBGC?

A diligent search must be made for each missing participant before information about the missing participant or payment is submitted to the PBGC (see Qs 16:57–16:58). A search is a diligent search only if it:

1. Begins not more than nine months before distributions are to be made and is carried on in such a manner that, if the individual is found, distribution to the individual can reasonably be expected to be made on or before the deemed distribution date;
2. Includes inquiry of any plan beneficiaries (including alternate payees) of the missing participant whose names and addresses are known to the plan administrator; or
3. Includes use of a commercial locator service to search for the missing participant if the benefit due to the participant is more than $50 per month, without charge to the missing participant or reduction of the missing participant's plan benefit (see Q 16:54). For benefits of less than $50 per month, only a records search is required.

The new regulations issued by the PBGC for plan terminations on or after January 1, 2018, expanded the above search requirements to include a search of plan records, records of the participant's most recent employer and any other retirement or welfare plan in which the participant participates, and a no-fee Internet search through a search engine or social media site. The regulation adds defined contribution plans and defined benefit plans not covered by the PBGC to the missing participant program as well as participants who can be located but are nonresponsive. The search for participants in defined contribution plans must be conducted following the requirements outlined in DOL's Field Assistance Bulletin No. 2014-01.

[PBGC Reg. § 4050.4(b); www.pbgc.gov/sites/default/files/form-mp100-instructions.pdf]

Q 16:57 What amount is paid to the PBGC after a diligent search for a missing participant fails?

The amount paid to the PBGC is called the *designated benefit*. In no event, however, may the designated benefit exceed the maximum lump sum permitted under Code Section 415 (see chapter 9). The provisions in the plan document dealing with the availability of lump-sum distribution will dictate the calculation of the designated benefit as shown below.

1. *Mandatory lump sum*. If a missing participant is required under the terms of the plan to receive a mandatory lump sum as of the deemed distribution date, the amount shall be the lump-sum payment that the plan administrator would have distributed to the missing participant as of the deemed distribution date. By law, this cannot exceed $5,000.
2. *De minimis lump sum*. If a missing participant is not described in paragraph 1 above, is not in pay status as of the deemed distribution date, and

has a *de minimis* benefit of $5,000 or less as of the deemed distribution date, the *missing participant lump-sum assumptions* and the "most valuable benefit" (Q 16:60) are used.

3. *No lump sum.* If the missing participant is not permitted under the terms of the plan to elect a lump sum, the *missing participant annuity assumptions* are used.
4. *Elective lump sum.* If the missing participant may, under the terms of the plan, elect a lump sum and the lump sum is greater than $5,000, then the greater of the amounts determined under paragraphs (1) or (3) is used.

The PBGC regulations for 2018 modify the calculation of the amount that is transferred to the PBGC for a missing participant. Under the regulations, the value is determined as of the transfer date using either the plan's assumptions or the PBGC missing participant assumptions, depending on whether the participant or spouse is required to consent to the distribution and if a lump sum can be elected. For participants who are not in pay status, the value of the benefit is determined as a life annuity beginning at an expected retirement age. The PBGC has posted an online spreadsheet that allows the plan's actuary to input the participant's information and have the spreadsheet compute the benefit transfer amount.

The regulations also break out the amount of missed benefit payments due to a participant from the participant's future benefit payments. The plan must transfer the missed payments plus interest (the plan make-up amount) due to a participant who is in pay status or a participant who is not in pay status but whose required beginning date under IRC § 401(a)(9) is prior to the benefit transfer date.

There is a $35 fee associated when a benefit valued at more than $250 is transferred to the PBGC.

[PBGC Reg. § 4050.5(a); www.pbgc.gov/sites/default/files/form-mp100-instructions.pdf]

Q 16:58 What are the missing participant annuity assumptions?

The *missing participant annuity assumptions* are the interest rate assumptions and actuarial methods (using the interest rates for annuity valuations in Table I of Appendix B to Section 4044 of the PBGC regulations) for valuing a benefit to be paid by the PBGC as an annuity applied:

1. As if the deemed distribution date were the termination date;
2. Using mortality rates that are a fixed blend of 50 percent of the healthy male mortality rates and 50 percent of the healthy female mortality rates found in PBGC Regulations Sections 4050 as found on the PBGC website at http://www.pbgc.gov/prac/mortality-retirement-and-pv-max-guarantee/erisa-mortality-tables/erisa-section-4050-mortality-table-for-2018-valuation-dates.html (see Appendix F);

3. Without using the expected retirement age assumptions in PBGC Regulation Sections 4044.55 through 4044.57;
4. Without making the adjustment for expenses provided for in PBGC Regulations Section 4044.52(d); and
5. By adding $300 as an adjustment (loading) for expenses for each missing participant whose designated benefit without such adjustment would be greater than $5,000.

[PBGC Reg. §§ 4050.2, 4050.5(b)(1); www.pbgc.gov/sites/default/files/form-mp100-instructions.pdf]

Q 16:59 How are missing participant lump-sum assumptions determined?

Missing participant lump-sum assumptions means the interest rate assumptions and actuarial methods for valuing a benefit to be paid by the PBGC as a lump sum and applied:

1. As if the deemed distribution date were the termination date;
2. Without using the expected retirement age assumptions in PBGC Regulation Sections 4044.55 through 4044.57;
3. Using mortality rates that are a fixed blend of 50 percent of the healthy male mortality rates and 50 percent of the healthy female mortality rates found in PBGC Regulations Sections 4050 as found on the PBGC website at http://www.pbgc.gov/prac/mortality-retirement-and-pv-max-guarantee/erisa-mortality-tables/erisa-section-4050-mortality-table-for-2018-valuation-dates.html (see Appendix F).
4. With no adjustment to reflect loading for expenses; and
5. Using the interest assumptions in Appendix B of PBGC Regulations Part 4022.

See Q 16:57 for the changes to the calculation for participants not in pay status under the 2018 PBGC regulations.

[PBGC Reg. § 4022.7(d); www.pbgc.gov/sites/default/files/form-mp100-instructions.pdf]

Q 16:60 What is the most valuable benefit for a missing participant?

For a missing participant who is in pay status as of the deemed distribution date, the most valuable benefit is the benefit being paid.

For a missing participant who is not in pay status as of the deemed distribution date, the most valuable benefit is the benefit payable at the age on or after the deemed distribution date (beginning with the participant's earliest early retirement age and ending with the participant's normal retirement age) for which the present value as of the deemed distribution date is the greatest.

The present value as of the deemed distribution date with respect to any age is determined by multiplying:

1. The monthly (or other periodic) benefit payable under the plan by
2. The present value, determined as of the deemed distribution date using the missing participant annuity assumptions, of a $1 monthly (or other periodic) annuity beginning at the applicable age.

See Q 16:57 for the changes to the calculation for participants not in pay status under the 2018 PBGC regulations.

[PBGC Reg. § 4050.5(b); www.pbgc.gov/sites/default/files/form-mp100-instructions.pdf]

Post-Distribution Certification

Q 16:61 What must be provided to the PBGC after benefits are distributed?

PBGC Form 501, *Post-Distribution Certification for Standard Termination,* must be prepared, signed by the plan administrator, and filed with the PBGC stating that all participants have received the benefits due them, either via a single sum or through the purchase of irrevocable commitments from an insurance carrier. If some participants could not be located, the plan administrator must purchase an annuity contract for the missing participants or the benefits payable are to be turned over to the PBGC in accordance with Qs 16:51–16:57. [ERISA § 4041(b)(3)(B); PBGC Reg. § 4041.29]

PBGC Form 501 should be filed no later than 30 days after completion of the distribution of assets in a standard termination. The form must be filed with the PBGC at:

Pension Benefit Guaranty Corporation
Standard Termination Compliance Division
Processing and Technical Assistance Branch
1200 K Street, NW
Washington, DC 20005-4026

The requirements for filing Form 501 were expanded after March 31, 2015, to include a copy of the plan document and documentation showing the actual payments to participants or annuity providers.

[PBGC Reg. § 4041.29; PBGC Standard Termination Filing Instructions]

Q 16:62 What are the penalties for failure to comply with the post-distribution certification requirements?

The PBGC may assess a penalty of up to $1,000 per day for late filing of a Form 501. However, PBGC will do so only to the extent the Form 501 is filed more than 90 days after the distribution deadline. [ERISA § 4071; PBGC Reg. § 4041.29]

Q 16:63 When must the distribution be completed?

The distribution of plan assets must be completed within 180 days after the 60-day review period expires or within 120 days of receipt of the IRS determination letter, if later (see Q 16:64), or within 180 days after the PBGC revokes its NONC. [PBGC Reg. § 4041.28(a)(1)] A failure to distribute assets within 180 days will nullify the termination, and all actions taken to effect the plan's termination will be null and void. The plan will then be treated as an ongoing plan. The plan administrator will then have to notify affected parties that the termination was invalid and a new NOIT will need to be issued. [PBGC Reg. § 4041.31(e)]

Q 16:64 May an extension of the 180-day period be granted?

Yes. The plan administrator will be entitled to an automatic extension to distribute assets to plan participants under these circumstances:

1. The plan administrator has submitted to the IRS a complete request for determination with respect to the plan's qualified status on or before the date the plan administrator files the standard termination notice with the PBGC.
2. The IRS determination letter is not received at least 60 days before the expiration of the 180-day period.

If the conditions for the automatic extension are satisfied, the time for distributing plan assets is extended until 120 days after receipt of a favorable determination letter from the IRS. [PBGC Reg. § 4041.30(c)]

Q 16:65 What if the plan administrator is unable to distribute assets for reasons other than the delay in issuance of a favorable determination letter from the IRS?

If a delay caused by, for example, the inability to obtain consent forms or illiquidity of plan assets causes the plan administrator to need more than 180 days, the plan administrator may request an extension from the PBGC. This is not an automatic extension; the PBGC has the authority to grant or deny it. The PBGC will consider the length of the delay and whether ordinary business care and prudence in attempting to meet the deadline has been exercised. Any request that is filed later than the 15th day before the deadline must include a justification for not filing the request earlier.

[PBGC Reg. § 4041.30]

Q 16:66 Where are requests for extension submitted?

All requests for extension must be sent, e-mailed, or faxed to:

Pension Benefit Guaranty Corporation
Standard Termination Compliance Division
Processing and Technical Assistance Branch
1200 K Street, NW
Washington, DC 20005-4026
e-mail: standard@pbgc.gov; Fax: (202) 326-4001

[PBGC Standard Termination Filing Instructions]

Spinoff/Termination Transaction Rules

Q 16:67 What is a spinoff/termination transaction?

A *spinoff/termination transaction* is a transaction in which a single defined benefit plan is split into two or more plans and there is a reversion of residual assets to an employer upon the termination of one or more but fewer than all of the resulting plans. [PBGC Reg. § 4041.23(c); PBGC Standard Termination Filing Instructions]

Q 16:68 Who are affected participants in a spinoff/termination transaction?

All participants, beneficiaries of deceased participants, and alternate payees in the original plan who are, as of the proposed termination date, covered by an ongoing plan are affected participants. [PBGC Reg. § 4041.23(c)]

Q 16:69 What notices must be provided to affected participants in a spinoff/termination transaction?

The following notices must be provided to affected participants:

1. NOIT (see Qs 16:9, 16:10);
2. NOPB (see Qs 16:37–16:42);
3. Notice of Annuity Information (see Qs 16:11–16:13).

[PBGC Reg. §§ 4041.23(c), 4041.24(f), 4041.27(a)(2)]

Q 16:70 What are the consequences of failure to provide the notices described above?

The PBGC will issue a NONC and the plan spinoff/termination transaction will be nullified. Note that the plan administrator may apply for reconsideration. [PBGC Reg. § 4041.31(a)(1)(v), (d)]

Final Returns/Reports

Q 16:71 When is the final Form 5500 due to be filed?

The due dates for Forms 5500, 5500-SF, or 5500-EZ are the last day of the seventh month after the date all assets were distributed. A 2½-month extension may be obtained by filing Form 5558 with the IRS. [2017 Instructions for Form 5500]

Q 16:72 How are the distributions to participants reported?

Form 1099-R is used to report distributions to participants. Form 1099-R must be provided to participants by January 31 in the calendar year following the calendar year of distribution. The plan reports income tax withholding on Form 945, which is also due by January 31 in the calendar year following the calendar year of distribution. (See chapter 27 for a detailed discussion of distribution reporting.)

Chapter 17

Underfunded Plans

When a qualified plan outlives its usefulness or can no longer be afforded, any plan sponsor generally wants to be rid of the plan and its administrative complexities. However, terminating an underfunded defined benefit plan, or an underfunded money purchase or target benefit plan, is not easy. Before the Employee Retirement Income Security Act (ERISA) was passed in 1974, underfunded defined benefit plans could be terminated and plan participants would simply lose their benefits.

This chapter does not address underfunded multiemployer plans. See the *Plan Termination Answer Book, Fifth Edition*, as supplemented by the 2017 Cumulative Supplement thereto [Bitzer; Wolters Kluwer Law & Business, 2017] for information related to underfunded multiemployer plans, including information on their termination.

Underfunded PBGC-Covered Defined Benefit Plans 17-1
Involuntary Terminations 17-20
PPA Requirements for Distress and Involuntary Terminations 17-21
Defined Benefit Plans Not Covered by the PBGC 17-24
Making Contributions to Meet Plan Liabilities 17-26
Underfunded Defined Contribution Plans 17-27

Underfunded PBGC-Covered Defined Benefit Plans

Q 17:1 What options are available to the plan sponsor of an underfunded Pension Benefit Guaranty Corporation (PBGC)-covered plan?

The plan sponsor has several options if plan assets are insufficient to satisfy benefit liabilities (underfunded) upon plan termination (see Q 17:2):

1. Make a contribution in an amount equal to the difference between benefit liabilities and plan assets. [PBGC Standard Termination Filing Instructions, Appendix D]

2. Continue the plan and continue making contributions to the plan until assets are at least as great as benefit liabilities and the plan can be terminated in a standard termination (see chapter 16). In most cases, it may be desirable to freeze future benefit accruals (see chapter 15).
3. Determine whether a majority owner or owners, if any, are willing to waive a portion of their accrued benefits so that the plan qualifies for a standard termination (see chapter 16).
4. If the plan is not severely underfunded and does not allow for lump-sum distributions, the plan sponsor may be able to find an annuity carrier to provide the full accrued benefits to all participants through the use of a terminal funding contract or amend the plan to permit lump-sum distributions if the rates for lump-sum distributions would produce a lower liability than the annuity purchase rates (see chapter 16).
5. Determine whether the plan sponsor qualifies for a distress termination (see Q 17:4).
6. Continue the plan and wait for the PBGC to take it over in an involuntary termination (see Q 17:32).

Q 17:2 How are benefit liabilities measured for plan termination purposes?

Generally speaking, plan liabilities are equal to the present value of the accrued benefit of all participants as of the date of termination. Plan liabilities include fixed and contingent liabilities, that is, benefits that may not yet be payable, because the participant has not reached a normal or early retirement age. [Treas. Reg. § 1.401-2(b)(2)] (Chapter 9 discusses the determination of the accrued benefit in a defined benefit plan.) The present value of accrued benefits is computed by applying the actuarial equivalence factors contained in the plan document. Those factors are limited to pre- and post-retirement interest and mortality assumptions. Note that there is a minimum lump sum actuarial equivalent of the accrued benefit as established by Code Section 417(e) within plans that offer a lump-sum benefit option. (See chapters 9, 15, and 16 for a detailed discussion of determining present value.)

Q 17:3 What steps are necessary to terminate a defined benefit plan in a PBGC distress termination?

In order to terminate a PBGC-covered plan in a distress termination, the plan administrator must take the following specific steps and meet specified deadlines as outlined below:

1. Select a proposed termination date (see Q 16:8).
2. Identify which of the four distress tests can be satisfied by each contributing sponsor and any controlled group members; each entity may separately satisfy a test (see Qs 17:4, 17:5).
3. Issue a Notice of Intent to Terminate (NOIT) to affected parties at least 60 days and no more than 90 days before the proposed termination date (see Qs 17:8, 17:9).

4. File Form 600 with the PBGC (see Qs 17:9, 17:10).
5. Beginning on the proposed termination date, reduce the benefits of participants in pay status to the estimated benefit levels guaranteed by the PBGC (see Qs 17:11–17:15).
6. File a Distress Termination Notice (PBGC Form 601 with Schedule EA-D) with the PBGC on or before the 120th day after the proposed termination date (see Q 17:10).
7. File participant and benefit information with the PBGC by the later of:
   a. 120 days after the proposed termination date; or
   b. 30 days after receipt of PBGC's determination that the requirements for a distress termination have been satisfied.
8. If the plan has sufficient assets to provide at least all guaranteed benefits (but not all plan liabilities), the plan administrator should proceed with the distribution of guaranteed benefits to plan participants and file PBGC Form 602, *Post-Distribution Certification*, with the PBGC.

[PBGC Reg. § 4041.41(a); PBGC Distress Termination Filing Instructions]

Q 17:4 How may the plan sponsor of a defined benefit plan qualify for a distress termination?

The PBGC has the authority to determine whether the plan sponsor qualifies for a distress termination. Each entity that is, as of the proposed termination date, a contributing sponsor of the plan or a member of the sponsor's controlled group must meet at least one of these criteria:

1. *Liquidation Test.* An entity has filed, or has had filed against it, as of the proposed termination date, a petition seeking liquidation in a case under Title 11, United States Code, or under any similar federal law or law of a state or political subdivision of a state and that case has not been dismissed as of the proposed termination date; or a reorganization case (described below) is converted to a liquidation case as of the proposed termination date.

   ERISA Section 4041(c)(B)(i) and Treasury Regulations Section 4041.41(c)(1) refer explicitly only to liquidation under federal bankruptcy or similar federal law or to liquidation under state insolvency law, and require that the liquidation case, as of the proposed termination date, not be dismissed. In determining whether an entity meets the liquidation *distress* test, the PBGC will consider a case in which liquidation was completed prior to the proposed termination date, or was achieved through a foreclosure by secured creditors (as a result of which the entity ceased operations and had all of its assets seized by such secured creditors) or through an assignment of all of the entity's assets for the benefit of creditors. (In any such case, however, the PBGC will find the liquidation test is met only if it concludes that there is no indication that a principal purpose of the liquidation is to evade liability with respect to the plan or the PBGC or otherwise to abuse the termination insurance program.)

2. *Reorganization Test.* An entity has filed, or has had filed against it, as of the proposed termination date, a petition seeking reorganization in a case under Title 11, United States Code, or under any similar law of a state or political subdivision of a state and that case has not been dismissed as of the proposed termination date. Such entity timely submits a copy of any requests for the approval of the bankruptcy court (or other appropriate court in a case under such similar law of a state or political subdivision) of the plan termination to the PBGC at the time the request is made. The court determines that, unless the plan is terminated, the entity will be unable to pay all of its debts pursuant to a plan of reorganization and will be unable to continue in business outside the Chapter 11 reorganization process and approves the termination.
3. *Business Continuation Test.* An entity demonstrates to the satisfaction of the PBGC that, unless a *distress* termination occurs, it will be unable to pay its debts when due and will be unable to continue in business.
4. *Unreasonably Burdensome Pension Costs Test.* An entity demonstrates to the satisfaction of the PBGC that the costs of providing pension coverage have become unreasonably burdensome to it solely as a result of a decline of its workforce covered as participants under all single-employer pension plans for which it is a contributing sponsor.

[PBGC Reg. § 4041.41(c); PBGC Distress Termination Filing Instructions]

Example 17-1: ABC Autos has sponsored a defined benefit plan since 1996. Employment was at an all-time high in 2008, when it reached 150 participants. However, because of a declining workforce, due in large part to an underperforming economy and reduced sales, ABC Autos can no longer afford the plan and wants to terminate it. If plan assets are insufficient to satisfy plan liabilities, ABC Autos may provide evidence to the PBGC that the cost of providing pension coverage has become unreasonably burdensome. If the PBGC is satisfied that ABC Autos has met the distress termination criteria, the plan sponsor may proceed.

Q 17:5 What information must be provided to the PBGC to support the request for a distress termination?

To substantiate a claim for a distress termination, the following documentation must be provided to the PBGC:

1. Liquidation test. A copy of the filed petition showing the court docket number or a copy of any documents showing a foreclosure by a secured creditor or an assignment for the benefit of creditors.
2. Reorganization test. A copy of the filed petition showing the court docket number, a copy of the notification to the PBGC of the request for approval of the plan termination by the federal bankruptcy or other federal court, or appropriate state court, and a copy of the court order (if any) approving termination.

3. Business continuation test. Audited financial statements of the entity must be provided for the five most recent fiscal years ending prior to the proposed termination date. If audited financial statements are not available, unaudited statements may be submitted together with a brief explanation of why audited statements are not available. The financial statements must be augmented as follows:
   a. Pension costs must be identified for each year for the pension plan that is the subject of the application. Pension costs should include an estimate of the annual and quarterly minimum funding requirements for the year in progress at the time of the application and for the next three years.
   b. If the entity has undergone or is in the process of undergoing a partial liquidation, include an estimate of the sales, gross profit, and operating profit that would have been reported for each of the five years covered by the financial statement for only the portion of the business that is currently expected to continue. State the significant assumptions made about the allocation of joint costs.
   c. State the estimated liquidation values for any assets related to discontinued operations or operations that are not expected to continue, along with the sources for the estimates.
   d. If financial statements are submitted that do not contain complete footnote disclosures, they must be augmented by a schedule identifying all outstanding indebtedness, including the name of the lender, the amount of the outstanding loan, schedule repayments, interest rate (collateral, significant covenants), and whether the loan is in default.
   e. Identify and explain any material changes in financial position since the date of the last financial statement.
   f. All business or operating plans prepared by or for management, including all explanatory text and schedules.
   g. All financial submissions, if any, made within the prior three years to a financial institution, government agency, or investment banker in support of possible outside financing or sale of the business.
   h. All recent financial analyses done by an outside party, with a certification by the company's chief executive officer that the information on which each analysis is based is accurate and complete.
   i. Any other relevant information.
4. Unreasonably burdensome pension costs test. The name and plan number of each single-employer defined benefit plan maintained by the contributing sponsor and each controlled group member must be included as well as the latest Form 5500, Schedule SB or MB, filed for each plan. A plan census for each plan showing total, active, and retired participants for the five most recent plan years ending prior to the proposed termination date (this data may be provided by submitting the relevant Form 5500, Schedule SB, or MB).

Audited financial statements for the entity's five most recent fiscal years ending prior to the proposed termination date, updated to show any material changes, with a breakout of the contributing sponsor's total pension cost, including any defined contribution plans, as a percentage of the entity's total wage costs and a statement of the total costs per plan. If audited financial statements are not available, submit unaudited statements and include a brief explanation of why audited statements are not available, as well as the reason(s) for a decline in workforce and any other relevant information.

[PBGC Distress Termination Filing Instructions]

Q 17:6 Should a plan sponsor who meets the distress criteria discussed in Q 17:4 always file for a distress termination with the PBGC?

No. A terminating plan that has sufficient assets to satisfy all benefit liabilities in a standard termination should file for a standard termination (see chapter 16). [PBGC Distress Termination Filing Instructions]

Q 17:7 What information must be provided to plan participants in a distress termination?

Before the plan sponsor asks the PBGC to review the request for a distress termination, the plan administrator must provide the 60-day NOIT to affected parties. [ERISA § 4041(c)(1)(A)]

Q 17:8 What information is contained in the NOIT?

At least 60 days and no more than 90 days before the proposed termination date, the plan administrator must issue to each affected party a written NOIT the plan. All of the following information should be included in the NOIT:

1. The name of the plan and contributing sponsor;
2. The employer identification number (EIN) of the contributing plan sponsor and the plan number (PN) assigned by the sponsor for Internal Revenue Service (IRS) and Department of Labor (DOL) disclosure (Form 5500, etc.). If there is no EIN or PN, the notice must indicate this;
3. The name, address, and telephone number of the person who may be contacted by an affected party with questions about the plan termination;
4. A statement that the plan administrator expects to terminate the plan in a distress termination on a specified proposed termination date;
5. A statement that benefit and service accruals will continue until the date of termination, or that benefit accruals were, or will be, frozen as of a specified date;
6. A statement providing information as to how an affected party can obtain a copy of the latest updated summary plan description;
7. A statement of whether plan assets are sufficient to pay all guaranteed benefits or all benefit liabilities;

8. A brief description of benefits guaranteed by the PBGC (e.g., if only a portion of the benefits is guaranteed because of the phase-in rule, that should be explained), and a statement that participants and beneficiaries may receive a portion of the benefits to which each is entitled under the terms of the plan in excess of guaranteed benefits; and
9. A statement, if applicable, that benefits may be subject to reduction because of the limitation on the amounts guaranteed by the PBGC or because plan assets are insufficient to pay for full benefits and that payments in excess of the amount guaranteed by the PBGC may be recouped by the PBGC.

[PBGC Reg. § 4041.43]

A model NOIT is contained in the PBGC Distress Termination Filing Instructions, Appendix B.

Q 17:9 Who are affected parties?

Affected parties, those who must receive the NOIT, fall into the following categories:

1. Each participant;
2. Each beneficiary of a deceased participant;
3. Each alternate payee under a qualified domestic relations order (QDRO) (see chapter 3);
4. Each employee organization that currently represents any group of participants;
5. For any group of participants not currently represented by an employee organization, the employee organization, if any, that last represented the group of participants within the last five years; and
6. The PBGC.

If an affected party has designated in writing that another individual is to receive the notice, the designated individual is the affected party. [ERISA § 4001(a)(21); PBGC Reg. § 4001.2]

Q 17:10 What information must be provided to the PBGC in a distress termination?

PBGC Form 600 is used to notify the PBGC that the plan sponsor intends to file for a distress termination. Form 600 is filed with the PBGC after the NOIT is provided to the other affected parties. General information that must be provided to the PBGC includes the proposed termination date, the estimated number of participants, any business changes occurring with the contributing plan sponsor, and information to substantiate the plan sponsor's claim that it qualified for a distress termination.

If the plan sponsor wishes to designate a representative to discuss the distress termination with the PBGC, Schedule REP-D may be filed with Form 600. If the plan sponsor wishes to designate a representative at a later time, Schedule REP-D can be filed at any time. It can also be used to revoke a prior designation.

As soon as practicable after the date on which the NOIT is provided to affected parties, the plan administrator must provide the following information to the PBGC:

1. Any information needed by the PBGC to substantiate that the business entity has met the *distress* criteria (see Q 17:4).
2. The amount, as of the proposed termination and distribution dates, of the current value of plan assets.
3. The actuarial present value of the benefit liabilities under the plan.
4. Whether or not the plan is sufficient for benefit liabilities.
5. The actuarial present value of benefits guaranteed under ERISA Section 4022 (see Qs 17:12–17:24).
6. Whether or not the plan is sufficient for guaranteed benefits.

If the plan is not sufficient for benefit liabilities, the plan administrator must provide the following information in an electronic format:

- Participant categories (retired, including beneficiaries receiving benefits from the plan; inactive participants entitled to future benefits; active participants with vested benefits; and active participants without vested benefits)
- Name of the participant; note substantial owners by inserting an asterisk (*) in front of the participant name (enter in parentheses each person's highest percentage of ownership during the 60-month period ending on the proposed termination date)
- Address
- Social Security number
- Marital status
- Gender
- Date of birth
- Beneficiaries (name, address, gender, date of birth, social security number)
- Retiree benefit information: For each retiree, provide the benefit commencement date, form of benefit, and the type of benefit (normal, early, late, or disability)
- Date of employment and date of participation in the plan
- Date of employment termination (if terminated before proposed termination date)
- Credited service: Provide the amount of all credited service as defined in the plan document. Show any breaks in service between the date of hire and date of termination of employment or proposed termination date.

- Compensation (if a factor in the calculation of the benefit, show all applicable compensation figures used in the determination of the benefits)
- Monthly plan accrued benefit at normal retirement age: This is the monthly benefit in the normal annuity form under the plan based on credited service as of the proposed termination date. If the monthly plan benefit is greater than the accrued benefit, show how the benefit is calculated. Provide any other information that is necessary to show the determination of each participant's plan benefit. If the plan is contributory, provide the total amount of each employee's contributions with and without interest credited by the plan and the portion of the normal retirement benefit attributable to employee contributions. If the accrued benefit is integrated using an offset or excess method, provide the offset or excess benefit and the data used in determining such amounts. If, before retirement, the accrued monthly benefit is determined from the cash value of the insurance or annuity contract, provide the cash value.
- Adjusted monthly accrued benefit: If, as of the proposed termination date, an individual is receiving or has elected to receive benefits in an optional form or at an early retirement age permitted by the plan, show the amount payable under that election.
- Plan adjustment factors
- Value of adjusted monthly plan benefit
- Vesting percentage (vested monthly adjusted benefit)
- Monthly vested adjusted plan benefit
  - Benefits are to be determined in accordance with all current Code and ERISA requirements, including:
    - Statutory hybrid plans final regulations and transitional guidance
    - USERRA rules
    - Code Section 436 benefit restrictions
- Monthly guaranteed benefit
- Value of monthly guaranteed benefit
- Title IV benefits
- Value of Title IV benefits
- Additional information requested by the PBGC

Further, the plan administrator must certify that:

1. The information on which the enrolled actuary based the certifications is accurate and complete, and
2. The information provided to the PBGC is accurate and complete.

The PBGC prefers that this information be provided in an electronic format. PBGC will provide the format for the preferred electronic information if and when it determines that the plan sponsor qualifies for a distress termination.

PBGC may be contacted at its Customer Contact Center for Plan Administrators and Pension Professionals at (800) 736-2444 or at distress@pbgc.gov.

[ERISA § 4041(c)(2); PBGC Distress Termination Filing Instructions]

Q 17:11 What is the next step if the PBGC determines that the plan sponsor is eligible for a distress termination?

The plan administrator files PBGC Form 601, *Distress Termination Notice, Single-Employer Plan Termination*, with Schedule EA-D (the enrolled actuary's certification). The filing must be sent in on or before the 120th day after the proposed termination date or, if later, 30 days after receipt of the PBGC's determination that the requirements for a distress termination have been satisfied. The filing may be sent by mail, by commercial delivery service, or by hand to:

Pension Benefit Guaranty Corporation
Distress Terminations
Suite 270
1200 K Street, NW
Washington, DC 20005-4026

The forms may *not* be faxed or e-mailed to the PBGC. However, questions may be e-mailed to distress@pbgc.gov.

A distress termination may fall into one of three categories:

1. *Assets sufficient to satisfy benefit liabilities*. The plan is eligible to file as a standard termination (see chapter 16) even though the contributing sponsor or members of the controlled group meet the requirements for a distress termination. The plan sponsor may request that the PBGC convert the request to a standard termination.
2. *Assets sufficient to satisfy guaranteed benefits* but insufficient to satisfy benefit liabilities. The plan sponsor proceeds to pay benefits to plan participants in accordance with ERISA Section 4041(c)(3)(B)(ii). (See Qs 17:12–17:24 for the determination of guaranteed benefits.)
3. *Assets insufficient to satisfy guaranteed benefits*. The PBGC becomes the trustee of the plan, responsible for the management of plan assets and the payment of plan benefits to participants (see Q 17:27).

[PBGC Distress Termination Filing Instructions]

Q 17:12 What benefits provided in a defined benefit plan are guaranteed by the PBGC?

In a PBGC-covered plan, accrued benefits, up to a specified level, are guaranteed by the PBGC if they are accrued and vested as of the date of termination of the plan. The vested amount is determined without reference to the termination of the plan. [ERISA § 4022(a)] (See chapter 8 regarding vesting determination.)

The maximum guaranteeable benefit is a benefit that has an actuarial value that does not exceed the actuarial value of a monthly benefit in the form of a life annuity beginning at age 65, equal to the lesser of:

1. The participant's average monthly gross income from his or her employer during the five consecutive highest calendar-year periods (or if less, during the number of calendar years in the period in which he or she actively participates in the plan); or
2. A dollar limit, adjusted each year (starting in 1974) by the cost-of-living adjustments to Social Security.

[ERISA § 4022(b)(3)]

Q 17:13 What are the dollar limits for each year?

The adjusted dollar limits since the start of ERISA in 1974 are:

Year	*Monthly Amount*
1974	$ 750.00
1975	$ 801.14
1976	$ 869.32
1977	$ 937.50
1978	$1,005.68
1979	$1,073.86
1980	$1,159.09
1981	$1,261.36
1982	$1,380.68
1983	$1,517.05
1984	$1,602.27
1985	$1,687.50
1986	$1,789.77
1987	$1,857.95
1988	$1,909.09
1989	$2,028.41
1990	$2,164.77
1991	$2,250.00
1992	$2,352.27
1993	$2,437.50
1994	$2,556.82
1995	$2,573.86
1997	$2,761.36
1998	$2,880.68

Year	*Monthly Amount*
1999	$3,051.14
2000	$3,221.59
2001	$3,392.05
2002	$3,579.55
2003	$3,664.77
2004	$3,698.86
2005	$3,801.14
2006	$3,971.59
2007	$4,125.00
2008	$4,312.50
2009	$4,500.00
2010	$4,500.00
2011	$4,500.00
2012	$4,653.41
2013	$4,789.77
2014	$4,943.18
2015	$5,011.36
2016	$5,011.36
2017	$5,369.32
2018	$5,420.45

[www.pbgc.gov]

Q 17:14 Are there any adjustments to the maximum guaranteed benefits?

Yes. Maximum guaranteed benefits may be adjusted for:

1. Actuarial equivalence for benefits beginning before, or after, age 65 or in a form other than a life annuity (see Qs 17:15–17:21);
2. Benefit increases due to a plan amendment within the 60 months preceding the termination of the plan (see Q 17:22); and
3. Benefits payable to a majority owner (see Qs 17:23, 17:24).

[ERISA § 4022(b)]

Q 17:15 How are maximum guaranteed benefits actuarially adjusted?

The PBGC prescribes certain factors for the actuarial adjustment of benefits. The plan's actuary will perform the calculations, and the PBGC generally will audit the results.

The types of adjustments made to the guaranteed benefits include the following:

1. Age adjustment (see Q 17:16);
2. Factors for benefits payable as a period certain and continuous annuity (see Q 17:17);
3. Factors for benefits payable as a joint and survivor annuity (contingent basis) (see Q 17:18);
4. Factors for benefits payable as a joint and survivor annuity (joint basis) (see Q 17:19);
5. Factors for age differences in joint and survivor annuities (see Q 17:20);
6. Factors for step-down life annuity (see Q 17:21).

[PBGC Reg. § 4022.23]

Q 17:16 How is the age adjustment to PBGC-guaranteed benefits made if benefits begin before or after age 65?

If benefits are to begin before age 65, the maximum guaranteed benefit is reduced as shown in Table 17-1.

Table 17-1. Reduction of Maximum Guaranteed Benefit

Time Period	*Adjustment Factor*
For each of the 60 months immediately preceding the 65th birthday	7/12 of 1 percent
For each of the 60 months immediately preceding the 60th birthday	4/12 of 1 percent
For each of the 120 months immediately preceding the 55th birthday	2/12 of 1 percent
For each of the 120 months immediately preceding the 45th birthday	1/12 of 1 percent
For each of the 120 months immediately preceding the 35th birthday	1/24 of 1 percent
For each of the 120 months immediately preceding the 25th birthday	1/48 of 1 percent

[PBGC Reg. § 4022.23(c)]

If benefits begin after age 65, guaranteed benefits are increased.

A chart that shows the 2018 and earlier annual and monthly maximum benefit guarantees for retirees from age 45 to 75 can be found at https://www.pbgc.gov/wr/benefits/guaranteed-benefits/maximum-guarantee.

Q 17:17 What adjustment factors are used for period certain and continuous annuities?

The monthly guaranteed benefit is reduced by the following amounts for each month of the period certain after the date of plan termination:

- For each month up to 60 months deduct 1/24 of 1 percent and
- For each month beyond 60 months deduct 1/12 of 1 percent.

A *cash refund annuity* is treated as a benefit payable for a period certain and continuous. The period of certainty is computed by dividing the amount of the lump-sum refund by the monthly amount to which the participant is entitled under the terms of the plan. An *installment refund annuity* is treated as a benefit payable for a period certain and continuous. The period of certainty is computed by dividing the amount of the remaining refund by the monthly amount to which the participant is entitled under the terms of the plan.

[PBGC Reg. § 4022.23(d)(1)]

Q 17:18 What adjustment factors are used for joint and survivor annuities (contingent basis)?

Such an annuity is paid on a contingent basis, meaning that the spouse of the participant receives reduced benefits when the participant dies. The monthly guaranteed benefit is reduced by an amount equal to 10 percent plus 2/10 of 1 percent for each percentage point in excess of 50 percent of the participant's benefit that will continue to be paid to the beneficiary. If the benefit payable to the beneficiary is less than 50 percent of the participant's benefit, the PBGC will provide the adjustment factors to be used.

[PBGC Reg. § 4022.23(d)(2)]

Q 17:19 What adjustment factors are used for a joint and survivor annuity (joint basis)?

A joint basis means that the annuity benefit continuing to the survivor is reduced at the first death (whether that be the participant's or their beneficiary's). The monthly guaranteed benefit is reduced by an amount equal to 4/10 of 1 percent for each percentage point in excess of 50 percent of the participant's original benefit that will continue to be paid to the survivor. If the benefit payable to the survivor is less than 50 percent of the participant's original benefit, the PBGC provides the adjustment factors to be used.

[PBGC Reg. § 4022.23(d)(3)]

Q 17:20 What adjustment factors are used for age differences in joint and survivor annuities?

When the beneficiary's age is different from the participant's age by 15 or fewer years, the monthly guaranteed benefit is adjusted by the following amounts:

- If the beneficiary is younger than the participant, deduct 1 percent for each year of the age difference; or

- If the beneficiary is older than the participant, add 1/2 of 1 percent for each year of the age difference.

In computing the difference in ages, years over 65 years of age are not counted. If the difference in age between the beneficiary and the participant is greater than 15 years, the PBGC will provide the adjustment factors to be used. [PBGC Reg. § 4022.23(e)]

Q 17:21 What adjustment factors are used for step-down life annuities?

If a reduced benefit is payable, generally after a participant becomes eligible for Social Security benefits, the PBGC guaranteed benefit is adjusted in accordance with the following steps:

1. The temporary additional amount payable under a step-down life annuity is converted to a life annuity payable in monthly installments by multiplying the appropriate factor based on the participant's age and the number of remaining years of the temporary additional benefit. The factors are set forth in Table 17-2.

Table 17-2. Step-Down Life Annuity Factors

Age/Years	*1*	*2*	*3*	*4*	*5*	*6*	*7*	*8*	*9*	*10*
45	.060	.117	.170	.220	.268	.315	.355	.395	.435	.475
46	.061	.119	.173	.224	.273	.321	.362	.403	.444	.485
47	.062	.121	.176	.228	.278	.327	.369	.411	.453	.495
48	.063	.123	.179	.232	.283	.333	.376	.419	.462	.505
49	.064	.125	.182	.236	.288	.339	.383	.427	.471	.515
50	.065	.127	.185	.240	.293	.345	.390	.435	.480	.525
51	.066	.129	.188	.244	.298	.651	.397	.443	.489	.535
52	.067	.131	.191	.248	.303	.357	.404	.451	.498	.545
53	.068	.133	.194	.252	.308	.363	.411	.459	.507	.555
54	.069	.135	.197	.256	.313	.369	.418	.467	.516	.565
55	.070	.137	.200	.260	.318	.375	.425	.475	.525	.575
56	.072	.141	.206	.268	.328	.387	.439	.491	.543	
57	.074	.145	.212	.276	.338	.399	.453	.507		
58	.076	.149	.218	.284	.348	.411	.467			
59	.078	.153	.224	.292	.358	.423				
60	.080	.157	.230	.300	.368					
61	.082	.161	.236	.308						
62	.084	.165	.242							
63	.086	.169								
64	.088									

The age of the participant is computed based on the age at his or her last birthday. If the benefit is payable for less than 1 year, the appropriate factor is obtained by multiplying the factor for 1 year by a fraction, the numerator of which is the number of months the benefit is payable, and the denominator of which is 12. If the benefit is payable for 1 or more whole years, plus an additional number of months less than 12, the appropriate factor is obtained by linear interpolation between the factor for the number of whole years the benefit is payable and the factor for the next year.

2. If a participant is entitled to and chooses to receive a step-down life annuity at an age younger than 65, the PBGC monthly guaranteed amount computed is adjusted by applying the age factors shown in Table 17-1.
3. If the level-life monthly benefit calculated pursuant to step (1) above exceeds the monthly amount calculated pursuant to step (2), then the monthly maximum benefit guaranteeable shall be a step-down life annuity under which the monthly amount of the temporary additional benefit and the amount of the monthly benefit payable for life shall bear the same ratio to the monthly amount of the temporary additional benefit and the monthly benefit payable for life provided under the plan, respectively, as the monthly benefit calculated pursuant to step (2) bears to the monthly benefit calculated pursuant to step (1).

[PBGC Reg. § 4022.23(f)]

Q 17:22 How are benefit increases treated for purposes of the PBGC maximum guarantees?

Effective for notices of intent to terminate filed on or after January 1, 2006, the definition of majority owner is expanded (see Q 17:23). The five-year phase-in of PBGC-guaranteed benefits does not apply to this expanded group (see 17:24).

A five-year phase-in of benefit guarantees for participants other than majority owners (Q 17:23) is provided by multiplying the amount of any benefit increase made within the last five years by the number of years the benefit increase has been in effect, and multiplying the product by the greater of:

1. 20 percent; or
2. $20 per month.

In computing the number of years that a benefit increase has been in effect, all complete 12-month periods before the date of termination are aggregated and treated as a single benefit increase.

However, any benefit increase is guaranteed only to the extent that the PBGC determines that the plan was terminated for reasonable business purposes, not for purposes of obtaining additional benefits from the PBGC.

[PBGC Reg. §§ 4022.24, 4022.25; PPA § 407; ERISA § 4022(b)(5)]

Q 17:23 Who are majority owners?

A majority owner is an individual who, at any time during the 60-month period ending on the date the determination is being made, directly or indirectly owns 50 percent or more of:

1. An unincorporated trade or business;
2. The capital interest or the profits interest in a partnership; or
3. The voting stock of a corporation or the value of all of the stock of a corporation.

The constructive ownership rules of Code Section 1563(e) apply, which attribute ownership to certain individuals, determined without regard to employer stock owned by a qualified plan.

[ERISA § 4022(b)(5)(A); PBGC § 4041.2]

Q 17:24 How are a majority owner's guaranteed benefits limited by the PBGC?

For a participant in a plan whose benefits have not been increased by reason of any plan amendments, and who is a majority owner, the amount of benefits guaranteed may not exceed the product of:

1. A fraction (not to exceed 1), the numerator of which is the number of years from the later of the effective date or the adoption date of the plan to the termination date, and the denominator of which is 10; and
2. The amount of the majority owner's monthly benefits guaranteed under the rules discussed in Qs 17:11–17:20.

For a participant in a plan in which benefit increases have occurred (within the last five years) and who is a majority owner, the amount of the benefit guaranteed is determined by treating each benefit increase attributable to a plan amendment as if it were provided under a new plan. However, in no event may the benefit guarantee exceed the amount computed above.

[PBGC Reg. § 4022.26; PPA § 407; ERISA § 4022(b)(5)]

> **Example 17-2:** Carlton is a majority owner of CDE Cars. He participates in the defined benefit plan, and the plan has been in effect for five years. The plan has not been amended since its inception. Carlton's maximum PBGC guaranteed benefit in 2018 is:
>
> $$5/10 \times \$5{,}420.45 = \$2{,}710.23$$

Q 17:25 How is a plan administered during the distress termination process?

After issuing the NOIT to plan participants, the plan administrator must follow these rules:

1. The plan administrator must continue to carry out normal operation of the plan, such as putting participants into pay status, collecting contributions to the plan, and investing plan assets;

2. New loans to plan participants (if permitted by the plan) may not be made, beginning on the first date the NOIT is issued;
3. No plan assets may be distributed, except for death benefits or payments in the form of an annuity;
4. Irrevocable commitments to purchase annuities from an insurance carrier may not be made; and
5. Existing annuity payments are reduced, if need be, to the PBGC's guaranteed benefits beginning on the proposed termination date (see Qs 17:12–17:24).

[PBGC Reg. § 4041.42]

Q 17:26 What steps are involved if the plan has sufficient assets to satisfy guaranteed benefits?

If the PBGC determines that the plan has sufficient assets to provide at least all guaranteed benefits, the PBGC will issue a distribution notice. Then, the plan administrator must take the following steps:

1. Issue a notice of benefit distribution to each participant or beneficiary no later than 60 days after receiving the distribution notice from the PBGC.
2. File a certification with the PBGC no later than 15 days after the notices of benefit distribution were issued.
3. Make a distribution of guaranteed benefits (and any additional benefits attributable to the remaining plan assets in accordance with ERISA Section 4044 (see Q 17:40)), no earlier than the 61st day and no later than the 240th day following the issue of the notice of benefit distribution.
4. File Form 602, *Post-Distribution Certification for Distress Termination*, with the PBGC within 30 days after the distribution of assets is completed.
5. Either the plan administrator or the plan sponsor must take steps to preserve and maintain plan records.

[PBGC Reg. §§ 4041.48, 4041.50; PBGC Distress Termination Filing Instructions]

Q 17:27 What happens if the plan has insufficient assets to pay guaranteed benefits?

The PBGC is required to institute trusteeship proceedings for the plan. [ERISA § 4042(d); PBGC Distress Termination Filing Instructions]

Q 17:28 What happens if the funded status of the plan changes after a distribution notice is issued?

The plan administrator must notify the PBGC promptly of that fact. If the plan becomes sufficient to satisfy benefit liabilities, the plan administrator may request the PBGC to convert the plan to a standard termination. If the plan is no longer sufficient to satisfy guaranteed benefits, no further action should be taken until the PBGC issues a notice of concurrence or non-concurrence with the plan administrator's findings. If the plan assets are sufficient for guaranteed benefits (see Qs 17:12–17:21) but not for benefit liabilities, the PBGC must be notified; however, the plan administrator may continue distributing benefits. [PBGC Reg. § 4041.49(c)]

Q 17:29 What amount is due and payable immediately upon a distress termination to the PBGC?

A dollar amount equaling the difference between the benefit liabilities and plan assets is due immediately to the PBGC as of the termination date, in cash or securities acceptable to the PBGC. To the extent that the liability exceeds 30 percent of the collective net worth of contributing plan sponsors or members of the controlled group, the balance may be paid over time on commercially reasonable terms. However, a plan sponsor may be able to demonstrate to the PBGC that the payment of such an amount may impose a severe hardship. If the PBGC determines that such a hardship exists and it believes that there is a reasonable possibility that the acceptable alternative terms will be met, a delay in such immediate payments will be permitted. [PBGC Reg. §§ 4062.3, 4062.9]

Example 17-3: CDE Cars has qualified for a distress termination and has insufficient assets to satisfy all benefit liabilities. The amount of the insufficiency is $10.2 million. However, 30 percent of the net worth of CDE Cars and the members of the controlled group is only $8.2 million. The $8.2 million is payable immediately to the PBGC in cash and securities; the remaining balance is due to the PBGC over time under commercially reasonable terms unless CDE Cars can demonstrate that this will be a severe hardship. In such case, the immediate payment may be delayed.

Q 17:30 Will plan participants recover their unfunded benefit liabilities if the plan sponsor makes payments to the PBGC?

Yes, participants, beneficiaries, and alternate payees will be paid a percentage of their unfunded benefit liabilities in excess of PBGC-guaranteed benefits equal to the percentage recovered by the PBGC. [ERISA § 4001(a)(18)]

Q 17:31 Because participants will generally not receive their full benefits in a distress termination, will such participants have standing to sue the plan fiduciaries?

On March 20, 2009, the Ninth Circuit Court of Appeals in San Francisco reviewed a spun-off defined benefit plan that was subsequently terminated in a distress termination and turned over to the PBGC. The court ruled that participants lacked standing under ERISA to sue for breach of fiduciary duty. The court also held that the PBGC's decision not to pursue an enforcement action against the plan's fiduciaries was not subject to judicial review. In a small victory for plan participants, the court held that ERISA did not preempt the participants' potential state law claim for professional negligence against the plan's actuary. [Paulsen v. CNF, Inc., 599 F.3d 1061 (9th Cir. 2009)]

Q 17:32 What happens if the PBGC determines that the requirements for a distress termination are not satisfied?

If the PBGC determines that the plan does not qualify for a distress termination, the termination is null and void and the plan remains an ongoing plan for all purposes. However, if the only reason that the PBGC determines that the plan does not qualify for a distress termination is that Form 601 is filed incomplete, the PBGC will advise the plan administrator of the missing information. In this case, the PBGC will consider the original filing complete if the missing information is filed with the PBGC no later than the 120th day after the proposed termination date or the 30th day after the date of PBGC's written notice, whichever is later.

The plan administrator may apply to the PBGC for reconsideration of its determination. After the reconsideration period has expired (or the plan administrator decides not to request a reconsideration):

1. The prohibition on applicable loans to plan participants ceases to apply;
2. Benefits may be paid in permitted forms other than an annuity;
3. Irrevocable commitments to buy annuities for retired participants may be made; and
4. Any benefits in excess of PBGC-guaranteed benefits not paid while a distress termination was being considered, must now be paid to plan participants with interest.

[PBGC Reg. §§ 4003.31, 4041.42(d); PBGC Distress Termination Filing Instructions]

Involuntary Terminations

Q 17:33 May the PBGC initiate a plan termination?

The PBGC may institute proceedings to terminate a plan whenever it determines that:

1. The plan has not met the minimum funding standard required under Code Sections 412 and 430.
2. The plan will be unable to pay benefits when due.
3. There has been a distribution under the plan to a majority owner (see Q 17:23) (This should generally not occur because of the existence of rules restricting lump-sum distributions to highly compensated employees. (see chapter 14)) and:
   a. The distribution had a value of $10,000 or more;
   b. The distribution was not made because of the death of the participant; and
   c. Immediately after the distribution, the plan had unfunded vested benefits.
4. The possible future liabilities of the PBGC with respect to the plan may be expected to increase unreasonably if the plan is not terminated.

The PBGC is required, as soon as practicable, to institute proceedings to terminate a single-employer plan whenever the PBGC determines that the plan does not have assets available to pay benefits that are currently due under the terms of the plan. The PBGC is permitted to prescribe simplified procedures to follow in terminating small plans, as long as those procedures include substantial safeguards for the rights of the participants and beneficiaries under the plans, and for the employers who maintain such plans. [ERISA §§ 4042(a), 4043(c)(7)]

Example 17-4: The PBGC receives notice that CDE Cars failed to meet minimum funding standards for its defined benefit plan for the plan year ending June 30, 2018. In reviewing its records and the reporting provided on annual Forms 5500, Schedule SB prepared by the enrolled actuary, the PBGC realizes that unfunded liabilities have been growing at an annual rate of 15 percent per year over the last five years. The plan does not qualify for a standard termination. The PBGC may take steps to terminate the plan through an involuntary termination. By doing this, the PBGC will be able to cease future benefit accruals, as one step to slow the 15 percent growth rate on the unfunded liabilities, and avoid related future increases in liability.

Q 17:34 What is the liability of the plan sponsor if plan assets are insufficient to cover benefit liabilities under a PBGC-initiated involuntary termination?

Under current PBGC rules, the plan sponsor is liable to the PBGC for payment of the entire difference between:

1. The actuarial present value of benefit liabilities (see Q 17:2) and
2. The current value of plan assets.

Under the previous PBGC rules, the plan sponsor's liability was limited to 30 percent of net worth, not the entire difference noted above. Now, the 30 percent of net worth measurement is relevant only for the following purposes:

1. In determining the value of the unfunded liability that is payable immediately at the date of termination; and
2. In determining the amount of the lien that may be imposed if the unfunded liability is unpaid.

[ERISA §§ 4062, 4001(a)(16)]

PPA Requirements for Distress and Involuntary Terminations

Q 17:35 What are the rights of an affected party with respect to receipt of information submitted to the PBGC in a distress or involuntary termination?

Not later than 15 days after receipt of a request from an affected party, the plan administrator of a terminating plan must provide the affected party with any information that was required to be submitted to the PBGC pursuant to the termination. The enhanced disclosure requirements apply to both involuntary and distress terminations. Plan administrators must not disclose the information in a manner that identifies an individual participant or beneficiary.

The final PBGC regulations make it clear that plan administrators in a distress and PBGC-initiated involuntary terminations, and plan sponsors in PBGC-initiated involuntary terminations, may charge a reasonable fee for any information provided in other than electronic format.

[PPA § 506(a); ERISA § 4041(c)(2)(D); PBGC Reg. § 4041.51, § 4041.51]

Q 17:36 What disclosures are required of the PBGC in a PBGC-initiated termination?

Not later than 15 days after receipt of a request from an affected party (see Q 17:35), the PBGC shall provide a copy of the administrative record, including the trusteeship decision record of termination of the plan. The right to request a copy of the administrative record arises only after a Notice of Determination that the plan should be terminated is received by the plan administrator.

[PBGC Reg. § 4042.5]

Q 17:37 Does a plan sponsor owe premiums to the PBGC in the event of a distress or involuntary termination?

Yes, a termination premium generally applies in the case of certain plan terminations occurring after 2005. An additional premium of $1,250 per participant is imposed generally for the year of the termination and each of the following two years. The premium applies in the case of:

1. An involuntary plan termination by the PBGC; or
2. A distress termination due to reorganization in bankruptcy, the inability of the employer to pay its debts when due, or a determination that a termination is necessary to avoid unreasonably burdensome pension costs caused solely by a decline in the workforce.

In the case of a termination due to reorganization, the liability for the premium does not arise until the employer is discharged from the reorganization proceeding. The premium does not apply with respect to a plan terminated during bankruptcy reorganization proceedings pursuant to a bankruptcy filing before October 18, 2005.

The premium is due within 30 days after the first day of the applicable plan year.

In February 2008, a bankruptcy court judge, Allan Gropper, ruled that the PBGC could not impose the post-termination premium of $1,250 per participant against Oneida, Ltd., which was in Chapter 11 bankruptcy reorganization. The PBGC appealed this ruling on the grounds that the fees were expressly authorized by the Deficit Reduction Act of 2005. [Oneida Ltd. v. Pension Benefit Guar. Corp., 372 B.R. 107, 111 (S.D.N.Y. 2007)]

The Second Circuit reversed the findings of the bankruptcy court and ruled that an employer that terminated a defined benefit plan while undergoing a bankruptcy reorganization could not avoid paying a termination premium to the PBGC by classifying the termination premium as an unsecured, pre-petition claim that was dischargeable. [PBGC v. Oneida, Ltd., 562 F.3d 154 (2d Cir. 2009)]

[PPA § 401; ERISA § 4006(a)(7)]

Q 17:38 Does a distress or involuntary termination have an impact on other plans of the plan sponsor?

Yes, nonqualified deferred compensation arrangements are subject to an excise tax if amounts are set aside for applicable covered employees during the restricted period. The restricted period is defined as:

1. Any period during which the plan is in at-risk status (as defined in Code Section 430(i));
2. Any period during which the plan sponsor is a debtor in a case under title 11, United States Code, or similar federal or state law; and
3. The 12-month period beginning on the date that is six months before the termination date of the plan if, as of the termination date, the plan is not sufficient for benefit liabilities (within the meaning of Section 4041 of the Employee Retirement Income Security Act of 1974).

In general, applicable covered employees include:

1. The chief executive officer (or individual acting in such capacity);
2. The four highest compensated officers for the taxable year (other than the chief executive officer); and
3. Individuals subject to Section 16(a) of the Securities Exchange Act of 1934.

An applicable covered employee includes any:

1. Covered employee of a plan sponsor;
2. Covered employee of a member of a controlled group which includes the plan sponsor; and
3. Former employee who was a covered employee at the time of termination of employment with the plan sponsor or a member of a controlled group that includes the plan sponsor.

A nonqualified deferred compensation plan is any plan that provides for the deferral of compensation other than a qualified employer plan or any bona fide vacation leave, sick leave, compensatory time, disability pay, or death benefit plan.

Any subsequent increases in the value of, or any earnings with respect to, transferred or restricted assets are treated as additional transfers of property. Interest at the underpayment rate plus one percentage point is imposed on the underpayments that would have occurred had the amounts been includible in income for the taxable year in which first deferred or, if later, the first taxable year not subject to a substantial risk of forfeiture. The amount required to be included in income is also subject to an additional 20 percent tax.

If an employer provides directly or indirectly for the payment of any federal, state, or local income taxes with respect to any compensation required to be included in income under the provision, interest is imposed on the amount of such payment in the same manner as if the payment were part of the deferred compensation to which it related. As under present law, such payment is included in income. In addition, such payment is subject to a 20 percent additional tax. The payment is also nondeductible by the employer.

[PPA § 116; I.R.C. § 409A(b)(3)]

Defined Benefit Plans Not Covered by the PBGC

Q 17:39 What happens if plan assets are not sufficient to satisfy the plan liabilities?

The plan sponsor of a plan not covered by the PBGC has the following options for terminating if plan assets are insufficient to satisfy all plan liabilities:

1. Make a contribution in an amount equal to the unfunded portion of the liability (see Q 17:40).
2. Continue the plan and continue making contributions to bring the plan assets up to the value of plan liabilities. In almost all cases, it may be desirable to cease future benefit accruals to contain plan liabilities as much as possible.
3. Provide for an ERISA Section 4044 allocation of plan assets, resulting generally in reduced benefits for some or all participants (see Q 17:42).
4. If the plan is not severely underfunded and does not allow for lump-sum distributions, the plan sponsor may be able to find an annuity carrier to provide the accrued benefits to all participants through the use of a terminal funding contract or amend the plan to permit lump-sum distributions if the rates for lump-sum distributions would produce a lower liability than the annuity purchase rates (see chapter 15 for a discussion of terminal funding contracts).

Q 17:40 When should a plan sponsor consider freezing and continuing an underfunded defined benefit plan?

A plan freeze should be considered when the plan no longer meets the plan sponsor's needs or objectives. In addition, if reducing future accrued benefits does not accomplish enough of a cost reduction and the plan sponsor cannot afford to make the plan sufficient for benefit liabilities, it should consider hard freezing future benefit accruals and maintaining the plan as a frozen plan. Doing so allows future contributions and investment earnings to grow plan assets sufficiently to cover plan liabilities. Freezing accrued benefits requires prior written notice to participants and other affected parties in accordance with ERISA Section 204(h) (see chapter 15).

Q 17:41 How does a plan sponsor terminate an underfunded defined benefit plan not subject to PBGC coverage?

A defined benefit plan (not covered by the PBGC) is underfunded if the actuarial present value of accrued benefits is greater than the value of plan assets. In such a case, the plan assets are to be allocated in accordance with ERISA Section 4044. [ERISA § 403(d)] Rev. Rul. 80-229 also provides guidance on the allocation of plan assets when a plan is underfunded upon plan termination. It relies on ERISA Section 4044 for the initial allocation of assets, but allows for other allocation methods as long as the percentage of the present value of accrued benefits payable to highly compensated employees is not more than the percentage for non-highly compensated employees. In other words, the entire reduction in benefits could be applied to only highly compensated employees.

Q 17:42 How are assets allocated under ERISA Section 4044?

In terminating a single-employer plan, the plan administrator must allocate the assets of the plan (i.e., those assets available to provide benefits) among the participants and beneficiaries of the plan in the following order:

1. To that portion of each individual's accrued benefit that is derived from the participant's contributions to the plan that are not mandatory contributions.
2. To that portion of each individual's accrued benefit that is derived from the participant's mandatory contributions.
3. For benefits payable as an annuity:
   a. In the case of benefits in pay status three years before the termination date, based on the lowest benefit under the plan's provisions in effect during the five-year period ending on that date, and
   b. In the case of other benefits that would have been in pay status three years before the termination date if the participant had retired and started receiving benefits prior to the beginning of that three-year period, based on the lowest benefit under the plan's provisions in effect during the five-year period ending on the termination date.
4. To all other benefits of individuals who would benefit if the plan were covered by the PBGC.
5. To all other nonforfeitable benefits under the plan.
6. To all other benefits under the plan.

[ERISA § 4044(a)]

Making Contributions to Meet Plan Liabilities

Q 17:43 May an employer make a contribution sufficient to satisfy plan liabilities?

Yes, a contribution sufficient to satisfy plan liabilities may be made. However, such contribution may not be fully deductible in the year in which it is contributed. [I.R.C. § 404] The deductibility of the contribution is the greatest of the amount determined under the following rules:

1. The normal deduction rules for ongoing plans (see Q 17:44).
2. The special deduction rule for PBGC-covered plans permitting a deduction for contributions to bring plan assets up to the level of the unfunded current liability (see Q 17:45).
3. A special rule for terminating plans permitting a deduction for contributions to bring plan assets up to the level of PBGC guaranteed benefits (see Q 17:46).

Q 17:44 What are the normal rules governing the maximum deductible limit for a defined benefit plan?

An employer may deduct contributions determined under the greatest of the following limits:

1. An amount necessary to satisfy the minimum funding standards under Code Section 430
2. The excess of:
   a. The sum of the funding target plus the target normal cost plus the cushion amount; over
   b. The actuarial value of plan assets

The funding target is equal to the present value of all benefit liabilities accrued at the beginning of the plan year. [I.R.C. § 430(d)(1)] The target normal cost is equal to the present value of the benefits accrued during the current year, including the increase in accrued benefits attributable to compensation increases. These present values are determined using the segment rates and a mortality table specified by the Treasury. [I.R.C. § 430(b)] The cushion amount for any plan year is the sum of:

1. 50 percent of the funding target for the plan year, and
2. The amount by which the funding target for the plan year would increase if the plan were to take into account:
   a. Increases in compensation which are expected to occur in succeeding plan years, or
   b. If the plan does not base benefits for service to date on compensation, increases in benefits that are expected to occur in succeeding plan years (determined on the basis of the average annual increase in benefits over the six immediately preceding plan years).

[I.R.C. § 404(o)(1), (3)]

Q 17:45 What is the special deduction limit for PBGC-covered plans with 100 or fewer participants?

A terminating defined benefit plan with 100 or fewer participants that is covered by the PBGC may deduct the amount needed to bring plan assets up to the level of benefit liabilities under ERISA Section 4041(d). See Chapter 16 for the determination of benefit liabilities. [I.R.C. § 404(o)(5) benefit liabilities under ERISA Section 4041(d)]

Q 17:46 What is the special deduction rule for terminating plans?

In the case of a standard termination (see chapter 16), contributions necessary to bring benefits up to the level guaranteed by the PBGC are fully deductible (see Qs 17:12–17:21 for a discussion of PBGC guaranteed benefits). [I.R.C. § 404(g)]

Q 17:47 What happens if an amount in excess of the deductible limit is contributed to a terminated plan?

Any contribution in excess of the plan year's deductible limit may be subject to a 10 percent excise tax. [I.R.C. § 4972] However, the plan sponsor may elect to be exempt from the 10 percent excise tax. [I.R.C. § 4972(c)(7)]

Underfunded Defined Contribution Plans

Q 17:48 What is an underfunded defined contribution plan?

A money purchase or target benefit plan that has not met the minimum funding standards under Code Section 412 for any plan year is considered an underfunded defined contribution plan. If the plan sponsor has not received a waiver of the minimum funding requirements, the sponsor is subject to an excise tax of 10 percent of the accumulated funding deficiency. If the accumulated funding deficiency is not corrected within the taxable period, an excise tax equal to 100 percent of the accumulated funding deficiency is imposed. [I.R.C. § 4971(b)] Because a plan sponsor would likely choose to contribute the accumulated funding deficiency to the plan (rather than pay the same amount to the IRS), an underfunded money purchase or target plan without a funding waiver is unlikely.

The funding waiver, if it is granted, is not a permanent forgiveness of the contribution requirement. The plan sponsor is required to amortize the waived amount in annual installments over five years. [I.R.C. § 412(b)(2)(C)]

Q 17:49 What interest rate is used to amortize the waived funding deficiency?

The interest rate used for the amortization payment is 150 percent of the federal mid-term rate (see Appendix A) in effect for the first month of the plan year of amortization. [I.R.C. § 412(d)(1)(A)]

Example 17-5: CDE Cars sponsors a money purchase plan that had a contribution requirement of $75,000 for the plan year that ended December 31, 2018. Because of financial hardship, CDE Cars applies for a waiver of the funding standards and receives approval from the IRS National Office. The $75,000 funding deficiency must be amortized over five plan years at 150 percent of the federal mid-term rate in effect at the beginning of the plan year. Assume that 150 percent of the federal mid-term rate in effect on January 1, 2019 (the first month of the plan year of amortization) is 4.50 percent. The annual installment required to repay the funding deficiency is $16,349, which is the annual amortization of $75,000 over five years at 4.50 percent interest.

Q 17:50 What happens when a money purchase or target plan is terminated before the funding waiver is entirely paid off?

As a condition of granting a funding waiver, the IRS will likely require an acceleration of payment of the accumulated funding deficiency at the time of plan termination. In some cases, the requirement of acceleration has applied only to the account balances of non-key employees or non-owner employees. [Rev. Rul. 78-223; Ltr. Ruls. 8950080, 8734057, 8430146]

In addition, there is a specific prohibition on amendments to the plan that change the rate at which benefits become nonforfeitable while a waiver is effective. If an amendment terminating the plan is adopted, such an amendment will likely accelerate the vesting to 100 percent for all participants. Under this scenario, the waiver is no longer valid and the accumulated funding deficiency becomes immediately due and payable. [I.R.C. §§ 412(a)(2), 430(e)(4)]

Part 4

Tax Treatment

Chapter 18

Taxation of Periodic Payments

This chapter explains and illustrates how periodic payments, or "amounts received as an annuity," made by a Code Section 401(a) qualified retirement plan are taxed. Periodic payments are amounts paid at regular intervals, such as weekly, monthly, or yearly, over a period of time greater than one year, for example, for a term of years or for life. Amounts received as an annuity under a qualified retirement plan (i.e., periodic payments) are includible in income in the taxable year received, except to the extent they represent the return of the recipient's investment in the contract (i.e., basis). A pro rata basis recovery rule called the "simplified method" applies, so that the portion of any annuity payment that represents a nontaxable return of basis is determined by applying an exclusion ratio equal to the employee's total investment in the contract as of the annuity starting date divided by the total expected payments over the term of the annuity. The amount of each annuity payment in excess of the portion representing a nontaxable return of basis is includible in income and taxed at ordinary income tax rates.

Internal Revenue Service (IRS) Notice 98-2 [1998-1 C.B. 266] explains certain changes to the annuity taxation rules under Code Section 72 that were made by the Small Business Job Protection Act of 1996 (SBJPA) and the Taxpayer Relief Act of 1997 (TRA '97). Notice 98-2 describes the simplified method provided by Code Section 72(d)(1) for determining the tax-free and taxable portions of certain annuity payments made from Section 401(a) qualified retirement plans and other retirement arrangements. IRS Publication 575, Pension and Annuity Income, also describes the simplified method.

In general, the simplified method applies to annuities with annuity starting dates after November 18, 1996. However, Notice 98-2 provided a transition rule for annuities that had annuity starting dates after November 18, 1996, and before January 1, 1997. Unlike the safe-harbor method in Notice 88-118 [1988-2 C.B. 450], which Notice 98-2 replaced, the simplified method is required by the Code (rather than optional), and distributees must use the simplified method in order to comply with Code Section 72(d), as amended by SBJPA and TRA '97. Payors also must use the simplified method to report the taxable portion of the annuity payments on IRS Form 1099-R. The simplified method described in Notice 98-2 does not apply if the annuity starting date was on or before November 18, 1996. If the annuity starting date was after July 1, 1986, but before November 19, 1996, distributees could use either the simplified method in effect prior to SBJPA or the "general rule" under Code 72 (described in IRS Publication 939, General Rule for Pensions and Annuities).

Understanding Basic Concepts 18-2
Simplified Method of Basis Recovery and Transition Rule 18-5
Fully Taxable Annuity Payments 18-14

Understanding Basic Concepts

Q 18:1 What is an annuity?

Generally, an annuity is a series of payments, beginning on a given date and continuing at regular intervals over a period of time greater than one full year, such as term of years, a lifetime, or a life expectancy. [I.R.S. Pub. 575]

Q 18:2 What are some common types of annuities?

The most common annuities payable under qualified retirement plans are:

- *Fixed-period annuity*. Pays definite amounts at regular intervals for a specified length of time.
- *Single life annuity*. Pays definite amounts, at regular intervals, for the life of one individual. The payments end at death.
- *Joint and survivor annuity*. The first annuitant receives a definite amount, at regular intervals, for life. After he or she dies, a second annuitant receives a definite amount, at regular intervals, for life. The amount paid to the second annuitant may or may not differ from the amount paid to the first annuitant.
- *Variable annuity*. Payments may vary in amount for a specified length of time or for life. The amount of the payments may depend upon such variables as profits earned by the pension or annuity funds, cost-of-living indexes, or earnings from a mutual fund.

- *Disability annuity*. Pays disability payments because the recipient retired upon disability and has not reached minimum retirement age under the plan.

[I.R.S. Pub. 575]

Q 18:3 When are distributions from qualified retirement plans treated as periodic payments, or "amounts received as an annuity"?

Distributions from a qualified retirement plan are treated as periodic payments, or amounts received as an annuity, only if these three conditions are satisfied:

1. They are received on or after the annuity starting date (i.e., the first day of the first period for which an amount is paid in the form of an annuity, as defined in Treas. Reg. § 1.72-4(b));
2. They are payable in periodic installments, at regular intervals (whether annually, semiannually, quarterly, monthly, weekly, or otherwise), over a period of more than one full year from the annuity starting date; and
3. The total of the amounts payable must be determinable at the annuity starting date: (a) directly, that is, from the terms of the contract or plan; or (b) indirectly, by the use of mortality tables, compound interest computations; or (c) both, in conjunction with the terms of the contract or plan and in accordance with sound actuarial theory.

[Treas. Reg. § 1.72-2(b)(2)]

Q 18:4 When is a variable annuity treated as periodic payments or "amounts received as an annuity"?

Variable payments may be considered periodic payments, and thus amounts received as an annuity, if they are paid under a contract or plan that provides that:

1. The amount of the periodic payments varies based on investment experience (as in certain profit sharing plans), cost-of-living indexes, or similar fluctuating criteria; or
2. The value of specified payments varies for income tax purposes, for example, any annuity payable in foreign currency.

[Treas. Reg. § 1.72-2(b)(3)]

Q 18:5 How are periodic payments (amounts received as an annuity) from a qualified retirement plan taxed?

Code Section 402(a) provides that the amount actually distributed to participants or other distributees by a qualified retirement plan is taxable to them in the year in which distributed, under the annuity taxation rules of Code Section 72. Code Section 72(b) provides that a portion of the annuity payments received in a taxable year may be excluded from gross income as a return of the distributee's investment (i.e., basis), if any, according to an exclusion ratio (see Q 18:6) determined at the annuity starting date. The numerator of the exclusion ratio is the employee's basis and the denominator is the expected return.

Code Section 72(e) contains rules relating to the taxability of amounts not received as annuities. Treasury Regulations Section 1.72-11(f) provides rules for the treatment of a single-sum withdrawal received on or after the annuity starting date.

IRS Notice 88-118 [1988-2 C.B. 450] provided a simplified safe-harbor method for determining the tax-free portion and taxable portion of certain annuity payments made from Section 401(a) qualified retirement plans, Section 403(a) qualified annuity plans, and Section 403(b) tax-sheltered annuity arrangements. Under that safe-harbor method, the exclusion ratio was determined by dividing the distributee's basis by an expected number of payments based upon the distributee's age. The result represented the tax-free portion of each payment. This safe-harbor method could be elected only if the distributee received monthly payments and it did not apply to installment payments that were not contingent upon life expectancy.

SBJPA amended Code Section 72(d) to *require* the use of a simplified method of basis recovery for most annuity distributions from Section 401(a) qualified retirement plans, Section 403(a) qualified annuity plans, and Section 403(b) tax-sheltered annuity arrangements. The simplified method in Code Section 72(d), and described in IRS Notice 98-2 [1998-2 I.R.B. 22], is similar to, but not the same as, the safe-harbor method in IRS Notice 88-118. SBJPA also provided a special rule where a single sum is received in connection with the commencement of annuity payments. In such a case, the single-sum payment is treated as if received before the annuity starting date. Generally, the SBJPA changes to Code Section 72(d) apply to distributions with annuity starting dates after November 18, 1996.

TRA '97 amended the simplified method of basis recovery under Code Section 72(d)(1)(B) and prescribed a different table if the annuity is payable based on the lives of more than one individual. That table applies to distributions with annuity starting dates after December 31, 1997. For annuities payable based on the life of only one individual, TRA '97 made no changes in the applicable table under the simplified method required by SBJPA.

Q 18:6 What is the *exclusion ratio*?

The *exclusion ratio* is the employee's investment in the contract, or cost basis under the plan, divided by his or her expected return under the plan (see Q 18:7). The excludable amount, if any, of each periodic payment is computed by multiplying the amount of the payment by the exclusion ratio.

Q 18:7 What is the employee's *expected return* under the plan?

The employee's *expected return* under the plan is the total amount receivable as an annuity under the plan. If the plan provides for payments over a lifetime, so that the total amount of expected payments depends, in whole or in part, on the life expectancy of one or more individuals, the expected return is computed based on actuarial tables provided by the IRS. However, if payments are made in a number of installments, the expected return is the aggregate of the amounts receivable under the plan as an annuity.

Example 18-1: Tom Joad, a participant in the Grapes of Wrath Corporation retirement plan, had a life expectancy of six years at his annuity starting date. Under the plan, Tom will receive $500 per month for life. During the years he participated in the plan, Tom contributed $3,600 worth of after-tax contributions to the plan (his cost basis, or investment in the contract). Tom's expected return under the plan is $36,000 ($6,000 per year for six years); thus, $50 (10 percent) of each monthly payment is excludable from his gross income [($3,600 ÷ $36,000) × $500].

Simplified Method of Basis Recovery and Transition Rule

Q 18:8 Must the simplified method of basis recovery always be used for calculating the taxable portion of annuity distributions from qualified retirement plans?

Yes. The simplified method of basis recovery in Code Section 72(d) and IRS Notice 98-2 [1998-1 C.B. 266] *must* be used by distributees to comply with Code Section 72, and by payors to report the taxable portion of annuity distributions on Form 1099-R. If payments are made on a non-monthly basis, the simplified method applies with appropriate adjustments. However, the simplified method does not apply if the annuitant is over age 75 and there are five or more years of guaranteed payments under the annuity.

In general, the simplified method of basis recovery applies to an annuity if the annuity starting date is after November 18, 1996. However, Notice 98-2 provided a transition rule (see Q 18:15) for annuities with starting dates that were after November 18, 1996, and before January 1, 1997. Unlike the safe-harbor method of basis recovery in Notice 88-118, the simplified method of basis recovery in Notice 98-2 is *required* by the Code (rather than optional) and distributees must use the simplified method in order to comply with Code Section 72(d) as amended by SBJPA and TRA '97. Payors must also use the simplified method to report the taxable portion of the annuity payments on Form 1099-R. The simplified method described in Notice 98-2 does not apply if the annuity starting date was on or before November 18, 1996.

Q 18:9 Which distributees and payors must use the simplified method of basis recovery for calculating the tax-free and taxable portions of each annuity payment made by qualified retirement plans?

The simplified method of basis recovery set forth in Code Section 72(d) and Notice 98-2 must be used by distributees and by payors to report the taxable portion of annuity distributions, if:

1. The annuity starting date is after November 18, 1996; and
2. On the annuity starting date, the distributee is under 75 years old or is entitled to fewer than five years of guaranteed annuity payments from the qualified plan. [I.R.S. Pub. 575]

However, if the distributee is age 75 or older on his or her annuity starting date and the annuity payments are guaranteed for at least five years, he or she must use the general rule of basis recovery described in IRS Publication 939. [I.R.S. Pub. 575]

There was a transition rule (see Q 18:15) for annuities that had annuity starting dates after November 18, 1996, and before January 1, 1997. Unlike the safe-harbor method of basis recovery described in Notice 88-118 [1988-2 C.B. 450], the simplified method of basis recovery described in Notice 98-2 is required by the Code to the extent it applies.

Q 18:10 How is the tax-free portion (the excluded amount) of each monthly annuity payment determined under the simplified method of basis recovery?

The Excluded Amount. Under the simplified method of basis recovery set forth in Code Section 72(d) and Notice 98-2, the distributee recovers his or her investment in the contract (i.e., basis) in level amounts over the expected number of monthly payments determined from Table 18-1 or 18-2, whichever applies (see Q 18:11). The portion of each annuity payment that is excluded from gross income by a distributee for income tax purposes is a level dollar amount determined by dividing the investment in the contract (i.e., basis) by the set number of annuity payments from the applicable table.

$$\frac{\text{Investment in the Contract}}{\text{Expected Number of Monthly Payments}} = \text{Tax-Free Portion of Monthly Annuity}$$

[Notice 98-2, 1998-1 C.B. 266, § III.B]

Application of Excluded Amount. The dollar amount determined above, as of the annuity starting date, will be excluded from each monthly annuity payment, even where the amount of the annuity payments changes. For example, the amount to be excluded from each annuity payment determined at the annuity starting date remains constant, even if payments increase, due to cost-of-living increases, or decrease, in the case of a reduced survivor annuity after the death of one of the annuitants.

If the amount to be excluded from each payment is greater than the amount of the annuity payment (for example, because of decreased survivor payments), then each annuity payment will be completely excluded from gross income until the entire investment in the contract (i.e., basis) is recovered. For those distributees with annuity starting dates after December 31, 1986, annuity payments received after the investment in the contract (i.e., basis) is recovered (generally, after the expected number of payments has been received) are fully includible in gross income. If annuity payments cease by reason of death, a deduction for the unrecovered investment in the contract (i.e., basis), if any, is allowed on the distributee's last income tax return.

Where two or more annuitants are receiving payments at the same time, each annuitant will exclude from each annuity payment a pro rata portion. The amount excluded is determined according to a ratio, the numerator of which is the amount of the beneficiary's annuity payment, and the denominator of which is the total amount of the monthly annuity payments to all beneficiaries. [Notice 98-2, 1998-1 C.B. 266, § III.E]

Adjustments for Non-Monthly Payments. In cases where annuity payments are not made monthly, an adjustment must be made to take into account the period on the basis of which the payments are made. One way to make this adjustment is to determine the number of expected payments by dividing the applicable expected number of months shown in Table 18-1 or 18-2, whichever applies (see Q 18:11) by the number of months in each period. Alternatively, use Table 18-1 or 18-2, whichever applies, to determine the tax-free portion of a monthly payment and then multiply the resulting dollar amount by the number of months in each period. The result is the same using either method. [Notice 98-2, 1998-1 C.B. 266, § III.F]

Q 18:11 How is the expected number of monthly annuity payments determined under the simplified method of basis recovery?

For Annuities with Starting Dates After November 18, 1996, and Before January 1, 1998. Under the simplified method of basis recovery described in Notice 98-2, for annuities with annuity starting dates after November 18, 1996, but before January 1, 1998, the total number of monthly payments expected to be received was based on the primary annuitant's age at the annuity starting date. The same expected number of payments applied whether the annuitant was receiving a single life annuity or a joint and survivor annuity. The expected number of payments is set forth in Table 18-1.

Table 18-1. Expected Number of Annuity Payments

Age of Primary Annuitant	*Expected Number of Payments*
55 and under	360
56–60	310
61–65	260
66–70	210
71 and over	160

[I.R.C. § 72(d)(1)(B)(iii); Notice 98-2, 1998-1 C.B. 266, § III.C.(1)]

For Annuities with Starting Dates After December 31, 1997. For annuities with annuity starting dates after December 31, 1997, the table used to determine the expected number of payments depends on whether the payments are based on the life of one individual or more than one individual. In the case of an annuity payable based on the life of only one individual, the total number of monthly payments expected to be received is based on the annuitant's age at the annuity starting date. An annuity payable over the life of one annuitant with a term certain feature is an annuity based on the life of that individual. Similarly, an annuity payable over the life of one annuitant with a temporary annuity payable to the annuitant's child until the child reaches an age specified in the plan (not more than age 25) is an annuity based on the life of that individual. The expected number of payments for an annuity based on the life of one individual is shown in Table 18-1.

In the case of an annuity payable based on the life of more than one individual, the total number of monthly payments expected to be received is based on the combined ages of the annuitants at the annuity starting date. If the annuity is payable to a primary annuitant and more than one survivor annuitant, the combined ages of the annuitants is the sum of the ages of the primary annuitant and the youngest survivor annuitant. If the annuity is payable to more than one survivor annuitant but there is no primary annuitant, the combined ages of the annuitants is the sum of the ages of the oldest survivor annuitant and the youngest survivor annuitant. In addition, any survivor annuitant whose entitlement to payments is contingent on an event other than the death of the primary annuitant is disregarded. The expected number of payments is shown in Table 18-2.

Table 18-2. Expected Number of Annuity Payments for More Than One Individual

Combined Ages of Annuitants	*Expected Number of Payments*
110 and under	410
111–120	360
121–130	310
131–140	260
141 and over	210

[I.R.C. § 72(d)(1)(B)(iv); Notice 98-2, 1998-1 C.B. 266, § III.C(2)]

Term Certain Annuities Without Life Contingencies. In the case of an annuity that does not depend in whole or in part on the life expectancy of one or more individuals, the expected number of payments is the number of monthly annuity payments under the contract. [Notice 98-2, 1998-1 C.B. 266, § III.C(3)]

Q 18:12 How is the investment in the contract (i.e., basis) calculated under the simplified method of basis recovery?

The investment in the contract (i.e., basis) is defined under Code Section 72(c)(1) as the aggregate premiums or other consideration paid (generally, the aggregate amount of after-tax contributions made to the plan), reduced by amounts received before the annuity starting date, that were excluded from gross income. In addition, Code Section 72(c)(2) provides that the investment in the contract (i.e., basis) must be adjusted to reflect the value of any refund feature. Under Code Section 72(d)(1)(C), as amended by SBJPA, for purposes of the simplified method of basis recovery, the investment in the contract (i.e., basis) is determined without regard to the adjustment for any refund feature as described in Code Section 72(c)(2).

Under prior law, in certain cases, the investment in the contract (i.e., basis) could be increased by any death benefit exclusion that was allowed under Code Section 101(b) if the employee's death benefits were paid to a survivor in the form of an annuity, other than a joint and survivor annuity. But Code Section 101(b) was repealed by SBJPA for decedents dying after August 20, 1996. Accordingly, surviving beneficiaries of decedents dying after August 20, 1996 may not increase the investment in the contract (i.e., basis) by the death benefit exclusion. [Notice 98-2, 1998-1 C.B. 266, § III.D] IRS Publication 575, *Pension and Annuity Income*, illustrates how investment in the contract (i.e., basis) is determined.

Q 18:13 Does the IRS provide any examples to illustrate how the simplified method of basis recovery is applied?

Yes. The simplified method of basis recovery is illustrated by examples supplied in IRS Notice 98-2. [1998-1 C.B. 266] In all examples, the investment in the contract (i.e., basis) is stated as the employee's after-tax contributions and with no adjustment for the refund feature.

Example 18-2: Upon retirement, Tom Joad, age 65, begins receiving retirement benefits in the form of a joint and 50 percent survivor annuity to be paid for the joint lives of Tom and his wife, Ma Joad, age 64. Tom's annuity starting date was January 1, 1997. Tom made $26,000 of after-tax contributions to the plan and received no distributions prior to the annuity starting date. Tom will receive a monthly retirement benefit of $1,000, and Ma will receive a monthly survivor benefit of $500 upon Tom's death.

Tom's investment in the contract is $26,000. Because the annuity starting date is prior to January 1, 1998, the expected number of monthly payments for a distributee who is age 65 is 260. The tax-free portion of each $1,000 monthly annuity payment to Tom is $100, determined by dividing Tom's investment ($26,000) by the expected number of payments (260).

$$\frac{\$26{,}000 \text{ investment}}{260 \text{ monthly payments}} = \$100 \text{ monthly return of investment}$$

Upon Tom's death, if Tom has not recovered the full $26,000 investment, Ma will also exclude $100 from each $500 monthly annuity payment.

Any annuity payments received after the 260 monthly payments have been made will be fully includible in gross income. If Tom and Ma die before 260 monthly payments have been made, a deduction is allowed for the last income tax return in the amount of the unrecovered investment in the contract (i.e., basis). [Notice 98-2, 1998-1 C.B. 266, § III.G(i), Ex. 1]

Example 18-3: Upon retirement, Tom Joad, age 65, begins receiving retirement benefits in the form of a joint and 50 percent survivor annuity to be paid for the joint lives of Tom and his wife, Ma Joad, age 64. Tom's annuity starting date was January 1, 1998. Tom contributed $26,000 to the plan, and received no distributions prior to the annuity starting date. Tom will receive a monthly retirement benefit of $1,000, and Ma will receive a monthly survivor benefit of $500 upon Tom's death.

Tom's investment in the contract is $26,000. The expected number of monthly payments is 310 for two distributees whose combined ages are 129. The tax-free portion of each $1,000 monthly annuity payment to Tom is $83.87, determined by dividing Tom's investment ($26,000) by the expected number of payments (310).

$$\frac{\$26{,}000 \text{ investment}}{310 \text{ monthly payments}} = \$83.87 \text{ monthly return of investment}$$

Upon Tom's death, if Tom has not recovered the full $26,000 investment, Ma will also exclude $83.87 from each $500 monthly annuity payment.

Any annuity payments received after the 310 monthly payments have been made will be fully includible in gross income. If Tom and Ma die before 310 monthly payments have been made, a deduction is allowed for the last income tax return in the amount of the unrecovered investment in the contract (i.e., basis). [Notice 98-2, 1998-1 C.B. 266, § III.G(ii), Ex. 2]

Example 18-4: Upon retirement, Tom Joad, age 66, begins receiving retirement benefits in the form of a joint and 50 percent survivor annuity to be paid for the joint lives of Tom and Tom's wife, Ma Joad, age 65. Tom's annuity starting date was January 1, 1997. Tom contributed $42,000 to the plan, and received no distributions prior to the annuity starting date. Tom will receive a quarterly retirement benefit of $6,000 and Tom's wife, Ma Joad, will receive a quarterly survivor benefit of $3,000 upon Tom's death.

Tom's investment in the contract is $42,000. Because the annuity starting date is prior to January 1, 1998, the expected number of monthly payments for a distributee who is age 66 is 210. Because Tom's annuity is paid quarterly, the appropriate adjustment is to divide the expected number of payments (210) by the number of months in the period (3), which equals 70. Thus, the tax-free portion of each $6,000 quarterly annuity payment to Tom is $600, determined by dividing Tom's investment ($42,000) by the expected number of quarterly payments (70).

$$\frac{\$42{,}000 \text{ investment}}{70 \text{ monthly payments}} = \$600 \text{ quarterly return of investment}$$

Alternatively, the appropriate adjustment can be made by dividing $42,000 by 210 and multiplying the resulting $200 per month by the number of months in the period, three (3), which equals a $600 return of investment per quarter.

$$\frac{\$42{,}000 \text{ investment}}{210 \text{ monthly payments}} \times 3 \text{ months per quarter} = \$600 \text{ quarterly return of investment}$$

[Notice 98-2, 1998-1 C.B. 266, § III.G(iii), Ex. 3]

Example 18-5: Upon retirement, Tom Joad, age 57, begins receiving retirement benefits in the form of a joint and 50 percent survivor annuity to be paid for the joint lives of Tom and Tom's wife, Ma Joad, age 57. Tom contributed $31,000 to the plan. Tom's annuity starting date was July 1, 1998. On Tom's annuity starting date, in connection with receiving the first annuity payment, Tom receives a single-sum payment of $10,000. Had the single-sum payment of $10,000 been received prior to Tom's annuity starting date, then under the rules of Code Section 72(e), $2,000 would have been considered as a recovery of Tom's investment in the contract. Tom will receive a monthly retirement benefit of $1,500 per month, and Ma will receive a monthly survivor benefit of $750 upon Tom's death.

Because the $10,000 is treated as if received before the annuity starting date, Tom will include $8,000 in income as a result of the single-sum payment ($10,000 minus $2,000) and for purposes of determining the tax-free portion of each annuity payment. Tom's investment in the contract is $29,000 (the after-tax contributions to the plan minus the $2,000 portion of the single-sum payment representing the recovery of Tom's investment in the contract). The expected number of monthly payments for two annuitants whose combined ages are 114 is 360. The tax-free portion of each $1,500 monthly annuity payment to Tom is $80.56, determined by dividing Tom's investment ($29,000) by the expected number of payments (360).

$$\frac{\$29{,}000 \text{ investment}}{360 \text{ monthly payments}} = \$80.56 \text{ monthly return of investment}$$

Upon Tom's death, if Tom has not recovered the full $29,000 investment, Ma will also exclude $80.56 from each $750 monthly annuity payment.

Any annuity payments received after the 360 monthly payments have been made will be fully includible in gross income. If Tom and Ma Joad die before 360 monthly payments have been made, a deduction is allowed for the last income tax return in the amount of the unrecovered investment in the contract (i.e., basis). [Notice 98-2, 1998-1 C.B. 266, § III.G(iv), Ex. 4] IRS Publication 575, *Pension and Annuity Income,* contains additional examples and worksheets illustrating the simplified method of basis recovery.

Q 18:14 What was the effective date of the simplified method of basis recovery?

The simplified method of basis recovery required by Code Section 72(d) and Notice 98-2 became generally effective for annuities with annuity starting dates after November 18, 1996. For annuities with annuity starting dates after December 31, 1997, if the annuity is payable based on the lives of more than one individual, the simplified method of basis recovery based on the combined ages of the annuitants is to be used. [Notice 98-2, 1998-1 C.B. 266, § IV]

Q 18:15 Was there a transition rule for payors and distributees who may have continued to use pre-SBJPA annuity taxation rules for annuities with annuity starting dates after November 18, 1996, and before January 1, 1997?

Yes. Some payors and distributees may have continued to use the law in effect prior to SBJPA (including the safe-harbor simplified method of basis recovery contained in Notice 88-118) for annuities with annuity starting dates after November 18, 1996, and before January 1, 1997. Notice 98-2 contains a transition rule for these payors and distributees.

Under this transition rule, the law in effect prior to SBJPA (including the safe-harbor simplified method of basis recovery contained in Notice 88-118) was permitted to be used to determine the taxable and tax-free portions of annuity payments received in 1996 and 1997. Accordingly, payors were not required to re-issue Forms 1099-R for 1996 (and 1997, if applicable) and distributees were not required to file amended income tax returns for 1996 (and 1997, if applicable), solely because they failed to take into account the changes to Code Section 72(d) made by SBJPA.

Nevertheless, a payor who reports the taxable portion of annuity payments on Form 1099-R must determine the taxable and tax-free portion of annuity payments using the transition method described below. The transition method must be applied to annuity payments made on and after January 1, 1998. However, payors may choose to apply the transition method for annuity payments made on an earlier date (for example, payments made on and after January 1, 1997). Under the transition method, the tax-free portion of each annuity payment made on and after the transition date is determined by dividing the remaining investment in the contract (i.e., basis) by the remaining number of expected payments. The remaining investment in the contract (i.e., basis) is the distributee's original investment in the contract (i.e., basis) as of the annuity starting date minus the amount of the investment in the contract (i.e., basis) treated as recovered after the annuity starting date and before the transition date. The remaining number of expected monthly payments is the total number as of the annuity starting date (as determined by using Table 18-1 or 18-2 as applicable) minus the number of payments made prior to the transition date. Where the payor does not report the taxable portion of annuity payments on Form 1099-R, a distributee who uses the transition rule must determine the taxable and tax-free portions of annuity payments using the transition method in Q 18:16. [Notice 98-2, 1998-1 C.B. 266, § V]

Q 18:16 Are there any examples that illustrate how the transition rule described in Q 18:15 was applied?

Yes. Assume the same facts as in Example 18-2 except that Tom's annuity starting date was December 1, 1996. The tax-free portion of each $1,000 monthly annuity payment to Tom was determined under the safe-harbor simplified method of basis recovery under Notice 88-118. This tax-free portion was $108.33, calculated as follows:

$$\frac{\$26{,}000 \text{ investment}}{240 \text{ monthly payments}} = \$108.33 \text{ monthly return of investment}$$

The $108.33 was treated as tax-free for the 1996 return. Under the transition rule, this treatment for 1996 was allowed. However, the taxable and tax-free portions had to be redetermined using the transition method with a transition date of January 1, 1998, or earlier.

Assume that Tom used January 1, 1997, as the transition date. For annuity payments received after December 31, 1996, determine the tax-free portion of each $1,000 annuity payment by dividing the remaining investment in the contract (i.e., basis) by the remaining number of expected payments as of the transition date, determined in accordance with Code Section 72(d) and Notice 98-2. Accordingly, the tax-free portion of each $1,000 payment received in 1997 and later years is $99.97, determined as follows:

$$\frac{\$25{,}891.67\ (\$26{,}000 - \$108.33)}{259 \text{ payments } (260 - 1)} = \$99.97 \text{ return of investment}$$

Under this method, the total amount of annuity payments that is tax-free is $26,000. [Notice 98-2, 1998-1 C.B. 266, § V(i)]

Fully Taxable Annuity Payments

Q 18:17 If the distributee has no investment in the contract (i.e., no basis) in his or her plan, will the annuity payments that he or she receives be fully taxable?

Yes. The annuity payments that the distributee receives are fully taxable if he or she has no investment in the contract (i.e., basis) in his or her plan because:

1. The distributee did not pay anything or is not considered to have paid anything into the plan;
2. The distributee's employer did not withhold contributions from the distributee's salary; or
3. The distributee got back all of his or her contributions tax-free in prior years before his or her annuity starting date.

A distributee who has no investment in the contract (i.e., basis) under his or her plan should report the entire amount of his or her annuity payments for the taxable year on Form 1040 or Form 1040A.

Q 18:18 How are distributions of deductible voluntary employee contributions (DVECs) taxed?

Distributions received that are based on accumulated deductible voluntary employee contributions (DVECs) are generally fully taxable in the year distributed. Accumulated DVECs include net earnings on the contributions. DVECs do not qualify for special five- or ten-year forward income averaging or capital gain treatment (see chapter 19).

Chapter 19

Taxation of Nonperiodic Payments

This chapter explains how nonperiodic payments from qualified retirement plans are taxed. Nonperiodic payments, also called "amounts not received as an annuity," are payments other than periodic payments (i.e., "amounts received as an annuity") (see chapter 18) and corrective distributions. The portion of a nonperiodic payment that is subject to tax depends on when the payment is made in relation to the annuity starting date. If the payment is made before the annuity starting date, its tax treatment depends on the type of contract or transaction from which it results.

Annuity Starting Date 19-1
Various Types of Taxable Distributions and Transfers 19-4
Lump-Sum Distributions 19-9
Five-Year Forward Income Averaging 19-23
Ten-Year Forward Income Averaging 19-29
Capital Gains Treatment 19-30
Special Lump-Sum Distribution Issues 19-33

Annuity Starting Date

Q 19:1 What is the tax treatment of a nonperiodic distribution received on or after the annuity starting date?

Generally, if a nonperiodic payment is made from a qualified retirement plan on or after the *annuity starting date* (see Q 18:3), all of the payment generally must be included in the recipient's gross income. [I.R.C. § 72(e)(2)(A)] For example, a cost-of-living increase in a pension after the annuity starting date is a nonperiodic payment (an amount not received as an annuity) and, therefore, is fully taxable. [I.R.S. Pub. 575]

Q 19:2 Can part of a nonperiodic payment received on or after the annuity starting date nevertheless be excluded from gross income if its payment reduces later annuity payments?

Yes. If the annuity payments a participant receives from a qualified retirement plan are reduced because he or she received a nonperiodic distribution from the plan, he or she can exclude part of the nonperiodic distribution from gross income. The excludable portion of the nonperiodic distribution equals the participant's *investment in the contract*, that is, his or her cost basis under the plan, reduced by any tax-free amounts that he or she previously received from the plan, multiplied by a fraction. The numerator of the fraction is the reduction in each annuity payment because of the nonperiodic distribution. The denominator is the full, unreduced amount of each annuity payment originally provided for. [I.R.S. Pub. 575]

Q 19:3 Can part of a nonperiodic payment received on or after the annuity starting date nevertheless be excluded from gross income if it is a distribution in full discharge of the plan's obligation to the participant?

Yes. A participant may receive a nonperiodic distribution on or after the annuity starting date that fully satisfies the plan's obligation to him or her. If that is the case, the nonperiodic payment is included in the participant's gross income only to the extent it exceeds his or her remaining cost basis under the plan. [I.R.S. Pub. 575]

Q 19:4 What is the tax treatment of a nonperiodic distribution that is received before the annuity starting date?

If a participant receives a nonperiodic distribution before the annuity starting date from a qualified retirement plan, he or she generally can allocate only part of it to his or her investment in the contract (i.e., basis) under the plan. The participant can exclude from gross income the part of the nonperiodic distribution that he or she allocates to his or her investment in the contract (i.e., basis). The remainder of the nonperiodic distribution is included in the participant's gross income. However, there are several exceptions to this general rule (see Q 19:5). For this purpose, a "qualified retirement plan" includes a Code Section 401(a) qualified retirement plan (or annuity contract purchased by such a plan), a Code Section 403(a) qualified annuity plan, or a Code Section 403(b) tax-sheltered annuity plan.

To determine the excludable amount of a nonperiodic distribution made by a qualified retirement plan before the annuity starting date, use the following formula:

$$\text{Amount of the nonperiodic distribution} \times \frac{\text{Investment in the contract (i.e., basis) under the plan}}{\text{Account balance}} = \text{Excludable amount}$$

For this purpose, the account balance includes only vested amounts.

Under a defined contribution plan, the participant's own contributions (and income allocable to them) may be treated as a separate plan in calculating the taxable portion of any nonperiodic distribution that is made before the annuity starting date. The employer's contributions (and income allocable to those contributions) would not be considered part of that separate contract. [I.R.S. Pub. 575]

Example 19-1: Before Doc's annuity starting date under the Western Biological Laboratory retirement plan, he received a $50,000 nonperiodic distribution from the plan. Doc's investment in the contract (i.e., basis) under the plan is $10,000, and his vested account balance is $100,000. He can exclude $5,000 of the $50,000 distribution, determined as follows:

$$\$50{,}000 \text{ amount of the nonperiodic distribution} \times \frac{\$10{,}000 \text{ investment in the contract (i.e., basis) under the plan}}{\$100{,}000 \text{ vested account balance}} = \$5{,}000 \text{ amount of the nonperiodic distribution that is excludable from gross income}$$

[I.R.S. Pub. 575]

Q 19:5 Are there limitations or exceptions to the general allocation rule described in Q 19:4?

Yes. There are one limitation and several exceptions to the general allocation rule described in Q 19:4 governing the tax treatment of nonperiodic distributions made from qualified retirement plans before the annuity starting date.

Limitation of the General Rule for Plans That Permitted Withdrawal of Employee Contributions. If, as of May 5, 1986, a qualified retirement plan permitted in-service withdrawals of employee contributions, the allocation rule described in Q 19:4 applies only to a limited extent. (In this context, employee contributions do not include employer contributions made under a salary reduction agreement.) The allocation rule applies only to the extent that the nonperiodic distribution received before the annuity starting date exceeded the participant's investment in the contract (i.e., basis) under the plan as of December 31, 1986. Any nonperiodic distribution that was received before the annuity starting date and that was equal to or less than the participant's investment in the contract (i.e., basis) under the plan as of December 31, 1986, was treated as a tax-free recovery of basis. [I.R.C. § 72(e)(8)(D); I.R.S. Pub. 575]

Exceptions to the General Allocation Rule. Certain nonperiodic distributions received before the annuity starting date are not subject to the general allocation rule described in Q 19:4. If a participant receives such a distribution, he or she includes it in gross income only to the extent that it exceeds his or her investment in the contract (i.e., basis) under the plan.

This exception to the general allocation rule applies to three types of distributions:

1. Distributions in full discharge of the plan's obligation to the recipient that are received as a refund of what the participant paid into the plan;
2. Distributions from a life insurance or endowment contract (other than a modified endowment contract described in Code Section 7702A) that are not received as an annuity under the contract; and
3. Distributions from certain plans in existence before August 14, 1982, to the extent that they are allocable to the participant's investment in the contract (i.e., basis) in the plan before August 14, 1982. [I.R.S. Pub. 575]

Example 19-2: Lee Chong established the Lee Chong Grocery Store retirement plan before August 14, 1982, and made after-tax employee contributions under the plan both before August 14, 1982, and after August 13, 1982. Any nonperiodic distribution made to Lee from the plan would be allocated to his investment in the contract (i.e., basis) or to his earnings under the plan in the following order:

1. The after-tax contributions (tax-free to him) that he made before August 14, 1982;
2. The earnings (taxable to him) on the after-tax contributions that he made before August 14, 1982;
3. The earnings (taxable to him) on the after-tax contributions that he made after August 13, 1982; and
4. The after-tax contributions (tax-free to him) that he made after August 13, 1982. [I.R.S. Pub. 575]

Various Types of Taxable Distributions and Transfers

Q 19:6 How are distributions of U.S. Savings Bonds from qualified retirement plans taxed?

The recipient must include in gross income the value of the bonds at the time of the distribution. The value of the bonds includes accrued interest. When the bonds are cashed in, Form 1099-INT will show the total interest accrued, including the part that was reported as gross income when the bonds were distributed from the qualified retirement plan. (For further information on how to adjust interest income for U.S. Savings Bond interest that has been reported previously, see "How to Report Interest Income," in Chapter 1 of IRS Publication No. 550, Investment Income and Expenses.) [I.R.S. Pub. 575]

Q 19:7 How are distributions of excess elective deferrals taxed?

If a participant's elective deferrals for a particular taxable year exceed that year's dollar limitation (e.g., $18,500 for 2018, plus $6,000 for catch-up contributions for individuals age 50 or older), then, generally, he or she must include that excess in his or her gross income for that taxable year. For this purpose, elective deferrals include elective contributions under Code Section 401(k) plans, Code Section 501(c)(18) plans (certain retirement plans funded only by employee contributions), salary-reduction simplified employee pension (SARSEP) plans, and Code Section 403(b) tax-sheltered annuities. (After December 31, 1996, employers are no longer allowed to establish SARSEPs. However, transition rules allow participants to continue to contribute to existing plans.) However, elective deferrals do not include employer contributions to a Code Section 403(b) tax-sheltered annuity if they are made under a one-time, irrevocable election that the employee makes as soon as he or she becomes eligible to participate in the 403(b) arrangement.

Excess elective deferrals are elective deferrals to all such plans and arrangements, for a given taxable year, that exceed that taxable year's dollar limitation.

If the plan document permits, the excess deferral can be distributed to the participant who made it. If the individual participates in only one plan, and the plan allows excess deferrals to be distributed, the participant must notify the plan (by the deadline specified in the plan) that he or she made excess deferrals for the taxable year. The plan must then distribute the excess deferrals, plus earnings, to the participant by April 15 of the following taxable year.

If an individual participates in more than one plan, he or she can have excess deferrals paid out of any of the plans that permit corrective distributions of excess deferrals. The participant must notify each plan by the date required by that plan of the amount that it must distribute. The plan must then distribute that amount, plus earnings, to the participant by April 15 of the following taxable year.

If the participant receives excess deferrals by that April 15, he or she does not have to include them again in his or her taxable income. (If the excess deferrals are distributed by April 15 of the taxable year following the taxable year for which they were made, they need only be included in gross income once: in the taxable year for which they were made.) However, any income on the excess deferrals is included in the participant's gross income for the taxable year in which the income is actually distributed. Neither the excess deferrals nor the income they earned while they were held in the plan is subject to the 10 percent additional income tax on pre-age-59½ distributions (see chapter 22).

If the excess deferrals and the earnings attributable to them are not distributed by the April 15 of the taxable year following the taxable year for which the elective deferrals were made, they are taxed twice, once in the taxable year in which they were made, and again, in the taxable year in which they are actually distributed.

Q 19:8 How are corrective distributions of excess elective contributions taxed?

This is discussed in chapter 5.

Q 19:9 How are corrective distributions of excess aggregate contributions taxed?

This is discussed in chapter 5.

Q 19:10 How are corrective distributions of excess annual additions taxed?

This is discussed in chapter 5.

Under Code Section 415, for years beginning after December 31, 2001, the annual addition to a defined contribution plan is generally limited to the lesser of 100 percent of the participant's Code Section 415(c)(3) compensation or $40,000 (indexed thereafter in $1,000 increments). For limitation years ending before January 1, 1998, Code Section 415(c)(3) "compensation" meant taxable compensation only. For limitation years beginning on or after January 1, 1998, Code Section 415(c)(3) "compensation" also includes salary reduction contributions under Code Sections 125, 132(f)(4), 401(k), 403(b), 457, simplified employee pension (SEP) plans, and 501(c)(18) plans. Under certain circumstances, contributions in excess of those limits, called excess annual additions, may be corrected by a distribution of the participant's elective deferrals, or a return of his or her after-tax contributions and attributable earnings.

A corrective distribution of excess annual additions consisting of elective deferrals or of earnings attributable to after-tax contributions is fully taxable in the year it is paid. It cannot be rolled over on a tax-free basis into another qualified plan or IRA. It is not, however, subject to the 10 percent additional income tax on early distributions. Any corrective distribution consisting solely of the participant's after-tax contributions is not taxable; it is a tax-free return of the participant's basis under the plan. [I.R.S. Pub. 575]

Q 19:11 When is a loan from a qualified retirement plan taxable as a nonperiodic distribution?

If a loan from a qualified retirement plan gives rise to a deemed distribution or a distribution of a plan loan offset amount, then either type of distribution is treated as a nonperiodic distribution (see chapter 2). [I.R.S. Pub. 575]

Q 19:12 How are transfers of annuity contracts treated under the nonperiodic distribution taxation rules?

If a participant transfers, without full and adequate consideration, an annuity contract issued after April 22, 1987, he or she is treated as having received a nonperiodic distribution. The amount of the nonperiodic distribution equals the cash surrender value of the contract at the time of the transfer minus the cost of the contract at that time.

This rule does not apply to transfers between spouses or transfers incident to a divorce.

No gain or loss is recognized if an annuity contract is exchanged for another if the insured or annuitant remains the same. However, the gain on the sale of an annuity contract is ordinary income to the extent that the gain is due to interest accumulated on the contract. Gain due to interest is ordinary income if the contract is exchanged for a life insurance or endowment contract. However, gain or loss is not recognized on the exchange of an annuity contract solely for another annuity contract. Nonrecognition generally applies only when one annuity contract is exchanged directly for another. [I.R.S. Pub. 575]

Q 19:13 How are distributions of annuity contracts from qualified retirement plans taxed?

The distribution of an annuity contract by a qualified retirement plan to a participant is not taxed to him or her (even if the contract has a cash surrender value) unless and until the participant surrenders the contract. [Treas. Reg. § 1.404(a)-1(a)(2)] However, the cash surrender value of an annuity contract that was issued after 1962 may be recovered tax-free only if it is nontransferable by the distributee. [Treas. Reg. § 1.401-9(b)(1); Treas. Reg. § 1.402(a)-1(a)(2)] However, even if an annuity contract that was issued after 1962 is transferable, its distribution is not taxable if the contract is made nontransferable within 60 days after the date it is distributed. [Treas. Reg. § 1.402(a)-1(a)(2)] If the distribution of the annuity contract is not taxable, annuity payments made under such a contract are taxable as amounts received as an annuity or periodic distributions (see chapter 18).

Q 19:14 What is the tax treatment of accident or health benefits provided under a qualified retirement plan?

Accident or health benefits that are provided under qualified retirement plans are taxed separately from the retirement benefits provided under such plans. For example, in addition to paying a pension at retirement, a qualified pension plan may pay an earlier pension if the participant becomes disabled. Or, a profit-sharing plan may provide for the periodic distribution of a participant's account balance during periods when the participant is absent from work because of personal injury or sickness, with the remainder of the account balance to be paid when he or she separates from service, as long as the accident and health benefit is "incidental" when compared with the separation benefit.

The annuity taxation rules under Code Section 72 do not apply to accident or health benefits received under a qualified retirement plan that "provides" for benefits that may be excludable from gross income as accident or health benefits under Code Section 104 or 105. A qualified retirement plan that pays amounts that are used for accident or health purposes may nonetheless not provide for accident or health benefits.

Retirement benefits that are received from a qualified retirement plan are taxed under the annuity rules of Code Section 72, without regard to the inclusion or exclusion in income of accident or health benefits. [Treas. Reg. § 1.72-15(e)]

However, any accident or health benefits that are excludable as attributable to employee contributions [I.R.C. § 104(a)(3)] are not included in the expected return, in determining the taxable portion of an amount received as an annuity. Any employee contributions that are used to provide accident or health benefits cannot be included in the employee's investment in the contract (i.e., basis).

Accident or health benefits received under a qualified retirement plan that are attributable to employer contributions are includible in an employee's gross income, unless they are excludable as an amount expended for medical care under Code Section 105(b), or are payments for certain disabilities or disfigurements under Code Section 105(c).

Q 19:15 What is the tax treatment of accident or health benefits provided under a qualified retirement plan to self-employed individuals?

All payments under a qualified retirement plan that provide for retirement and accident and health benefits to, or on behalf of, a self-employed individual are taxed under the annuity taxation rules of Code Section 72.

However, for accident or health benefits provided through an insurance contract or a similar arrangement, the payments are excludable from income to the extent that the self-employed individual is considered to have paid for the insurance coverage himself or herself under Code Section 104(a)(3). [Treas. Reg. § 1.72-15(g)]

Q 19:16 What is the tax treatment of medical benefits provided for retired employees under qualified retirement plans?

The payment of medical benefits to retired employees under a qualified retirement plan from an account described in Code Section 401(h) is treated in the same manner as a payment of accident or health benefits attributable to employer contributions, or employer-provided coverage under an accident or health plan. Accordingly, amounts applied for the payment of accident or health benefits, or for the payment of accident or health coverage, from a Code Section 401(h) account are not includible in the gross income of the participant on whose behalf such contributions were made to the extent they are excludable from gross income under Code Section 104, 105, or 106. [Treas. Reg. § 1.402(a)-1(e)(2)]

Q 19:17 What is the tax treatment of trustee-to-trustee transfers made between qualified retirement plans?

A benefit is taxable only when it is actually distributed from a qualified retirement plan. A direct transfer of a participant's benefit by the trustee of one qualified retirement plan to the trustee of another such plan (i.e., a trustee-to-trustee transfer) is not considered either a distribution or a rollover; therefore, the transfer is not taxable to the participant.

Q 19:18 What is the tax treatment of distributions of deductible qualified voluntary employee contributions that were contributed to qualified plans before 1987?

A deductible qualified voluntary employee contribution (QVEC) was any deductible qualified voluntary employee contribution made after 1981 but before 1987 that was allowed as a deduction for any year under Code Section 219(a).

The term accumulated QVECs means pre-1987 QVECs, plus the amount of income or gain allocable to them, minus allocable losses, expenses, and distributions of such contributions to the participant. [I.R.C. § 72(o)(5)(B)]

Any deductible QVECs that a participant made to a qualified retirement plan before 1987 are taxable when they are distributed to the participant, and they are not includible in any lump-sum distribution from the plan. [I.R.C. § 402(d)(4)(A), as in effect prior to amendment by SBJPA § 1401(a)] Distributions of accumulated QVECs are includible in gross income, unless they are rolled over, on a tax-free basis, into an IRA or another qualified retirement plan and are separately accounted for under the IRA or plan as deductible employee contributions. [I.R.C. § 402(a)]

Under a special ordering rule, unless the plan document provides otherwise, the accumulated QVECs are not considered distributed until all other amounts to the credit of the participant have been distributed.

QVECs are not included in the participant's cost basis under the plan.

Although distributions of QVECs (which were deductible when made) may be rolled over tax-free into an IRA or another qualified plan, a distribution of nondeductible employee contributions may not. [I.R.C. § 402(c)(2)] This is because the maximum amount of a qualified plan distribution that may be rolled over tax-free to an IRA or another qualified plan is that portion of the distribution that would be included in the recipient's gross income if it were received currently, and not rolled over. A distribution of accumulated QVECs would be taxable if received, but a distribution of nondeductible (after-tax) employee contributions (but not attributable earnings) would be excludable from income if received.

Because accumulated QVECs may not be included in any lump-sum distribution from a qualified plan, forward averaging and capital gains treatments, to the extent available, cannot be applied to them.

Lump-Sum Distributions

Q 19:19 What changes did the Small Business Job Protection Act of 1996 make to the rules affecting the taxation of lump-sum distributions from qualified retirement plans?

The Small Business Job Protection Act of 1996 (SBJPA) repealed special five-year forward averaging for lump-sum distributions from qualified retirement plans, effective for lump-sum distributions received in taxable years beginning after December 31, 1999. However, SBJPA retained a Tax Reform Act of 1986 (TRA '86) grandfather provision allowing individuals who were 50 years of age or older on January 1, 1986, to elect even more favorable 10-year averaging treatment.

Q 19:20 What is a lump-sum distribution from a qualified retirement plan?

A lump-sum distribution from a qualified retirement plan is a distribution or payment, within one taxable year of the recipient, of the balance to the credit of an employee, which becomes payable to the recipient:

1. On account of the employee's death;
2. After the employee attains age 59½;
3. On account of a common law employee's separation from service; or
4. After a self-employed individual becomes totally and permanently disabled.

[I.R.C. § 402(d)(4)(A), before amendment by SBJPA, for taxable years beginning before January 1, 2000; I.R.C. § 402(e)(4)(D), as amended by SBJPA § 1401(b)(1), effective for taxable years beginning after December 31, 1999]

Q 19:21 When is a self-employed individual totally and permanently disabled for purposes of the lump-sum distribution rules?

A self-employed individual is disabled if he or she is unable to engage in any substantial gainful activity by reason of any medically determinable physical or mental impairment that can be expected to result in death or to be of long-continued and indefinite duration. The participant is not considered disabled unless he or she furnishes proof of the existence of the disability in a form and manner satisfactory to the I.R.S. [I.R.C. § 72(m)(7)]

Q 19:22 How is the distribution of an annuity contract treated?

A distribution of an annuity contract from a qualified plan is treated as a lump-sum distribution. [I.R.C. § 402(d)(4)(A), as in effect prior to amendment by SBJPA, for taxable years beginning before January 1, 1996.]

Q 19:23 What distributions do not qualify as lump-sum distributions?

The following distributions do not qualify as lump-sum distributions:

1. The part of a distribution not rolled over if the distribution is partially rolled over to another qualified plan or IRA.
2. Any distribution if an earlier election to use either the five- or ten-year tax option had been made after 1986 for the same plan participant.

3. U.S. Retirement Plan Bonds distributed with a lump-sum distribution.
4. Any distribution made during the first five taxable years that the participant was in the plan, unless it was made because the participant died.
5. The current actuarial value of any annuity contract included in the lump-sum distribution. (This value is used to compute tax on the ordinary income portion of the distribution under the five- or ten-year forward averaging method, to the extent these methods are available.)
6. A distribution to a 5 percent owner that is subject to penalties under Code Section 72(m)(5)(A) because it exceeds the benefits provided under the plan's benefit formula.
7. A distribution from an IRA.
8. A distribution from a Code Section 403(b) tax-sheltered annuity plan.
9. A distribution of the redemption proceeds of bonds rolled over tax-free to a qualified plan from a qualified bond purchase plan.
10. A distribution from a qualified plan if (a) the participant or his or her surviving spouse previously received an eligible rollover distribution from the same plan (or another plan of the employer that must be combined with that plan under the lump-sum distribution rules) and (b) the previous distribution was rolled over tax-free into another qualified plan or to an IRA.
11. A distribution from a qualified plan that received a rollover after 2001 from an IRA (other than a conduit IRA), a Code Section 457 governmental plan, or a Code Section 403(b) plan on behalf of the participant.
12. A distribution from a qualified plan that received a rollover after 2001 from another qualified plan on behalf of that plan participant's surviving spouse.
13. A corrective distribution of excess elective deferrals, excess contributions, excess aggregate contributions, or excess annual additions.
14. A lump-sum credit or payment from the Federal Civil Service Retirement System (or the Federal Employees Retirement System).

[I.R.S. Pub. 575]

Q 19:24 Can a distribution be a lump-sum distribution if it is not made from a tax-exempt trust that forms a part of a qualified retirement plan?

No. A distribution cannot be a lump-sum distribution unless it is made from a tax-exempt trust, described under Code Section 501(a), that forms a part of a Code Section 401(a) qualified retirement plan or a Code Section 403(a) qualified annuity plan. [I.R.C. § 402(d)(4)(A), as in effect prior to amendment by SBJPA, for taxable years beginning before January 1, 2000; I.R.C. § 402(e)(4)(D), as amended by SBJPA § 1401(b)(1), effective for taxable years beginning after December 31, 1999]

However, a lump-sum distribution may be made directly by an insurance company if benefits under the plan are funded by a group annuity contract issued by that insurer. [Rev. Rul. 59-401, 1959-2 C.B. 121, obsolete on other issues; Rev. Rul. 88-85, 1988-2 C.B. 333]

Q 19:25 What happens if a distribution is made under a trust that is tax-exempt in the distribution year but not in a prior year?

If a trust that forms part of a qualified retirement plan is tax-exempt for the taxable year of the distribution but was not tax-exempt for one or more taxable years before the year of distribution, the employer contributions that were included in the employee's gross income in the years when the trust was nonexempt are treated as part of the consideration paid by the employee (see chapter 26). [Treas. Reg. § 1.402(a)-1(a)(1)(iv)]

Q 19:26 Must an employee have been a plan participant for at least five years before any lump-sum distribution received during a taxable year beginning before January 1, 2000, could qualify for special forward averaging treatment?

Yes. No lump-sum distribution received by an employee from a qualified retirement plan could have been eligible for special forward averaging treatment unless the employee had been a participant in the plan for five or more taxable years before the taxable year of the distribution. [I.R.C. § 402(d)(4)(F), as in effect prior to amendment by SBJPA, for taxable years beginning before January 1, 2000]

However, the five-year participation requirement does not apply for distributions made to a deceased employee's beneficiary. [I.R.S. Pub. 575]

If the entire balance to the credit of the employee under one qualified plan of an employer is transferred to another qualified plan of the same employer, the five-year participation rule is satisfied if the employee participates in either or both plans for five taxable years before the taxable year of the distribution. This is called service-tacking. [Ltr. Rul. 8531078] If less than the entire balance to the employee's credit is transferred from one qualified plan to the other, only the employee's years of participation under the plan making the distribution are counted in determining whether the five-year participation requirement has been met. [Ltr. Rul. 8531078]

The five-year requirement was met when an employee's account balance was transferred, in a trustee-to-trustee transfer, from one employer's plan to the plan of a later employer, and the employee participated in either plan for a total of five taxable years before the taxable year of the distribution from the transferee plan. [Ltr. Ruls. 8934051, 8247068]

The same tacking rule applied for the five-year participation requirement, when a participant was an active participant in one employer's plan that merged into a different employer's plan. [Ltr. Rul. 7835062]

Q 19:27 Must a distribution represent the entire balance to the credit of an employee to qualify as a lump-sum distribution?

Yes. A distribution must represent the entire balance to the credit of an employee to qualify as a lump-sum distribution. [I.R.C. § 402(d)(4)(A), as in effect prior to amendment by SBJPA, for taxable years beginning before January 1, 2000; I.R.C. § 402(e)(4)(D), as amended by SBJPA § 1401(b)(1), effective for taxable years beginning after December 31, 1999]

The balance to an employee's credit is determined as of the first distribution received after the event that qualifies the distribution as a lump-sum distribution (e.g., the employee's death or separation from service). [Notice 89-25, 1989-1 C.B. 662, Q&A-6] Amounts distributed to the employee before any such event are disregarded. [Rev. Rul. 69-495, 1969-2 C.B. 100] Also, additional amounts that are credited to the employee after the date his or her balance is determined may, but are not required to, be treated as part of the balance to his or her credit under the plan.

> **Example 19-3:** If, in 2019, employee Mary Talbot receives $100,000, which represents her entire vested balance as of January 1, 2019, she is treated as having received the entire balance to her credit, even though an additional $5,000 is allocated to her account on December 31, 2019, because of her service in 2019.

A distribution, on account of separation from service, of the balance to the credit of an employee was a lump-sum distribution, even though the employee, who was over 70½, had already begun receiving minimum required distributions (see chapter 4) under the plan during the years before he or she retired. [Ltr. Rul. 9143078]

Q 19:28 Which qualified retirement plans must be aggregated in determining whether a distribution represents the balance to the credit of an employee?

All qualified retirement plans of the same type that are maintained by the same employer must be aggregated and treated as a single plan in determining whether a distribution represents the balance to the credit of an employee under the lump-sum distribution rules. All pension plans (meaning all defined benefit, money purchase, cash balance, and target benefit plans) maintained by the same employer must be aggregated and treated as a single plan. All profit-sharing plans, including profit-sharing plans that have a 401(k) feature, maintained by the same employer must be aggregated and treated as a single plan; and all stock bonus plans, including any plan with a 401(k) feature, maintained by the same employer must be aggregated and treated as a single plan. [I.R.C. § 402(d)(4)(C), as in effect prior to amendment by SBJPA, for taxable years beginning before January 1, 2000; I.R.C. § 402(e)(4)(D)(ii), as amended by SBJPA, effective for taxable years beginning after December 31, 1999]

The IRS has held that this aggregation rule applies not only to all single-employer pension plans that an employer maintains but also to all multiemployer pension plans to which the employer contributes.

The IRS has held that all employers who are parties to a collectively bargained multiemployer plan are treated as a single employer. Therefore, if an employee's present employer contributes to such a plan on his or her behalf, and the employee's previous employer contributed to a different multiemployer plan under the same collective bargaining agreement, the two plans are considered maintained by the same employer in determining the balance to the credit of the employee. [Ltr. Rul. 8412081]

All trusts (other than nonqualified trusts) and annuity contracts (other than those which do not satisfy the requirements of Code Section 404(a)(2)) that are part of the same qualified retirement plan must be aggregated and treated as a single trust in determining the balance to the credit of the employee. [I.R.C. § 402(d)(4)(C)(i), as in effect prior to amendment by SBJPA, for taxable years beginning before January 1, 2000; I.R.C. § 402(e)(4)(D)(ii)(II), as amended by SBJPA, effective for taxable years beginning after December 31, 1999]

Q 19:29 What amounts are excluded from the balance to the credit of an employee in determining whether a distribution qualifies as a lump-sum distribution?

The balance to the credit of an employee, in determining whether a particular distribution from a qualified retirement plan qualifies as a lump-sum distribution, does not include:

1. Any accumulated deductible QVECs that the employee made before 1987;
2. Any amount payable to an alternate payee under a qualified domestic relations order (QDRO);
3. Any amount transferred from a defined contribution plan to a qualified cost-of-living arrangement (COLA) under a defined benefit plan (as described in Code Section 415(k)(2));
4. Certain forfeitable amounts (see Q 19:32);
5. U.S. Retirement Plan Bonds that are distributed with a lump-sum distribution; and
6. Amounts that have accrued to an employee's benefit under the plan but that have not been included in his or her benefit in the year of the distribution under the plan's most recent accounting.

Q 19:30 Does the balance to the credit of an employee include amounts payable to an alternate payee under a QDRO?

No. Therefore, a distribution that is made from a qualified retirement plan to an employee may still qualify as a lump-sum distribution, even if a portion of the amount that would otherwise have been includible in his or her account balance was previously distributed to an alternate payee under a QDRO.

A payment or distribution to an alternate payee under a QDRO is treated as a lump-sum distribution in the hands of the alternate payee if the payment or distribution of the balance to the credit of the employee is treated as a lump-sum distribution. [I.R.C. § 402(d)(4)(J), as in effect prior to amendment by SBJPA, for taxable years beginning before January 1, 2000; I.R.C. § 402(e)(4)(D)(v), as amended by SBJPA, effective for taxable years beginning after December 31, 1999] In determining whether the distribution to the alternate payee consists of the balance to the credit of the alternate payee, the amount payable to the employee under the plan is not taken into account. [I.R.C. § 402(d)(4)(J), as in effect prior to amendment by SBJPA, for taxable years beginning before January 1, 2000; I.R.C. § 402(e)(4)(D)(v), as amended by SBJPA, effective for taxable years beginning after December 31, 1999]

Q 19:31 What types of contingent plan interests are excluded from the balance to the credit of the employee in determining whether a distribution qualifies as a lump-sum distribution?

The balance to the credit of the employee, in determining whether a distribution qualifies as a lump-sum distribution, does not include the participant's contingent interest in a pending litigation account under the qualified plan. Therefore, a participant who receives a distribution of the balance to his or her credit under the plan, excluding the contingent interest, receives the balance to his or her credit under the plan. If that balance, without the contingent interest, is distributed to the participant within a single taxable year, it is a lump-sum distribution. [Ltr. Rul. 9028103]

Plan funds that have been impounded by a court, and that would be released to participants if the lawsuit were resolved in their favor, are contingent interests that are not included in the participants' balance under the plan. [Rev. Rul. 83-57, 1983-1 C.B. 92]

Q 19:32 If a plan fails to distribute the balance to the credit of an employee within a single taxable year because it cannot liquidate certain illiquid assets necessary to fund the distribution, does the distribution qualify as a lump-sum distribution?

No. If the plan fails to distribute the balance to the credit of an employee within a single taxable year because poor market conditions make it impossible for the plan to liquidate illiquid assets that are necessary to fund the distribution, the distribution to the employee, if made over more than a single taxable year, does not qualify as a lump-sum distribution. For example, distributions received by participants in a profit-sharing plan were not lump-sum distributions when the distributions did not include the participants' interest in a real estate fund in which the plan had invested that had not been liquidated when the participants' distributions were made. In this situation, the IRS held that if a participant's interest in the illiquid real estate fund were not distributed within the same taxable year as the other liquid plan assets, the distribution of the liquid assets would not qualify for lump-sum treatment. [Ltr. Rul. 9316047]

However, even if the plan cannot liquidate certain of its assets, it can nevertheless preserve lump-sum distribution status if it uses an intermediary trust. For example, the plan sponsor of a qualified plan whose assets include illiquid assets (e.g., real estate, limited partnership interests, guaranteed investment contracts (GICs) issued by insurance companies that have been placed under state receivership) may, in connection with the termination and liquidation of its plan, create a separate nonqualified trust (i.e., a *liquidating* or *wasting trust*) to hold the illiquid plan assets. Plan participants under the terminating plan will then receive a distribution of their entire benefit under the plan, consisting of both liquid plan assets and a certificate of participation in the liquidating or wasting trust. The liquidating or wasting trust continues to exist, after the qualified plan and trust terminate and make the distributions just described, and collects both income and liquidation proceeds as its illiquid assets are liquidated, and typically distributes such income and proceeds periodically to the trust's beneficiaries until the illiquid assets are completely liquidated.

The IRS has approved the use of liquidating or wasting trusts to facilitate the termination and winding up of several types of qualified plans. [Ltr. Ruls. 9726032 (use of a wasting trust in connection with the termination of a combined money purchase and profit-sharing plan that held illiquid real estate, i.e., mostly unimproved land, when it terminated), 9421042 (use of a wasting trust in connection with termination of a profit-sharing plan whose assets included significant real estate holdings when it terminated in a depressed real estate market), 9418028 (use of a wasting trust in connection with the termination of a profit sharing/401(k) plan with assets, at the time of the plan terminated, included a GIC that had been issued by an insurance company that had been placed under state receivership), 9417041 (use of a wasting trust in connection with the termination of a qualified plan whose assets at termination included interests in real estate limited partnerships), 9104038 (use of a wasting trust in connection with the termination of a profit-sharing plan whose assets at termination included real property that could not be sold at a reasonable price when the plan terminated because of unfavorable market conditions), 895006 (use of a wasting trust in connection with the termination of a collectively bargained money purchase pension plan whose assets at termination included real estate interests that were not readily marketable when the plan terminated because they could be sold only at unreasonable discounts or because their sale would violate the terms of agreements between the plan and certain real estate investment funds, and because the plan was involved in litigation against the manager of one such fund for alleged breaches of fiduciary duties under Title I of ERISA)]

When a liquidating or wasting trust is established to facilitate the termination of a qualified plan that holds illiquid assets when it terminates, participants will be able to receive single-sum distributions from the terminating plan, consisting of their vested account balances or accrued benefits (less the participant's share of the wasting trust's interest in the plan's illiquid assets), plus a certificate of participation in the illiquid trust, which they may then directly roll over into an IRA or another qualified plan, or take into current income.

Q 19:33 Under what circumstances will there be a recapture of any tax benefit derived from the taxation of a distribution as a lump-sum distribution?

An employee who is treated as having received the balance to his or her credit under a plan as a lump-sum distribution because amounts in which he or she was not vested were not treated as part of the balance (see Q 19:31) is subject to recapture if the same employer later reemploys him or her. There will be a recapture of any tax benefit derived from the taxation of the distribution as a lump-sum distribution if all of these four circumstances exist:

1. An amount is treated as a lump-sum distribution;
2. Lump-sum treatment applies to the distribution;
3. The employee is later reemployed by the same employer; and
4. As a result of services performed after being so reemployed, there is an increase in the employee's vesting for benefits accrued before he or she separated from the employer's service.

[I.R.C. § 402(d)(6)(B), before amendment by SBJPA, for taxable years beginning before January 1, 2000]

If all of the above conditions are met, the recapture occurs in the following manner: The taxpayer's income tax for the taxable year in which the increase in vesting first occurs is increased by the reduction in tax that resulted from applying the lump-sum taxation rules. [I.R.C. § 402(d)(6)(B), as in effect prior to amendment by SBJPA, for taxable years beginning before January 1, 2000]

Q 19:34 Is a distribution a lump-sum distribution, if it otherwise qualifies, even though part of it is "restricted" under the early termination rules that affect the distribution of benefits to the 25 highest-paid employees if the plan is terminated within the first 10 years of its existence?

Yes. Even though the restricted portion may have to be refunded to the plan, and thus is received subject to this contingency, the recipient nevertheless is treated as having received the entire balance to his or her credit under the plan, and will qualify for lump-sum treatment (see chapter 15). [Rev. Rul. 81-135, 1981-1 C.B. 203; Ltr. Ruls. 7910069, 7910032]

Q 19:35 Does a delay in distribution prevent lump-sum treatment?

It may not. For example, a distribution was delayed because a plan had administrative problems. The total amount of the distribution, that is, the amount standing to the employee's credit under the plan when he separated from service, plus any additional increment accruing from that date until the date of distribution, was distributed within a single taxable year of the employee as soon as administratively possible after his separation from service. The IRS treated the distribution as a lump-sum distribution. The payment was made to the separated employee four years after he separated from service, but it nevertheless was made within a single taxable year. [Rev. Rul. 60-292, 1960-2 C.B. 153]

Similarly, an employee's election to delay receiving his account under the plan to a later year did not prevent meeting the "within one taxable year of the recipient" rule, because the taxable year in which the total distribution is ultimately made does not have to be the year of, or even the year immediately following, the year the employee separates from service. [Ltr. Rul. 8203095]

Q 19:36 Are there circumstances in which additional amounts can be credited to an employee's account under a plan that will not disqualify an earlier distribution from lump-sum treatment?

Yes. To qualify for lump-sum treatment, the balance to the credit of an employee must be distributed within a single taxable year of the recipient. The balance is determined as of the first distribution after the event that is the basis for the lump-sum distribution.

The distribution of any additional amounts that are credited to an employee's account after a lump-sum distribution has already been made does not disqualify the original distribution from lump-sum treatment. For example, a distribution made by a profit-sharing plan in the year the employee separated from service qualified for lump-sum treatment even though an additional amount, representing the employee's allocable share of the employer's profits for the year the employee separated from service, was distributed to the employee in the following year. However, the distribution of that additional amount in the following year did not qualify for lump-sum treatment. [Rev. Rul. 56-558, 1956-2 C.B. 290]

When a profit-sharing plan made a distribution in the year after an employee's separation from service, and the distribution included both the employee's balance under the plan at separation and his allocable share of the employer's profits for the year in which he separated from service, the entire distribution qualified for lump-sum treatment. [Rev. Rul. 62-190, 1962-2 C.B. 130]

When an employee who reached age 59½ received a distribution of the balance to his credit under the plan, determined by an accounting at the end of the previous year, any additional amounts that could have been credited to the employee's account after the date of a later accounting may, but need not, have been treated as part of the balance to the credit of the employee for that year. [Notice 89-25, 1989-1 C.B. 662, Q&A-6] The following example illustrates this point:

Example 19-4: In 2019, employee Frank Battle receives $100,000, which represents his entire balance under the Battle Farm profit-sharing plan as of January 1, 2019. He will be treated as having received the entire balance to his credit under the plan, even though an additional $5,000 is allocated to his account on December 31, 2019, on account of his service during 2019.

Q 19:37 Under what circumstances are distributions treated as lump-sum distributions made on account of an employee's death?

A distribution payable by a plan on account of an employee's death qualifies as a lump-sum distribution if the other requirements for lump-sum treatment are met. Therefore, a distribution made by a plan on account of an employee's death to an *inter vivos* trust that the employee had established for the benefit of his or her surviving spouse and children was a distribution made on account of the employee's death, and would qualify as a lump-sum distribution, if all other requirements for lump-sum treatment were met. [Rev. Rul. 83-121, 1983-2 C.B. 74]

Also, a distribution made by a plan to an employee's beneficiary on account of the employee's death after separation from service or retirement qualifies as a lump-sum distribution. Therefore, distributions that a plan makes to an employee before he or she died do not preclude an amount paid to his or her beneficiary on account of the employee's death from qualifying for lump-sum treatment. [Rev. Rul. 69-495, 1969-2 C.B. 100] However, a distribution from the plan to a contingent beneficiary upon the death of the primary beneficiary is not a distribution on account of the employee's death, and thus does not qualify for lump-sum treatment. [Gunnison v. Comm'r, 461 F.2d 496, 29 AFTR 2d 72-1052, 72-1 U.S.T.C. ¶ 9389 (7th Cir. 1972), *aff'g* 54 T.C. 1766 (1970)]

Q 19:38 Under what circumstances are distributions treated as lump-sum distributions made on account of an employee's separation from service?

A distribution made by a plan on account of a common law employee's separation from service qualifies for lump-sum treatment if the other requirements for lump-sum treatment have been met (see Q 19:20).

An employee who elects not to participate any longer in his or her employer's plan, but who continues to work for the employer, has not separated from service. [Rev. Rul. 56-214, 1956-1 C.B. 196]

When an employee separated from the service of his first employer and rolled over a lump-sum distribution from that employer's plan into his new employer's plan, any distribution from the current employer's plan while the employee was still employed by the current employer would not qualify for lump-sum treatment because the employee had not yet separated from the service of his new employer. [Ltr. Rul. 8247068]

When an employee was employed by two separate corporations, whose separate qualified pension plans were funded through a single tax-exempt trust, terminated his employment with one of the corporations, a distribution constituting the balance to the employee's credit under the plan of his former employer qualified as a lump-sum distribution because it represented the balance to his credit under that particular, separate plan. [Rev. Rul. 80-128, 1980-1 C.B. 86]

A distribution from a plan may be made on account of an employee's separation from service, even if the distribution actually occurs before the employee's separation date. For example, distributions that were made within one taxable year were treated as made on account of a separation from service arising from a business liquidation that did not actually occur until three years later. [Patty Smith v. United States, 460 F.2d 1005 (6th Cir. 1972)] Also, a plan distribution was made on account of a separation from service when a corporation, in anticipation of its liquidation, terminated its qualified retirement plan and made distributions to the participants, who remained employed by the company for several months until the business finally wound up its affairs. [Snow v. United States, DC-WA, 75-2 U.S.T.C. ¶ 9618 (July 7, 1975)]

Q 19:39 At what time is an employee considered to have separated from his or her employer's service for purposes of the lump-sum distribution rules?

An employee is considered separated from an employer's service only when there is a complete severance of the employment relationship. An employee who continues to work without pay does not separate from service. It is the rendering of services, or being engaged to render services, and not the payment of compensation, that determines whether or not there has been a separation from service under the lump-sum distribution rules. [Rev. Rul. 57-115, 1957-1 C.B. 160]

An employee separates from an employer's service only if the employee dies, retires, resigns, or is discharged. [Rev. Rul. 79-336, 1979-2 C.B. 187]

A change in status from an employee to an independent contractor is not a separation from service, particularly if the individual renders the same services before and after the change in status. [Reinhardt, 85 T.C. 511 (1985)]

Similarly, there was no separation from service when an employee of a partnership became a partner, because he continued to render services in the ongoing business. [Rev. Rul. 81-26, 1981-1 C.B. 200]

A shareholder-employee who sold his shares in a corporation but who remained employed by the company as its adviser, did not separate from service, even though the company never called upon him to render services. [Bolden, 39 T.C. 829 (1963)]

However, in another instance, the IRS ruled that a separation from service had occurred when an employee retired and became chairman of his former employer's board of directors and agreed to render part-time consulting services to the company, as an independent contractor, under a five-year consulting contract under which his former employer had no power to direct or control his services. [Ltr. Rul. 8931054]

Simply changing the form of ownership of an employer does not cause a separation from service. [Rev. Rul. 79-336, 1979-2 C.B. 187]

The termination of a plan is not, by itself, a separation from service under the lump-sum distribution rules. However, if an employee actually ceases to render services to his or her former employer, there is a separation from service, regardless of whether or not the plan terminates simultaneously with or immediately after that separation. [Judkins, 31 T.C. 1022 (1959)]

Q 19:40 If a recipient receives a lump-sum distribution from a qualified retirement plan after 1999, what are the various options for treating the taxable portion of the distribution?

If a recipient receives a lump-sum distribution from a qualified retirement plan after 1999, there are various options for how the recipient can treat the taxable portion of the distribution. Five are described below. The recipient can:

1. Roll over all or part of the lump-sum distribution. No tax is currently due on the part that is rolled over. Any part that is not rolled over would be reported as ordinary income (see chapter 21);
2. Report the entire taxable portion of the lump-sum distribution as ordinary income on his or her tax return;
3. Report the part of the taxable portion of the lump-sum distribution that is attributable to participation in the plan before 1974 as a capital gain (if he or she qualifies), and the portion that is attributable to post-1973 plan participation as ordinary income;
4. Use the special 10-year averaging method (see Qs 19:50 and 19:61), if he or she qualifies, to figure the tax on the ordinary income portion of the distribution (from plan participation after 1973). Report the capital gain portion of the lump-sum distribution (from plan participation before 1974) on Form 4972, Part II (if the recipient qualifies); or
5. Use the special 10-year averaging method to figure the tax on the total taxable amount (if the recipient qualifies).

[I.R.S. Pub. No. 575]

Q 19:41 How are lump-sum distributions made after 1999 from qualified retirement plans taxed?

Generally, a lump-sum distribution from a qualified retirement plan to an employee or his or her beneficiaries is taxable as ordinary income. (Special five-year forward averaging is not available for lump-sum distributions received in taxable years beginning after December 31, 1999.) Plan participants who reached age 50 before 1986 and who receive a lump-sum distribution in a taxable year beginning after December 31, 1999, may elect 10-year forward averaging or a flat 20 percent capital gains tax on any portion of the lump-sum distribution that is attributable to plan participation before 1974.

Q 19:42 What elections are available to an employee who reached age 50 before 1986?

For a lump-sum distribution received by an employee who reached age 50 before 1986 (or received by an individual, estate, or trust with respect to such an employee), the following elections may be made: (1) an election may be made to use one of three tax treatments if the lump-sum distribution is received in a taxable year beginning before January 1, 2000, and (2) an election may be made to use one of two tax treatments if the lump-sum distribution is received in a taxable year beginning after December 31, 1999. The election may be made even if the employee did not attain age 59½ (which is otherwise required).

However, for a distribution to be eligible for capital gains treatment, it must be a lump-sum distribution. Thus, if the employee has not yet reached age 59½, the distribution must have been made on account of separation from service, death, or, in the case of self-employed individuals, disability.

Lump-Sum Distributions Received in a Taxable Year Beginning Before January 1, 2000. The three tax treatments that may be elected for a lump-sum distribution received, in a taxable year beginning before January 1, 2000, by (or with respect to) an employee who was born before 1936 (and thus, who reached age 50 before 1986) are:

1. Special five-year forward income averaging, either of the entire amount of the taxable portion of the lump-sum distribution or of only the ordinary income portion (for which capital gains treatment was not available);
2. Special 10-year forward income averaging, either of the entire amount of the taxable portion of the lump-sum distribution or of only the ordinary income portion (for which capital gains treatment was not available); or
3. A flat 20 percent tax on the long-term capital gains portion of the lump-sum distribution, that is, the portion that is attributable to the employee's pre-1974 participation under the plan.

Lump-Sum Distributions Received in a Taxable Year Beginning After December 31, 1999. The two tax treatments that may be elected for a lump-sum distribution received, in a taxable year beginning after December 31, 1999, by (or with respect to) an employee who was born before 1936 (and thus, who reached age 50 before 1986) are:

1. Special 10-year forward averaging, either of the entire amount of the taxable portion of the lump-sum distribution or of only the ordinary income portion (for which capital gain treatment was not available); or
2. A flat 20 percent tax on the long-term capital gains portion of the lump-sum distribution, that is, the portion that is attributable to the employee's pre-1974 participation under the plan.

Q 19:43 How is the tax computed for an individual who elects capital gains treatment?

If an individual who reached age 50 before 1986 made the one-time election for lump-sum distributions and elected pre-1974 capital gains treatment, the tax on that individual's lump-sum distribution would be figured as follows:

1. The taxable portion of the lump-sum distribution, minus the portion attributable to the employee's pre-1974 participation under the plan,

constitutes ordinary income includible in income for the taxable year of the distribution. [TRA '86 § 1122(h)(3)(B)] Special five-year forward income averaging (at the tax rates in the year of the distribution) or special 10-year forward income averaging (at 1986 rates) may be used to determine the income tax on the ordinary income portion of the distribution, for lump-sum distributions received in taxable years beginning before January 1, 2000 [TRA '86 § 1122(h)(5)]; only special 10-year forward income averaging is available for taxable years beginning after December 31, 1999. The tax on the ordinary income portion of the lump-sum distribution is then added to the tax determined under (2) below.

2. The pre-1974 portion of the lump-sum distribution is taxed at the flat capital gains rate of 20 percent.

Q 19:44 May more than one election of this special tax treatment be made?

No more than one election of special 10-year forward income averaging or capital gains treatment may be made by, or with respect to, an employee who reached age 50 before 1986. [TRA '86 § 1122(h)(3)(C)] Also, if this election is made, no other special forward income averaging election can be made by, or with respect to, that employee. [TRA '86 § 12(h)(3)(C)] Therefore, if an employee who reached age 50 before 1986 makes such an election before he or she reaches age 59½, he or she may not later elect special five-year forward income averaging for any lump-sum distribution received after he or she reaches age 59½. The election may be made only once by, or with respect to, an employee who reached age 50 before 1986. Thus, if that employee has died, his or her beneficiary need not have reached age 50 before 1986, as long as the deceased employee did.

Five-Year Forward Income Averaging

Q 19:45 Generally, when may the special five-year forward income averaging method have been applied to a lump-sum distribution?

A recipient of a lump-sum distribution received in a taxable year beginning before January 1, 2000, may have elected to have the total taxable portion of the distribution taxed under the five-year forward averaging rules. [I.R.C. § 402(d)(1)(A), as in effect prior to amendment by SBJPA, for taxable years beginning before January 1, 2000] However, five-year forward averaging is not available for any lump-sum distribution received in a taxable year beginning after December 31, 1999. The five-year income averaging tax (to the extent five-year forward income averaging was available) was figured using the tax rate for an unmarried individual (other than surviving spouses and heads of households). The five-year income averaging tax was (to the extent five-year forward income averaging was available) separate from, and in addition to, the regular tax on the taxpayer's other income. [I.R.C. § 402(d)(1)(A), as in effect prior to amendment by SBJPA, for taxable years beginning after December 31, 1999]

Special Five-Year Forward Income Averaging for Lump-Sum Distributions Received in Taxable Years Beginning Before January 1, 2000. The following discussion of special five-year forward income averaging in this Chapter 19 applies only to lump-sum distributions received in taxable years beginning before January 1, 2000. The total taxable amount is allowed as a deduction from gross income (whether or not the taxpayer itemizes) to the extent that the total taxable amount is included in gross income. [I.R.C. § 402(d)(3), as in effect prior to amendment by SBJPA, for taxable years beginning before January 1, 2000] Thus, the lump-sum distribution is taxed twice: once, under the special five-year forward income averaging computation, and a second time as an amount included in the taxpayer's regular taxable income.

For distributions with respect to employees who reached age 50 before 1986, the five-year forward income averaging election can be modified to be a 10-year forward income averaging election. For distributions for which the 10-year forward averaging election is made, 10-year averaging is applied using the same rules as five-year averaging, but with the differences in calculation described in Q 19:58.

Special five-year forward averaging was available to a recipient of a lump-sum distribution, received in a taxable year beginning before January 1, 2000, from a qualified retirement plan only if all these conditions were satisfied:

1. The distribution was received on or after the employee has reached age 59½ (except for recipients making the election for employees who reached age 50 before 1986);
2. The recipient elected special five-year forward averaging for the taxable year for all lump-sum distributions received during that taxable year; and
3. No lump-sum distribution from the same plan was rolled over tax-free into an IRA or another qualified plan.

The election of special five-year forward income averaging could have been made only if the distribution was received on or after the employee had reached age 59½. [I.R.C. § 402(d)(4)(B)(i), as in effect prior to amendment by SBJPA, for taxable years beginning before January 1, 2000] Therefore, when the employee died before reaching age 59½ beneficiary received a lump-sum distribution of the employee's benefit before the employee would have reached age 59½ had the employee lived, the beneficiary was not entitled to elect five-year forward averaging. [Cebula, 101 T.C. 70 (1993)] However, a beneficiary was permitted to make the election to apply special five-year forward income averaging well after the employee has died, if the employee would have been age 59½ or older at the time of the distribution, had he or she lived.

Q 19:46 Could five-year forward averaging have been used for a lump-sum distribution if any portion of that distribution had been rolled over tax-free into another qualified plan or an IRA?

No. If any such distribution to an employee was rolled over tax-free, special forward income averaging could not be used for any later distribution from that plan, or from any plan that had to have been aggregated with that plan. [I.R.C. § 402(c)(10), as in effect for taxable years beginning before January 1, 2000, prior to repeal by SBJPA § 1401(b)(2)] (For distributions made before 1993, forward averaging was available for distributions following an eligible rollover of qualified total distributions from the plan in prior years, because Code Section 402(c)(10) was not in effect at that time. However, Code Section 402(c)(10) was repealed by SBJPA Section 1401(b)(2), effective for taxable years beginning after December 31, 1999.)

Q 19:47 How often was an employee permitted to elect to use five-year forward income averaging for lump-sum distributions?

An election to use special five-year forward income averaging, with respect to a lump-sum distribution received in a taxable year beginning before January 1, 2000, was permitted to be made only once by, or with respect to, any employee. [I.R.C. § 402(d)(4)(B), as in effect prior to amendment by SBJPA, for taxable years beginning before January 1, 2000] Thus, a participant could not elect five-year forward averaging for any distributions he or she received in any taxable year (beginning before January 1, 2000) after the one in which he or she elected five-year averaging.

Q 19:48 Who was permitted to elect to apply five-year forward income averaging to a lump-sum distribution made from a qualified retirement plan?

Special five-year forward income averaging was permitted to be applied to a lump-sum distribution from a qualified retirement plan only if the taxpayer made the five-year averaging election and received the distribution in a taxable year beginning before January 1, 2000. [I.R.C. § 402(d)(4)(B), as in effect prior to amendment by SBJPA, for taxable years beginning before January 1, 2000] Only individuals, estates, and trusts who received a lump-sum distribution from a qualified retirement plan in a taxable year beginning before January 1, 2000, were permitted to make the special five-year forward income averaging election. [I.R.C. § 402(d)(4)(B), as in effect prior to amendment by SBJPA, for taxable years beginning before January 1, 2000]

Q 19:49 Who was liable to pay the separate five-year averaging tax?

The recipient of the distribution received in a taxable year beginning before January 1, 2000, was liable to pay the separate five-year averaging tax. [I.R.C. § 402(d)(1)(D), as in effect prior to amendment by SBJPA, for taxable years beginning before January 1, 2000]

A beneficiary of a trust to which a lump-sum distribution is made is treated as the recipient of the distribution if the beneficiary is now (1) an employee (including a self-employed individual) with respect to the plan that made the distribution or (2) treated as the owner of the trust under the grantor trust and other trust ownership rules. [I.R.C. § 671 et seq.]

Q 19:50 Were estates or trusts that received lump-sum distributions from qualified retirement plans eligible to make the five-year forward averaging election?

Yes. Estates or trusts that received lump-sum distributions in a taxable year beginning before January 1, 2000, were eligible to elect five-year forward income averaging. [I.R.C. § 402(d)(4)(B), as in effect prior to amendment by SBJPA, for taxable years beginning before January 1, 2000] When two or more trusts received such a distribution with respect to an employee (including a self-employed individual), only the employee, or his or her personal representative if he or she had died, was permitted to make this election. [Treas. Reg. § 1.402(e)(4)(B)-1(b)]

Q 19:51 How did a recipient of a lump-sum distribution received from a qualified retirement plan elect special five-year forward income averaging?

A recipient of a lump-sum distribution received in a taxable year beginning before January 1, 2000, elected special five-year forward income averaging by filing Form 4972 as part of his or her income tax return. [Treas. Reg. § 1.402(e)(4)(B)-1(c)(2)] This included an employee (or a self-employed individual) with respect to whom a lump-sum distribution was received by two or more trusts. In the case of a deceased employee, the employee's personal representative made the election.

If there was more than one recipient, each recipient (when not all of the recipients are trusts) made the five-year forward averaging election by filing Form 4972 with his or her income tax return (see the instructions to Form 4972). When an election of special five-year forward averaging treatment was to be made for a year after the income tax return for that year had been filed (but before the expiration of the period for making the averaging election), the election was made by filing Form 4972 with an amended income tax return.

A five-year averaging election was required to be made for the taxable year for which it applied, and the election was required to cover all lump-sum distributions received during that taxable year.

Q 19:52 When did the special five-year forward income averaging election have to be made with respect to a lump-sum distribution?

The special five-year forward income averaging election was required to be made, with respect to such a distribution, at any time before the expiration of the refund claim period (including any extension) for the year to which the election was to apply.

Q 19:53 When could the special five-year forward averaging election be revoked with respect to a lump-sum distribution?

The special five-year forward income averaging election was permitted to be revoked, with respect to such a distribution, within the refund claim period, if an amended income tax return was filed for the year of the election. The amended return was required to contain a statement revoking the election and was required to be accompanied by payment of any tax attributable to the revocation. If an election for a taxable year was revoked, another election for that year was permitted to be made under the regular election rules.

Q 19:54 How was the separate five-year averaging tax determined with respect to a lump-sum distribution?

The separate five-year averaging tax for any such taxable year was an amount equal to five times the tax that would have been imposed if the taxpayer had been an unmarried individual and the taxable income had been an amount equal to: one-fifth of the excess of the total taxable amount (see Q 19:56) of the lump-sum distribution for the tax year [I.R.C. § 402(d)(1)(B)(i), as in effect prior to amendment by SBJPA, for taxable years beginning before January 1, 2000], minus the minimum distribution allowance (see Q 19:57). [I.R.C. § 402(d)(1)(B)(ii), as in effect prior to amendment by SBJPA, for taxable years beginning before Jan. 1, 2000]

A seven-step method was used in determining the separate five-year averaging tax on a lump-sum distribution received in a taxable year beginning before January 1, 2000:

Step 1. Compute the total taxable amount of the distribution (see Q 19:55).

Step 2. If a portion of the participant's benefit is attributable to pre-1974 participation, and the election described in Q 19:40 or Q 19:42 has been made, determine the ordinary income portion of the distribution (see Q 19:65).

Step 3. If there is a death benefit exclusion, reduce the amount in Step 2 by the death benefit exclusion. If the death benefit exclusion applies and an election of capital gains treatment for pre-1974 participation is made (see Q 19:42), the exclusion must be adjusted. [Note that the death benefit exclusion is no longer available with respect to decedents dying after August 20, 1996, the enactment date of SBJPA]

Step 4. If there is an estate tax amount attributable to the lump-sum distribution, reduce the taxable amount by the estate tax deduction attributable to the distribution (see Q 19:57). If an amount of the estate tax is attributable to the distribution and an election of capital gains treatment for pre-1974 plan participation is made (see Q 19:42), the amount of this reduction must be adjusted (see Q 19:56).

Step 5. Reduce the taxable amount by the minimum distribution allowance (see Q 19:57).

Step 6. Determine the tax on one-fifth of the total taxable income in Step 1, as reduced in Steps 2–5, using the tax rates for the year of the distribution.

Step 7. Multiply the amount in Step 6 by five. (This is the separate five-year averaging tax on the lump-sum distribution received in a taxable year beginning before January 1, 2000.)

Q 19:55 How was the total taxable amount of a lump-sum distribution computed?

The total taxable amount of a lump-sum distribution (Step 1 in Q 19:54) was the total amount of the lump-sum distribution, reduced by the sum of:

1. The amounts considered contributed by the employee in excess of previous distributions that were not includible in gross income [I.R.C. § 402(d)(4)(D)(i), as in effect prior to amendment by SBJPA, for taxable years beginning before January 1, 2000]; and
2. The net unrealized appreciation (NUA) attributable to that part of the distribution that consisted of securities of the employer corporation. [I.R.C. § 402(d)(4)(D)(ii), as in effect prior to amendment by SBJPA, for taxable years beginning before January 1, 2000] The term "securities of the employer corporation" means shares of stock, bonds, and debentures (with interest coupons or in registered form) issued by the employer (including its parent owning 50 percent or more of the voting power of its shares or subsidiary). [I.R.C. § 402(d)(4)(L), as in effect prior to amendment by SBJPA, for taxable years beginning before January 1, 2000]

The amount of all lump-sum distributions for the taxable year was required to be aggregated.

Q 19:56 Under what circumstances was the total taxable amount of lump-sum distribution reduced by the allocable estate tax deduction?

If a lump-sum distribution received by a participant's beneficiary in a taxable year beginning before January 1, 2000, was subject to the five-year forward averaging computation, the total taxable amount of the distribution was required to be reduced by the estate tax deduction attributable to the total taxable amount of the distribution (before reduction by the estate tax deduction; see Step 4 in Q 19:54). [I.R.C. § 691(c)(5)]

Q 19:57 How was the minimum distribution allowance computed in figuring the separate five-year forward averaging tax?

The total taxable amount (computed in Step 1 in Q 19:54) was reduced by the minimum distribution allowance. [I.R.C. § 402(d)(1)(B), as in effect prior to amendment by SBJPA, for taxable years beginning before January 1, 2000] The minimum distribution allowance for the taxable year was:

1. The lesser of ½ × "t" or $10,000 [I.R.C. § 402(d)(1)(C)(i), as in effect prior to amendment by SBJPA, for taxable years beginning before January 1, 2000], *minus*
2. 20 percent × "t" × $20,000, or zero if "t" is less than $20,000 [I.R.C. § 402(d)(1)(C)(ii)],

where "t" is the total taxable income.

The minimum distribution allowance, however, could not be less than zero. [I.R.C. § 402(d)(1)(C)(i), as in effect prior to amendment by SBJPA, for taxable years beginning before January 1, 2000]

Q 19:58 How was the separate five-year averaging tax calculated when a lump-sum distribution included the distribution, received in a taxable year beginning before January 1, 1996, of an annuity contract?

When such a lump-sum distribution included an annuity contract, the total taxable amount of the distribution (see Q 19:55) that was applicable to the contract included the current actuarial value of the contract, determined on the date of the distribution. [I.R.C. § 402(d)(2)(C), as in effect prior to amendment by SBJPA, for taxable years beginning before January 1, 2000]

The amount of the separate five-year averaging tax (computed on the total taxable amount, including the annuity contract) was then reduced (but not below zero) by the portion of the tax that was attributable to the annuity contract. [I.R.C. § 402(d)(2)(A), as in effect prior to amendment by SBJPA, for taxable years beginning before Jan uary 1, 2000]

Ten-Year Forward Income Averaging

Q 19:59 What is 10-year forward income averaging?

If an employee reached age 50 before 1986, then he or she may elect to have the entire taxable portion of his or her lump-sum distribution, or that part of the taxable portion for which capital gains treatment is not elected, taxed under the 10-year averaging method. Ten-year forward income averaging is available, under these circumstances, in any taxable year. The 10-year separate averaging tax on lump-sum distributions is separate from, and in addition to, the regular tax on the taxpayer's other taxable income. Thus, the amount of the distribution that is taxed under the 10-year averaging method is not included in the taxpayer's adjusted gross income. [I.R.C. § 62(a)(8)] If the amount of the distribution is included in gross income, adjusted gross income is computed by subtracting the amount taxed under 10-year forward averaging.

Even though it is referred to as an averaging method, the 10-year averaging method is a formula for figuring the tax on a lump-sum distribution only for the taxable year of receipt. The taxpayer pays the separate 10-year averaging tax only once, not over 10 years. [I.R.S. Pub. 575]

If an employee chooses the 10-year averaging method, the separate 10-year averaging tax is computed on Form 4972 using the special 1986 tax rates shown in the instructions to the Form 4972. [I.R.S. Pub. 575] The recipient of the lump-sum distribution is liable for the separate 10-year averaging tax.

Q 19:60 Under what circumstances is 10-year averaging available to the recipient of a lump-sum distribution?

Ten-year forward averaging is available to the recipient of a lump-sum distribution from a qualified retirement plan only if:

1. The distribution is received by, or on behalf of, an employee who reached age 50 before 1986, that is, who was born before 1936 and did not die before reaching age 50;
2. The recipient elects 10-year forward averaging for the taxable year for all lump-sum distributions received during that year; and
3. No part of the lump-sum distribution was rolled over tax-free to another qualified plan or to an IRA.

An election to use 10-year forward averaging may be made only once with respect to any employee. [TRA '86 § 1122(h)(C)(3)] These rules were not changed by SBJPA.

Q 19:61 How is the separate 10-year forward averaging tax computed?

For a lump-sum distribution made with respect to an employee who reached age 50 before 1986 and for which a 10-year forward averaging election is made, the 10-year averaging tax is computed the same way as the five-year forward averaging tax was computed, but substituting "ten times" for "five times," and "1/10" for "1/5," and using 1986 tax rates provided by the IRS in the instructions to Form 4972. [TRA '86 § 1122(h)(5)] These rules were not changed by SBJPA.

Capital Gains Treatment

Q 19:62 Under what circumstances can an election be made to treat the portion of a lump-sum distribution attributable to pre-1974 plan participation as a capital gain, subject to the flat 20 percent capital gains tax?

If an employee who receives a lump-sum distribution reached age 50 before 1986, he or she can elect to treat the portion of the distribution to which "existing capital gains provisions" apply at the flat 20 percent capital gains rate.

[TRA '86 § 1122(h)(3)(B)(ii)] Existing capital gains provisions apply to that portion of the lump-sum distribution attributable to pre-1974 participation in the plan. Thus, 20 percent of the amount of the portion of a lump-sum distribution attributable to pre-1974 plan participation, for which capital gains treatment is elected, is effectively treated as a separate tax added to the tax on regular taxable income. [TRA '86 § 1122(h)(3)(B)(ii)] Alternatively, the capital gain portion of a lump-sum distribution may also be treated as ordinary income for purposes of a forward averaging method, as long as capital gains treatment is not also elected for that portion. [I.R.S. Pub. 575]

Q 19:63 How often can a recipient of a lump-sum distribution from a qualified retirement plan elect to apply capital gains treatment to the portion of the distribution attributable to pre-1974 plan participation?

Only one election may be made to treat an employee's pre-1974 participation benefit as a long-term capital gain, taxable at the 20 percent capital gain rate. If an employee elects to treat his or her pre-1974 participation benefit as a long-term capital gain taxable at the 20 percent rate, he or she will be treated as having exhausted the one-time lump-sum election and, therefore, will not be able to elect five-year (to the extent it is available) or ten-year forward income averaging for any other future lump-sum distributions. [TRA '86 § 1122(h)(3)(C)]

Q 19:64 What are the existing capital gains provisions that apply to recipients who elect to apply capital gains treatment to the pre-1974 portion of a lump-sum distribution?

The existing capital gains provisions are defined with reference to the repealed capital gains provisions under former Code Section 402(a)(2), as in effect on the day before it was repealed by the TRA '86. [TRA '86 § 1122(h)(6)] Thus, under TRA '86, the allocation of the lump-sum distribution between its capital gains portion and its ordinary income portion is made under the repealed version of Code Section 402(a)(2).

Q 19:65 How are the capital gains and the ordinary income portions of a lump-sum distribution determined?

To determine the portion of a lump-sum distribution that is attributable to the employee's pre-1974 participation under the plan, and thus eligible for long-term capital gains treatment, the total taxable amount of the lump-sum distribution is multiplied by the following fraction:

$$\frac{\text{Months of active participation by the employee in the plan before 1974}}{\text{Total months of active participation by the employee in the plan}}$$

The portion of the lump-sum distribution that is ordinary income, and thus not eligible for long-term capital gains treatment, is determined by multiplying the taxable portion of the lump-sum distribution by the following fraction:

$$\frac{\text{Months of active participation by the employee in the plan after 1973}}{\text{Total months of active participation by the employee in the plan}}$$

or, more simply:

Ordinary income portion = Total taxable amount − Capital gains portion

[I.R.S. Pub. 575]

In computing the months of active participation before 1974, any part of a calendar year in which an employee was an active participant under the plan is counted as 12 months; for active participation after 1973, any portion of a calendar month in which the employee is an *active participant* under the plan is counted as one month. [Ltr. Rul. 7922109; I.R.S. Pub. 575]

Allocating the Death Benefit Exclusion. If the recipient of the lump-sum distribution can take the death benefit exclusion (to the extent it is available) and make the capital gain treatment election, he or she must allocate the death benefit exclusion between the ordinary income and capital gains portions of the lump-sum distribution. (The death benefit exclusion is not available with respect to decedents dying after August 20, 1996, the enactment date of the Small Business Job Protection Act of 1996.) The allocation is determined pursuant to Form 4972's instructions.

Allocating Federal Estate Tax. If any federal estate tax is attributable to the lump-sum distribution and the recipient makes the capital gain election, he or she must allocate the federal estate tax between the ordinary income and capital gains portions of the lump-sum distribution. He or she should follow the Form 4972 instructions to determine the allocation. If the capital gain election is not made, the estate tax attributable to both parts of the lump-sum distribution must be entered on the form. For more information on how to determine the estate tax attributable to the lump-sum distribution, see the instructions to Form 706.

Q 19:66 What rules apply when choosing to use the special five-year or ten-year forward averaging method or the capital gain method for a lump-sum distribution from a qualified retirement plan?

A recipient can choose to use the special five-year (to the extent it is available) or ten-year forward averaging method or the capital gain method only once after 1986 for any plan participant. (Five-year forward averaging is not available with respect to lump-sum distributions received in taxable years beginning after December 31, 1999.) If the recipient chooses to use any of these special methods, he or she cannot use any such method for any distributions received with respect to the participant in a later taxable year.

A recipient must complete Form 4972, *Tax on Lump Sum Distributions*, and attach it to Form 1040 if he or she wants to use any of the special taxation methods. If the recipient received more than one lump-sum distribution for a plan participant during the taxable year, he or she must add them together in using the special method.

If the recipient and his or her spouse are filing a joint tax return and each has received a lump-sum distribution, each must complete a separate Form 4972. Then, the separate taxes from the separate Forms 4972 should be added together, and the total should be entered on Form 1040 of their joint tax return.

Q 19:67 What is the time frame for making a decision on a special method of taxation?

The recipient of a lump-sum distribution must decide to use the special method before the end of the time, including extensions, for making a claim for a credit or a refund of taxes. This is usually three years after the date the return was filed or two years after the date the tax was paid, whichever is later. (Returns filed before April 15 are considered filed on April 15 for this purpose.)

The recipient can change his or her mind and decide not to use the special method within the time period just discussed. If the recipient changes his or her mind, he or she must file Form 1040X, *Amended U.S. Individual Income Tax Return*, with a statement saying that he or she does not want to use the special method. The recipient must pay any additional taxes due to the change with the Form 1040X.

Special Lump-Sum Distribution Issues

Q 19:68 What portion of a lump-sum distribution can be recovered tax-free?

The portion of the lump-sum distribution that represents the participant's investment in the contract (i.e., basis) under the plan may be recovered tax-free. In general, the participant's investment in the contract (i.e., basis) consists of:

1. The participant's total nondeductible contributions to the plan;
2. The total of the participant's taxable costs of any life insurance contract distributed (see chapter 6);
3. Any employer contributions that were taxable to the participant;
4. Repayments of loans that were taxable to the participant (see chapter 2);
5. The NUA in employer's securities distributed (see Q 19:53); and
6. The death benefit exclusion, if applicable. (The death benefit exclusion is not available with respect to decedents dying after August 20, 1996, the enactment date of SBJPA.)

The investment in the contract (i.e., basis) must be reduced by amounts previously distributed from the plan tax-free.

The total taxable amount of the lump-sum distribution is the portion that represents the employer's contribution and income earned on the account under the plan. [I.R.S. Pub. 575]

Q 19:69 Can the recipient claim a loss on his or her tax return if the lump-sum distribution he or she receives is less than his or her investment in the contract (i.e., basis) in the lump-sum distribution?

Yes. The recipient may be able to take a loss on his or her tax return if the lump-sum distribution amount is less than the plan participant's investment in the contract (i.e., basis) in the lump-sum distribution. The recipient must receive the distribution entirely in cash or worthless securities for this purpose.

To claim the loss, the recipient must itemize deductions on Schedule A (Form 1040). He or she must show the loss as a miscellaneous itemized deduction (subject to the "2 percent of adjusted gross income" limit). The amount that may be claimed as a loss is the difference between the plan participant's investment in the contract (i.e., basis) and the cash amount of the lump-sum distribution. [I.R.S. Pub 575]

Q 19:70 What is the tax treatment of lump-sum distributions that include employer securities?

If the lump-sum distribution from the employer's qualified retirement plan includes securities in the employer's company, the securities may have increased in value during the time they were held under the plan. Securities for this purpose include stocks, bonds, registered debentures, and debentures with interest coupons attached. The increase in the value of the securities is called NUA. If the distribution from the plan is a lump-sum distribution, the recipient is not taxed on the NUA when he or she receives the securities. If the distribution is not a lump-sum distribution, the tax deferral applies only to the extent the NUA results from employee contributions. This treatment does not apply to a distribution based on deductible QVECs. The NUA on which income tax is deferred should be shown on the Form 1099-R that the recipient receives from the payor of the distribution.

The recipient can elect to be taxed on the NUA, if he or she desires. The election is made on the tax return on which the recipient has to include the distribution. (See the instructions to Form 4972.)

Q 19:71 What happens when the recipient later sells or exchanges the employer securities?

When the recipient sells or exchanges the employer securities with untaxed NUA, any gain that is realized is long-term capital gain up to the amount of the NUA. This is true no matter how long the securities have been held. Any gain that is more than the NUA is a long-term or short-term capital gain, depending upon how long the securities have been held after they were distributed from the qualified plan.

If the recipient receives only worthless securities, he or she can claim a loss of the plan participant's total contributions to the qualified plan. To do so, the recipient must itemize his or her deductions on Schedule A (Form 1040) and claim the loss as a miscellaneous deduction (subject to the "2 percent of adjusted gross income" limit).

The recipient cannot claim a loss if all he or she receives is stock with a fair market value that is less than the plan participant's total contributions to the plan. The recipient can claim a loss only if he or she sells or exchanges the stock for less than the plan participant's contributions. [I.R.S. Pub. 575]

Determining the Capital Gain and Ordinary Income Portions of a Lump-Sum Distribution. Generally, the capital gain and ordinary income portions of a lump-sum distribution are determined by using the following formulas:

$$\text{Total taxable amount} \times \frac{\text{Months of active participation before 1974}}{\text{Total months of active participation}} = \text{Capital gain}$$

$$\text{Total taxable amount} \times \frac{\text{Months of active participation after 1973}}{\text{Total months of active participation}} = \text{Ordinary income}$$

In figuring the months of active participation before 1974, count as 12 months any part of a calendar year in which the plan participant actively participated under the plan. For active participation after 1973, count as one month any part of a calendar month in which the participant actively participated in the plan.

The capital gain portion of the lump-sum distribution should be shown on Form 1099-R, *Distributions from Pensions, Annuities, Retirement or Profit Sharing Plans, IRAs, Insurance Contracts, etc.*, or other statement given to the recipient by the payor of the distribution.

Chapter 20

Additional Taxes

Federal tax law imposes additional income and excise taxes on certain distributions from qualified retirement plans and individual retirement arrangements (IRAs) to discourage the use of benefits for nonretirement purposes. This chapter discusses the 10 percent additional income tax on early distributions from qualified retirement plans and the 50 percent excise tax on the amount by which annual distributions from qualified retirement plans fall short of the required minimum distribution (RMD) for the calendar year.

The Taxpayer Relief Act of 1997 (TRA '97) repealed the former 15 percent excise tax on excess distributions, effective with respect to excess distributions received after December 31, 1996, as well as the former 15 percent additional estate tax on excess retirement accumulations, effective with respect to the estates of decedents dying after December 31, 1996.

The Pension Protection Act of 2006 (PPA) exempted the following two types of distributions from the 10 percent additional income tax on early distributions: (1) qualified reservist distributions (and the HEART Act of 2008 made that exemption permanent for individuals who are ordered or called to active duty on or after December 31, 2007) and (2) distributions from governmental plans to qualified public safety employees who separate from service after age 50. [I.R.C §§ 72(t)(2)(G), 72(t)(10)] Internal Revenue Service (IRS) Notice 2007-7, 2007-5 I.R.B. 395, provides additional guidance on the exemption for qualified public safety employees. IRS Notice 2010-15, 2010-6 I.R.B. 390, provides additional guidance on the HEART Act of 2008 amendments to Code Section 72(t)(2)(G). Those amendments deleted the previous reference to December 31, 2007, so that the exemption from the 10 percent additional income tax for qualified reservist distributions no longer has an expiration date. The Defending Public Safety Employees' Retirement Act (enacted on June 29, 2015) and the Protecting Americans from Tax Hikes Act of 2015 (PATH Act) (enacted on December

18, 2015), each applicable to distributions made after December 31, 2015, collectively broadened the definition of "qualified public safety employees" under Code Section 72(t)(10)(B)(ii). The Defending Public Safety Employees' Retirement Act also amended Code Section 72(t)(10)(A) so that the exemption from the 10 percent additional income tax on early distributions to qualified public safety employees from governmental plans applies not just to governmental defined benefit plans but also to governmental defined contribution plans. Finally, the Defending Public Safety Employees' Retirement Act amended Code Section 72(t)(4)(A)(ii) so that a distribution from a governmental plan to a qualified public safety employee under Code Section 72(t)(10) will not be treated as a modification to a series of substantially equal payments for purposes of Code Section 72(t)(4), which exempts from the 10 percent additional income tax any distributions that are part of a series of substantially equal periodic payments made not less frequently than annually for the life (or the life expectancy) of the employee or the joint lives (or joint life expectancies) of the employee and his or her designated beneficiary.

The Tax Cuts and Jobs Act of 2017 (TCJA) (Pub. L. No. 115-97, enacted on December 22, 2017), exempted "qualified 2016 disaster distributions" and the Bipartisan Budget Act of 2018 (BBA) (Pub. L. No. 115-123, enacted on February 9, 2018), exempted "qualified wildfire distributions" from the 10 percent additional income tax on early distributions.

Additional 10 Percent Income Tax on Early Distributions 20-2
Fifty Percent Excise Tax on Failure to Make RMDs 20-14

Additional 10 Percent Income Tax on Early Distributions

Q 20:1 When is the 10 percent additional income tax on early distributions from qualified retirement plans imposed?

The 10 percent additional income tax is imposed on early distributions from any qualified retirement plan as defined by Code Section 401(a), qualified annuity plan as defined by Code Section 403(a), an annuity contract described in Code Section 403(b), or an individual retirement account or annuity (IRA) described in Code Section 408(a) or 408(b). [I.R.C. §§ 72(t), 4974(c)] The 10 percent additional income tax does not apply, however, to early distributions from eligible deferred compensation plans maintained by tax-exempt employers or state and local governments, as defined by Code Section 457(b). The 10 percent tax is imposed on the portion of the early distribution that is includible in gross income. However, several early distributions are exempt from the application of the 10 percent additional income tax (see Q 20:2).

The 10 percent additional income tax applies to the taxable portion of any nonexempt early distribution, including lump-sum distributions, regardless of whether they are made with the participant's consent. Thus, the 10 percent additional income tax applies to involuntary cash-outs of benefits of $5,000 or less, unless the amounts distributed are rolled over, on a tax-deferred basis, into an eligible retirement plan.

Q 20:2 Which distributions from qualified plans are not subject to the 10 percent additional income tax?

The following qualified plan distributions are not subject to the 10 percent additional income tax on early distributions:

1. Distributions that are made on or after the date the employee attains age 59½ [I.R.C. § 72(t)(2)(A)(i)];
2. Distributions that are made to a beneficiary (or to the employee's estate) on or after the employee's death [I.R.C. § 72(t)(2)(A)(ii)];
3. Distributions that are attributable to an employee's becoming totally and permanently disabled within the meaning of Code Section 72(m)(7) (see Q 20:3) [I.R.C. § 72(t)(2)(A)(iii)];
4. Distributions that are part of a series of substantially equal periodic payments made not less frequently than annually for the life (or the life expectancy) of the employee or the joint lives (or joint life expectancies) of the employee and his or her designated beneficiary (see Q 20:4) [I.R.C. § 72(t)(2)(A)(iv)];
5. Distributions made to an employee following separation from service after reaching age 55 (this exception does not apply to IRAs) [I.R.C. § 72(t)(2)(A)(v)];
6. Distributions that are dividends paid on stock of a corporation held in an ESOP [I.R.C. § 72(t)(2)(A)(vi)];
7. Distributions made on account of an IRS levy under Code Section 6331 on the qualified retirement plan. [I.R.C. § 72(t)(2)(vii)] (See Q 20:12.) (This exception, enacted under the Internal Revenue Service Restructuring and Reform Act of 1998, became effective for levy distributions made after December 31, 1999.)
8. Payments under a phased retirement annuity or a composite retirement annuity. [I.R.C. § 72(t)(2)(A)(viii)]
9. Distributions made to an employee (other than those described in (1) through (8), above, or in (10), below) to the extent that they do not exceed the amount allowable as a medical expense deduction under Code Section 213 to the employee for amounts paid during the taxable year for

medical care (determined without regard to whether the employee itemizes deductions for that taxable year) [I.R.C. § 72(t)(2)(B)];

10. Distributions that are made to alternate payees under qualified domestic relations orders (QDROs) (this exception does not apply to IRAs) [I.R.C. § 72(t)(2)(C)];
11. Transfers of assets from a terminated defined benefit plan to a 401(k) plan maintained by the same employer, which are not treated as distributions from the terminated plan [Ltr. Rul. 8531078];
12. Distributions that are rolled over, on a tax-deferred basis, into an eligible retirement plan, because the 10 percent additional income tax applies only to that portion of a nonexemptedearly distribution that is includible in gross income [Ltr. Rul. 9010007];
13. Employer contributions and trust income that are treated as having been applied to the purchase of life insurance protection for a plan participant, even though these amounts are includible in the participant's gross income [Notice 89-25, 1989-1 C.B. 662, Q&A-11];
14. Distributions of elective deferrals and employee contributions that exceed the annual limitations imposed under Code Section 415;
15. Corrective distributions of excess aggregate contributions, which are employer matching contributions, employee after-tax contributions, and certain other contributions that exceed the amounts allowed for the plan year under the actual contribution percentage (ACP) test described in Code Section 401(m);
16. Corrective distributions of excess contributions, which are the amounts of elective deferrals made by highly compensated participants under a 401(k) plan that exceed the limits prescribed for the plan year by the actual deferral percentage (ADP) test described in Code Section 401(k);
17. Corrective distributions of excess elective deferrals, which are elective deferrals made by an individual in excess of the applicable dollar limit established under Code Section 402(g) for the taxable year in question;
18. Qualified reservist distributions [I.R.C. § 72(t)(2)(G)] (see Q 20:8);
19. Distributions from governmental defined benefit plans or defined contribution plans to qualified public safety employees who separate from service after age 50 [I.R.C. § 72(t)(10)] (see Q 20:9);
20. Distributions made in 2016 and 2017 that are "qualified 2016 disaster distributions" made to victims of Hurricanes Harvey, Irma, and Maria [TCJA § 11028(b)(1)(A)]; and
21. "Qualified wildfire distributions" made on or after October 8, 2017, and before January 1, 2019, to victims of the California wildfires [BBA § 20102(a)(1)].

Q 20:3 How is the term *disabled* defined for purposes of the exception to the 10 percent additional income tax for distributions that are attributable to an employee's becoming disabled?

An individual is considered *disabled*, under Code Section 72(m)(7), if he or she is unable to engage in any substantial gainful activity by reason of any medically determinable physical or mental impairment that can be expected to result in death or be of a long-continued and indefinite duration. An individual is not considered disabled unless he or she furnishes proof of the existence of disability in the form and manner that the IRS prescribes. [Code § 72(m)(7)]

Q 20:4 What is a "series of substantially equal periodic payments" for purposes of the provision that exempts these payments from the 10 percent additional income tax on early distributions?

Generally, the 10 percent additional income tax is imposed on the portion of early distributions from qualified plans that is includible in gross income. However, under one of the several exceptions to that general rule, the tax does not apply to distributions that are part of a series of substantially equal periodic payments made not less frequently than annually for the life (or life expectancy) of the employee, or the joint lives (or joint life expectancies) of the employee and his or her beneficiary.

However, if the series of periodic payments is subsequently modified (other than by death, disability, or a distribution to which Code Section 72(t)(10) applies (i.e., a distribution from a governmental defined benefit or defined contribution plan to a qualified public safety employee)) within five years after the date the first payment in the series is made (or, if later, by the date an employee reaches age 59½), the exception to the 10 percent additional income tax no longer applies, and the taxpayer's tax for the year in which the series of payments has been modified would be increased by the amount that would have been imposed, but for this exception, plus interest.

IRS Notice 89-25 [1989-1 C.B. 662, Q&A-12], as modified by Revenue Ruling 2002-62 [2002-2 C.B. 710], provides three payment methods that satisfy the substantially equal periodic payment test and that would therefore be exempt from the 10 percent additional income tax:

1. *The RMD Method.* Under this method, the annual payment for each year is determined by dividing the account balance for that year by the number from the chosen life expectancy table for that year. Under this method, the account balance, the number from the chosen life expectancy table, and the resulting annual payments are redetermined for each year. If this method is chosen, there will not be deemed to be a modification in the series of substantially equal periodic payments, even if the amount of payments changes from year to year, provided there is not a change to another method of determining the payment.
2. *The Fixed Amortization Method.* Under this method, the annual payment for each year is determined by amortizing in level amounts the account

balance over a specific number of years determined using the chosen life expectancy table and the chosen interest rate. Under this method, the account balance, the number from the chosen life expectancy table, and the resulting annual payment are determined once for the first distribution year and the annual payment is the same amount in each succeeding year.

3. *The Fixed Annuitization Method.* Under this method, the annual payment for each year is determined by dividing the account balance by an annuity factor that is the present value of an annuity of $1 per year beginning at the taxpayer's age and continuing for the life of the taxpayer (or the joint lives of the individual and the beneficiary). Under this method, the account balance, the annuity factor, the chosen interest rate, and the resulting annual payment are determined once for the first distribution year and the annual payment is the same amount in each succeeding year.

[Notice 89-25, 1989-1 C.B. 662, Q&A-12; Rev. Rul. 2002-62, 2002-2 C.B. 710]

Example 20-1: Horace Abbeville, 50 years old with a life expectancy of 33.11 years, has a $100,000 account balance under the Cannery Row Corporation profit sharing plan. Assuming an interest rate of 8 percent, the plan could satisfy this requirement by distributing $8,679 annually to Horace, which is derived from amortizing $100,000 over 33.1 years at 8 percent interest.

Payments are substantially equal periodic payments if the amount to be distributed annually is determined by dividing the individual's account balance under the plan by an annuity factor (the present value of an annuity of $1 per year beginning at the individual's age attained in the first distribution year and continuing for life) with the annuity factor derived using a reasonable mortality table and an interest rate that does not exceed a reasonable interest rate on the date payments begin. If substantially equal periodic payments are being determined, the individual's account balance under the plan would be divided by an annuity factor equal to the present value of an annuity of $1 per month beginning at the individual's age attained in the first distribution year and continuing for life.

Example 20-2: Assume the annuity factor for a $1 per year annuity for Lee Chong, who is 50 years old, is 11.109 (assuming an interest rate of 8 percent and using the UP-1984 Mortality Table). If Lee has a $100,000 account under the Lee Chong Grocery Company profit sharing plan, he would receive an annual distribution of $9,002 ($100,000 ÷ 11.109 = $9,002).

On October 21, 2002, the IRS released Revenue Ruling 2002-62 [2002-2 C.B. 710] in order to help taxpayers preserve their retirement savings when there is an unexpected drop in the value of those savings. Some taxpayers began receiving fixed payments from their retirement plans based on the value of their accounts at the time they started receiving payments. Under Revenue Ruling 2002-62, those taxpayers may make a one-time switch—without penalty—to a method of determining the amount of their payments based on the value of their accounts as it changes from year to year. Revenue Ruling 2002-62 was intended to help many taxpayers to preserve their retirement savings by allowing them to slow their distributions down in the event of unexpected market downturns. [I.R.S. News Release I.R. 2002-104 (Oct. 3, 2002)]

IRS Revenue Ruling 2002-62 allows an individual who begins distributions in a year using either the fixed amortization method or the fixed annuitization method to switch, in any subsequent year, to the RMD method to determine the payment for the year of the switch and all subsequent years, and the change in method will not be treated as a modification within the meaning of Code Section 72(t)(4). Once a change is made, however, the RMD method must be followed in all subsequent years. Any subsequent change in method will be a modification for purposes of Code Section 72(t)(4). [Rev. Rul. 2002-62, 2002-2 C.B. 710]

The IRS will issue a general information letter in response to a taxpayer who requests additional information on the methodologies used in Notice 89-25, Q&A-12, to calculate substantially equal periodic payments for purposes of the exception to the 10 percent income tax on early distributions granted under Code Section 72(t)(2)(A)(iv).

The three methods of distribution described above are not the only methods that meet the requirements of the substantially equal periodic payment exception to the 10 percent additional income tax. [Ltr. Rul. 9008073] Another method may be used in a private letter ruling request, but, of course, it would be subject to individual analysis. [FAQs regarding Rev. Rul. 2002-62] For example, the IRS has ruled that the following three methods of distribution satisfy the substantially equal periodic payment exception and thus do not invoke the 10 percent additional income tax:

1. Payment of an individual's IRA account balance over his or her life expectancy (as of his or her attained age in the calendar year in which the payments begin), using an assumed interest rate of 120 percent of the long-term applicable federal rate (AFR), rounded to the nearest 0.2 percent for the month before the distributions were to begin [Ltr. Rul. 8946045];
2. Payment of an individual's account balance as of the month before the first payment over a number of months equal to the joint life and last survivor expectancy of the participant and his or her beneficiary and multiplied by 12, assuming an annual interest rate of 9 percent, compounded monthly. The annual periodic payment, once determined, would not change, except if the employee or his or her spouse died. The IRS also has approved a feature that allows the survivor of the two to elect to have the amount of the distribution in the year following the year of the other's death recalculated, using the survivor's life expectancy only, and distributed monthly [Ltr. Rul. 8919052]; and
3. Payment of the participant's account balance over his or her life expectancy, using an 8 percent interest rate for calculating the first year's distribution amount. For subsequent years, the prior year's distribution amount is multiplied by a fraction, the numerator of which is that year's dollar limitation under Code Section 415(b)(1)(A), and the denominator of which is the prior year's limitation. [Ltr. Rul. 9047043]

Q 20:5 Will the 10 percent additional income tax be imposed, despite the exception for substantially equal periodic payments, if the series of payments is modified after it has begun?

Yes. The 10 percent additional income tax will be imposed, even if it did not apply when the payments began because they were part of a series of substantially equal periodic payments, if the series of payments is later modified (other than because of death, disability, or a distribution to which Code Section 72(t)(10) applies (i.e., a distribution from a governmental defined benefit or defined contribution plan to a qualified public safety employee)) and if the method of distribution is changed before the later of:

1. The close of the five-year period beginning with the date of the first payment and continuing until after the employee reaches age 59½; or
2. The date the employee reaches age 59½.

When the series of substantially equal periodic payments is later modified, the 10 percent additional income tax is imposed for the first taxable year in which the modification occurred. The amount of the tax is the amount that would have been imposed had the substantially equal periodic payments exception not applied, plus interest for the so-called deferral period. The deferral period is the period beginning with the taxable year in which the distribution would have been subject to the 10 percent additional income tax (were it not for the substantially equal periodic payments exception) and ending with the taxable year in which the modification of that distribution method occurs.

Examples 20-3 and 20-4 illustrate how the rules in (1) and (2), above, apply.

Example 20-3: Mack begins receiving payments, in substantially equal installments, at age 56, from the Palace Flophouse and Grill profit sharing plan. Before he reaches age 61 (which would be the close of the five-year period beginning with his first payment), Mack changes his method of distribution to a method that no longer satisfies the substantially equal periodic distribution exception. As a result, the 10 percent additional income tax on early distribution is imposed on any amounts Mack receives from the plan before he reaches age 59½, just as if the exception had never applied.

Example 20-4: When she is age 50, Dora retires and begins to receive distributions from the Bear Flag Restaurant retirement plan under a method that provides for substantially equal payments over her life expectancy. When she reaches age 58, she elects to receive her remaining benefits in the form of a single sum. The 10 percent additional income tax applies on the amount that has already been distributed to her and, if she receives the single sum before she reaches age 59½, to that distribution as well.

As Example 20-4 illustrates, the 10 percent additional income tax does not apply to amounts that are distributed after the taxpayer reaches age 59½. Example 20-5 further illustrates this point.

Example 20-5: Doc begins receiving distributions in substantially equal installments, at age 57, from the Western Biological Corporation retirement plan. When he is 61 years old, Doc changes the method of distribution to one that no longer satisfies the substantially equal periodic payment exception. As a result, the 10 percent additional income tax is imposed on amounts that had been distributed to Doc before he reached age 59½, but it does not apply to any amount that is distributed to him after he reaches age 59½.

Q 20:6 Is a reduction in the amount of payment the kind of modification of a series of substantially equal periodic payments that would cause that exception no longer to apply?

Yes. A reduction in the amount of payments is the kind of modification that invokes the 10 percent additional income tax on early distributions. The IRS has ruled [Ltr. Rul. 8921099] that a taxpayer who was 51 years old when he began to receive substantially equal periodic payments from a plan could not reduce the amount of those payments, before he reached age 59½, without incurring the 10 percent additional income tax.

Q 20:7 Does the 10 percent additional income tax apply if the distribution is made after the employee separates from service after reaching age 55?

No. The 10 percent additional income tax does not apply to distributions made to an employee after he or she separates from service after reaching age 55. [I.R.C. § 72(t)(2)(A)(v)] A distribution from a qualified plan to an employee is treated as meeting this exception if these two conditions are satisfied:

1. The distribution is made after the employee separates from the service of the employer maintaining the plan; and
2. The separation from service occurs during or after the calendar year in which he or she reaches age 55.

[Notice 87-13, 1987-1 C.B. 432, Q&A-20]

This exception continues to apply even if the employee is reemployed by the same (or a different) employer, as long as he or she in fact separated from the service of the employer maintaining the plan before his or her distributions had begun. The IRS closely scrutinizes short-term separations from service to see whether they are true separations.

The exception to the 10 percent additional income tax under Code Section 72(t)(2)(A)(v) applies only if the participant is at least age 55 when he or she separates from service. The Tax Court has held that a participant who was 53 years old when she separated from service and 55 years old when she received distributions from her former employer's qualified retirement plan was not eligible for the exception (and therefore, was liable for the 10 percent additional income tax) because she was not at least age 55 when she separated from service. [Watson v. Commissioner, T.C. Summary Op. 2011-113 (Sept. 28, 2011)]

Q 20:8 Does the 10 percent additional income tax apply to qualified reservist distributions?

No. The 10 percent additional income tax on early distributions does not apply to qualified reservist distributions. [I.R.C. § 72(t)(2)(G), as added by PPA § 827 and amended by the HEART Act of 2008 § 107] A *qualified reservist distribution* from a Code Section 401(a) plan is a distribution (1) attributable to elective deferrals under a Code Section 401(k) plan, (2) made to an individual who (by reason of being a member of a reserve component as defined in Section 101 of Title 37 of the U.S. Code) was ordered or called to active duty for a period in excess of 179 days or for an indefinite period, and (3) made during the period beginning on the date of such order or call to duty and ending at the close of the active duty period. A 401(k) plan will not violate the distribution restrictions applicable to such plans if it includes a provision permitting qualified reservist distributions. An individual who receives a qualified reservist distribution may, at any time during the two-year period beginning on the day after the end of the active duty period, make one or more contributions to an IRA of such individual in an aggregate amount not to exceed the amount of such distribution. The dollar limitations otherwise applicable to contributions to IRAs do not apply to any contribution made pursuant to a 401(k) plan's qualified reservist distribution provision. No deduction is allowed, however, for any IRA contribution made under the provision. The exception from the 10 percent additional income tax on early distributions for qualified reservist distributions was added to Code Section 72(t) by PPA, and it applied to distributions made after September 11, 2001, to individuals ordered or called to active duty after September 11, 2001, and before December 31, 2007. The exception was made permanent by the HEART Act of 2008, with respect to individuals who are ordered or called to active duty on or after December 31, 2007. [I.R.C. § 72(t)(2)(G), as added by PPA § 827, and as amended by the HEART Act of 2008 § 107; IRS Notice 2010-15, 2010-6 I.R.B. 390]

Q 20:9 Does the 10 percent additional income tax on early distributions apply to distributions from governmental defined benefit or defined contribution plans to qualified public safety employees who separate from service after age 50?

No. The 10 percent additional income tax on early distributions does not apply to distributions from a governmental defined benefit or defined contribution plan (as defined in Code Section 414(d)) to any qualified public safety employee who separates from service after attainment of age 50. This exception to the 10 percent additional income tax applies to distributions made from governmental defined benefit plans after August 17, 2006 [I.R.C. § 72(t)(10), as added by PPA § 828; IRS Notice 2007-7, 2007-5 I.R.B. 395, § IV, Q&A-6], and to distributions from governmental defined contribution plans after December 31, 2015 [I.R.C. § 72(t)(10)(A), as amended by § 2(b) of the Defending Public Safety Employees' Retirement Act, Pub. L. No. 114-26 (2015)].

Qualified Public Safety Employee. For these purposes, the term *qualified public safety employee* means (1) any employee of a state or a political subdivision of a state (such as a county or city) whose principal duties include services requiring specialized training in the area of police protection, firefighting services, or emergency medical services for any area within the jurisdiction of the state or the political subdivision of the state, or (2) any federal law enforcement officer described in Section 8331(20) or 8401(17) of Title 5 of the U.S. Code, any federal customs and border protection officer described in Section 8331(31) or 8401(36) of Title 5, any federal firefighter described in Section 8331(21) or 8401(14) of Title 5, any air traffic controller described in Section 8331(30) or 8401(35) of Title 5, any nuclear materials courier described in Section 8331(27) or 8401(33) of Title 5, any member of the United States Capitol Police, any member of the United States Supreme Court Police, or any diplomatic security special agent of the United States Department of State. [I.R.C. § 72(t)(10)(B), as amended by § 2(a) of the Defending Public Safety Employees' Retirement Act, Pub. L. No. 114-26 (enacted on June 29, 2015, and applicable to distributions made after December 31, 2015), and by § 308 of the Protecting Americans from Tax Hikes Act of 2015 (PATH Act) (enacted on December 18, 2015, and also applicable to distributions made after December 31, 2015); IRS Notice 2007-2, 2007-5 I.R.B. 395, § IV]

Qualifying for the Exception to the 10 Percent Additional Tax. In order to qualify for the exception to the 10 percent additional tax under Code Section 72(t)(10), the following are necessary:

1. A qualified public safety employee must have received the distribution from a governmental defined benefit or defined contribution plan after separating from service with the employer maintaining the plan; and
2. The separation from service must have occurred during or after the calendar year in which the qualified public safety employee attained age 50.

For example, a qualified public safety employee who separated from service on June 30, 2006, and attained age 50 on December 12, 2006, is eligible for the exception under Code Section 72(t)(10) with respect to distributions made after August 17, 2006. [I.R.C. § 72(t)(10), as added by PPA § 828; IRS Notice 2007-7, 2007-5 I.R.B. 395, § IV, Q&A-7]

Consequences of Post-August 17, 2006, Modification of Substantially Equal Periodic Payments. If, before August 18, 2006, a qualified public safety employee began receiving substantially equal periodic payments that qualified for the exception to the 10 percent additional tax described in Code Section 72(t)(2)(A)(iv) and then modified the periodic payments after August 17, 2006, as long as the modified payments satisfy the requirements described in items 1 and 2 above, the payments received by the qualified public safety employee after August 17, 2006, would qualify for the exception to the 10 percent additional tax under Code Section 72(t)(10). [IRS Notice 2007-7, 2007-5 I.R.B. 395, § IV, Q&A-8]

Exception to 10 Percent Additional Tax Applies Only to Distributions from Defined Benefit and Defined Contribution Plans. The exception to the 10 percent additional tax under Code Section 72(t)(10) applies only to amounts distributed from a governmental defined benefit or defined contribution plan and does not apply to distributions from an IRA. Thus, the exception to the 10 percent additional tax under Code Section 72(t)(10) does not apply to an early distribution from an IRA if the qualified public safety employee rolls over distributions from a governmental defined benefit plan into a defined contribution plan or an IRA and subsequently takes an early distribution from the defined contribution plan or the IRA. [I.R.C. § 72(t)(10)(A); IRS Notice 2007-7, 2007-5 I.R.B. 395, § IV, Q&A-9]

Reporting Distributions. A payer reports distributions that qualify for the exception to the 10 percent additional tax in Box 7 of IRS Form 1099-R, using distribution code 2 (early distribution, exception applies). However, a payer also is permitted to use distribution code 1 (early distribution, no known exception) in Box 7 of IRS Form 1099-R if the payer does not know whether the exception under Code Section 72(t)(10) applies. For further information on reporting, see chapter 27. [IRS Notice 2007-7, 2007-5 I.R.B. 395, § IV, Q&A-10]

Q 20:10 Is a distribution that is otherwise subject to the 10 percent additional income tax on early distributions exempt if it is involuntary?

No. A distribution that is otherwise subject to the 10 percent additional income tax on early distributions is not excepted simply because the recipient had no control over when it was paid.

Q 20:11 Does the 10 percent additional income tax on early distributions apply to distributions that are made pursuant to a designation in effect under Tax Equity and Fiscal Responsibility Act of 1982 (TEFRA) Section 242(b)(2)?

No. The 10 percent additional income tax on early distributions does not apply to distributions that are otherwise subject to the tax if those distributions are made pursuant to a designation that is in effect under Section 242(b)(2) of the Tax Equity and Fiscal Responsibility Act of 1982 (TEFRA). However, if the TEFRA designation ceases to be in effect for those benefits for whatever reason, later distributions will be subject to the 10 percent additional income tax. [Notice 87-13, 1987-1 C.B. 432, Q&A-22]

Q 20:12 When did the 10 percent additional income tax on early distributions become effective?

The 10 percent additional income tax on early distributions applies to non-exempted, early distributions that are made in taxable years beginning after 1986. However, certain transitional rules do apply (see Q 20:13).

Q 20:13 What transitional rules under TRA '86 protect certain early distributions from the application of the 10 percent additional income tax?

First, the 10 percent additional income tax does not apply to distributions to any employee from a plan maintained by his or her employer if these three conditions are met:

1. As of March 1, 1986, the employee had separated from the service of that employer;
2. As of March 1, 1986, the employee's accrued benefit was in pay status under a written election providing a specific schedule for the distribution of his or her entire accrued benefit; and
3. His or her distribution is made under that written election. If distributions that began to be made in accordance with the employee's written election as of March 1, 1986, are no longer made in accordance with that election, then any later distributions that are otherwise subject to the 10 percent additional income tax are no longer shielded from that tax by this transitional rule.

Second, another transitional rule applied under TRA '86 to any employee who died, separated from service, or became disabled before January 1, 1987, and received a lump-sum distribution before March 16, 1987. The employee was allowed to treat the lump-sum distribution as if he or she received it at the time of separation from service and would thereby avoid the 10 percent additional income tax. In addition, any individual, trust, or estate that received a lump-sum distribution with respect to an employee who would have been eligible for this transitional rule could also elect the protection of the rule and not be subject to the tax.

Q 20:14 Does the 10 percent additional income tax apply if the distribution is made from a plan that is subject to an IRS levy under Code Section 6331?

No. The 10 percent additional income tax does not apply to amounts that are withdrawn from a qualified plan (or IRA) that is subject to a levy by the IRS under Code Section 6331. [I.R.C. § 72(t)(2)(A)(vii)] The exception applies only if the plan (or IRA) is levied; it does not apply, for example, if the taxpayer withdraws funds to pay taxes in the absence of a levy, in order to release a levy on other interests. This rule is effective for levy distributions made after December 31, 1999. [I.R.C. § 72(t)(2)(A)(vii), as added by § 3436 of the IRS Restructuring and Reform Act of 1998; *Conference Report on Internal Revenue Service Restructuring and Reform Act of 1998* (H.R. Rpt. 105-599), at 57]

Q 20:15 How should a taxpayer report the 10 percent additional income tax on early distributions?

If the 10 percent additional income tax is the only special additional tax that the taxpayer owes, and if his or her Form 1099-R reporting the early distribution shows distribution code 1 in Box 7, he or she will simply enter 10 percent of the taxable portion of the distribution on the applicable line of his or her Form 1040 and write "No" on the dotted line next to that line. Under these circumstances, the taxpayer does not also have to file Form 5329, *Additional Taxes on Qualified Plans (Including IRAs) and Other Tax-Favored Accounts*.

However, even if the 10 percent additional income tax on early distributions is the only tax the taxpayer owes, he or she may have to file Form 5329 if he or she receives an early distribution and his or her Form 1099-R does not show distribution code 1 in Box 7.

Fifty Percent Excise Tax on Failure to Make RMDs

Q 20:16 Is any tax imposed on a payee if the amount distributed during the taxable year is less than the RMD for that year?

Yes. If the amount distributed to a payee from any qualified retirement plan (see Q 20:17) or any eligible deferred compensation plan (defined in Code Section 457(b)) for a calendar year is less than the RMD for that year, a 50 percent nondeductible excise tax is imposed on the payee (under Code Section 4974) for the taxable year beginning with or within the calendar year during which the amount is required to be distributed.

The excise tax equals 50 percent of the amount by which the RMD exceeds the actual amount distributed during the calendar year. The payee must pay the tax. For a qualified retirement plan described in Code Section 401(a), RMD means the minimum amount required to be distributed under Code Section 401(a)(9) and the related Treasury regulations. (See chapter 4.) [Treas. Reg. § 54.4974-2, Q&A-1]

Q 20:17 What is a qualified retirement plan for purposes of the 50 percent excise tax rules?

Under the 50 percent excise tax rules, each of the following is a qualified retirement plan:

1. A qualified retirement plan under Code Section 401(a), which includes a tax-exempt trust described in Code Section 501(a);
2. A qualified annuity plan described in Code Section 403(a);
3. An annuity contract, custodial account, or retirement income account described in Code Section 403(b)(1), 403(b)(7), and 403(b)(9);
4. An IRA described in Code Section 408(a) or 408(b) (including a Roth IRA described in Code Section 408A); or
5. Any other plan, contract, account, or annuity that, at any time, has been treated as a plan, account, or annuity described in items 1 through 4 above, whether or not such plan, contract, account, or annuity currently satisfies the applicable requirements for such treatment. [Treas. Reg. § 54.4974-2, Q&A-2]

This chapter, however, focuses on how the 50 percent excise tax rules apply to qualified retirement plans described in Code Section 401(a).

Q 20:18 If a payee's interest under a qualified retirement plan is in the form of an individual account and that account is not being distributed from a purchased annuity contract, how is the RMD for a given calendar year determined for purposes of calculating the 50 percent excise tax under Code Section 4974?

General Rule. In calculating the 50 percent excise tax, the RMD for any calendar year is the minimum amount required to be distributed for that calendar year to satisfy the minimum distribution requirements of Treasury Regulations Section 1.401(a)(9)-5. [Treas. Reg. § 54.4974-2, Q&A-3(a)]

Default Provisions. Unless the plan document provides otherwise, the default provisions described in Treasury Regulations Section 1.401(a)(9)-3, Q&A-4(a), apply in determining the RMD for purposes of calculating the 50 percent excise tax.

Five-Year Rule. If the five-year rule of Code Section 401(a)(9)(B)(ii) (see chapter 4) applies to the distribution of the individual account to a payee, no RMD has to be made until the calendar year that contains the fifth anniversary of the employee's death. In that calendar year, the RMD is the payee's entire remaining interest in the plan. [Treas. Reg. § 54.4974-2, Q&A-3(c)]

> **Example 20-6:** Adam Trask, a participant in the East of Eden Company profit sharing plan, dies on April 5, 2019, with a $100,000 account under the plan. Adam's beneficiary, Cal, elects the five-year rule (see chapter 4) to govern the payment from the plan. No RMD has to be made from the plan for calendar years 2019 through 2023, inclusive. The RMD that must be paid to Cal for calendar year 2024 is the amount, on December 31, 2024, of Cal's entire interest in the plan.

Q 20:19 If the payee's interest under a Section 401(a) qualified retirement plan is distributed in the form of an annuity, how is the RMD determined for purposes of calculating the 50 percent excise tax under Code Section 4974?

If a payee's interest in a qualified retirement plan is distributed in the form of an annuity (either directly from the plan, in the case of a defined benefit plan, or under an annuity contract purchased from an insurance company), the amount of the RMD in calculating the 50 percent excise tax under Code Section 4974 is determined as follows.

Permissible Annuity Distribution Option. The RMD for each calendar year is the amount that the annuity contract (or the defined benefit plan's distribution option) will distribute if distributions are being made under a "permissible annuity distribution option." A permissible annuity distribution option is an annuity contract (or a distribution option under a defined benefit plan) that specifically provides for distributions that equal or exceed the RMD for every calendar year. [Treas. Reg. § 54.4974-2, Q&A-4(a)]

If the annuity contract (or the distribution option under a defined benefit plan) under which distributions to the payee are being made is a permissible annuity distribution option, an amount equal to or exceeding the RMD for any given calendar year will be distributed, and so the 50 percent excise tax will not apply.

Example 20-7: The Salinas Valley Corporation defined benefit plan offers participant Samuel Hilton the distribution option of a single life annuity paying $1,000 per month or a joint and survivor annuity paying $750 per month. Each option satisfies the RMD rules under Code Section 401(a)(9). If Samuel elects the single life annuity, his RMD, to avoid the 50 percent excise tax, is $12,000 (12 × $1,000) per calendar year. If he elects the joint and survivor annuity, his RMD is $9,000 (12 × $750) per calendar year.

Impermissible Annuity Distribution Option. If the purchased annuity contract (or the distribution option under the defined benefit plan) provides for payments that would be less than the RMD for every calendar year, then it is an "impermissible annuity distribution option," and the 50 percent excise tax on underpayments will apply. [Treas. Reg. § 54.4974-2, Q&A-4(b)]

Q 20:20 If the annuity contract (or the defined benefit plan's distribution option) provides an impermissible annuity distribution option, how is the RMD for each calendar year, for purposes of calculating the 50 percent excise tax, determined for defined benefit plans?

For distributions from defined benefit plans that begin before the employee dies, if there is a designated beneficiary under the impermissible annuity distribution option for purposes of the RMD rules, the permissible annuity distribution option, which will pay the RMD for purposes of calculating the 50 percent excise tax, is the plan's joint and survivor annuity option, payable for the lives of the employee and his or her designated beneficiary in a manner that provides the greatest level amount for each year. If the plan does not provide such an option or there is no designated beneficiary under the impermissible annuity distribution option, the permissible annuity distribution option is the life annuity option under the plan payable for the employee's life, in level amounts, with no survivor benefits. [Treas. Reg. § 54.4974-2, Q&A-4(b)(1)(i)]

For distributions from defined benefit plans that begin after the employee dies, if there is a designated beneficiary under an impermissible annuity distribution option, the permissible annuity distribution option (that is, the distribution option that will pay the RMD for the calendar year, for purposes of calculating the 50 percent excise tax) is the life annuity option payable, in level amounts, for the life of the designated beneficiary. [Treas. Reg. § 54.4974-2, Q&A-4(b)(1)(ii)]

If there is no designated beneficiary, the five-year rule (see chapter 4) applies. If the five-year rule applies, no distribution is required until the calendar year that includes the fifth anniversary of the employee's death. In that calendar year, the payee's entire remaining interest in the annuity contract must be distributed. If it is not, the RMD rules are not met, and the 50 percent excise tax on underpayments applies.

Q 20:21 If a defined contribution plan distributes a purchased annuity contract that is an impermissible annuity distribution option, which does not pay at least the RMD for any calendar year, what rules would apply?

In such a case, the RMD rules would not be met, and the 50 percent excise tax on underpayments would apply.

The RMD, for purposes of calculating the 50 percent excise tax, is the amount that would have been distributed each calendar year under a purchased annuity contract that is a permissible annuity distribution option that pays the RMD each calendar year. The permissible annuity distribution option is determined under the same rules that apply to defined benefit plans. [Treas. Reg. § 54.4974-2, Q&A-4(b)(2)]

Q 20:22 If there is any remaining benefit with respect to an employee after any calendar year in which his or her entire remaining benefit had to be distributed from a qualified retirement plan under the RMD rules, what is the amount of the RMD for each calendar year after that calendar year?

The RMD is the entire remaining benefit. If the entire remaining benefit is not distributed in any calendar year, the 50 percent excise tax on underpayments is imposed on that benefit. [Treas. Reg. § 54.4974-2, Q&A-5]

Q 20:23 For which calendar year is the 50 percent excise tax imposed when the amount not distributed is an amount required to be distributed by April 1 of a calendar year?

If the amount not paid is an amount that had to be paid by April 1 of a calendar year (the "required beginning date," described in chapter 4), then that amount is the RMD for the previous calendar year (the "first distribution calendar year," described in chapter 4). However, the 50 percent excise tax is imposed for the calendar year containing the required beginning date, even though the preceding calendar year is the calendar year for which the RMD had to be made. [Treas. Reg. § 54.4974-2, Q&A-6]

Q 20:24 Are there any circumstances under which the 50 percent excise tax on underpayments may be waived?

Yes, the 50 percent excise tax may be waived by the IRS or automatically, if certain conditions are met.

Waiver by the IRS. The IRS may waive the 50 percent excise tax on underpayments if the payee establishes, to the IRS's satisfaction, that:

1. The shortfall between the amount that was actually distributed for a particular calendar year and the RMD for that year was the result of reasonable error; and
2. Reasonable steps are being taken to remedy the shortfall. [Treas. Reg. § 4974-2, Q&A-7(a)]

To obtain a waiver of the 50 percent excise tax from the IRS, the payee must file Form 5329, *Additional Taxes on Qualified Plans (Including IRAs) and Other Tax-Favored Account*, pay the tax, and attach a letter explaining why the waiver should be granted. If the IRS grants the waiver request, it will send the taxpayer a refund. [Form 5329 and Instructions]

Automatic Waiver. The 50 percent excise tax on underpayments will be waived automatically, unless the IRS determines otherwise, if:

1. The payee is an individual who is the sole beneficiary and whose RMD amount for a calendar year is determined under the life expectancy rule under Treasury Regulations Section 1.401(a)(9)-3, Q&A-3, in the case of an employee's death before the employee's required beginning date; and
2. The employee's entire benefit to which that beneficiary is entitled is distributed by the end of the fifth calendar year following the calendar year that contains the employee's date of death.

[Treas. Reg. § 54.4974-2, Q&A-7(b)]

Chapter 21

Direct Rollovers

This chapter explains the rules governing direct rollovers from qualified retirement plans, as described in Section 401(a)(31) of the Internal Revenue Code. Those rules were modified by the Economic Growth and Tax Relief Reconciliation Act of 2001 (EGTRRA), which significantly increased pension portability and encouraged taxpayers to keep their retirement savings in tax-favored retirement plans. The changes effected by EGTRRA generally began to apply to distributions made after December 31, 2001. The automatic rollover provisions, which were also added to the Code by EGTRRA, became effective for mandatory distributions made on or after March 28, 2005.

Final regulations and guidance issued by the IRS in recent years regarding particular aspects of direct rollovers are also considered in this chapter.

The Pension Protection Act of 2006 (PPA) also made a number of changes to the direct rollover rules: (1) it increased the portability of employee after-tax contributions (and attributable earnings) by allowing such amounts to be directly rolled over in taxable years beginning after December 31, 2006; (2) it permitted nonspouse beneficiaries to directly roll over qualified retirement plan distributions made after December 31, 2006, into inherited IRAs; (3) it allowed qualified retirement plans to make direct rollovers, after December 31, 2007, into Roth IRAs, under the same conversion rules that apply to conversions of traditional IRAs into Roth IRAs; (4) it increased, from a maximum of 90 days to a maximum of 180 days, the earliest date prior to the date of distribution by which a Code Section 402(f) rollover notice may be provided to a distributee, effective for years beginning after December 31, 2006; and (5) it prohibited States from reducing the unemployment compensation of individuals who have received rollover distributions from certain employer-sponsored retirement plans or IRAs, effective for weeks beginning on or after PPA's August 17, 2006, enactment date. [PPA §§ 822, 824, 829, 1102, 1105]

The Worker, Retiree, and Employer Recovery Act of 2008 (WRERA) made some technical changes to PPA's provisions dealing with direct rollovers made by nonspouse beneficiaries. As mentioned above, PPA permitted nonspouse beneficiaries to directly roll over qualified retirement plan distributions made after December 31, 2006 into inherited IRAs. In Notice 2007-7, 2007-5 I.R.B. 395, however, the IRS stated that this PPA provision was optional (i.e., that plans were not required to offer a direct rollover opportunity to a nonspouse beneficiary) and that the mandatory 20 percent withholding requirements of Code Section 3405(c) and the rollover notice requirements of Code Section 402(f) did not apply to such distributions. WRERA amended PPA to provide that, for plan years beginning after December 31, 2009 (i.e., January 1, 2010 for calendar-year plans), plans are required to give nonspouse beneficiaries the opportunity to directly roll over eligible rollover distributions into inherited IRAs, and such distributions are subject to the same rules as all other eligible rollover distributions, including mandatory 20 percent withholding and rollover notice requirements. [I.R.C. §§ 402(c)(11) and 402(f)(2)(A), as amended by WRERA § 108(f)]

IRS Notice 2009-68, 2009-39 I.R.B. 423 contains two safe-harbor rollover notices that satisfy the rollover notice requirement of Code Section 402(f). The first safe-harbor rollover notice applies to a distribution not from a designated Roth account (as described in Code Section 402A), and the second safe-harbor rollover notice applies to a distribution from a designated Roth account. The safe-harbor rollover notices published in Notice 2009-68 update the safe-harbor rollover notices that were published in Notice 2002-3, to reflect changes in the law. IRS Notice 2014-74, 2014-50 I.R.B. 937 amends the two safe-harbor rollover notices in Notice 2009-68, 2009-2 C.B. 423, that can be used to satisfy the requirement under Code Section 402(f) that certain information be provided to recipients of eligible rollover distributions.

IRS Notice 2009-75, 2009-39 I.R.B. 436 describes the federal income tax consequences of rolling over an eligible rollover distribution from a Code Section 401(a) qualified retirement plan, a Code Section 403(a) annuity plan, a Code Section 403(b) plan, or a Code Section 457(b) eligible governmental plan to a Roth IRA described in Code Section 408A.

IRS Notice 2010-84, 2010-51 I.R.B. 872 provides guidance under Code Section 402A(c)(4) relating to rollovers from 401(k) plans to designated Roth accounts in the same plan (i.e., "in-plan Roth rollovers"), as added by Section 2112 of the Small Business Jobs Act of 2010 (SBJA). (The guidance in Notice

2010-84 also generally applies to in-plan Roth rollovers under Section 403(b) plans.)

Revenue Ruling 2012-4, 2012-8 I.R.B. 386 describes whether a qualified defined benefit pension plan that accepts a direct rollover of an eligible rollover distribution from a qualified defined contribution plan maintained by the same employer satisfied Code Sections 411 and 415 in a case in which the defined benefit plan provides an annuity resulting from the direct rollover.

Revenue Ruling 2014-09, 2014 I.R.B. 975 describes two situations in which the plan administrator of a Code Section 401(a) qualified retirement plan may reasonably conclude that a potential rollover contribution is a valid rollover contribution under Treasury Regulations Section 1.401(a)(31)-1, Q&A-14(b)(2).

IRS Notice 2014-54, 2014-41 I.R.B. 670 provides rules for allocating pre-tax and after-tax amounts among distributions that are made to multiple destinations from a Code Section 401(a) qualified retirement plan. The rules also apply to disbursements from Code Section 403(b) tax-sheltered annuity plans and Code Section 457(b) governmental deferred compensation plans. Prior to the issuance of IRS Notice 2014-54, the IRS treated disbursements from a retirement plan that were rolled over to multiple destinations as separate distributions to each destination, with each distribution treated as containing a pro rata portion of pre-tax and after-tax amounts. IRS Notice 2014-54, issued on September 18, 2014, provides that all disbursements from a retirement plan scheduled to be made at the same time are treated as a single distribution even if they are sent to multiple destinations. As a result of IRS Notice 2014-54, taxpayers with pre-tax and after-tax amounts in their plan, for example, can transfer through direct rollovers the pre-tax portion of the distribution (including earnings on after-tax amounts) to a traditional IRA and the after-tax portion of the distribution to a Roth IRA. (Previous interpretations allowed accomplishing this result through 60-day rollovers but not direct rollovers.) The guidance in IRS Notice 2014-54 generally became effective on January 1, 2015; however, transitional rules included in IRS Notice 2014-54 permit taxpayers to use the new rules prior to the effective date. Specifically, plan sponsors may apply the guidance in IRS Notice 2014-54 to distributions made on or after September 18, 2014, and apply a reasonable interpretation of the guidance for distributions made before that date.

IRS Notice 2014-74, 2014-50 I.R.B. 937 amends the two safe-harbor rollover notices in IRS Notice 2009-68, 2009-2 C.B. 423, that can be used to satisfy the requirement under Code

Section 402(f) that certain information be provided to recipients of eligible rollover distributions. Amendments to the safe-harbor rollover notices reflected in IRS Notice 2014-74 relate to the allocation of pre-tax and after-tax amounts (under IRS Notice 2014-54), distributions in the form of in-plan Roth rollovers, and certain other clarifications to the two safe-harbor rollover notices. The amendments to the safe-harbor rollover notices (and the model rollover notices) in IRS Notice 2014-74 may be used for plans that apply the guidance in Section III of IRS Notice 2014-54 with respect to the allocation of pre-tax and after-tax amounts.

The Protecting Americans from Tax Hikes Act of 2015 (PATH Act), enacted on December 18, 2015, as part of the Consolidated Appropriations Act, 2016, amended Code Section 408(p)(1)(B) to permit rollover contributions to be made after December 18, 2015 from qualified retirement plans or IRAs to SIMPLE retirement accounts, as follows: (1) during the first two years of an individual's participation in a SIMPLE retirement account, he or she may roll over amounts from one SIMPLE retirement account into another SIMPLE retirement account; and (2) after the first two years of an individual's participation in a SIMPLE retirement account, he or she may roll over amounts from a SIMPLE retirement account, a qualified retirement plan, or an IRA into a SIMPLE retirement account.

On May 17, 2016, the IRS issued final regulations [81 Fed. Reg. 31165] modifying Treasury Regulations Section 1.402A-1 (designated Roth accounts) that remove the allocation rule and treat distributions from a Roth account made to multiple destinations as a single distribution. The regulations apply to distributions from designated Roth accounts made on or after January 1, 2016, and taxpayers are required to follow the allocation rules described in IRS Notice 2014-54. The regulations also preserve the separate distribution rule for distributions made prior to the January 1, 2016 applicability date, except that a taxpayer is permitted to choose not to apply the separate distribution rule to distributions that are made on or after September 18, 2014 and before January 1, 2016. Taxpayers who chose not to apply the separate distribution rule to distributions made during that transition period were required to apply a reasonable interpretation of the last sentence of Code Section 402(c)(2) (generally requiring that pre-tax amounts be treated as rolled over first) to allocate pre-tax and after-tax amounts among disbursements made to multiple destinations. For this purpose, a reasonable interpretation of the last sentence of Code Section 402(c)(2) includes the rules described in IRS Notice 2014-54. [81 Fed. Reg. 31165]

On August 24, 2016, the IRS issued Revenue Procedure 2016-47, 2016-37 I.R.B. 346, which provided self-certification procedures designed to help recipients of retirement plan distributions who inadvertently miss the 60-day time limit for properly rolling such distributions over into another retirement plan or IRA. Revenue Procedure 2016-34 explains how eligible taxpayers, encountering a variety of mitigating circumstances, can qualify for a waiver of the 60-day time limit and avoid possible early distribution taxes. In addition, Revenue Procedure 2016-47 includes a sample self-certification letter that a taxpayer can use to notify the administrator or trustee of a retirement plan or IRA receiving the rollover that they qualify for the waiver. Normally, an eligible distribution from a qualified retirement plan or IRA can qualify for tax-free rollover treatment only if it is contributed to another retirement plan or IRA by the 60th day after it was received. In most cases, taxpayers who fail to meet the 60-day time limit could only obtain a waiver by requesting a private letter ruling from the IRS. A taxpayer who missed the 60-day time limit will now ordinarily qualify for a waiver if one or more of the 11 mitigating circumstances listed in Revenue Procedure 2016-47 apply to him or her. The listed circumstances include a distribution check that was misplaced and never cashed, severe damage to the taxpayer's home, the death of a family member, the serious illness of the taxpayer or a family member, the taxpayer's incarceration, or restrictions imposed by a foreign country. Ordinarily, the IRS and plan administrators and trustees will honor a taxpayer's truthful self-certification that they qualify for a waiver under these circumstances. Moreover, even if a taxpayer does not self-certify, the IRS has the authority to grant a waiver during a subsequent examination. Other requirements, along with a copy of the sample self-certification letter, can be found in Revenue Procedure 2016-47. Taxpayers wishing to transfer retirement plan or IRA distributions to another retirement plan or IRA could consider requesting that the administrator or trustee make a direct trustee-to-trustee transfer, rather than doing a 60-day rollover. The IRS also issued FAQs relating to waivers of the 60-day rollover requirement, available at https://www.irs.gov/retirement-plans/retirement-plans-faqs-relating-to-waivers-of-the-60-day-rollover-requirement.

The Tax Cuts and Jobs Act (TCJA), enacted on December 22, 2017, extended the indirect rollover period for qualified plan loan offset amounts from 60 days after the offset to the affected participant's tax filing deadline (including extensions) for the year of the offset.

Direct Rollover Option Required 21-6
Eligible Rollover Distributions 21-22
Section 402(f) Rollover Notice 21-42
Rollover Contributions by Employees Not Yet Eligible to
Participate in a Qualified Plan 21-44
Other Direct Rollover Issues 21-45

Direct Rollover Option Required

Q 21:1 What are the direct rollover requirements under Code Section 401(a)(31)?

To satisfy Code Section 401(a)(31), as added by the Unemployment Compensation Amendments of 1992 (UCA), a qualified retirement plan must provide that if the distributee of any eligible rollover distribution (see Q 21:22) elects to have the distribution paid directly to an eligible retirement plan (see Q 21:21) and specifies the eligible retirement plan to which the distribution is to be paid, the distribution will be paid to that plan in a direct rollover (see Q 21:2). The qualified retirement plan must give the distributee the option of having his or her distribution paid in a direct rollover to an eligible retirement plan specified by the distributee.

Note, however, that Code Section 401(a)(31)(E) limits the types of qualified trusts that are treated as eligible retirement plans to defined contribution plans that accept eligible rollover distributions; therefore, a plan will not fail to satisfy Code Section 401(a)(31) solely because the plan will not permit a direct rollover to a qualified trust that is part of a defined benefit plan. On the other hand, if a distributee elects a direct rollover of an eligible rollover distribution to a qualified annuity plan described in Code Section 403(a), that distribution must be paid to the annuity plan, even if the recipient annuity plan is a defined benefit plan. [Treas. Reg. § 1.401(a)(31)-1, Q&A-2]

Notice Requirement. Code Section 402(f) requires the plan administrator of a qualified retirement plan to provide, within a reasonable period of time before making an eligible rollover distribution, a written explanation (i.e., a rollover notice) to the distributee of the distributee's right to elect a direct rollover and the withholding consequences (see below) of not making that election. The explanation is also required to provide certain other relevant information relating to the taxation of distributions (see Qs 21:37–21:41).

Mandatory Withholding. If the distributee of an eligible rollover distribution does not elect to have the eligible rollover distribution paid directly from the plan to an eligible retirement plan in a direct rollover under Code Section 401(a)(31), the eligible rollover distribution is subject to 20 percent income tax withholding under Code Section 3405(c) (see chapter 24).

Q 21:2 What is a direct rollover that satisfies Code Section 401(a)(31), and how is it accomplished?

A direct rollover that satisfies Code Section 401(a)(31) is an eligible rollover distribution that is paid directly to an eligible retirement plan for the benefit of the distributee.

A direct rollover may be accomplished by any reasonable means of direct payment to an eligible retirement plan. Reasonable means of direct payment include, for example, a wire transfer or the mailing of a check to the eligible retirement plan; if the payment is made by wire transfer, the wire transfer must be directed only to the trustee of the eligible retirement plan and the check must be negotiable only by the trustee of the eligible retirement plan. In the case of an eligible retirement plan that does not have a trustee, the custodian of the plan or issuer of the contract under the plan, as appropriate, is treated as the trustee for such purposes. [Treas. Reg. § 1.401(a)(31)-1, Q&A-3]

Providing the distributee with a check and instructing the distributee to deliver the check to the eligible retirement plan is also a reasonable means of direct payment, provided that the check is made payable as follows: "[Name of the trustee] as trustee of [name of the eligible retirement plan]." For example, if the name of the eligible retirement plan is "Individual Retirement Account of Tom Joad," and the name of the trustee is the "Grapes of Wrath Bank," the payee line of a check would read "Grapes of Wrath Bank as trustee of Individual Retirement Account of Tom Joad." The check also must indicate that it is for the benefit of the distributee, unless the name of the distributee is included in the name of the eligible retirement plan. If the eligible retirement plan is not an IRA, the payee line of the check need not identify the trustee by name. For example, the payee line of a check for the benefit of distributee Pa Joad might read, "Trustee of Salinas Valley Corporation Savings Plan FBO Pa Joad." [Treas. Reg. § 1.401(a)(31)-1, Q&A-4]

Q 21:3 Is a distribution that is directly rolled over currently includible in gross income or subject to 20 percent withholding?

No. An eligible rollover distribution that is paid to an eligible retirement plan in a direct rollover is not currently includible in the distributee's gross income under Code Section 402(c). Further, it is exempt from the 20 percent withholding imposed under Code Section 3405(c)(2). However, when any portion of the eligible rollover distribution is subsequently distributed from the eligible retirement plan, that portion will be includible in gross income to the extent required under Code Section 402, 403, or 408. [Treas. Reg. § 1.401(a)(31)-1, Q&A-5]

Q 21:4 What procedures may a plan administrator prescribe for electing a direct rollover?

A plan administrator may prescribe any procedure for a distributee to elect a direct rollover under Code Section 401(a)(31), provided the procedure is reasonable. The procedure may include any reasonable requirement for information or documentation from the distributee in addition to the items of adequate information specified below. For example, it would be reasonable for the plan administrator to require that the distributee provide a statement from the designated recipient plan that the plan will accept the direct rollover for the benefit of the distributee and that the recipient plan is, or is intended to be, an individual retirement account (IRA, a qualified retirement plan under Code Section 401(a)) or a qualified annuity plan under Code Section 403(a), whichever applies. In the case of a designated recipient plan that is a qualified retirement plan under Code Section 401(a), it would also be reasonable for the plan administrator to require a statement that the qualified retirement plan is not excepted from the definition of an eligible retirement plan by Code Section 401(a)(31)(E) (that is, the plan is not a defined benefit plan).

Impermissible Procedures. A qualified retirement plan will fail to satisfy Code Section 401(a)(31), however, if the plan administrator prescribes any unreasonable procedure or requires information or documentation that effectively eliminates or substantially impairs the distributee's ability to elect a direct rollover. For example, it would effectively eliminate or substantially impair the distributee's ability to elect a direct rollover if:

1. The recipient plan required the distributee to obtain an opinion of counsel stating that the eligible retirement plan receiving the rollover is a qualified retirement plan or IRA;
2. The distributing plan required a letter from the recipient eligible retirement plan stating that, upon request by the distributing plan, the recipient plan will automatically return any direct rollover amount that the distributing plan advises the recipient plan was paid incorrectly; or
3. The distributing plan required, as a condition for making a direct rollover, a letter from the recipient eligible retirement plan indemnifying the distributing plan for any liability arising from the distribution.

[Treas. Reg. § 1.401(a)(31)-1, Q&A-6]

Q 21:5 May a plan administrator treat a distributee as having made an election under a default procedure when the distributee does not affirmatively elect to make or not to make a direct rollover within a certain time period?

Yes. A plan administrator may establish a default procedure whereby any distributee who fails to make an affirmative election within a specified time frame is treated as having made or not made a direct rollover election. The plan administrator may not, however, make a distribution under any default procedure unless (1) the distributee has received an explanation of the default procedure and an explanation of the direct rollover option (i.e., a rollover notice) as required under Code Section 402(f) (see Q 21:36), and (2) the timing requirements for both explanations have been satisfied (see Q 21:45). [Treas. Reg. § 1.401(a)(31)-1, Q&A-7]

Q 21:6 How did EGTRRA change the rules regarding the default option for mandatory distributions?

EGTRRA made direct rollovers the default option for mandatory distributions (i.e., those whose present value does not exceed $5,000) that exceed $1,000 and are eligible rollover distributions from a qualified retirement plan (as described in Code Section 401(a)). That is, such a distribution must be rolled over automatically to a designated IRA—unless the participant affirmatively elects to have the distribution transferred to a different IRA or a qualified retirement plan or to receive it directly. [I.R.C. § 401(a)(31)(B); Notice 2005-5, 2005-3 I.R.B. 337]

Qualified retirement plans may make mandatory distributions of vested account balances or benefits of $5,000 or less without the participant's consent following termination of employment. Effective March 28, 2005, mandatory distributions of more than $1,000 that are eligible rollover distributions and that are made on or after that date must be automatically rolled over into an individual retirement account or annuity (IRA) selected by the plan administrator for the participant's benefit, unless the participant affirmatively elects to receive the mandatory distribution currently or to directly roll it over into another employer's plan or into an IRA of his or her own choosing. [I.R.C. § 401(a)(31)(B); Notice 2005-5, 2005-3 I.R.B. 337]

On September 28, 2004, the U.S. Department of Labor (DOL) issued final regulations providing compliance "safe harbors" for fiduciaries of ERISA-subject plans under which (1) the fiduciary's selection of an IRA provider to receive the plan's automatic rollovers, and (2) the initial investment choices for the rolled-over funds, would be deemed to satisfy ERISA's fiduciary responsibility requirements. The DOL safe harbors apply to automatic rollovers of mandatory distributions of more than $1,000 but not more than $5,000, as well as to automatic rollovers of mandatory distributions of $1,000 or less. [69 Fed. Reg. 58018]

On January 18, 2005, the IRS issued Notice 2005-5, providing guidance on how qualified retirement plans must be amended and operated to comply with EGTRRA's automatic rollover rules. The IRS's automatic rollover requirements apply to mandatory distributions over $1,000, but not to such distributions of $1,000 or less. [Notice 2005-5, 2005-3 I.R.B. 337]

DOL Safe Harbor. The DOL's safe-harbor regulations provide that a fiduciary of an ERISA-subject plan will be deemed to have satisfied his or her ERISA fiduciary duties in connection with the plan's automatic rollover of a mandatory distribution that is made to a plan participant who fails to affirmatively elect to receive the distribution currently or to directly roll it over into another employer's plan or into an IRA of his or her own choosing (sometimes referred to as a "nonelecting participant"), with respect to both the fiduciary's selection of an IRA provider to receive the automatic rollover and the initial investment choices for the rolled-over funds, but only if the following requirements are met:

1. The value of the mandatory distribution does not exceed $5,000 (rollover contributions need not be included in determining whether the $5,000 distribution threshold has been met);

2. The mandatory distribution must be rolled over into an IRA;
3. The plan fiduciary must enter into a written agreement with the IRA provider stating that:
   a. The rolled-over funds must be invested in an investment product designed to preserve principal and provide a reasonable rate of return, whether or not guaranteed, consistent with liquidity;
   b. The investment product selected for the rolled-over funds must seek to maintain, over the term of the investment, a dollar value that is equal to the amount invested in the product by the IRA;
   c. The investment product selected for the rolled-over funds must be offered by a state or federally regulated financial institution, which must be either: a bank or savings association, the deposits of which are insured by the Federal Deposit Insurance Corporation (FDIC); a credit union, the member accounts of which are insured within the meaning of Section 101(7) of the Federal Credit Union Act; an insurance company, the products of which are protected by state guaranty associations; or an investment company (registered under the Investment Company Act of 1940);
   d. All fees and expenses relating to the IRA, including investments by the IRA (e.g., establishment charges, maintenance fees, investment expenses, termination costs, and surrender charges) must not exceed the fees and expenses charged by the IRA provider for comparable IRAs established for reasons other than the receipt of automatic rollovers of mandatory distributions; and
   e. The plan participant on whose behalf the fiduciary makes an automatic rollover must have the right to enforce the terms of the written contract establishing the IRA, with regard to his or her rolled-over funds, against the IRA provider;
4. Plan participants have been furnished a summary plan description (SPD), or a summary of material modifications (SMM), that describes the plan's automatic rollover rules for mandatory distributions, including an explanation that the mandatory distribution will be invested in an investment product designed to preserve principal and provide a reasonable rate of return and liquidity, a statement indicating how fees and expenses attendant to the IRA will be allocated (i.e., the extent to which expenses will be borne by the IRA account holder alone or shared with the distributing plan or plan sponsor), and the name, address, and telephone number of a plan contact (to the extent not otherwise provided in the SPD or SMM) for further information concerning the plan's automatic rollover provisions, the IRA provider, and the fees and expenses relating to the IRA; and
5. Both the fiduciary's selection of an IRA and the investment of rolled-over funds under the IRA must not result in any nonexempt prohibited transaction under ERISA. (The DOL has issued a prohibited transaction class exemption (PTCE) permitting banks and other financial institutions that maintain qualified retirement plans to designate themselves as the IRA

providers to receive automatic rollovers of mandatory distributions from their own plans, provided certain conditions are met.)

[69 Fed. Reg. 58018]

IRS Notice 2005-5. Notice 2005-5 provided the following guidance to sponsors of qualified retirement plans so that they could amend their plan documents and operate their plans in compliance with EGTRRA's automatic rollover rules:

1. EGTRRA's automatic rollover rules only apply to qualified retirement plans that provide for mandatory distributions (i.e., plans that distribute vested account balances or benefits of $5,000 or less without the participant's consent following termination of employment). EGTRRA's automatic rollover rules apply to any mandatory distribution that is more than $1,000 and that is an "eligible rollover distribution" subject to the direct rollover requirements of Code Section 401(a)(31). (However, an eligible rollover distribution in the form of a plan loan offset amount is not subject to these automatic rollover rules.)
2. A *mandatory distribution* is a distribution made, without the participant's consent, before he or she reaches the later of age 62 or normal retirement age. A distribution to a surviving spouse or to a qualified domestic relations order (QDRO) alternate payee is not a mandatory distribution for purposes of the automatic rollover rules. Although the Code generally prohibits mandatory distributions of vested account balances or benefits of more than $5,000, the automatic rollover rules apply without regard to the amount of the distribution as long as the amount exceeds $1,000.
3. In order to satisfy the automatic rollover rules, a qualified retirement plan must provide that, when making a mandatory distribution that exceeds $1,000 and that is an eligible rollover distribution, if, after receiving a Code Section 402(f) rollover notice, a participant fails to affirmatively elect to receive the mandatory distribution currently or have it directly rolled over into another employer's plan or into an IRA of his or her own choosing, the mandatory distribution automatically will be rolled over into an IRA selected by the plan administrator and then rolled-over funds will be invested in IRA investments selected by the plan administrator.
4. The automatic rollover rules generally apply to mandatory distributions made on or after March 28, 2005, although there are delayed effective dates for certain governmental plans and church plans (see below).
5. The automatic rollover rules apply not only to Code Section 401(a) qualified retirement plans, but also to Code Section 414(d) governmental plans and to Code Section 457(b) eligible governmental plans, but these types of governmental plans do not have to comply with the rules prior to the close of the first regular legislative session of the legislative body with the authority to amend the plan that begins on or after January 1, 2006. The automatic rollover rules do not apply, however, to nongovernmental Code Section 457(b) plans.

6. The automatic rollover rules also apply to Code Section 403(b) plans (i.e., Code Section 403(b)(1) annuity contracts, 403(b)(7) custodial accounts, and 403(b)(9) retirement income accounts). If the 403(b) plan is a governmental plan (e.g., a 403(b) plan maintained by a public school district), then the delayed compliance date described in item 5, above, applies.
7. The automatic rollover rules also apply to Code Section 414(e) church plans that have not elected under Code Section 410(d) to have ERISA apply to them (i.e., "non-electing church plans"), but these types of plans do not have to comply with the rules prior to 60 days after the close of the earliest church convention with the authority to amend the plan that occurs on or after January 1, 2006.
8. A plan will not be treated as disqualified merely because it delays mandatory rollovers for nonelecting participants due to lack of sufficient administrative procedures for automatic rollovers, including establishing IRAs to accept automatic rollovers, provided the mandatory rollovers are made on or before December 31, 2005.
9. The plan administrator may execute the necessary documents to establish an IRA with a financial institution it has selected on behalf of a nonelecting participant. For these purposes, the plan administrator may use the nonelecting participant's most recent mailing address in the records of the employer and plan administrator. The IRA trustee or issuer must provide an IRA disclosure statement to the nonelecting participant and provide the required revocation period. However, the IRA trustee or issuer will not be treated as failing to satisfy the disclosure requirements merely because the U.S. Postal Service (USPS) returns the disclosure statement as undeliverable after it was mailed to the nonelecting participant using the address for such participant provided by the plan administrator as such participant's most recent mailing address in the records of the employer and plan administrator.
10. A mandatory distribution may be paid to an IRA, such as a deemed Roth IRA, that is part of the plan that is making the distribution.
11. A plan sponsor may amend its plan to eliminate the plan's mandatory distribution provisions, and such an amendment will not violate the Code's anti-cutback rules.
12. Any plan that requires a participant's consent to distribute a vested account balance or benefit of more than $1,000 but not more than $5,000 does not have to comply with spousal consent requirements with respect to such distributions, even if the plan otherwise is subject to the qualified joint and survivor annuity (QJSA) for distributions exceeding $5,000.
13. The plan administrator must notify a participant in writing (either separately or as part of the Section 402(f) rollover notice) that, absent an affirmative election otherwise, his or her mandatory distribution will be automatically rolled over into an IRA. The notice must identify the IRA trustee or issuer, and it may be sent electronically provided certain requirements are met. The plan administrator will not be treated as

failing this notice requirement merely because the USPS returns the notice as undeliverable after the notice was mailed to the participant using the participant's most recent mailing address in the records of the employer and plan administrator.

14. A plan that provides for mandatory distributions had to adopt a "good faith" plan amendment, reflecting the automatic rollover requirements, by the end of the first plan year ending after March 28, 2005 (for example, by December 31, 2005, for calendar-year plans, or by the applicable delayed effective dates for governmental and church plans). Notice 2005-5 included a sample amendment that plan sponsors could use for this purpose. A plan that does not provide for mandatory distributions does not have to be amended to comply with the automatic rollover rules.

[Notice 2005-5, 2005-3 I.R.B. 337]

DOL Prohibited Transaction Class Exemption. On September 28, 2004, the DOL issued a PTCE that permits a fiduciary of a plan who is also the employer maintaining the plan to establish, on behalf of its separated employees, an individual retirement plan (i.e., an IRA) at a financial institution that is the employer or an affiliate, in connection with an automatic rollover of a mandatory cash-out under Code Section 401(a)(31)(B). The PTCE also permits a plan fiduciary to select a proprietary product as the initial investment for such individual retirement plans. Finally, the PTCE also provides relief for the receipt of certain fees by the individual retirement plan provider in connection with the establishment or maintenance of the plan and the initial investment of the mandatory cash-out.

Pre-EGTRRA Rules. The pre-EGTRRA rules are specified in Revenue Ruling 2000-36 [2000-2 C.B. 140], in which the IRS ruled that the sponsor of a qualified defined contribution plan could amend its plan to change the existing default method of payment (i.e., single-sum cash payment) to a direct rollover either to another qualified plan or to an IRA for involuntary distributions (i.e., those of $5,000 or less) without violating either the direct rollover rules of Code Section 401(a)(31) or the anti-cutback rules of Code Section 411(d)(6). The plan amendment provided that in the case of a default direct rollover the plan administrator would select an IRA trustee, custodian, or issuer that is unrelated to the plan sponsor, establish the IRA with that trustee, custodian, or issuer on behalf of any separating employee who fails affirmatively to elect a direct rollover or a cash payment, and make the initial investment choices for the account. The DOL advised the IRS that in the context of a default direct rollover described in Revenue Ruling 2000-36, the participant will cease to be a participant covered under the plan within the meaning of D.O.L. Regulations Section 2510.3-3(d)(2)(ii)(B) (relating to participants covered under an ERISA employee pension plan) and the distributed assets will cease to be plan assets within the meaning of D.O.L. Regulations Section 2510.3-101 (the definition of plan assets) if the distribution constitutes the entire benefit rights of the participant. The DOL also noticed that the selection of an IRA trustee, custodian, or issuer and IRA investment for purposes of a default direct rollover would constitute a fiduciary act subject to the general fiduciary standards and prohibited transaction provisions of ERISA. In addition, the plan provisions governing the default direct rollover of distributions, including the participant's ability to affirmatively opt out of the arrangement, must be described in the SPD furnished to participants and beneficiaries.

Q 21:7 What change did EGTRRA make with regard to the cash-out rule?

Under EGTRRA, which became effective for distributions made after December 31, 2001, a plan may provide that the present value of a participant's vested account is determined without regard to the portion of such benefit that is attributable to rollover contributions (and any earnings allocable thereto), for purposes of the cash-out rule. [EGTRRA § 648]

Q 21:8 May a plan administrator establish a deadline after which a distributee may not revoke an election to make or not make a direct rollover?

Yes. However, a plan administrator is not permitted to prescribe any deadline or time period with respect to revocation of a direct rollover election that is more restrictive for the distributee than that which otherwise applies under the plan to revocation of the form of distribution elected by the distributee. [Treas. Reg. § 1.401(a)(31)-1, Q&A-8]

Q 21:9 Must a plan administrator permit a distributee to have a portion of an eligible rollover distribution paid to an eligible retirement plan in a direct rollover and the remainder paid to the distributee?

Yes, a plan administrator must permit a distributee to elect to have a portion of an eligible rollover distribution paid to an eligible retirement plan in a direct rollover and the remainder paid to the distributee. A plan administrator may require, however, that if the distributee elects to have only a portion of an eligible rollover distribution paid to an eligible retirement plan in a direct rollover, that portion be equal to at least a specified minimum amount, as long as the specified minimum amount is less than or equal to $500 or any greater amount as prescribed by the IRS. Furthermore, if the entire amount of the eligible rollover distribution is less than or equal to the specified minimum amount, the plan administrator need not allow the distributee to divide the distribution. [Treas. Reg. § 1.401(a)(31)-1, Q&A-9]

Q 21:10 Must a plan administrator allow a distributee to divide an eligible rollover distribution and have it paid in direct rollovers to two or more eligible retirement plans?

No. A plan administrator is not required (but is allowed) to permit a distributee to divide an eligible rollover distribution into separate distributions to be paid to two or more eligible retirement plans in direct rollovers. In other words, a plan administrator may require that a distributee select a single eligible retirement plan to which the eligible rollover distribution (or portion thereof) will be distributed in a direct rollover. [Treas. Reg. § 1.401(a)(31)-1, Q&A-10]

Q 21:11 May a qualified retirement plan refuse to permit a distributee to elect a direct rollover if his or her eligible rollover distributions during a year are reasonably expected to total less than $200?

Yes. A qualified retirement plan will satisfy Code Section 401(a)(31) even though the plan administrator does not permit any distributee to elect a direct rollover with respect to eligible rollover distributions during a year that are reasonably expected to total less than $200 or any lower minimum amount specified by the plan administrator. The rules relating to whether withholding under Code Section 3405(c) is required for an eligible rollover distribution that is less than $200 (see Qs 24:4–24:32), also apply for purposes of determining whether a direct rollover election under Code Section 401(a)(31) must be provided for an eligible rollover distribution that is less than $200 or the lower specified amount. [Treas. Reg. § 1.401(a)(31)-1, Q&A-11]

Q 21:12 May a plan administrator apply a distributee's election to make (or not to make) a direct rollover with respect to one payment in a series of periodic payments to all subsequent payments in the series?

Yes. A plan administrator is permitted to apply a distributee's election to make (or not to make) a direct rollover with respect to one payment in a series of periodic payments to all subsequent payments in the series, provided that:

1. The employee is permitted at any time to change, with respect to subsequent payments, a previous election to make (or not to make) a direct rollover; and
2. The written explanation provided under Code Section 402(f) (i.e., the rollover notice; see Q 21:46) explains that the election to make (or not to make) a direct rollover will apply to all future payments unless the employee later changes the election.

[Treas. Reg. § 1.401(a)(31)-1, Q&A-12]

Q 21:13 Must the eligible retirement plan designated by a distributee to receive a direct rollover distribution accept the distribution?

No. Although Code Section 401(a)(31) requires qualified retirement plans to provide distributees the option to make a direct rollover of their eligible rollover distributions to an eligible retirement plan, it imposes no requirement that any eligible retirement plan accept rollovers. Thus, a plan may refuse to accept rollovers. Alternatively, a plan may limit the circumstances under which it will accept rollovers. For example, a plan may limit the types of plans from which it will accept a rollover or limit the types of assets it will accept in a rollover (such as accepting only cash or its equivalent). [Treas. Reg. § 1.401(a)(31)-1, Q&A-13]

Q 21:14 How is an invalid rollover contribution treated for purposes of applying the qualification requirements of Code Section 401(a) to the receiving plan?

An invalid rollover contribution will be treated (for purposes of applying the qualification requirements of Code Section 401(a) to the receiving plan) as if it were a valid rollover contribution, if the following two conditions are satisfied:

1. When accepting the amount from the employee as a rollover contribution, the plan administrator of the receiving plan reasonably concludes that the contribution is a valid rollover contribution. (Although evidence that the distributing plan is the subject of a determination letter from the IRS indicating that it is qualified would be useful to the receiving plan administrator in reasonably concluding that the contribution is a valid rollover contribution, it is not necessary for the distributing plan to have such a determination letter in order for the receiving plan administrator to reach that conclusion.) [Treas. Reg. § 1.401(a)(31)-1, Q&A-14(a)] Revenue Ruling 2014-09, 2014 I.R.B. 975, discussed below, describes two situations in which the administrator of a Code Section 401(a) qualified retirement plan may reasonably conclude that a potential rollover contribution is a valid rollover contribution.
2. If the plan administrator of the receiving plan later determines that the contribution was an invalid rollover contribution, the amount of such contribution, plus any earnings attributable thereto, is distributed to the employee within a reasonable time after that determination. [Treas. Reg. § 1.401(a)(31)-1, Q&A-14(a)]

For purposes of the rule under discussion, an *invalid rollover contribution* is an amount that is accepted by a plan as a direct rollover within the meaning of Treasury Regulations Section 1.402(c)-2, Q&A-1 or as an indirect rollover from a conduit IRA within the meaning of Code Section 408(d)(3), but that is not an eligible rollover distribution from a qualified plan (or a conduit IRA) or that does not satisfy the other requirements of Code Sections 401(l)(31), 402(c), or 408(d)(3) for treatment as a rollover or a rollover contribution. [Treas. Reg. § 1.401(a)(31)-1, Q&A-14(b)(1)]

A *valid rollover contribution* is a contribution that is accepted by a plan as a rollover and that satisfies the requirements of Code Sections 401(a)(31), 402(c), or 408(d)(3) for treatment as a rollover or a rollover contribution. [Treas. Reg. § 1.401(a)(31)-1, Q&A-14(b)(2)]

The following examples illustrate the relief from disqualification that Treasury Regulations Section 1.401(a)(31)-1, Q&A-14, provides to plans that accept invalid rollover contributions.

Example 21-1: The Salinas Valley Corporation maintains the Salinas Valley Corporation Retirement Plan, a profit sharing plan qualified under Code

Section 401(a). The plan provides that any employee of the corporation may make a rollover contribution to the plan. Tom Joad, an employee of the corporation, will not have attained age 70½ by the end of the year, and has a vested account balance in the Grapes of Wrath Corporation Plan (a plan maintained by Tom's previous employer). Tom elects a single-sum distribution from the Grapes of Wrath Corporation Plan and elects that it be paid to the Salinas Valley Corporation Retirement Plan in a direct rollover. Tom provides the plan administrator of the Salinas Valley Corporation Retirement Plan with a letter from the plan administrator of the Grapes of Wrath Corporation Plan stating that the Grapes of Wrath Corporation Plan has received a determination letter from the IRS indicating that the Grapes of Wrath Corporation Plan is qualified. In light of that letter, absent facts to the contrary, the plan administrator may reasonably conclude that the Grapes of Wrath Corporation Plan is qualified and that the amount paid as a direct rollover is an eligible rollover distribution. [Treas. Reg. § 1.401(a)(31)-1, Q&A-14, Ex. 1]

Example 21-2: The facts are the same as in Example 21-1, except that instead of a determination letter from the IRS, Tom gives the plan administrator of the Salinas Valley Corporation Retirement Plan a letter from the plan administrator of the Grapes of Wrath Corporation Plan representing that such plan satisfies the requirements of Code Section 401(a) (or representing that such plan is intended to satisfy such requirements and the plan administrator is not aware of any plan provision or operation that would result in the disqualification of the plan). In light of that letter, absent facts to the contrary, the plan administrator may reasonably conclude that the Grapes of Wrath Corporation Plan is qualified and that the amount paid as a direct rollover is an eligible rollover distribution. [Treas. Reg. § 1.401(a)(31)-1, Q&A-14, Ex. 2]

Example 21-3: The facts are the same as in Example 21-1, except that Tom elects to receive the distribution from the Grapes of Wrath Corporation Plan and wishes to make a rollover contribution described in Code Section 402 (i.e., a 60-day rollover) rather than a direct rollover. When making the rollover contribution, Tom certifies that, to the best of his knowledge, he is entitled to the distribution as an employee and not as a beneficiary, the distribution from the Grapes of Wrath Corporation Plan to be contributed to the Salinas Valley Corporation Retirement Plan is not one of a series of periodic payments, the distribution from the Grapes of Wrath Corporation Plan was received by him not more than 60 days before the date of the rollover contribution, and the entire amount of the rollover contribution would be includible in gross income if it were not being rolled over.

As support for those certifications, Tom provides the plan administrator of the Salinas Valley Corporation Retirement Plan with two statements from the Grapes of Wrath Corporation Plan. The first is a letter from the plan administrator of the Grapes of Wrath Corporation Plan, as described in Example 21-1, stating that the Grapes of Wrath Corporation Plan has received a determination letter from the IRS indicating that the Grapes of Wrath Corporation Plan is qualified. The second is the distribution statement that accompanied the distribution check. The distribution statement indicates that the distribution is being made by the Grapes of Wrath Corporation Plan to Tom, indicates the gross amount of the distribution, and indicates that the amount withheld as federal income tax is 20 percent of the gross amount of the distribution. Tom contributes to the Salinas Valley Corporation Retirement Plan an amount not greater than the gross amount of the distribution stated in the letter from the Grapes of Wrath Corporation Plan, and the contribution is made within 60 days of the date of the distribution statement from the Grapes of Wrath Corporation Plan.

Based on the certifications and documentation provided by Tom, absent facts to the contrary, the plan administrator may reasonably conclude that the Grapes of Wrath Corporation Plan is qualified and that the distribution otherwise satisfies the requirements of Code Section 402(c) for treatment as a rollover contribution. [Treas. Reg. § 1.401(a)(31)-1, Q&A-14, Ex. 3]

Example 21-4: The facts are the same as in Example 21-3, except that, rather than contributing the distribution from the Grapes of Wrath Corporation Plan to the Salinas Valley Corporation Retirement Plan, Tom contributes the distribution from the Grapes of Wrath Corporation Plan to his IRA, an individual retirement account described in Code Section 408(a). After the contribution of the distribution from the Grapes of Wrath Corporation Plan to the IRA, but before the year in which Tom attains age 70½, Tom requests a distribution from the IRA and decides to contribute it to the Salinas Valley Corporation Retirement Plan as a rollover contribution. To make the rollover contribution, Tom endorses the check received from the IRA as payable to the Salinas Valley Corporation Retirement Plan.

In addition to providing the certifications described in Example 21-3 with respect to the distribution from the Grapes of Wrath Corporation Plan, Tom certifies that, to the best of his knowledge, the contribution to the IRA was made not more than 60 days after the date he received the distribution from the Grapes of Wrath Corporation Plan, no amount other than the distribution from the Grapes of Wrath Corporation Plan has been contributed to the IRA, and the distribution from the IRA was received not more than 60 days earlier than the rollover contribution to the Salinas Valley Corporation Retirement Plan.

As support for those certifications, in addition to the two statements from the Grapes of Wrath Corporation Plan described in Example 21-3, Tom provides copies of statements from the IRA. The statements indicate that the account is identified as an IRA, the account was established within 60 days of the date of the letter from the Grapes of Wrath Corporation Plan informing Tom that an amount had been distributed, and the opening balance in the IRA does not exceed the amount of the distribution described in the letter from the Grapes of Wrath Corporation Plan. There is no indication in the statements that any additional contributions have been made to the IRA since the account was opened. The date on the check from the IRA is less than 60 days before the date that Tom makes the contribution to the Salinas Valley Corporation Retirement Plan.

Based on the certifications and documentation provided by Tom, absent facts to the contrary, the plan administrator may reasonably conclude that the Grapes of Wrath Corporation Plan is qualified and that the contribution by Tom is a rollover contribution described in Code Section 408(d)(3)(A)(ii) that satisfies the other requirements of Code Section 408(d)(3) for treatment as a rollover contribution. [Treas. Reg. § 1.401(a)(31)-1, Q&A-14, Ex. 4]

To satisfy the first condition for a *valid rollover* described in item 1 above, when accepting the amount from the employee as a rollover contribution, the plan administrator of the receiving plan must reasonably conclude that the contribution is a valid rollover contribution. (Although evidence that the distributing plan is the subject of a determination letter from the IRS indicating that it is qualified would be useful to the receiving plan administrator in reasonably concluding that the contribution is a valid rollover contribution, it is not necessary for the distributing plan to have such a determination letter in order for the receiving plan administrator to reach that conclusion.) [Treas. Reg. § 1.401(a)(31)-1, Q&A-14(a)] Revenue Ruling 2014-09, 2014 I.R.B. 975 describes two situations in which the administrator of a Code Section 401(a) qualified retirement plan may reasonably conclude that a potential rollover contribution is a valid rollover contribution:

Situation 1: Receiving a Rollover from an Employer Plan. Under the facts in Situation 1 of Revenue Ruling 2014-09, Employer X maintains Plan M, a Code Section 401(a) qualified profit sharing plan that covers a class of its employees. Plan M provides that any employee of Employer X who is in the covered class may make a rollover contribution to Plan M. Plan M does not accept rollover contributions of after-tax amounts or amounts attributable to designated Roth contributions. Employee A is an employee of Employer X who is eligible to make rollover contributions to Plan M. Employee A has a vested account balance in Plan O (a retirement plan maintained by Employee A's prior employer) and is eligible for a distribution under the terms of Plan O.

In 2014, Employee A requests a distribution of her vested account balance in Plan O and elects that it be paid to Plan M in the form of a direct rollover. The trustee for Plan O distributes Employee A's vested account balance in a direct rollover to Plan M by issuing a check payable to the trustee of Plan M for the benefit of Employee A, and provides the check to Employee A. Employee A provides the plan administrator for Plan M with the name of Employee A's prior employer and delivers the check, with an attached check stub that identifies Plan O as the source of the funds, to the plan administrator. Employee A also certifies that the distribution from Plan O does not include after-tax contributions or amounts attributable to designated Roth contributions.

The plan administrator for Plan M accesses the EFAST2 database maintained by the DOL at www.efast.dol.gov and searches the most recently filed Form 5500 for Plan O. The latest Form 5500 for Plan O that the plan administrator for Plan M locates in the database is the Form 5500 filed for the plan year beginning January 1, 2012 and ending December 31, 2012. On that filing, line 8a does not include code 3C (for a plan not intended to be qualified under Code Section 401, 403, or 408).

The IRS analyzed that, by completing the Form 5500 in this manner, the plan administrator for Plan O made a representation that Plan O is intended to be a plan qualified under Code Section 401, 403, or 408. As a result of this filing, it is reasonable for the plan administrator for Plan M to conclude that Plan O is intended to be a qualified plan. The trustee for Plan O issued a check payable to the trustee for Plan M for the benefit of Employee A, which indicates that the plan administrator for Plan O treated the distribution as an eligible rollover distribution to be directly rolled over. Accordingly, it is reasonable for the plan administrator for Plan M to conclude that the potential rollover contribution is an eligible rollover distribution from Plan O. The IRS further stated that, for example, if the distribution had occurred during or after the year in which Employee A had attained age 70½, it would be reasonable for the plan administrator for Plan M to conclude that, in accordance with Treasury Regulations Section 1.402(c)-2, Q&A-7, Plan O distributed the required minimum amount under Code Section 401(a)(9) prior to making the direct rollover.

The IRS concluded, on the basis of the facts and analysis in Situation 1 of Revenue Ruling 2014-09, that absent any evidence to the contrary, it would be reasonable for the plan administrator for Plan M to conclude that the potential rollover contribution to Plan M of the distribution from Plan O was a *valid rollover contribution*.

Situation 2: Receiving a Rollover from an IRA. The facts in Situation 2 of Revenue Ruling 2014-09 are the same as Situation 1, except that Employee A has an account balance in IRA N, which is titled "IRA of Employee A." IRA N is a traditional IRA within the meaning of Treasury Regulations Section 1.408A-8, Q&A-1(a)(2) (rather than a Roth IRA or a SIMPLE IRA as described in Code Section 408(p)), and is not an inherited IRA within the meaning of Code Section 408(d)(3)(C)(ii). Employee A requests a distribution of her account balance in the form of a direct payment from IRA N to Plan M. The trustee for IRA N issues a check payable to the trustee for Plan M for the benefit of Employee A and provides the check to Employee A. Employee A delivers the check, including a check stub that identifies "IRA of Employee A" as the source of the funds, to the plan administrator for Plan M. Employee A certifies that her distribution from IRA N includes no after-tax amounts. Employee A also certifies that she will not have attained age 70½ by the end of the year in which the check is issued.

The IRS analyzed that, in Situation 2, the trustee for IRA N issued a check payable to the trustee for Plan M for the benefit of Employee A, which indicated that the trustee for IRA N treated the distribution as a rollover contribution paid directly to Plan M. Because the check stub indicated that the distributing account was titled "IRA of Employee A," the plan administrator for Plan M can reasonably conclude that the source of the funds is a traditional, non-inherited IRA.

In addition, Employee A certified that the distribution included no after-tax amounts and that she would not attain age 70½ by the end of the year of the transfer. Therefore, it was reasonable for the plan administrator for Plan M to conclude that the distribution from IRA N was a distribution that could be rolled over.

The IRS concluded, on the basis of the facts and analysis in Situation 2, that absent any evidence to the contrary, it would be reasonable for the plan administrator for Plan M to conclude that the potential rollover contribution to Plan M of the distribution from IRA N was a *valid rollover contribution*. If Employee A had attained age 70½ or older by the end of the year in which the check was issued, the plan administrator could not reasonably conclude that the potential rollover contribution was a *valid rollover contribution* absent additional information indicating that Code Section 408(a)(6) or Code Section 408(b)(3) had been satisfied with respect to IRA N in the year in which the check was issued.

The IRS further concluded that results in Situation 1 and Situation 2 would be the same if there had been no check stub identifying the source of the funds, as long as the check itself identified the source of the funds as Plan O or IRA N, respectively. The IRS also concluded that, similarly, the results would be the same if the rollover had been accomplished through a wire transfer or other electronic means, provided that the plan administrator or trustee for the sending plan or IRA had communicated to the plan administrator for Plan M the same information regarding the source of the funds. [IRS Rev. Rul. 2014-09, 2014-17 I.R.B. 975]

Q 21:15 For plan qualification purposes, is an eligible rollover distribution that is paid to an eligible retirement plan in a direct rollover a distribution and rollover, or is it a transfer of assets and liabilities?

For purposes of applying the plan qualification requirements of Code Section 401(a), a direct rollover is a distribution and rollover of the eligible rollover distribution and not a transfer of assets or liabilities. Thus, for example, if the consent requirements under Code Section 411(a)(11) or Code Sections 401(a)(11) and 417(a)(2) apply to the distribution, they must be met before the eligible rollover distribution may be distributed in a direct rollover. On the other hand, the direct rollover is not a transfer of assets and liabilities that must satisfy the requirements of Code Section 414(l). Also, a direct rollover is not an elective transfer of benefits for purposes of applying the anti-cutback requirements under Code Section 411(d)(6), as described in Treasury Regulations Section 1.411(d)-4, Q&A-3. Therefore, for example, the eligible retirement plan is not required to provide, with respect to amounts paid to it in a direct rollover, the same optional forms of benefits that were provided under the plan that made the direct rollover. The direct rollover requirements of Code Section 401(a)(31) do not affect the ability of a qualified plan to make an elective or nonelective transfer of assets and liabilities to another qualified plan in accordance with applicable law (such as the merger rules under Code Section 414(l)). [Treas. Reg. § 1.401(a)(31)-1, Q&A-15]

Q 21:16 Must a direct rollover option be provided for an eligible rollover distribution that is in the form of a plan loan offset amount?

No. A plan will not fail to satisfy Code Section 401(a)(31) merely because the plan does not permit a distributee to elect a direct rollover of an eligible rollover distribution in the form of a plan loan offset amount. In general, a plan loan offset amount is a distribution that occurs when, under the terms governing a plan loan, the participant's accrued benefit is reduced (offset) in order to repay the loan. (See Q 21:28; chapter 14.) [see Treas. Reg. § 1.402(c)-2(b), Q&A-9] A plan administrator is permitted to allow a direct rollover of a participant note for a plan loan to a qualified plan. [Treas. Reg. § 1.401(a)(31)-1, Q&A-16]

Q 21:17 Must a direct rollover option be provided for an eligible rollover distribution from a qualified plan distributed annuity contract?

Yes. If any amount to be distributed under a qualified plan distributed annuity contract is an eligible rollover distribution (in accordance with Treasury Regulations Section 1.402(c)-2, Q&A-10), the annuity contract must satisfy Code Section 401(a)(31) in the same manner as a qualified plan under Code Section 401(a)(31). A qualified plan distributed annuity contract is an annuity contract purchased for the participant, and distributed to the participant, by a qualified plan. [see Treas. Reg. § 1.402(c)-2, Q&A-10] In the case of a qualified plan distributed annuity contract, the payor under the contract is treated as the plan administrator. [Treas. Reg. § 1.401(a)(31)-1, Q&A-17]

Q 21:18 What assumptions may a plan administrator make regarding whether a benefit is an eligible rollover distribution?

For purposes of Code Section 401(a)(31), a plan administrator may make the following assumptions in determining the amount of a distribution that is an eligible rollover distribution for which a direct rollover option must be provided:

1. *$5,000 Death Benefit.* A plan administrator is permitted to assume that a distribution from the plan, in respect of a decedent who died on or before August 20, 1996 (the enactment date of the Small Business Job Protection Act of 1996), that qualifies for the death benefit exclusion under Code Section 101(b) is the only death benefit being paid with respect to such a decedent that qualifies for that exclusion. Thus, to the extent that such a distribution would be excludable from gross income based on this assumption, the plan administrator may assume that it is not an eligible rollover distribution.
2. *Determination of Designated Beneficiary.* For the purpose of determining the amount of the minimum distribution required to satisfy Code Section 401(a)(9) for any calendar year, the plan administrator may assume that there is no designated beneficiary. [Treas. Reg. § 1.401(a)(31)-1, Q&A-18]

Eligible Rollover Distributions

Q 21:19 What rules are in effect regarding distributions that may be rolled over to an eligible retirement plan under EGTRRA?

EGTRRA significantly increased pension portability, effective for distributions made after December 31, 2001. In general, EGTRRA allows eligible rollover distributions from Code Section 401(a) qualified retirement plans, Code Section 403(b) annuities, and Code Section 457(b) eligible governmental plans to be rolled over to *any* such plan or arrangement. (Note, however, that hardship distributions from Section 457(b) eligible governmental plans are not eligible rollover distributions.) Distributions from a traditional IRA also may generally be rolled over into a Code Section 401(a) qualified plan, a Code Section 403(b) annuity, or a Code Section 457(b) eligible governmental plan. As under pre-EGTRRA law, Code Section 401(a) qualified plans, Code Section 403(b) annuities, and Code Section 457(b) plans are not required to accept rollovers. [EGTRRA §§ 641–643, 649]

The pre-EGTRRA direct rollover and withholding rules were extended to distributions from a Code Section 457(b) eligible governmental plan and such plans are required to provide written notification (i.e., the rollover notice) to participants regarding eligible rollover distributions (see Q 21:20). Furthermore, amounts distributed from a Code Section 457(b) plan are subject to the 10 percent premature distribution penalty to the extent the distribution consists of amounts attributable to rollovers from another type of plan; Section 457(b) plans must separately account for such amounts. [EGTRRA § 649]

After-Tax Contributions. EGTRRA permits employee after-tax contributions to be rolled over to another qualified retirement plan (as described in Code Section 401(a)) or a traditional IRA. After-tax contributions (including nondeductible contributions to an IRA) may not, however, be rolled over from an IRA to a qualified plan, a Section 403(b) annuity, or a Section 457(b) plan. When a rollover is made from one qualified retirement plan to another, it must be accomplished only by means of a direct rollover. Furthermore, a qualified retirement plan may not accept rollovers of after-tax contributions unless the plan provides separate accounting for such contributions (and earnings on those contributions). [EGTRRA § 643]

Spousal Rollovers. Under EGTRRA, a surviving spouse may roll over distributions into a qualified retirement plan (as described in Code Section 401(a)), a Section 403(b) annuity, or a Section 457(b) plan in which the surviving spouse participates. [EGTRRA § 641(d)]

Q 21:20 What rule was in effect regarding distributions that may be rolled over to an eligible retirement plan before the enactment of EGTRRA?

Under Code Section 402(c) (as it existed before the enactment of EGTRRA), any portion of a distribution from a qualified plan that was an eligible rollover distribution described in Code Section 402(c)(4) could be rolled over to an eligible retirement plan described in Code Section 402(c)(8)(B). (See Qs 21:1–21:19, 21:36; chapter 24.)

Q 21:21 What is an eligible retirement plan, and what is a qualified trust?

An *eligible retirement plan*, under Code Section 402(c)(8)(B), is an individual retirement account described in Code Section 408(a), an individual retirement annuity described in Code Section 408(b) (other than an endowment contract), a qualified trust, an annuity plan described in Code Section 403(a), an eligible governmental plan described in Code Section 457(b), and an annuity contract described in Code Section 403(b). For purposes of Code Section 402(c), a *qualified trust* is an employees' trust described in Code Section 401(a) that is exempt from tax under Code Section 501(a). An individual retirement plan is an IRA described in Code Section 408(a) or an individual retirement annuity (other than an endowment contract) described in Code Section 408(b). [Treas. Reg. § 1.402(c)-2, Q&A-2]

Q 21:22 What is an eligible rollover distribution?

Unless specifically excluded, an *eligible rollover distribution* is any distribution to an employee (or to a spousal distributee) of all or any portion of the balance to the credit of the employee in a qualified plan. Thus, except as specifically provided otherwise (see Q 21:23), any amount distributed to an employee (or a spousal distributee) from a qualified plan is an eligible rollover distribution, regardless of whether it is a distribution of a benefit that is protected under Code Section 411(d)(6). [Treas. Reg. § 1.402(c)-2, Q&A-3]

WRERA amended Code Sections 402(c)(11) and 402(f)(2)(A) to provide that, for plan years beginning on or after January 1, 2010, distributions to designated nonspouse beneficiaries must be treated as eligible rollover distributions for the purpose of making a direct rollover into an inherited IRA. Such eligible rollover distributions, like all other eligible rollover distributions, are subject to the 20 percent mandatory withholding requirement under Code Section 3405(c) and the rollover notice requirement of Code Section 402(f). Under Notice 2007-7, 2007-5 I.R.B. 395, the IRS had taken the view that the nonspouse beneficiary rollover provision (which had been added by PPA and had become effective for the 2007 plan year) was merely optional and that the other direct rollover requirements (i.e., the 20 percent mandatory withholding requirement and the rollover notice requirement) did not apply.

Q 21:23 What amounts are not eligible rollover distributions?

The following are not eligible rollover distributions:

1. Any distribution that is one of a series of substantially equal periodic payments made (not less frequently than annually) over any one of the following periods—
   a. The life of the employee (or the joint lives of the employee and the employee's designated beneficiary),
   b. The life expectancy of the employee (and the employee's designated beneficiary), or
   c. A specified period of 10 years or more.
2. Any distribution to the extent the distribution is a required minimum distribution (RMD) under Code Section 401(a)(9).

3. The portion of any distribution that is not includible in gross income (determined without regard to the exclusion for net unrealized appreciation described in Code Section 402(e)(4)). Thus, for example, an eligible rollover distribution does not include the portion of any distribution that is excludable from gross income under Code Section 72 as a return of the employee's investment in the contract (e.g., a return of the employee's after-tax contributions) but does include net unrealized appreciation. [Treas. Reg. § 1.402(c)-2, Q&A-3] However, such portions may be eligible rollover distributions if transferred to an IRA or transferred via a direct trustee-to-trustee transfer to a qualified trust or 403(b) annuity contract and such trust or contract provides for separate accounting (including earnings). [I.R.C. § 402(c)(2)]
4. A hardship distribution made after December 31, 1998, from a 401(k) plan or a Section 403(b) arrangement [I.R.C. §§ 402(c)(4)(C), 403(b)(8)(B), as added and amended by RRA § 6005(c)(2)(B), RRA § 6005(c)(2)(C)] (although the IRS has provided transitional relief [Notice 99-5, 1999-3 I.R.B. 10] and some permanent relief [Notice 2000-32, 2000-26 I.R.B. 1274] from this exception).
5. Elective deferrals as defined in Code Section 402(g)(3) that, pursuant to Treasury Regulations Section 1.415-6(b)(6)(iv), are returned as a result of the application of the Section 415 limits, together with the income allocable to the corrective distributions.
6. Corrective distributions of excess deferrals as described in Treasury Regulations Section 1.402(g)-1(e)(3), together with the income allocable to the corrective distributions.
7. Corrective distributions of excess contributions under a qualified cash or deferred arrangement described in Treasury Regulations Section 1.401(k)-2(b)(2) and excess aggregate contributions described in Treasury Regulations Section 1.401(m)-2(b)(2), together with the income allocable to the distributions.
8. Loans that are treated as deemed distributions pursuant to Code Section 72(p).
9. Dividends paid on employer securities as described in Code Section 404(k).
10. The costs of life insurance coverage (PS-58 costs).
11. Similar items designated by the IRS.

[Treas. Reg. § 1.402(c)-2, Q&A-3 and Q&A-4]

Q 21:24 How is it determined whether a series of payments is a series of substantially equal periodic payments over a specified period?

Generally, whether a series of payments is a series of substantially equal periodic payments over a period specified in Code Section 402(c)(4)(A) is determined by following the principles of Code Section 72(t)(2)(A)(iv) at the time payments begin, without regard to contingencies or modifications that have not yet occurred. Thus, for example, a joint and 50 percent survivor annuity will be treated as a series of substantially equal payments at the time payments commence, as will a joint and survivor annuity that provides for increased payments to the employee if the employee's beneficiary dies before the employee. Similarly, when determining if a disability benefit payment is part of a series of substantially equal payments for a period described in Code Section 402(c)(4)(A), any contingency under which payments cease upon recovery from the disability may be disregarded.

Certain Social Security Supplements Disregarded. For purposes of determining whether a distribution is one of a series of payments that are substantially equal, Social Security supplements described in Code Section 411(a)(9) are disregarded. For example, if a distributee receives a life annuity of $500 per month, plus a Social Security supplement consisting of payments of $200 per month until the distributee reaches the age at which Social Security benefits of not less than $200 a month begin, the $200 supplemental payments are disregarded; therefore, each monthly payment of $700 made before the Social Security retirement age (SSRA) and each monthly payment of $500 made after the SSRA is treated as one of a series of substantially equal periodic payments for life. A series of payments that are not substantially equal solely because the amount of each payment is reduced upon attainment of SSRA (or, alternatively, upon commencement of Social Security early retirement, survivor, or disability benefits) will also be treated as substantially equal as long as the reduction in the actual payments is level and does not exceed the applicable Social Security benefit.

Changes in the Amount of Payments or the Distributee. If the amount (or, if applicable, the method of calculating the amount) of the payments changes so that subsequent payments are not substantially equal to previous payments, a new determination must be made as to whether the remaining payments are a series of substantially equal periodic payments over a specified period. Such a determination is made without taking into account payments made or the years of payment that elapsed before the change. However, a new determination is not made merely because, upon the death of the participant, the spouse or former spouse of the participant becomes the distributee. That is, once distributions commence over a period that is at least as long as either the first annuitant's life or 10 years (e.g., as provided by a life annuity with a five-year- or ten-year-certain guarantee), then substantially equal payments to the survivor are not eligible rollover distributions even though the payment period remaining after the death of the participant is or may be less than the period described in Code Section 402(c)(4)(A). For example, substantially equal periodic payments made under a life annuity with a five-year term certain would not be an eligible rollover distribution even when paid after the death of the participant with three years remaining under the term certain.

Defined Contribution Plans. The following rules apply in determining whether a series of payments from a defined contribution plan constitute substantially equal periodic payments for a period described in Code Section 402(c)(4)(A):

1. *Declining Balance of Years.* A series of payments from an account balance under a defined contribution plan will be considered substantially equal payments over a specified period if, for each year, the amount of the distribution is calculated by dividing the account balance by the number of years remaining in the period. For example, a series of payments will be considered substantially equal payments over 10 years if the series is determined as follows. In year 1, the annual payment is the account balance divided by 10; in year 2, the annual payment is the remaining account balance divided by 9; and so on until year 10 when the entire remaining balance is distributed.
2. *Reasonable Actuarial Assumptions.* If a participant's account balance under a defined contribution plan is to be distributed in annual installments of a specified amount until the account balance is exhausted, the period of years over which the installments will be distributed must be determined using reasonable actuarial assumptions. For example, if a participant has an account balance of $100,000, elects distributions of $12,000 per year until the account balance is exhausted, and the future rate of return is assumed to be 8 percent per year, the account balance will be exhausted in approximately 14 years. Similarly, if the same participant elects a fixed annual distribution amount and the fixed annual amount is less than or equal to $10,000, it is reasonable to assume that a future rate of return will be greater than 0 percent and thus the account will not be exhausted in less than 10 years.

[Treas. Reg. § 1.402(c)-2, Q&A-5]

Q 21:25 What types of variations in the amount of a payment cause the payment not to be part of a series of substantially equal periodic payments?

Except as provided below, a payment is treated as independent of the payments in a series of substantially equal payments, and thus as not part of the series, if the payment is substantially larger or smaller than the other payments in the series. An independent payment is an eligible rollover distribution if it is not otherwise excepted from the definition of eligible rollover distribution. That is so regardless of whether the payment is made before, with, or after payments in the series. For example, if a participant elects a single payment of half of the account balance with the remainder of the account balance paid over the life expectancy of the distributee, the single payment is treated as independent of the payments in the series and is an eligible rollover distribution unless otherwise excepted. Similarly, if a participant's surviving spouse receives a survivor life annuity of $1,000 per month plus a single payment on account of death of $7,500, the single payment is treated as independent of the payments in the annuity and is an eligible rollover distribution unless otherwise excepted.

The following special rules apply:

1. *Administrative Error or Delay.* If, due solely to reasonable administrative error or delay in payment, there is an adjustment after the annuity starting

date to the amount of any payment in a series of payments that otherwise would constitute a series of substantially equal payments described in Code Section 402(c)(4)(A), the adjusted payment or payments will be treated as part of the series of substantially equal periodic payments and will not be treated as independent of the payments in the series. For example, if, due solely to reasonable administrative delay, the first payment of a life annuity is delayed by two months and reflects an additional two months' worth of benefits, that payment will be treated as a substantially equal payment in the series rather than as an independent payment. The result will not change merely because the amount of the adjustment is paid in a separate supplemental payment.

2. *Supplemental Payments for Annuitants.* A supplemental payment from a defined benefit plan to annuitants (e.g., retirees or beneficiaries) will be treated as part of a series of substantially equal payments, rather than as an independent payment, provided that the following conditions are met:
   a. The supplement is a benefit increase for annuitants;
   b. The amount of the supplement is determined in a consistent manner for all similarly situated annuitants;
   c. The supplement is paid to annuitants who are otherwise receiving payments that would constitute substantially equal periodic payments; and
   d. The aggregate supplement is less than or equal to the greater of 10 percent of the annual rate of payment for the annuity, or $750 (or any higher amount prescribed by the IRS).
3. *Final Payment in a Series.* If a payment in a series of payments from an account balance under a defined contribution plan represents the remaining balance to the credit and is substantially less than the other payments in the series, the final payment must nevertheless be treated as a payment in the series of substantially equal payments. It may not be treated as an independent payment if the other payments in the series are substantially equal and the payments are for a period described in Code Section 402(c)(4)(A) based on the applicable rules (see Q 21:24). Thus, such final payment will not be an eligible rollover distribution.

[Treas. Reg. § 1.402(c)-2, Q&A-6]

Q 21:26 When is a distribution from a plan an RMD under Code Section 401(a)(9)?

General Rule. Except as provided below, if a minimum distribution is required for a calendar year, the amounts distributed during that calendar year are treated as RMDs under Code Section 401(a)(9), to the extent that the total RMD under Code Section 401(a)(9) for the calendar year has not been satisfied. Accordingly, such amounts are not eligible rollover distributions.

For example, if a participant is required under Code Section 401(a)(9) to receive an RMD for a calendar year of $5,000 and the participant receives a total of $7,200 in that year, the first $5,000 distributed will be treated as the RMD and will not be an eligible rollover distribution; the remaining $2,200 will be an eligible rollover distribution if it otherwise qualifies. If the total Section 401(a)(9) RMD for a calendar year is not distributed in that calendar year (e.g., when the distribution for the calendar year is made on the following April 1), the amount that was required but not distributed is added to the amount required to be distributed for the next calendar year in determining the portion of any distribution in the next calendar year that is an RMD.

Distribution Before Age 70½. Any amount that is paid before January 1 of the year in which the employee attains (or would have attained) age 70½ will not be treated as required under Code Section 401(a)(9) and thus is an eligible rollover distribution if it otherwise qualifies.

Special Rule for Annuities. In the case of annuity payments from a defined benefit plan, or under an annuity contract purchased from an insurance company (including a qualified plan distributed annuity contract; see Q 21:29), the entire amount of any such annuity payment made on or after a participant's required beginning date will be treated as an amount required under Code Section 401(a)(9) and thus will not be an eligible rollover distribution.

[Treas. Reg. § 1.402(c)-2, Q&A-7]

Q 21:27 How are amounts that are not includible in gross income allocated for purposes of determining the RMD?

If a plan has not yet satisfied Code Section 401(a)(9) for the year with respect to a participant, a distribution is made to the participant that exceeds the amount required and a portion of that distribution is excludable from gross income. For purposes of determining the amount of the distribution that is an eligible rollover distribution, the portion of the distribution that is excludable from gross income is first allocated toward satisfaction of Code Section 401(a)(9); the remaining portion of the RMD, if any, is satisfied from the portion of the distribution that is includible in gross income.

For example, if a participant is required under Code Section 401(a)(9) to receive an RMD for a calendar year of $4,000 and the participant receives a $4,800 distribution, of which $1,000 is excludable from income as a return of basis, the $1,000 return of basis is allocated toward satisfying the RMD. The remaining $3,000 of the RMD is satisfied from the $3,800 of the distribution that is includible in gross income, so that the remaining balance of the distribution, $800, is an eligible rollover distribution if it otherwise qualifies.

[Treas. Reg. § 1.402(c)-2, Q&A-8]

Q 21:28 Can a qualified plan loan offset amount be rolled over into another eligible retirement plan or IRA?

Yes. A "qualified plan loan offset amount" due to a plan termination or default due to severance from employment may be rolled over into another eligible retirement plan or IRA by the participant's tax filing deadline (including extensions) for the year of the offset. [I.R.C. § 402(c)(3)(C)(i), as added by TCJA § 13613(a), effective with respect to qualified plan loan offset amounts that are treated as distributed in taxable years beginning after December 31, 2017] Under the law as in effect before TCJA, a loan offset was eligible to be rolled over into another qualified retirement plan or IRA only if it was rolled over within 60 days after the offset. Under the TCJA, a "qualified plan loan offset amount" means a "plan loan offset amount" that is treated (deemed) as distributed from a qualified employer plan to a participant or beneficiary solely by reason of:

1. The termination of the qualified employer plan, or
2. The failure to meet the repayment terms of the loan from the plan because of the participant's severance from employment. [I.R.C. § 402(c)(3)(C)(ii), as added by TCJA § 13613(a), effective with respect to plan loan offset amounts that are treated as distributed in taxable years beginning after December 31, 2017]

A "plan loan offset amount" means the amount by which the participant's accrued benefit (e.g., the participant's account under a 401(k) plan) is reduced in order to repay a loan from the plan [I.R.C. § 402(c)(3)(C)(iii), as added by TCJA § 13613(a), effective with respect to plan loan offset amounts that are treated as distributed in taxable years beginning after December 31, 2017]

The TCJA's extended rollover period for "qualified plan loan offset amounts" applies to Code Section 401(a) qualified plans, 403(b) plans, and governmental 457(b) plans that offer loans.

A distribution of a plan loan offset amount is an eligible rollover distribution if it satisfies certain requirements (see Q 21:22). Thus, an amount equal to the plan loan offset amount may be rolled over by the participant (or spousal distributee) to an eligible retirement plan no later than the participant's tax filing deadline (including extensions) for the taxable year of the offset unless the plan loan offset amount fails to be an eligible rollover distribution for another reason. (See Q 21:16 for guidance concerning the offering of a direct rollover of a plan loan offset amount; see chapter 24 for guidance concerning special withholding rules with respect to plan loan offset amounts.) [I.R.C. § 402(c)(3)(C)(i), as added by TCJA § 13613(a), effective with respect to plan loan offset amounts that are treated as distributed in taxable years beginning after December 31, 2017; Treas. Reg. § 1.402(c)-2, Q&A-9(a)]

For purposes of Code Section 402(c), a *distribution of a plan loan offset amount* is a distribution that occurs when, under the plan terms governing a plan loan, a participant's accrued benefit is reduced (offset) in order to repay the loan (including the enforcement of the plan's security interest in the participant's accrued benefit). A distribution of a plan loan offset amount can occur in a variety of circumstances (e.g., where the terms governing a plan loan require that, in the event of the participant's termination of employment or request for a distribution, the loan be repaid immediately or treated as in default). A distribution of a plan loan offset amount also occurs when, under the terms governing the plan loan, the loan is canceled, accelerated, or treated as if it were in default (e.g., where the plan treats a loan as in default upon a participant's termination of employment or within a specified period thereafter). A distribution of a plan loan offset amount is an actual distribution, not a deemed distribution under Code Section 72(p). [Treas. Reg. § 1.402(c)-2, Q&A-9(b)]

Example 21-5: In 2019, Adam Trask has an account balance of $10,000 in the East of Eden Corporation plan, of which $3,000 is invested in a plan loan to Adam that is secured by his account balance under the plan. Adam has made no after-tax employee contributions to the plan. The plan does not provide any direct rollover option with respect to plan loans. Upon termination of employment in 2019, Adam, who has not yet reached his required beginning date, elects a distribution of his entire account balance in the plan, and his outstanding loan is offset against the account balance on distribution. Adam elects a direct rollover of the distribution.

In order to satisfy Code Section 401(a)(31), the plan must pay $7,000 directly to the eligible retirement plan chosen by Adam in a direct rollover. When Adam's account balance was offset by the amount of the $3,000 unpaid loan balance, he received a plan loan offset amount (equivalent to $3,000) that is an eligible rollover distribution. The plan satisfies Code Section 401(a)(31), even though a direct rollover option was not provided with respect to the $3,000 plan loan offset amount.

No withholding is required under Code Section 3405(c) on account of the distribution of the $3,000 plan loan offset amount because no cash or other property (other than the plan loan offset amount) is received by Adam from which to satisfy the withholding. Adam may roll over $3,000 to an eligible retirement plan within the 60-day period provided in Code Section 402(c)(3). [Treas. Reg. § 1.402(c)-2, Q&A-9, Ex. 1]

Example 21-6: The facts are the same as in Example 21-5, except that the terms governing the plan loan to Adam provide that, upon termination of employment, Adam's account balance is automatically offset by the amount of any unpaid loan balance to repay the loan. Adam terminates employment but does not request a distribution from the plan. Nevertheless, pursuant to the terms governing the plan loan, Adam's account balance is automatically offset by the amount of the $3,000 unpaid loan balance.

The $3,000 plan loan offset amount attributable to the plan loan in this example is treated in the same manner as the $3,000 plan loan offset amount in Example 21-5. [Treas. Reg. § 1.402(c)-2, Q&A-9, Ex. 2]

Example 21-7: The facts are the same as in Example 21-6, except that, instead of providing for an automatic offset upon termination of employment to repay the plan loan, the terms governing the plan loan require full repayment of the loan by Adam within 30 days of termination of employment. Adam terminates employment, does not elect a distribution from the plan, and also fails to repay the plan loan within 30 days. The plan administrator of the plan declares the plan loan to Adam in default and executes on the loan by offsetting Adam's account balance by the amount of the $3,000 unpaid loan balance.

The $3,000 plan loan offset amount attributable to the plan loan in this example is treated in the same manner as the $3,000 plan loan offset amount in Example 21-5 and in Example 21-6. The result in this example is the same even though the plan administrator treats the loan as in default before offsetting Adam's accrued benefit by the amount of the unpaid loan. [Treas. Reg. § 1.402(c)-2, Q&A-9, Ex. 3]

Example 21-8: The facts are the same as in Example 21-5, except that Adam elects to receive the distribution of the account balance that remains after the $3,000 offset to repay the plan loan, instead of electing a direct rollover of the remaining account balance.

In this case, the amount of the distribution received by Adam is $10,000, not $3,000. Because the amount of the $3,000 offset attributable to the loan is included in determining the amount that equals 20 percent of the eligible rollover distribution received by Adam, withholding in the amount of $2,000 (20 percent of $10,000) is required under Code Section 3405(c). The $2,000 is required to be withheld from the $7,000 to be distributed to Adam in cash, so that he actually receives a check for $5,000. [Treas. Reg. § 1.402(c)-2, Q&A-9, Ex. 4]

Example 21-9: The facts are the same as in Example 21-8, except that the $7,000 distribution to Adam after the offset to repay the loan consists solely of employer securities within the meaning of Code Section 402(e)(4)(E). In this case, no withholding is required under Code Section 3405(c) because the distribution consists solely of the $3,000 plan loan offset amount and the $7,000 distribution of employer securities. That is the result because the total amount required to be withheld does not exceed the sum of the cash and the fair market value of other property distributed, excluding plan loan offset amounts and employer securities. Adam may roll over the employer securities and $3,000 to an eligible retirement plan within the rollover period provided in Code Section 402(c)(3)(C)(i). [I.R.C. § 402(c)(3)(C)(i), as added by TCJA § 13613(a), effective with respect to plan loan offset amounts that are treated as distributed in taxable years beginning after December 31, 2017; Treas. Reg. § 1.402(c)-2, Q&A-9, Ex. 5]

Example 21-10: Cal Trask, who is age 40, has an account balance in the Salinas Valley Company Plan, a profit sharing plan qualified under Code Section 401(a) that includes a qualified cash or deferred arrangement described in Code Section 401(k). The plan provides for no after-tax employee contributions. In 2011, Cal receives a loan from the plan, the terms of which satisfy Code Section 72(p)(2), and which is secured by elective contributions subject to the distribution restrictions in Code Section 401(k)(2)(B). In 2019, the loan fails to satisfy Code Section 72(p)(2) because Cal stops repayment. In that year, pursuant to Code Section 72(p), Cal is taxed on a deemed distribution equal to the amount of the unpaid loan balance. The deemed distribution is not an eligible rollover distribution. Because Cal has not separated from service or experienced any other event that permits the distribution under Code

Section 401(k)(2)(B) of the elective contributions that secure the loan, the plan is prohibited from executing on the loan. Accordingly, Cal's account balance is not offset by the amount of the unpaid loan balance at the time Cal stops repayment on the loan. Thus, there is no distribution of an offset amount that is an eligible rollover distribution in 2019. [Treas. Reg. § 1.402(c)-2, Q&A-9, Ex. 6]

Q 21:29 What is a qualified plan distributed annuity contract, and how is an amount paid under such a contract treated for purposes of Code Section 402(c)?

A *qualified plan distributed annuity contract* is an annuity contract purchased for a participant, and distributed to the participant, by a qualified plan.

Amounts paid under a qualified plan distributed annuity contract are payments of the balance to the credit of the employee for purposes of Code Section 402(c) and are eligible rollover distributions, if they otherwise qualify. Thus, for example, if a participant surrenders a contract for a single-sum payment of its cash surrender value, the payment would be an eligible rollover distribution to the extent it is includible in gross income and not an RMD under Code Section 401(a)(9). This rule applies even if the annuity contract is distributed in connection with a plan termination. (See Q 21:17 and chapter 24 concerning the direct rollover requirements and 20 percent withholding requirements, respectively, that apply to eligible rollover distributions from such an annuity contract.) [Treas. Reg. § 1.402(c)-2, Q&A-10]

Q 21:30 If a participant contributes all or part of an eligible rollover distribution to an eligible retirement plan within 60 days, is the amount contributed not currently includible in gross income?

Yes. The amount contributed is not currently includible in gross income, provided that it is contributed to the eligible retirement plan no later than the 60th day following the day on which the participant received the distribution. If more than one distribution is received by a participant from a qualified plan during a taxable year, the 60-day rule applies separately to each distribution.

Because the amount withheld as income tax under Code Section 3405(c) is considered an amount distributed under Code Section 402(c), an amount equal to all or any portion of the amount withheld may be contributed as a rollover to an eligible retirement plan within the 60-day period, in addition to the net amount of the eligible rollover distribution actually received by the employee. However, if all or any portion of an amount equal to the amount withheld is not contributed as a rollover, it is included in the employee's gross income to the extent required under Code Section 402(a) and also may be subject to the 10 percent premature distribution penalty under Code Section 72(t). [Treas. Reg. § 1.402(c)-2, Q&A-11]

Q 21:31 How did EGTRRA modify the 60-day rule?

Distributions from an IRA or a qualified retirement plan (as described in Code Section 401(a)) may be rolled over tax-free if the rollover is accomplished no later than the 60th day following the day on which the distributee received the distribution (the 60-day rollover period does not apply to qualified plan loan offset amounts, see Q 21:28). EGTRRA permits the Secretary of the Treasury to waive the 60-day period if imposing it would be against equity or good conscience. [EGTRRA § 644] Under prior law, the Secretary could only waive the 60-day requirement during military service in a combat zone or by reason of a presidentially declared disaster. [EGTRRA § 644] Under EGTRRA, which began to apply to distributions made after December 31, 2001, the Secretary's discretion is extended to other events beyond the reasonable control of the individual subject to the 60-day requirement. Among those events are death, disability, hospitalization, incarceration, errors committed by a financial institution, postal error, and restrictions imposed by a foreign country. [EGTRRA § 644]

On January 27, 2003, the IRS issued Revenue Procedure 2003-16 [2003-1 I.R.B. 359], which provides guidance on applying to the IRS for a hardship waiver of the 60-day rollover requirement. It also provides for an automatic waiver under certain circumstances. Unless the conditions for an automatic waiver are satisfied, a taxpayer must apply for a hardship exception to the 60-day rollover requirement, using the same procedure as that outlined in Revenue Procedure 2003-4 for private letter rulings, and must pay a user fee. Revenue Procedure 2009-4, 2009-1 I.R.B. 118 contains a sample letter ruling request format (in Appendix A) and a checklist of information (in Appendix B) that should be submitted with ruling requests made under the revenue procedure.

The IRS will issue a ruling waiving the 60-day rollover requirement in cases where the failure to waive it would be against equity or good conscience, including casualty, disaster, or other events beyond the reasonable control of the taxpayer. In determining whether to grant a waiver, the IRS will consider all relevant facts and circumstances, including (1) errors committed by a financial institution (other than certain errors which would support an automatic approval of a waiver of the 60-day requirement), (2) inability to complete a rollover due to death, disability, hospitalization, incarceration, restrictions imposed by a foreign country, or postal error, (3) the use of the amount distributed (for example, in the case of payment by check, whether the check was cashed), and (4) the time elapsed since the distribution occurred. [Rev. Proc. 2003-16, 2003-1 I.R.B. 359, §§ 3.01 and 3.02]

Under the procedures relating to automatic approval of a waiver of the 60-day requirement, no application to the IRS is required if a financial institution receives funds on behalf of a taxpayer prior to the expiration of the 60-day rollover period, the taxpayer follows all procedures required by the financial institution for depositing the funds into an eligible retirement plan within the 60-day period (including giving instructions to deposit the funds into an eligible retirement plan) and, solely due to an error on the part of the financial institution, the funds are not deposited into an eligible retirement plan within the 60-day rollover period. Automatic approval is granted only (1) if the funds are deposited into an eligible retirement plan within one year from the beginning of the 60-day rollover period, and (2) if the financial institution had deposited the funds as instructed, it would have been a valid rollover.

In order to be eligible for a waiver of the 60-day rollover period, either automatic or through application to the IRS, the distribution must have occurred after December 31, 2001, and the rules regarding the amount of money or other property that can be rolled over into an eligible retirement plan within the 60-day rollover period apply to deposits made pursuant to a waiver of the 60-day rollover period (thus, if a taxpayer received $6,000 in cash from his or her IRA, the most that could be deposited into an eligible retirement plan pursuant to a waiver of the 60-day rollover period is $6,000). Also, the rules for waiver of the 60-day rollover period became effective on January 27, 2003. [Rev. Proc. 2003-16, 2003-1 I.R.B. 359, §§ 3.04 and 4] Revenue Procedure 2003-16 was modified by Revenue Procedure 2016-47, 2016-37 I.R.B. 346, described below.

On August 24, 2016, the IRS issued Revenue Procedure 2016-47, 2016-37 I.R.B. 346, which provides self-certification procedures designed to help recipients of retirement plan distributions who inadvertently miss the 60-day time limit for properly rolling such distributions over into another retirement plan or IRA. Revenue Procedure 2016-47 became effective on August 24, 2016. [Rev. Proc. 2016-46, 2016-37 I.R.B. 346, § 5]

Revenue Procedure 2016-47 provides guidance concerning waivers of the 60-day rollover requirement in Code Sections 402(c)(3) and 408(d)(3). Specifically, it provides for a self-certification procedure (subject to verification on audit) that may be used by a taxpayer claiming eligibility for a waiver under Code Section 402(c)(3)(B) or 408(d)(3)(I) with respect to a rollover into a plan or an IRA. Revenue Procedure 2016-47 provides that a plan administrator or an IRA trustee, custodian or issuer ("IRA trustee") may rely on the certification in accepting and reporting receipt of a rollover contribution. It also modifies IRS Revenue Procedure 2003-16, by providing that the IRS may grant a waiver during an examination of the taxpayer's income tax return. The Appendix to Revenue Procedure 2016-47 contains a model letter that a taxpayer may use for self-certification. [Rev. Proc. 2016-46, 2016-37 I.R.B. 346, § 1]

Self-Certification Requirements. Revenue Procedure 2016-47's self-certification requirements are as follows:

Written Self-Certification. A taxpayer may make a written certification to a plan administrator or an IRA trustee that a contribution satisfies the conditions for self-certification set forth in Section 3.02 of Revenue Procedure 2016-47, described below. The taxpayer's self-certification has the effects described in Section 3.04 of Revenue Procedure 2016-47, also described below. Taxpayers may make the certification by using the model letter in the Appendix to Revenue Procedure 2016-47 on a word-for-word basis or by using a letter that is substantially similar in all material respects. A copy of the certification should be kept in the taxpayer's files and be available if requested by the IRS on audit. [Rev. Proc. 2016-47, 2016-37 I.R.B. 346, § 3.01]

Conditions for Self-Certification. Self-certification is available only if certain conditions are met. First, the IRS must not have previously denied a waiver request with respect to a rollover of all or part of the distribution to which the contribution relates. [Rev. Proc. 2016-47, 2016-37 I.R.B. 346, § 3.02(1)] Second, the taxpayer must have missed the 60-day deadline because of the taxpayer's inability to complete a rollover due to one or more of the following reasons:

1. An error was committed by the financial institution receiving the contribution or making the distribution to which the contribution relates;
2. The distribution, having been made in the form of a check, was misplaced and never cashed;
3. The distribution was deposited into and remained in an account that the taxpayer mistakenly thought was an eligible retirement plan;
4. The taxpayer's principal residence was severely damaged;
5. A member of the taxpayer's family died;
6. The taxpayer or a member of the taxpayer's family was seriously ill;
7. The taxpayer was incarcerated;
8. Restrictions were imposed by a foreign country;
9. A postal error occurred;
10. The distribution was made on account of a levy under Code Section 6331 (relating to levy and distraint) and the proceeds of the levy have been returned to the taxpayer; or
11. The party making the distribution to which the rollover relates delayed providing information that the receiving plan or IRA required to complete the rollover despite the taxpayer's reasonable efforts to obtain the information. [Rev. Proc. 2016-47, 2016-37 I.R.B. 346, § 3.02(2)]

Contributions As Soon As Practicable, with a 30-Day Safe Harbor. The contribution must be made to the plan or the IRA as soon as practicable after the reason or reasons listed above no longer prevent the taxpayer from making the contribution. This requirement is deemed to be satisfied if the contribution is made within 30 days after the reason or reasons no longer prevent the taxpayer from making the contribution. [Rev. Proc. 2016-47, 2016-37 I.R.B. 346, § 3.02(3)]

Reporting on IRS Form 5498 (IRA Contribution Information). The IRS has modified the Instructions to Form 5498 to require that an IRA trustee that accepts a rollover contribution after the 60-day deadline report that the contribution was accepted after the 60-day deadline. [Rev. Proc. 2016-47, 2016-37 I.R.B. 346, § 3.03]

Effects of Self-Certification. Self-certification has the following two effects:

1. *Effect on Plan Administrator or IRA Trustee.* For purposes of accepting and reporting a rollover contribution into a plan or an IRA, a plan administrator or an IRA trustee may rely on a taxpayer's self-certification in determining whether the taxpayer has satisfied the conditions for a waiver of the 60-day rollover requirement under Code Section 402(c)(3)(B) or

408(d)(3)(I). However, a plan administrator or an IRA trustee may not rely on the self-certification for other purposes or if the plan administrator or the IRA trustee has actual knowledge that is contrary to the self-certification. [Rev. Proc. 2016-47, 2016-37 I.R.B. 346, § 3.04(1)]

2. *Effect on Taxpayer.* A self-certification is not a waiver by the IRS of the 60-day rollover requirement. However, a taxpayer may report the contribution as a valid rollover unless later informed otherwise by the IRS. The IRS, in the course of an examination, may consider whether a taxpayer's contribution meets the requirement for a waiver. For example, the IRS may determine that the requirements for a waiver were not met because of a material misstatement in the self-certification, the reason or reasons claimed by the taxpayer for missing the 60-day deadline did not prevent the taxpayer from completing the rollover within 60 days following receipt, or the taxpayer failed to make the contribution as soon as practicable after the reason or reasons no longer prevented the taxpayer from making the contribution. In such a case, the taxpayer may be subject to additions to income or penalties, such as the penalty for failure to pay the proper amount of tax under Code Section 6651 (relating to the failure to file a return or to pay tax). [Rev. Proc. 2016-47, 2016-37 I.R.B. 346, § 3.04(2)]

Additional Waivers During Examination. In addition to automatic waivers and waivers through application to the IRS under Section 3 of Revenue Procedure 2003-16 [2003-1 I.R.B. 359] (discussed above), the IRS, in the course of examining a taxpayer's individual income tax return, may determine that the taxpayer qualifies for a waiver of the 60-day rollover requirement in Code Section 402(c)(30)(B) or 408(d)(3)(I). [Rev. Proc. 2016-47, 2016-47 I.R.B. 346, § 4]

For general information about IRS waivers of the 60-day rollover requirement, see "Retirement Plans FAQs relating to Waivers of the 60-Day Rollover Requirement," available at https://www.irs.gov/Retirement-Plans/Retirement-Plans-FAQs-relating-to-Waivers-of-the-60-Day-Rollover-Requirement.

Q 21:32 How does Code Section 402(c) apply to a distributee who is not the participant?

Spousal Distributee. If any distribution attributable to a participant is paid to the participant's surviving spouse, Code Section 402(c) applies to the distribution in the same manner as if the spouse were the participant. The same rule applies if any distribution attributable to a participant is paid in accordance with a QDRO (as defined in Code Section 414(p)) to the participant's spouse or former spouse who is an alternate payee. Therefore, a distribution to the surviving spouse of a participant (or to a spouse or former spouse who is an alternate payee under a QDRO), including a distribution of ancillary death benefits attributable to the participant, is an eligible rollover distribution if it meets the requirements of Code Sections 402(c)(2) and (4). [Treas. Reg. § 1.402(c)-2, Q&A-12(a)]

Non-Spousal Distributee. Under Code Section 402(c)(11) (which was added by PPA Section 829), if a direct trustee-to-trustee transfer of any portion of a distribution from an eligible retirement plan is made to an IRA that is established for the purpose of receiving the distribution on behalf of a designated beneficiary who is a nonspouse beneficiary, the transfer is treated as a direct rollover of an eligible rollover distribution for purposes of Code Section 402(c). The IRA of the nonspouse beneficiary is treated as an inherited IRA within the meaning of Code Section 408(d)(3)(C). PPA's nonspouse direct rollover rules began to apply to distributions made after December 31, 2006. [Code § 402(c)(11); IRS Notice 2007-7, 2007-5 I.R.B. 395, § V]

WRERA made some technical changes to PPA's provisions dealing with direct rollovers made by nonspouse beneficiaries. As mentioned above, PPA permitted nonspouse beneficiaries to directly roll over qualified plan distributions made after December 31, 2006 into inherited IRAs. In Notice 2007-7, 2007-5 I.R.B. 395, however, the IRS stated that this PPA provision was optional (i.e., that plans were not required to offer a direct rollover opportunity to a nonspouse beneficiary) and that the mandatory 20 percent withholding requirement of Code Section 3405(c) and the rollover notice requirement of Code Section 402(f) did not apply to such distributions. WRERA amended PPA to provide that, for plan years beginning after December 31, 2009 (i.e., January 1, 2010 for calendar-year plans), plans are required to give nonspouse beneficiaries the opportunity to directly roll over eligible rollover distributions into inherited IRAs, and such distributions are subject to the same rules as all other eligible rollover distributions, including mandatory 20 percent withholding and rollover notice requirements. [I.R.C. §§ 402(c)(11) and 402(f)(2)(A), as amended by WRERA § 108(f)]

Q 21:33 Must a participant's (or distributee's) election to treat a contribution of an eligible rollover distribution to an individual retirement plan as a rollover contribution be irrevocable?

In general, yes. For a contribution of an eligible rollover distribution to an individual retirement plan to constitute a rollover and thus to qualify for current exclusion from gross income, a distributee must elect, at the time the contribution is made, to treat the contribution as a rollover contribution. Such an election is made by informing the trustee, issuer, or custodian of the eligible retirement plan that the contribution is a rollover contribution and the election is irrevocable.

Once any portion of an eligible rollover distribution has been contributed to an individual retirement plan and designated as a rollover distribution, taxation of the withdrawal of the contribution from the individual retirement plan is determined under Code Section 408(d) rather than under Code Section 402 or 403. Therefore, the eligible rollover distribution is not eligible for capital gains treatment, five-year or ten-year averaging (to the extent available), or the exclusion from gross income for net unrealized appreciation on employer stock.

Direct Rollover. If an eligible rollover distribution is paid to an individual retirement plan in a direct rollover at the election of the distributee, the distributee is deemed to have irrevocably designated that the direct rollover is a rollover contribution. [Treas. Reg. § 1.402(c)-2, Q&A-13]

Q 21:34 How is the $5,000 death benefit exclusion under Code Section 101(b) treated for purposes of determining the amount that is an eligible rollover distribution?

To the extent that a death benefit is a distribution from a qualified plan, the portion of the distribution that is excluded from gross income under Code Section 101(b) is not an eligible rollover distribution. Since the Small Business Job Protection Act (SBJPA) was passed in 1996, however, the death benefit exclusion is not available with respect to decedents dying after August 20, 1996. [Treas. Reg. § 1.402(c)-2, Q&A-14; see Treas. Reg. § 1.401(e)(31)-1, Q&A-17 regarding assumptions that a plan administrator may make with respect to whether and to what extent a distribution of a survivor benefit is excludable from gross income under Code § 101(b)]

Q 21:35 May a participant (or distributee) roll over more than the plan administrator determines to be an eligible rollover distribution using permissible assumptions?

Yes. The portion of any distribution that a participant (or distributee) may roll over as an eligible rollover distribution under Code Section 402(c) is determined based on the application of Code Section 402 and other relevant provisions of the Internal Revenue Code. The application of these provisions may produce different results from any assumption used by the plan administrator (see Q 21:18). [Treas. Reg. § 1.402(c)-2, Q&A-15]

Q 21:36 How is a rollover from a qualified plan to an IRA treated for purposes of the one-year look-back rollover limitation of Code Section 408(d)(3)(B)?

A distribution from a qualified plan that is rolled over to an IRA is not treated for purposes of Code Section 408(d)(3)(B) as an amount received by an individual from an IRA that is not includible in gross income because of the application of Code Section 408(d)(3).

Q 21:37 May distributions from a Code Section 401(a) qualified retirement plan be rolled over into a Roth IRA?

Yes. The rollover may be made through a direct rollover from the plan to the Roth IRA, or an amount may be distributed from the plan and contributed (rolled over) to the Roth IRA within 60 days. In either case, the amount rolled over must be an eligible rollover distribution (as defined in Code Section 402(c)(4)) and, pursuant to the conversion rules under Code Section 408A(d)(3)(A), there must be included in gross income any amount that would be includible if the distribution were not rolled over. For taxable years beginning in 2010 only, however, the taxable amount of a rollover or a conversion to a Roth IRA that otherwise would have been includible in gross income for the taxable year beginning in 2010 is includible half in the taxable year beginning in 2011 and half in the taxable year beginning in 2012, unless the taxpayer elected to include the entire taxable amount in the taxable year beginning in 2010. In addition, for taxable years beginning before January 10, 2010, an individual cannot make a qualified rollover contribution from an eligible retirement plan other than a Roth IRA if, for the year the eligible rollover distribution is made, he or she has a modified adjusted gross income exceeding $100,000 or is married and files a separate return. [I.R.C. § 408A(e), as amended by PPA § 824; IRS Notice 2008-30, 2008-12 I.R.B. 638, § II, Q&A-1] The $100,000 limit and the requirement that a married distributee file a joint return do not apply to distributions made on or after January 1, 2010. [IRS Notice 2009-75, 2009-39 I.R.B. 436]

IRS Notice 2009-75, which modified and clarified Notice 2008-30, describes the federal income tax consequences of rolling over an eligible rollover distribution from a Code Section 401(a) qualified retirement plan, a Code Section 403(a) annuity plan, a Code Section 403(b) plan, or a Code Section 457(b) eligible governmental plan to a Code Section 408A Roth IRA.

Rollovers to a Roth IRA of Distributions That Are Not Made from a Designated Roth Account. If an eligible rollover distribution from an eligible employer plan (i.e., a 401(a), 403(a), 403(b), or 457(b) eligible governmental plan) is rolled over to a Roth IRA and the distribution is *not* made from a designated Roth account under such a plan, then the amount that would be includible in gross income were it not part of a qualified rollover contribution is included in the distributee's gross income for the year of the distribution. For this purpose, the amount included in gross income is equal to the amount rolled over, reduced by the amount of any after-tax contributions that are included in the amount rolled over, in the same manner as if the distribution had been rolled over to a non-Roth IRA that was the participant's only non-Roth IRA and that non-Roth IRA had then been immediately converted to a Roth IRA. [IRS Notice 2009-75, 2009-39 I.R.B. 436, Q&A-1(a)] An eligible rollover distribution made before January 1, 2010 from a non-Roth account under an eligible employer plan may not be rolled over to a Roth IRA unless, for the year of the distribution, the distributee's modified adjusted gross income does not exceed $100,000 and, in the case of a married distributee, the distributee files a joint federal income tax return with his or her spouse. The $100,000 limit and the requirement that a married distributee file a joint return do not apply to such distribution made on or after January 1, 2010. If an eligible rollover distribution made before 2010 is ineligible to be rolled over to a Roth IRA either because the distributee's modified adjusted gross income exceeds $100,000 or because a married distributee does not file a joint return, the distribution may be rolled over into a non-Roth IRA and then the non-Roth IRA may be converted, on or after January 1, 2010, into a Roth IRA. [IRS Notice 2009-75, 2009-39 I.R.B. 436, Q&A-2(a)]

Rollovers to a Roth IRA of Distributions That Are *Made from a Designated Roth Account.* If an eligible rollover distribution made from a designated Roth account in an eligible employer plan (described above) is rolled over to a Roth IRA, the amount rolled over is not includible in the distributee's gross income, whether or not the distribution is a qualified distribution from the designated Roth account. [IRS Notice 2009-75, 2009-39 I.R.B. 436, Q&A-1(b)] There are no restrictions based on the modified adjusted gross income limitations and joint filing requirements that apply to a rollover of an eligible rollover distribution made from a designated Roth account under an eligible employer plan to a Roth IRA. [IRS Notice 2009-75, 2009-39 I.R.B. 436, Q&A-2(b)]

Q 21:38 Can distributions from other types of retirement plans (other than Code Section 401(a) qualified retirement plans) be rolled over into a Roth IRA?

Subject to the limitations described in Q 21:37, the definition of a qualified rollover contribution in Code Section 408A(e) includes distributions from Code Section 403(a) and Code Section 403(b) annuity plans and from Code Section 457(b) eligible governmental plans. [IRS Notice 2008-30, 2008-12 I.R.B. 638, § II, Q&A-2; IRS Notice 2009-75, 2009-39 I.R.B. 436]

Q 21:39 Does the 10 percent additional tax under Code Section 72(t) apply to a qualified rollover contribution from an eligible retirement plan other than a Roth IRA?

No. Pursuant to Code Section 408A(d)(3)(A)(ii), the 10 percent additional tax under Code Section 72(t) does not apply to rollovers from an eligible retirement plan other than a Roth IRA. However, as with conversions, if a taxable amount rolled over into a Roth IRA from an eligible retirement plan other than a Roth IRA is distributed within five years, Code Section 72(t) would apply to such distribution as if it were includible in gross income. (See I.R.C. § 408A(d)(3)(F).) [IRS Notice 2008-30, 2008-12 I.R.B. 638, § II, Q&A-3]

Q 21:40 Under Code Section 401(a)(31)(A), must a plan permit a distributee of an eligible rollover distribution to elect a direct rollover into a Roth IRA?

Yes. Code Section 401(a)(31)(A) requires that a plan follow a distributee's election to have an eligible rollover distribution paid in a direct rollover to an eligible retirement plan specified by the distributee. [IRS Notice 2008-30, 2008-12 I.R.B. 638, § II, Q&A-4]

Q 21:41 Is the plan administrator responsible for ensuring that the distributee is eligible to make a rollover into a Roth IRA?

No. The plan administrator is not responsible for ensuring that the distributee is eligible to make a rollover to a Roth IRA. However, a distributee that is ineligible to make a rollover to a Roth IRA may recharacterize the contribution pursuant to Code Section 408A(d)(6). [IRS Notice 2008-30, 2008-12 I.R.B. 638, § II, Q&A-5]

Q 21:42 What are the withholding requirements for an eligible rollover distribution that is rolled over into a Roth IRA?

An eligible rollover distribution paid to an employee or the employee's spouse is subject to 20 percent mandatory withholding under Code Section 3405(c).

Pursuant to Code Section 3405(c)(2), an eligible rollover distribution that a distributee elects, under Code Section 401(a)(31)(A), to have paid directly to an eligible retirement plan (including a Roth IRA) is not subject to mandatory withholding, even if the distribution is includible in gross income. Also, a distribution that is directly rolled over into a Roth IRA by a nonspouse beneficiary pursuant to Code Section 402(c)(11) (see Q 21:43) is not subject to mandatory withholding. However, a distributee and a plan administrator are permitted to enter into a voluntary withholding agreement with respect to an eligible rollover distribution that is directly rolled over from an eligible retirement plan into a Roth IRA. (See I.R.C. § 3402(p) and the regulations thereunder relating to voluntary withholding.) [IRS Notice 2008-30, 2008-12 I.R.B. 638, § II, Q&A-6; IRS Notice 2009-75, 2009-39 I.R.B. 436]

Q 21:43 Can beneficiaries make qualified rollover contributions to Roth IRAs?

Yes. In the case of a distribution from an eligible retirement plan other than a Roth IRA, the modified adjusted gross income and filing status of the beneficiary are used to determine eligibility to make a qualified rollover contribution to the Roth IRA. Pursuant to Code Section 402(c)(11), a plan must permit rollovers by nonspouse beneficiaries, and a rollover by a nonspouse beneficiary must be made by a direct trustee-to-trustee transfer. A nonspouse beneficiary that is ineligible to make a qualified rollover contribution to a Roth IRA may recharacterize the contribution pursuant to Code Section 408A(d)(6).

Section 402(f) Rollover Notice

Q 21:44 What were the requirements for a written direct rollover notice under Code Section 402(f) before the enactment of EGTRRA?

Under Code Section 402(f), the plan administrator of a qualified plan is required, within a reasonable period of time before making an eligible rollover distribution, to provide the distributee with the written explanation described in Code Section 402(f) (Section 402(f) notice). The Section 402(f) notice must be designed to be easily understood and must explain the following: the rules under which the distributee may elect that the distribution be paid in the form of a direct rollover to an eligible retirement plan; the rules that require the withholding of tax on the distribution if it is not paid in a direct rollover; the rules under which the distributee may defer tax on the distribution if it is contributed in a rollover to an eligible retirement plan within 60 days of the distribution; and, if applicable, certain special rules regarding the taxation of the distribution as described in Code Section 5402(d) (averaging, to the extent available, with respect to lump-sum distributions) and 402(e) (other rules including treatment of net unrealized appreciation). (See Q 21:5 for additional information that must be provided if a plan provides a default procedure regarding the election of a direct rollover.)

Model Section 402(f) Notice. Code Section 402(f) applies to eligible rollover distributions made after December 31, 1992. A plan administrator will be deemed to have complied with the requirements relating to the contents of the Section 402(f) notice if the plan administrator provides the applicable model Section 402(f) notice published by the IRS. [see Notice 2009-68, 2009-39 I.R.B. 423, as modified by Notice 2014-74, 2014-50 I.R.B. 937]

Q 21:45 When must a plan administrator provide the Code Section 402(f) notice to a distributee?

A plan administrator must provide the Code Section 402(f) notice to a distributee no less than 30 days and no more than 180 days before the date of a distribution. However, if the distributee, after having received the notice, affirmatively elects a distribution, a plan will not fail to satisfy Code Section 402(f) merely because the distribution is made less than 30 days after the notice was provided. However, the plan administrator must clearly indicate that the distributee has a right to consider the decision of whether or not to elect a direct rollover for at least 30 days after the notice is provided. The plan administrator may use any method to inform the distributee of the relevant time period, provided that the method is reasonably designed to attract the attention of the distributee. For example, the information could be either included in the Section 402(f) notice or stated in a separate document (attached to the election form) that is provided at the same time as the notice. For purposes of satisfying these requirements, the plan administrator may substitute the annuity starting date, within the meaning of Treasury Regulations Section 1.401(a)-20, Q&A-10, for the date of the distribution. [PPA § 1102(a)(1)(B); Treas. Reg. § 1.402(f)-1, Q&A-2(a)]

Alternatively, a plan administrator may:

1. Provide a distributee with the Code Section 402(f) notice;
2. Provide the distributee with a summary of the Section 402(f) notice within the time period described above. The summary must set forth the principal provisions of the Section 402(f) notice, must refer the distributee to the most recent version of the Section 402(f) notice (and, in the case of a notice provided in any document containing information in addition to the notice, must identify that document and must provide a reasonable indication of where the notice may be found in that document, such as by index reference or by section heading), and must advise the distributee that, upon request, a copy of the Section 402(f) notice will be provided without charge.
3. If the distributee so requests after receiving such summary, provide the Section 402(f) notice to the distributee without charge and no less than 30 days before the date of a distribution (or the annuity starting date), subject to the rules for distributee's waiver of that 30-day period.

[PPA § 1102(a)(1)(B); Treas. Reg. § 1.402(f)-1, Q&A-2(b)]

Q 21:46 Must a plan administrator provide a separate Section 402(f) notice for each distribution in a series of periodic payments that are eligible rollover distributions?

No. In the case of a series of periodic payments that are eligible rollover distributions, the plan administrator may satisfy Code Section 402(f) with respect to each payment in a series by providing the Section 402(f) notice before the first payment in the series, in accordance with the rules (see Q 21:45), and providing the notice at least once annually for as long as the payments continue. (But see Q 21:12.) [Treas. Reg. § 1.402(f)-1, Q&A-3]

Q 21:47 May a plan administrator post the Section 402(f) notice as a means of providing it to distributees?

No. Posting the Section 402(f) notice will not be considered provision of the notice. The written notice must be provided individually to any distributee of an eligible rollover distribution within the specified time period (see Qs 21:45 and 21:46). [Treas. Reg. § 1.402(f)-1, Q&A-4]

Q 21:48 Must the Section 402(f) notice always be a written paper document?

No. A plan administrator may provide a distributee with the Section 402(f) notice or a summary notice (see Q 21:45) either on a written paper document or through an electronic medium reasonably accessible to the distributee. If the notice or summary is provided through an electronic medium, the applicable requirements of Treasury Regulations Section 1.401(a)-21 must be met.

[Treas. Reg. § 1.402(f)-1, Q&A-5]

Rollover Contributions by Employees Not Yet Eligible to Participate in a Qualified Plan

Q 21:49 If employees who have not satisfied a qualified retirement plan's minimum age and service requirements are allowed to make rollover contributions to the plan, to what extent are those employees taken into account under the plan for purposes of the minimum coverage and nondiscrimination requirements?

The extent to which such employees are taken into account under the plan for purposes of the minimum coverage requirements of Code Section 410(b) and the nondiscrimination requirements of Code Sections 401(a)(4), 401(k)(3), and 401(m)(2) are illustrated by the example below.

Example 21-11: The Salinas Valley Corporation maintains the Salinas Valley Corporation Plan, a profit sharing plan qualified under Code Section 401(a) that includes a 401(k) feature and that provides for matching and nonelective contributions. The plan does not accept after-tax employee contributions. The corporation consists of the Harvesting Division and the Canning Division. Employees of the Harvesting Division are eligible to participate in the plan—that is, to make salary deferral contributions and receive allocations of matching and nonelective contributions—when they have completed one year of service with the corporation. Employees of the Harvesting Division who have satisfied the plan's minimum one year of service requirement are also permitted to make rollover contributions to the plan. Effective January 1, 2019, the plan is amended to allow all employees of the Harvesting Division, including employees who have not completed one year of service, to make rollover contributions to the plan at any time after they begin their employment with the corporation.

Based on the above facts, the extent to which any employees who make rollover contributions to the plan before they have completed the plan's one year of service requirement are taken into account for purposes of the minimum coverage and nondiscrimination requirements is as follows:

1. The plan may treat such employees as excludable employees for purposes of the minimum coverage requirements of Code Section 410(b).
2. Also, these employees are not taken into account in applying the actual deferral percentage (ADP) test under Code Section 401(k)(3) to the portion of the plan that is a 401(k) plan, the actual contribution percentage (ACP) test to the portion of the plan that is a 401(m) plan, or the nondiscrimination in amount of contributions or benefit requirement under Code Section 401(a)(4) to the portion of the plan that consists of nonelective contributions.
3. The plan must separately satisfy the nondiscriminatory availability requirement of Treasury Regulations Section 1.401(a)(4)-1(b)(3) with respect to the right of such employees to make rollover contributions to the plan. The plan is treated as separately satisfying this requirement because it satisfies the requirements of the design-based safe harbor described in Revenue Ruling 96-48. [1996-2 C.B. 31]

Furthermore, for purposes of the top-heavy minimum contribution and benefit requirements of Code Section 416(c), employees such as those described in Example 21-11 are not participants for a plan year merely because they make (or are eligible to make) rollover contributions under the plan. Such employees, therefore, are not required to accrue minimum benefits or receive minimum allocations for years in which the plan is top heavy. [Rev. Rul. 96-48, 1996-2 C.B. 31]

Other Direct Rollover Issues

Q 21:50 If a plan separately accounts for amounts attributable to rollover contributions to the plan, will distributions of those amounts be subject to the restrictions on permissible timing that apply to distributions of other amounts from the plan?

No. If an eligible retirement plan separately accounts for amounts attributable to rollover contributions to the plan, distributions of those amounts are not subject to the restrictions on permissible timing that apply, under the applicable requirements of the Code, to distributions of other amounts from the plan. Accordingly, the plan may permit the distribution of amounts attributable to rollover contributions at any time an individual requests them.

Thus, for example, if the receiving plan is a money purchase pension plan and the plan separately accounts for amounts attributable to rollover contributions, a plan provision permitting the in-service distribution of those amounts will not cause the plan to fail to satisfy the pension plan requirements of Treasury Regulations Section 1.401-1(b)(1)(i).

However, a distribution of amounts attributable to rollover contributions is subject to the QJSA and Qualified Preretirement Survivor Annuity requirements of Code Sections 401(l)(11) and 417, the minimum distribution requirements of Code Section 401(a)(9), and the additional income tax on premature distributions under Code Section 72(t), as applicable to the receiving plan. Thus, for example, if a distribution from an IRA is rolled over into a Code Section 401(a) qualified plan, any distribution from the qualified plan of amounts attributable to the rollover would be subject to the exceptions from the Code Section 72(t) tax that apply to qualified plans and not the exceptions that apply to IRAs.

These rules do not apply to amounts received by a qualified plan as a result of a merger, consolidation, or transfer of plan assets under Code Section 414(l). [Rev. Rul. 2004-12, 2004-1 C.B. 478]

Q 21:51 May an ESOP direct certain rollovers of distributions of S corporation stock to an IRA in accordance with a distributee's election without terminating the corporation's S election?

Yes. The IRS will accept the position that an S corporation's election is not affected as a result of an employee ownership plan's (ESOP's) distribution of S corporation stock where the participant directs that such stock be distributed to an IRA in a direct rollover, provided that:

1. The terms of the ESOP require that the S corporation repurchase its stock immediately upon the ESOP's distribution of the stock to an IRA;
2. The S corporation actually repurchases the S corporation stock contemporaneously with, and effective on the same day as, the distribution; and
3. No income (including tax-exempt income), loss, deduction, or credit attributable to the distributed S corporation stock under Code Section 1366 is allocated to the participant's IRA.

Satisfaction of these three conditions ensures that the ESOP distributing the S corporation stock will meet the direct rollover requirements of Code Section 401(a)(3) and that the IRA receiving the direct rollover will not hold S corporation stock, since IRA trustees or custodians are not permissible S corporation shareholders under Code Sections 1361(b) and (c)(6). [Rev. Proc. 2003-23, 2003-11 I.R.B. 599]

Q 21:52 Under what circumstances may a defined benefit pension plan accept a direct rollover of an eligible rollover distribution from a qualified defined contribution plan maintained by the same employer where the defined benefit plan provides an annuity resulting from the direct rollover?

In Revenue Ruling 2012-4, 2012-8 I.R.B. 386, the IRS described whether a qualified defined benefit pension plan that accepted a direct rollover of an eligible rollover distribution from a qualified defined contribution plan maintained by the same employer satisfied the minimum vesting standards of Code Section 411 and the annual limitations requirements of Code Section 415 in a case where the defined benefit plan provided an annuity resulting from the direct rollover. The holdings of Revenue Ruling 2012-4 (described below) do not apply to rollovers made before January 1, 2013; however, plan sponsors may rely on the holdings of Revenue Ruling 2012-4 with respect to rollovers made before January 1, 2013.

In Revenue Ruling 2012-4, the IRS ruled that under the facts presented:

1. A qualified defined benefit plan that accepts a direct rollover of an employee's or former employee's benefit from a qualified defined contribution plan maintained by the same employer does not violate the minimum vesting standards of Code Section 411 or the annual limitations requirements of Code Section 415 if the defined benefit plan provides an annuity resulting from the direct rollover that is determined by converting the amount directly rolled over into an actuarially equivalent immediate annuity using the applicable interest rate and applicable mortality table under Code Section 417(e);
2. If a defined benefit plan were to provide an annuity resulting from the rollover amount that is determined using a *less favorable* actuarial basis than that required under the rules of Code Section 411(c) (so that the annuity is *smaller* than required under the rules of Code Section 411(c)), then the plan would *not* satisfy the minimum vesting standard of Code Section 411(a)(1); and
3. If a defined benefit plan were to provide an annuity resulting from the rollover amount that is determined using a *more favorable* actuarial basis than that required under the rules of Code Section 411(c) (so that the annuity is *larger* than required under the rules of Code Section 411(c)), then the portion of the benefit resulting from the amount directly rolled over that exceeds the benefit derived from that rolled over amount under the rules of Code Section 411(c)(2)(B) would be subject to the minimum vesting rules applicable to benefits derived from employer contributions and would be included in the annual benefit for purposes of the annual limitations requirements of Code Section 415(b) (limitation for defined benefit plans).

Q 21:53 What are the rules for allocating pre-tax and after-tax amounts among distributions that are made to multiple destinations from a Code Section 401(a) qualified retirement plan?

If a participant's account balance in a Code Section 401(a) qualified retirement plan includes both pre-tax and after-tax amounts, then distributions from the account generally are considered to include a pro rata share of both pre-tax and after-tax amounts. For example, if a participant's account balance is $100,000, and consists of $80,000 in pre-tax amounts and $20,000 in after-tax amounts, and the participant requests a distribution of $50,000, his or her distribution would consist of $40,000 of pre-tax amounts and $10,000 of after-tax amounts.

Prior to the issuance of IRS Notice 2014-54, 2014-41 I.R.B. 670, the IRS treated distributions from a retirement plan that were rolled over to multiple destinations as separate distributions to each destination, with each distribution treated as containing a pro rata portion of the pre-tax and after-tax amounts. Notice 2014-54, which was issued on September 18, 2014, provides that all disbursements from a retirement plan scheduled to be made at the same time are treated as a single distribution even if they are sent to multiple destinations. The new rule provided in Notice 2014-54 is referred to as the "single distribution rule."

As a result of Notice 2014-54, participants with pre-tax and after-tax amounts in their retirement plan, for example, can transfer through direct rollovers the pre-tax portion of the distribution (including earnings on after-tax amounts) to a traditional IRA and the after-tax portion of the distribution to a Roth IRA. (Previous interpretations allowed accomplishing this result through 60-day rollovers but not direct rollovers.) The guidance provided in Notice 2014-54 applies only to distributions from Code Section 401(a) qualified retirement plans (such as profit sharing and 401(k) plans), Code Section 403(b) tax-sheltered annuity plans, and Code Section 457(b) governmental plans. The guidance in Notice 2014-54 generally became effective January 1, 2015; however, transitional rules included in Notice 2014-54 permitted taxpayers to use the new rules provided in Notice 2014-54 prior to that general effective date. The guidance in Notice 2014-54 does not apply to distributions from IRAs. [Notice 2014-54, 2014-41 I.R.B. 670]

The IRS received a number of questions following the issuance of Notice 2014-54, and provided FAQs (https://www.irs.gov/Retirement-Plans/Rollovers-of-After-Tax-Contributions-in-Retirement-Plans) to assist taxpayers in applying Notice 2014-54:

1. In one of these FAQs, the IRS stated that a plan participant may not roll over just the after-tax amount in his or her plan account to a Roth IRA and leave the remaining amounts in the plan (i.e., take a partial distribution of just the after-tax amounts). The IRS explained that the guidance in Notice 2014-54 does not alter the requirement that each distribution from a retirement plan must include a proportional share of the pre-tax and after-tax amounts in the participant's account. Accordingly, any partial distribution from the plan must include some of the pre-tax amounts in the participant's account; that is, the participant cannot take a distribution of only

the after-tax amounts and leave the pre-tax amounts in the plan. In order to roll over all of the participant's after-tax contributions to a Roth IRA, the participant could take a distribution of the full amount (all pre-tax and after-tax amounts) in his or her account, roll over all of the pre-tax amounts in a direct rollover to a traditional IRA or another eligible retirement plan, and roll over all the after-tax amounts in a direct rollover to a Roth IRA. [IRS FAQs on Rollovers of After-Tax Contributions in Retirement Plans, available at https://www.irs.gov/Retirement-Plans/Rollovers-of-After-Tax-Contributions-in-Retirement-Plans]

2. In another of these FAQs, the IRS stated that a retirement plan participant could roll over his or her after-tax contributions from the plan to a Roth IRA and roll over earnings on his or her after-tax contributions to a traditional IRA. The IRS explained that earnings associated with the participant's after-tax contributions to his or her retirement plan are pre-tax amounts in the participant's plan account. Thus, after-tax contributions in the participant's plan account could be rolled over to a Roth IRA without also including the earnings on those contributions. The IRS further explained that, under Notice 2014-54, all pre-tax amounts in a distribution may be rolled over to a traditional IRA and, in that case, would not be included in income until distributed from the IRA. [IRS FAQs on Rollovers of After-Tax Contributions in Retirement Plans, available at https://www.irs.gov/Retirement-Plans/Rollovers-of-After-Tax-Contributions-in-Retirement-Plans]

Chapter 22

State Income Tax Withholding and FICA and FUTA Treatment

This chapter surveys the different state individual income tax withholding rules that apply to qualified plan distributions.

Survey of State Income Tax Withholding Rules 22-1
FICA and FUTA Treatment of Qualified Plan Distributions 22-5
State "Source" Taxation of Retirement Benefits 22-5

Survey of State Income Tax Withholding Rules

Q 22:1 What are the states' rules on income tax withholding?

Like the federal government, most states impose individual income taxes. Not only is there federal income tax withholding from qualified plan distributions (see chapter 24), but, in many cases, there is state income tax withholding as well.

Alabama. The state income tax withholding rules for qualified plan distributions are the same as the federal income tax withholding rules (see chapter 24).

Alaska. Alaska does not impose an individual income tax, and so qualified plan distributions are not subject to state income tax withholding.

Arizona. Individuals who receive qualified plan distributions may request state income tax withholding.

Arkansas. The state income tax withholding rules for qualified plan distributions are the same as the federal income tax withholding rules (see chapter 24).

California. Individuals who receive qualified plan distributions may request state income tax withholding.

Colorado. Individuals who receive qualified plan distributions may request state income tax withholding.

Connecticut. Payors of pensions and annuities must notify Connecticut residents that withholding is available and must withhold if the payee submits a request in writing. The minimum withholding amount is $10 per payment, and the amount withheld must be a whole dollar amount. Form CT-W4P, *Withholding Certificate for Pension or Annuity Payments*, should be completed.

Delaware. The state income tax withholding rules for qualified plan distributions are the same as the federal income tax withholding rules (see chapter 24).

District of Columbia. Withholding is required (at the highest individual income tax rate) from lump-sum distributions, but not (1) any portion of a lump-sum payment that was previously subject to tax or (2) an eligible rollover distribution. Recipients may request employers to withhold District of Columbia income tax; Form 8-1806 should be used.

Florida. Florida does not impose an individual income tax, and so qualified plan distributions are not subject to state income tax withholding.

Georgia. Recipients of qualified plan distributions may choose whether to have Georgia income tax withholding. Form G-4P should be used to elect withholding preferences. Nonperiodic payments are not subject to withholding.

Hawaii. Hawaii does not impose an individual income tax, and so qualified plan distributions are not subject to state income tax withholding.

Idaho. Individuals who receive qualified plan distributions may request state income tax withholding.

Illinois. No state income tax withholding is required for qualified plan distributions.

Indiana. No state income tax withholding is required for qualified plan distributions. Indiana payors must withhold if requested by the recipient. Non-Indiana payors may choose to withhold at the request of the recipient. Recipient must complete Form WH-4P, *Annuitant's Request for State Income Tax Withholding.*

Iowa. No state income tax withholding is required for qualified plan distributions paid to nonresidents of Iowa. For Iowa residents, state income taxes are withheld at a rate of 5 percent or in accordance with formulas or tables, unless the distributions are not subject to tax, distributions are under $250, or the taxable amount per year is less than $3,000. Recipients may be entitled to exemptions of up to $3,000.

Kansas. State income tax withholding is required on qualified plan distributions paid from Kansas sources subject to federal income tax withholding.

Kentucky. Recipients of qualified plan distributions may voluntarily elect state income tax withholding.

Louisiana. Recipients of qualified plan distributions may voluntarily elect state income tax withholding.

Maine. No state income tax withholding is required for qualified plan distributions paid to nonresidents. State income tax withholding is required on qualified plan distributions paid to residents if federal income tax withholding is required.

Maryland. The state income tax withholding rules for qualified plan distributions are the same as the federal income tax withholding rules (see chapter 24). Recipients may voluntarily elect state income tax withholding on distributions not subject to mandatory state income tax withholding; voluntary withholding must be a whole dollar amount and at least $5 per month.

Massachusetts. The state income tax withholding rules for qualified plan distributions are the same as the federal income tax withholding rules (see chapter 24). Withholding is required on qualified plan distributions paid to Massachusetts residents who have not elected to be exempt from federal income tax withholding. Form TA-1 should be used to register and pay the tax withheld.

Michigan. Recipients of qualified plan distributions may voluntarily elect state income tax withholding; voluntary withholding must be at least $5 per month. Pension withholding tables have been issued.

Minnesota. Recipients of qualified plan distributions may voluntarily elect state income tax withholding. Form W-4P, *Withholding Certificate for Pension or Annuity Payments*, should be completed.

Mississippi. Qualified plan distributions, whether or not they are subject to mandatory 20 percent federal income tax withholding, generally are not subject to state income tax withholding.

Missouri. Recipients of qualified plan distributions may voluntarily elect state income tax withholding. Form MO W-4P, *Withholding Certificate for Pension or Annuity Payments*, should be used.

Montana. Recipients of qualified plan distributions may voluntarily elect state income tax withholding.

Nebraska. Recipients of qualified plan distributions may voluntarily elect state income tax withholding.

Nevada. Nevada does not impose an individual income tax, and so qualified plan distributions are not subject to state income tax withholding.

New Hampshire. New Hampshire does not impose an individual income tax, and so qualified plan distributions are not subject to state income tax withholding.

New Jersey. Recipients of qualified plan distributions may voluntarily elect state income tax withholding; voluntary withholding must be at least $10 per payment. Recipients should complete Form NJ-W-4P, *Certificate of Voluntary Withholding of New Jersey Gross Income Tax from Pension and Annuity Payments*.

New Mexico. Recipients of qualified plan distributions may voluntarily elect state income tax withholding.

New York. Recipients of qualified plan distributions may voluntarily elect state income tax withholding; voluntary withholding must be at least $5 per month. Recipients should complete Form IT-2104-P, *Annuitant's Request for Income Tax Withholding.*

North Carolina. Recipients of qualified plan distributions may voluntarily elect state income tax withholding.

North Dakota. Recipients of qualified plan distributions may voluntarily elect state income tax withholding.

Ohio. Recipients of qualified plan distributions may voluntarily elect state income tax withholding.

Oklahoma. The state income tax withholding rules for qualified plan distributions are the same as the federal income tax withholding rules (see chapter 24).

Oregon. The state income tax withholding rules for qualified plan distributions are the same as the federal income tax withholding rules (see chapter 24).

Pennsylvania. State income tax withholding is required from any portion of the distribution that was not taxed previously.

Rhode Island. Recipients of qualified plan distributions may voluntarily elect state income tax withholding.

South Carolina. Recipients of qualified plan distributions may voluntarily elect state income tax withholding.

South Dakota. South Dakota does not impose an individual income tax, and so qualified plan distributions are not subject to state income tax withholding.

Tennessee. Tennessee does not impose an individual income tax, and so qualified plan distributions are not subject to state income tax withholding.

Texas. Texas does not impose an individual income tax, and so qualified plan distributions are not subject to state income tax withholding.

Utah. Recipients of qualified plan distributions may voluntarily elect state income tax withholding.

Vermont. State income tax withholding is not required on qualified plan distributions unless federal income tax is withheld. State income tax withholding also is required if federal income tax withholding is voluntarily elected.

Virginia. The state income tax withholding rules for qualified plan distributions are the same as the federal income tax withholding rules (see chapter 24). The recipient may elect no withholding if: (1) the same choice was made for federal purposes; (2) the recipient is a nonresident; (3) the recipient expects to have no tax liability; or (4) the recipient's adjusted gross income is less than the applicable dollar threshold for the given year.

Washington. Washington does not impose an individual income tax, and so qualified plan distributions are not subject to state income tax withholding.

West Virginia. Recipients of qualified plan distributions may voluntarily elect state income tax withholding. Form IT-104, *Employee's Withholding Exemption Certificate*, should be completed.

Wisconsin. State income tax withholding is not required for qualified plan distributions received by nonresidents after retirement for services performed in Wisconsin. Payors must withhold state income tax from qualified plan distribution at the recipient's request.

Wyoming. Wyoming does not impose an individual income tax, and so qualified plan distributions are not subject to state income tax withholding.

FICA and FUTA Treatment of Qualified Plan Distributions

Q 22:2 How are distributions from qualified plans treated?

Distributions from qualified plans are not wages for purposes of the Federal Insurance Contributions Act (FICA) or the Federal Unemployment Tax Act (FUTA) and so are not subject to FICA or FUTA taxes. [I.R.C. §§ 3121(a)(13), 3306(b)(10)]

State "Source" Taxation of Retirement Benefits

Q 22:3 What is the State Taxation of Pension Income Act of 1995, and what effect does it have on qualified plan distributions?

The State Taxation of Pension Income Act of 1995 [Pub. L. No. 104-95] prohibits any state from taxing pension distributions made to individuals who have moved out of the state where they earned the pension. The act protects all distributions from qualified retirement plans (including, for this purpose, plans described under Code Section 401(a) or 401(k), simplified employee pensions (SEPs), individual retirement accounts or annuities (IRAs), tax-sheltered annuities under Code Section 403(b), nonqualified deferred compensation plans under Code Section 457, governmental plans, and Section 501(c)(18) trusts). The act also protects distributions from nonqualified plans, but only if they:

1. Are made over 10 or more years, or over the life or life expectancy of the employee (or the joint life or joint life expectancy of the employee and his or her beneficiary); or
2. Are received after the employee terminates employment under an excess benefit, mirror, or wraparound plan; that is, a plan that is designed to provide benefits over the limitations set forth in Code Sections 401(a)(17), 401(m), 402(g), 403(b), 408(k), or 415.

Chapter 23

Plan Disqualification and Self-Correction Programs

The disqualification of a qualified retirement plan may result in adverse tax consequences for the plan's sponsoring employer, the plan's underlying trust, and plan participants. IRS Revenue Procedure 2016-51 [2016-42 I.R.B. 465] updates the comprehensive system of correction programs for sponsors of retirement plans that are intended to satisfy the requirements of Code Section 401(a), 403(a), 403(b), 408(k), or 408(p) but that have not met those requirements for a period of time. This system, the Employee Plans Compliance Resolution System (EPCRS), permits plan sponsors to correct these failures and thereby continue to provide their employees with retirement benefits on a tax-favored basis. The components of EPCRS are the Self-Correction Program (SCP), the Voluntary Correction Program (VCP), and the Audit Closing Agreement Program (Audit CAP). This chapter covers EPCRS as it applies to Section 401(a) qualified retirement plans. Revenue Procedure 2016-51 modified and superseded Revenue Procedure 2013-12 [2013-4 I.R.B. 313], which was the prior consolidated statement of the correction programs under EPCRS. Revenue Procedure 2016-51 also modified and superseded Revenue Procedure 2015-17 [2015-16 I.R.B. 914] and Revenue Procedure 2015-28 [2015-16 I.R.B. 920], each of which had modified Revenue Procedure 2013-12. Section 2.04 of Revenue Procedure 2016-51 describes most of the modifications to Revenue Procedure 2013-12 that are reflected in Revenue Procedure 2016-51. Some of the key changes reflected in Revenue Procedure 2016-51 are as follows:

- Determination letter applications are no longer permitted when applying for correction programs under EPCRS.
- The fees associated with the VCP program are now user fees and are no longer set forth in the EPCRS revenue procedure. Instead, the VCP user fees are found in the annual IRS

Employee Plans revenue procedure that sets forth user fees. For example, for VCP submissions made in 2017, the applicable VCP fees are set forth in Revenue Procedure 2017-4 [2017-1 I.R.B. 146], Appendix A.08.

- The availability of SCP for significant failures has been modified to provide that, for qualified individually designed plans, a determination letter need not be current to satisfy the favorable letter requirement.

The Pension Protection Act of 2006 (PPA) clarified that the Secretary of the Treasury has the full authority to establish and implement EPCRS (or any successor program) and any other employee plans correction policies, including the authority to waive income, excise, or other taxes to ensure that any tax, penalty, or sanction is not excessive and bears a reasonable relationship to the nature, extent, and severity of the failure. [PPA § 1101(a)] In addition, PPA directed the Secretary of the Treasury to continue to update and improve EPCRS (or any successor program), giving special attention to (1) increasing the awareness and knowledge of small employers concerning the availability and use of EPCRS; (2) taking into account special concerns and circumstances that small employers face with respect to compliance and correction of compliance failures; (3) extending the duration of the self-correction period under SCP for significant compliance failures; (4) expanding the availability to correct insignificant compliance failures under SCP during audit; and (5) assuring that any tax, penalty, or sanction that is imposed by reason of a compliance failure is not excessive and bears a reasonable relationship to the nature, extent, and severity of the failure. [PPA § 1101(b)] The PPA provisions relating to EPCRS became effective on August 17, 2006, PPA's enactment date.

In Revenue Procedure 2013-12, the IRS asked for comments on EPCRS improvements, including: (1) how to correct failures to implement automatic enrollment for elective deferrals in a Code Section 401(k) or 403(b) plan; (2) whether Appendix A.05(2)(d)(ii) to Revenue Procedure 2013-12 should also be applied to a Code Section 401(k)(13) safe harbor plan that has automatic escalation in elective deferrals; and (3) how to resolve specific issues relating to safe harbor notices and designated Roth contributions. [Rev. Proc. 2012-13, § 2.05] Revenue Procedure 2013-12 was modified and superseded by Revenue Procedure 2016-51.

On March 27, 2015, the IRS issued Revenue Procedure 2015-27, which modified Revenue Procedure 2013-12 and made miscellaneous changes to improve EPCRS, such as reducing VCP compliance fees relating to failures to meet the requirements of

Code Section 72(p) with respect to participant loans, and clarifying that, for certain "overpayments," as defined in Sections 5.01(3)(c) and 5.02(4) of Revenue Procedure 2013-12, a plan may use correction methods other than those set forth in the applicable sections of Revenue Procedure 2013-12. [Rev. Proc. 2015-27, § 1] The other modifications to Revenue Procedure 2013-12 are described in Section 3.03 of Revenue Procedure 2015-27. Revenue Procedure 2015-27 modifies, but does not supersede, Revenue Procedure 2013-12. [Rev. Proc. 2015-27, § 3.01] Revenue Procedure 2015-27 is generally effective July 1, 2015, but plan sponsors are permitted, at their option, to apply the provisions of Revenue Procedure 2015-27 on or after March 27, 2015, the date the IRS issued Revenue Procedure 2015-27. [Rev. Proc. 2015-27, § 6] In Revenue Procedure 2015-27, the Treasury Department and the IRS continued to invite further comments on how to improve EPCRS. [Rev. Proc. 2015-27, § 2.03] Revenue Procedure 2015-27 was modified and superseded by Revenue Procedure 2016-51.

In addition, on April 2, 2015, the IRS issued Revenue Procedure 2015-28, which further modified Revenue Procedure 2013-12 by (1) adding new safe harbor EPCRS correction methods relating to automatic contribution features (including automatic enrollment and automatic escalation of elective deferrals under Code Section 401(k) and 403(b) plans and (2) adding special safe harbor correction methods for plans (including those with automatic contribution features) that have failures that are of limited duration and involve elective deferrals. As in Revenue Procedure 2015-27, the Treasury Department and the IRS continued, in Revenue procedure 2015-28, to invite further comments on how to improve EPCRS. [Rev. Proc. 2015-28, § 2.06] Like Revenue Procedure 2015-27, Revenue Procedure 2015-28 modifies, but does not supersede, Revenue Procedure 2013-12. [Rev. Proc. 2015-28, § 3.01] Revenue Procedure 2015-28 became effective on April 2, 2015. [Rev. Proc. 2015-28, § 6] Revenue Procedure 2015-28 was modified and superseded by Revenue Procedure 2016-51.

On August 10, 2015, the IRS issued Announcement 2015-19, 2015-32 I.R.B. 157, which sharply curtailed the IRS's determination letter program for individually designed qualified retirement plans. In Announcement 2015-19, the IRS requested comments on a number of issues, including what changes should be made to other IRS programs, including EPCRS, to facilitate the changes described in the announcement. Revenue Procedure 2016-51 reflects the curtailment of the IRS determination letter program for individually designed qualified retirement plans.

In Revenue Procedure 2018-4, 2018-1 I.R.B. 146, the IRS changed the system for determining VCP user fees under EPCRS, effective for VCP submissions made on or after January 2, 2018. Under the new system, most VCP submissions made on or after January 2, 2018, are subject to a simplified VCP user fee structure based solely upon the amount of total net assets in the retirement plan, determined from the plan's most recently filed Form 5500 series return.

Disqualification Events 23-4
Alternatives to Plan Disqualification—SCP, VCP, and Audit CAP 23-7
Program Eligibility 23-7
Self-Correction Program (SCP) Requirements 23-13
Voluntary Correction Program (VCP) Requirements 23-17
Audit Closing Agreement Program (Audit CAP) Requirements 23-21
Consequences of Plan Disqualification 23-24

Disqualification Events

Q 23:1 What events may cause a qualified retirement plan to become disqualified?

Any number of circumstances may cause a qualified retirement plan to fail to meet the qualification requirements. Just one operational violation of the provisions of Code Section 401(a) may cause the plan to become disqualified. Selected provisions of Code Section 401(a) are shown in the chart below, with possible violations.

Code Section	*Description of Requirements*	*Possible Violations*
401(a)	Exclusive benefit rule	Ineligible employees are enrolled as participants under the plan.
401(a)(2)	Reversion of contributions to the employer before benefits paid to participants	Plan sponsor borrows 90% of plan assets.
401(a)(3)	Minimum coverage rules of Code Section 410(b)	Plan fails ratio percentage test and average benefits test.
401(a)(4)	Contributions or benefits must not discriminate in favor of HCEs	A plan fails nondiscrimination rules.

Code Section	*Description of Requirements*	*Possible Violations*
401(a)(5)	Permitted disparity rules	A defined contribution plan only allocates contributions on earnings above $100,000.
401(a)(7)	Minimum vesting rules	A plan contains a 20-year cliff vesting schedule.
401(a)(9)	Minimum distribution rules	A plan fails to distribute benefits to an employee who has reached his or her required beginning date.
401(a)(10)	Top-heavy rules	A plan sponsor with a top-heavy defined benefit plan (as its only plan) fails to provide top-heavy minimum benefits to non-key employees.
401(a)(11)	Qualified joint and survivor annuity rules and preretirement survivor annuities	A plan fails to secure the consent of the participant's spouse when a lump-sum distribution of $150,000 is made.
401(a)(13)	Anti-assignment and anti-alienation rules	A participant assigns his or her interest in a plan as collateral for a home mortgage.
401(a)(14)	Latest time for commencement of benefits	A plan sponsor fails to distribute benefits at age 65 when the participant has terminated employment and has passed the fifth anniversary of commencement of participation.
401(a)(16)	Benefits and contributions limited by Code Section 415	A plan sponsor contributes $60,000 in 2017 to the account of a participant in a defined contribution plan.
401(a)(17)	$275,000 compensation cap (in 2018)	All of a participant's compensation of $300,000 is used in determining benefits under a plan for the 2018 plan year.
401(a)(19)	Nonforfeiture of employee contributions	Mandatory contributions of $5,000 from an employee are forfeited.
401(a)(22)	Purchase of employer securities	A money purchase or target plan uses 50% of its assets to buy employer securities.

Code Section	Description of Requirements	Possible Violations
401(a)(26)	Minimum participation requirements	A defined benefit plan fails to cover 40% of all nonexcludable employees and covers fewer than 50 employees.
401(a)(28)	ESOP diversification requirements	An ESOP fails to provide an option to diversify investments to a participant who has reached age 55 and has at least 10 years of participation in the plan.
401(a)(29)	Security requirement for underfunded defined benefit plan making plan amendment	Plan underfunded by 50% amends plan to increase benefits without posting security.
401(a)(30)	Limits on elective deferrals	401(k) plan allows a participant to defer $30,000 in the calendar year 2018.
401(a)(31)	Direct rollovers	Plan distributes $20,000 directly to participant, despite participant's request to directly roll over to IRA.
401(a)(33)	Prohibitions on benefit increases while plan sponsor is in bankruptcy	A defined benefit plan (where the plan sponsor has filed under Chapter 11) amends its plan to increase benefits by 10%.

Other problems that may cause a qualified retirement plan to lose its qualified status are:

1. Failure to maintain documents in compliance with applicable law;
2. Failure to follow the terms of the plan; and
3. Failure to operate the plan's trust in accordance with the exclusive benefit rule.

Example 23-1: The profit-sharing plan and trust of the Pastures of Heaven Corporation have been in existence for nearly 10 years; the trust assets total nearly $600,000, with 10 employees currently participating. Meredith decides to renovate her barn and removes all the funds from the plan to pay the contractors for building supplies. It is likely that an IRS auditor would examine this plan and determine that it is not operated for the exclusive benefit of the participants and beneficiaries. The plan would likely be disqualified. Meredith would also be subject to the prohibited transaction rules of ERISA.

Alternatives to Plan Disqualification—SCP, VCP, and Audit CAP

Q 23:2 What programs are available to a plan sponsor who wants to lessen the financial impact of plan disqualification?

The IRS has three programs to help qualified retirement plans lessen the financial effects of plan disqualification. The two voluntary programs are the SCP and the VCP with IRS approval, and the correction on audit program is the Audit CAP.

1. *SCP.* A plan sponsor that has established compliance practices and procedures may, at any time and without paying any fee or sanction, correct insignificant operational failures. In addition, in the case of a qualified plan that meets the applicable SCP eligibility requirements, the plan sponsor generally may correct even significant operational failures without payment of any fee or sanction.
2. *VCP.* A plan sponsor, at any time before audit, may pay a limited fee and receive the IRS's approval for correction of a qualified plan failure. Under VCP, there are special procedures for anonymous submissions and group submissions.
3. *Audit CAP.* If a failure (other than a failure corrected through SCP or VCP) is identified on audit, the plan sponsor may correct the failure under Audit CAP and pay a sanction. The sanction imposed will bear a reasonable relationship to the nature, extent, and severity of the failure, taking into account the extent to which correction occurred before audit.

[Rev. Proc. 2016-51, § 1.03]

Program Eligibility

Q 23:3 What qualified retirement plan failures may be corrected under SCP?

Operational Failures. SCP is available only for operational failures. Qualified retirement plans are eligible for SCP with respect to significant and insignificant operational failures. [Rev. Proc. 2016-51, § 4.01(1)]

With respect to a qualified retirement plan, an "operational failure" means a qualification failure (other than an employer eligibility failure) that arises solely from the failure to follow plan provisions. A failure to follow the terms of the plan providing for the satisfaction of the requirements of Code Section 401(k) and Code Section 401(m) is considered to be an operational failure. A plan does not have an operational failure to the extent the plan may be amended retroactively to reflect the plan's operations (e.g., pursuant to Code Section 401(b)). In the situation where a plan sponsor timely adopted an amendment and the plan was not operated in accordance with the terms of the amendment, the plan is considered to have an operational failure. [Rev. Proc. 2016-51, § 5.01(2)(b)]

Effect of Examination. If a plan or plan sponsor is under IRS examination, insignificant operational failures can be corrected under SCP and, if correction of significant operational failures has been completed or substantially completed before the plan or plan sponsor is under examination, correction of those failures can be completed under SCP. [Rev. Proc. 2016-51, § 4.02]

Favorable Letter Requirement. The provisions of SCP relating to significant operational failures are available for a qualified retirement plan only if, as of the date of correction, the plan is the subject of a favorable letter. [Rev. Proc. 2016-51, § 4.03(1)] With respect to an individually designed qualified retirement plan, the term "favorable letter" means a determination letter issued with respect to the plan (there is no longer any requirement that the determination letter be a "current" determination letter). [Rev. Proc. 2016-51, §§ 4.03(1) and 5.01(4)(a)] For a qualified retirement plan that is a master or prototype or volume submitter plan, the term "favorable letter" means a current favorable opinion letter (for a master or prototype plan) or a current favorable advisory letter (for a volume submitter plan). [Rev. Proc. 2016-51, §§ 4.03(2) and 5.01(4)(b)]

Established Practices and Procedures. To be eligible for SCP, the plan sponsor or administrator of a plan must have established practices and procedures (formal or informal) reasonably designed to promote and facilitate overall compliance in form and operation with applicable Code requirements. For example, the plan administrator of a qualified retirement plan that may be top-heavy under Code Section 416 may include in its plan operating manual a specific annual step to determine whether the plan is top heavy and, if so, to ensure that the minimum contribution requirements of the top-heavy rules are satisfied. A plan document alone does not constitute evidence of established procedures. In order for a plan sponsor or administrator to use SCP, these established procedures must have been in place and routinely followed, and an operational failure must have occurred through an oversight or mistake in applying them. SCP may also be used in situations where the operational failure occurred because the procedures that were in place, while reasonable, were not sufficient to prevent the occurrence of the failure. A plan that provides for elective deferrals and nonelective employer contributions that are not matching contributions is not treated as failing to have established practices and procedures to prevent the occurrence of a Code Section 415(c) violation if, under the plan, excess annual additions under Code Section 415(c) are regularly corrected by return of elective deferrals to the affected employee within nine and one-half months after the end of the plan's limitation year. The correction, however, should not violate another applicable Code requirement. In the case of a failure that relates to transferred assets or to a plan assumed in connection with a corporate merger, acquisition, or other similar employer transaction between the plan sponsor and the sponsor of the transferor plan or the prior plan sponsor of an assumed plan, the plan is considered to have established practices and procedures for the transferred assets if such practices and procedures are in effect for the transferred assets by the end of the first plan year that begins after the corporate merger, acquisition, or similar transaction. [Rev. Proc. 2016-51, § 4.04]

Availability of Correction by Plan Amendment. A qualified retirement plan sponsor may use SCP to correct an operational failure by plan amendment in order to conform the plan document to the plan's prior operations only to correct the operational failures listed in Section 2.07 of Appendix B to Revenue Procedure 2016-51 (i.e., Code Section 401(a)(17) failures, hardship distribution failures, plan loan failures, and early inclusion of otherwise eligible employee failures). These failures must be corrected in accordance with the correction methods set forth in Section 2.07 of Appendix B to Revenue Procedure 2016-51. SCP is not otherwise available for a plan sponsor to correct an operational failure by plan amendment. Any plan amendment must comply with the requirements of Code Section 401(a), including the requirements of Code Sections 401(a)(4), 410(b), and 411(d)(6). If a plan sponsor corrects an operational failure in accordance with the approved correction methods under Appendix B to Revenue Procedure 2016-51, it may amend the plan to reflect the corrective action. For example, if the plan failed to satisfy the actual deferral percentage (ADP) test required under Code Section 401(k)(3) and the plan sponsor makes qualified nonelective contributions (QNECs) not already provided for under the plan, the plan may be amended to provide for QNECs. SCP is not otherwise available for a plan sponsor to correct an operational failure by plan amendment. [Rev. Proc. 2016-51, § 4.05(2)]

SCP Not Available to Correct an Employer Eligibility Failure. SCP is not available for a plan sponsor to correct an employer eligibility failure. [Rev. Proc. 2015-51, § 4.06] The term "employer eligibility failure" in this context means the adoption of a plan intended to include a qualified cash or deferred arrangement under Code Section 401(k) by an employer that fails to meet the employer eligibility requirements to establish a Code Section 401(k) plan. [Rev. Proc. 2016-51, § 5.01(2)(d)]

SCP Not Available to Correct an Orphan Plan. SCP is not available for correcting failures in orphan plans. [Rev. Proc. 2016-51, § 4.08] An "orphan plan" includes a qualified retirement plan with respect to which an eligible party has determined that the plan sponsor no longer exists, cannot be located, or is unable to maintain the plan. The term "orphan plan," however, does not include any plan subject to Title I of ERISA that is terminated pursuant to DOL Regulations Section 2578.1, which governs the termination of abandoned individual account plans. [Rev. Proc. 2016-51, § 5.03(1)]

Egregious Failures. SCP is not available to correct operational failures that are egregious. [Rev. Proc. 2016-51, § 4.10(2)] An "egregious failure" would include any case in which the IRS concludes that the parties controlling the plan recognized that the action taken would constitute a qualification failure and the failure either involves a substantial number of participants or beneficiaries or involves participants who are predominantly highly compensated employees (HCEs). [Rev. Proc. 2016-51, § 4.10(3)] VCP is available to correct egregious failures. [Rev. Proc. 2016-51, § 4.10(3)]

Diversion or Misuse of Plan Assets. SCP is not available to correct failures relating to the diversion or misuse of plan assets. [Rev. Proc. 2016-51, § 4.11]

Abusive Tax Avoidance Transactions. If the plan or plan sponsor has been a party to an abusive tax avoidance transaction (as defined in Revenue Procedure 2016-51, Section 4.12(2)), SCP is not available to correct any operational failure that is directly or indirectly related to the abusive tax avoidance transaction. [Rev. Proc. 2016-51, § 4.12(1)(a)]

Q 23:4 What qualified retirement plan failures may be corrected under VCP?

VCP provides general procedures for correction of *all* qualification failures: operational failures (see Q 23:3), plan document failures, demographic failures, and employer eligibility failures (see Q 23:3). VCP also provides general procedures for the correction of participant loans that did not comply with the requirements of Code Section 72(p)(2). [Rev. Proc. 2016-51, § 4.01(2)]

With respect to a qualified retirement plan, the term "plan document failure" means a plan provision (or the absence of a plan provision) that, on its face, violates the requirements of Code Section 401(a). A plan document failure includes any qualification failure that is a violation of the requirements of Code Section 401(a) and that is not an operational failure (as defined in Revenue Procedure 2016-51, § 5.01(2)(b)), a demographic failure (as defined in Revenue Procedure 2016-51, § 5.01(2)(c)), or an employer eligibility failure (as defined in Revenue Procedure 2016-51, § 5.01(2)(d)). [Rev. Proc. 2016-51, § 5.01(2)(a)(i)] The term "plan document failure" includes a nonamender failure (as defined in Revenue Procedure 2016-51, § 5.01(2)(a)(ii)(C)), a failure to adopt good faith amendments (as defined in Revenue Procedure 2016-51, § 5.01(2)(a)(ii)(A)), and a failure to adopt interim amendments (as defined in Revenue Procedure 2016-51, § 5.01(2)(a)(ii)(B)). On the other hand, a failure to adopt a discretionary amendment by the plan adoption deadline set forth in Section 8.02 of Revenue Procedure 2016-37 [2016-29 I.R.B. 136] (or, prior to January 1, 2017, Section 5.05(2) of Revenue Procedure 2007-44 [2007-28 I.R.B. 54], which was superseded by Revenue Procedure 2016-37), is not considered a "plan document failure." [Rev. Proc. 2016-51, § 5.01(2)(a)(i)]

Effect of Examination. If the plan or plan sponsor is under examination (as defined in Revenue Procedure 2016-51, Section 5.08) by the IRS, VCP is not available. [Rev. Proc. 2016-51, § 4.02]

Availability of Correction by Plan Amendment. A plan sponsor of a qualified plan may use VCP to correct plan document, demographic, and operational failures by a plan amendment, including correcting an operational failure by a plan amendment to conform the terms of the plan to the plan's prior operations, provided that the amendment complies with the applicable requirements of Code Section 401(a), including the nondiscrimination requirements of Code Section 401(a)(4), the minimum coverage requirements of Code Section 410(b), and the anti-cutback rules of Code Section 411(d)(6). In addition, a plan sponsor may adopt a plan amendment to reflect the corrective action. For example, if the plan failed to satisfy the ADP test required under Code Section 401(k)(3) and the plan sponsor must make QNECs not already provided for under the plan, the plan may be amended to provide for QNECs. The issuance of a compliance statement constitutes a determination that the failure identified has been corrected, but does not constitute a determination that the terms of the plan, including the corrective plan amendment, satisfy the qualification requirements in form. [Rev. Proc. 2016-51, § 4.05(1)]

Availability of Correction for a Terminated Plan. Correction of qualification failures in a terminated plan may be made under VCP, whether or not the plan trust or contract is still in existence. [Rev. Proc. 2016-51, § 4.07]

Availability of Correction for an Orphan Plan. A failure in an orphan plan that is terminating may be corrected only under VCP and Audit CAP, provided that the party acting on behalf of the plan is an eligible party (as defined in Section 5.03(2) of Revenue Procedure 2016-51). SCP is not available for correcting failures in orphan plans. [Rev. Proc. 2016-51, § 4.08] An "orphan plan" includes a qualified retirement plan with respect to which an eligible party has determined that the plan sponsor no longer exists, cannot be located, or is unable to maintain the plan. The term "orphan plan," however, does not include any plan subject to Title I of ERISA that is terminated pursuant to DOL Regulations Section 2578.1, governing the termination of abandoned individual account plans. [Rev. Proc. 2016-51, § 5.03(1)]

Egregious Failures. VCP is available to correct egregious failures. However, the IRS reserves the right to impose a sanction that may be larger than the user fee described in the annual IRS revenue procedure that sets forth user fees, including VCP user fees (for example, Revenue Procedure 2017-4, 2017-1 I.R.B. 146). For this purpose, an "egregious failure" would include any case in which the IRS concludes that the parties controlling the plan recognized that the action taken would constitute a failure and the failure either involves a substantial number of participants or beneficiaries or involves participants who are predominantly HCEs. [Rev. Proc. 2016-51, § 4.10(3)]

Diversion or Misuse of Plan Assets. VCP is not available to correct failures relating to the diversion or misuse of plan assets. [Rev. Proc. 2016-51, § 4.11]

Abusive Tax Avoidance Transactions. With respect to VCP, if the IRS determines that a plan or plan sponsor was, or may have been, a party to an abusive tax avoidance transaction (as defined in Section 4.12(2) of Revenue Procedure 2016-51), then the matter will be referred to the IRS Employee Plans Tax Shelter Coordinator. Upon receiving a response from the Tax Shelter Coordinator, the IRS may determine that the plan or the plan sponsor has been a party to an abusive tax avoidance transaction, and that the failures addressed in the VCP submission are related to that transaction. In those situations, the IRS will conclude the review of the VCP submission without issuing a compliance statement and will refer the case for examination. However, if the Tax Shelter Coordinator determines that the plan failures are unrelated to the abusive tax avoidance transaction or that no abusive tax avoidance transaction occurred, then the IRS will continue to address the failures identified in the VCP submission, and may issue a compliance statement with respect to those failures. In no event may a compliance statement be relied on for the purpose of concluding that the plan or plan sponsor was not a party to an abusive tax avoidance transaction. In addition, even if it is concluded that the failures can be addressed pursuant to a VCP submission, the IRS reserves the right to make a referral of the abusive tax avoidance transaction matter for examination. [Rev. Proc. 2016-51, § 4.12(1)(b)]

Q 23:5 What qualified retirement plan failures may be corrected under Audit CAP?

Unless otherwise provided in Revenue Procedure 2016-51, Audit CAP is available to qualified retirement plans for correction of all failures found on IRS examination that have not been corrected in accordance with SCP or VCP. Audit CAP also provides general procedures for the correction of participant loans that did not comply with the requirements of Code Section 72(p)(2). [Rev. Proc. 2016-51, § 4.01(3)]

Availability of Correction by Plan Amendment. A qualified retirement plan sponsor may use Audit CAP to correct plan document, demographic, and operational failures by a plan amendment, including correcting an operational failure by a plan amendment to conform the terms of the plan to the plan's prior operations, provided that the amendment complies with the applicable requirements of Code Section 401(a), including the nondiscrimination requirements of Code Section 401(a)(4), the minimum coverage requirements of Code Section 410(b), and the anti-cutback rules of Code Section 411(d)(6). In addition, a plan sponsor may adopt a plan amendment to reflect the corrective action. For example, if the plan failed to satisfy the ADP test required under Code Section 401(k)(3) and the plan sponsor must make QNECs not already provided for under the plan, the plan may be amended to provide for QNECs. The issuance of a compliance statement constitutes a determination that the failure identified has been corrected, but does not constitute a determination that the terms of the plan, including the corrective amendment, satisfy the qualification requirements in form. [Rev. Proc. 2016-51, § 4.05(1)]

Availability of Correction for a Terminated Plan. Correction of qualification failures in a terminated plan may be made under Audit CAP, whether or not the plan trust or contract is still in existence. [Rev. Proc. 2016-51, § 4.07]

Availability of Correction for an Orphan Plan. A failure in an orphan plan that is terminating may be corrected only under Audit CAP and VCP, provided that the party acting on behalf of the plan is an eligible party. SCP is not available for correcting failures in orphan plans. [Rev. Proc. 2016-51, § 4.08] An "orphan plan" includes a qualified retirement plan with respect to which an eligible party has determined that the plan sponsor no longer exists, cannot be located, or is unable to maintain the plan. The term "orphan plan," however, does not include any plan subject to Title I of ERISA that is terminated pursuant to DOL Regulations Section 2578.1, which governs the termination of abandoned individual account plans. [Rev. Proc. 2016-51, § 5.03(1)]

Egregious Failures. Audit CAP is available to correct egregious failures. [Rev. Proc. 2016-51, § 4.10(4)]

Diversion or Misuse of Plan Assets. Audit CAP is not available to correct failures relating to the diversion or misuse of plan assets. [Rev. Proc. 2016-51, § 4.11]

Abusive Tax Avoidance Transactions. For plans under examination, if the IRS determines that the plan or plan sponsor was, or may have been, a party to an abusive tax avoidance transaction, the matter may be referred to the IRS Employee Plans Tax Shelter Coordinator. With respect to plans under examination, an abusive tax avoidance transaction includes a transaction described in Section 4.12(2) of Revenue Procedure 2016-51 and any other transaction that the IRS determines was designed to facilitate the impermissible avoidance of tax. Upon receiving a response from the Tax Shelter Coordinator, the following may occur: (1) if the IRS determines that a failure is related to the abusive tax avoidance transaction, the IRS reserves the right to conclude that neither Audit CAP nor SCP is available for that failure, or (2) if the IRS determines that satisfactory corrective actions have not been taken with regard to the transaction, the IRS reserves the right to conclude that neither Audit CAP nor SCP is available for the plan. [Rev. Proc. 2016-51, § 4.12(1)(c)]

Self-Correction Program (SCP) Requirements

Q 23:6 How are insignificant operational failures corrected under SCP?

SCP is available to correct an insignificant operational failure (see Q 23:3) even if the plan or plan sponsor is under IRS examination and even if the operational failure is discovered by an IRS agent on examination. [Rev. Proc. 2016-51, § 8.01]

Factors Considered. The factors to be considered in determining whether or not an operational failure under a plan is insignificant include, but are not limited to:

1. Whether other failures occurred during the period being examined (for this purpose, a failure is not considered to have occurred more than once merely because more than one participant is affected by the failure);
2. The percentage of plan assets and contributions involved in the failure;
3. The number of years the failure occurred;
4. The number of participants affected relative to the total number of participants in the plan;
5. The number of participants affected as a result of the failure relative to the number of participants who could have been affected by the failure;
6. Whether correction was made within a reasonable time after discovery of the failure; and
7. The reason for the failure (e.g., data errors, such as errors in the transcription of data, the transposition of numbers, or minor arithmetic errors).

No single factor is determinative. Additionally, factors 2, 4, and 5 above should not be interpreted to exclude small businesses. [Rev. Proc. 2016-51, § 8.02]

Multiple Failures. In the case of a plan with more than one operational failure in a single year, or operational failures that occur in more than one year, the operational failures are eligible for correction under SCP only if all the operational failures are insignificant in the aggregate. Operational failures that have been corrected under that portion of SCP that covers the correction of significant operational failures, or operational failures that have been corrected under VCP, are not taken into account for purposes of determining if operational failures are insignificant in the aggregate. [Rev. Proc. 2016-51, § 8.03]

Examples. The following examples illustrate the application of SCP to self-correct insignificant operational failures. Each example assumes that the eligibility requirements of Revenue Procedure 2016-51 relating to SCP (for example, the requirements in Section 4.04 of Revenue Procedure 2016-51 relating to established practices and procedures) have been satisfied and that no operational failures occurred except the ones identified.

Example 23-2: In 2016, Pastures of Heaven, Inc. established The Pastures of Heaven Plan, a profit-sharing plan that satisfies the requirements of Code Section 401(a) in form. In 2018, the benefits of 50 of the 250 participants in the plan were limited by Code Section 415(c). However, when the IRS examined the plan in 2019, it discovered that, during the 2018 limitation year, the annual additions allocated to the accounts of three employees exceeded the maximum limits under Code Section 415(c). The employer contributed $3.5 million to the plan for the plan year. The amount of the excesses totaled $4,550. Because the number of participants affected by the failure relative to the total number of participants who could have been affected by the failure, and the monetary amount of the failure relative to the total employer contribution to the plan for the 2018 plan year are insignificant, the Section 415(c) failure in the plan that occurred in 2018 would be eligible for correction under the portion of SCP that covers the self-correction of insignificant operational failures. [Rev. Proc. 2016-51, § 8.04, Ex. 1]

Example 23-3: The facts are the same as in Example 23-2, except that the failure to satisfy Code Section 415 occurred during each of the 2017 and 2018 limitation years. In addition, the three participants affected by the Section 415 failure were not identical each year. The fact that the Section 415 failures occurred during more than one limitation year did not cause the failures to be significant; accordingly, the failures are still eligible for correction under the portion of SCP that covers the self-correction of insignificant operational failures. [Rev. Proc. 2016-51, § 8.04, Ex. 2]

Example 23-4: The facts are the same as in Example 23-2, except that the annual additions of 18 of the 50 employees whose benefits were limited by Code Section 415(c) nevertheless exceeded the maximum limits under Code Section 415(c) during the 2018 limitation year, and the amount of the excesses ranged from $1,000 to $9,000 and totaled $150,000. Under these facts, taking into account the number of participants affected by the failure relative to the total number of participants who could have been affected by the failure for the 2018 limitation year (and the monetary amount of the failure relative to the total employer contribution), the failure is significant. Accordingly, the Code Section 415(c) failure in the plan that occurred in 2018 is ineligible for correction under the portion of SCP that covers the self-correction of insignificant operational failures. [Rev. Proc. 2016-51, § 8.04, Ex. 3]

Example 23-5: The Monterey Company maintains the Monterey Company Money Purchase Pension Plan, established in 2015. The plan document satisfies the requirements of Code Section 401(a). The formula under the plan provides for an employer contribution equal to 10 percent of compensation, as defined in the plan. During its examination of the plan for the 2019 plan year, the IRS discovered that the employee responsible for entering data into the employer's computer made minor arithmetic errors in transcribing the compensation data with respect to six of the plan's 40 participants, resulting in excess allocations to those six participants' accounts. Under these facts, the number of participants affected by the failure relative to the number of participants that could have been affected is insignificant, and the failure is due to minor data errors. Thus, the failure occurring in 2019 would be insignificant and therefore eligible for correction under the portion of SCP that covers the self-correction of insignificant operational failures. [Rev. Proc. 2016-51, § 8.04, Ex. 4]

Q 23:7 How are significant operational failures corrected under SCP?

The SCP requirements for self-correction of significant operational failures are satisfied if the significant operational failure is corrected and the correction is either completed or substantially completed (in accordance with Section 9.03 of Revenue Procedure 2016-51) by the last day of the correction period (described in Section 9.02 of Revenue Procedure 2016-51). [Rev. Proc. 2016-51, § 9.01]

End of the Correction Period. The last day of the correction period for an operational failure is the last day of the second plan year following the plan year in which the failure occurred. However, in the case of a failure to satisfy the ADP requirements of Code Section 401(k)(3), the ACP requirements of Code Section 401(m)(2), or, for plan years beginning on or before December 31, 2001, the multiple use test of Code Section 401(m)(9), the correction period does not end until the last day of the second plan year following the plan year that includes the last day of the additional period for correction permitted under Code Section 401(k)(8) or 401(m)(6). Section 6.02(5)(d)(ii) of Revenue Procedure 2016-51 provides a limited extension of the correction period for plan sponsors taking action to locate lost participants. [Rev. Proc. 2016-51, § 9.02(1)]

Extension of Correction Period for Transferred Assets. In the case of an operational failure that relates only to transferred assets, or to a plan assumed in connection with a corporate merger, acquisition, or other similar employer transaction, the correction period does not end until the last day of the first plan year that begins after the corporate merger, acquisition, or similar employer transaction between the plan sponsor and the sponsor of the transferor plan or the prior sponsor of an assumed plan. [Rev. Proc. 2016-51, § 9.02(2)]

Effect of Examination. Generally, the correction period for an operational failure that occurs for any plan year ends, in any event, on the first date the plan or the plan sponsor is under IRS examination for that plan year. [Rev. Proc. 2016-51, § 9.02(3)]

Substantial Completion of Correction. Correction of an operational failure is substantially completed by the last day of the correction period only if either of the following requirements is satisfied:

1. During the correction period, the plan sponsor is reasonably prompt in identifying the operational failure, formulating a correction method, and initiating correction in a manner that demonstrates a commitment to completing correction of the operational failure as expeditiously as practicable, and within 120 days after the last day of the correction period, the plan sponsor completes correction of the operational failure.
2. During the correction period, correction is completed with respect to 65 percent of all participants affected by the operational failure, and, thereafter, the plan sponsor completes correction of the operational failure with respect to the remaining affected participants in a diligent manner.

[Rev. Proc. 2016-51, § 9.03]

Examples. The following examples illustrate the application of the self-correction of significant operational failures under SCP. The examples assume that the eligibility requirements for use of SCP have been met.

Example 23-6: The Wicks Corporation established a qualified defined contribution plan in 2015 and received a favorable determination letter. During 2019, while doing a self-audit of the operation of the plan for the 2018 plan year, the plan administrator discovered that, despite established practices and procedures established by the corporation with respect to the plan, several eligible employees were excluded from participation. The administrator also found that for 2018 operational failures occurred because the elective deferrals of additional employees exceeded the Code Section 402(g) limit and the corporation failed to make the required top-heavy minimum contribution. In addition, during the review of the administration for the 2018 plan year, it was found that the plan administrator intended to implement a correction for the failure to satisfy the ADP test (as described in Code Section 401(k)(3)) for the 2017 plan year. During the 2020 plan year, the plan sponsor made corrective contributions on behalf of the excluded employees, distributed the excess deferrals to the affected participants, and made a top-heavy minimum contribution for all participants entitled to that contribution for the 2018 plan year. Each corrective contribution and distribution was credited with earnings at a rate appropriate for the plan from the date the corrective contribution or distribution should have been made to the date of correction. The failed ADP test for 2017 was corrected by making corrective contributions, adjusted for earnings, on behalf of non-highly compensated employees (NHCEs) using the method described in Appendix A.03 of Revenue Procedure 2016-51. Under these facts, the plan sponsor has corrected the ADP test for the 2017 plan year and the operational failures for the 2018 plan year within the correction period and thus satisfied the requirements for self-correction of significant operational failures under SCP. [Rev. Proc. 2016-51, § 9.04, Ex. 1]

Example 23-7: The Whiteside Company established a qualified defined contribution plan in 2005 and received a favorable determination letter for the applicable law changes. In April 2019, Whiteside purchased all of the stock of the Salinas Company, a wholly owned subsidiary of the Monterey Company. Employees of the Salinas Company participated in a qualified defined contribution plan sponsored by the Monterey Company, the Monterey Company Defined Contribution Plan. Following the Whiteside Company's review of the Monterey Plan, the Whiteside Company and the Monterey Company agreed that the Whiteside Company Plan would accept a transfer of plan assets attributable to the account balances of the employees of the Salinas Company who had participated in the Monterey Company Plan. As part of this agreement, the Monterey Company represented to the Whiteside Company that the Monterey Company Plan was tax qualified. The Whiteside Company and the Monterey Company also agreed that such transfer would be in accordance with the plan merger requirements of Code Section 414(l) and Treasury Regulations Section 1.414(l)-1 and addressed issues related to costs associated with the transfer. Following the transaction, the employees of the Salinas Company began participation in the Whiteside Company Plan. Effective July 1, 2019, the Whiteside Company Plan accepted the transfer of plan assets from the Monterey Company Plan. After the transfer, the Whiteside Company determined that all the participants in one division of the Salinas Company had been incorrectly excluded from allocation of the profit-sharing contributions for the 2014 and 2015 plan years. During 2020, the Whiteside Company made corrective contributions on behalf of the affected participants. The corrective contributions were credited with earnings at a rate appropriate for the plan from the date the corrective contribution should have been made to the date of correction and the Whiteside Company otherwise complied with the requirements of SCP. Under these facts, the Whiteside Company has, within the correction period, corrected the operational failures for the 2014 and 2015 plan years with respect to the assets transferred to the Whiteside Company Plan and thus satisfied the requirements of SCP with respect to the self-correction of significant operational failures. [Rev. Proc. 2016-51, § 9.04, Ex. 2]

Voluntary Correction Program (VCP) Requirements

Q 23:8 What are the VCP requirements?

VCP Requirements. The VCP requirements are satisfied with respect to failures submitted in accordance with the requirements of Section 10 of Revenue Procedure 2016-51 if the plan sponsor pays the required user fee and implements the corrective actions and satisfies any other conditions in the VCP compliance statement. [Rev. Proc. 2016-51, § 10.01] The submission procedures for VCP are set forth in Section 11 of Revenue Procedure 2016-51.

Identification of Failures. VCP is not based upon an IRS examination of the plan. Only the failures raised by the plan sponsor or failures identified by the IRS in processing the VCP application are addressed under VCP, and only those failures are covered by a VCP compliance statement. The IRS will not make any investigation or finding under VCP concerning whether there are failures. [Rev. Proc. 2016-51, § 10.02]

Effect of VCP Submission on Examination. Because VCP does not arise out of an IRS examination, consideration under VCP does not preclude or impede (under Code Section 7605(b) or any administrative provisions adopted by the IRS) a subsequent IRS examination of the plan sponsor or the plan with respect to the taxable year (or years) involved with respect to matters that are outside the VCP compliance statement. However, a plan sponsor's statements describing failures are made only for purposes of VCP and will not be regarded by the IRS as an admission of a failure for purposes of any subsequent examination. [Rev. Proc. 2016-51, § 10.03]

No Concurrent Examination Activity. Except in unusual circumstances, a plan that has been properly submitted under VCP will not be examined by the IRS while the submission is pending. Notwithstanding the above, a plan that is eligible for a group submission under EPCRS (as described in Section 10.10 of Revenue Procedure 2016-51) may be examined by the IRS while the group submission is pending with respect to issues not identified in the group submission at the time such plan comes under examination. In addition, if it is determined that either the plan or the plan sponsor was, or may have been, a party to an abusive tax avoidance transaction (as defined in Section 4.12(2) of Revenue Procedure 2016-51), the IRS may authorize the examination of the plan, even if a submission pursuant to VCP is pending. This practice regarding concurrent examination does not extend to other plans of the plan sponsor. Thus, any plan of the plan sponsor that is not pending under VCP could be subject to IRS examination. [Rev. Proc. 2016-51, § 10.04]

Determination Letter Application for Plan Amendments Not Related to a VCP Submission. The IRS may process a determination letter application (including an application requested on IRS Form 5310, *Application for Determination for Terminating Plan*) submitted under the determination letter program (as set forth in Revenue Procedure 2017-7, 2017-1 I.R.B. 146, and Revenue Procedure 2016-37, 2016-29 I.R.B. 136, and any subsequent guidance issued in the Internal Revenue Bulletin) while separately processing a VCP submission for the same plan. Generally, issuance of the determination letter in response to an application made on IRS Form 5310 will be suspended pending the closure of the VCP submission. [Rev. Proc. 2016-51, § 10.05(1)] A submission of a plan under the determination letter program does not constitute a submission under VCP. If the plan sponsor discovers a failure, the failure may not be corrected as part of the determination letter process. The plan sponsor may use SCP and VCP instead, as applicable. If the IRS, in connection with a determination letter application, discovers failures, the IRS may issue a closing agreement with respect to the failures identified or, if appropriate, refer the case to Employee Plans Examinations. In such a case, the VCP user fee structure does not apply. Except as provided in Section 10.05(3) of Revenue Procedure 2016-51, the sanction in Section 14.01 of Revenue Procedure 2016-51, relating to Audit CAP, applies. [Rev. Proc. 2016-51, § 10.05(2)]

Compliance Statement. The compliance statement issued by the IRS for a VCP submission only addresses the failures identified in the submission, the terms of correction (including any revision of administrative procedures), and the time period within which proposed corrections must be implemented (including any changes in administrative procedures). The compliance statement also provides that the IRS will not treat the plan as failing to satisfy the applicable requirements of the Code on account of the failures described in the compliance statement if the conditions of the compliance statement are satisfied. The reliance provided by a compliance statement is limited to the specific failures and years specified and does not provide reliance for any other failure or year. [Rev. Proc. 2016-51, § 10.07(1)]

- *Interim Amendment Failures.* With respect to a failure to amend a plan timely for interim amendments, as described in Section 5.01(2)(a)(ii)(B) of Revenue Procedure 2016-51, the issuance of a compliance statement will result in the corrective amendments being treated as if they had been adopted timely for the purpose of determining the availability of the remedial amendment period described in Revenue Procedure 2007-44 and Revenue Procedure 2016-37. However, the issuance of such a compliance statement does not constitute a determination as to whether the interim amendment, as drafted, complies with the change in qualification requirement. The compliance statement does not constitute a determination that the terms of the plan, including the corrective plan amendment, satisfy the qualification requirements in form. [Rev. Proc. 2016-51, § 10.07(2)(a)]
- *Nonamender Failures.* With respect to a failure to amend a plan timely for disqualifying provisions or a failure to timely adopt applicable required amendments provided in the IRS's Required Amendments List, as described in Section 5.01(2)(a)(ii)(C) of Revenue Procedure 2016-51, the issuance of a compliance statement will result in the corrective amendments being treated as if they had been timely adopted during the applicable remedial amendment period. However, the issuance of such a compliance statement does not constitute a determination as to whether the corrective plan amendment as drafted complies with the change in qualification requirement. The compliance statement does not constitute a determination as to whether the corrective plan amendment conforms the terms of the plan to the plan's prior operations or whether the terms of the plan, including the corrective plan amendment, satisfy the qualification requirements in form. [Rev. Proc. 2016-51, § 10.07(2)(b)]
- *Operational Failures.* If a plan sponsor submits a VCP filing correcting an operational failure through a plan amendment and the plan amendment is

accepted as a proper correction of the operational failure, then the compliance statement issued under VCP constitutes a determination that the operational failure has been corrected, but it is not a determination that the terms of the plan, including the corrective plan amendment, satisfy the qualification requirements in form. [Rev. Proc. 2016-51, § 10.07(2)(c)]

Where current procedures are inadequate for operating the plan in conformance with the applicable requirements of the Code, the compliance statement will be conditioned upon the implementation of stated administrative procedures. The IRS may prescribe appropriate administrative procedures in the compliance statement. [Rev. Proc. 2016-51, § 10.07(3)]

The compliance statement is conditioned on (1) there being no misstatement or omission of material facts in connection with the submission and (2) the implementation of the specific corrections and satisfaction of any other conditions in the compliance statement. [Rev. Proc. 2016-51, § 10.07(4)]

Effect of Compliance Statement on Examination. The compliance statement is binding upon both the IRS and the plan sponsor with respect to the specific tax matters identified in the statement for the periods specified, but does not preclude or impede an IRS examination of the plan relating to matters outside the compliance statement, even with respect to the same taxable year or years to which the compliance statement relates. [Rev. Proc. 2016-51, § 10.08]

Q 23:9 What special rules apply to anonymous (John Doe) submissions under VCP?

Special Rules Relating to Anonymous (John Doe) Submission Procedures. The Anonymous Submission procedure described in Section 10.09 of Revenue Procedure 2016-51 permits submission of a qualified plan under VCP without initially identifying the plan or the plan sponsor. The requirements for VCP procedures under Revenue Procedure 2016-51 apply to Anonymous Submissions. However, information identifying the plan or the plan sponsor may be redacted (and the power of attorney statement and the penalty of perjury statement need not be included with the initial submission). For purposes of processing the Anonymous Submission, the state of the plan sponsor must be identified in the initial submission. All Anonymous Submissions must be numbered or labeled on the first page of the VCP submission by the plan sponsor or its representative to facilitate identification and tracking of the submission. Once the IRS and the plan representative reach an agreement with respect to the Anonymous Submission, the IRS will contact the plan representative in writing indicating the terms of the agreement. The plan sponsor will have 21 calendar days from the date of the letter of agreement to identify the plan and plan sponsor. If the plan sponsor does not submit the identifying material (including the power of attorney statement and the penalty of perjury statement) within 21 calendar days of the letter of agreement, the matter will be closed and the user fee will not be returned. [Rev. Proc. 2016-51, § 10.09(1)]

Until the plan and the plan sponsor are identified to the IRS, an Anonymous Submission does not preclude or impede an IRS examination of the plan sponsor or its plans. Thus, a plan submitted under the Anonymous Submission procedure that comes under IRS examination prior to the date the IRS receives the identifying materials of the plan and plan sponsor will no longer be eligible under VCP. [Rev. Proc. 2016-51, § 10.09(2)]

Q 23:10 What special rules apply to group submissions under VCP?

An eligible organization may submit a VCP request for a qualified plan under the VCP Group Submission procedure for operational and plan document failures. [Rev. Proc. 2016-51, § 10.10] The special rules that govern Group Submissions under VCP are set forth in Section 10.10 of Revenue Procedure 2016-51.

Q 23:11 What are the VCP user fees?

Beginning in 2017 and each year thereafter, the user fees for VCP submissions are published as part of the annual IRS revenue procedure that sets forth user fees, including VCP user fees. Plan sponsors should refer to the annual IRS revenue procedure in effect at the time they file their VCP submission with the IRS to determine the VCP user fee. [Rev. Proc. 2016-51, § 12.01(2)] For example, the VCP user fees for VCP submissions filed with the IRS on or after January 2, 2018, are determined under Revenue Procedure 2018-4, Appendix A.09. In Revenue Procedure 2018-4, the IRS announced a change in the system for determining VCP fees. Under the new system, most VCP submissions made in 2018 are subject to a new simplified fee structure under which fees range from $1,500 to $3,500 based solely upon the amount of total net assets in the retirement plan, determined from the plan's most recently filed Form 5500 series return. A description of the VCP user fees is available at https://www.irs.gov/retirement-plans/voluntary-correction-program-fees.

Audit Closing Agreement Program (Audit CAP) Requirements

Q 23:12 What is the Audit CAP program?

Audit CAP is the audit correction program under EPCRS, and it is available for all types of qualification failures found on IRS examination that cannot be corrected under SCP or VCP. If such a failure is identified on audit, the plan sponsor may correct the failure and pay a sanction. The sanction imposed will bear a reasonable relationship to the nature, extent, and severity of the failure, taking into account the extent to which correction occurred before the audit.

Audit CAP Requirements. If the IRS identifies a qualification failure (other than a failure that has been corrected in accordance with SCP or VCP) upon an IRS Employee Plans or Exempt Organizations examination of a qualified retirement plan, the plan sponsor must correct the failure, pay a sanction (see Q 23:13), satisfy any additional requirements of Section 13.03 of Revenue Procedure 2016-51, and enter into a closing agreement with the IRS. [Rev. Proc. 2016-51, § 13.01]

Payment of Sanction. Payment of the sanction generally is required at the time the closing agreement is signed. All sanction amounts should be submitted by certified or cashier's check made payable to the United States Treasury. However, at the plan sponsor's option, the sanction may be paid by credit or debit card or directly from a checking or savings account through www.pay.gov. [Rev. Proc. 2016-51, § 13.02]

Additional Requirements. Depending on the nature of the failure, the IRS will discuss the appropriateness of the plan's existing administrative procedures with the plan sponsor. If existing administrative procedures are inadequate for operating the plan in conformance with the applicable requirements of the Code, the closing agreement may be conditioned upon the implementation of stated procedures. [Rev. Proc. 2016-51, § 13.03]

Failure to Reach Resolution. If the IRS and the plan sponsor cannot reach an agreement with respect to the correction of the failure(s) or the amount of the sanction, the plan will be disqualified. [Rev. Proc. 2016-51, § 13.04]

Effect of Closing Agreement. A closing agreement constitutes an agreement between the IRS and the plan sponsor that is binding with respect to the tax matters identified for the periods specified. [Rev. Proc. 2016-51, § 13.05]

Other Procedural Rules. The procedural rules for Audit CAP are set forth in Internal Revenue Manual (IRM) 7.2.2., EPCRS. [Rev. Proc. 2016-51, § 13.06]

Q 23:13 What is the Audit CAP sanction?

Determination of Sanction. The sanction under Audit CAP is a negotiated amount that is based on the facts and circumstances, including the relevant factors described in Section 14.02 of Revenue Procedure 2016-51. Sanctions will not be excessive and will bear a reasonable relationship to the nature, extent, and severity of the failures, based on the factors described below. The sanction generally will not be less than the VCP user fee applicable to the plan. [Rev. Proc. 2016-51, § 14.01]

Factors Considered. Factors considered when calculating the amount of the sanction include:

1. The steps taken by the plan sponsor to ensure that the plan had no failures;
2. The steps taken to identify failures that may have occurred;
3. The extent to which correction had progressed before the examination was initiated, including full correction;
4. The number and type of employees affected by the failure;
5. The number of NHCEs who would be adversely affected if the plan were not treated as qualified;
6. Whether the failure is a failure to satisfy the nondiscrimination requirements of Code Section 401(a)(4), the minimum participation requirements of Code Section 401(a)(26), or the minimum coverage requirements of Code Section 410(b);
7. Whether the failure is solely an employer eligibility failure;

8. The period over which the failure(s) occurred (e.g., the time that has elapsed since the end of the applicable remedial amendment period under Code Section 401(b) for a plan document failure);
9. The reason for the failure(s) (e.g., data errors such as errors in the transcription of data, the transposition of numbers, or minor arithmetic errors); and
10. The "maximum payment amount," as defined in Section 5.01(5) of Revenue Procedure 2016-51.

[Rev. Proc. 2016-51, § 14.02(1)]

Additional factors are considered when determining the sanction for nonamender failures in qualified retirement plans, and also for participant loan failures. [Rev. Proc. 2016-51, § 14.02(2) and (3)]

Transferred Assets. If the examination involves a plan with transferred assets and the IRS determines that no new incidents of the failures that relate to the transferred assets occur after the end of the second year that begins after the corporate merger, acquisition, or other similar employer transaction occurred, the sanction under Audit CAP will not exceed the sanction that would apply if the transferred assets were maintained as a separate plan. [Rev. Proc. 2016-51, § 14.03]

Q 23:14 How are Audit CAP sanctions paid?

Audit CAP sanctions should generally be paid by parties other than the plan's related trust: contributing employers, responsible fiduciaries, or their insurers. In limited cases, Audit CAP sanctions may come from plan participants and trust assets.

Plan Participants. When the party responsible for the disqualifying defect (e.g., the trustee or 100 percent owner of the business) is also a participant in the plan, this party may offer to pay the Audit CAP sanction and costs from a distribution of his or her accrued benefit under the plan if:

- The participant is currently entitled to a distribution under the terms of the plan.
- The consent requirements of Code Sections 411(a)(11) and 417 have been satisfied (see chapter 11).
- The portion of the distribution that the participant directs to be paid to the IRS as an Audit CAP sanction is paid in a revocable arrangement that meets the requirements of Treasury Regulations Section 1.401(a)-13(e).

Such amounts are treated as taxable distributions and are subject to additional tax under Code Section 72.

Trust Assets. Any sanction paid by the trust must not exceed the tax liability of the trust alone upon disqualification. In some cases, the employer or other parties responsible for the disqualifying violation may lack the funds to pay the costs imposed under Audit CAP. Under the following conditions, trust assets may be used in such cases to help meet the cost of sanction and correction if:

- The employer has insufficient assets to pay due to significant financial distress;
- The employer's tax liability upon disqualification would be nominal, or relatively insignificant compared to that of the trust; and
- The adverse consequences of plan disqualification would fall most heavily on non-highly compensated participants.

The IRS must consult with the DOL in determining whether Audit CAP sanctions may be paid from the trust assets. [I.R.S. Field Directive, Payment of CAP Sanctions from Trust Assets, Feb. 21, 1995]

Consequences of Plan Disqualification

Q 23:15 What are the consequences of plan disqualification?

In general, plan disqualification causes:

1. Loss of tax deductions by the employer for contributions made to the plan;
2. Immediate taxation of trust income; and
3. Immediate taxation of all or a portion of the accrued benefit of employees (in some cases, the impact may be limited to highly compensated employees (HCEs)).

Q 23:16 For what period of time may the IRS disqualify a previously qualified plan?

Depending on whether the violation is an operational or form (i.e., plan document) defect, the IRS may retroactively disqualify a plan. In the case of a form defect, if the plan sponsor has received a favorable determination letter from the IRS, the plan will not be disqualified until the plan is amended or required to be amended due to law changes.

The IRS may disqualify a plan retroactively:

- From the plan's inception;
- For a certain number of years; or
- From a certain date.

The plan will remain disqualified until remedial action is taken to correct the problem. [I.R.C. § 7805(b)]

Q 23:17 Are there any limits on retroactive plan disqualification?

If the IRS determines that retroactive disqualification of a plan is the appropriate course of action, the disqualification can be retroactive to tax years (of the trust and participants) for which the statute of limitations has not run. The IRS is limited to three years in which to assess taxes on an employer who sponsored, or an employee who participated in, a disqualified plan. [I.R.C. § 6501(a)] For a tax-exempt trust, the statutory period expires three years after the later of:

1. The date an employer or administrator files its Form 5500 series return, or
2. The last day allowed by law or regulation for filing the returns.

Q 23:18 What are the tax consequences to the employee if a plan is disqualified?

Employer contributions made on behalf of an employee, during a taxable year of the employer that ends within or with a taxable year of the nonexempt trust, are includible as compensation in the gross income of the employee of the taxable year during which the contributions are made, but only if the employee's interest in that contribution is "substantially vested" at the time the contribution is made. [Treas. Reg. § 1.402(b)-1(a)(1)] (See Q 23:25 for certain exceptions to these rules.)

Q 23:19 How are employer contributions determined for purposes of the rule discussed in Q 23:18?

For a defined contribution plan, employer contributions are simply the amount of employer contributions allocated during the plan year to the employee. For a defined benefit plan (in which the amount of the employer contributions attributable to a participant is generally not known), employer contributions are the differences between:

1. The amount determined in accordance with the formula described in Treasury Regulations Section 1.403(b)-1(d)(4) as of the end of the taxable year, *minus*
2. The amount determined in accordance with the formula described in Treasury Regulations Section 1.403(b)-1(d)(4) as of the end of the prior taxable year.

As an alternative, the amount of employer contributions may be determined under any other method that uses recognized actuarial principles consistent with the provisions of the plan under which the contributions are made *and* the method adopted by the employer for funding the benefits under the plan. [Treas. Reg. § 1.402(b)-1(a)(2)]

Q 23:20 How are employer contributions computed for defined benefit plans under the Section 403(b) rules?

The contributions made by the employer are deemed to be the product of the amounts described in items 1 through 4:

1. The projected annual amount of the employee's pension (as of the end of the taxable year) to be provided at normal retirement age (from employer contributions), based upon the provisions of the plan in effect at such

time and upon the assumption of the employee's continued employment with the present employer at the present rate of salary.

2. The value, from Table 23-2, below, at normal retirement age of an annuity of $1.00 per annum payable in equal monthly installments during the life of the employee, based upon normal retirement age as defined in the plan.
3. The value, from Table 23-4, below (representing the level annual contribution that will accumulate to $1.00 at normal retirement age), for the sum of:

Note: If the normal form of retirement benefit under the plan is other than a straight life annuity, the value from Table 23-2 should be divided by the amount determined from Table 23-3.

a. The number of years remaining from the end of the taxable year to normal retirement age; and
b. The lesser of the number of years of service credited through the end of the taxable year *or* the number of years that the plan has been in existence at such time.

Table 23-2. Value at Normal Retirement Ages of Annuity of $1.00 per Annum Payable in Equal Monthly Installments During the Life of the Employee

Age	*Value*	*Age*	*Value*
40	11.49	61	8.79
41	11.40	62	8.62
42	11.31	63	8.44
43	11.22	64	8.25
44	11.12	65	8.08
45	11.01	66	7.86
46	10.91	67	7.70
47	10.79	68	7.50
48	10.68	69	7.29
49	10.56	70	7.10
50	10.43	71	6.88
51	10.30	72	6.68
52	10.18	73	6.46
53	10.04	74	6.25
54	9.89	75	6.03
55	9.75	76	5.82
56	9.60	77	5.61
57	9.44	78	5.40
58	9.28	79	5.20
59	9.13	80	4.99
60	8.96		

1. The lesser of the number of years of service credited through the end of the taxable year *or* the number of years that the plan has been in existence at such time.

[Treas. Reg. § 1.403(b)-1(d)(4)]

Table 23-3. Deductions for Benefits in Non-Life Annuity Form

Annuity for 5 years certain and life thereafter	0.97
Annuity for 10 years certain and life thereafter	0.90
Annuity for 15 years certain and life thereafter	0.80
Annuity for 20 years certain and life thereafter	0.70
Life annuity with installment refund	0.80
Life annuity with cash refund	0.75

Note: The term *cash refund* to refund of accumulated employer contributions does not refer to refund of employee contributions only, often referred to as "modified cash refund."

Table 23-4. Level Annual Contribution That Will Accumulate to $1.00 at the End of Number of Years

Number of Years	*Amount*	*Number of Years*	*Amount*
1	$1.0000	17	.0296
2	.4806	18	.0267
3	.3080	19	.0241
4	.2219	20	.0219
5	.1705	21	.0198
6	.1363	22	.0180
7	.1121	23	.0164
8	.0940	24	.0150
9	.0801	25	.0137
10	.0690	26	.0125
11	.0601	27	.0114
12	.0527	28	.0105
13	.0465	29	.0096
14	.0413	30	.0088
15	.0368	31	.0081
16	.0330	32	.0075

Table 23-4. Level Annual Contribution That Will Accumulate to $1.00 at the End of Number of Years (cont'd)

Number of Years	*Amount*	*Number of Years*	*Amount*
33	.0069	42	.0033
34	.0063	43	.0030
35	.0058	44	.0028
36	.0053	45	.0026
37	.0049	46	.0024
38	.0045	47	.0022
39	.0042	48	.0020
40	.0039	49	.0019
41	.0036	50	.0017

Example 23-8: Meredith participates in the East of Eden Corporation defined benefit plan, which has a normal retirement age of 65. Benefits are provided in life annuity form, and Meredith is age 45. She has been a participant since the plan started 10 years ago. The plan is disqualified for the calendar year 2019. Meredith is 100 percent vested, and her projected benefit under the plan has increased from $30,000 per year to $36,000 during 2019. Using Treasury Regulations Section 1.403(b)-1(d)(4), the value of the employer contributions for Meredith in 2019 is computed as follows:

1. Projected annual benefit: $36,000
2. Value from Table 23-1 at normal retirement age 65: $8.08
3. Value from Table 23-2—sum of years remaining to normal retirement (20) and years that the plan has been in existence (10): .0088
4. The number of years the plan has been in existence: 10

The value as of December 31, 2019, is:

(1) × (2) × (3) × (4) = $36,000 × $8.08 × .0088 × 10 – $25,597.44

The value as of December 31, 2018, is computed in a similar manner:

(1) × (2) × (3) × (4) = $30,000 × $8.08 × .0088 × 9 – $19,198.08

The employer contributions attributable to the 2019 disqualified year are simply the difference between the 2018 and 2019 values, or $6,399.36. Therefore, Meredith will have an additional taxable income of $6,399.36 reported to her in 2019.

Q 23:21 What other methods may be used in determining employer contributions for defined benefit plans?

Although there is no written guidance, a method that computes the actuarial present value of the increase in the accrued benefit for the taxable year would likely be reasonable. The present value computation could be done using the actuarial assumptions of interest and mortality that are used in funding the plan for purposes of Code Section 412 (see chapter 9).

Q 23:22 What does "substantially vested" mean for purposes of inclusion in gross income?

A participant's accrued benefit is substantially vested when it is not subject to a substantial risk of forfeiture. In other words, the contribution is included in income to the extent it is vested at the time of contribution. [Treas. Reg. § 1.83-3(b)]

Q 23:23 What happens if the employee's interest in the trust changes from nonvested to vested?

If the employee's previously nonvested interest becomes vested during an employee's tax year and a non-tax-exempt year of the trust ends with or within that employee's tax year, the value of the employee's interest in the trust on the date of change in vested status must be included in gross income. This is only to the extent that the previously nonvested amount is attributable to employer contributions and attributable income. [Treas. Reg. § 1.402(b)-1(b)(1), (3)]

Example 23-9: The Chicago Novelties Corporation profit-sharing plan is disqualified for plan and calendar years 2018 and 2019 (because of failure to make top-heavy minimum contributions). Employer contributions were made and allocated to Meredith, an NHCE, as follows:

Year	*Employer Contribution*
2018	$3,600
2019	$4,000

The plan uses a vesting schedule of 20 percent per year of service, and Meredith has four years of vesting service as of the end of 2018. The amount of the employer contribution taxable to Meredith in 2018 is equal to:

Employer contribution × Vested percentage = $3,600 × 80% – $2,880

In 2019, Meredith becomes fully vested, so the entire $4,000 contributed for her benefit is taxable. In addition, the nonvested amount from 2018 of $720 (20% × $3,600) is also included in taxable income in 2019. If $300 of earnings were credited to Meredith's account (attributable to the 2018 contribution of $3,600), an additional $720 (20% × $3,600) would also be taxable to Meredith in 2019.

Q 23:24 Are there any exceptions to the inclusion-of-income rule discussed in Q 23:18?

Yes. If one of the reasons a trust is not exempt from tax under Code Section 501 is the failure of the plan to meet the minimum participation requirements [I.R.C. § 401(a)(26)], the minimum coverage requirements [I.R.C. § 410(b)], or the nondiscrimination rules [I.R.C. § 401(a)(4)], then the only employees subject to the inclusion-of-income rules are HCEs who were either:

- Highly compensated during the taxable year; or
- Highly compensated during any preceding period for which service was creditable to the employee under the plan.

(See Appendix G for definition of HCEs.) It is important to note that for these purposes, the inclusion-of-income rule is expanded to include the entire vested account balance or accrued benefit. [I.R.C. § 402(b)(4); Preamble to Treas. Reg. § 1.401(a)(4)]

> **Example 23-10:** Scout participates in the New England Novelties, Inc. money purchase plan. During her year of entry into the plan, 2015, Scout was an HCE. She was also highly compensated during 2016, but ceased to be an HCE for taxable years 2017 through 2019. The money purchase plan is disqualified for 2018 because of a failure to meet the minimum coverage requirements of Code Section 410(b). Scout's entire vested account balance will be treated as taxable income.

Q 23:25 How are amounts previously taxed due to plan disqualification treated when amounts are later distributed from the qualified plan?

Such amounts are not taxed twice and are treated as an investment in the contract, excluded from tax when actually distributed from the plan. [Treas. Reg. § 1.402(b)-1(b)(5)]

> **Example 23-11:** Meredith retires at age 65 from the New England Viola Makers Corporation. Her vested account balance in the corporation's profit-sharing plan is $450,000. The plan was disqualified for tax years 2016 through 2019, and as a result, Meredith realized taxable income of $150,000 for that period. The $150,000 amount that was previously taxed may not be rolled over to an IRA, nor may it be included in taxable income if Meredith takes a lump-sum distribution.

Q 23:26 What happens if a lump-sum distribution is made from a disqualified plan?

If a previously qualified plan becomes disqualified, and the trust that is part of the plan is not exempt at the time a lump-sum distribution is received or made available, the distribution is taxed as ordinary income. This result is true even if the trust was exempt for a substantial portion of the time that funds were accumulated. [Treas. Reg. § 1.402(a)-1(a)(1)(v); Ltr. Rul. 8133014]

Part 5

Administrative Requirements

Chapter 24

Federal Income Tax Withholding

Payments from qualified retirement plans that are eligible rollover distributions (see chapter 21) are subject to mandatory withholding of federal income taxes at the 20 percent rate if they are not directly rolled over into an eligible retirement plan. Payments that are not eligible rollover distributions are subject to federal income tax withholding as wages if they are periodic payments; if they are not, the withholding rate is 10 percent. Recipients may elect not to have federal income taxes withheld from certain payments that are not eligible rollover distributions. For a description of state income tax withholding rules, see chapter 22.

A few general rules about federal income tax withholding from qualified retirement plan distributions are (1) federal income taxes are withheld only with respect to the taxable portion of a qualified retirement plan distribution; (2) federal income taxes are not required to be withheld from that portion of a distribution that the payor reasonably believes is not includible in the recipient's gross income; (3) the wage bracket method or the percentage method may be used to determine the amount of federal income taxes that must be withheld from a periodic payment; (4) withholding at the 20 percent rate is mandatory for any qualified retirement plan distribution that is eligible for direct rollover treatment (i.e., an eligible rollover distribution), but that is not rolled over directly into an eligible retirement plan; and (5) in general, payors or plan administrators are liable for federal income tax withholding.

Federal Income Tax Withholding on Eligible Rollover Distributions That Are Not Rolled Over 24-2
Federal Income Tax Withholding on Periodic and Nonperiodic Payments That Are Not Eligible Rollover Distributions 24-9
Rules Applicable to Periodic Payments 24-9
Rules Applicable to Nonperiodic Payments 24-20

Federal Income Tax Withholding on Eligible Rollover Distributions That Are Not Rolled Over

Q 24:1 What are the withholding requirements under Code Section 3405 for eligible rollover distributions from qualified retirement plans?

General Rule. Code Section 3405(c), added by the Unemployment Compensation Amendments of 1992 (UCA), provides that any designated distribution that is an eligible rollover distribution (as defined in Code Section 402(f)(2)(A)) from a qualified retirement plan (see Q 21:21) is subject to income tax withholding at the rate of 20 percent, unless the distributee elects to have the distribution paid directly to an eligible retirement plan in a direct rollover. If a designated distribution is not an eligible rollover distribution, it is subject to the elective withholding provisions of Code Section 3405(a) (relating to periodic payments) and is not subject to the mandatory withholding provisions of Code Section 3405(c).

Statutory Effective Date—General Rule. Code Section 3405(c), as added by UCA, began to apply to eligible rollover distributions made on or after January 1, 1993, even if the employee's employment with the employer maintaining the plan terminated before January 1, 1993, and even if the eligible rollover distribution is part of a series of payments that began before January 1, 1993.

Regulatory Effective Date. The final Treasury regulations under Code Section 3405(c) apply to eligible rollover distributions made on or after October 19, 1995. For eligible rollover distributions that were made on or after January 1, 1993, and before October 19, 1995, temporary Treasury regulations applied. However, for any distributions that were made on or after January 1, 1993, but before October 19, 1995, a plan administrator or payor may have complied with the withholding requirements of Code Section 3405(c) by substituting any or all provisions of the final Treasury regulations. [Treas. Reg. § 31.3405(c)-1, Q&A-1]

Q 24:2 May a distributee elect under Code Section 3405(c) not to have federal income tax withheld from an eligible rollover distribution?

No. The 20 percent income tax withholding imposed under Code Section 3405(c)(1) applies to any eligible rollover distribution that is not paid directly to an eligible retirement plan in a direct rollover. However, the 20 percent income tax will not apply to any eligible rollover distribution that the distributee elects under Code Section 401(a)(31) to have paid directly to an eligible retirement plan in a direct rollover. [Treas. Reg. § 31.3405(c)-1, Q&A-2]

Q 24:3 May a distributee elect to have more than 20 percent federal income tax withheld from an eligible rollover distribution?

Yes. Under Code Section 3402(p), a distributee of an eligible rollover distribution and the plan administrator or payor may enter into an agreement to provide for withholding in excess of 20 percent from an eligible rollover distribution. The agreement must be made in accordance with applicable forms and instructions. However, no request for withholding will be effective between the plan administrator or payor and the distributee until the plan administrator or payor accepts the request by commencing to withhold from the amounts with respect to which the request was made. An agreement under Code Section 3402(p) shall be effective for such period as the plan administrator or payor and the distributee mutually agree upon. However, either party to the agreement may terminate the agreement prior to the end of such period by furnishing a signed written notice to the other. [Treas. Reg. § 31.3405(c)-1, Q&A-3]

Q 24:4 Who has responsibility for complying with Code Section 3405(c) relating to the 20 percent income tax withholding on eligible rollover distributions?

Code Section 3405(d) generally requires the plan administrator of a qualified retirement plan to withhold under Code Section 3405(c)(1) an amount equal to 20 percent of the portion of an eligible rollover distribution that the distributee does not elect to have paid in a direct rollover. When an amount is paid under a qualified plan distributed annuity contract (as defined in Q 21:28), the payor is treated as the plan administrator. [Treas. Reg. § 31.3405(c)-1, Q&A-4]

Q 24:5 May the plan administrator shift the withholding responsibility to the payor and, if so, how?

Yes. The plan administrator may shift the withholding responsibility to the payor by following the procedures set forth in Treasury Regulations Section 35.3405-1, Q&A E-2 through E-5 (relating to elective withholding on pensions, annuities, and certain other deferred income), with appropriate adjustments, including the plan administrator's identification of amounts that constitute required minimum distributions (RMDs). [Treas. Reg. § 31.3402(c)-1, Q&A-5]

Q 24:6 How does the 20 percent withholding requirement under Code Section 3405(c) apply if a distributee elects to have a portion of an eligible rollover distribution paid to an eligible retirement plan in a direct rollover and to have the remainder of that distribution paid to the distributee?

If a distributee elects to have a portion of an eligible rollover distribution paid to an eligible retirement plan in a direct rollover and to receive the remainder of the distribution, the 20 percent withholding requirement under Code Section 3405(c) applies only to the portion of the eligible rollover distribution that the distributee receives and not to the portion that is paid in a direct rollover. [Treas. Reg. § 31.3405(c)-1, Q&A-6]

Q 24:7 Will the plan administrator be subject to liability for tax, interest, or penalties for failure to withhold 20 percent from an eligible rollover distribution that, because of erroneous information provided by a distributee, is not paid to an eligible retirement plan even though the distributee elected a direct rollover?

General Rule. If the plan administrator reasonably relied on adequate information provided by the distributee (as described below), the plan administrator will not be subject to liability for taxes, interest, or penalties for failure to withhold income tax from an eligible rollover distribution solely because the distribution is paid to an account or plan that is not an eligible retirement plan. Although the plan administrator is not required to verify independently the accuracy of information provided by the distributee, the plan administrator's reliance on the information furnished must be reasonable. For example, it is not reasonable for the plan administrator to rely on information that is clearly erroneous on its face.

Adequate Information. The plan administrator has obtained from the distributee adequate information on which to rely in making a direct rollover if the distributee furnishes to the plan administrator the name of the eligible retirement plan; a representation that the recipient plan is an individual retirement plan or a qualified retirement plan, as appropriate; and any other information that is necessary in order to permit the plan administrator to accomplish the direct rollover by the means it has selected. This information must include any information needed to comply with the specific requirements of Qs 24:3 and 24:4. For example, if the direct rollover is to be made by mailing a check to the trustee of an individual retirement account, the plan administrator must obtain, in addition to the name of the individual retirement account and the representation described above, the name and address of the trustee of the individual retirement account. [Treas. Reg. § 31.3405(c)-1, Q&A-7]

Q 24:8 Is an eligible rollover distribution that is paid to a qualified defined benefit plan subject to 20 percent withholding?

No. If an eligible rollover distribution is paid in a direct rollover to an eligible retirement plan within the meaning of Code Section 402(c)(8), including a qualified defined benefit plan, it is reasonable to believe that the distribution is not includible in gross income pursuant to Code Section 402(c)(1). Accordingly, pursuant to Code Section 3405(e)(1)(B), the distribution is not a designated distribution and is not subject to 20 percent withholding. [Treas. Reg. § 31.3405(c)-1, Q&A-8]

Q 24:9 If property other than cash, employer securities, or plan loans is distributed, how is the 20 percent income tax withholding required under Code Section 3405(c) accomplished?

When all or a portion of an eligible rollover distribution subject to 20 percent income tax withholding under Code Section 3405(c) consists of property other than cash, employer securities, or plan loan offset amounts, the plan administrator or payor must apply Treasury Regulations Section 35.3405-1, Q&A F-2, and may apply Treasury Regulations Section 35.3405-1, Q&A F-3, in determining how to satisfy the withholding requirements. [Treas. Reg. § 31.3405(c)-1, Q&A-9]

Q 24:10 What assumptions may a plan administrator make regarding whether a benefit is an eligible rollover distribution for purposes of determining the amount of a distribution that is subject to 20 percent mandatory withholding?

For purposes of determining the amount of a distribution that is subject to 20 percent mandatory withholding, a plan administrator may make the assumptions described below in determining the amount of a distribution that is an eligible rollover distribution and a designated distribution. (Q 28:17 provides assumptions for purposes of complying with Code Section 401(a)(31).)

$5,000 Death Benefit Exclusion No Longer Available. The former $5,000 death benefit exclusion does not apply to a distribution paid with respect to any decedent who dies after August 20, 1996, the Small Business Job Protection Act (SBJPA) enactment date. Thus, a plan administrator may not assume that $5,000 of any such distribution is not an eligible rollover distribution.

RMDs. The plan administrator is permitted to determine the amount of the minimum distribution required to satisfy Code Section 401(a)(9)(A) for any calendar year by assuming that there is no designated beneficiary.

Valuation of Property. In the case of a distribution that includes property, in calculating the amount of the distribution for purposes for applying Code Section 3405(c), the value of the property may be determined in accordance with Treasury Regulations Section 35.3405-1, Q&A F-1. [Treas. Reg. § 31.3405(c)-1, Q&A-10]

Q 24:11 Are there any special rules for applying the 20 percent withholding requirement to employer securities and a plan loan offset amount distributed in an eligible rollover distribution?

Yes. The maximum amount to be withheld on any designated distribution (including any eligible rollover distribution) under Code Section 3405(c) must not exceed the sum of the cash and the fair market value of the property (excluding employer securities) received in the distribution. The amount of the sum is determined without regard to whether any portion of the cash or property is a designated distribution or an eligible rollover distribution. For purposes of this rule, any plan loan offset amount (see Q 21:15) is treated in the same manner as employer securities. Thus, although employer securities and plan loan offset amounts must be included in the amount that is multiplied by 20 percent, the total amount required to be withheld for an eligible rollover distribution is limited to the sum of the cash and the fair market value of property received by the distributee, excluding any amount of the distribution that is a plan loan offset amount or that is distributed in the form of employer securities. For example, if the only portion of an eligible rollover distribution that is not paid in a direct rollover consists of employer securities or a plan loan offset amount, withholding is not required. In addition, if a distribution consists solely of employer securities and cash (not in excess of $200) in lieu of fractional shares, no amount is required to be withheld as income tax from the distribution under Code Section 3405 (including Code Section 3405(c)). For purposes of Code Section 3405, employer securities are securities of the employer corporation within the meaning of Code Section 402(e)(4)(E)(ii). [Treas. Reg. § 31.3405(c)-1, Q&A-11]

Q 24:12 How does the mandatory withholding rule apply to net unrealized appreciation from employer securities?

An eligible rollover distribution can include net unrealized appreciation (NUA) from employer securities, within the meaning of Code Section 402(e)(4), even if the net unrealized appreciation is excluded from gross income under Code Section 402(e)(4). However, to the extent that it is excludable from gross income pursuant to Code Section 402(e)(4), net unrealized appreciation is not a designated distribution pursuant to Code Section 3405(e)(1)(B) because it is reasonable to believe that it is not includible in gross income. Thus, to the extent that net unrealized appreciation is excludable from gross income pursuant to Code Section 402(e)(4), net unrealized appreciation is not included in the amount of an eligible rollover distribution that is subject to 20 percent withholding. [Treas. Reg. § 31.3405(c)-1, Q&A-12]

Q 24:13 Does the 20 percent withholding requirement apply to eligible rollover distributions from a qualified plan distributed annuity contract?

The 20 percent withholding requirement applies to eligible rollover distributions from a qualified plan distributed annuity contract as defined in Q 21:28. In the case of an eligible rollover distribution from such an annuity contract, the payor is treated as the plan administrator for purposes of Code Section 3405. (See Q 21:16 concerning the direct rollover requirements that apply to distributions from such an annuity contract and see Q 21:28 concerning the treatment of distributions from such annuity contracts as eligible rollover distributions.) [Treas. Reg. § 31.3405(c)-1, Q&A-13]

Q 24:14 Must a payor or plan administrator withhold federal income tax from an eligible rollover distribution for which a direct rollover election was not made if the amount of the distribution is less than $200?

No. However, all eligible rollover distributions received within one taxable year of the distributee under the same plan must be aggregated for purposes of determining whether the $200 floor is reached. If the plan administrator or payor does not know at the time of the first distribution (that is less than $200) whether there will be additional eligible rollover distributions during the year for which aggregation is required, the plan administrator need not withhold from the first distribution. If distributions are made within one taxable year under more than one plan of an employer, the plan administrator or payor may, but need not, aggregate distributions for purposes of determining whether the $200 floor is reached. However, once the $200 threshold has been reached, the sum of all payments during the year must be used to determine the applicable amount to be withheld from subsequent payments during the year. [Treas. Reg. § 31.3405(c)-1, Q&A-14]

Q 24:15 If eligible rollover distributions are made from a qualified retirement plan, who has responsibility for making the returns and reports required under applicable regulations?

Generally, the plan administrator, as defined in Code Section 414(g), is responsible for maintaining the records and making the required reports with respect to eligible rollover distributions from qualified retirement plans. However, if the plan administrator fails to keep the required records and make the required reports, the employer maintaining the plan is responsible for the reports and returns. [Treas. Reg. § 31.3405(c)-1, Q&A-15]

Q 24:16 What eligible rollover distributions must be reported on Form 1099-R?

Each eligible rollover distribution, including each eligible rollover distribution that is paid directly to an eligible retirement plan in a direct rollover, must be reported on Form 1099-R in accordance with the instructions for Form 1099-R. (See chapter 27.) For purposes of the reporting required under Code Section 6047(e), a direct rollover is treated as a distribution that is immediately rolled over to an eligible retirement plan. Distributions that are not eligible rollover distributions are subject to the reporting requirements set forth in Treasury Regulations Section 35.3405-1 and applicable forms and instructions. [Treas. Reg. § 31.3405(c)-1, Q&A-16]

Q 24:17 Must the plan administrator, trustee, or custodian of the eligible retirement plan report amounts received in a direct rollover?

IRA. If a distributee elects to have an eligible rollover distribution paid to an IRA in a direct rollover, the eligible rollover distribution is reported on Form 5498 as a rollover contribution to the IRA, in accordance with the instructions for Form 5498.

Qualified Retirement Plan. If a distributee elects to have an eligible rollover distribution paid to a qualified retirement plan (see Q 21:5), the recipient plan or annuity is not required to report the receipt of the rollover contribution. [Treas. Reg. § 31.3405(c)-1, Q&A-17]

Q 24:18 How does the payor of an eligible rollover distribution from which federal income taxes have been withheld report those withholdings to the IRS?

Payors that withhold federal income taxes from nonpayroll items (for example, eligible rollover distributions from qualified retirement plans) must report those withholdings to the IRS on Form 945, *Annual Return of Withheld Federal Income Tax*, generally by January 31, following the taxable year for which the withholdings were made. (However, if the payor has deposited the withholdings on time with the applicable Federal Reserve Bank, in full payment of the taxes for the year, it may file Form 945 by February 10, following the taxable year for which the withholdings were made.)

As a general rule, all federal income tax withholdings shown on Forms 1099 (e.g., Form 1099-R, Distribution from Pensions, Annuities, Retirement or Profit-Sharing Plans, IRAs, Insurance Contracts, etc.) must be reported to the IRS on Form 945. Certain federal income tax depositors must file Form 945-A, *Annual Record of Federal Tax Liability*, along with Form 945.

A payor must file its first Form 945 for the first calendar year that it incurs a nonpayroll tax liability. Thereafter, the payor must file Form 945 only for a calendar year in which it is required to withhold federal income tax from nonpayroll payments.

The withholdings that are reported to the IRS on Form 945 are actually deposited with the applicable Federal Reserve bank using Form 8109 or 8109-B, Federal Tax Deposit Coupon. However, income taxes withheld from qualified plan distributions may have to be deposited, by electronic funds transfer (EFT) instead of by paper coupons, through the Electronic Federal Tax Payment System (EFTPS). Employers that had employment tax obligations in excess of $200,000 in 1998 had to begin to deposit withheld employment taxes electronically, through EFTPS, by January 1, 2000. Employers that first exceed the threshold in 1999 or a subsequent year similarly are required to deposit by EFT beginning in the second succeeding calendar year. An employer that exceeds the threshold will not be permitted to resume making paper coupon deposits if its deposits fall below $200,000 in a subsequent year. Employers that are currently required to deposit by EFT will be given a fresh start and will not be required to use EFT unless they exceed the $200,000 threshold in 1998 or a subsequent calendar year. [Treas. Reg. § 31.6302-1(h)(2)] The requirement to deposit payroll withheld taxes through EFTPS also applies to nonpayroll withheld taxes, including federal income taxes withheld from qualified plan distributions. [Treas. Reg. §§ 31.6302-1(h)(3), 31.6302-4(b)(4)]

Circular E, Employer's Tax Guide, explains the rules for withholding, depositing, and reporting federal income tax. IRS Publication 15-A, Employer's Supplemental Tax Guide, includes information on income tax withholding from pensions and annuities.

Federal Income Tax Withholding on Periodic and Nonperiodic Payments That Are Not Eligible Rollover Distributions

Rules Applicable to Periodic Payments

Q 24:19 What is a *periodic payment* for purposes of the federal income tax withholding rules?

A *periodic payment* is an annuity or similar periodic payment whether paid by a licensed life insurance company, a financial institution, or a retirement plan. The term *annuity* means a series of payments payable over a period greater than one year and taxable under Code Section 72 as amounts received as an annuity, whether or not the payments are variable in amount. [I.R.C. § 3405(e)(2); Treas. Reg. § 35.3405-1T, Q&A A-9]

Q 24:20 How is federal income tax withheld from a periodic payment?

Amounts are withheld as if the periodic payments were payments of wages by an employer to an employee for the appropriate payroll period. If the payee has not filed a withholding certificate (IRS Form W-4P), the amount of federal income tax to be withheld is calculated by treating the payee as a married individual claiming three withholding allowances. [I.R.C. §§ 3405(a)(1), 3405(a)(4); Treas. Reg. § 35.3405-1T, Q&A A-10]

Code Section 3405(a)(4), as in effect before 2018, provided that, in the case of a payee entitled to periodic payments with respect to which a withholding certificate (IRS Form W-4P) had not been furnished, the amount to be withheld from each such payment "shall be determined by treating the payee as a married individual claiming three withholding exemptions." Section 11041(c)(2)(G) of the Tax Cuts and Jobs Act (P.L. 115-97, enacted on December 22, 2017), amended Code Section 3405(a)(4) to provide that the withholding rate when no withholding certificate (IRS Form W-4P) is furnished "shall be determined under rules prescribed by the Secretary." On February 12, 2018, the IRS issued Notice 2018-14, 2018-7 I.R.B. 353, which provides that, for 2018, the rules for withholding when no withholding certificate (IRS Form W-4P) is furnished with respect to periodic payments under Code Section 3405(a)(4) will parallel the rules for prior years and be based on treating the payee as a married individual claiming three withholding allowances.

Q 24:21 Do these withholding rules apply to periodic payments made from a qualified retirement plan to the surviving spouse or other beneficiary of a deceased payee?

Yes. The federal income tax withholding rules apply to periodic payments made from a qualified retirement plan to a deceased payee's surviving spouse or other beneficiary. [Treas. Reg. § 35.3405-1T, Q&A A-17]

Q 24:22 Who is required to withhold federal income tax from periodic payments made by a qualified retirement plan?

The plan administrator must withhold, and is liable for payment of, the withheld federal income tax, unless the plan administrator directs the payor to withhold the tax and furnishes the payor with any information that may be required by the IRS. These rules apply to qualified retirement plans as well as once-qualified retirement plans that are no longer qualified. [I.R.C. § 3405(d)(2); Treas. Reg. § 35.3405-1T, Q&A A-13] (See Q 24:25 for a description of the material that the plan administrator must furnish to the payor.)

Q 24:23 Who is a *plan administrator* for purposes of these withholding rules?

The plan administrator, for these purposes, is the plan administrator as defined in Code Section 414(g). [I.R.C. § 3405(e)(7)] Under Code Section 414(g), the plan administrator is the person specifically designated as the plan administrator by the terms of the plan or trust. If the plan or trust does not specifically designate the plan administrator (as provided in Treasury Regulations Section 1.414(g)-1(a)), then the plan administrator is generally determined as follows:

1. In the case of a plan maintained by a single employer, the employer is the plan administrator.
2. In the case of a plan maintained by two or more employers or jointly by one or more employers and one or more employee organizations (i.e., unions), the association, committee, joint board of trustees, or other similar group of representatives who maintain the plan is the plan administrator.
3. In any case in which (1) or (2) above does not apply, the person actually responsible for the control, disposition, or management of the assets is the plan administrator. [Treas. Reg. § 35.3405-1T, Q&A A-14]

Q 24:24 How may the plan administrator of a qualified retirement plan transfer the duty to withhold federal income taxes to a payor?

A plan administrator of a qualified retirement plan may transfer the liability for withholding federal income taxes by (1) directing the payor in writing to withhold the tax and (2) providing the payor with any required information. This direction is presumed to remain in effect until the plan administrator revokes it in writing. [Treas. Reg. § 35.3405-1T, Q&A E-2]

Q 24:25 What information must the plan administrator provide to the payor in order to transfer liability for federal income tax withholding?

The general rule is that the plan administrator must provide the payor with all information necessary to compute correctly the withholding tax liability. To satisfy this requirement, the plan administrator must explicitly inform the payor

(1) of the information that would be reportable on the Form W-2P or 1099-R or (2) that such information is not applicable to a particular payee or to any payments under the plan. For example, if the plan administrator is silent with respect to any employee contributions, the plan administrator has not satisfied his or her reporting obligations even if there are no employee contributions to the plan. Thus, the plan administrator is expected to provide the payee with the following minimum information:

1. The name, address, and social security number of the payee and the payee's spouse or other beneficiary if applicable;
2. The existence and amount of any employee contributions;
3. The amount of accumulated deductible employee contributions;
4. The payee's cost basis in any employer securities and the current fair market value of the securities;
5. The existence and amount of any premiums paid for the current cost of life insurance that were previously includible in income;
6. A statement of the reason (e.g., death, disability, or retirement) for the payment of the distribution;
7. The date on which payments commence and the amount and frequency of payments;
8. The age of the payee and of the payee's spouse or designated beneficiary, if applicable; and
9. Any other information required by Form W-2P or 1099-R.

[Treas. Reg. § 35.3405-1T, Q&A E-3]

Q 24:26 If the plan administrator does not notify the payor of the amount of employee contributions with respect to one payee, has federal income tax liability shifted to the payor?

Yes. The plan administrator satisfies the requirements described in Q 24:25 as to the information that must be supplied to the payor so long as the failure to provide the required information occurs on an infrequent basis or the plan administrator informs that payor in writing that the plan administrator has made a good faith effort to supply all the required information but that the amount of employee contributions as to a particular payee is unavailable. [Treas. Reg. § 35.3405-1T, Q&A E-4]

Q 24:27 If the plan administrator fails to supply the payor with any information concerning the existence or amount of any employee contributions, has withholding liability shifted to the payor?

No. The plan administrator has not satisfied his reporting obligation as described in Q 24:25 as to employee contributions even if there are no employee contributions unless the plan administrator affirmatively states that there are no employee contributions or states that the reporting of this item is not applicable in determining the payee's tax liability. [Treas. Reg. § 35.3405-1T, Q&A E-5]

Q 24:28 May a recipient of a periodic payment (other than an eligible rollover distribution) elect out of federal income tax withholding?

Yes. A recipient of periodic payments (other than eligible rollover distributions) may elect out of federal income tax withholding (except with respect to certain payments made outside of the United States) (see Q 24:32). The election out of federal income tax withholding will remain in effect until it is revoked. [I.R.C. § 3405(a)(2)] The election and any revocation of the election take effect in the manner provided under Code Section 3402(f)(3), regarding wage withholding exemption certificates. [I.R.C. § 3405(a)(3); Treas. Reg. § 35.3405-1T, Q&A D-1] The payor is required to provide each payee with notice of the right to elect not to have withholding apply and of the right to revoke the election. [Treas. Reg. § 35.3405-1T, Q&A D-1]

Q 24:29 In the case of a distribution made on account of the death of an employee, who makes the election not to have federal income tax withholding apply?

The election may be made by the beneficiary of the benefits specified by the decedent in accordance with plan procedures or, if there is no designated beneficiary, by the beneficiary specified under the terms of the plan. If there is no designated beneficiary and the terms of the plan do not specify a beneficiary, then the election may be made by the executor or the personal representative of the decedent. [Treas. Reg. § 35.3405-1T, Q&A D-2]

Q 24:30 Who is required to provide notice to the payee of the payee's right not to have withholding apply?

The payor must provide notice to the payee of the payee's right to elect not to have withholding apply. Thus, even if the plan administrator has failed to transfer liability for withholding to the payor, the payor must provide notice to the payee. [I.R.C. § 3405(d)(10)(B); Treas. Reg. § 35.3405-1T, Q&A D-3]

Q 24:31 When must notice of the right to elect not to have withholding apply be given for periodic payments?

In the case of periodic payments, notice of the election must be provided not earlier than six months before the first payment and not later than when making the first payment. However, even if notice is provided at a date before the first payment, notice must also be given when making the first payment. Therefore, notice must be provided at least once each calendar year of the right to make the election and to revoke the election. [I.R.C. § 3405(e)(10)(B)(i); Treas. Reg. § 35.3405-1T, Q&A D-4]

Q 24:32 Must notice of the right to elect not to have federal income tax withholding be provided to those payees whose annual payments are less than $5,400?

Yes. However, under Code Section 3405(e), notice is required to be provided only when making the first payment. Therefore, a payor may provide notice to a payee with annual payments less than $5,400 by indicating to the payee when making the first payment that no federal income tax will be withheld unless the payee chooses to have withholding apply by filing a withholding certificate (Form W-4P), if the payor also provides information concerning where a withholding certificate may be obtained. [Treas. Reg. § 35.3405-1T, Q&A D-5]

Q 24:33 Must notice of the right to elect not to have federal income tax withholding apply be provided in the same manner to all payees?

No. If the payor provides notice to all payees when making the first payment, the payor may, in addition, provide earlier notice as provided in Code Section 3405(d)(10)(B)(i)(I) to selected groups of payees, such as those payees whose annual payments are over $5,400. [Treas. Reg. § 35.3405-1T, Q&A D-6]

Q 24:34 Must notice be attached to the first payment to satisfy the requirement that the notice be provided when making the first payment?

No. Because many payees utilize EFT to deposit their pension or annuity checks, notice does not have to be attached physically to the check. [Treas. Reg. § 35.3405-1T, Q&A D-7]

Q 24:35 If a payee utilizes electronic funds transfer and notice is mailed directly to the payee at the same time the check is issued, is the notice requirement satisfied even though the payee receives the notice 15 days after the check is deposited?

Yes. Although it is desirable that the notice reaches the payee immediately prior to or concurrent with the receipt of the check, the notice requirement is deemed to be satisfied if the payee receives the notice within 15 days before or after receipt of the first payment. [Treas. Reg. § 35.3405-1T, Q&A D-8]

Q 24:36 If the payor of a periodic payment timely provides notice of the election not to have federal income tax withholding apply, may the payor specify a time prior to distribution by which the election must be made?

Yes. The election not to have federal income tax withholding apply is generally given effect as provided in Code Section 3402(f)(3) for a withholding certificate (Form W-4P) filed to replace an existing certificate. However, the payor may require that the election be made up to 30 days before the first payment to be effective for the first payment. [Treas. Reg. § 35.3405-1T, Q&A D-11]

Q 24:37 If notice is provided to a payee prior to the first payment of a periodic payment, why must it also be provided at the time of the first payment?

Notice must be provided at the time of the first payment because Code Section 3405(d)(10)(B)(i)(II) requires such notice. In addition, because the payee has the right to make an election or to revoke a prior election at any time before the beginning of the payment period, notice must be provided when making the first payment in order to offer the payee ample opportunity to make or revoke an election not to have withholding apply even if the election will not be effective until later payments. [Treas. Reg. § 35.3405-1T, Q&A D-14]

Q 24:38 Must a payor provide notice if it is reasonable to believe that the entire amount payable is excludable from the payee's gross income?

No. Amounts that it is reasonable to believe are not includible in federal gross income are not distributions for purposes of the elective withholding rules. Therefore, no notice is required of the ability to elect not to have withholding apply. [Treas. Reg. § 35.3405-1T, Q&A D-16]

Q 24:39 What information concerning the election not to have federal income tax withholding apply must be provided by the payor to the payee?

Notice to a payee must contain the following information: (1) notice of the payee's right to elect not to have federal income tax withholding apply to any payment or distribution and information on how to make that election; (2) notice of the payee's right to revoke such an election at any time and a statement that the election remains effective until revoked; and (3) a statement to advise payees that penalties may be incurred under the estimated tax payment rules if the payments of estimated tax are not adequate and sufficient tax is not withheld from the payment.

In the event that the payor does not know what portion of a distribution is includible in gross income and treats these payments, in their entirety, as includible in federal gross income, the following additional statements must be included with the notice: (1) federal income tax will be withheld on the gross amount of the payment even though the payee may be receiving amounts that are not subject to withholding because they are excludable from gross income; (2) this withholding procedure may result in excess withholding on the payment; and (3) the payee may adjust his or her allowances claimed on the withholding certificate (Form W-4P) if the payee wants a lesser amount withheld from each payment or the payee may provide the payor with the information necessary to calculate the taxable portion of each payment. [Treas. Reg. § 35.3405-1T, Q&A D-18 and A-33]

Q 24:40 Is there any non-required information that is desirable to include in the notice to payees?

Yes. It is desirable to include a statement in the notice to payees that the election not to have withholding apply is prospective only and that any election made after a payment to the payee is not an election with respect to that payment. [Treas. Reg. § 35.3405-1T, Q&A D-19]

Q 24:41 May the plan administrator provide the notice to payees on behalf of the payor?

Yes. The plan administrator may provide the notice on behalf of the payor. However, the payor has sole responsibility for providing this notice whether or not the plan administrator has shifted the liability for withholding to the payor, and if the plan administrator fails to provide adequate notice, the payor is responsible. [Treas. Reg. § 35.3405-1T, Q&A D-20]

Q 24:42 Is there a sample notice that can be used to satisfy the notice requirement for periodic payments?

Yes. Any payor who uses the following sample notice is deemed to satisfy the notice requirement if notice is timely provided:

NOTICE OF WITHHOLDING ON PERIODIC PAYMENTS

The [pension] OR [annuity] payments you receive from the [insert name of plan or company] will be subject to federal income tax withholding unless you elect not to have withholding apply. Withholding will only apply to the portion of your [pension] OR [annuity] payment that is already included in your income subject to federal income tax and will be like wage withholding. Thus, there will be no withholding on the return of your own nondeductible contributions to the [plan] OR [contract].

You may elect not to have withholding apply to your [pension] OR [annuity] payments by returning the signed and dated election [manner may be specified] to [insert name and address]. Your election will remain in effect until you revoke it. You may revoke your election at any time by returning the signed and dated revocation to [insert appropriate name or address]. Any election or revocation will be effective no later than the January 1, May 1, July 1, or October 1 after it is received, so long as it is received at least 30 days before that date. You may make and revoke elections not to have withholding apply as often as you wish. Additional elections may be obtained from [insert name and address].

If you do not return the election form by [insert date], federal income tax will be withheld from the taxable portion of your [pension] OR [annuity] payments as if you were a married individual claiming three withholding allowances. As a result, no federal income tax will be withheld if the taxable portion of your annual [pension] OR [annuity] payments is less than $5,400.

If you elect not to have withholding apply to your [pension] OR [annuity] payments, or if you do not have enough federal income tax withheld from your [pension] OR [annuity] payments, you may be responsible for payment of estimated tax. You may incur penalties under the estimated tax rules if your withholding and estimated tax payments are not sufficient.

[Treas. Reg. § 35.3405-1T, Q&A D-21]

Q 24:43 Is there sample language that may be used to elect not to have federal income tax withholding apply or to revoke a prior election not to have withholding apply?

Yes. A payee may elect not to have withholding apply or may revoke a prior election in any manner that clearly shows the payee's intent. The following language would suffice.

ELECTION FOR RECIPIENTS OF PERIODIC PAYMENTS

Instructions. Check Box A if you do not want any federal income tax withheld from your [pension] OR [annuity]. Check Box B to revoke an election not to have withholding apply. Return the signed and dated election to [insert name and address].

Even if you elect not to have federal income tax withheld, you are liable for payment of federal income tax on the taxable portion of your [pension] OR [annuity]. You also may be subject to tax penalties under the estimated tax payment rules if your payments of estimated tax and withholding, if any, are not adequate.

A ☐ do not want to have federal income tax withheld from my [pension] OR [annuity].

B ☐ want to have federal income tax withheld from my [pension] OR [annuity].

Signed: ________ ________
Name Date

Return your completed election to: [insert name and address].

[Treas. Reg. § 35.3405-1T, Q&A D-22]

Q 24:44 May the payee's election be combined with a withholding certificate (Form W-4P)?

Yes. The payor may provide a single statement for the payee to fill out and return that would enable the payee to elect not to have federal income tax withholding apply or to revoke a previous election and, at the same time, would enable the payee to claim the number of withholding allowances and the dollar amount the payee wants withheld. [Treas. Reg. § 35.3405-1T, Q&A D-23]

Q 24:45 Will a notice mailed to the payee's last-known address fulfill the notice requirement?

Yes. A notice mailed to the payee's last-known address will fulfill Code Section 3405(d)(10)(B)'s notice requirement. [Treas. Reg. § 35.3405-1T, Q&A D-24]

Q 24:46 If the payor provides notice before making the first payment, can an abbreviated notice be used to satisfy the requirement that a notice be given when making the first payment?

Yes. It is permissible to provide with the payment a statement that the payee has the right to elect out of federal income tax withholding. For example, the following sample notice may be used to satisfy the notice requirement if the payor has provided notice previously:

If federal income taxes have been withheld from the [pension] OR [annuity] payment you are receiving and if you do not wish to have taxes withheld, you should notify [insert name and address]. However, if you elect not to have withholding apply to your [pension] OR [annuity] payments, or if you do not have enough federal income tax withheld from your pension OR [annuity] payment, you may be responsible for payment of estimated tax. You may incur penalties under the estimated tax rules if your withholding and estimated tax payments are not sufficient.

If federal income taxes are not being withheld from your [pension] OR [annuity] payment because you have elected not to have withholding apply and if you wish to revoke that election and have federal income taxes withheld from your [pension] OR [annuity] payments, you should notify [insert name and address].

[Treas. Reg. § 35.3405-1T, Q&A D-27]

Q 24:47 Is the payor of periodic payments required to aggregate those payments with a payee's compensation to determine the amount of federal income taxes that must be withheld?

No. Although the payor must withhold from any periodic payment the amount that has to be withheld if the payment were a payment of wages by an employer to an employee for a payroll period, the amount of federal income taxes that must be withheld is calculated separately from the actual wages to the payee for the same period. [Treas. Reg. § 35.3405-1T, Q&A B-1]

Q 24:48 Can either the percentage method or the wage bracket method be used to determine the federal income tax withholding liability on a periodic payment?

Yes. Withholding on a periodic payment is accomplished by treating the payment as if it were wages. Therefore, unless the employee has elected not to have withholding apply (only in cases where the periodic payment is not an eligible rollover distribution), any method of withholding that is an appropriate method for withholding on wages is also an appropriate method for withholding on periodic payments. Refer to the Employer's Tax Guide (Circular E) for the general procedures on withholding, deposit, payment, and reporting of federal income tax withheld. Note, however, that any specific procedures contained in the Treasury regulations governing withholding [Treas. Reg. § 35.3405-1 et seq.] take precedence over any contrary rules in Circular E. [Treas. Reg. § 35.3405-1T, Q&A B-2]

Q 24:49 Do rules similar to those for wage withholding apply to the filing of a withholding certificate for periodic payments?

Yes. Unless the special withholding rules for pensions, annuities, and certain other deferred income in Code Section 3405 specifically conflict with the wage withholding rules under Code Section 3402, the rules for withholding on periodic payments will parallel the rules for wage withholding. Thus, if a withholding certificate (Form W-4P) is filed by a payee, it will generally take effect as provided in Code Section 3402(f)(3), relating to withholding exemptions for certificates filed to replace existing certificates. If a withholding certificate is furnished by a payee on or before the date on which payments commence, withholding takes effect with respect to payments made more than 30 days after the certificate is furnished, unless the payor elects to make it effective at an earlier date. If a payee furnishes a withholding certificate after the date on which payments commence, the withholding takes effect with respect to payments made on or after the status determination date (January 1, May 1, July 1, or October 1) that is at least 30 days after the date the certificate is filed, unless the payor elects to make it effective at an earlier date. If no withholding certificate (Form W-4P) is filed, the amount withheld is determined as if the payee were a married person claiming three withholding allowances. [Treas. Reg. § 35.3405-1T, Q&A B-3]

Q 24:50 If no withholding certificate has been filed and the payor is aware that the payee is single, is it still appropriate to base withholding on a married individual claiming three allowances?

Yes. If no withholding certificate (Form W-4P) is filed, the payor is not required or permitted to base withholding on the amount of allowances the payee actually is entitled to claim. Thus, the payor must base withholding on the rates for a married person with three withholding allowances. [Treas. Reg. § 35.3405-1T, Q&A B-4]

Code Section 3405(a)(4), as in effect before 2018, provided that, in the case of a payee entitled to periodic payments with respect to which a withholding certificate (IRS Form W-4P) had not been furnished, the amount to be withheld from each such payment "shall be determined by treating the payee as a married individual claiming three withholding exemptions." Section 11041(c)(2)(G) of the Tax Cuts and Jobs Act (P.L. 115-97, enacted on December 22, 2017), amended Code Section 3405(a)(4) to provide that the withholding rate when no withholding certificate (IRS Form W-4P) is furnished "shall be determined under rules prescribed by the Secretary." On February 12, 2018, the IRS issued Notice 2018-14, 2018-7 I.R.B. 353, which provides that, for 2018, the rules for withholding when no withholding certificate (IRS Form W-4P) is furnished with respect to periodic payments under Code Section 3405(a)(4) will parallel the rules for prior years and be based on treating the payee as a married individual claiming three withholding allowances.

Q 24:51 May a payor determine whether payments to an individual are subject to withholding based on the amount of the first periodic payment for the year?

No. Periodic payments can vary during a calendar year because of make-up or past-due payments, variable rates of payments, or cost-of-living adjustments, so that withholding based on the first payment within a year may be an inaccurate measure of withholding on total payments for the year. Therefore, the amount to be withheld is determined each payment period in the same manner as applies to withholding on wages (see the Employer's Tax Guide (Circular E) and the Treasury Regulations under Code Section 3402, regarding wage withholding). [Treas. Reg. § 35.3405-1T, Q&A B-5]

Q 24:52 If a payment period is specified by the terms of a commercial annuity contract, must that period be used as the appropriate period for determining the amount to be withheld?

Yes. Similarly, if the payment period is designated in a plan administrator's report, this period must be used as the appropriate payment period. [Treas. Reg. § 35.3405-1T, Q&A B-6]

Q 24:53 If the payor received no report from the plan administrator or beneficiary concerning the payment period, but knows the frequency of payments, can the known frequency be used as the appropriate payment period?

Yes. However, if no report is received and the payor has no knowledge of the frequency of payments, then the payor must treat the distribution as a nonperiodic distribution (see Q 24:55). Therefore, a distribution cannot be a periodic payment unless the frequency of payments is known. [Treas. Reg. § 35.3405-1T, Q&A B-7]

Q 24:54 If a payee receives a one-time payment that is a makeup payment resulting from an insurance company's incorrect calculation of a monthly annuity amount, is the one-time payment part of a series of periodic payments?

Yes. Because the onetime payment is a catch-up of prior amounts due as periodic payments, it is treated as part of a series of periodic payments. These payments are treated for withholding purposes in a manner similar to the treatment of supplemental wage payments in Treasury Regulations Section 31.3402(g)-1. [Treas. Reg. § 35.3405-1T, Q&A B-8]

Rules Applicable to Nonperiodic Payments

Q 24:55 What is a nonperiodic distribution?

A nonperiodic distribution is any designated distribution that is not a periodic payment. [I.R.C. § 3405(e)(3)]

For qualified retirement plan distributions made after 1992, mandatory federal income tax withholding is imposed at the rate of 20 percent on any distribution that is an eligible rollover distribution, but that is not directly rolled over into an eligible retirement plan. [I.R.C. § 3405(c)(1)(B)] Recipients cannot elect out of the 20 percent withholding, as they can for withholding on periodic distributions that are not eligible rollover distributions (see Q 24:2).

Nonperiodic distributions that are *not* eligible rollover distributions are subject to federal income tax withholding at the 10 percent rate. [I.R.C. § 3405(b)(1)] A recipient of any nonperiodic distribution (other than an eligible rollover distribution) may elect exemption from the 10 percent withholding, except for certain payments made outside the United States. The election is made on a distribution-by-distribution basis. However, to the extent permitted under applicable Treasury regulations, the election out of the 10 percent withholding may apply to later nonperiodic distributions made by the payor to the payee under the same plan. [I.R.C. § 3405(b)(2)(B)]

The Treasury Regulations under Code Section 3405 set forth the time and manner for making the election out of 10 percent withholding. Those regulations provide the following sample election form, which the payor can furnish, along with the notice to the payee of the payee's right to elect out of the 10 percent withholding (see Q 24:56). The payee can sign and then return the election form to the payor.

ELECTION FOR PAYEES OF NONPERIODIC PAYMENTS

Instructions. If you do not want any federal income tax withheld from your [distribution] OR [withdrawal], sign and date this election and return it to [insert name and address].

Even if you elect not to have federal income tax withheld, you are liable for payment of federal income tax on the taxable portion of your [distribution] or [withdrawal]. You also may be subject to tax penalties under the estimated tax payment rules if your payments of estimated tax and withholding, if any, are not adequate.

I do not want to have federal income tax withheld from my [distribution] OR [withdrawal].

Signed: ________ ________
Name Date

Return your completed election to: [insert name and address].

[Treas. Reg. § 35.3405-1T, Q&A D-26]

Q 24:56 Must the payor of a nonperiodic distribution (other than an eligible rollover distribution) notify the payee of his or her right to elect out of the 10 percent federal income tax withholding?

Yes. The payor of a nonperiodic distribution (other than an eligible rollover distribution) must notify each payee of his or her right to elect out of the 10 percent federal income tax withholding. The notice must be furnished at the time the nonperiodic distribution is made, or at an earlier time, if the Treasury regulations so prescribe. [I.R.C. § 3405(e)(10)(B)(ii)]

The payor should furnish the notice at a time sufficiently prior to the distribution date that the payee has reasonable time to elect out of withholding and the payor can receive that election and act upon it before the distribution is made. The facts and circumstances of each case will determine what a reasonable time is for furnishing the notice. [Treas. Reg. § 35.3405-1T, Q&A D-9] A notice that the plan administrator includes with the payee's application for benefits satisfies the reasonable time requirement. [Treas. Reg. § 35.3405-1T, Q&A D-10]

A payor may impose a deadline on the time the payee has to elect out of withholding, so as to ensure timely payment of the distribution, in the correct amount, but the payor must accept any election out of withholding or any revocation of that election right up to the time of distribution. [Treas. Reg. § 35.3405-1T, Q&A D-12]

A payor that furnishes the following sample notice of the right to elect out of the 10 percent federal income tax withholding is deemed to satisfy the notice requirement, provided the notice is timely provided. [Treas. Reg. § 35.3405-1T, Q&A D-25]

NOTICE OF WITHHOLDING ON DISTRIBUTIONS OR WITHDRAWALS FROM ANNUITIES, IRAs, PENSION, PROFIT SHARING, STOCK BONUS, AND OTHER DEFERRED COMPENSATION PLANS

The [distributions] OR [withdrawals] you receive from the [insert name of plan or company] are subject to federal income tax withholding unless you elect not to have withholding apply. Withholding will only apply to the portion of your [distribution] OR [withdrawal] that is included in your income subject to federal income tax. Thus, for example, there will be no withholding on the return of your own nondeductible contributions to the [plan] OR [contract].

You may elect not to have withholding apply to your [distribution] OR [withdrawal] payments by signing and dating the attached election and returning it [manner may be specified] to [insert name and address].

If you do not return the election by [insert date], receipt of your payments may be delayed. If you do not respond by the date your [distribution] OR [withdrawal] is scheduled to begin, federal income tax will be withheld from the taxable portion of your [distribution] OR [withdrawal]. [Insert information on rates if desired.]

If you elect not to have withholding apply to your [distribution] OR [withdrawal] payments, or if you do not have enough federal income tax withheld from your [distribution] OR [withdrawal], you may be responsible for payment of estimated tax. You may incur penalties under the estimated tax rules if your withholding and estimated tax payments are not sufficient.

No federal income tax withholding is required [Treas. Reg. 35.3405-1T, Q&A F-6], and as a result, no notice of the right to elect out of withholding need be given to a payee [Treas. Reg. § 35.3405-1T, Q&A F-7] if a nonperiodic distribution is under $200. Payments from several plans of the same employer may, but need not, be aggregated to determine if the $200 threshold has been reached. If the payor or plan administrator does not know, at the time a first payment of $200 or less is made, whether there will be more payments during the year for which aggregation of plans is required, the payor or plan administrator is not required to withhold federal income taxes from the first payment.

[Treas. Reg. § 35.3405-1T, Q&A F-6]

Q 24:57 What withholding rules apply to qualified retirement plan distributions that are paid outside the United States?

Distributions to nonresident aliens that do not qualify as an annuity are generally subject to tax at a rate of 30 percent. [I.R.C. §§ 871(a), 1441; Treas. Reg. § 1.1441-1, 2] However, an income tax treaty to which the United States is a party may provide for a reduced rate of tax. [Treas. Reg. § 1.1441-6(a); https://www.irs.gov/retirement-plans/plan-distributions-to-foreign-persons-require-withholding] Payors of qualified retirement plan distributions must generally withhold 30 percent from a plan distribution paid to a foreign payee unless the payor can readily associate the payment with valid documentation that establishes the payee is either a U.S. person or a foreign person entitled to a rate of withholding lower than 30 percent. Documentation can include Form W-9 (Request for Taxpayer Identification Number and Certification), Form W-8BEN (Certificate of Status of Beneficial Owner for United States Tax Withholding and Reporting (Entities)), or other appropriate sources. If the payor cannot reliably document the status of a retirement plan distribution recipient as a U.S. person or a foreign person entitled to lower withholding, the payor should apply the presumption rules in IRS Regulation Section 1.1441-1(b)(3)(iii)(C). Under those presumption rules, a retirement plan distribution is presumed to be made to a U.S. person only if the withholding agent has a record of a Social Security number for the payee, and relies on a payee mailing address that is in the United States or in the foreign country with which the United States has an income tax treaty in effect giving its residents exemption from U.S. tax of payments of this type. A payment that does not meet these presumption rules is presumed to be made to a foreign person. [see Treas. Reg. § 1.1441-1(b)(3)(iii)(C) for the complete rule] Plan sponsors and third-party administrators are withholding agents and may be liable for taxes and penalties for improper withholding. [see "Plan Distributions to Foreign Persons Require Withholding," available at https://www.irs.gov/retirement-plans/plan-distributions-to-foreign-persons-require-withholding]

Effective for payments made after December 31, 2000, payors of distributions from qualified retirement plans to nonresident aliens are required to withhold from the distributions in accordance with the 30 percent flat rate of Code Section 1441, rather than the graduated withholding rate of Code Section 3405, that is applicable to pension distributions to citizens of the United States. [Treas. Reg. § 1.1441-4(b)(1)(ii), (g); Notice 99-25, 1999-1 C.B. 1070] The rule will apply to payments from any trust under Code Section 401(a), annuity plan under Code Section 403(a), or annuity, custodial account, or retirement account under Code Section 403(b) made to nonresident aliens.

Lump-sum distributions, which would be subject to long-term capital gains treatment made to nonresident aliens, are subject to withholding. [Treas. Reg. § 1.1441-2(b)] However, the pension withholding rules do not apply to amounts paid to nonresident aliens if the amounts are subject to the withholding of tax on nonresident aliens or would be subject to such withholding but for a tax treaty. [I.R.C. § 3405(e)(1)(B)(iii)]

Chapter 25

Distributions In-Kind

Distributing assets in-kind (property other than cash) may be a convenience or a requirement, depending on the type of plan involved. Employee stock ownership plan (ESOP) participants, for example, generally have a right to demand a distribution in the form of employer securities. Participants in other types of plans may have the right to choose an in-kind distribution if the plan sponsor has agreed to assume the responsibility of the added complexity of such distributions under the plan.

In General 25-1
Optional Form of Benefit Rules 25-2
Operational Rules 25-6
Tax Withholding Requirements 25-7
Rollover Rules 25-9
Treatment of Life Insurance and Annuity Contracts 25-11
Distribution of Employer Securities 25-16

In General

Q 25:1 Who chooses to distribute in-kind?

Any plan sponsor maintaining a qualified plan may provide that distributions from the plan may be in cash or kind. If in-kind distributions are available, the plan sponsor must generally offer the option to receive an in-kind distribution to participants eligible to receive a distribution.

Q 25:2 Why would a plan sponsor choose to allow in-kind distributions?

There are a number of reasons why a plan sponsor may allow in-kind distributions. For example, many, if not most, 401(k) and other defined contribution plans permit participant investment direction among a selected menu of investments for the plan. Such plans may allow the participant to maintain his or her current investment strategy after distribution by directly transferring vested investment shares to an individual retirement account (IRA). Under this arrangement, a participant can choose when to sell a fund without being subject to market risk (i.e., the stock market and mutual fund may be low in value at the time of distribution). Otherwise, a participant who wishes to receive his or her vested balance may be forced to sell at a poor time and may incur significant losses. Also, if a plan does not allow in-kind distributions and a participant wants to invest in his or her current investments after the distribution, the participant may be forced to incur transaction charges to liquidate assets for distribution and then again when the participant buys the same holdings again after distributions.

Another example occurs when an individual life insurance contract or guaranteed investment contract (GIC) held in the plan may not be able to be liquidated due to an insolvency or financial difficulty of an insurance carrier. If the contract is distributed in-kind to the participant, the participant may later receive some value from the contract.

Further, plan sponsors that provide a death benefit through individual life insurance contracts may choose to reduce or eliminate the coverage. In such a case, the participant may want to assume all or a portion of the contract by continuing to pay the premiums personally. Similarly, a participant who is terminating employment may wish to continue the life insurance coverage offered in the retirement plan because replacement life insurance may be prohibitively expensive or unavailable due to his or her current health condition. It would be valuable to participants in these situations to be able to receive their life insurance policy as an in-kind distribution.

Certain plan assets, other than insurance contracts, may also be illiquid due to current market conditions. These could include real estate, collectibles, limited partnership interests, or securities of a corporation in bankruptcy or similar financial distress.

Optional Form of Benefit Rules

Q 25:3 Is the right to receive an in-kind distribution a protected optional form of benefit?

Yes, the right of a participant to receive an in-kind distribution is considered an optional form of benefit. As such, this option is a protected benefit and cannot be eliminated or made subject to employer discretion. The rights to receive cash or receive in-kind distributions are treated as two separate optional forms of benefit. Even though in-kind distribution is a protected right, that protection applies only to prior accruals; a plan sponsor can amend the plan to eliminate in-kind distributions for future accruals. [Treas. Reg. § 1.411(d)-4, Q&A-1(b)(1)]

Example 25-1: ABC Medical Clinic sponsors a 401(k) plan that offers participants the right to receive distributions in cash or in-kind. ABC Medical Clinic decides on January 1, 2018, that distributing in-kind creates too much paperwork and wants to eliminate the right to distribute in-kind. However, the participants will still retain the right to receive an in-kind distribution of benefits accrued on or before January 1, 2018, when this right is eliminated for future accruals. Sue leaves her job in December 2018 with a vested account balance of $160,000. Her account balance as of December 31, 2017, was $111,500; therefore, ABC Medical Clinic must offer Sue the right to receive an in-kind distribution of $111,500 (plus earnings attributable to the $111,500) based on this account balance.

Q 25:4 What nondiscrimination rules apply to in-kind distributions?

The right to an in-kind distribution is an optional form of benefit and is subject to the nondiscriminatory availability rules (see chapter 10). In general, this means that in-kind distribution may not be more available to highly compensated employees (HCEs) than non-highly compensated employees (NHCEs). [Treas. Reg. § 1.401(a)(4)-4(e)(1)(i)] The plan's in-kind distribution feature must satisfy two tests: a current availability test and an effective availability test. [Treas. Reg. § 1.401(a)(4)-4(a)]

Q 25:5 How is the current availability test satisfied?

The current availability requirement is satisfied if the group of employees for whom an in-kind distribution is available during a plan year satisfies the minimum coverage requirements of Code Section 410(b) by passing either the ratio percentage test or the nondiscriminatory classification test. [Treas. Reg. § 1.410(b)-4] The ratio percentage test is performed by looking at the percentage of NHCEs and HCEs who currently have the opportunity (if they were to leave employment) to receive a distribution in-kind as follows:

$$\frac{\text{NHCEs entitled to in-kind distribution/Total nonexcludable NHCEs}}{\text{HCEs entitled to in-kind distribution/Total nonexcludable HCEs}}$$

(See Appendix G for the determination of HCEs.) If the above ratio is 70 percent or greater, the plan satisfies the ratio percentage test. If the ratio is less than 70 percent, an alternate test, known as the *nondiscriminatory classification test,* may be used. The required 70 percent ratio is reduced to a lower threshold, based on the concentration of NHCEs. The concentration of NHCEs is the percentage of all employees of the employer who are NHCEs, taking into account only nonexcludable employees (see Q 25:6). Table 25-1 shows the safe- and unsafe-harbor percentages to meet the nondiscriminatory classification test for each NHCE concentration percentage.

Table 25-1.

NHCE Concentration Percentage	*Safe-Harbor Percentage*	*Unsafe-Harbor Percentage*
0–60%	50.00%	40.00%
61%	49.25%	39.25%
62%	48.50%	38.50%
63%	47.75%	37.75%
64%	47.00%	37.00%
65%	46.25%	36.25%
66%	45.50%	35.50%
67%	44.75%	34.75%
68%	44.00%	34.00%
69%	43.25%	33.25%
70%	42.50%	32.50%
71%	41.75%	31.75%
72%	41.00%	31.00%
73%	40.25%	30.25%
74%	39.50%	29.50%
75%	38.75%	28.75%
76%	38.00%	28.00%
77%	37.25%	27.25%
78%	36.50%	26.50%
79%	35.75%	25.75%
80%	35.00%	25.00%
81%	34.25%	24.25%
82%	33.50%	23.50%
83%	32.75%	22.75%
84%	32.00%	22.00%
85%	31.25%	21.25%
86%	30.50%	20.50%
87%	29.75%	20.00%
88%	29.00%	20.00%
89%	28.25%	20.00%
90%	27.50%	20.00%
91%	26.75%	20.00%
92%	26.00%	20.00%
93%	25.25%	20.00%

Table 25-1. *(cont'd)*

NHCE Concentration Percentage	*Safe-Harbor Percentage*	*Unsafe-Harbor Percentage*
94%	24.50%	20.00%
95%	23.75%	20.00%
96%	23.00%	20.00%
97%	22.25%	20.00%
98%	21.50%	20.00%
99%	20.75%	20.00%

A plan that exceeds its safe-harbor percentage will meet the current availability test; a plan that is below its unsafe-harbor percentage will not meet the current availability test. Plans falling between the safe-harbor and unsafe-harbor percentages must satisfy a facts and circumstances test. This would involve making a request to the IRS for a determination of whether this optional form of benefit is nondiscriminatory. [Treas. Reg. § 1.401(a)(4)-4(b)]

Q 25:6 Who is a nonexcludable HCE or NHCE?

A *nonexcludable HCE* or *NHCE* is any employee who will be counted in current availability testing because he or she does not fit into at least one of these four categories of excludable employees:

1. Employees who fail to meet the minimum age and service conditions of the plan.
2. Nonresident aliens who receive no U.S.-source income from the employer.
3. Collectively bargained employees with respect to a plan that solely benefits noncollectively bargained employees.
4. Employees of qualified separate lines of business as defined in Treasury Regulations Section § 1.414(r)-1(b).

[Treas. Reg. § 1.410(b)-6]

Q 25:7 When is the effective availability test satisfied for in-kind distributions?

Based on all of the facts and circumstances, the group of employees to whom an in-kind distribution is available must not substantially favor HCEs. [Treas. Reg. § 1.401(a)(4)-4(c)(1)] (See Appendix G for the determination of HCEs.)

Operational Rules

Q 25:8 How does the plan sponsor ensure that the nondiscriminatory availability rules for in-kind distribution are satisfied?

In-kind distributions, if available, should generally be offered to all participants in the plan. If it is not feasible to offer that option to all participants, the group of participants to whom in-kind distributions are offered must not include a disproportionate number of HCEs (see Qs 25:4–25:7).

Example 25-2: CDE Pharmacy terminates its profit sharing plan. The plan does not allow participants to direct the investments in their account. The plan permits distributions to be made in-kind. The plan owns a piece of real estate currently valued by an independent appraiser at $250,000, and total plan assets are $1 million. The real estate has been on the market for several months, and there is no buyer in sight. Joe, the 100 percent owner of CDE Pharmacy, decides that he would like to distribute the real estate in-kind to himself. Joe's account balance is $650,000, and if permitted, he could receive the entire parcel of real estate as part of his distribution. However, this would violate the current availability rules, because the four other participants in the plan (all NHCEs) would not be offered the opportunity to receive their distributions in-kind. Joe offers the option of an in-kind distribution of a portion of the real estate to Sue, Sally, and Sheila. Sue, Sally, and Sheila decide they are not interested in real estate as a part of their distribution. However, Joe did not amend the plan to offer real estate to Simon. By offering the option to 75 percent (three of four) of the NHCEs, Joe has likely satisfied the effective availability rules.

Q 25:9 How does a distribution in-kind work?

The methods for distributing plan assets in-kind will vary, depending on the circumstances:

1. In a participant investment-directed defined contribution plan, the securities held in a participant's account could be offered to the participant as an in-kind distribution. This could occur at any distributable event such as termination of employment, retirement, or termination of the plan.
2. In a defined benefit plan or employer investment-directed defined contribution plan, if in-kind distributions are not permitted, plan assets sufficient to make a distribution will generally be liquidated immediately before distribution. If some assets are not liquid or there are particular assets that participants are interested in keeping, the plan sponsor may decide to distribute these assets in-kind, if the plan so provides or is amended to so provide.
3. In an ESOP or stock bonus plan, the participant is entitled to receive a distribution of the employer securities, and share certificates of the employer securities will be distributed to the participant (see chapter 13). [I.R.C. §§ 409(h), 401(a)(23)] However, an S corporation ESOP may

distribute cash to plan participants in lieu of distributing employer securities. [I.R.C. § 409(h)(2)(B)]

Q 25:10 What happens if NHCEs accept the offer of in-kind distributions and the property cannot be divided?

In several private letter rulings, the IRS has allowed the establishment of a nonqualified trust to hold the plan's illiquid assets. The amount transferred to the trust is taxable income to the participant. When the illiquid assets become marketable, the independent trustee of the nonqualified trust sells those assets and distributes them on a pro rata basis. [Ltr. Ruls. 8950006, 9041075, 9226066, 9305027, 9421041]

Example 25-3: Assume the same facts as in Example 25-2, except that Joe does not want to receive the real estate as an in-kind distribution. Further assume that the real estate parcel has been on the market for the last two years and has not been sold. Joe, as the plan sponsor, could establish a nonqualified trust (with an independent trustee) to hold the parcel of real estate until it is sold. Each participant would have a pro rata share in the nonqualified trust based on the ratio of his or her account balance to the total of all account balances. Thus, Joe's pro rata share of the nonqualified trust would be 65 percent ($650,000 ÷ $1,000,000). When the real estate is eventually sold, Joe will receive 65 percent of the proceeds.

Q 25:11 How are assets distributed in-kind valued?

Assets distributed in-kind must be valued at their fair market value. [Treas. Reg. § 1.402(a)-1(a)(1)(iii)] If the securities or other assets are not publicly traded, an independent third party should appraise the assets.

Example 25-4: ABC Medical Clinic is terminating a defined benefit plan that contains the shares of a privately held corporation, DEF. Mary, the trustee of the plan and sole participant, is reluctant to sell the shares of DEF because of the success of the corporation, and she does not want to incur the transaction costs of selling the shares and then buying them personally. Mary should obtain an independent appraisal of the shares of DEF before proceeding with the distribution.

Tax Withholding Requirements

Q 25:12 What are the federal income tax withholding requirements for assets distributed in-kind?

If assets distributed in-kind are not transferred into an IRA or another qualified plan via a direct rollover (see chapter 21), the distribution is generally subject to the tax withholding requirements. One exception, employer securities, is discussed in chapter 24. An eligible rollover distribution, whether it is in cash or in-kind, is subject to mandatory 20 percent federal tax withholding (see chapter 24). The amount subject to withholding depends on the relative amounts of in-kind assets and cash distributed:

1. If the cash is sufficient to cover the entire amount of the tax withholding, the entire in-kind asset may be distributed to the plan participant, with applicable taxes being paid.
2. If the cash is insufficient to cover the entire amount of tax withholding due, the participant may be requested to pay the trustee of the plan in cash for the amount of the insufficiency.
3. If the participant does not provide the cash necessary to cover the balance of the withholding, the trustee must then sell a portion (or all if part cannot be sold) of the in-kind assets to cover the withholding.

[Treas. Reg. § 35.3405-1T, Q&As F-2, F-3]

Example 25-5: CDE Pharmacy sponsors a profit sharing plan that permits in-kind distribution of assets. Jan quits and requests that shares of FGH High Risk Growth Fund (FGH HRGF) be distributed to her, as well as the cash in her account. Jan's distribution consists of the following:

Cash	$20,000
FGH HRGF	$60,000
Total	$80,000

The mandatory tax withholding requirements provide that 20 percent of the distributable amount, or $16,000 (20% × $80,000), be withheld from Jan's account. Jan will receive a total of $64,000 ($80,000 − $16,000), which will consist of shares of FGH HRGF, which are valued at $60,000 and $4,000 in cash.

Example 25-6: Brandon terminates employment from CDE Pharmacy. He requests that he receive the FGH HRGF and the IJK Government Securities Fund (IJK GSF) shares in-kind. His distribution will consist of:

FGH HRGF	$40,000
IJK GSF	$70,000
Cash	$15,000
Total	$125,000

Brandon's tax withholding requirement is $25,000 (20% × $125,000), and his cash distribution of $15,000 is insufficient to cover the withholding. Brandon may pay the balance of $10,000 to the trustee in cash, or, if he declines, the trustee must sell sufficient mutual fund shares to raise the $10,000 needed to cover the withholding.

Q 25:13 What happens if the plan administrator or trustee cannot determine the value of the property without delaying payment to the participant?

In many situations, the plan administrator or payer will not be able to determine the value of property to be distributed as of the date of distribution without delaying payment to the participant. In those cases, the plan administrator or trustee may determine the value of the property to be distributed as of the last preceding valuation date before the date of distribution, as long as the valuation is made at least once each year. If the most recent valuation date occurred within the 90 days immediately preceding the date of distribution, the next most recent valuation date may be used. [Treas. Reg. § 35.3405-1T, Q&A F-1]

> **Example 25-7:** Bryan is to receive 90 shares of DEF as part of his distribution, plus $12,500 in cash. DEF is a closely held business, and an annual appraisal is performed on March 31 of each year. Bryan receives the distribution of shares in August 2018. On March 31, 2018, DEF was valued in an independent appraisal at $510 per share. In calculating the tax withholding requirements, the DEF shares are valued at $45,900 (90 shares × $510 per share). The withholding due is 20 percent of $58,400 ($12,500 + $45,900), or $11,680.

Rollover Rules

Q 25:14 Can assets distributed in-kind be rolled over into an IRA or another qualified plan?

Yes, assets distributed in-kind generally may be transferred via direct rollover into an IRA or another qualified plan (see chapter 21 for rollover requirements). However, the trustee or custodian of the IRA or the trustee of the qualified plan must be willing to accept such assets. Often, a participant must undergo a long search to secure an IRA trustee or custodian willing to accept unusual assets such as limited partnership interests, real estate, or closely held stock of a private corporation. An IRA may not hold life insurance contracts and an IRA trustee is prohibited from accepting or holding collectibles, including:

- Any work of art
- Any rug or antique
- Any metal or gem
- Stamps or coins (exceptions are provided for certain gold, silver, platinum, state coins, and gold, silver, platinum, or palladium bullion)
- Any alcoholic beverage
- Any other tangible personal property specified by the Secretary of the Treasury

[I.R.C. § 408(m)]

Q 25:15 May a participant roll over in-kind assets received from a qualified plan if it is not rolled over as part of a direct rollover?

Yes, the participant may roll over in-kind assets received directly (i.e., not in a direct rollover) from a qualified plan to an IRA or another qualified plan within 60 days after receipt. [I.R.C. § 402(c)(3)] However, the mandatory 20 percent tax withholding requirements will apply to the distribution. (see Qs 25:12, 25:13). If the participant receives property as a distribution, the property must be properly and timely rolled over to receive tax-free treatment. [I.R.C. § 402(c)(1)(C)]

Example 25-8: Shannon receives a distribution of 300 shares of the FGH Fund, worth $40,000 at the date of distribution, July 2, 2018. Her cash distribution was $10,000, but that was used to satisfy the 20 percent tax withholding obligation. Shannon decides on July 31, 2018, that she would like to defer taxation on the entire distribution. She can roll over the 300 FGH shares, and she can replenish the $10,000 applied as a tax withholding from her personal funds if she wants to avoid taxable income on that $10,000 in 2018.

Q 25:16 May a participant who receives a distribution of property sell it and roll it over into an IRA?

Yes, the property may be sold and the proceeds rolled over into an IRA or another qualified plan, even if the sales proceeds are greater than the amount of the initial distribution. If a loss is incurred and the entire proceeds of the sale are rolled over, the participant will not be taxed on the amount of the loss. [I.R.C. § 402(c)(6)]

Example 25-9: Erika receives a distribution of 300 shares of the IJK Fund, worth $45,000 at the date of distribution, July 2, 2018. On July 31, 2018, Erika sells the 300 shares of IJK that she received for $56,000. The entire $56,000 may be rolled over tax-free to an IRA on or before August 31, 2018 (60 days from July 2, 2018).

Example 25-10: Jordan is not so fortunate with the 200 shares of the FGH Fund worth $35,000 that he received on July 5, 2018. He sells the shares on August 17, 2018, for a substantial loss, as the shares are now worth only $15,000. Jordan may roll over $15,000 to an IRA on or before September 3, 2018. The $20,000 amount that was not rolled over because of the drop in value will not be taxable to Jordan, as long as all of the proceeds on the sale of FGH are rolled over.

Q 25:17 What if less than the full amount of the property received is rolled over?

A pro rata gain or loss must be recognized in gross income, unless the participant designates otherwise. The designation may be made by the due date (including extensions) of the participant's individual tax return. [I.R.C. § 402(c)(6)(C)]

Example 25-11: Bernie participates in the CDE Pharmacy 401(k) plan. As part of her distribution (after withholding), she receives, on September 6, 2018, shares of the FGH mutual fund valued at $40,000. Bernie sells the FGH mutual fund shares for $50,000 on October 15, 2018, and opts to roll over only $45,000 into an IRA on October 31, 2018. Unless Bernie designates otherwise by the due date of her personal return, a pro rata gain must be recognized in her 2018 gross income, calculated as follows:

Pro rata gain	=	(Gain ÷ Sales proceeds) × Amount not rolled over
	=	($10,000 ÷ $50,000) × $5,000
	=	$1,000

However, Bernie could designate that the entire $5,000 that was not rolled over be treated as a gain instead of income.

Treatment of Life Insurance and Annuity Contracts

Q 25:18 Can life insurance and annuity contracts be distributed in-kind?

Yes, individual life insurance and annuity contracts may be distributed directly to the participant. If a distribution of the contract from a pension plan occurs while the participant is currently employed, the plan's qualified status may be in jeopardy, unless in-service distributions are permitted (see chapter 1). Alternatively, if the insurance or annuity contract is sold to the participant (with the proceeds from the sale being deposited into the plan), a prohibited transaction may occur. Fortunately, the Department of Labor recognized this catch-22 situation and issued a prohibited-transaction-class exemption (P.T.C.E. 77-8), which was later modified by P.T.C.E. 92-6, to permit the sale of individual life insurance contracts to any of the following:

1. A plan participant insured under the contract;
2. A relative of the insured participant who is a beneficiary under the contract;
3. An employer, any of whose employees are covered by the plan; or
4. Another employee benefit plan.

The sales price is the fair market value of the contract (which may be the cash surrender value), provided certain conditions are met. [P.T.C.E. 92-6, 56 Fed. Reg. 31679] Rev. Proc. 2005-25 provides guidance from the IRS on the fair market value of insurance contracts for such transactions.

Q 25:19 What conditions must be satisfied for the sale of an insurance contract to a participant or relative to be exempt from the prohibited transaction rules?

The following conditions must be satisfied:

1. The participant is insured under the contract.

2. If the sale is to a relative, the relative must be a member of the family (including brothers or sisters) and a beneficiary under the contract.
3. The contract, if it had not been sold, would have been surrendered by the plan.
4. The amount received by the plan as consideration for the sale is at least equal to the amount necessary to put the plan in the same cash position as it would have been in had it retained the contract, surrendered it, and made any distribution owing to the participant of his or her vested interest under the plan.
5. The plan must not, with respect to the sale, discriminate in form or in operation in favor of plan participants who are officers, shareholders, or HCEs.

[P.T.C.E. 92-6, 56 Fed. Reg. 31679]

Q 25:20 Under what circumstances would a plan typically sell a life insurance contract to a participant or a relative of the participant?

The usual situations that cause a plan to offer to sell a life insurance contract to the participant (or a relative of the participant) are:

1. The insurance contract exceeds the incidental limits, and the contract must be reduced to retain the plan's qualified status. In this case, the insurance company may split the contract into two contracts, one that will be retained by the plan and the other maintained by the participant. If the participant chooses not to maintain the policy, the existing contract will simply be reduced.
2. The plan sponsor decides to eliminate life insurance in the plan entirely. This can also occur when a Code Section 412(e)(3) plan is converted to a traditional defined benefit plan.
3. The participant terminates or retires and would like to continue to maintain the life insurance on his or her own personal basis. This may happen for many reasons (e.g., the participant has a health problem and is uninsurable).
4. The plan terminates (see chapter 15) and the participant would like to maintain the insurance on a personal basis.

Q 25:21 How is the sale price for the purchase of the contract determined?

The insurance company will determine the cash surrender value of the contract at the time of the transfer. The participant (or relative of the participant) will then pay to the plan the amount of the cash surrender value. Alternatively, if the participant cannot afford to pay the cash surrender value, but still would like to receive the policy personally, the plan sponsor could request a maximum policy loan. If the cash surrender value of the contract is greater than the policy loan, the difference would be due from the participant. [Rev. Proc. 2004-16, 2004-10 I.R.B. 559] Note that the IRS guidance on determining the fair market value of the contract is found in Rev. Proc. 2005-25.

Example 25-12: Greg participates in the defined benefit plan sponsored by ABC Medical Clinic. The plan has a life insurance policy with a face amount of $250,000 maintained on his life. The Clinic decides that it does not want to continue maintaining life insurance coverage in the defined benefit plan. Greg is in need of this life insurance protection, but cannot afford to pay the $65,000 cash surrender value in the contract. Greg requests that the policy be transferred to him after a maximum policy loan is taken by the plan. The maximum policy loan is $62,500. Thus, Greg must pay $2,500 ($65,000 − $62,500) to the ABC Medical Clinic defined benefit plan before the insurance policy may be distributed to him. After the transfer, Greg will be responsible for the interest on the policy loan and if the policy loan is not repaid, it will be deducted from any proceeds payable upon his death.

Q 25:22 Are there circumstances under which the taxable amount of the insurance contract distributed will exceed the cash surrender value?

Yes, a so-called springing cash value contract, under which the reserves of the contract are substantially higher than its cash surrender value, will result in taxable income to the participant in an amount equal to the reserves in the contract. This type of contract became popular in the early 1980s as a means to reduce the surplus in a defined benefit plan. A similar type of contract was used in aggressively funded fully insured plans under Code Section 412(i), which has been replaced by Code Section 412(e)(3). The mechanism was to purchase a life insurance contract that had extremely low cash surrender values in the first three to five years (as compared with the premiums paid). Then, the policy was distributed to the participant for a relatively low cash surrender value, and the participant personally surrendered the policy later, after the low value period expired, for a significantly increased value. Notice 89-25 revised the valuation of such contracts. [Notice 89-25, Q&A-10]

However, in response to Notice 89-25, life insurance contracts were marketed that were structured in a manner that resulted in a temporary period during which neither a contract's reserves nor its cash surrender value represented the fair market value of the contract. For example, some life insurance contracts provided for large surrender charges (and other charges that were not expected) to be paid with future elimination or reversal. This future elimination or reversal was not always reflected in the calculation of the contract's reserve. If such a contract was distributed prior to the elimination or reversal of those charges, both the cash surrender value and the reserve under the contract significantly understated the fair market value of the contract. For example, it would not be appropriate to use a contract's reserve or the net surrender value of the contract as fair market value at the time of distribution if, under that contract, those amounts are significantly less than the aggregate of:

1. The premiums paid from the date of issue through the date of distribution, plus

2. Any amounts credited (or otherwise made available) to the policyholder with respect to those premiums (including interest, dividends, and similar income items) or, in the case of variable contracts, all adjustments made with respect to the premiums paid during that period that reflect investment return and the current market value of segregated asset accounts, minus
3. Reasonable mortality charges and reasonable charges (other than mortality charges) actually charged from the date of issue to the date of distribution and expected to be paid.

The regulations are to be applicable to any distribution of a transferable retirement income, endowment, or other life insurance contract occurring on or after February 13, 2004.

[Rev. Proc. 2005-25; Treas. Reg. § 1.402(a)-1(a)(2)]

Example 25-13: Alan participates in a CDE Pharmacy Defined Benefit Plan. In Year 1, the plan acquired a life insurance contract on Alan's life that was not a variable contract and had a face amount of $1,400,000. In that year and for the next four years, the plan paid premiums of $100,000 per year on the contract. The contract provided for a surrender charge that was fixed for the first five years of the contract and then decreased ratably to zero at the end of 10 years. The contract also imposed reasonable mortality and other charges.

The contract provided a stated cash surrender value for each of the first 10 years (the first five years are guaranteed), as set forth in the table below. The reserves under the contract, including life insurance reserves and reserves for advance premiums, and dividend accumulations at the end of the fifth year were $150,000.

Year	*Premium*	*Net Surrender Value*	*Cash Value Determined Without Reduction for Surrender Charge*
1	$100,000		
2	$100,000		
3	$100,000		
4	$100,000		
5	$100,000	$100,000	$450,000
6		$195,000	$475,000
7		$290,000	$500,000
8		$385,000	$525,000
9		$480,000	$550,000
10		$575,000	$575,000

At the end of Year 5, Alan retired and received a distribution of the insurance contract that was purchased on his life.

The contract was included in Alan's income at its fair market value of $450,000, rather than the $100,000 cash surrender value. Furthermore, Alan could not treat the $150,000 reserve as of the end of the fifth year as the fair market value, because this amount is less than the amount a willing buyer would pay a willing seller for such a contract, with neither party being under a compulsion to buy and sell and both having reasonable knowledge of the relevant facts.

Q 25:23 What are the tax consequences of distributing an insurance contract?

Generally, the distribution of a life insurance contract will be taxed to the participant as ordinary income unless it is a part of a lump-sum distribution that is eligible for favorable tax treatment. (See chapter 19 for a discussion of lump-sum treatment.) However, the participant may receive a credit for the cumulative PS-58 costs (see chapter 6) previously taxed to the participant (see Q 25:27). [Treas. Reg. § 1.402(a)-1(a)(2)]

Q 25:24 May an insurance contract be rolled over into an IRA?

No, a life insurance contract may not be rolled over into an IRA, either by direct rollover or subsequent rollover by the participant after receiving the contract. [I.R.C. § 408(a)(3); Rev. Rul. 81-275]

Q 25:25 May the participant roll over a life insurance contract into another qualified plan?

Yes, if the subsequent plan accepts rollovers and permits the investment in life insurance, the participant may roll over a life insurance contract into that plan.

Q 25:26 May the participant surrender the life insurance contract and then roll over the proceeds into an IRA?

Yes, the rules on the sale of property (other than cash) apply in this situation (see Qs 25:15, 25:16).

Q 25:27 May a participant receive credit for the PS-58 costs taxable in prior years?

Yes, the previously taxed PS-58 costs may be credited against the taxable amount when the contract is distributed to the participant. [Treas. Reg. § 1.72-16(b)] However, the PS-58 credit will not apply if the following is true:

1. The life insurance policy was surrendered by the plan and the proceeds were distributed to the participant. In this case, the cumulative PS-58 costs may not be recoverable by the participant. [see Ltr. Rul. 8721083]
2. The life insurance policy was stripped of all value up to the amount of the cumulative PS-58 costs by the plan and then distributed to the participant.

In this case, the cumulative PS-58 costs would be recoverable by the participant.

[Treas. Reg. § 1.72-16(b)(4); Ltr. Rul. 8539066]

Q 25:28 May an annuity contract be distributed in-kind to a participant?

Yes, but the annuity contract must be nontransferable; that is, the contract may not be transferred to any other individual after it is distributed to the participant. [I.R.C. § 402(b)(2); Treas. Reg. §§ 1.401(a)-1(a)(2), 1.402(c)-2, Q&A-10] The distribution of the annuity contract must also comply with the spousal consent requirements. (See chapter 19 for a discussion of the tax treatment of distributions of annuity contracts and chapter 11 for a discussion of the spousal consent requirements.)

Q 25:29 May an annuity contract be exchanged for another annuity contract with a different insurer without creating taxable income?

Yes, the nontransferability requirements are not violated if an annuity contract received as a distribution is exchanged for a *materially* similar contract with another insurer. There will be no income tax consequences as a result of the exchange. However, if the contracts are not materially similar, the fair market value of the new contract is immediately taxable. [G.C.M. 39882 (May 27, 1992)]

Example 25-14: Jonell, a participant in the target benefit plan of ABC Medical Clinic, terminates employment and receives an annuity contract as part of her distribution. Her spouse consents to the distribution. Jonell is concerned about the viability of the insurer and requests that the contract be exchanged for a materially similar annuity contract with an AAA-rated insurance company. The new contract is nontransferable and contains spousal consent requirements. Jonell does not realize any taxable income upon the exchange of this contract.

Distribution of Employer Securities

Q 25:30 May employer securities be distributed in-kind?

Yes, an ESOP or qualified stock bonus plan must generally permit the distribution of employer securities. A distribution of employer securities within a lump-sum distribution (see chapter 19) directly to a participant may provide some tax advantages over a rollover to the participant's IRA or another qualified plan because the net unrealized appreciation (NUA) is not considered gross income at the time of distribution. [I.R.C. § 402(e)(4); Treas. Reg. § 1.402(a)-1(b)(1)(i)(a)]

Q 25:31 What is NUA?

Net realized appreciation is the difference, if positive, between the fair market value of the employer securities and the plan's cost basis for the securities. The amount of NUA is computed by the plan and reported to the participant on Form 1099-R (see chapter 27). The plan must track the cost basis of the employer securities as they are acquired by the ESOP or stock bonus plan. [Treas. Reg. § 1.402(a)-1(b)(2)(i)]

Q 25:32 May the participant choose not to have the rules on NUA apply?

Yes, the participant may choose, on his or her personal tax return, not to defer the gain on the NUA. By making such an election, the participant is choosing to pay the tax currently, rather than defer the gain until the time when the employer securities are sold. [I.R.C. § 402(e)(4)(B)]

Q 25:33 How is the cost basis determined?

The cost basis of the employer securities is computed in accordance with one of the following rules. If Rule 1 is not applicable, then Rule 2 must be applied. If Rule 2 is inapplicable, then Rule 3 applies. Finally, if Rule 3 is inapplicable, Rule 4 applies.

Rule 1. If the employer security was allocated to the account of the participant at the time it was contributed to, or purchased by, the trust, cost basis is used. [Treas. Reg. § 1.402(a)-1(b)(2)(ii)(a)]

Rule 2. If, as of the close of each taxable year of the trust, the trust allocates to the accounts of the participants all securities acquired during the year (exclusive of securities that are not allocated due to a requirement that only whole shares be allocated), the cost basis for securities purchased during the year is the average cost of the securities acquired during the year. [Treas. Reg. § 1.402(a)-1(b)(2)(ii)(b)]

Rule 3. If neither Rule 1 nor Rule 2 is applicable, if the trust fund is exclusively invested in a single type of employer security, and if during the year none of the employer securities has been sold (except to pay benefits under the trust), the cost basis of employer securities is the total amount of contributions credited to the account of the participant, reduced by amounts that are not invested in employer securities. [Treas. Reg. § 1.402(a)-1(b)(2)(ii)(c)]

Rule 4. If none of the above methods can be used, the basis of employer securities is determined on an average cost basis. A first in, first out (FIFO) basis or a moving average may be used, as chosen by the plan sponsor. [Treas. Reg. § 1.402(a)-1(b)(2)(ii)(d)]

Example 25-15: *Method 1.* The CDE Pharmacy stock bonus plan allocates employer securities to the accounts of the participants at the time the plan acquires the securities. Bob has 120 shares allocated to his account at the time of his termination of employment, with a current market value of $12,000. The cost basis for Bob's shares, based on the plan accounting, is $5,000. If Bob receives a lump-sum distribution including 120 shares in-kind, the NUA is computed as follows:

NUA - Fair market value of employer securities − Cost basis
- $12,000 − $5,000
- $7,000

Example 25-16: *Method 2.* The ABC Medical Clinic ESOP allocates employer securities acquired during the year as of the last day of the plan year and determines the corresponding cost basis using the average purchase price. The ESOP, for the plan year ended December 31, 2018, acquires the following amounts of shares at the prices indicated:

Date	*Number of Shares*	*Purchase Price*
May 6, 2018	200	$15,000
July 7, 2018	400	$35,000
September 19, 2018	600	$46,000
Totals	1,200	$96,000

The average cost of the shares purchased during the year is $80 ($96,000 ÷ 1,200). Mitzi has 100 shares allocated to her account during 2018. The cost basis of the shares acquired during 2018, for Mitzi is $8,000 ($80 × 100 shares).

Example 25-17: *Method 3.* The CDE Pharmacy ESOP cannot use Method 1 or 2 because the plan does not allocate employer securities at the time of acquisition or annually. Fred had contributions allocated to his account in the following years:

Year	*Amount of Contribution*
1	$1,250
2	$1,750
3	$3,500
4	$4,500
5	$6,000
Total	$17,000

At the time Fred leaves, he has 550 shares of CDE Pharmacy allocated to his account and $1,000 in cash. The market value of the shares at the time of distribution is $33,500. The NUA is calculated as follows:

NUA - Market value of shares − Employer contributions − Unallocated cash
- $33,500 − $17,000 − $1,000
- $15,500

Example 25-18: *Method 4.* The DEF Nurses ESOP uses the rolling cost method and recomputes the average cost whenever employer securities are acquired or sold. The following acquisitions and sales have occurred since the ESOP was instituted:

Date	*Shares Acquired/(Sold)*	*Acquisition/(Sales) Cost*
May 2, 2011	1,500	$300,000
July 25, 2012	2,500	$550,000
August 14, 2013	(500)	($125,000)
March 27, 2014	1,000	$250,000
April 13, 2016	(1,000)	($275,000)
May 26, 2017	2,000	$550,000
Totals	5,500	$1,250,000

When Bob receives a distribution from the ESOP of 1,000 shares worth $250,000, his cost basis is computed by looking at the average acquisition price of $227.27 ($1,250,000 ÷ 5,500 shares). His NUA is computed as follows:

NUA - Market value of employer securities − Cost basis
- $250,000 − (1,000 × $227.27)
- $250,000 − $227,270
- $22,730

Q 25:34 What happens if the employer securities decline in value?

If the market value of the employer securities is less than the cost basis, no loss is realized until the employer securities are actually sold. The cost basis is maintained, so the participant may still have the opportunity to recoup losses. There is an exception, however, for employer securities that are worthless. The participant is allowed an ordinary loss deduction (to the extent of his or her after-tax contributions) for a distribution of worthless securities. [Rev. Rul. 72-328]

Q 25:35 If the participant chooses to defer tax on the NUA, what taxable results occur when the employer securities are sold?

When the former participant sells or exchanges the employer securities with untaxed NUA, any gain that is realized is long-term capital gain up to the amount of the NUA. This is true no matter how long the securities have been held. Any gain that is more than the NUA is a long-term or short-term capital gain, depending upon how long the securities have been held after they were distributed from the qualified plan. [Notice 98-24]

For gains in excess of NUA, the Tax Increase Prevention and Reconciliation Act of 2005, enacted in May 2006, provided a two-year extension, from 2008 to 2010 (which was extended by President Obama from 2010 to 2012), of the reduced 15 percent tax rate on long-term capital gains. For individuals in the 10 percent and 15 percent income tax brackets, the tax rate on long-term capital gains is 0 percent. For 2012, generally speaking, individuals earning less than $34,000 and married couples (filing jointly) earning less than $68,000 would qualify for the 0 percent rate. [I.R.C. § 1]

For the most part, the American Taxpayer Relief Act of 2012 maintained the 2012 rates, but it changed the top marginal tax rate on long-term capital gains to 20 percent for individuals with taxable income over $400,000 (subject to indexing) or married couples with taxable income over $450,000 (subject to indexing). The Tax Cuts and Jobs Act (TCJA) (Pub. L. No. 115-97, enacted on December 22, 2017) effective in 2018 still has three tax rates for long-term capital gains with the 20 percent rate applying to individuals with taxable income over $425,801.

> **Example 25-19:** Annette participates in the ABC Medical Clinic ESOP and receives a distribution of 5,000 shares of employer securities in 2018. Her NUA is $65,000, on which she chooses to defer tax until the employer securities are sold. If she sells the securities later in 2018 and realizes a gain of $75,000, the NUA of $65,000 is subject to capital gains rates, while the $10,000 (in excess of NUA) is treated as short-term gain. If she sells the securities in 2019 (after holding them for at least one year) and realizes a gain of $100,000, the entire $100,000 will be taxable as capital gains at a 15 percent tax rate, assuming that Annette and her spouse are in a tax bracket higher than 15 percent and have less than $479,001 (as indexed) taxable income.

> **Example 25-20:** Greg also participates in the ABC Medical Clinic ESOP and directly rolls over 10,000 shares of employer securities. His NUA is $130,000 at the time of the rollover. The stock continues to appreciate in value, and the total appreciation when Greg sells the employer securities is $278,000. Greg decides to receive a distribution from the IRA of $365,000, which represents the entire proceeds from the sale of employer securities. This amount is subject to ordinary income tax; capital gains treatment is not available for Greg.

Chapter 26

Trustee-to-Trustee Transfers

This chapter explains the rules governing certain transfers made directly from one retirement plan to another (trustee-to-trustee transfers), including (1) so-called elective transfers of benefits between plans that result in the elimination or reduction of Section 411(d)(6) protected benefits but do not violate the anti-cutback rules, provided certain requirements are met, and (2) transfers of plan assets and liabilities in connection with plan mergers, consolidations, and asset transfers. It should be emphasized that a trustee-to-trustee transfer is not a direct rollover (see chapter 21).

Retirement Plan Mergers, Consolidations, and Asset Transfers 26-1
Application of the Merger, Consolidation, and Transfer Requirements to Retirement Plan Spinoffs 26-2
Retirement Plan Mergers or Consolidations 26-3

Retirement Plan Mergers, Consolidations, and Asset Transfers

Q 26:1 What rules under the Code and ERISA apply to retirement plan mergers, consolidations, and transfers of assets?

The Code and ERISA protect participants' benefits when qualified retirement plans are merged or consolidated or when assets are transferred from one plan to another. [I.R.C. §§ 401(a)(12), 414(l)(1); ERISA § 208]

ERISA Protections. Under ERISA, plan participants are protected against losing accrued benefits by a guarantee that their benefits after a merger, consolidation, or transfer of assets will be equal to or greater than their benefits immediately before any such transaction, if the plan had then terminated. [ERISA § 208]

Code Protections. The two relevant Code provisions provide similar protections. Code Section 414(l) provides that a trust forming part of a plan will not be a qualified trust unless each participant would receive, if the plan terminated immediately after the merger, consolidation, or transfer, a benefit equal to or greater than the benefit he or she would have received if the plan had terminated immediately before the merger, consolidation, or transfer. [I.R.C. § 414(l)(1)]

Similarly, Code Section 401(a)(12) requires a plan to provide that each participant shall be entitled to a benefit after the merger, consolidation, or transfer of assets that is equal to or greater than the benefit he or she would have received immediately before the merger. Code Section 401(a)(12) specifies provisions to be contained in the plan document, whether or not such a transaction ever takes place, but Code Section 414(l) applies only when such a transaction occurs.

These rules do not apply to multiemployer plans, which are subject to their own rules. [I.R.C. § 414(l)(1), last sentence; I.R.C. § 401(a)(12), last sentence; ERISA § 208, last sentence]

The plan benefits that are subject to the merger, consolidation, and transfer rules under the Code and ERISA are those provided exclusively by plan assets, under the priority allocation rules of ERISA Section 4044, if the plan had then terminated. [Treas. Reg. § 1.414(l)-1(b)(5)] Therefore, protected benefits do not include benefits guaranteed by the Pension Benefit Guaranty Corporation (PBGC) but not provided by the assets of the plan.

Q 26:2 Are there any exceptions to the merger, consolidation, and transfer rules?

Yes. Except to the extent provided in PBGC regulations, the merger, consolidation, and transfer rules do not apply when (1) a multiemployer plan is split into two or more plans, one or more of which is not a multiemployer plan, or (2) a single employer plan is merged into a multiemployer plan. [Treas. Reg. § 1.414(l)-1(c)(2)] This exception does not apply to multiple employer plans.

Application of the Merger, Consolidation, and Transfer Requirements to Retirement Plan Spinoffs

Q 26:3 Do the merger, consolidation, and transfer of asset rules apply to retirement plan spinoffs?

Yes. The merger, consolidation, and transfer of asset rules also apply to a retirement plan "spinoff," that is, a single plan split into two or more spinoff plans. [Treas. Reg. §§ 1.414(l)-1(b)(4), 1.414(l)-1(m), (n)]

Q 26:4 How do the merger, consolidation, and transfer of asset rules apply to defined contribution plan spinoffs?

After a defined contribution plan spinoff, the requirements of the merger, consolidation, and transfer of asset rules are met if the following two conditions are satisfied:

1. The account balance of each participant in a resulting plan (or the sum of his or her account balances if he or she participates in more than one resulting plan) equals his or her account balance in the original plan, before the spinoff; and
2. Immediately after the spinoff, the value of the assets of each resulting plan equals the sum of all participant account balances under that plan.

[ERISA § 208; Treas. Reg. § 1.414(l)-1(m)]

Q 26:5 How do the merger, consolidation, and transfer of asset rules apply to defined benefit plan spinoffs?

General Rule. With the exception of small spinoffs (see below), if a defined benefit plan is spun off, the requirements of the merger, consolidation, and transfer of asset rules are met if both of the following conditions are satisfied:

1. All of the accrued benefits of each participant are allocated to only one of the resulting plans; and
2. The value of the assets allocated to each resulting plan is not less than the present value of benefits accumulated before the spinoff. Present value is determined on a termination basis.

[I.R.C. § 414(l)(2); ERISA § 208; Treas. Reg. § 1.414(l)-1(n)(1)]

Exception for De Minimis *Spinoffs*. The merger, consolidation, and transfer of asset rules will be deemed to be satisfied if both of the following conditions are met:

1. The value of the assets that are spun off equals the present value of the accrued benefits that are spun off (whether or not vested); and
2. The value of the assets that are spun off, when combined with any assets that are transferred in other spinoffs during the same plan year, is less than 3 percent of the assets of the pre-spinoff plan on at least one day in that plan year.

Spinoffs that happen in previous or later plan years are ignored if they are not part of a single spinoff designed to occur, in steps, over more than one plan year. [Treas. Reg. § 1.414(l)-1(n)(2)]

Retirement Plan Mergers or Consolidations

Q 26:6 What is a "merged" or "consolidated" retirement plan?

A retirement plan merger or consolidation occurs when two or more plans are combined into a single plan. [Treas. Reg. § 1.414(l)-1(b)(2)] A plan is considered a single plan only if, on an ongoing basis, all of the plan assets are available to pay benefits to covered employees and their beneficiaries. [Treas. Reg. § 1.414(l)-1(b)(1)]

Q 26:7 How are the merger rules satisfied when two or more defined contribution plans merge?

The plan merger rules will be satisfied when two or more defined contribution plans merge if all of the following three conditions are met:

1. The sum of the account balances in each plan equals the fair market value (determined as of the date of the merger) of the entire plan's assets.
2. The assets of each plan are combined to form the assets of the merged plan.
3. Immediately after the merger, each participant in the merged plan has an account balance equal to the sum of the account balances he or she had in the plans immediately before the merger. [Treas. Reg. § 1.414(l)-1(d)] When two defined contribution plans are merged, forfeitures attributable to either pre-merger plan may be allocated among all participants in the merged plan. [T.I.R. No. 1408, Q-17 (Oct. 30, 1975)]

Q 26:8 How are the merger rules satisfied when two or more defined benefit plans are merged?

After the merger of two or more defined benefit plans, the merger rules are applied by comparing the benefits on a termination basis before and after the merger. [Treas. Reg. § 1.414(l)-1(e)] "Benefits on a termination basis" are the benefits that would be provided exclusively by plan assets pursuant to ERISA Section 4044 and the regulations thereunder, if the plan is terminated, which sets forth the rules governing the allocation of plan assets by priority categories. [Treas. Reg. § 1.414(l)-1(b)(5)] Thus, the term "benefits on a termination basis" does not include benefits that are guaranteed by the PBGC, but not provided by plan assets. [Treas. Reg. § 414(l)-1(b)(5)]

At times, for some participants, the benefits provided on a termination basis for the resulting merged plan would differ from the benefits provided on a termination basis in the pre-merger plans if the plan's assets were simply combined and if each participant retained an accrued benefit. [Treas. Reg. § 1.414(l)-1(e)(2)] If this were the case, some participants would get smaller benefits after the merger than before the merger. This would violate the merger rules under Code Section 414(l), unless the distribution of benefits on termination, under ERISA Section 4044, were changed. Thus, the Treasury regulations modify the application of ERISA Section 4044 through the use of a special schedule of benefits. [Treas. Reg. § 1.414(l)-1(e)(2), (f)]

If a defined benefit plan is merged with a defined contribution plan, one of the plans before the merger should be converted into the other kind of plan. [Treas. Reg. § 1.414(l)-1(l)] The rules described in this Q 26:8 would apply if the defined contribution plan were converted into a defined benefit plan, and those described in Q 26:7 would apply if the defined benefit plan were converted into a defined contribution plan.

Q 26:9 Must the IRS be notified if there is a retirement plan merger or consolidation, spinoff, or transfer of plan assets or liabilities?

Yes, unless an exception to the IRS notification rules applies (see Q 26:12). Generally, not less than 30 days before a retirement plan merger or consolidation, spinoff, or transfer of plan assets or liabilities of one plan to another plan, the sponsor or plan administrator of each plan involved in the transaction must file a notice with the IRS, on Form 5310-A, *Notice of Plan Merger or Consolidation, Spinoff, or Transfer of Plan Assets or Liabilities*; *Notice of Qualified Separate Lines of Business*. [I.R.C. § 6058(b); Treas. Reg. § 301.6058-1(e)]

Q 26:10 What is the purpose of Form 5310-A?

IRS Form 5310-A is used by retirement plan sponsors or plan administrators to give the IRS an advance notice of:

1. *Plan merger or consolidation.* A plan merger or consolidation that is the combining of two or more plans into a single plan.
2. *Plan spinoff.* A plan spinoff that is the splitting of a single plan into two or more spinoff plans.
3. *Transfer of plan assets or liabilities to another plan.* A plan transfer of assets or liabilities that is the splitting off of a portion of the assets or liabilities of the transferor plan and the concurrent acquisition or assumption of these split-off assets or liabilities by the transferee plan. [Instructions to Form 5310-A]

An IRS determination letter will not be issued when a Form 5310-A is filed. [Instructions to Form 5310-A]

Note: In September 1994, Form 5310-A was revised to include the notice employers must file if they wish to be treated as operating qualified separate lines of business (QSLOBs) for plan years beginning after 1993. See IRS Revenue Procedure 93-40 [1993-2 C.B. 535] and the Instructions to IRS Form 5310-A. Note also that an IRS determination letter will not be issued when a Form 5310-A is filed as a QSLOB notice. [Instructions to IRS Form 5310-A]

Q 26:11 Who must file Form 5310-A with the IRS?

Unless an exception to the IRS notification rules applies (see Q 26:12), the sponsor or plan administrator (as defined in Code § 414(g)) of a pension, profit sharing, or other deferred compensation plan (except a multiemployer plan covered by PBGC insurance) must file IRS Form 5310-A for a plan merger or consolidation, a spinoff, or a transfer of plan assets or liabilities to another plan. [I.R.C. § 6058(b); Treas. Reg. § 301.6058-1(e); Instructions to Form 5310-A]

IRS Form 5310-A must be filed for each plan with a separate employer identification number (EIN) and plan number (PN) if that plan is involved in a merger or transfer of plan assets or liabilities. This includes plans that were not in existence before the plan merger and plans that cease to exist after the plan merger. In the case of a plan spinoff, Form 5310-A should be filed only for the plan in existence before the spinoff. [Instructions to Form 5310-A]

Q 26:12 Are there any situations in which Form 5310-A does not have to be filed with the IRS?

Yes. Form 5310-A does not have to be filed with the IRS in any of the situations described below.

Direct Rollover. Form 5310-A does not have to be filed for an eligible rollover distribution that is paid directly to an eligible retirement plan in a direct rollover described in Code Section 401(a)(31). [Instructions to Form 5310-A]

Certain Plan Mergers, Consolidations, or Spinoffs. Form 5310-A does not have to be filed with the IRS if the plan merger or consolidation, spinoff, or transfer of plan assets or liabilities complies with Treasury Regulations Section 1.414(l)-1(d), (h), (m), or (n)(2). Generally, those requirements will be satisfied in the following four situations:

1. *Two or more defined contribution plans are merged and all of the following conditions are met—*
   a. The sum of the account balances in each plan prior to the merger (including unallocated forfeitures, an unallocated suspense account for excess annual additions, and an unallocated suspense account for an employee stock ownership plan (ESOP)) equals the fair market value of the entire plan assets. (For example, neither plan has an outstanding Code Section 412(d) minimum funding waiver balance.)
   b. The assets of each plan are combined to form the assets of the plan as merged.
   c. Immediately after the merger, each participant in the plan as merged has an account balance equal to the sum of the account balances the participant had in the plans immediately prior to the merger.
2. *There is a spinoff of a defined contribution plan and all of the following conditions are met—*
   a. The sum of the account balances in the plan prior to the spinoff equals the fair market value of all plan assets. (For example, the plan does not have an outstanding Code Section 412(d) minimum funding waiver balance.)
   b. The sum of the account balances for each of the participants in the resulting plan(s) equals the account balance of the participants in the plan before the spinoff.
   c. The assets in each of the plans immediately after the spinoff equal the sum of the account balances for all participants in that plan. (For example, the plan does not have unallocated accounts.)
3. *Two or more defined benefit plans are merged into one defined benefit plan and both of the following conditions are met—*

a. The total liabilities (the present value of benefits whether or not vested) that are merged into the larger plan involved in the merger are less than 3 percent of the assets of the larger plan. This condition must be satisfied on at least one day in the larger plan's year during which the merger occurs. All previous mergers (including transfers from another plan) occurring in the same plan year are taken into account in determining the percentage of assets. For example, assume that a merger involving almost 3 percent of the assets of the larger plan occurs in the first month of the larger plan's plan year. In the fourth month of that year, a second merger occurs involving liabilities equal to 2 percent of the assets of the larger plan. The total of both mergers exceeds 3 percent of the assets of the larger plan. As a result of the second merger, both mergers must be reported to the IRS on Form 5310-A. Also, mergers occurring in previous plan years are taken into account in determining the percentage of assets above if the series of mergers is, in substance, one transaction with the merger occurring during the current plan year. Aggregating mergers may cause a merger, for which a Form 5310-A was not initially required to be filed, to become reportable as a result of a subsequent merger. In this case, the merger(s) must be reported on the Form 5310-A filed for the subsequent merger.

b. The provisions of the larger plan that allocate assets at the time of termination must provide that in event of a spinoff or termination of the plan within five years following the merger, plan assets will be allocated first for the benefits of the participants in the other plan(s) to the extent of their benefits on a termination basis just prior to the merger.

4. *There is a spinoff of a defined benefit plan into two or more defined benefit plans and both of the following conditions are met—*

a. For each plan that results from the spinoff, other than the spunoff plan with the greatest value of plan assets after the spinoff, the value of the assets spun off is not less than the present value of the benefits spun off (whether or not vested).

b. The value of the assets spun off to all the resulting spunoff plans (other than the spunoff plan with the greatest value of plan assets after the spinoff) plus other assets previously spun off (including transfers to another plan) during the plan year in which the spinoff occurs is less than 3 percent of the assets of the plan before the spinoff as of at least one day in that plan's plan year. For example, assume that a spinoff involving less than 3 percent of the assets of the plan occurs in the first month of the plan year. In the fourth month of the plan year, a second spinoff occurs, involving liabilities equal to 2 percent of the assets of the plan. The total of both spinoffs exceeds 3 percent of the plan assets. As a result of the second spinoff, Form 5310-A must be filed to report both spinoffs.

Spinoffs occurring in previous or subsequent plan years are taken into account in determining the percentage of assets spun off for purposes of determining whether a single transaction greater than

3 percent (of plan assets) has occurred if such spinoffs are, in substance, one transaction with the spinoff occurring during the current plan year.

Aggregating spinoffs may cause a spinoff for which a Form 5310-A was not initially required to be filed to become reportable as a result of a subsequent spinoff. In this case, report the spinoff(s) on the Form 5310-A filed for the subsequent spinoff. In this case, the spinoffs would be reported on the Form 5310-A filed for the subsequent spinoff.

Transfers of Plan Assets or Liabilities. A transfer of plan assets or liabilities is considered a combination of separate plan spinoffs and mergers.

Form 5310-A does not have to be filed with the IRS for (1) the transferor plan in a transfer transaction if the assets transferred satisfy the spinoff conditions in situation 2 or 4 above, or (2) the transferee plan in a transfer transaction if the plan liabilities transferred satisfy the merger conditions in situation 1 or 3 above.

Thus, in some situations, the transferor plan may have to file Form 5310-A but not the transferee plan, or the transferee plan may have to file but not the transferor plan. [Instructions to Form 5310-A]

Q 26:13 If a Form 5310-A must be filed with the IRS, when must it be filed?

If a Form 5310-A is required to be filed with the IRS, it must be filed at least 30 days prior to a plan merger or consolidation, spinoff, or transfer of plan assets or liabilities to another plan. [Instructions to Form 5310-A]

Q 26:14 Are there penalties for filing a Form 5310-A late?

Yes. If the Form 5310-A is being filed with the IRS to report a plan merger or consolidation, spinoff, or transfer of plan assets or liabilities, there is a penalty for late filing. The penalty is $25 a day for each day the Form 5310-A is late (up to a maximum of $15,000). The Form 5310-A is late if it is not filed at least 30 days before the plan merger or consolidation, spinoff, or transfer of plan assets or liabilities. [Instructions to Form 5310-A]

Chapter 27

Reporting Distributions: IRS Form 1099-R

When funds are distributed from a qualified retirement plan, the trustee or plan administrator must provide an IRS Form 1099-R to report the taxable income to the IRS and to the participant. All Form 1099-Rs are then transmitted by the payer to the IRS. This chapter discusses the reporting of distributions from qualified retirement plans.

Overview 27-1
General Requirements 27-2
Line-by-Line Explanation 27-10
Electronic Filing 27-20
Correcting Form 1099-R 27-25
Combined Federal/State Filing Program 27-26

Overview

Q 27:1 What is IRS Form 1099-R?

IRS Form 1099-R (Form 1099-R), *Distributions from Pension, Annuities, Retirement or Profit-Sharing Plans, IRAs, Insurance Contracts, etc.*, is used to report distributions from qualified plans (including § 457(b) state and local government plans), whether or not the distribution is taxable or the payer withheld federal income tax. (See chapter 24 for a discussion of withholding tax.) Any distribution over $10 must be reported on Form 1099-R. The entire distribution must be reported even though some of the distribution may not be taxable. See Q 27:17 for different types of distributions that are reported on Form 1099-R.

[2018 Instructions for Forms 1099-R and 5498, at 1]

Q 27:2 Is military retirement pay reported on Form 1099-R?

Yes. Payments to military retirees are reported on Form 1099-R. Military retirement pay awarded in a property settlement to a former spouse is reportable under the name and taxpayer identification number (TIN) of the recipient, not the military retiree. Payments of military survivor benefit annuities are also reported on Form 1099-R. [2018 Instructions for Forms 1099-R and 5498, at 2]

Q 27:3 How are payments to an alternate payee under a QDRO reported?

Payments to an alternate payee (who is a spouse or former spouse of the participant) under a qualified domestic relations order (QDRO) are reported on Form 1099-R using the name and TIN of the alternate payee. If the alternate payee under a QDRO is not a spouse or former spouse, the name and TIN of the participant are used. (See chapter 3.) [2018 Instructions for Forms 1099-R and 5498, at 9]

Q 27:4 How are payments to nonresident aliens reported?

If income tax is withheld under Code Section 3405 on any distribution to a nonresident alien, the distribution and withholding are reported on Form 1099-R.

If income tax is not withheld under Code Section 3405, income tax must be withheld under Code Section 1441, generally at a 30 percent rate (see chapter 24). Such distributions and withholding must be reported on IRS Form 1042, *Annual Withholding Tax Return for U.S. Source Income of Foreign Persons*, and IRS Form 1042-S, *Foreign Person's U.S. Source Income Subject to Withholding*.

[2018 Instructions for Forms 1099-R and 5498, at 9]

General Requirements

Q 27:5 Who must file Form 1099-R?

The payer, trustee, or plan administrator must file Form 1099-R, using the same name and employer identification number (EIN) used to deposit any tax withheld and to file the annual withholding tax return, Form 945. [2018 Instructions for Forms 1099-R and 5498, at 9]

Q 27:6 When must Form 1099-R be given to the participant?

Form 1099-R must be given to the participant by January 31 of the calendar year following the calendar year of distribution. If that date is on a Saturday, Sunday, or legal holiday, the Form 1099-R will be due on the next business day. A business day is any day that is not a Saturday, Sunday, or legal holiday. For 2018, the due date is January 31, 2019. [2018 General Instructions for Forms 1097, 1098, 1099, 3921, 3922, 5498, and W-2G, at 15]

Q 27:7 May an extension be granted to provide Form 1099-Rs to participants?

Yes, a payer may request an extension of time by sending a letter to:

Internal Revenue Service

Information Returns Branch

Attn: Extension of Time Coordinator

240 Murall Drive

Mail Stop 4360

Kearneysville, WV 25430

The letter must include the payer's name, TIN, address, an indication that the request is for an extension for filing Form 1099-R, the reason for the delay, and the signature of the payer or authorized agent. The request must be postmarked by January 31 of the year following the year of distribution. If that date is a Saturday, Sunday, or legal holiday, the extension request will be due on the next business day. If the request for extension is approved, up to 30 extra days will be granted to furnish Form 1099-R to the participants. [2018 General Instructions for Forms 1097, 1098, 1099, 3921, 3922, 5498, and W-2G, at 16]

Q 27:8 When must Form 1099-R and Form 1096 be filed with the IRS?

Paper Forms 1099-R and 1096, *Annual Summary and Transmittal of U.S. Information Returns*, must be filed with the IRS by the last day of February in the calendar year following the calendar year of distributions. If that date is a Saturday, Sunday, or legal holiday, the forms will be due on the next business day. If the payer is filing electronically, the due date is March 31 in the calendar year following the calendar year of distributions. (See Q 27:40 for filing electronically.) If that date is a Saturday, Sunday, or legal holiday, the forms will be due on the next business day. If 250 or more forms are to be filed, electronic filing is required unless there is a hardship waiver granted. The IRS encourages electronic filing even though fewer than 250 forms are filed. [2018 General Instructions for Forms 1097, 1098, 1099, 3921, 3922, 5498, and W-2G, at 6]

Q 27:9 May an extension to file Form 1099-R with the IRS be granted?

Yes. The payer may request an extension by filing IRS Form 8809, *Request for Extension of Time to File Information Returns*. The request must be made on or before the due date for filing IRS Form 1096 (Form 1096) (see Q 27:8). The extension is automatic and gives the payer an additional 30 days to file. Under certain hardship conditions, one additional request for a 30-day extension may be made. The form may be submitted on paper or through the Filing Information Returns Electronically (FIRE) system (see Q 27:15) either as a fill-in form or as an electronic file.

If the request for an extension is for more than 10 filers, Form 8809 must be completed either online or electronically. If the request is for 10 or fewer filers, Form 8809 may be completed, filed on paper, and mailed. The forms should be mailed to the location below, based on the state in which the trustee or custodian is located:

Location of Principal Business or Legal Residence of Trustee or Custodian	*Mailing Address*
Alabama, Arizona, Arkansas, Connecticut, Delaware, Florida, Georgia, Kentucky, Louisiana, Maine, Massachusetts, Mississippi, New Hampshire, New Jersey, New Mexico, New York, North Carolina, Ohio, Pennsylvania, Rhode Island, Texas, Vermont, Virginia, West Virginia	Department of the Treasury Internal Revenue Service Center Austin, TX 73301
Alaska, California, Colorado, District of Columbia, Hawaii, Idaho, Illinois, Indiana, Iowa, Kansas, Maryland, Michigan, Minnesota, Missouri, Montana, Nebraska, Nevada, North Dakota, Oklahoma, Oregon, South Carolina, South Dakota, Tennessee, Utah, Washington, Wisconsin, Wyoming	Department of the Treasury Internal Revenue Service Center Kansas City, MO 64999
No U.S. principal place of business or legal residence	Department of the Treasury Internal Revenue Service Center Austin, TX 73301

[2018 General Instructions for Forms 1097, 1098, 1099, 3921, 3922, 5498, and W-2G, at 7, Form 8809]

Q 27:10 What are the penalties for failure to file Form 1099-Rs with the IRS on a timely basis?

The penalty for failure to timely file Form 1099-Rs is determined by the timing of the late filing of Form 1099-Rs, according to the following chart based on a due date of February 28:

Timing	*Penalty*	*Small Business Penalty*
By March 30	$50 per return; maximum of $547,000 per year	$50 per return; maximum of $191,000 per year
Between March 31 and August 1	$100 per return; maximum of $1,641,000 per year	$100 per return; maximum of $547,000 per year
After August 1 or no filing	$260 per return; maximum of $3,282,500 per year	$270 per return; maximum of $1,094,000 per year

For purposes of these penalties, a *small business* is defined as a business (the words presumably also apply to a pension or profit sharing trust) with average annual gross receipts of $5 million or less for the three most recent tax years (or for its period of existence, if shorter) ending before the calendar year in which the information returns were due.

If failure to file a correct information return is due to intentional disregard of the filing or correct information requirements, the penalty is at least $270 per information return, with no maximum penalty.

[I.R.C. §§ 6721(a), 6721(b), 6721(c), 6721(e); 2018 General Instructions to Forms 1097, 1098, 1099, 3921, 3922, 5498, and W-2G, at 18]

Q 27:11 Are there any exceptions to the penalties for failure to file correct Form 1099-Rs?

Penalties will not be applied in the following circumstances:

1. If the payer can show that the failure was due to reasonable cause and not to willful neglect, the penalties will not be applied. The payer must demonstrate that the failure was due to events beyond his or her control or due to significant mitigating factors. The payer must also show that he or she acted in a responsible manner and took steps to avoid the failure in the future.
2. An inconsequential error or omission is not considered a failure to include correct information. An inconsequential error or omission is defined as a mistake that does not prevent or hinder the IRS from processing the return, from correlating the information required to be shown on the return with the information shown on the payee's tax return, or from otherwise putting the return to its intended use. The following errors and omissions are *never* considered inconsequential:
   a. An incorrect TIN;
   b. A payee's surname; and
   c. Any money amount.
3. If the payer cannot show reasonable cause, the penalty for failure to file correct information returns will not apply to the greater of 10 information returns or ½ of 1 percent of the total number of information returns that the payer is required to file for the calendar year, if all the following conditions are met:
   a. The payer filed Form 1099-R;
   b. The payer either failed to include all the information required on a return or included incorrect information; and
   c. The payer filed corrected Form 1099-Rs by August 1 of the year the return was due to be filed.

[2018 General Instructions to Forms 1097, 1098, 1099, 3921, 3922, 5498, and W-2G, at 18–19]

Q 27:12 What are the penalties for failure to furnish correct Form 1099-R to a participant?

The penalty for failure to furnish a correct Form 1099-R to a participant without reasonable cause is based on when the correct Form 1099-R is furnished and follows the same schedule as in Q 27:10. [I.R.C. § 6722] If failure to provide a correct Form 1099-R is due to intentional disregard of the requirements to furnish a correct payee Form 1099-R, the penalty is at least $540 per payee statement, with no maximum penalty. [I.R.C. § 6722(c); 2018 General Instructions to Forms 1097, 1098, 1099, 3921, 3922, 5498, and W-2G, at 19]

Q 27:13 Are there any exceptions to the penalties for failure to furnish correct Form 1099-R to a participant?

An inconsequential error or omission is not considered a failure to include correct information on a Form 1099-R. An inconsequential error or omission is defined as a mistake that does not prevent or hinder the payee from timely receiving correct information and reporting it on his or her income tax return or from otherwise putting the Form 1099-R to its intended use. The following errors and omissions are *never* considered inconsequential:

- Any dollar amount
- A significant item in a payee's address
- The appropriate Form 1099-R (i.e., whether the form is an acceptable substitute for the official IRS Form 1099-R)
- Whether the statement was furnished in person or by "statement mailing" when required.

[2018 General Instructions to Forms 1097, 1098, 1099, 3921, 3922, 5498, and W-2G, at 18–19]

Q 27:14 Where should paper returns for Forms 1099-R and 1096 be filed with the IRS?

The forms should be filed based on the state in which the trustee or custodian is located:

Location of Principal Business or Legal Residence of Trustee or Custodian	*Mailing Address*
Alabama, Arizona, Arkansas, Connecticut, Delaware, Florida, Georgia, Kentucky, Louisiana, Maine, Massachusetts, Mississippi, New Hampshire, New Jersey, New Mexico, New York, North Carolina, Ohio, Pennsylvania, Rhode Island, Texas, Vermont, Virginia, West Virginia	Department of the Treasury Internal Revenue Service Center Austin, TX 73301

Location of Principal Business or Legal Residence of Trustee or Custodian	*Mailing Address*
Alaska, California, Colorado, District of Columbia, Hawaii, Idaho, Illinois, Indiana, Iowa, Kansas, Maryland, Michigan, Minnesota, Missouri, Montana, Nebraska, Nevada, North Dakota, Oklahoma, Oregon, South Carolina, South Dakota, Tennessee, Utah, Washington, Wisconsin, Wyoming	Department of the Treasury Internal Revenue Service Center Kansas City, MO 64999
No U.S. principal place of business or legal residence	Department of the Treasury Internal Revenue Service Center Austin, TX 73301

[2018 General Instructions for Forms 1097, 1098, 1099, 3921, 3922, 5498, and W-2G, at 7]

Q 27:15 Where should electronic returns be filed?

Electronic submissions are filed using the FIRE System, which operates 24 hours per day, seven days per week. Software that can produce the proper format for the FIRE System is needed. The FIRE System is accessed on the Internet at:

https://fire.irs.gov

IRS Publication 1220 provides more in-depth information regarding the use of the FIRE System.

[2018 General Instructions for Forms 1097, 1098, 1099, 3921, 3922, 5498, and W-2G, at 8–9]

Q 27:16 How should information returns be delivered to the IRS?

Information returns that are filed on paper will be considered timely filed if the form is properly addressed and mailed on or before the due date (see addresses in Q 27:14).

In addition to the U.S. Postal Service, private delivery services designated by the IRS will meet the "timely mailing as timely filing" rule for information returns. The list contains the following services:

- *DHL Express (DHL):* DHL "Same Day" Service
- *Federal Express (FedEx):* FedEx Priority Overnight, FedEx Standard Overnight, FedEx 2 Day, FedEx International Priority, and FedEx International First; and
- *United Parcel Service (UPS):* UPS Next Day Air, UPS Next Day Air Saver, UPS 2nd Day Air, UPS 2nd Day Air A.M., UPS Worldwide Express Plus, and UPS Worldwide Express

Private delivery services can arrange to provide written proof of the mailing date to the filer.

[2018 General Instructions for Forms 1097, 1098, 1099, 3921, 3922, 5498, and W-2G, at 6]

Q 27:17 What types of retirement plan distributions are reported on Form 1099-R?

The following types of retirement plan distributions are reported on Form 1099-R (the chapters where more detail can be found are shown in parentheses):

1. In-service withdrawals from profit sharing or 401(k) plans, including from permissible eligible automatic contribution arrangements (chapter 1);
2. In-service distributions from pension plans, including defined benefit, money purchase, and target benefit plans (chapter 1);
3. Employee stock ownership plan (ESOP) paid Code Section 404(k) dividends (chapter 1);
4. In-service ESOP distributions made pursuant to the diversification requirement after age 55 (chapter 1);
5. Deemed distributions under the participant loan rules (chapter 2);
6. Distributions made pursuant to QDROs (chapter 3);
7. Corrective distributions of excess contributions, excess deferrals, excess aggregate contributions, and 415 excess annual additions (chapter 5);
8. Taxable cost of life insurance (commonly known as PS-58 cost);
9. Amounts payable as an annuity, either from an annuity contract or directly from the plan (chapter 18);
10. Installment payments (chapter 19);
11. Single-sum payments, whether or not they qualify for lump-sum treatment (chapter 19);
12. Direct rollovers to an IRA or another qualified plan (chapter 21);
13. Distributions from a deductible voluntary employee contribution (DVEC) account (chapter 19);
14. Designated Roth account rollovers or distributions, including in-plan (chapter 19);
15. Distributions under Employee Plans Compliance Resolution System (EPCRS);
16. Reportable death benefits under Section 6050Y.

[2018 Instructions for Forms 1099-R and 5498, at 1–9]

Q 27:18 How are ESOP dividends reported?

Distribution of Code Section 404(k) dividends from an ESOP are reported on Form 1099-R. Distribution other than Code Section 404(k) dividends from an ESOP must be reported on a separate Form 1099-R. Section 404(k) dividends paid directly from the corporation to participants or beneficiaries are reported on IRS Form 1099-DIV. [2018 Instructions for Forms 1099-R and 5498, at 2]

Q 27:19 How is a distribution from a DVEC account reported?

Under rules in place before the Tax Reform Act of 1986, a plan could permit DVECs, within certain limits. If a distribution from a retirement plan includes a distribution of DVECs, two Form 1099-Rs should be filed, one to report the DVEC and the other to report the balance of the funds. For a direct rollover of funds that include DVECs, file only one Form 1099-R to report the direct rollover of the entire amount. [2018 Instructions for Forms 1099-R and 5498, at 4]

Q 27:20 How is a *direct rollover* reported?

A *direct rollover* is the direct payment from a qualified plan to an IRA or other eligible retirement plan. A direct rollover must be reported on Form 1099-R. (See chapter 21 for a discussion of direct rollovers.) Starting in 2008, a non-spouse designated beneficiary can roll over a deceased participant's benefits to an IRA (see chapter 21).

[2018 Instructions for Forms 1099-R and 5498, at 4–5]

Q 27:21 Are trustee-to-trustee transfers reported on Form 1099-R?

No. Transfers that are between trustees of qualified plans or between a trustee and issuer (with the exception of direct rollovers; see Q 27:20), and that involve no payment or distribution of funds to the participant, are not reported on Form 1099-R. For example, if a defined benefit pension plan purchased an insurance company group annuity contract to provide annuity benefits elected by retired participants, this transaction would not be reported on a Form 1099-R.

[2018 Instructions for Forms 1099-R and 5498, at 6]

Q 27:22 What happens if excess contributions or excess aggregate contributions are discovered after a total distribution?

If a 401(k) plan fails the actual deferral percentage (ADP) or actual contribution percentage (ACP) (see chapter 5), a permitted correction is to refund excess contributions or excess aggregate contributions to applicable highly compensated employees (HCEs). If a total distribution has been made to an HCE before this discovery, part of the distribution must be recharacterized as an excess contribution or excess aggregate contribution. This recharacterization could occur long after the Form 1099-R has been issued to the participant.

The following steps must be completed to reflect this recharacterization:

1. File a corrected Form 1099-R for the correct amount of the total distribution, *excluding* the amount treated as an excess contribution or excess aggregate contribution (plus earnings related to the excess).

2. File a *new* Form 1099-R for the excess contributions or excess aggregate contribution and allocable earnings.
3. To avoid a late filing penalty (if the new Form 1099-R is prepared after February 28 of the applicable year or after March 31 if filed electronically), enter in the bottom margin of Form 1096 the words "Filed to Correct Excess (or Excess Aggregate) Contributions."
4. Issue copies of the corrected and new Form 1099-Rs to the plan participant with an explanation of why these new forms are being issued.

[2018 Instructions for Forms 1099-R and 5498, at 7]

Line-by-Line Explanation

Q 27:23 What information must be reported on Form 1099-R?

The following information should be provided on Form 1099-R:

1. Payer's name and address.
2. Payer's federal identification number.
3. Recipient's social security number (see Q 27:24).
4. Recipient's name.
5. Recipient's street address (including apartment number).
6. Recipient's city, state, and zip code.
7. Account number (optional for use by payer).
8. Box 1 Gross distribution (see Q 27:25).
9. Box 2a Taxable amount (see Q 27:26).
10. Box 2b Whether taxable amount has not been determined. Whether the distribution is a total distribution (see Q 27:27).
11. Box 3 Capital gains portion of the distribution reported in Box 2a (see Q 27:28).
12. Box 4 Federal income tax withheld (see Q 27:29).
13. Box 5 Employee contribution, designated Roth contributions, or insurance premiums (see Q 27:30).
14. Box 6 Net unrealized appreciation (NUA) in employer's securities (see Q 27:31).
15. Box 7 Distribution code and box to check whether IRA, SEP, or SIMPLE distribution (see Q 27:32).
16. Box 8 Actuarial value of annuity contract, reduced by certain amounts. (If annuity contract is part of a distribution to multiple recipients, show a percentage (see Q 27:33).)
17. Box 9a Participant's percentage of the total distribution (see Q 27:34).
18. Box 9b Total employee contributions (Q 27:35).

19. Box 10 Amount allocable to In-plan Roth Rollover (IRR) within 5 years (IRS Notice 2010-84) (Q 27:36).
20. Box 11 First year of designated Roth Contribution (see Q 27:37).
21. Box 12 State tax withheld (see Q 27:38).
22. Box 13 State/payer's state number (see Q 27:38).
23. Box 14 State distribution (see Q 27:38).
24. Box 15 Local tax withheld (see Q 27:38).
25. Box 16 Name of locality withholding local tax (see Q 27:38).
26. Box 17 Local distribution (see Q 27:38).

Note that a negative number may not be entered in any box on Form 1099-R.

[2018 Instructions for Forms 1099-R and 5498, at 10–18]

Q 27:24 How is an employee's Social Security number reported on Form 1099-R?

The Social Security number may be truncated on the paper Form 1099-R for payees. Filers may replace the first five digits of an employee's Social Security number with asterisks (*) or Xs; that is, either of the following formats would be acceptable:

1. ***-**-9999
2. XXX-XX-9999

A filer may not truncate a recipient's Social Security number on any forms filed with the IRS or with state or local governments. A payer's federal identification number may not be truncated. [2018 Instructions for Forms 1099-R and 5498, at 1; 2018 General Instructions for Certain Information Returns (Forms 1097, 1098, 1099, 3921, 3922, 5498, and W-2G), at 12]

Q 27:25 How is Box 1 of Form 1099-R completed?

The total gross amount of the distribution, before deduction for income tax or other items, should be reported in Box 1 of Form 1099-R. Include direct rollovers and premiums paid by a trustee or custodian for current life insurance protection (PS-58 cost), in this box. The value of U.S. savings bonds distributed from the plan should also be reported in this box. If U.S. savings bonds are distributed, a separate statement (not a Form 1099-R) should be furnished to the participant showing the value of each bond at the time of distribution. This will allow the participant to compute the interest income on each bond when it is redeemed. [2018 Instructions for Forms 1099-R and 5498, at 10]

> **Example 27-1:** Tony directly rolls over a distribution of $55,000 from the ABC 401(k) plan to an IRA that he has established. Although the $55,000 is not taxable to Tony, the $55,000 distribution must be reported on Form 1099-R, and Box 1 must show the $55,000 figure.

Q 27:26 How is Box 2a of Form 1099-R completed?

The payer should show the amount includible as taxable income to the payee. If the payer cannot reasonably obtain the data needed to determine the taxable amount, this box may be left blank. Do not include amounts that are excludable from tax or amounts that are reported in Boxes 5, 6, and 8. If the 1099-R is being used to report the annual PS-58 cost, Box 2a should contain the same number as Box 1. If a distribution was made in the same year that PS-58 costs are being reported, file separate Form 1099-Rs for the distribution and the PS-58 costs. For a direct rollover from a qualified plan to an IRA or another qualified plan, enter "-0-" (zero) in Box 2a.

If periodic distributions were made and such distributions started in 1998 or later, a simplified method is used to figure the taxable amount. (See chapter 18 for an explanation of these rules, particularly Qs 18:8–18:16.)

If the distribution resulted in a loss to the participant (e.g., the value of the employer stock distributed is less than the employees after-tax contributions), report the value of the employer stock in Box 1, leave Box 2a blank, and enter the after-tax contributions in Box 5. A participant's account balance may sustain a loss as the result of market fluctuations, but such a loss is not reported on Form 1099-R, as long as there are no after-tax employee contributions.

Generally, it is not necessary to compute the taxable amount of a traditional IRA, SEP, or SIMPLE IRA distribution. The total amount distributed from a traditional IRA, SEP, or SIMPLE IRA as reported in Box 1 is the same amount as should be reported in Box 2a.

[2018 Instructions for Forms 1099-R and 5498, at 10–11]

Q 27:27 How is Box 2b of Form 1099-R completed?

This line actually contains two boxes:

1. Taxable amount not determined and
2. Total distribution.

The first box, *Taxable amount not determined*, should be checked if the payer is unable to reasonably obtain the data needed to compute the taxable amount or if the payer is reporting a traditional IRA, SEP, or SIMPLE IRA distribution. If the box is marked, Box 2a should be left blank unless reporting a traditional IRA, SEP, or SIMPLE IRA distribution.

The second box, *Total distribution*, is checked only if the distribution is a total distribution. Two types of distributions qualify as total distributions for purposes of this box:

1. One or more distributions within an individual's tax year in which the entire balance of the account is distributed, or
2. The last of a series of periodic or installment payments in the year the final payment is made.

[2018 Instructions for Forms 1099-R and 5498, at 12]

Q 27:28 How is Box 3 of Form 1099-R completed?

For lump-sum distributions only, the amount of the distribution reported in Box 2a that is eligible for capital gains treatment is reported in Box 3 (see chapter 19). This special tax treatment is generally applicable only if both of the following are true:

1. The participant was born on or before January 1, 1936, and
2. The participant was an active participant in the plan before 1974.

This box should not be completed for a direct rollover (see chapter 21). [2018 Instructions for Forms 1099-R and 5498, at 12–13]

Q 27:29 How is Box 4 of Form 1099-R completed?

The amount of federal income tax withheld from the distribution should be reported in Box 4 (see chapter 24). [2018 Instructions for Forms 1099-R and 5498, at 13–14]

Q 27:30 How is Box 5 of Form 1099-R completed?

Box 5 consists of amounts that represent the after-tax contributions (including designated Roth contributions) that have been previously taxed to the employee, including:

1. Voluntary or mandatory after-tax employee contributions;
2. The cumulative PS-58 cost, but only if the contract was distributed;
3. The portion of a participant loan that has been previously taxed as a deemed distribution; or
4. Designated Roth contributions.

The portion of the employee's basis that has been distributed from a designated Roth account must be reported on a separate Form 1099-R.

If the trustee or plan administrator cannot reasonably obtain the data necessary to complete Box 5, it may be left blank. Also, leave Box 2a blank and check Box 2b: *Taxable amount not determined.* [2018 Instructions for Forms 1099-R and 5498, at 14]

Example 27-2: Sue has participated in the ABC thrift savings plan. She receives a single-sum distribution of $95,000, including an insurance contract with a cash value of $25,000. Sue has previously paid taxes on the following amounts:

Source	*Amount*
After-tax employee contributions	$20,000
Cumulative PS-58 costs	$10,000
Participant loan-deemed distribution	$5,000
Total amount previously taxed	$35,000

Sue will receive a Form 1099-R showing $35,000 in Box 5.

Q 27:31 How is Box 6 of Form 1099-R completed?

Box 6 is completed if a distribution of employer securities of the plan sponsor (or securities of the sponsor's parent or subsidiary) is made to the participant. The NUA is reported if it can be determined. All the NUA should be reported if the distribution is a lump-sum distribution. If it is not a lump-sum distribution, only the NUA of employer securities attributable to employee contributions may be shown. [Treas. Reg. § 1.402(a)-1(b); Notice 89-25, 1989-1 C.B. 662, Q&A-1] The NUA should be shown in Box 1, but not Box 2a. This item need not be completed if the participant makes a direct rollover. [2018 Instructions for Forms 1099-R and 5498, at 14]

> **Example 27-3:** Keith receives a lump-sum distribution, including employer securities from the ABC Employee Stock Ownership Plan. He receives 100 shares with a current market value of $275,000. However, the cost basis as computed by the plan administrator is $175,000. Keith has the difference, or $100,000, reported in Box 6 of Form 1099-R as NUA.

Q 27:32 How are the codes in Box 7 of Form 1099-R determined?

The following rules should be followed in completing Box 7:

1. Three numeric combinations are permitted on a single Form 1099-R: Codes 1 and 8, Codes 2 and 8, or Codes 4 and 8.
2. If different parts of a distribution require different codes, a separate Form 1099-R should be prepared for each part of a distribution requiring a different code.
3. If only part of an eligible rollover distribution is paid in a direct rollover and part is not, a separate Form 1099-R is filed for each part.
4. If part of a distribution is a minimum required distribution under Code Section 401(a)(9) (see chapter 4), two separate Form 1099-Rs must be filed.
5. For a direct rollover to an IRA for the surviving spouse of a deceased participant, enter Codes 4 and G.
6. If the distribution is of excess deferrals, excess contributions, or excess aggregate contributions, parts of the distribution may be taxable in two or three different years. File separate Form 1099-Rs using Code 8 or P to indicate the year the amount is taxable.
7. Although the participant may be age 59½ or older, use Code 1 if a series of substantially equal periodic payments was modified within five years of the date of the first payment.

The following codes are to be used for a distribution from a qualified plan (the related chapters in this book are also shown):

Code	*Description*	*Chapter*	*Use with Codes:*
1	*Early Distribution:* Use this code if the participant has **not** reached age 59½ **and** if it is not known if any of the exceptions under Codes 2, 3, or 4 apply. Use Code 1 even if the distribution is made for medical expenses, health insurance premiums, first-time home purchase, qualified higher education expenses, or a qualified reservist distribution under Code Section 72(t). Use this code also if a taxpayer is age 59½ or over and has modified a series of substantially equal periodic payments prior to the end of the five-year period.	20	8, B, D, K, L, M, or P
2	Participant has not reached age 59½, and one of the exceptions below applies: a. A Roth IRA conversion (an IRA converted to a Roth IRA); b. A distribution made from a qualified retirement plan because of an IRS levy under Code Section 6331; c. A distribution from a qualified retirement plan after separation from service when the participant has reached age 55; d. A Section 457(b) distribution *and* not subject to the additional 10% tax; e. A distribution from a governmental defined benefit plan to a public safety employee after separation from service in or after the year the employee has reached age 50; f. A distribution that is part of a series of substantially equal periodic payments as described in Code Section 72(q), (t), (u), or (v); g. A distribution that is a permissible withdrawal under an eligible automatic contribution arrangement; h. Any other distribution subject to an exception under Code Section 72(q), (t), (u), or (v) that is not required to be reported using Code 1, 3, or 4.	20	8, B, D, K, L, M, or P

Code	Description	Chapter	Use with Codes:
3	Disability.	20	D
4	Death: Use this code regardless of the age of the participant to indicate payment to a deceased participant's beneficiary, including an estate or trust.	20	8, A, B, D, G, H, K, L, M, or P
5	Prohibited transaction.	N/A	None
6	Section 1035 exchange: Use this code to indicate the tax-free e-exchange of life insurance, annuity, long-term care insurance, or endowment contracts under Section 1035.	N/A	W
7	*Normal Distribution:* Use this code if the participant was at least age 59½. Also, use Code 7 if no other code applies.	20	A, B, D, K, L, or M
8	Excess deferrals, excess contributions, or excess aggregate contributions deferrals (all plus earnings) taxable in the current year.	5	1, 2, 4, B, J, or K
9	*PS-58 Costs*: Use this code to report taxable amounts for current life insurance protection.	6	None
A	Eligible for 10-year income averaging: Use this code to indicate that the distribution is eligible for 10-year averaging on a lump-sum distribution.	19	4 or 7
B	Designated Roth account distribution. Use Code B for a distribution from a designated Roth account that is not a qualified distribution, Code E for a Section 415 excess under EPCRS or Code H for a direct rollover to a Roth IRA.	N/A	1, 2, 4, 7, 8, G, L, M, P, or U
C	Reportable death benefits under Section 6050Y. Use Code C for a distribution to report payments of reportable death benefits.	N/A	D
D	Distributions from nonqualified annuity plan and for distributions from life insurance contract subject to tax under Section 1411.	N/A	1, 2, 3, 4, 7, or C

Code	*Description*	*Chapter*	*Use with Codes:*
E	Distributions under Employee Plans Compliance Resolution System.	5, 23	None
F	Charitable gift annuity.	N/A	None
G	Direct rollover to IRA.	21	4, B, or K
H	Direct rollover of a designated Roth account distribution to a Roth IRA.	21	4
J	Early distribution from a Roth IRA when Code Q or Code T does not apply. Use Code 2 for an IRS levy and Code 5 for a prohibited transaction.	N/A	8 or P
K	Distribution of IRA assets not having a readily available FMV.	N/A	1, 2, 4, 7, 8, or G
L	Loans treated as deemed distributions under Code Section 72(p): Do not use Code L to report a loan offset.	2	1, 2, 4, 7, or B
M	Qualified plan loan offset. Use Code M for a qualified plan loan offset distribution due to severance from employment or termination of the plan.	N/A	1, 2, 4, 7, or B
N	Recharacterized IRA contribution made for the current year.	N/A	None
P	Excess contributions or excess deferrals (plus earnings) taxable in prior year.	5	1, 2, 4, B, or J
Q	Qualified distribution from a Roth IRA.	N/A	None
R	Recharacterized IRA contribution made for prior year.	N/A	None
S	Early distribution from a SIMPLE IRA in first two years, no known exception: Use Code S only if the distribution is from a SIMPLE IRA in the first two years; the employee is not yet age 59, and none of the exceptions under Code Section 72(t) are known to apply. The two-year period begins on the day contributions are first deposited in the individual's SIMPLE IRA by the employer. Do not use Code	N/A	None

Code	Description	Chapter	Use with Codes:
	S if Code 3 (disability) or Code 4 (death) applies.		
T	Roth IRA distribution; exception applies.	N/A	None
U	Dividends distributed from an ESOP under Code Section 404(k). Dividends paid directly by the corporation to plan participants are reported on Form 1099-DIV.	1	B
W	Charges or payments for purchasing qualified long-term care insurance contracts under combined arrangements, which are excludible under Code Section 72(e)(11) against the cash value of an annuity contract or the cash surrender value of a life insurance contract.	N/A	6

New for 2018 are the codes for reportable death benefits under Section 6050Y (C) and loan offsets at severance from employment or plan termination (M) which is reported separately from a loan default resulting in a deemed distribution (L).

[2018 Instructions for Forms 1099-R and 5498, at 16–18]

Example 27-4: Maureen, age 35, terminates employment from the ABC defined benefit plan and receives a distribution of $2,500 that is not directly rolled over to an IRA. None of the exceptions to the 10 percent additional income tax on early distributions applies. Code 1 is reported on Form 1099-R.

Example 27-5: Nancy, age 42, becomes totally disabled and starts receiving annuity payments from the ABC profit sharing plan. Code 3 is reported on Form 1099-R.

Example 27-6: ABC has a 401(k) plan and distributes (before April 15, 2019) an excess deferral plus earnings of $1,250 to Sam because he contributed too much in 2018. Although this amount is distributed in 2019, it is taxable in 2018 and is reported on a 2018 Form 1099-R as Code P.

Example 27-7: ABC sponsors a 401(k) plan with a calendar year end. For the calendar year ended December 31, 2018, the plan fails its ADP test and must distribute $2,700 to a HCE, Linda. The distribution is made to Linda in 2019, and will be taxable in 2019, and reported on a 2019 Form 1099-R as Code 8.

Example 27-8: Jeff receives a payment, as an alternative payee under a QDRO, from the ABC profit sharing plan. Because this distribution is not subject to the 10 percent additional income tax on early distributions, Code 7 is reported on Form 1099-R.

Example 27-9: Dan participates in the ABC defined benefit plan. The plan provides Dan with a $275,000 death benefit funded by life insurance. Dan must report annual taxable income of $1,249 as his PS-58 cost in 2018. Code 9 is shown on his 2018 Form 1099-R.

Example 27-10: Dixie, who was born in 1935 and has participated in the ABC defined benefit plan since 1971, retires and receives a lump-sum distribution of $578,908. Code A is reported on Form 1099-R.

Example 27-11: Lynn, a participant in the ABC profit sharing plan, is age 75 and wants to retire and roll over a distribution of $250,000 from the plan to an IRA. However, she must receive a minimum required distribution of $20,000 from the plan before the rollover can occur. Two separate Form 1099-Rs are prepared for Lynn, one reflecting a direct rollover (Code G) of $230,000 and the other reflecting the minimum required distribution of $20,000 (Code 7).

Example 27-12: Bob receives a dividend of $350 from the ABC ESOP during 2018. This dividend is not an eligible rollover distribution. He terminates employment later in 2018 and receives a distribution of $350,000. The $350,000 distribution is not rolled over to an IRA or other eligible plan. Bob is 46 years old, and none of the exceptions to the 10 percent additional income tax on early distributions applies to him. Thus, two Form 1099-Rs are furnished to Bob: the $350 dividend with a Code U and the single-sum distribution of $350,000 with a Code 1.

Example 27-13: Ed borrows $9,000 from his 401(k) plan during 2018. He fails to make required quarterly installments on his loan and the loan is in default and considered a deemed distribution. Code L is used on Form 1099-R. Since Ed is age 45, Code 1 is also used.

Example 27-14: Norman began receiving payments that qualified for the exception as part of a series of substantially equal periodic payments under Code Section 72(t)(A)(iv) when he was 58. Norman modified the series of payments at age 61. Although Norman is older than 59½, Code 1 must be used because Norman modified the series of payments within the first five years.

Q 27:33 How is Box 8 of Form 1099-R completed?

The current actuarial value of an annuity contract that is part of a lump sum is shown in Box 8. The amount reported in Box 8 should not be included in Boxes 1 and 2a. In determining the value of the annuity contract, show the value as an amount equal to the current actuarial value of the annuity contract, reduced by an amount equal to the excess of the employee's contributions over the cash and other property (not including the annuity contract) distributed. If an annuity contract is part of a distribution to multiple recipients in a lump sum, enter the percentage of the total annuity contract each Form 1099-R represents. [2018 Instructions for Forms 1099-R and 5498, at 15]

Q 27:34 How is Box 9a of Form 1099-R completed?

If the distribution is a total distribution that is made to more than one person, show the percentage received by the person whose name appears as the recipient on Form 1099-R. This box does not have to be completed for a direct rollover. [2018 Instructions for Forms 1099-R and 5498, at 15]

Q 27:35 How is Box 9b of Form 1099-R completed?

The payer is not required to enter the total employee contribution in Box 9b. Because the information might be helpful to the payee, however, the payer may continue to report it. If the payer chooses to report employee contributions, amounts recovered tax-free in prior years should not be included in Box 9b. For a total distribution, Box 5 is used to report employee contributions.

The same holds true for designated Roth account contributions. This is not a required entry on Form 1099-R. If the payer chooses to report total designated Roth account contributions, previously recovered tax-free amounts from prior years should not be included. For a total distribution, report the total designated Roth account contributions in Box 5 rather than in Box 9b. [2018 Instructions for Forms 1099-R and 5498, at 15]

Q 27:36 How is Box 10 completed?

Box 10 is completed by inserting the amount of the distribution allocable to any IRR made within the five-year period beginning with the first day of the year in which the rollover was made. [IRS Notice 2010-84, Q/A 13; 2018 Instructions for Forms 1099-R and 5498, at 15–16]

Q 27:37 How is Box 11 completed?

Box 11 is completed by inserting the first year of the five-taxable-year period. For example, the first year that a designated Roth contribution could be made was 2006. [2018 Instructions for Forms 1099-R and 5498, at 16]

Q 27:38 How are Boxes 12 through 17 of Form 1099-R completed?

These boxes are for the convenience of the payer and the recipient. If state and/or local income tax has been withheld, it may be shown in Boxes 12 and/or 15, as appropriate. In Box 13, enter the abbreviated name of the state and the payer's state identification number, if applicable. In Box 16, enter the name of the locality, if applicable. Boxes 14 and 17 may be used to enter the amount of the state or local distribution, respectively, if applicable. Copy 1 of Form 1099-R may be used to provide information to the state or local tax department. Copy 2 of Form 1099-R may be used as the recipient's copy in filing a state or local income tax return. [2018 Instructions for Forms 1099-R and 5498, at 16]

Electronic Filing

Q 27:39 May Form 1099-R be filed electronically with the IRS?

Yes, electronic submissions should be filed using the FIRE System. The FIRE System operates 24 hours a day, seven days a week and is accessed via the Internet at FIRE.IRS.gov. [2018 General Instructions for Forms 1097, 1098, 1099, 3921, 3922, 5498, and W-2G, at 8–9]

Q 27:40 What is the due date for electronic filing of Form 1099-R?

The due date for electronic filing is March 31. If that date is a Saturday, Sunday, or legal holiday, the forms will be due on the next business day. The FIRE system operates 24 hours a day, seven days a week, except Wednesdays from 2:00 AM to 5:00 AM (EST). The FIRE System is generally unavailable the last two weeks of December through the middle of January for annual updates. [2018 General Instructions for Forms 1097, 1098, 1099, 3921, 3922, 5498, and W-2G, at 8; Pub. 1220]

Q 27:41 Is there a requirement for filing electronically?

Yes, a payer that is required to file 250 or more Form 1099-Rs must file electronically. Even if the payer has fewer than 250 forms to file, the IRS encourages payers to file electronically. [2018 General Instructions for Forms 1097, 1098, 1099, 3921, 3922, 5498, and W-2G, at 8]

Q 27:42 Must IRS approval be obtained to file electronically?

Yes, the payer must file IRS Form 4419, *Application for Filing Information Returns Electronically*, at least 30 days before the due date of Form 1099-R. Once the payer has received approval, he or she need not reapply each year. The IRS will respond, in writing, usually within 30 days, to notify the payer of approval or provide further instructions to obtain approval. It is important to note that Box 3 must contain an EIN. The IRS will no longer issue Transmitter Control Codes to a Social Security number. [2018 General Instructions for Forms 1097, 1098, 1099, 3921, 3922, 5498, and W-2G, at 8; IRS Form 4419 (rev. Apr. 2016); Rev. Proc. 2009-30]

Q 27:43 May a waiver from filing electronically be granted?

Yes. To receive a waiver from the required filing of Form 1099-R electronically, the payer should submit IRS Form 8508, *Request for Waiver from Filing Information Returns Electronically*, requesting a hardship waiver from filing electronically. The waiver request must be filed at least 45 days before the due date of Form 1099-R. A payer may receive approval of a waiver request for a one-year period only. If more waivers are needed, the payer must reapply each year.

If a waiver for filing electronically is obtained, this waiver also applies to any corrections to Form 1099-R. If original returns are submitted electronically, a waiver must be obtained to file corrections on paper if there are 250 or more corrections. [2018 General Instructions for Forms 1097, 1098, 1099, 3921, 3922, 5498, and W-2G, at 8–9; IRS Form 8508 (rev. Nov. 2016)]

Example 27-15: The ABC Bank acts as trustee for a number of qualified plans. For the first time, the bank must prepare over 250 Form 1099-Rs in 2018. Unfortunately, the bank is changing computer systems, making electronic filing quite difficult. The bank may apply for a waiver for 2018, on or before January 14, 2019 (note the due date in 2019 is February 28, 2019).

Q 27:44 What is the penalty for failure to file electronically?

If a payer is required to file electronically but fails to do so and does not have an approved waiver on record, the payer may be subject to a penalty of up to $270 per information return unless reasonable cause can be established. To minimize the $270 penalty, the payer may file the first 250 Form 1099-Rs on paper. [2018 General Instructions for Forms 1097, 1098, 1099, 3921, 3922, 5498, and W-2G, at 8–9]

Example 27-16: Through an oversight, ABC Bank fails to request a waiver of the electronic filing requirements. Because it has to file 300 Form 1099-Rs, 250 of those forms may be filed on paper. The balance, or 50 forms, will be subject to a penalty of up to $270 each.

Q 27:45 May Form 1099-R be furnished electronically to a plan participant?

The payee copy of Form 1099-R may be furnished electronically for pension plans.

Copy B of Form 1099-R may be furnished to the payee electronically rather than on paper. If the payer meets the requirements listed below, the payer is treated as furnishing Form 1099-R on a timely basis to the payee:

Consent. The payee must consent in the affirmative and not have withdrawn the consent before the statement is furnished. The consent by the payee must be made electronically in a way that shows that he or she can access the statement in the electronic format in which it will be furnished. The payer must notify the payee of any hardware or software changes prior to furnishing the statement. A new consent to receive the statement electronically is required after the new hardware or software is put into service.

Before furnishing the statements electronically, the payer must provide the payee with a prominent display of the following information:

- Formats available. If the payee does not consent to receive the statement electronically, a paper copy will be provided.
- The scope and duration of the consent. For example, whether the consent applies to every year the statement is furnished or only for the January 31 immediately following the date of the consent.
- How to obtain a paper copy after giving the consent for electronic receipt of the statement.

- How to withdraw the consent. The consent may be withdrawn at any time by furnishing the withdrawal in writing (electronically or on paper) to the person whose name appears on the statement. Confirmation of the withdrawal also will be in writing (electronically or on paper).
- Notice of termination. The notice must state under what conditions the statements will no longer be furnished to the payee electronically.
- Procedures to update the payee's information.
- A description of the hardware and software required to access, print and retain a statement, and a date the statement will no longer be available on the website.

Format, posting, and notification. Additionally, the payer must:

- Ensure that the electronic format contains all the required information and complies with the applicable revenue procedure for substitute statements to payees. [see IRS Pub. 1179]
- Post the applicable statement on a website accessible to the payee on or before the January 31 due date, through at least October 15 of that year.
- Inform the payee, electronically or by mail, of the posting and how to access and print the statement.

[2018 General Instructions for Forms 1097, 1098, 1099, 3921, 3922, 5498, and W-2G, at 16]

Q 27:46 What are common errors in preparing Form 1099-R?

The IRS finds the following errors to be most common in the preparation of Form 1099-R:

1. Duplicate filings;
2. Payer's name, address, or TIN on Form 1099-R does not match with the information on Form 1096;
3. The decimal point to show dollars and cents is omitted (e.g., "2435.00" is correct, but "2435" is not);
4. Two or more types of returns submitted with one Form 1096 (e.g., IRS Forms 1099-INT and 1099-MISC with one Form 1096). A separate Form 1096 must be submitted with each type of return.

[2018 General Instructions for Forms 1097, 1098, 1099, 3921, 3922, 5498, and W-2G, at 11]

Q 27:47 What are the administrative rules for paper filing of Form 1099-R?

Paper forms are read by optical character recognition equipment. Payers must follow these instructions or be subject to a penalty of $50 for each incorrectly filed document:

1. Use the original forms supplied by the IRS or an approved vendor; photocopies are not acceptable.

2. Do not cut or separate the forms that are printed two or three to a sheet. If at least one form is completed, the entire page should be submitted.
3. Do not fold the forms; send them to the IRS in a flat mailing envelope.
4. Do not staple, tear, or tape any of the forms.
5. Pinfeed holes on Form 1099-R are not acceptable. If the pinfeed holes are outside the 8½-by-11-inch area, remove the strips containing the pinfeed holes. Substitute forms prepared in continuous or strip form must be burst and stripped to conform to the size specified for a single sheet (8½-by-11-inch) before they are filed with the IRS.
6. Do not change the title of any box on Form 1099-R. Do not use Form 1099-R to report items that are not properly reportable on Form 1099-R.
7. Submit only Copy A to the IRS.
8. Do not use a prior year's form unless prior-year information is being submitted.
9. If substitute forms are used, follow the guidelines contained in IRS Publication 1179, "General Rules and Specifications for Substitute Forms 1096, 1098, 1099, 5498, W-2G, and 1042-S." If substitute forms do not meet the current specifications and are not machine scannable, the payer may be subject to a penalty of $50 for each return for improper format.
10. Do not use dollar signs ($), ampersands (&), asterisks (*), commas (,) or other special characters in money amount boxes on the payee name line.

[2018 General Instructions for Forms 1097, 1098, 1099, 3921, 3922, 5498, and W-2G, at 9]

Q 27:48 What format does the IRS suggest for the completion of Form 1099-Rs?

These suggestions allow the IRS to process the submitted Form 1099-R in the most economical manner:

1. Type or machine print data entries using 12 pitch Courier black type. Use black print, not script, characters. Entries should not be handwritten. Insert data in the middle of the blocks well separated from other printing and guidelines, and take other measures to guarantee a dark black, clear, sharp image.
2. Do not enter "-0-" or "none" in money amount boxes when no entry is required. Leave the boxes blank unless the instructions specifically require that you enter a zero.
3. For the convenience of the payer, an account number may be designated on the form. This number must not appear anywhere else on the form.
4. Do not enter number signs (#) or dollar signs ($).

[2018 General Instructions for Forms 1097, 1098, 1099, 3921, 3922, 5498, and W-2G, at 9–10]

Q 27:49 How are Form 1099-Rs submitted to the IRS?

If fewer than 250 Form 1099-Rs are filed and the payer is filing paper documents, Form 1096, *Annual Summary and Transmittal of U.S. Information Returns*, is used as a transmittal form. If the payer is filing electronically, the guidelines for the FIRE System are contained in IRS Publication 1220. [2018 General Instructions for Forms 1097, 1098, 1099, 3921, 3922, 5498, and W-2G, at 9–10]

Correcting Form 1099-R

Q 27:50 How is an incorrect Form 1099-R corrected?

If fewer than 250 corrections are needed, paper returns may be prepared that reflect the correct information. The box on the top of Form 1099-R marked "Corrected" should be checked. All forms should be transmitted with a Form 1096 (see Q 27:51). If 250 or more Form 1099-Rs need to be corrected, the corrections must be done electronically and sent to the IRS via the FIRE System. [2018 General Instructions for Forms 1097, 1098, 1099, 3921, 3922, 5498, and W-2G, at 10]

Q 27:51 What are the procedures for filing corrected returns on paper?

The procedures vary, depending on the nature of the error. The payer should identify the error type (1 or 2) and then follow the applicable instructions summarized below. (See Table 27-1.)

Table 27-1.

Error Type 1	*Correction*
Incorrect money amounts(s), code, or checkbox, or **Incorrect address,** or **Incorrect payee name,** or **A return was filed when one should not have been filed.** These errors require only one return to make the correction. **Caution**: If you must correct a TIN and/or a name and address, follow the instructions under Error Type 2.	**A. Form 1099-R** 1. Prepare a new information return. 2. Enter an "X" in the "CORRECTED" box (and date (optional)) at the top of the form. 3. Correct any recipient information such as money amounts and address. Report other information as per original return. **B. Form 1096** 1. Prepare a new transmittal Form 1096. 2. Provide all requested information on the form as it applies to Part A, 1 and 2. 3. File Form 1096 and Copy A of the return with the appropriate service center. 4. Do not include a copy of the original return that was filed incorrectly.

Table 27-1.*(cont'd)*

Error Type 2	*Correction*
No payee TIN (SSN, or EIN), or **Incorrect payee TIN**, or **Incorrect name and address**, or **Original return filed using wrong type of return** (for example, a Form 1099-DIV was filed when a Form 1099-R should have been filed).	**Step 1.** Identify incorrect return submitted. 1. Prepare a new information return. 2. Enter an "X" in the "CORRECTED" box (and date (optional)) at the top of the form. 3. Enter the payer, recipient, and account number information exactly as it appeared on the original incorrect return; however, enter 0 (zero) for all money amounts. **Step 2.** Report correct information.
Two separate returns are required to make the correction properly. Follow all instructions for both Steps 1 and 2.	**A. Form 1099-R** a. Prepare a new information return. b. Do not enter an "X" in the "CORRECTED" box at the top of the form. Prepare the new return as though it is an original. c. Include all the correct information on the form including the correct TIN, name, and address. **B. Form 1096** a. Prepare a new transmittal Form 1096. b. Enter the words "Filed to Correct TIN," "Filed to Correct Name and Address," or "Filed to Correct Return" in the bottom margin of the form. c. Provide all requested information on the form as it applies to the returns prepared in Steps 1 and 2. d. File Form 1096 and Copy A of the return with the appropriate service center. e. Do not include a copy of the original return that was filed incorrectly.

[2018 General Instructions for Forms 1097, 1098, 1099, 3921, 3922, 5495, and W-2G, at 10–11]

Q 27:52 May an incorrect Form 1099-R be voided?

Yes, an incorrect Form 1099-R may be eliminated by checking the "void" box at the top of the form. This option is available only for returns that have not yet been filed with the IRS. If the IRS has already been sent the incorrect Form 1099-R, the methods discussed in Q 27:50 must be used. [2018 General Instructions for Forms 1097, 1098, 1099, 3921, 3922, 5498, and W-2G, at 10]

Combined Federal/State Filing Program

Q 27:53 What is the Combined Federal/State Filing Program?

The Combined Federal/State Filing Program (CF/SF) Program was established to simplify information returns filing for the payer. Under the program, the IRS/IRB (IRS/Information Returns Branch) will forward the information on Form 1099-Rs to participating states free of charge for approved filers. This is only applicable to original and corrected Form 1099-Rs that are filed electronically. Separate reporting to those states is not required. [Rev. Proc. 2012-30]

Q 27:54 What is the procedure for a payer to obtain approval to use the CF/SF Program?

The filer must submit a test file coded for the CF/SF program. The test file must consist of a sample of Form 1099-R:

1. Transmitter "T" record
2. Payer "A" record (must not be fictitious data)
3. Multiple Payee "B" records (at least 11 "B" records per each "A" record)
4. End of Payer "C" record
5. State Totals "K" record
6. End of Transmission "F" record

A test file is required only for the first year of filing, but it is recommended that a test file be sent each year that the payer participates in the CF/SF Program.

Electronic filers must log on to the FIRE System within two business days to check the acceptability of their test file.

If a payee has a reporting requirement for more than one state, separate "B" records must be created for each state. Some states require separate notification that the payer is filing in this manner. Check with the appropriate states for further information.

[Rev. Proc. 2012-30, at 24]

Q 27:55 What is the deadline for requesting approval to participate in the CF/SF Program?

An electronic test file coded for this program (see Q 27:56) must be submitted to IRS/IRB between November 1 and February 15. The earliest date (November 1) will be in the year that the combined filing is requested. For example, for

2018 tax year filings (returns to be filed in 2019), the window to request approval would be between November 1, 2018, and February 15, 2019. See Q 27:40 for the availability of the FIRE System during this time frame.

[Rev. Proc. 2012-13, at 24]

Q 27:56 What states are participating in this program?

The participating states and their codes are shown in Table 27-2.

Table 27-2. Participating States and Their Codes

*State**	*Code*
Alabama	01
Arizona	04
Arkansas	05
California	06
Colorado	07
Connecticut	08
Delaware	10
Georgia	13
Hawaii	15
Idaho	16
Indiana	18
Kansas	20
Louisiana	22
Maine	23
Maryland	24
Massachusetts	25
Michigan	26
Minnesota	27
Mississippi	28
Missouri	29
Montana	30
Nebraska	31
New Jersey	34
New Mexico	35
North Carolina	37
North Dakota	38

Table 27-2. Participating States and Their Codes (*cont'd*)

State	*Code*
Ohio	39
Oklahoma	40
South Carolina	45
Wisconsin	55

*The codes listed above are correct for the IRS Combined Federal/State Filing Program and may not correspond to the state codes of other agencies or programs.

[IRS Pub. 1220 at 25 (see 2018 version).]

Part 6

Distribution Planning

Chapter 28

Rollovers

Using rollovers to an eligible retirement plan (see Q 28:5) to defer taxation on amounts distributed from qualified plans has been an option since the passage of the Employee Retirement Income Security Act of 1974 (ERISA) in 1974. The availability of this option was significantly enhanced by the Unemployment Compensation Amendments Act of 1992 (UCA). Even greater opportunities presented themselves with rollovers to Roth IRAs as a result of the Taxpayer Relief Act of 1997 (TRA '97), the Economic Growth and Tax Relief Reconciliation Act of 2001 (EGTRRA), the Tax Increase Prevention and Reconciliation Act of 2005 (TIPRA), the Pension Protection Act of 2006 (PPA), Worker, Retiree, and Employer Recovery Act of 2008 (WRERA), and the Small Business Jobs and Credit Act of 2012 (SBJCA).

Review of the Basics 28-1
Challenges in IRA Rollovers 28-5
Advantages and Disadvantages of IRA Rollovers 28-11
Roth IRAs 28-12

Review of the Basics

Q 28:1 What is an eligible rollover distribution?

Except as otherwise provided (see Q 28:2), an eligible rollover distribution means any distribution of all or any portion of the balance to the credit of the employee (see Q 28:3) in a qualified plan. [Treas. Reg. § 1.402(c)-2, Q&A-3]

WRERA amended Code Sections 402(c)(11) and 402(f)(2)(A) to provide that, for plan years beginning on or after January 1, 2010, distributions to designated nonspouse beneficiaries must be treated as eligible rollover distributions for the purpose of making a direct rollover into an inherited IRA. Such eligible rollover distributions, like all other eligible rollover distributions, are subject to the

20 percent mandatory tax withholding requirement under Code Section 3405(c) (when the amounts are not rolled over into an eligible retirement plan (see Q 28:5)) and the rollover notice requirement of Code Section 402(f). Under Notice 2007-7, the IRS had taken the view that the nonspouse beneficiary rollover provision (which had been added by PPA and had become effective for the 2007 plan year) was merely optional and that the other direct rollover requirements (i.e., the 20 percent mandatory tax withholding requirement and the rollover notice requirement) did not apply. [IRS Notice 2007-5] The distribution rules and notice requirements have been updated by Notices 2009-68, 2014-54, and 2014-74.

Q 28:2 Are there amounts that are not eligible rollover distributions?

An eligible rollover distribution does not include any of the following items:

1. Any distribution that is one of a series of substantially equal periodic payments made (not less frequently than annually) over any one of the following periods:
   a. The life of the employee (or the joint lives of the employee and the employee's designated beneficiary),
   b. The life expectancy of the employee (or the joint life and last survivor expectancy of the employee and the employee's designated beneficiary), or
   c. A specified period of 10 years or more;
2. Any required minimum distribution (RMD) under Code Section 401(a)(9) (see chapter 4);
3. The portion of any part of a distribution that is not includible in gross income, determined without regard to the exclusion for net unrealized appreciation (for example, a return of an employee's after-tax contributions) However, such portions may be eligible rollover distributions if transferred to an IRA or transferred via a direct trustee-to-trustee transfer to a qualified trust or 403(b) annuity contract and such trust or contract provides for separate accounting (including earnings) [I.R.C. § 402(c)(2)];
4. A hardship distribution made after December 31, 1998, from a 401(k) plan or a Section 403(b) arrangement [I.R.C. §§ 402(c)(4)(C), 403(b)(8)(B), as added and amended by RRA § 6005(c)(2)(B), RRA § 6005(c)(2)(C)] (although the IRS has provided transitional relief [Notice 99-5] and some permanent relief [Notice 2000-32] from this exception);
5. Returns of Section 401(k) elective deferrals that are returned as a result of the Section 415 limitations on annual additions (see chapter 5);
6. Corrective distributions of excess deferrals as described in Treasury Regulations Section 1.402(g)-1(e)(3), together with the income allocable to the corrective distributions (see chapter 5);
7. Corrective distributions of excess contributions and excess deferrals under qualified cash-or-deferred arrangements and corrective distributions of excess aggregate contributions, together with the income allocable to those corrective distributions (see chapter 5);

8. Loans in default that are deemed distributions—in contrast to actual offset distributions, which are includible in eligible rollover distributions (see chapter 2);
9. Dividends paid on employer securities, as described in Code Section 404(k) (see chapter 1);
10. The costs of life insurance coverage (PS-58 costs; see chapter 6); and
11. Similar items designated by the IRS in revenue rulings, notices, and other guidance of general applicability.

[Treas. Reg. § 1.402(c)-2, Q&As-3 to -4]

Q 28:3 How is the balance to the credit of the participant defined?

The vested account balance in a defined contribution plan or the vested accrued benefit in a defined benefit plan is generally treated as the balance to the credit of the participant. The balance to the credit of a participant excludes:

1. Qualified voluntary employee contributions (would have been contributed between 1982 and 1986) [I.R.C. § 72(o)(5)];
2. Amounts payable to an alternate payee under a qualified domestic relations order (QDRO) (see chapter 3); and
3. Amounts transferred from a defined contribution plan to a qualified cost-of-living arrangement under a defined benefit plan. [I.R.C. § 415(k)(2)]

[I.R.C. §§ 402(c)(4), 402(e)(4)(D)(vi), 402(e)(4)(D)(vii)]

Q 28:4 What happens if an eligible rollover distribution is received in cash by the participant?

The distribution is subject to 20 percent mandatory income tax withholding (see chapter 24) and is taxable to the participant in the year of distribution. However, if the participant rolls the distribution into an eligible retirement plan within 60 days of receipt, the amount rolled over would not be subject to tax. The participant, however, would have to come up with the cash necessary to replace the tax withheld to avoid taxation on any part of the distribution. For this reason, it generally makes sense for the participant to roll the entire eligible rollover distribution directly into an eligible retirement plan (see Q 28:5). [I.R.C. §§ 402(c)(3), 3405(c)]

Example 28-1: Larry receives an eligible rollover distribution of $150,000 from the ABC Art defined benefit plan. Because he is subject to mandatory tax withholding, the net cash that Larry receives in the distribution is $120,000 ($150,000 − (20% × $150,000)). If Larry rolls the cash received of $120,000 into an IRA within 60 days of receipt, he does not have to pay tax on $120,000. However, he is subject to tax on the tax withheld of $30,000. If Larry has an additional $30,000 in personal funds, however, and rolls the total eligible rollover distribution of $150,000 to an IRA within 60 days of receipt of his distribution, he does not currently have to pay any tax. The withheld amount of $30,000 is considered prepaid income tax when Larry files his personal tax return.

Q 28:5 What is considered an eligible retirement plan under the rollover rules?

An eligible retirement plan, as defined under Code Section 402(c)(8)(B), means an individual retirement plan or a qualified plan. An individual retirement plan is an IRA described in Code Section 408(a) or an individual retirement annuity (other than an endowment contract) described in Code Section 408(b). A qualified plan is a qualified defined contribution or defined benefit plan described in Code Section 401(a) that accepts rollover contributions, or an annuity plan described in Code Section 403(a). [Treas. Reg. § 1.402(c)-2, Q&A-2]

Eligible retirement plans also include Section 457 and Section 403(b) plans, if they permit rollovers. [I.R.C. § 402(c)(8)(B)]

Q 28:6 What are the consequences of a rollover into an IRA more than 60 days after receipt of the distribution?

A rollover that is rolled into an eligible retirement plan after more than 60 days from receipt of a distribution is subjected to income tax. In addition, because the late deposit into the IRA is not a rollover contribution, it is treated as a regular IRA contribution and is subject to the usual limits. Any amount of the late rollover that exceeds the normal IRA limits, if not removed by April 15 of the year following the year of rollover, is subject to a 6 percent annual excise tax until the excess is removed from the IRA. [I.R.C. § 408(d)(4), (5)]

Example 28-2: Katherine (who has attained age 70½) receives a distribution of $480,000 from the ABC Art 401(k) plan in October 2018. She elects a direct rollover of the entire amount to an IRA. $20,000 of the $480,000 distribution represents her RMD under Code Section 401(a)(9). Assume that Katherine does not qualify to make a deductible IRA contribution for 2018. As an RMD, the $20,000 is not an eligible rollover distribution and is, therefore, an excess IRA contribution. If $20,000 is not removed from the IRA by April 15, 2019, it is subject to a 6 percent excise tax each calendar year until it is removed from the IRA.

Q 28:7 May an individual other than the participant roll over funds into an IRA?

Yes. The following are circumstances in which a non-participant may roll funds over into an IRA:

1. The surviving spouse of a deceased participant may roll over the eligible qualified plan death proceeds into an IRA, a qualified plan, 403(b) annuity, or a governmental 457 plan. [I.R.C. § 402(c)(9)]
2. A former spouse or current spouse who is an alternate payee under a QDRO (see chapter 3) may roll an eligible rollover distribution into an IRA. [Treas. Reg. § 1.402(c)-2, Q&A-12; Ltr. Rul. 9109052]
3. A nonspouse beneficiary is permitted to roll over benefits, in a trustee-to-trustee transfer, to an IRA. This treats the IRA as an inherited IRA and allows the nonspouse beneficiary to satisfy the minimum distribution

requirements under Code Section 401(a)(9) from the IRA. This is effective for distributions made after 2006. Under WRERA, this is a mandated provision in a retirement plan for plan years beginning after December 31, 2009. [PPA § 829; I.R.C. § 402(c)(11)(A)(i); WRERA Sec. 108(f)]

Challenges in IRA Rollovers

Q 28:8 What problems may be encountered in attempting a direct rollover to an IRA?

This discussion focuses on direct rollovers as a means to accomplish a tax-free rollover to an IRA. Although it is possible to distribute funds directly to the participant from a qualified plan, which are then rolled over to an IRA within 60 days for receipt of the distribution, this needlessly subjects the distribution to a 20 percent mandatory tax withholding (see chapter 24). Some of the problems that a participant or trustee may encounter when attempting a direct rollover to an IRA include:

1. An IRA custodian may be unwilling to accept unusual assets (see Q 28:9).
2. An IRA custodian will be unable to accept collectibles (see Q 28:10).
3. The trustee of the qualified plan may need to first distribute a portion of the account balance directly to the participant if the participant has reached age 70½ (see Q 28:13).
4. The participant electing a direct rollover may have made an election under the Tax Equity and Fiscal Responsibility Act of 1982 (TEFRA) Section 242(b) (see Q 28:14).

Q 28:9 What type of assets are IRA custodians often unwilling to accept?

In the case of a distribution in kind from a qualified plan (see chapter 25), a direct rollover to an IRA may be accomplished only by directly transferring plan assets in kind. Many IRA custodians are not willing to act as a custodian for certain types of assets, including real estate, limited partnerships, securities of closely held corporations, and trust deeds. Reasons for the lack of willingness to accept such types of assets include the difficulty in transferring the asset in kind, the expense of valuation, and potential recordkeeping issues. Through a diligent search, however, a participant can generally find an IRA custodian willing to accept such assets (for a fee) in a direct rollover.

Q 28:10 May an IRA custodian accept collectibles in a direct rollover?

Although it is uncommon for a qualified plan to invest in collectibles, because of the fiduciary requirements of ERISA, some plans do, in fact, have such investments. However, an IRA trustee is prohibited from accepting collectibles, including any:

- Work of art
- Rug or antique
- Metal or gem
- Stamp or coin (with certain exceptions as noted below)
- Alcoholic beverage
- Other tangible personal property specified by the Secretary of the Treasury

The term *collectible* does *not* include:

- A gold coin described in Code Section 5112(a)(7), (8), (9), or (10)
- A silver coin described in Code Section 5112(e)
- A platinum coin described in Code Section 5112(k)
- A coin issued under the laws of any state, or
- Any gold, silver, platinum, or palladium bullion of a fineness equal to or exceeding the minimum fineness that a contract market requires for metals that may be delivered in satisfaction of a regulated futures contract, if such bullion is in the physical possession of an IRA trustee.

[I.R.C. § 408(m)]

In the case of a collectible that may not be rolled over to an IRA, the trustee of the qualified plan must either sell the collectible and distribute the cash in a direct rollover to the IRA or distribute the collectible directly to the participant. If the collectible is distributed in kind directly to the participant, special problems will occur with respect to mandatory tax withholding (see Q 28:11).

Q 28:11 How do the mandatory tax withholding rules operate when collectibles are distributed in kind?

Any distribution (with the exception of employer stock), whether it is in cash or property, is subject to mandatory 20 percent tax withholding (see chapter 24). If some cash is distributed along with the collectible, mandatory tax withholding will be easier to accomplish. The following rules apply when distributing collectibles to a participant:

1. If the cash distributed along with the collectibles is sufficient to cover the entire amount of the withholding, the entire collectible asset may be distributed to the plan participant.
2. If the cash distributed along with the collectibles is insufficient to cover the entire amount of withholding due, the participant may be requested to pay the trustee of the plan in cash for the amount of the tax withholding insufficiency.
3. If the participant does not provide the cash necessary to cover the balance of the withholding, the trustee must then sell all or a portion of the collectible asset to cover the withholding.

   An exception exists if a distribution includes property that is not includible in a designated distribution, such as the distribution of U.S.

Savings Bonds or an annuity contract; such property need not be sold or redeemed to meet any withholding obligation.

[Treas. Reg. § 35.3405-1T, F-2, F-3]

Example 28-3: Bernie participates in the ABC Art profit-sharing plan. The plan has invested part of its assets in a painting. Bernie, the only remaining participant in the plan, retires and elects a direct transfer of her account balance to an IRA. The IRA custodian accepts all other assets in Bernie's account, but cannot accept the painting because it is a collectible (see Q 28:10). The trustee of the profit-sharing plan has the painting appraised at $25,000. To distribute the painting directly to Bernie, Bernie must either:

- Pay $5,000 ($25,000 × 20%) directly to the trustee out of her personal assets to cover the mandatory tax withholding; or
- Ask the profit-sharing trustee to distribute $6,250 in cash from Bernie's account to cover the mandatory tax withholding (20% × ($25,000 + $6,250) = $6,250) before the balance is directly transferred to an IRA.

If Bernie is unwilling to accept either choice, the profit-sharing trustee must sell the painting and distribute cash to Bernie. Note that if the collectible assets were divisible, for example, coins, a portion of the collectible asset could potentially be sold to cover the amount of the mandatory tax withholding.

Q 28:12 How does an individual lose flexibility after electing a direct rollover?

In the period between age 55 and age 59½, an individual may lose the opportunity to withdraw unlimited funds from an IRA without incurring a penalty. An individual who terminates employment after age 55 may receive a distribution of his or her entire account balance from a qualified plan without being subject to the additional 10 percent income tax on early distributions (see chapter 20). However, if that same individual makes a direct rollover to an IRA, amounts withdrawn before age 59½ are subject to the additional 10 percent income tax on early distributions, unless one of these three exceptions apply:

1. The participant dies;
2. The participant becomes disabled within the meaning of Code Section 72(m)(7); or
3. The distribution is part of a series of substantially equal periodic payments (not less frequently than annually) made for the life (i.e., the life expectancy) of the participant or the joint lives (or the joint life expectancies) of the participant and his or her designated beneficiary (see Qs 30:6–30:11).

[I.R.C. § 72(t)(1), (2), (3)]

Example 28-4: Upon termination of employment from CDE Crafts, Danny elects a direct rollover of $175,000 from the CDE Crafts 401(k) plan to an IRA. Danny is age 56 and could have directly received the entire distribution as a lump-sum distribution. The distribution would have been exempt from the additional 10 percent income tax on early distributions because Danny was over age 55 at the time of his termination of employment. Two years after the direct rollover to an IRA, when he is age 58, Danny needs $125,000 to start a new business. If Danny withdraws $125,000 from the IRA, the withdrawal will be subject to an additional 10 percent income tax on early distributions because he is younger than age 59½.

Q 28:13 What happens if an employee who is older than age 70½ elects a direct rollover?

An employee who is older than age 70½ may elect a direct rollover, but the minimum distribution requirements of Code Section 401(a)(9) (see chapter 4) must first be satisfied, because a minimum required distribution is not an eligible rollover distribution. [Treas. Reg. § 1.402(c)-2, Q&A-3(b)(2)] The amount of the minimum required distribution (not eligible for rollover) will depend on the year of the rollover and whether distributions have begun:

1. *First distribution calendar year.* This is the calendar year in which the employee turns age 70½ or, if later, the year in which the individual terminates employment (if he or she is not a 5 percent owner). Although minimum required distributions need not begin until April 1 of the calendar year following the first distribution calendar year, the direct rollover may not include the amount of the minimum required distribution for the first distribution calendar year.
2. *Second distribution calendar year.* This is the calendar year immediately following the first distribution calendar year. If distributions have not begun, the minimum required distribution for the first and second distribution calendar years must be made before the direct rollover is completed in the second distribution calendar year. If the first distribution has already been made (generally before April 1 of the second distribution calendar year), the second distribution must be made before the direct rollover is completed.
3. *Third distribution calendar year and later.* If the minimum required distribution for the calendar year has not been made, the distribution must be made before the direct rollover is completed.

[Treas. Reg. § 1.401(a)(9)-7, Q&A-3] (See chapter 4 for detailed rules on minimum required distributions.)

Example 28-5: Deb, who turned age 70½ in 2019, terminates employment in 2019 and elects a direct rollover of her account balance of $153,000 in the CDE Crafts' 401(k) plan to an IRA. Her minimum required distribution for 2019, based on her 2018 account balance and single life expectancy, is $9,000. Only $144,000 may be directly rolled over into an IRA; the remaining $9,000 must be distributed to Deb. The $9,000 is taxable but is not subject to 20 percent income tax withholding as it is not a distribution that can be rolled over.

Example 28-6: Mary (who owns a 10 percent interest in CDE Crafts) turned age 70½ in 2018, terminates employment in February of 2019, and elects a direct rollover of her account balance of $680,000 in the CDE Crafts' 401(k) plan to an IRA. She has not received her minimum required distribution for the 2018 or 2019 calendar years. Therefore, Mary must directly receive her minimum required distributions for both 2018 and 2019 before the direct rollover of the remainder is made to an IRA.

Q 28:14 How does a direct rollover affect an election under TEFRA 242(b)?

Participants in qualified plans as of December 31, 1983, were able to make an election that allowed them the opportunity to delay receiving benefits later than required under Code Section 401(a)(9) (see chapter 4). Essentially, participants could defer receipt of benefits later than age 70½. A direct rollover to an IRA or another qualified plan has the following implications for participants with valid elections under TEFRA Section 242(b)(2):

1. Distributions under the receiving plan must be distributed in accordance with the minimum distribution requirements of Code Section 401(a)(9), not the TEFRA Section 242(b)(2) election; and
2. If the amount rolled over was not distributed in accordance with the election under TEFRA Section 242(b)(2), the election is revoked and a make-up distribution must be made under Code Section 401(a)(9) (see Q 28:15).

[TEFRA § 242(b)(2); Treas. Reg. § 1.401(a)(9)-8, Q&A-13]

In a private letter ruling, however, the IRS stated that an in-service withdrawal of funds from a profit-sharing plan in accordance with the terms of the plan would not invalidate the TEFRA Section 242(b) election. In the case in question, an individual participated in a profit-sharing plan and had made a valid election under Section 242(b) before December 31, 1983. The profit-sharing plan permitted in-service withdrawals if such withdrawals were at least $1,000. The IRS ruled that the in-service withdrawal of a portion of the account balance did not invalidate the Section 242(b) election with respect to the remaining balance, because the TEFRA 242(b) election covered only post-employment distributions. [Ltr. Rul. 200034031]

Q 28:15 When must distributions begin if the participant is older than age 70½ when the TEFRA Section 242(b) election is revoked?

Make-up distributions must be made by the end of the calendar year following the calendar year in which revocation occurs. Further, an additional amount may be required to be distributed to satisfy the minimum distribution incidental death benefit requirement under Treasury Regulations Section 1.401(a)(9)-2. If the entire balance to the credit of the participant was directly rolled over into an IRA or another qualified plan, it appears that the receiving plan must pay the make-up distribution. [Treas. Reg. § 1.401(a)(9)-8, Q&A-16]

Example 28-7: Rachel made a valid election under TEFRA Section 242(b) in 1983. She owns 10 percent of the stock in CDE Crafts and participates in its profit-sharing plan. Under the election Rachel made, distributions are to begin at age 80, to be paid over her life expectancy. Rachel retires in 2018, at age 77 and elects a direct rollover of her account balance of $475,000 to an IRA in 2018. By reason of the direct rollover, she has revoked the election made under TEFRA Section 242(b), and retroactive payments back to the time of her required beginning date, April 1, 2011, must be made on or before December 31, 2019 (the calendar year following the year of revocation). Rachel has elected payments based on the Uniform Lifetime Table with annual recalculation. The calculation of the retroactive payments is shown below.

Distribution Calendar Year	*Account Balance Date*	*Relevant Account Balance*	*Uniform Lifetime Table Factor*	*Minimum Required Distribution*
2010	12/31/2009	$303,000	27.4	$11,058
2011	12/31/2010	$323,000	26.5	$12,189
2012	12/31/2011	$356,000	25.6	$13,906
2013	12/31/2012	$389,000	24.7	$15,749
2014	12/31/2013	$402,000	23.8	$16,891
2015	12/31/2014	$415,000	22.9	$18,122
2016	12/31/2015	$400,000	22.0	$18,182
2017	12/31/2016	$385,000	21.2	$18,160
2018	12/31/2017	$405,000	20.3	$19,951
Total				$144,208

The account balance each year is reduced by the amounts previously required to be distributed. The total amount to be distributed before December 31, 2019, as a result of the revocation of the TEFRA Section 242(b) election, is $144,208. In addition, the minimum required distribution for distribution calendar year 2019 must also be distributed from the IRA. Had Rachel elected to receive her account balance as an in-service distribution prior to her year of retirement, she would not have revoked her TEFRA Section 242(b) election and could have transferred the entire balance to an IRA avoiding the immediate taxation on $144,208.

Advantages and Disadvantages of IRA Rollovers

Q 28:16 What are the advantages of an IRA rollover?

An IRA rollover's basic advantage is that it allows the participant to continue to defer payment of federal, state, and local taxes. In a tax-sheltered environment of an IRA, taxation on investment earnings is also deferred and the distribution is generally able to grow faster than it would if it were distributed in cash directly to the participant and subject to current taxation.

A participant in an IRA also has the advantage of total investment control. A participant in a defined contribution plan (e.g., 401(k) plan) will often have some degree of choice in his or her investment, but it is generally limited to a range of funds selected by the plan trustees. Participants in other qualified plans (e.g., defined benefit plans) will generally not have any discretion relative to their interests in the plan. But an IRA participant may invest money freely, subject only to the limitations imposed by the IRA trustee.

Lastly, a participant can avoid the imposition of 20 percent mandatory income tax withholding by rolling eligible amounts over into an IRA and later withdrawing the funds. Amounts withdrawn from an IRA are subject to voluntary income tax withholding at a 10 percent rate, not a 20 percent mandatory tax withholding. [I.R.C. § 3405(b)(1)]

Q 28:17 Is there an advantage in a direct rollover to an IRA for a participant who is entitled to a lump-sum distribution in a defined benefit plan?

Yes, but defined benefit plans must restrict the payment of lump-sum benefits to certain highly compensated employees (HCEs), if plan assets are less than 110 percent of current liabilities (see chapter 14). An employee whose lump-sum availability is restricted may still receive a direct rollover, if permitted by the plan document, provided that an agreement has been established to secure repayment to the plan of any amount necessary for the distribution of assets upon plan termination. [Rev. Rul. 92-76]

Example 28-8: Norman, a restricted highly compensated employee, retires in 2018 at age 55 from ABC Art. Norman's lump sum under the ABC Art defined benefit plan is $425,000. Because the plan assets are not greater than 110 percent of current liabilities and the value of Norman's benefit is more than 1 percent of the plan's total current liability, Norman would generally not be eligible to receive the lump-sum benefit. If he still wishes to rollover his lump-sum benefit to an IRA, Norman can still receive a distribution if he posts an acceptable bond equal to at least 100 percent of the restricted amount, as permitted in the ABC Art defined benefit plan. By doing this, the ABC Art defined benefit plan would be repaid if the plan were underfunded at the time it was terminated.

Q 28:18 What are the disadvantages of an IRA rollover?

Investment control is a double-edged sword: With complete investment discretion, participants now have additional responsibility to invest wisely. The professional expertise available to plan sponsors with millions of dollars to invest is generally not available to small investors. This can be particularly problematic for an individual who does not have any experience managing money. Fortunately, as defined contribution plans in which participants direct the investments of their accounts have become prevalent and participant investment education has improved, participants are becoming more sophisticated investors.

However, there are also a number of disadvantages to IRA rollovers from a tax standpoint:

1. A participant who was born before 1936 loses the ability to income average;
2. If a participant who was born before 1936 participated in a plan before 1974, the special capital gains treatment available for such participation is permanently lost by rolling over into an IRA; and
3. If employer securities are part of the IRA rollover, the ability to defer tax on the net unrealized appreciation is permanently lost.

There are also a number of financial disadvantages to an IRA rollover. Loans are not permitted from an IRA. Any amounts borrowed from an IRA are treated as a prohibited transaction and the entire IRA balance becomes immediately taxable. [I.R.C. § 408(e)(2)] A participant may not maintain a life insurance contract within an IRA, so if the insurance coverage cannot be maintained within a qualified plan, the participant must maintain it on a personal basis.

Roth IRAs

Q 28:19 What is a Roth IRA?

A Roth IRA (named after former Sen. William V. Roth (R-Del.)) is an individual retirement plan that is designated at the time of establishment as a Roth IRA. No deduction is allowed under Code Section 219 for any contributions to a Roth IRA. In certain circumstances, a qualified rollover contribution may be made from an individual retirement plan (other than a Roth IRA) to a Roth IRA. [I.R.C. § 408A(b), (c)(1), (c)(3)(B)]

Q 28:20 Who qualifies for a Roth IRA rollover?

WRERA has changed the rules regarding who is eligible for a rollover to a Roth IRA. Effective for tax years after December 31, 2009, participants may roll over their designated Roth accounts in a qualified retirement plan to a Roth IRA without regard to income limitations. [I.R.C. § 408A(c)(3)(B)]

However, an individual is not allowed to make a qualified rollover contribution to a Roth IRA from an individual IRA (other than a Roth IRA) in either of the following circumstances:

1. The taxpayer's adjusted gross income for such taxable year exceeds $100,000; or
2. The taxpayer is a married individual filing a separate return.

Effective for tax years beginning after December 31, 2009, the adjusted gross income limitations are removed.

[I.R.C. § 408A(c)]

Q 28:21 How is an existing IRA converted into a Roth IRA?

When an existing IRA is converted into a Roth IRA, its assets are deemed to be distributed to the IRA owner and are then rolled over into the Roth IRA. The entire amount of the existing IRA (excluding nondeductible contributions) is taxable in the year of conversion. In the case of a conversion to a Roth IRA that occurred before January 1, 1999, the taxable amount was determined by spreading the taxable income ratably over four years, beginning with the taxable year in which the conversion occurred. [I.R.C. § 408A(d)(3)(A)]

Example 28-9: Carolyn, age 45, made a rollover contribution to an IRA of $110,000 in 1997, from the ABC Art's 401(k) Plan. In 1998, she converted her existing IRA, now worth $125,000, to a Roth IRA. Her adjusted gross income for 1998 was less than $100,000, so she qualified for a Roth IRA conversion. Because the conversion was done in 1998, Carolyn was able to spread the additional $125,000 in taxable income ratably over four years at the rate of $31,250 per year. If her marginal tax rate was 28 percent, Carolyn paid additional taxes of $8,750 (28% × $31,250) each year for four years.

Example 28-10: Revising Example 28-9, Carolyn waited until 2018 to convert her existing IRA to a Roth IRA, rather than converting it in 1998. The IRA was worth $175,000 upon conversion in 2018. Carolyn's adjusted gross income for 2018 is more than $100,000, but she qualifies for the conversion due to the WRERA changes. Assuming a marginal 28 percent tax rate, the total tax payable due to the conversion would have been $49,000 ($175,000 × 28%). Because Carolyn did not make the conversion before January 1, 1999, the entire $49,000 was due for 2018.

Q 28:22 Is the Roth IRA conversion subject to the 10 percent additional income tax on early distributions for individuals who are younger than age 59½ at the time of conversion?

No. [I.R.C. § 408A(d)(3)(A)(ii)]

Q 28:23 Are investment earnings ever taxed when distributions are made from Roth IRAs?

Yes. Accumulated investment earnings on Roth IRAs will be subject to taxation unless the distribution is made:

1. After the five-taxable-year period beginning with the first taxable year during which the Roth IRA conversion occurred; or
2. After attainment of age 59½, death, disability, or a first-time home purchase.

[I.R.C. § 408A(d)(2)]

Q 28:24 Does it make sense to roll over a distribution from a qualified plan to a Roth IRA?

Effective in 2010 (without regard to the adjusted gross income limitations discussed in Q 28:20), plan distributions may be rolled over directly to Roth IRAs. It may make sense for an individual to consider paying taxes now, rather than later, knowing that the total account (including investment earnings) will never be taxed (if the requirements in Q 28:23 are met). Generally, individuals in a position to leave the money untouched for many years may find the Roth IRA conversion cost-effective, especially if tax rates increase.

Also, it appears that net unrealized appreciation from employer securities will never be taxed if such securities are directly rolled over to a Roth IRA. Notice 2008-30 contains language similar to the Code and states:

> In either case, the amount rolled over must be an eligible rollover distribution (as defined in § 402(c)(4)) and, pursuant to § 408A(d)(3)(A), there is included in gross income any amount that *would be includible* if the distribution were not rolled over. [Emphasis added.]

Thus, if employer securities are directly rolled over to a Roth IRA, it appears that only the cost basis will be taxable.

In Notice 2014-54, the IRS provided some clarification on the ability to roll-over after-tax money in a qualified plan to a Roth IRA and the pre-tax money in a qualified plan to a regular IRA. This Notice clarified the use of pro rata transfers when a distribution included both pre-tax and after-tax funds. However, the Notice did not provide an example where the qualified plan distribution only included after-tax money, which leaves open the question that if only after-tax money is subject to distribution, can the entire distribution be transferred to a Roth IRA.

For more details on rollovers to Roth IRAs, see chapter 21.

[Notice 2014-54; PPA § 824; I.R.C. § 408A(e); Notice 2008-30, IRB 2008-12 (Mar. 24, 2008), Q&A-1]

> **Example 28-11:** Jack, age 43, terminates employment with CDE Crafts in 2019 and receives a distribution from the CDE Crafts' 401(k) plan. Part of his distribution is 1,000 shares of employer securities, currently valued at $560,000. The cost basis of the shares is $60,000. If Jack had the shares

directly transferred to him personally, he would be immediately taxed on the cost basis of $60,000. He would likely be eligible for capital gains treatment at a reduced rate when he sells the shares at a later time. Instead, Jack rolls over the distribution of employer securities directly to a Roth IRA. He is taxed immediately on the cost basis of the shares of $60,000. It is likely that the increase in the value of the shares over the cost basis will never be taxed.

Q 28:25 When might a Roth IRA conversion not make sense?

If the payment of the taxes for conversion to a Roth IRA causes cash flow difficulties, it may not make sense to convert. Also, if the individual or his or her tax advisor expects that their future tax rates will decline steeply, a Roth IRA conversion may not be advisable.

Example 28-12: Caroline is considering the conversion of her existing 401(k) account to a Roth IRA. She speaks with her tax advisor who believes that a flat tax rate of 17 percent will be applicable when Caroline needs to withdraw her retirement savings. Caroline is currently in a federal tax bracket of 35 percent, so a Roth IRA conversion may not make sense.

Q 28:26 How did the Tax Increase Prevention and Reconciliation Act of 2005 (TIPRA) and WRERA change the rules regarding Roth IRA conversions?

WRERA changed the rules regarding who is eligible for a rollover to a Roth IRA. Due to this law, effective for plan years after December 31, 2009, participants may roll over their designated Roth accounts to a Roth IRA without regard to income limitations. [I.R.C. § 408A(c)(3)(B)]

Under prior law, in order to be able to convert from a traditional IRA to a Roth IRA, the taxpayer's adjusted gross income (AGI) for the year must not have exceeded $100,000. The $100,000 limit applied to the combined income of a married couple filing jointly.

Under TIPRA, the income limit was eliminated, effective for tax years beginning after December 31, 2009. Thus, taxpayers would be permitted to make such conversions without regard to their AGI. Under the bill, taxpayers could elect to pay tax on amounts converted in 2010 in equal installments in 2011 and 2012. However, income inclusion would be accelerated if converted amounts were distributed before 2012.

Taxpayers who convert their IRAs in 2011 and beyond would have one year to pay the resulting tax. This provision does not sunset. [TIPRA § 512]

Example 28-13: Jill has an IRA with an account balance of $100,000. In 2010, Jill converts her IRA to a Roth IRA. Jill has the ability to pay the tax in equal installments in 2011 and 2012. Alternatively, she may choose to pay the entire tax in 2010, if she believes that tax rates will significantly increase. If Jill takes a distribution from the Roth IRA in 2010 or 2011, her tax will be recomputed for 2010.

Chapter 29

Lump-Sum Distributions

A qualified plan participant who chooses to receive a lump-sum distribution in cash from a plan must make a number of choices. This chapter explores the advantages and disadvantages of electing a cash lump-sum distribution.

Review 29-1
Calculating Taxable Amounts 29-3
Economic Issues 29-9
Impact of Other Taxes 29-10
Advantages and Disadvantages of Lump-Sum Distributions 29-10

Review

Q 29:1 What is a lump-sum distribution?

A distribution made from a qualified plan qualifies for lump-sum treatment if it meets each of these requirements:

1. The distribution or distributions to the recipient are made within one taxable year.
2. The distribution represents the balance to the credit of the participant.
3. The distribution is made on account of:
   a. The participant's death,
   b. Attainment of at least age 59½,
   c. Separation from service (applicable only to participants who are not self-employed), or
   d. Total and permanent disability (applicable to a self-employed participant).

[I.R.C. § 402(e)(4)(D)]

Q 29:2 How is disability defined for lump-sum purposes?

A self-employed individual is considered disabled if he or she is unable to engage in any substantial gainful activity by reason of any medically determinable physical or mental impairment that can be expected to result in death or to be of long-continued and indefinite duration. An individual is not considered disabled unless he or she furnishes proof of the existence of the disability in a form or manner required by the IRS. [I.R.C. § 72(m)(7)]

Q 29:3 What plans are aggregated for purposes of the lump-sum distribution rules?

All pension plans (defined benefit, money purchase, and target benefit plans) of the employer are aggregated and treated as a single plan. All profit sharing and 401(k) plans are aggregated and treated as a single plan. All stock bonus plans and employee stock ownership plans (ESOPs) are aggregated and treated as a single plan. [I.R.C. § 402(e)(4)(D)(ii)]

Q 29:4 How is the balance to the credit of the participant defined?

The vested account balance in a defined contribution plan or the vested present value of the accrued benefit in a defined benefit plan is generally treated as the balance to the credit of the participant. The balance to the credit of a participant excludes:

1. Accumulated qualified voluntary employee contributions (QVECs); [I.R.C. § 72(o)(5)]
2. Amounts payable to an alternate payee under a qualified domestic relations order (QDRO) (see chapter 3); and
3. Amounts transferred from a defined contribution plan to a qualified cost-of-living arrangement under a defined benefit plan. [I.R.C. § 415(k)(2)]

[I.R.C. § 402(e)(4)(D)]

Q 29:5 Is favorable tax treatment available to all individuals who qualify for lump-sum treatment?

No. Most individuals will have their entire lump-sum distributions treated as ordinary income, and they will not be able to use any forward averaging. Others could have had their entire lump-sum distributions treated as ordinary income, but were only able to use five-year forward averaging *if* the distribution occurred before December 31, 1999. Other individuals, if they were grandfathered under the Tax Reform Act of 1986 (TRA '86), have the most favorable options. Tax treatment options available to participants who qualify for lump-sum treatment (or, if deceased, their spouses) are shown in Table 29-1.

Table 29-1. Availability of Tax Treatment

Criteria		
Over Age 59½?	*Born On or Before 1/1/36?*	*Tax Treatment*
No	No	Ordinary income
Yes	No	Ordinary income
N/A	Yes	Choice of: (1) ordinary income; (2) 10-year averaging; (3) capital gains/10-year averaging

[I.R.C. § 402(e)(4)(D); Pub. L. No. 99-514, § 1122(h)(3)(A)(ii)]

Q 29:6 When may the participant elect special tax treatment?

If the individual is grandfathered under TRA '86, this special tax treatment is available upon death, separation from service (in the case of individuals who are not self-employed), or disability (including for self-employed individuals). [Pub. L. No. 99-514, § 1122(h)(3)(A)(ii)]

Q 29:7 If an individual rolls over a portion of a lump-sum distribution to an IRA or another qualified plan, will favorable tax treatment be available for the remaining portion?

No. The amounts retained will be subject to ordinary income tax. [I.R.C. § 402(e)(4)(D)]

Calculating Taxable Amounts

Q 29:8 How is the total taxable amount determined?

The total taxable amount is the amount received in the taxable year, less:

1. The investment in the contract (e.g., after-tax employee contributions, PS-58 costs (for taxable life insurance coverage), deemed loan distributions under Code Section 72(p) (see chapter 19); and
2. The net unrealized appreciation (NUA) in employer securities (see chapter 25).

[2018 Instructions for Forms 1099-R and 5498]

Q 29:9 How is the minimum distribution allowance (MDA) computed?

The minimum distribution allowance (MDA) provides for a reduction in the taxable amount for small distributions to participants born before January 2, 1936, that are less than $70,000. The reduction or MDA for a taxable year is equal to:

1. The lesser of $10,000 or one-half of the total taxable amount of the lump-sum distribution *reduced by* (but not below zero)
2. 20 percent of the amount (if any) by which the total taxable amount exceeds $20,000.

[Prop. Treas. Reg. § 1.402(e)-2(b)(3); Pub. L. No. 104-188, § 1401(c)(2)]

The MDA at various taxable income thresholds is as follows:

Taxable Amount	*MDA*
$5,000	$2,500
$10,000	$5,000
$15,000	$7,500
$20,000	$10,000
$25,000	$9,000
$30,000	$8,000
$35,000	$7,000
$40,000	$6,000
$45,000	$5,000
$50,000	$4,000
$55,000	$3,000
$60,000	$2,000
$65,000	$1,000
$70,000	$ 0

Q 29:10 How does the computation change if the lump-sum distribution is paid to the beneficiary of a deceased participant?

If a lump-sum distribution made to a participant's (who was born before January 2, 1936) beneficiary is subject to the five-year averaging computation, the total taxable amount of the distribution must be reduced by the estate tax deduction attributable to the total taxable amount of the distribution. [I.R.C. § 691(c)(4)]

Q 29:11 Who is eligible for grandfather treatment under TRA '86?

If a participant had reached age 50 on or before January 1, 1986 (born on or before January 2, 1936), and receives a lump-sum distribution, under the grandfather provisions of TRA '86, that participant has five choices on the taxation of his or her distribution:

1. Ordinary income on the entire portion of the distribution;
2. Ten-year forward averaging on the entire distribution;
3. Capital gains treatment on a portion of the distribution, 10-year forward averaging on the balance;

4. Capital gains treatment on a portion of the distribution, ordinary income on the balance; and
5. Roll the entire distribution (or a portion) over to an IRA, in which case the portion that is not rolled over is subject to ordinary income tax.

An individual may choose to use 10-year forward averaging only once after 1986. Form 4972 should be completed and attached to Form 1040 if options 2 or 3 are chosen.

[Pub. L. No. 100-647, § 1011A(b)(13)-(15); IRS Pub. 575]

Q 29:12 How is the capital gains portion of the distribution determined?

The capital gains treatment is only available to a participant (or beneficiary of a participant) who participated in the plan before 1974. The portion of the taxable amount of the distribution taxed as long-term capital gain is determined by multiplying the taxable portion of the distribution by the following ratio:

$$\frac{\text{Number of months of plan participation before 1974}}{\text{Total number of months of plan participation}}$$

In figuring the months of active participation before 1974, any portion of a calendar year in which the employee actively participated is counted as 12 months. In figuring active participation after 1973, any portion of a calendar month in which the employee actively participated is counted as one month. [IRS Pub. No. 575 at 21; Prop. Treas. Reg. § 1.402(e)-2(d)(3)]

Example 29-1: Kevin retired at age 76 on April 25, 2011, from ABC Music. He receives a lump-sum distribution of $900,000 from the defined benefit plan and is entitled to receive capital gains treatment on a portion of the distribution. Kevin has been an active participant in the plan since July 1, 1959. The number of months of active participation before 1974 is 180 months (15 years, counting 1959 as a full year), and the number of months of active participation after 1973 is 448 months (37 full years and four months). The capital gains portion of Kevin's distribution is computed as follows:

$$\$900{,}000 \times 180 \div (180 + 448) = \$257{,}962$$

The remainder of the distribution, or $642,038, is eligible for 10-year forward averaging.

Q 29:13 How is the capital gains portion of the distribution taxed?

The capital gains portion is taxed at a flat 20 percent rate. [Pub. L. No. 99-514, § 1122(h)(3)(B)(ii)]

Example 29-2: In Example 29-1, the capital gains portion of Kevin's distribution was $257,962. The tax on this portion of the distribution is $51,592 (20% × $257,962).

Q 29:14 How is 10-year income averaging computed?

Ten-year income averaging is computed as follows:

Step 1. Compute the total taxable amount of the distribution.

Step 2. If there is a death benefit exclusion, reduce the amount in Step 1 by the death benefit exclusion.

Step 3. If there is an estate tax amount attributable to the lump-sum distribution, reduce the taxable amount by the estate tax deduction attributable to the distribution.

Step 4. Reduce the taxable amount by the MDA (see Q 29:9).

Step 5. Determine the tax on 1/10 of the total taxable income [Step 1–Step 2–Step 3–Step 4] using 1986 tax rates (see the table below).

Step 6. Multiply the result in Step 5 by 10.

[Pub. L. No. 99-514, § 1122(h)(5); Form 4972]

1986 Tax Rate Schedule for Single Individuals

Amounts of at least:	*But not over:*	*Tax is equal to:*	*Of the amount over:*
-0-	$ 1,190	11%	-0-
$ 1,190	$ 2,270	$ 130.90 + 12%	$ 1,190
$ 2,270	$ 4,530	$ 260.50 + 14%	$ 2,270
$ 4,530	$ 6,690	$ 576.90 + 15%	$ 4,530
$ 6,690	$ 9,170	$ 900.90 + 16%	$ 6,690
$ 9,170	$11,440	$ 1,297.70 + 18%	$ 9,170
$11,440	$13,710	$ 1,706.30 + 20%	$11,440
$13,710	$17,160	$ 2,160.30 + 23%	$13,710
$17,160	$22,880	$ 2,953.80 + 26%	$17,160
$22,880	$28,600	$ 4,441.00 + 30%	$22,880
$28,600	$34,320	$ 6,157.00 + 34%	$28,600
$34,320	$42,300	$ 8,101.80 + 38%	$34,320
$42,300	$57,190	$11,134.20 + 42%	$42,300
$57,190	$85,790	$17,388.00 + 48%	$57,190
$85,790	–	$31,116.00 + 50%	$85,790

Example 29-3: Bill, age 76, receives a lump-sum distribution of $45,000 from the ABC Music profit sharing plan. Bill was over age 50 on January 1, 1986, and has participated in the plan for more than five years. He elects 10-year income averaging treatment on the entire taxable distribution of $45,000. His taxes on the distribution are computed as follows:

$$MDA = \$10,000 - 20\% \times (\$45,000 - \$20,000) = \$5,000$$

$$\text{Taxable amount: } \$45,000 - \$5,000 = \$40,000$$

Bill's tax rate is based on 1/10 of $40,000, or $4,000; the tax is computed as $260.50 plus 14 percent of the excess over $2,270 (see the table above), multiplied by 10. The total taxes payable are:

$$\begin{aligned}\text{Total Taxes} &= 10 \times [\$260.50 + 14\% \times (\$4,000 - \$2,270)] \\ &= 10 \times (\$260.50 + \$242.20) \\ &= \$5,027\end{aligned}$$

Example 29-4: Roanne receives a lump-sum distribution of $650,000 from ABC Music. Her net distribution, after 20 percent mandatory withholding, is $520,000. She is eligible for 10-year income averaging, but decides after 45 days that she wants to roll over all but $20,000 into an IRA. Roanne has lost the ability to use 10-year income averaging; therefore, the $20,000 remaining and the $130,000 withheld are subject to ordinary income tax.

Example 29-5: Lloyd receives a lump-sum distribution of $60,000 in December 2018 from the CDE Radio profit sharing plan. Lloyd has no investment in the contract or NUA from employer securities. Lloyd has terminated employment and was born on January 15, 1934, so he is eligible for grandfathering under TRA '86. His MDA is calculated as follows:

$$\$10,000 - 20\% \times (\$60,000 - \$20,000) = \$2,000$$

The net taxable distribution to Lloyd is $58,000 ($60,000 − $2,000). Ten-year averaging is computed using Form 4972. The taxable amount is computed by taking 10 percent of the net taxable distribution of $58,000, or $5,800. Using 1986 tax rates (see Q 29:14), the tax on income of $5,800 is $576.90 plus 15 percent of the excess over $4,530. The taxable amount is computed as follows:

$$\text{Tax on } \$5,800 = \$576.90 + 15\% \times (\$5,800 - \$4,530) = \$767.40$$

$$10 \times \$767.40 = \$7,674$$

This amount is then added to Line 44 of 2018 Form 1040.

Example 29-6: Bob receives a lump-sum distribution of $540,000 from the CDE Radio profit sharing plan. Bob has participated in the plan for over five years and is eligible for grandfather treatment under TRA '86. The net taxable amount to Bob is $540,000 because he is not eligible for the MDA (because his distribution exceeds $70,000). Bob's taxes, using $540,000 as the taxable amount, are:

$$\begin{aligned}\text{Tax on 1/10 of } \$54,000 &= \$11,134.20 + 42\% \times (\$54,000 - \$42,300) \\ &= \$16,048.20 \\ \text{Tax on Entire Distribution} &= 10 \times \$16,048.20 = \$160,482.00\end{aligned}$$

Q 29:15 How does the distribution of an annuity affect the taxation of a lump-sum distribution?

When a lump-sum distribution includes an annuity contract, the total taxable amount of the distribution is computed by adding in the actuarial value of the annuity contract. Then, the tax attributable to the annuity contract is subtracted from the amount computed to come up with the net taxable amount. In computing the tax, the following steps are taken:

Step 1. Determine the amount of the lump-sum distribution without taking into account the annuity contract received.

Step 2. Determine the current actuarial value of the annuity received as part of the lump-sum distribution.

Step 3. Add the amounts in Step 1 and Step 2. This is the adjusted total taxable amount.

Step 4. Determine the amount of the MDA (see Q 29:9).

Step 5. Subtract the amount in Step 4 from the amount in Step 3.

Step 6. Multiply the amount in Step 5 by 10 percent.

Step 7. Determine the tax on the amount in Step 6.

Step 8. Multiply the amount in Step 7 by 10. This is the amount of the separate tax on the lump-sum distribution, including the annuity contract.

Step 9. Divide the current actuarial value of the annuity by the amount in Step 3. This amount can be no more than one.

Step 10. Multiply the amount in Step 8 by the amount in Step 9. This is the portion of the separate tax that is attributable to the annuity contract.

Step 11. Subtract the amount in Step 10 from the amount in Step 8. This is the 10-year averaging tax on the distribution.

[IRS Pub. 575]

Example 29-7: Rosina receives a lump-sum distribution from the ABC Music defined benefit plan. Rosina, age 76, has participated in the plan for more than five years. Rosina's total distribution is $750,000, comprising a non-transferable annuity contract with an actuarial value of $250,000 and cash of $500,000. Rosina is grandfathered under TRA '86, and is entitled to 10-year income averaging on the distribution. The tax (using 1986 tax rates) is computed as follows:

Step 1. Lump-sum distribution without the annuity contract = $500,000

Step 2. Actuarial value of annuity contract = $250,000

Step 3. Adjusted total taxable amount = $500,000 + $250,000 = $750,000

Step 4. MDA is not applicable because distribution exceeds $70,000

Step 5. Net taxable amount = $750,000

Step 6. 1/10 × $750,000 = $75,000

Step 7. Tax on 75,000 = $17,388 + 48% × ($75,000 − $57,190) = $25,936.80

Step 8. Tax on $750,000 = 10 × $25,936.80 = $259,368

Step 9. Actuarial value of annuity/Step 3 = $250,000/$750,000 = 33.33%

Step 10. Step 8 × Step 9 = $259,368 × 33.33% = $86,447.35

Step 11. Ten-year income averaging tax = Step 8 − Step 10 = $259,368 − $86,447.35 = $172,920.65

Economic Issues

Q 29:16 Should a participant take advantage of the availability of capital gains treatment or income average the entire distribution?

That depends on the relative length of time the participant has participated in the plan. The table below illustrates when it makes sense to use capital gains rather than ordinary income treatment for a lump-sum distribution (based on 2010 tax rates and termination of employment in December 2009).

Year of Entry	*Capital Gains Breakpoint*	*Ordinary Income Breakpoint*
1955	$148,122	$1,979,367
1960	$143,811	$1,410,760
1965	$138,890	$1,040,660
1970	$137,100	$ 762,305
1975 or later	N/A	$ 602,121

Example 29-8: Becky, grandfathered for special tax treatment under TRA '86, participated in the CDE Radio's profit sharing plan since 1970 and received a lump-sum distribution in 2010 after terminating employment in December 2009. If the distribution was less than $137,100, Becky minimized her taxes by electing 10-year income averaging. If the distribution was more than $137,100 but less than $762,305, Becky minimized her taxes by electing 10-year income averaging on the post-1973 portion of the distribution and capital gains treatment on the pre-1974 portion of the distribution. If the distribution was more than $762,305, Becky minimized her taxes by electing ordinary income treatment.

Note: When amounts were below the capital gains breakpoint, it generally made sense to elect 10-year income averaging to minimize taxes. When amounts were above the capital gains breakpoint (but below the ordinary income breakpoint), it made more sense to elect capital gains treatment in conjunction with 10-year income averaging. When amounts were above the ordinary income breakpoint, it made economic sense to elect ordinary income treatment. For amounts below $70,000, the MDA (in conjunction with 10-year income averaging) will generally produce the least amount of taxes.

Impact of Other Taxes

Q 29:17 Must other taxes be taken into consideration when a participant receives a lump-sum distribution?

Yes. The 10 percent additional income tax on early distributions before age 59½ may apply (see Q 29:18). [I.R.C. § 72(t)]

Q 29:18 How does the 10 percent additional income tax on early distributions affect the calculation of the taxes on a lump-sum distribution?

A participant who is younger than age 59½ and who receives a lump-sum distribution is subject to a 10 percent additional income tax on an early distribution unless he or she meets one of these three exceptions:

1. Death;
2. Disability as defined in Code Section 72(m)(7) (see Q 29:2); or
3. Separation from service after reaching age 55.

The penalty of 10 percent additional income tax is imposed on the entire taxable portion of the distribution. [I.R.C. § 72(t)(1)]

> **Example 29-9:** Steve retires at age 45 and receives a lump-sum distribution of $434,000 from the ABC Music pension plan. He is not grandfathered under TRA '86 and is not disabled and must pay ordinary income tax on the entire distribution plus the 10 percent additional income tax penalty of $43,400 since he received it prior to attaining age 59½.

Advantages and Disadvantages of Lump-Sum Distributions

Q 29:19 What are the advantages to the participant of receiving a lump-sum distribution?

A participant may find a lump-sum distribution to be advantageous as compared with annuity distributions or installments for a number of reasons:

1. The participant may be in need of the spendable cash (after the applicable income tax and any related tax penalty) available in a lump-sum distribution.
2. The participant may want complete flexibility in dealing with his or her retirement funds and may not want to have to request funds when needed from an IRA or qualified plan trustee.
3. The participant may not want to deal with the complications of leaving money in a qualified environment (e.g., mandatory distributions after age 70½).
4. The participant may wish to take advantage of NUA in employer securities held within the qualified plan.

Q 29:20 What are the disadvantages of a lump-sum distribution?

In some cases, notably many defined benefit plans, a lump-sum distribution may not be a permitted form of payment under the plan.

If available, a lump-sum distribution has some disadvantages, when compared with IRA rollover, installment, or annuity payment options:

1. The lump-sum distribution will generally not accumulate as fast outside a qualified plan environment, due to the current taxation of the earnings.
2. If tax rates decrease in the future, the participant would not have the opportunity to timely withdraw funds from an IRA (compared to a rollover).
3. The participant is effectively prepaying applicable federal, state, and local taxes when taking a lump-sum distribution.
4. The participant runs the risk of outliving his or her money (compared to an annuity).
5. In the current low interest rate environment, the lump-sum distribution from a defined benefit plan, even when computed using the applicable interest rates and mortality table under IRC § 417(e), may not be sufficient for the participant to purchase an individual annuity that would replicate the monthly benefit provided by the plan.

Q 29:21 When does a lump-sum distribution make economic sense?

From the participant's standpoint, a lump-sum distribution may maximize the spendable retirement dollars available to a participant and his or her family under the following sample circumstances:

1. If a defined benefit plan permits lump-sum distributions (and does not condition such distributions on the participant's health), a terminally ill participant (and beneficiary) will receive far greater benefits than by annuitizing the benefits.

   Example 29-10: Leonard, age 65, who is terminally ill with cancer, retires and chooses a qualified joint and 50 percent survivor annuity of $2,400 per month. He dies two months later, and his spouse, Anna, age 60, receives a benefit of $1,200 per month for the rest of her life. However, had Leonard chosen a lump-sum distribution, he would have received a single sum of approximately $266,000. Had the distribution been rolled over to an IRA, Anna could have received a life annuity benefit of approximately $2,350 per month, rather than the $1,200 per month she is currently receiving.

2. If the lump-sum distribution is less than $70,000, the MDA may significantly reduce the taxable income of the participant (see Q 29:9).
3. If the participant has significant participation in the plan before 1974 and is entitled to a distribution greater than approximately $130,000, the 20 percent tax rate on the capital gains portion of the distribution will significantly reduce the taxes (see Q 29:16).

4. A lump-sum distribution that includes employer securities with substantial NUA may result in a significant deferral of taxes on the NUA (see Q 29:22).

Q 29:22 How are employer securities in a lump-sum distribution treated?

A distribution of employer securities in a lump sum (see chapter 19) to a participant may provide significant tax advantages to the participant because the NUA is not taxable at the time of distribution. See chapter 28 for a discussion of NUA and the direct rollover of employer securities to a Roth IRA. [I.R.C. § 402(e)(4); Treas. Reg. § 1.402(a)-1(b)(1)(i)(a)]

> **Example 29-11:** Annette participates in the CDE Radio ESOP and receives a distribution of 5,000 shares of employer securities worth $265,000 in 2018. Her NUA is $65,000, which she chooses to defer tax on until the employer securities are sold. Annette is taxed on the difference, or $200,000, as a lump-sum distribution in 2018. If she sells the securities in 2018 and realizes a gain of $100,000 (including the original NUA of $65,000), the entire $100,000 will likely be subject to capital gains tax.

Q 29:23 What happens if the estate of a deceased participant receives employer securities?

The NUA that was not taxed when employer securities were distributed is includible in the estate's gross income as taxable income in respect of a decedent in the taxable year in which the executor sells the employer securities. The gain is treated as a long-term capital gain, and the estate is allowed a deduction for any estate tax paid. [Rev. Rul. 69-297]

Appendix A

120 Percent of Federal Midterm Rate

Some calculations relating to pension distributions use 120 percent of the Federal Midterm rate, including the following:

1. Calculation of the interest due on repayment of a distribution under a defined benefit plan (see chapters 8 and 9);
2. Calculation of the amount of the accrued benefit attributable to mandatory employee contributions under a defined benefit plan (see chapter 9);
3. As an option in the calculation of the interest rate for purposes of the "substantially equal period payment" rules (discussed in chapters 20 and 28).

Year	*1987*	*1988*	*1989*	*1990*	*1991*	*1992*	*1993*
Jan	8.34%	10.61%	11.11%	9.57%	9.78%	8.10%	7.63%
Feb	8.35%	10.52%	11.36%	9.70%	9.64%	7.64%	7.50%
Mar	8.39%	9.82%	11.22%	10.27%	9.41%	8.06%	7.08%
Apr	8.45%	9.66%	11.58%	10.54%	9.50%	8.43%	6.56%
May	8.82%	10.04%	11.68%	10.61%	9.62%	8.56%	6.57%
June	9.95%	10.47%	11.26%	10.97%	9.53%	8.47%	6.41%
July	10.31%	10.77%	10.54%	10.53%	9.66%	8.25%	6.67%
Aug	9.87%	10.66%	10.01%	10.44%	9.87%	7.82%	6.40%
Sept	10.20%	10.94%	9.68%	10.28%	9.59%	7.19%	6.44%
Oct	10.73%	11.08%	10.10%	10.63%	9.08%	6.96%	6.02%
Nov	11.49%	10.73%	10.07%	10.59%	8.69%	6.83%	5.91%
Dec	10.79%	10.61%	9.70%	10.25%	8.51%	7.40%	6.10%

Year	*1994*	*1995*	*1996*	*1997*	*1998*	*1999*	*2000*
Jan	6.40%	9.54%	6.89%	7.34%	7.13%	5.59%	7.47%
Feb	6.42%	9.59%	6.75%	7.68%	6.84%	5.67%	7.90%
Mar	6.45%	9.34%	6.56%	7.72%	6.72%	5.80%	8.19%
Apr	7.08%	8.84%	7.08%	7.82%	6.85%	6.35%	8.08%
May	7.74%	8.58%	7.65%	8.25%	6.84%	6.28%	7.70%
June	8.33%	8.22%	7.93%	8.19%	6.95%	6.46%	7.96%
July	8.22%	7.56%	8.12%	8.00%	6.83%	7.01%	7.96%
Aug	8.49%	7.27%	8.24%	7.07%	6.70%	7.16%	7.62%
Sept	8.49%	7.68%	7.99%	7.69%	6.67%	7.19%	7.50%
Oct	8.56%	7.59%	8.09%	7.63%	6.16%	7.25%	7.33%
Nov	8.97%	7.35%	7.94%	7.34%	5.42%	7.32%	7.23%
Dec	9.33%	7.12%	7.59%	7.25%	5.43%	7.46%	7.07%

Year	*2001*	*2002*	*2003*	*2004*	*2005*	*2006*
Jan	6.75%	5.40%	4.12%	4.23%	4.53%	5.39%
Feb	6.10%	5.58%	3.93%	4.13%	4.60%	5.29%
Mar	6.10%	5.43%	3.89%	4.01%	4.60%	5.42%
Apr	5.95%	5.60%	3.56%	3.80%	4.92%	5.68%
May	5.73%	6.01%	3.82%	3.81%	5.15%	5.82%
June	6.04%	5.71%	3.68%	4.67%	4.82%	6.09%
July	6.16%	5.53%	3.06%	4.94%	4.63%	6.08%
Aug	6.01%	5.10%	3.25%	4.81%	4.71%	6.27%
Sept	5.79%	4.51%	4.12%	4.61%	5.04%	6.03%
Oct	5.52%	4.16%	4.39%	4.36%	4.91%	5.74%
Nov	4.97%	3.68%	3.99%	4.26%	5.09%	5.65%
Dec	4.78%	3.98%	4.26%	4.28%	5.43%	5.70%

Year	*2007*	*2008*	*2009*	*2010*	*2011*	*2012*
Jan	5.51%	4.31%	2.48%	2.95%	2.33%	1.40%
Feb	5.65%	4.22%	1.98%	3.39%	2.80%	1.34%
Mar	5.84%	3.57%	2.33%	3.23%	2.94%	1.40%
Apr	5.54%	3.45%	2.59%	3.25%	2.98%	1.38%
May	5.56%	3.29%	2.47%	3.45%	2.94%	1.57%
June	5.59%	3.84%	2.71%	3.27%	2.73%	1.28%
July	5.96%	4.14%	3.32%	2.83%	2.40%	1.10%
Aug	6.13%	4.26%	3.37%	2.62%	2.28%	1.06%

Year	*2007*	*2008*	*2009*	*2010*	*2011*	*2012*
Sept	5.76%	4.16%	3.45%	2.32%	1.95%	1.01%
Oct	5.23%	3.81%	3.20%	2.07%	1.44%	1.12%
Nov	5.28%	3.57%	3.10%	1.91%	1.45%	1.07%
Dec	4.97%	3.43%	3.16%	1.83%	1.53%	1.14%

Year	*2013*	*2014*	*2015*	*2016*	*2017*
Jan	1.04%	2.10%	2.10%	2.17%	2.36%
Feb	1.21%	2.36%	2.04%	2.18%	2.53%
Mar	1.31%	2.21%	1.76%	1.77%	2.47%
Apr	1.31%	2.17%	2.04%	1.74%	2.55%
May	1.20%	2.31%	1.83%	1.71%	2.45%
June	1.14%	2.29%	1.92%	1.70%	2.35%
July	1.47%	2.18%	2.12%	1.71%	2.27%
Aug	1.95%	2.27%	2.18%	1.43%	
Sept	1.99%	2.23%	2.12%	1.47%	
Oct	2.31%	2.22%	2.00%	1.56%	
Nov	2.07%	2.28%	1.91%	1.61%	
Dec	1.98%	2.06%	2.01%	1.76%	

Appendix B

Pre-GATT Section 417(e) Interest Rates

These are the pre-GATT 417(e) interest rates, which PBGC continues to publish at:

https://www.pbgc.gov/prac/interest/vls

For purposes of determining the lump-sum equivalent of a monthly annuity benefit, the following rules and interest rates shall apply:

1. For benefits for which the participant or beneficiary is entitled to be in pay status on the valuation date, the immediate annuity rate shall apply.
2. For benefits for which the deferral period is y years (y is an integer and 0 < y < n1), interest rate i1 shall apply from the valuation date for a period of y years; thereafter the immediate annuity rate shall apply.
3. For benefits for which the deferral period is y years (y is an integer and n1 < y < n1 + n2), interest rate i2 shall apply from the valuation date for a period of y − n1 years, interest rate i1 shall apply for the following n1 years; thereafter the immediate annuity rate shall apply.
4. For benefits for which the deferral period is y years (y is an integer and y > n1 + n2), interest rate i3 shall apply from the valuation date for a period of y − n1 − n2 years, interest rate i2 shall apply for the following n2 years, interest rate i1 shall apply for the following n1 years; thereafter the immediate annuity rate shall apply.

For Plans with a Valuation Date		*Immediate Annuity*	*Deferred Annuities (Percent)*			*Years*	
On or After	*Before*	*Rate*	*i(1)*	*i(2)*	*i(3)*	*n(1)*	*n(2)*
9-2-74	10-1-75	8.00%	1.0725	1.0575	1.0425	7	8
10-1-75	1-1-76	7.75%	1.0725	1.0575	1.0425	7	7
1-1-76	3-1-76	8.00%	1.0725	1.0525	1.0400	7	10
3-1-76	6-1-76	7.25%	1.0700	1.0500	1.0400	7	10
6-1-76	9-1-76	7.25%	1.0675	1.0475	1.0350	7	10
9-1-76	12-1-76	7.00%	1.0600	1.0475	1.0350	8	10
12-1-76	3-1-77	7.00%	1.0625	1.0475	1.0375	7	10

For Plans with a Valuation Date		*Immediate Annuity*	*Deferred Annuities (Percent)*			*Years*	
On or After	*Before*	*Rate*	*i(1)*	*i(2)*	*i(3)*	*n(1)*	*n(2)*
3-1-77	6-1-77	7.00%	1.0600	1.0475	1.0350	8	10
6-1-77	12-1-77	6.75%	1.0625	1.0450	1.0375	8	10
12-1-77	3-1-78	6.75%	1.0625	1.0450	1.0375	8	10
3-1-78	6-1-78	7.00%	1.0625	1.0475	1.0375	7	10
6-1-78	9-1-78	7.25%	1.0675	1.0475	1.0350	7	10
9-1-78	3-1-79	7.25%	1.0675	1.0475	1.0350	7	10
3-1-79	6-1-79	7.50%	1.0675	1.0550	1.0400	7	8
6-1-79	9-1-79	7.50%	1.0675	1.0550	1.0400	7	8
9-1-79	12-1-79	7.75%	1.0700	1.0575	1.0400	7	8
12-1-79	3-1-80	8.50%	1.0775	1.0650	1.0400	7	8
3-1-80	6-1-80	8.75%	1.0800	1.0675	1.0400	7	8
6-1-80	9-1-80	8.75%	1.0800	1.0675	1.0400	7	8
9-1-80	12-1-80	9.00%	1.0825	1.0700	1.0400	7	8
12-1-80	1-1-81	9.25%	1.0850	1.0725	1.0400	7	8
1-1-81	2-1-81	9.50%	1.0875	1.0750	1.0400	7	8
2-1-81	4-1-81	9.75%	1.0900	1.0775	1.0400	7	8
4-1-81	6-1-81	10.00%	1.0925	1.0800	1.0400	7	8
6-1-81	7-1-81	10.25%	1.0950	1.0825	1.0400	7	8
7-1-81	8-1-81	10.50%	1.0975	1.0850	1.0400	7	8
8-1-81	10-1-81	10.25%	1.0950	1.0825	1.0400	7	8
10-1-81	11-1-81	10.50%	1.0975	1.0850	1.0400	7	8
11-1-81	12-1-81	10.75%	1.1000	1.0875	1.0400	7	8
12-1-81	1-1-82	11.00%	1.1025	1.0900	1.0400	7	8
1-1-82	2-1-82	10.50%	1.0975	1.0850	1.0400	7	8
2-1-82	3-1-82	10.75%	1.1000	1.0875	1.0400	7	8
3-1-82	6-1-82	11.00%	1.1025	1.0900	1.0400	7	8
6-1-82	8-1-82	10.75%	1.1000	1.0875	1.0400	7	8
8-1-82	10-1-82	11.00%	1.1025	1.0900	1.0400	7	8
10-1-82	11-1-82	10.75%	1.1000	1.0875	1.0400	7	8
11-1-82	12-1-82	10.50%	1.0975	1.0850	1.0400	7	8
12-1-82	1-1-83	10.25%	1.0950	1.0825	1.0400	7	8
1-1-83	2-1-83	10.00%	1.0925	1.0800	1.0400	7	8
2-1-83	4-1-83	9.75%	1.0900	1.0775	1.0400	7	8
4-1-83	6-1-83	9.50%	1.0875	1.0750	1.0400	7	8
6-1-83	9-1-83	9.25%	1.0850	1.0725	1.0400	7	8

For Plans with a Valuation Date		Immediate Annuity	Deferred Annuities (Percent)			Years	
On or After	*Before*	*Rate*	*i(1)*	*i(2)*	*i(3)*	*n(1)*	*n(2)*
9-1-83	2-1-84	9.50%	1.0875	1.0750	1.0400	7	8
2-1-84	3-1-84	9.75%	1.0900	1.0775	1.0400	7	8
3-1-84	4-1-84	9.50%	1.0875	1.0750	1.0400	7	8
4-1-84	5-1-84	9.75%	1.0900	1.0775	1.0400	7	8
5-1-84	7-1-84	10.00%	1.0925	1.0800	1.0400	7	8
7-1-84	8-1-84	10.50%	1.0975	1.0850	1.0400	7	8
8-1-84	9-1-84	10.75%	1.1000	1.0875	1.0400	7	8
9-1-84	11-1-84	10.50%	1.0975	1.0850	1.0400	7	8
11-1-84	12-1-84	10.25%	1.0950	1.0825	1.0400	7	8
12-1-84	1-1-85	10.00%	1.0925	1.0800	1.0400	7	8
1-1-85	3-1-85	9.75%	1.0900	1.0775	1.0400	7	8
3-1-85	4-1-85	9.50%	1.0875	1.0750	1.0400	7	8
4-1-85	5-1-85	9.75%	1.0900	1.0775	1.0400	7	8
5-1-85	6-1-85	10.00%	1.0925	1.0800	1.0400	7	8
6-1-85	7-1-85	9.75%	1.0900	1.0775	1.0400	7	8
7-1-85	10-1-85	9.25%	1.0850	1.0725	1.0400	7	8
10-1-85	1-1-86	9.00%	1.0825	1.0700	1.0400	7	8
1-1-86	2-1-86	8.75%	1.0800	1.0675	1.0400	7	8
2-1-86	4-1-86	8.50%	1.0775	1.0650	1.0400	7	8
4-1-86	5-1-86	8.00%	1.0725	1.0600	1.0400	7	8
5-1-86	10-1-86	7.75%	1.0700	1.0575	1.0400	7	8
10-1-86	11-1-86	7.50%	1.0675	1.0550	1.0400	7	8
11-1-86	12-1-86	7.75%	1.0700	1.0575	1.0400	7	8
12-1-86	3-1-87	7.50%	1.0675	1.0550	1.0400	7	8
3-1-87	6-1-87	7.25%	1.0650	1.0525	1.0400	7	8
6-1-87	7-1-87	7.50%	1.0675	1.0550	1.0400	7	8
7-1-87	10-1-87	7.75%	1.0700	1.0575	1.0400	7	8
10-1-87	11-1-87	8.00%	1.0725	1.0600	1.0400	7	8
11-1-87	3-1-88	8.25%	1.0750	1.0625	1.0400	7	8
3-1-88	4-1-88	8.00%	1.0725	1.0600	1.0400	7	8
4-1-88	6-1-88	7.75%	1.0700	1.0575	1.0400	7	8
6-1-88	9-1-88	8.00%	1.0725	1.0600	1.0400	7	8
9-1-88	11-1-88	8.25%	1.0750	1.0625	1.0400	7	8
11-1-88	4-1-89	7.75%	1.0700	1.0575	1.0400	7	8
4-1-89	6-1-89	8.00%	1.0725	1.0600	1.0400	7	8

For Plans with a Valuation Date		*Immediate Annuity*	*Deferred Annuities (Percent)*			*Years*	
On or After	*Before*	*Rate*	*i(1)*	*i(2)*	*i(3)*	*n(1)*	*n(2)*
6-1-89	8-1-89	7.75%	1.0700	1.0575	1.0400	7	8
8-1-89	9-1-89	7.50%	1.0075	1.0550	1.0400	7	8
9-1-89	10-1-89	7.25%	1.0650	1.0525	1.0400	7	8
10-1-89	12-1-89	7.50%	1.0675	1.0550	1.0400	7	8
12-1-89	3-1-90	7.25%	1.0650	1.0525	1.0400	7	8
3-1-90	6-1-90	7.50%	1.0675	1.0550	1.0400	7	8
6-1-90	7-1-90	7.75%	1.0700	1.0575	1.0400	7	8
7-1-90	9-1-90	7.50%	1.0675	1.0550	1.0400	7	8
9-1-90	10-1-90	7.25%	1.0650	1.0525	1.0400	7	8
10-1-90	11-1-90	7.50%	1.0675	1.5500	1.0400	7	8
11-1-90	12-1-90	7.75%	1.0700	1.0575	1.0400	7	8
12-1-90	1-1-91	7.50%	1.0675	1.0550	1.0400	7	8
1-1-91	3-1-91	7.25%	1.0650	1.0525	1.0400	7	8
3-1-91	6-1-91	7.00%	1.0625	1.0500	1.0400	7	8
6-1-91	7-1-91	6.75%	1.0600	1.0475	1.0400	7	8
7-1-91	10-1-91	7.00%	1.0625	1.0500	1.0400	7	8
10-1-91	1-1-92	6.75%	1.0600	1.4750	1.0400	7	8
1-1-92	2-1-92	6.50%	1.0575	1.0450	1.0400	7	8
2-1-92	3-1-92	6.25%	1.0550	1.0425	1.0400	7	8
3-1-92	7-1-92	6.50%	1.0575	1.0450	1.0400	7	8
7-1-92	8-1-92	6.25%	1.0550	1.0425	1.0400	7	8
8-1-92	9-1-92	6.00%	1.0525	1.0400	1.0400	7	8
9-1-92	12-1-92	5.75%	1.0500	1.0400	1.0400	7	8
12-1-92	1-1-93	6.00%	1.0525	1.0400	1.0400	7	8
1-1-93	2-1-93	5.75%	1.0500	1.0400	1.0400	7	8
2-1-93	3-1-93	5.50%	1.0475	1.0400	1.0400	7	8
3-1-93	4-1-93	5.25%	1.0450	1.0400	1.0400	7	8
4-1-93	8-1-93	5.00%	1.0425	1.0400	1.0400	7	8
8-1-93	10-1-93	4.75%	1.0400	1.0400	1.0400	7	8
10-1-93	11-1-93	4.25%	1.0400	1.0400	1.0400	7	8
11-1-93	12-1-93	4.25%	4.00	4.00	4.00	7	8
12-1-93	1-1-94	4.25%	4.00	4.00	4.00	7	8
1-1-94	2-1-94	4.50%	4.00	4.00	4.00	7	8
2-1-94	3-1-94	4.50%	4.00	4.00	4.00	7	8
3-1-94	4-1-94	4.50%	4.00	4.00	4.00	7	8

For Plans with a Valuation Date		*Immediate Annuity*	*Deferred Annuities (Percent)*			*Years*	
On or After	*Before*	*Rate*	*i(1)*	*i(2)*	*i(3)*	*n(1)*	*n(2)*
4-1-94	5-1-94	4.75%	4.00	4.00	4.00	7	8
5-1-94	6-1-94	5.25%	4.50	4.00	4.00	7	8
6-1-94	7-1-94	5.25%	4.50	4.00	4.00	7	8
7-1-94	8-1-94	5.50%	4.75	4.00	4.00	7	8
8-1-94	9-1-94	5.75%	5.00	4.00	4.00	7	8
9-1-94	10-1-94	5.50%	4.75	4.00	4.00	7	8
10-1-94	11-1-94	5.50%	4.75	4.00	4.00	7	8
11-1-94	12-1-94	6.00%	5.25	4.00	4.00	7	8
12-1-94	1-1-95	6.25%	5.50	4.25	4.00	7	8
1-1-95	2-1-95	6.00%	5.25	4.00	4.00	7	8
2-1-95	3-1-95	6.00%	5.25	4.00	4.00	7	8
3-1-95	4-1-95	6.00%	5.25	4.00	4.00	7	8
4-1-95	5-1-95	5.75%	5.00	4.00	4.00	7	8
5-1-95	6-1-95	5.50%	4.75	4.00	4.00	7	8
6-1-95	7-1-95	5.50%	4.75	4.00	4.00	7	8
7-1-95	8-1-95	4.75%	4.00	4.00	4.00	7	8
8-1-95	9-1-95	4.75%	4.00	4.00	4.00	7	8
9-1-95	10-1-95	5.00%	4.25	4.00	4.00	7	8
10-1-95	11-1-95	4.75%	4.00	4.00	4.00	7	8
11-1-95	12-1-95	4.75%	4.00	4.00	4.00	7	8
12-1-95	1-1-96	4.50%	4.00	4.00	4.00	7	8
1-1-96	2-1-96	4.50%	4.00	4.00	4.00	7	8
2-1-96	3-1-96	4.25%	4.00	4.00	4.00	7	8
3-1-96	4-1-96	4.25%	4.00	4.00	4.00	7	8
4-1-96	5-1-96	4.75%	4.00	4.00	4.00	7	8
5-1-96	6-1-96	5.00%	4.25	4.00	4.00	7	8
6-1-96	7-1-96	5.00%	4.25	4.00	4.00	7	8
7-1-96	8-1-96	5.00%	4.25	4.00	4.00	7	8
8-1-96	9-1-96	5.25%	4.50	4.00	4.00	7	8
9-1-96	10-1-96	5.25%	4.50	4.00	4.00	7	8
10-1-96	11-1-96	5.25%	4.50	4.00	4.00	7	8
11-1-96	12-1-96	5.00%	4.25	4.00	4.00	7	8
12-1-96	1-1-97	4.75%	4.00	4.00	4.00	7	8
1-1-97	2-1-97	4.50%	4.00	4.00	4.00	7	8
2-1-97	3-1-97	4.75%	4.00	4.00	4.00	7	8

For Plans with a Valuation Date		*Immediate Annuity*	*Deferred Annuities (Percent)*			*Years*	
On or After	*Before*	*Rate*	*i(1)*	*i(2)*	*i(3)*	*n(1)*	*n(2)*
3-1-97	4-1-97	5.00%	4.25	4.00	4.00	7	8
4-1-97	5-1-97	4.75%	4.00	4.00	4.00	7	8
5-1-97	6-1-97	5.00%	4.25	4.00	4.00	7	8
6-1-97	7-1-97	5.25%	4.50	4.00	4.00	7	8
7-1-97	8-1-97	5.25%	4.50	4.00	4.00	7	8
8-1-97	9-1-97	4.75%	4.00	4.00	4.00	7	8
9-1-97	10-1-97	4.50%	4.00	4.00	4.00	7	8
10-1-97	11-1-97	4.75%	4.00	4.00	4.00	7	8
11-1-97	12-1-97	4.50%	4.00	4.00	4.00	7	8
12-1-97	1-1-98	4.50%	4.00	4.00	4.00	7	8
1-1-98	2-1-98	4.25%	4.00	4.00	4.00	7	8
2-1-98	3-1-98	4.25%	4.00	4.00	4.00	7	8
3-1-98	4-1-98	4.25%	4.00	4.00	4.00	7	8
4-1-98	5-1-98	4.25%	4.00	4.00	4.00	7	8
5-1-98	6-1-98	4.25%	4.00	4.00	4.00	7	8
6-1-98	7-1-98	4.25%	4.00	4.00	4.00	7	8
7-1-98	8-1-98	4.00%	4.00	4.00	4.00	7	8
8-1-98	9-1-98	4.00%	4.00	4.00	4.00	7	8
9-1-98	10-1-98	4.00%	4.00	4.00	4.00	7	8
10-1-98	11-1-98	4.00%	4.00	4.00	4.00	7	8
11-1-98	12-1-98	3.75%	4.00	4.00	4.00	7	8
12-1-98	1-1-99	4.00%	4.00	4.00	4.00	7	8
1-1-99	2-1-99	4.00%	4.00	4.00	4.00	7	8
2-1-99	3-1-99	4.00%	4.00	4.00	4.00	7	8
3-1-99	4-1-99	4.00%	4.00	4.00	4.00	7	8
4-1-99	5-1-99	4.25%	4.00	4.00	4.00	7	8
5-1-99	6-1-99	4.25%	4.00	4.00	4.00	7	8
6-1-99	7-1-99	4.25%	4.00	4.00	4.00	7	8
7-1-99	8-1-99	4.50%	4.00	4.00	4.00	7	8
8-1-99	9-1-99	5.00%	4.25	4.00	4.00	7	8
9-1-99	10-1-99	5.00%	4.25	4.00	4.00	7	8
10-1-99	11-1-99	5.00%	4.25	4.00	4.00	7	8
11-1-99	12-1-99	5.00%	4.25	4.00	4.00	7	8
12-1-99	1-1-00	5.25%	4.50	4.00	4.00	7	8
1-1-00	2-1-00	5.00%	4.25	4.00	4.00	7	8

For Plans with a Valuation Date		*Immediate Annuity*	*Deferred Annuities (Percent)*			*Years*	
On or After	*Before*	*Rate*	*i(1)*	*i(2)*	*i(3)*	*n(1)*	*n(2)*
2-1-00	3-1-00	5.25%	4.50	4.00	4.00	7	8
3-1-00	4-1-00	5.25%	4.50	4.00	4.00	7	8
4-1-00	5-1-00	5.25%	4.50	4.00	4.00	7	8
5-1-00	6-1-00	5.25%	4.50	4.00	4.00	7	8
6-1-00	7-1-00	5.25%	4.50	4.00	4.00	7	8
7-1-00	8-1-00	5.50%	4.75	4.00	4.00	7	8
8-1-00	9-1-00	5.25%	4.50	4.00	4.00	7	8
9-1-00	10-1-00	5.00%	4.25	4.00	4.00	7	8
10-1-00	11-1-00	5.00%	4.25	4.00	4.00	7	8
11-1-00	12-1-00	5.25%	4.50	4.00	4.00	7	8
12-1-00	1-1-01	5.25%	4.50	4.00	4.00	7	8
1-1-01	2-1-01	5.00%	4.25	4.00	4.00	7	8
2-1-01	3-1-01	4.75%	4.00	4.00	4.00	7	8
3-1-01	4-1-01	4.75%	4.00	4.00	4.00	7	8
4-1-01	5-1-01	4.75%	4.00	4.00	4.00	7	8
5-1-01	6-1-01	4.75%	4.00	4.00	4.00	7	8
6-1-01	7-1-01	5.00%	4.25	4.00	4.00	7	8
7-1-01	8-1-01	5.00%	4.25	4.00	4.00	7	8
8-1-01	9-1-01	4.75%	4.00	4.00	4.00	7	8
9-1-01	10-1-01	4.50%	4.00	4.00	4.00	7	8
10-1-01	11-1-01	4.50%	4.00	4.00	4.00	7	8
11-1-01	12-1-01	4.75%	4.00	4.00	4.00	7	8
12-1-01	1-1-02	4.50%	4.00	4.00	4.00	7	8
1-1-02	2-1-02	4.50%	4.00	4.00	4.00	7	8
2-1-02	3-1-02	4.75%	4.00	4.00	4.00	7	8
3-1-02	4-1-02	4.50%	4.00	4.00	4.00	7	8
4-1-02	5-1-02	4.25%	4.00	4.00	4.00	7	8
5-1-02	6-1-02	4.75%	4.00	4.00	4.00	7	8
6-1-02	7-1-02	4.50%	4.00	4.00	4.00	7	8
7-1-02	8-1-02	4.50%	4.00	4.00	4.00	7	8
8-1-02	9-1-02	4.25%	4.00	4.00	4.00	7	8
9-1-02	10-1-02	4.25%	4.00	4.00	4.00	7	8
10-1-02	11-1-02	4.00%	4.00	4.00	4.00	7	8
11-1-02	12-1-02	3.75%	4.00	4.00	4.00	7	8
12-1-02	1-1-03	4.00%	4.00	4.00	4.00	7	8

For Plans with a Valuation Date		Immediate Annuity	Deferred Annuities (Percent)			Years	
On or After	Before	Rate	i(1)	i(2)	i(3)	n(1)	n(2)
1-1-03	2-1-03	4.00%	4.00	4.00	4.00	7	8
2-1-03	3-1-03	3.75%	4.00	4.00	4.00	7	8
3-1-03	4-1-03	3.75%	4.00	4.00	4.00	7	8
4-1-03	5-1-03	3.50%	4.00	4.00	4.00	7	8
5-1-03	6-1-03	3.50%	4.00	4.00	4.00	7	8
6-1-03	7-1-03	3.50%	4.00	4.00	4.00	7	8
7-1-03	8-1-03	3.00%	4.00	4.00	4.00	7	8
8-1-03	9-1-03	3.00%	4.00	4.00	4.00	7	8
9-1-03	10-1-03	3.50%	4.00	4.00	4.00	7	8
10-1-03	11-1-03	3.50%	4.00	4.00	4.00	7	8
11-1-03	12-1-03	3.25%	4.00	4.00	4.00	7	8
12-1-03	1-1-04	3.25%	4.00	4.00	4.00	7	8
1-1-04	2-1-04	3.25%	4.00	4.00	4.00	7	8
2-1-04	3-1-04	3.25%	4.00	4.00	4.00	7	8
3-1-04	4-1-04	3.00%	4.00	4.00	4.00	7	8
4-1-04	5-1-04	3.00%	4.00	4.00	4.00	7	8
5-1-04	6-1-04	3.00%	4.00	4.00	4.00	7	8
6-1-04	7-1-04	3.50%	4.00	4.00	4.00	7	8
7-1-04	8-1-04	3.50%	4.00	4.00	4.00	7	8
8-1-04	9-1-04	3.50%	4.00	4.00	4.00	7	8
9-1-04	10-1-04	3.25%	4.00	4.00	4.00	7	8
10-1-04	11-1-04	3.00%	4.00	4.00	4.00	7	8
11-1-04	12-1-04	2.75%	4.00	4.00	4.00	7	8
12-1-04	1-1-05	2.75%	4.00	4.00	4.00	7	8
1-1-05	2-1-05	3.00%	4.00	4.00	4.00	7	8
2-1-05	3-1-05	3.00%	4.00	4.00	4.00	7	8
3-1-05	4-1-05	2.75%	4.00	4.00	4.00	7	8
4-1-05	5-1-05	2.75%	4.00	4.00	4.00	7	8
5-1-05	6-1-05	2.75%	4.00	4.00	4.00	7	8
6-1-05	7-1-05	2.50%	4.00	4.00	4.00	7	8
7-1-05	8-1-05	2.50%	4.00	4.00	4.00	7	8
8-1-05	9-1-05	2.25%	4.00	4.00	4.00	7	8
9-1-05	10-1-05	2.50%	4.00	4.00	4.00	7	8
10-1-05	11-1-05	2.25%	4.00	4.00	4.00	7	8
11-1-05	12-1-05	2.50%	4.00	4.00	4.00	7	8

For Plans with a Valuation Date		Immediate Annuity	Deferred Annuities (Percent)			Years	
On or After	Before	Rate	i(1)	i(2)	i(3)	n(1)	n(2)
12-1-05	1-1-06	2.75%	4.00	4.00	4.00	7	8
1-1-06	2-1-06	2.75%	4.00	4.00	4.00	7	8
2-1-06	3-1-06	2.75%	4.00	4.00	4.00	7	8
3-1-06	4-1-06	2.75%	4.00	4.00	4.00	7	8
4-1-06	5-1-06	2.75%	4.00	4.00	4.00	7	8
5-1-06	6-1-06	3.00%	4.00	4.00	4.00	7	8
6-1-06	7-1-06	3.25%	4.00	4.00	4.00	7	8
7-1-06	8-1-06	3.50%	4.00	4.00	4.00	7	8
8-1-06	9-1-06	3.50%	4.00	4.00	4.00	7	8
9-1-06	10-1-06	3.25%	4.00	4.00	4.00	7	8
10-1-06	11-1-06	3.00%	4.00	4.00	4.00	7	8
11-1-06	12-1-06	2.75%	4.00	4.00	4.00	7	8
12-1-06	1-1-07	3.00%	4.00	4.00	4.00	7	8
1-1-07	2-1-07	2.75%	4.00	4.00	4.00	7	8
2-1-07	3-1-07	3.00%	4.00	4.00	4.00	7	8
3-1-07	4-1-07	3.00%	4.00	4.00	4.00	7	8
4-1-07	5-1-07	2.75%	4.00	4.00	4.00	7	8
5-1-07	6-1-07	3.00%	4.00	4.00	4.00	7	8
6-1-07	7-1-07	3.00%	4.00	4.00	4.00	7	8
7-1-07	8-1-07	3.25%	4.00	4.00	4.00	7	8
8-1-07	9-1-07	3.50%	4.00	4.00	4.00	7	8
9-1-07	10-1-07	3.25%	4.00	4.00	4.00	7	8
10-1-07	11-1-07	3.25%	4.00	4.00	4.00	7	8
11-1-07	12-1-07	3.25%	4.00	4.00	4.00	7	8
12-1-07	1-1-08	3.00%	4.00	4.00	4.00	7	8
1-1-08	2-1-08	3.00%	4.00	4.00	4.00	7	8
2-1-08	3-1-08	3.25%	4.00	4.00	4.00	7	8
3-1-08	4-1-08	3.00%	4.00	4.00	4.00	7	8
4-1-08	5-1-08	3.25%	4.00	4.00	4.00	7	8
5-1-08	6-1-08	3.25%	4.00	4.00	4.00	7	8
6-1-08	7-1-08	3.25%	4.00	4.00	4.00	7	8
7-1-08	8-1-08	3.50%	4.00	4.00	4.00	7	8
8-1-08	9-1-08	3.25%	4.00	4.00	4.00	7	8
9-1-08	10-1-08	3.50%	4.00	4.00	4.00	7	8
10-1-08	11-1-08	3.25%	4.00	4.00	4.00	7	8

For Plans with a Valuation Date		*Immediate Annuity*	*Deferred Annuities (Percent)*			*Years*	
On or After	*Before*	*Rate*	*i(1)*	*i(2)*	*i(3)*	*n(1)*	*n(2)*
11-1-08	12-1-08	3.75%	4.00	4.00	4.00	7	8
12-1-08	1-1-09	4.75%	4.00	4.00	4.00	7	8
1-1-09	2-1-09	4.00%	4.00	4.00	4.00	7	8
2-1-09	3-1-09	3.00%	4.00	4.00	4.00	7	8
3-1-09	4-1-09	3.50%	4.00	4.00	4.00	7	8
4-1-09	5-1-09	3.25%	4.00	4.00	4.00	7	8
5-1-09	6-1-09	3.50%	4.00	4.00	4.00	7	8
6-1-09	7-1-09	3.75%	4.00	4.00	4.00	7	8
7-1-09	8-1-09	3.75%	4.00	4.00	4.00	7	8
8-1-09	9-1-09	3.00%	4.00	4.00	4.00	7	8
9-1-09	10-1-09	3.00%	4.00	4.00	4.00	7	8
10-1-09	11-1-09	2.50%	4.00	4.00	4.00	7	8
11-1-09	12-1-09	2.25%	4.00	4.00	4.00	7	8
12-1-09	1-1-10	2.50%	4.00	4.00	4.00	7	8
1-1-10	2-1-10	2.50%	4.00	4.00	4.00	7	8
2-1-10	3-1-10	2.75%	4.00	4.00	4.00	7	8
3-1-10	4-1-10	2.75%	4.00	4.00	4.00	7	8
4-1-10	5-1-10	2.75%	4.00	4.00	4.00	7	8
5-1-10	6-1-10	3.00%	4.00	4.00	4.00	7	8
6-1-10	7-1-10	2.75%	4.00	4.00	4.00	7	8
7-1-10	8-1-10	2.50%	4.00	4.00	4.00	7	8
8-1-10	9-1-10	2.25%	4.00	4.00	4.00	7	8
9-1-10	10-1-10	2.25%	4.00	4.00	4.00	7	8
10-1-10	11-1-10	1.75%	4.00	4.00	4.00	7	8
11-1-10	12-1-10	1.75%	4.00	4.00	4.00	7	8
12-1-10	1-1-11	2.25%	4.00	4.00	4.00	7	8
1-1-11	2-1-11	2.25%	4.00	4.00	4.00	7	8
2-1-11	3-1-11	2.50%	4.00	4.00	4.00	7	8
3-1-11	4-1-11	2.50%	4.00	4.00	4.00	7	8
4-1-11	5-1-11	2.50%	4.00	4.00	4.00	7	8
5-1-11	6-1-11	2.50%	4.00	4.00	4.00	7	8
6-1-11	7-1-11	2.50%	4.00	4.00	4.00	7	8
7-1-11	8-1-11	2.25%	4.00	4.00	4.00	7	8
8-1-11	9-1-11	2.25%	4.00	4.00	4.00	7	8
9-1-11	10-1-11	2.25%	4.00	4.00	4.00	7	8

For Plans with a Valuation Date		Immediate Annuity	Deferred Annuities (Percent)			Years	
On or After	Before	Rate	i(1)	i(2)	i(3)	n(1)	n(2)
10-1-11	11-1-11	1.75%	4.00	4.00	4.00	7	8
11-1-11	12-1-11	1.50%	4.00	4.00	4.00	7	8
12-1-11	1-1-12	1.50%	4.00	4.00	4.00	7	8
1-1-12	2-1-12	1.25%	4.00	4.00	4.00	7	8
2-1-12	3-1-12	1.25%	4.00	4.00	4.00	7	8
3-1-12	4-1-12	1.25%	4.00	4.00	4.00	7	8
4-1-12	5-1-12	1.25%	4.00	4.00	4.00	7	8
5-1-12	6-1-12	1.50%	4.00	4.00	4.00	7	8
6-1-12	7-1-12	1.25%	4.00	4.00	4.00	7	8
7-1-12	8-1-12	1.00%	4.00	4.00	4.00	7	8
8-1-12	9-1-12	1.00%	4.00	4.00	4.00	7	8
9-1-12	10-1-12	0.75%	4.00	4.00	4.00	7	8
10-1-12	11-1-12	0.75%	4.00	4.00	4.00	7	8
11-1-12	12-1-12	0.75%	4.00	4.00	4.00	7	8
12-1-12	1-1-13	0.75%	4.00	4.00	4.00	7	8
1-1-13	2-1-13	0.75%	4.00	4.00	4.00	7	8
2-1-13	3-1-13	0.75%	4.00	4.00	4.00	7	8
3-1-13	4-1-13	1.00%	4.00	4.00	4.00	7	8
4-1-13	5-1-13	1.00%	4.00	4.00	4.00	7	8
5-1-13	6-1-13	1.00%	4.00	4.00	4.00	7	8
6-1-13	7-1-13	0.75%	4.00	4.00	4.00	7	8
7-1-13	8-1-13	1.25%	4.00	4.00	4.00	7	8
8-1-13	9-1-13	1.75%	4.00	4.00	4.00	7	8
9-1-13	10-1-13	1.50%	4.00	4.00	4.00	7	8
10-1-13	11-1-13	1.75%	4.00	4.00	4.00	7	8
11-1-13	12-1-13	1.75%	4.00	4.00	4.00	7	8
12-1-13	1-1-14	1.75%	4.00	4.00	4.00	7	8
1-1-14	2-1-14	1.75%	4.00	4.00	4.00	7	8
2-1-14	3-1-14	1.75%	4.00	4.00	4.00	7	8
3-1-14	4-1-14	1.50%	4.00	4.00	4.00	7	8
4-1-14	5-1-14	1.50%	4.00	4.00	4.00	7	8
5-1-14	6-1-14	1.50%	4.00	4.00	4.00	7	8
6-1-14	7-1-14	1.25%	4.00	4.00	4.00	7	8
7-1-14	8-1-14	1.25%	4.00	4.00	4.00	7	8
8-1-14	9-1-14	1.25%	4.00	4.00	4.00	7	8

For Plans with a Valuation Date		*Immediate Annuity*	*Deferred Annuities (Percent)*			*Years*	
On or After	*Before*	*Rate*	*i(1)*	*i(2)*	*i(3)*	*n(1)*	*n(2)*
9-1-14	10-1-14	1.25%	4.00	4.00	4.00	7	8
10-1-14	11-1-14	1.00%	4.00	4.00	4.00	7	8
11-1-14	12-1-14	1.25%	4.00	4.00	4.00	7	8
12-1-14	1-1-15	1.00%	4.00	4.00	4.00	7	8
1-1-15	2-1-15	1.00%	4.00	4.00	4.00	7	8
2-1-15	3-1-15	1.00%	4.00	4.00	4.00	7	8
3-1-15	4-1-15	0.50%	4.00	4.00	4.00	7	8
4-1-15	5-1-15	0.75%	4.00	4.00	4.00	7	8
5-1-15	6-1-15	0.75%	4.00	4.00	4.00	7	8
6-1-15	7-1-15	0.75%	4.00	4.00	4.00	7	8
7-1-15	8-1-15	1.25%	4.00	4.00	4.00	7	8
8-1-15	9-1-15	1.50%	4.00	4.00	4.00	7	8
9-1-15	10-1-15	1.25%	4.00	4.00	4.00	7	8
10-1-15	11-1-15	1.25%	4.00	4.00	4.00	7	8
11-1-15	12-1-15	1.25%	4.00	4.00	4.00	7	8
12-1-15	1-1-16	1.25%	4.00	4.00	4.00	7	8
1-1-16	2-1-16	1.25%	4.00	4.00	4.00	7	8
2-1-16	3-1-16	1.25%	4.00	4.00	4.00	7	8
3-1-16	4-1-16	1.25%	4.00	4.00	4.00	7	8
4-1-16	5-1-16	1.00%	4.00	4.00	4.00	7	8
5-1-16	6-1-16	1.00%	4.00	4.00	4.00	7	8
6-1-16	7-1-16	0.75%	4.00	4.00	4.00	7	8
7-1-16	8-1-16	0.75%	4.00	4.00	4.00	7	8
8-1-16	9-1-16	0.50%	4.00	4.00	4.00	7	8
9-1-16	10-1-16	0.50%	4.00	4.00	4.00	7	8
10-1-16	11-1-16	0.50%	4.00	4.00	4.00	7	8
11-1-16	12-1-16	0.50%	4.00	4.00	4.00	7	8
12-1-16	1-1-17	0.75%	4.00	4.00	4.00	7	8
1-1-17	2-1-17	1.25%	4.00	4.00	4.00	7	8
2-1-17	3-1-17	1.00%	4.00	4.00	4.00	7	8
3-1-17	4-1-17	1.00%	4.00	4.00	4.00	7	8
4-1-17	5-1-17	1.00%	4.00	4.00	4.00	7	8
5-1-17	6-1-17	1.00%	4.00	4.00	4.00	7	8
6-1-17	7-1-17	1.00%	4.00	4.00	4.00	7	8
7-1-17	8-1-17	1.00%	4.00	4.00	4.00	7	8

Appendix C

30-Year Treasury Securities Rates

Historical RPA (GATT) interest rates may be found on the Internet at:

www.irs.gov/retirement-plans/interest-rates-tables

Month/Year	*Interest Rate Percentage*	*Month/Year*	*Interest Rate Percentage*
July 1994	7.58%	May 1996	6.93%
August 1994	7.49%	June 1996	7.06%
September 1994	7.71%	July 1996	7.03%
October 1994	7.94%	August 1996	6.84%
November 1994	8.08%	September 1996	7.03%
December 1994	7.87%	October 1996	6.81%
January 1995	7.85%	November 1996	6.48%
February 1995	7.61%	December 1996	6.55%
March 1995	7.45%	January 1997	6.83%
April 1995	7.36%	February 1997	6.69%
May 1995	6.95%	March 1997	6.93%
June 1995	6.57%	April 1997	7.09%
July 1995	6.72%	May 1997	6.94%
August 1995	6.86%	June 1997	6.77%
September 1995	6.55%	July 1997	6.51%
October 1995	6.37%	August 1997	6.58%
November 1995	6.26%	September 1997	6.50%
December 1995	6.06%	October 1997	6.33%
January 1996	6.05%	November 1997	6.11%
February 1996	6.24%	December 1997	5.99%
March 1996	6.60%	January 1998	5.81%
April 1996	6.79%	February 1998	5.89%

Month/Year	*Interest Rate Percentage*	*Month/Year*	*Interest Rate Percentage*
March 1998	5.95%	March 2001	5.34%
April 1998	5.92%	April 2001	5.65%
May 1998	5.93%	May 2001	5.78%
June 1998	5.70%	June 2001	5.67%
July 1998	5.68%	July 2001	5.61%
August 1998	5.54%	August 2001	5.48%
September 1998	5.20%	September 2001	5.48%
October 1998	5.01%	October 2001	5.32%
November 1998	5.25%	November 2001	5.12%
December 1998	5.06%	December 2001	5.48%
January 1999	5.16%	January 2002	5.45%
February 1999	5.37%	February 2002	5.40%
March 1999	5.58%	March 2002	5.71%
April 1999	5.55%	April 2002	5.68%
May 1999	5.81%	May 2002	5.65%
June 1999	6.04%	June 2002	5.52%
July 1999	5.98%	July 2002	5.39%
August 1999	6.07%	August 2002	5.08%
September 1999	6.07%	September 2002	4.76%
October 1999	6.26%	October 2002	4.93%
November 1999	6.15%	November 2002	4.96%
December 1999	6.35%	December 2002	4.92%
January 2000	6.63%	January 2003	4.94%
February 2000	6.23%	February 2003	4.81%
March 2000	6.05%	March 2003	4.80%
April 2000	5.85%	April 2003	4.90%
May 2000	6.15%	May 2003	4.53%
June 2000	5.93%	June 2003	4.37%
July 2000	5.85%	July 2003	4.93%
August 2000	5.72%	August 2003	5.31%
September 2000	5.83%	September 2003	5.14%
October 2000	5.80%	October 2003	5.16%
November 2000	5.78%	November 2003	5.12%
December 2000	5.49%	December 2003	5.07%
January 2001	5.54%	January 2004	4.98%
February 2001	5.45%	February 2004	4.93%

Month/Year	*Interest Rate Percentage*	*Month/Year*	*Interest Rate Percentage*
March 2004	4.74%	March 2007	4.72%
April 2004	5.14%	April 2007	4.87%
May 2004	5.42%	May 2007	4.90%
June 2004	5.41%	June 2007	5.20%
July 2004	5.22%	July 2007	5.20%
August 2004	5.06%	August 2007	5.11%
September 2004	4.90%	September 2007	4.93%
October 2004	4.86%	June 2007	4.79%
November 2004	4.89%	October 2007	4.77%
December 2004	4.86%	November 2007	4.52%
January 2005	4.73%	December 2007	4.53%
February 2005	4.55%	January 2008	4.33%
March 2005	4.78%	February 2008	4.52%
April 2005	4.65%	March 2008	4.39%
May 2005	4.49%	April 2008	4.44%
June 2005	4.29%	May 2008	4.60%
July 2005	4.41%	June 2008	4.69%
August 2005	4.46%	July 2008	4.57%
September 2005	4.47%	August 2008	4.50%
October 2005	4.68%	September 2008	4.27%
November 2005	4.73%	October 2008	4.17%
December 2005	4.65%	November 2008	4.00%
January 2006	4.59%	December 2008	2.87%
February 2006	4.58%	January 2009	3.13%
March 2006	4.73%	February 2009	3.59%
April 2006	5.06%	March 2009	3.64%
May 2006	5.20%	April 2009	3.76%
June 2006	5.16%	May 2009	4.23%
July 2006	5.13%	June 2009	4.52%
August 2006	5.00%	July 2009	4.41%
September 2006	4.85%	August 2009	4.37%
October 2006	4.85%	September 2009	4.19%
November 2006	4.69%	October 2009	4.19%
December 2006	4.68%	November 2009	4.31%
January 2007	4.85%	December 2009	4.49%
February 2007	4.82%	January 2010	4.60%

Month/Year	*Interest Rate Percentage*	*Month/Year*	*Interest Rate Percentage*
February 2010	4.62%	February 2013	3.17%
March 2010	4.65%	March 2013	3.16%
April 2010	4.69%	April 2013	2.93%
May 2010	4.29%	May 2013	3.11%
June 2010	4.13%	June 2013	3.40%
July 2010	3.99%	July 2013	3.61%
August 2010	3.80%	August 2013	3.76%
September 2010	3.77%	September 2013	3.79%
October 2010	3.87%	October 2013	3.68%
November 2010	4.19%	November 2013	3.80%
December 2010	4.42%	December 2013	3.89%
January 2011	4.52%	January 2014	3.77%
February 2011	4.65%	February 2014	3.66%
March 2011	4.51%	March 2014	3.62%
April 2011	4.50%	April 2014	3.52%
May 2011	4.29%	May 2014	3.39%
June 2011	4.23%	June 2014	3.42%
July 2011	4.27%	July 2014	3.33%
August 2011	3.65%	August 2014	3.20%
September 2011	3.18%	September 2014	3.26%
October 2011	3.13%	October 2014	3.04%
November 2011	3.02%	November 2014	3.04%
December 2011	2.98%	December 2014	2.83%
January 2012	3.03%	January 2015	2.46%
February 2012	3.11%	February 2015	2.57%
March 2012	3.28%	March 2015	2.63%
April 2012	3.18%	April 2015	2.59%
May 2012	2.93%	May 2015	2.96%
June 2012	2.70%	June 2015	3.11%
July 2012	2.59%	July 2015	3.07%
August 2012	2.77%	August 2015	2.86%
September 2012	2.88%	September 2015	2.95%
October 2012	2.90%	October 2015	2.89%
November 2012	2.80%	November 2015	3.03%
December 2012	2.88%	December 2015	2.97%
January 2013	3.08%	January 2016	2.86%

Month/Year	*Interest Rate Percentage*	*Month/Year*	*Interest Rate Percentage*
February 2016	2.62%	November 2016	2.86%
March 2016	2.68%	December 2016	3.11%
April 2016	2.62%	January 2017	3.02%
May 2016	2.63%	February 2017	3.03%
June 2016	2.45%	March 2017	3.08%
July 2016	2.23%	April 2017	2.94%
August 2016	2.26%	May 2017	2.96%
September 2016	2.35%	June 2017	2.80%
October 2016	2.50%	July 2017	2.88%

Appendix D

Single Life Table

The final regulations under Code Section 401(a)(9) contain a Single Life Table as shown below [Treas. Reg. § 1.401(a)(9)-9, Q&A-1]:

Age	*Multiple*	*Age*	*Multiple*	*Age*	*Multiple*
0	82.4	23	60.1	46	37.9
1	81.6	24	59.1	47	37.0
2	80.6	25	58.2	48	36.0
3	79.7	26	57.2	49	35.1
4	78.7	27	56.2	50	34.2
5	77.7	28	55.3	51	33.3
6	76.7	29	54.3	52	32.3
7	75.8	30	53.3	53	31.4
8	74.8	31	52.4	54	30.5
9	73.8	32	51.4	55	29.6
10	72.8	33	50.4	56	28.7
11	71.8	34	49.4	57	27.9
12	70.8	35	48.5	58	27.0
13	69.9	36	47.5	59	26.1
14	68.9	37	46.5	60	25.2
15	67.9	38	45.6	61	24.4
16	66.9	39	44.6	62	23.5
17	66.0	40	43.6	63	22.7
18	65.0	41	42.7	64	21.8
19	64.0	42	41.7	65	21.0
20	63.0	43	40.7	66	20.2
21	62.1	44	39.8	67	19.4
22	61.1	45	38.8	68	18.6

Age	*Multiple*	*Age*	*Multiple*	*Age*	*Multiple*
69	17.8	84	8.1	99	3.1
70	17.0	85	7.6	100	2.9
71	16.3	86	7.1	101	2.7
72	15.5	87	6.7	102	2.5
73	14.8	88	6.3	103	2.3
74	14.1	89	5.9	104	2.1
75	13.4	90	5.5	105	1.9
76	12.7	91	5.2	106	1.7
77	12.1	92	4.9	107	1.5
78	11.4	93	4.6	108	1.4
79	10.8	94	4.3	109	1.2
80	10.2	95	4.1	110	1.1
81	9.7	96	3.8	111 +	1.0
82	9.1	97	3.6		
83	8.6	98	3.4		

Table for determining distribution period. The following table, referred to as the Uniform Lifetime Table, is used for determining the distribution period for lifetime distributions to an employee in situations in which the employee's spouse is either not the sole designated beneficiary or is the sole designated beneficiary but is not more than ten years younger than the employee. [Treas. Reg. § 1.401(a)(9)-9, Q&A-2]

Age of Employee	*Distribution Period*	*Age of Employee*	*Distribution Period*
70	27.4	84	15.5
71	26.5	85	14.8
72	25.6	86	14.1
73	24.7	87	13.4
74	23.8	88	12.7
75	22.9	89	12.0
76	22.0	90	11.4
77	21.2	91	10.8
78	20.3	92	10.2
79	19.5	93	9.6
80	18.7	94	9.1
81	17.9	95	8.6
82	17.1	96	8.1
83	16.3	97	7.6

Age of Employee	*Distribution Period*	*Age of Employee*	*Distribution Period*
98	7.1	107	3.9
99	6.7	108	3.7
100	6.3	109	3.4
101	5.9	110	3.1
102	5.5	111	2.9
103	5.2	112	2.6
104	4.9	113	2.4
105	4.5	114	2.1
106	4.2	115+	1.9

Appendix E

Joint Life and Last Survivor Table

The final regulations under Code Section 401(a)(9) contain a Joint and Last Survivor Table as shown below. [Treas. Reg. § 1.401(a)(9)-9, Q&A-3]

Ages	*0*	*1*	*2*	*3*	*4*	*5*	*6*	*7*	*8*	*9*
0	90.0	89.5	89.0	88.6	88.2	87.8	87.4	87.1	86.8	86.5
1	89.5	89.0	88.5	88.1	87.6	87.2	86.8	86.5	86.1	85.8
2	89.0	88.5	88.0	87.5	87.1	86.6	86.2	85.8	85.5	85.1
3	88.6	88.1	87.5	87.0	86.5	86.1	85.6	85.2	84.8	84.5
4	88.2	87.6	87.1	86.5	86.0	85.5	85.1	84.6	84.2	83.8
5	87.8	87.2	86.6	86.1	85.5	85.0	84.5	84.1	83.6	83.2
6	87.4	86.8	86.2	85.6	85.1	84.5	84.0	83.5	83.1	82.6
7	87.1	86.5	85.8	85.2	84.6	84.1	83.5	83.0	82.5	82.1
8	86.8	86.1	85.5	84.8	84.2	83.6	83.1	82.5	82.0	81.6
9	86.5	85.8	85.1	84.5	83.8	83.2	82.6	82.1	81.6	81.0
10	86.2	85.5	84.8	84.0	83.5	82.8	82.2	81.6	81.1	80.6
11	85.9	85.2	84.5	83.8	83.1	82.5	81.8	81.2	80.7	80.1
12	85.7	84.9	84.2	83.5	82.8	82.1	81.5	80.8	80.2	79.7
13	85.4	84.7	84.0	83.2	82.5	81.8	81.1	80.5	79.9	79.2
14	85.2	84.5	83.7	83.0	82.2	81.5	80.8	80.1	79.5	78.9
15	85.0	84.3	83.5	82.7	82.0	81.2	80.5	79.8	79.1	78.5
16	84.9	84.1	83.3	82.5	81.7	81.0	80.2	79.5	78.8	78.1
17	84.7	83.9	83.1	82.3	81.5	80.7	80.0	79.2	78.5	77.8
18	84.5	83.7	82.9	82.1	81.3	80.5	79.7	79.0	78.2	77.5
19	84.4	83.6	82.7	81.9	81.1	80.3	79.5	78.7	78.0	77.3
20	84.3	83.4	82.6	81.8	80.9	80.1	79.3	78.5	77.7	77.0
21	84.1	83.3	82.4	81.6	80.8	79.9	79.1	78.3	77.5	76.8
22	84.0	83.2	82.3	81.5	80.6	79.8	78.9	78.1	77.3	76.5

Ages	*0*	*1*	*2*	*3*	*4*	*5*	*6*	*7*	*8*	*9*
23	83.9	83.1	82.2	81.3	80.5	79.6	78.8	77.9	77.1	76.3
24	83.8	83.0	82.1	81.2	80.3	79.5	78.6	77.8	76.9	76.1
25	83.7	82.9	82.0	81.1	80.2	79.3	78.5	77.6	76.8	75.9
26	83.6	82.8	81.9	81.0	80.1	79.2	78.3	77.5	76.6	75.8
27	83.6	82.7	81.8	80.9	80.0	79.1	78.2	77.4	76.5	75.6
28	83.5	82.6	81.7	80.8	79.9	79.0	78.1	77.2	76.4	75.5
29	83.4	82.6	81.6	80.7	79.8	78.9	78.0	77.1	76.2	75.4
30	83.4	82.5	81.6	80.7	79.7	78.8	77.9	77.0	76.1	75.2
31	83.3	82.4	81.5	80.6	79.7	78.8	77.8	76.9	76.0	75.1
32	83.3	82.4	81.5	80.5	79.6	78.7	77.8	76.8	75.9	75.0
33	83.2	82.3	81.4	80.5	79.5	78.6	77.7	76.8	75.9	74.9
34	83.2	82.3	81.3	80.4	79.5	78.5	77.6	76.7	75.8	74.9
35	83.1	82.2	81.3	80.4	79.4	78.5	77.6	76.6	75.7	74.8
36	83.1	82.2	81.3	80.3	79.4	78.4	77.5	76.6	75.6	74.7
37	83.0	82.2	81.2	80.3	79.3	78.4	77.4	76.5	75.6	74.6
38	83.0	82.1	81.2	80.2	79.3	78.3	77.4	76.4	75.5	74.6
39	83.0	82.1	81.1	80.2	79.2	78.3	77.3	76.4	75.5	74.5
40	82.9	82.1	81.1	80.2	79.2	78.3	77.3	76.4	75.4	74.5
41	82.9	82.0	81.1	80.1	79.2	78.2	77.3	76.3	75.4	74.4
42	82.9	82.0	81.1	80.1	79.1	78.2	77.2	76.3	75.3	74.4
43	82.9	82.0	81.0	80.1	79.1	78.2	77.2	76.2	75.3	74.3
44	82.8	82.9	81.0	80.0	79.1	78.1	77.2	76.2	75.2	74.3
45	82.8	81.9	81.0	80.0	79.1	78.1	77.1	76.2	75.2	74.3
46	82.8	81.9	81.0	80.0	79.0	78.1	77.1	76.1	75.2	74.2
47	82.8	81.9	80.9	80.0	79.0	78.0	77.1	76.1	75.2	74.2
48	82.8	81.9	80.9	80.0	79.0	78.0	77.1	76.1	75.1	74.2
49	82.7	81.8	80.9	79.9	79.0	78.0	77.0	76.1	75.1	74.1
50	82.7	81.8	80.9	79.9	79.0	78.0	77.0	76.0	75.1	74.1
51	82.7	81.8	80.9	79.9	78.9	78.0	77.0	76.0	75.1	74.1
52	82.7	81.8	80.9	79.9	78.9	78.0	77.0	76.0	75.0	74.1
53	82.7	81.8	80.8	79.9	78.9	77.9	77.0	76.0	75.0	74.0
54	82.7	81.8	80.8	79.9	78.9	77.9	76.9	76.0	75.0	74.0
55	82.6	81.8	80.8	79.8	78.9	77.9	76.9	76.0	75.0	74.0
56	82.6	81.7	80.8	79.8	78.9	77.9	76.9	75.9	75.0	74.0
57	82.6	81.7	80.8	79.8	78.9	77.9	76.9	75.9	75.0	74.0
58	82.6	81.7	80.8	79.8	78.8	77.9	76.9	75.9	74.9	74.0
59	82.6	81.7	80.8	79.8	78.8	77.9	76.9	75.9	74.9	74.0

Ages	*0*	*1*	*2*	*3*	*4*	*5*	*6*	*7*	*8*	*9*
60	82.6	81.7	80.8	79.8	78.8	77.8	76.9	75.9	74.9	73.9
61	82.6	81.7	80.8	79.8	78.8	77.8	76.9	75.9	74.9	73.9
62	82.6	81.7	80.7	79.8	78.8	77.8	76.9	75.9	74.9	73.9
63	82.6	81.7	80.7	79.8	78.8	77.8	76.8	75.9	74.9	73.9
64	82.5	81.7	80.7	79.8	78.8	77.8	76.8	75.9	74.9	73.9
65	82.5	81.7	80.7	79.8	78.8	77.8	76.8	75.8	74.9	73.9
66	82.5	81.7	80.7	79.7	78.8	77.8	76.8	75.8	74.9	73.9
67	82.5	81.7	80.7	79.7	78.8	77.8	76.8	75.8	74.9	73.9
68	82.5	81.6	80.7	79.7	78.8	77.8	76.8	75.8	74.8	73.9
69	82.5	81.6	80.7	79.7	78.8	77.8	76.8	75.8	74.8	73.9
70	82.5	81.6	80.7	79.7	78.8	77.8	76.8	75.8	74.8	73.9
71	82.5	81.6	80.7	79.7	78.7	77.8	76.8	75.8	74.8	73.8
72	82.5	81.6	80.7	79.7	78.7	77.8	76.8	75.8	74.8	73.8
73	82.5	81.6	80.7	79.7	78.7	77.8	76.8	75.8	74.8	73.8
74	85.2	81.6	80.7	79.7	78.7	77.8	76.8	75.8	74.8	73.8
75	82.5	81.6	80.7	79.7	78.7	77.8	76.8	75.8	74.8	73.8
76	82.5	81.6	80.7	79.7	78.7	77.7	76.8	75.8	74.8	73.8
78	82.5	81.6	80.7	79.7	78.7	77.7	76.8	75.8	74.8	73.8
79	82.5	81.6	80.7	79.7	78.7	77.7	76.8	75.8	74.8	73.8
80	82.4	81.6	80.7	79.7	78.7	77.7	76.8	75.8	74.8	73.8
81	82.4	81.6	80.7	79.7	78.7	77.7	76.8	75.8	74.8	73.8
82	82.4	81.6	80.7	79.7	78.7	77.7	76.8	75.8	74.8	73.8
83	82.4	81.6	80.7	79.7	78.7	77.7	76.8	75.8	74.8	73.8
84	82.4	81.6	80.6	79.7	78.7	77.7	76.8	75.8	74.8	73.8
85	82.4	81.6	80.6	79.7	78.7	77.7	76.8	75.8	74.8	73.8
86	82.4	81.6	80.6	79.7	78.7	77.7	76.7	75.8	74.8	73.8
87	82.4	81.6	80.6	79.7	78.7	77.7	76.7	75.8	74.8	73.8
88	82.4	81.6	80.6	79.7	78.7	77.7	76.7	75.8	74.8	73.8
89	82.4	81.6	80.6	79.7	78.7	77.7	76.7	75.8	74.8	73.8
90	82.4	81.6	80.6	79.7	78.7	77.7	76.7	75.8	74.8	73.8
91	82.4	81.6	80.6	79.7	78.7	77.7	76.7	75.8	74.8	73.8
92	82.4	81.6	80.6	79.7	78.7	77.7	76.7	75.8	74.8	73.8
93	82.4	81.6	80.6	79.7	78.7	77.7	76.7	75.8	74.8	73.8
94	82.4	81.6	80.6	79.7	78.7	77.7	76.7	75.8	74.8	73.8
95	82.4	81.6	80.6	79.7	78.7	77.7	76.7	75.8	74.8	73.8
96	82.4	81.6	80.6	79.7	78.7	77.7	76.7	75.8	74.8	73.8
97	82.4	81.6	80.6	79.7	78.7	77.7	76.7	75.8	74.8	73.8

Ages	0	1	2	3	4	5	6	7	8	9
98	82.4	81.6	80.6	79.7	78.7	77.7	76.7	75.8	74.8	73.8
99	82.4	81.6	80.6	79.7	78.7	77.7	76.7	75.8	74.8	73.8
100	82.4	81.6	80.6	79.7	78.7	77.7	76.7	75.8	74.8	73.8
101	82.4	81.6	80.6	79.7	78.7	77.7	76.7	75.8	74.8	73.8
102	82.4	81.6	80.6	79.7	78.7	77.7	76.7	75.8	74.8	73.8
103	82.4	81.6	80.6	79.7	78.7	77.7	76.7	75.8	74.8	73.8
104	82.4	81.6	80.6	79.7	78.7	77.7	76.7	75.8	74.8	73.8
105	82.4	81.6	80.6	79.7	78.7	77.7	76.7	75.8	74.8	73.8
106	82.4	81.6	80.6	79.7	78.7	77.7	76.7	75.8	74.8	73.8
107	82.4	81.6	80.6	79.7	78.7	77.7	76.7	75.8	74.8	73.8
108	82.4	81.6	80.6	79.7	78.7	77.7	76.7	75.8	74.8	73.8
109	82.4	81.6	80.6	79.7	78.7	77.7	76.7	75.8	74.8	73.8
110	82.4	81.6	80.6	79.7	78.7	77.7	76.7	75.8	74.8	73.8
111	82.4	81.6	80.6	79.7	78.7	77.7	76.7	75.8	74.8	73.8
112	82.4	81.6	80.6	79.7	78.7	77.7	76.7	75.8	74.8	73.8
113	82.4	81.6	80.6	79.7	78.7	77.7	76.7	75.8	74.8	73.8
114	82.4	81.6	80.6	79.7	78.7	77.7	76.7	75.8	74.8	73.8
115+	82.4	81.6	80.6	79.7	78.7	77.7	76.7	75.8	74.8	73.8

Ages	10	11	12	13	14	15	16	17	18	19
10	80.0	79.6	79.1	78.7	78.2	77.9	77.5	77.2	76.8	76.5
11	79.6	79.0	78.6	78.1	77.7	77.3	76.9	76.5	76.2	75.8
12	79.1	78.6	78.1	77.6	77.1	76.7	76.3	75.9	75.5	75.2
13	78.7	78.1	77.6	77.1	76.6	76.1	75.7	75.3	74.9	74.5
14	78.2	77.7	77.1	76.6	76.1	75.6	75.1	74.7	74.3	73.9
15	77.9	77.3	76.7	76.1	75.6	75.1	74.6	74.1	73.7	73.3
16	77.5	76.9	76.3	75.7	75.1	74.6	74.1	73.6	73.1	72.7
17	77.2	76.5	75.9	75.3	74.7	74.1	73.6	73.1	72.6	72.1
18	76.8	76.2	75.5	74.9	74.3	73.7	73.1	72.6	72.1	71.6
19	76.5	75.8	75.2	74.5	73.9	73.3	72.7	72.1	71.6	71.1
20	76.3	75.5	74.8	74.2	73.5	72.9	72.3	71.7	71.1	70.6
21	76.0	75.3	74.5	73.8	73.2	72.5	71.9	71.3	70.7	70.1
22	75.8	75.0	74.3	73.5	72.9	72.2	71.5	70.9	70.3	69.7
23	75.5	74.8	74.0	73.3	72.6	71.9	71.2	70.5	69.9	69.3
24	75.3	74.5	73.8	73.0	72.3	71.6	70.9	70.2	69.5	68.9
25	75.1	74.3	73.5	72.8	72.0	71.3	70.6	69.9	69.2	68.5
26	75.0	74.1	73.3	72.5	71.8	71.0	70.3	69.6	68.9	68.2

Ages	*10*	*11*	*12*	*13*	*14*	*15*	*16*	*17*	*18*	*19*
27	74.8	74.0	73.1	72.3	71.6	70.8	70.0	69.3	68.6	67.9
28	74.6	73.8	73.0	72.2	71.3	70.6	69.8	69.0	68.3	67.6
29	74.5	73.6	72.8	72.0	71.2	70.4	69.6	68.8	68.0	67.3
30	74.4	73.5	72.7	71.8	71.0	70.2	69.4	68.6	67.8	67.1
31	74.3	73.4	72.5	71.7	70.8	70.0	69.2	68.4	67.6	66.8
32	74.1	73.3	72.4	71.5	70.7	69.8	69.0	68.2	67.4	66.6
33	74.0	73.2	72.3	71.4	70.5	69.7	68.8	68.0	67.2	66.4
34	73.9	73.0	72.2	71.3	70.4	69.5	68.7	67.8	67.0	66.2
35	73.9	73.0	72.1	71.2	70.3	69.4	68.5	67.7	66.8	66.0
36	73.8	72.9	72.0	71.1	70.2	69.3	68.4	67.6	66.7	65.9
37	73.7	72.8	71.9	71.0	70.1	69.2	68.3	67.4	66.6	65.7
38	73.6	72.7	71.8	70.9	70.0	69.1	68.2	67.3	66.4	65.6
39	73.6	72.7	71.7	70.8	69.9	69.0	68.1	67.2	66.3	65.4
40	73.5	72.6	71.7	70.7	69.8	68.9	68.0	67.1	66.2	65.3
41	73.5	72.5	71.6	70.7	69.7	68.8	67.9	67.0	66.1	65.2
42	73.4	72.5	71.5	70.6	69.7	68.8	67.8	66.9	66.0	65.1
43	43.4	72.4	71.5	70.6	69.6	68.7	67.8	66.8	65.9	65.0
44	73.3	72.4	71.4	70.5	69.6	68.6	67.7	66.8	65.9	64.9
45	73.3	72.3	71.4	70.5	69.5	68.6	67.6	66.7	65.8	64.9
46	73.3	72.3	71.4	70.4	69.5	68.5	67.6	66.6	65.7	64.8
47	73.2	72.3	71.3	70.4	69.4	68.5	67.5	66.6	65.7	64.7
48	73.2	72.2	71.3	70.3	69.4	68.4	67.5	66.5	65.6	64.7
49	73.2	72.2	71.2	70.3	69.3	68.4	67.4	66.5	65.6	64.6
50	73.1	72.2	71.2	70.3	69.3	68.4	67.4	66.5	65.5	64.6
51	73.1	72.2	71.2	70.2	69.3	68.3	67.4	66.4	65.5	64.5
52	73.1	72.1	71.2	70.2	69.2	68.3	67.3	66.4	65.4	64.5
53	73.1	72.1	71.1	70.2	69.2	68.3	67.3	66.3	65.4	64.4
54	73.1	72.1	71.1	70.2	69.2	68.2	67.3	66.3	65.4	64.4
55	73.0	72.1	71.1	70.1	69.2	68.2	67.2	66.3	65.3	64.4
56	73.0	72.1	71.1	70.1	69.1	68.2	67.2	66.3	65.3	64.3
57	73.0	72.0	71.1	70.1	69.1	68.2	67.2	66.2	65.3	64.3
58	73.0	72.0	71.0	70.1	69.1	68.1	67.2	66.2	65.2	64.3
59	73.0	72.0	71.0	70.1	69.1	68.1	67.2	66.2	65.2	64.3
60	73.0	72.0	71.0	70.0	69.1	68.1	67.1	66.2	65.2	64.2
61	73.0	72.0	71.0	70.0	69.1	68.1	67.1	66.2	65.2	64.2
62	72.9	72.0	71.0	70.0	69.0	68.1	67.1	66.1	65.2	64.2
63	72.9	72.0	71.0	70.0	69.0	68.1	67.1	66.1	65.2	64.2

Ages	10	11	12	13	14	15	16	17	18	19
64	72.9	71.9	71.0	70.0	69.0	68.0	67.1	66.1	65.1	64.2
65	72.9	71.9	71.0	70.0	69.0	68.0	67.1	66.1	65.1	64.2
66	72.9	71.9	70.9	70.0	69.0	68.0	67.1	66.1	65.1	64.1
67	72.9	71.9	70.9	70.0	69.0	68.0	67.0	66.1	65.1	64.1
68	72.9	71.9	70.9	70.0	69.0	68.0	67.0	66.1	65.1	64.1
69	72.9	71.9	70.9	69.9	69.0	68.0	67.0	66.1	65.1	64.1
70	72.9	71.9	70.9	69.9	69.0	68.0	67.0	66.0	65.1	64.1
71	72.9	71.9	70.9	69.9	69.0	68.0	67.0	66.0	65.1	64.1
72	72.9	71.9	70.9	69.9	69.0	68.0	67.0	66.0	65.1	64.1
73	72.9	71.9	70.9	69.9	68.9	68.0	67.0	66.0	65.0	64.1
74	72.9	71.9	70.9	69.9	68.9	68.0	67.0	66.0	65.0	64.1
75	72.8	71.9	70.9	69.9	68.9	68.0	67.0	66.0	65.0	64.1
76	72.8	71.9	70.9	69.9	68.9	68.0	67.0	66.0	65.0	64.1
78	72.8	71.9	70.9	69.9	68.9	67.9	67.0	66.0	65.0	64.0
79	72.8	71.9	70.9	69.9	68.9	67.9	67.0	66.0	65.0	64.0
80	72.8	71.9	70.9	69.9	68.9	67.9	67.0	66.0	65.0	64.0
81	72.8	71.9	70.9	69.9	68.9	67.9	67.0	66.0	65.0	64.0
82	72.8	71.8	70.9	69.9	68.9	67.9	67.0	66.0	65.0	64.0
83	72.8	71.8	70.9	69.9	68.9	67.9	67.0	66.0	65.0	64.0
84	72.8	71.8	70.9	69.9	68.9	67.9	67.0	66.0	65.0	64.0
85	72.8	71.8	70.9	69.9	68.9	67.9	66.9	66.0	65.0	64.0
86	72.8	70.9	70.9	69.9	68.9	67.9	66.9	66.0	65.0	64.0
87	72.8	70.9	70.9	69.9	68.9	67.9	66.9	66.0	65.0	64.0
88	72.8	70.9	70.9	69.9	68.9	67.9	66.9	66.0	65.0	64.0
89	72.8	71.8	70.9	69.9	68.9	67.9	66.9	66.0	65.0	64.0
90	72.8	71.8	70.9	69.9	68.9	67.9	66.9	66.0	65.0	64.0
91	72.8	71.8	70.9	69.9	68.9	67.9	66.9	66.0	65.0	64.0
92	72.8	71.8	70.9	69.9	68.9	67.9	66.9	66.0	65.0	64.0
93	72.8	71.8	70.9	69.9	68.9	67.9	66.9	66.0	65.0	64.0
94	72.8	71.8	70.8	69.9	68.9	67.9	66.9	66.0	65.0	64.0
95	72.8	71.8	70.8	69.9	68.9	67.9	66.9	66.0	65.0	64.0
96	72.8	71.8	70.8	69.9	68.9	67.9	66.9	66.0	65.0	64.0
97	72.8	71.8	70.8	69.9	68.9	67.9	66.9	66.0	65.0	64.0
98	72.8	71.8	70.8	69.9	68.9	67.9	66.9	66.0	65.0	64.0
99	72.8	71.8	70.8	69.9	68.9	67.9	66.9	66.0	65.0	64.0
100	72.8	71.8	70.8	69.9	68.9	67.9	66.9	66.0	65.0	64.0
101	72.8	71.8	70.8	69.9	68.9	67.9	66.9	66.0	65.0	64.0

Ages	10	11	12	13	14	15	16	17	18	19
102	72.8	71.8	70.8	69.9	68.9	67.9	66.9	66.0	65.0	64.0
103	72.8	71.8	70.8	69.9	68.9	67.9	66.9	66.0	65.0	64.0
104	72.8	71.8	70.8	69.9	68.9	67.9	66.9	66.0	65.0	64.0
105	72.8	71.8	70.8	69.9	68.9	67.9	66.9	66.0	65.0	64.0
106	72.8	71.8	70.8	69.9	68.9	67.9	66.9	66.0	65.0	64.0
107	72.8	71.8	70.8	69.9	68.9	67.9	66.9	66.0	65.0	64.0
108	72.8	71.8	70.8	69.9	68.9	67.9	66.9	66.0	65.0	64.0
109	72.8	71.8	70.8	69.9	68.9	67.9	66.9	66.0	65.0	64.0
110	72.8	71.8	70.8	69.9	68.9	67.9	66.9	66.0	65.0	64.0
111	72.8	71.8	70.8	69.9	68.9	67.9	66.9	66.0	65.0	64.0
112	72.8	71.8	70.8	69.9	68.9	67.9	66.9	66.0	65.0	64.0
113	72.8	71.8	70.8	69.9	68.9	67.9	66.9	66.0	65.0	64.0
114	72.8	71.8	70.8	69.9	68.9	67.9	66.9	66.0	65.0	64.0
115+	72.8	71.8	70.8	69.9	68.9	67.9	66.9	66.0	65.0	64.0

Ages	20	21	22	23	24	25	26	27	28	29
20	70.1	69.6	69.1	68.7	68.3	67.9	67.5	67.2	66.9	66.6
21	69.6	69.1	68.6	68.2	67.7	67.3	66.9	66.6	66.2	65.9
22	69.1	68.6	68.1	67.6	67.2	66.7	66.3	65.9	65.6	65.2
23	68.7	68.2	67.6	67.1	66.6	66.2	65.7	65.3	64.9	64.6
24	68.3	67.7	67.2	66.6	66.1	65.6	65.2	64.7	64.3	63.9
25	67.9	67.3	66.7	66.2	65.6	65.1	64.6	64.2	63.7	63.3
26	67.5	66.9	66.3	65.7	65.2	64.6	64.1	63.6	63.2	62.8
27	67.2	66.6	65.9	65.3	64.7	64.2	63.6	63.1	62.7	62.2
28	66.9	66.2	65.6	64.9	64.3	63.7	63.2	62.7	62.1	61.7
29	66.6	65.9	65.2	64.6	63.9	63.3	62.8	62.2	61.7	61.2
30	66.3	65.6	64.9	64.2	63.6	62.9	62.3	61.8	61.2	60.7
31	66.1	65.3	64.6	63.9	63.2	62.6	62.0	61.4	60.8	60.2
32	65.8	65.1	64.3	63.6	62.9	62.2	61.6	61.0	60.4	59.8
33	65.6	64.8	64.1	63.3	62.6	61.9	61.3	60.6	60.0	59.4
34	65.4	64.6	63.8	63.1	62.3	61.6	60.9	60.3	59.6	59.0
35	65.2	64.4	63.6	62.8	62.1	61.4	60.6	59.9	59.3	58.6
36	65.0	64.2	63.4	62.6	61.9	61.1	60.4	59.6	59.0	58.3
37	64.9	64.0	63.2	62.4	61.6	60.9	30.1	59.4	58.7	58.0
38	64.7	63.9	63.0	62.2	61.4	60.6	59.9	59.1	58.4	57.7
39	64.6	63.7	62.9	62.1	61.2	60.4	59.6	58.9	58.1	57.4
40	64.4	63.6	62.7	61.9	61.1	60.2	59.4	58.7	57.9	57.1

Ages	*20*	*21*	*22*	*23*	*24*	*25*	*26*	*27*	*28*	*29*
41	64.3	63.5	62.6	61.7	60.9	60.1	59.3	58.5	57.7	56.9
42	64.2	63.3	62.5	61.6	60.8	59.9	59.1	58.3	57.5	56.7
43	64.1	63.2	62.4	61.5	60.6	59.8	58.9	58.1	57.3	56.5
44	64.0	63.1	62.2	61.4	60.5	59.6	58.8	57.9	57.1	56.3
45	64.0	63.0	62.2	61.3	60.4	59.5	58.6	57.8	56.9	56.1
46	63.9	63.0	62.1	61.2	60.3	59.4	58.5	57.7	56.8	56.0
47	63.8	62.9	62.0	61.1	60.2	59.3	58.4	57.5	56.7	55.8
48	63.7	62.8	61.9	61.0	60.1	59.2	58.3	57.4	56.5	55.7
49	63.7	62.8	61.8	60.9	60.0	59.1	58.2	57.3	56.4	55.6
50	63.6	62.7	61.8	60.8	59.9	59.0	58.1	57.2	56.3	55.4
51	63.6	62.6	61.7	60.8	59.9	58.9	58.0	57.1	56.2	55.3
52	63.5	62.6	61.7	60.7	59.8	58.9	58.0	57.1	56.1	55.2
53	63.5	62.5	61.6	60.7	59.7	58.8	57.9	57.0	56.1	55.2
54	63.5	62.5	61.6	60.6	59.7	58.8	57.8	56.9	56.0	55.1
55	63.4	62.5	61.5	60.6	59.6	58.7	57.8	56.8	55.9	55.0
56	63.4	62.4	61.5	60.5	59.6	58.7	57.7	56.8	55.9	54.9
57	63.4	62.4	61.5	60.5	59.6	58.6	57.7	56.7	55.8	54.9
58	63.3	62.4	61.4	60.5	59.5	58.6	57.6	56.7	55.8	54.8
59	63.3	62.3	61.4	60.4	59.5	58.5	57.6	56.7	55.7	54.8
60	63.3	62.3	61.4	60.4	59.5	58.5	57.6	56.6	55.7	54.7
61	63.3	62.3	61.3	60.4	59.4	58.5	57.5	56.6	55.6	54.7
62	63.2	62.3	61.3	60.4	59.4	58.4	57.5	56.5	55.6	54.7
63	63.2	62.3	61.3	60.3	59.4	58.4	57.5	56.5	55.6	54.6
64	63.2	62.2	61.3	60.3	59.4	58.4	57.4	56.5	55.5	54.6
65	63.2	62.2	61.3	60.3	59.3	58.4	57.4	56.5	55.5	54.6
66	63.2	62.2	61.2	60.3	59.3	58.4	57.4	56.4	55.5	54.5
67	63.2	62.2	61.2	60.3	59.3	58.3	57.4	56.4	55.5	54.5
68	63.1	62.2	61.2	60.2	59.3	58.3	57.4	56.4	55.4	54.5
69	63.1	62.2	61.2	60.2	59.3	58.3	57.3	56.4	55.4	54.5
70	63.1	62.2	61.2	60.2	59.3	58.3	57.3	56.4	55.4	54.4
71	63.1	62.1	61.2	60.2	59.2	58.3	57.3	56.4	55.4	54.4
72	63.1	62.1	61.2	60.2	59.2	58.3	57.3	56.3	55.4	54.4
73	63.1	62.1	61.2	60.2	59.2	58.3	57.3	56.3	55.4	54.4
74	63.1	62.1	61.2	60.2	59.2	58.2	57.3	56.3	55.4	54.4
75	63.1	62.1	61.1	60.2	59.2	58.2	57.3	56.3	55.3	54.4
76	63.1	62.1	61.1	60.2	59.2	58.2	57.3	56.3	55.3	54.4
77	63.1	62.1	61.1	60.2	59.2	58.2	57.3	56.3	55.3	54.4
78	63.1	62.1	61.1	60.2	59.2	58.2	57.3	56.3	55.3	54.4

Ages	*20*	*21*	*22*	*23*	*24*	*25*	*26*	*27*	*28*	*29*
79	63.1	62.1	61.1	60.2	59.2	58.2	57.2	56.3	55.3	54.3
80	63.1	62.1	61.1	60.1	59.2	58.2	57.2	56.3	55.3	54.3
81	63.1	62.1	61.1	60.1	59.2	58.2	57.2	56.3	55.3	54.3
82	63.1	62.1	61.1	60.1	59.2	58.2	57.2	56.3	55.3	54.3
83	63.1	62.1	61.1	60.1	59.2	58.2	57.2	56.3	55.3	54.3
84	63.0	62.1	61.1	60.1	59.2	58.2	57.2	56.3	55.3	54.3
85	63.0	62.1	61.1	60.1	59.2	58.2	57.2	56.3	55.3	54.3
86	63.0	62.1	61.1	60.1	59.2	58.2	57.2	56.2	55.3	54.3
87	63.0	62.1	61.1	60.1	59.2	58.2	57.2	56.2	55.3	54.3
88	63.0	62.1	61.1	60.1	59.2	58.2	57.2	56.2	55.3	54.3
89	63.0	62.1	61.1	60.1	59.1	58.2	57.2	56.2	55.3	54.3
90	63.0	62.1	61.1	60.1	59.1	58.2	57.2	56.2	55.3	54.3
91	63.0	62.1	61.1	60.1	59.1	58.2	57.2	56.2	55.3	54.3
92	63.0	62.1	61.1	60.1	59.1	58.2	57.2	56.2	55.3	54.3
93	63.0	62.1	61.1	60.1	59.1	58.2	57.2	56.2	55.3	54.3
94	63.0	62.1	61.1	60.1	59.1	58.2	57.2	56.2	55.3	54.3
95	63.0	62.1	61.1	60.1	59.1	58.2	57.2	56.2	55.3	54.3
96	63.0	62.1	61.1	60.1	59.1	58.2	57.2	56.2	55.3	54.3
97	63.0	62.1	61.1	60.1	59.1	58.2	57.2	56.2	55.3	54.3
98	63.0	62.1	61.1	60.1	59.1	58.2	57.2	56.2	55.3	54.3
99	63.0	62.1	61.1	60.1	59.1	58.2	57.2	56.2	55.3	54.3
100	63.0	62.1	61.1	60.1	59.1	58.2	57.2	56.2	55.3	54.3
101	63.0	62.1	61.1	60.1	59.1	58.2	57.2	56.2	55.3	54.3
102	63.0	62.1	61.1	60.1	59.1	58.2	57.2	56.2	55.3	54.3
103	63.0	62.1	61.1	60.1	59.1	58.2	57.2	56.2	55.3	54.3
104	63.0	62.1	61.1	60.1	59.1	58.2	57.2	56.2	55.3	54.3
105	63.0	62.1	61.1	60.1	59.1	58.2	57.2	56.2	55.3	54.3
106	63.0	62.1	61.1	60.1	59.1	58.2	57.2	56.2	55.3	54.3
107	63.0	62.1	61.1	60.1	59.1	58.2	57.2	56.2	55.3	54.3
108	63.0	62.1	61.1	60.1	59.1	58.2	57.2	56.2	55.3	54.3
109	63.0	62.1	61.1	60.1	59.1	58.2	57.2	56.2	55.3	54.3
110	63.0	62.1	61.1	60.1	59.1	58.2	57.2	56.2	55.3	54.3
111	63.0	62.1	61.1	60.1	59.1	58.2	57.2	56.2	55.3	54.3
112	63.0	62.1	61.1	60.1	59.1	58.2	57.2	56.2	55.3	54.3
113	63.0	62.1	61.1	60.1	59.1	58.2	57.2	56.2	55.3	54.3
114	63.0	62.1	61.1	60.1	59.1	58.2	57.2	56.2	55.3	54.3
115+	63.0	62.1	61.1	60.1	59.1	58.2	57.2	56.2	55.3	54.3

Ages	*30*	*31*	*32*	*33*	*34*	*35*	*36*	*37*	*38*	*39*
30	60.2	59.7	59.2	58.8	58.4	58.0	57.6	57.3	57.0	56.7
31	59.7	59.2	58.7	58.2	57.8	57.4	57.0	56.6	56.3	56.0
32	59.2	58.7	58.2	57.7	57.2	56.8	56.4	56.0	55.6	55.3
33	58.8	58.2	57.7	57.2	56.7	56.2	55.8	55.4	55.0	54.7
34	58.4	57.8	57.2	56.7	56.2	55.7	55.3	54.8	53.4	54.0
35	58.0	57.4	56.8	56.2	55.7	55.2	54.7	54.3	53.8	53.4
36	57.6	57.0	56.4	55.8	55.3	54.7	54.2	53.7	53.3	52.8
37	57.3	56.6	56.0	55.4	54.8	54.3	53.7	53.2	52.7	52.3
38	57.0	56.3	55.6	55.0	54.4	53.8	53.3	52.7	52.2	51.7
39	56.7	56.0	55.3	54.7	54.0	53.4	52.8	52.3	51.7	51.2
40	56.4	55.7	55.0	54.3	53.7	53.0	52.4	51.8	51.3	50.8
41	56.1	55.4	54.7	54.0	53.3	52.7	52.0	51.4	50.9	50.3
42	55.9	55.2	54.4	53.7	53.0	52.3	51.7	51.1	50.4	49.9
43	55.7	54.9	54.2	53.4	52.7	52.0	51.3	50.7	50.1	49.5
44	55.5	54.7	53.9	53.2	52.4	51.7	51.0	50.4	49.7	49.1
45	55.3	54.5	53.7	52.9	52.2	51.5	50.7	50.0	49.4	48.7
46	55.1	54.3	53.5	52.7	52.0	51.2	50.5	49.8	49.1	48.4
47	55.0	54.1	53.3	52.5	51.7	51.0	50.2	49.5	48.8	48.1
48	54.8	54.0	53.2	52.3	51.5	50.8	50.0	49.2	48.5	47.8
49	54.7	53.8	53.0	52.2	51.4	50.6	49.8	49.0	48.2	47.5
50	54.6	53.7	52.9	52.0	51.2	50.4	49.6	48.8	48.0	47.3
51	54.5	53.6	52.7	51.9	51.0	50.2	49.4	48.6	47.8	47.0
52	54.4	53.5	52.6	51.7	50.9	50.0	49.2	48.4	47.6	46.8
53	54.3	53.4	52.5	51.6	50.8	49.9	49.1	48.2	47.4	46.6
54	54.2	53.3	52.4	51.5	50.6	49.8	48.9	48.1	47.2	46.4
55	54.1	53.2	52.3	51.4	50.5	49.7	48.8	47.9	47.1	46.3
56	54.0	53.1	52.2	51.3	50.4	49.5	48.7	47.8	47.0	46.1
57	54.0	53.0	52.1	51.2	50.3	49.4	48.6	47.7	46.8	46.0
58	53.9	53.0	52.1	51.2	50.3	49.4	48.5	47.6	46.7	45.8
59	53.8	52.9	52.0	51.1	50.2	49.3	48.4	47.5	46.6	45.7
60	53.8	52.9	51.9	51.0	50.1	49.2	48.3	47.4	46.5	45.6
61	53.8	52.8	51.9	51.0	50.0	49.1	48.2	47.3	46.4	45.5
62	53.7	52.8	51.8	50.9	50.0	49.1	48.1	47.2	46.3	45.4
63	53.7	52.7	51.8	50.9	49.9	49.0	48.1	47.2	46.3	45.3
64	53.6	52.7	51.8	50.8	49.9	48.9	48.0	47.1	46.2	45.3
65	53.6	52.7	51.7	50.8	49.8	48.9	48.0	47.0	46.1	45.2
66	53.6	52.6	51.7	50.7	49.8	48.9	47.9	47.0	46.1	45.1

Ages	*30*	*31*	*32*	*33*	*34*	*35*	*36*	*37*	*38*	*39*
67	53.6	52.6	51.7	50.7	49.8	48.8	47.9	46.9	46.0	45.1
68	53.5	52.6	51.6	50.7	49.7	48.8	47.8	46.9	46.0	45.0
69	53.5	52.6	51.6	50.6	49.7	48.7	47.8	46.9	45.9	45.0
70	53.5	52.5	51.6	50.6	49.7	48.7	47.8	46.8	45.9	44.9
71	53.5	52.5	51.6	50.6	49.6	48.7	47.7	46.8	45.9	44.9
72	53.5	52.5	51.5	50.6	49.6	48.7	47.7	46.8	45.8	44.9
73	53.4	52.5	51.5	50.6	49.6	48.6	47.7	46.7	45.8	44.8
74	53.4	52.5	51.5	50.5	49.6	48.6	47.7	46.7	45.8	44.8
75	53.4	52.5	51.5	50.5	49.6	48.6	47.7	46.7	45.7	44.8
76	53.4	52.4	51.5	50.5	49.6	48.6	47.6	46.7	45.7	44.8
77	53.4	52.4	51.5	50.5	49.5	48.6	47.6	46.7	45.7	44.8
78	53.4	52.4	51.5	50.5	49.5	48.6	47.6	46.6	45.7	44.7
79	53.4	52.4	51.5	50.5	49.5	48.6	47.6	46.6	45.7	44.7
80	53.4	52.4	51.4	50.5	49.5	48.5	47.6	46.6	45.7	44.7
81	53.4	52.4	51.4	50.5	49.5	48.5	47.6	46.6	45.7	44.7
82	53.4	52.4	51.4	50.5	49.5	48.5	47.6	46.6	45.6	44.7
83	53.4	52.4	51.4	50.5	49.5	48.5	47.6	46.6	45.6	44.7
84	53.4	52.4	51.4	50.5	49.5	48.5	47.5	46.6	45.6	44.7
85	53.3	52.4	51.4	50.4	49.5	48.5	47.5	46.6	45.6	44.7
86	53.3	52.4	51.4	50.4	49.5	48.5	47.5	46.6	45.6	44.6
87	53.3	52.4	51.4	50.4	49.5	48.5	47.5	46.6	45.6	44.6
88	53.3	52.4	51.4	50.4	49.5	48.5	47.5	46.6	45.6	44.6
89	53.3	52.4	51.4	50.4	49.5	48.5	47.5	46.6	45.6	44.6
90	53.3	52.4	51.4	50.4	49.5	48.5	47.5	46.6	45.6	44.6
91	53.3	52.4	51.4	50.4	49.5	48.5	47.5	46.6	45.6	44.6
92	53.3	52.4	51.4	50.4	49.5	48.5	47.5	46.6	45.6	44.6
93	53.3	52.4	51.4	50.4	49.5	48.5	47.5	46.6	45.6	44.6
94	53.3	52.4	51.4	50.4	49.5	48.5	47.5	46.6	45.6	44.6
95	53.3	52.4	51.4	50.4	49.5	48.5	47.5	46.6	45.6	44.6
96	53.3	52.4	51.4	50.4	49.5	48.5	47.5	46.5	45.6	44.6
97	53.3	52.4	51.4	50.4	49.5	48.5	47.5	46.5	45.6	44.6
98	53.3	52.4	51.4	50.4	49.5	48.5	47.5	46.5	45.6	44.6
99	53.3	52.4	51.4	50.4	49.5	48.5	47.5	46.5	45.6	44.6
100	53.3	52.4	51.4	50.4	49.5	48.5	47.5	46.5	45.6	44.6
101	53.3	52.4	51.4	50.4	49.5	48.5	47.5	46.5	45.6	44.6
102	53.3	52.4	51.4	50.4	49.5	48.5	47.5	46.5	45.6	44.6
103	53.3	52.4	51.4	50.4	49.5	48.5	47.5	46.5	45.6	44.6

Ages	*30*	*31*	*32*	*33*	*34*	*35*	*36*	*37*	*38*	*39*
104	53.3	52.4	51.4	50.4	49.5	48.5	47.5	46.5	45.6	44.6
105	53.3	52.4	51.4	50.4	49.4	48.5	47.5	46.5	45.6	44.6
106	53.3	52.4	51.4	50.4	49.4	48.5	47.5	46.5	45.6	44.6
107	53.3	52.4	51.4	50.4	49.4	48.5	47.5	46.5	45.6	44.6
108	53.3	52.4	51.4	50.4	49.4	48.5	47.5	46.5	45.6	44.6
109	53.3	52.4	51.4	50.4	49.4	48.5	47.5	46.5	45.6	44.6
110	53.3	52.4	51.4	50.4	49.4	48.5	47.5	46.5	45.6	44.6
111	53.3	52.4	51.4	50.4	49.4	48.5	47.5	46.5	45.6	44.6
112	53.3	52.4	51.4	50.4	49.4	48.5	47.5	46.5	45.6	44.6
113	53.3	52.4	51.4	50.4	49.4	48.5	47.5	46.5	45.6	44.6
114	53.3	52.4	51.4	50.4	49.4	48.5	47.5	46.5	45.6	44.6
115 +	53.3	52.4	51.4	50.4	49.4	48.5	47.5	46.5	45.6	44.6

Ages	*40*	*41*	*42*	*43*	*44*	*45*	*46*	*47*	*48*	*49*
40	50.2	49.8	49.3	48.9	48.5	48.1	47.7	47.4	47.1	46.8
41	59.8	49.3	48.8	48.3	47.9	47.5	47.1	46.7	46.4	46.1
42	49.3	48.8	48.3	47.8	47.3	46.9	46.5	46.1	45.8	45.4
43	48.9	48.3	47.8	47.3	46.8	46.3	45.9	45.5	45.1	44.8
44	48.5	47.9	47.3	46.8	46.3	45.8	45.4	44.9	44.5	44.2
45	48.1	47.5	46.9	46.3	45.8	45.3	44.8	44.4	44.0	43.6
46	47.7	47.1	46.5	45.9	45.4	44.8	44.3	43.9	43.4	43.0
47	47.4	46.7	46.1	45.5	44.9	44.4	43.9	43.4	42.9	42.4
48	47.1	46.4	45.8	45.1	44.5	44.0	43.4	42.9	42.4	41.9
49	46.8	46.1	45.4	44.8	44.2	43.6	43.0	42.4	41.9	41.4
50	46.35	45.8	45.1	44.4	43.8	43.2	42.6	42.0	41.5	40.9
51	46.3	45.5	44.8	44.1	43.5	42.8	42.2	41.6	41.0	40.5
52	46.0	45.3	44.6	43.8	43.2	42.5	41.8	41.2	40.6	40.1
53	45.8	45.1	44.3	43.6	42.9	42.2	41.5	40.9	40.3	39.7
54	45.6	44.8	44.1	43.3	42.6	41.9	41.2	40.5	39.9	39.3
55	45.5	44.7	43.9	43.1	42.4	41.6	40.9	40.2	39.6	38.9
56	45.3	44.5	43.7	42.9	42.1	41.4	40.7	40.0	39.3	38.6
57	45.1	44.3	43.5	42.7	41.9	41.2	40.4	39.7	39.0	38.3
58	45.0	44.2	43.3	42.5	41.7	40.9	40.2	39.4	38.7	38.0
59	44.9	44.0	43.2	42.4	41.5	40.7	40.0	39.2	38.5	37.8
60	44.7	43.9	43.0	42.2	41.4	40.6	39.8	39.0	38.2	37.5
61	44.6	43.8	42.9	42.1	41.2	40.4	39.6	38.8	38.0	37.3
62	44.5	43.7	42.8	41.9	41.1	40.3	39.4	38.6	37.8	37.1

Ages	*40*	*41*	*42*	*43*	*44*	*45*	*46*	*47*	*48*	*49*
63	44.5	43.6	42.7	41.8	41.0	40.1	39.3	38.5	37.7	36.9
64	44.4	43.5	42.6	41.7	40.8	40.0	39.2	38.3	37.5	36.7
65	44.3	43.4	42.5	41.6	40.7	39.9	39.0	38.2	37.4	36.6
66	44.2	43.3	42.4	41.5	40.6	39.8	38.9	38.1	37.2	36.4
67	44.2	43.2	42.3	41.4	40.6	39.7	38.8	38.0	37.1	36.3
68	44.1	43.1	42.3	41.4	40.5	39.6	38.7	37.9	37.0	36.2
69	44.1	43.1	42.2	41.3	40.4	39.5	38.6	37.8	36.9	36.0
70	44.0	43.1	42.2	41.3	40.3	39.4	38.6	37.7	36.8	35.9
71	44.0	43.0	42.1	41.2	40.3	39.4	38.5	37.6	36.7	35.9
72	43.9	43.0	42.1	41.1	40.2	39.3	38.5	37.5	36.6	35.8
73	43.9	43.0	42.0	41.1	40.2	39.3	38.4	37.5	36.6	35.7
74	43.9	42.9	42.0	41.1	40.1	39.2	38.4	37.4	36.5	35.6
75	43.8	42.9	42.0	41.0	40.1	39.2	38.3	37.4	36.5	35.6
76	43.8	42.9	41.9	41.0	40.1	39.1	38.3	37.3	36.4	35.5
77	43.8	42.9	41.9	40.9	40.0	39.1	38.2	37.3	36.4	35.5
78	43.8	42.8	41.9	40.9	40.0	39.1	38.2	37.2	36.3	35.4
79	43.8	42.8	41.9	40.9	40.0	39.1	38.1	37.2	36.3	35.4
80	43.7	42.8	41.8	40.9	40.0	39.0	38.1	37.2	36.3	35.4
81	43.7	42.8	41.8	40.9	39.9	39.0	38.1	37.2	36.2	35.3
82	43.7	42.8	41.8	40.9	39.9	39.0	38.1	37.1	36.2	35.3
83	43.7	42.8	41.8	40.9	39.9	39.0	38.0	37.1	36.2	35.3
84	43.7	42.7	41.8	40.8	39.9	39.0	38.0	37.1	36.2	35.3
85	43.7	42.7	41.8	40.8	39.9	38.9	38.0	37.1	36.2	35.2
86	43.7	42.7	41.8	40.8	39.9	38.9	38.0	37.1	36.1	35.2
87	43.7	42.7	41.8	40.8	39.9	38.9	38.0	37.0	36.1	35.2
88	43.7	42.7	41.8	40.8	39.9	38.9	38.0	37.0	36.1	35.2
89	43.7	42.7	41.7	40.8	39.8	38.9	38.0	37.0	36.1	35.2
90	43.7	42.7	41.7	40.8	39.8	38.9	38.0	37.0	36.1	35.2
91	43.7	42.7	41.7	40.8	39.8	38.9	37.9	37.0	36.1	35.2
92	43.7	42.7	41.7	40.8	39.8	38.9	37.9	37.0	36.1	35.1
93	43.7	42.7	41.7	40.8	39.8	38.9	37.9	37.0	36.1	35.1
94	43.7	42.7	41.7	40.8	39.8	38.9	37.9	37.0	36.1	35.1
95	43.6	42.7	41.7	40.8	39.8	38.9	37.9	37.0	36.1	35.1
96	43.6	42.7	41.7	40.8	39.8	38.9	37.9	37.0	36.1	35.1
97	43.6	42.7	41.7	40.8	39.8	38.9	37.9	37.0	36.1	35.1
98	43.6	42.7	41.7	40.8	39.8	38.9	37.9	37.0	36.0	35.1
99	43.6	42.7	41.7	40.8	39.8	38.9	37.9	37.0	36.0	35.1

Ages	*40*	*41*	*42*	*43*	*44*	*45*	*46*	*47*	*48*	*49*
100	43.6	42.7	41.7	40.8	39.8	38.8	37.9	37.0	36.0	35.1
101	43.6	42.7	41.7	40.8	39.8	38.8	37.9	37.0	36.0	35.1
102	43.6	42.7	41.7	40.8	39.8	38.8	37.9	37.0	36.0	35.1
103	43.6	42.7	41.7	40.8	39.8	38.8	37.9	37.0	36.0	35.1
104	43.6	42.7	41.7	40.8	39.8	38.8	37.9	37.0	36.0	35.1
105	43.6	42.7	41.7	40.8	39.8	38.8	37.9	37.0	36.0	35.1
106	43.6	42.7	41.7	40.8	39.8	38.8	37.9	37.0	36.0	35.1
107	43.6	42.7	41.7	40.8	39.8	38.8	37.9	37.0	36.0	35.1
108	43.6	42.7	41.7	40.8	39.8	38.8	37.9	37.0	36.0	35.1
109	43.6	42.7	41.7	40.7	39.8	38.8	37.9	37.0	36.0	35.1
110	43.6	42.7	41.7	40.7	39.8	38.8	37.9	37.0	36.0	35.1
111	43.6	42.7	41.7	40.7	39.8	38.8	37.9	37.0	36.0	35.1
112	43.6	42.7	41.7	40.7	39.8	38.8	37.9	37.0	36.0	35.1
113	43.6	42.7	41.7	40.7	39.8	38.8	37.9	37.0	36.0	35.1
114	43.6	42.7	41.7	40.7	39.8	38.8	37.9	37.0	36.0	35.1
115+	43.6	42.7	41.7	40.7	39.8	38.8	37.9	37.0	36.0	35.1

Ages	*50*	*51*	*52*	*53*	*54*	*55*	*56*	*57*	*58*	*59*
50	40.4	40.0	39.5	39.1	38.7	38.3	38.0	37.6	37.3	37.1
51	40.0	39.5	39.0	38.5	38.1	37.7	37.4	37.0	36.7	36.4
52	39.5	39.0	38.5	38.0	37.6	37.2	36.8	36.4	36.0	35.7
53	39.1	38.5	38.0	37.5	37.1	36.6	36.2	35.8	35.4	35.1
54	38.7	38.1	37.6	37.1	36.6	36.1	35.7	35.2	34.8	34.5
55	38.3	37.7	37.2	36.6	36.1	35.6	35.1	34.7	34.3	33.9
56	38.0	37.4	36.8	36.2	35.7	35.1	34.7	34.2	33.7	33.3
57	37.6	37.0	36.4	35.8	35.2	34.7	34.2	33.7	33.2	32.8
58	37.3	36.7	36.0	35.4	34.8	34.3	33.7	33.2	32.8	32.3
59	37.1	36.4	35.7	35.1	34.5	33.9	33.3	32.8	32.3	31.8
60	36.8	36.1	35.4	34.8	34.1	33.5	32.9	32.4	31.9	31.3
61	36.6	35.8	35.1	34.5	33.8	33.2	32.6	32.0	31.4	30.9
62	36.3	35.6	34.9	34.2	33.5	32.9	32.2	31.6	31.1	30.5
63	36.1	35.4	34.6	33.9	33.2	32.6	31.9	31.3	30.7	30.1
64	35.9	35.2	34.4	33.7	33.0	32.3	31.6	31.0	30.4	29.8
65	35.8	35.0	34.2	33.5	32.7	32.0	31.4	30.7	30.0	29.4
66	35.6	34.8	34.0	33.3	32.5	31.8	31.1	30.4	29.8	29.1
67	35.5	34.7	33.9	33.1	32.3	31.6	30.9	30.2	29.5	28.8
68	35.3	34.5	33.7	32.9	32.1	31.4	30.7	29.9	29.2	28.6

Ages	*50*	*51*	*52*	*53*	*54*	*55*	*56*	*57*	*58*	*59*
69	35.2	34.4	33.6	32.8	32.0	31.2	30.5	29.7	29.0	28.3
70	35.1	34.3	33.4	32.6	31.8	31.1	30.3	29.5	28.8	28.1
71	35.0	34.2	33.3	32.5	31.7	30.9	30.1	29.4	28.6	27.9
72	34.9	34.1	33.2	32.4	31.6	30.8	30.0	29.2	28.4	27.7
73	34.8	34.0	33.1	32.3	31.5	30.6	29.8	29.1	28.3	27.5
74	34.8	33.9	33.0	32.2	31.4	30.5	29.7	28.9	28.1	27.4
75	34.7	33.8	33.0	32.1	31.3	30.4	29.6	28.8	28.0	27.2
76	34.6	33.8	33.9	32.0	31.2	30.3	29.5	28.7	27.9	27.1
77	34.6	33.7	32.8	32.0	31.1	30.3	29.4	28.6	27.8	27.0
78	34.5	33.6	32.8	31.9	31.0	30.2	29.3	28.5	27.7	26.9
79	34.5	33.6	32.7	31.8	31.0	30.1	29.3	28.4	27.6	26.8
80	34.5	33.6	32.7	31.8	30.9	30.1	29.2	28.4	27.5	26.7
81	34.4	33.5	32.6	31.8	30.9	30.0	29.2	28.3	27.5	26.6
82	34.4	33.5	32.6	31.7	30.8	30.0	29.1	28.3	27.4	26.6
83	34.4	33.5	32.6	31.7	30.8	29.9	29.1	28.2	27.4	26.5
84	34.3	33.4	32.5	31.7	30.8	29.9	29.0	28.2	27.3	26.5
85	34.3	33.4	32.5	31.6	30.7	29.8	29.0	28.1	27.3	26.4
86	34.3	33.4	32.5	31.6	30.7	29.8	29.0	28.1	27.2	26.4
87	34.3	33.4	32.5	31.6	30.7	29.8	28.9	28.1	27.2	26.4
88	34.3	33.4	32.5	31.6	30.7	29.8	28.9	28.0	27.2	26.3
89	34.3	33.3	32.4	31.5	30.7	29.8	28.9	28.0	27.2	26.3
90	34.2	33.3	32.4	31.5	30.6	29.8	28.9	28.0	27.1	26.3
91	34.2	33.3	32.4	31.5	30.6	29.7	28.9	28.0	27.1	26.3
92	34.2	33.3	32.4	31.5	30.6	29.7	28.8	28.0	27.1	26.2
93	34.2	33.3	32.4	31.5	30.6	29.7	28.8	28.0	27.1	26.2
94	34.2	33.3	32.4	31.5	30.6	29.7	28.8	27.9	27.1	26.2
95	34.2	33.3	32.4	31.5	30.6	29.7	28.8	27.9	27.1	26.2
96	34.2	33.3	32.4	31.5	30.6	29.7	28.8	27.9	27.0	26.2
97	34.2	33.3	32.4	31.5	30.6	29.7	28.8	27.9	27.0	26.2
98	34.2	33.3	32.4	31.5	30.6	29.7	28.8	27.9	27.0	26.2
99	34.2	33.3	32.4	31.5	30.6	29.7	28.8	27.9	27.0	26.2
100	34.2	33.3	32.4	31.5	30.6	29.7	28.8	27.9	27.0	26.1
101	34.2	33.3	32.4	31.5	30.6	29.7	28.8	27.9	27.0	26.1
102	34.2	33.3	32.4	31.4	30.5	29.7	28.8	27.9	27.0	26.1
103	34.2	33.3	32.4	31.4	30.5	29.7	28.8	27.9	27.0	26.1
104	34.2	33.3	32.4	31.4	30.5	29.6	28.8	27.9	27.0	26.1
105	34.2	33.3	32.4	31.4	30.5	29.6	28.8	27.9	27.0	26.1

Ages	50	51	52	53	54	55	56	57	58	59
106	34.2	33.3	32.3	31.4	30.5	29.6	28.8	27.9	27.0	26.1
107	34.2	33.3	32.3	31.4	30.5	29.6	28.8	27.9	27.0	26.1
108	34.2	33.3	32.3	31.4	30.5	29.6	28.8	27.9	27.0	26.1
109	34.2	33.3	32.3	31.4	30.5	29.6	28.7	27.9	27.0	26.1
110	34.2	33.3	32.3	31.4	30.5	29.6	28.7	27.9	27.0	26.1
111	34.2	33.3	32.3	31.4	30.5	29.6	28.7	27.9	27.0	26.1
112	34.2	33.3	32.3	31.4	30.5	29.6	28.7	27.9	27.0	26.1
113	34.2	33.3	32.3	31.4	30.5	29.6	28.7	27.9	27.0	26.1
114	34.2	33.3	32.3	31.4	30.5	29.6	28.7	27.9	27.0	26.1
115 +	34.2	33.3	32.3	31.4	30.5	29.6	28.7	27.9	27.0	26.1

Ages	60	61	62	63	64	65	66	67	68	69
60	30.9	30.4	30.0	29.6	29.2	28.8	28.5	28.2	27.9	27.6
61	30.4	29.9	29.5	29.0	28.6	28.3	27.9	27.6	27.3	27.0
62	30.0	29.5	29.0	28.5	28.1	27.7	27.3	27.0	26.7	26.4
63	29.6	29.0	28.5	28.1	27.6	27.2	26.8	26.4	26.1	25.7
64	29.2	28.6	28.1	27.6	27.1	26.7	26.3	25.9	25.5	25.2
65	28.8	28.3	27.7	27.2	26.7	26.2	25.8	25.4	25.0	24.6
66	28.8	27.9	27.3	26.8	26.3	25.8	25.3	24.9	24.5	24.1
67	28.2	27.6	27.0	26.4	25.9	25.4	24.9	24.4	24.0	23.6
68	27.9	27.3	26.7	26.1	25.5	25.0	24.5	24.0	23.5	23.1
69	27.6	27.0	26.4	25.7	25.2	24.6	24.1	23.6	23.1	22.6
70	27.4	27.6	26.1	25.4	24.8	24.3	23.7	23.2	22.7	22.2
71	27.2	26.5	25.8	25.2	24.5	23.9	23.4	22.8	22.3	21.8
72	27.0	26.3	25.6	24.9	24.3	23.7	23.1	22.5	22.0	21.4
73	26.8	26.1	25.4	24.7	24.0	23.4	22.8	22.2	21.6	21.1
74	26.6	25.9	25.2	24.5	23.8	23.1	22.5	21.9	21.3	20.8
75	26.5	25.7	25.0	24.3	23.6	22.9	22.3	21.6	21.0	20.5
76	26.3	25.6	24.8	24.1	23.4	22.7	22.0	21.4	20.8	20.2
77	26.2	25.4	24.7	23.9	23.2	22.5	21.8	21.2	20.6	19.9
78	26.1	25.3	24.6	23.8	23.1	22.4	21.7	21.0	20.3	19.7
79	26.0	25.2	24.4	23.7	22.9	22.2	21.5	20.8	20.1	19.5
80	25.9	25.1	24.3	23.6	22.8	22.1	21.3	20.6	20.0	19.3
81	25.8	25	24.2	23.4	22.7	21.9	21.2	20.5	19.8	19.1
82	25.8	24.9	24.1	23.4	22.6	21.8	21.1	20.4	19.7	19.0
83	2537	24.9	24.1	23.3	22.5	21.7	21.0	20.2	19.5	18.8
84	25.6	24.8	24.0	23.2	22.4	21.6	20.9	20.1	19.4	18.7

Ages	60	61	62	63	64	65	66	67	68	69
85	25.6	24.8	23.9	23.1	22.3	21.6	20.8	20.1	19.3	18.6
86	25.5	24.7	23.9	23.1	22.3	21.5	20.7	20.0	19.2	18.5
87	25.5	24.7	23.8	23.0	22.2	21.4	20.7	19.9	19.2	18.4
88	25.5	24.6	23.8	23.0	22.2	21.4	20.6	19.8	19.1	18.3
89	25.4	24.6	23.8	22.9	22.1	21.3	20.5	19.8	19.0	18.3
90	25.4	24.6	23.7	22.9	22.1	21.3	20.5	19.7	19.0	18.2
91	25.4	24.5	23.7	22.9	22.1	21.3	20.5	19.7	18.9	18.2
92	25.4	24.5	23.7	22.9	22.0	21.2	20.4	19.6	18.9	18.1
93	25.4	24.5	23.7	22.8	22.0	21.2	20.4	19.6	18.8	18.1
94	25.3	24.5	23.6	22.8	22.0	21.2	20.4	19.6	18.8	18.0
95	25.3	24.5	23.6	22.8	22.0	21.1	20.3	19.6	18.8	18.0
96	25.3	24.5	23.6	22.8	21.9	21.1	20.3	19.5	18.8	18.0
97	25.3	24.5	23.6	22.8	21.9	21.1	20.3	19.5	18.7	18.0
98	25.3	24.4	23.6	22.8	21.9	21.1	20.3	19.5	18.7	17.9
99	25.3	24.4	23.6	22.7	21.9	21.1	20.3	19.5	18.7	17.9
100	25.3	24.4	23.6	22.7	21.9	21.1	20.3	19.5	18.7	17.9
101	25.3	24.4	23.6	22.7	21.9	21.1	20.2	19.4	18.7	17.9
102	25.3	24.4	23.6	22.7	21.9	21.1	20.2	19.4	18.6	17.9
103	25.3	24.4	26.6	22.7	21.9	21.0	20.2	19.4	18.6	17.9
104	25.3	24.4	23.5	22.7	21.9	21.0	20.2	19.4	18.6	17.8
105	25.3	24.4	23.5	22.7	21.9	21.0	20.2	19.4	18.6	17.8
106	25.2	24.4	23.5	22.7	21.9	21.0	20.2	19.4	18.6	17.8
107	25.2	24.4	23.5	22.7	21.8	21.0	20.2	19.4	18.6	17.8
108	25.2	24.4	23.5	22.7	21.8	21.0	20.2	19.4	18.6	17.8
109	25.2	24.4	23.5	22.7	21.8	21.0	20.2	19.4	18.6	17.8
110	25.2	24.4	23.5	22.7	21.8	21.0	20.2	19.4	18.6	17.8
111	25.2	24.4	23.5	22.7	21.8	21.0	20.2	19.4	18.6	17.8
112	25.2	24.4	23.5	22.7	21.8	21.0	20.2	19.4	18.6	17.8
113	25.2	24.4	23.5	22.7	21.8	21.0	20.2	19.4	18.6	17.8
114	25.2	24.4	23.5	22.7	21.8	21.0	20.2	19.4	18.6	17.8
115+	25.2	24.4	23.5	22.7	21.8	21.0	20.2	19.4	18.6	17.8

Ages	70	71	72	73	74	75	76	77	78	79
70	21.8	21.3	20.9	20.6	20.2	19.9	19.6	19.4	19.1	18.9
71	21.3	20.9	20.5	20.1	19.7	19.4	19.1	18.8	18.5	18.3
72	20.9	20.5	20.0	19.6	19.3	18.9	18.6	18.3	18.0	17.7
73	20.6	20.1	19.6	19.2	18.8	18.4	18.1	17.8	17.5	17.2

Ages	*70*	*71*	*72*	*73*	*74*	*75*	*76*	*77*	*78*	*79*
74	20.2	19.7	19.3	18.8	18.4	18.0	17.6	17.3	17.0	16.7
75	19.9	19.4	18.9	18.4	18.0	17.6	17.2	16.8	16.5	16.2
76	19.6	19.1	18.6	18.1	17.6	17.2	16.8	16.4	16.0	15.7
77	19.4	18.8	18.3	17.8	17.3	16.8	16.4	16.0	15.6	15.3
78	19.1	18.5	18.0	17.5	17.0	16.5	16.0	15.6	15.2	14.9
79	18.9	18.3	17.7	17.2	16.7	16.2	15.7	15.3	14.9	14.5
80	18.7	18.1	17.5	16.9	16.4	15.9	15.4	15.0	14.5	14.1
81	18.5	17.9	17.3	16.7	16.2	15.6	15.1	14.7	14.2	13.8
82	18.3	17.7	17.1	16.5	15.9	15.4	14.9	14.4	13.9	13.5
83	18.2	17.5	16.9	16.3	15.7	15.2	14.7	14.2	13.7	13.2
84	18.0	17.4	16.7	16.1	15.5	15.0	14.4	13.9	13.4	13.0
85	17.9	17.3	16.6	16.0	15.4	14.8	14.3	13.7	13.2	12.8
86	17.8	17.1	16.5	15.8	15.2	14.6	14.1	13.5	13.0	12.5
87	17.7	17.0	16.4	15.7	15.1	14.5	13.9	13.4	12.9	12.4
88	17.6	16.9	16.3	15.6	15.0	14.4	13.8	13.2	12.7	12.2
89	17.6	16.9	16.2	15.5	14.9	14.3	13.7	13.1	12.6	12.0
90	17.5	16.8	16.1	15.4	14.8	14.2	13.6	13.0	12.4	11.9
91	17.4	16.7	16.0	15.4	14.7	14.1	13.5	12.9	12.3	11.8
92	17.4	16.7	16.0	15.3	14.6	14.0	13.4	12.8	12.2	11.7
93	17.3	16.6	15.9	15.2	14.6	13.9	13.3	12.7	12.1	11.6
94	17.3	16.6	15.9	15.2	14.5	13.9	13.2	12.6	12.0	11.5
95	17.3	16.5	15.8	15.1	15.5	13.8	13.2	12.6	12.0	11.4
96	17.2	16.5	15.8	15.1	14.4	13.8	13.1	12.5	11.9	11.3
97	17.2	16.5	15.8	15.1	14.4	13.7	13.1	12.5	11.9	11.3
98	17.2	16.4	15.7	15.0	14.3	13.7	13.0	12.4	11.8	11.2
99	17.2	16.4	15.7	15.0	14.3	13.6	13.0	12.4	11.8	11.2
100	17.1	16.4	15.7	15.0	14.3	13.6	12.9	12.3	11.7	11.1
101	17.1	16.4	15.6	14.9	14.2	13.6	12.9	12.3	11.7	11.1
102	17.1	16.4	15.6	14.9	14.2	13.5	12.9	12.2	11.6	11.0
103	17.1	16.3	15.6	14.9	14.2	13.5	12.9	12.2	11.6	11.0
104	17.1	16.3	15.6	14.9	14.2	13.5	12.8	12.2	11.6	11.0
105	17.1	16.3	15.6	14.9	14.2	13.5	12.8	12.2	11.5	10.9
106	17.1	16.3	15.6	14.8	14.1	13.5	12.8	12.2	11.5	10.9
107	17.0	16.3	15.6	14.8	14.1	13.4	12.8	12.1	11.5	10.9
108	17.0	16.3	15.5	14.8	14.1	13.4	12.8	12.1	11.5	10.9
109	17.0	16.3	15.5	14.8	14.1	13.4	12.8	12.1	11.5	10.9
110	17.0	16.3	15.5	14.8	14.1	13.4	12.7	12.1	11.5	10.9

Ages	70	71	72	73	74	75	76	77	78	79
111	17.0	16.3	15.5	14.8	14.1	13.4	12.7	12.1	11.5	10.8
112	17.0	16.3	15.5	14.8	14.1	13.4	12.7	12.1	11.5	10.8
113	17.0	16.3	15.5	14.8	14.1	13.4	12.7	12.1	11.4	10.8
114	17.0	16.3	15.5	14.8	14.1	13.4	12.7	12.1	11.4	10.8
115+	17.0	16.3	15.5	14.8	14.1	13.4	12.7	12.1	11.4	10.8

Ages	80	81	82	83	84	85	86	87	88	89
80	13.8	13.4	13.1	12.8	12.6	12.3	12.1	11.9	11.7	11.5
81	13.4	13.1	12.7	12.4	12.2	11.9	11.7	11.4	11.3	11.1
82	13.1	12.7	12.4	12.1	11.8	11.5	11.3	11.0	10.8	10.6
83	12.8	12.4	12.1	11.7	11.4	11.1	10.9	10.6	10.4	10.2
84	12.6	12.2	11.8	11.4	11.1	10.8	10.5	10.3	10.1	9.9
85	12.3	11.9	11.5	11.1	10.8	10.5	10.2	9.9	9.7	9.5
86	12.1	11.7	11.3	10.9	10.5	10.2	9.9	9.6	9.4	9.2
87	11.9	11.4	11.0	10.6	10.3	9.9	9.6	9.4	9.1	8.9
88	11.7	11.3	10.8	10.4	10.1	9.7	9.4	9.1	8.8	8.6
89	11.5	11.1	10.6	10.2	9.9	9.5	9.2	8.9	8.6	8.3
90	11.4	10.9	10.5	10.1	9.7	9.3	9.0	8.6	8.3	8.1
91	11.3	10.8	10.3	9.9	9.5	9.1	8.8	8.4	8.1	7.9
92	11.2	10.7	10.2	9.8	9.3	9.0	8.6	8.3	8.0	7.7
93	11.2	10.6	10.1	9.6	9.2	8.8	8.5	8.1	7.8	7.5
94	11.0	10.5	10.0	9.5	9.1	8.7	8.3	8.0	7.6	7.3
95	10.9	10.4	9.9	9.4	9.0	8.6	8.2	7.8	7.5	7.2
96	10.8	10.3	9.8	9.3	8.9	8.5	8.1	7.7	7.4	7.1
97	10.7	10.2	9.7	9.2	8.8	8.4	8.0	7.6	7.3	6.9
98	10.7	10.1	9.6	9.2	8.7	8.3	7.9	7.5	7.1	6.8
99	10.6	10.1	9.6	9.1	8.6	8.2	7.8	7.4	7.0	6.7
100	10.6	10.0	9.5	9.0	8.5	8.1	7.7	7.3	6.9	6.6
101	10.5	10.0	9.4	9.0	8.5	8.0	7.6	7.2	6.9	6.5
102	10.5	9.9	9.4	8.9	8.4	8.0	7.5	7.1	6.8	6.4
103	10.4	9.9	9.4	8.8	8.4	7.9	7.5	7.1	6.7	6.3
104	10.4	9.8	9.3	8.8	8.3	7.9	7.4	7.0	6.6	6.3
105	10.4	9.8	9.3	8.8	8.3	7.8	7.4	7.0	6.6	6.2
106	10.3	9.8	9.2	8.7	8.2	7.8	7.3	6.9	6.5	6.2
107	10.3	9.8	9.2	8.7	8.2	7.7	7.3	6.9	6.5	6.1
108	10.3	9.7	9.2	8.7	8.2	7.7	7.3	6.8	6.4	6.1
109	10.3	9.7	9.2	8.7	8.2	7.7	7.2	6.8	6.4	6.0

Ages	*80*	*81*	*82*	*83*	*84*	*85*	*86*	*87*	*88*	*89*
110	10.3	9.7	9.2	8.6	8.1	7.7	7.2	6.8	6.4	6.0
111	10.3	9.7	9.1	8.6	8.1	7.6	7.2	6.8	6.3	6.0
112	10.2	9.7	9.1	8.6	8.1	7.6	7.2	6.7	6.3	5.9
113	10.2	9.7	9.1	8.6	8.1	7.6	7.2	6.7	6.3	5.9
114	10.2	9.7	9.1	8.6	8.1	7.6	7.1	6.7	6.3	5.9
115+	10.2	9.7	9.1	8.6	8.1	7.6	7.1	6.7	6.3	5.9

Ages	*90*	*91*	*92*	*93*	*94*	*95*	*96*	*97*	*98*	*99*
90	7.8	7.6	7.4	7.2	7.1	6.9	6.8	6.6	6.5	6.4
91	7.6	7.4	7.2	7.0	6.8	6.7	6.5	6.4	6.3	6.1
92	7.4	7.2	7.0	6.8	6.6	6.4	6.3	6.1	6.0	5.9
93	7.2	7.0	6.8	6.6	6.4	6.2	6.1	5.9	5.8	5.6
94	7.1	6.8	6.6	6.4	6.2	6.0	5.9	5.7	5.6	5.4
95	6.9	6.7	6.4	6.2	6.0	5.8	5.7	5.5	5.4	5.2
96	6.8	6.5	6.3	6.1	5.9	5.7	5.5	5.3	5.2	5.0
97	6.6	6.4	6.1	5.9	5.7	5.5	5.3	5.2	5.0	4.9
98	6.5	6.3	6.0	5.8	5.6	5.4	5.2	5.0	4.8	4.7
99	6.4	6.1	5.9	5.6	5.4	5.2	5.0	4.9	4.7	4.5
100	6.3	6.0	5.8	5.5	5.3	5.1	4.9	4.7	4.5	4.4
101	6.2	5.9	5.6	5.4	5.2	5.0	4.8	4.6	4.4	4.2
102	6.1	5.8	5.5	5.3	5.1	4.8	4.6	4.4	4.3	4.1
103	6.0	5.7	5.4	5.2	5.0	4.7	4.5	4.3	4.1	4.0
104	5.9	5.6	5.4	5.1	4.9	4.6	4.4	4.2	4.0	3.8
105	5.8	5.6	5.3	5.0	4.8	4.5	4.3	4.1	3.9	3.7
106	5.8	5.5	5.2	4.9	4.7	4.5	4.2	4.0	3.8	3.6
107	5.7	5.4	5.1	4.9	4.6	4.4	4.2	3.9	3.7	3.5
108	5.7	5.4	5.1	4.8	4.6	4.3	4.1	3.9	3.7	3.5
109	5.7	5.3	5.0	4.8	4.5	4.3	4.0	3.8	3.6	3.4
110	5.6	5.3	5.0	4.7	4.5	4.2	4.0	3.8	3.5	3.3
111	5.6	5.3	5.0	4.7	4.4	4.2	3.9	3.7	3.5	3.3
112	5.6	5.3	4.9	4.7	4.4	4.1	3.9	3.7	3.5	3.2
113	5.6	5.2	4.9	4.6	4.4	4.1	3.9	3.6	3.4	3.2
114	5.6	5.2	4.9	4.6	4.3	4.1	3.9	3.6	3.4	3.2
115+	5.5	5.2	4.9	4.6	4.3	4.1	3.8	3.6	3.4	3.1

Ages	*100*	*101*	*102*	*103*	*104*	*105*	*106*	*107*	*108*	*109*
100	4.2	4.1	3.9	3.8	3.7	3.5	3.4	3.6	3.3	3.2
101	4.1	3.9	3.7	3.6	3.5	3.4	3.2	3.1	3.1	3.0

Ages	*100*	*101*	*102*	*103*	*104*	*105*	*106*	*107*	*108*	*109*
102	3.9	3.7	3.6	3.4	3.3	3.2	3.1	3.0	2.9	2.8
103	3.8	3.6	3.4	3.3	3.2	3.0	2.9	2.8	2.7	2.6
104	3.7	3.5	3.3	3.2	3.0	2.9	2.7	2.6	2.5	2.4
105	3.5	3.4	3.2	3.0	2.9	2.7	2.6	2.5	2.4	2.3
106	3.4	3.2	3.1	2.9	2.7	2.6	2.4	2.3	2.2	2.1
107	3.3	3.1	3.0	2.8	2.6	2.5	2.3	2.2	2.1	2.0
108	3.3	3.1	2.9	2.7	2.5	2.4	2.2	2.1	1.9	1.8
109	3.2	3.0	2.8	2.6	2.4	2.3	2.1	2.0	1.8	1.7
110	3.1	2.9	2.7	2.5	2.3	2.2	2.0	1.9	1.7	1.6
111	3.1	2.9	2.7	2.5	2.3	2.1	1.9	1.8	1.6	1.5
112	3.0	2.8	2.6	2.4	2.2	2.0	1.9	1.7	1.5	1.4
113	3.0	2.8	2.6	2.4	2.2	2.0	1.8	1.6	1.5	1.3
114	3.0	2.7	2.5	2.3	2.1	1.9	1.8	1.6	1.4	1.3
115+	2.9	2.7	2.5	2.3	2.1	1.9	1.7	1.5	1.4	1.2

Ages	*110*	*111*	*112*	*113*	*114*	*115+*
110	1.5	1.4	1.3	1.2	1.1	1.1
111	1.4	1.2	1.1	1.1	1.0	1.0
112	1.3	1.1	1.0	1.0	1.0	1.0
113	1.2	1.1	1.0	1.0	1.0	1.0
114	1.1	1.0	1.0	1.0	1.0	1.0
115+	1.1	1.0	1.0	1.0	1.0	1.0

Appendix F

Mortality Tables

Notice 2008-85 provides the static mortality tables that many pension plans will use to calculate their minimum funding obligations for 2009 through 2013 plan years. The Notice also includes a modified "unisex" version of the mortality tables to be used for calculating lump-sum distributions during that same period. The unisex mortality tables are shown below. [I.R.B. 2008-42, Oct. 20, 2008] Notice 2013-49 provides the static mortality tables that many pension plans will use to calculate their minimum funding obligations for 2014 through 2015 plan years. The Notice also includes a modified "unisex" version of the mortality tables to be used for calculating lump-sum distributions during that same period. The unisex mortality tables are shown below along with tables for 2016 and 2017. [I.R.B. 2013-32, Aug. 5, 2013]

The PBGC rates used in the calculation of liabilities for distress and involuntary plan terminations are shown below. The PBGC mortality tables used for the calculation of amounts due for missing participants are also shown below.

Age	2009	2010	2011	2012	2013	2014	2015
1	0.000372	0.000365	0.000358	0.000350	0.000343	0.000337	0.000329
2	0.000247	0.000242	0.000237	0.000233	0.000228	0.000223	0.000219
3	0.000196	0.000192	0.000188	0.000184	0.000181	0.000177	0.000174
4	0.000150	0.000147	0.000144	0.000141	0.000138	0.000136	0.000133
5	0.000137	0.000134	0.000131	0.000129	0.000126	0.000124	0.000121
6	0.000129	0.000127	0.000124	0.000122	0.000120	0.000117	0.000115
7	0.000123	0.000121	0.000118	0.000116	0.000114	0.000111	0.000109
8	0.000112	0.000110	0.000108	0.000105	0.000103	0.000101	0.000099
9	0.000108	0.000105	0.000104	0.000101	0.000100	0.000097	0.000095
10	0.000109	0.000107	0.000104	0.000103	0.000100	0.000098	0.000097
11	0.000112	0.000109	0.000108	0.000105	0.000103	0.000101	0.000099
12	0.000116	0.000114	0.000112	0.000109	0.000107	0.000105	0.000103
13	0.000122	0.000120	0.000117	0.000115	0.000112	0.000110	0.000108

Age	*2009*	*2010*	*2011*	*2012*	*2013*	*2014*	*2015*
14	0.000133	0.000130	0.000128	0.000125	0.000123	0.000121	0.000119
15	0.000143	0.000141	0.000138	0.000135	0.000133	0.000130	0.000128
16	0.000151	0.000149	0.000146	0.000144	0.000141	0.000139	0.000136
17	0.000161	0.000158	0.000156	0.000153	0.000150	0.000148	0.000145
18	0.000167	0.000164	0.000161	0.000158	0.000156	0.000153	0.000151
19	0.000171	0.000168	0.000165	0.000162	0.000159	0.000157	0.000154
20	0.000174	0.000171	0.000168	0.000165	0.000162	0.000159	0.000156
21	0.000179	0.000176	0.000173	0.000170	0.000167	0.000164	0.000161
22	0.000186	0.000182	0.000179	0.000176	0.000173	0.000171	0.000168
23	0.000197	0.000194	0.000191	0.000188	0.000185	0.000182	0.000179
24	0.000208	0.000205	0.000202	0.000199	0.000197	0.000194	0.000191
25	0.000222	0.000219	0.000217	0.000214	0.000212	0.000210	0.000207
26	0.000244	0.000242	0.000240	0.000238	0.000236	0.000234	0.000233
27	0.000253	0.000251	0.000249	0.000248	0.000246	0.000244	0.000242
28	0.000262	0.000261	0.000259	0.000257	0.000255	0.000253	0.000251
29	0.000276	0.000273	0.000272	0.000270	0.000268	0.000266	0.000264
30	0.000301	0.000299	0.000297	0.000295	0.000293	0.000291	0.000289
31	0.000348	0.000346	0.000344	0.000342	0.000340	0.000337	0.000335
32	0.000394	0.000391	0.000389	0.000387	0.000384	0.000382	0.000380
33	0.000438	0.000436	0.000433	0.000430	0.000427	0.000425	0.000422
34	0.000482	0.000479	0.000476	0.000473	0.000469	0.000466	0.000463
35	0.000525	0.000521	0.000518	0.000514	0.000510	0.000507	0.000503
36	0.000566	0.000561	0.000557	0.000553	0.000549	0.000545	0.000541
37	0.000604	0.000599	0.000594	0.000590	0.000585	0.000581	0.000576
38	0.000630	0.000625	0.000619	0.000614	0.000609	0.000604	0.000599
39	0.000657	0.000651	0.000644	0.000638	0.000632	0.000626	0.000620
40	0.000691	0.000684	0.000677	0.000669	0.000662	0.000655	0.000649
41	0.000729	0.000721	0.000713	0.000705	0.000697	0.000689	0.000682
42	0.000775	0.000765	0.000756	0.000747	0.000738	0.000730	0.000721
43	0.000826	0.000815	0.000805	0.000795	0.000785	0.000775	0.000765
44	0.000885	0.000873	0.000862	0.000850	0.000839	0.000828	0.000817
45	0.000940	0.000926	0.000913	0.000900	0.000887	0.000875	0.000862
46	0.000994	0.000980	0.000964	0.000950	0.000936	0.000921	0.000907
47	0.001054	0.001037	0.001021	0.001004	0.000987	0.000972	0.000956
48	0.001130	0.001112	0.001093	0.001074	0.001056	0.001038	0.001021
49	0.001215	0.001194	0.001173	0.001153	0.001133	0.001113	0.001094
50	0.001323	0.001300	0.001277	0.001254	0.001232	0.001211	0.001189

Age	2009	2010	2011	2012	2013	2014	2015
51	0.001423	0.001398	0.001373	0.001349	0.001325	0.001302	0.001279
52	0.001570	0.001543	0.001516	0.001490	0.001464	0.001440	0.001415
53	0.001764	0.001736	0.001707	0.001680	0.001653	0.001626	0.001600
54	0.001990	0.001959	0.001930	0.001901	0.001872	0.001844	0.001816
55	0.002346	0.002313	0.002282	0.002251	0.002220	0.002191	0.002161
56	0.002818	0.002783	0.002750	0.002716	0.002684	0.002651	0.002619
57	0.003243	0.003206	0.003171	0.003135	0.003101	0.003066	0.003033
58	0.003706	0.003666	0.003627	0.003588	0.003550	0.003513	0.003475
59	0.004206	0.004161	0.004116	0.004072	0.004029	0.003986	0.003944
60	0.004803	0.004752	0.004701	0.004651	0.004601	0.004553	0.004505
61	0.005576	0.005519	0.005462	0.005407	0.005352	0.005298	0.005244
62	0.006405	0.006339	0.006274	0.006211	0.006148	0.006085	0.006023
63	0.007444	0.007372	0.007300	0.007229	0.007158	0.007089	0.007021
64	0.008410	0.008328	0.008247	0.008167	0.008088	0.008009	0.007932
65	0.009508	0.009415	0.009324	0.009233	0.009143	0.009055	0.008967
66	0.010866	0.010766	0.010666	0.010567	0.010469	0.010373	0.010277
67	0.012108	0.011995	0.011884	0.011774	0.011665	0.011557	0.011451
68	0.013316	0.013185	0.013056	0.012928	0.012802	0.012678	0.012555
69	0.014742	0.014598	0.014455	0.014313	0.014174	0.014036	0.013900
70	0.016160	0.015993	0.015829	0.015666	0.015506	0.015347	0.015192
71	0.017803	0.017611	0.017422	0.017234	0.017049	0.016866	0.016686
72	0.019833	0.019619	0.019407	0.019199	0.018993	0.018790	0.018589
73	0.021968	0.021720	0.021476	0.021234	0.020995	0.020760	0.020527
74	0.024500	0.024223	0.023950	0.023680	0.023414	0.023151	0.022892
75	0.027315	0.027008	0.026703	0.026402	0.026105	0.025811	0.025522
76	0.030348	0.030005	0.029667	0.029332	0.029002	0.028675	0.028352
77	0.034204	0.033851	0.033502	0.033157	0.032815	0.032478	0.032144
78	0.038256	0.037881	0.037510	0.037143	0.036779	0.036420	0.036064
79	0.042806	0.042409	0.042016	0.041627	0.041242	0.040860	0.040483
80	0.047905	0.047487	0.047073	0.046663	0.046257	0.045854	0.045454
81	0.053861	0.053421	0.052986	0.052553	0.052125	0.051700	0.051278
82	0.060545	0.060085	0.059630	0.059177	0.058729	0.058283	0.057841
83	0.067380	0.066869	0.066362	0.065858	0.065358	0.064863	0.064371
84	0.075650	0.075120	0.074594	0.074072	0.073553	0.073039	0.072527
85	0.084660	0.084103	0.083549	0.082999	0.082452	0.081909	0.081370
86	0.094731	0.094148	0.093568	0.092992	0.092420	0.091851	0.091285
87	0.106954	0.106403	0.105854	0.105309	0.104766	0.104226	0.103690

Age	2009	2010	2011	2012	2013	2014	2015
88	0.119811	0.119262	0.118716	0.118173	0.117631	0.117093	0.116557
89	0.133578	0.133024	0.132472	0.131923	0.131375	0.130831	0.130289
90	0.148759	0.148226	0.147696	0.147168	0.146641	0.146117	0.145594
91	0.162589	0.162008	0.161428	0.160851	0.160276	0.159703	0.159132
92	0.178330	0.177795	0.177261	0.176729	0.176200	0.175671	0.175144
93	0.193878	0.193379	0.192881	0.192385	0.191890	0.191396	0.190903
94	0.207982	0.207446	0.206912	0.206380	0.205848	0.205319	0.204791
95	0.223718	0.223270	0.222824	0.222378	0.221934	0.221490	0.221047
96	0.236930	0.236456	0.235983	0.235511	0.235040	0.234570	0.234101
97	0.251111	0.250715	0.250319	0.249924	0.249530	0.249136	0.248743
98	0.265340	0.265075	0.264810	0.264545	0.264280	0.264016	0.263752
99	0.276338	0.276062	0.275786	0.275510	0.275234	0.274959	0.274684
100	0.286390	0.286104	0.285818	0.285532	0.285247	0.284961	0.284676
101	0.301731	0.301731	0.301731	0.301731	0.301731	0.301731	0.301731
102	0.313092	0.313092	0.313092	0.313092	0.313092	0.313092	0.313092
103	0.324542	0.324542	0.324542	0.324542	0.324542	0.324542	0.324542
104	0.335529	0.335529	0.335529	0.335529	0.335529	0.335529	0.335529
105	0.345501	0.345501	0.345501	0.345501	0.345501	0.345501	0.345501
106	0.353906	0.353906	0.353906	0.353906	0.353906	0.353906	0.353906
107	0.361363	0.361363	0.361363	0.361363	0.361363	0.361363	0.361363
108	0.368721	0.368721	0.368721	0.368721	0.368721	0.368721	0.368721
109	0.375772	0.375772	0.375772	0.375772	0.375772	0.375772	0.375772
110	0.382309	0.382309	0.382309	0.382309	0.382309	0.382309	0.382309
111	0.388123	0.388123	0.388123	0.388123	0.388123	0.388123	0.388123
112	0.393008	0.393008	0.393008	0.393008	0.393008	0.393008	0.393008
113	0.396754	0.396754	0.396754	0.396754	0.396754	0.396754	0.396754
114	0.399154	0.399154	0.399154	0.399154	0.399154	0.399154	0.399154
115	0.400000	0.400000	0.400000	0.400000	0.400000	0.400000	0.400000
116	0.400000	0.400000	0.400000	0.400000	0.400000	0.400000	0.400000
117	0.400000	0.400000	0.400000	0.400000	0.400000	0.400000	0.400000
118	0.400000	0.400000	0.400000	0.400000	0.400000	0.400000	0.400000
119	0.400000	0.400000	0.400000	0.400000	0.400000	0.400000	0.400000
120	1.000000	1.000000	1.000000	1.000000	1.000000	1.000000	1.000000

Age	*2016*	*2017*
1	0.000323	0.000317
2	0.000215	0.000210
3	0.000170	0.000167
4	0.000130	0.000128
5	0.000119	0.000116
6	0.000112	0.000110
7	0.000107	0.000105
8	0.000097	0.000095
9	0.000094	0.000091
10	0.000094	0.000093
11	0.000097	0.000095
12	0.000101	0.000099
13	0.000106	0.000104
14	0.000116	0.000114
15	0.000126	0.000124
16	0.000134	0.000132
17	0.000143	0.000140
18	0.000148	0.000146
19	0.000151	0.000148
20	0.000153	0.000151
21	0.000158	0.000156
22	0.000165	0.000162
23	0.000176	0.000174
24	0.000189	0.000186
25	0.000205	0.000203
26	0.000231	0.000229
27	0.000240	0.000239
28	0.000249	0.000248
29	0.000262	0.000260
30	0.000287	0.000285
31	0.000333	0.000331
32	0.000377	0.000375
33	0.000419	0.000416
34	0.000460	0.000457
35	0.000500	0.000496
36	0.000537	0.000533
37	0.000572	0.000567

Age	*2016*	*2017*
38	0.000593	0.000588
39	0.000614	0.000608
40	0.000642	0.000635
41	0.000674	0.000666
42	0.000712	0.000704
43	0.000756	0.000747
44	0.000806	0.000795
45	0.000850	0.000838
46	0.000893	0.000880
47	0.000940	0.000925
48	0.001004	0.000987
49	0.001075	0.001056
50	0.001168	0.001148
51	0.001256	0.001234
52	0.001391	0.001366
53	0.001574	0.001549
54	0.001789	0.001762
55	0.002131	0.002103
56	0.002588	0.002557
57	0.002999	0.002967
58	0.003438	0.003402
59	0.003903	0.003861
60	0.004457	0.004410
61	0.005191	0.005139
62	0.005963	0.005902
63	0.006953	0.006886
64	0.007855	0.007780
65	0.008880	0.008795
66	0.010183	0.010089
67	0.011345	0.011241
68	0.012433	0.012313
69	0.013765	0.013631
70	0.015037	0.014884
71	0.016507	0.016331
72	0.018391	0.018195
73	0.020297	0.020071
74	0.022635	0.022382
75	0.025235	0.024952

Age	*2016*	*2017*
76	0.028033	0.027718
77	0.031814	0.031488
78	0.035712	0.035363
79	0.040109	0.039738
80	0.045059	0.044667
81	0.050860	0.050446
82	0.057403	0.056967
83	0.063883	0.063398
84	0.072020	0.071516
85	0.080834	0.080302
86	0.090724	0.090166
87	0.103156	0.102625
88	0.116023	0.115492
89	0.129748	0.129211
90	0.145074	0.144554
91	0.158563	0.157996
92	0.174618	0.174095
93	0.190412	0.189922
94	0.204264	0.203738
95	0.220605	0.220163
96	0.233633	0.233165
97	0.248351	0.247959
98	0.263488	0.263225
99	0.274409	0.274135
100	0.284392	0.284107
101	0.301731	0.301731
102	0.313092	0.313092
103	0.324542	0.324542
104	0.335529	0.335529
105	0.345501	0.345501
106	0.353906	0.353906
107	0.361363	0.361363
108	0.368721	0.368721
109	0.375772	0.375772
110	0.382309	0.382309
111	0.388123	0.388123
112	0.393008	0.393008

Age	*2016*	*2017*
113	0.396754	0.396754
114	0.399154	0.399154
115	0.400000	0.400000
116	0.400000	0.400000
117	0.400000	0.400000
118	0.400000	0.400000
119	0.400000	0.400000
120	1.000000	1.000000

PBGC Mortality Tables for Distress and Involuntary Plan Terminations

These mortality tables are used to determine the present value of annuities in involuntary terminations and distress terminations of single-employer plans in 2014 through 2017, as discussed in PBGC Regulations Section 4044:

Mortality Rates for Year 2014 Valuation Dates Under Section 4044

Age	*Healthy Male*	*Healthy Female*	*SS-Disabled Male*	*SS-Disabled Female*	*Non-SS Disabled Male*	*Non-SS Disabled Female*
15	0.000209	0.000144	0.022010	0.007777	0.000278	0.000192
16	0.000237	0.000166	0.022502	0.008120	0.000293	0.000191
17	0.000260	0.000184	0.023001	0.008476	0.000307	0.000188
18	0.000278	0.000192	0.023519	0.008852	0.000331	0.000184
19	0.000293	0.000191	0.024045	0.009243	0.000358	0.000186
20	0.000307	0.000188	0.024583	0.009650	0.000402	0.000193
21	0.000331	0.000184	0.025133	0.010076	0.000453	0.000199
22	0.000358	0.000186	0.025697	0.010521	0.000526	0.000205
23	0.000402	0.000193	0.026269	0.010984	0.000625	0.000220
24	0.000453	0.000199	0.026857	0.011468	0.000673	0.000226
25	0.000526	0.000205	0.027457	0.011974	0.000698	0.000235
26	0.000625	0.000220	0.028071	0.012502	0.000721	0.000248
27	0.000673	0.000226	0.028704	0.013057	0.000742	0.000279
28	0.000698	0.000235	0.029345	0.013632	0.000760	0.000315
29	0.000721	0.000248	0.029999	0.014229	0.000776	0.000336
30	0.000742	0.000279	0.030661	0.014843	0.000785	0.000346
31	0.000760	0.000315	0.031331	0.015473	0.000786	0.000357
32	0.000776	0.000336	0.032006	0.016103	0.000787	0.000369

Mortality Rates for Year 2014 Valuation Dates Under Section 4044 *(cont'd)*

Age	*Healthy Male*	*Healthy Female*	*SS-Disabled Male*	*SS-Disabled Female*	*Non-SS Disabled Male*	*Non-SS Disabled Female*
33	0.000785	0.000346	0.032689	0.016604	0.000798	0.000383
34	0.000786	0.000357	0.033405	0.017121	0.000824	0.000400
35	0.000787	0.000369	0.034184	0.017654	0.000843	0.000421
36	0.000798	0.000383	0.034981	0.018204	0.000871	0.000445
37	0.000824	0.000400	0.035796	0.018770	0.000906	0.000485
38	0.000843	0.000421	0.036634	0.019355	0.000948	0.000525
39	0.000871	0.000445	0.037493	0.019957	0.000996	0.000564
40	0.000906	0.000485	0.038373	0.020579	0.001043	0.000599
41	0.000948	0.000525	0.039272	0.021219	0.001092	0.000630
42	0.000996	0.000564	0.040189	0.021880	0.001146	0.000645
43	0.001043	0.000599	0.041122	0.022561	0.001213	0.000664
44	0.001092	0.000630	0.042071	0.023263	0.001298	0.000694
45	0.001146	0.000645	0.043033	0.023988	0.001393	0.000752
46	0.001213	0.000664	0.044007	0.024734	0.001495	0.000816
47	0.001298	0.000694	0.044993	0.025504	0.001608	0.000918
48	0.001393	0.000752	0.045989	0.026298	0.001737	0.001039
49	0.001495	0.000816	0.046993	0.027117	0.001885	0.001221
50	0.001608	0.000918	0.048004	0.027961	0.002102	0.001428
51	0.001737	0.001039	0.049021	0.028832	0.002334	0.001658
52	0.001885	0.001221	0.050042	0.029730	0.002676	0.001938
53	0.002102	0.001428	0.051067	0.030655	0.003086	0.002300
54	0.002334	0.001658	0.052093	0.031609	0.003588	0.002701
55	0.002676	0.001938	0.053120	0.032594	0.004175	0.003108
56	0.003086	0.002300	0.054144	0.033608	0.004699	0.003574
57	0.003588	0.002701	0.055089	0.034655	0.005286	0.004107
58	0.004175	0.003108	0.056068	0.035733	0.006140	0.004711
59	0.004699	0.003574	0.057080	0.036846	0.006933	0.005395
60	0.005286	0.004107	0.058118	0.037993	0.008081	0.006177
61	0.006140	0.004711	0.059172	0.039176	0.009115	0.007050
62	0.006933	0.005395	0.060232	0.040395	0.010239	0.007990
63	0.008081	0.006177	0.061303	0.041653	0.011793	0.008968
64	0.009115	0.007050	0.062429	0.042950	0.013095	0.009958
65	0.010239	0.007990	0.063669	0.044287	0.013989	0.010882
66	0.011793	0.008968	0.065082	0.045666	0.015306	0.011757

Mortality Rates for Year 2014 Valuation Dates Under Section 4044 *(cont'd)*

Age	*Healthy Male*	*Healthy Female*	*SS-Disabled Male*	*SS-Disabled Female*	*Non-SS Disabled Male*	*Non-SS Disabled Female*
67	0.013095	0.009958	0.066724	0.046828	0.016214	0.012702
68	0.013989	0.010882	0.068642	0.048070	0.017732	0.013423
69	0.015306	0.011757	0.070834	0.049584	0.019461	0.014816
70	0.016214	0.012702	0.073284	0.051331	0.021319	0.015976
71	0.017732	0.013423	0.075979	0.053268	0.023267	0.017751
72	0.019461	0.014816	0.078903	0.055356	0.026212	0.019170
73	0.021319	0.015976	0.082070	0.057573	0.028780	0.021400
74	0.023267	0.017751	0.085606	0.059979	0.032801	0.024705
75	0.026212	0.019170	0.088918	0.062574	0.037586	0.027633
76	0.028780	0.021400	0.092208	0.065480	0.043104	0.030799
77	0.032801	0.024705	0.095625	0.068690	0.049335	0.034312
78	0.037586	0.027633	0.099216	0.072237	0.056253	0.038280
79	0.043104	0.030799	0.103030	0.076156	0.063826	0.042810
80	0.049335	0.034312	0.107113	0.080480	0.069723	0.047778
81	0.056253	0.038280	0.111515	0.085243	0.078049	0.053110
82	0.063826	0.042810	0.116283	0.090480	0.084691	0.060805
83	0.069723	0.047778	0.121464	0.096224	0.092140	0.069707
84	0.078049	0.053110	0.127108	0.102508	0.103832	0.080112
85	0.084691	0.060805	0.133262	0.109368	0.117474	0.089453
86	0.092140	0.069707	0.139974	0.116837	0.129014	0.102773
87	0.103832	0.080112	0.147292	0.124948	0.145812	0.114241
88	0.117474	0.089453	0.155265	0.133736	0.155265	0.126509
89	0.129014	0.102773	0.163939	0.143234	0.163939	0.139502
90	0.145812	0.114241	0.173363	0.153477	0.173363	0.153477
91	0.159473	0.126509	0.183585	0.164498	0.183585	0.164498
92	0.179107	0.139502	0.194653	0.176332	0.194653	0.176332
93	0.194938	0.157894	0.206615	0.189011	0.206615	0.189011
94	0.211945	0.172826	0.219519	0.202571	0.219519	0.202571
95	0.236547	0.188557	0.234086	0.217045	0.234086	0.217045
96	0.254676	0.205088	0.248436	0.232467	0.248436	0.232467
97	0.272199	0.229204	0.263954	0.248870	0.263954	0.248870
98	0.297680	0.248047	0.280803	0.266289	0.280803	0.266289
99	0.314396	0.267873	0.299154	0.284758	0.299154	0.284758
100	0.331030	0.288444	0.319185	0.303433	0.319185	0.303433

Mortality Rates for Year 2014 Valuation Dates Under Section 4044 *(cont'd)*

Age	*Healthy Male*	*Healthy Female*	*SS-Disabled Male*	*SS-Disabled Female*	*Non-SS Disabled Male*	*Non-SS Disabled Female*
101	0.358560	0.318956	0.341086	0.327385	0.341086	0.327385
102	0.376699	0.340960	0.365052	0.359020	0.365052	0.359020
103	0.396884	0.364586	0.393102	0.395842	0.393102	0.395842
104	0.418855	0.389996	0.427255	0.438360	0.427255	0.438360
105	0.440585	0.415180	0.469531	0.487816	0.469531	0.471493
106	0.460043	0.438126	0.521945	0.545886	0.492807	0.483473
107	0.475200	0.456824	0.586518	0.614309	0.497189	0.492436
108	0.485670	0.471493	0.665268	0.694884	0.499394	0.498054
109	0.492807	0.483473	0.760215	0.789474	0.500000	0.500000
110	0.497189	0.492436	1.000000	1.000000	0.500000	0.500000
111	0.499394	0.498054			0.500000	0.500000
112	0.500000	0.500000			0.500000	0.500000
113	0.500000	0.500000			0.500000	0.500000
114	0.500000	0.500000			0.500000	0.500000
115	0.500000	0.500000			0.500000	0.500000
116	0.500000	0.500000			0.500000	0.500000
117	0.500000	0.500000			1.000000	1.000000
118	0.500000	0.500000				
119	0.500000	0.500000				
120	1.000000	1.000000				

Mortality Rates for Year 2015 Valuation Dates Under Section 4044

Age	*Healthy Male*	*Healthy Female*	*SS-Disabled Male*	*SS-Disabled Female*	*Non-SS Disabled Male*	*Non-SS Disabled Female*
15	0.000205	0.000141	0.022010	0.007777	0.000273	0.000189
16	0.000232	0.000163	0.022502	0.008120	0.000287	0.000188
17	0.000255	0.000182	0.023001	0.008476	0.000301	0.000185
18	0.000273	0.000189	0.023519	0.008852	0.000325	0.000181
19	0.000287	0.000188	0.024045	0.009243	0.000351	0.000183
20	0.000301	0.000185	0.024583	0.009650	0.000396	0.000190
21	0.000325	0.000181	0.025133	0.010076	0.000447	0.000196
22	0.000351	0.000183	0.025697	0.010521	0.000521	0.000202

Mortality Rates for Year 2015 Valuation Dates Under Section 4044 *(cont'd)*

Age	*Healthy Male*	*Healthy Female*	*SS-Disabled Male*	*SS-Disabled Female*	*Non-SS Disabled Male*	*Non-SS Disabled Female*
23	0.000396	0.000190	0.026269	0.010984	0.000622	0.000217
24	0.000447	0.000196	0.026857	0.011468	0.000669	0.000223
25	0.000521	0.000202	0.027457	0.011974	0.000694	0.000232
26	0.000622	0.000217	0.028071	0.012502	0.000717	0.000245
27	0.000669	0.000223	0.028704	0.013057	0.000738	0.000276
28	0.000694	0.000232	0.029345	0.013632	0.000756	0.000313
29	0.000717	0.000245	0.029999	0.014229	0.000772	0.000333
30	0.000738	0.000276	0.030661	0.014843	0.000781	0.000343
31	0.000756	0.000313	0.031331	0.015473	0.000782	0.000353
32	0.000772	0.000333	0.032006	0.016103	0.000783	0.000365
33	0.000781	0.000343	0.032689	0.016604	0.000794	0.000378
34	0.000782	0.000353	0.033405	0.017121	0.000820	0.000395
35	0.000783	0.000365	0.034184	0.017654	0.000838	0.000415
36	0.000794	0.000378	0.034981	0.018204	0.000865	0.000439
37	0.000820	0.000395	0.035796	0.018770	0.000899	0.000478
38	0.000838	0.000415	0.036634	0.019355	0.000939	0.000517
39	0.000865	0.000439	0.037493	0.019957	0.000986	0.000556
40	0.000899	0.000478	0.038373	0.020579	0.001032	0.000590
41	0.000939	0.000517	0.039272	0.021219	0.001078	0.000621
42	0.000986	0.000556	0.040189	0.021880	0.001131	0.000634
43	0.001032	0.000590	0.041122	0.022561	0.001196	0.000653
44	0.001078	0.000621	0.042071	0.023263	0.001278	0.000681
45	0.001131	0.000634	0.043033	0.023988	0.001371	0.000739
46	0.001196	0.000653	0.044007	0.024734	0.001470	0.000802
47	0.001278	0.000681	0.044993	0.025504	0.001579	0.000903
48	0.001371	0.000739	0.045989	0.026298	0.001704	0.001023
49	0.001470	0.000802	0.046993	0.027117	0.001847	0.001204
50	0.001579	0.000903	0.048004	0.027961	0.002060	0.001411
51	0.001704	0.001023	0.049021	0.028832	0.002287	0.001641
52	0.001847	0.001204	0.050042	0.029730	0.002625	0.001922
53	0.002060	0.001411	0.051067	0.030655	0.003031	0.002286
54	0.002287	0.001641	0.052093	0.031609	0.003527	0.002687
55	0.002625	0.001922	0.053120	0.032594	0.004109	0.003092

Mortality Rates for Year 2015 Valuation Dates Under Section 4044 *(cont'd)*

Age	*Healthy Male*	*Healthy Female*	*SS-Disabled Male*	*SS-Disabled Female*	*Non-SS Disabled Male*	*Non-SS Disabled Female*
56	0.003031	0.002286	0.054144	0.033608	0.004624	0.003556
57	0.003527	0.002687	0.055089	0.034655	0.005202	0.004086
58	0.004109	0.003092	0.056068	0.035733	0.006048	0.004688
59	0.004624	0.003556	0.057080	0.036846	0.006829	0.005368
60	0.005202	0.004086	0.058118	0.037993	0.007968	0.006146
61	0.006048	0.004688	0.059172	0.039176	0.008987	0.007015
62	0.006829	0.005368	0.060232	0.040395	0.010095	0.007950
63	0.007968	0.006146	0.061303	0.041653	0.011639	0.008923
64	0.008987	0.007015	0.062429	0.042950	0.012925	0.009908
65	0.010095	0.007950	0.063669	0.044287	0.013793	0.010828
66	0.011639	0.008923	0.065082	0.045666	0.015091	0.011698
67	0.012925	0.009908	0.066724	0.046828	0.015971	0.012638
68	0.013793	0.010828	0.068642	0.048070	0.017466	0.013342
69	0.015091	0.011698	0.070834	0.049584	0.019169	0.014727
70	0.015971	0.012638	0.073284	0.051331	0.020999	0.015864
71	0.017466	0.013342	0.075979	0.053268	0.022918	0.017627
72	0.019169	0.014727	0.078903	0.055356	0.025845	0.019016
73	0.020999	0.015864	0.082070	0.057573	0.028378	0.021229
74	0.022918	0.017627	0.085606	0.059979	0.032374	0.024532
75	0.025845	0.019016	0.088918	0.062574	0.037135	0.027439
76	0.028378	0.021229	0.092208	0.065480	0.042630	0.030583
77	0.032374	0.024532	0.095625	0.068690	0.048842	0.034072
78	0.037135	0.027439	0.099216	0.072237	0.055747	0.038012
79	0.042630	0.030583	0.103030	0.076156	0.063315	0.042511
80	0.048842	0.034072	0.107113	0.080480	0.069165	0.047443
81	0.055747	0.038012	0.111515	0.085243	0.077502	0.052738
82	0.063315	0.042511	0.116283	0.090480	0.084098	0.060440
83	0.069165	0.047443	0.121464	0.096224	0.091495	0.069358
84	0.077502	0.052738	0.127108	0.102508	0.103209	0.079792
85	0.084098	0.060440	0.133262	0.109368	0.116887	0.089095
86	0.091495	0.069358	0.139974	0.116837	0.128369	0.102465
87	0.103209	0.079792	0.147292	0.124948	0.145229	0.113898
88	0.116887	0.089095	0.155265	0.133736	0.155265	0.126130
89	0.128369	0.102465	0.163939	0.143234	0.163939	0.139083

Mortality Rates for Year 2015 Valuation Dates Under Section 4044 *(cont'd)*

Age	*Healthy Male*	*Healthy Female*	*SS-Disabled Male*	*SS-Disabled Female*	*Non-SS Disabled Male*	*Non-SS Disabled Female*
90	0.145229	0.113898	0.173363	0.153477	0.173363	0.153477
91	0.158835	0.126130	0.183585	0.164498	0.183585	0.164498
92	0.178570	0.139083	0.194653	0.176332	0.194653	0.176332
93	0.194353	0.157579	0.206615	0.189011	0.206615	0.189011
94	0.211309	0.172480	0.219519	0.202571	0.219519	0.202571
95	0.236074	0.188180	0.234086	0.217045	0.234086	0.217045
96	0.254167	0.204678	0.248436	0.232467	0.248436	0.232467
97	0.271654	0.228975	0.263954	0.248870	0.263954	0.248870
98	0.297382	0.247799	0.280803	0.266289	0.280803	0.266289
99	0.314082	0.267605	0.299154	0.284758	0.299154	0.284758
100	0.330699	0.288156	0.319185	0.303433	0.319185	0.303433
101	0.358560	0.318956	0.341086	0.327385	0.341086	0.327385
102	0.376699	0.340960	0.365052	0.359020	0.365052	0.359020
103	0.396884	0.364586	0.393102	0.395842	0.393102	0.395842
104	0.418855	0.389996	0.427255	0.438360	0.427255	0.438360
105	0.440585	0.415180	0.469531	0.487816	0.469531	0.471493
106	0.460043	0.438126	0.521945	0.545886	0.492807	0.483473
107	0.475200	0.456824	0.586518	0.614309	0.497189	0.492436
108	0.485670	0.471493	0.665268	0.694884	0.499394	0.498054
109	0.492807	0.483473	0.760215	0.789474	0.500000	0.500000
110	0.497189	0.492436	1.000000	1.000000	0.500000	0.500000
111	0.499394	0.498054			0.500000	0.500000
112	0.500000	0.500000			0.500000	0.500000
113	0.500000	0.500000			0.500000	0.500000
114	0.500000	0.500000			0.500000	0.500000
115	0.500000	0.500000			0.500000	0.500000
116	0.500000	0.500000			0.500000	0.500000
117	0.500000	0.500000			1.000000	1.000000
118	0.500000	0.500000				
119	0.500000	0.500000				
120	1.000000	1.000000				

Mortality Rates for Year 2016 Valuation Dates Under Section 4044

Age	*Healthy Male*	*Healthy Female*	*SS-Disabled Male*	*SS-Disabled Female*	*Non-SS Disabled Male*	*Non-SS Disabled Female*
15	0.000201	0.000139	0.022010	0.007777	0.000268	0.000187
16	0.000228	0.000161	0.022502	0.008120	0.000282	0.000186
17	0.000251	0.000179	0.023001	0.008476	0.000295	0.000182
18	0.000268	0.000187	0.023519	0.008852	0.000319	0.000178
19	0.000282	0.000186	0.024045	0.009243	0.000345	0.000180
20	0.000295	0.000182	0.024583	0.009650	0.000390	0.000187
21	0.000319	0.000178	0.025133	0.010076	0.000441	0.000193
22	0.000345	0.000180	0.025697	0.010521	0.000515	0.000199
23	0.000390	0.000187	0.026269	0.010984	0.000618	0.000215
24	0.000441	0.000193	0.026857	0.011468	0.000666	0.000220
25	0.000515	0.000199	0.027457	0.011974	0.000691	0.000230
26	0.000618	0.000215	0.028071	0.012502	0.000714	0.000242
27	0.000666	0.000220	0.028704	0.013057	0.000734	0.000273
28	0.000691	0.000230	0.029345	0.013632	0.000752	0.000310
29	0.000714	0.000242	0.029999	0.014229	0.000768	0.000330
30	0.000734	0.000273	0.030661	0.014843	0.000777	0.000340
31	0.000752	0.000310	0.031331	0.015473	0.000778	0.000349
32	0.000768	0.000330	0.032006	0.016103	0.000779	0.000361
33	0.000777	0.000340	0.032689	0.016604	0.000790	0.000374
34	0.000778	0.000349	0.033405	0.017121	0.000816	0.000390
35	0.000779	0.000361	0.034184	0.017654	0.000833	0.000410
36	0.000790	0.000374	0.034981	0.018204	0.000859	0.000432
37	0.000816	0.000390	0.035796	0.018770	0.000892	0.000470
38	0.000833	0.000410	0.036634	0.019355	0.000931	0.000509
39	0.000859	0.000432	0.037493	0.019957	0.000976	0.000547
40	0.000892	0.000470	0.038373	0.020579	0.001021	0.000581
41	0.000931	0.000509	0.039272	0.021219	0.001066	0.000612
42	0.000976	0.000547	0.040189	0.021880	0.001116	0.000624
43	0.001021	0.000581	0.041122	0.022561	0.001180	0.000642
44	0.001066	0.000612	0.042071	0.023263	0.001259	0.000669
45	0.001116	0.000624	0.043033	0.023988	0.001349	0.000725
46	0.001180	0.000642	0.044007	0.024734	0.001445	0.000787
47	0.001259	0.000669	0.044993	0.025504	0.001551	0.000887
48	0.001349	0.000725	0.045989	0.026298	0.001671	0.001006

Mortality Rates for Year 2016 Valuation Dates Under Section 4044 *(cont'd)*

Age	*Healthy Male*	*Healthy Female*	*SS-Disabled Male*	*SS-Disabled Female*	*Non-SS Disabled Male*	*Non-SS Disabled Female*
49	0.001445	0.000787	0.046993	0.027117	0.001810	0.001187
50	0.001551	0.000887	0.048004	0.027961	0.002019	0.001394
51	0.001671	0.001006	0.049021	0.028832	0.002241	0.001625
52	0.001810	0.001187	0.050042	0.029730	0.002575	0.001907
53	0.002019	0.001394	0.051067	0.030655	0.002976	0.002272
54	0.002241	0.001625	0.052093	0.031609	0.003467	0.002674
55	0.002575	0.001907	0.053120	0.032594	0.004043	0.003077
56	0.002976	0.002272	0.054144	0.033608	0.004550	0.003538
57	0.003467	0.002674	0.055089	0.034655	0.005118	0.004066
58	0.004043	0.003077	0.056068	0.035733	0.005958	0.004664
59	0.004550	0.003538	0.057080	0.036846	0.006727	0.005342
60	0.005118	0.004066	0.058118	0.037993	0.007856	0.006115
61	0.005958	0.004664	0.059172	0.039176	0.008862	0.006980
62	0.006727	0.005342	0.060232	0.040395	0.009954	0.007910
63	0.007856	0.006115	0.061303	0.041653	0.011488	0.008878
64	0.008862	0.006980	0.062429	0.042950	0.012757	0.009859
65	0.009954	0.007910	0.063669	0.044287	0.013600	0.010774
66	0.011488	0.008878	0.065082	0.045666	0.014880	0.011640
67	0.012757	0.009859	0.066724	0.046828	0.015732	0.012575
68	0.013600	0.010774	0.068642	0.048070	0.017204	0.013262
69	0.014880	0.011640	0.070834	0.049584	0.018881	0.014639
70	0.015732	0.012575	0.073284	0.051331	0.020684	0.015753
71	0.017204	0.013262	0.075979	0.053268	0.022574	0.017503
72	0.018881	0.014639	0.078903	0.055356	0.025483	0.018864
73	0.020684	0.015753	0.082070	0.057573	0.027980	0.021059
74	0.022574	0.017503	0.085606	0.059979	0.031953	0.024361
75	0.025483	0.018864	0.088918	0.062574	0.036690	0.027247
76	0.027980	0.021059	0.092208	0.065480	0.042161	0.030369
77	0.031953	0.024361	0.095625	0.068690	0.048353	0.033833
78	0.036690	0.027247	0.099216	0.072237	0.055245	0.037746
79	0.042161	0.030369	0.103030	0.076156	0.062809	0.042213
80	0.048353	0.033833	0.107113	0.080480	0.068612	0.047111
81	0.055245	0.037746	0.111515	0.085243	0.076960	0.052369

Mortality Rates for Year 2016 Valuation Dates Under Section 4044 *(cont'd)*

Age	*Healthy Male*	*Healthy Female*	*SS-Disabled Male*	*SS-Disabled Female*	*Non-SS Disabled Male*	*Non-SS Disabled Female*
82	0.062809	0.042213	0.116283	0.090480	0.083510	0.060077
83	0.068612	0.047111	0.121464	0.096224	0.090855	0.069011
84	0.076960	0.052369	0.127108	0.102508	0.102590	0.079473
85	0.083510	0.060077	0.133262	0.109368	0.116302	0.088739
86	0.090855	0.069011	0.139974	0.116837	0.127727	0.102157
87	0.102590	0.079473	0.147292	0.124948	0.144648	0.113556
88	0.116302	0.088739	0.155265	0.133736	0.155265	0.125751
89	0.127727	0.102157	0.163939	0.143234	0.163939	0.138666
90	0.144648	0.113556	0.173363	0.153477	0.173363	0.153477
91	0.158200	0.125751	0.183585	0.164498	0.183585	0.164498
92	0.178034	0.138666	0.194653	0.176332	0.194653	0.176332
93	0.193770	0.157263	0.206615	0.189011	0.206615	0.189011
94	0.210675	0.172135	0.219519	0.202571	0.219519	0.202571
95	0.235601	0.187804	0.234086	0.217045	0.234086	0.217045
96	0.253659	0.204268	0.248436	0.232467	0.248436	0.232467
97	0.271111	0.228746	0.263954	0.248870	0.263954	0.248870
98	0.297085	0.247551	0.280803	0.266289	0.280803	0.266289
99	0.313768	0.267337	0.299154	0.284758	0.299154	0.284758
100	0.330368	0.287868	0.319185	0.303433	0.319185	0.303433
101	0.358560	0.318956	0.341086	0.327385	0.341086	0.327385
102	0.376699	0.340960	0.365052	0.359020	0.365052	0.359020
103	0.396884	0.364586	0.393102	0.395842	0.393102	0.395842
104	0.418855	0.389996	0.427255	0.438360	0.427255	0.438360
105	0.440585	0.415180	0.469531	0.487816	0.469531	0.471493
106	0.460043	0.438126	0.521945	0.545886	0.492807	0.483473
107	0.475200	0.456824	0.586518	0.614309	0.497189	0.492436
108	0.485670	0.471493	0.665268	0.694884	0.499394	0.498054
109	0.492807	0.483473	0.760215	0.789474	0.500000	0.500000
110	0.497189	0.492436	1.000000	1.000000	0.500000	0.500000
111	0.499394	0.498054			0.500000	0.500000
112	0.500000	0.500000			0.500000	0.500000
113	0.500000	0.500000			0.500000	0.500000
114	0.500000	0.500000			0.500000	0.500000

Mortality Rates for Year 2016 Valuation Dates Under Section 4044 *(cont'd)*

Age	*Healthy Male*	*Healthy Female*	*SS-Disabled Male*	*SS-Disabled Female*	*Non-SS Disabled Male*	*Non-SS Disabled Female*
115	0.500000	0.500000			0.500000	0.500000
116	0.500000	0.500000			0.500000	0.500000
117	0.500000	0.500000			1.000000	1.000000
118	0.500000	0.500000				
119	0.500000	0.500000				
120	1.000000	1.000000				

Mortality Rates for Year 2017 Valuation Dates Under Section 4044

Age	*Healthy Male*	*Healthy Female*	*SS-Disabled Male*	*SS-Disabled Female*	*Non-SS Disabled Male*	*Non-SS Disabled Female*
15	0.000197	0.000137	0.022010	0.007777	0.000263	0.000184
16	0.000224	0.000159	0.022502	0.008120	0.000277	0.000183
17	0.000246	0.000176	0.023001	0.008476	0.000289	0.000179
18	0.000263	0.000184	0.023519	0.008852	0.000313	0.000175
19	0.000277	0.000183	0.024045	0.009243	0.000340	0.000177
20	0.000289	0.000179	0.024583	0.009650	0.000384	0.000184
21	0.000313	0.000175	0.025133	0.010076	0.000436	0.000190
22	0.000340	0.000177	0.025697	0.010521	0.000510	0.000197
23	0.000384	0.000184	0.026269	0.010984	0.000614	0.000212
24	0.000436	0.000190	0.026857	0.011468	0.000663	0.000218
25	0.000510	0.000197	0.027457	0.011974	0.000687	0.000227
26	0.000614	0.000212	0.028071	0.012502	0.000710	0.000239
27	0.000663	0.000218	0.028704	0.013057	0.000731	0.000271
28	0.000687	0.000227	0.029345	0.013632	0.000748	0.000308
29	0.000710	0.000239	0.029999	0.014229	0.000764	0.000328
30	0.000731	0.000271	0.030661	0.014843	0.000773	0.000337
31	0.000748	0.000308	0.031331	0.015473	0.000774	0.000346
32	0.000764	0.000328	0.032006	0.016103	0.000776	0.000357
33	0.000773	0.000337	0.032689	0.016604	0.000786	0.000369
34	0.000774	0.000346	0.033405	0.017121	0.000812	0.000385
35	0.000776	0.000357	0.034184	0.017654	0.000828	0.000404
36	0.000786	0.000369	0.034981	0.018204	0.000853	0.000426

Mortality Rates for Year 2016 Valuation Dates Under Section 4044 *(cont'd)*

Age	*Healthy Male*	*Healthy Female*	*SS-Disabled Male*	*SS-Disabled Female*	*Non-SS Disabled Male*	*Non-SS Disabled Female*
37	0.000812	0.000385	0.035796	0.018770	0.000885	0.000463
38	0.000828	0.000404	0.036634	0.019355	0.000922	0.000502
39	0.000853	0.000426	0.037493	0.019957	0.000966	0.000539
40	0.000885	0.000463	0.038373	0.020579	0.001009	0.000573
41	0.000922	0.000502	0.039272	0.021219	0.001053	0.000602
42	0.000966	0.000539	0.040189	0.021880	0.001102	0.000614
43	0.001009	0.000573	0.041122	0.022561	0.001163	0.000631
44	0.001053	0.000602	0.042071	0.023263	0.001240	0.000657
45	0.001102	0.000614	0.043033	0.023988	0.001327	0.000712
46	0.001163	0.000631	0.044007	0.024734	0.001420	0.000773
47	0.001240	0.000657	0.044993	0.025504	0.001523	0.000872
48	0.001327	0.000712	0.045989	0.026298	0.001640	0.000990
49	0.001420	0.000773	0.046993	0.027117	0.001774	0.001171
50	0.001523	0.000872	0.048004	0.027961	0.001979	0.001377
51	0.001640	0.000990	0.049021	0.028832	0.002196	0.001608
52	0.001774	0.001171	0.050042	0.029730	0.002526	0.001892
53	0.001979	0.001377	0.051067	0.030655	0.002922	0.002259
54	0.002196	0.001608	0.052093	0.031609	0.003408	0.002660
55	0.002526	0.001892	0.053120	0.032594	0.003978	0.003061
56	0.002922	0.002259	0.054144	0.033608	0.004477	0.003521
57	0.003408	0.002660	0.055089	0.034655	0.005036	0.004045
58	0.003978	0.003061	0.056068	0.035733	0.005868	0.004641
59	0.004477	0.003521	0.057080	0.036846	0.006626	0.005315
60	0.005036	0.004045	0.058118	0.037993	0.007746	0.006085
61	0.005868	0.004641	0.059172	0.039176	0.008738	0.006945
62	0.006626	0.005315	0.060232	0.040395	0.009815	0.007870
63	0.007746	0.006085	0.061303	0.041653	0.011339	0.008834
64	0.008738	0.006945	0.062429	0.042950	0.012591	0.009809
65	0.009815	0.007870	0.063669	0.044287	0.013410	0.010720
66	0.011339	0.008834	0.065082	0.045666	0.014672	0.011582
67	0.012591	0.009809	0.066724	0.046828	0.015496	0.012512
68	0.013410	0.010720	0.068642	0.048070	0.016946	0.013183
69	0.014672	0.011582	0.070834	0.049584	0.018598	0.014551
70	0.015496	0.012512	0.073284	0.051331	0.020374	0.015643

Mortality Rates for Year 2016 Valuation Dates Under Section 4044 *(cont'd)*

Age	*Healthy Male*	*Healthy Female*	*SS-Disabled Male*	*SS-Disabled Female*	*Non-SS Disabled Male*	*Non-SS Disabled Female*
71	0.016946	0.013183	0.075979	0.053268	0.022235	0.017381
72	0.018598	0.014551	0.078903	0.055356	0.025126	0.018713
73	0.020374	0.015643	0.082070	0.057573	0.027589	0.020890
74	0.022235	0.017381	0.085606	0.059979	0.031538	0.024190
75	0.025126	0.018713	0.088918	0.062574	0.036249	0.027056
76	0.027589	0.020890	0.092208	0.065480	0.041697	0.030157
77	0.031538	0.024190	0.095625	0.068690	0.047870	0.033596
78	0.036249	0.027056	0.099216	0.072237	0.054748	0.037482
79	0.041697	0.030157	0.103030	0.076156	0.062306	0.041917
80	0.047870	0.033596	0.107113	0.080480	0.068063	0.046782
81	0.054748	0.037482	0.111515	0.085243	0.076421	0.052002
82	0.062306	0.041917	0.116283	0.090480	0.082925	0.059717
83	0.068063	0.046782	0.121464	0.096224	0.090219	0.068666
84	0.076421	0.052002	0.127108	0.102508	0.101974	0.079155
85	0.082925	0.059717	0.133262	0.109368	0.115721	0.088384
86	0.090219	0.068666	0.139974	0.116837	0.127088	0.101851
87	0.101974	0.079155	0.147292	0.124948	0.144069	0.113215
88	0.115721	0.088384	0.155265	0.133736	0.155265	0.125374
89	0.127088	0.101851	0.163939	0.143234	0.163939	0.138250
90	0.144069	0.113215	0.173363	0.153477	0.173363	0.153477
91	0.157567	0.125374	0.183585	0.164498	0.183585	0.164498
92	0.177500	0.138250	0.194653	0.176332	0.194653	0.176332
93	0.193189	0.156949	0.206615	0.189011	0.206615	0.189011
94	0.210043	0.171791	0.219519	0.202571	0.219519	0.202571
95	0.235130	0.187428	0.234086	0.217045	0.234086	0.217045
96	0.253151	0.203860	0.248436	0.232467	0.248436	0.232467
97	0.270569	0.228517	0.263954	0.248870	0.263954	0.248870
98	0.296788	0.247304	0.280803	0.266289	0.280803	0.266289
99	0.313454	0.267070	0.299154	0.284758	0.299154	0.284758
100	0.330037	0.287580	0.319185	0.303433	0.319185	0.303433
101	0.358560	0.318956	0.341086	0.327385	0.341086	0.327385
102	0.376699	0.340960	0.365052	0.359020	0.365052	0.359020
103	0.396884	0.364586	0.393102	0.395842	0.393102	0.395842
104	0.418855	0.389996	0.427255	0.438360	0.427255	0.438360

Mortality Rates for Year 2017 Valuation Dates Under Section 4044 *(cont'd)*

Age	*Healthy Male*	*Healthy Female*	*SS-Disabled Male*	*SS-Disabled Female*	*Non-SS Disabled Male*	*Non-SS Disabled Female*
105	0.440585	0.415180	0.469531	0.487816	0.469531	0.471493
106	0.460043	0.438126	0.521945	0.545886	0.492807	0.483473
107	0.475200	0.456824	0.586518	0.614309	0.497189	0.492436
108	0.485670	0.471493	0.665268	0.694884	0.499394	0.498054
109	0.492807	0.483473	0.760215	0.789474	0.500000	0.500000
110	0.497189	0.492436	1.000000	1.000000	0.500000	0.500000
111	0.499394	0.498054			0.500000	0.500000
112	0.500000	0.500000			0.500000	0.500000
113	0.500000	0.500000			0.500000	0.500000
114	0.500000	0.500000			0.500000	0.500000
115	0.500000	0.500000			0.500000	0.500000
116	0.500000	0.500000			0.500000	0.500000
117	0.500000	0.500000			1.000000	1.000000
118	0.500000	0.500000				
119	0.500000	0.500000				
120	1.000000	1.000000				

ERISA Section 4050 Mortality Rates for 2014 to 2017 Valuation Dates

This mortality table is used as part of the "missing participant annuity assumptions" as discussed in PBGC Regulations Section 4050.

	50/50 Male/Female Blend			
Age	*2014*	*2015*	*2016*	*2017*
15	0.000177	0.000173	0.000170	0.000167
16	0.000202	0.000198	0.000195	0.000192
17	0.000222	0.000219	0.000215	0.000211
18	0.000235	0.000231	0.000228	0.000224
19	0.000242	0.000238	0.000234	0.000230
20	0.000248	0.000243	0.000239	0.000234
21	0.000258	0.000253	0.000249	0.000244
22	0.000272	0.000267	0.000263	0.000259
23	0.000298	0.000293	0.000289	0.000284
24	0.000326	0.000322	0.000317	0.000313

50/50 Male/Female Blend

Age	2014	2015	2016	2017
25	0.000366	0.000362	0.000357	0.000354
26	0.000423	0.000420	0.000417	0.000413
27	0.000450	0.000446	0.000443	0.000441
28	0.000467	0.000463	0.000461	0.000457
29	0.000485	0.000481	0.000478	0.000475
30	0.000511	0.000507	0.000504	0.000501
31	0.000538	0.000535	0.000531	0.000528
32	0.000556	0.000553	0.000549	0.000546
33	0.000566	0.000562	0.000559	0.000555
34	0.000572	0.000568	0.000564	0.000560
35	0.000578	0.000574	0.000570	0.000567
36	0.000591	0.000586	0.000582	0.000578
37	0.000612	0.000608	0.000603	0.000599
38	0.000632	0.000627	0.000622	0.000616
39	0.000658	0.000652	0.000646	0.000640
40	0.000696	0.000689	0.000681	0.000674
41	0.000737	0.000728	0.000720	0.000712
42	0.000780	0.000771	0.000762	0.000753
43	0.000821	0.000811	0.000801	0.000791
44	0.000861	0.000850	0.000839	0.000828
45	0.000896	0.000883	0.000870	0.000858
46	0.000939	0.000925	0.000911	0.000897
47	0.000996	0.000980	0.000964	0.000949
48	0.001073	0.001055	0.001037	0.001020
49	0.001156	0.001136	0.001116	0.001097
50	0.001263	0.001241	0.001219	0.001198
51	0.001388	0.001364	0.001339	0.001315
52	0.001553	0.001526	0.001499	0.001473
53	0.001765	0.001736	0.001707	0.001678
54	0.001996	0.001964	0.001933	0.001902
55	0.002307	0.002274	0.002241	0.002209
56	0.002693	0.002659	0.002624	0.002591
57	0.003145	0.003107	0.003071	0.003034
58	0.003642	0.003601	0.003560	0.003520
59	0.004137	0.004090	0.004044	0.003999
60	0.004697	0.004644	0.004592	0.004541

50/50 Male/Female Blend

Age	*2014*	*2015*	*2016*	*2017*
61	0.005426	0.005368	0.005311	0.005255
62	0.006164	0.006099	0.006035	0.005971
63	0.007129	0.007057	0.006986	0.006916
64	0.008083	0.008001	0.007921	0.007842
65	0.009115	0.009023	0.008932	0.008843
66	0.010381	0.010281	0.010183	0.010087
67	0.011527	0.011417	0.011308	0.011200
68	0.012436	0.012311	0.012187	0.012065
69	0.013532	0.013395	0.013260	0.013127
70	0.014458	0.014305	0.014154	0.014004
71	0.015578	0.015404	0.015233	0.015065
72	0.017139	0.016948	0.016760	0.016575
73	0.018648	0.018432	0.018219	0.018009
74	0.020509	0.020273	0.020039	0.019808
75	0.022691	0.022431	0.022174	0.021920
76	0.025090	0.024804	0.024520	0.024240
77	0.028753	0.028453	0.028157	0.027864
78	0.032610	0.032287	0.031969	0.031653
79	0.036952	0.036607	0.036265	0.035927
80	0.041824	0.041457	0.041093	0.040733
81	0.047267	0.046880	0.046496	0.046115
82	0.053318	0.052913	0.052511	0.052112
83	0.058751	0.058304	0.057862	0.057423
84	0.065580	0.065120	0.064665	0.064212
85	0.072748	0.072269	0.071794	0.071321
86	0.080924	0.080427	0.079933	0.079443
87	0.091972	0.091501	0.091032	0.090565
88	0.103464	0.102991	0.102521	0.102053
89	0.115894	0.115417	0.114942	0.114470
90	0.130027	0.129564	0.129102	0.128642
91	0.142991	0.142483	0.141976	0.141471
92	0.159305	0.158827	0.158350	0.157875
93	0.176416	0.175966	0.175517	0.175069
94	0.192386	0.191895	0.191405	0.190917
95	0.212552	0.212127	0.211703	0.211279
96	0.229882	0.229423	0.228964	0.228506

50/50 Male/Female Blend

Age	*2014*	*2015*	*2016*	*2017*
97	0.250702	0.250315	0.249929	0.249543
98	0.272864	0.272591	0.272318	0.272046
99	0.291135	0.290844	0.290553	0.290262
100	0.309737	0.309428	0.309118	0.308809
101	0.338758	0.338758	0.338758	0.338758
102	0.358830	0.358830	0.358830	0.358830
103	0.380735	0.380735	0.380735	0.380735
104	0.404426	0.404426	0.404426	0.404426
105	0.427883	0.427883	0.427883	0.427883
106	0.449085	0.449085	0.449085	0.449085
107	0.466012	0.466012	0.466012	0.466012
108	0.478582	0.478582	0.478582	0.478582
109	0.488140	0.488140	0.488140	0.488140
110	0.494813	0.494813	0.494813	0.494813
111	0.498724	0.498724	0.498724	0.498724
112	0.500000	0.500000	0.500000	0.500000
113	0.500000	0.500000	0.500000	0.500000
114	0.500000	0.500000	0.500000	0.500000
115	0.500000	0.500000	0.500000	0.500000
116	0.500000	0.500000	0.500000	0.500000
117	0.500000	0.500000	0.500000	0.500000
118	0.500000	0.500000	0.500000	0.500000
119	0.500000	0.500000	0.500000	0.500000
120	1.000000	1.000000	1.000000	1.000000

Appendix G

Determination of HCEs

The determination of highly compensated employees is of critical importance for a number of reasons relating to distributions from retirement plans. The determination of HCEs plays in part in the following rules:

- The determination of excess contributions and excess aggregate contributions (see chapter 5)
- The determination of whether a participant in a defined benefit plan is restricted from receiving a lump sum distribution or other accelerated payment (see chapter 14)
- The determination of whether the option for a distribution in kind discriminates in favor of HCEs (see chapter 25)
- The determination of whether the allocation of surplus assets in an overfunded plan discriminates in favor of HCEs (see chapter 15)
- The determination of whether an optional form of benefit discriminates in favor of HCEs (see chapter 10)

Q G:1 How are HCEs defined?

HCEs are determined under Code Section 414(q). These eight questions must be answered in making the determination (see Qs G:2–G:18):

1. What entities are treated as part of the employer? (Q G:2)
2. Who is treated as an employee? (Q G:3)
3. What period is being tested? (Qs G:4, G:5)
4. What groups of employees are considered? (Qs G:6–G:8)
5. What is the compensation of each employee? (Q G:9)
6. Who are considered 5 percent owners? (Q G:10)
7. How are members of top-paid group determined? (Qs G:11–G:15)
8. Who are highly compensated former employees (HCFEs)? (Qs G:16–G:18)

Q G:2 What entities are treated as part of the employer?

The employer includes not only the employers who sponsor the plan but all entities required to be aggregated with the employer under the aggregation rules of Code Sections 414(b), (c), (m), and (o). These four following entities are treated as a single employer in determining HCEs:

1. All Corporations that are members of a controlled group of corporations (as defined in Code Section 414(b)) that includes the sponsoring entity;
2. All trades or businesses (whether or not incorporated) that are under common control (as defined in Code Section 414(c)) including the sponsoring entity;
3. All organizations (whether or not incorporated) that are members of an affiliated service group (as defined in Code Section 414(m)) including the sponsoring entity; and
4. Any other entities required to be aggregated with the employing entity under Code Section 414(o) and the regulations.

The line-of-business rules under Code Section 414(r) do not apply. Thus, qualified separate lines of business do not separately test each entity in determining the group of HCEs. [Treas. Reg. § 1.414(q)-1T Q&A-6]

Example G-1: The LN Homes Corporation is owned 50 percent by MLM and 50 percent by CRV, two unrelated individuals. LN Homes Corporation sponsors a defined benefit plan and covers employees who are employed by LN Homes Corporation. MLM and CRV also each own 50 percent of Yellow Paddleboats, Inc. Yellow Paddleboats, Inc. does not sponsor a qualified plan. LN Homes Corporation and Yellow Paddleboats, Inc. are a controlled group of corporations under Code Section 414(b). Both corporations are treated as a single entity in determining the highly compensated employees covered by the LN Homes Corporation defined benefit plan.

Q G:3 Who is treated as an employee?

"Employee" refers to individuals who perform services for the employer and are either common-law employees of the employer or self-employed individuals who are treated as employees under Code Section 401(c)(1). [Treas. Reg. § 1.414(q)-1T Q&A-7]

Q G:4 What periods are used for testing a plan to determine HCEs?

Two periods are used for testing, (1) the determination year and (2) the look-back year. Generally, the determination year is based on the plan year and the look-back year is the 12-month period immediately preceding the determination year. If an employer sponsors two plans with different plan years, separate calculations must be done for each of the two plans. The look-back year may never be less than a 12-month period. [Treas. Reg. § 1.414(q)-1T Q&A-14(a)]

Example G-2: Ben's Guitar Store, Inc. sponsors a defined benefit plan and a 401(k) plan. The 401(k) plan is on a calendar-year basis, and the defined benefit plan year runs from July 1 to June 30 each year. For plan years ending in 2016, these look-back and determination periods are used:

Plan	*Look-Back Year*	*Determination Year*
401(k)	1/1/2015–12/31/2015	1/1/2016–12/31/2016
Defined Benefit Plan	7/1/2014–6/30/2015	7/1/2015–6/30/2016

Q G:5 Are simpler methods available for determining the look-back and determination years?

Yes. Under the calendar-year data election, the calendar year beginning with or within the look-back year (the 12-month period preceding the determination year) is treated as the look-back year. If the plan has a calendar year as its determination year, then the immediately preceding calendar year is the look-back year for the plan. This is the case whether or not a calendar-year data election is made. Thus, a calendar-year data election would have no effect on the HCE determination for a calendar-year plan. [Notice 97-45, 1997-33 I.R.B. 7, § V(2)]

Notification or filing with the IRS of a calendar-year data election is not required in order for the election to be valid. Under certain circumstances, plan amendments may be required to reflect the election. [Notice 97-45]

Example G-3: Ben's Guitar Store, Inc. sponsors a defined benefit plan and a 401(k) plan. The 401(k) plan is on a calendar-year basis, and the defined benefit plan year runs from July 1 to June 30 each year. Ben's Guitar Store, Inc. makes the calendar-year data election. For plan years ending in 2016, the following look-back and determination periods are used:

Plan	*Look-Back Year*	*Determination Year*
401(k)	1/1/2015–12/31/2015	1/1/2016–12/31/2016
Defined Benefit Plan	1/1/2015–12/31/2015	7/1/2015–6/30/2016

Q G:6 Who is an HCE?

The group of employees who are highly compensated consists of highly compensated active employees (see Q G:7) and highly compensated former employees (HCFEs) (see Q G:16). [Treas. Reg. § 1.414(q)-1T Q&A-2]

Q G:7 Who is a highly compensated active employee?

A highly compensated active employee is any employee who performs services during the determination year and is described in either of the following groups:

I LOOK-BACK YEAR

Five Percent Owner. The employee is considered a 5 percent owner at any time during the look-back year (see Q G:10).

Compensation Above $80,000. The employee received compensation in excess of $80,000 (see Q G:8) during the look-back year (see Q G:4, Q G:5). Note that a top-paid group election may be made to limit the number of employees in this group (see Q G:11).

II DETERMINATION YEAR

Five Percent Owner. The employee is considered a 5 percent owner at any time during the determination year (Q G:10).

[Treas. Reg. § 1.414(q)-1T Q&A-3].

Q G:8 How is the $80,000 threshold indexed?

The $80,000 threshold is indexed at the same time and in the same manner as the Section 415(b)(1)(A) dollar limits for defined benefit plans. [Treas. Reg. § 1.414(q)-1T Q&A-3(c)(1)] For 2015 plan years, the threshold is $120,000. For 2015 determination years, the look-back year would be 2014 when the limit was $115,000. [IRS Announcement, IR-2014-99, October 23, 2014]

Q G:9 How is compensation determined in establishing the group of HCEs?

"Compensation" includes compensation within the meaning of Code Section 415(c)(3) (basically, total taxable compensation) plus elective or salary reduction contributions to a cafeteria plan [I.R.C. § 125], cash or deferred arrangement [I.R.C. § 402(a)(8)], or a tax-sheltered annuity. [I.R.C. § 403(b)] Elective deferrals under a Section 457 plan or pick-up contributions under a Section 414(h)(2) plan are not included in compensation. [Treas. Reg. § 1.414(q)-1T Q&A-13]

> **Example G-4:** Gladys earns $121,000 during 2015 from the Wagner Corporation. She participates in the defined benefit and 401(k) plans (calendar year) sponsored by the company and electively contributes $15,000 to the 401(k) plan. Although her taxable compensation for 2015 is $106,000 ($121,000 − $15,000), her compensation for determining whether she is highly compensated is $121,000 for the 2015 calendar year. She will be a highly compensated employee for the 2016 plan year.

Q G:10 Who is considered a 5 percent owner of the employer?

An employee is considered a 5 percent owner of the employer for the determination or look-back year if, at any time during the year, the employee is a 5 percent owner as defined in the top-heavy rules of Code Section 416. A 5 percent owner is defined as an individual who:

1. If the employer is a corporation, owns (or is considered as owning with the stock attribution rules of Code Section 318) more than 5 percent of the outstanding stock of the corporation or stock possessing more than 5 percent of the total combined voting power of all stock of the corporation; or
2. If the employer is not a corporation, owns more than 5 percent of the capital or profits interest in the employer.

Although the attribution rules in Code Section 318(a)(2) require that 50 percent or more of the value of the stock be owned by an individual before the attribution rules apply, the 5 percent owner rules reduce this threshold to 5 percent. Also, in determining the 5 percent threshold, only ownership in a single entity is considered; the controlled group and affiliated service group rules of Code Sections 414(b), (c), and (m) are ignored. [I.R.C. §§ 416(i)(1), 318(a)(2)(C)]

It is important to note that the calendar-year data election (Q G:5) has no impact on the determination of a 5 percent owner. If an employee is a 5 percent owner in either the look-back year or the determination year, then the employee is an HCE. [Notice 97-45, § V(2)(b)]

Example G-5: Beth owns 6 percent of the stock of Brookfield Resources Corporation, which is a part of a controlled group with Scott's Diagnostic Centers, Inc. Although Beth owns less than 2 percent of the value of all the stock in the controlled group of corporations, she is considered a 5 percent owner by virtue of the fact that she owns more than 5 percent of the stock of Brookfield Resources Corporation.

Example G-6: Jack owns 4 percent of the stock of Wacky Jack's Toys, Inc. His children also own stock in the corporation; Ben owns 2 percent and Grace owns 1 percent. Jack is considered a 5 percent owner, because he owns his 4 percent plus the 3 percent owned by his children. Ben also is considered a 5 percent owner, because the stock of his father is attributed to him (4 percent plus 2 percent); Grace's stock is not attributable to Ben as a sibling. Grace is not considered a 5 percent owner, because the stock attributable to her is not greater than 5 percent (4 percent plus 1 percent).

Example G-7: John, the 100 percent owner of Pa's Lawn Service, Inc., sells his entire interest to Dolly, who is unrelated to him, in April 2015. Pa's Lawn Service, Inc. sponsors a defined benefit plan with a plan year that runs from March 1 to February 28. Pa's Lawn Service, Inc. makes a calendar-year data election for the plan year ended February 28, 2016. For purposes of determining who meets the $80,000 threshold, the look-back year is the calendar year 2015. However, for purposes of determining who is a 5 percent owner, the look-back year is March 1, 2015 through February 28, 2016. Because John was a 5 percent owner during the look-back year, he is treated as an HCE for the plan year ended February 28, 2016.

Q G:11 How are the members of the top-paid group determined?

An employee is in the top-paid group for a look-back year if the employee is one of the top 20 percent of the employer's employees, ranked on the basis of amount of compensation received from the employer during the look-back year. Identifying employees in the top-paid group requires two steps:

Step 1. Determining the number of employees that corresponds to 20 percent of the employer's employees; and

Step 2. Identifying the particular employees who are among the number of employees who receive the most compensation during the look-back year.

Employees who perform no services for the employer during a year are not included in making either of the above determinations. [Treas. Reg. § 1.414(q)-1T Q&A-9(a)]

Q G:12 How are the number of employees in the top-paid group calculated?

The starting point for calculating the number of employees in the top-paid group is the total number of active employees of the employer during the look-back year, without regard to whether any of the active employees are eligible to participate in the plan. The following two categories of employees may be excluded from the count (without regard to the fact that they may be covered under the plan):

Category 1. Employees who fit the description of any one of these service or age criteria:

1. Employees who have completed fewer than six months of service by the end of the year;
2. Employees who normally work fewer than 17 hours per week;
3. Employees who have not reached age 21 by the end of the year; or
4. Employees who normally work fewer than six months during any year.

Category 2. Collectively bargained employees, when both of the two following conditions are satisfied:

1. At least 90 percent of the employees of the employer are collectively bargained employees; and
2. The plan covers only noncollectively bargained employees.

The employer may choose to substitute a shorter period of service or lower age, or choose not to apply any exclusions at all. It is important to note that, by modifying the allowable exclusions, the top-paid group becomes larger and, potentially, a larger number of employees might be considered HCEs. [Treas. Reg. § 1.414(q)-1T, Q&A-9(b)]

Example G-8: Jen's Sailing Centers, Inc. maintains a defined benefit plan. The total number of employees who worked for the company during the look-back year (December 31, 2015) is 200. Although the company employs

50 union employees (who are not covered by the plan), the company may not exclude the union employees from the number in the top-paid group, because they constitute less than 90 percent of all employees of Jen's Sailing Centers, Inc. However, the following categories of employees may be excluded:

Category 1. Employees who fit the description of any one of these service or age criteria:

1. Employees who have completed fewer than six months of service by the end of the year;
2. Employees who normally work fewer than 17 hours per week;
3. Employees who have not reached age 21 by the end of the year; or
4. Employees who normally work fewer than six months during any year.

Category 2. Collectively bargained employees, when both of the two following conditions are satisfied:

1. At least 90 percent of the employees of the employer are collectively bargained employees; and
2. The plan covers only noncollectively bargained employees.

The computation of the top-paid group is shown below:

(200 − 30 − 40 − 10) × 20% = 24 employees.

Therefore, 24 employees are in the top-paid group.

Q G:13 Once the number in the top-paid group is determined, how are the particular employees identified?

All employees (except for collectively bargained employees who are excluded under the rules described in Q G:12) are then ranked in order of compensation. Although certain employees may have been excluded from the determination of the number of employees in the top-paid group, those same employees may still be included in the actual top-paid group. [Treas. Reg. § 1.414(q)-1T Q&A-9(c)]

Example G-9: Jen's Sailing Centers, Inc. from Example G-8 employs two expert sailors, Sophie and Caroline, who are the highest-paid employees (earning $200,000 each), but work only three months during the year. Although Sophie and Caroline are excluded in counting the number of top-paid employees (24), they are still treated as HCEs in the top-paid group.

Q G:14 What if an employee is highly compensated by virtue of being in more than one of the highly compensated categories discussed in Q G:6?

An employee who is in more than one category is treated as highly compensated and is not disregarded in determining whether another individual is highly compensated. Thus, for example, the fact that an individual is considered a

5 percent owner does not exclude that individual from being a member of the top-paid group. [Treas. Reg. § 1.414(q)-1T Q&A-3(d)]

Example G-10: Jody, a 5 percent owner of Jen's Sailing Centers, Inc. in Example G-9 earns $150,000 per year. She is *not* excluded from the top-paid group because she is a 5 percent owner.

Q G:15 How are family members treated in applying the HCE rules?

Family members are no longer aggregated and treated as a single HCE. Those rules were repealed, effective for plan years beginning on or after January 1, 1997, under SBJPA. [SBJPA § 1431(b)(3)]

Q G:16 Who are HCFEs?

A person who performs no service for the employer during the determination year is treated as a former employee. A former employee will be treated as an HCFE if that employee:

1. Had a separation year before the determination year; or
2. Was a highly compensated active employee in the separation year or in any determination year ending on or after the employee's 55th birthday.

Because the pre-SBJPA $50,000 and $75,000 limits (as indexed) were not effective until plan years beginning in 1987, the highly compensated employee rules require the application of the $50,000 and $75,000 thresholds for separation years beginning before 1987 in determining whether an employee was highly compensated at the time of separation from service. In lieu of making that determination (particularly, the determination of the top-paid group in a pre-1987 year), the employer may choose, in the plan document, to treat the following individuals as HCFEs, if the employee separated from service before January 1, 1987, and was in either or both of the following groups during (1) the employee's separation year (or the year preceding the separation year) or (2) during any year ending on or after the employee's 55th birthday (or the last year ending before the employee's 55th birthday):

1. The employee was a 5 percent owner of the employer at any time during the year; or
2. The employee received compensation in excess of $50,000 during the year.

The determinations may be made on the basis of the calendar year, the plan year, or any other 12-month period selected by the employer and applied on a reasonable and consistent basis. [Treas. Reg. § 1.414(q)-1T Q&A-4(d)].

Q G:17 What is a separation year and how is it used in determining HCFEs?

A separation year can be the actual determination year in which the employee separates from service or the deemed separation year. An employee is deemed to have a separation year if, in a determination year before age 55, the employee earns significantly less compensation than in prior years. This rule applies whether or not the reduction in compensation occurs due to a leave of absence.

In determining the "significant" threshold described above, an employee earning compensation that is less than 50 percent of his or her average compensation earned during the three prior calendar years will have a deemed separation year. If the employee has less than three years of service with the employer, then those lesser years will be averaged.

An employee who has been designated as an HCFE will cease to be an HCFE if:

1. He or she returned to employment (in the case of an actual separation from service) and has increased compensation; or
2. He or she has a deemed resumption of employment (in the case of a deemed separation) and has increased compensation.

Whether the compensation increase is sufficient to remove the designation of HCFE is a facts and circumstances test. To the extent that such compensation increase would not result in a deemed separation year (i.e., the increase results in compensation greater than 50 percent of the three year average), the HCFE designation is removed. [Treas. Reg. § 1.414(q)-1T, Q&A-5]

Example G-11: Irene is an HCE of Rene's Cookie Creations, Inc. During each of the years 2012, 2013, and 2014, she earned $150,000. In 2015, she decided to cut back her hours to spend more time with her family and only earned $40,000. Because her compensation during the determination year (2015) is less than 50 percent of the average annual compensation earned in her three consecutive highest paid years ($150,000), Irene has a deemed separation year in 2015. Irene is treated as an HCFE in 2016 and future years, unless she experiences a deemed or actual resumption of employment.

Q G:18 How are HCFEs treated in determining highly compensated active employees?

HCFEs are not included in the top-paid group (see Q G:11). In addition, HCFEs are not counted in determining the number of employees in the top-paid group. [Treas. Reg. § 1.414(q)-1T Q&A-4(e)(2)]

Appendix H

Minimum Present Value Segment Rates

Generally for plan years beginning after December 31, 2007, the applicable interest rates under Code Section 417(e)(3)(D) are segment rates computed without regard to a 24-month average. For plan years beginning in 2008 through 2011, the applicable interest rate was the monthly spot segment rate blended with the applicable rate under Code Section 417(e)(3)(A)(ii)(II) as in effect for plan years beginning in 2007. For plan years beginning in the stated year, the following rates are the applicable interest rates for the month and year listed for minimum present value computations under Code Section 417(e)(3)(D). The most current rates can be found on the IRS website at:

http://www.irs.gov/retirement-plans/minimum-present-value-segment-rates

For Plan Years Beginning In	*Month/ Year*	*First Segment*	*Second Segment*	*Third Segment*
All	Jul-17	1.97	3.66	4.37
All	Jun-17	1.96	3.60	4.39
All	May-17	1.96	3.77	4.62
All	Apr-17	1.96	3.78	4.66
All	Mar-17	2.06	3.95	4.75
All	Feb-17	1.96	3.91	4.69
All	Jan-17	2.00	3.91	4.66
All	Dec-16	2.04	4.03	4.82
All	Nov-16	1.79	3.80	4.71
All	Oct-16	1.57	3.45	4.39
All	Sep-16	1.47	3.34	4.30
All	Aug-16	1.39	3.27	4.18
All	Jul-16	1.36	3.26	4.16
All	Jun-16	1.44	3.46	4.48
All	May-16	1.50	3.60	4.62

For Plan Years Beginning In	*Month/ Year*	*First Segment*	*Second Segment*	*Third Segment*
All	Apr-16	1.47	3.65	4.62
All	Mar-16	1.68	3.87	4.84
All	Feb-16	1.71	3.98	5.03
All	Jan-16	1.78	4.08	5.02
All	Dec-15	1.82	4.12	5.01
All	Nov-15	1.76	4.15	5.13
All	Oct-15	1.61	4.02	5.03
All	Sep-15	1.69	4.11	5.07
All	Aug-15	1.68	4.05	4.98
All	Jul-15	1.63	4.14	5.13
All	Jun-15	1.59	4.13	5.20
All	May-15	1.38	3.88	4.98
All	Apr-15	1.27	3.52	4.47
All	Mar-15	1.38	3.58	4.50
All	Feb-15	1.35	3.52	4.47
All	Jan-15	1.33	3.46	4.40
All	Dec-14	1.48	3.77	4.79
All	Nov-14	1.40	3.88	4.96
All	Oct-14	1.29	3.81	4.88
All	Sep-14	1.40	3.98	5.04
All	Aug-14	1.24	3.86	4.96
All	Jul-14	1.26	3.94	5.02
All	Jun-14	1.23	4.01	5.09
All	May-14	1.17	3.98	5.01
All	Apr-14	1.24	4.13	5.15
All	Mar-14	1.23	4.23	5.31
All	Feb-14	1.17	4.29	5.36
All	Jan-14	1.24	4.42	5.40
All	Dec-13	1.25	4.57	5.60
All	Nov-13	1.19	4.53	5.66
All	Oct-13	1.24	4.47	5.52
All	Sep-13	1.40	4.66	5.62
All	Aug-13	1.36	4.60	5.58
All	Jul-13	1.34	4.45	5.44
All	Jun-13	1.24	4.25	5.43

For Plan Years Beginning In	*Month/ Year*	*First Segment*	*Second Segment*	*Third Segment*
All	May-13	0.97	3.76	5.01
All	Apr-13	0.93	3.61	4.88
All	Mar-13	0.97	3.82	5.11
All	Feb-13	0.99	3.82	5.02
All	Jan-13	1.00	3.73	4.89
2011	Dec-12	1.38	3.43	4.39
2012	Dec-12	1.00	3.57	4.77
2013	Dec-12	1.00	3.57	4.77
2011	Nov-12	1.34	3.36	4.24
2012	Nov-12	0.97	3.50	4.60
2013	Nov-12	0.97	3.50	4.60
2011	Oct-12	1.35	3.44	4.24
2012	Oct-12	0.96	3.57	4.58
2013	Oct-12	0.96	3.57	4.58
2011	Sep-12	1.39	3.54	4.31
2012	Sep-12	1.02	3.71	4.67
2013	Sep-12	1.02	3.71	4.67
2011	Aug-12	1.46	3.52	4.17
2012	Aug-12	1.13	3.71	4.52
2013	Aug-12	1.13	3.71	4.52
2011	Jul-12	1.49	3.45	4.12
2012	Jul-12	1.22	3.66	4.50
2011	Jun-12	1.82	3.72	4.48
2012	Jun-12	1.60	3.97	4.93
2011	May-12	1.86	3.88	4.62
2012	May-12	1.59	4.12	5.04
2011	Apr-12	1.87	4.08	4.75
2012	Apr-12	1.54	4.30	5.14
2011	Mar-12	1.91	4.14	4.80
2012	Mar-12	1.57	4.36	5.18
2011	Feb-12	1.87	4.04	4.69
2012	Feb-12	1.56	4.27	5.08
2011	Jan-12	2.08	4.09	4.76
2012	Jan-12	1.84	4.36	5.19
2011	Dec-11	2.25	4.16	4.79

For Plan Years Beginning In	*Month/ Year*	*First Segment*	*Second Segment*	*Third Segment*
2012	Dec-11	2.07	4.45	5.24
2010	Nov-11	2.40	3.89	4.36
2011	Nov-11	2.20	4.18	4.81
2012	Nov-11	1.99	4.47	5.26
2010	Oct-11	2.51	3.99	4.55
2011	Oct-11	2.30	4.27	5.03
2012	Oct-11	2.09	4.56	5.50
2010	Sep-11	2.46	3.97	4.75
2011	Sep-11	2.22	4.23	5.28
2012	Sep-11	1.98	4.49	5.80
2010	Aug-11	2.57	4.23	5.07
2011	Aug-11	2.21	4.43	5.55
2012	Aug-11	1.85	4.62	6.02
2010	Jul-11	2.74	4.69	5.48
2011	Jul-11	2.23	4.83	5.88
2010	Jun-11	2.71	4.69	5.49
2011	Jun-11	2.21	4.84	5.91
2010	May-11	2.75	4.72	5.44
2011	May-11	2.23	4.86	5.83
2010	Apr-11	2.96	4.94	5.66
2011	Apr-11	2.44	5.08	6.05
2010	Mar-11	2.95	4.94	5.68
2011	Mar-11	2.43	5.09	6.07
2010	Feb-11	3.07	5.06	5.78
2011	Feb-11	2.55	5.20	6.16
2010	Jan-11	2.97	4.96	5.66
2011	Jan-11	2.45	5.10	6.04
2010	Dec-10	2.96	4.91	5.68
2011	Dec-10	2.47	5.07	6.10
2010	Nov-10	2.67	4.62	5.59
2011	Nov-10	2.16	4.77	6.05
2009	Oct-10	2.95	4.21	4.81
2010	Oct-10	2.48	4.39	5.28
2011	Oct-10	2.02	4.56	5.75
2009	Sep-10	2.96	4.16	4.67

For Plan Years Beginning In	Month/ Year	First Segment	Second Segment	Third Segment
2010	Sep-10	2.55	4.36	5.13
2011	Sep-10	2.15	4.55	5.58
2009	Aug-10	3.00	4.20	4.63
2010	Aug-10	2.61	4.41	5.05
2011	Aug-10	2.21	4.61	5.46
2009	Jul-10	3.22	4.43	4.84
2010	Jul-10	2.83	4.66	5.26
2009	Jun-10	3.42	4.62	4.99
2010	Jun-10	3.06	4.86	5.43
2009	May-10	3.51	4.74	5.08
2010	May-10	3.12	4.97	5.47
2009	Apr-10	3.73	5.05	5.40
2010	Apr-10	3.26	5.24	5.76
2009	Mar-10	3.71	5.05	5.42
2010	Mar-10	3.23	5.25	5.81
2009	Feb-10	3.69	5.08	5.42
2010	Feb-10	3.22	5.31	5.83
2009	Jan-10	3.68	5.02	5.35
2010	Jan-10	3.23	5.22	5.72
2009	Dec-09	3.63	4.95	5.27
2010	Dec-09	3.21	5.19	5.67
2008	Nov-09	3.92	4.56	4.71
2009	Nov-09	3.53	4.81	5.10
2010	Nov-09	3.13	5.07	5.50
2008	Oct-09	3.87	4.47	4.57
2009	Oct-09	3.55	4.75	4.94
2010	Oct-09	3.24	5.02	5.32
2008	Sep-09	3.90	4.48	4.57
2009	Sep-09	3.61	4.77	4.94
2010	Sep-09	3.31	5.05	5.32
2008	Aug-09	4.11	4.68	4.74
2009	Aug-09	3.85	5.00	5.11
2010	Aug-09	3.60	5.31	5.47
2008	Jul-09	4.21	4.78	4.82
2009	Jul-09	4.00	5.16	5.23

For Plan Years Beginning In	*Month/ Year*	*First Segment*	*Second Segment*	*Third Segment*
2008	Jun-09	4.39	4.93	4.93
2009	Jun-09	4.27	5.35	5.33
2008	May-09	4.24	4.78	4.74
2009	May-09	4.25	5.34	5.25
2008	Apr-09	4.03	4.44	4.39
2009	Apr-09	4.30	5.12	5.02
2008	Mar-09	4.05	4.42	4.48
2009	Mar-09	4.46	5.20	5.32
2008	Feb-09	3.92	4.29	4.29
2009	Feb-09	4.25	4.98	4.99
2008	Jan-09	3.54	3.86	3.77
2009	Jan-09	3.96	4.60	4.40
2008	Dec-08	3.64	3.72	3.57
2009	Dec-08	4.41	4.57	4.27
2008	Nov-08	4.62	4.85	4.68
2009	Nov-08	5.24	5.69	5.37
2008	Oct-08	4.81	5.06	4.79
2009	Oct-08	5.44	5.95	5.41
2008	Sep-08	4.59	4.89	4.79
2009	Sep-08	4.91	5.50	5.31
2008	Aug-08	4.64	4.97	4.98
2009	Aug-08	4.78	5.45	5.46
2008	Jul-08	4.69	5.03	5.06
2008	Jun-08	4.75	5.08	5.14
2008	May-08	4.61	4.95	5.03
2008	Apr-08	4.47	4.81	4.94
2008	Mar-08	4.37	4.79	4.91
2008	Feb-08	4.44	4.85	5.03
2008	Jan-08	4.34	4.67	4.81
2008	Dec-07	4.61	4.85	4.96
2008	Nov-07	4.60	4.82	4.91
2008	Oct-07	4.85	5.02	5.09
2008	Sep-07	4.89	5.06	5.14
2008	Aug-07	5.02	5.18	5.28

Table of Cases

[*References are to question numbers.*]

Administrative Comm. of the Sea Ray Employees' Stock Ownership and Profit Sharing Plan v. Daniel Robinson, ... 8:78
Bolden, ... 19:39
Borda v. Hardy, Lewis, Pollard & Page, P.C., ... 8:70
Borst v. Chevron Corp., ... 8:76, 8:80
Carter v. Pension Plan of A. Finkl & Sons Co. for Eligible Office Employees, ... 8:71
Cebula, ... 19:45
Central Laborers Pension Fund v. Heinz, ... 10:25
Collingnon v. Reporting Servs. Co., ... 8:76
Commonwealth Edison Co. v. Vega, ... 15:49
Conkright v. Frommert, ... 13:32
Firestone Tire & Rubber Co. v. Bruch, ... 13:32
Frias v. Comm'r, ... 2:7
Goodin v. Innovative Tech. Solutions, Inc., ... 13:8
Gulf Pension Litig., In re, ... 8:76, 8:80
Gunnison v. Commissioner, ... 19:37
Halliburton Co. v. Commissioner, ... 8:78
Heinz v. Central Laborers' Pension Fund, ... 8:58
Judkins, ... 19:39
Kelli Goodin v. Innovative Technical Solutions, Inc., ... 13:8
Lindsay v. Thiokol Corp., ... 12:1
Matz v. Household Int'l Tax Reduction Inv. Plan, ... 8:76, 8:78
Nash v. Halliburton Co., ... 8:78
Oneida Ltd. v. Pension Benefit Guar. Corp., ... 17:37
Patterson v. Shumate, ... 7:1
Patty Smith v. United States, ... 19:38
Paulsen v. CNF, Inc., ... 17:31
PBGC v. Oneida, Ltd., ... 17:37
Reinhardt, ... 19:39
Smith v. United States, ... 19:38
Snow v. United States, ... 19:38
Tipton & Kalmbach, Inc. v. Commissioner, ... 8:76, 8:77
Watson v. Commissioner, T.C. Summary Op., ... 20:7
Weil v. Terson Co. Ret. Plan Comm., ... 8:76, 8:77, 8:79

Table of Internal Revenue Code Sections

[*References are to question numbers.*]

IRC §

1 .... 25:35
1.401(a)(4)-2(b) 15:19
1.401(a)(4)-3(b) 15:19
22(e)(3) 12:43
41(a) 1:29
41(c)(2) 1:29
41(c)(4) 1:29
62(a)(8) 19:59
72 .... 2:13, 2:24, 4:33, 5:8, 5:44, 18:5, 18:8, 19:14–19:15, 21:23, 23:14, 24:19
72(b) 18:5
72(c)(1) 18:12
72(c)(2) 18:12
72(d) 18:5, 18:8, 18:9, 18:10, 18:14, 18:15, 18:16
72(d)(1)(B) 18:5
72(d)(1)(B)(iii) 18:11
72(d)(1)(B)(iv) 18:11
72(d)(1)(C) 18:12
72(d)(2) 4:57
72(e) 1:42, 2:13, 2:16, 18:5, 18:13
72(e)(2)(A) 19:1
72(e)(8)(D) 19:5
72(e)(11) 27:32
72(m)(3)(B) 6:2
72(m)(5) 2:13
72(m)(5)(A) 19:23
72(m)(7) 4:48, 12:36, 19:21, 20:2, 20:3, 28:12, 29:2, 29:18
72(m)(10) 3:57
72(o)(5) 28:3, 29:4
72(o)(5)(B) 19:18
72(p) 2:1–2:3, 2:10–2:17, 2:19–2:22, 2:24, 2:27, 2:32, 4:33, 7:2, 21:23, 21:28, 27:32, 29:8
72(p)(1) 2:1
72(p)(1)(A) 2:1, 2:3

IRC §

72(p)(1)(B) 2:1
72(p)(2) 2:1, 2:8, 2:11, 2:15, 2:23, 21:28, 23:4, 23:5, 23:11, 23:13
72(p)(2)(A) 2:1, 2:3, 2:4, 2:7, 2:15, 2:23, 14:8
72(p)(2)(A)(i) 2:3
72(p)(2)(B) 2:1, 2:3, 2:5, 2:7, 2:8, 2:11, 2:23, 2:33
72(p)(2)(B)(i) 2:3
72(p)(2)(B)(ii) 2:3, 2:5, 2:23
72(p)(2)(C) 2:1, 2:3, 2:6–2:8, 2:11, 2:23, 2:33
72(p)(2)(D) 2:3
72(p)(5) 2:1
72(q) 27:32
72(t) 2:7, 2:13, 5:14, 5:29, 5:43, 5:46, 12:38, 20:1, 20:8, 21:30, 21:39, 21:50, 27:32, 29:17
72(t)(1) 28:12, 29:18
72(t)(2) 28:12
72(t)(2)(A)(i) 20:2
72(t)(2)(A)(ii) 20:2
72(t)(2)(A)(iii) 20:2
72(t)(2)(A)(iv) 11:47, 20:2, 20:4, 20:9, 21:24, 27:32
72(t)(2)(A)(v) 20:2, 20:7
72(t)(2)(A)(vi) 1:44, 20:2
72(t)(2)(A)(vii) 20:2, 20:14
72(t)(2)(A)(viii) 20:2
72(t)(2)(B) 20:2
72(t)(2)(C) 3:59, 20:2
72(t)(2)(G) 20:2, 20:8
72(t)(3) 28:12
72(t)(4) 20:4
72(t)(10) 20:2, 20:4, 20:5, 20:9
72(t)(10)(A) 20:9
72(t)(10)(B) 1:17, 12:2, 20:9
72(u) 27:32

IRC §

72(v) . . . 27:32
83 . . . 9:62
83(b) . . . 9:62
101(b) . . . 18:12, 21:18, 21:34
104 . . . 19:14, 19:16
104(a)(3) . . . 19:14, 19:15
105 . . . 19:14, 19:16
105(b) . . . 19:14
105(c) . . . 19:14
106 . . . 19:16
108(f) . . . 21:32
121 . . . 2:5
125 . . . 1:13, 9:62, 19:10, App. G:9
132(f)(4) . . . 19:10
152 . . . 1:6, 1:11
152(b)(1) . . . 1:11
152(b)(2) . . . 1:11
152(d)(1)(B) . . . 1:11
163(h)(3)(B) . . . 2:5
165 . . . 1:11
165(h)(5) . . . 1:11
213 . . . 1:11, 20:2
217 . . . 9:62
219 . . . 28:19
219(a) . . . 19:18
318 . . . 8:31, 13:4, App. G:10
318(a)(2) . . . 8:31, 13:4, App. G:10
318(a)(2)(C) . . . 8:31, 13:4, App. G:10
401 . . . 2:11, 7:1–7:3, 10:30, 15:30, 15:68, 21:14
401(a) . . . 1:2, 1:3, 1:17, 2:2, 2:11, 2:49, 3:63, 4:2, 4:4, 4:27, 4:47, 4:64, 4:72, 5:8, 8:70, 10:28, 10:34–10:36, 11:1, 15:2, 15:3, 15:18, 15:32, 16:1, 18:5, 19:4, 20:1, 20:8, 20:16, 20:17, 20:19, 21:4, 21:6, 21:14, 21:15, 21:19, 21:21, 21:28, 21:31, 21:37, 21:38, 21:49, 21:50, 21:53, 22:3, 23:1, 23:3–23:6, 23:8, 24:1, 24:57, 28:5
401(a)(2) . . . 23:1
401(a)(3) . . . 21:51, 23:1
401(a)(3)(A) . . . 11:21
401(a)(4) . . . 5:8, 5:10, 5:25, 5:30, 5:35, 5:39, 8:15, 8:20, 8:21, 8:61, 9:18, 10:1–10:4, 10:24, 10:27, 10:30, 10:33, 10:34, 10:36–38, 12:19, 14:1, 14:2, 14:5, 15:17, 15:33, 16:36, 21:49, 23:1, 23:3–23:5, 23:8, 23:13, 23:24
401(a)(5) . . . 23:1
401(a)(7) . . . 8:74, 23:1
401(a)(8) . . . 8:60
401(a)(9) . . . 1:19, 3:20, 3:21, 4:3, 4:4, 4:6, 4:8, 4:10, 4:17, 4:19, 4:21, 4:22, 4:24, 4:28, 4:30, 4:31, 4:33–4:35, 4:37, 4:40, 4:45–4:48, 4:50–4:51, 4:53, 4:55–4:63, 4:65–4:67, 4:69–4:71, 5:29, 5:45, 10:29, 10:30, 10:34, 12:22, 12:23, 12:74, 12:78, 12:81, 13:2, 13:5, 13:19, 16:57, 20:16, 20:19, 21:14, 21:18, 21:23, 21:26, 21:27, 21:29, 21:50, 23:1, 23:11, 27:32, 28:2, 28:6, 28:7, 28:13, 28:14, App. D, App. E
401(a)(9)(A) . . . 4:5, 4:61, 24:10
401(a)(9)(A)(i) . . . 4:9, 4:23
401(a)(9)(A)(ii) . . . 4:9, 4:10, 4:11, 4:23, 4:34, 4:43, 4:47, 4:61
401(a)(9)(B) . . . 4:61, 4:66
401(a)(9)(B)(i) . . . 4:9, 4:10, 4:61
401(a)(9)(B)(ii) . . . 4:3, 4:10–4:12, 4:14, 4:15, 4:20, 4:61, 12:81, 20:18
401(a)(9)(B)(iii) . . . 4:3, 4:10, 4:11, 4:13–4:15, 4:20, 4:23, 4:31, 4:34, 4:36, 4:60, 4:61, 4:66
401(a)(9)(B)(iii)(II) . . . 4:44
401(a)(9)(B)(iv) . . . 4:10, 4:11, 4:14, 4:15, 4:20, 4:23, 4:31, 4:34, 4:36, 4:60, 4:61
401(a)(9)(B)(iv)(II) . . . 4:15, 4:16, 4:20, 4:44
401(a)(9)(C) . . . 13:3
401(a)(9)(C)(ii) . . . 1:16
401(a)(9)(C)(iii) . . . 4:41, 4:42, 13:19
401(a)(9)(E) . . . 4:17
401(a)(9)(F) . . . 4:47
401(a)(9)(G) . . . 4:4, 4:5, 4:23, 4:35
401(a)(9)(H) . . . 4:4
401(a)(10) . . . 10:34, 23:1
401(a)(11) . . . 1:35, 1:36, 2:45, 3:19, 4:18, 4:59, 4:61, 4:68, 10:21, 10:30, 10:34, 11:2–11:7, 11:12, 11:15, 11:21, 11:24, 11:25, 11:33, 11:36, 11:38, 11:40, 11:41, 11:43–11:46, 11:50, 11:51, 11:56, 12:54, 12:56, 21:15, 23:1
401(a)(11)(B) . . . 4:59
401(a)(11)(B)(iii) . . . 2:48, 11:5, 11:16
401(a)(11)(B)(iii)(I) . . . 11:5, 10:30, 11:3
401(a)(11)(B)(iii)(II) . . . 11:3, 11:5
401(a)(11)(B)(iii)(III) . . . 11:5
401(a)(12) . . . 26:1
401(a)(13) . . . 2:19, 3:1, 3:63, 23:1
401(a)(13)(B) . . . 3:1, 3:20, 3:50, 3:52
401(a)(14) . . . 13:1, 23:1
401(a)(16) . . . 23:1
401(a)(17) . . . 3:19, 9:59, 22:3, 23:1, 23:3
401(a)(19) . . . 23:1
401(a)(20) . . . 11:1
401(a)(22) . . . 23:1
401(a)(23) . . . 25:9
401(a)(25) . . . 10:28, 10:35, 10:36
401(a)(26) . . . 10:4, 23:1, 23:4, 23:13, 23:24
401(a)(28) . . . 10:30, 23:1
401(a)(28)(B) . . . 1:24, 10:30
401(a)(28)(B)(i) . . . 10:25, 10:30
401(a)(28)(B)(ii) . . . 1:27
401(a)(28)(B)(ii)(I) . . . 10:25
401(a)(28)(B)(ii)(1) . . . 10:30
401(a)(28)(B)(iii) . . . 1:25, 10:21
401(a)(28)(B)(iv) . . . 1:26

IRC §

401(a)(28)(C) 1:38
401(a)(29) 23:1
401(a)(30) 23:1
401(a)(31) ... 2:11, 2:12, 10:34, 21:1, 21:2, 21:4, 21:11, 21:13–21:18, 21:28, 21:40, 23:1, 24:2, 24:10, 26:12
401(a)(31)(A) 21:40, 21:42
401(a)(31)(B) 15:79, 21:6
401(a)(31)(C) 10:34
401(a)(31)(E) 21:1, 21:4
401(a)(33) 23:1
401(a)(35) 10:25, 10:30
401(a)(36) 1:17, 12:27
401(b) 23:3, 23:4, 23:8, 23:13
401(c)(1) .... App. G:3
401(c)(2) 9:62
401(d)(6) 1:17
401(h) 10:39, 19:16
401(k) ... 2:7, 2:11, 5:8, 5:15, 5:18, 5:31, 8:6, 9:2, 10:34, 11:5, 15:19, 19:7, 19:10, 20:2, 20:8, 21:28, 21:49, 22:3, 23:3, 28:2, App. G:2, App. G:3
401(k)(2)(B) 2:11, 5:44, 21:28
401(k)(2)(B)(i)(IV) 1:6, 1:13
401(k)(3) 5:35, 21:49, 23:3–23:5, 23:7
401(k)(3)(A)(ii) 5:46
401(k)(8) 4:33, 23:7
401(k)(8)(A)(i) 5:11, 5:26
401(k)(8)(B) 5:1
401(k)(8)(C) 5:7
401(k)(12)(B) 9:2
401(k)(12)(C) 9:2
401(k)(13) 8:12, 8:13
401(k)(13)(D)(iii)(I) 8:12
401(k)(13)(D)(iii)(I) 1:9
401(l)(11) 21:50
401(k)(14)(B) 1:13
401(l)(31) 21:14
401(m) 2:16, 15:19, 20:2, 22:3, 23:3
401(m)(2) 21:49, 23:7
401(m)(2)(A) 5:16
401(m)(6) 4:33, 5:23, 23:7
401(m)(6)(A) 5:25
401(m)(9) 23:7
401(p)(3) 3:20
401(p)(4)(A)(iii) 3:50
402 .... 2:11, 21:3, 21:14, 21:33, 21:35
402(a) 3:55, 18:5, 19:18, 21:30
402(a)(1) 2:19
402(a)(2) 19:64
402(a)(6)(F) 3:60
402(a)(6)(F)(iii) 3:60
402(a)(8) .... App. G:9
402(b)(2) 25:28
402(b)(4) 23:24

IRC §

402(c) ... 4:34, 7:1, 7:5, 21:3, 21:14, 21:20, 21:21, 21:28–21:30, 21:32, 21:35
402(c)(1) 24:8
402(c)(1)(C) 25:15
402(c)(2) 19:18, 21:23, 21:32, 28:2
402(c)(2)(C) 2:11, 2:12
402(c)(3) 2:11, 2:12, 21:28, 25:15, 28:4
402(c)(3)(C) 2:11, 2:12
402(c)(3)(C)(i) 2:11, 21:28
402(c)(3)(C)(ii) 21:28
402(c)(3)(C)(iii) 21:28
402(c)(4) 21:20, 21:32, 21:37, 28:3, 28:24
402(c)(4)(A) 21:24, 21:25
402(c)(4)(C) 1:5, 21:23, 28:2
402(c)(6) 3:60, 25:16
402(c)(6)(C) 25:17
402(c)(8) 24:8
402(c)(8)(B) 1:15, 3:63, 21:20, 21:21, 28:5
402(c)(9) 28:7
402(c)(10) 19:46
402(c)(11) 12:75, 21:22, 21:32, 21:42, 21:43, 28:1
402(c)(11)(A)(i) 28:7
402(d) 15:81
402(d)(1)(A) 19:45
402(d)(1)(B) 19:57
402(d)(1)(B)(i) 19:54
402(d)(1)(B)(ii) 19:54
402(d)(1)(C)(i) 19:57
402(d)(1)(C)(ii) 19:57
402(d)(1)(D) 19:49
402(d)(2)(A) 19:58
402(d)(2)(C) 19:58
402(d)(3) 19:45
402(d)(4)(A) 19:18, 19:20, 19:22, 19:24, 19:27
402(d)(4)(B) 19:47, 19:48, 19:50
402(d)(4)(B)(i) 19:45
402(d)(4)(C) 19:28
402(d)(4)(C)(i) 19:28
402(d)(4)(D)(i) 19:55
402(d)(4)(D)(ii) 19:55
402(d)(4)(F) 19:26
402(d)(4)(J) 19:30
402(d)(4)(L) 19:55
402(d)(6)(B) 19:33
402(e) 15:81, 21:44
402(e)(1)(A) 3:55, 3:60
402(e)(1)(B) 3:60
402(e)(3) 12:68
402(e)(4) 21:23, 24:12, 25:30, 29:22
402(e)(4)(B) 25:32
402(e)(4)(D) ... 3:61, 14:18, 19:20, 19:24, 19:27, 29:1, 29:4, 29:5, 29:7
402(e)(4)(D)(ii) 19:28, 29:3

IRC §

402(e)(4)(D)(ii)(II) 19:28
402(e)(4)(D)(v) 19:30
402(e)(4)(D)(vi) 28:3
402(e)(4)(D)(vii) 28:3
402(e)(4)(E) 2:11, 21:28
402(e)(4)(E)(ii) 10:30, 24:11
402(e)(4)(O) 3:61
402(e)(6) 7:5
402(f) 15:81–15:84, 21:1, 21:5, 21:6, 21:12, 21:22, 21:32, 21:44–21:48, 28:1
402(f)(2)(A) 12:75, 21:22, 21:32, 24:1, 28:1
402(g) 5:31, 5:34, 5:44, 5:48, 20:2, 22:3, 23:7
402(g)(1) 5:32, 5:33
402(g)(2)(A)(ii) 5:40
402(g)(3) 10:26, 21:23
402(g)(4) 5:32
403 .... 7:1–7:3, 21:3, 21:14, 21:33
403(a) 2:2, 4:2, 4:27, 4:47, 15:18, 18:5, 19:4, 19:24, 20:1, 20:17, 21:1, 21:4, 21:21, 21:37, 21:38, 24:57, 28:5
403(a)(4) 7:5
403(a)(5) 7:5
403(b) .... 2:2, 2:49, 4:2, 4:27, 5:31, 7:2, 7:3, 9:62, 12:30, 18:5, 19:4, 19:7, 19:10, 19:23, 20:1, 21:6, 21:19, 21:21, 21:28, 21:37, 21:38, 21:53, 22:3, 23:20, 24:57, 28:2, 28:5, App. G:9
403(b)(1) 20:17, 21:6
403(b)(7) 20:17, 21:6
403(b)(8) 7:5
403(b)(8)(B) 21:23, 28:2
403(b)(9) 20:17, 21:6
404 .... 5:8, 5:13, 5:28, 5:35, 15:74, 16:51, 17:43
404(a) 1:2
404(a)(2) 19:28
404(a)(6) 1:2, 1:29
404(e) 6:2
404(g) 17:46
404(k) 1:12, 1:13, 4:33, 21:23, 27:17, 27:18, 27:32, 28:2
404(k)(1) 1:42
404(k)(2)(A) 1:43
404(k)(2)(A)(iii)(II) 4:33
404(n) 5:13
404(o)(1) 17:44
404(o)(3) 17:44
404(o)(5) 17:45
408 .... 4:27, 7:1, 7:2, 7:3, 7:5, 21:3, 21:14
408(a) 4:2, 16:2, 20:1, 20:17, 21:14, 21:21, 28:5
408(a)(3) 25:24
408(a)(6) 21:14
408(b) 4:2, 7:5, 16:2, 20:1, 20:17, 21:21, 28:5
408(b)(3) 21:14

IRC §

408(d) 21:33
408(d)(3) 21:14, 21:36
408(d)(3)(A)(ii) 21:14
408(d)(3)(B) 21:36
408(d)(3)(C) 21:32
408(d)(3)(C)(ii) 21:14
408(d)(4) 28:6
408(d)(5) 28:6
408(e)(2) 28:18
408(k) 22:3
408(m) 25:14, 28:10
408(p) 7:5
408(p)(2)(C)(i) 9:60
408A 4:2, 7:1–7:3, 7:5, 20:17, 21:37
408A(b) 28:19
408A(c) 28:20
408A(c)(1) 28:19
408A(c)(3)(B) 28:19, 28:20, 28:26
408A(d)(2) 28:23
408A(d)(3)(A) 21:37, 28:21, 28:24
408A(d)(3)(A)(ii) 21:39, 28:22
408A(d)(3)(F) 21:39
408A(d)(6) 21:41, 21:43
408A(e) 21:37, 21:38, 28:24
409 .... 5:8
409(a) 10:32
409(h) 10:32, 10:33, 25:9
409(h)(1) 13:8
409(h)(1)(B) 10:32
409(h)(2)(B) 13:8, 25:9
409(h)(3) 13:13
409(h)(4) 13:10
409(h)(5) 13:11
409(h)(6) 13:12
409(n) 10:21
409(o)(1)(A) 13:14
409(o)(1)(B) 13:14
409(o)(1)(C) 13:14
409A 9:62
409A(b)(3) 14:27, 17:38
410(a)(11) 11:35
410(a)(31) 7:1
410(b) 8:20, 8:21, 10:4, 10:6, 12:18, 15:23, 15:27, 15:33, 21:49, 23:1, 23:3–23:5, 23:13, 23:24, 25:5
410(b)(6)(C) 10:17
410(d) 16:2, 21:6
410(d)(1) 8:2
411 .... 1:17, 4:41, 4:42, 5:8, 5:35, 8:82, 9:85, 10:25, 11:1, 11:13, 11:22, 13:1, 21:52
411(a) 8:1, 8:11, 9:22, 10:25, 10:39, 12:32
411(a)(1) 8:6, 21:52
411(a)(2)(A) 8:8
411(a)(2)(B) 8:8, 8:10
411(a)(3)–(11) 10:25, 10:39

IRC §

411(a)(3)(A) 11:16, 12:53
411(a)(3)(B) 10:39, 11:13, 13:17
411(a)(4) 8:46
411(a)(5)(A) 8:38
411(a)(6)(B) 8:53
411(a)(6)(C) 8:53, 8:59
411(a)(6)(D) 8:53, 10:39
411(a)(6)(E) 8:54
411(a)(7) 4:47, 10:29, 10:34
411(a)(7)(A)(ii) 9:1
411(a)(7)(C) 8:64, 10:29
411(a)(8) 8:5, 12:1
411(a)(8)(B)(i) 9:21
411(a)(9) 1:17, 10:23, 10:26, 10:39, 12:3, 21:24
411(a)(10) 1:17, 10:39, 12:3
411(a)(10)(A) 8:55, 10:39
411(a)(10)(B) 8:56, 10:39
411(a)(11) 4:59, 5:12, 5:27, 5:42, 8:62, 9:9, 9:78, 10:35, 11:12, 13:6, 15:84, 21:15, 23:14
411(a)(11)(C) 1:45
411(a)(12) 8:9
411(a)(13) 8:13
411(a)(13)(A) 16:21
411(b) 12:24
411(b)(1) 9:23
411(b)(1)(A) 9:26
411(b)(1)(B) 9:25
411(b)(1)(C) 9:24
411(b)(1)(H) 12:21, 12:24
411(b)(1)(H)(ii) 9:43
411(b)(1)(H)(iii) 12:25
411(b)(5)(B) 9:79
411(c) 21:52
411(c)(2)(A) 8:6
411(c)(2)(B) 9:30, 9:31, 21:52
411(c)(2)(C) 9:32, 9:46
411(d) 10:39
411(d)(1) 8:15
411(d)(3) 8:69, 8:72, 8:73, 8:75
411(d)(5) 9:30
411(d)(6) 1:7, 1:17, 1:35, 1:36, 3:52, 4:67, 8:58, 8:71, 10:15, 10:17, 10:23, 10:25, 10:26, 10:28–10:31, 10:33–10:39, 11:6, 11:45, 12:3, 12:32, 12:66, 13:8, 13:16, 14:7, 14:17, 15:33, 15:77, 15:85, 21:6, 21:15, 21:22, 23:3–23:5, 23:8
411(d)(6)(A) 10:22, 10:25, 10:28, 10:39
411(d)(6)(B) 4:67, 10:25, 10:39–10:41, 10:43
411(d)(6)(B)(i) 10:22
411(d)(6)(B)(ii) 10:25
411(d)(6)(D) 10:25
411(d)(6)(E) 10:25
411(e)(1) 8:2

IRC §

412 .... 5:8, 5:35, 8:4, 8:23, 8:69, 8:70, 9:16, 9:27, 10:30, 11:3, 11:6, 11:29, 11:36, 12:69, 17:33, 17:48, 23:21
412(a)(2) 17:50
412(b)(2)(C) 9:16, 17:48
412(c)(8) 10:25, 10:39
412(d) 26:12
412(d)(1)(A) 9:16, 17:49
412(e)(3) 9:23, 9:27, 12:68–12:70, 25:20, 25:22
412(i) 25:22
412(l)(7) 14:9, 14:10
412(l)(7)(B)(ii) 10:21
413(c) 15:24, 15:66
414 .... 7:1, 7:2, 7:3
414(a)(1) 8:49
414(a)(6)(A) 11:24
414(b) .... 2:3, 4:27, 8:31, 8:34, 8:40, 9:36, 13:4, 14:7, 16:26, App. G:2, App. G:10
414(c) .... 2:3, 4:27, 8:31, 8:34, 8:40, 9:36, 13:4, 14:7, 16:26, App. G:2, App. G:10
414(d) ... 1:17, 4:6, 4:40, 4:47, 4:49, 7:2, 7:3, 8:2, 10:4, 12:2, 20:9, 21:6
414(d)(6) 1:35
414(e) 16:2, 21:6
414(e)(1) 8:2
414(f) 15:10
414(g) 3:13, 24:15, 24:23, 26:11
414(h)(2) .... App. G:9
414(k) 4:56, 9:89–9:91
414(l) 1:35, 4:26, 10:4, 10:17, 10:34, 10:39, 21:15, 21:50, 23:7, 26:1, 26:8
414(l)(1) 10:34, 26:1
414(l)(2) 26:5
414(m) ... 2:3, 4:27, 8:31, 8:34, 8:40, 9:36, 13:4, 14:7, 15:19, App. G:2, App. G:10
414(n) 15:19
414(o) .... 4:27, 8:40, 9:36, 14:7, App. G:2
414(p) 4:18, 4:34, 4:47, 4:61, 11:47, 21:32
414(p)(1)–(3) 3:41
414(p)(1) 3:3, 3:4
414(p)(1)(A) 3:62
414(p)(1)(A)(i) 3:5, 3:16
414(p)(1)(A)(ii) 3:5
414(p)(1)(B) 3:2
414(p)(2) 3:21, 3:45
414(p)(2)(A) 3:5
414(p)(2)(B)–(D) 3:17
414(p)(2)(B) 3:5, 3:31
414(p)(2)(C) 3:5, 3:35
414(p)(2)(D) 3:5, 3:9, 3:36
414(p)(3) 3:16, 3:21
414(p)(3)(A) 3:5, 3:23, 3:31
414(p)(3)(B) 3:5, 3:23, 3:31
414(p)(3)(C) 3:5, 3:37

IRC §

414(p)(4) 3:16, 3:21, 3:25
414(p)(4)(A)(i) 3:24
414(p)(4)(A)(ii) 3:24
414(p)(4)(A)(iii) 3:5, 3:20, 3:24, 3:50
414(p)(4)(B) 3:25
414(p)(5) 3:19
414(p)(5)(A) 3:26
414(p)(6) 3:40
414(p)(6)(A) 3:46
414(p)(6)(A)(ii) 3:12, 3:47, 3:49
414(p)(6)(B) 3:39
414(p)(7) 3:40, 3:48, 4:62
414(p)(7)(A) 4:62
414(p)(7)(D) 3:48
414(p)(7)(E) 4:62
414(p)(8) 3:6
414(q) .... 2:35, App. G:1
414(q)(4) 8:32
414(r) .... App. G:2
414(s) 10:24
414(u) 2:8
414(u)(4) 2:8
414(v) 5:32
414(w)(3) 5:15, 5:30
415 ...... 3:30, 4:33, 4:46, 5:8, 5:13, 5:28, 5:35, 5:44, 5:48, 8:25, 9:47, 9:56, 9:59, 9:70, 9:71, 10:30, 10:34, 11:47, 12:19, 12:52, 12:65, 15:27, 16:2, 16:57, 19:10, 20:2, 21:23, 21:52, 22:3, 23:1, 23:3, 23:6, 27:32, 28:2
415(b) 9:57, 9:69, 10:30, 21:52
415(b)(1) 9:56
415(b)(1)(A) .... 20:4, App. G:8
415(b)(1)(B) 10:41
415(b)(2)(A) 9:57
415(b)(2)(B) 9:57, 11:47
415(b)(2)(C) 9:58
415(b)(2)(D) 9:59
415(b)(2)(E) 9:67, 9:68, 9:69
415(b)(2)(E)(vi) 9:60
415(b)(3) 9:69, 10:41
415(b)(4) 9:64
415(b)(5)(A) 9:63
415(b)(5)(B) 9:63
415(c) 5:48, 9:94, 9:95, 23:3, 23:6
415(c)(2)(B) 2:16
415(c)(3) .... 10:41, 19:10, App. G:9
415(c)(3)(C) 12:42, 12:44
415(d) 8:33, 12:52
415(d)(6) 10:30
415(k)(2) 19:29, 28:3, 29:4
416 ..... 1:16, 4:6, 5:35, 8:31, 13:4, 15:27, 23:3, App. G:10
416(b)(1) 8:17
416(c) 21:49
416(c)(1)(C) 9:50
416(c)(1)(C)(iii) 15:63
416(g)(1) 8:18
416(g)(1)(B) 8:20
416(g)(2)(A)(i) 8:20
416(g)(3) 8:26
416(g)(4)(B) 8:27
416(g)(4)(C) 8:19
416(g)(4)(E) 8:27
416(i) 8:33
416(i)(1) .... 8:31, 13:4, App. G:10
416(i)(1)(A) 8:30, 8:35
416(i)(1)(D) 8:32
417 ..... 2:45, 3:19, 4:18, 4:46, 4:59, 4:61, 4:68, 5:8, 5:12, 5:27, 5:42, 10:25, 10:30, 10:34, 10:39, 11:1, 11:2, 11:4–11:7, 11:9, 11:12, 11:15, 11:21, 11:25, 11:35, 11:47, 11:54, 11:56, 12:54, 12:56, 21:50, 23:14
417(a) 4:68, 11:5, 11:9, 11:10, 11:47
417(a)(1) 11:37
417(a)(1)(A)(i) 11:37, 11:47
417(a)(2) 2:45, 11:3, 11:24, 11:37, 11:47, 15:80, 21:15
417(a)(2)(B) 2:45, 11:24
417(a)(3) 10:39, 10:42, 11:47, 11:50
417(a)(3)(A) 11:47
417(a)(3)(A)(i) 12:62
417(a)(3)(B) 11:47, 11:49
417(a)(3)(B)(i) 11:43
417(a)(3)(B)(ii) 11:47
417(a)(5)(A) 11:5
417(a)(6) 11:47
417(a)(6)(A) ... 11:4, 11:11, 11:12, 11:17, 11:37
417(a)(7) 11:47
417(b) 11:47
417(c)(1) 12:62
417(c)(2) 11:4
417(c)(3) 11:52
417(e) .... 4:47, 4:59, 4:68, 9:32, 9:33, 9:52, 9:57, 9:59, 9:68, 9:69, 9:78, 10:30, 10:34, 10:35, 10:39, 11:9, 11:10, 12:65, 13:7, 14:13, 15:52–15:54, 15:56, 15:71, 16:20, 16:21, 16:23, 16:45, 17:2, 21:52, 29:20, 29:21, App. B
417(e)(3), ... 9:31, 9:60, 9:65, 9:69, 9:70, 9:79, 11:17, 11:47, 11:52, 11:54, 15:54, 16:21
417(e)(3)(A)(ii)(I) 10:39
417(e)(3)(A)(ii)(II) .... 10:39, App. H
417(e)(3)(D) .... 9:79, App. H
417(g) 11:38, 11:39, 11:46
430 .... 9:27, 14:23, 17:33, 17:44
430(b) 15:61, 16:32, 17:44
430(d)(1) 14:11, 17:44
430(e)(4) 17:50
430(h)(2)(C)(iii) 9:79

IRC §

430(i) 14:27, 17:38
436 .... 16:10
436(b) 14:20
436(d) 14:24
436(d)(2) 10:30
436(d)(5) 14:21
436(f) 14:25, 14:26
436(j)(2) 14:22
457 .... 7:1–7:3, 19:10, 12:30, 19:23, 22:3, 28:5, App. G:9
457(b) 2:49, 4:2, 4:27, 20:1, 20:16, 21:6, 21:19, 21:21, 21:28, 21:37, 21:38, 21:53, 27:1, 27:32
457(f)(1)(A) 9:62
501 .... 8:2, 23:24
501(a) 2:2, 7:1, 19:24, 20:17, 21:21
501(c) 7:2, 7:3
501(c)(8) 16:2
501(c)(9) 16:2
501(c)(18) 5:31, 16:2, 19:7, 19:10, 22:3
541(c)(2) 7:1
633 .... 20:2
671 et seq. 19:49
691(c)(4) 29:10
691(c)(5) 19:56
731(c)(2) 10:30
871(a) 24:57
1034 .... 2:1
1361 .... 10:32
1361(b) 21:51
1361(c)(6) 21:51
1366 .... 21:51
1441 .... 24:57, 27:4
1563(e) 16:3, 17:23
1563(e)(3)(C) 16:3
2039 .... 4:31
2518 .... 4:20
3121(a)(13) 22:2
3121(w)(3)(A) 4:6, 4:40
3121(w)(3)(B) 4:6, 4:40
3306(b)(10) 22:2
3402 .... 24:49, 24:51
3402(f)(3) 24:28, 24:36, 24:49
3402(p) 21:42, 24:3
3405 ..... 24:11, 24:13, 24:49, 24:55, 24:57, 27:4
3405(a) 24:1
3405(a)(1) 24:20
3405(a)(2) 24:28
3405(a)(3) 24:28
3405(a)(4) 24:20, 24:50
3405(b)(1) 24:55, 28:16
3405(b)(2)(B) 24:55
3405(c) 2:11, 2:17, 3:60, 21:1, 21:11, 21:22, 21:28, 21:30, 21:32, 21:42, 24:1, 24:6, 24:9–24:11, 28:1, 28:4

IRC §

3405(c)(1) 2:19, 24:2, 24:4
3405(c)(1)(B) 24:55
3405(c)(2) 21:3, 21:42
3405(d) 24:4
3405(d)(2) 24:22
3405(d)(10)(B) 24:30, 24:45
3405(d)(10)(B)(i)(I) 24:33
3405(d)(10)(B)(i)(II) 24:37
3405(e) 24:32
3405(e)(1)(B) 24:8, 24:12
3405(e)(1)(B)(iii) 24:57
3405(e)(1)(B)(iv) 1:46
3405(e)(2) 24:19
3405(e)(3) 24:55
3405(e)(7) 24:23
3405(e)(10)(B)(i) 24:31
3405(e)(10)(B)(i)(I) 24:36
3405(e)(10)(B)(ii) 24:56
4281 .... 10:25
4971(b) 17:48
4972 .... 17:47
4974 ..... 4:22, 12:81, 20:16, 20:18, 20:19, 23:11
4974(c) .... 20:1, 4974(c)(7)17:47
4975 .... 2:3, 2:21, 2:22, 2:35, 2:37
4975(a) 2:34
4975(b) 2:34
4975(c)(1)(B) 2:34, 2:35
4975(d)(1) 2:19, 2:34, 2:35
4975(d)(1)(A)–(E) 2:1, 2:34
4975(e)(2) 2:34, 2:35
4975(e)(7) 10:30, 10:32, 10:34
4975(f)(4) 2:34
4975(f)(4)(A) 2:34
4975(f)(5) 2:34
4979 .... 5:15, 5:30
4979(f)(1) 5:15
4979(f)(2) 5:14, 5:29, 5:30
4980 .... 1:30, 15:74, 16:51
4980(c)(3)(B) 1:30
4980(d)(1) 15:72, 16:49
4980(d)(2) 15:73, 16:50
4980(d)(3) 15:75, 16:52
4980F 1:17, 12:3
4980F(c)(3) 15:15
4980F(e) 10:39
5112(a)(7) 28:10
5112(a)(8) 28:10
5112(a)(9) 28:10
5112(a)(10) 28:10
5112(e) 28:10
5112(k) 28:10
5402(d) 21:44
6047(e) 24:16
6057 .... 8:70
6058 .... 8:70

IRC §

6058(b) 26:9, 26:11
6059 .... 8:70
6321 .... 3:63
6331 .... 20:14, 27:32
6343 .... 3:63
6501(a) 23:17
6721(a) 27:10
6721(b) 27:10
6721(c) 27:10
6721(e) 27:10
6722 .... 27:12
6722(c) 27:12
7476(b)(3) 15:28, 15:67
7605(b) 23:8
7701(a)(37) 15:90
7702A 19:5
7805 .... 7:1
7805(b) 23:16

Table of Treasury Regulations

[References are to question numbers.]

Treas. Reg. §

1.46-8(e)(10) 1:33
1.72-2(b)(1) 1:20
1.72-2(b)(2) 1:20, 18:3
1.72-2(b)(3) 18:4
1.72-4(b) 18:3
1.72-11(f) 18:5
1.72-15(e) 19:14
1.72-15(g) 19:15
1.72-16(b) 6:1, 25:27
1.72-16(b)(3) 6:3
1.72-16(b)(4) 6:2, 25:27
1.72(p)-1 .... 2:1, 2:2
1.72(p)-1(18)(b) 2:22
1.72(p)-1, Q&A-1(a) 2:1
1.72(p)-1, Q&A-1(b) 2:1
1.72(p)-1, Q&A-2 .... 2:2
1.72(p)-1, Q&A-3(b) 2:1, 2:3, 2:7, 2:11
1.72(p)-1, Q&A-3(b)(2) 2:1
1.72(p)-1, Q&A-4(a) 2:3
1.72(p)-1, Q&A-4(b) 2:3
1.72(p)-1, Q&A-4(b), Ex. 1 .... 2:3
1.72(p)-1, Q&A-4(b), Ex. 2 .... 2:3
1.72(p)-1, Q&A-4(b), Ex. 3 .... 2:3
1.72(p)-1, Q&A-4(b), Ex. 4 .... 2:3
1.72(p)-1, Q&A-5 .... 2:5
1.72(p)-1, Q&A-6 .... 2:5
1.72(p)-1, Q&A-7 .... 2:5
1.72(p)-1, Q&A-8(a) 2:5
1.72(p)-1, Q&A-8(b), Ex. 2:5
1.72(p)-1, Q&A-9(a) 2:8
1.72(p)-1, Q&A-9(b) 2:8
1.72(p)-1, Q&A-9(d), Ex. 1 .... 2:8
1.72(p)-1, Q&A-9(d), Ex. 2 .... 2:8
1.72(p)-1, Q&A-10 .... 2:3
1.72(p)-1, Q&A-10(a) 2:3, 2:7
1.72(p)-1, Q&A-10(b) 2:7
1.72(p)-1, Q&A-10(c) 2:3
1.72(p)-1, Q&A-11 .... 2:3

Treas. Reg. §

1.72(p)-1, Q&A-11(a) 2:13
1.72(p)-1, Q&A-11(b) 2:13
1.72(p)-1, Q&A-12 .... 2:11, 2:12
1.72(p)-1, Q&A-13(a) 2:11
1.72(p)-1, Q&A-13(a)(2) 2:11
1.72(p)-1, Q&A-13(b) 2:11
1.72(p)-1, Q&A-14 .... 2:14
1.72(p)-1, Q&A-15 .... 2:17
1.72(p)-1, Q&A-16 .... 2:21
1.72(p)-1, Q&A-17 .... 2:20
1.72(p)-1, Q&A-18 .... 2:3
1.72(p)-1, Q&A-18(a) 2:22
1.72(p)-1, Q&A-18(b) 2:22
1.72(p)-1, Q&A-18(c) 2:22
1.72(p)-1, Q&A-18(d) 2:22
1.72(p)-1, Q&A-19(a) 2:15
1.72(p)-1, Q&A-19(b)(1) 2:15
1.72(p)-1, Q&A-19(b)(2) 2:15
1.72(p)-1, Q&A-19(b)(3) 2:15
1.72(p)-1, Q&A-20(a)(1) 2:23
1.72(p)-1, Q&A-20(b), Ex. 1 .... 2:23
1.72(p)-1, Q&A-20(b), Ex. 2 .... 2:23
1.72(p)-1, Q&A-21(a) 2:16
1.72(p)-1, Q&A-21(b), Ex. 2:16
1.72(p)-1, Q&A-22(a) 2:24
1.72(p)-1, Q&A-22(b) 2:24
1.72(p)-1, Q&A-22(c)(1) 2:24
1.72(p)-1, Q&A-22(c)(2)(i) 2:24
1.72(p)-1, Q&A-22(c)(2)(ii) 2:24
1.72(p)-1, Q&A-22(c)(2)(iii) 2:24
1.72(p)-1, Q&A-22(c)(2)(iv) 2:24
1.72(p)-1, Q&A-22(c)(3), Ex. 1 .... 2:24
1.72(p)-1, Q&A-22(c)(3), Ex. 2 .... 2:24
1.72(p)-1, Q&A-22(c)(3), Ex. 3 .... 2:24
1.72(p)-1, Q&A-22(c)(3), Ex. 4 .... 2:24
1.72(p)-1, Q&A-22(d) 2:24
1.72(p)-2, Q&A-20(a)(2) 2:23
1.83-3(b) 23:22

Treas. Reg. §

1.170A-13(c)(5) 1:41, 1:42
1.401-1(b) 15:18
1.401-1(b)(1) 23:3, 23:4
1.401-1(b)(1)(i) 4:35, 10:39, 10:43, 12:17, 12:64, 12:66, 21:50
1.401-1(b)(1)(ii) 1:1–1:3
1.401-1(b)(2) 15:3
1.401-2(b)(2) 17:2
1.401-4(c) 14:1
1.401-6(b)(2) 8:74, 8:80
1.401(a)-1 .... 1:20
1.401(a)-1(a)(2) 25:28
1.401(a)-1(b)(1)(i) 1:20
1.401(a)-1(b)(2) 1:20, 12:2
1.401(a)-1(b)(2)(i) 1:20
1.401(a)-1(b)(2)(ii) 1:20
1.401(a)-1(b)(2)(iii) 1:20
1.401(a)-1(b)(2)(iv) 1:20
1.401(a)-1(b)(2)(v) 1:20
1.401(a)-1(b)(3) 1:20, 12:28
1.401(a)-1(b)(4) 1:20, 12:2
1.401(a)-9(b)(1) 19:13
1.401(a)-11(g) 5:4
1.401(a)-13(b)(1) 3:1
1.401(a)-13(e) 23:14
1.401(a)-13(g)(4)(i)(B)(1) 3:26
1.401(a)-13(g)(4)(i)(B)(2) 3:26
1.401(a)-13(g)(4)(ii) 3:26
1.401(a)-13(g)(4)(iii)(A) 3:27
1.401(a)-13(g)(4)(iii)(B) 3:28
1.401(a)-13(g)(4)(iii)(C) 3:29
1.401(a)-13(g)(4)(iv) 3:30
1.401(a)-14(c) 12:16
1.401(a)-20, Q&A-1 .... 11:1
1.401(a)-20, Q&A-2 .... 11:2
1.401(a)-20, Q&A-3 .... 11:25, 12:54
1.401(a)-20, Q&A-3(a) 11:3
1.401(a)-20, Q&A-3(a)(1)–(3) 11:3
1.401(a)-20, Q&A-3(a)(3)(b)(1) 11:3
1.401(a)-20, Q&A-3(a)(3)(b)(2) 11:3
1.401(a)-20, Q&A-3(b)(1) 11:3
1.401(a)-20, Q&A-4 .... 11:4, 12:55
1.401(a)-20, Q&A-5 .... 1:39, 12:56
1.401(a)-20, Q&A-5(a) 11:6
1.401(a)-20, Q&A-5(b) 11:6
1.401(a)-20, Q&A-6 .... 11:7
1.401(a)-20, Q&A-7 .... 11:8
1.401(a)-20, Q&A-8(a) 11:9
1.401(a)-20, Q&A-8(b) 11:9
1.401(a)-20, Q&A-8(c) 11:9
1.401(a)-20, Q&A-8(d) 11:9
1.401(a)-20, Q&A-9 .... 12:59
1.401(a)-20, Q&A-9(a) 11:10
1.401(a)-20, Q&A-9(b) 11:10
1.401(a)-20, Q&A-10 .... 12:63, 21:45

Treas. Reg. §

1.401(a)-20, Q&A-10(a) 11:11
1.401(a)-20, Q&A-10(b)(1) 11:12
1.401(a)-20, Q&A-10(b)(2) 11:12
1.401(a)-20, Q&A-10(b)(3) 11:12
1.401(a)-20, Q&A-10(b)(4) 11:12
1.401(a)-20, Q&A-10(b)(5) 11:12
1.401(a)-20, Q&A-10(c) 11:13
1.401(a)-20, Q&A-10(c)(2)(i) 11:13
1.401(a)-20, Q&A-10(c)(2)(ii) 11:13
1.401(a)-20, Q&A-10(d)(1) 11:13
1.401(a)-20, Q&A-10(d)(2) 11:13
1.401(a)-20, Q&A-11 .... 11:14
1.401(a)-20, Q&A-12(a) 11:3, 11:15
1.401(a)-20, Q&A-12(b) 11:3, 11:15
1.401(a)-20, Q&A-13 .... 11:16
1.401(a)-20, Q&A-16 .... 11:17, 11:29, 11:42
1.401(a)-20, Q&A-17 .... 11:27
1.401(a)-20, Q&A-17(a) 11:18
1.401(a)-20, Q&A-17(b)(2) 11:18
1.401(a)-20, Q&A-17(b)(3) 11:18
1.401(a)-20, Q&A-17(b)(4) 11:18
1.401(a)-20, Q&A-18 .... 11:19
1.401(a)-20, Q&A-19 .... 11:20
1.401(a)-20, Q&A-20 .... 11:21, 12:54
1.401(a)-20, Q&A-21 .... 11:22
1.401(a)-20, Q&A-22(a) 11:23
1.401(a)-20, Q&A-22(b) 11:23
1.401(a)-20, Q&A-24(a)(1) 2:45, 11:24
1.401(a)-20, Q&A-24(a)(2) 11:24
1.401(a)-20, Q&A-24(b) 2:46, 11:24
1.401(a)-20, Q&A-24(c) 2:47, 11:24
1.401(a)-20, Q&A-24(d) 2:48, 11:24
1.401(a)-20, Q&A-24(e) 11:24
1.401(a)-20, Q&A-25(a) 11:25
1.401(a)-20, Q&A-25(b)(1) 11:26
1.401(a)-20, Q&A-25(b)(2)(i) 11:26
1.401(a)-20, Q&A-25(b)(2)(ii) 11:26
1.401(a)-20, Q&A-25(b)(3) 11:26
1.401(a)-20, Q&A-26 .... 11:28
1.401(a)-20, Q&A-27 .... 11:29
1.401(a)-20, Q&A-28 .... 11:30
1.401(a)-20, Q&A-29 .... 11:31
1.401(a)-20, Q&A-30 .... 11:32
1.401(a)-20, Q&A-31(a) 11:34
1.401(a)-20, Q&A-31(b)(1) 11:34
1.401(a)-20, Q&A-31(b)(2) 11:34
1.401(a)-20, Q&A-31(b)(3) 11:34
1.401(a)-20, Q&A-31(c) 11:34
1.401(a)-20, Q&A-32(a) 11:35
1.401(a)-20, Q&A-32(b) 11:35
1.401(a)-20, Q&A-33(a) 11:36
1.401(a)-20, Q&A-33(b) 11:36
1.401(a)-20, Q&A-34 .... 11:48
1.401(a)-20, Q&A-35(a) 11:49, 11:50
1.401(a)-20, Q&A-35(b) 11:49

Treas. Reg. §

1.401(a)-20, Q&A-35(c) 11:49
1.401(a)-20, Q&A-37 .... 11:50
1.401(a)-20, Q&A-38(a)(1) 11:58
1.401(a)-20, Q&A-38(a)(2), Ex. 1 .... 11:58
1.401(a)-20, Q&A-38(a)(2), Ex. 2 .... 11:58
1.401(a)-20, Q&A-38(b) 11:58
1.401(a)-21 .... 2:1, 11:50, 11:56, 21:48
1.401(a)-21(f), Ex. 3 .... 11:56
1.401(a)-21(g) 11:56
1.401(a)(4) 10:34, 23:24
1.401(a)(4)-1–13 .... 10:4
1.401(a)(4)-1 .... 10:2
1.401(a)(4)-1(b)(2) 10:1, 10:4
1.401(a)(4)-1(b)(3) 10:1, 21:49
1.401(a)(4)-1(b)(4) 10:1
1.401(a)(4)-1(c)(2) 10:2
1.401(a)(4)-1(c)(3) 10:3
1.401(a)(4)-1(c)(4)(i) 10:4
1.401(a)(4)-1(c)(4)(ii) 10:4
1.401(a)(4)-1(c)(4)(iii) 10:4
1.401(a)(4)-1(c)(5) 10:4
1.401(a)(4)-1(c)(6) 10:4
1.401(a)(4)-1(c)(7) 10:4
1.401(a)(4)-1(c)(8) 10:4
1.401(a)(4)-1(c)(9) 10:4
1.401(a)(4)-1(c)(10) 10:4
1.401(a)(4)-1(c)(11) 10:4
1.401(a)(4)-1(c)(12) 10:4
1.401(a)(4)-1(c)(13) 10:4
1.401(a)(4)-1(c)(16) 10:4
1.401(a)(4)-3(b)(2)(iii) 12:17, 12:18
1.401(a)(4)-3(f)(4) 12:19
1.401(a)(4)-3(f)(4)(iii) 10:19
1.401(a)(4)-4 .... 10:1, 10:24, 10:34
1.401(a)(4)-4(a) 10:5, 25:4
1.401(a)(4)-4(b) 10:5, 25:5
1.401(a)(4)-4(b)(1) 10:6
1.401(a)(4)-4(b)(2) 12:18
1.401(a)(4)-4(b)(2)(i) 10:6
1.401(a)(4)-4(b)(2)(ii)(A)(1) 10:7
1.401(a)(4)-4(b)(2)(ii)(A)(2) 10:8
1.401(a)(4)-4(b)(2)(ii)(B) 10:9
1.401(a)(4)-4(b)(2)(ii)(C) 10:10
1.401(a)(4)-4(b)(2)(ii)(D) 10:11
1.401(a)(4)-4(b)(2)(ii)(E) 10:12
1.401(a)(4)-4(b)(3)(i) 10:13
1.401(a)(4)-4(b)(3)(ii)(A) 10:14
1.401(a)(4)-4(b)(3)(ii)(B) 10:15
1.401(a)(4)-4(c) 10:5
1.401(a)(4)-4(c)(1) 10:16, 25:7
1.401(a)(4)-4(c)(2), Ex. 1 .... 10:16
1.401(a)(4)-4(c)(2), Ex. 2 .... 10:16
1.401(a)(4)-4(c)(2), Ex. 3 .... 10:16
1.401(a)(4)-4(d) 10:5
1.401(a)(4)-4(d)(1) 10:17

Treas. Reg. §

1.401(a)(4)-4(d)(1)(iii) 10:17
1.401(a)(4)-4(d)(2) 10:18
1.401(a)(4)-4(d)(3) 10:19
1.401(a)(4)-4(d)(4) 10:20
1.401(a)(4)-4(d)(4)(i)(A) 10:39
1.401(a)(4)-4(d)(4)(iii), Ex. 1 .... 10:20
1.401(a)(4)-4(d)(4)(iii), Ex. 2 .... 10:20
1.401(a)(4)-4(d)(5) 10:21
1.401(a)(4)-4(d)(6) 10:21
1.401(a)(4)-4(d)(7) 10:21
1.401(a)(4)-4(e) 10:5
1.401(a)(4)-4(e)(1) 10:20
1.401(a)(4)-4(e)(1)(i) 10:22, 25:4
1.401(a)(4)-4(e)(1)(ii)(A) 10:22
1.401(a)(4)-4(e)(1)(ii)(B) 10:22
1.401(a)(4)-4(e)(1)(ii)(D) 10:22
1.401(a)(4)-4(e)(1)(iii), Ex. 1 .... 10:22
1.401(a)(4)-4(e)(1)(iii), Ex. 2 .... 10:22
1.401(a)(4)-4(e)(1)(iii), Ex. 3 .... 10:22
1.401(a)(4)-4(e)(2) 10:23
1.401(a)(4)-4(e)(3) 10:34
1.401(a)(4)-4(e)(3)(i) 10:24
1.401(a)(4)-4(e)(3)(ii)(A)-(I) 10:24
1.401(a)(4)-5 .... 14:16
1.401(a)(4)-5(b) 14:18
1.401(a)(4)-5(b)(1) 14:2
1.401(a)(4)-5(b)(2) 14:5
1.401(a)(4)-5(b)(3)(i) 14:6
1.401(a)(4)-5(b)(3)(i)(A) 14:13
1.401(a)(4)-5(b)(3)(i)(B) 14:13
1.401(a)(4)-5(b)(3)(ii) 14:7
1.401(a)(4)-5(b)(3)(iii) 14:8
1.401(a)(4)-5(b)(3)(iv) 14:9
1.401(a)(4)-5(b)(3)(v) 14:12
1.401(a)(4)-5(b)(4) 14:17
1.401(a)(4)-8(b)(3)(i)(B) 8:60
1.401(a)(4)-8(c)(3)(i) 9:73
1.401(a)(4)-8(c)(3)(vi) 9:78, 9:80
1.401(a)(4)-8(c)(3)(vii) 9:78
1.401(a)(4)-8(d)(1) 12:57
1.401(a)(4)-8(d)(1)(vii) 9:86
1.401(a)(4)-9(b) 10:4
1.401(a)(4)-9(b)(2)(v) 10:1
1.401(a)(4)-9(c) 10:4
1.401(a)(4)-10 .... 10:4
1.401(a)(4)-11(b) 10:4
1.401(a)(4)-11(c) 10:4
1.401(a)(4)-11(d) 10:4
1.401(a)(4)-11(d)(2) 8:45, 9:41
1.401(a)(4)-11(g) 10:3
1.401(a)(4)-12 .... 10:22, 10:26, 10:39, 12:20
1.401(a)(4)-13 .... 10:2
1.401(a)(9)-1–9 .... 4:4
1.401(a)(9)-1, Q&A-1 .... 4:2
1.401(a)(9)-1, Q&A-2(a) 4:3

Treas. Reg. §

1.401(a)(9)-1, Q&A-2(b)(1) 4:3
1.401(a)(9)-1, Q&A-2(b)(2) 4:3
1.401(a)(9)-1, Q&A-2(c) 4:3
1.401(a)(9)-1, Q&A-2(d) 4:6, 4:40, 4:49
1.401(a)(9)-1, Q&A-3(a) 4:4
1.401(a)(9)-1, Q&A-3(b) 4:4
1.401(a)(9)-1, Q&A-3(c) 4:4
1.401(a)(9)-2 . . . . 28:15
1.401(a)(9)-2, Q&A-1(a) 4:5
1.401(a)(9)-2, Q&A-1(b) 4:5
1.401(a)(9)-2, Q&A-1(c) 4:5
1.401(a)(9)-2, Q&A-2 . . . . 13:4
1.401(a)(9)-2, Q&A-2(a) 4:6
1.401(a)(9)-2, Q&A-2(b) 4:6
1.401(a)(9)-2, Q&A-2(c) 4:6
1.401(a)(9)-2, Q&A-2(d) 4:6
1.401(a)(9)-2, Q&A-2(e) 4:6
1.401(a)(9)-2, Q&A-3 . . . . 4:7
1.401(a)(9)-2, Q&A-4 . . . . 4:8
1.401(a)(9)-2, Q&A-5 . . . . 4:9
1.401(a)(9)-2, Q&A-6(a) 4:10
1.401(a)(9)-2, Q&A-6(b) 4:10
1.401(a)(9)-3 . . . . 4:4, 4:10, 4:23
1.401(a)(9)-3(e) 4:26
1.401(a)(9)-3, Q&A-1 . . . . 12:74
1.401(a)(9)-3, Q&A-1(a) 4:11
1.401(a)(9)-3, Q&A-2 . . . . 4:12, 4:20, 12:77
1.401(a)(9)-3, Q&A-3 . . . . 4:16, 12:76, 20:24
1.401(a)(9)-3, Q&A-3(a) 4:13, 4:23, 4:34
1.401(a)(9)-3, Q&A-3(b) 4:13, 4:34
1.401(a)(9)-3, Q&A-4 . . . . 12:78
1.401(a)(9)-3, Q&A-4(a) 4:14, 20:18
1.401(a)(9)-3, Q&A-4(c) 4:14
1.401(a)(9)-3, Q&A-5 . . . . 4:15, 4:20
1.401(a)(9)-4 . . . . 4:3, 4:14
1.401(a)(9)-4(b) 4:14
1.401(a)(9)-4, Q&A-1 . . . . 4:17
1.401(a)(9)-4, Q&A-2 . . . . 4:18
1.401(a)(9)-4, Q&A-3 . . . . 4:19, 4:31, 12:79
1.401(a)(9)-4, Q&A-4 . . . . 12:82
1.401(a)(9)-4, Q&A-4(a) 4:20
1.401(a)(9)-4, Q&A-4(b) 4:20
1.401(a)(9)-4, Q&A-4(c) 4:20
1.401(a)(9)-4, Q&A-5 . . . . 12:80, 12:81
1.401(a)(9)-4, Q&A-5(a) 4:21
1.401(a)(9)-4, Q&A-5(b) 4:21
1.401(a)(9)-4, Q&A-6 . . . . 12:81
1.401(a)(9)-4, Q&A-6(a) 4:22
1.401(a)(9)-4, Q&A-6(b) 4:22
1.401(a)(9)-4, Q&A-6(c)(1) 4:22
1.401(a)(9)-4, Q&A-6(c)(2) 4:22
1.401(a)(9)-5 . . . . 4:3, 4:5, 4:23, 4:45, 20:18
1.401(a)(9)-5, Q&A-1 . . . . 4:23
1.401(a)(9)-5, Q&A-1(a) 4:23
1.401(a)(9)-5, Q&A-1(b) 4:23

Treas. Reg. §

1.401(a)(9)-5, Q&A-1(c) 4:23
1.401(a)(9)-5, Q&A-1(d) 4:23
1.401(a)(9)-5, Q&A-1(e) 4:24
1.401(a)(9)-5, Q&A-2 . . . . 4:25
1.401(a)(9)-5, Q&A-3(a) 4:26
1.401(a)(9)-5, Q&A-3(b) 4:26
1.401(a)(9)-5, Q&A-3(c) 4:26
1.401(a)(9)-5, Q&A-3(d) 4:26, 4:27
1.401(a)(9)-5, Q&A-4(a) 4:28
1.401(a)(9)-5, Q&A-4(b)(1) 4:28
1.401(a)(9)-5, Q&A-4(b)(2) 4:28
1.401(a)(9)-5, Q&A-5(a) 4:29
1.401(a)(9)-5, Q&A-5(b) 4:29, 4:36
1.401(a)(9)-5, Q&A-5(c)(1) 4:29
1.401(a)(9)-5, Q&A-5(c)(2) 4:29
1.401(a)(9)-5, Q&A-5(c)(3) 4:28
1.401(a)(9)-5, Q&A-6 . . . . 4:29
1.401(a)(9)-5, Q&A-7 . . . . 4:62
1.401(a)(9)-5, Q&A-7(a)(1) 4:31
1.401(a)(9)-5, Q&A-7(a)(2) 4:31
1.401(a)(9)-5, Q&A-7(b) 4:31
1.401(a)(9)-5, Q&A-7(c)(1) 4:31
1.401(a)(9)-5, Q&A-7(c)(2) 4:31
1.401(a)(9)-5, Q&A-7(c)(3), Ex. 1 . . . . 4:31
1.401(a)(9)-5, Q&A-7(c)(3), Ex. 2 . . . . 4:31
1.401(a)(9)-5, Q&A-8 . . . . 4:32, 4:62, 4:63
1.401(a)(9)-5, Q&A-9 . . . . 4:33
1.401(a)(9)-5, Q&A-9(a) 4:33
1.401(a)(9)-6 . . . . 4:3, 4:5, 4:6, 4:20, 4:24, 4:27, 4:37, 4:40, 4:45, 4:46, 4:49
1.401(a)(9)-6, Q&A-1–15 . . . . 4:50
1.401(a)(9)-6, Q&A-1 . . . . 4:47–4:48
1.401(a)(9)-6, Q&A-1(a) 4:34, 4:47
1.401(a)(9)-6, Q&A-1(b) 4:34
1.401(a)(9)-6, Q&A-1(b)(1)(i) 4:34
1.401(a)(9)-6, Q&A-1(c) 4:27, 4:34
1.401(a)(9)-6, Q&A-1(d)(1) 4:34
1.401(a)(9)-6, Q&A-1(d)(2) 4:34
1.401(a)(9)-6, Q&A-1(e) 4:34
1.401(a)(9)-6, Q&A-1(f) 4:34
1.401(a)(9)-6, Q&A-2 . . . . 4:35
1.401(a)(9)-6, Q&A-2(a) 4:35
1.401(a)(9)-6, Q&A-2(b) 4:35
1.401(a)(9)-6, Q&A-2(c) 4:35
1.401(a)(9)-6, Q&A-2(c)(2) 4:35
1.401(a)(9)-6, Q&A-2(c)(3) 4:35
1.401(a)(9)-6, Q&A-2(d) 4:35
1.401(a)(9)-6, Q&A-2(e) 4:35
1.401(a)(9)-6, Q&A-3(a) 4:36
1.401(a)(9)-6, Q&A-3(b)(1) 4:36
1.401(a)(9)-6, Q&A-3(b)(2) 4:36
1.401(a)(9)-6, Q&A-4 . . . . 4:24
1.401(a)(9)-6, Q&A-4(a) 4:37
1.401(a)(9)-6, Q&A-5 . . . . 4:38
1.401(a)(9)-6, Q&A-6 . . . . 4:16, 4:39, 4:63

Treas. Reg. §

1.401(a)(9)-6, Q&A-7 .... 13:19
1.401(a)(9)-6, Q&A-7(a) 4:40
1.401(a)(9)-6, Q&A-7(b) 4:40
1.401(a)(9)-6, Q&A-7(c) 4:40
1.401(a)(9)-6, Q&A-7(d) 4:40
1.401(a)(9)-6, Q&A-8 .... 4:41
1.401(a)(9)-6, Q&A-9 .... 4:42, 13:19
1.401(a)(9)-6, Q&A-10 .... 4:10, 4:11, 4:36
1.401(a)(9)-6, Q&A-10(a) 4:43
1.401(a)(9)-6, Q&A-10(b) 4:43
1.401(a)(9)-6, Q&A-11 .... 4:16, 4:44
1.401(a)(9)-6, Q&A-12(a) 4:45
1.401(a)(9)-6, Q&A-12(b) 4:45
1.401(a)(9)-6, Q&A-12(c)(1) 4:45
1.401(a)(9)-6, Q&A-12(c)(2) 4:45
1.401(a)(9)-6, Q&A-12(c)(3) 4:45
1.401(a)(9)-6, Q&A-13 .... 4:46
1.401(a)(9)-6, Q&A-13, Ex. 2 .... 4:46
1.401(a)(9)-6, Q&A-13, Ex. 3 .... 4:46
1.401(a)(9)-6, Q&A-13(b) 4:46
1.401(a)(9)-6, Q&A-13(c) 4:46
1.401(a)(9)-6, Q&A-13(c)(1) 4:46
1.401(a)(9)-6, Q&A-13(c)(2) 4:46
1.401(a)(9)-6, Q&A-13(c)(3) 4:46
1.401(a)(9)-6, Q&A-13(d), Ex. 1 .... 4:46
1.401(a)(9)-6, Q&A-14 .... 4:34, 4:47
1.401(a)(9)-6, Q&A-14(a)(1)-(6) 4:47
1.401(a)(9)-6, Q&A-14(a)(4) 4:47
1.401(a)(9)-6, Q&A-14(b) 4:34, 4:47
1.401(a)(9)-6, Q&A-14(c) 4:34, 4:47
1.401(a)(9)-6, Q&A-14(c)(3) 4:47
1.401(a)(9)-6, Q&A-14(c)(4) 4:47
1.401(a)(9)-6, Q&A-14(d) 4:34, 4:47
1.401(a)(9)-6, Q&A-14(d)(1) 4:47
1.401(a)(9)-6, Q&A-14(e) 4:47
1.401(a)(9)-6, Q&A-14(e)(1) 4:47
1.401(a)(9)-6, Q&A-14(e)(2) 4:47
1.401(a)(9)-6, Q&A-14(e)(3) 4:47
1.401(a)(9)-6, Q&A-14(f), Ex. 1 .... 4:47
1.401(a)(9)-6, Q&A-14(f), Ex. 2 .... 4:47
1.401(a)(9)-6, Q&A-14(f), Ex. 3 .... 4:47
1.401(a)(9)-6, Q&A-14(f), Ex. 4 .... 4:47
1.401(a)(9)-6, Q&A-14(f), Ex. 5 .... 4:47
1.401(a)(9)-6, Q&A-14(f), Ex. 6 .... 4:47
1.401(a)(9)-6, Q&A-14(f), Ex. 7 .... 4:47
1.401(a)(9)-6, Q&A-14(f), Ex. 8 .... 4:47
1.401(a)(9)-6, Q&A-14(f), Ex. 9 .... 4:47
1.401(a)(9)-6, Q&A-15 .... 4:47
1.401(a)(9)-6, Q&A-16 .... 4:50
1.401(a)(9)-6, Q&A-17 .... 4:26, 4:27
1.401(a)(9)-6, Q&A-17(a)(1) 4:27
1.401(a)(9)-6, Q&A-17(a)(2) 4:27
1.401(a)(9)-6, Q&A-17(a)(3) 4:27
1.401(a)(9)-6, Q&A-17(a)(4) 4:27
1.401(a)(9)-6, Q&A-17(a)(5) 4:27

Treas. Reg. §

1.401(a)(9)-6, Q&A-17(a)(6) 4:27
1.401(a)(9)-6, Q&A-17(b) 4:27
1.401(a)(9)-6, Q&A-17(b)(1) 4:27
1.401(a)(9)-6, Q&A-17(b)(2)(i) 4:27
1.401(a)(9)-6, Q&A-17(b)(2)(ii) 4:27
1.401(a)(9)-6, Q&A-17(b)(3) 4:27
1.401(a)(9)-6, Q&A-17(b)(3)(i) 4:27
1.401(a)(9)-6, Q&A-17(b)(3)(ii) 4:27
1.401(a)(9)-6, Q&A-17(c) 4:27
1.401(a)(9)-6, Q&A-17(d) 4:27
1.401(a)(9)-6, Q&A-17(d)(1)(i) 4:27
1.401(a)(9)-6, Q&A-17(d)(1)(ii)(A) 4:27
1.401(a)(9)-6, Q&A-17(d)(1)(ii)(B) 4:27
1.401(a)(9)-6, Q&A-17(d)(1)(ii)(C) 4:27
1.401(a)(9)-6, Q&A-17(d)(1)(iii) 4:27
1.401(a)(9)-6, Q&A-17(d)(2)(i) 4:27
1.401(a)(9)-6, Q&A-17(d)(2)(ii) 4:27
1.401(a)(9)-6, Q&A-17(d)(2)(iii) 4:27
1.401(a)(9)-6, Q&A-17(d)(3)(i) 4:27
1.401(a)(9)-6, Q&A-17(d)(4)(i) 4:27
1.401(a)(9)-6, Q&A-17(d)(4)(ii) 4:27
1.401(a)(9)-6, Q&A-17(d)(5) 4:27
1.401(a)(9)-6, Q&A-17(e)(1) 4:27
1.401(a)(9)-6, Q&A-17(e)(2) 4:27
1.401(a)(9)-7, Q&A-1 .... 4:51
1.401(a)(9)-7, Q&A-2 ..... 4:26, 4:27, 4:52, 4:54
1.401(a)(9)-7, Q&A-3 .... 4:26, 4:55, 28:13
1.401(a)(9)-7, Q&A-3(a) 4:53
1.401(a)(9)-7, Q&A-3(b) 4:53
1.401(a)(9)-7, Q&A-4 .... 4:26, 4:54, 4:55
1.401(a)(9)-7, Q&A-5 .... 4:55
1.401(a)(9)-8, Q&A-1 .... 4:56
1.401(a)(9)-8, Q&A-2 .... 4:31, 12:79
1.401(a)(9)-8, Q&A-2(a)(1) 4:57
1.401(a)(9)-8, Q&A-2(a)(2) 4:57
1.401(a)(9)-8, Q&A-2(a)(3) 4:24
1.401(a)(9)-8, Q&A-3 .... 4:31, 4:58, 12:79
1.401(a)(9)-8, Q&A-4 .... 4:59
1.401(a)(9)-8, Q&A-5 .... 4:60
1.401(a)(9)-8, Q&A-6(a) 4:61
1.401(a)(9)-8, Q&A-6(b)(1) 4:61
1.401(a)(9)-8, Q&A-6(b)(2) 4:61
1.401(a)(9)-8, Q&A-6(c) 4:61
1.401(a)(9)-8, Q&A-8 .... 4:63
1.401(a)(9)-8, Q&A-9 .... 4:64
1.401(a)(9)-8, Q&A-10 .... 4:65
1.401(a)(9)-8, Q&A-11 .... 4:66
1.401(a)(9)-8, Q&A-12 .... 4:67
1.401(a)(9)-8, Q&A-13 .... 4:68, 13:5, 28:14
1.401(a)(9)-8, Q&A-14(a) 4:69
1.401(a)(9)-8, Q&A-14(b) 4:69
1.401(a)(9)-8, Q&A-14(c) 4:69
1.401(a)(9)-8, Q&A-15 .... 4:70
1.401(a)(9)-8, Q&A-16 .... 4:71, 28:15
1.401(a)(9)-9, Q&A-1 .... 4:30, 4:47, App. D

Treas. Reg. §

1.401(a)(9)-9, Q&A-2 .... 4:28, 4:36, App. D
1.401(a)(9)-9, Q&A-3 .... 4:30, App. E
1.401(a)(9)-9, Q&A-A 4:47
1.401(a)(31)-1, Q&A-2 .... 21:1
1.401(a)(31)-1, Q&A-3 .... 10:34, 21:2
1.401(a)(31)-1, Q&A-4 .... 21:2
1.401(a)(31)-1, Q&A-5 .... 21:3
1.401(a)(31)-1, Q&A-6 .... 21:4
1.401(a)(31)-1, Q&A-7 .... 21:5
1.401(a)(31)-1, Q&A-8 .... 21:8
1.401(a)(31)-1, Q&A-9 .... 21:9
1.401(a)(31)-1, Q&A-10 .... 21:10
1.401(a)(31)-1, Q&A-11 .... 21:11
1.401(a)(31)-1, Q&A-12 .... 21:12
1.401(a)(31)-1, Q&A-13 .... 21:13
1.401(a)(31)-1, Q&A-14 .... 10:34, 21:14
1.401(a)(31)-1, Q&A-14(a) 21:14
1.401(a)(31)-1, Q&A-14(b)(1) 21:14
1.401(a)(31)-1, Q&A-14(b)(2) 21:14
1.401(a)(31)-1, Q&A-14, Ex. 1 .... 21:14
1.401(a)(31)-1, Q&A-14, Ex. 2 .... 21:14
1.401(a)(31)-1, Q&A-14, Ex. 3 .... 21:14
1.401(a)(31)-1, Q&A-14, Ex. 4 .... 21:14
1.401(a)(31)-1, Q&A-15 .... 21:15
1.401(a)(31)-1, Q&A-16 .... 21:16
1.401(a)(31)-1, Q&A-17 .... 21:17
1.401(a)(31)-1, Q&A-18 .... 21:18
1.401(a)(31)-1(b), Q&A-15 .... 2:12
1.401(b)-1 .... 1:20, 12:3
1.401(e)(31)-1, Q&A-17 .... 21:34
1.401(k)-1(a)(3)(iv) 5:31
1.401(k)-1(d)(1)(ii) 1:6
1.401(k)-1(d)(3) 1:6, 10:30
1.401(k)-1(d)(3)(i) 1:7
1.401(k)-1(d)(3)(ii) 1:8, 1:9
1.401(k)-1(d)(3)(iii)(A) 1:6, 1:10
1.401(k)-1(d)(3)(iii)(B) 1:6
1.401(k)-1(d)(3)(iii)(B)(1)–(6) 1:11
1.401(k)-1(d)(3)(iii)(B)(1) 1:6
1.401(k)-1(d)(3)(iii)(B)(3) 1:6
1.401(k)-1(d)(3)(iii)(B)(5) 1:6
1.401(k)-1(d)(3)(iv)(A) 1:12
1.401(k)-1(d)(3)(iv)(B) 1:12
1.401(k)-1(d)(3)(iv)(C) 1:6, 1:12
1.401(k)-1(d)(3)(iv)(D) 1:6
1.401(k)-1(d)(3)(iv)(E) 1:12, 1:13
1.401(k)-1(d)(3)(iv)(E)(2) 1:13
1.401(k)-1(d)(3)(iv)(F) 1:13
1.401(k)-1(d)(3)(v) 1:11, 1:13
1.401(k)-1(d)(5)(iii) 2:11
1.401(k)-1(f)(1)(i) 10:24
1.401(k)-2(b)(1)(i) 5:2
1.401(k)-2(b)(1)(ii) 5:3
1.401(k)-2(b)(1)(iii) 5:4
1.401(k)-2(b)(2) 21:23
1.401(k)-2(b)(2)(ii) 5:6
1.401(k)-2(b)(2)(ii)(A) 5:1
1.401(k)-2(b)(2)(iii) 5:7
1.401(k)-2(b)(2)(iv) 5:25
1.401(k)-2(b)(2)(iv)(A) 5:10
1.401(k)-2(b)(2)(iv)(B) 5:10
1.401(k)-2(b)(2)(iv)(C) 5:10
1.401(k)-2(b)(2)(iv)(D) 5:11
1.401(k)-2(b)(2)(v) 5:9
1.401(k)-2(b)(2)(vi)(A) 5:14, 5:29
1.401(k)-2(b)(2)(vi)(C) 5:14
1.401(k)-2(b)(2)(vii)(A) 5:12
1.401(k)-2(b)(2)(vii)(B) 5:13
1.401(k)-2(b)(2)(vii)(D) 5:5
1.401(k)-2(b)(3) 5:8
1.401(k)-2(b)(5)(i) 5:15
1.401(k)-2(b)(5)(ii) 5:15
1.401(k)-2(b)(5)(iii) 5:15
1.401(k)-6 .... 8:6, 9:2, 10:24
1.401(l)-3(e)(2) 12:19
1.401(l)-3(e)(3) 12:20
1.401(m)-1(a)(2) 10:24
1.401(m)-1(a)(3) 10:24
1.401(m)-1(e)(1)(i) 10:24
1.401(m)-2(a)(4)(ii) 5:22
1.401(m)-2(b)(1)(i) 5:17
1.401(m)-2(b)(1)(ii) 5:18
1.401(m)-2(b)(1)(iii) 5:19
1.401(m)-2(b)(2) 5:21, 21:23
1.401(m)-2(b)(2)(ii)(A) 5:16
1.401(m)-2(b)(2)(iv)(A) 5:25
1.401(m)-2(b)(2)(iv)(B) 5:25
1.401(m)-2(b)(2)(iv)(C) 5:25
1.401(m)-2(b)(2)(iv)(D) 5:25, 5:26
1.401(m)-2(b)(2)(iv)(E) 5:25
1.401(m)-2(b)(2)(v) 5:24
1.401(m)-2(b)(2)(vi)(A) 5:29
1.401(m)-2(b)(3)(i) 5:27
1.401(m)-2(b)(3)(ii) 5:28
1.401(m)-2(b)(3)(iii) 5:29
1.401(m)-2(b)(3)(iv) 5:20
1.401(m)-2(b)(3)(v) 5:29
1.401(m)-2(b)(4)(ii) 5:30
1.401(m)-2(b)(4)(iii) 5:30
1.401(m)-2(c) 10:24
1.401(m)-5 .... 5:16
1.402(a)-1(a)(1)(iii) 25:11
1.402(a)-1(a)(1)(iv) 19:25
1.402(a)-1(a)(1)(v) 23:26
1.402(a)-1(a)(2) 19:13, 25:22, 25:23
1.402(a)-1(b) 27:31
1.402(a)-1(b)(1)(i)(a) 25:30, 29:22
1.402(a)-1(b)(2)(i) 25:31
1.402(a)-1(b)(2)(ii)(a) 25:33
1.402(a)-1(b)(2)(ii)(b) 25:33

Treas. Reg. §

1.402(a)-1(b)(2)(ii)(c) 25:33
1.402(a)-1(b)(2)(ii)(d) 25:33
1.402(a)-1(e)(2) 19:16
1.402(b)-1(a)(1) 23:18
1.402(b)-1(a)(2) 23:19
1.402(b)-1(b)(1) 23:23
1.402(b)-1(b)(3) 23:23
1.402(b)-1(b)(5) 23:25
1.402(c)-2, Q&A-1 ..... 21:14, 28:5
1.402(c)-2, Q&A-2 ..... 21:21, 28:5
1.402(c)-2, Q&A-3 ..... 2:12, 21:22, 21:23, 28:2
1.402(c)-2, Q&A-3(a) 28:1
1.402(c)-2, Q&A-3(b)(2) 28:13
1.402(c)-2, Q&A-4 ..... 21:23, 28:2
1.402(c)-2, Q&A-4(d) 2:11, 2:12
1.402(c)-2, Q&A-5 ..... 21:24
1.402(c)-2, Q&A-6 ..... 21:25
1.402(c)-2, Q&A-7 ..... 21:14, 21:26
1.402(c)-2, Q&A-8 ..... 21:27
1.402(c)-2, Q&A-9 ..... 2:17
1.402(c)-2, Q&A-9(a) 2:12, 21:28
1.402(c)-2, Q&A-9(b) 2:11, 21:28
1.402(c)-2, Q&A-9(c) 2:11
1.402(c)-2, Q&A-9(c), Ex. 1 ..... 2:11, 21:28
1.402(c)-2, Q&A-9(c), Ex. 2 ..... 2:11, 21:28
1.402(c)-2, Q&A-9(c), Ex. 3 ..... 2:11, 21:28
1.402(c)-2, Q&A-9(c), Ex. 4 ..... 2:11, 21:28
1.402(c)-2, Q&A-9(c), Ex. 5 ..... 2:11, 21:28
1.402(c)-2, Q&A-9(c), Ex. 6 ..... 2:11, 21:28
1.402(c)-2, Q&A-10 ..... 21:17, 21:29, 25:28
1.402(c)-2, Q&A-11 ..... 21:30
1.402(c)-2, Q&A-12 ..... 28:7
1.402(c)-2, Q&A-12(a) 21:32
1.402(c)-2, Q&A-13 ..... 21:33
1.402(c)-2, Q&A-14 ..... 21:34
1.402(c)-2, Q&A-15 ..... 21:35
1.402(c)-2(b), Q&A-9 ..... 21:16
1.402(e)(4)(B)-1(b) 19:50
1.402(e)(4)(B)-1(c)(2) 19:51
1.402(f)-1 ..... 15:84
1.402(f)-1, Q-1 ..... 15:83
1.402(f)-1, Q-2 ..... 15:84
1.402(f)-1, Q&A-1 ..... 15:81
1.402(f)-1, Q&A-2(a) 21:45
1.402(f)-1, Q&A-2(b) 21:45
1.402(f)-1, Q&A-3 ..... 21:46
1.402(f)-1, Q&A-4 ..... 21:47
1.402(f)-1, Q&A-5 ..... 21:48
1.402(f)-1(b) 15:82
1.402(g)-1(a) 5:31
1.402(g)-1(b) 5:31
1.402(g)-1(c) 5:31
1.402(g)-1(d) 5:32
1.402(g)-1(e)(1)(i) 5:34
1.402(g)-1(e)(1)(ii) 5:35

Treas. Reg. §

1.402(g)-1(e)(2)(i) 5:36
1.402(g)-1(e)(2)(ii) 5:36
1.402(g)-1(e)(3) 4:33, 21:23, 28:2
1.402(g)-1(e)(3)(i)(A) 5:37
1.402(g)-1(e)(3)(i)(B) 5:37
1.402(g)-1(e)(3)(i)(C) 5:37
1.402(g)-1(e)(3)(ii) 5:37
1.402(g)-1(e)(4) 5:38
1.402(g)-1(e)(5) 5:39
1.402(g)-1(e)(5)(i) 5:39
1.402(g)-1(e)(5)(ii) 5:39
1.402(g)-1(e)(6) 5:41
1.402(g)-1(e)(7) 5:42
1.402(g)-1(e)(8) 5:44
1.402(g)-1(e)(8)(i) 5:43
1.402(g)-1(e)(9) 5:45
1.402(g)-1(e)(10) 5:46
1.402(g)-1(e)(11) 5:46
1.402(g)-1(e)(11), Ex. 3 ..... 5:46
1.403(b)-1(d)(4) 23:19, 23:20
1.403(b)-6(e)(2) 4:6, 4:40, 4:49
1.403(b)-6(e)(8) 4:6, 4:40, 4:49
1.404(a)-1(a)(2) 19:13
1.404(e)-1A(g) 6:2
1.408A-8, Q&A-1(a)(2) 21:14
1.410(a)-7(d)(1) 8:41
1.410(b)-2(b)(2) 10:16
1.410(b)-2(b)(7) 10:4
1.410(b)-2(f) 10:34
1.410(b)-4 ..... 25:5
1.410(b)-4(c)(4) 12:18
1.410(b)-5 ..... 10:6
1.410(b)-6 ..... 25:6
1.410(b)-6(d) 15:24
1.410(b)-7(c) 10:4
1.410(b)-7(d) 10:4, 10:21
1.410(b)-9 ..... 15:24
1.411(a)-1(a) 8:4
1.411(a)-4(a) 8:16
1.411(a)-4(b)(2) 13:20
1.411(a)-4(c) 8:16
1.411(a)-5 ..... 8:46
1.411(a)-5(a) 8:51
1.411(a)-5(b)(1) 8:47
1.411(a)-5(b)(2) 8:48
1.411(a)-5(b)(3) 8:49
1.411(a)-5(b)(3)(v) 8:50
1.411(a)-7(b)(1) 12:4
1.411(a)-7(c) 12:7
1.411(a)-7(c)(3) 12:8
1.411(a)-7(c)(4) 12:9
1.411(a)-7(d)(2)(ii) 9:46
1.411(a)-7(d)(2)(ii)(B) 8:65
1.411(a)-7(d)(4) 8:62, 9:9, 9:11
1.411(a)-7(d)(4)(iv) 9:11

Treas. Reg. §

1.411(a)-7(d)(4)(iv)(C) 9:46
1.411(a)-7(d)(4)(v) 8:66, 9:12
1.411(a)-7(d)(4)(vi) 9:11
1.411(a)-7(d)(5) 2:11
1.411(a)-7(d)(5)(iii)(A) 8:68, 9:15
1.411(a)-7(d)(5)(iii)(B) 8:68, 9:15
1.411(a)-7(d)(6)(iii)(C) 8:67, 9:13
1.411(a)-8 .... 10:39
1.411(a)-11(c)(3)(ii) 10:30, 11:9
1.411(a)-11(e)(1) 15:77
1.411(b)-1(a)(1) 9:1
1.411(b)-1(d)(1) 9:43
1.411(b)-1(d)(2) 9:28
1.411(b)-1(e)(2) 8:53
1.411(b)-2(b)(1)(i) 12:24
1.411(b)-2(b)(4) 12:33
1.411(c)-1(b) 9:2
1.411(c)-1(c) 8:7
1.411(d)-1(f)(1) 10:43
1.411(d)-1(g)(5) 10:43
1.411(d)-2 .... 8:72
1.411(d)-2(a)(1) 8:69
1.411(d)-2(a)(2)(i) 8:79
1.411(d)-2(a)(2)(ii) 8:79
1.411(d)-2(a)(2)(iii) 8:79
1.411(d)-2(b) 8:74, 8:75, 8:76
1.411(d)-2(b)(1) 8:72
1.411(d)-2(b)(2) 8:72, 8:80
1.411(d)-2(b)(3) 8:72
1.411(d)-2(c) 8:70
1.411(d)-2(d) 8:80, 8:83
1.411(d)-2(d)(1) 8:83
1.411(d)-3 ...., 10:29, 10:39, 10:43, 11:45
1.411(d)-3(a) 10:39
1.411(d)-3(a)(1) 10:39
1.411(d)-3(a)(2)(i) 10:39
1.411(d)-3(a)(2)(ii) 10:39
1.411(d)-3(a)(2)(iii) 10:39
1.411(d)-3(a)(3) 8:56, 8:58, 10:25, 12:32, 13:16
1.411(d)-3(a)(3)(i) 10:39
1.411(d)-3(a)(3)(ii) 10:39
1.411(d)-3(a)(4), Ex. 1 .... 10:39
1.411(d)-3(a)(4), Ex. 2 .... 10:39
1.411(d)-3(a)(4), Ex. 3 .... 10:39
1.411(d)-3(a)(4), Ex. 4 .... 10:39
1.411(d)-3(b)(1)(i) 10:39
1.411(d)-3(b)(1)(ii) 10:39
1.411(d)-3(b)(1)(iii) 10:39
1.411(d)-3(b)(2) 10:39
1.411(d)-3(b)(2)(ii) 10:39
1.411(d)-3(b)(3)(ii) 10:39
1.411(d)-3(b)(4), Ex. 1 .... 10:39
1.411(d)-3(b)(4), Ex. 2 .... 10:39
1.411(d)-3(b)(4), Ex. 3 .... 10:39

Treas. Reg. §

1.411(d)-3(c) 10:39
1.411(d)-3(c)(2)(ii) 10:39
1.411(d)-3(c)(3)(i) 10:39
1.411(d)-3(c)(3)(ii)(A) 10:39
1.411(d)-3(c)(3)(ii)(B) 10:39
1.411(d)-3(c)(3)(ii)(C) 10:39
1.411(d)-3(c)(4)(i) 10:39
1.411(d)-3(c)(4)(ii) 10:39
1.411(d)-3(c)(4)(iii) 10:39
1.411(d)-3(c)(4)(iv) 10:39
1.411(d)-3(c)(4)(v) 10:39
1.411(d)-3(c)(4)(vi) 10:39
1.411(d)-3(c)(5) 10:39
1.411(d)-3(d)(1) 10:40
1.411(d)-3(d)(2)(i) 10:40
1.411(d)-3(d)(2)(ii) 10:40
1.411(d)-3(d)(2)(iii) 10:40
1.411(d)-3(d)(2)(iv) 10:40
1.411(d)-3(d)(2)(v) 10:40
1.411(d)-3(e)(1) 10:41
1.411(d)-3(e)(2)(i)(A) 10:41
1.411(d)-3(e)(2)(i)(B) 10:41
1.411(d)-3(e)(2)(i)(C) 10:41
1.411(d)-3(e)(2)(i)(D), Ex. 10:41
1.411(d)-3(e)(2)(ii)(A) 10:41
1.411(d)-3(e)(2)(ii)(B) 10:41
1.411(d)-3(e)(2)(iii) 10:41
1.411(d)-3(e)(3)(i) 10:41
1.411(d)-3(e)(3)(ii) 10:41
1.411(d)-3(e)(4) 10:41
1.411(d)-3(e)(5) 10:41
1.411(d)-3(e)(6) 10:39
1.411(d)-3(e)(6)(i) 10:41
1.411(d)-3(e)(6)(ii) 10:41
1.411(d)-3(e)(6)(ii)(B) 10:41
1.411(d)-3(e)(6)(ii)(C) 10:41
1.411(d)-3(e)(6)(iii) 10:41
1.411(d)-3(f)(1) 10:42
1.411(d)-3(f)(3) 10:42
1.411(d)-3(f)(4) 10:42
1.411(d)-3(f)(5) 10:42
1.411(d)-3(g) 10:42
1.411(d)-3(g)(2) 10:39
1.411(d)-3(g)(4) 10:39
1.411(d)-3(g)(5) 10:39, 10:42
1.411(d)-3(g)(6)(i) 10:25
1.411(d)-3(g)(6)(ii) 10:27
1.411(d)-3(g)(6)(ii)(A) 10:39
1.411(d)-3(g)(6)(ii)(B) 10:39
1.411(d)-3(g)(6)(iii) 10:39
1.411(d)-3(g)(6)(iv) 10:25
1.411(d)-3(g)(8) 10:39, 10:42
1.411(d)-3(g)(9) 10:39, 10:42
1.411(d)-3(g)(11) 10:39
1.411(d)-3(g)(13) 10:39

Treas. Reg. §

1.411(d)-3(g)(14) 10:39
1.411(d)-3(g)(15) 10:39
1.411(d)-3(g)(16) 10:39
1.411(d)-3(h), Ex. 1 .... 10:43
1.411(d)-3(h), Ex. 2 .... 10:43
1.411(d)-3(h), Ex. 3 .... 10:43
1.411(d)-3(h), Ex. 4 .... 10:43
1.411(d)-3(h), Ex. 5 .... 10:43
1.411(d)-3(j)(3)(i) 12:32, 13:16
1.411(d)-4 .... 1:7, 10:25, 10:29, 10:30, 10:39
1.411(d)-4, Q&A-1 .... 10:15, 10:25
1.411(d)-4, Q&A-1–3 .... 10:25
1.411(d)-4, Q&A-1 .... 10:15, 10:25
1.411(d)-4, Q&A-1(b)(1) 10:27, 25:3
1.411(d)-4, Q&A-1(b)(2), Ex. 1 .... 10:27
1.411(d)-4, Q&A-1(b)(2), Ex. 2 .... 10:27
1.411(d)-4, Q&A-1(b)(2), Ex. 3 .... 10:27
1.411(d)-4, Q&A-1(b)(2), Ex. 4 .... 10:27
1.411(d)-4, Q&A-1(b)(2), Ex. 5 .... 10:27
1.411(d)-4, Q&A-1(b)(2), Ex. 6 .... 10:27
1.411(d)-4, Q&A-1(b)(2), Ex. 7 .... 10:27
1.411(d)-4, Q&A-1(b)(2), Ex. 8 .... 10:27
1.411(d)-4, Q&A-1(b)(2), Ex. 9 .... 10:27
1.411(d)-4, Q&A-1(b)(2), Ex. 10 .... 10:27
1.411(d)-4, Q&A-1(c)(1) 10:28
1.411(d)-4, Q&A-1(d) 10:26
1.411(d)-4, Q&A-2 .... 10:38
1.411(d)-4, Q&A-2(a)(1) 10:29
1.411(d)-4, Q&A-2(a)(2)(i) 10:29
1.411(d)-4, Q&A-2(a)(2)(ii) 10:29
1.411(d)-4, Q&A-2(a)(2)(iii) 10:29
1.411(d)-4, Q&A-2(a)(2)(iv), Ex. 1 .... 10:29
1.411(d)-4, Q&A-2(a)(2)(iv), Ex. 2 .... 10:29
1.411(d)-4, Q&A-2(a)(3)(i) 10:29
1.411(d)-4, Q&A-2(a)(3)(ii) 10:29
1.411(d)-4, Q&A-2(a)(3)(ii)(B), Ex. 1 .... 10:29
1.411(d)-4, Q&A-2(a)(3)(ii)(B), Ex. 2 .... 10:29
1.411(d)-4, Q&A-2(a)(4) 10:29
1.411(d)-4, Q&A-2(b)(1) 10:30
1.411(d)-4, Q&A-2(b)(2) 10:30
1.411(d)-4, Q&A-2(b)(2)(i) 10:30
1.411(d)-4, Q&A-2(b)(2)(ii) 10:30
1.411(d)-4, Q&A-2(b)(2)(iii)(A) 10:30
1.411(d)-4, Q&A-2(b)(2)(iii)(B) 10:30
1.411(d)-4, Q&A-2(b)(2)(iii)(C) 10:30
1.411(d)-4, Q&A-2(b)(2)(iii)(D), Ex. 1 .... 10:30
1.411(d)-4, Q&A-2(b)(2)(iii)(D), Ex. 2 .... 10:30
1.411(d)-4, Q&A-2(b)(2)(iii)(D), Ex. 3 .... 10:30
1.411(d)-4, Q&A-2(b)(2)(iv) 10:30
1.411(d)-4, Q&A-2(b)(2)(v) 10:30, 10:40
1.411(d)-4, Q&A-2(b)(2)(vi)(B), Ex. 1 .... 10:30
1.411(d)-4, Q&A-2(b)(2)(vi)(B), Ex. 2 .... 10:30
1.411(d)-4, Q&A-2(b)(2)(vii) 10:30
1.411(d)-4, Q&A-2(b)(2)(viii) 10:30

Treas. Reg. §

1.411(d)-4, Q&A-2(b)(2)(ix) 10:30
1.411(d)-4, Q&A-2(b)(2)(x) 1:7, 10:30
1.411(d)-4, Q&A-2(b)(2)(xi) 10:30
1.411(d)-4, Q&A-2(b)(2)(xii) 10:25, 10:30
1.411(d)-4, Q&A-2(c)(1) 10:31
1.411(d)-4, Q&A-2(c)(2) 10:31
1.411(d)-4, Q&A-2(d)(1)(i) 10:32
1.411(d)-4, Q&A-2(d)(1)(iii) 10:32
1.411(d)-4, Q&A-2(d)(1)(iv) 10:32
1.411(d)-4, Q&A-2(d)(2)(i) 10:33
1.411(d)-4, Q&A-2(d)(2)(ii) 10:33
1.411(d)-4, Q&A-2(e) 10:25
1.411(d)-4, Q&A-2(e)(1) 10:30
1.411(d)-4, Q&A-2(e)(2) 10:30
1.411(d)-4, Q&A-2(e)(3), Ex. 10:30
1.411(d)-4, Q&A-3 .... 21:15
1.411(d)-4, Q&A-3(a)(1) 10:34
1.411(d)-4, Q&A-3(a)(3) 10:34
1.411(d)-4, Q&A-3(a)(4) 10:34
1.411(d)-4, Q&A-3(b) 10:4, 10:34
1.411(d)-4, Q&A-3(b)(1)(i) 10:34
1.411(d)-4, Q&A-3(b)(1)(ii) 10:34
1.411(d)-4, Q&A-3(b)(1)(iii) 10:34
1.411(d)-4, Q&A-3(b)(2) 10:34
1.411(d)-4, Q&A-3(b)(3)(i) 10:34
1.411(d)-4, Q&A-3(b)(3)(ii) 10:34
1.411(d)-4, Q&A-3(c) 10:34
1.411(d)-4, Q&A-3(c)(1)(i)-(vi) 10:34
1.411(d)-4, Q&A-3(c)(2)(i) 10:34
1.411(d)-4, Q&A-3(c)(3)(ii) 10:34
1.411(d)-4, Q&A-4 .... 10:35
1.411(d)-4, Q&A-4(a) 10:35
1.411(d)-4, Q&A-5 .... 10:36
1.411(d)-4, Q&A-6(a)(1) 10:37
1.411(d)-4, Q&A-6(a)(2) 10:37
1.411(d)-4, Q&A-6(b) 10:37
1.411(d)-4, Q&A-7 .... 10:38
1.411(d)-4, Q&A-8 .... 10:38
1.411(d)-4, Q&A-12 .... 1:20, 12:3
1.414(g)-1 .... 3:13
1.414(g)-1(a) 24:23
1.414(*l*)-1 .... 4:55, 23:7
1.414(*l*)-1(b) 4:69
1.414(*l*)-1(b)(1) 26:6
1.414(*l*)-1(b)(2) 26:6
1.414(*l*)-1(b)(4) 26:3
1.414(l)-1(b)(5) 26:1, 26:8
1.414(*l*)-1(c)(2) 26:2
1.414(*l*)-1(d) 1:39, 26:7, 26:12
1.414(*l*)-1(e) 26:8
1.414(*l*)-1(e)(2) 26:8
1.414(*l*)-1(f) 26:8
1.414(*l*)-1(h) 26:12
1.414(*l*)-1(l) 26:8
1.414(*l*)-1(m) 26:3, 26:4, 26:12

Treas. Reg. §

1.414(*l*)-1(n) 26:3
1.414(*l*)-1(n)(1) 26:5
1.414(*l*)-1(n)(2) 26:5, 26:12
1.414(r)-1(b) 25:6
1.414(v)-1 .... 5:32
1.415-3(c)(2)(ii) 12:52
1.415-3(c)(2)(iii) 12:52
1.415-6(b)(6)(iv) 4:33, 21:23
1.415(b)-1(a)(1)(ii) 9:61, 9:69
1.415(b)-1(a)(5) 9:59
1.415(b)-1(b)(1)(i) 9:58
1.415(b)-1(c)(3)(i) 9:67
1.415(b)-1(f) 9:64
1.415(c)-1 .... 5:47
1.415(c)-1(a) 5:47
1.415(c)-2(b) 9:62
1.416-1, M-2 .... 9:50
1.416-1, M-3 .... 9:51
1.416-1, M-12 .... 9:49, 9:53
1.416-1, M-13 .... 9:54
1.416-1, M-17 .... 9:28
1.416-1, Q&A T-7 .... 8:21
1.416-1, Q&A T-13 .... 8:34
1.416-1, Q&A T-14 .... 8:35
1.416-1, Q&A T-23 .... 8:22
1.416-1, Q&A T-24 .... 8:23
1.416-1, Q&A T-25 .... 8:24
1.416-1, Q&A T-26 .... 8:25
1.416-1, Q&A T-30 .... 8:26
1.416-1, Q&A T-31 .... 8:28
1.416-1, Q&A T-32 .... 8:26, 8:29
1.416-1, Q&A V-3 .... 8:36
1.416-1, Q&A V-7 .... 8:37
1.417(a)(3)-1 .... 11:43, 11:50, 11:55
1.417(a)(3)-1(a)(1) 11:50
1.417(a)(3)-1(a)(2) 11:50
1.417(a)(3)-1(a)(3) 11:50, 11:54, 11:56
1.417(a)(3)-1(a)(4) 11:50
1.417(a)(3)-1(b) 11:51
1.417(a)(3)-1(b)(1) 11:51
1.417(a)(3)-1(b)(2) 11:51
1.417(a)(3)-1(c) 11:51
1.417(a)(3)-1(c)(1)(i)–(v) 11:52
1.417(a)(3)-1(c)(2) 11:52
1.417(a)(3)-1(c)(2)(ii)(A) 11:52
1.417(a)(3)-1(c)(2)(ii)(B) 11:52
1.417(a)(3)-1(c)(2)(ii)(C) 11:52
1.417(a)(3)-1(c)(2)(iii)(A) 11:52
1.417(a)(3)-1(c)(2)(iii)(B) 11:52
1.417(a)(3)-1(c)(2)(iii)(C) 11:52, 11:55
1.417(a)(3)-1(c)(2)(iv)(A) 11:52
1.417(a)(3)-1(c)(2)(iv)(B) 11:52
1.417(a)(3)-1(c)(2)(v)(A) 11:52
1.417(a)(3)-1(c)(2)(v)(B) 11:52
1.417(a)(3)-1(c)(2)(v)(C) 11:52

Treas. Reg. §

1.417(a)(3)-1(c)(3)(i) 11:52
1.417(a)(3)-1(c)(3)(ii) 11:52
1.417(a)(3)-1(c)(3)(iii) 11:52
1.417(a)(3)-1(c)(4) 11:52
1.417(a)(3)-1(c)(5)(ii) 11:52
1.417(a)(3)-1(c)(5)(ii)(A) 11:52
1.417(a)(3)-1(c)(5)(ii)(B) 11:52
1.417(a)(3)-1(c)(5)(ii)(C) 11:52
1.417(a)(3)-1(c)(5)(ii)(D) 11:52
1.417(a)(3)-1(c)(5)(iii) 11:52
1.417(a)(3)-1(d) 11:51
1.417(a)(3)-1(d)(1) 11:53
1.417(a)(3)-1(d)(2)(i) 11:53
1.417(a)(3)-1(d)(2)(ii) 11:53
1.417(a)(3)-1(d)(2)(iii) 11:53
1.417(a)(3)-1(d)(3) 11:53
1.417(a)(3)-1(d)(4) 11:53
1.417(a)(3)-1(d)(4)(i) 11:53
1.417(a)(3)-1(d)(4)(ii) 11:53
1.417(a)(3)-1(d)(5) 11:53
1.417(a)(3)-1(e), Ex. 1 .... 11:54
1.417(a)(3)-1(e), Ex. 2 .... 11:54
1.417(a)(3)-1(e), Ex. 3 .... 11:54
1.417(a)(3)-1(e), Ex. 4 .... 11:54
1.417(a)(3)-1(f)(1)(i) 11:55
1.417(a)(3)-1(f)(1)(ii) 11:55
1.417(a)(3)-1(f)(2)(i) 11:55
1.417(a)(3)-1(f)(2)(ii) 11:55
1.417(a)(3)-1(f)(2)(iii) 11:55
1.417(a)(3)-1(j)(4) 11:55
1.417(e)-1 .... 15:54
1.417(e)-1(b)(1) 15:78
1.417(e)-1(b)(2) 2:45
1.417(e)-1(b)(3)(i) 11:47
1.417(e)-1(b)(3)(ii) 10:39, 10:42, 11:50
1.417(e)-1(b)(3)(ii)(A) 11:47
1.417(e)-1(b)(3)(ii)(B) 11:47
1.417(e)-1(b)(3)(ii)(C) 11:47
1.417(e)-1(b)(3)(ii)(D) 11:47
1.417(e)-1(b)(3)(iii) 11:47
1.417(e)-1(b)(3)(iv)(A)–(E) 11:47
1.417(e)-1(b)(3)(v)(A) 11:47
1.417(e)-1(b)(3)(v)(B) 11:47
1.417(e)-1(b)(3)(v)(C) 11:47
1.417(e)-1(b)(3)(vi) 11:47
1.417(e)-1(d) 11:52
1.417(e)-1(d)(2) 11:52, 11:54, 11:55
1.417(e)-1(d)(3) 9:33, 9:34, 9:66, 11:52, 11:55
1.417(e)-1(d)(4) 9:66, 15:55, 16:22
1.417(e)-1(d)(10)(ii) 15:56, 16:23
1.430(d)-1(b)(1) 15:61, 16:32
1.430(h)-1 .... 16:21
1.436-1(d)(3)(iii)(C) 14:20
1.436-1(d)(4) 14:21

Treas. Reg. §

1.436-1(f)(2) 14:25
1.436-1(f)(3) 14:25
1.436-1(g)(2)(ii) 14:26
1.436-1(j)(1) 14:22
1.436-1(j)(1) 14:22
1.436-1(j)(1)(ii)(B) 14:24
1.436-1(j)(1)(ii)(D) 14:24
1.436-1(j)(2) 14:23
1.436-1(j)(6) 14:21
1.1441-1 .... 24:57
1.1441-1(b)(3)(iii)(C) 24:57
1.1441-2 .... 24:57
1.1441-2(b) 24:57
1.1441-4(b)(1)(ii) 24:57
1.1441-4(g) 24:57
1.1441-6(a) 24:57
1.6047-2 .... 4:27
1.6047-2(e) 4:27
1.7476-1 .... 15:31
1.7476-1(b)(5) 15:30
31.3402(c)-1, Q&A-5 .... 24:5
31.3402(g)-1 .... 24:54
31.3405-1, Q&A E-2–5 .... 24:5
31.3405(c)-1, Q&A-1 .... 24:1
31.3405(c)-1, Q&A-2 .... 24:2
31.3405(c)-1, Q&A-3 .... 24:3
31.3405(c)-1, Q&A-4 .... 24:4
31.3405(c)-1, Q&A-6 .... 24:6
31.3405(c)-1, Q&A-7 .... 24:7
31.3405(c)-1, Q&A-8 .... 24:8
31.3405(c)-1, Q&A-9 .... 2:17, 24:9
31.3405(c)-1, Q&A-10 .... 24:10
31.3405(c)-1, Q&A-11 .... 2:17, 9:6, 24:11
31.3405(c)-1, Q&A-12 .... 24:12
31.3405(c)-1, Q&A-13 .... 24:13
31.3405(c)-1, Q&A-14 .... 24:14
31.3405(c)-1, Q&A-15 .... 24:15
31.3405(c)-1, Q&A-16 .... 24:16
31.3405(c)-1, Q&A-17 .... 24:17
31.6302-1(h)(2) 24:18
31.6302-1(h)(3) 24:18
31.6302-4(b)(4) 24:18
35.3405-1 et seq. 24:48
35.3405-1 .... 24:16
35.3405-1, F-4 .... 2:17
35.3405-1, F-5 .... 2:17
35.3405-1, Q&A F-1 .... 24:10
35.3405-1, Q&A F-2 .... 24:9
35.3405-1, Q&A F-3 .... 24:9
53.4941(e)-1(c)(1) 2:21
53.4941(e)-1(e)(1)(i) 2:34
54.4974-2, Q&A-1 .... 20:16
54.4974-2, Q&A-2 .... 20:17
54.4974-2, Q&A-3(a) 20:18
54.4974-2, Q&A-3(c) 20:18
54.4974-2, Q&A-4(a) 20:19
54.4974-2, Q&A-4(b) 20:19
54.4974-2, Q&A-4(b)(1)(i) 20:20
54.4974-2, Q&A-4(b)(1)(ii) 20:20
54.4974-2, Q&A-4(b)(2) 20:21
54.4974-2, Q&A-5 .... 20:22
54.4974-2, Q&A-6 .... 20:23
54.4974-2, Q&A-7(a) 20:24
54.4974-2, Q&A-7(b) 20:24
54.4974-7(b) 20:24
54.4975-7(b)(1)(iv) 13:9
54.4975-7(b)(10) 13:9
54.4979-1 .... 5:15, 5:30
54.4980F-1 .... 15:12, 10:39
54.4980F-1, Q&A-3 .... 16:30
54.4980F-1, Q&A-9 .... 15:10, 15:59, 16:30
54.4980F-1, Q&A-10 .... 15:9
54.4980F-1, Q&A-11 .... 15:13
54.4980F-1, Q&A-13 .... 15:11, 15:12, 16:34
54.4980F-1, Q&A-13(a) 15:10
54.4980F-1(b), Q&A-14(a)(2) 15:15
54.4980F-1(b), Q&A-15(b) 15:15
141.4975-13 .... 2:21
301.6058-1(e) 26:9, 26:11
4041.41(c)(1) 17:4

Temp. Treas. Reg. §

1.411(a)-8T 8:37
1.411(a)-8T(b)(2) 8:57
1.414(q)-1T Q&A-2 .... App. G:6
1.414(q)-1T Q&A-3 .... App. G:7
1.414(q)-1T Q&A-3(c)(1) .... App. G:8
1.414(q)-1T Q&A-3(d) .... App. G:14
1.414(q)-1T Q&A-4(d) .... App. G:16
1.414(q)-1T Q&A-4(e)(2) .... App. G:18
1.414(q)-1T Q&A-5 .... App. G:17
1.414(q)-1T Q&A-6 .... App. G:2
1.414(q)-1T Q&A-7 .... App. G:3
1.414(q)-1T Q&A-9(a) .... App. G:11
1.414(q)-1T Q&A-9(b) .... App. G:12
1.414(q)-1T Q&A-9(c) .... App. G:13
1.414(q)-1T Q&A-13 .... App. G:9
1.414(q)-1T Q&A-14(a) .... App. G:4
35.3405-1T, Q&A A-9 .... 24:19
35.3405-1T, Q&A A-10 .... 24:20
35.3405-1T, Q&A A-13 .... 24:22
35.3405-1T, Q&A A-14 .... 24:23
35.3405-1T, Q&A A-17 .... 24:21
35.3405-1T, Q&A A-33 .... 24:39
35.3405-1T, Q&A B-1 .... 24:47
35.3405-1T, Q&A B-2 .... 24:48
35.3405-1T, Q&A B-3 .... 24:49
35.3405-1T, Q&A B-4 .... 24:50
35.3405-1T, Q&A B-5 .... 24:51
35.3405-1T, Q&A B-6 .... 24:52

Temp. Treas. Reg. §

35.3405-1T, Q&A B-7 .... 24:53
35.3405-1T, Q&A B-8 .... 24:54
35.3405-1T, Q&A D-1 .... 24:28
35.3405-1T, Q&A D-2 .... 24:29
35.3405-1T, Q&A D-3 .... 24:30
35.3405-1T, Q&A D-4 .... 24:31
35.3405-1T, Q&A D-5 .... 24:32
35.3405-1T, Q&A D-6 .... 24:33
35.3405-1T, Q&A D-7 .... 24:34
35.3405-1T, Q&A D-8 .... 24:35
35.3405-1T, Q&A D-9 .... 24:56
35.3405-1T, Q&A D-10 .... 24:56
35.3405-1T, Q&A D-11 .... 24:36
35.3405-1T, Q&A D-12 .... 24:56
35.3405-1T, Q&A D-14 .... 24:37
35.3405-1T, Q&A D-16 .... 24:38
35.3405-1T, Q&A D-18 .... 24:39–24:45
35.3405-1T, Q&A D-19 .... 24:40
35.3405-1T, Q&A D-20 .... 24:41
35.3405-1T, Q&A D-21 .... 24:42
35.3405-1T, Q&A D-22 .... 24:43
35.3405-1T, Q&A D-23 .... 24:44
35.3405-1T, Q&A D-24 .... 24:45
35.3405-1T, Q&A D-25 .... 24:56
35.3405-1T, Q&A D-26 .... 24:55
35.3405-1T, Q&A D-27 .... 24:46
35.3405-1T, Q&A E-2 .... 24:24

Temp. Treas. Reg. §

35.3405-1T, Q&A E-3 .... 24:25
35.3405-1T, Q&A E-4 .... 24:26
35.3405-1T, Q&A E-5 .... 24:27
35.3405-1T, Q&A F-1 .... 25:13
35.3405-1T, Q&A F-2 .... 25:12, 28:11
35.3405-1T, Q&A F-3 .... 25:12, 28:11
35.3405-1T, Q&A F-4 .... 2:17
35.3405-1T, Q&A F-5 ....
35.3405-1T, Q&A F-6 .... 24:56
35.3405-1T, Q&A F-7 .... 24:56

Prop. Treas. Reg. §

1.401(a)(9)-5 .... 12:31
1.401(a)(9)-6 .... 12:30
1.401(a)-20, Q&A-4 .... 11:4
1.402(e)-2(b)(3) 29:9
1.402(e)-2(d)(3) 29:12
1.411(a)(13)-1(c)(1) 8:14
1.411(b)(5)-1(c) 9:55, 7:75
1.411(b)(5)-1(d) 9:79
1.411(b)-2 .... 12:32
1.411(b)-2(b)(1)(i) 12:24
1.411(b)-2(b)(4) 12:26, 12:33, 13:21
1.412(b)-4(b) 16:32
1.417(e)-1(b)(3)(i) 11:44
417(e)-1(d)(7) 9:65

Index

[References are to question numbers.]

A

Abandoned defined contribution plans, termination of plan
- Audit CAP correction, 23:5
- contents of notice to DOL, 15:94
- DOL guidance, 15:89
- lost participants, locating, 15:92
- 90-day period, 15:93
- notice, 15:94, 15:95
- qualified termination administrators, 15:89–15:96
- requirements for QTA, 15:90
- Special Terminal Report for Abandoned Plans, 15:96
- tasks in winding up orphan plan, 15:95
- VCP fees, waiver of, 23:11
- when considered abandoned, 15:91
- when orphan plan deemed to be terminated, 15:93

Accident or health benefits, non-periodic payments, 19:14
- retired employees, 19:16
- self-employed individuals, 19:15

Account balances, determination of
- cash-out rules, 9:15
  - nonvested portion of account benefit, 8:59
  - no vested account benefit by participant, 8:63
- defined benefit plans, 9:20–9:34
  - accumulated employee mandatory contributions, 9:32, 9:33
  - applicable interest rates under Section 417(e), 9:34
  - cash balance plans, 9:29
  - employee contributions, 9:30, 9:31
  - floor offset plans, 9:29
  - fractional rule, 9:24
  - mandatory employee contributions, 9:30
  - minimum accrual requirements, 9:23
  - normal retirement age, 9:21, 9:22
  - 133 1/3 percent rule, 9:25
  - pre-GATT Section 417(e) interest rates, App. B
  - Section 412(e)(3) plans, 9:27, 9:28
  - 3 percent method of benefit accrual, 9:26
  - traditional, 9:20
- defined contribution plans, 9:1–9:8
  - accrued benefit, defined, 9:1
  - daily valued plans, 9:8
  - immediate100 percent vesting, 9:2
  - loans, effect on, 9:6
  - salary deferrals, 9:7
  - underfunded plans, 9:17–9:19
  - updating of account balances, 9:3, 9:7
  - valuation date, 9:4, 9:5
- 401(k) plans, updating of account balances, 9:7
- steps involved in determining, 9:19

Accrued benefits
- cash balance plans for nondiscrimination testing purposes, 9:80
- cash-out rules
  - nonvested portion of accrued benefit, 8:59
  - no vested accrued benefit by participant, 8:63, 9:10
- computation of, 9:47
- defined benefit plans
  - accumulated employee mandatory contributions, 9:33
  - actuarial increase, 4:40–4:42
  - benefit formula, change by plan sponsor, 9:55
  - determination of, 9:20–9:34
  - lump sum determinations, 9:71
  - minimum benefit requirements, 9:48
  - top-heavy minimum benefits, 9:50

Accrued benefits *(cont'd)*
defined benefit plans *(cont'd)*
2 percent minimum, 9:51
traditional, 9:20
defined contribution plans, determination of account balances, 9:1
late retirement, 12:24–12:26
adjustment to accrued benefits, 12:25
defined benefit plans, 12:24
defined contribution plans, 12:23
delayed retirement accrued benefits, 12:25, 12:26
optional form of benefits, decrease by plan amendment, 10:39
present value of. *See* Present value of accrued benefits (PVAB)
termination of employment, cessation of accruals, 16:9
top-heavy minimum benefits
comparability approach, 9:49, 9:53
defined benefit plans, 9:50
5 percent of pay, contributions of, 9:54
floor-offset approach, 9:49, 9:52
generally, 9:49

Accrued service, determination of, 9:35–9:46
cash-out rules, 9:44–9:46
classifications of employees, different service crediting methods for, 9:41
days of service, 9:40
hours of service
defined, 9:36
equivalency methods, 9:39, 9:40
1,000 hours of service, 9:42
recordkeeping requirements, 9:38
months, equivalencies, 9:40
periods of employment, equivalency methods, 9:40
recordkeeping requirements, alleviation of, 9:38
semimonthly period, 9:40
weeks of service, 9:40
years of service
defined, 9:35
disregarding of certain, 9:43
elapsed time method for determining, 9:37
methods for determining, 9:37

ACP test. *See* Actual compensation percentage (ACP) test

Acquisitions. *See* Mergers and acquisitions

Actual benefit percentage (ABP) test, 10:6

Actual compensation percentage (ACP) test, 5:21, 27:22
excess aggregate contributions, deemed ACP, 5:23

Actual deferral percentage (ADP) test
highly compensated employees, excess contributions, 5:6, 5:22, 5:23, 27:22

Actuarial assumptions
defined benefit plan accrued benefit, 4:40–4:42
eligible rollover distributions, substantially equal periodic payments, 21:24
maximum annual benefit, 9:60
missing participants, 16:58, 16:59

Additional taxes, Ch. 20

Adjusted funding target attainment percentage (AFTAP), 14:22, 14:23

Administrative determination of benefits, Ch. 9. *See also* specific topics for detailed treatment
account balances, determination of
defined benefit plans, 9:20–9:34
defined contribution plans, 9:1–9:8
accrued service, determination of, 9:35–9:46
benefit minimums and limitations, 9:47–9:64
cash balance plans, 9:73–9:83
cash-out rules, 9:9–9:15
defined benefit plans, determination of account balances, 9:20–9:34
defined contribution plans
account balances, determination of, 9:1–9:8
underfunded plans, 9:16–9:19
floor offset plans, 9:84–9:88
lump sum determinations, 9:65–9:71
nontraditional plans, 9:72
pension equity plans, 9:92, 9:93
Section 414(k) plans (defined benefit plans, benefits derived from employer contributions), 9:89–9:91
Section 415 limitations on benefits and contributions, 9:56–9:64
lump sum distributions, 9:67
target benefit plans, 9:94–9:96

ADP test. *See* Actual deferral percentage (ADP) test

Affiliated service groups, vesting
hours of service, defined, 8:40
officers of corporations, 8:34

After-tax contributions
Form 1099-R, 18:15, 27:30

Age 55
direct rollovers, 28:12
exemption, early distributions, additional 10 percent income tax, 20:7

Age 59½
direct rollovers, 28:12
distributions prior to. *See* Early distributions, additional 10 percent income tax

Age 70½
attainment of, 4:7
direct rollovers, 28:13, 28:15
required minimum distributions
actuarial increase in accrued benefit under defined benefit plan, 4:40–4:42
age 70½ attainment date, 4:7

Age Discrimination in Employment Act (ADEA), 12:21

Aggregated plans
balance to the credit of an employee, lump sum distributions, 19:28
lump sum distributions, 19:28, 29:3
nondiscrimination, minimum coverage rules, 10:4
top-heavy plans, vesting, 8:21, 8:22

Aggregation of certain benefits, rights, or features. *See* Benefits, rights, and features generally

Aggregation rules and HCEs, App. G:2

Alternate payees
DROs, 3:6
last known mailing address, 3:10
nonperiodic payments, balance to the credit of an employee, lump sum distributions, 19:30
QDROs. *See* Qualified domestic relations orders
QJSA rules, 11:12
QPSA rules, 11:12

Amendment of plan. *See* Plan amendment, 25:35

Amortization
loans from plan by participant, 2:6

Amounts received as annuity treated as. *See* Periodic payments

Ancillary benefits
optional forms of benefits, 10:23
taxable life insurance costs, nondiscrimination rules, 6:7

Annuities. *See* specific topic

Annuity contracts
commercial, withholding on periodic payments not eligible rollover distributions, 24:52
elective deferrals/matching accounts into deferred annuity contract, 12:55
eligible rollover distributions
direct rollovers, 21:17
qualified plan distributed annuity contract, 21:29
withholding on distributions that are not rolled over, 24:13
Form 1099-R, 18:15, 27:33
fully taxable annuity payments, 18:17, 18:18
in-kind distributions, insurance contracts, 25:18, 25:28, 25:29
insurance company, purchase from, 4:37, 4:47
lump sum distributions, nonperiodic payments, 19:22
5-year averaging tax, 19:58
missing participants, terminated plan, 16:54–16:60
nonperiodic payments
distributions of, 19:13
lump sum distributions, 19:22, 19:58
transfers treated as, 19:12
QJSA and, 11:2
QLAC and, 12:30
QPSA and, 11:2
required minimum distributions
annuity contracts purchased from insurance company, distributions from, 4:37, 4:63
calendar years 2003, 2004, and 2005, 4:50
defined contribution plan requirements, satisfying, 4:24
delay in annuity contract issued by life insurance company in delinquency proceedings, 4:63
distributions before required beginning date, 4:43, 4:44
50 percent excise tax on failure to make, 20:19, 20:20
individual account not yet annuitized, 4:45
purchased from insurance company, distributions from, 4:63
Section 411(d)(6) rules, 10:29
termination of plan, annuity purchase for missing participant, 16:55

Annuity payments
cost-of-living index, 4:47
increases, 4:47
minimum distribution incidental benefit requirement, 4:35
required minimum distributions as
acceleration of payments, defined, 4:47
actuarial gain, defined, 4:47
actuarial increase in accrued benefit under defined benefit plan, 4:40–4:43
change of payment period, 4:46

Annuity payments (*cont'd*)
required minimum distributions as (*cont'd*)
commencement of payments, 4:44
defined benefit plans, 4:34, 4:38
definitions, 4:47
distribution for purposes of Section 401(a)(9), 4:34–4:50
distributions before required beginning date, 4:43
distributions from annuity contract purchased from insurance company, 4:37
increase, 4:47
individual account not yet annuitized, 4:45
surviving spouse, distributions before required beginning date, 4:44
total future expected payments, defined, 4:47
unvested portion, effect, 4:39

Annuity starting date
death benefits, defined benefit plans, 12:61, 12:63
disability benefits
QJSA rules, 11:13
QPSA rules, 11:13
nonperiodic payments, 19:1–19:5
general allocation rule, exceptions to, 19:5
on or after starting date, tax treatment of payments received, 19:1
part of payment received on or after starting date, 19:2, 19:3
permitted withdrawal of employee contributions, 19:5
before starting date, tax treatment of payment received, 19:5
QJSA rules, 11:11–11:13
annuity payments, 11:12
disability benefits, 11:13
relevance of, 11:11
retroactive annuity starting date, 11:47
survivor annuity requirements, 11:12
QPSA rules, 11:11–11:13
annuity payments, 11:12
disability benefits, 11:13
relevance of, 11:11
retroactive annuity starting date, 11:47
survivor annuity requirements, 11:12
retroactive annuity starting date, 11:47

Anonymous (John Doe) submission procedures under VCP, 23:9

Anti-alienation rules
exceptions, 3:1–3:63

Anticutback rules
Section 411(d)(6) rules and, 10:32, 10:34, 10:36, 10:43

Appeals
termination of employment, claims for benefits, 13:28, 13:29

Art works
acceptance of by trustee, 25:14
assets IRA custodians are unwilling to accept, 28:10

Assets. *See* specific topic

Assignment of benefits
exceptions, 3:1–3:63

Audit
favorable determination letter protecting against future audit, 15:20

Audit Closing Agreement Program (Audit CAP)
alternatives to plan disqualification, 15:37, 23:2
defined, 23:12
determination letter, 23:5
egregious failures, 23:5
failures corrected under, 23:5
orphan plans, correction, 23:5
payment of sanction, 23:14
plan amendment corrections, 23:5
program eligibility, 23:5, 23:12–23:14
requirements, 23:12
sanctions, 23:12–23:14

B

Balance to the credit of the participant
lump sum distributions
definition, 29:4
nonperiodic payments, 19:27–19:32
rollovers, 28:3

Bankruptcy
BAPCPA requirements. *See also* Bankruptcy Abuse Prevention and Consumer Protection Act of 2005, Ch. 7
distress termination, defined benefit plans, 17:4
legislation, Ch. 7

Bankruptcy Abuse Prevention and Consumer Protection Act of 2005 (BAPCPA), Ch. 7
automatic stay provisions, changes, 7:2
Chapter 13 plans, 7:4
direct transfers, 7:1
eligible rollover distributions, 7:1
loans from plan by participant, 7:3

protection for tax-favored retirement plans, expansion, 7:1
Roth IRA assets, cap on assets, 7:5
withholding, 7:2

Beneficiaries. *See* Designated beneficiaries; *specific topic*

Benefit accruals. *See* Accrued benefits

Benefit limits. *See* Limitations on benefits and contributions under qualified plans (Section 415); Minimum benefit requirements

Benefits, rights, and features generally. *See also* specific plan
age and service conditions, disregarding of, 10:7, 10:8
aggregation of certain benefits, rights, or features, 10:20
current availability rules
age and service conditions, disregarding of, 10:7, 10:8
conditions disregarded in determining eligibility for, 10:9–10:12
dollar limits disregarded in determining availability, 10:11
elimination of benefits, rights or features, 10:13, 10:14
nonprotected benefits, 10:15
permissive aggregation of certain benefits, rights, and features, 10:20
plan loans, availability of, 10:12
early retirement window benefits, testing rules, 10:19
effective availability, 10:5, 10:16
permissive aggregation of certain benefits, rights, and features, 10:20
frozen participants, 10:18
generally, 10:5
nondiscrimination rules. *See* Nondiscrimination rules
nonprotected benefits, 10:15
spousal benefits, 10:21
testing rules, 10:17–10:19
early retirement window benefits, 10:19
frozen participants, 10:18
mergers and acquisitions, 10:17

Breaks in service. *See* Vesting

Bridge benefits, 12:9

Business continuation test
distress termination, underfunded plans, 17:4, 17:5

Buybacks
nondiscrimination rules, 10:4
Section 411(d)(6) rules, 10:29

C

CAP. *See* Audit Closing Agreement Program

Capital gains
employer securities, NUA sales, 25:35
lump sum distributions, 29:12, 29:13, 29:16
nonperiodic payments, 19:62–19:68

Career average defined benefit plans, 9:74

Cash balance plans
account balances, determination of, 9:29
accrued benefits, computation of, 9:80, 9:82
nondiscrimination testing purposes, 9:80
administrative determination of benefits, 9:73–9:83
career average defined benefit plans, 9:74
defined, 9:73
defined benefit plans and Section 414(k) plans, differences, 9:90
hypothetical account balance, interest rate used to increase, 9:81
interest rate, 9:81
interest rate whipsaw, 9:78, 9:79
nondiscrimination testing purposes, determination of accrued benefits, 9:80
payment in alternative forms at normal retirement age, 9:83
percentage of pay credited to, 9:76, 9:77
PPA requirements
interest rate whipsaw, 9:79
Section 414(k) plans and defined benefit plans, differences, 9:90
traditional defined benefit plan, conversion of, 9:75
vesting
portion of benefit determined under defined benefit formula, 8:14
rules for, 8:13

Cash-out rules, 9:9–9:15
account balance, determination of, 9:15
defined, 9:9
defined benefit plans, 9:44–9:46
defined contribution plans
interest rate charged on amounts repaid, 9:12
repayment provisions, 9:11
direct rollovers, 21:7
employers without cash-out rules, 9:14, 9:15
forfeited funds, restoration of, 9:13
interest rate, defined benefit plans, 9:46
repayment provisions
defined contribution plans, 9:11, 9:12
forfeited funds, restoration of, 9:13

Cash-out rules (*cont'd*)
repayment provisions (*cont'd*)
funds, permissible restoration of, 9:13
interest rate charged on amounts repaid, 9:12
vesting and
generally, 8:62
nonvested portion of account balance or accrued benefit, 8:59
no vested account balance or accrued benefit by participant, 8:63, 9:10
sources of restoration, 8:67

Cash refund annuity, underfunded plans, 17:17

Chapter 13 plans
BAPCPA requirements, 7:4

Child support, QDRO issued, 3:4

Church plans
defined, 4:6
required minimum distributions, 4:6
termination of plan, 16:2

Closing Agreement Program. *See* Audit Closing Agreement Program

Code sections. *See* headings starting with "Section"

Coins, silver, gold or platinum
assets IRA custodians are unwilling to accept, 28:10

Collateral agreements
distributions, restrictions, 14:14–14:19

Collectibles, individual retirement accounts (IRAs)
acceptance of by trustee, 25:14
assets IRA custodians are unwilling to accept, 28:10
in-kind distributions, mandatory tax withholding, 28:11

Collectively bargained plans
nondiscrimination rules, 10:4
vesting, delayed effective date, 8:11

Commencement of benefits. *See* specific topic

Commercial annuity contracts, periodic payments, 24:52

Common-law employee, separation from service, 19:38

Comparability analysis
top-heavy minimum benefits, 9:49

Compliance. *See* specific topic

Consent
required minimum distributions, 4:59

Consolidations
required minimum distributions, 4:55, 4:69
trustee-to-trustee transfers
ERISA, rules under, 26:1
exceptions to rules, 26:2
Form 5310-A, 26:10, 26:14
generally, 26:1
spinoffs, application to, 26:3–26:5, 26:11, 26:12

Constructive ownership rules
termination of plan, 16:3
underfunded plans, 17:23

Continuous annuities
underfunded plans, 17:17

Contributions. *See* specific topic

Controlled groups
taxable life insurance costs, nondiscrimination rules, 6:8
vesting
hours of service, defined, 8:40
officers of corporations, 8:34

Corporations. *See* specific topic

Correction of plan failures. *See* Disqualification of plan

Corrective distributions, 5:1–5:48
employer contributions, treatment as, 5:28
excess aggregate contributions, 5:16–5:30
allocation of income, 5:25
combination of correction methods, 5:18
consent not required, 5:27
defined, 5:16
early distributions, exemption from additional 10 percent income tax, 20:2
excess contributions, coordination with correction of, 5:22
failure to correct on a timely basis, 5:30
highly compensated employees, 5:21, 5:29
how accomplished, 5:24
impermissible correction methods, 5:19
partial correction, 5:20
permissible methods of correcting, 5:17
voluntary correction program, 5:30
excess annual additions
correction methods for, 5:47
defined, 5:47
nonperiodic payments, 19:10
on or after January 1, 2009, 5:48
excess contributions, 5:1–5:7, 5:9
ACP test, satisfaction of, 5:21, 5:23
ADP test, satisfaction of, 5:6, 5:22, 5:23
allocations of income, 5:10
combination of correction methods, 5:3
consent not required, 5:12

defined, 5:1
determination of, 5:6
early distributions, exemption from additional 10 percent income tax, 20:2
employer contributions, treatment as, 5:13
excess aggregate contributions, coordination with correction of, 5:22
failure to make corrections, 5:15
gap period income, allocating, 5:11
highly compensated employees, 5:5–5:7, 5:9, 5:14
impermissible methods of correcting, 5:4
leveling, 5:6, 5:23
partial correction, 5:5
permissible methods of correcting, 5:2
recharacterization of, 5:8
excess elective contributions, 5:31–5:46
annual dollar limitation, 5:32
consent, 5:42
coordination with distribution or recharacterization of elective contributions, 5:41
defined, 5:33
elective contributions defined, 5:31
employer contributions, treatment as, 5:35
gap period income, allocating, 5:40
income allocation, 5:39
irrevocable elections, 5:31
minimum distribution requirements, reduction of, 5:45
partial correction, 5:46
plan distribution requirements, 5:38
recharacterization of elective contributions, 5:41
required minimum distributions, 5:43
tax treatment, 5:43, 5:44
tax year, 5:36, 5:37
treatment under qualified plan, 5:34
excess income, 5:9
how accomplished, 5:24
gap period income distributions, 5:26
restricted employee, distributions to, 14:19
rollovers, 28:2
voluntary correction program, excess aggregate contributions, 5:30

Cost-of-living arrangements
transfers from defined contribution plan to defined benefit plans, 28:3

Cost-of-living index
annuity payments, 4:47

Crediting service, nondiscrimination rules, 10:4

Current availability requirement, nondiscrimination rules. *See* Nondiscrimination rules

Curtailment of plan, vesting, 8:82

D

Death benefits
defined benefit plans, 12:60–12:73
annuity starting date, 12:63
50 percent test, satisfaction of, 12:72
incidental limits for life insurance, 12:71
lump sum equivalent benefit, determination of, 12:65
100 times monthly benefit, benefit equal, 12:66, 12:67, 12:73
provision of benefits, 12:60
QPSA rules, 12:62
Section 412(e)(3) requirements, 12:69–12:71
small plans, 12:68
types of benefits provided, 12:61, 12:64
defined contribution plans, 12:53–12:59
annuity, benefits paid in the form of, 12:58
life annuity, benefits paid in form of, 12:55
offset plan, 12:57
profit sharing plan not subject to survivor annuity requirement, 12:55
provision of benefits, 12:53
QJSA rules, 12:59
QPSA rules, 12:54, 12:59
transferee plan, 12:56
designated beneficiaries
determination of, 12:82
estate as, 12:79
trust as, 12:80, 12:81
eligible rollover distributions, $5,000 exclusion, 21:34, 24:10
estate as designated beneficiary, 12:79
5-year rule, 4:61, 4:66, 12:74, 12:77, 12:78
life expectancy rule, 12:74, 12:76, 12:78
required minimum distributions, 12:74–12:82
estate as designated beneficiary, 12:79
5-year rule, 12:74, 12:77, 12:78
IRA rollovers, 12:75
life expectancy rule, 12:74, 12:76, 12:78
timing of benefit payments, 12:74
trusts as designated beneficiary, 12:80, 12:81
Section 412(e)(3) plans, 12:70
timing of benefit payments, 12:74

Death benefits *(cont'd)*
top-heavy plans, treatment as distributions, 8:28
trust as designated beneficiary, 12:80, 12:81

Death of beneficiary, required minimum distributions
surviving spouse, 4:13

Death of beneficiary, required minimum distributions, surviving spouse
death of, 4:15

Death of participant, minimum required distributions
applicable distribution period, 4:29
death before required beginning date
5-year rule, 4:11, 4:12, 4:14, 4:15
life expectancy rule, 4:11, 4:13–4:15
surviving spouse, 4:15
distribution of interest, 4:11
distributions beginning during a participant's lifetime, 4:9
payments after participant's death, 4:67
required beginning date, death before, 4:11–4:16

Deductible voluntary employee contribution
Form 1099-R, 27:19
taxation of distributions, 18:18

Deemed distributions
eligible rollover distributions, 21:23
hardship distributions, 1:11
loans from plan by participant
accrued interest as indirect loan, 2:15
defined, 2:11
failure to make installment payments, 2:7
federal tax basis, 2:13, 2:16
prior loans, to repay, 2:23
prohibited transactions, 2:21
refinancing, 2:23
repayments after deemed distributions, 2:16
reporting requirements, 2:14
rollovers, 2:12
subsequent loans, effect on, 2:15
withholding, 2:17

Default on participant loans. *See* Loans from plan by participant

Deferred compensation plans
minimum distribution requirements. *See* Required minimum distributions
required minimum distributions, 20:16

Defined benefit plans
account balances, determination of, 9:20–9:34
accrued benefit, determination of, 9:20
accumulated employee mandatory contributions, 9:32, 9:33
applicable interest rates under Section 417(e), 9:34
cash balance plans, 9:29
employee contributions, 9:30, 9:31
floor offset plans, 9:29
fractional rule, 9:24
hybrid plan, 9:29
mandatory employee contributions, 9:30
minimum accrual requirements, 9:23
normal retirement age, 9:21, 9:22
133 1/3 percent rule, 9:25
pre-GATT Section 417(e) interest rates, App. B
Section 412(e)(3) plans, 9:27, 9:28
3 percent method of benefit accrual, 9:26
traditional, 9:20
accrued benefits
benefit formula, change by plan sponsor, 9:55
cash-out rules, 9:44
determination of, 9:20–9:34
lump sum determinations, 9:71
minimum benefit requirements, 9:48
top-heavy minimum benefits, 9:50
2 percent minimum, 9:51
accumulated employee mandatory contributions
accrued benefit, conversion into, 9:33
determination of, 9:32
annuity starting date, death benefits, 12:61, 12:63
career average defined benefit plans, 9:74
cash balance plans. *See also* Cash balance plans
account balances, determination of, 9:29
vesting, 3-year cliff minimum schedule, 8:14
cash-out rules, 9:44–9:46
death benefits, 12:60–12:73
annuity starting date, 12:63
50 percent test, satisfaction of, 12:72
incidental limits for life insurance, 12:71
lump sum equivalent benefit, determination of, 12:65
100 times monthly benefit, benefit equal, 12:66, 12:67, 12:73
provision of benefits, 12:60
Section 412(e)(3) requirements, 12:69
small plans, 12:68
types of benefits provided, 12:61, 12:64
defined contribution plans, transfers between optional forms of benefits, 10:30, 10:34

direct rollovers, 21:52
disability benefits, 12:46–12:52
  commencement of benefits, 12:46, 12:51
  limitations, 12:52
  lump sum distribution, determination of, 12:48
  monthly benefit, determination of, 12:49
  payment of benefits, 12:47
  subsidized benefit defined, 12:50
distributions, restrictions, 14:2
eligible rollover distributions, withholding on distributions not rolled over, 24:8
employer contributions, 23:20, 23:21
employer contributions, benefits derived from (Section 414(k) plans), 9:89–9:91
  cash balance plans, differences, 9:90
  defined, 9:89
  determination of benefits, 9:91
floor offset plans
  account balances, determination of, 9:29
  defined contribution plan used to offset defined benefit plan, 9:86
401(k) plans, transfers to, early distribution penalty exception, 20:2
fractional rule, determination of account balances, 9:24
governmental plans, distributions to public safety employees, 20:2, 20:9
in-kind distributions
  insurance contracts, 25:22
  operational rules, 25:9
in-service distributions, continuation of accrual of benefits, 1:22, 1:23
insurance contracts, in-kind distributions, 25:22
life insurance, incidental limits, 12:71
lump sum distributions, benefits payable as
  accrued benefits, 9:71
  advantages of, 29:21
  disability benefits, 12:48
  disadvantages of, 29:20
  PFEA requirements, 9:67
  PPA requirements, 9:67
  required minimum distributions, 4:34
  RPA ’94 provisions, 9:67
  SBJPA ’96 provisions, 9:67
  WRERA requirements, 9:67
mandatory employee contributions, 9:31
maximum annual benefit, 9:56
mergers and acquisitions, trustee-to-trustee transfers, 26:8, 26:12
minimum accrual requirements, 9:23
minimum benefit requirements
  benefit formula, change by plan sponsor, 9:55
  generally, 9:48
  Section 415 limits, 9:64
  2 percent minimum, 9:51
normal retirement age, 12:2, 12:7
  defined, 9:21
  principal significance of, 9:22
133 1/3 percent rule, determination of account balances, 9:25
optional forms of benefits
  accrual method, differences in, 10:22
  benefit formula, differences in, 10:22
  Section 411(d)(6) rules, 10:34
  uniform normal retirement age, differences attributable to, 10:22
payments to surviving child, 4:48
protected benefits, Section 411(d)(6) rules, 10:34
provide early retirement, with no subsidy, 12:15
public safety employees, distributions to, 20:2
  separation from service after age 50, 20:9
QDROs
  alternate payees, 3:33
  termination of plan, 3:54
QJSA benefits, 11:15
  defined, 12:62
  generally, 11:3
  QDRO benefits, 3:33
  rules governing, 11:19
QPSA benefits, 11:15
  defined, 11:62
  generally, 11:3
  100 times monthly benefit, benefit equal to plus QPSA, 12:66
  participant charged for benefit, 11:22
  rules governing, 11:19, 11:20
  surviving spouse, beginning of distributions to, 11:23
qualified cost-of-living arrangements, transfers from defined contribution plan, 28:3
required minimum distributions, 4:38–4:42, 4:57
  annuity distributions from to satisfy, 4:38
  annuity payments, as, 4:34
  50 percent excise tax on failure to make, 20:20
  life expectancies, 4:30–4:31
  portion of employee benefit not vested, 4:39
  segregated shares, 4:57, 4:58
  separate accounts, 4:58
retirement
  disability benefits, 12:46–12:52
  late retirement, 12:21, 12:24

Defined benefit plans (*cont'd*)
retirement (*cont'd*)
suspension-of-benefit rules, minimum vesting standards, 12:32
Section 412(e)(3) plans, 9:27, 9:28
Section 414(k) plans, 9:89–9:91
single-employer plans to eliminate single-sum distribution option, amendment of, 10:30
spinoffs, trustee-to-trustee transfers, 26:5
surplus assets, termination of plans, 15:71–15:75, 16:46–16:49
taxable life insurance costs, 6:2
termination of employment. *See* Termination of employment
termination of plan
assets of plan, insufficiency, 15:57, 15:58
cessation of benefit accruals, notice of, 15:62
determination whether may be terminated, 15:52
excise taxes, benefit increases to qualify for reduction in reversion, 16:52
generally, 15:53
information gathering, 15:63, 15:64, 16:35, 16:36
interest rates for terminating plans, 15:55, 15:56
IRS submission, 15:65–15:68
liability contributed by plan sponsor, 15:60, 16:31
PBGC process, 16:29, 16:31, 17:2
rates for terminating plans, 15:54
sponsor of plan, actions of, 15:59–15:61, 16:29, 16:31
steps involved, 15:51
surplus assets, 15:72–15:75, 16:46–16:49
terminal funding contracts, 15:58
3 percent method of benefit accrual, determination of account balances, 9:26
top-heavy plans, vesting, 8:18, 8:24, 8:25
trustee-to-trustee transfers
mergers and acquisitions, 26:8, 26:12
spinoffs, 26:5
204(h) notice, 15:62
underfunded plans, Ch. 17
adjustments, maximum guaranteed benefits, 17:14–17:15
allocation of assets under ERISA, 17:42
benefit increases and maximum guaranteed benefits, 17:22
benefit liability measurement, plan termination, 17:2
cash refund annuities, 17:17
continuation of, 17:40
distress termination, 17:4–17:11, 17:26, 17:29, 17:31, 17:32
dollar limits for each year, 17:13
frozen plan, 17:40
guaranteed benefits, 17:24, 17:26
installment refund annuities, 17:17
joint and survivor annuities, 17:20
joint and survivor annuities (contingent basis), 17:18
joint and survivor annuities (joint basis), 17:19
majority owners, 17:23, 17:24
maximum deductible limit, 17:45
maximum guaranteed benefits, 17:14–17:15, 17:22
not covered by PBGC, 17:39–17:42
PBGC, benefits guaranteed by, 17:12
step-down life annuities, 17:21
vesting
account balances value, 8:27
application of rules, 8:3
breaks in service, 8:53
employee-derived accrued benefit, 8:7
forfeitures, 8:60, 8:65
maximum interest rate, forfeitures, 8:65
present value of accrued benefits, 8:24, 8:27
top-heavy plans, 8:18, 8:24, 8:25

Defined contribution plans
abandoned plans. *See* Abandoned defined contribution plans
account balances, determination of, 9:1–9:8
accrued benefit, defined, 9:1
daily valued plans, 9:8
immediate 100 percent vesting, 9:2
loans, effect on, 9:6
salary deferrals, 9:7
underfunded plans, 9:17–9:19
updating of account balances, 9:3, 9:7
valuation date, 9:4, 9:5
cash balance plans. *See* Cash balance plans
cash-out rules
interest charged on amounts repaid, 9:12
repayment provisions, 9:11
collateral agreements, use of, 14:17
death benefits, 12:53–12:59
annuity, benefits paid in the form of, 12:58
life annuity, benefits paid in form of, 12:55
offset plan, 12:57
profit sharing plan not subject to survivor annuity requirement, 12:55
QJSA, account balance subject to, 12:59
QPSA, account balance subject to, 12:59
transferee plan, 12:56
death benefits, provision of, 12:53
defined benefit plans, transfers between, 10:30, 10:34

direct rollovers, 21:2
  annuity benefit, 9:57
eligible rollover distributions
  accomplishing, 21:2
  substantially equal periodic payments, 21:24, 21:46
employee-directed defined contribution plan, in-kind distributions, 25:9
employer contributions, 23:19
floor offset plans, defined benefit plans offset by defined contribution plans, 9:86
immediate allocation method to determine adjusted account balance, 9:18
individual accounts, required minimum distributions, 4:24
in-kind distributions, 25:9
in-service distributions
  continuation of accrual of benefits, 1:22
  continuation of contributions, 1:24
  transfers of shares to other defined contribution plans from ESOP, 1:38–1:40
maximum annual benefit, 9:56
mergers and acquisitions, trustee-to-trustee transfers, 26:7, 26:8
minimum funding standards
  QJSA rules, 11:3, 11:4
  QPSA rules, 11:3, 11:4
  Section 412, 11:28
normal retirement age, 12:6
offset plan, death benefits, 12:57
optional forms of benefits, 10:34
  allocation formula, differences in, 10:22
orphan plans. *See* Abandoned defined contribution plans
protected benefits, 10:34
QDROs
  allocation of determination expenses, 3:42
  alternate payees, 3:32
QJSA requirements
  benefits, 11:15
  taxable life insurance costs, incidental limits, generally, 11:3
QPSA requirements
  account balance subject to, 12:59
  benefits, 11:15
  forfeitures on account of death, 11:16
  forfeitures on death, 11:20, 11:21
  generally, 11:3
  portion of death benefit paid as, 12:54
  rules governing, 11:20, 11:21
  surviving spouse, beginning of distributions to, 11:23
qualified cost-of-living arrangements under defined benefit plans, transfers, 28:3
required minimum distributions, 4:23–4:33
  amounts not taken into account, 4:33
  amounts used for determining, 4:26
  annuity contracts, use to satisfy, 4:24
  applicable distribution period, 4:28, 4:29
  calendar year distributions, 4:23, 4:25
  50 percent excise tax on failure to make, 20:21
  individual accounts, 4:32, 4:33
  life expectancies, 4:30
  qualifying longevity annuity contract (QLAC), 4:27
  uniform lifetime table, 4:28
  unvested portion of individual account, 4:32
retirement
  disability benefits, 12:40–12:45
  late retirement, 12:21, 12:23
Section 411(d)(6) protected benefits, 10:25
spinoffs, trustee-to-trustee transfers, 26:4
survivor annuity requirements, transferee plans, 11:6
suspense account method to determine adjusted account balance, 9:18
taxable life insurance costs, incidental limits, 6:3
termination of employment, determination of present value of vested accrued benefits, 13:7
termination of plan, 15:6–15:50
  abandoned plans. *See* Abandoned defined contribution plans
  final disclosure forms, 15:49, 15:50
  final stages, 15:40–15:41
  information gathering, 15:16, 15:17, 15:21
  IRS submission, 15:18–15:33
  liability contributed by plan sponsor in year of termination, 15:8
  liquidating plan assets, 15:38, 15:39
  lost participants, 15:43
  missing participants, 16:54
  plan sponsor adopting resolution to terminate plan, 15:7
  problem-solving options, 15:34–15:37
  procedural steps, 15:6
  204(h) notice, 15:9–15:15
  underfunded defined contribution plans, 15:25
top-heavy plans, vesting, 8:18, 8:23
transferee plans, survivor annuity requirements, 11:6
trustee-to-trustee transfers
  mergers and acquisitions, 26:7, 26:8, 26:12
  spinoffs, 26:4
204(h) notice, 15:9–15:15
  contents of, 15:13
  delivery of, 15:11

Defined contribution plans (*cont'd*)
204(h) notice (*cont'd*)
electronic delivery of, 15:12
failure to provide, penalties, 15:15
provision of, 15:10
reason for, 15:9
when must be provided, 15:14
underfunded plans, 9:16–9:19
account balances, determination of, 9:16–9:19
defined, 9:16, 17:48
immediate allocation method to determine adjusted account balance, 9:18
suspense account method to determine adjusted account balance, 9:18
unrestricted distribution method to determine adjusted account balance, 9:18
unrestricted distribution method to determine adjusted account balance, 9:18
valuation date of account balances
adjustments made between, 9:4
underlying investments, rapid change in value, 9:5
vesting
account balances value, determination of, 8:23
application of rules, 8:3
breaks in service, 8:53
cash-out/repayment rules, 8:67
forfeitures, 8:61, 8:68
100 percent vesting of benefits, 8:6
restoration of accrued benefit, 8:66
top-heavy minimum schedules, 8:10
top-heavy plans, 8:18, 8:23

Delinquency proceedings, life insurance company issuing annuity contract, 4:63

Department of Labor (DOL)
abandoned defined contribution plans, guidance, 15:89
rollovers, safe harbors for fiduciaries, final regulations, 21:6
suspension of benefits, noncompliance with requirements, 12:33
termination of employment
claims for benefits, 13:24
suspension of benefits, 13:21

Depository option
restrictions on distributions to, 14:4

Designated beneficiaries
death benefits
determination of beneficiary, 12:82
estate or trust as, 12:79–12:81
defined, 4:17
eligible rollover distributions, direct rollovers, 21:18
estate or trust as, 4:19, 4:66
QDRO alternate payees, 3:28
required minimum distributions, 4:3. *See also* Required minimum distributions
affirmative election, 4:18
deceased beneficiary, 4:20
defined contribution plans, distribution period after participant's death, 4:29
distribution calendar year, 4:20
no designated beneficiary, 4:29
when determined, 4:20

Designated Roth account distributions
reporting requirements, 27:30, 27:35, 27:37

Determination date, vesting in top-heavy plans, 8:19

Determination letters
audit closing agreement program, 23:5
self-correction program, 23:3
termination of plan, 15:4, 15:18–15:21
PBGC process, 16:65
voluntary correction program, 23:4, 23:8

Determination of life expectancy. *See* Life expectancies

Diligent search
PBGC definition, 16:56

Directors of corporations
loans from plan by participant, disproportionate availability to, 2:39

Direct rollovers, Ch. 21
age 70½, 28:13, 28:15
annuity benefit, defined contribution plan, 9:57
cash-out rule, 21:7
defined benefit plans accepts, 21:52
eligible rollover distributions, 21:18–21:36
acceptance of distribution, requirement of, 21:13
administrative error or delay, 21:25
after-tax allocation rules, 21:53
amounts that are not eligible rollover distributions, 21:23
annuities, RMD, 21:26
annuity contracts, 21:17
assumptions regarding whether benefit is eligible rollover distribution, 21:18
checks, payment by, 21:2
death benefit, 21:18
deceased participant's retirement plan, 12:75
default procedure, 21:5
defined, 21:22
designated beneficiary, determination of, 21:18

as distribution and rollover or transfer of assets and liabilities, 21:15
eligible retirement plan, defined, 21:21
excess contributions, corrective distributions, 21:23
final payment in a series, 21:25
$5,000 death benefit, 21:18, 21:34
general rule, 21:22
gross income inclusion, 21:3, 21:27
independent payments, 21:25
individual retirement account (IRA) plans, 21:36
ineligible amounts, 21:23
information provided by distributee, 21:4
invalid rollover contribution, 21:14
irrevocability of election to treat contribution of eligible rollover distribution to individual retirement plan as rollover, 21:33
loans from plan by participant, offset amounts used to repay, 21:16, 21:28
multiple destinations, tax amount distribution, 21:53
nonspousal distributee, 21:32
offset amounts used to repay plan loans, 21:16, 21:28
1-year look-back rollover limitation, 21:36
periodic payments, 21:12, 21:24, 21:46
permissible procedures, 21:4
portion paid to eligible retirement plan, remainder paid to distributee, 21:9
pre-tax allocation rules, 21:53
procedures for electing, 21:4
qualified plan distributed annuity contract, 21:29
qualified retirement plan, 21:53
qualified trust defined, 21:21
reporting requirements, 24:16, 24:17
required minimum distribution, 21:26, 21:27
revocation of election, 21:8
separate distributions, division into, 21:10
60-day rule, 21:30, 21:31
spousal distributee, 21:32
substantially equal periodic payments, 21:24, 21:25, 21:46
supplemental payments for annuitants, 21:25
transfer of assets and liabilities *vs.* distribution, 21:15
$200, distributions less than, 21:11
20 percent withholding and, 21:3
withholding, 24:6, 24:7, 24:14
written explanation, 21:44–21:48
employees not yet eligible to participate in a qualified plan, 21:49
ESOPs, 21:51
flexibility lost by individual, 28:12
Form 1099-R, 27:20
IRAs
advantages of, 28:17
problems, 28:8
mandatory distributions, 21:6
mandatory tax withholding, 21:1
minimum coverage and nondiscrimination requirements, 21:49
notice requirements, 21:1
plan loan note, 2:19
revocation of TEFRA election after age 70½, 28:15
Section 401(a)(31), direct rollover requirements, Ch. 21
Section 411(d)(6) rules, 10:34
separate accounting for amounts attributable to rollover contributions, 21:50
TEFRA, designations in effect under, 28:14, 28:15

Disability benefits
defined benefit plans
commencement of benefits, 12:46, 12:51
limitations, 12:52
lump sum distributions, 12:49
monthly benefit, 12:49
payment of benefits, 12:47
retirement, 12:46–12:52
subsidized benefit defined, 12:50
defined contribution plans
long-term disability insurance, 12:45
retirement, 12:40–12:45
definition of disability, 19:21
lump sum distributions, 29:2
early distributions, exemption from additional 10 percent income tax
definition of disabled, 20:3
transitional rules, 20:13
lump sum distributions
defined benefit plans, 12:48
definition of disability, 19:21, 29:2
normal retirement age, qualified disability benefit defined, 12:8
payment of benefits, 12:47
QJSA starting date, 11:13
QPSA starting date, 11:13
qualified disability benefit defined, 12:8
retirement, 12:34–12:52
commencement of benefits, 12:46, 12:51
conditions required for, 12:39
defined benefit plans, 12:46–12:52
defined contribution plans, 12:40–12:45
definitions of disability, 12:35–12:38
determination of disability, 12:35

Disability benefits *(cont'd)*
retirement *(cont'd)*
limitations, 12:52
monthly benefit, determination of, 12:49
narrow definitions, 12:37
normal retirement age for commencement of benefits, 12:51
qualified plan, provision by, 12:34
Social Security definition of disability, 12:36, 12:38
subsidized benefit defined, 12:50
total and permanent disability, 12:43

Disclosures
QDROs, alternate payees, 3:51

Discontinuance of plan contributions
vesting, 8:83

Discretionary profit sharing plans, information gathering, 15:16

Disqualification of plan
alternatives to. *See* specific programs for detailed treatment
consequences of plan disqualification, 23:15–23:26
amounts previously taxed, 23:25
distribution of previously taxed amounts, 23:25
employee's interest in trust, 23:23
employer contributions, 23:18–23:21
generally, 23:15
inclusion-of-income rule, 23:18, 23:24
interest in trust changes from nonvested to vested, 23:23
limits on retroactive plan disqualification, 23:17
lump sum distribution, 23:26
period of disqualification, 23:16
substantially vested, 23:22
tax consequences, 23:18
vesting considerations, 23:22, 23:23
disqualification events, 23:1
early distributions, 4:64
inclusion-of-income rule, 23:18, 23:24
relief from, TEFRA Section 242(b)(2), 4:68
required minimum distributions, 4:64
self-correction procedures. *See* specific programs

Distress terminations
amount due and payable upon, 17:29
business combination test, 17:4, 17:5
defined benefit plans, 17:4–17:11, 17:26, 17:29, 17:31, 17:32
determination of eligibility by PBGC, 17:11
filing requirement, 17:6
Form 601, 17:11
information, rights of affected party to receipt of, 17:35
information provided to plan participants, 17:7
liquidation test, 17:4, 17:5
other plans, impact on, 17:38
PBGC, information provided to, 17:5, 17:10
pension costs test, 17:4, 17:5
plan administration during, 17:26
PPA requirements, 17:35–17:38
premiums owed by plan sponsor, 17:37
reorganization test, 17:4, 17:5
steps involved, 17:3

Distributions
deemed distributions. *See* Deemed distributions
early distributions. *See* Early distributions, additional 10 percent income tax
in-kind distributions. *See* In-kind distributions
in-service distributions. *See* In-service distributions
lump sum. *See* Lump sum distributions
reporting. *See* Form 1099-R
required minimum distributions. *See* Required minimum distributions
restrictions, Ch. 14
accumulated amount, 14:13
adjusted funding target attainment percentage (AFTAP), determination, 14:21–14:23
application of restrictions, 14:6
benefits included, 14:8
benefit restriction rules, 14:5–14:13
benefits subject to, 14:8
bond option, posting collateral with plan trustee, 14:4
Code Section 436, 14:20–14:27
collateral, posting with plan trustee, 14:4
collateral agreements, use of, 14:14–14:19
current assets, 14:12
current liabilities, 14:10, 14:12
defined benefit plans, 14:2
defined contribution plans, collateral agreements, use of, 14:17
depository option, 14:4
disqualifying defect, correction by plan sponsor, 14:19
employee defined, 14:7
escrow option, 14:4
exceptions to rule, 14:9
fully funded plans, 14:24
funding target, 14:11, 14:12
"high 25" limit, 14:7
historical perspective, 14:1–14:4

how benefits are restricted, 14:5
IRA escrow option, posting collateral with plan trustee, 14:4
letter of credit option, posting collateral with plan trustee, 14:4
life annuity, amounts in excess excepted, 14:9
lump sum distributions, 14:18
multiple employer plans, 14:9
original rules, restriction of benefits under, 14:3
prohibited payments, 14:21
recomputation of restricted amounts each year, 14:13
restricted employee defined, 14:7
scope of rules, 14:27
security for larger distributions, 14:23, 14:25, 14:26
substantial owners, 14:3
termination of employment, 14:5
termination of plan within ten years after establishment, 14:3
TRA '86, 14:2
unpredictable contingent event benefits, 14:10
rollovers. *See* Eligible rollover distributions

Distributions in kind. *See* In-kind distributions

Diversification requirements
ESOPs
amounts in excess of those required, 1:37
appraisers, valuation of employer securities, 1:42
December 31, 1986, securities acquired after, 1:33
employer securities subject to, 1:31–1:34
how plan meets requirements, 1:30
in-service distributions, 1:27–1:43
January 1, 1987, securities acquired before, 1:32
portion of qualified participant's account subject to, 1:36
qualified election period, 1:29
qualified participant defined, 1:28
rollovers, 1:43
simplified methods for determining number of employer securities subject to, 1:34
small account balances and, 1:35
transfers of shares to other defined contribution plans from ESOP, 1:38–1:40
valuation of employer securities for purposes of, 1:41, 1:42
protected benefits, 10:30
TRASOPs, 1:32, 1:42
simplified methods for determining number of employer securities subject to, 1:34
small account balances and, 1:35
small account balances subject to requirements, 1:35
valuation of employer securities, 1:41

Dividends, ESOPs
employer securities, 1:44–1:49
Form 1099-R, 27:18

Divorce
QDRO as part of decree, 3:3, 3:4
QJSA rules, 11:26
QPSA rules, 11:26

DOL. *See* Department of Labor

Domestic relations orders (DROs). *See also* Qualified domestic relations orders (QDROs)
advisory opinions, 3:14
alteration of form or amount of benefits, disallowance, 3:23
alternate payees, 3:6
last known mailing address, 3:10
retirement plan benefits payable to another alternate payee under prior QDRO, 3:37
state agency, benefits paid to, 3:8
defective, rejection of, 3:45
defined, 3:2
determination if order is QDRO, 3:12
divorce proceeding, not issued as part of, 3:4
failure to qualify as QDRO, 3:22
failure to specify factual identifying information, 3:45
notice of determination, 3:49
procedures to follow after retirement plan receives DRO, 3:46–3:54
property settlement, as part of, 3:3
requirements, 3:4
state law and, 3:44
time to determine whether DRO is QDRO, 3:47
written procedures for determining status
amendment of retirement plan document to implement QDRO, 3:38
design of procedures, generally, 3:40
reasonable written procedures, 3:39

DVEC. *See* Deductible voluntary employee contribution

E

Early distributions, additional 10 percent income tax
disabled individuals
exemptions for, 20:3
transitional rules, 20:13

Early distributions, additional 10 percent income tax *(cont'd)*
effective date, 20:12
ESOPs, payment of dividends, 1:47
exceptions
disability, 20:3
generally, 20:2
involuntary distributions, 20:10
mandatory distributions, 21:6
separation from service, 20:7
excess elective contributions, 5:43
loans from plan by participant, 2:13
lump sum distributions, calculation of taxable amounts, 29:18
QDROs, 3:59
qualified reservist distributions, 20:8
public safety employees, separation from service after age 50, 20:9
separation from service after age 50, 20:9
qualified retirement plans, when tax imposed, 20:1
reporting requirements, 20:15
Roth IRA rollovers and, 28:7
TEFRA, designations in effect under, 20:11
transitional rules, 20:13

Early retirement. *See* Retirement

EBSA. *See* Employee Benefits Security Administration

Economic Growth and Tax Relief Reconciliation Act of 2001 (EGTRRA)
defined contribution plan, Section 411(d)(6) protected benefits, 10:25
direct rollovers
cash-out rule, 21:7
eligible rollover distribution assumptions, 21:19
mandatory distributions, 21:6
pre-EGTRRA, 21:20
Section 402(f) notice, 21:44–21:48
60-day rollover rule, 21:31
plan loans to owner-employee, 2:1
termination of plan
204(h) notice, contents of, 15:13

Educational expenses, hardship distributions from 401(k) plans to pay, 1:11

Effective availability requirement, nondiscrimination rules. *See* Nondiscrimination rules

EFT. *See* Electronic funds transfer

EGTRRA. *See* Economic Growth and Tax Relief Reconciliation Act of 2001

Elapsed time method for determining years of service, 8:41

Elections. *See* specific topic

Electronic Federal Tax Payment System (EFTPS)
eligible rollover distributions, withholding, 24:18

Electronic filing
Form 1099-R, 27:39–27:45
approval for, 27:42
failure to file, penalty, 27:44
IRS submission, 27:49
place for filing, 27:15
requirements, 27:41
time for filing, 27:8, 27:40
waiver, 27:43
notice of suspension of benefits and claim denial, 13:27
204(h) notice, 15:12
QPSA and QJSA administration, 11:56

Electronic funds transfer (EFT)
eligible rollover distributions, withholding, 24:18
periodic payments that are not eligible rollover distributions, 24:35

Electronic Signatures in Global and National Commerce Act (E-SIGN), 11:56

Eligible automatic contribution arrangements. *See* Corrective distributions

Eligible cost-of-living index, defined, 4:47

Eligible rollover distributions, 21:18–21:36
bankruptcy, BAPCPA requirements, 7:1
cash, received in, 28:4
death benefits, $5,000 exclusion, 21:18, 21:34, 24:10
defined, 28:1
direct rollovers, 21:11
acceptance of distribution, requirement of, 21:13
actuarial assumptions, 21:24
administrative error or delay, 21:25
after-tax allocation rules, 21:53
amounts that are not eligible rollover distributions, 21:23
annuities, RMD, 21:26
annuity contracts, 21:17
assumptions regarding whether benefit is eligible rollover distribution, 21:18, 21:19
checks, payment by, 21:2
death benefit, 21:18
default procedure, 21:5
defined, 21:22
designated beneficiary, determination of, 21:18
direct rollovers, 21:2
eligible retirement plan, defined, 21:21

excess contributions, corrective distributions, 21:23
final payment in a series, 21:25
$5,000 death benefit, 21:18, 21:34
general rule, 21:20
gross income inclusion, 21:3, 21:27
impermissible procedures, 21:4
independent payments, 21:25
individual retirement account (IRA) plans, 21:21, 21:36
ineligible amounts, 21:23
information provided by distributee, 21:4
irrevocability of election to treat contribution of eligible rollover distribution to individual retirement plan as rollover, 21:33
loans from plan by participant, offset amounts used to repay, 21:16, 21:28
more than administrator determines to be eligible, 21:35
multiple destinations, tax amount distribution, 21:53
offset amounts used to repay plan loans, 21:16, 21:28
1-year look-back rollover limitation, 21:36
periodic payments, 21:12, 21:25, 21:46
permissible procedures, 21:4
portion paid to eligible retirement plan, remainder paid to distributee, 21:9
pre-tax allocation rules, 21:53
procedures for electing, 21:4
qualified trust, defined, 21:21
required minimum distribution, 21:26
revocation of election, 21:8
Section 401(a)(31), satisfaction of requirements, 21:2
separate distributions, division into, 21:10
60-day rule, 21:30, 21:31
spousal distributee, 21:32
substantially equal periodic payments, 21:24, 21:25, 21:46
supplemental payments for annuitants, 21:25
transfer of assets and liabilities *vs.* distribution, 21:15
$200, distributions less than, 21:11
20 percent withholding and, 21:3
written explanation, 21:44–21:48
EFT, withholding, 24:18
eligible retirement plan defined, 28:5
employer securities, withholding on distributions that are not rolled over, 24:11, 24:12
ineligible items, 28:2
loans from plan by participant, 2:13
deemed distributions, 21:23
offset amount distributed in eligible rollover distribution, 24:11
withholding, 2:17
mandatory tax withholding, distribution received in cash, 28:4
plan administrator, withholding on eligible rollover distributions that are not rolled over
liability of, 24:7
payor, shifting of responsibility to, 24:5
withholding rules, 24:23–24:27
required minimum distribution
generally, 21:26
gross income, amount not includable in, 21:27
20 percent withholding rule
amount, determination of, 24:10
annuity contract, 24:13
defined benefit plan, distribution paid to, 24:8
generally, 24:3
plan loan offset amount, 24:11
portion of distribution paid in direct rollover, 24:6
property other than cash distributed, 24:9
$200, distribution less than withholding, 24:14
UCA provisions, 24:1
withholding on eligible rollover distributions that are not rolled over, 24:1–24:18
adequate information, 24:7
annuity contracts, 24:13
compliance, responsibility for, 24:4
death benefit exclusion, 24:10
defined benefit plan, distribution paid to, 24:8
effective dates, 24:1
election not to have federal income tax withheld, 24:2
Form 1099-R, 24:16
liability of plan administrator, 24:7
plan administrator, shifting of responsibility to payor, 24:5
property other than cash distributed, 24:9
required minimum distributions, 24:10
returns, responsibility for, 24:15
$200, distribution less than, 24:14
20 percent withholding rule, 24:3–24:13
UCA provisions, 24:1

Employee Benefits Security Administration (EBSA), abandoned defined contribution plans
guidance, 15:89
Special Terminal Report for Abandoned Plans, 15:96

Employee contributions. *See also* Defined contribution plans
defined benefit plans, account balances, 9:30, 9:31
QJSA, benefits from, 11:14
QPSA, benefits from, 11:14
vesting years, determination of mandatory employee contributions, 8:48

Employee Retirement Income Security Act of 1974 (ERISA)
defined benefit plans, underfunded plans, 17:41, 17:42
electronic filing, 11:56
loans from plan by participant, prohibited transaction rules, 2:1
notice and disclosure requirements, new technologies, 11:56
optional forms of benefits, Section 411(d)(6) rules, 10:25
paperless filing and record keeping, 11:56
spousal consent requirement, 11:27
termination of employment, claims for benefits, 13:23, 13:30
remedies available, 13:31
trustee-to-trustee transfers, 26:8
vesting rules
generally, 8:1
minimum vesting standards, 8:2
partial terminations, 8:73
purpose of rule, 8:74

Employee stock ownership plans (ESOPs)
direct rollovers, 21:51
diversification requirements
amounts in excess of those required, 1:37
appraisers, valuation of employer securities, 1:42
December 31, 1986, securities acquired after, 1:33
employer securities subject to, 1:31–1:34
how plan meets requirements, 1:30
portion of qualified participant's account subject to, 1:36
qualified election period, 1:29
qualified participant defined, 1:28
rollovers of amounts distributed as part of diversification election, 1:43
simplified methods for determining employer securities subject to, 1:34
small account balances and, 1:35
transfers of shares to other defined contribution plans from ESOP, 1:38–1:40
valuation of employer securities, 1:41, 1:42
dividends on employer securities
early distribution penalty, 1:47
generally, 1:44
mandatory tax withholding, 1:49
payment of, 1:45–1:49
spousal consent for dividends in excess of $5,000, 1:48
employer securities
diversification requirements, 1:31–1:34
readily tradable, 10:32, 13:9
Form 1099-R, reporting of dividends, 27:18
in-kind distributions, 25:9
in-service distributions, 1:26–1:49
diversification requirements, 1:27–1:43
dividends on employer securities, 1:44–1:49
when distribution may be made, 1:26
investment requirement, 10:33
nondiscrimination rules
Section 411(d)(6) rules and, 10:33
spousal benefits, 10:21
optional forms of benefits
Section 411(d)(6) rules, 10:32, 10:33
spousal benefits, 10:21
put options, termination of employment
exceptions to requirements, 13:13
fair market value of securities, 13:11
installment payments elected for vested ESOP balance, 13:12
length of time must be offered to participant, 13:10
Section 411(d)(6) rules, nondiscrimination rules and, 10:33
termination of employment, 13:8–13:15
employer securities, determination if readily tradable, 13:9
installment payments elected for vested ESOP balance, 13:12
options available to participant, 13:8
time distributions must begin, 13:14, 13:15

Employee welfare benefit plans
termination of plan, 16:2

Employer contributions
corrective distributions, treatment as, 5:28
disqualification of plan, consequences of, 23:19
forfeited contributions, 5:28
life insurance contracts, use to purchase, 20:2
pre-2007 matching contributions, accelerated vesting, 8:9
QJSA, benefits from, 11:14
QPSA, benefits from, 11:14

Employer securities, 25:30–25:35

EPCRS
distributions to restricted employee, 14:19

ERISA. *See* Employee Retirement Income Security Act of 1974

Escrow option
distributions to restricted employee, 14:4

E-SIGN (Electronic Signatures in Global and National Commerce Act), 11:56

ESOPs. *See* Employee stock ownership plans

Estates and trusts
annuity payments from qualified trust, 4:47
death benefits
estate as designated beneficiary, 12:79
trust as designated beneficiary, 12:80, 12:81
disqualification of plan, 23:23
employer securities, receipt of by estate, 29:23
life insurance contracts, early distributions, exemption from additional 10 percent income tax, 20:2
lump sum distributions, 5-year forward averaging election, nonperiodic payments, 19:50
payment by plan to, required minimum distributions, 4:66
required minimum distributions
estate as designated beneficiary, 4:19
payment by plan to estate or trust, 4:66
trust as designated beneficiary, 4:3, 4:19, 4:21, 4:22

Estate tax
lump sum distributions, flat 20 percent capital gains tax on nonperiodic payments, 19:65

Eviction, hardship distributions from 401(k) plans to prevent, 1:11

Excess aggregate contributions
corrective distributions, 5:16–5:30

Excess aggregate contributions, corrective distributions
allocation of income, 5:25
combination of correction methods, 5:18
consent not required, 5:27
defined, 5:16
early distributions, exemption from additional 10 percent income tax, 20:2
excess contributions, coordination with correction of, 5:22
failure to correct on a timely basis, 5:30
Form 1099-R reporting, 27:22
highly compensated employees, 5:21, 5:29
how accomplished, 5:24
impermissible correction methods, 5:19
permissible methods of correcting, 5:17
voluntary correction program, 5:30

Excess annual additions, corrective distributions, 5:47
correction methods for, 5:47
nonperiodic payments, 19:10

Excess benefit plans
termination of plan, 16:2

Excess contributions
corrective distributions, 5:1–5:7

Excess contributions, corrective distributions
ACP test, satisfaction of, 5:21, 5:23
ADP test, satisfaction of, 5:6, 5:22, 5:23
allocations of income, 5:10
combination of correction methods, 5:3
consent not required, 5:12
definition of excess contribution, 5:1
determination of, 5:6
early distributions, exemption from additional 10 percent income tax, 20:2
employer contributions, treatment as, 5:13
excess aggregate contributions, coordination with correction of, 5:22
failure to make corrections, 5:15
Form 1099-R reporting, 27:22
gap period income, allocating, 5:11
highly compensated employees, 5:5–5:7, 5:9, 5:14
how accomplished, 5:24
impermissible methods of correcting, 5:4
leveling, 5:6, 5:23
partial correction, 5:5
permissible methods of correcting, 5:2
recharacterization of excess contribution, 5:8

Excess deferrals, nonperiodic payments, 19:7

Excess distributions
individual accounts, credit, 4:25
loans from plan by participant, additional 10 percent tax on deemed distributions, 2:13
restrictions, 14:19

Excess elective contributions
corrective distributions, 5:31–5:46
annual dollar limitation, 5:32
consent not required, 5:42
definition of excess contributions, 5:33
elective contributions defined, 5:31
gap period income, allocating, 5:40
income allocation, 5:39
irrevocable elections, 5:31
recharacterization of elective contributions, 5:41
tax treatment, 5:43
treatment under qualified plan, 5:34
nonperiodic payments, 19:7

Excess income
corrective distributions, 5:24

Excise tax
excess distributions, additional 10 percent tax on loans from plan by participant, 2:13
required minimum distributions
annuity, payee's interest in form of, 20:19
default provisions, 20:18
deferred compensation plans, 20:16
5-year rule, 20:18, 20:20
individual account, payee's interest in form of, 20:18
qualified retirement plans, 20:16, 20:17
required beginning date, 20:23
waiver of tax, 20:24
termination of plan
benefit in defined benefit plan increases to qualify for reduction in taxes, 16:52
reduction in reversion from 50 percent to 20 percent, 15:75, 16:52

F

Fair market value of securities, ESOPs, 1:41, 13:11

Family members as HCEs, App. G:15

Federal income tax. *See* Withholding; specific topics

Federal midterm rate, 120 percent of, App. A

Federal Truth-in-Lending Act, 2:49

FICA taxes
qualified plan distributions, treatment of, 22:2

Financial need
hardship distributions from plans. *See* Hardship distributions

5 percent owners
HCEs and, App. G:10, App. G:14
required minimum distributions, 13:4
required beginning date, 4:6
vesting, 8:30, 8:31

5-year averaging. *See* Lump sum distributions; Nonperiodic payments

5-year rule, required minimum distributions, 4:11, 4:12, 4:14, 4:15
death benefits, 12:74, 12:77, 12:78

Fixed number of years, in-service distributions, 1:2

Fixed-period annuities, defined, 18:2

Flat-dollar benefit plans
termination of plan, information gathering, 15:63, 16:35

Floor offset plans
account balances, determination of, 9:29
defined, 9:84
defined contribution plan used to offset defined benefit plan, 9:86
minimum benefit requirements, top-heavy minimum benefits, 9:49, 9:52
operation of, 9:87
special requirements, 9:85
vested benefits, 9:88

Foreclosure, hardship distributions from 401(k) plans to prevent, 1:11

Forfeitures
death, on, 11:16, 11:20, 11:21
survivor annuity benefits, upon death, 11:12
vesting and
defined benefit plans, 8:60
defined contribution plans, 8:61, 8:68
nonvested portion of account balance or accrued benefit, 8:59
plan repayment provisions, 8:64
target benefit plans, 8:60
treatment of forfeitures, 8:60

Form 500
termination of plan, PBGC process, 16:16, 16:17

Form 501
termination of plan, PBGC process, 16:61

Form 601, 17:11, 17:32

Form 945
eligible rollover distributions, withholding, 24:18

Form 945-A
eligible rollover distributions, withholding, 24:18

Form 1040
early distributions, additional 10 percent income tax, 20:15
nonperiodic payments
lump sum distributions, 19:66, 19:69

Form 1040X
nonperiodic payments, lump sum distributions, 19:68

Form 1096, 27:49
time for filing, 27:8

Form 1099-INT
U.S. Savings Bonds, nonperiodic payments, 19:6

Form 1099-R, Ch. 27
- administrative rules for paper filing, 27:47
- after-tax contributions, 27:30
- alternate payee, QDRO under, 27:3
- annuity contracts, 18:15, 27:33
- combined federal/state filing program, 27:53–27:56
  - approval deadline, 27:54
  - approval procedure, 27:54
  - deadline for requesting approval, 27:55
  - participating states, 27:56
- common preparation errors, 27:46
- completion of, format suggested by IRS, 27:48
- corrections to
  - common preparation errors, 27:46
  - generally, 27:50
  - procedures for correcting on paper, 27:51
  - voiding an incorrect form, 27:52
- deductible voluntary employee contribution, 27:19
- designated Roth account distributions, 27:30, 27:35, 27:37
- direct rollovers, 27:20
- early distributions, additional 10 percent income tax, 20:15
- electronic filing, 27:39–27:45
  - approval for, 27:42
  - due date, 27:40
  - failure to file, penalty, 27:44
  - IRS submission, 27:49
  - place for filing, 27:15
  - requirements, 27:41
  - waiver, 27:43
- electronic version furnished to participants, 27:45
- eligible rollover distributions, withholding, 24:16
- ESOPs, reporting of dividends, 27:18
- extensions of time
  - filing, 27:9
  - participant, given to, 27:7
- failure to file
  - electronically, penalty, 27:44
  - exceptions to penalties, 27:11, 27:13
  - on timely basis, 27:10
  - penalties, 27:12
- Form 8508 and, 27:43
- general requirements, 27:3–27:22
- in-plan Roth rollover, 27:36
- IRS submission, 27:49
- line-by-line explanation, 27:23–27:38
- lump sum distributions, 27:28, 27:31, 27:33
- military retirement pay, 27:2
- net unrealized appreciation, 27:31
- overview, 27:1–27:3
- PBGC plan terminations, 16:72
- periodic payments, 27:27
  - from qualified plan, 27:27
- place for filing, 27:14
  - electronic returns, 27:15
- PS-58 costs, 27:26
- QDRO, alternate payee under, 27:3
- Social Security number, 27:24
- taxable life insurance costs, 6:11
- termination of plan, distributions to participants, 15:88
- time for filing
  - due date, 27:8
  - electronic filing, 27:40
  - extensions of time, 27:9
  - failure to file on timely basis, 27:10
- time to give to participant, 27:6
  - extension of time, 27:7
- total distributions made to more than one person, 27:34
- trustee-to-trustee transfers, 27:21
- types of distributions reported on, 27:17, 27:32
- U.S. Savings Bonds, 27:25
- voiding an incorrect form, 27:52
- who must file, 27:5

Form 2848
- generally, 15:21
- purpose, 15:26

Form 4419
- electronic filing, 27:42

Form 4972
- lump sum distributions, nonperiodic payments, 19:65, 19:66

Form 5310
- generally, 15:21
- information provided, 15:23
- termination of plan, IRS submission, 15:65

Form 5310-A, 26:10–26:14
- penalties for late filing, 26:14
- purpose of, 26:10
- time to file, 26:14
- trustee-to-trustee transfers
  - consolidations, 26:10, 26:14
  - exceptions for, 26:12
  - spinoffs, 26:10, 26:12, 26:13
  - who must file, 26:11
- who must file, 26:12

Form 5329, 20:15
- early distributions, additional 10 percent income tax, 20:15
- required minimum distributions, 20:24

Form 5498
eligible rollover distributions, withholding, 24:17

Form 5500, termination of plan
final form due, 15:49, 15:87, 16:71

Form 5500-EZ, termination of plan
final form due, 15:49, 15:87, 16:71

Form 5500-SF, termination of plan
final form due, 15:49, 15:87, 16:71

Form 6088
completion of, 15:66
generally, 15:21
termination of plan, IRS submission, 15:24, 15:66

Form 8109
eligible rollover distributions, withholding, 24:18

Form 8109-B
eligible rollover distributions, withholding, 24:18

Form 8508
electronic filing, waiver, 27:43

Form 8717
described, 15:22
generally, 15:21
termination of plan, IRS submission, 15:65

Former employees
highly compensated former employees, determining, App. G
nondiscrimination rules, 10:4

Form W-4P, 24:44, 24:49

401(k) plans
account balances, determination of, 9:7
additional relief, for, 1:15
corrective distributions reporting, 27:22
defined benefit plans, transfers from, early distribution penalty exception, 20:2
eligible retirement plans, relief for, 1:16
hardship distributions
amount necessary to satisfy need, determination, 1:12
deemed hardship rule, 1:11
determination of need, 1:7
educational expenses, payment of, 1:11
eligible rollover distributions, 21:23
employer reliance on employee representation, 1:12
eviction, distributions to prevent, 1:11
foreclosure, distributions to prevent, 1:11
generally, 1:4–1:13, 1:6
immediate and heavy financial need, 1:7–1:8
limitations on amount, 1:8
maximum distributable amount, 1:9
medical expenses, 1:11
necessity of distribution deemed by plan, 1:13
no alternative means available, 1:12
primary residence, purchase of, 1:11
qualified matching contributions, 1:9
qualified nonelective contributions, 1:9
relief to taxpayers, 1:14
repair of primary residence, 1:11
rules, 1:14
safe-harbor standard, 1:13
tuition expenses, payment of, 1:11
in-service distributions, 1:1–1:13
nonperiodic payments, excess deferrals, 19:7
salary deferrals, 9:7
termination of plan, information gathering, 15:16
top-heavy plans, vesting, 8:23
vesting
account balances value, determination of, 8:23
top-heavy plans, 8:23

402(h) notice. *See* Eligible rollover distributions

415 limitations. *See* Limitations on benefits and contributions under qualified plans (Section 415)

Fraternal beneficiary society
vesting, minimum vesting requirements, 8:2

Fresh-start rules, nondiscrimination rules, 10:4

Frozen participants, benefits, rights, and features, 10:18

Frozen plans
QJSA rules, 11:7
QPSA rules, 11:7

Fully insured plans
defined benefit plans, 9:27, 9:28
death benefits, 12:69–12:71
lump sum distributions, 9:70

FUTA taxes
qualified plan distributions, treatment of, 22:2

G

Gold coins or bullion
assets IRA custodians are unwilling to accept, 28:10

Governmental plans
defined benefit pension plans, distributions to public safety employees, 20:2
separation from service after age 50, 20:9
nondiscrimination rules, 10:4
required minimum distributions
failure to satisfy RMD rules, 4:49
required beginning date, defined, 4:6
termination of plan, 16:2
vesting, minimum vesting requirements, 8:2

Grandfather rules, benefits accruing before TRA '86. *See* specific topic

Guaranteed lifetime withdrawal benefit (GLWB) 10:24

Guaranteed minimum withdrawal benefits (GMWB) 10:24

Guidance documents
abandoned defined contribution plans, 15:89
QDROs, 3:62

H

Hardship distributions
401(k) plans, 1:4–1:13
amount necessary to satisfy need, determination, 1:12
deemed hardship rule, 1:11
determination of need, 1:7
educational expenses, payment of, 1:11
eligible rollover distribution, 21:23
employer reliance on employee representation, 1:12
eviction, distributions to prevent, 1:11
foreclosure, distributions to prevent, 1:11
generally, 1:6
immediate and heavy financial need, 1:7–1:8
limitations on amount, 1:8
maximum distributable amount, 1:9
medical expenses, 1:11
necessity of distribution deemed by plan, 1:13
no alternative means available, 1:12
primary residence, purchase of, 1:11
qualified matching contributions, 1:9
qualified nonelective contributions, 1:9
repair of primary residence, 1:11
safe-harbor standard, 1:13
tuition expenses, payment of, 1:11
immediate and heavy financial need, 1:7, 1:8
determination of, 1:10
maximum distributable amount, 1:9
profit sharing plans
generally, 1:4
maximum distributable amount, 1:9
qualified matching contributions, 1:9
qualified nonelective contributions, 1:9
taxation of, 1:5
protected benefits, amendment of standards, 10:30
rollover distributions, eligibility, 21:23, 28:2
stock bonus plans
generally, 1:4
taxation of, 1:5

Hardship waivers
direct rollovers, 60-day rollover rule, 21:31

HCEs. *See* Highly compensated employees

Highly compensated employees. *See also* Key employees
active employees, App. G:7
compensation, determination of, App. G:9
corrective distributions
excess aggregate contributions, 5:21, 5:29
excess contributions, 5:5–5:7, 5:9, 5:14, 5:22, 5:23
defined, App. G:1, App. G:6
determination of, App. G
determination years, App. G:5
employee, defined, App. G:3
entities treated as part of employer, App. G:2
excess aggregate contributions, corrective distributions, 5:21
excess contributions
ADP test, 5:6, 5:22, 5:23, 27:22
corrective distributions, 5:7
excess aggregate contributions, 5:22–5:24
family members as, App. G:15
five percent owner of company, App. G:10, App. G:14
former employees, App. G:6, App. G:16–G:18
"high 25" limit, 19:34
in-kind distributions, 25:3–25:7
loans from plan by participant, disproportionate availability to, 2:39
look-back years, App. G:5
nondiscrimination rules, vesting, 8:15
periods used in testing plans for, App. G:4
restrictions on distributions to. *See also* Nondiscrimination rules
"high 25" limit, 19:34
threshold amount indexed, App. G:8
top paid group, determination of, App. G:11–G:13
vesting, nondiscrimination rules, 8:15

Home. *See* Primary residence

Hours of service. *See* Accrued service, determination of; Vesting

Hurricanes Katrina, Rita, Sandy, or Wilma, losses suffered from
loans from plan by participant, 2:26, 2:27

Hurricane Matthew in 2016 or 2017,
special plan loan rules for taxpayers, 2:29
Disaster Tax Relief and Airport and Airway Extension Act of 2017, 2:33
Hurricane Irma, by, 2:31
Hurricane Harvey, by, 2:30
Hurricane Maria or the California Wildfires, 2:32

I

Incidental limits
taxable life insurance costs. *See* Life insurance

Income taxes. *See* specific topic

Independent appraiser
ESOPs, valuation of employer securities, 1:42

Individual accounts
annuity contracts, required minimum distributions, 4:45
calendar year distributions, 4:25
defined contribution plans, required minimum distributions, 4:32, 4:33
excess distributions, credit for, 4:25
required minimum distributions
amount used for determining, 4:26
annuity contract used to satisfy, 4:24
defined contribution plans, calendar year distributions, 4:23
excess distributions, credit for, 4:25
50 percent excise tax on failure to make, 20:18
rollovers, 4:51
separate accounts, required minimum distributions, 4:58

Individual retirement accounts (IRAs)
bankruptcy, cap on assets, 7:5
coins, silver, gold or platinum, assets custodians are unwilling to accept, 28:10
collectibles
acceptance by trustee, 25:14
assets custodians are unwilling to accept, 28:10
in-kind distributions, mandatory tax withholding, 28:11
direct rollovers
advantages of, 28:17
challenges, 28:8–28:15
eligible distributions, 21:36
problems, 28:8
distributions, restrictions, 14:4, 14:15
minimum distribution requirement. *See* Required minimum distributions
rollovers, 14:15
early distributions, additional 10 percent income tax imposition, 20:1
payment of account balance, exemptions for, 20:4
eligible rollover distributions, one-year-look-back rollover limitation, 21:36
gold coins or bullion, assets custodians are unwilling to accept, 28:10
in-kind distributions, rollovers
collectibles, acceptance by trustee, 25:14
distribution of property received by participant, 25:16
insurance contracts, 25:24
life insurance contracts and, 25:26
works of art, acceptance by trustee, 25:14
investment transferred to IRA, in-kind distributions, 25:2
mandatory tax withholding, collectibles, 28:11
qualified voluntary employee contributions, 19:18
rollovers
advantages of, 28:16
assets custodians are unwilling to accept, 28:9, 28:10
challenges, 28:8–28:15
disadvantages of, 28:18
5-year forward averaging election, use of, 19:46
individual other than participant, 28:7
more than 60 days after receipt of distribution, 28:6
nonspouse beneficiary, 12:75, 21:22, 21:32, 28:7
problems in attempting rollovers, 28:8
qualified voluntary employee contributions, into, 19:18
Roth IRAs. *See* Roth IRAs
silver coins or bullion, assets custodians are unwilling to accept, 28:10
termination of plan, 16:2
works of art
acceptance by trustee, 25:14
assets custodians are unwilling to accept, 28:10

Information returns
delivery to IRS, 27:16

In-kind distributions, Ch. 25
annuity contracts
insurance contracts and, 25:18, 25:28, 25:29
assets, rollovers, 25:14, 25:15
collectibles
IRAs, 28:11
rollover rules, 25:14
defined benefit plans, 25:9
defined contribution plans, 25:9
employee-directed defined contribution plan, 25:9
employer securities, 25:30–25:35
cost basis, determination of, 25:33
decline in value, 25:34
deferring tax on net unrealized appreciation, 25:35
generally, 25:30
net unrealized appreciation, 25:31, 25:35
generally, 25:1–25:2
highly compensated employees, nondiscrimination rules, 25:3–25:7
insurance contracts, 25:18–25:29
annuity contracts and, 25:18, 25:28, 25:29
cash surrender value of contract, 25:21, 25:22
defined benefit plans, 25:22
prohibited-transaction-class exemption, 25:18, 25:19
rollover rules, 25:24–25:26
sales of life insurance contracts, typical, 25:20
springing cash value contracts, 25:22
tax consequences, 25:23
investment, transfers to IRA, 25:2
IRAs, collectibles, 28:11
life insurance contracts, additional, 25:2
nondiscrimination rules
current availability test, 25:5
effective availability test, 25:7
non-highly compensated employees
nondiscriminatory availability rules, 25:8
nonexcludable highly compensated employee or non-highly compensated employee, 25:6
operational rules, 25:10
operational rules, 25:8–25:11
defined benefit plans, 25:9
defined contribution plans, 25:9
employee-directed defined contribution plan, 25:9
ESOPs, 25:9
nondiscriminatory availability rules, 25:8
stock bonus plans, 25:9
valuation of assets, 25:11
optional forms of benefits rules, 25:3–25:7
nondiscrimination rules, 25:3–25:7
right to receive as optional forms of benefits, 25:3
PS-58 costs, credit for costs taxable in prior years, 25:27
reasons for choice of, 25:2
rollover rules, 25:14–25:17
generally, 25:14
insurance contracts, 25:24–25:26
less than full amount of property rolled over, 25:17
qualified plan, assets received from, 25:15
sale of property and rollover, 25:16
stock bonus plans, 25:9
tax withholding requirements
determination of value of property delays payment to participant, 25:13
generally, 25:12
mandatory tax withholding, 25:12
termination of plan, elimination or reduction of benefits, 10:30
valuation of assets, 25:11

In-service distributions, 1:1–1:49
continuation of accrual of benefits, 1:22
defined benefit plans, 1:22
continuation of accrual of benefits, 1:23
defined contribution plans
continuation of accrual of benefits, 1:22
continuation of contributions, 1:24
transfers of shares to other plans from ESOP, 1:38–1:40
ESOPs, 1:26–1:49
diversification requirements, 1:27–1:43
dividends on employer securities, 1:44–1:49
when distribution may be made, 1:26
fixed number of years defined, 1:2
401(k) plans, 1:1–1:13
pension plans, 1:18–1:25
continuation of accrual of benefits, 1:22, 1:23
earliest time active participant may begin receiving benefits, 1:20
lump sum distribution received before termination of employment, tax treatment, 1:25
normal retirement age requirement, 1:20
payment of benefits, 1:21
required beginning date, 1:19
required minimum distribution rules, 1:19
rules for, 1:18
profit sharing plans
fixed number of years defined, 1:2
generally, 1:1

In-service distributions *(cont'd)*
profit sharing plans *(cont'd)*
hardship distributions, 1:4
2-year rule for withdrawals, exceptions, 1:3
TRASOPs
dividends on employer securities, 1:44–1:49
employer securities subject to diversification requirements, 1:31–1:34
when distribution may be made, 1:26
vesting, value of account balances and present value of accrued benefits, 8:26

Installment payments
ESOP balance at termination of employment, 13:12
loans from plan by participant, failure to make payments, 2:3, 2:7

Installment refund annuities
underfunded plans, 17:17

Insurance contracts
actuarial gain, defined, 4:47
in-kind distributions, 25:18–25:29
annuity contracts and, 25:18, 25:28, 25:29
cash surrender value of contract, 25:21, 25:22
defined benefit plans, 25:22
prohibited-transaction-class exemption, 25:18, 25:19
PS-58 cost, credit for, 25:27
rollover rules, 25:24–25:26
sales of life insurance contracts, typical, 25:20
springing cash value contracts, 25:22
tax consequences, 25:23
long-term disability benefits, defined contribution plan, 12:45
springing cash value contracts, 25:22
termination of PBGC plan, 16:55

Interest rates
account balances, determination of
applicable interest rates under Section 417(e), 9:34
pre-GATT Section 417(e) interest rates, App. B
cash balance plans, 9:81
interest rate whipsaw, 9:78, 9:79
cash-out rules
defined benefit plans, 9:46
defined contribution plans, 9:12
defined benefit plans
cash-out rules, 9:46
forfeitures, vesting and, 8:65
maximum interest rate, forfeitures, 8:65
terminating plans, 15:55, 15:56
Federal Midterm rate, 120 percent of, App. A
loans from plan by participant, 2:42
lump sum determinations, 9:65
minimum present value segment rates, App. H
pre-GATT Section 417(e) interest rates, App. B
terminating plans, 15:54, 16:21–16:24
30-year Treasury securities rates, App. C

Internal Revenue Code. *See* specific Section

Internal Revenue Service (IRS)
plan operational failures or qualification defects found during review, 15:34–15:37

Internal Revenue Service Restructuring and Reform Act of 1998 (IRRA)
tax on early distributions because of IRS levy, 20:2, 20:14

Investment in the contract
lump sum distributions, nonperiodic payments, 19:68
periodic payments, 18:5, 18:12
QDROs, allocation to alternate payees, 3:57, 3:58

Involuntary distributions
early distributions, additional 10 percent income tax, exemption from, 20:10
elimination or reduction of benefits, 10:30

Involuntary termination. *See* Termination of plan

IRAs. *See* Individual retirement accounts

IRRA. *See* Internal Revenue Service Restructuring and Reform Act of 1998

J

John Doe submission procedures under VCP, 23:9

Joint and survivor annuities
age differences, underfunded plans, 17:20
contingent basis, underfunded plans, 17:18
defined, 18:2
joint basis, underfunded plans, 17:19
minimum distribution incidental benefit requirement, 4:35
Section 411(d)(6) rules, elimination or reduction of benefits, 10:30
underfunded plans
age differences, 17:20
contingent basis, 17:18
joint basis, 17:19

Joint Life and Last Survivor Table, App. E

K

Katrina Emergency Tax Relief Act of 2005 (KETRA)
loans from plan by participant, 2:26

Key employees. *See also* Highly compensated employees
vesting, 8:30–8:35
annual compensation, 8:30
defined, 8:30
5 percent owners, 8:30, 8:31
includable officers, 8:30, 8:33–8:35
1 percent owners, 8:30, 8:32
top-heavy plans, participation in more than one plan, 8:20

L

Labor Department. *See* Department of Labor (DOL)

Late retirement. *See* Retirement

Leave of absence
loans from plan by participant, effect on, 2:8

Letter-forwarding programs for missing participants, 15:42–15:45

Letter of credit option, posting collateral with plan trustee, 14:4

Level amortization requirement. *See* Loans from plan by participant

Levy, IRS
income tax on early distributions, 20:2, 20:14

Life annuities
defined benefit plans, required minimum distributions, 4:34
minimum distribution incidental benefit requirement, 4:35
restrictions on distributions, exceptions, 14:9
single life annuities, defined, 18:2
step-down, 17:21

Life expectancies. *See also* Mortality tables
applicability of rule, determination, 12:78
death benefits, compliance with rule, 12:76
death of participant, minimum required distributions, 4:13–4:15
required minimum distributions
beneficiaries, 4:30–4:31
death benefits, 12:74
multiple beneficiaries, 4:31
period certain under annuity contract, 4:35, 4:36

Life insurance
defined benefit plans, incidental limits, 12:71
distributions used to purchase contracts, exemption from additional 10 percent income tax, 20:2
in-kind distributions, surrender and then rollover into IRA, 25:26
joint and survivor protection premiums, 6:12
PS-58 costs. *See* PS-58 costs
reporting requirements, 6:11
self-employed individuals, 6:2
survivor whole life contracts, 6:12
taxable life insurance costs, Ch. 6
calculation of, 6:1–6:12
termination of employment, 6:7
termination of qualified plan, 15:85
universal life contracts, 6:10

Limitations on benefits and contributions under qualified plans (Section 415)
actuarial assumptions, 9:60
age 65, distribution after, 9:59
annual benefit defined, 9:57
benefits payable, 9:69
compensation
average compensation defined, 9:61
defined, 9:62
defined benefit plans
disability benefits, 12:51
maximum benefit, 9:56
minimum benefit, 9:64
defined contribution plans, maximum benefit, 9:56
disability benefits, 12:51
early distribution of benefits, 9:58
maximum annual benefit
average compensation defined, 9:61
short-service employees, 9:63
Social Security retirement age, benefits beginning before, 9:59
minimum benefit, defined benefit plans, 9:64
mortality tables to be used for adjustments, 9:68
PFEA requirements, 9:67
PPA requirements, 9:67
RPA '94 and, 9:67
SBJPA '96 and, 9:67
short-service employees, reduction in maximum benefits, 9:63
Social Security retirement age, benefits beginning before
maximum benefits, increase of, 9:59
reduction of benefits, 9:58
WRERA requirements, 9:67

Liquidating trust
illiquid plan assets, 19:32

Liquidation
distress termination test, 17:4, 17:5
plan assets, termination of plan. *See* Termination of plan

Loans from plan by participant, 2:1–2:49
amortization, 2:6
availability of loans on reasonably equivalent basis, 2:38, 2:40
bankruptcy, discharge, 7:3
current availability rules, 10:12
deemed distributions
federal tax basis, 2:13, 2:16
installment payments, failure to make, 2:7
interest as indirect loan, 2:15
prior loans, loans that repay and have later repayment date, 2:23
prohibited transactions, 2:21
refinancing, 2:23
repayments after, 2:16
reporting requirements, 2:14
rollovers, 2:12
subsequent loans, effect on, 2:15
withholding, 2:17
default
elimination or reduction of benefits, 10:30
protected benefits, Section 411(d)(6) rules, 10:30
unpaid loan balance offset against participant's accrued balance, 2:46
defined contribution plan account balances, effect on determination of, 9:6
discharge, bankruptcy, 7:3
distributions attributable to, treatment of, 2:1–2:27
early distributions, additional 10 percent income tax, 2:13
eligible rollover distributions
deemed distributions, 21:23
offset amount, withholding on distributions that are not rolled over, 24:11
withholding, 2:17, 24:11
express or tacit understanding that loan will not be repaid, 2:20
extension of loan, spousal consent, 2:47
Federal Truth-in-Lending Act, 2:49
5-year repayment rule, 2:5
highly compensated employees, disproportionate availability to, 2:39
home loans, exceptions to repayment rule, 2:5
installment payments, failure to make, 2:3, 2:7
interest rate, 2:42
IRS documentation requirements, 2:1
leave of absence, 2:8
level amortization requirement, 2:7, 2:8
limits on amount, 2:4
military service, 2:8
multiple loans, 2:23
nonperiodic payments, taxable as, 19:11
offset amount
distribution of, 2:11
repayment of loans, 2:12, 21:16, 21:28
withholding, 2:17
withholding, eligible rollover distributions, 24:11
owner-employee, 2:1
participant loan, defined, 2:37
prior loans, to repay, 2:23
prohibited transaction rules, 2:1, 2:34–2:44
applicable rules, 2:35
availability of loans on reasonably equivalent basis, 2:38, 2:40
definitions, 2:34
ERISA rules, 2:35–2:37
fiduciary prohibitions, relief under ERISA section 408(b)(1), 2:36
highly compensated employees, officers, or shareholders, disproportionate availability to, 2:39
participant loan, defined, 2:37
party in interest, defined, 2:35
repayments as "plan assets," 2:44
QJSA rules, 11:24
outstanding loan when participant dies, effect, 2:48
QPSA rules, 11:24
outstanding loan when participant dies, effect, 2:48
qualified employer plan, defined, 2:2
refinancing, 2:23
relief to taxpayers, 2:25
renegotiation of loan, spousal consent, 2:47
renewal of loan, spousal consent, 2:47
repayments
amortization, 2:6
"plan assets," as, 2:44
replacement loans, 2:23
residential mortgage loans, 2:22
rollovers, plan loan note, 2:19

Section 72(p) rules, 2:1
amortization, 2:6
deemed distributions, 2:7, 2:12–2:17
distributions attributable to loans, treatment of, 2:1–2:27
effective date, 2:24
failure to make installment payments, 2:7
failure to meet requirements, 2:3
5-year repayment rule, 2:5
home loans, exceptions to repayment rule, 2:5
Hurricanes Katrina, Rita, Sandy, or Wilma, losses suffered from, 2:26, 2:27
leave of absence, 2:8
level amortization requirement, 2:3, 2:8
limits on amount, 2:4
military service, 2:8
qualified employer plan, defined, 2:2
term of loan, 2:5
security for, 2:43
sham loans, 2:20
special loan rules, 2:25, 2:28
specific provisions for, 2:41
spousal consent
default, unpaid loan balance offset against participant's accrued balance, 2:46
extension of loan, 2:47
QJSA, effect, 2:48
QPSA, effect, 2:48
renegotiation of loan, 2:47
renewal of loan, 2:47
survivor annuity requirements, plans subject to, 2:45–2:48
taxable distributions, treatment as, 2:1–2:10
significant rules, 2:1
termination of employment
acceleration of repayment, 2:9
outstanding loan balanced carried after, 2:10
term of loan, 2:5
transfers of assets and liabilities between plans, 2:18
transfers of plan loan notes, 2:18
withholding requirements for distributions, 2:17

Longevity annuities, defined, 12:29

Lost participants. *See* Termination of plan

Louisiana storms in 2016 and 2017, special plan loan rules for taxpayers, 2:28

Lump sum distributions, 9:65–9:71, Ch. 29
advantages of, 29:19
age 50 reached before 1986, 10-year forward averaging election, 19:59
aggregation of plans, 29:3
annuity, distribution of, 29:15
balance to the credit of an employee, 29:4
aggregation of plans, 19:28
alternate payees, inclusion of amounts payable to, 19:30
contingent plan interests excluded, 19:31
excluded amounts, 19:29
failure to distribute within single taxable year, 19:32
nonperiodic payments, 19:27–19:32
QDROs, amounts payable to alternate payee under, 19:30
beneficiary of deceased participant, distribution paid to, 29:10
calculations of taxable amounts, 29:8–29:15
annuity, distribution of, 29:15
beneficiary of deceased participant, distribution paid to, 29:10
capital gains portion, 29:12, 29:13, 29:16
early distributions, additional 10 percent income tax, effect of, 29:18
minimum distribution allowance, computation of, 29:9
10-year averaging, 29:14
total taxable amount determined, 29:8
capital gains treatment, 29:12, 29:13, 29:16
cash balance plans, interest rate whipsaw, 9:78
death benefits
defined benefit plans, 12:65
nonperiodic payments, 19:37
defined, 29:1
defined benefit plans
accrued benefits, 9:71
advantages of, 29:21
death benefits, 12:65
disability benefits, 12:48
disadvantages of, 29:20
PFEA requirements, 9:67
PPA requirements, 9:67
required minimum distributions, 4:34
RPA '94 provisions, 9:67
SBJPA '96 provisions, 9:67
WRERA requirements, 9:67
disability, defined, 19:21, 29:2
disadvantages of, 29:20
disqualified plan, 23:26
early distributions, additional 10 percent income tax
effect on calculation of taxes, 29:18
imposition of tax, 20:1
economic issues, 29:16
employer securities
deceased employee, receipt by, 29:23
generally, 29:22
net unrealized amount, 29:21–29:23
nonperiodic payments, 19:70, 19:71

Lump sum distributions (*cont'd*)
5-year forward averaging election, nonperiodic payments
age 50 reached before 1986, 19:41–19:54
annuity contracts, distribution of, 19:58
choice to use, 19:66
computation of total taxable amount, 19:55
determination of tax, 19:54
estates or trusts, 19:50
frequency of use, 19:47
how to elect, 19:51
minimum distribution allowance, computation of, 19:57
more than one election, permissibility of, 19:44
portion of distribution rolled over to other qualified plan or IRA, 19:46
reduction of total taxable amount, 19:56
revocation of election, 19:53
separate five-year averaging tax, 19:49
time to elect, 19:52
when method may be applied, 19:45
who may elect, 19:48
flat 20 percent capital gains tax on nonperiodic payments
choice to use, 19:66
death benefit exclusion, allocation of, 19:65
determination of, 19:65
estate tax, allocation of, 19:65
existing capital gains provisions and, 19:63
frequency of application, 19:63
time frame for choosing, 19:68
Form 1099-R, 27:28–27:32
fully insured plans, 9:70
grandfather rule, benefits accruing before TRA '86
eligibility for, 9:12
generally, 29:5, 29:11
Group Annuity Reserving Table, 14:18
interest rates, 9:65
determination of, 9:66
limitations on benefits and contributions under qualified plans (Section 415)
calculation changes in major laws, 9:67
PFEA requirements, 9:67
PPA requirements, 9:67
RPA '94 provisions, 9:67
SBJPA '96 provisions, 9:67
WRERA requirements, 9:67
minimum benefit, 9:65
interest rates, 15:54
minimum distribution allowance, computation of, 29:9
missing participants, 16:57, 16:59
mortality tables, 9:65
nonperiodic payments, 19:19–19:71
additional amounts permitted to be credit to employee's account, 19:36
annuity contracts, 19:22, 19:58
capital gains treatment, 19:62–19:68
common-law employee, separation from service, 19:38
death of employee, distributions treated as lump sum distributions, 19:37
December 31, 1999, received after, 19:19
definition of lump sum distribution, 19:20, 19:21
delays in distribution that do not prevent lump sum treatment, 19:35
disability defined, 19:21
early termination rules, restriction under, 19:34
employer securities, inclusion of, 19:70, 19:71
5-year forward averaging election, 19:41, 19:45–19:58
5-year participation rule, 19:26
investment in the contract, 19:68
losses, claim of if less than investment in the contract (i.e., basis) received, 19:69
net unrealized appreciation, 19:55, 19:70, 19:71
nonqualifying distributions, 19:23
recapture of tax benefits, 19:33
reemployment, later, 19:33
SBJPA, changes, 19:19
separation from service, 19:38, 19:39
special issues, 19:68–19:71
taxable portion of distribution, options for treating, 19:40
tax-exempt trust, distributions not made from, 19:24
tax-free portion, 19:68
10-year forward averaging election, 19:40–19:44
termination of plan, 19:34
trust tax-exempt in distribution year but not in prior year, 19:25
notice of plan benefits (NOPB), 16:41
PPA requirements
interest rates and mortality tables, 15:54
minimum under Section 417(e), 15:54
QDROs, alternate payees, 3:59, 3:61
retirement, disability benefits, 12:48
review, 29:1–29:7
rollovers to IRA or other plan, 29:7

self-employed individual, definition of disability, 19:21, 29:2
Small Business Job Protection Act of 1996 (SBJPA '96)
annuity contracts, 19:22
balance to the credit of the employee, 19:27
changes made to rules, 19:19
definition of lump sum distribution, 19:20
distributions not made from trust, 19:24
TRA '86, grandfathered provisions, 1:25
trust tax-exempt in distribution year but not in prior year, 19:25
taxes, impact of, 29:17, 29:18
tax treatment options, 29:5
10-year averaging, 29:14
10-year forward averaging election, nonperiodic payments, 19:40–19:42
age 50 reached before 1986, 19:59–19:61
choice to use, 19:66
circumstances of, 19:60
separate ten-year forward averaging tax, computation of, 19:61
when participant may elect special tax treatment, 29:6

M

Magnetic media. *See* Electronic filing

Majority owners
underfunded plans, 17:23, 17:24

Mandatory distributions
direct rollovers, default rules, 21:6

Mandatory tax withholding
eligible rollover distributions
cash, received in, 28:4
net unrealized appreciation, distributions not rolled over, 24:12
ESOPs, dividends on employer securities, 1:49
in-kind distributions, 25:12
IRAs, collectibles, 28:11
rollovers, collectibles, 28:11

Master or prototype plans
termination of plan, determination letters, 15:21

Matching contributions
hardship distributions, 1:9
vesting, pre-2007 employer contributions, 8:9

Maternity or paternity absences, breaks in service
vesting, 8:54

Maximum benefits
limitations on benefits and contributions under qualified plans. *See* Limitations on benefits and contributions under qualified plans (Section 415)

MDIB (minimum distribution incidental benefit). *See* Required minimum distributions

Medical benefits. *See* Accident or health benefits, non-periodic payments

Medical expenses
early distributions, exemption from additional 10 percent income tax, 20:2
hardship distributions from 401(k) plans, 1:11

Mergers and acquisitions
benefits, rights, and features, testing rules, 10:17
optional forms of benefits, 10:29
QDROs, rights of alternate payees, 3:52
QJSA rules, 11:6
QPSA rules, 11:6
required minimum distributions, 4:55
trustee-to-trustee transfers, 26:6–26:12
defined benefit plans, merger of two or more, 26:8, 26:12
defined contribution plans, merger of two or more, 26:7, 26:12
definition of merger, 26:6
ERISA, rules under, 26:1
generally, 26:1
notification to IRS, 26:9
spinoffs, application to, 26:3–26:5
trustee-to-trustee transfers, exceptions to rules, 26:2

Military service
loans from plan by participant, 2:8

Military service, loans from plan by participant
retirement pay, Form 1099-R, 27:2

Minimum benefit requirements
defined benefit plans
benefit formula, change by plan sponsor, 9:55
generally, 9:48
top-heavy minimum benefits, 9:50, 9:51
2 percent minimum, 9:51
top-heavy minimum benefits
comparability approach, 9:49, 9:53
defined benefit plans, 9:50, 9:51

Minimum benefit requirements (*cont'd*)
top-heavy minimum benefits (*cont'd*)
5 percent of pay, contributions of, 9:54
floor-offset approach, 9:49, 9:52
generally, 9:49

Minimum coverage rules, nondiscrimination rules, 10:4, 21:49

Minimum distribution incidental benefit (MDIB). *See* Required minimum distributions

Minimum funding standards
defined benefit plans
QJSA rules, 11:3
QPSA rules, 11:3
defined contribution plans
QJSA rules, 11:3, 11:4
QPSA rules, 11:3, 11:4

Minimum present value segment rates, App. H

Minimum required contribution
termination of plan, application to entire year, 16:32

Minimum required distributions. *See* Required minimum distributions

Missing participants
annuity assumptions, 16:58
annuity purchase, 16:55
de minimis lump sum payments, 16:57
elective lump sum payments, 16:57
failure to find, 16:57
fiduciary of ERISA plan, 15:42
letter-forwarding programs, 15:42–15:45
lump sum assumptions, 16:59
lump sum payments, 16:57
mandatory lump sum payments, 16:57
method of locating, 16:54
most valuable benefit, 16:60
no lump sum payments, 16:57
pay status benefit, 16:60
present value of accrued benefits, 16:60

Money purchase plans
in-service distributions, continuation of accrual of benefits, 1:22
QPSA and QJSA requirements, portions subject to each, 11:10
termination of plan, information gathering, 15:16
top-heavy plans, vesting, 8:23
underfunded plans, 9:16, 17:48
funding waiver, 17:50
vesting
account balances value, determination of, 8:23
top-heavy plans, 8:23

Mortality tables, App. F
life expectancy adjustments, 9:68
lump sum determinations, 9:65
single life table, App. D
terminating plans, rates, 15:54

Multiemployer plans
optional forms of benefits rules, 10:9
termination of employment, suspension of benefits, 13:17
trustee-to-trustee transfers, 26:2

Multiple employer plans
distributions, restrictions, 14:9

Multiple plan participant
required minimum distributions, 4:56

N

Net unrealized amount, employer securities
lump sum distributions, 29:21–29:23

Net unrealized appreciation (NUA)
employer securities
deferral of tax on net unrealized appreciation, 25:35
eligible rollover distributions, mandatory tax withholding on distributions that are not rolled over, 24:12
in-kind distributions, 25:31, 25:32, 25:35
Form 1099-R, 27:31
in-kind distributions, employer securities, 25:31, 25:32, 25:35
lump sum distributions
calculation of taxable amount, 29:8
nonperiodic payments, 19:55, 19:70, 19:71

NOIT. *See* Notice of intent to terminate

NONC. *See* Notice of Noncompliance

Nondiscrimination rules
age and service conditions, disregard of, 10:7, 10:8
aggregated plans, minimum coverage rules, 10:4
aggregation of certain benefits, rights, or features, 10:20
amendment to plan, 10:1
average benefit percentage (ABP) test, 10:6
benefits, rights, and features, 10:1, 10:5
buybacks, 10:4
cash balance plans, determination of accrued benefits, 9:80
collectively bargained plans, 10:4
contributions, 10:1

crediting service, 10:4
current availability requirement, 10:6–10:15
age and service conditions, disregarding of, 10:7, 10:8
average benefit percentage (ABP) test, 10:6
early retirement window benefits, 12:18
safe and unsafe harbor percentages, 6:8
satisfaction of, 6:8, 10:6
direct rollovers, 21:49
earnings, allocation of, 10:4
effective availability requirement, optional forms of benefits rules, 10:5, 10:16
effective dates, 10:4
ESOPs
Section 411(d)(6) rules, 10:33
spousal benefits, 10:21
former employees, 10:4
fresh-start rules, 10:4
generally, 10:1, 10:5
governmental plans, 10:4
highly compensated employees
in-kind distributions, 25:3–25:7
taxable life insurance costs, 6:8
vesting, 8:15
in-kind distributions
current availability test, 25:5
effective availability test, 25:7
nonexcludable highly compensated employee or non-highly compensated employee, 25:6
operational rules, 25:8
interpretation of, 10:2
life insurance. *See this heading:* taxable life insurance costs
minimum coverage rules, 10:4
optional forms of benefits
effective availability requirement, 10:5, 10:16
unpredictable contingent event benefits, 10:21
plan year, application on basis of, 10:3
ratio percentage test, taxable life insurance costs, 6:8
requirements, 10:1
restructuring of plan, 10:4
rollovers, 10:4, 21:49
scope and application of, 10:1–10:4
spousal benefits, 10:21
testing for, 10:17–10:19
early retirement window benefits, 10:19
frozen participants, 10:18
mergers and acquisitions, 10:17
transfers, 10:4
unpredictable contingent event benefits, 10:21
vesting, minimum requirements, coordination with, 8:15

Nonelective contributions
hardship distributions and, 1:9

Non-highly compensated employees
in-kind distributions
nondiscriminatory availability rules, 25:8
nonexcludable highly compensated employee or non-highly compensated employee, 25:6
operational rules, 25:10
nondiscrimination rules, in-kind distributions, 25:6, 25:8
taxable life insurance costs, 6:8

Nonperiodic payments, Ch. 19
accident or health benefits
generally, 19:14
retired employees, 19:16
self-employed individuals, 19:15
age 50 reached before 1986, 10-year forward averaging election, 19:59–19:61
annuity contracts
distributions of, 19:13
lump sum distributions, 19:22, 19:58
transfers of, 19:12
annuity starting date, 19:1–19:5
general allocation rule, exceptions to, 19:5
on or after starting date, tax treatment of payments received, 19:1
part of payment received on or after starting date, 19:2, 19:3
permitted withdrawal of employee contributions, 19:5
balance to the credit of an employee, lump sum distributions
aggregation of plans, 19:28
alternate payees, inclusion of amounts payable to, 19:31
contingent plan interests excluded, 19:31
excluded amounts, 19:29
failure to distribute within single taxable year, 19:32
generally, 19:27
QDROs, amounts payable to alternate payee under, 19:30
employer securities, lump sum distributions, 19:70, 19:71
excess annual additions, taxation of, 19:10
excess deferrals, 19:7
excess elective contributions, taxation of, 19:7
5-year forward averaging election
age 50 reached before 1986, 19:41–19:54
annuity contracts, distribution of, 19:58

Nonperiodic payments (*cont'd*)
5-year forward averaging election (*cont'd*)
choice to use, 19:66
computation of total taxable amount, 19:55
December 31, 1999, payments received after, 19:19
December 31, 1999, payments received before, 19:41–19:54
determination of tax, 19:54
estates or trusts, 19:50
frequency of use, 19:47
generally, 19:42
how to elect, 19:51
minimum distribution allowance, computation of, 19:57
more than one election, permissibility of, 19:44
portion of distribution rolled over to other qualified plan or IRA, 19:46
revocation of election, 19:53
separate five-year averaging tax, 19:49
time to elect, 19:52
when method may be applied, 19:45
who may elect, 19:48
5-year participation rule, lump sum distributions, 19:26
flat 20 percent capital gains tax on lump sum distributions
age 50 reached before 1986, 19:59–19:61
choice to use, 19:66
death benefit exclusion, allocation of, 19:65
determination of, 19:65
estate tax, allocation of, 19:65
existing capital gains provisions and, 19:64
frequency of application, 19:63
ordinary income portion, determination of, 19:65
time frame for choosing, 19:68
loans from plan by participant taxable as, 19:11
lump sum distributions, 19:19–19:71
additional amounts permitted to be credited to employee's account, 19:36
annuity contracts, 19:22, 19:58
capital gains treatment, 19:62–19:68
common-law employee, separation from service, 19:38
death benefits, 19:37, 19:68
death of employee, distributions treated as lump sum distributions, 19:37
December 31, 1999, received after, 19:19
defined, 19:20
delays in distribution that do not prevent lump sum treatment, 19:35
disability defined, 19:21
early termination rules, restriction under, 19:34
employer securities, inclusion of, 19:70, 19:71
5-year forward averaging election, 19:41–19:58
5-year participation rule, 19:26
investment in the contract, 19:68
losses, claim of if less than investment in the contract (i.e., basis) received, 19:69
net unrealized appreciation, 19:55, 19:70, 19:71
nonqualifying distributions, 19:23
recapture of tax benefits, 19:33
reduction of total taxable amount, 19:56
reemployment, later, 19:33
SBJPA '96 changes, 19:19
separation from service, 19:38, 19:39
special issues, 19:68–19:71
tax computed for an individual, 19:43
taxable portion of distribution, options for treating, 19:40
tax-exempt trusts, distributions not made from, 19:24
tax-free portion, 19:68
termination of plan, 19:34
trust tax-exempt in distribution year but not in prior year, 19:25
qualified voluntary employee contributions, 19:18
taxation of, Ch. 19
10-year forward averaging election, lump sum distributions, 19:40–19:44
age 50 reached before 1986, 19:61
choice to use, 19:66
circumstances of, 19:60
generally, 19:59
separate ten-year forward averaging tax, computation of, 19:61
trustee-to-trustee transfers, tax treatment, 19:17
U.S. Savings Bonds, 19:6
withholding
definition of nonperiodic payment, 24:55
outside U.S., qualified plan distributions, 24:57
10 percent withholding, right to elect out of, 24:55–24:57

Nontraditional plans
administrative determination of benefits, 9:72

NOPB. *See* Notice of plan benefits

Normal retirement age, *See also* Written explanations 12:1–12:9.

account balances, determination of, 9:21, 9:22
cash balance plans, 9:83
date of retirement, determination of, 12:5
defined, 9:21, 12:1
defined benefit plans, 12:2, 12:7
defined contribution plans, 12:6
disability benefits, commencement of benefits, 12:51
earlier than permissible under regulations, 12:3
in-service pension plan distributions, requirement, 1:20
not specified in plan, 12:4
100 percent vesting of benefits, 8:5
pension plans, 12:1
principal significance of, 9:22
qualified disability benefit defined, 12:8
required minimum distributions, 4:64
Social Security supplement, 12:9
uniform normal retirement age, differences attributable to, 10:22

Notice
direct rollovers, 21:1
DROs, determination, 3:49
employee, suspension of benefits, 13:18
periodic payments that are not eligible rollover distributions, withholding, 24:30–24:46
QDROs, determination, 3:49
QJSA rules, 11:47–11:56
QPSA rules, 11:47–11:56
termination of plan
abandoned defined contribution plans, 15:94, 15:95
annuity information, 16:10, 16:12
cessation of benefit accruals, 15:62
contents of, 15:13
delivery of, 15:11, 16:34
distributee, when Section 402(f) notice must be provided to, 15:84
final stages, 15:40–15:41
interested parties, defined, 15:30
IRS submission, 15:29, 15:31, 15:32, 15:68
language used for Section 402(f) notice, 15:82, 15:83
notice of intent, 16:9–16:14
plan benefits, notice of, 16:37–16:42
reason for notice, 15:9, 16:33
standard termination notice, 16:15
when must be provided, 15:14

Notice of intent to terminate (NOIT)
PBGC process, 16:9–16:14
underfunded plans
affected parties, 17:9
information contained in, 17:7, 17:8
PBGC, information provided to, 17:10

Notice of noncompliance (NONC), 16:18, 16:19

Notice of plan benefits (NOPB), 16:37–16:42
contents, 16:38
defined, 16:37
de minimis benefits, 16:41
information provided, 16:39
lump sum payments, 16:41
participants in pay status, 16:40
participants not in pay status, 16:42
participants retiring, 16:41

NUA. *See* Net unrealized appreciation

O

OBRA (Omnibus Budget Reconciliation Act)
late retirement benefits, 12:21

Officers of corporations
loans from plan, disproportionate availability to, 2:39
vesting, includable officers, 8:30
activities causing treatment as officer, 8:34
defined, 8:33
limits on number included, 8:35

Offsets
loans from plan by participant
offset amounts used to repay, 2:11, 2:12, 21:16, 21:28
withholding, eligible rollover distributions, 24:11
withholding requirements for distributions, 2:17
QDROs, offsets of retirement plan benefits, 3:63
QJSA rules, 11:6
QPSA rules, 11:6
TRA '97 provisions allowing, 3:63

Omnibus Budget Reconciliation Act (OBRA)
late retirement benefits, 12:21

100 percent vesting of benefits. *See* Vesting

133 1/3 percent rule, determination of account balances
defined benefit plans, 9:25

1 percent owners
vesting, 8:30, 8:32

Optional forms of benefits, Ch. 10
accrual method, differences in, 10:22
accrued benefits, decrease by plan amendment, 10:39
actuarial value, 10:41
present value, reductions in, 10:43
aggregation of certain benefits, rights, or features, 10:20
allocation formula, differences in, 10:22
ancillary benefits, defined, 10:23
annuity starting date, defined, 10:41
average benefit percentage (ABP) test, 10:6
benefit formula, differences in, 10:22
burdensome, elimination or reduction in benefits, 10:41
contingent benefits, 10:39
core options, 10:40
current availability requirement
age and service conditions, disregarding of, 10:7, 10:8
generally, 10:6
permissive aggregation of certain benefits, rights, and features, 10:20
satisfaction of requirement, 10:6
definitions, 10:22–10:24
accrual method, differences in, 10:22
allocation formula, differences in, 10:22
ancillary benefits, 10:23
benefit formula, differences in, 10:22
optional forms of benefits, 10:22
other right or feature, 10:24
uniform normal retirement age, differences attributable to, 10:22
de minimis rules, application of, 10:43
de minimis value, elimination or reduction in benefits, 10:41
early retirement window benefits, 10:19
effective availability, 10:5, 10:16
permissive aggregation of certain benefits, rights, and features, 10:20
ESOPs
Section 411(d)(6) rules, 10:32, 10:33
spousal benefits, 10:21
families of optional forms of benefits, 10:39
in-kind distributions, 25:3–25:7
nondiscrimination rules, 25:3–25:7
right to receive as optional forms of benefits, 25:3
installment optional form of benefit, 10:32
joint and contingent options, 10:39
level installment payment options, 10:39
multiemployer plans, 10:9
multiple plan amendments, 10:39
core option rule, applicability, 10:40
modifying optional forms of benefits, 10:31
noncore optional forms of benefits, 10:43
elimination if core options offered, 10:40
nondiscrimination rules
age and service conditions, disregarding of, 10:7, 10:8
aggregation of certain benefits, rights, or features, 10:20
benefits, rights and features, 10:5
current availability, 10:6–10:15
effective availability, 10:16
spousal benefits, 10:21
unpredictable contingent event benefits, 10:21
other right or feature defined, 10:24
plan amendments
accrued benefit decreased by, 10:39
elimination or reduction of Section 411(d)(6)(B) protected benefits, 10:41
multiple amendments modifying optional forms of benefits, 10:31
repeated amendments, 10:28
plant shutdown benefits, 10:39
QJSA, waivers by participant, 11:34
redundant, as, 10:43
refund of employee contributions, 10:39
repeated plan amendments, 10:28
retirement-type subsidies, 10:25
Section 411(d)(6) rules
annuity contracts, 10:29
anticutback rules and, 10:32, 10:34, 10:36, 10:43
beneficiary, benefits payable to, 10:29
benefits not Section 411(d)(6) protected benefits, 10:26
buyback rule, 10:29
defaulted loans, 10:30
defined, 10:27
defined benefit plans and defined contribution plans, transfers between, 10:30, 10:34
defined contribution plans, 10:34
de minimis change in timing, 10:30
direct rollovers, 10:34
diversification requirement, coordination with, 10:30
elimination of benefits, 10:29, 10:30, 10:39, 10:41
ESOPs, 10:32, 10:33
hardship distribution standards, amendment of, 10:30
in-kind distributions, 10:30
installment optional form of benefit, 10:32
involuntary distributions, 10:30
joint and survivor annuities, 10:30
multiple plan amendments modifying optional forms of benefits, 10:31

objective conditions, permissibility of, 10:37
plan mergers and benefit transfers, 10:29
profit sharing plans, 10:30
protected benefits, 10:29
readily tradable employer securities, 10:32
reduction of benefits, 10:29, 10:30
repeated plan amendments, 10:28
single-sum optional form of benefit, 10:32
spouse, benefits payable to, 10:29
statutory requirements, change in, 10:30
stock bonus plans, 10:32, 10:33
termination of plan, 10:32
waiver prohibition, 10:34
short life expectancy, 10:40
single-sum distributions, 10:40
Social Security leveling, 10:39
spousal benefits, 10:21
stock bonus plans, 10:32, 10:33
testing rules
early retirement window benefits, 10:19
frozen participants, 10:18
mergers and acquisitions, 10:17
uniform normal retirement age, differences attributable to, 10:22
utilization test, 10:42

Ordinary income
lump sum distributions, flat 20 percent capital gains tax on nonperiodic payments, 19:65

Orphan plans. *See* Abandoned defined contribution plans

Other right or feature defined, 10:24

P

Partial terminations
definitions, 8:75
determinative factors and circumstances, 8:76–8:78, 8:80
ERISA requirements, 8:73
percentage reduction in participation, 8:76, 8:78
purpose of rule, 8:74
request for IRS determination, 8:81
significant reduction in number of participants, 8:75
vested account balance or benefit, determining, 8:79

Partnerships
termination of plan, 16:3

PBGC. *See* Pension Benefit Guaranty Corporation

Penalties. *See* specific topic

Pension Benefit Guaranty Corporation (PBGC)
missing participants, 15:86, 16:54–16:60
QDROs
guidance, 3:62
termination of defined benefit plan and, 3:54
QPSA and, 11:8
qualified joint and survivor annuity and, 11:8
single-employer defined benefit plans, amendment of, 10:30
termination of plan, Ch. 16
actuary, certification by, 16:16
affected parties, NOIT, 16:14
assets of plan, insufficiency, 16:25–16:28
benefit election forms and notices, distributions of, 16:53
benefit liabilities, measurement of, 16:20–16:24
coverage, 16:1–16:4
defined benefit plans, 16:29, 16:31
determination letters, 16:65
distress termination, 17:25, 17:29, 17:31, 17:32
excess benefit plans, 16:2
excise taxes, benefit increases in defined benefit plan to qualify for reduction in reversion, 16:52
exemption from coverage, 16:2
final stages, 16:43–16:45
flat-dollar benefit plans, 16:35
guarantee, extinguishment of, 16:9
information gathering, 16:35, 16:36
insurance contracts, 16:35
interest rates, determination, 16:21–16:24
lost participants, 16:54–16:60
majority owners, 16:26, 16:27
measurement of benefit liabilities, 16:20–16:24
missing participants, 15:86, 16:54–16:60
mortality rates, determination, 16:21
noncompliance, notice of, 16:18, 16:19
notice of intent to terminate (NOIT), 16:9–16:14
notice of plan benefits, 16:37–16:42
partnerships, 16:3
percentage-of-pay benefit plans, 16:35
plan administered during, 16:11
plan benefits, notice of, 16:37–16:42
post-distribution certification, 16:61–16:66
preliminary information for PBGC, 16:15–16:19
present value of accrued benefits, 16:45
professional individuals defined, 16:4
proposed termination date, 16:8

Pension Benefit Guaranty Corporation (PBGC) *(cont'd)*
termination of plan *(cont'd)*
qualified replacement plan defined, 16:50
reporting of distributions (Form 1099-R), 16:72
small plans, what constitutes, 16:30
spinoff/termination rules, 16:67–16:70
sponsor of plan, actions by, 16:29–16:32
standard terminations, 16:5, 16:6, 16:15–16:19, 16:27
steps, 16:5–16:8
substantial owner defined, 16:3
sufficiency requirement, 16:9
surplus assets, 16:46–16:49
terminal funding contracts, 16:28
top-heavy plans, 16:35
204(h) notice, 16:30, 16:33, 16:34
who determines, 16:7
underfunded plans, 17:1–17:50
termination of plan, initiation by PBGC, 17:33

Pension costs test
distress termination, underfunded plans, 17:4, 17:5

Pension equity plans, 9:92, 9:93

Pension Funding Equity Act of 2004 (PFEA)
lump sum determinations, 9:67

Pension plans. *See also* Profit sharing plans; Qualified retirement plans
in-service distributions, 1:18–1:25
continuation of accrual of benefits, 1:22
earliest time active participant may begin receiving benefits, 1:20
lump sum distribution received before termination of employment, tax treatment, 1:25
payment of benefits, 1:21
required beginning date, 1:19
required minimum distribution rules, 1:19
rules for, 1:18
minimum distribution requirements. *See* Required minimum distributions
normal retirement age, 12:1

Pension Protection Act of 2006 (PPA), 9:78
cash balance plans
interest rates, 9:79
vesting, 8:13
collectively bargained plans, vesting, 8:11
defined benefit plans
QPSA rules, 12:62
substantial owners not majority owners, 17:22
underfunded plans, 17:22
defined contribution plans, vesting, 8:10
hardship withdrawal provisions, 1:6
in-service distributions, 1:20
lump sum distributions
Section 415 limits, 9:67
maximum annual benefit, actuarial assumptions, 9:60
minimum vesting requirements, exceptions to, 8:8
phased retirement, 12:28
QOSA requirements, 11:38–11:46
QPSA rules, defined benefit plans, 12:62
termination of plan,
interest rates, minimum lump sum, 15:54
underfunded defined benefit plans, 17:22
vesting
cash balance plans, 8:13
collectively bargained plans, 8:11
defined contribution plans, 8:10

Percentage-of-pay benefit plans
termination of plan, information gathering, 15:63, 16:35

Periodic payments, Ch. 18
amounts received as annuity
distributions from qualified retirement plans treated as, 18:3
variable annuities treated as, 18:4
annuity contracts, fully taxable annuity payments, 18:17, 18:18
annuity defined, 18:1
deductible voluntary employee contribution, 18:18
defined, 24:19
eligible rollover distributions, direct rollovers, 21:12, 21:25, 21:46
exclusion ratio, 18:6
expected return under plan, 18:7
fixed amortization method, 20:4
fixed annuitization method, 20:4
fixed-period annuities, 18:2
Form 1099-R, 27:27
generally, 18:3, 18:5
investment in the contract, 18:5, 18:12
joint and survivor annuities, 18:2
series of substantially equal periodic payments, 20:4
simplified method of basis recovery, 18:8–18:16
effective date, 18:14
examples of application, 18:13
expected number of monthly annuity payments, 18:11
generally, 18:8
taxable portion, calculating, 18:9
tax-free portion, calculating, 18:9, 18:10
transition rule, 18:15, 18:16
single life annuities, 18:2

substantially equal periodic payments, exemption from additional 10 percent income tax
fixed amortization method, 20:4
fixed annuitization method, 20:4
generally, 20:4
modification of payments, 20:5, 20:6
reduction in amount of payment as modification of series, 20:6
required minimum distribution method, 20:4
series of substantially equal periodic payments, 20:4
taxation of, Ch. 18
variable annuities
defined, 18:2
generally, 18:4
withholding on periodic payments that are not eligible rollover distributions, 24:19–24:54
abbreviated notice, 24:46
aggregation of payments, 24:47
beneficiaries of deceased employee, 24:21
commercial annuity contract, payment period specified in terms of, 24:52
death of employee, distribution made on account of, 24:29
definition of periodic payment, 24:19
EFT, 24:35
failure of plan administrator to notify payor, 24:26, 24:27
first periodic payment of year, 24:51
$5,400, annual payments less than, 24:32
Form W-4P, combination of notice with, 24:44
frequency of payments used as payment period, 24:53
gross income, entire amount excludable from, 24:38
how tax is withheld, 24:20
information provided by plan administrator to payor, 24:25–24:27
insurance company's incorrect calculation of monthly annuity amount, 24:54
language of notice, 24:43
mailing of notice, 24:45
notice of right not to have withholding apply, 24:30–24:46
payment period, 24:53
payor, notice to payees on behalf of, 24:41
payors of, 24:47
plan administrators, 24:23–24:27
recipients of, 24:28, 24:54
sample notice, 24:42
surviving spouse, payments made to, 24:21
transfers of duties, 24:24
wage bracket method of determining withholding, 24:48
who is required to withhold, 24:22
withholding certificate, 24:49, 24:50

Permissive aggregation group (PAG), vesting of top-heavy plans, 8:21, 8:22

Permitted disparity
early retirement, 12:20

PFEA. *See* Pension Funding Equity Act of 2004

Plan amendment
Audit CAP correction, 23:5
defined contribution plan, reducing accrued benefits, 10:25
employer discretion or conditions restricting availability of protected benefits, 10:29, 10:38
nondiscrimination rules, 10:1
optional forms of benefits
accrued benefit decreased by plan amendment, 10:39
elimination or reduction of Section 411(d)(6)(B) protected benefits, 10:41
multiple plan amendments modifying optional forms of benefits, 10:31
repeated plan amendments, 10:28
Section 411(d)(6) rules, 10:30
QDROs, rights of alternate payees, 3:52
QOSA requirements, 11:45
required minimum distributions, benefit options eliminated, 4:67
self-correction program, 23:3
voluntary correction program, 23:4, 23:8

Plan disqualification. *See* Disqualification of plan

Plan loans. *See* Loans from plan by participant

Plan-to-plan transfers, vested benefits, 8:29

Plant shutdown benefits
optional forms of benefits, 10:39

PPA. *See* Pension Protection Act of 2006

Predecessor plan defined
vesting years, determination of, 8:50

Pre-GATT Section 417(e) interest rates, App. B

Premature distributions. *See* Early distributions, additional 10 percent income tax

Prenuptial agreements, 11:30

Present value of accrued benefits (PVAB)
termination of plan, recalculation of PVAB, 15:71, 16:45
vesting
defined benefit plans, 8:24, 8:25
top-heavy plans, 8:17–8:27

Primary residence, purchase or repair of
hardship distributions from 401(k) plans, 1:11
loans from plan by participant, exceptions to repayment rule, 2:5

Professional individuals
termination of plan, PBGC process, 16:4

Professional service employers
termination of plan, PBGC process, 16:4

Profit sharing plans. *See also* Pension plans; Qualified retirement plans
elimination or reduction of benefits, Section 411(d)(6) rules, 10:30
hardship distributions
distributable amount, 1:9
generally, 1:4
qualified matching contributions, 1:9
qualified nonelective contributions, 1:9
taxation of, 1:5
in-service distributions
fixed number of years defined, 1:2
generally, 1:1
hardship distributions, 1:4
2-year rule for withdrawals, exceptions, 1:3
long-term disability insurance, 12:45
minimum distribution requirements. *See* Required minimum distributions
survivor annuity requirements, 11:3, 11:4
taxable life insurance costs, 6:4
termination of plan
information gathering, 15:16
plan sponsor adopting resolution to terminate defined contribution plan, 15:7
reason for considering, 15:1
top-heavy plans, vesting, 8:23
vesting
account balances value, determination of, 8:23
top-heavy plans, 8:23

Prohibited transactions
in-kind distributions, insurance contracts, 25:18, 25:19
loans as, 2:1, 2:34–2:44
applicable rules, 2:34, 2:35
deemed distributions, 2:21
definitions, 2:34
ERISA rules, 2:35–2:37
fiduciary prohibitions, relief under ERISA section 408(b)(1), 2:36
highly compensated employees, officers, or shareholders, disproportionate availability to, 2:39
participant loan, defined, 2:37
party in interest, defined, 2:35
reasonably equivalent basis, loans considered to be available on, 2:38, 2:40
repayments withheld, as "plan assets," 2:44

Property settlement
QDRO as part of, 3:3

Protected benefits, Ch. 10. *See also* Nondiscrimination rules
aggregation of certain benefits, rights, or features. *See* Benefits, rights, and features generally
current availability rules. *See* Benefits, rights, and features generally
effective availability. *See* Benefits, rights, and features generally
installment optional form of benefit, 10:32
retirement-type subsidies, 10:25
Section 411(d)(6) rules
annuity contracts, 10:29
anticutback rules and, 10:32, 10:34, 10:36, 10:43
benefits that are not Section 411(d)(6) protected benefits, 10:26
buyback rule, 10:29
defaulted loans, 10:30
defined benefit plans, 10:30, 10:34
defined contribution plans, 10:30, 10:34
denial of protected benefit, 10:35
direct rollovers, 10:34
diversification requirement, coordination with, 10:30
elimination of benefits, 10:29, 10:30, 10:39, 10:41
ESOPs, 10:32, 10:33
generally, 10:25
hardship distribution standards, amendment of, 10:30
in-kind distributions, 10:30
installment optional form of benefit, 10:32
involuntary distributions, 10:30
joint and survivor annuities, 10:30
mandatory distributions, 21:6
multiple plan amendments modifying optional forms of benefits, 10:31
objective conditions, permissibility of, 10:37
plan amendment to allow employer discretion to restrict, 10:38
plan mergers and benefit transfers, 10:29
profit sharing plans, 10:30
provision of benefits under terms of plan only, 10:28
readily tradable employer securities, 10:32
reduction of benefits, 10:29, 10:30
repeated plan amendments, 10:28
single-sum optional form of benefit, 10:32

spouse, benefits payable to, 10:29
statutory requirements, change in, 10:30
stock bonus plans, 10:32, 10:33
termination of plan, 10:30
vesting, 8:58
waiver prohibition, 10:34
spousal benefits. *See* Benefits, rights, and features generally
stock bonus plans
credit for, in-kind distributions, 25:27
Section 411(d)(6) rules, 10:32, 10:33
vesting, Section 411(d)(6) rules, 8:58

PS-58 costs, 6:1–6:12
age used in determining, 6:6
cash value exceeding face amount, 6:9
computation of annual cost, 6:3
contracts subject to treatment as, 6:1
credit for costs taxable in prior years, 25:27
in-kind distributions, credit for costs taxable in prior years, 25:27
joint and survivor protection premiums, 6:12
new life insurance contracts issued during year, 6:8
rates used in determining, 6:4, 6:5
reporting requirements, 6:11, 27:26
self-employed individuals, 6:2
survivor whole life contracts, 6:12
tables used in determining, 6:4
joint and survivor protection, 6:12
termination of employment, 6:7
universal life contracts, 6:10

Public safety employees, distributions from defined contribution plans, 20:2
separation from service after age 50, 20:9

Put options, ESOPs, termination of employment
exceptions to requirements, 13:13
fair market value of securities, 13:11
installment payments elected for vested ESOP balance, 13:12
length of time must be offered to participant, 13:10

PVAB. *See* Present value of accrued benefits

Q

QACAs. *See* Qualified automatic contribution arrangements

QDIA. *See* Qualified default investment alternative

QDROs. *See* Qualified domestic relations orders

QJSA. *See* Qualified joint and survivor annuity

QPSA. *See* Qualified preretirement survivor annuity

QTAs. *See* Qualified termination administrators

Qualified automatic contribution arrangements (QACAs)
vesting requirements, 8:12

Qualified default investment alternative (QDIA) 10:24

Qualified domestic relations orders (QDROs), 3:1–3:63. *See also* Domestic relations orders (DROs)
administration of plan
administrator, 3:13
effect of QDRO on, 3:50
alteration of form or amount of benefits, disallowance
earliest retirement age, 3:25
exceptions, 3:24
former spouse, treatment as surviving spouse, 3:26, 3:29
timing of benefit payments, 3:25
alternate payees
additional benefits, 3:27
alteration of payment retirement plan benefits, 3:24
amount given to, 3:16
change of prior assignment of retirement plan benefits to, 3:34
defined, 3:6
defined benefit plans, 3:33
defined contribution plans, 3:32
designation of beneficiary, 3:28
disclosure rights, 3:51
early distributions, additional 10 percent income tax, 3:59
form in which alternate payee's benefits will be paid, 3:20
Form 1099-R, 27:3
generally, 3:5
guardian of, payment to, 3:7
income, inclusion of benefits, 3:55, 3:56
income-averaging of lump sum distribution by spouse or former spouse, 3:61
information required to be provided by plan administrator, 3:41
investment in the contract, allocation, 3:57, 3:58
lump sum distributions, 3:61
mailing address, 3:10
nonspouse, 3:56, 3:58
required minimum distributions, 4:61, 4:62

Qualified domestic relations orders (QDROs), *(cont'd)*
alternate payees *(cont'd)*
retirement plan benefits payable to another alternate payee under prior QDRO, 3:37
rollovers, 3:60
specification of benefits, 3:31–3:34
spouse or former spouse, 3:55, 3:57, 3:61
state agency, benefits paid to, 3:8
vesting, additional, 3:27
when benefits will be received, 3:21
wrongful payment of retirement plan benefits to participant, 3:48
amendment, 3:52
annual limitations on contributions and benefits, 3:30
anti-alienation rules, 3:1
assignment rules, 3:1
balance to the credit of participant, 28:3
benefit period, specification of, 3:30
child support, 3:4
defined, 3:5
defined benefit plans
alternate payees, 3:33
termination of plan, 3:54
defined contribution plans
allocation of determination expenses, 3:42
alternate payees, 3:32
determination if order is QDRO, 3:12
advisory opinions, 3:14
allocation of expenses, 3:42
division of plan benefits
best way, 3:15
reasons for, 3:17
type of retirement plan and, 3:18
divorce decree, as part of, 3:3, 3:4
drafting, 3:62
earliest retirement age, 3:25
early distributions, additional 10 percent income tax
alternate payee, 3:59
exemption from, 20:2
former spouse, treatment as surviving spouse, 3:26
death of, 3:29
guardian of alternate payee, payment to, 3:7
guidance documents, 3:62
income-averaging treatment, 3:61
investment in the contract, allocation between participant and alternate payees, 3:57, 3:58
lump sum distributions
alternate payees, 3:61, 19:30
balance to the credit of an employee, 19:30
mailing address of alternate payee, 3:10
mergers, 3:52
model forms, 3:43
modification of, 3:34
multiple retirement plans, coverage of, 3:9
notice of determination, 3:49
offsets of retirement plan benefits, 3:63
payments, specification of number of, 3:35
PBGC as trustee upon termination of plan, 3:54
plan, specification of, 3:36
provisions required, 3:11
reasonable written procedures, 3:39
required minimum distributions, 4:60–4:62
to alternate payee, 4:61, 4:62
reviewing, guidance, 3:62
rollovers by alternate payees, 3:60
successor employer, maintained by, 3:52
survivor benefits, described, 3:19
taxation of distributions under, 3:55–3:61
income-averaging of lump sum distribution by spouse or former spouse, 3:61
spouse or former spouse, 3:55, 3:57
termination of retirement plan and, 3:53
defined benefit plans, 3:54
time to determine whether DRO is QDRO, 3:47
written procedures for determining status
amendment of retirement plan document to implement QDRO, 3:38
design of procedures, generally, 3:40
wrongful payment of retirement plan benefits to participant, 3:48

Qualified employer plan. *See* specific topic

Qualified joint and survivor annuity (QJSA), Ch. 11
additional accruals, 11:13
alternate payees, 11:12
annuity contracts purchased and distributed to participant or spouse, 11:2
annuity starting date, 11:11–11:13
administrative delays, 11:12
disability benefit, 11:13
relevance of, 11:11
retroactive, 11:47
application to unmarried participants, surviving spouses, participants with change in marital status, 11:25, 11:26
benefits, 11:14–11:17
change in status, survivor annuity requirements and, 11:24

defined benefit plans
  benefits applicable to, 11:15
  defined, 12:62
  generally, 11:3
  QDRO benefits, 3:33
  rules governing, 11:19
defined contribution plans
  account balance subject to, 12:59
  benefits applicable to, 11:15
  generally, 11:3
disability benefit, annuity starting date, 11:13
divorce, survivor annuity requirements, 11:26
earliest retirement age, 11:18
electronic filing, 11:56
employer contributions, benefits from, 11:14
frozen plans, 11:7
fully subsidized benefits, 11:57, 11:58
loans from plan by participant, 2:48, 11:24
  application, 11:24
mandatory distributions, 11:9
mergers, 11:6
minimum funding requirements, 11:28
offset plans, 11:6
1-year marriage rule, 11:26
  defined contribution plan, vested account balance, 11:28
optional forms of benefits, waivers by participant, 11:34
participants, application to retirement plan, 11:9
payments in form of, 11:9
PBGC, administration by, 11:8
plans subject to, 11:3, 11:4
  benefits applicable to, 11:15
portions of benefits under retirement plan subject to, 11:10
prenuptial agreements, spousal consent, 11:30
profit-sharing plan, deferred annuity contract purchased under, 11:5
QDROs and, 3:19
  former spouse, treatment as surviving spouse, 3:26, 3:29
REA 1984 requirements added to Code and ERISA, 11:1
remarriage, survivor annuity requirements, 11:26
renegotiation, survivor annuity requirements and, 11:24
separation before age 35, 11:49
spinoffs, 11:6
spousal consent, 11:27–11:33
  generally, 11:17
  loans from plan by participant, survivor annuity requirements and, 11:24
  prenuptial agreements, 11:30
  revocability, 11:32
  waiver of, 11:29, 11:31, 11:35
subsidized survivor benefits, 11:57, 11:58
suspension of benefits, 11:13
terminated retirement plan, 11:7
timing of distributions, 11:18
transferee plans, 11:6
unmarried participant
  generally, 11:17
  survivor annuity requirements, application to, 11:25, 11:26
waivers
  generally, 11:9
  participant, by, 11:33–11:37
  right to waive, 11:37
  rules governing, 11:34
written explanation of coverage (notice requirements), 11:47–11:56
  effective dates, 11:55
  examples, 11:54
  generally applicable information requirements, satisfaction of, 11:53
  information to be provided, 11:51–11:53
  married and unmarried individuals, 11:52
  nonvested participants, 11:48
  participant-specific information requirements, 11:52
  purpose of, 11:47
  reasonable period for providing, 11:49
  relative values, determination of, 11:52
  satisfaction of requirements, 11:50
  separation before age 35, 11:49
  when required, 11:49

Qualified matching contributions
  hardship distributions, 1:9

Qualified nonelective contributions, hardship distributions, 1:9

Qualified optional survivor annuity (QOSA)
  effective date of requirements, 11:46
  implementation by plans, 11:40
  level of spouse survivor annuity to be provided, 11:39
  plan amendments, 11:45
  PPA requirements, 11:38–11:46
  preretirement survivor annuities and, 11:44
  single life annuity, actuarially equivalent to, 11:41
  spousal consent for distribution by participant, 11:42
  written explanations of terms and conditions, 11:43

Qualified plan. *See* specific topic

Qualified preretirement survivor annuity (QPSA), 11:1–11:58
additional accruals, 11:13
alternate payees, 11:12
amount of, rules governing, 11:20
annuity contracts purchased and distributed to participant or spouse, 11:2
annuity starting date, 11:11–11:13
administrative delays, 11:12
disability benefit, 11:13
relevance of, 11:11
retroactive, 11:47
benefits, 11:14–11:17
benefits to which survivor annuity rules apply, 11:26
change in status, survivor annuity requirements and, 11:24, 11:26
defined benefit plans, 12:62
benefits applicable to, 11:15
generally, 11:3
100 times monthly benefit, benefit equal to plus QPSA, 12:66
participant charged for benefit, 11:22
rules governing, 11:19, 11:20
surviving spouse, beginning of distributions to, 11:23
defined contribution plans
account balance subject to, 12:59
benefits applicable to, 11:15
forfeitures on death, 11:16, 11:21
generally, 11:3
portion of death benefit paid as, 12:54
rules governing, 11:20, 11:21
disability benefit, annuity starting date, 11:13
divorce, survivor annuity requirements, 11:26
earliest retirement age, 11:20
electronic filing, 11:56
employee contributions, benefits from, 11:14
forfeitability
death, on, 11:12, 11:16
generally, 11:20
frozen plans, 11:7
fully subsidized benefits, 11:57, 11:58
loans from plan by participant, application, 11:24
mandatory distributions, 11:9
mergers, 11:6
offset plans, 11:6
1-year marriage rule, 11:26
defined contribution plan, vested account balance, 11:28
participants, application to retirement plan, 11:9
payments in form of, 11:9
PBGC, administration by, 11:8
plans subject to, 11:3, 11:4
benefits, 11:15
portions of benefits under retirement plan subject to, 11:10
PPA requirements, defined benefit plans, 12:62
prenuptial agreements, spousal consent, 11:30
profit-sharing plan, deferred annuity contract purchased under, 11:5
QDROs and, 3:19
former spouse, treatment as surviving spouse, 3:26, 3:29
REA 1984 requirements added to Code and ERISA, 11:1
remarriage, survivor annuity requirements, 11:26
renegotiation, survivor annuity requirements and, 11:24
rules governing, 11:19–11:23
Section 401(a)(11) requirements, plans subject to
defined contribution plans, 11:21
loans from plan by participant, 11:24
waiver of spousal benefit, time and manner of, 11:36
Section 412 minimum funding requirements, 11:28, 11:36
Section 417 requirements, plans subject to
defined contribution plans, 11:21
loans from plan by participant, 11:24
separation before age 35, 11:49
spinoffs, 11:6
spousal consent
loans from plan by participant, survivor annuity requirements and, 11:24
prenuptial agreements, 11:30
revocability, 11:32
waiver of, 11:29, 11:31, 11:35
subsidized survivor benefits, 11:57, 11:58
surviving spouses, 11:25, 11:26
beginning of distributions to, 11:23
suspension of benefits, 11:13
terminated retirement plan, 11:7
transferee plans, 11:6
unmarried participants, application, 11:25, 11:26
waivers
generally, 11:9
participant, by, 11:33–11:37

right to waive, 11:37
rules governing, 11:34
time and manner of waiver, 11:36
written explanation of coverage (notice requirements), 11:47–11:56
effective dates, 11:55
generally applicable information requirements, satisfaction of, 11:53
information to be provided, 11:51
nonvested participants, 11:48
purpose of, 11:47
reasonable period for providing, 11:49
satisfaction of requirements, 11:50
separation before age 35, 11:49
when required, 11:49

Qualified replacement plans
defined, 15:73, 16:50
transfers to, 15:74, 16:51

Qualified reservist distributions, 20:2
10 percent additional income tax, 20:8
public safety employees, separation from service after age 50, 20:9
separation from service after age 50, 20:9

Qualified retirement plans
benefits, rights, and features, nondiscrimination rules, 10:5
direct rollovers by employees not yet eligible to participate, 21:49
distributed annuity contract, 21:29
distributions from. *See* Form 1099-R
excise tax, required minimum distributions, 20:17, 20:22

Qualified Social Security supplements, 10:22

Qualified termination administrators (QTAs)
abandoned defined contribution plans, 15:89–15:96

Qualified termination administrators (QTAs), abandoned defined contribution plans
contents of notice to DOL, 15:94
lost participants, locating, 15:92
requirements, 15:90
Special Terminal Report for Abandoned Plans, 15:96
tasks in winding up orphan plan, 15:95
when orphan plan deemed to be terminated, 15:93
when plan considered abandoned, 15:91

Qualified voluntary employee contributions (QVECs)
nonperiodic payments, 19:18

Qualifying longevity annuity contract (QLAC) 12:30
defined, 4:27

R

Railroad Retirement Act, 16:2

Ratio percentage test, nondiscrimination rules
taxable life insurance costs, 6:8

REA 1984. *See* Retirement Equity Act of 1984

Recordkeeping requirements
accrual service, determination of, 9:38
new technology to satisfy, 11:56
vesting years, determination of, 8:42

Reduction of benefits
Section 411(d)(6) rules, 10:29, 10:30

Reliance on employee representation by employer
hardship distributions from 401(k) plans, 1:12

Religious denomination, plan established and maintained for minimum vesting requirements, 8:2

Remarriage, survivor annuity requirements, 11:26

Reorganization test
distress termination, underfunded plans, 17:4, 17:5

Repair of primary residence
hardship distributions from 401(k) plans, 1:11

Reporting requirements
designated Roth account distributions, 27:30, 27:35, 27:37
early distributions, additional 10 percent income tax, 20:15
eligible rollover distributions, responsibility for, 24:1–24:18
Form 1099-R. *See* Form 1099-R
loans from plan by participant as deemed distributions, 2:14
nonresident aliens, 27:4
PS-58 costs, 6:11, 27:26
qualified retirement plans, distributions from. *See* Form 1099-R
taxable life insurance costs, 6:11

Reporting requirements *(cont'd)*
termination of plan
final disclosure forms, distributions to participants, 15:88
PBGC process, 16:72

Required aggregation group (RAG), vesting of top-heavy plans, 8:20–8:22

Required beginning date. *See* Required minimum distributions

Required minimum distributions (RMDs)
account balances subject to, 4:3
age 70½, attainment of
commencement of distributions, 4:10
distribution period, calculation of, 4:28
generally, 4:7
annuities
acceleration of payments, defined, 4:47
actuarial gain, defined, 4:47
calendar years 2003, 2004, and 2005, 4:50
cost-of-living index, 4:47
definitions, 4:47
delay in issuance of contract by life insurance company in delinquency proceedings, 4:63
distributions, 4:65
distributions before required beginning date, 4:43, 4:44
distributions from contract purchased from insurance company, 4:37
50 percent excise tax on failure to make, 20:19, 20:20
individual account not yet annuitized, 4:45
MDIB requirement, 4:35
payment period, change of, 4:46
total value being annuitized, defined, 4:47
trust, payments from, 4:47
unvested portion, effect, 4:39
annuity payments under defined benefit plans, 4:38
commencement, 4:34
distribution for purposes of Section 401(a)(9), 4:34–4:50
generally, 4:34
life annuity with period certain, 4:34
benefits subject to, 4:3
calendar year of distribution, 4:20
annuities, 4:50
annuity distributions under a defined benefit plan, 4:38
unvested portion, 4:39
church plans, defined, 4:6
consolidations, 4:55, 4:69
corrective distributions, excess elective contributions, 5:45
cost-of-living index, 4:47
death benefits
defined benefit plan distributions, 4:34
estate as designated beneficiary, 12:79
5-year rule, 4:66, 12:74, 12:77, 12:78
life expectancy rule, 12:74, 12:76, 12:78
optional benefits, 4:67
timing of benefit payments, 12:74
trust as designated beneficiary, 12:80, 12:81
death of participant
distribution period, calculation of, 4:29
5-year rule, 4:11, 4:12, 4:14, 4:15
before required beginning date, 4:11–4:16
defined benefit plans, 4:34, 4:57
actuarial increase in accrued benefit, 4:40–4:43
segregated shares, 4:57, 4:58, 4:61
separate accounts, 4:61
defined contribution plans, 4:23–4:33
amounts not taken into account, 4:33
amount used for determining, 4:26
annuity contracts, use to satisfy, 4:24
applicable distribution period, 4:28, 4:29
calendar year distributions, 4:25
qualifying longevity annuity contract (QLAC), 4:27
unvested portion of individual account, 4:32
designated beneficiaries, 4:3
affirmative election, 4:18
commencement of distributions, 4:20
commencement of distributions to surviving spouse, 4:16
contingent beneficiary, 4:31
defined, 4:17
distribution calendar year, 4:20
distribution period, 4:29
estate or trust as, 4:19
life expectancy rule, 4:13
multiple, life expectancy determination, 4:31
nonspouse, 4:29
person other than an individual, 4:19
spouse, 4:29
successor beneficiary, 4:31
trust as, 4:21, 4:22
when determined, 4:20
direct rollovers, eligible distributions, 21:26, 21:27
distributions after age 70½, 4:64
distributions beginning during a participant's lifetime, 4:5–4:10
commencement of distributions, 4:10
distributions after participant's death, 4:9
required beginning date, defined, 4:6

eligible rollover distributions withholding on distributions not rolled over, 24:10
employee account balances and benefits, 4:3
Employee Plans (EP) examinations
employees, IRS issuing field directive to, 4:72
excess elective contributions, corrective distributions, 5:43
5 percent owner
  generally, 13:4
  required beginning date, 4:6
50 percent excise tax on failure to make, 20:16–20:24
  annuity, payee's interest in form of, 20:19
  default provisions, 20:18
  deferred compensation plans, 20:16
  defined benefit plans, payee's interest in form of annuity, 20:20
  defined contribution plans, payee's interest in form of annuity, 20:21
  entire remaining benefit, 20:22
  5-year rule, 20:18, 20:20
  generally, 20:16
  individual account, payee's interest in form of, 20:18
  qualified retirement plans defined, 20:17
  required beginning date, 20:23
  waiver of tax, 20:24
5-year rule, death of participant before required beginning date, 4:11, 4:12, 4:14, 4:15
governmental plans
  failure to satisfy RMD rules, 4:49
  required beginning date, defined, 4:6
individual accounts under defined contribution plans, calendar year distributions, 4:23
joint and survivor annuities, MDIB requirement, 4:35
life annuities, MDIB requirement, 4:35
life expectancies, designated beneficiaries, 4:31
life expectancy rule, 4:13–4:15
MDIB requirements
  distributions in form of life or joint and survivor annuity, 4:35
  individual accounts under defined contribution plans, calendar year distributions, 4:23
  joint and survivor annuities, 4:35
  life annuity, distributions in form of, 4:35
  multiple beneficiaries, 4:35
  TEFRA, accordance with, 4:68
mergers, 4:55
more than one qualified plan, participation in, 4:56
multiple beneficiaries, MDIB requirement, 4:35
participants not subject to, 13:5
payment after participant's death, estate or trust as beneficiary, 4:66
pension plans, in-service distributions, normal retirement age, 4:64
period certain annuities
  length of period certain, 4:36
  MDIB requirement, 4:35
post-death distributions, default rule, 4:4
provisions of qualified plans, 4:4
QDROs, 4:60–4:62
QLAC
  application to, 12:31
  defined, 4:27
required beginning date, 13:3
  annuity payments, 4:43
  death of participant before, 4:11–4:16
  defined, 4:6
  defined benefit plan, annuity distributions, 4:38
  distributions before, 4:6
  failure by employee or spouse to consent to distribution while it is immediately distributable, 4:59
  generally, 4:6
  TEFRA election, revocation after, 4:71
  unvested portion of individual account, 4:32
retirement plans, 4:2
rollovers, 4:51, 4:52, 4:70
segregated shares, 4:57, 4:61
separate accounts, 4:57, 4:58, 4:61
spinoffs, 4:55
spouse defined, 4:60
substantially equal periodic payments, exemption from additional 10 percent income tax, 20:4
surviving spouse
  defined, 4:60
  distributions before required beginning date, 4:44
TEFRA
  MDIB requirements, 4:68
  Section 242(b)(2) election, 4:71
  transfers, effect on election, 4:69
termination of employment
  5 percent owner, 13:4
  participants not subject to rules, 13:5
  required beginning date, 13:3
transfers, 4:55, 4:69
  TEFRA election, effect of transfer from one plan to another, 4:69
  transferee plan, 4:54, 4:55, 4:69
  transferor plan, 4:53, 4:55, 4:69

Required minimum distributions (RMDs) (*cont'd*)
trust as designated beneficiary, documentation, 4:3
waiver for 2009, 4:1
withholding on eligible rollover distributions that are not rolled over, 24:10

Residential mortgage loans
loans from plan by participant, 2:22

Residential property. *See* Primary residence, purchase or repair of

Restructuring of plan, nondiscrimination rules, 10:4

Retirement. *See also* Qualified retirement plans
bridge benefit, 12:9
current availability requirement, early retirement window benefits, 12:18
defined benefit plans, late retirement, 12:21
defined contribution plans
disability benefits, 12:40–12:45
late retirement, 12:21, 12:23
disability benefits
commencement of benefits, 12:46, 12:51
compensation, determination of, 12:44
defined benefit plans, 12:46–12:52
defined contribution plans, 12:40–12:45
limitations, 12:52
lump sum distributions, 12:48
monthly benefit, determination of, 12:49
normal retirement age for commencement of benefits, 12:51
payment of benefits, 12:47
subsidized benefit defined, 12:50
total and permanent disability, 12:43
early retirement, 12:10–12:20
age requirements, 12:13
availability of option before early retirement age, 12:16
choice of, reasons, 12:12
earliest retirement age, QJSA and, 11:18
eligibility requirements, 12:13
no subsidy, defined benefit plan provided, 12:15
permitted disparity, restrictions in plans using, 12:20
provision of option, reasons for, 12:11
requirements, 12:19
Section 411(d)(6)(B) protected benefits, elimination of, 12:16
service requirements, 12:13
subsidies, types of, 12:14
types of subsidies provided, 12:14
early retirement window benefits
current availability requirement, 12:18
generally, 12:17
optional forms of benefits rules, 10:19
late retirement, 12:21–12:26
Age Discrimination in Employment Act, 12:21
defined benefit plans, 12:21, 12:24
defined contribution plans, 12:21, 12:23
delayed retirement accrued benefits, 12:25, 12:26
issues determining, 12:22
mandatory retirement age, 12:21
normal retirement age. *See* Normal retirement age
phased retirement, 12:27, 12:28
Social Security retirement age, benefits beginning before maximum benefits, increase of, 9:59
reduction of benefits, 9:58
Social Security supplement, 12:9
suspension of benefits, 12:32
noncompliance with DOL requirements, 12:33

Retirement Equity Act of 1984 (REA 1984)
protected benefits, 10:25
QJSA and QPSA coverage, notice requirements, 11:47
spousal consent requirement, 11:27
survivor annuity requirements, 11:1

Retirement Protection Act of 1994 (RPA '94), lump sum determinations
changes to limits, 9:67

Retirement-type subsidies
elimination of Section 411(d)(6)(B) protected benefits, 10:41
protected benefits, 10:25

Returns
eligible rollover distributions, responsibility for, 24:15

Rollovers, Ch. 28. *See also* Direct rollovers; Eligible rollover distributions
automatic rollover rules, 21:6
balance to the credit of the participant, 28:3
corrective distributions, 28:2
early distributions, exemption from additional 10 percent income tax, 20:2
ESOPs, diversification election amounts distributed as part of, 1:43
individual accounts, required minimum distributions, 4:51, 4:52
in-kind distributions, 25:14–25:17
generally, 25:14
insurance contracts, 25:24–25:26

less than full amount of property rolled over, 25:17
qualified plan, assets received from, 25:15
sale of property and rollover, 25:16
IRAs
advantages of, 28:16, 28:17
assets custodians are unwilling to accept, 28:9, 28:10
challenges, 28:8–28:15
deceased participant's retirement plan, 12:75
disadvantages of, 28:18
individual other than participant, 28:7
more than 60 days after receipt of distribution, 28:6
nonspouse beneficiary, 12:75, 21:22, 21:32, 28:7
problems in attempting rollovers, 28:8
restricted distributions, 14:15
loans from plan by participant, eligible rollover distributions, 2:12, 2:17
mandatory tax withholding, collectibles, 28:11
nondiscrimination rules, 10:4
QDRO alternate payees, by, 3:60
required minimum distributions, 4:51, 4:52, 4:70
Roth IRAs. *See* Roth IRAs
termination of plan, written explanation requirement, 15:81
vested benefits, 8:29

Roth IRAs
conversion of traditional IRA to, 28:21, 28:22, 28:25
changes, 28:26
early distribution penalty and, 28:7
defined, 28:19
reporting requirements, designated distributions, 27:30, 27:35, 27:37
rollovers, 21:37–21:43, 28:19–28:26
bankruptcy, cap on assets, 7:5
election by distributee of eligible rollover distribution, 21:40, 21:41
investment earnings, 28:23
other types of retirement plans, from, 21:38
qualification, 28:20
qualified contributions, 21:43
rationale, 28:24, 28:25
Section 401(a) plan, from, 21:37, 21:53
Tax Increase Prevention and Reconciliation Act of 2005, 28:26
10 percent additional tax under Section 72(t), applicability, 21:39
withholding requirements, 21:42

RPA '94. *See* Retirement Protection Act of 1994

S

Safe harbors
defined contribution plans, transfers of shares to other plans from ESOP, 1:38–1:40
direct rollovers, 21:6
401(k) plans, hardship distributions, 1:11, 1:13
in-service pension plan distributions, retirement age requirement, 1:20
qualified retirement plan, taxation of periodic annuity payments, 18:5
tax-sheltered annuity arrangements, 18:5
taxable life insurance costs, current availability test, 6:8

Salary-reduction simplified employee pension (SARSEP) plans
nonperiodic payments, excess deferrals, 19:7

SBJPA '96. *See* Small Business Job Protection Act of 1996

Schedule EA-S
termination of plan, PBGC process, 16:16, 16:17

Schedule REP-S
termination of plan, PBGC process, 16:15

Section 401(a)(9), required minimum distributions. *See* Required minimum distributions

Section 401(a)(31), direct rollover requirements, Ch. 21

Section 401(a)(4) requirements. *See* Nondiscrimination rules

Section 401(a)(11) requirements, plans subject to. *See* Qualified joint and survivor annuity (QJSA); Qualified preretirement survivor annuity

Section 3405(c)
eligible rollover distributions, withholding on distributions that are not rolled over. *See* Eligible rollover distributions

Section 501(c)(18) plans
nonperiodic distributions, excess deferrals, 19:7

Section 411(d)(6) rules. *See* Optional forms of benefits; Protected benefits

Section 412(e)(3) plans. *See* Fully insured plans

Section 412(j) requirements. *See* Defined benefit plans

Section 414(k) plans, 9:89–9:91

Section 415 limitations. *See* Limitations on benefits and contributions under qualified plans (Section 415)

Section 412 minimum funding requirements, 11:3, 11:28, 11:36

Section 72(p) rules, loans from plan by participant
amortization, 2:6
deemed distributions, 2:7, 2:12–2:17
distributions attributable to loans, treatment of, 2:11–2:27
effective date, 2:24
failure to make installment payments, 2:7
failure to meet requirements, 2:3
5-year repayment rule, 2:5
generally, 2:1
home loans, exceptions to repayment rule, 2:5
Hurricanes Katrina, Rita, Sandy, or Wilma, losses suffered from, 2:26, 2:27
leave of absence, 2:8
level amortization requirement, 2:3, 2:8
limits on amount, 2:4
military service, 2:8
prohibited transaction rules, 2:34–2:44
qualified employer plan, defined, 2:2
term of loan, 2:5

Section 417 requirements, plans subject to. *See* Qualified joint and survivor annuity (QJSA); Qualified preretirement survivor annuity

Securities Exchange Act of 1984, 13:9

Securities rates
30-year Treasury, App. C

Security for participant's loans, 2:43

Segregated shares, required minimum distributions, 4:57, 4:58, 4:61

Self-correction programs. *See also* specific program names
correction period, 23:7
determination letters, 23:3
effect of examination, 23:3
egregious failures, 23:3
established practices and procedures, 23:3
excess contributions, 5:30
failures outside remedies, 23:3
insignificant operational failures, 23:6
lessening impact of plan disqualification, 23:2
multiple failures, 23:6
operational failures, 23:3
orphan plans, correction, 23:3
plan amendment, 23:3, 23:7
program eligibility, 23:3, 23:6, 23:7
significant operational failures, 23:7
termination of plan, problem-solving options, 15:34–15:37

Self-employed individuals
accident or health benefits, nonperiodic payments, 19:15
compensation defined, limitations on benefits and contributions under qualified plans (Section 415), 9:62
disability defined for purposes of lump sum distributions, 19:21, 29:2
taxable life insurance costs, 6:2

Separate accounts, required minimum distributions, 4:57, 4:58, 4:61

Separation from service
early distributions, additional 10 percent income tax
exemption from, 20:7
transitional rules, 20:13
nonperiodic payments, lump sum distributions, 19:38, 19:39
public safety employees, qualified reservist distributions, 20:9

Sham loans, 2:20

Shareholders
loans from plan, disproportionate availability to, 2:39

Short-service employees
maximum annual benefit, 9:63

Silver coins or bullion
assets IRA custodians are unwilling to accept, 28:10

Simplified method of basis recovery, periodic payments. *See* Periodic payments

Single life annuities
defined, 18:2
QOSA, actuarially equivalent to, 11:41

Single Life Table, App. D

Small Business Job Protection Act of 1996 (SBJPA '96)
annuity contracts, five-year forward averaging election, 19:58
death benefits, $5,000 exclusion, 21:18
in-service distributions, 1:25
limitations on benefits and contributions under qualified plans (Section 415), lump sum distributions, 9:67

lump sum distributions, nonperiodic payments
annuity contracts, 19:22
balance to the credit of the employee, 19:27, 19:28
changes made to rules, 19:21
death benefit exclusions, 19:68
definition of lump sum distribution, 19:20
5-year forward averaging election, 19:54, 19:55, 19:57, 19:58
flat 20 percent capital gains tax, 19:65
recapture of tax benefits, 19:33
reemployment, later, 19:33
tax-exempt trusts, distributions not made from, 19:24
TRA '86, grandfathered provisions, 19:19
trust tax-exempt in distribution year but not in prior year, 19:25
nonperiodic payments
lump sum distributions, 19:19
qualified voluntary employee contributions, 19:18
QDROs, income-averaging treatment of lump sum distribution, 3:61
qualified voluntary employee contributions, nonperiodic payments, 19:18
simplified method of basis recovery, periodic payments
generally, 18:8
recovering investment in contract, 18:5
transition rule, 18:15, 18:16

Social Security Administration (SSA) Program
letter-forwarding program, 15:44, 16:54
termination of plan, location of missing participant, 15:44, 16:54

Social Security benefits
disability, defined, 12:36, 12:38
leveling, 10:39
retirement age, benefits beginning before
maximum benefits, increase of, 9:59
reduction of benefits, 9:58

Social Security supplement
normal retirement age and, 12:9
Qualified Social Security supplements, 10:22

Soldiers' and Sailors' Civil Relief Act Amendments of 1942, 2:8

SPDs (summary plan descriptions)
mandatory distributions, 21:6

Spinoffs
QJSA rules, 11:6
QPSA rules, 11:6
required minimum distributions, 4:55
spinoff/termination transaction rules
affected participants, 16:68
definition, 16:67
failure to provide notices, 16:70
notices to affected participants, 16:69
trustee-to-trustee transfers, 26:3–26:5
Form 5310-A, 26:10, 26:12, 26:13

Sponsor of plan. *See* specific topic

Spousal consent
corrective distributions, excess contributions, 5:42
electronic filing, 11:56
ESOPs, dividends in excess of $5,000, 1:48
loans from plan by participant, survivor annuity requirements, 2:45–2:48
new technologies to satisfy requirements, 11:56
QJSA rules, 11:27–11:33
general consent, 11:35
generally, 11:17
loans from plan by participant, survivor annuity requirements and, 11:24
prenuptial agreements, 11:30
revocability, 11:32
waivers, 11:35
QOSA distribution by participant, for, 11:42
QPSA rules
general consent, 11:35
waivers, 11:29, 11:31, 11:33, 11:35
required minimum distributions, 4:59
termination of plan, form of benefit other than QJSA, 15:80

Spouse. *See* Spousal consent; Surviving spouse; *specific topic*

Springing cash value insurance contracts, 25:22

SSA Program. *See* Social Security Administration (SSA) Program

State agencies
DRO benefits paid to, 3:8

State law and regulation
DROs, state domestic relations law and, 3:44
income tax withholding, 22:1
source taxation of retirement benefits, 22:3

State Taxation of Pension Income Act of 1995,

Step-down life annuities
underfunded plans, 17:21

Stock bonus plans
elimination or reduction of benefits, Section 411(d)(6) rules, 10:30

Stock bonus plans *(cont'd)*
hardship distributions
generally, 1:4
taxation of, 1:5
in-kind distributions, 25:9
minimum distribution requirements. *See* Required minimum distributions
optional forms of benefits, Section 411(d)(6) rules, 10:32, 10:33
protected benefits, Section 411(d)(6) rules, 10:32, 10:33
Section 411(d)(6) rules, 10:30
survivor annuity requirements, 11:3, 11:4
top-heavy plans, vesting, 8:23
vesting
account balances value, determination of, 8:23
top-heavy plans, 8:23

Subsidized benefit defined, 12:50

Substantially equal periodic payments
direct rollovers, 21:24, 21:25, 21:46
exemption from additional 10 percent income tax
generally, 20:4
modification of payments after beginning, 20:5, 20:6
reduction in amount of payment as modification of series, 20:6
series of substantially equal periodic payments, 20:4

Substantial owners
defined, termination of plan, 16:3

Successor employer, QDRO maintained by, 3:52

Summary of material modifications
mandatory distributions, 21:6

Summary plan descriptions (SPDs)
mandatory distributions, 21:6

Surplus assets
termination of plan. *See* Termination of plan

Surviving spouse
QJSA rules. *See* Qualified joint and survivor annuity
QOSA requirements. *See* Qualified optional survivor annuity
QPSA. *See* Qualified preretirement survivor annuity
required minimum distributions, 4:13
annuity distributions before required beginning date, 4:44
commencement of distributions, 4:16
death of spouse before distributions begin, 4:15
definition of surviving spouse, 4:60
distribution period, 4:20
sole beneficiary, spouse as, 4:28
withholding on periodic payments that are not eligible rollover distributions, 24:21

Survivor annuity requirements
QJSA. *See* Qualified joint and survivor annuity
QOSA. *See* Qualified optional survivor annuity
QPSA. *See* Qualified preretirement survivor annuity

Survivor benefits and QDROs, 3:19

Suspension of benefits
noncompliance with DOL requirements, 12:33
retirement, 12:32
survivor annuities, 11:13
termination of employment. *See* Termination of employment

T

Target benefit plans
defined, 9:94
determination of benefits, 9:96
in-service distributions, continuation of accrual of benefits, 1:22
operation of, 9:95
termination of plan, 16:2
information gathering, 15:16
top-heavy plans, vesting, 8:23
underfunded plans, 9:16, 17:48
funding waiver, 17:50
vesting
account balances value, determination of, 8:23
forfeitures, 8:60
top-heavy plans, 8:23

Target date funds (TDFs) 10:24

Taxation. *See* specific topics and types of taxation

Tax credit employee stock ownership plans (TRASOPs)
diversification requirements, 1:31–1:34, 1:41
appraisers, valuation of employer securities subject to, 1:42
December 31, 1986, securities acquired after, 1:33
January 1, 1987, securities acquired before, 1:32

portion of qualified participant's account subject to, 1:36
simplified methods for determining employer securities subject to diversification rules, 1:34
small account balances subject to, 1:35
valuation of employer securities subject to, 1:41
in-service distributions
dividends on employer securities, 1:44–1:49
employer securities subject to diversification requirements, 1:27
when distribution may be made, 1:26
termination of employment
options available to participant, 13:8
put options, exceptions to requirements, 13:13

Tax Equity and Fiscal Responsibility Act of 1982 (TEFRA)
direct rollovers, 28:14, 28:15
early distributions, additional 10 percent income tax, 20:11
required minimum distributions
rollovers, 4:70
Section 242(b)(2) election, 4:68, 4:71
termination of employment, 13:5
transfers, 4:69

Tax Increase Prevention and Reconciliation Act of 2006
employer securities, capital gains tax reduction, 25:35
Roth IRA rollovers, conversion, 28:26

Taxpayer Relief Act of 1997 (TRA '97)
electronic filing, 11:56
new technologies, 11:56
offsets of retirement plan benefits permitted, 3:63
simplified method of basis recovery, periodic payments
generally, 18:8
98-2 notice, 18:8
recovering investment in contract, 18:5
tax-sheltered annuity arrangements, 18:5

Tax Reform Act of 1984 (TRA '84)
required minimum distributions, 4:68

Tax Reform Act of 1986 (TRA '86)
deductible voluntary employee contribution, 27:19
distributions, restrictions, 14:2
early distributions, additional 10 percent income tax, transitional rules, 20:13
in-service distributions, 1:25
loans from plan by participant, distributions attributable to, 2:19
lump sum distributions
eligibility for grandfather treatment, 29:11
grandfather rule, benefits accruing before TRA '86, eligibility for, 9:12
nonperiodic payments, 19:19
tax treatment, 29:5, 29:6
survivor annuity requirements, 11:1

Tax Reform Act of 1997 (TRA '97)
lump sum distributions, nonperiodic payments, 10:4

Tax withholding. *See* Withholding

TDFs. *See* Target date funds

TEFRA. *See* Tax Equity and Fiscal Responsibility Act of 1982

10 percent additional income tax on early distributions. *See* Early distributions, additional 10 percent income tax

10-year averaging. *See* Lump sum distributions; Nonperiodic payments

Terminal funding contracts, 15:58, 16:28

Termination of employment, Ch. 13
claims for benefits, 13:22–13:32
arbitrary and capricious standard, 13:32
criminal penalties for violation of ERISA, 13:31
defined, 13:24
denial of, 13:25–13:29
de novo standard, 13:32
electronic notice of suspension of benefits and claim denial, 13:27
failure to comply with claims procedure requirements, penalty, 13:30, 13:31
filing of claim, 13:22, 13:24
requirements for procedure, 13:23, 13:30
review by courts, 13:32
deferral of payments, time frame
participant, by, 13:2
plan, by, 13:1
distributions, restrictions, 14:2, 14:3
ESOPs, 13:8–13:15
employer securities, determination if readily tradable, 13:9
installment payments elected for vested ESOP balance, 13:12
options available to participant, 13:8
time when distributions must begin, 13:14, 13:15
general considerations, 13:1–13:7
loans from plan by participant
acceleration of repayment, 2:9

Termination of employment (*cont'd*)
loans from plan by participant (*cont'd*)
outstanding loan balanced carried after termination, 2:10
minimum required distribution
5 percent owner, 13:4
participants not subject to, 13:5
required beginning date, 13:3
suspension of benefits, 13:16–13:21
employee again terminates employment after payment of benefits has been suspended, 13:19
failure to comply with DOL requirements, 13:21
generally, 13:16
multiemployer plans, 13:17
notice to employee, 13:18
repayment of amounts withheld, 13:20
taxable life insurance costs, 6:7
TRASOPs, options available to participant, 13:8
vested benefits
immediate distribution of, 13:6
present value of vested accrued benefit, determination of, 13:7

Termination of plan, Ch. 15
abandoned defined contribution plans, 15:89–15:96
contents of notice to DOL, 15:94
DOL guidance, 15:89
lost participants, locating, 15:92
90-day period, 15:93
notice, 15:94, 15:95
qualified termination administrators, 15:89–15:96
requirements for QTA, 15:90
Special Terminal Report for Abandoned Plans, 15:96
tasks in winding up orphan plan, 15:95
when considered abandoned, 15:91
when orphan plan deemed to be terminated, 15:93
account balances in defined contribution plan, updating from last valuation date, 15:40
ACP test
distribution of, 15:41
assets of plan, insufficiency
generally, 15:57
majority owners, 16:26, 16:27
PBGC process, 16:25–16:28
standard terminations, 16:5, 16:6, 16:27
terminal funding contract, 15:58, 16:28
business reasons, 15:2, 15:3
church plans, 16:2
compliance with qualification requirements, 15:5
constructive ownership rules, 16:3
defined benefit plans
assets of plan, insufficiency, 15:57, 15:58
cessation of benefit accruals, notice of, 15:62
determination of whether plan may be terminated, 15:52
excise taxes, benefit increases to qualify for reduction in reversion, 16:52
information gathering, 15:63, 16:35, 16:36
interest rates for terminating plans, 15:55, 15:56
IRS submission, 15:65–15:68
liability contributed by plan sponsor, 15:60, 16:31
PBGC process, 16:29, 16:31
rates for terminating plans, 15:54
sponsor of plan, actions of, 15:59–15:61, 16:29, 16:31
steps involved, 15:51
surplus assets, 15:72–15:75, 16:46–16:49
underfunded PBGC-covered plans, benefit liability measurement, 17:2
defined contribution plans, 15:6–15:50
abandoned plans, 15:89–15:96
final disclosure forms, 15:49, 15:50
final stages, 15:40–15:41
information gathering, 15:21
IRS submission, 15:18–15:33
liability contributed by plan sponsor in year of termination, 15:8
liquidating plan assets, 15:38, 15:39
lost participant, 15:43
plan sponsor adopting resolution to terminate plan, 15:7
problem-solving options, 15:34–15:37
procedural steps, 15:6
sponsor of plan, actions of, 15:7, 15:8
204(h) notice, 15:9–15:15
underfunded defined contribution plans, 15:25
determination letters, 15:4, 15:18–15:21
discretionary profit sharing plans, information gathering, 15:16
distress terminations. *See* Distress terminations
distributions, restrictions, 14:6
election forms, distribution of
benefit election forms, 15:41, 15:76, 15:77, 16:53
$5,000, distributions less than, 15:79
form of benefit other than QJSA, 15:78, 15:80
language used for Section 402(f) notice, 15:82, 15:83
life insurance coverage in qualified plan, 15:85

lost participants, 15:86
spousal consent to form of benefit other than QJSA, 15:80
written explanation requirements, eligibility for rollover treatment, 15:81
employee welfare benefit plans, 16:2
excess benefit plans, 16:2
excise taxes, benefit increases in defined benefit plan to qualify for reduction in reversion, 16:52
final disclosure forms
distributions to participants, 15:50, 15:88, 16:72
5500 series forms, due date, 15:49, 15:87, 16:71
final stages
account balances in defined contribution plan, updating from last valuation date, 15:40
benefit election forms, distribution of, 15:41
conversion of plan assets to cash, 16:43
notice, 15:41
PBGC process, 16:43–16:45
starting of liquidation process, 16:44
$5,000, distributions less than, 15:79
flat-dollar benefit plans, information gathering, 15:63, 16:35
401(k) plans, information gathering, 15:16
frequency of valuation, information on, 15:16
general requirements, 15:1–15:5
governmental plans, 16:2
horizontal plan termination, 8:72
individual insurance contracts, information on
defined benefit plans, 15:63
defined contribution plans, 15:16
information gathering, 15:16, 15:17, 16:36
data, type of, 15:63, 16:35
PBGC process, 16:35, 16:36
in-kind distributions, elimination or reduction of benefits, 10:30
insurance contracts, information gathering, 15:63, 16:35
interested parties
additional information to, 15:33
defined, 15:30
notice to, 15:31, 15:32
interest rates, 15:54, 16:21–16:24
involuntary terminations, underfunded plans, 17:33, 17:34
information, rights of affected party to receipt of, 17:35
other plans, impact on, 17:38
PPA requirements, 17:35–17:38
premiums owed by plan sponsor, 17:37
IRAs, 16:2
IRS submission
additional information, 15:33
determination letters, 15:18–15:21
Form 2848, 15:26
Form 5310, 15:23
Form 6088, 15:24, 15:25, 15:66
Form 8717, 15:22, 15:65
information necessary, 15:21, 15:27, 15:65
length of time for favorable determination letter, 15:28, 15:67
notice to participants, 15:29
purpose of, 15:18
underfunded defined contribution plans, 15:25
user fees, 15:22
language used for Section 402(f) notice, 15:82, 15:83
liabilities of plan, measurement of, 15:53–15:56, 16:20–16:24
life insurance coverage in qualified plan, 15:85
liquidation of plan assets
generally, 15:69, 16:44
present value of accrued benefits, recalculation of, 15:71
when process should be started, 15:39, 15:70, 16:44
lost participants
abandoned defined contribution plans, 15:92
fiduciary of ERISA plan, 15:42
Internet resources, 15:46, 16:54
IRS Program used to locate, 15:43
letter-forwarding programs, 15:42–15:45
methods to locate, 15:86, 16:54
PBGC missing participant program, 15:47, 15:86
private locator programs, 15:45, 16:54
SSA program used to locate, 15:44, 16:54
unclaimed benefits, 15:48
lump sum distributions, nonperiodic payments, 19:34
master or prototype plans, determination letters, 15:21
measurement of benefit liabilities, 16:20–16:24
measurement of plan liabilities, 15:53–15:56
minimum funding standard, application of, 15:61
minimum required contribution, application of, 16:32
money purchase plans, information gathering, 15:16
mortality rates, 15:54, 16:21

Termination of plan (*cont'd*)
notice
abandoned defined contribution plans, 15:94, 15:95
annuity information, 16:10, 16:12
cessation of benefit accruals, 15:62
contents of, 15:13
delivery of, 15:11, 16:34
distributee, when Section 402(f) notice must be provided to, 15:84
final stages, 15:41
intent to terminate. *See* Notice of intent to terminate (NOIT)
IRS submission, 15:29, 15:31, 15:32, 15:68
language used for Section 402(f) notice, 15:82, 15:83
PBGC process, 16:9–16:14
penalties for failure to provide, 15:15
plan benefits, notice of, 16:37–16:42
reason for, 15:9, 16:33
standard termination notice, 16:15
when must be provided, 15:14
partial terminations, vesting, 8:69, 8:72
PBGC missing participant program, 15:47, 15:86
PBGC process, Ch. 16
actuary, certification by, 16:16
affected parties, NOIT, 16:14
benefit election forms and notices, distributions of, 16:53
benefit liabilities, measurement of, 16:20–16:24
coverage, 16:1–16:4
defined benefit plans, 16:29, 16:31
determination letters, 16:65
excess benefit plans, 16:2
excise taxes, benefit increases in defined benefit plan to qualify for reduction in reversion, 16:52
exemption from coverage, 16:2
final stages, 16:43–16:45
flat-dollar benefit plans, 16:35
guarantee, extinguishment of, 16:9
information gathering, 16:35, 16:36
insurance contracts, 16:35
interest rates, determination, 16:21–16:24
lost participants, 16:54–16:60
majority owners, 16:26, 16:27
measurement of benefit liabilities, 16:20–16:24
minimum required contribution, application to entire year, 16:32
missing participants, 16:54–16:60
mortality rates, determination, 16:21
noncompliance, notice of, 16:18, 16:19
notice of intent to terminate (NOIT), 16:9–16:14
partnerships, 16:3
plan administered during, 16:11
plan benefits, notice of, 16:37–16:42
post-distribution certification, 16:61–16:66
preliminary information for, 16:15–16:19
present value of accrued benefits, 16:45
professional individuals defined, 16:4
professional service employers defined, 16:4
proposed termination date, 16:8
qualified replacement plan defined, 16:50
reporting requirements, 16:72
small plans, what constitutes, 16:30
spinoff/termination transaction rules, 16:67–16:70
sponsor of plan, actions by, 16:29–16:32
standard terminations, 16:5, 16:6, 16:15–16:19, 16:27
steps, 16:5–16:8
substantial owner defined, 16:3
sufficiency requirement, 16:9
surplus assets, 16:46–16:49
terminal funding contracts, 16:28
top-heavy plans, 16:35
204(h) notice, 16:33, 16:34
underfunded PBGC-covered defined benefit plans, benefit liability measurement, 17:2
who determines, 16:7
percentage of pay plans, information gathering, 15:63, 16:36
post-distribution certification
determination letter, delay in issuance of, 16:65
failure to comply, penalties, 16:62
generally, 16:61
180-day period, 16:64
requests for extension, 16:66
when must be completed, 16:63
interest rates, minimum lump sum, 15:54
missing participant program, 15:47
present value of accrued benefits, recalculation of, 15:71, 16:45
private locator programs used to locate lost participants, 15:45, 16:54
profit sharing plans
information gathering, 15:16
plan sponsor adopting resolution to terminate defined contribution plan, 15:7
reason for considering, 15:1
QDROs, rights and, 3:53
defined benefit plans, 3:54
QJSA rules, 11:7
QPSA rules, 11:7
qualified plans, 15:2
qualified replacement plans, 15:73, 16:50

remedial amendment period, 15:5, 15:64
reporting requirements, distributions to participants, 15:88
rollover treatment, eligibility for, 15:81
small plans, what constitutes, 16:30
sponsor of plan, actions by
defined benefit plan, 15:59–15:61
defined contribution plans, 15:7, 15:8
minimum funding standard, application of, 15:61
minimum required contribution, application of, 16:32
SSA program used to locate lost participants, 15:44, 16:54
standard terminations, 16:15–16:19
surplus assets
excise tax, reduction in reversion from 50 percent to 20 percent, 15:75, 16:52
generally, 15:72, 16:49
PBGC process, 16:46–16:49
present value of accrued benefits, recalculation of, 15:71, 16:45
qualified replacement plans, 15:74, 16:50, 16:51
ratable distribution of, 16:47, 16:48
reversions, rules governing, 16:46
target benefit plans, 16:2
terminal funding contracts, 15:58, 16:28
top-heavy plans, information gathering, 15:63, 16:35
204(h) notice, 15:9–15:15
contents of, 15:13
delivery of, 15:11, 16:34
electronic delivery of, 15:12
failure to provide, penalties, 15:15
PBGC process, 16:30, 16:33, 16:34
provision of, 15:10
reason for, 15:9, 16:33
when must be provided, 15:14
unclaimed benefits, lost participants, 16:54–16:60
underfunded plans, 17:33, 17:34
distress terminations. *See* Distress terminations
information, rights of affected party to receipt of, 17:35
other plans, impact on, 17:38
PPA requirements, 17:35–17:38
premiums owed by plan sponsor, 17:37
unwritten plans, 16:2
valid business reason requirement, 15:2, 15:3
vertical plan termination, 8:72
vesting
generally, 8:69
horizontal plan termination, 8:72
partial terminations, 8:69, 8:72
reversed plan termination, 8:71
significant percentage of participants dropped, 8:75
vertical plan termination, 8:72
when plan is considered terminated, 8:70

30-year Treasury securities rates, App. C

3 percent method of benefit accrual, determination of account balances
defined benefit plans, 9:26

Top-heavy minimum benefits
comparability approach, 9:49, 9:53
defined benefit plans, 9:50, 9:51
5 percent of pay, contributions of, 9:54
floor-offset approach, 9:49, 9:52
generally, 9:49

Top-heavy plans
death benefits treated as distributions, 8:28
direct rollover before meeting minimum participation, 21:49
termination of plan, information gathering, 15:63, 16:35
vesting, 8:17–8:27
account balances value, determination of, 8:23, 8:26, 8:27
aggregation of plans, 8:21, 8:22
cessation of plan as top-heavy, 8:37
death benefits, payment of, 8:28
defined benefit plans, 8:18, 8:24, 8:25
defined contribution plans, 8:18, 8:23
definition of top-heavy plan, 8:18
determination date, 8:19
determination of top-heavy status, 8:23–8:27
401(k) plans, 8:23
money purchase plans, 8:23
more than one plan, participation by key employee in, 8:20
permissive aggregation group, 8:21, 8:22
present value of accrued benefits, determination of, 8:24–8:27
profit sharing plans, 8:23
required aggregation group, 8:20–8:22
schedules, 8:36, 8:37
6-year graded vesting, 8:17
stock bonus plans, 8:23
target benefit plans, 8:23
3-year cliff vesting, 8:17

TRA '84 (Tax Reform Act of 1984)
required minimum distributions, 4:68

TRA '86. *See* Tax Reform Act of 1986

TRA '97 (Tax Reform Act of 1997)
lump sum distributions, nonperiodic payments, 10:4

Transferee plans
defined contribution plan death benefits, 12:56
survivor annuity requirements, 11:6

Transfers. *See also* Trustee-to-trustee transfers
defined contribution plan, benefit reduction or elimination, 10:25
nondiscrimination rules, 10:4
required minimum distributions
eligible rollover distribution as, 21:15
mergers, 4:69
spinoffs, 4:69
TEFRA election, effect of rollover or transfer from one plan to another, 4:69
transferee plan, 4:54, 4:55, 4:69
transferor plan, 4:53, 4:55, 4:69
terminated plan's surplus assets to qualified replacement plan, 15:74, 16:51

TRASOPs. *See* Tax credit employee stock ownership plans

Trustee-to-trustee transfers, Ch. 26
assets, 26:10
ERISA, rules under, 26:1
exceptions to rules, 26:2
generally, 26:1
spinoffs, application to, 26:3–26:5
consolidations
ERISA, rules under, 26:1
exceptions to rules, 26:2
Form 5310-A, 26:10, 26:14
generally, 26:1
retirement plan, 26:6
spinoffs, application to, 26:3–26:5
defined benefit plans
mergers and acquisitions, 26:8, 26:12
spinoffs, 26:5
ERISA provisions, 26:8
Form 5310-A, 26:10–26:12
Form 1099-R, 27:21
mergers and acquisitions, 26:6–26:14
defined, 26:6
defined benefit plans, 26:8, 26:12
defined contribution plans, 26:7, 26:8, 26:12
ERISA, rules under, 26:1
generally, 26:1
notification to IRS, 26:9
retirement plan, 26:6
spinoffs, application to, 26:3–26:5
termination benefits, 26:8
multiemployer plans, 26:2
nonperiodic payments, 19:17
spinoffs, 26:3–26:5
defined benefit plans, 26:5
defined contribution plans, 26:4
de minimis rules, 26:5
Form 5310-A, 26:10, 26:12, 26:13

Trusts. *See* Estates and trusts

204(h) notice (Notice of Cessation of Benefit Accrual). *See* Termination of plan

U

UCA. *See* Unemployment Compensation Amendments of 1992

Underfunded plans, 17:1–17:50
actuarial adjustments of maximum guaranteed benefits, 17:14
age adjustments for maximum guaranteed benefits, 17:15, 17:16
benefit liabilities
measurement for plan termination purposes, 17:2
plan assets insufficient to cover, 17:34
recovery of, 17:30
cash refund annuity, 17:17
change in funded status, 17:28
constructive ownership rules, 17:23
defined benefit plans, Ch. 17
adjustments, maximum guaranteed benefits, 17:14, 17:15
allocation of assets under ERISA, 17:42
benefit increases and maximum guaranteed benefits, 17:22
cash refund annuities, 17:17
continuation of, 17:40
distress termination, 17:4–17:11, 17:25, 17:29, 17:31, 17:32
dollar limits for each year, 17:13
frozen plan, 17:40
guaranteed benefits, 17:24, 17:26
installment refund annuities, 17:17
joint and survivor annuities (contingent basis), 17:18
joint and survivor annuities (joint basis), 17:19
joint and survivor annuities, age differences, 17:20
majority owners, 17:23, 17:24
maximum deductible limit, 17:44
maximum guaranteed benefits, 17:14, 17:15, 17:22
measurement for plan termination purposes, 17:2
PBGC, benefits guaranteed by, 17:12
single-employer plans, 17:42
step-down life annuities, 17:21
defined contribution plans, 9:16–9:19
account balances, determination of, 9:16–9:19

defined, 9:16, 17:48
immediate allocation method to determine adjusted account balance, 9:18
suspense account method to determine adjusted account balance, 9:18
unrestricted distribution method to determine adjusted account balance, 9:18
distress terminations. *See* Distress terminations
dollar limits for each year, 17:13
excess contributions, 17:47
funded status, change in, 17:28
guaranteed benefits
insufficient assets for, 17:27
majority owners, 17:24
sufficient assets for, 17:26
installment refund annuities, 17:17
interest rate, waived funding deficiency, 17:49
involuntary terminations
deduction limit, plans with over 100 participants, 17:45
employer contribution to pay liabilities, 17:43
insufficient assets to pay liabilities, 17:39
PPA requirements, 17:35–17:38
joint and survivor annuities
age differences, 17:20
contingent basis, 17:18
joint basis, 17:19
majority owners, 17:24
guaranteed benefits, 17:24
money purchase plans, 9:16, 17:48, 17:50
notice of intent to terminate (NOIT)
affected parties, 17:9
information contained in, 17:7, 17:8
PBGC, information provided to, 17:10
single-employer plans, 17:42
special deduction rules, 17:46
target benefit plans, 9:16, 17:48
funding waiver, 17:50
termination of plan, involuntary, 17:33, 17:34
distress terminations. *See* Distress terminations
information, rights of affected party to receipt of, 17:35
other plans, impact on, 17:38
PPA requirements, 17:35–17:38
premiums owed by plan sponsor, 17:37
waived funding deficiency, interest rate, 17:49

Unemployment Compensation Amendments of 1992 (UCA)
eligible rollover distributions, 24:1
QDROs, rollovers by alternate payees, 3:60

Uniformed Services Employment and Reemployment Rights Act of 1994 (USERRA)
loans, level amortization requirement during leave of absence, 2:8

Uniform lifetime table
required minimum distributions, 4:28

Unpredictable contingent event benefits, 14:10
nondiscrimination rules, 10:21

Unwritten plans
termination of plan, 16:2

U.S. Department of Labor. *See* Department of Labor (DOL)

U.S. Savings Bonds
Form 1099-R, 27:25
nonperiodic payments, 19:6

User fees
termination of plan, IRS submission, 15:22

USERRA (Uniformed Services Employment and Reemployment Rights Act of 1994)
loans, level amortization requirement during leave of absence, 2:8

V

Variable annuities
amount received as annuity, treatment as, 18:4
defined, 18:2

VCP program. *See* Voluntary Correction with IRS Approval (VCP) program

VEBAs (voluntary employees' beneficiary associations), vesting requirements, 8:2

Vesting, 8:1–8:83
account balances value, top-heavy plans
defined contribution plans, 8:23
disregarding of, 8:27
distributions taken into account, 8:26
401(k) plans, 8:23
money purchase plans, 8:23
profit sharing plans, 8:23
stock bonus plans, 8:23
target benefit plans, 8:23
amendments in schedules
future vesting and, 8:56
generally, 8:55
reasonable election period, 8:57
regulations, 8:58
Section 411(d)(6), effect of, 8:58
application of rules, 8:3

Vesting (*cont'd*)
breaks in service
determination of vesting service, 8:53
5-year rule, 8:53
generally, 8:51–8:53
maternity or paternity absences, 8:54
1-year break, 8:52, 8:54
1-year holdout rule, 8:53
rule of parity, 8:53
cash balance plans
portion of benefit determined under defined benefit formula, 8:14
rules for, 8:13
cash-out rules
generally, 8:62
no vested account balance or accrued benefit by participant, 8:63, 9:10
sources of restoration, 8:67
classifications of employees, different service-crediting methods for, 8:45
collectively bargained plans, delayed effective date, 8:11
curtailment of plan, 8:82
defined benefit plans
breaks in service, 8:53
employee-derived accrued benefit, 8:7
forfeitures, 8:60, 8:65
maximum interest rate, forfeitures, 8:65
present value of accrued benefits, 8:24, 8:25
unvested portion, effect on required minimum distribution, 4:39
defined contribution plans
account balances value, determination of, 8:23
application of rules, 8:3
breaks in service, 8:53
cash-out/repayment rules, 8:67
forfeitures, 8:61, 8:68
immediate 100 percent vesting, 9:2
100 percent vesting of benefits, 8:6
PPA change, 8:10
required minimum distributions, unvested portion of individual account, 4:32
restoration of accrued benefit, 8:66
top-heavy minimum schedules, 8:10
discontinuance of plan contributions, 8:83
disqualified plan, 23:22, 23:23
elapsed time method for determining years of service, 8:41
employee-derived account balances and accrued benefit
defined benefit plans with mandatory employee contributions, 8:7
minimum vesting requirements, 8:8
equivalency methods to determine vesting years, 8:43, 8:44
5-year cliff, employer-derived account balances and accrued benefits, 8:8
floor offset plans, 9:88
forfeitures
cause, for, 8:16
defined benefit plans, 8:60, 8:65
defined contribution plans, 8:61, 8:68
nonvested portion of account balance or accrued benefit, 8:59
plan repayment provisions, 8:64
target benefit plans, 8:60
treatment of, 8:60
401(k) plans, account balances value, determination of, 8:23
fraternal beneficiary society, 8:2
future vesting, amendments in schedules and, 8:56
general rules, 8:1–8:9
governmental plans, minimum vesting requirements, 8:2
highly compensated employees, nondiscrimination rules, 8:15
hours of service, defined, 8:40
key employees, 8:30–8:35
annual compensation, 8:30
defined, 8:30
5 percent owners, 8:30, 8:31
includable officers, 8:30, 8:33–8:35
1 percent owners, 8:30, 8:32
top-heavy plans, participation in more than one plan, 8:20
minimum vesting requirements
accelerated vesting schedules, 8:9
employee-derived account balances and accrued benefit, 8:8
ERISA, under, 8:2
nondiscrimination rules, coordination with, 8:15
money purchase plans, account balances value, 8:23
nondiscrimination rules, 8:15
normal retirement age, 8:5, 12:1
100 percent vesting of benefits
determination of, 8:5
generally, 8:4
normal retirement age, 8:5
separate accounts not maintained, 8:6
types of contributions, 8:6
partial terminations
definitions, 8:75
determinative factors and circumstances, 8:76–8:78, 8:80
ERISA requirements, 8:73
percentage reduction in participation, 8:76, 8:78
purpose of rule, 8:74

request for IRS determination, 8:81
significant reduction in number of participants, as, 8:75
vested account balance or benefit, determining, 8:79
plan-to-plan transfers, 8:29
predecessor plan defined, 8:50
pre-2007 matching employer contributions, 8:9
present value of accrued benefits, top-heavy plans
actuarial assumptions used to determine, 8:25
defined benefit plans, 8:24, 8:25
disregarding of, 8:27
distributions taken into account, 8:26
profit sharing plans, account balances value, 8:23
QACAs, 8:12
recordkeeping requirements, alternatives to alleviate, 8:42
religious denomination, plan established and maintained for, 8:2
rollovers, 8:29
Section 401(a)(4) requirements, 8:15
simplified computation method, 8:44
6-year graded vesting, top-heavy plans, 8:17
stock bonus plans, account balances value, 8:23
target benefit plans
account balances value, determination of, 8:23
forfeitures, 8:60
termination of employment
ESOPs, installment payments elected for vested ESOP balance, 13:12
immediate distribution of vested benefits, 13:6
termination of plan
generally, 8:69
horizontal plan termination, 8:72
partial terminations, 8:69, 8:72
reversed plan termination, 8:71
significant percentage of participants dropped, 8:75
vertical plan termination, 8:72
when plan is considered terminated, 8:70
3- to 7-year vesting, employer-derived account balances and accrued benefits, 8:8
3-year cliff
cash balance plans, portion of benefit under defined benefit formula, 8:14
top-heavy plans, 8:17
top-heavy plans, 8:17–8:27
account balances value, determination of, 8:23, 8:26, 8:27
aggregation of plans, 8:21, 8:22
cessation of plan as top-heavy, 8:37
death benefits, payment of, 8:28
defined, 8:18
defined benefit plans, 8:24, 8:25
defined contribution plans, 8:23
determination date, 8:19
determination of top-heavy status, 8:23–8:27
401(k) plans, 8:23
money purchase plans, 8:23
more than one plan, participation by key employee in, 8:20
permissive aggregation group, 8:21, 8:22
present value of accrued benefits, determination of, 8:24–8:27
profit sharing plans, 8:23
required aggregation group, 8:20–8:22
schedules, 8:36, 8:37
6-year graded vesting, 8:17
stock bonus plans, 8:23
target benefit plans, 8:23
3-year cliff vesting, 8:17
years of service, vesting percentage, 8:17
vesting years, determination of, 8:38–8:53
age 18, before, 8:47
classifications of employees, different service-crediting methods for, 8:45
computation period, change of, 8:39
days, 8:44
elapsed time method for determining years of service, 8:41
equivalency methods, 8:43, 8:44
hours of service, defined, 8:40
mandatory employee contributions, 8:48
months, 8:44
predecessor plan defined, 8:50
recordkeeping requirements, alternatives, 8:42
semimonthly period, 8:44
simplified computation method, 8:44
weeks, 8:44
year of service defined, 8:38
years before plan maintained, 8:49
years of service taken into account, 8:46
voluntary employees' beneficiary associations, 8:2
years of service
age 18, before, 8:47
defined, 8:38
elapsed time method, 8:41
mandatory employee contributions, 8:48
taken into account, 8:46
vesting percentage, 8:8
years before plan maintained, 8:49

Voluntary Correction with IRS Approval (VCP) program
anonymous (John Doe) submission procedures, 23:9
compliance statement, 23:8
corrective distributions, excess aggregate contributions, 5:30
determination letters, 23:4, 23:8
effect of examination, 23:4
effect of submission on examination, 23:8
egregious failures, 23:4, 23:11
failures corrected under, 23:4
group submissions, 23:10, 23:11
lessening impact of plan disqualification, 23:2
no concurrent examination activity, 23:8
orphan plans, correction, 23:4
plan amendment, 23:4
plan assets, diversion or misuse of, 23:4
program eligibility, 23:8–23:11
requirements, 23:8–23:11
user fees, 23:11

Voluntary employees' beneficiary associations (VEBAs), vesting requirements, 8:2

W

Waivers
Form 1099-R, electronic filing requirement, 27:43
QJSA rules
participant, by, 11:34–11:37
right to waive, 11:37
spousal consent, 11:29, 11:31, 11:33, 11:35
QPSA rules
manner of waiver, 11:36
participant, by, 11:34–11:37
right to waive, 11:37
spousal consent, 11:29, 11:31, 11:33, 11:35
required minimum distributions, 4:1, 20:24

Walk-in CAP. *See* Audit Closing Agreement Program

Wasting trust, 19:32

Withholding. *See also* Mandatory tax withholding
annuity contracts
commercial annuity contracts, withholding on periodic payments that are not eligible rollover distributions, 24:52
eligible rollover distributions, 24:13
bankruptcy, 7:2
eligible rollover distributions, direct rollovers
Roth IRAs, into, 21:42
20 percent withholding, 21:3
eligible rollover distributions that are not rolled over, 24:1–24:18
adequate information, 24:7
annuity contracts, 24:13
compliance, responsibility for, 24:4
death benefit exclusion, 24:10
defined benefit plan, distribution paid to, 24:8
effective dates, 24:1
election not to have federal income tax withheld, 24:2
employer securities, 24:11
Form 1099-R, 24:16
liability of plan administrator, 24:7
loans from plan by participant, offset amount distributed in eligible rollover distribution, 24:11
plan administrator, shifting of responsibility to payor, 24:5
property other than cash distributed, 24:9
reports, responsibility for, 24:1–24:18
required minimum distributions, 24:10
returns, responsibility for, 24:15
$200, distribution less than, 24:14
20 percent withholding rule, 24:1–24:13
UCA provisions, 24:1
valuation of property, 24:10
employer securities, eligible rollover distributions, 24:11
federal income tax, Ch. 24
in-kind distributions
determination of value of property delays payment to participant, 25:13
generally, 25:12
loans from plan by participant, 2:17
nonperiodic payments, 24:55–24:57
defined, 24:55
outside U.S., qualified plan distributions, 24:57
10 percent withholding, right to elect out of, 24:56
periodic payments that are not eligible rollover distributions, 24:19–24:54
abbreviated notice, 24:46
aggregation of payments, 24:47
beneficiaries of deceased employee, 24:21
commercial annuity contract, payment period specified in terms of, 24:52, 24:53
death of employee, distribution made on account of, 24:29
defined, 24:19
EFT, 24:35
failure of plan administrator to notify payor, 24:26, 24:27
first periodic payment of year, 24:51

$5,400, annual payments less than, 24:32
Form W-4P, combination of notice with, 24:44
frequency of payments used as payment period, 24:53
gross income, entire amount excludable from, 24:38
how federal income tax withheld, 24:20
information provided by plan administrator to payor, 24:25–24:27
insurance company's incorrect calculation of monthly annuity amount, 24:54
language of notice, 24:43
mailing of notice, 24:45
notice of right not to have withholding apply, 24:30–24:46
payment period, 24:53
payor, notice to payees on behalf of, 24:41
payors of, 24:47
percentage method of determining withholding, 24:48
plan administrators, 24:23–24:27
recipients of, 24:28, 24:54
sample notice, 24:42
transfers of duties, 24:24
wage bracket method of determining withholding, 24:48
who is required to withhold, 24:22
withholding certificate, 24:49, 24:50
state income taxes, rules of specific states, 22:1
20 percent withholding, rollover distributions, 21:3
wage bracket method of determining withholding, periodic payments not eligible rollover distributions, 24:48

Withholding certificate
periodic payments that are not eligible rollover distributions, 24:49

Withholding certificate, periodic payments that are not eligible rollover distributions
no certificate filed, 24:50

Worker, Retiree, and Employer Recovery Act of 2008 (WRERA)
lump sum determinations, 9:67
required minimum distributions, waiver for 2009, 4:1
rollovers to nonspouse beneficiaries, 12:75, 28:7
Roth IRA rollovers, eligibility, 28:20, 28:26

Works of art
acceptance of by trustee, 25:14
assets IRA custodians are unwilling to accept, 28:10

WRERA. *See* Worker, Retiree, and Employer Recovery Act of 2008

Written explanations
eligible rollover distributions, 21:44–21:48
alternatives to written paper document, 21:46
to distributee, 21:45
posting of notice, 21:47
requirements pre-EGTRRA, 21:44
separate notice for periodic payments, 21:46
written format, 21:48
QJSA rules, 11:47–11:56
effective dates, 11:55
examples, 11:54
generally applicable information requirements, satisfaction of, 11:53
information to be provided, 11:51–11:53
married and unmarried individuals, 11:52
nonvested participants, 11:48
participant-specific information requirements, 11:52
purpose of, 11:47
reasonable period for providing, 11:49
relative values, determination of, 11:52
satisfaction of requirements, 11:50
separation before age 35, 11:49
when required, 11:49
QOSA terms and conditions, 11:43
QPSA rules, 11:47–11:56
effective dates, 11:55
generally applicable information requirements, satisfaction of, 11:53
information to be provided, 11:51
nonvested participants, 11:48
purpose of, 11:47
reasonable period for providing, 11:49
satisfaction of requirements, 11:50
separation before age 35, 11:49
when required, 11:49
termination of plan, eligibility for rollover treatment, 15:81

Y

Years of service. *See* Accrued service, determination of; Vesting